CONTRIBUTING EDITORS

1900–1904	James B. Ayres, *University of Texas*
1905–1909	Charles D. Peavy, *University of Houston*
1910–1914	Virginia T. Herrin, *East Carolina University*
1915–1919	Eugene N. James, *Northern Illinois University*
1920–1924	Mary Devine, *University of Massachusetts, at Salem*
1925–1929	Arthur R. Huseboe, *Augustana College*
1930–1934	Richard Dolezal, *Latin School of Chicago*
1935–1939	Stuart Wilson, *State University of New York, at Fredonia*
1940–1944	Amy M. Charles, *University of North Carolina, Greensboro*
1945–1949	Richard Morton, *McMaster University, Hamilton, Ontario*
1950–1954	Robert C. Steensma, *University of Utah*
1955–1959	L. P. Goggin, *Duquesne University*
1961–1965	Edmund Napieralski, *and* Jean Westbrook, *Loyola University, Chicago*
1965–1967	Edmund Napieralski, *Georgetown University*

Restoration and Eighteenth Century

THEATRE RESEARCH

A *Bibliographical Guide,*

1900-1968

Edited by

CARL J. STRATMAN, C.S.V.
DAVID G. SPENCER, and
MARY ELIZABETH DEVINE

SOUTHERN ILLINOIS UNIVERSITY PRESS
Carbondale and Edwardsville

FEFFER & SIMONS, INC.
London and Amsterdam

CONTENTS

INTRODUCTION

At the Convention of the Modern Language Association which met in Chicago during December of 1961, a special Conference was devoted to the topic of 17th and 18th century drama and theatre. As a result of this particular Conference the members voted: 1) to continue this Conference; and 2) to publish a form of newsletter under the aegis of the Modern Language Association and Loyola University.

Although the Conference devoted to 17th and 18th century drama and theatre--later, Restoration and 18th century theatre--has not been held for several years, the publication which began as a newsletter developed into the biannual journal, Restoration and 18th Century Theatre Research. One of the main features of the journal has been the publication of an annual bibliography, in the November issue, covering publications of the preceding year which have to do with Restoration and 18th century theatre. The first issue of the bibliography appeared in 1962.

Because of the ever widening interest in the area 1660-1800, and because of the success of the yearly bibliography, it seemed that there was a special need for a bibliography of Restoration and 18th century theatre studies covering the years prior to 1961. In order to help alleviate this need it was decided to publish a bibliography of works appearing in the 20th century which were devoted to Restoration and 18th century theatre. An appeal for contributing editors appeared in several issues of Restoration and 18th Century Theatre Research asking each potential editor to undertake the task of collecting material published in a single five-year period from 1900 to 1960. By 1964 various scholars had volunteered and had begun the actual work of collecting titles. Delays occurred, however, when some editors, for various reasons, had to resign and other editors had to be found.

Almost two years ago all the entries had been received by the general editor. He noticed, in studying the entries for the various five-year segments, that a number of basic works seemed to be missing in some periods. It then became his task to attempt to fill these gaps. Further, he also noticed that the original format for the entries was not always followed. So, with the collaboration of Mary Devine, he attempted to bring about a closer uniformity of format among the completed entries. At long last the task is finished.

The bibliography itself contains over six thousand entries devoted to studies of all phases of dramatic and theatrical activity in the British Isles during the Restoration and 18th century. The work limits itself to studies, as well as editions of plays, published between 1900 and 1968. Further, the bibliography is limited to material which relates in some way to the Restoration and 18th century; earlier writers, works, or dramatic activities are introduced only if the material is related in some way to the period of 1660-1800. Thus, Shakespeare's or Ben Jonson's names appear in the bibliography only when a specific work has bearing on the Restoration or 18th century. For example, Hazelton Spencer's book, Shakespeare Improved; the Restoration Versions in Quarto and on the Stage, is included, as is David Nicol Smith's work, Shakespeare in the Eighteenth Century, because both works are specifically related to the Restoration or the 18th century.

The Bibliography is divided into 780 subject headings, arranged in an alphabetical sequence. Included are 432 categories devoted to the names of actors, musicians, playwrights, scene painters, stage managers, and other people connected with theatrical activity. The other 348 subject headings cover such diverse topics as audiences, cities, echo device, friendship, guns, Hugenots, leisure, London Fairs, marriage, Methodism, negro, taste, and wits. Under each category the entries are placed in chronological order. When entries have subdivisions, as happens particularly in the case of popular authors, the arrangement is chronological within each subdivision.

An attempt was made to annotate as many entries as possible. The ideal, of course, would have been to annotate every entry, but quite early in the project it was realized that some items would not actually be seen by the compiler. For example, most masters' theses, as well as most early doctoral dissertations, were to be found only at the university where written, and thus out of the reach of most compilers. In addition, a number of books and articles, culled by the compiler from standard reference sources, e.g., the annual bibliographies of PMLA and MHRA, would not be at his particular university, or at the other libraries available to him. In spite of these limitations, however, some 5,359, or 81.6 per cent of all entries are annotated. These annotations are descriptive of the purpose and contents of books and articles rather than critical.

Finally, the Index is arranged in one continuous alphabet so as to include not only proper names of actors, musicians, playwrights, etc., but also to cover the various categories. Because of the numerous and complicated problems which would arise if we attempted to cope with

all the individual plays written during the 140 year period of the
Restoration and 18th century, it was decided not to make the names
of the plays a particular concern of the Index.

A word of caution may be in order at this time. The editor realizes
that even with his attempts to correct errors of fact, to make the
format uniform throughout, and personally to add almost a thousand
entries to the entire bibliography, that there will be omissions and
errors in a volume of this size. All he can do is to beg the indulgence
of those who use the book, and ask them to call such omissions or errors to his attention.

Such a bibliography is a cooperative project and many helped in its
preparation. Thanks are due primarily, of course, to the various compilers for, without their labors and industry this work would not have
appeared. Grateful acknowledgment is made to Loyola University, which
contributed funds towards the typing of the manuscript, and to Mrs.
Marion McCann of Loyola University Press, who typed the entire manuscript. For undertaking the arduous task of preparing the Index, I wish
to thank Mrs. Ralph F. Kenyon of Southern Illinois University Press.
For his continuing interest and encouragement, although he had to with-
draw from full participation in the project somewhat early due to medical
reasons, I am grateful to David G. Spencer.

Finally, may I say that I hope the bibliography will be of some assistance and service to the ever growing number of scholars who devote
their interests to the theatre of the Restoration and the 18th century.

Restoration and Eighteenth Century

THEATRE RESEARCH

Acting

1 Armstrong, Cecil Ferard. The Actor's Companion. With an Introduction by Arthur Bourchier, M.A., and Chapters by Clarence
  Derwent and Frederick James. London: Mills & Boon, Limited
  [1912]. 186 pp.
      Conditions and opportunities for those determined to be
  actors.
2 Colby, Elbridge. "Strolling Players in the Eighteenth Century."
  Notes and Queries, 11th Ser., XII (December 11, 1915), 454-
  457.
      A document in the British Museum (Add. MS. 33, 488) adds
  to our knowledge of strolling players in the 18th century by
  showing that the actors played many parts, that receipts were
  scanty, that the enterprise was run on a shoestring, and that
  the companies were haphazardly thrown together.
3 Campbell, Lily Bess. "The Rise of a Theory of Stage Presentation
  in England During the Eighteenth Century." Publications of the
  Modern Language Association, XXXIII (1917), 163-200.
      History of acting in the 18th century according to the idea
  that theories of acting follow the general artistic theory of
  the day.
4 Graves, Thornton S. "Some Aspects of Extemporal Acting."
  Studies in Philology, XIX (1922), 429-456.
      Discusses precedents for actors adding to the script in
  performance, such as Shakespeare, the Italian commedia
  dell'arte. Numerous references to 18th-century plays and
  actors with many anecdotal illustrations.
5 MacMillan, Dougald, and Howard Mumford Jones, Eds. Plays
  of the Restoration and Eighteenth-Century As They Were
  Acted At the Theatres-Royal by Their Majesties' Servants.
  New York: Henry Holt, 1931. 896 pp.
      Attempts to recreate the conventions of staging and acting
  as they were at the Theatres-Royal.
6 Hahn, Eugene. "Theories of Acting in Eighteenth-Century England." Ph.D. University of Wisconsin, 1935.

7 Henderson, John. "Theories of Acting in Eighteenth Century
       England." Ph.M. University of Wisconsin, 1935.
8 Trudeau, Tressa. "The 18th Century Attitude toward Life in
       England As Reflected in the Acting of the Period." M.A.
       Wayne University, 1938.
9 Vardac, Alexander Nicholas. "From Garrick to Griffith: Transi-
       tion from Stage to Screen." Ph.D. Yale University, 1942.
10 Downer, Alan S. "Nature to Advantage Dressed. Eighteenth-
       Century Acting." Publications of the Modern Language Asso-
       ciation, LVIII (December, 1943), 1002-1037.
           Differentiates the manner of Betterton, Cibber, Booth,
       Wilks, Macklin, Garrick, and Kemble.
11 Harvey, Sir John Martin. "The Player and His Art." Royal
       Society of Literature of the United Kingdom, London. Essays
       by Divers Hands, being the Transactions. New [3rd] Ser.,
       XX (1943), [99]-112.
           This discussion deals with the responsibilities and rewards
       of actors and includes references to Garrick, among others.
12 Smalley, Beryl. "An Anonymous Poem of the Eighteenth Century."
       Review of English Studies, XIX (January, 1943), 70.
           Discusses ["The Actor's Epitomé"], an anonymous poem
       "in a hand of the first quarter of the eighteenth century"
       written in a copy of Rowe's 1709 edition of Shakespeare
       presented by Arthur Rogers to the Bodleian Library.
13 Cooke, Anne M. "An Analysis of the Acting Styles of Garrick,
       Siddons, and Edmund Kean in Relation to the Dominant Trends
       in Art and Literature of the Eighteenth Century." Ph.D. Yale
       University, 1944.
14 -----. "Eighteenth Century Acting Styles." Phylon: The Atlantic
       University Review of Race and Culture, V (Third Quarter,
       1944), 219-224.
           Reviews the acting styles of David Garrick, Mrs. Siddons
       and Edmund Kean. Author feels that the comparative individual-
       ity of their acting styles affected "the force of the conventions
       in various art forms."
15 Hughes, Leo. "'The Actor's Epitome.'" Review of English Studies,
       XX (1944), 306-307.
           Concerned with Hill's versified treatment of the art of
       acting.
16 Downer, Alan S. "Players and Painted Stage: Nineteenth Century
       Acting." Publications of the Modern Language Association,
       LXI (1946), 522-576.
           A major study, in continuance of the classic "Nature to
       Advantage Dressed: Eighteenth Century Acting" (PMLA,
       LVII, 1943), which constantly makes reference to techniques

of eighteenth century acting and analyses the place of
eighteenth century plays in the repertory of the nineteenth
century.

17 -----. "Mr. Dangle's Defense: Acting and Stage History."
English Institute Essays (1947), 159-190.
   A general survey of English stage history.

18 Wasserman, Earl R. "The Sympathetic Imagination in Eighteenth-
Century Theories of Acting." Journal of English and Germanic
Philology, XLVI (July, 1947), 264-272.
   Suggests that the eighteenth century theatre was significant
for the growing imaginative understanding of the actor's
creative function. The roles of conscious artifice and native
insight in acting are debated during the period.

19 Oubre, Juanita Bernice. "A Beginning of a Study on English Acting
Techniques 1700-1725." M.A. State University of Iowa, 1948.

20 "A Theatrical Ghost." Times Literary Supplement, February
28, 1948, p. 121.
   An editorial on the actor's art, alluding briefly to the
eighteenth century.

21 Cole, Toby, and Helen Krick Chinoy, eds. Actors on Acting:
The Theories, Techniques, and Practices of the Great Actors
of All Times As Told in Their Own Words. New York: Crown,
1949. xiv, 596 pp.
   Includes quotations from Betterton, Cibber, Garrick, and
others of the period.

22 Vardac, A. Nicholas. Stage to Screen: Theatrical Method from
Garrick to Griffith. Cambridge: Harvard University Press,
1949. xxvi, 283 pp.
   The growth of realism in acting and production is seen to
grow from Garrick's pictorial staging.

23 Adams, William Wall. "Relationships between the Principles of
Acting and Rhetorical Delivery in Eighteenth-Century England."
Ph.D. University of Illinois, 1954. 146 pp. (Publication No.
9023).
   Based on primary sources, this study attempts to discover
the relationships between acting and rhetorical delivery and
to locate their origins in the milieu of the period.

24 Wilson, John Harold. "Rant, Cant and Tone on the Restoration
Stage." Studies in Philology, LII (1955), 592-598.
   Gives instances from plays where exaggerated tone was
called for to give satiric effect; describes the acting style
on the Restoration stage.

25 Hopkins, Robert H. "Rigor Mortis and Eighteenth Century
Tragedy." Notes and Queries, New Ser., VI (1959), 411-412.
   Actors portraying corpses wrongly stiffened when carried
off.

26 Joseph, Bertram. The Tragic Actor. London: Routledge and Kegan
    Paul, 1959. xvi, 415 pp.

27 Lund, Clyde W. "English Comedy Acting Style, 1750-1800." M.A.
    Saint Cloud State College, 1960.

28 Schaal, David G. "The English Background of American Rehearsal-
    Direction Practices in the Eighteenth Century." Educational
    Theatre Journal, XII (1960), 262-269.
        Most actors in America were English.

29 Golding, Alfred. "The Theory and Practice of Presentational
    Acting in the Serious Drama of France, England, and Germany
    During the 18th and 19th Centuries." Ph.D. Columbia University,
    1962.
        Includes a description of the theory and practice of 18th
    Century acting through a study of actors' memoirs and trea-
    tises for novice players.

30 Jensby, Wesley Joe. "A Historical Study of the Characteristics
    of Acting During the Restoration Period in England (1660-
    1710)." Ph.D. University of Southern California, 1963. (Order
    No. 63-6327).
        Examines the characteristics of Restoration acting through
    a study of contemporary remarks and criticisms of acting, of
    the relationship between Restoration and Elizabethan acting,
    and of the influence of Restoration acting on eighteenth cen-
    tury theatrics.

31 Woodbury, Lael J. "Death on the Romantic Stage." Quarterly
    Journal of Speech, XLIX (February, 1963), 57-61.
        Contrasts 19th century styles of acting with those employed
    in the neo-classical age. The eighteenth century "fostered an
    acting style which expressed the ideals of order and ideality
    then in vogue."

32 Angus, William. "Acting Shakespeare." Queen's Quarterly,
    LXXII (1965), 313-333.
        Brief section on the acting styles of Betterton, Garrick,
    and Macklin.

33 Hunt, Hugh. "Restoration Acting." Restoration Theatre. Edited
    by John Russell Brown and Bernard Harris. (Stratford-Upon-
    Avon Studies, 6). (London: Edward Arnold, 1965; New York:
    St. Martin's Press, 1965), 179-192.
        Discusses the introduction of actresses and movable scenery
    to the stage.

34 Downer, Alan S. "Nature to Advantage Dressed: Eighteenth Cen-
    tury Acting." Restoration Drama: Modern Essays in Criticism.
    (A Galaxy Book). Edited by John Loftis. (New York: Oxford
    University Press, 1966), 328-371.
        Reprinted from PMLA, LVIII (1943), 1002-1037. A study

of four "schools" of acting in the 18th century: Betterton,
Cibber-Booth-Wilks, Macklin-Garrick, and Kemble.

35 Henshaw, Nancy Wandalie. "Graphic Sources for a Modern
Approach to the Acting of Restoration Comedy." Ph.D.
University of Pittsburgh, 1967. (Order No. 68-9743).

Uses seventeenth-century engravings, handbooks of
deportment, memoirs, diaries, and satires to present
guides for the realistic method of acting that should be employed in modern productions of Restoration comedies.

Acting Companies

36 Leech, Clifford. "A Restoration Touring Company." London Times
Literary Supplement, May 31, 1934, p. 392.

Suggests that a license issued April 14, 1662, from the Office of Revels may have authorized the first Restoration provincial touring company.

37 Duncan, Barry. "A Worcestershire Company." Theatre Notebook, II (July, 1948), 76-78.

A tour of Mr. Phillips and his Company of Comedians in
1778.

38 Gerold, A. W. "The Organisation of Representative Acting Companies since Elizabethan Times." M.A. Columbia University,
1948.

39 Hoppe, Harry R. "English Acting Companies at the Court of
Brussels in the Seventeenth Century." Review of English Studies,
New Ser., VI (1955), 26-33.

Identifies companies and players who travelled to Brussels.
Information based on three account books of the royal court
preserved in the General Archives (records from 1612-1618
and mid-1647 to 1652.)

40 Rosenfeld, Sybil. Foreign Theatrical Companies in Great Britain
in the 17th and 18th Centuries. London: Printed for the Society,
1955. vi, 42 pp. (Society for Theatre Research Pamphlet
Series, No. 4, 1954-55.)

A study of those foreign companies--who sang or acted--
who came to Great Britain in troupes from 1629 to 1776. The
material is arranged chronologically and is divided into discussion of each year's activity.

41 Langhans, Edward A. "New Restoration Theatre Accounts, 1682-
1692." Theatre Notebook, XVII (Summer, 1963), 118-134.

Two documents in the Chancery Masters Exhibits at the
Public Record Office give valuable information on performance
dates and schedules of the United Company.

42 Burner, Sandra A. "A Provincial Strolling Company of the 1670's."
    Theatre Notebook, XX (Winter, 1965/6), 74-78.
    Suggests the possibility of a touring company, a contingent
    from the Nursery, active in Norwich and the provinces in the
    early 1670's.

Actors

43 Robins, Edward. Twelve Great Actors. New York: G. P. Putnam's
    Sons, 1900. 460 pp.
    Brief character sketches of Garrick, John Philip Kemble, and
    Edmund Kean.
44 Armstrong, Cecil Ferard. A Century of Great Actors, 1750-1850.
    London: Mills & Boon, Ltd., 1912. [8], 412 pp. Bibliography,
    pp. 411-412.
    Chapters devoted to the following 18th century actors: David
    Garrick, Sprange Barry, John Henderson, George F. Cooke,
    John Philip Kemble, Charles Macklin, and Joseph Shepherd
    Munden.
45 Graham, Harry. "The Infant Roscius." Splendid Failures. (Lon-
    don: Edward Arnold, 1913), 122-154.
    On the career, 1802-1808, of William Henry West Betty,
    the child actor who played Osman, Norval, Hamlet, and
    Macbeth to packed houses in Ireland, the English provinces,
    at Covent Garden and Drury Lane with Barrymore, Hargrave,
    Mrs. Siddons, and Charles Kemble in supporting roles.
46 Grundy, C. Reginald. "Two Mezzotints by John Smith." Con-
    noisseur, XXXV (January-April, 1913), 239-244.
    Impress of Garrick's seal and some original lines sent to
    Patty More by Garrick on back of a mezzopint of Kneller's
    self portrait, which Garrick fancied looked like himself.
47 Douglas, William. "Moss, an Actor." Notes and Queries, 11th
    Ser., IX (April 25, 1914), 335.
    Appearances at Covent Garden and the Haymarket. Member
    of the Edinburg Company, manager at Dumfries and at White-
    haven.
48 Lawrence, W. J. "An English Comedian at the Court of Louis XIV
    (Joe Haines)." Notes and Queries, VIII (1921), 401.
    A brief biography of Joe Haines who went to France in the
    entourage of the Duke of Buckingham in 1670.
49 Colby, Elbridge. "Strolling Players of the 18th Century." Notes
    and Queries, 12th Ser., IX (August, 1921), 168.
    A brief bibliography of books, essays and contemporaneous
    comments on strolling players.
50 C., G. "Italian Actor in England in the 17th Century." Notes and

Queries, 12th Ser., XII (February, 1923), 155.

A correction of the spelling of Tiberio Fiurelli's name to
Fiorelli.

51 Graves, Thornton S. "Strolling Players in the Eighteenth Century."
Notes and Queries, 13th Ser., I (July 7, 1923), 6-7.

A list of works (plays, memoirs, etc.) bearing on the history
of strolling players in the 18th century. Items cover the years
1727-1825 and are arranged chronologically. Supplements the
one by Colby in Notes and Queries (1921), p. 168.

52 Colby, Elbridge. "A Supplement on Strollers." Publications of
the Modern Language Association, XXXIX (1924), 642-654.

A supplement to Alwin Thaler's article, "Strolling Players
and Provincial Drama after Shakespeare" (q.v.) offering
further documentation of the miserable existence of the strolling players.

53 Von Platen, Carl. Sceniska artister från Shaksperes tid till våra
dagar. 2a omarbetande upplagan. Stockholm: P.A. Norstedt &
Söner, 1924.

A biographical dictionary of actors and actresses of several
countries.

54 Skinner, Otis. "His Majestie's Servant." Scribner's Magazine,
LXXXII (October, 1927), 396-403.

Biographical sketches of Thomas Betterton, Nell Gwyn, with
an imaginary description of an evening's performance of Betterton's Hamlet. Portraits of Betterton, Gwyn, and Elizabeth Barry.

55 -----. Mad Folk of the Theatre: Ten Studies in Temperment.
Indianapolis: The Bobbs-Merrill Company [1928]. 297 pp.

This work contains a series of ten sketches of actors who
appeared from the time of Charles II to the Victorian era. Of
interest here are those dealing with Thomas Betterton, Nell
Gwynn, James Quin, George Anne Bellamy, John Wilkinson,
Dorothy Jordan, George Cooke, and Edmund Kean.

56 Boas, F. S. "The University of Oxford and the Professional
Players." Times Literary Supplement, March 14, 1929, p.
206.

Performances at Oxford must have been without the University walls, and the evidence is against "academic hospital-
ity" to players (see R. C. Rhodes, TLS, February 21, 1929).

57 Coad, Oral Sumner and Mims, Edwin, Jr. The American Stage.
New Haven: Yale University Press, 1929. 362 pp.

This pictorial history depicts the transference to the American stage of English plays, players and acting traditions.
Other European influences as well as the growth of the uniquely
American theatre are covered in a history that ranges from 18th
century productions to the early 20th century.

58 Rhodes, R. Crompton. "The King's Players at Oxford, 1661-
    1712." London Times Literary Supplement, February 21,
    1929, p. 140.
      Throughout the 17th century Oxford University gave con-
    tinuous encouragement to the performance of plays.

59 -----. "The King's Players at Oxford." London Times Literary
    Supplement, April 11, 1929, p. 295.
      Replies to F. S. Boas (TLS, March 14, 1929) that only
    Royal companies were granted academic hospitality from
    1661 to 1713. After that time Parliamentary opposition to
    players' visits to Oxford was due to the character of the
    actresses.

60 Wood, Frederick T. "Strolling Actors in the Eighteenth Century."
    Englische Studien, LXVI (1931), 16-53.
      Describes type of actors, audience, organization of com-
    panies, theatres, stock, repertoire, from information culled
    from memoirs of various strollers, including Tate Wilkinson,
    Charlotte Charke, Tony Aston, Sylvester Daggerwood, and
    others.

61 Avery, Emmett L. "Two French Children on the English Stage,
    1716-1719." Philological Quarterly, XIII (1934), 78-82.
      Tells of the appearances of the French dancers Mlle Marie
    Sallé and her brother in England between 1716 and 1719 when
    they were approximately nine and eleven years old, respectively.

62 Ormsbee, Helen. Backstage with Actors, from the Time of
    Shakespeare to the Present Day. New York: Thomas Y.
    Crowell Company, 1938. xiv, 343 pp.
      A popular biography of various actors, including Betterton
    and Garrick. Most of the content is commonplace, superficial,
    and oversimplified.

63 Wilson, Willard. "The Life of the British Actor in the Eighteenth
    Century." Ph.D. University of Southern California, 1939.
      This study provides a coherent view of the lot of actors and
    actresses during the period from 1698 to 1814. Consideration
    of every major aspect of the actor's life indicates that con-
    ditions outside the theatre were not as contemptible as some
    have believed.

64 Brooking, Cecil. "Stage Folk in Dighton Prints." Notes and Queries,
    CLXXIX (1940), 403-407; CLXXIX (1940), 438-440.
      Brief accounts of actors and actresses of whom Robert
    Dighton drew and printed caricatures.

65 Baker, Herschel C. "Strolling Actors in Eighteenth Century Eng-
    land." University of Texas Studies in English (1941), 100-200.

66 Grundell, H. W. "Actors and Actresses in XVIIIth-Century
    Comedy." Notes and Queries, CCXXX (1941), 44-45.

According to a Restoration stage tradition that extended into the eighteenth century, an actor was occasionally expected
to play a minor female role.

67 Aylesbury, Vale of. "Peg Woffington and Mrs. Cholmondeley."
Notes & Queries, CLXXXIII (1942), 170.
Mrs. Cholmondeley, the sister of Peg Woffington, apparent-
ly knew Fanny Burney. See also the article by James Seton-
Anderson, pp. 264-265, of the same year.

68 Rosenfeld, Sybil. "Some Notes on the Players in Oxford, 1661-
1713." Review of English Studies, XIX (October, 1943), 366-
375.
A chronologically arranged account of the companies which
played in Oxford, 1661-1713; discusses the plays they performed
and other relevant material.

69 Angus, William. "Actors and Audiences in Eighteenth-Century
London." Studies in Speech and Drama in Honor of Alexander
W. Drummond. Edited by Donald C. Bryant, Bernard Hewitt,
Karl R. Wallace, and Herbert A. Wichelns. (Ithaca, N.Y.:
Cornell University Press, 1944), 123-138.
Considers the importance of the theatre manager--and the
influence the audience exercised upon him and his players.
Discusses the composition of the audience and suggests that,
if the member of the audience in the theatre "was one of a
large group or family, like the modern subscribers at the
opera," his behavior was "more like that of spectators at a
baseball game today."

70 Fuchs, Max. Lexique des Troupes de Comédiends au XVIIIe
Siècle. In Bibliothèque de la Société des Historiens du Théâtre.
Vol. XIX. Paris: E. Droz, 1944. xviii, 231 pp.
This lists, alphabetically, members of comedy troupes who
travelled through France and Europe from the death of Louis
XIV to the Revolution. When such information is available,
entries include biographical data and material pertaining to
the performer's various theatrical engagements.

71 Scott, W. S. The Georgian Theatre. London: Westhouse, 1946.
Contains short biographies of major theatrical figures
from the eighteenth century.

72 Price, Cecil. "An Eighteenth-Century Theatrical Agreement."
Theatre Notebook, II (January, 1948), 31-34.
Describes the terms of contract for a company of actors in
the 1780's.

73 Darlington, William Aubrey. The Actor and His Audience. London: Phoenix House, 1949. 188 pp.
A definition of the ideal tragic actor, deriving from a study
of the great English actors, including Betterton and Garrick.

74 Reynolds, James. "Ghosts in Old Irish Theatres." Theatre Arts, XXXIII (July, 1949), 42-45, 100.

Anecdotes of Peg Woffington, Spranger Barry, George-Anne Bellamy and other Irish theatre people.

75 Brook, Donald. A Pageant of English Actors. London: Rockliff [1950], 286 pp.

Biographies which attempt to discuss the actors's interpretations of various roles. Includes discussion of Thomas Betterton, David Garrick, and John Kemble.

76 Hogan, Charles B. "18th-century Actors in the D.N.B.--Additions and Corrections." Theatre Notebook, VI (1951-1952), 45-48, 66-71, 87-96.

Hogan includes new or corrected information on over one hundred actors and actresses.

77 Sprague, Arthur Colby. Shakespearian Players and Performances. Cambridge: Harvard University Press, 1953. 222 pp.

Sprague discusses the following Restoration and eighteenth-century actors and actresses: Betterton as Hamlet (pp. 9-20), Garrick as Lear (pp. 21-40), Kemble as Hamlet (pp. 41-56), and Mrs. Siddons as Lady Macbeth (pp. 57-70).

78 Brown, A. Stuart. "The Peer and the Players." Theatre Notebook, IX (1955), 76-78.

Discusses John Howe, Baron Chedworth, 1754-1804, and his legacies to several performers, Thomas Penrice, Mary Taylor, Edward Seymour, Harriet Bedell, Mary-Ann Kent, Elizabeth Edmead, John Powell. Some basic details of lives and careers of the actors are given.

79 Varey, J. E. "Notes on English Theatrical Performers in Spain: Part II (1583-1868)," Theatre Notebook, X (1956), 74-79.

80 Findlater, Richard. Six Great Actors. David Garrick, John Philip Kemble, Edmund Kean, W. C. Macready, Sir Henry Irving, Sir Johnston Forbes-Robertson. London: Hamish Hamilton, 1957. 191, [1] pp.

Through a resumé of the careers of David Garrick and John Philip Kemble the writer attempts to understand them in relation to their own period.

81 Hogan, Charles Beecher. "Eighteenth-Century Actors in the D.N.B.: Additions and Corrections (Second Series)." Theatre Notebook, XI (1957), 113-121.

82 Jones, Claude E. "Isaac Reed's 'Theatrical Obituary.'" Notes & Queries, New Ser., IV (1957), 390-392.

18th century actors. Compiled ca. 1799.

83 Schrickx, W. "Betrekkingen von het Vlaamse Geestesleven met de Engelse en Amerikaanse Letteren." Levende Talen, No. 197 (December, 1958), 641-656.

Touches on English actors in Flanders in the 17th Century.

84 Leathers, Victor. British Entertainers in France. Toronto: University of Toronto Press, 1959. 179 pp.

A record of visits to France, 1600-1900, by British entertainers with reports of their receptions by the critics, the artists, and the public. About four chapters are devoted to the Restoration and 18th century.

85 Highfill, Philip H. "Actors' Wills." Theatre Notebook, XV (1960), 7-15.

A study of some forty actors' wills reveals that principal actors were generally quite prosperous and that even midling actors were often closely connected with the affluent classes.

86 Riewald, J. G. "New Light on the English Actors in the Netherlands, c. 1590-c. 1660." English Studies, XLI (1960), 65-92.

After about 1650, wandering English acting troupes, which entered Europe via the Low Countries and which had been reinforced by native players to form the "Engelache commedianten," gradually merged into the various national theatres.

87 Bridges-Adams, W. "When Did Respectability Begin?" Drama, No. 67 (Winter, 1962), pp. 26-28.

Actor's position in society. Some notes on Restoration and Eighteenth Century performers.

88 Highfill, Philip H., Jr. "A Biographical Dictionary of Performers, 1660-1801." 17th and 18th Century Theatre Research, I (May, 1962), 20-22.

Announcement concerning the editors, future publication, and contents of the dictionary.

89 -----. "Extra." Theatre Notebook, XVII (Spring, 1963), 103-104.

The term 'Extra' in theatre jargon was in familiar use by 1781 according to BM. Add 40,166 which gives salary regulations for the Manchester and Liverpool Theatres.

90 Wilson, John Harold. "The Duchess of Portsmouth's Players." Notes and Queries, New Ser., X (1963), 106-107.

Argues that the Duchess of Portsmouth Players never existed. The Indian Emperor was produced by a group of amateurs before September 30, 1675.

91 Wilson, John Harold. "Players' Lists in the Lord Chamberlain's Registers." Theatre Notebook, XVIII (Autumn, 1963), 25-30.

Reprint of Players' Lists from October 6, 1660 to November 14, 1698. The names of Thomas Betterton, Colley Cibber, Nathaniel Lee, and other playwrights are found among the actors' names.

92 Wagenknecht, Edward. Merely Players. Norman: University of Oklahoma Press, 1966. 270 pp.

Biographies of David Garrick, Edmund Kean, William
Charles Macready, Edwin Forrest, Edwin Booth, Sir Henry
Irving, Joseph Jefferson, and Richard Mansfield.

93 Coleman, William S. E. "Post-Restoration Shylocks Prior to
Macklin." Theatre Survey, VIII (1967), 17-36.

Questions the common assumption that a comedic approach
to Shylock prevailed in the early 18th century. Examines the
roles of Thomas Dogget, Benjamin Griffin, Anthony Boheme,
John Ogden, Anthony Aston, and John Arthur.

94 Engel, Glorianne. "The Comic Actor in the Age of Garrick:
His Style and Craftsmanship." Ph.D. University of Pittsburgh,
1967. (Order No. 68-7520).

Discusses the criticism and acting treatises of the period and
studies the careers of nine comic actors in depth: David Garrick,
Henry Woodward, Edward Shuter, Richard Yates, Kitty Clive,
Peg Woffington, Mrs. Abington, Samuel Foote, and Thomas
Weston.

Actresses

95 Robins, Edward. Twelve Great Actresses. New York: G. P.
Putnam's Sons, 1900. 431 pp.

Brief character sketches of Anne Bracegirdle, Anne Oldfield, Margaret Woffington, Frances Abington, Sarah Siddons,
Dora Jordan, and Mary (Mrs. Perdita Robinson) Darby.

96 Fyvie, John. Comedy Queens of the Georgian Era. New York: E.
P. Dutton and Company, 1907. xi, 445 pp.

A series of biographical sketches, based mostly on eighteenth
century memoirs, of Lavinia Fenton, Charlotte Charke, Cath-
erine Clive, Margaret Woffington, George Anne Bellamy,
Frances Abington, Sophia Baddeley, Elizabeth Farren, Mary
"Perdita" Robinson, Mary Sumbel, Dora Jorday, and Harriet
Mellon. A 1906 edition was published in London.

97 -----. Tragedy Queens of the Georgian Era. London: Methuen;
New York: Dutton, 1909. x, 316 pp.

Traces the careers of actresses of 18th and early 19th
centuries, e.g., Elizabeth Barry, Anne Bracegirdle, Anne
Oldfield, Mary Porter, Susannah Ciber, Elizabeth Inchbald,
Sarah Siddons, Hannah Pritchard, Mary Ann Yates, Anne
Crawford, Julia Glover, Miss O'Neill (Lady Becher).

98 Douglas, William. "Restoration Characters." Notes and Queries,
11th Ser., I (January 15, 1910), 57.

According to MS notes of James Winston, once co-manager
of the Haymarket theatre, Jane Long acted the roles of Flora,
Zarma, and Mrs. Nell in Davenant's company in 1662--still

living in 1670. Her portrait included in Colnaghi's Catalogue in 1827.

99 Collins, Charles Williams. Great Love Stories of the Theatre: A Record of Theatrical Romance. London and New York: Duffield, 1911. 327 pp.

Romances of Nell Gwynn and Charles II, Elizabeth Barry and Thomas Otway, Peg Woffington, "Perdita" Robinson, and Becky Wells.

100 Burwash, Ida. "English Play-Actresses from Anne to Victoria." The Canadian Magazine, XXXVIII (1912), 261-271.

The triumphs of English actresses who worked with Betterton and Garrick: Gwynn, Barry, Bracegirdle, Oldfield, Woffington, Clive, Bellamy, and Siddons.

101 Metcalf, Cranstown. Peeresses of the Stage. With 24 portraits. London: Andrew Melrose, 1913. xi, 264 pp.

A popular history of the marriages of various actresses into the nobility. Chapter I treats three 18th century actresses--Anastasia Robinson (Countess of Peterborough), Lavinia Fenton (Duchess of Bolton), Elizabeth Farren (Countess of Derby).

102 Simpson, Harold, and Mrs. Charles Brau. Century of Famous Actresses, 1750-1850. London: Mills and Boon, 1913. 380 pp.

Sketches of the lives and careers of the major actresses of the period. The Appendix lists the play, author, and character played for the major performances of each actress.

103 Izard, Forrest. Heroines of the Modern Stage. New York: Sturgis, 1915. 390 pp.

The Appendix contains an essay on the first English actresses and the change in the actors' social status.

104 "Costumes a la Mode." Theatre Arts Monthly, X (July, 1926), 471.

Portraits of Mrs. Abington (1737-1815), Mrs. Pope (1740-1797), and Mrs. Yates (1728-1787), costumed for various Shakespearean plays.

105 Gilder, Rosamond. "Enter Ianthe, Veil'd." Theatre Arts Monthly, XI (January, 1927), 49-58.

On the first actresses on the English stage; the first serious heroic part was that of Ianthe in Davenant's The Siege of Rhodes. With a portrait of Margaret Hughes.

106 Henrich, Royla. "English Actresses of the Eighteenth Century." M.A. University of Wisconsin, 1929.

107 Melville, Lewis [Lewis Saul Benjamin]. More Stage Favourites of the Eighteenth Century. London: Hutchinson, 1929. 286 pp.

Biographical sketches of Frances Abington, Sarah Siddons, Mary Anne "Perdita" Robinson, and Dorothy Jordan.

108 Lanier, Henry Wysham. The First English Actresses, from the Initial Appearance of Women on the Stage in 1660 till 1700.

New York: The Players, 1930. 104 pp.

This illustrated monograph of "feminine beginnings on our
stage" depicts the history and personalities of the first ladies
of the English stage whose characters and performances "eventual
ly gave dignity and position to the craft." It includes chapters on
Mary Saunderson and Mrs. Bracegirdle as well as a table of 17th
century British actresses.

109 Gilder, Rosamond. Enter the Actress; the First Woman in the
Theatre. London: George G. Harrap & Co. [1931]. 313 pp.

This book offers a view of the adventures of "the true in-
novators who dared to face a hostile tradition and earn their
living or try out their new ideas in a new profession."

110 Hachmuth, Doris Juanita. "A Historical Study of Certain Great
English Actresses." M.A. University of Southern California,
1935.

111 Brooking, Cecil. "Actresses on the Tiles." Notes and Queries,
CLXXIX (1940), 330-334.

Short accounts of the lives of eighteenth-century actresses
whose portraits appear on theatrical tiles transferred from
drawings in Bell's British Theatre.

112 Troubridge, St. Vincent. "Helena in All's Well That Ends Well."
Notes and Queries, CLXXXI (1941), 109-110.

Lists actresses who have played Helena: Mrs. Giffard, Mrs.
Woffington, Mrs. Pritchard, Miss Macklin, Mrs. Palmer, Mrs.
Mattocks, Miss Farren, Mrs. Jordan.

113 Rogers, Francis. "Some Prima Donnas of the Latter Eighteenth
Century." Musical Quarterly, XXX (April, 1944), 147-162.

A continuation of "Handel and the Five Prima Donnas,"
(Musical Quarterly, XXIX (April, 1943), 214-224): Caterina
Gabrielli, Lucrezia Agujari, Elizabeth Bellington, Guiseppina
Grassini, and Angelica Catalani.

114 MacQueen-Pope, W. Lady's [sic] First; the Story of Woman's
Conquest of the British Stage. London: W. H. Allen, 1952.
xiv, 384 pp.

A popular history of actresses since the Restoration, at
least as devoted to their private lives and to their careers.

115 Gagen, Jean Elizabeth. The New Woman: Her Emergence in English Drama, 1600-1730. New York: Twayne Publishers, 1954.
193 pp.

The new trends of thought regarding woman's inherent
nobility and dignity found their way into the drama of this period.

116 Wilson, John Harold. "Lord Oxford's 'Roxalana.'" Theatre Notebook, XII (1957), 14-16.

117 de la Torre, Lillian. Actress: Being the Story of Sarah Siddons.
New York: Nelson, 1958. 223 pp.

Biography for young readers.

118 Wilson, John Harold. All the Kings' Ladies: Actresses of the
Restoration. Chicago: University of Chicago Press, 1958. x,
206 pp.

Background discussion plus biographical dictionary.

119 Bushnell, George H. "The Original Lady Randolph." Theatre
Notebook, XIII (1959), 119-123.

Sarah Ward in Home's Douglas, Edinburgh, 1756.

120 Pendleton, Frances J. "Morality Among Actresses: An Investi-
gation of the Moral Reputation of Actresses from Their First
Appearances to the End of the Seventeenth Century with Special
Emphasis on the English Restoration Period." M.A. Sacramento
State College, 1959.

121 Haskell, George D., Jr. "Complicated Charms, The Literary
Activities of Eighteenth Century Actresses." Ph.D. Fordham
University, 1960.

122 Marinacci, Barbara. Leading Ladies, A Gallery of Famous Actresses.
New York: Dodd, Mead, & Co., 1961. xiii, 306 pp.

An account of eleven famous actresses from Mary Betterton,
Charlotte Cushman, Eleanora Duse, to Gertrude Lawrence.
Interpretative studies.

123 Reed, Sally Lou. "The Advent of Actresses on the English Public Stage and Subsequent Effects on the Female Role in Restoration Drama." M.A. University of Southern California, 1961.

124 Wilson, John Harold. "Biographical Notes on Some Restoration
Actresses." Theatre Notebook, XVIII (Winter, 1963/4), 43-47.

Corrections and supplement to the author's All the King's
Ladies, 1958, Appendix A, The Actresses, 1660-1689. Notes on
Katherine Corey, Mrs. Knepp, the two Mrs. Prices, Elizabeth
Roche, the two Mrs. Knights and others.

Adams, Charles

125 Guest, Alan D. "Charles Adams and John Gilbert-Cooper."
Theatre Notebook, XI (1957), 135-141.

Actor and playwright, ca. 1762.

Adaptations

126 Hughes, Leo and Arthur H. Scouten. "Some Theatrical Adaptations of a Picaresque Tale." Studies in English, Department
of English, The University of Texas, 1945-46. (Austin: University of Texas Press, 1946), 98-114.

A story used in William Percy's Cuck-Queanes and Cuckolds
Errants and Marston's The Dutch Courtezan is traced through

Restoration and eighteenth century drama.

127 Ashin, Mark. "Restoration Adaptations of Jacoblan and Caroline
Comedy." Ph.D. Chicago University, 1950.

Addison, Joseph

general works

128 Addison, Joseph. Selections from the Writings of Joseph Addison.
Edited, with introduction and notes by Barrett Wendell and
Chester Noyes Greenough. Athenaeum Press Series. Boston:
Ginn & Co. [c. 1905]. lxi, 346 pp.
"Introduction" covers the life and writings of Addison with
emphasis on the periodical writings and includes a bibliography
of Addison's works, biography and criticism. Selections include
Cato, Act V (pp. 23-33), Spectator No. 5, "The Opera" (pp. 66-
69), Spectator No. 39, "Modern Tragedy" (pp. 89-93), Spectator
No. 40, "The Same Subject, continued" (pp. 94-97), and Spec-
tator No. 335, "Sir Roger at the Theatre" (pp. 196-199).

129 -----. The Miscellaneous Works of Joseph Addison. Edited by A.
C. Guthkelch. 2 vols. London: G. Bell and Sons, Ltd., 1914.
Reprints Tickell's "Preface" to Addison's Works (1721);
Vol. I contains Rosamond (pp. 293-330), Cato (pp. 335-422),
The Drummer (pp. 423-490). Each play is preceeded by a
note stating which text has been reprinted and which have been
collated and dealing very briefly with bibliography pertinent
to the work.

letters

130 [Addison, Joseph]. The Letters of Joseph Addison. Edited by Walter
Graham. Oxford: at the Clarendon Press, 1941. 527 pp.
Contains a history of Addison's correspondence, a list of
letters, the letters printed both in full and in abstract and
about fifty pages of letters addressed to Addison (including one
from John Gay). Although the letters are primarily "public,"
there is some correspondence between Addison and Congreve.

bibliography and criticism

131 Saude, Emil. Die Grundlagen der literarischen Kritik bei Joseph
Addison. Weimar, 1906, 67 pp.
Inaugural dissertation, Friederich-Wilhelms-Universität.
Pages 44-49 discuss Addison's critical views of the drama
(tragedy, tragicomedy, comedy, and the opera).

132 Courthope, William John. Addison. English Men of Letters.
     London: Macmillan and Co., Ltd., 1911. vi, 197 pp.
         Treats the state of English society and letters after the
     Restoration and within this, Addison's writings--including a
     lengthy analysis of Cato.

133 Hegnauer, Adolphe G. Der Einfluss von Addisons "Cato" die
     dramatische Literatur England's und des Sentiments in der 1.
     Hälfte des 18 Jahrhunderts. Hamburg: M. Lange, 1912. 157 pp.
         The success of Cato in the 18th century in London and Smock
     Alley in Dublin, and in Edinburgh, its influence on the revenge
     tragedies of Young, Motley, Fenton, Thomson. With Addison's
     Cato manners, morals, and respectability came into their own.

134 Boume, Paul. "Die Stellung von Addison und Steele zum Theater
     in den Moralischen Wochenschriften." Münster Dissertation,
     1920.

135 Fletcher, Edward Garland. "Records and History of Theatrical
     Activities in Pittsburgh, Pennylvania from Their Beginning to
     1861." Ph.D., Harvard University, 1931.
         A discussion of the beginnings of theatrical activity in
     Pittsburgh in the eighteenth century; the first known performance
     was one of Cato in April, 1790.

136 Greenough, Chester Noyes. "Did Joseph Addison Write The Play-
     house?" Harvard Studies and Notes in Philology and Literature,
     XVII (1935), 55-66.
         Examines the old surmise that Addison wrote this satiric
     attack upon Covent Garden Theatre, finds valid evidence
     wanting, and concludes that the poem was neither "written
     nor revised" by Addison.

137 Zeitvogel, Albert. Addisons Cato. Eine geschichtliche und
     dramatische Quellenuntersuchung. Inaugural Dissertation.
     Münster, 1936. 65 pp.
         A study of Addison's tragedy with almost exclusive em-
     phasis upon its historical and dramatic sources.

138 Saer, H. A. "Notes on the Use of Themes Taken from the
     'Spectator' in Eighteenth-Century French Plays." Modern
     Languages, XXI (1939), 5-16, 55-61.

139 Morris, Robert L. "Joseph Addison's Literary Criticism."
     Ph.D. University of Iowa, 1940.

140 Noack, F. E. Die bürgerlichen Züge in Addisons "Cato."
     Berlin: Funk, 1940. 48 pp.
         Influence of Addison's dramatic theory in Cato and in the
     Spectator.

141 H., C. E. "The Death of Addison." Notes and Queries, CLXXX
     (1941), 211.
         What is the history of a story concerning Addison's death-

bed exhortation, "See in what peace a Christian can die?"

142 Salmon, David. "Addison in Pembrokeshire." Notes and Queries, CLXXXI (August 2, 1941), 61; (August 16, 1941), 94.

Perhaps Addison once stayed at Haroldston, the Perrot family home in Pembrokeshire.

143 Atkins, Stuart. "Addison's Cato: I.i.47-53." Philological Quarterly, XXI (October, 1942), 430-433.

Corrects the punctuation of these lines to bring them into conformity with Addison's "piety" and "his taste." Atkins offers evidence from the quartos to show that his reading is correct.

144 Summers, Silas E. "Addison's Conception of Tragedy." College English, VIII (February, 1947), 245-248.

His theory of tragedy is pieced together from various Spectator papers. For the most part he agrees with Aristotle.

145 Halsband, Robert. "Addison's Cato and Lady Mary Wortley Montagu." Publications of the Modern Language Association, LXV (1950), 1122-1129.

Addison revised Cato in light of a pre-performance critique by Lady Mary.

146 Wheatley, Katherine E. "Addison's Portrait of the Neoclassical Critic." Review of English Studies, New Ser., I (1950), 245-247.

The words and actions of Addison's Sir Timothy Tittle (Tatler, No. 165) resemble those of characters in Moliere's Critique de l'École des Femmes.

147 Smithers, Peter. The Life of Joseph Addison. Oxford: The Clarendon Press, 1954. viii, 491 pp.

The first full-length biography of Joseph Addison deals extensively with Addison's time, life and works. See especially the chapter entitled "Cato in the Wilderness."

148 Edelen, Georges. "Joseph Glanvill, Henry More, and the Phantom Drummer of Tedworth." Harvard Library Bulletin, X (1956), 186-192.

Relates to Addison's The Drummer.

149 Baker, Donald C. "Witchcraft, Addison and The Drummer." Studia Neophilologica, XXXI (1959), 174-181.

Argues that "it seems quite probable that Addison saw in a comedy of this sort [The Drummer] an opportunity to delineate a common-sense view of the matter [witchcraft], a rational view, still without denying the supernatural."

150 Bond, Richmond P. New Letters to the "Tatler" and "Spectator." Austin: University of Texas Press, 1959. 232 pp.

Subjects include the theatre.

151 Montgomery, Henry C. "Addison's Cato and George Washington."

Classical Journal, LV (1960), 210-212.

Washington liked the theatre and in particular the political idealism of Cato, a play popular in America in the mid-1700's. There is also discussion of the play itself and the ideals expressed.

152 Stratman, Carl J., C.S.V. "Unrecorded Editions of Addison's Cato, Published before 1756." Theatre Notebook, XV (1961), 102.

Lists some ten editions which do not appear in the Cambridge Bibliography of English Literature, or in Allardyce Nicoll's A History of English Drama, 1660-1900.

153 Elioseff, Lee Andrew. The Cultural Milieu of Addison's Literary Criticism. Austin: University of Texas Press, 1963. 252 pp.

A thorough investigation of Addison's debt to 18th century culture. Addison's literary criticism was moulded by the period's "political and national loyalties, literary and theatrical practices and shifts in taste..." Important chapters on tragedy and the Italian opera.

154 Kelsall, M. M. "Addison and Classical Rome: an Investigation of the Importance of the Literature of the Roman World in the English Works of Joseph Addison. B. Litt. Oxford University (Brasenose), 1964.

155 -----. "The Meaning of Addison's Cato." Review of English Studies, XVII (1966), 149-162.

Addison's intention was to give a preeminent example of "Roman virtue" and also an example of the virtues of Roman republican liberty.

156 Kenny, Shirley Strum. "Two Scenes by Addison in Steele's Tender Husband." Studies in Bibliography: Papers of the Bibliographical Society of the University of Virginia, XIX (1966), 217-226.

Addison wrote parts of Acts III, i and V, i.

157 Litto, Frederic M. "Addison's Cato in the Colonies." William and Mary Quarterly, XXIII (1966), 431-449.

The many editions and performances of the play in the 18th century America demonstrate that the work was considered a classic. Its most meaningful popularity occurred when it was used as an instrument of political propaganda.

158 Dobrée, Bonamy. Essays in Biography, 1680-1726. Freeport, New York: Books for Libraries Press, 1967. 362 pp.

A reprint of the 1925 edition contains biographies of Etherege, Vanbrugh and Addison.

Advertisements

159 Avery, Emmett L. "The Dramatists in the Theatrical Advertise-

ments, 1700-09." Modern Language Quarterly, VIII (1947),
448-454.

Theatrical information derived from newspaper advertisements.

160 Payne, William L. An Index to Defoe's "Review." New York:
Columbia University Press, 1949. 144 pp.

Contains an appendix listing play advertisements in the
journal.

Aesthetics

161 Draper, John W. Eighteenth-century English Aesthetics, a Bibliography. Heidelberg: Carl Winters, 1931. 140 pp. ("Antlistische
Forschungen," Heft 71).

An annotated bibliography, arranged alphabetically within
sections. See, "Literature and Drama," pp. 61-115.

African Princes

162 Sypher, Wylie. "The African Prince in London." Journal of the
History of Ideas, II (April, 1941), 237-247.

"Describes several literary treatments of African princes
which seem to be based upon visits to London by negroes of
high rank."

After-Pieces

163 Jones, Bertrand L. "Introduction to the History of the After-Piece
and the Curtain-Raiser of the English Stage from Their Beginning to 1740." M.A. University of Chicago, 1913.

164 Baskervill, Charles R. "Play-Lists and Afterpieces of the Mid-
Eighteenth Century." Modern Philology, XXIII (1926), 445-
464.

Calls attention to the importance of the lists of current plays
contained in the periodical publications such as the Gentleman's
Magazine, especially for the information they give in reward to
afterpieces.

Aickin, James

165 McKenzie, Jack. "James Aickin." Theatre Notebook, X (1956), 63.
Actor.

America

166 Isaac, Edith J. R. "1620--The Puritans and the Theatre--1920."
    Theatre Arts Monthly, IV (1920), 280-285.
        A consideration of Puritanism and the American theatre which
    concentrates on the years before 1800.

Amusements

167 Boulton, William B. The Amusements of Old London. Being a
    Survey of the Sports and Pastimes, Tea Gardens and Parks,
    Playhouses, and other Diversions of the People of London
    from the 17th to the beginning of the 19th Century. 2 vols.
    London: John C. Nimmo, 1901. 272 pp.
        A survey of amusements of Londoners, with anecdotes and
    comments of famous people, including sections on bear and
    bull baiting, al fresco entertainments, The Mulberry Garden,
    masquerades, fairs, gambling, etc. Vol. I, Ch. VI, pp. 207-
    272 on plays and operas.

168 Chancellor, Edwin Beresford. The Pleasure Haunts of London
    During Four Centuries. London: Constable & Co., Ltd., 1925.
    466 pp.
        Discusses theaters, gardens, fairs, "shows," and spas,
    and gambling, pastimes, and musical affairs from Tudor
    times till publication. Illustrated with engravings from rare
    sources, and well indexed.

Ancients and Moderns

169 Malas. "La Querelle des Anciens et des Modernes en Angleterre
    jusqu'a Swift." MS. University of Paris (Sorbonne), 1922.

Anecdotes

170 Engelbach, Arthur Harold, Compiler. Anecdotes of the Theatre;
    Collected and Arranged. London: Grant Richards, Ltd., 1914.
    271 pp.
        A collection of anecdotes primarily devoted to the English
    theatre. There is no perceptible order of arrangement.

Anonymous Literature

171 Halkett, Samuel, and John Laing. Dictionary of Anonymous and
    Pseudonymous English Literature. New and enlarged edition
    by James Kennedy, W. A. Smith, and A. F. Johnson. London

and Edinburgh: Oliver and Boyd, Vol. I, A-C, 1926; Vol. II,
D-G, 1926; Vol. III, H-L, 1928; Vol. IV, M-P, 1928; Vol. V,
Q-S, 1929.

Lists plays and the like by title, with the author's name and
the source of the attribution. Index in Vol. VII (1934).

Applause

172 Graves, Thornton S. "Organized Applause." South Atlantic Quarterly, XIX (July, 1920), 236-248.
A discussion of the appearances of and references to "leaders
of applause," (claques) in the Restoration and 18th-century
theatre.

Apprentices

173 Newlin, Claude M. "The Theatre and the Apprentices." Modern
Language Notes, XLV (1930), 451-454.
Studies the on-the-job-training given to aspiring thespians.

Arbuthnot, John

174 Sherburn, George. "The Fortunes and Misfortunes of Three Hours
after Marriage." Modern Philology, XXIV (August, 1926), 91-
109.
A discussion of the farce by Pope, Gay, and Arbuthnot, assembling much contemporary evidence and correcting several
misconceptions.

Architecture

175 Macomber, Philip Alan. "The Iconography of London Theatre
Auditorium Architecture, 1660-1800." Ph.D. The Ohio Uni-
versity, 1959.
Study of about 700 pictures selected from 3,500.

Aristotle

176 McMahon, A. Philip. "Seven Questions on Aristotelian Definitions
of Tragedy and Comedy." Harvard Studies in Classical Philology, XL (1929), 97-198.
The last question (VII) summarizes attitudes of three play-
wrights--Shadwell, Dryden, and Steele--toward Aristotle.

177 Herrick, Marvin Theodore. The Poetics of Aristotle in England.
New Haven: Yale University Press, 1930. 196 pp. (Cornell

Studies in English, XVII).

Especially valuable in tracing the application or misapplication of Aristotle's Poetics to the drama.

178 Dacier, A[ndre]. The Preface to Aristotle's Art of Poetry (1705). Introduction by Samuel Holt Monk. Los Angeles: William Andrews Clark Memorial Library, University of California, 1959. (Augustan Reprint Society, Publication No. 76).

This is the first English translation of Dacier's 1692 French treatise. Monk's introduction places Dacier in the history of commentaries on Aristotle, and discusses Dacier's orthodox position on the rules and on the nature of tragedy.

Arne, Thomas

text

179 Arne, Thomas Augustine. Artaxerxes. Introduction by William Gillis. The Augustan Reprint Society, Publication No. 99. Los Angeles: William Andrews Clark Memorial Library, 1963. vii, 47 pp.

Text a facsimile of the 1761 edition; introduction discusses the background and production of Artaxerxes.

biography and criticism

180 Flood, W. H. Grattan. "Dr. Arne's Visit to Dublin." The Musical Antiquary, I (1909-1910), 215-233.

Production of series of musicals and operas--Tom Thumb, Acis and Galatea, Rosamund, The Beggar's Opera--at Aungier Street Theatre and Theatre Royal in Smock Alley, 1742-1759.

181 Cummings, William H. "Dr. Arne." Proceedings of the Musical Association, XXXVIII (March 15, 1910), 75-90.

A history of Arne's career with emphasis upon his compositions for the stage.

182 Scott, Hugh Arthur. "Sidelights on Thomas Arne." Musical Quarterly, XXI (1935), 301-310.

A series of biographical notes about Arne with primary emphasis upon a definition of his character.

183 Sands, Mollie. "The Bicentenary of Arne's Songs in As You Like It." Notes and Queries, CLXXIX (1940), 416-417.

December 20, 1940, marks two hundred years since Thomas Lowe sang T. A. Arne's versions of two Shakespeare songs at Drury Lane in As You Like It.

184 Roscoe, P. C. "Arne and The Guardian Outwitted." Music and Letters, XXIV (1943), 237-245.

Gives an overview of the critical reaction to The Guardian
Outwitted and the satirical and deprecatory ballads it inspired,
including one of unknown authorship.

185 Cudworth, Charles. "Boyce and Arne: 'The Generation of 1710.'"
     Music and Letters, XLI (1960), 136-145.
          Parallel careers.

186 Herbage, Julian. "Arne's Theatrical Masques." Listener, LXIV
     (1960), 489.
          Herbage provides a short statement of Arne's career and
     theatrical masques.

Arrowsmith, Joseph

187 Love, Harold. "A Lost Comedy by Joseph Arrowsmith." Notes
     and Queries, New Ser., XIV (1967), 217-218.
          Arrowsmith probably wrote a play performed before Charles
     II on October 4, 1671 in Cambridge and The Reformation, a
     comedy attacking the heroic play.

Arthurian

188 Brinkley, Roberta Florence. Arthurian Legend in the Seventeenth
     Century. Baltimore: The Johns Hopkins Press, 1932.
          Chapter III, "Trojan and Saxon in Literature," describes
     the use of the politically important Arthur legend in Restoration
     drama, among other literary forms. Among the plays discussed
     are Ravenscroft's King Edgar and Alfreda and Thomas Rymer's
     play about Edgar.

Aston, Anthony

text

189 Aston, Anthony. "The Fool's Opera." National Society of the
     Colonial Dames of America. Pennsylvania. . . Church Music
     and Musical Life in Pennsylvania in the Eighteenth Century
     . . . Prepared by the Committee on Historical Research . . .
     3 vols. Philadelphia: Printed for the Society, 1926-1947.
          Volume three, part one, of this series deals essentially
     with English musical life in the American colonies and con-
     tains the libretto of The Fool's Opera as well as sections
     dealing with music in The Beggar's Opera and The Harlequin's
     Opera.

biography and criticism

190 Nicholson, Watson. Anthony Aston, Stroller and Adventurer; to
      which is appended Aston's Brief Supplement to Cibber's Lives.
      South Haven, Michigan: Published by the Author, 1920. 98 pp.
           A biography of Anthony Aston, the noted strolling player
      and performer of medleys, based on Aston's Sketch of his life,
      discovered in the British Museum by Nicholson.
191 Graves, Thornton S. "Some Facts about Anthony Aston." Journal
      of English and Germanic Philology, XX (1921), 391-396.
           An attempt to point out and correct errors made by Nichol-
      son (q.v.) in his statements and interpretations relating to
      Aston.
192 Griffith, R. H. "Tony Aston's Fool's Opera." Journal of English
      and Germanic Philology, XXI (1922), 188-189.
           Fixes the date of publication of the Fool's Opera as April 1,
      1731.

Atkyns, Charlotte

193 Tisdall, E. E. P. Mrs. 'Pimpernel' Atkyns: The Strange Story of
      a Drury Lane Actress Who Was the Only Heroine of the French
      Revolution. London: Jarrolds, 1965. 290 pp.
           A popular biography dealing for the most part with the
      revolutionary activities of Charlotte Walpole Atkyns (1758-
      1836). Chapter two concerns her acting career in London and
      her relationship to Sheridan and Garrick.

Attacks on the Theatre

194 Trace, Arthur S., Jr. "The Continuity of Opposition to the Theater
      in England from Gosson to Collier." Ph.D. Stanford University,
      1954. 376 pp. (Publication No. 9513).
           Although the continuity of opposition is apparent, important
      differences are discernible between Elizabethan and Restoration
      attacks on the theatre.

Attributions

195 Troubridge, St. Vincent. "Late Eighteenth-Century Plays."
      Theatre Notebook, I (October, 1946), 62.
           Notes on the authorship of plays listed under "unknown
      authors" by Nicoll.

Audience

196   Mark, Jeffrey. "The Problem of Audiences." Music and Letters,
      IV (1923), 348-355.
         A discussion of the attitudes and behavior of the audience
      in the playhouse, especially at the opera, with consideration
      of Restoration and 18th-century English audiences, among
      others.

197   Allen, Robert J. The Clubs of Augustan London. Harvard Studies
      in English, Vol. VII. Cambridge: Harvard University Press,
      1933. 305 pp.
         An account of the people who made up the clubs in London;
      this book peripherally studies the playwrights and the audience
      of eighteenth-century drama.

198   Ross, Julian L. "Dramatist vs. Audience in the Early Eighteenth
      Century." Philological Quarterly, XII (1933), 78-81.
         An amusing account of the commercial problems of drama-
      tists.

199   Thomas, Carl A. "The Restoration Theater Audience--A Critical
      and Historical Evaluation of the London Playgoers of the Late
      Seventeenth Century, 1660-1700." Ph.D. University of Southern
      California, 1952. 432 pp.
         Thomas attempts to establish the size, composition, taste,
      and behavior of the Restoration audiences in the London theatres.

200   Lynch, James J. Box, Pit, and Gallery: Stage and Society in John-
      son's London. Berkeley and Los Angeles: University of Calif-
      ornia Press, 1953. 362 pp.
         By means of the known facts of the mid-eighteenth-century
      theatre, Lynch attempts "to discover what the repertory re-
      veals about contemporary society." Historical study, limited
      to 1737-1777.

201   Smith, Dane Farnsworth. The Critics in the Audience of the
      London Theatres from Buckingham to Sheridan: A Study of
      Neoclassicism in the Playhouse, 1671-1779. Albuquerque:
      University of New Mexico Press, 1953. 287 pp.
         By means of passages from plays, prologues, and epilogues,
      audience attitudes and behavior are clearly shown.

202   Bevan, Ian. Royal Performance: The Story of Royal Theatre-
      Going. London: Hutchinson, 1954. 280 pp.
         Pages 80-139 covers the Restoration and eighteenth century.

203   Zitner, Sheldon P. "The English Theatre Audience 1660-1700."
      Ph.D. Duke University, 1955.

204   Kinsley, William Benton. "Satiric Audiences in the Augustan Age."
      Ph.D. Yale University, 1965. (Order No. 65-14, 684.)
         "The subtlety and complexity of much Augustan satire gave

its audience an important, and sometimes crucial, role in
determining its meaning in social contexts."

205 Avery, Emmett L. "The Restoration Audience." Philological
     Quarterly, XLV (1966), 54-61.
     A study of some known spectators reveals the wide social
     and intellectual range of the Restoration audience.

206 Love, Harold. "The Myth of the Restoration Audience." Komos,
     I (1967), 49-56.

Augustan

207 Johnson, James William. "The Meaning of 'Augustan.'" Journal
     of the History of Ideas, XIX (1958), 507-522.
     Discusses analogues of English Augustan Age with the
     Augustan Age of Rome and points out that the specific con-
     notations of the term varied with its application to different
     aspects of the English scene, literary, political, and social.

208 Erskine-Hill, Howard. "Augustans on Augustanism: England,
     1665-1759." Renaissance and Modern Studies, XI (1967), 55-83.
     Examines some of the more important passages in which
     Augustans use the word "Augustan," express their understand-
     ing of it, and explicitly or implicitly apply it to their own age.
     Includes references to Dryden, Rowe and Goldsmith.

Austen, Jane

209 Gleason, George Donald. "Dramatic Affinities in the Life and
     Work of Jane Austen." Ph.D. State University of Iowa, 1958.
     Her acquaintance with and interest in the theatre, especial-
     ly school and private theatricals.

Bagley, G.

210 Leech, Clifford. "A Restoration Touring Company." Times
     Literary Supplement, May 31, 1934, p. 392.
     Leech quotes from a license, dated April 14, 1662, granting
     Bagley's company permission to perform Noah's Flood in the
     provinces and suggests that Bagley might be "leader of the first
     licensed touring company of the Restoration." He also comments
     on the apparent appropriateness of the subject matter insofar
     as the more puritanical provinces were concerned.

Baillie, Joanna

211 MacCunn, Florence A. Sir Walter Scott's Friends. Edinburgh
      and London: William Blackwood and Sons, 1909. xiii, 448 pp.
         Includes a chapter on Joanna Baillie as Scott's friend and
      as playwright.
212 Pieszczek, Rudolf [Karl]. Joanna Baillie, ihr Leben, ihre drama-
      tischen Theorien, und ihre Leidenschaftsspiele. Berlin: G. Schade,
      1910. 70, [2] pp.
213 Badstuber, Alfred. Joanna Baillie's Plays. Vienna und Leipzig:
      W. Braumüller, 1911. 119 pp.
         "The Plays on the Passions" analyzed and then judged by
      her dramatic theory of 1798. Her method of characterization
      influenced by books of "characters."
214 Plarr, Victor C. "Sir Walter Scott and Joanna Baillie." The
      Edinburgh Review, CCXVI (October, 1912), 355-371; CCXVII
      (January, 1913), 170-181.
         Prints previously unpublished letters (as of 1913), of Sir
      Walter Scott to Joanna Baillie with comments and explanation
      by the editor from the collection in the Library of the Royal
      College of Surgeons of England. Contains allusions to Joanna's
      plays, particularly The Family Legend.
215 Sears, Lloyd. "The Relation of Joanna Baillie to the English
      Romantic Movement." M.A. University of Kansas, 1921.
216 Meynell, Mrs. Alice. "Joanna Baillie." Second Person Singular
      and Other Essays. 2nd impression. (London, New York:
      Humphrey Milford, Oxford University Press, 1922), 56-61.
         Mrs. Meynell's essay on Joanna Baillie's Plays on the
      Passions concentrates on the comedies, especially The Trial.
217 Carhart, Margaret Sprague. The Life and Work of Joanna Baillie.
      Yale Studies in English, LXIV. New Haven: Yale University
      Press, 1923. 215 pp.
         Presentation of Mrs. Baillie's life, the literary background
      of her works, her dramatic theory, and the stage history of
      her plays. Concludes that Joanna Baillie stands "as the greatest
      Scotch dramatist."
218 Livengood, Bernice I. "Critical Edition of Joanna Baillie's The
      Bride." M.A. University of Kansas, 1927.

Baker, Thomas

219 Baker, Thomas. The Fine Lady's Airs (1709). Edited, with an
      Introduction by John Harrington Smith. Los Angeles: William
      Andrews Memorial Library, 1951. Augustan Reprint Society,
      Publication No. 25.

Introduction is a discussion of Baker's life and career, followed by the text of the play which, in type, resembles Restoration comedy.

Ballad Opera

220 Squire, W. Barclay. "An Index of Tunes in The Ballad Operas."
     The Musical Antiquary, II (October, 1910--July, 1911), 1-17.
     Index of 39 operas (printed editions) 1728-1750 arranged
     alphabetically by title followed by a list of songs alphabetically
     by title of tune and with cross references to the operas.
221 Flood, William H. Grattan. "Irish Musical Bibliography."
     Sammelbände der Internationalen Musikgesellschaft, XIII
     (1911-1912), 458-462.
     List of printed works from 1725-1905. Includes about 100
     titles containing Irish folk melodies scattered through the
     English ballad operas from 1728 through 1748.
222 Sonneck, O. G. [Note]. The Musical Antiquary, II (April, 1911),
     181.
     Calls attention to the fact that The Wedding was omitted
     from Squires' list. The two editions of The Wedding are both
     in the Library of Congress.
223 Tufts, George. "A Bibliography of Ballad Opera." Typewritten
     manuscript. Cambridge, Massachusetts, 1911.
224 Mark, Jeffrey. "Ballad Opera and Its Significance in the History
     of English Stage-Music." London Mercury, VIII (1923), 265-
     278.
     An examination of ballad opera in the early and middle 18th
     century, beginning with late 17th century imitations of Italian
     operas; Mark's conclusion is that ballad opera was successful
     because the form was one with which the English people were
     instinctively sympathetic.
225 Gagey, Edmond McAdoo. Ballad Opera. (Columbia University
     Studies in English and Comparative Literature, No. 130). New
     York: Columbia University Press, 1937. xii, 259 pp.
     Describing the history of the ballad opera as a process of
     "degeneration" after Gay's Beggar's Opera, Gagey traces the
     fortunes of the form on the 18th century stage. Contains a
     bibliography of published and unpublished ballad operas.
226 -----. Ballad Opera. New York: Benjamin Blom, 1964. 259 pp.
     A reprint of the 1937 edition.

Ballet

227 Prunières, Henri. Le Ballet de Cour en France, Avant Benserade

et Lully. Paris: Henri Laurens, 1914. vi, 280 pp.

A study of the development and decline of the Ballet de Cour in the 16th and 17th centuries; the influence of the Pléiade and Italian drama, and the English extension of the genre in the masque; the staging, poetry, and music of the Ballet de Cour. Includes text of "Ballet de la Deliverance de Renaud."

228 McPharlin, Paul. "Eighteenth Century Ballet Masks." Notes and Queries, CLIII (September 24, 1927), 225.

Gaetan Vestris and Jean Georges Noverre are credited with dispensing with the mask.

229 Beaumont, Cyril William. Five Centuries of Ballet Design. London: The Studio, Ltd. [1939]. 136 pp.

Intended as a companion volume to Design for the Ballet. This work attempts to trace "the evolution of design for Ballet from the Italian Renaissance to 1922. The work is profusely illustrated.

230 -----. Ballet Design Past and Present. Privately printed, 1946. xxxi, 216 pp.

A general survey, with comment on the period in England (pp. xxiv-xxv) and illustrations from D'Avenant's masques (pp. 4-5).

231 Haskell, Arnold. Ballet: A Reader's Guide. Published for the National Book League by Cambridge University Press, 1947. 12 pp.

This bibliography, compiled by Arnold Haskell and W. A. Munford, contains a brief introduction on the elements important to a critic of ballet and a bibliography--annotated-- of books designed to introduce the reader to the essential works on the subject. Includes several entries on the history of the ballet.

232 Fletcher, Ifan Kyrle. "An Unpublished Letter of Dauberval." Theatre Notebook, IV (October, 1949), 5-6.

A letter of 1796, referring to contemporary ballet dancers.

Bancroft, John

233 Ticknor, Margaret. "John Bancroft, a Seventeenth Century Dramatist." M.A. George Washington University, 1941.

Banks, John

text

234 Banks, John. The Unhappy Favourite; Or, The Earl of Essex.

Edited by Thomas M. H. Blair. New York: Columbia University Press, 1939. xiv, 143 pp.

This edition presents a facsimile reproduction of the 1682 quarto of the play frequently viewed as the prototype of the "she-tragedy." Included in the volume are a critical biography of Banks, an analysis of the source and tradition of the play, extensive notes to the text, and a bibliography.

biography and criticism

235 Rietmann, Adolphe. The Earle of Essex and Mary Stuart: Two of John Banks' Tragedies, with a Side Reference to Two German Plays on the Same Subjects by Hermann Müller ... Wetzikon: Wirz, 1915. 76 pp.

236 Backus, E. N. "The MS. Play, Anna Bullen." Publications of the Modern Language Association, XLVII (1932), 741-752.

An anonymous manuscript play, Anna Bullen, apparently a copy of an earlier heroic tragedy, may be the source for John Banks' Vertue Betray'd; or, Anna Bullen.

237 [Tupper, Fred Salisbury.] "The Influence of Shakespeare on John Banks." By Thomas Lee [pseud.]. Winthrop Sargent Prize Essay. Harvard University, 1934. 47 pp.

A discussion of the twelve of shakespeare's plays which influenced Banks and how they colored significantly every aspect of the work.

238 -----. "John Banks: A Study in the Origins of the Pathetic Tragedy." Ph.D. Harvard University Press, 1935.

A biographical and critical study of Banks and his plays with emphasis upon the development of a "philosophy of sentimentalism." An analysis of Banks' influence and reputation after 1677 is included.

239 Lumiansky, R. M. "A Note on Blair's Edition of The Unhappy Favourite." Modern Language Notes, LVI (April, 1941), 280-282.

Corrects a reading in The Secret History of the Most Renowned Queen Elizabeth and the Earl of Essex, printed in 12°, London, 1680, which was the source for Banks' The Unhappy Favourite.

240 Bowers, Fredson. "The Variant Sheets in John Banks' Cyrus the Great, 1699." Studies in Bibliography, IV (1951-1952), 174-182.

Bowers discusses the order of setting and printing these variant sheets.

241 Hochuli, Hans. John Banks: Eine Studie zum Drama des späten 17. Jahrhunderts. Bern: A. Francke, 1952. 95 pp.

Banks' plays illustrate the transition from late-seventeenth-

century baroque to the classicism of the early eighteenth
century.

242 Knepler, Henry W. "Maxwell Anderson: A Historical Parallel-
Problems for the Poetic Dramatist." Queen's Quarterly, LXIV
(1957), 250-263.
Parallels with John Banks.

243 Devlin, James J. "The Albion Queens by John Banks: A Critical
Edition." Ph.D. University of Pennsylvania, 1958.

244 -----. "The Dramatis Personae and the Dating of John Banks'
The Albion Queens." Notes and Queries, New Ser., X (1963),
213-215.
Corrects the list of actors for the 1704 production at Drury
Lane. Additional remarks on the date of publication.

Barry, Elizabeth

245 Ham, Roswell G. "Thomas Otway, Rochester, and Mrs. Barry."
Notes and Queries, CXLIX (September 5, 1925), 165-167.
Discusses references to Barry's career and relations with
Otway and Rochester.

246 Summers, Montague. "Betterton and Mrs. Barry in Hamlet."
London Times Literary Supplement, March 29, 1934, p. 229.
[Corr. by C. K. Adams, April 5, 1934, p. 244.]
Controversy over which actor and actress is represented
in Garrick Club paintings Nos. 115, 439.

247 Hook, Lucyle. "Mrs. Elizabeth Barry and Mrs. Anne Bracegirdle,
Actresses, Their Careers from 1672 to 1695, A Study in Influences." Ph.D. New York University, 1945.

248 -----. Mrs. Elizabeth Barry and Mrs. Anne Bracegirdle Actresses,
Their Careers from 1672 to 1695: A Study in Influences. New
York: New York University Press, 1950. 13 pp.
This is an abstract of an earlier thesis (1945).

249 Shaaber, M. A. "A Letter from Mrs. Barry." University of Pennsylvania Library Chronicle, XVI (1950), 46-49.
Publishes a letter from Elizabeth Barry to Lady Lisburne
dated January 5, 1699.

250 Hook, Lucyle. "Portraits of Elizabeth Barry and Anne Brace-
girdle." Theatre Notebook, XV (Summer, 1961), 129-137.
The two actresses, identified as Britannia and Flora in
Kneller's large Equestrian Picture of William III, now in
Hampton Court. Traces source of engravings in The Biograph-
ical Mirrour.

Barry, Spranger

251 Montague-Smith, P. W. "Ancestry of the Actor, Spranger Barry."
     Notes and Queries, CXCIII (October 2, 1948), 432-433.
        Genealogical study.
252 Sadleir, Thomas U. "Ancestry of the Actor, Spranger Barry."
     Notes and Queries, CXCIV (April 2, 1949), 150.
        Additional genealogical detail.

Bath

253 Barbeau, A. Life and Letters at Bath in the XVIIIth Century . . .
     With a Preface by Austin Dobson. London: W. Heinemann,
     1904. xxxi, 328 pp.
        A scholarly history of happenings in Bath, from the end of
     the 17th century to the middle of the 19th, with emphasis on
     the activities of literary persons. Full list of sources quoted,
     and heavy documentation in notes, though little incorporated
     in text.
254 [Melville, Lewis Saul Benjamin]. Bath Under Beau Nash. London:
     E. Nash, 1907. 321 pp.
        An account of life at Bath within the context of Nash's
     biography; draws heavily on sources, such as letters, not
     available to Goldsmith while writing Nash's life. Includes Dr.
     Oliver's "A Faint Sketch of the Life, Character and Manners
     of the Late Mr. Nash," and Nash's epitaph by William King.
255 Price, Cecil. "Some Movements of the Bath Company, 1729-
     1734." Theatre Notebook, I (October, 1946), 55-56.
        A calendar of performances through the West Country.
256 Wood, Frederick Thomas. "Theatrical Performances at Bath in
     the Eighteenth Century." Notes and Queries, CXCII (November
     1, 1947), 477-478; (November 15, 1947), 486-490; (December
     13, 1947), 539-541; (December 27, 1947), 552-558; CXCIII
     (January 24, 1948), 38-40; (March 6, 1948), 92-93; (June 12,
     1948), 253-255.
        A day by day listing of performances, derived from play-
     bills, local papers, and the Bath Theatre MS register for 1770
     and other sources.

Beattie, James

257 Beattie, James. London Diary, 1773. Edited by Ralph S. Walker.
     Aberdeen University Studies, No. 122. Aberdeen: University of
     Aberdeen Press, 1946. 146 pp.

A general view of London life and conditions by a little
known member of the Burney - Garrick - Johnson circle.
Frequent references are made to theatrical events.

258 -----. James Beattie's Day-Book, 1773-1798. Edited, with an
Introduction and Notes, by Ralph S. Walker. Aberdeen: Printed
for The Third Spalding Club, 1948. VII, 9-227, [1], 14 pp.
Gives a picture of the cost of living and travel in Scotland
and beyond.

Beaumont and Fletcher

259 Sprague, Arthur C. Beaumont and Fletcher on the Restoration
Stage. Cambridge: Harvard University Press, 1926. xx, 298 pp.
An excellent though limited stage history of the plays from
1660 to the death of Betterton in 1710. Discusses twenty adaptations of the plays during the same period, but does not discuss
the influence of Beaumont and Fletcher on Restoration drama.

260 Wilson, John Harold. The Influence of Beaumont and Fletcher on
Restoration Drama. Ohio State University Press, 1928. vii,
156 pp.
There are two main parts--a survey of the stage history
of the Beaumont-Fletcher dramas between 1660 and 1710 and
an analysis of the alterations and adaptations of those dramas.
A widespread filching of ideas by Restoration playwrights from
the elder dramatists.

261 Warren, Austin. "Pope's Index to Beaumont and Fletcher." Modern
Language Notes, XLVI (1931), 515-517.
Describes a MS. in the British Museum containing three
sheets of an incomplete index to the 1679 folio of Beaumont
and Fletcher by Pope. Describes some of Pope's annotations
and concludes that Pope at one time entertained the idea of
editing Shakespeare's contemporaries.

262 Van Lennep, William. "'The New-Made Nobleman.'" Times
Literary Supplement, June 20, 1936, p. 523.
The play referred to by this title and performed in 1661
was actually Beaumont and Fletcher's Noble Gentleman.

263 Bennett, Charles H. "A Boswell Reference." Times Literary
Supplement, May 18, 1940, p. 248.
Treats Boswell's reference to the collaboration of
Beaumont and Fletcher.

264 Wallis, Lawrence B. Fletcher, Beaumont and Company: Entertainers to the Jacobean Gentry. New York: King's Crown
Press, 1947. xii, 315 pp.
Includes various comments on the reputation of Beaumont
and Fletcher during the Restoration period.

265 Rulfs, Donald J. "Beaumont and Fletcher on the London Stage,
      1776-1833." Publications of the Modern Language Association,
      LXIII (1948), 1245-1264.
         Notes the revivals during the period and describes the re-
      visions in the plays to suit contemporary tastes.
266 Appleton, William W. Beaumont and Fletcher: A Critical Study.
      London: George Allen and Unwin; Fair Lawn, N.J.: Essential
      Books, 1956. 131 pp.
         Contains chapters on Restoration and 18th Century.
267 Sprague, Arthur Colby. Beaumont and Fletcher on the Restoration
      Stage. New York: Benjamin Blom, 1965. 229 pp.
         A reprint of the 1926 edition. History of the plays between
      1660 and 1710.
268 Wilson, John Harold. The Influence of Beaumont and Fletcher on
      Restoration Drama. New York: Benjamin Blom, 1967. 162 pp.
         Reprint of the 1928 edition.

Beeston, William

269 Nicoll, Allardyce. "Some Notes on William Beeston." Times
      Literary Supplement, November 22, 1923, p. 789.
         A biographical sketch of William Beeston, manager of the
      Salisbury Court theatre during the reign of Charles II.
270 -----. "The Rights of Beeston and D'Avenant in Elizabethan Plays."
      Review of English Studies, I (January, 1925), 84-91.
         Davenant's actors, descendants of William Beeston's company,
      considered themselves as inheritors of certain prompt copies
      of Shakespeare's plays in Beeston's possession.

Behn, Aphra

works

271 Summers, Montague, ed. The Works of Aphra Behn. 6 vols. Lon-
      don: William Heinemann, 1915.
         First modern edition of Mrs. Behn's work. In a memoir in
      the first volume, tries to clear up some of the mysteries con-
      nected with her life: her maiden name, father's profession,
      place of birth, moral character, and collaborator (does not
      believe Ravenscroft was). Presents her as a writer of comedies
      that should give her high place in our literature. Plays are in-
      cluded in first four volumes, together with arguments, source,
      theatrical history, and notes.
272 Behn, Aphra. The Works of Aphra Behn. Edited by Montague Sum-
      mers. 6 vols. New York: Phaeton Press, 1967.
         Facsimile of 1915 edition.

selected writings

273 -----. Selected Writings of the Ingenious Mrs. Aphra Behn . . .
Together with a Critical Portrait by Robert Phelps by way of
Introduction. [New York]: Grove Press [1950]. 243 pp.
   Contains the text of four novels and the comedy The Dutch
Lover, unedited, with the accompanying "Epistle to the Reader."
The introduction is concerned largely with Aphra Behn's bio-
graphy in relation to the background of her times and with her
works, especially her views on theatre.

single texts

274 -----. The Rover. Edited by Frederick M. Link. (Regents
Restoration Drama Series). Lincoln: University of Nebraska
Press, 1967.
   Includes introduction, notes and chronology.

biography and criticism

275 Siegel, P. "Aphra Behns Gedichte und Prosawerke." Anglia, XXV
(1902), 329-385.
276 Bernbaum, E. "Mrs. Behn's Biography a Fiction." Publications of
the Modern Language Association, XXVIII (1913), 432-453.
   Life and Memoirs of Mrs. Behn is worthless as a biographical
document but important for the history of fiction. Anticipates
the method of Defoe.
277 Matthews, Albert. [Correspondence.] Notes and Queries, 11th
Ser., IX (February 7, 1914), 116.
   Suggests the possibility that the book referred to in Mrs.
Behn's The Feign'd Curtizans as being by Cartwright is The
Preacher's Travels by John Cartwright of Magdalene College,
Oxford, published in 1611 and later revised.
278 Norman, William. "Mrs. Behn's Emperor of the Moon." Notes
and Queries, 11th Ser., IX (April 4, 1914), 275.
   Says production in 1777 at the Patagonian Theatre was a
revival. Identifies location of the theatre as being in Exeter
Change on a portion of the site of Burleigh House. Last record
of performance in 1779 was "The Apothesis of Punch. A Satyri-
cal Masque with a Monody on the Death of the Late Master
Punch."
279 S., M. [Correspondence.] Notes and Queries, 11th Ser., IX
(March 21, 1914), 231.
   Emperor of the Moon by Mrs. Behn, "after lying dormant
for many years was acted with considerable alterations at the
Patagonian Theatre in 1777."

280 -----. "Mrs. Behn's Emperor of the Moon." Notes and Queries,
    11th Ser., IX (May 16, 1914), 394.
        Traces the origin of the farce to the French Arlequin Em-
    pereur and to Italian commedia dell'arte.
281 Blashfield, Evangeline. Portraits and Backgrounds; Hrotsvitha,
    Aphra Behn, Aissé, Rosalba Carriera. New York: G. Scribner's
    Sons, 1917. vi, 493 pp.
        Of the four women depicted here, only Mrs. Aphra Behn's
    portrait holds interest for the student of Restoration drama.
    She is called the inventor of the novel with a purpose and the
    first woman who made a livelihood through her writings, in-
    cluding her dramatic works. Contains interesting references to
    contemporary playwrights.
282 Benjamins, H. D. "Een Koninklijke Slaaf in Suriname: Roman
    Door Aphra Behn, Aanteekewing Betreffende de Schrijfster."
    De West-Indische Eids (1919), 474-480.
        A short biography of Aphra Behn, together with an apprecia-
    tion of Oroonoko, or The Royal Slave, especially as an abolition-
    ist work.
283 More, Paul Elmer. "A Restoration Bluestocking." With the Wits.
    Shelburne Essays, Tenth Series. (Boston: Houghton Mifflin
    Company, 1919), 69-97.
        An essay on Mrs. Aphra Behn maintaining that her judgment
    that ". . . comedy was never meant either for a converting or
    a conforming ordinance" is closer to the truth about her own
    plays and others of the period than the one which claims the
    Restoration dramatists were moral censors of the age.
284 Johnson, Edwin D. "Aphra Behn's 'Oroonoko.'" Journal of Negro
    History, X (July, 1925), 334-342.
        On the historical validity of the novel (dramatized by Southerne).
285 Bennett, R. E. "A Bibliographical Correction." Review of English
    Studies, III (October, 1927), 450-451.
        Explains an allusion in Mrs. Aphra Behn's play (1687).
286 Sackville-West, V. Aphra Behn: The Incomparable Astrea. Lon-
    don: Gerald Howe, 1927. 93 pp.
        A memoir of Aphra Behn (1640-1689), "the first woman in
    England to earn her living by her pen."
287 Gilder, Rosamond. "Aphra Behn." Theatre Arts Monthly, XII
    (June, 1928), 397-409.
        A sketch of the career of the "first and foremost" of wo-
    men playwrights in the Restoration, with her portrait by Lely
    and a portrait of Killigrew by Abbey.
288 Jerrold, Walter and Clare Jerrold. Five Queer Women. New York,
    London: Brentano, 1929. xii, 356 pp.

Aphra Behn, Mary Manley, Susanna Centlivre, Eliza Haywood, and Letitia Pilkington.

289 Donald, H. G. "A Critical Analysis of the Writings of Aphra
     Behn." M.A. McGill University, 1930.

290 Sackville-West, V. Six Brilliant English Women. London:
     Gerald Howe, 1930.
          Some 80 pages are devoted to a brief biography of Aphra
     Behn, attempting to prove that Mrs. Behn was a lady of great
     accomplishments. Highly romantic in tone. Provides a biblio-
     graphy of Mrs. Behn's works.

291 Harris, Brice. "Aphra Behn's Bajazet to Gloriana." Times
     Literary Supplement, February 9, 1933, p. 92.
          Seeks to prove that Aphra Behn is indeed the author of
     Bajazet to Gloriana, as had been only suggested hitherto.

292 Platt, H. G. "Astrea and Celadon: an Untouched Portrait of Aphra
     Behn." Publications of the Modern Language Association,
     XLIX (1934), 544-559.
          Mr. Platt attempts to provide a biography of Mrs. Behn not
     based on her own words, as most others have been. Astrea
     and Celadon are pseudonyms for William Scot (son of the
     regicide, Thomas Scot) and Aphra Behn.

293 Graham, C. B. "An Echo of Jonson in Aphra Behn's Sir Patient
     Fancy." Modern Language Notes, LIII (1938), 278-279.
          Mrs. Behn borrowed three lines from Volpone.

294 Mathews, Ernest G. "Montfleury's Ecole des Jaloux and Aphra
     Behn's The False Count." Modern Language Notes, LIV
     (1939), 438-439.
          Comment on the similarities and differences between Mrs.
     Behn's play and its French source.

295 Van Lennep, William. "Two Restoration Comedies." Times
     Literary Supplement, January 28, 1939, pp. 57-58.
          Bibliographical data about the anonymous comedy, The
     Revenge (1680), and Mrs. Behn's The False Count (1682).

296 Bowman, Wayne. "The Comedies of Mrs. Aphra Behn." M.A.
     University of North Carolina, 1940.

297 Summers, Montague. "Aphra Behn and Montfleury." Modern
     Language Notes, LVI (November, 1941), 562.
          Calls attention to his article in Notes and Queries (CLIX
     [October 18, 1930], 274-275) stating that Mrs. Behn's The
     False Count is derived from Antoine Montfleury's L'Ecole
     des Jaloux, sometimes played in the 18th century as La
     Fausse Turquie.

298 Baker, Herschel. "Mrs. Behn Forgets." University of Texas
     Studies in English, XXII (1942), 121-123.

299 Hill, Rowland M. "Aphra Behn's Use of Setting." Modern

Language Quarterly, VII (1946), 189-203.

Mainly about the novels, describing her growing interest in location and background description.

300 ·Geyer, Richard B. "Aphra Behn: Restoration Dramatist." M.A. Miami University, 1947.

301 Woodcock, George. The Incomparable Aphra. London: Boardman, 1948. 248 pp.

A thorough study of Mrs. Behn, with particular attention to her comic techniques.

302 Wakefield-Richmond. "The Life and Works of Mrs. Aphra Behn, with a Special Study of Oroonoko." B. Litt. Oxford University (St. Hilda's), 1949.

303 Hahn, Emily. Aphra Behn. London: Jonathan Cape [1951]. 319 pp.

A light biography which pays little attention to the plays.

304 Mundy, P. D. "Aphra Behn, Novelist and Dramatist (1640?-1689)." Notes and Queries, CXCIX (1954), 199-201.

The exact identity of Aphra Behn's father is still in doubt.

305 Hogan, Floriana T. "The Spanish Comedia and the English Comedy of Intrigue with Special Reference to Aphra Behn." Ph.D. Boston University, 1955.

306 Mundy, P. D. "Aphra Behn (1640?-1689)." Notes and Queries, CC (1955), 23.

Biographical information on Mrs. Aphra Behn, focusing on the problem of parentage.

307 Hamblen, Abigail Ann. "Lady Who Lived By Her Wits." Dalhousie Review, XXXVII (1957), 52-56.

Very little related to her plays.

308 Wermuth, Paul C. "Bacon's Rebellion in the London Theatre." Virginia Cavalcade, VII (Summer, 1957), 38-39.

Discusses Mrs. Behn's The Widdow Ranter; or, The History of Bacon in Virginia (with prologue and epilogue by Dryden) and compares the play with the historical event.

309 Cameron, W. J. "George Cranville and the 'Remaines' of Aphra Behn." Notes and Queries, CCIV (1959), 88-92.

310 Sheffey, Ruthe Turner. "The Literary Reputation of Aphra Behn." Ph.D. University of Pennsylvania, 1959.

311 Cameron, William James. New Light on Aphra Behn: An Investigation into the Facts and Fictions Surrounding her Journey to Surinam in 1663 and her Activities as a Spy in Flanders in 1666. University of Auckland. Monographs, No. 5. [Auckland], 1961. 106 pp.

Discusses Mrs. Behn's possible journey to Surinam, her work as a royalist agent in Antwerp, and her first biographies ---to illuminate the autobiographical information in Oroonoko and The Fair Jilt. Concludes that her statements about her

life should not be dismissed as mere fiction though they are
not yet established as fact.

312 Hargreaves, Henry Allen. "The Life and Plays of Mrs. Aphra
    Behn." Ph.D. Duke University, 1961.

       Examines Mrs. Behn's plays, in order to determine some
of the characteristics which make them successful in the
Restoration theatre.

313 Andrew, Richard H. "Social Themes in the Plays of Aphra Behn."
    M.A. Bowling Green State University, 1965.

314 Barrett, Alberta Gregg. "Plot, Characterization, and Theme in
    the Plays of Aphra Behn." Ph.D. University of Pennsylvania,
    1965. (Order No. 66-4599).

       Analyzes the works of Aphra Behn from the standpoint of
their dramatic potentiality, ability to portray human nature,
and satiric import.

Bell, John

315 Morison, Stanley. John Bell, 1745-1831, Bookseller, Printer,
    Publisher, Typefounder, Journalist. Cambridge: Cambridge
    University Press, 1930. xi, 166 pp.

       Contains descriptions and illustrations of Bell's editions
of several books pertaining to theatre, e.g., the acting edition
of Shakespeare's plays, British Theatre, Nipclose's The
Theatres, and Rowe's Tamerlane.

Bellamy, George

316 Dissell, Dorothy G. "An Apology for the Life of George Ann
    Bellamy, a Mingled Yarn." Ph.D. Boston University, 1954.

317 Hartmann, Cyril Hughes. Enchanting Bellamy. London: Wm.
    Heinemann, Ltd., 1956. xi, 339 pp.

       A biography based on George Ann Bellamy's own An Apology
for the Life of George Ann Bellamy, late of Covent Garden.
Brief bibliography and index.

318 Sewell, Rev. Brocard, O. Carm. "George Anne Bellamy." Wise-
    man Review, CCXXXV (1961), 56-59.

       A brief biography of the eighteenth century London actress
George Anne Bellamy.

Benefit Performance

319 McKenty, David Edward. "The Benefit System in Augustan Drama."
    Ph.D. University of Pennsylvania, 1966. (Order No. 66-10,
    643).

Augustan poets and performances were paid not with cash
but with the opportunity to risk capital in hope of great gain.
The effects of this "benefit system" on the playwrights, actors,
and the selection of plays are studied.

Berkeley, John

320 Falk, Bernard. The Berkeleys of Berkeley Square and Some of
     Their Kinsfolk. With 33 illustrations. London, New York,
     Melbourne: Hutchinson & Co., Ltd., 1944. 284 pp.
          Concerns Sir John Berkeley (1607?-1678), and the various
     descendants. The use of Pepys material, and reference to the
     theatre, can be found in the Diary.

Betterton, Thomas

single texts

321 Purcell, Henry. Dioclesian. Edited by Sir Frederick J. Bridge
     and John Pointer. London: Novello and Company, Ltd., 1900.
     xviii, 159 pp.
          The text of The Prophetess; or, The History of Dioclesian
     adapted by Thomas Betterton from Beaumont and Fletcher's
     play of the same title, and Purcell's complete score for the
     opera edited from the original published in 1691; also three
     songs written for a revival of the work in 1691 and 1692.

biography and criticism

322 Kopp, Wilhelm. "Das Tragödien-Kostuem von Betterton bis Kem-
     ble in seiner Entwicklung zur historischen Treue, 1660-
     1817." Ph.D. Bonn Dissertation, 1930.
323 Paul, Henry N. "Players' Quartos and Duodecimos of Hamlet."
     Modern Language Notes, XLIX (1934), 369-375.
          A description of Theobald's stage edition of 1743, and the
     Betterton text of 1683.
324 Summers, Montague. "Betterton and Mrs. Barry in Hamlet."
     London Times Literary Supplement, March 29, 1934, p. 229.
          Controversy over which actor and actress is represented
     in Garrick Club paintings Nos. 115, 439. See also article by
     C. K. Adams, April 5, 1934, p. 244.
325 Snodgrass, A. E. "The Best Actor in the World." Cornhill
     Magazine, CLII (December, 1935), 719-722.
          A brief portrait and eulogy of Betterton's acting abilities.

326 Heil, Liselotte. "Die Darstellung der englischen Tragödie zur
     Zeit Bettertons, 1660-1710. Theater, Bühnenreform, In-
     szenierungs-und Schauspielerstil." Inaugural Dissertation.
     Berlin, 1936.

327 Summers, Montague. "The Comedies of Thomas Betterton."
     Notes and Queries, CLXX (1936), 454-456.
          Bibliographical and critical commentary upon Betterton's
     comedies with emphasis upon The Amorous Widow (c. 1670),
     The Woman Made a Justice (c. 1670), and The Revenge (c.
     1680).

328 Seely, Frederick Franklin. "Thomas Betterton, Dramatist."
     Ph.D. University of Iowa, 1942.

329 Sprague, Arthur Colby. "Did Betterton Chant?" Theatre Notebook,
     I (October, 1946), 54-55.
          The evidence that he did is not quite conclusive.

330 Bottomly, Gordon. "Did Betterton Chant?" Theatre Notebook, I
     (January, 1947), 75.
          Additions to A. C. Sprague's note (I, October, 1946).

331 Dent, Edward, John Stead and Gordon Bottomly. "Did Betterton
     Chant?" Theatre Notebook, I (July, 1947), 115-116.
          Continuing controversy over A. C. Sprague's note (I,
     October, 1946).

332 Sands, Mollie. "Did Betterton Chant?" Theatre Notebook, I
     (April, 1947), 99-100.
          Additions to A. C. Sprague's note (I, October, 1946).

333 Armstrong, William A. "The Acting of Thomas Betterton."
     English, X (1954-1955), 55-57.
          Betterton's long career on the stage (1659-1710) represented
     the Restoration theatre's highest achievements in acting and
     stagecraft.

334 Bowers, Fredson. "A Bibliographical History of the Fletcher-
     Betterton Play, The Prophetess, 1690." Library, 5th ser.,
     XVI (1961), 169-175.
          A bibliographical study of the first and second edition, to-
     gether with the issues, of Thomas Betterton's opera, based on
     Fletcher's Prophetess, and published by Jacob Tonson in 1690.

335 Dickens, Louis George. "The Story of Appius and Virginia in
     English Literature." Ph.D. University of Rochester, 1963.
     (Order No. 63-7762).
          Includes a discussion of the dramatic versions of Betterton
     and Dennis.

336 Bartholomeusz, Dennis. "The Davenant-Betterton Macbeth."
     Komos, I (1967), 41-48.

Betty, Master

337 Altick, Richard D. "The Marvelous Child of the English Stage."
      College English, VII (October, 1945), 78-85.
          Master Betty's performances in 1803-1805 and their
      rhapsodic reception are analyzed, so as to reveal the low
      level of theatrical taste in the last decades of the 18th century.

Bibiena Family

338 Mayor, Alpheus Hyatt. The Bibiena Family. New York: Bittner,
      1945. 37 pp.
          A study of the family of stage designers, with illustrations
      and genealogical tables.
339 Isaacs, Edith J.R. "The Bibiena Family." Theatre Arts, XXX
      (May, 1946), 305-309.
          A study of the family of theatrical designers, motivated by
      the appearance of A. Hyatt Mayor's book The Bibiena Family
      (1945).

Bible

340 Coleman, Edward Davidson. "The Bible in English Drama; an
      Annotated List of Plays Dealing with Biblical Themes, in-
      cluding Translations from Other Languages." Bulletin of the
      New York Public Library, XXXIV (1930), 695; 785; 839; XXXV
      (1931), 31; 103; 167.
          Following an interesting introduction on the use of the Bible
      in English drama are annotated lists of English plays based on
      Biblical themes, including translations to be found at the New
      York Public Library, The Library of Congress, The British
      Museum and other sources.
341 Roston, M. "The Use in English Drama of Themes from the Old
      Testament and Its Apocrypha." Ph.D. London University (Ex-
      ternal), 1961.

Bibliography

342 Daly, Augustin. Catalogue of the Valuable Literary and Art Pro-
      perty Gathered by the Late Augustin Daly, To Be Disposed of
      At Absolute Public Sale. Part 2. New York, 1900.
          The main catalog is in dictionary form, authors, titles
      and subjects in one alphabet. Other sections list separately
      autographs, plays, etc. Entries include publication informa-
      tion, format, and brief description of illustrations. Bound with
      list of prices realized.

343 Greg, Walter Wilson. A List of English Plays Written Before
     1643 and Printed Before 1700. London: Printed for the Biblio-
     graphical Society by Blades, East and Blades, 1900. [ix]-xi,
     158 pp.
          A descriptive bibliography arranged alphabetically by author,
     with plays of each author listed chronologically. Editions of
     separate plays subsequent to a collected edition are omitted,
     as are the numerous reprints of Shakespeare, Beaumont and
     Fletcher, and Jonson.

344 McKee, Thomas Jefferson. Catalogue of the Library of the Late
     Thomas Jefferson McKee...to be Sold at Auction...by John
     Anderson, Jr. 9 parts in 3 vols. [New York: D. Taylor and Co.,
     1900-1906.]
          Part II covers the drama in its histories, biographies and
     controversies--a collection of biographical, critical, and
     historical material pertinent to darma. Part III contains mater-
     ial on English plays of the 16th, 17th and 18th centuries. Gives
     full bibliographical information for each work, a description of
     the book, and sometimes additional notes.

345 Reader's Guide to Periodical Literature. New York: H. W. Wilson
     Co., 1900--.

346 Lefferts, Marshall Clifford. A Check-list of the Library of Mr.
     Marshall C. Lefferts ... Purchased and for sale by George H.
     Richmond. New York, 1901. 103 pp.
          Three sections, "Americana," "English Literature," and
     "Dramatic Works, and Plays," with items listed alphabetically
     by author, entries including title, date, and very brief description
     of size and binding. A number of 17th century editions of Restor-
     ation plays are listed.

347 Dix, E. R. McC., Compiler. The List of Books, Tracts, Broad-
     sides, &c., Printed in Dublin From 1601 to 1700. [Parts 3 and
     4. 1651-1700]. Dublin: T. G. O'Donoghue; London: B. Dobell,
     1902-1905. 2 Parts.
          Each page is divided into six columns, giving the date, author,
     title, size, printer, owner or reference.

348 Greg, Walter Wilson. A List of Masques, Pageants, &c., Sup-
     plementary to a List of English Plays. London: Printed for the
     Bibliographical Society by Blades, East and Blades, 1902. [vii]-
     xi, 35, [i]-[xxxi] pp.
          A descriptive bibliography, the works listed chronologically
     within an alphabetical arrangement by author. Also contains
     an essay introducing the subject of dramatic bibliography,
     advertisement lists, the early play lists, and addenda and cor-
     rigenda to A List of English Plays.

349 Toedteberg, Augustus. Catalogue of the Collection of Augustus
     Toedteberg... To Be Sold at Auction...by the Anderson Auction
     Company. 34 vols. [New York: D. Taylor & Co., 1903-1904].
          Primarily prints, drawings, autographs and playbills, books
     included in Part I. Arranged alphabetically for selling sessions.
     Numerous Restoration items.
350 Courtney, William Pridaux. A Register of National Bibliography.
     With a Selection of the Chief Bibliographical Books and Articles
     Printed in Other Countries. 3 vols. London: Archibald Constable
     and Company, 1905-1912.
          The first two volumes contain a list of bibliographies published
     before 1905; volume three is a supplement with approximately
     10,000 added references.
351 Nettleton, G. H. "The Books of Lydia Languish's Circulating Library."
     Journal of English and Germanic Philology, V (1905), 492-500.
          This study, based solely upon contemporary book notices and
     reviews in English periodicals, is intentionally confined to the
     books never previously located, those located incorrectly by
     previous critics, and "a few unfamiliar books about which new
     material from contemporary sources can be profitably supplied."
352 Poole, Lucius. Catalogue of the Dramatic Collection of the Late
     Lucius Poole, etc., of Boston, Comprising Many Rare and In-
     teresting Books Relating to the Biography and History of the Stage.
     Libbie & Co., Auctioneers. For sale April 20-21, 1905. 125 pp.
          Arranged alphabetically by author. Brief description of format,
     with extra notes on particularly rare or extensively illustrated
     items. Some 18th century items about the stage.
353 Terry, William. Catalogue of the Dramatic and American His-
     torical Library of W. H. Terry. To be sold, June 14 and 15,
     [21 and 22], 1906, by the Anderson Auction Co. [New York,
     1906]. 2 parts.
          A few 18th century editions of Restoration plays. Some
     playbills and extra illustrated volumes on lives of American
     and English players.
354 O'Donoghue, Freeman. British Museum Catalogue; Catalogue of
     Engraved British Portraits Preserved in the Department of
     Prints and Drawings in the British Museum. 6 vols. London:
     The British Museum, 1908-1925.
          Alphabetical listing of subjects with brief description of
     portrait and name of the painter and/or engraver. Vol. VI is
     a supplement with indexes of painters and engravers.
355 Clarence, Reginald pseud. for H. J. Eldredge. The Stage Cyclo-
     paedia. A Bibliography of Plays. An Alphabetical List of Plays
     and Other Stage Pieces of Which Any Record Can Be Found
     Since the Commencement of The English Stage, Together with

Descriptions, Authors' Names, Dates and Places of Production,
and Other Useful Information, Comprising in All Nearly 50,000
Plays and Extending Over a Period of Upwards of 500 Years.
London: The Stage, 1909. 503 pp.

The number of entries is closer to 30,000. A number of
errors throughout, but still of value for quick reference.

356 Old English Plays: Noted Bibliographically and Biographically. A
Catalogue with Selling Prices Affixed, of a Very Extensive Collection of Old English Plays, Offered for Sale by Pickering
and Chatto, London. London: Pickering and Chatto [1909].

A listing of 1450 entries, arranged by author, with full title
and description of book annotations for most entries of biographical and historical information. An addenda appeared in
the same year.

357 Casaide, Seamus. "Bibliography of Local Printing." The Irish Book
Lover, II (1910), 4-6.

A bibliography of bibliographies of 17th and 18th century
books and newspapers printed in Irish towns.

358 Drama Index. 40 Vols. Boston, Massachusetts: F. W. Faxon Co.,
1910-1952.

Part II of the Annual Magazine Subject Index, 1907-1952.

359 Greg, Walter W. "Notes on Dramatic Bibliographers." Malone
Society Collections. Oxford: University Press, 1911. Vol. 29,
Parts IV and V, pp. 324-340. Also, Library, 4th ser., XI,
No. 2 (1930), 162-172.

Description and evaluation of the work of 17th and 18th century compilers of lists and catalogues of stage plays and biographies of players.

360 Drama League of America. A Selected List of Essays and Books
About the Drama and the Theatre, Exclusive of Biography...
Arranged by Frank Choteau Brown. [Tufts College, Mass.:
Tufts College Press, ᶜ1912]. 27 pp.

The bibliography is a highly selective list of works which
appeared between 1875 and 1911. The general subject category
of each work is indicated.

361 Materials for the Study of the English Drama (Excluding Shakespeare). Chicago, Illinois: The University of Chicago Press,
1912. 89 pp.

A selected list of books in the Newberry library.

362 Newberry Library, Chicago. Materials for the Study of the English
Drama (excluding Shakespeare), a Selected List of Books in
the Newberry Library. Chicago: The Newberry Library [1912].
vii, 89 pp.

This list represents works deemed most useful to the largest
number of persons studying English drama. Works are listed

under nine subject classifications. The listings provide publication facts and a few brief annotations.

363 Peddie, Robert A. National Bibliographies. London: Grafton and
Co., 1912. vi, 34 pp.
A descriptive catalogue of the works which register the
books published in each country.

364 Bibliothek Weisstein. Edited by Fedor von Zobeltitz. Im Aufrage
des Konigl. 2 vols. Baurats Herman Weisstein fur die Gesellschaft der Bibliophelen, 1913.
Vol. II contains a bibliographical listing of English works in
Weisstein's library.

365 Drama League of America. A Selective List of Essays and Books
About the Theatre, Exclusive of Biography, and of Five Plays
Printed in English During 1912. Arranged by Frank Choteau
Brown. [Tufts College, Mass.: Tufts College Press, ᶜ1913.]
16 pp.
A brief bibliography includes some works on Restoration
and 18th-century theatre.

366 Eyre, George E. B. A Transcript of the Registers of the Worship-
ful Company of Stationers from 1640-1708 A.D. 3 vols. London:
Privately Printed, 1913-1914.

367 Rondel, Auguste. Conférence sur la Bibliographie Dramatique et
sur les Collections du Théâtre, Donneé, le 4 decembre 1912.
[Lille: impr. Lefebvre-Ducrocq, 1913.] 31 pp.
A speech by M. Rondel indicating the need for bibliographical
investigation of theatre, possible sources of material. Though
the emphasis is on French theatre, there is discussion of the
need for work on foreign theatre.

368 Taylor, Douglas. Catalogue of Library Autographs, Prints and
Playbills, Including the Fine Collection of Extra-illustrated
Books of the Late Douglas Taylor, Esq. . . . To be Sold
Nov. 24, 25, 26 and 28, 1913. New York: The Anderson Auction
Company [1913]. 231 pp.
The catalogue is arranged alphabetically in four daily lots,
and includes autographs from 18th century actors and actresses.
Item entries give dates, brief description, and indication of
rarity.

369 Catalogo. Museo Teatrale alla Scala. Milano: Alfieri e Lacroix,
1914. 116 pp.

370 Club of Odd Volumes, Boston. Exhibition: Prints, Playbills, Advertisements, and Autograph Letters to Illustrate the History
of the Boston Stage from 1791 to 1825. From the collection of
Mr. Robert Gould Shaw. April 20 to April 25, 1914, open from
2 p.m. to 6 p.m. [Boston, 1914].

A total of 172 items described in detail. Includes many
relevant to Restoration and eighteenth-century theatre (e.g.,
an advertisement for a production of The Mourning Bride
[1799]; a playbill for a production of Cato [1795]. There are
biographical sketches of some performers.

371 A Guide to the Reports of Manuscripts of Private Families,
Corporations, and Institutions in Great Britain, and Ireland.
2 vols. in 3. London: W. M. Stationery Office for the Historical Manuscripts Commission, 1914-1938.

372 Sonneck, Oscar George Theodore. Catalogue of Opera Librettos
Printed before 1800. 2 Vols. Washington, D.C.: U. S. Government Printing Office, 1914.
"About 6,000 entries arranged alphabetically under title,
accompanied by historical, descriptive, and bibliographical
notes."

373 Subject Index to Periodicals. London: Library Association.
1915--.
Annual.

374 Leach, Howard Seavoy. A Union List of Collections of English
Drama in American Libraries... Princeton, N.J.: The University Library, 1916. 12 pp.
Anthologies and collections arranged alphabetically by editor
or compiler; library locations are given. Contents of the antholog
or collection not described.

375 Lower, Henry Eastman, and George Heron Milne, Compilers.
The Dramatic Books and Plays (in English) Published during
1915. Boston: Boston Book Co., 1916. 62 pp.
Issued as an appendix to The Dramatic Index, 1915. Author
index with full publication information; title index of plays for
reference. Includes essays and criticism as well as editions of
plays.

376 Baugh, Albert C. "A Seventeenth-Century Play List." Modern
Language Review, XIII (1918), 401-411.
This is a brief history and catalogue of 17th century plays
owned by a Mr. Horne, a Fellow of Oriel College. The list
probably dates from the period 1675-1680.

377 A Catalogue Of The Allen A. Brown Collection Of Books Relating
To The Stage In The Public Library Of The City of Boston.
Boston: Published by the Trustees, 1919. viii, 952 pp.
The main section is a catalogue of books on the history of
the stage, arranged in dictionary form, with authors, titles
and subjects. Plays and books about drama listed separately
by author. Each entry includes complete publication information, and some entries contain special notes on authenticity
or condition of the edition.

378 Wendell, Evert Jansen. Catalogue of the Literary and Artistic
  Property of the Late E. J. Wendell Other Than That Taken
  by Harvard University. To be sold October 15-25, by Thomas
  E. Kirby of the American Art Association. [New York: American Art Association, 1919.]
    The first six parts of the catalogue include dramatic books
  and tracts and dramatic prints. 4927 items, arranged by author
  or subject (portraits) or under general subject categories (e.g.,
  autographs). Large number of items relevant to Restoration
  and 18th century.

379 Dobell, Percy John. Books of the Time of the Restoration. Being
  a Collection of Plays, Poems and Prose Works Produced between the Years 1660 and 1700, by the Contemporaries of John
  Dryden. A priced catalogue. London: [P. J. & A. E. Dobell],
  1920. 2, 56 pp.
    This is a catalogue, described and annotated by Dobell, ar-
  ranged in alphabetical order, of books which he has for sale.
  As the prices are given it is of historical interest. There are
  627 numbered entries.

380 Modern Humanities Research Association. Annual Bibliography
  of English Language and Literature. [1920--]. Cambridge,
  1921--.
    The MHRA Bibliography." Standard reference.

381 O'Neill, James J. A Bibliographical Account of Irish Theatrical
  Literature: Part I: General Theatrical History, Players and
  Theatrical Periodicals. Dublin: John Falconer, 1920.
    A list of books and pamphlets dealing with the history of
  the Irish stage, the players, and the periodicals, arranged
  alphabetically; divided into--1) General Works, Pamphlets,
  etc.; 2) Players; 3) Periodicals.

382 The Ashley Library, A Catalogue Of Printed Books, MSS. and
  Autograph Letters, Collected by Thomas James Wise. 11
  vols. London: Printed for Private Circulation Only, 1922-1936.
    An annotated descriptive bibliography which includes many
  18th century authors. Arranged alphabetically. Vol. VII records
  plays by Nahum Tate, Sir Samuel Tuke, and Sir John Vanbrugh.
  Vol. VIII records works by William Wycherley, Joseph Addison,
  Aphra Behn, William Congreve, John Dryden, John Gay, Oliver
  Goldsmith, Nathaniel Lee, Richard B. Sheridan, Richard
  Steele.

383 "MLA International Bibliography of Books and Articles on the
  Modern Languages and Literatures." PMLA, 1922--.
    Annual bibliography. Before 1956 it included books and
  articles only by American writers. Standard. Most complete
  annual bibliography.

384 Cox, E. M. H., compiler. The Library of Edmund Gosse, Being
     a Descriptive and Bibliographical Catalogue of a Portion of His
     Collections. With an introductory essay by Mr. Gosse. London:
     Dulau &Co., Ltd., 1924. 300 pp.
         This listing of much of Sir Edmund Gosse's extensive library
     includes works of interest to the student of eighteenth-century
     and Restoration drama.

385 Maggs Brothers. Autograph Letters, Historical Documents and
     Author's Original Manuscripts. London: Maggs Brothers, 1925.
     (Catalogue No. 459).
         795 numbered entries, arranged in alphabetical order, by
     name of the writer. The entries are annotated so as to identify
     each item as fully as possible. Some 18th century items.

386 Northup, Clark Sutherland, et al. A Register of Bibliographies
     of the English Language and Literature. New Haven: Yale Uni-
     versity Press; London: Humphrey Milford, Oxford University
     Press, 1925. [12], 507 pp.
         Alphabetical arrangement. "Drama," pp. 121-146. Various
     dramatic writers are listed. Of some value, although largely
     superseded by the Cambridge Bibliography of English Literature.

387 "English Literature, 1660-1800: A Current Bibliography [1925--].
     Philological Quarterly, 1926--.
         An annual, annotated bibliography. Standard.

388 Hawkes, Arthur John. Lancashire Printed Books: A Bibliography of
     All the Books Printed in Lancashire Down to the Year 1800.
     Wigan: Printed for the Public Libraries Committee, 1925.
     xxviii, 155 pp.
         A descriptive, annotated bibliography, arranged chronologicall
     which catalogues Lancashire books according to the towns in which
     they were printed. Contains some dramatic works published in
     the 18th century.

389 Pollard, Alfred W., and G. R. Redgrave. Short-Title Catalogue of
     Books Printed in England, Scotland, and Ireland, and of English
     Books Printed Abroad, 1475-1640. London: Bibliographical
     Society, 609 pp.
         26,143 entries are arranged in alphabetical order by author.
     Library locations are given. For additional American holdings
     see, William W. Bishop, A Checklist of American Copies of
     "Short-title Catalogue" Books. 2nd ed. Ann Arbor, Michigan:
     University of Michigan, 1950. See also, Cecil K. Edmonds,
     "Huntington Library Supplement to the Record of Its Books in
     the Short-title Catalogue..." Huntington Library Bulletin, No.
     4, 1933.

390 Stonehill, Charles A., Jr., Andrew Block, and H. W. Stonehill.
     Anonyma and Pseudonyma. 4 vols., 2nd ed. London: C. A.

Stonehill, 1927.
    Lists plays, etc. by title, with the author's name. Vol. IV
    contains an author index.

391 Gamble, William Burt, compiler. The Development of Scenic
     Art and Stage Machinery: A List of References in the New York
     Public Library. Revised with Additions. New York: The New
     York Public Library, 1928. [8], 231 pp.
        The revision of the 1920 edition lists 3339 works owned by
     the library as of May 1, 1927. It includes indexes of authors,
     persons, subjects, and theatres and Stage Organizations.

392 Babcock, R. W. "A Preliminary Bibliography of Eighteenth-
     Century Criticism of Shakespeare." Studies in Philology,
     Extra Series, No. 1 (May, 1929), 58-76.
        Checklist of texts and studies.

393 National Operatic and Dramatic Association. Plays: A Guide to
     the Works in the Library of the National Operatic and Dramatic
     Association. Issued by Authority of the Council. London: Noda
     Ltd., 1929. 167 pp.
        Separate listings of dramatic and musical works. Dramatic
     entries are alphabetical by title. Musical entries are alphabet-
     ical by title.

394 Catholic Periodical Index. A Cumulative Author and Subject Index
     to a Selected List of Catholic Periodicals. Washington, D.C.:
     Catholic Library Association. 1930--.
        Quarterly, with annual and four-year cumulation.

395 Hall, Lillian Arvilla. Catalogue of Dramatic Portraits in the
     Theatre Collection of the Harvard College Library. Cambridge,
     Massachusetts: Harvard University Press, 1930.
        Arranged alphabetically by subject of portrait with artist
     and engraver and description of portrait.

396 Hayward, John. "Reader's Bibliography. Life and Letters after
     the Restoration." Life and Letters, IV (1930), 485-491.
        A reading list, with brief annotations of several dozen
     works which deal with the literary and social life from 1660-
     1700.

397 Kent, Violet, compiler. The Player's Library and Bibliography
     of the Theatre. With introductions by Geoffrey Whitworth and
     Frederick S. Boas. British Drama League Library. 2 vols.
     London: Gollancz, Ltd., 1930. Supplements.
        Catalogue of the library's holdings, divided into plays, ar-
     ranged alphabetically by author, and books about the theatre,
     arranged by subject. Play entries include indication of type,
     scene changes, costume, number of acts, and outstanding or
     unusual points in setting. Title index of all plays, which in-
     cludes references to collections. Entries for other theatre

books give only author, title, publisher, and date.

398 Catalogue of the Very Extensive and Well-Known Library of English Poetry, Drama, and Other Literature, Principally of the XVII and Early XVIII Centuries, Formed by the Late George Thorn-Drury, Esq. K. C. London: Sotheby, 1931. 175 pp.

This, the third portion of the catalogue, is devoted to the sales on the sixth, seventh, and eighth days, pp. 177-274. Nos. 1484-2360. The arrangement is alphabetical. The full title, etc., is given for each work, as well as the name of the buyer and the price.

399 Gilder, Rosamond. A Theatre Library. New York: Theatre Arts, Inc., for National Theatre Conference, 1932. xiv, 74 pp.

A basic, annotated bibliography of 100 books relating to theatre, arranged by countries. Entries 18 through 34 deal with English drama; several of these treat Restoration and 18th-century drama.

400 Baker, Blanch (Merritt). Dramatic Bibliography. An Annotated List of Books on the History and Criticism of the Drama and Stage and on the Allied Arts of the Theatre. New York: The H. W. Wilson Co., 1933. xvi, 320 pp.

The avowed purpose of this book is to provide a list of books "that would cover every phase of the arts of the theatre." It includes about 4000 books written during the "past 50 years," which represent a wide variety of opinions from "authorities and specialists."

401 Hammond, William A., comp. and ed. A Bibliography of Aesthetics and of the Philosophy of the Fine Arts from 1900 to 1932. Revised and enlarged edition. New York: Longmans, Green & Co., 1933. viii, 183 pp.

A bibliography of titles selected "with exclusive reference to their philosophical content." While several of the subject divisions will be of interest, it should be noted that the section on "Literature of the Drama and Theatre" contains 1001 titles listed alphabetically by author; sometimes there is a brief annotation. Several of the titles touch Restoration and 18th-century drama and theatre.

402 Templeman, William D. "Contributions to the Bibliography of Eighteenth-Century Aesthetics." Modern Philology, XXX (1933), 309-316.

A listing of 18th-century works--alphabetically by author-- which treat aesthetics; serves as addition to Draper's Eighteenth-Century English Aesthetics: A Bibliography.

403 Essay and General Literature Index. New York: H. W. Wilson Co. 1934--

Two issues a year, with annual and five-year cumulation.

404 Morgan, William Thomas. A Bibliography of British History
(1700-1715), with Special Reference to the Reign of Queen
Anne. Vol. I. 1700-1707. Bloomington, Indiana, 1934. xvii,
524 pp.

Of value to students concerned with the cultural and social
changes which were taking place in England in Queen Anne's
reign.

405 Summers, Montague. A Bibliography of the Restoration Drama.
London: The Fortune Press [1934]. 143 pp.

This book attempts to provide a complete alphabetical list
of "all plays, acted and unacted, printed and unprinted, belonging to the Restoration Theatre (1660-1700)." Includes
licensing and performance dates where available.

406 Van Patten, Nathan. An Index to Bibliographies and Bibliographical
Contributions Relating to the Work of American and British
Authors 1923-1932. Stanford, California: Stanford University
Press, 1934. vii, 324 pp.

407 Washington (State) University Department of Dramatic Art.
A Catalogue of the Division of Drama Library, University of
Washington. Seattle: University of Washington Book Store [1934].
69 pp.

A bibliography of criticism and acting editions of plays. Plays
arranged by subject, criticism by subject matter.

408 Harbage, Alfred. "Elizabethan and Seventeenth-Century Play Manuscripts." Publications of the Modern Language Association, L
(1935), 687-699.

A finding list of over 200 MSS dating from 1558 to 1700. Included are plays by Behn, Boyle, Dryden, D'Urfey, Settle, and
Wilmot, along with a large number of anonymous plays.

409 Boas, F. S. "Old Plays in Columbia University." Times Literary
Supplement, April 25, 1936, p. 360.

Boas records a number of Restoration plays in the Columbia
rare book department. Summers, in the May 2, 1936 (p. 379)
issue of the Supplement clarifies author and source of Neglected
Virtue (1696). Van Lennep and Robert Gale Noyes, in the June
6, 1936 (p. 480) correct and add to Boas and Summers. Finally,
in the June 13, 1936 (p. 500) issue of the Supplement Boas and
Summers add final words.

410 Day, Cyrus L., and Eleanore B. Murrie. English Song-Books,
1651-1702, and Their Publishers. London: The Bibliographical
Society, 1936. [355]-401 pp.

Reprinted from The Library, 4th Ser., XVI (1936), [355]-
401. A progress report. The work of John Playford is discussed
in some detail.

411 Gilder, Rosamond, and George Freedley. Theatre Collections
in Libraries and Museums. New York: Theatre Arts, 1936.
182 pp.
An invaluable guide to locations and contents of the principal
collections of materials related to the theatre. Worldwide in
scope, the volume includes an essay on the care and preservation of fugitive material by Mr. Freedley.

412 MacMillan, Dougald. "Unrecorded Eighteenth Century Plays."
Notes and Queries, CLXX (1936), 337.
Clarifies and corrects some of the attributions made by
F. T. Wood in Notes and Queries (1936), 56-58.

413 Wood, F. T. "Unrecorded Eighteenth-Century Plays." Notes and
Queries, CLXX (1936), 56-58, 319; CLXXII (1937), 43; CLXXIV
(1938), 383-384.
A list of 110 plays, most of them afterpieces, along with
other information compiled from provincial playbills and newspapers of the late 18th century.

414 Harbage, Alfred. "Elizabethan and Seventeenth-Century Play
Manuscripts: Addenda." Publications of the Modern Language
Association, LII (1937), 905-907.
Additional MSS by D'Urfey, Shadwell, and Wilmot, among
others, which supplement the finding list of MSS in PMLA, L
(1935), 687-699.

415 Lovett, Robert W. An Outline of Restoration and 18th Century
Plays (1660-1789). Boston, Massachusetts: Student Outlines Co.,
1937. 216 pp.
Primarily intended for students. Forty-two plays. Dramatis
personae, scene by scene summary of the action, brief critical
comment. A very brief introduction to the drama and theatre
of each period.

416 McCabe, William H. "The Play-List of the English College at St.
Omers, 1592-1762." Revue de Littérature Comparée. XVII
(1937), 355-375.
A list of plays, most of them in Latin, performed by English students at the Jesuit college, Pas de Calais.

417 Miller, Frances Schouler. "Notes on Some Eighteenth-Century
Dramas." Modern Language Notes, LII (1937), 203-206.
Provides some supplemental and corrective facts for Nicoll's
History of English Drama, Vols. II, III.

418 Wood, Frederick T. "The Attack on the Stage in the Eighteenth
Century." Notes and Queries, CLXIII (1937), 218-222.
A selective bibliography of items related to the controversy
over the morality of the stage that began with Jeremy Collier
and continued throughout the century.

419 Bibliographic Index. New York: H. W. Wilson Co. 1938--.
Two issues a year with annual cumulation.

420 Gray, Philip H., Jr. "Lenten Casts and the Nursery: Evidence
for the Dating of Certain Restoration Plays." Publications of
the Modern Language Association, LIII (1938), 781-794.
Distinguishing between the apprentice actors of the Nursery
operated jointly by the King's and Duke's Companies, and the
"'young men and women'" who were hirelings rather than actor-
sharers, Gray shows that when casts are made up entirely of
hireling actors, there is a "strong probability" that the plays
were acted during Lent because only at this period were such
groups given the exclusive right of performance.

421 MacMillan, Dougald. Drury Lane Calendar, 1747-1776. Oxford:
Clarendon Press, 1938. xxxiii, 364 pp.
An invaluable guide to dramatic activity at Drury Lane:
Part I is a calendar of performances, Part II an alphabetical
list of plays. The volume includes a concise account of Gar-
rick's managership and an index of actors and playwrights.

422 Giraud, Jeanne. Manuel de bibliographie littéraire pour les XVIe,
XVIIe et XVIIIe siècles francais: 1921-1935. Paris: Vrin, 1939.
v, 304 pp. (Publications de la Faculté des Lettres de l'Université de Lille, II).
Of value for students of comparative literature, with a
general section on "rapports intellectuels avec l'étranger."

423 MacMillan, Dougald. Catalogue of the Larpent Plays in the Huntington Library. (Huntington Library Lists, No. 4). San Marino,
California: Huntington Library, 1939. xv, 442 pp.
A catalogue of most of the new plays performed between
June 24, 1737, and January 18, 1824, based upon records of
plays sent to the office of the Examiner of Plays by the theatre
managers. Included are 2,399 plays, 102 unidentified items,
and an index of authors and titles.

424 Tobin, James E. Eighteenth Century English Literature and Its
Cultural Background. New York: Fordham University Press,
1939. vii, 190 pp.
A selective secondary bibliography with a separate section
on the 18th century drama and individual entries for all the
major dramatists and for many of the minor ones.

425 Harbage, Alfred. Annals of English Drama, 975-1700. An Analytical Record of All Plays, Extant or Lost, Chronologically Arranged and Indexed by Authors, Titles, Dramatic Companies,
etc. Philadelphia: University of Pennsylvania Press; London:
Humphrey Milford, 1940. 264 pp.
See the revised edition, 1964.

426 Magg Brothers. A Catalogue of Books Printed in England, Scotland,

and Ireland and of English Books Printed Abroad, 1640-1700.
Part I, A-L, No. 696; Part II, M-Z, No. 699. London, Maggs
Brothers, Ltd., 1940-1941. 226 pp.

A catalogue arranged alphabetically, by author of subject
treated, giving the full title, place of publication, publisher
or printer, date of publication, edition and price. Each work
is identified as fully as possible, and reference made to authorities when such exist. Of value for Restoration and 18th century
theatre and drama.

427 Metzdorf, Robert F., Compiler. Catalogue of the Autograph Collection of the University of Rochester. Rochester, New York:
The University of Rochester Library, 1940. 176 pp. Index.

Descriptions of the 1031 autographs from the collection in
the University's Treasure Room. The all-time "who's who"
collection is listed alphabetically according to signer. Letters,
cards, marginalia, mss., and scraps of paper make up the
bulk of miscellaneous items.

428 Smith, William C., Compiler. Catalogue of Printed Music Published
before 1801 Now in the British Museum. Second Supplement.
London: British Museum, By Order of the Trustees, 1940. 85 pp.

Contains titles acquired since the publication of the previous
catalogue, 1912; descriptive; alphabetically arranged.

429 Bateson, F. W., ed. The Cambridge Bibliography of English Literature. 4 vols. New York: Macmillan Co., 1941. Also Vol. V:
Supplement: A.D. 600-1900. Edited by George Watson. New
York and London: Cambridge University Press, 1957. xiv, 710
pp.

Attempts "to record, as far as possible in chronological
order, the authors, titles and editions, with relevant critical
matter, of all the writings in book-form (whether in English
or Latin) that can still be said to possess some literary interest, by natives of what is now the British Empire, up to the
year 1900."

430 [Bentley, Gerald Eades]. "A Rough Check-List of the University
of Chicago Libraries' Holdings in Seventeenth-Century Editions
of Plays in English." [Chicago, 1941]. [Typescript.]

A short-title index arranged alphabetically by author. Gives
only author, play's title, and date of the first edition.

431 Morgan, William Thomas, and Chlo Siner Morgan. A Bibliography of British History (1700-1715) with Special Reference
to the Reign of Queen Anne. Vols. IV and V. Bloomington: University of Indiana Press, 1941, 1942.

432 Paine, Clarence C. The Comedy of Manners (1660-1700): A Reference Guide to the Comedy of the Restoration. Boston, F. W.

Faxon Company, 1941. 51 pp.

397 numbered items listed in this reference guide for under-graduate and beginning graduate students. Citations are intended to include all references to secondary sources, critical, historical, and biographical. Various editions of plays are excluded together with references contained in general and special dictionaries and encyclopaedias.

433 Taylor, Archer. Renaissance Reference Books: A Checklist of Some Bibliographies Printed Before 1700. Berkeley and Los Angeles: University of California Press, 1941. 24 pp.

434 Bond, Donald F. "The New Cambridge Bibliography." Modern Philology, XXXIX (1942), 303-312.

An important review article on the CBEL, adding hundreds of titles. Particularly valuable on Anglo-French relationships in the eighteenth century.

435 Hackett, E. Byrne. Second Supplement to A Catalogue of the Renaissance (Part Two: England): English Drama, etc. to 1725. Special List, No. 17. New York: Brick Row Book Shop, 1942. 243 pp.

436 MacPike, E. F. "English, Scottish, and Irish Diaries, Journals, Commonplace-books, etc., 1500-1900. A Bibliographical Guide to Selected Material." Bulletin of Bibliography and Dramatic Index, XVII (1942), 183-185; XVII (1943), 213-215.

437 Offor, R. A Collection of Books in the University Library, Leeds, Printed Before the Nineteenth Century, Containing (a) Translations from English into French, (b) French Books on Great Britain. Part 5, 1660-1686. Leeds: Chorley and Pickersgill, 1942. (Reprinted from Proceedings of the Leeds Philosophical Society, V, part v [1942], 277-293.)

438 Ottemiller, John Henry. Index to Plays in Collections; an Author and Title Index to Plays Appearing in Collections Published between 1900 and 1942. Preface by George Freedley. New York: The H. W. Wilson Co., 1943. 130 pp.

Exhaustive index to English and American play collections and anthologies, 1900-1942. It includes a "List of Collections analyzed" (with contents), and complete bibliography of indexes to collections of the kinds of plays omitted. Only full texts are indexed.

439 Pearce, Ethel. "The Larpent Plays: Additions and Corrections." Huntington Library Quarterly, VI (1943), 491-494.

Supplements MacMillan's 1939 Catalogue; prints additions and corrections, numbered corresponding to the Catalogue.

440 Pane, Remigio Ugo. English Translations from the Spanish, 1484-1943. A Bibliography. New Brunswick: Rutgers University Press, 1944. 218 pp.

441 Sherman, Robert L. Drama Cyclopedia: a Bibliography of Plays
    and Players. Chicago: The Author [c. 1944]. 612 pp.
        Alphabetical listing of nearly every play produced in Amer-
    ica by a professional company from 1750 to 1940. The listings
    include the year in which each play was produced, its author, and
    a principal player.
442 Tobin, James E. "Three Eighteenth-Century Plays." Notes and
    Queries, CLXXXVI (1944), 18.
        Adds to and corrects Nicoll's History of Early Eighteenth
    Century Drama.
443 Woehl, Arthur L. "Some Plays in the Repertories of the Patent
    Houses." Studies in Speech and Drama in Honor of Alexander
    W. Drummond. Edited by Donald C. Bryant, Bernard Hewitt,
    Karl R. Wallace, and Herbert A. Wichelns. Ithaca, N.Y.:
    Cornell University Press, 1944, 105-122.
        Attempts to show, by examination of the plays presented at
    the two patent houses during the first decade of the Restoration,
    that there was more continuity between Elizabethan theatre and
    Restoration theatre than is generally supposed.
444 "Selective Current Bibliography for Aesthetics and Related Fields
    [1945--]. Journal of Aesthetics and Art Criticism, 1945/6--.
    Annual. Standard.
445 Wing, Donald G. A Short-title Catalogue of Books Printed in Eng-
    land, Scotland, Ireland, Wales, and British America, and of
    English Books Printed in Other Countries, 1641-1700. 3 vols.
    New York: Columbia University Press, 1945-1951 [i.e., 1952].
        This work continues the Pollard and Redgrave Short-title
    Catalogue. For corrections and additions, see: 1) Alden,
    John. Bibliographica Hibernica: Additions and Corrections to
    Wing. Charlottesville, Virginia, 1956; 2) Alden, John. Wing
    Addenda and Corrigenda: Some Notes on Materials in the
    British Museum. Charlottesville, Virginia, 1958; 3) Fry,
    Mary Isabel, and Godfrey Davies. "Supplement to the Short-
    title Catalogue, 1641-1700." Huntington Library Quarterly,
    XVI (1953), 393-436; 4) Hiscock, W. G. The Christ Church
    Holdings in Wing's Short-title Catalogue. Oxford, 1956.
446 Woodward, Gertrude L. and James G. McManaway. A Check
    List of English Plays, 1641-1700. Chicago: The Newberry
    Library, 1945. 156 pp.
        The standard check list, recording holdings in American
    libraries.
447 Baugh, Albert C., ed. "American Bibliography for 1946: English
    Language and Literature." Publications of the Modern Language
    Association, LXI (1946), 1226-1288.
        The standard annual check-list of studies.

448 Dick, Hugh G. "The English Drama to 1700." William Andrews
     Clark Memorial Library: Report of the First Decade 1934-
     1944. (Berkeley and Los Angeles: University of California,
     1946), 26-33.
        Notes the library's extensive holdings in Restoration drama,
     making the library one of the richest in the country in this
     area.
449 Hooker, Edward Niles. "The Eighteenth Century." William Andrews
     Clark Memorial Library: Report of the First Decade 1934-1944.
     (Berkeley and Los Angeles: University of California, 1946), 43-
     48.
        Describes the holdings of some of the dramatists in the
     earlier part of the century.
450 Hustvedt, Sigurd B. "The Age of Dryden." William Andrews Clark
     Memorial Library: Report of the First Decade 1934-1944.
     (Berkeley and Los Angeles: University of California, 1946),
     34-42.
        Describes the library's holdings in Dryden and Drydeniana.
451 Mack, Maynard. "Gay Augustan." Yale University Library Gazette,
     XXI (July, 1946), 6-10.
        A survey of the Chauncy Brewster Tinker collection at Yale,
     containing many dramatic items.
452 The Pierpont Morgan Library: English Drama from the Mid-Sixteenth
     to the Later Eighteenth Century. New York: The Pierpont Morgan
     Library, 1946. 96 pp.
        A survey of the Library's holdings.
453 Troubridge, St. Vincent. "Late Eighteenth-Century Plays." Theatre
     Notebook, I (April, 1947), 96.
        Some unrecorded plays of the period are noted.
454 Bowers, Fredson Thayer. "Certain Basic Problems in Descriptive
     Bibliography." Papers of the Bibliographical Society of America,
     XLII (1948), 211-228.
        Outlining some of the procedures in his forthcoming biblio-
     graphy of Restoration plays.
455 Crinò, Anna Maria. "Notizia di Una Piccola Collezione di Commedie
     e Tragedie Inglesi del Settecento." Anglica, II (September, 1948),
     40-58.
        Bibliographical descriptions and critical comments on plays
     in the author's possession.
456 Loewenberg, Alfred. The Theatre of the British Isles, Excluding
     London: a Bibliography. London, 1950. ix, 75 pp. (Society for
     Theatre Research. First Annual Publication, 1948-1949).
        The bibliography is divided into two sections. Part one,
     "General Section," contains books dealing with the whole
     countries; entries are arranged chronologically and include

author, title, publication facts, and some content annotations. Part two, also listed chronologically and containing the same sort of information, has the material listed alphabetically under places.

457 Miller, C. William. "'In the Savoy': A Study of Post-Restoration Imprints." Papers of the Bibliographical Society of the University of Virginia, I (1948), 41-46.

Attempts to identify the printers who used the imprint "In the Savoy." Numerous playbooks are discussed.

458 Smith, William C., Compiler. A Bibliography of the Musical Works Published by John Walsh During the Years 1695-1720. London: The Bibliographical Society, 1948. 215 pp.

A list of catalogues issued by John Walsh and his successors and a bibliography of the musical works published by Walsh, arranged chronologically. Includes music and songs from operas and plays, often indicating singers.

459 Bowers, Fredson Thayer. "Bibliographical Evidence from the Printer's Measure." Papers of the Bibliographical Society of the University of Virginia, II (1949), 153-167.

A study based on Restoration play quartos, which gives details on the printing of plays by Crowne, Southerne, Dryden, Shadwell and others.

460 -----. Principles of Bibliographical Description. Princeton: Princeton University Press, 1949. xvii, 503 pp.

A detailed and classic analysis of bibliographical problems, including, as illustration, many references to Restoration plays by Congreve, Dryden, Killigrew and others.

461 -----. A Supplement to the Woodward and McManaway Check-List of English Plays, 1641-1700. Charlottesville: The Bibliographical Society of the University of Virginia, 1949. 22 pp.

A mimeographed supplement to the check-list published in 1945 by the Newberry Library.

462 Dawson, Giles E. "The Resources and Policies of the Folger Shakespeare Library." Library Quarterly, XIX (1949), 178-185.

A general survey, with relevance to the collection of drama of the period.

463 Miller, C. William. Henry Herringman Imprints: a Preliminary Checklist. Charlottesville: Bibliographical Society of the University of Virginia, 1949.

A mimeographed list, including numerous play-books.

464 Smith, John Harrington and William G. B. Carson. "Genest's Additions and Corrections to The English Stage." Theatre Notebook, IV (1949-1950), 28-32.

In a copy of his own work now held by Washington University
(St. Louis) Genest recorded additions and corrections which he
may have intended for a second edition, which never appeared.

465 Bristol, England, Public Libraries. Index to Plays Available in The
Bristol Public Libraries. Bristol, 1950.

Single index includes title listings, and each title also appears under the author's name; the number of acts and characters is the only information given in the listing.

466 [Burnham, Margaret, Compiler, under the direction of the librarian
Mary Garnham]. The Player's Library; the Catalogue of the
Library of the British Drama League. With an introduction by
Frederick S. Boas. [London]: Published for the British Drama
League by Faber [1950]. xvi, 1115 pp.

Play titles arranged alphabetically under author; title index,
for plays and collections, also included. Complete entry gives
author's dates, type of play, number and sex of characters,
number of act and scene changes, costume appropriate to play.
Catalogue by subject of books on the theater, followed by author
index to catalogue. Excludes titles in the William Archer and
Gordon Craig Collections, and plays in foreign languages.

467 Fletcher, Ifan Kyrle. British Theatre, 1530-1900; an Exhibition
of Books, Prints, Drawings, Manuscripts and Playbills Organized
by Ifan Kyrle Fletcher for the National Book League, Oct.-Dec.,
1950. Cambridge, England: Published for the National Book League
by Cambridge University Press, 1950. 72 pp.

428 numbered entries, divided into 1) Plays, 2) Books about
the plays, 3) History and Criticism, 4) Actors and acting,
5) Theatres and their architecture, 6) Scenery and costume,
7) Pantomime, 8) Periodicals. Many items from the Restoration
and 18th century.

468 Loewenberg, Alfred. The Theatre of the British Isles Excluding
London: A Bibliography. London: Society for Theatre Research,
1950 [for 1949]. ix, 75 pp.

Standard check-list of sources and references to the provincial theatre.

469 "A Selective Check List of Bibliographical Scholarship [1949--]."
Studies in Bibliography, 1950/51--.

470 Ottemiller, John. Index to Plays in Collections; an Author and Title
Index to Plays Appearing in Collections Published between 1900
and 1950. Preface by George Freedley. 2nd edition, revised
and enlarged. Washington: Scarecrow Press, 1951. 386 pp.

In addition to the author and title indexes, the book includes
a key to symbols which list contents of collections analyzed.
Only complete texts of full-length plays are included.

471 "Annual Bibliography [of Comparative Literature, 1949--].
Yearbook of Comparative and General Literature, 1952--.
Standard.
472 Baker, Blanch. Theatre and Allied Arts. A guide to books dealing with the history, criticism, and technic of the drama and
theatre, and related arts and crafts. New York: Wilson, 1952.
xiii, 536 pp.
"Out of the mass of literature on drama and theatre subjects published between 1885 and 1948, about six thousand
volumes have been examined and selected . . . as reference
aids . . . in the history, theory, criticism, technic [sic]
and production of drama and other forms of stage entertainment."
473 Wilkinson, C. H. "English Plays in Worcester College Library."
Theatre Notebook, VIII (1953-1954), 15-17.
The library at Worcester College has "probably the largest
collection of Restoration plays in England outside the British
Museum and the Bodleian Library."
474 Wikelund, Philip. "Restoration Literature: An Annotated Bibliography." Folio (University of Indiana), XIX (1954), 135-155.
In this selective bibliography sections XII, XIII, and XIV
cover the drama and the playwrights.
475 Besterman, Theodore. A World Bibliography of Bibliographies
and of Bibliographical Catalogues, Calendars, Abstracts,
Digests, Indexes, and the Like. 3rd ed. Geneva: Societas
Bibliographica, 1955-1956.
First Edition 1939-1940; Second Edition, 1947-1949;
Fourth Edition, 1966-1967. A classified list of published
bibliographies.
476 Blagden, Cyprian. "The Missing Term Catalogue." Studies in
Bibliography, VII (1955), 185-190.
Reconstruction of list of titles (first published or reprinted
June-November, 1695) that would have been included.
477 Birley, Robert. "The History of Eton College Library." Library,
XI (1956), 231-261.
Includes acquisitions, 1660-1800.
478 Linton, Marion. "The Bute Collection of English Plays." Times
Literary Supplement, December 21, 1956, p. 772.
Includes 49 owned by Lady Mary Wortley Montagu.
479 Schwanbeck, Gisela. Bibliographie der deutschsprachighen
Hochschulschriften zur Theaterwissenschaft von 1885 bis
1960. Selbstverlag der Gesellschaft für Theatergeschichte,
Berlin, 1956. 536 pp.
Arranged in three sections: geographical, historical-geo-
graphical, and general topics. Entries include author, complete title, printer (if any), number of pages, university and
division, year presented.

480 Vowles, Richard B. Dramatic Theory: A Bibliography. New York:
The New York Public Library, 1956. 59 pp.
A bibliography, covering 1930-1956, of material related to
study of dramatic theory. A long section on the Poetics, followed by sections on form, content, genre, mode, language
and poetry in the theatre, audience and illusion, and dramatic
criticism.

481 Belknap, S. Yancey, Compiler. Guide to the Musical Arts: An
Analytical Index of Articles and Illustrations, 1953-56. New
York: The Scarecrow Press, Inc., 1957. [c. 1000 photolitho-
printed pages.]
Part I indexes articles in thirteen of the "world's leading
journals dealing with music, opera, the dance, and the theatre,"
including Musical Quarterly, Theatre Notebook, and Toute La
Danse.

482 "Bibliographie." Revue d'Histoire du Théâtre, Nos. 1 and 2 (1957),
83-128.
Lists works on theatre, 1956.

483 Blagden, Cyprian. "The English Stock of the Stationers Company in
the Time of the Stuarts." Library, XII (1957), 167-186.
Deals with the investment, management, account books and
income of the Stationers' Register Company's trade in English
language books during the Restoration. Includes representative
tables of expenditure and income.

484 English Literature in the Seventeenth Century: Guide to An Exhibition Held in 1957. Oxford: Bodleian Library, 1957. 167 pp.

485 Freudenberg, Anne, and Rudolf Hirsch, Lucy Clark, Fredson
Bowers, and Howell J. Heaney. "A Selective Check List of
Bibliographical Scholarship, 1949-1955." Studies in Bibliography,
X (1957), 1-192.
A separate volume. Studies of plays and critical works in-
dexed.

486 McManaway, James G. "The Theatrical Collectanea of Daniel
Lysons." Publications of the Bibliographic Society of America,
LI (1957), 333-334.
Five volumes of dramatic material in the Folger Library.

487 Morton, Richard. "Textual Problems in Restoration Broadsheet
Prologues and Epilogues." Library, XII (1957), 197-203.
Compares the broadsheet and quarto versions of several
prologues and epilogues and concludes that, "though we must
question the authority of some of the broadsheet texts, we may
feel certain that through them we can at times approach nearer
the original spoken version."

488 Clifford, James L. "The Eighteenth Century." Contemporary

Literary Scholarship. Edited by Lewis Leary. (New York: Appleton-Century-Crofts, 1958), 83-108.

Includes mention of some studies of playwrights.

489 Freedley, George. "The 26 Principal Theatre Collections in American Libraries and Museums." Bulletin of the New York Public Library, LXII (1958), 319-329.

26 collections listed alphabetically by state, with detailed descriptions (in most cases) of the quality and strengths of the collections relative to texts of plays, criticism, dramatic prints and other subjects related to the study of drama and theatre.

490 Horn-Monval, Madeleine. Répertoire Bibliographique des Traductions et Adaptations Francaises du Théatre Etranger du XVe Siècle a Nos Jours. Preface de Julien Cain. Paris: Centre National de la Recherche Scientifique, 1958--.

Part I is arranged alphabetically by author and then alphabetically by English title. Translations are divided into types (e.g., "manuscrit radiophonique," "traductions imprimées"); much additional information is given with each entry including location symbols for French libraries. Part VI is an index of English authors' works by English titles. Finally, there is an index of translators and adapters. (Vol. V, published in 1963, covers English and American theatre.)

491 Laird, Charlton. "Comparative Literature." Contemporary Literary Scholarship, ed. Lewis Leary. (New York: Appleton-Century-Crofts, 1958), 339-368.

Mentions studies touching upon drama and theatre, 1660-1800, passim.

492 Linton, Marion D. "The Bute Collection of English Plays." Stechert-Hafner Book News, XII (1958), 89-91.

Mostly 17th and 18th century plays now in the National Library of Scotland.

493 McCall, John Joseph. "Gerard Langbaine's An Account of the English Dramatick Poets (1691): Edited with an Introduction and Notes. Ph.D. Florida State University, 1958.

Compares earlier lists; discusses influence.

494 Popkin, Henry. "The Drama." Contemporary Literary Scholarship. Edited by Lewis Leary. (New York: Appleton-Century-Crofts, 1958), 289-337.

Survey of studies, 1660-1800, pp. 313-321.

495 Stratman, Carl J., C.S.V. "Unpublished Dissertations in the History and Theory of Tragedy, 1889-1957." Bulletin of Bibliography, XXII (1958), 161-164, 190-192, 214-216, 237-240; XXIII (1960), 15-20.

For the Seventeenth and Eighteenth centuries, see pages

191-192, 214-216. The arrangement is alphabetical by major writer.

496 Watson, George, ed. The Concise Cambridge Bibliography of English Literature, 600-1950. Cambridge: Cambridge University Press, 1958. xi, 272 pp.

497 Bunch, Antonia. "Playbills and Programmes in Guild-hall Library," Theatre Notebook, XIV (1959-60), 66-67.
　　1760 to 1924.

498 Dobrée, Bonamy. English Literature in the Early Eighteenth Century, 1700-1740. Oxford History of English Literature, Vol. VII. Oxford: Clarendon Press, 1959. xii, 701 pp.

499 Melnitz, William W. Theatre Arts Publications in the United States, 1947-52; a Five Year Bibliography. [Dubuque, 1959]. xiii, 91 pp. (American Educational Theatre Association. Monograph 1).
　　Primarily a subject index to books, magazine and newspaper articles, concerning all aspects of drama; listings include only information necessary to locate item.

500 Nicoll, Allardyce. A History of English Drama, 1600-1900. Vol. VI: A Short-Title Alphabetical Catalogue of Plays Produced or Printed in England from 1660-1900. 2nd ed. Cambridge: Cambridge University Press, 1959. xii, 565 pp.

501 Schmitt, Albert R. "The Programmschriften Collection." Library Library Chronicle, XXV (1959), 29-42.
　　Lists German scholarly papers, 1850-1918, some related to English Restoration drama.

502 Baldensperger, F. and Werner P. Friederich. A Bibliography of Comparative Literature. New York: Russell & Russell, 1960. 701 pp.
　　This is a reprint of the 1950 edition.

503 Cairo, Egypt. National Library. A Bibliography of Works about Music, Theatre Arts and Cinema. Cairo: National Library Press, 1960. 269, 82 pp.
　　Presumably a catalogue of holdings. The section on theatre has author and title index. Text in English and Arabic.

504 Craig, Hardin. "Textual Degeneration of Elizabethan and Stuart Plays: An Examination of Plays in Manuscript." The Rice Institute Pamphlet, XLVI (1960), 71-84.
　　Cites printings of plays after 1640.

505 "Letters of English Authors from the Collection of Robert H. Taylor." Princeton University Library Chronicle, XXI (1960), 200-236.
　　Numerous Restoration and 18th century people represented. Fragments of letters are printed.

506 McElroy, Davis D. and L. A. Four Centuries of Sea Plays, 1550-

1950; Being a Representative List of Theatrical Productions Involving Sailors, Ships, and the Sea, Arranged to Illustrate the History of Nautical Drama in Great Britain. To Which Is Added a Chronological List of Some Non-theatrical Pageants and Royal Shows of Nautical Interest . . . for Distribution by the Library of the British Drama League. London, 1960.

Alphabetical author listing, with plays listed alphabetically under author; gives date of production and wherever play has been examined, particular elements of nautical interest. Plays of unknown authorship listed chronologically.

507 Rojek, Hans Jurgen. Bibliographie der deutschsprachigen Hochschulschriften zur Theaterwissenschaft von 1953 bis 1960. Berlin: Selbstverlag der Gesellschaft für Theatergeschichte, 1960. 170 pp.

Continuation of Schwanbeck.

508 Sen, Sailendra Kumar. Capell and Malone, and Modern Critical Bibliography. Calcutta: K. L. Mukhopadhyay, 1960. 52 pp.

Methods in editing plays.

509 Smith, William C., assisted by Charles Humphries Handel. A Descriptive Catalogue of the Early Editions. London: Cassell [1960]. xxiii, 366 pp.

Works catalogued according to genre, alphabetically arranged within sections, the various editions of a work listed chronologically.

510 "The Virginia and Richard Ehrlich Collection." Boston Public Library Quarterly, XII (1960), 103-109.

Notes additions of items by Sheridan, among others.

511 Greene, Donald J. "Recent Studies in the Restoration and Eighteenth Century." Studies in English Literature, I (Summer, 1961), 115-141.

The essay analyzes several works--including literary histories, social histories, biographies, and critical works. Pp. 140-141 list and briefly describe works on Restoration and 18th-century drama; publication facts are given and, in some instances, annotations.

512 Hamer, Philip M., ed. A Guide to Archives and Manuscripts in the United States. Compiled for the National Historical Publications Commission. New Haven: Yale University Press, 1961. xxiii, 775 pp.

Invaluable reference tool. The index lists twenty-five libraries in the United States with theatre manuscript holdings. Some 1300 depositories in the 50 states appear in the work.

513 Scouten, Arthur H. The London Stage 1660-1800. A Calendar of Plays, Entertainments, and Afterpieces. Together with Casts, Box-Receipts and Contemporary Comment. Compiled from the

Playbills, Newspapers and Theatrical Diaries of the Period.
Part 3: 1729-1747. Carbondale, Illinois: Southern Illinois University Press, 1961. 2 vols. paged continuously. 1315 pp. Index
at end of each volume.

    The Introduction discusses the Playhouses, Licensing Act,
Theatrical Accommodations and Practices, Administration
and Management, Advertising, the Benefit Performance, Cos-
tumes, Scenery, Actors and Acting, Repertory, Dancing,
Music, Singing, Specialty Acts, the Audience, and Production.
Very valuable work.

514 Stratman, Carl J., C.S.V. "Problems in The Prompter, A Guide
to Plays." Papers of the Bibliographical Society of America, LV
(1961), 36-40.

    An attempt to solve the problems in The Prompter, which is
a bibliography of plays, having some 5,017 entries for English
drama from the beginnings to 1813.

515 -----. "A Survey of the Huntington Library's Holdings in the Field
of English Printed Drama." The Huntington Library Quarterly,
XXIV (1961), 171-174.

    Notes the total number of tragedies in the various centuries
as held by the Huntington and seven other representative libraries.

516 Van Lennep, William. "Plays on the English Stage, 1669-1672."
Theatre Notebook, XVI (Autumn, 1961), 12-20.

    Five play lists recently acquired by the Harvard Theatre Col-
lection. Provides a supplement to Nicoll's History of the Restoration Drama (1952).

517 Wolf, Erwin. "Englische Literatur im 18 Jahrhundert: Ein Fors-
chungsbericht (1950-1960)." Deutsche Vierteljahrsschrift für
Literaturwissenschaft und Geitesgeschichte, XXXV, Heft 3
(1961), 280-297.

    Includes a brief glimpse at a few of the leading books on
eighteenth century drama published between 1950 and 1960.

518 Belknap, S. Yancey. Guide to the Performing Arts 1961. New York:
The Scarecrow Press, 1962. 451 pp.

    Valuable reference work for all phases of theatre. The rea-
son for including the work is that it lists material published in
1961.

519 "Bibliography for 1961." 17th and 18th Century Theatre Research,
I (November, 1962), 5-26.

    Annotated bibliography of works dealing with Restoration
and Eighteenth Century theatre. Includes items for Nineteenth
Century theatre.

520 Stone, George Winchester, Jr., ed. The London Stage, 1660-1800:
A Calendar of Plays, Entertainments and Afterpieces, Together
with Casts, Box-Receipts, and Contemporary Comment . . .

Part 4: 1747-1776. Carbondale: Southern Illinois University
Press, 1962. 3 vols.

A day by day listing of the plays staged at the London theatres, together with the names of the actors in each piece. A
valuable Introduction discusses such matters as topical references, playhouses, theatrical financing, management and operation, advertising, make-up of the theatrical company, actors
and acting, the benefit performance, costume and scenery,
theatrical music.

521 Stratman, Carl J., C.S.V. "Unpublished Dissertations in the History and Theory of Tragedy, 1889-1957.-- Addenda." Bulletin
of Bibliography, XXIII (1962), 162-165, 187-192.

For the 17th and 18th centuries, see pp. 165, 187-188.

522 Bergquist, G. William, Editor. Three Centuries of English and
American Plays: A Checklist. England: 1500-1800; United
States: 1714-1830. New York and London: Hafner Publishing
Company, 1963. xii, 281 pp.

Basically an index of the Microprint edition of the Three
Centuries of English and American Plays. See the review, with
corrections, in Restoration and Eighteenth Century Theatre
Research, III (May, 1964), 50-56.

523 Halsband, Robert. "Recent Studies in the Restoration and Eighteenth
Century." Studies in English Literature, 1500-1900, III (1963),
433-447.

Discusses important recent studies on Dryden, Fielding,
Johnson and others.

524 Napieralski, Edmund A., and Jean C. Westbrook. "Restoration
and 18th Century Theatre Research Bibliography for 1962."
Restoration and Eighteenth Century Theatre Research, II
(November, 1963), 3-19.

An annual bibliography, beginning in 1963 and continuing to
the date of publication of this work. Jean Westbrook continued
as a collaborator through 1966. This is the only bibliography
published which is concerned only with Restoration and 18th
century theatre material.

525 Robinson, John. "Revision of Lowe's Bibliography." Restoration
and 18th Century Theatre Research, II (May, 1963), 8-12.

Editor Robinson lists four types of revisions: additions of
unknown entries, extension of bibliography to 1900, more detailed bibliographical descriptions, and correction of Lowe's
notes.

526 Schoenbaum, Samuel. "Research Opportunities in Late 17th Century Drama." Restoration and 18th Century Theatre Research,
II (May, 1963), 5-8.

Textual and bibliographical problems in 17th Century theatre
which merit investigation.

527 Stratman, Carl J., C.S.V. "Theses and Dissertations in Restoration and 18th Century Theatre." Restoration and 18th Century Theatre Research, II (1963), 20-45.

342 numbered entries, plus nine addenda, are arranged in alphabetical order in 102 categories, of which sixty-four are devoted to individual dramatists. The time span is, 1897-1962.

528 Cumulated Magazine Subject Index 1907-1949. A Cumulation of The F. W. Faxon Company's Annual Magazine Subject Index. Edited by Frederick Winthrop Faxton 1907-1935; Mary E. Bates 1936-1944; Anne C. Sutherland 1942-1949. Cumulated by G. K. Hall & Co. 2 vols. Boston, Massachusetts: G. K. Hall & Co., 1964.

This is a cumulation of the forty-three volumes of the Annual Magazine Subject Index. Alphabetical arrangement by topic or subject treated. Three columns to a page.

529 Day, Cyrus L. "The W. N. H. Harding Music Collection." Restoration and 18th Century Theatre Research, III (May, 1964), 23-24.

On editions and copies of Restoration and Augustan dramas, operas, and pantomimes in the private library of the Chicago book collector Harding.

530 Harbage, Alfred. Annals of English Drama, 975-1700. Revised by S. Schoenbaum. London: Methuen, 1964. 321 pp.

This revised edition of Harbage's 1940 compilation of dramatic pieces written for the English stage lists adaptations, translations, works composed in foreign languages, as well as descriptions of royal entertainments. Arranged chronologically and indexed according to playwright, title, and dramatic company. Several appendices note doctoral dissertation editions, the location of extant play manuscripts, and the names of theatres in operation during the period.

531 Napieralski, Edmund A. and Jean E. Westbrook. "Restoration and 18th Century Theatre Research Bibliography for 1963." Restoration and 18th Century Theatre Research, III (November, 1964), 3-24.

An annotated list of works published in 1963 which deal with Restoration and 18th Century Theatre. 151 entries.

532 Ottenmiller, John Henry. Index to Plays in Collections; an Author and Title Index to Plays Appearing in Collections Published between 1900 and 1962. 4th ed., revised and enlarged. New York: Scarecrow Press, 1964. 370 pp.

Author index includes author's dates, titles, date of first production, and references from variant titles, with collections in which plays may be found. Includes also list of collections analyzed and their contents.

533 Spacks, Patricia M. "Recent Studies in the Restoration and Eighteenth Century." Studies in English Literature, 1500-1900, IV (1964), 497-517.

Reviews important scholarly books and articles on Dryden, Garrick, and Murphy.

534 Stratman, Carl J., C.S.V. "A Survey of the Bodleian Library's Holdings in the Field of English Printed Tragedy." The Bodleian Library Record, VII (1964), 133-143.

For the 18th century there is a table which gives the number of editions, authors, tragedies, first editions, etc., which are located at the Bodleian. In addition, the article lists the authors of the Restoration and 18th century for whom the Bodleian has the first edition of all tragedies.

535 Besterman, Theodore. A World Bibliography of Bibliographies and of Bibliographical Catalogues, Calendars, Abstracts, Digests, Indexes, and the Like. 4th ed. 5 vols. Geneve: Societas Bibliographica, 1965-1966.

536 Dukore, Bernard F., ed. A Bibliography of Theatre Arts Publications in English, 1963. Compiled by the Bibliography Project of the American Educational Theatre Association. [Evanston, Ill., 1965]. vi, 82 pp.

This index is arranged alphabetically by author and, if anonymous, by title; entries include author and/or title, periodical title (when germane) and available publication facts. The subject index contains sections on 17th- and 18th-century British theatre; items are classified variously, as "general," "plays," "playwrights," "actors," etc.

537 Grieder, Theodore. "Annotated Checklist of the British Drama, 1789-99." Restoration and Eighteenth Century Theatre Research, IV (May, 1965), 21-47.

492 items compiled for the most part from the dramas in the Reader Microprint Series, Three Centuries of Drama: English and American. Annotations provide information on the historical context and social milieu of the plays.

538 International Index to Periodicals. New York: H. W. Wilson Co., 1907-1965. Then, Social Sciences and Humanities Index. 1965--.

Quarterly, with annual and three-year cumulation.

539 Napieralski, Edmund A., and Jean E. Westbrook. "Restoration and 18th Century Theatre Research Bibliography for 1964." Restoration and Eighteenth Century Theatre Research, IV (November, 1965), 11-38.

An annotated list of works published in 1964 that deal with Restoration and 18th Century Theatre. 166 items.

540 Price, Martin. "Recent Studies in the Restoration and Eighteenth Century." Studies in English Literature, 1500-1900, V (1965), 553-574.

This review article of major critical works published in 1964-

1965 contains references to studies on Dryden, Fielding, and Wycherley.

541 Watson, George. The Concise Bibliography of English Literature, 600-1950. Second Edition. New York: Cambridge University Press, 1965. 270 pp.

Complete revision of the 1958 text. Contains both primary and secondary material for the period 1660-1800.

542 Van Lennep, William, editor. The London Stage, 1660-1800. Part 1: 1660-1700. Critical Introduction by Emmett L. Avery and Arthur H. Scouten. Carbondale: Southern Illinois University Press, 1965. 532 pp.

The eighth volume of this invaluable calendar lists plays performed during the Restoration. A fine Introduction is devoted to a discussion of theatrical financing and production, playhouse construction, and audience response.

543 Bowers, Fredson. "Bibliography and Restoration Drama." Bibliography: Papers Read at a Clark Library Seminar, May 7, 1966. Edited by Fredson Bowers and Lyle H. Wright. (Los Angeles: Clark Memorial Library, U.C.L.A., 1966), 3-25.

Reviews bibliographies of Restoration plays and discusses the contribution methods of bibliography can make to an orderly account of Restoration drama.

544 Stratman, Carl J., C.S.V. Bibliography of English Printed Tragedy, 1565-1900. Carbondale and Edwardsville: Southern Illinois University Press, 1966. xx, 843 pp.

6852 numbered entries, and 285 anthologies. At least six hundred different tragedies, and all their editions, are listed for the period of the Restoration and 18th century. Library locations are given for each edition. A chronological table also. There are indications of the number of performances for each play.

545 -----. Dramatic Play Lists: 1591-1963. New York: The New York Public Library, 1966. 44 pp.

Thirty-three of the ninety-nine annotated lists of plays are printed in the Restoration and 18th century. Many of the other play lists, although printed later than 1799, give the plays published in the Restoration and 18th century.

546 Wilson, Stuart. "Restoration and 18th Century Theatre Research Bibliography for 1935-1939." Restoration and 18th Century Theatre Research, V (May, 1966), 40-58.

A list of works published from 1935 to 1939 that deal with Restoration and 18th century theatre. 345 items.

547 Brack, O. M., Jr., William J. Farrell, Charles N. Fifer, Donald T. Torchiana, and Curt A. Zimansky. "English Literature, 1660-1800: A Current Bibliography." Philological Quarterly, XLVI (1967), 289-384.

A comprehensive bibliography of books, articles, and reviews published in 1966 that pertain to Restoration and Augustan Literature. Arranged alphabetically according to author, within six major classifications.

548 Napieralski, Edmund A. "Restoration and 18th Century Theatre Research Bibliography for 1966." Restoration and Eighteenth Century Theatre Research, VI (November, 1967), 1-36.

An annotated list of works published in 1966 that deal with Restoration and 18th century theatre. 234 items.

549 Paulson, Ronald H. "Recent Studies in the Restoration and Eighteenth Century." Studies in English Literature, 1500-1900, VII (1967), 531-558.

A review article of major critical works published in 1966-67 contains information on studies of Behn, Cibber, Congreve, Dryden, Gay, Fielding, Farquhar, Lillo, Shadwell, Murphy, Steele, and Wycherley.

550 Tobin, J. E. Eighteenth Century English Literature and Its Cultural Background: A Bibliography. New York: Biblo and Tannen, 1967. 190 pp.

A reprint of the 1939 edition. Chapter VIII of Part I is devoted to works dealing with the cultural and critical backgrounds of 18th century drama; Part II contains bibliographies of critical works on individual authors.

551 Vernon, P. F. "Theses and Dissertations in Restoration and 18th Century Theatre: Addenda." Restoration and Eighteenth Century Theatre Research, VI (May, 1967), 55-56.

Twenty-two theses and dissertations in the University of London Library. The list is an addendum to the list published by Carl J. Stratman, C.S.V., in Restoration and Eighteenth Century Theatre Research, II (November, 1963), 20-45.

552 McNamee, Lawrence F. Dissertations in English and American Literature. Theses Accepted by American, British and German Universities, 1865-1964. New York, London: R. R. Bowker Company, 1968. xi, [1], 1124 pp.

A list of 14,262 dissertations covering all fields of English and American literature. The work is divided by centuries, and then by types. Within each section entries are arranged in chronological order.

553 Palmer, Helen H., and Anne Jane Dyson. European Drama Criticism. Hamden, Connecticut: The Shoe String Press, Inc., 1968. [8], 460 pp.

The Restoration and 18th century writers are listed, together with criticisms of their various plays in books and periodicals. The coverage for each author is not complete but, for a number of writers, more than has appeared to date.

Bickerstaffe, Isaac

single texts

554 Bickerstaffe, Isaac. Lionel and Clarissa. A comic opera as it is
     performed at the Lyric Theatre in Hammersmith. London:
     Secker, 1925. 89 pp.
         The text of the play.
555 -----. Love in a Village. A comic opera: as it is performed at
     the Lyric Theatre in Hammersmith. London: Secker, 1928.
     74 pp.
         The text of the play.

biography and criticism

556 Guiet, René. "An English Imitator of Favart: Isaac Bickerstaffe."
     Modern Language Notes, XXXVIII (1923), 54-56.
         A discussion of the Sultan or a Peep into the Seraglio (staged
     Dec. 12, 1775), as modelled on (sometimes plagiarized from)
     Favart's Trois Sultanes.
557 Macmillan, Ethel. "The Plays of Isaac Bickerstaffe in America."
     Philological Quarterly, V (January, 1926), 58-69.
         Traces the performances of the 13 of Bickerstaffe's 19 plays
     produced in America.
558 Sypher, Feltus Wylie. "The Anti-Slavery Movement to 1800 in
     English Literature Exclusive of the Periodical." Ph.D. Harvard
     University, 1937.
         Isaac Bickerstaffe's Love in the City, and Cumberland's
     West Indian are included in this study of the slavery controversy.
559 Russell, Howard H. "The Five Chief Works of Isaac Bickerstaffe."
     Ph.D. University of North Dakota, 1939.
560 Ure, Peter. "The Widow of Ephesus. Some Reflections on an Inter-
     national Theme." Durham University Journal, XLIX [New Ser.,
     XVIII] (1956-1957), 1-9.
         A chronological survey. The Ephesian Matron by "Isaac
     Bickerstaffe" plays down the antifeminist element of the story.
     During the eighteenth century the story was popular in vaude-
     ville, opera, and farce.

Biographia Dramatica

561 Powell, L. F. "George Steevens and Isaac Reed's Biographia
     Dramatica." Review of English Studies, V (July, 1929), 288-
     293.
         On contributions by Reed, cancelled by Steevens because of
     their malice.

562 Chancellor, E. Beresford. Annals of Fleet Street. New York:
Fred A. Stokes Company [c. 1910?]. 343 pp.
Some of the famous men and women associated with Fleet
Street are Dryden, Otway, Shadwell, and Lee.

563 Fyvie, John. Noble Dames and Notable Men of the Georgian Era.
New York: John Lane, 1911. 256 pp.
Six character sketches of eccentric 18th century personalities.
Chapter two is a sketch of Sir Henry Bate-Dudley, "fighting par-
son," journalist, writer of comic operas, and discoverer of
William Shield, composer. The sketch includes an account of
the riot at the performance of Bate-Dudley's The Blackamoor
Washed White at Drury Lane, and some facts in the life of his
sister-in-law, Mrs. Hartley, the actress.

564 Dobson, Austin. At Prior Park and Other Papers. New York:
Frederick A. Stokes Company, 1912. 305 pp.
Essays on eighteenth century personalities and their work
in England and France.

565 Historical Portraits 1700-1850. The Lives by C. R. L. Fletcher.
The Portraits Chosen by Emery Walker. With an Introduction
by C. F. Bell. Oxford: At the Clarendon Press, 1919. 2 vols.
A series of brief lives of the famous personalities of the
day, including William Congreve, Henry Fielding, John Gay,
Horace Walpole, Oliver Goldsmith, Samuel Johnson, Tobias
Smollett, and David Garrick. For each writer there are a
few clichés, titles of some of the works, and a photograph.

566 Chancellor, E. Beresford. The Lives of the Rakes. Vol. II: The
Restoration Rakes. London: Philip Allan & Co., 1924. 272 pp.
Vol. II contains biographies, concentrating on the subjects'
lives of pleasure, of the Duke of Buckingham, the Earl of
Rochester, Sir Charles Sedley, Etherege, Wycherley, and
others.

567 Dobrée, Bonamy, ed. From Anne to Victoria. New York:
Scribner's, 1937. x, 630 pp.
A collection of essays, primarily biographical, about
various figures of the 18th and early 19th centuries. Of parti-
cular interest are essays on Addison and Steele by Willard
Connely, Handel by Newman Flower, Fielding and Sterne by
Graham Greene, David Garrick by James Laver, and R. B.
Sheridan by W. A. Darlington.

568 Stauffer, Donald A. "A Parasitical Form of Biography." Modern
Language Notes, LV (April, 1940), 289-292.
"Eighteenth-century biographies inspired by current plays."

569 Venn, J. A., Compiler. Alumni Cantabrigienses: A Biographical
List of All Known Students, Graduates and Holders of Office

at the University of Cambridge from the Earliest Times to 1900.
Part II, from 1752 to 1900. Vol. I, Abbey-Challis. Cambridge:
The University Press, 1940. xii, 550 pp.

Provides academic history, honors, activities, information
concerning marriage, family, profession, public offices, date
and place of death.

570 Stauffer, Donald Alfred. The Art of Biography in Eighteenth-Century
England. Princeton, N.J.: Princeton University Press; London:
Humphrey Milford; Oxford University Press, 1941. 572 pp.

The first chapter (pp. 9-64) covers "Biography and the Drama";
it treats the influence of the stage on biography (both fortunate
and unfortunate) and examines the memoirs of several actors:
Cibber, Garrick, George Anne Bellamy, Sophia Baddeley, Tate
Wilkinson.

571 Magee, Grace Miriam. English Biography During the Restoration
Period. Los Angeles: University of Southern California Press,
1944.

572 Venn, J. A., Compiler. Alumni Cantabrigiensis. A Biographical
List of All Known Students, Graduates, and Holders of Office
at the University of Cambridge, from the Earliest Times to
1900. Part II. From 1752 to 1900. Vol. II. Chalmers-Fytche.
Cambridge: University Press, 1944. 593 pp.

Birch, Samuel

573 Troubridge, St. Vincent. "Date of Play Wanted." Notes and Queries,
CLXXXVI (1944), 165-166.

"Allardyce Nicoll lists The Smugglers, a melodrama by
Samuel Birch, produced at Drury Lane on 13 April, 1796."

Birkhead, Henry

574 Wagner, Bernard M. "Annals of English Drama." Times Literary
Supplement, October 22, 1964, p. 966.

Corrects an error in Harbage's work. Attributes The Female
Rebellion to Henry Birkhead who founded by endowment the Pro-
fessorship of Poetry at Oxford.

Birmingham

575 Cunningham, John E. Theatre Royal: The History of the Theatre
Royal, Birmingham. Oxford: George Ronald, 1950. 158 pp.

Chapters I and II contain some material pertinent to the
Restoration and eighteenth century.

Blackmore, Richard

576 R., G. R. Y. "Sir Richard Blackmore." Notes and Queries,
     CXLIX (September 5, 1925), 177.
         A Richard Blackmore was married on Feb. 9, 1685/6.
577 Blackmore, Sir Richard. Essay uponWit (1716). Edited with
     Joseph Addison's Freeholder (No. 45, 1716), by Richard
     C. Boys. Ann Arbor: Augustan Reprint Society, May, 1946.
         The Essay zealously attacks the immorality of the
     stage, and Boys' introduction provides background mater-
     ials.

Blow, John

578 Clarke, Henry Leland. "John Blow." Ph.D. Harvard University,
     1947.

Boaden, Charles

579 Woods, Charles B. "Captain B---'s Play." Harvard Studies
     and Notes in Philology and Literature, XV (1933), 243-
     255.
         Woods presents reasons for thinking the Modish Couple
     (thought to be written by Charles Boden) was written by
     Lord Hervey.

Booth, Mrs.

580 B., W. C. "Mrs. Booth, Actress." Notes and Queries, 11th
     Ser., III (February 25, 1911), 146-147.
         Memoirs of Richard Treffry, 1840, records the announce-
     ment in a sermon of 1803 by the Reverend Joseph Benson,
     Methodist of the "conversion and happy death" of Mrs. Booth.

Boswell, James

581 Boswell, James. On the Profession of a Player: Three Essays.
     Now first reprinted from the London Magazine for August,
     September, and October, 1770. London: E. Mathew and Marrot,
     1929. 43 pp.
         Boswell differs radically from Johnson in his estimate of
     acting, which should "be ranked among the learned professions."
582 Tillinghast, A. J. "Boswell Playing a Part." Renaissance and
     Modern Studies (University of Nottingham), IX (1965), 86-97.
583 Lustig, Irma S. "Boswell's Literary Criticism in The Life of

Johnson." Studies in English Literature, 1500-1900, VI
(1966), 529-541.
A review of Boswell's occasional literary opinions in The
Life includes his observation on Othello and on Gay's The
Beggar's Opera.

Bowen, William

584 Taylor, Aline Mackenzie. "Some New Light on William Bowen
(1666-1718): Actor and Customs Officer." Tulane Studies in
English, VI (1956), 31-56.
A detailed study of the theatrical career of William Bowen,
an Irish actor who is best remembered for having been killed
in a duel by James Quin.

Boyce, William

585 Cudworth, Charles. "Boyce and Arne: 'The Generation of 1710.'"
Music and Letters, XLI (1960), 136-145.
Parallel careers.

Boyer, Abel

586 Boyer, Abel. "Excerpts from The English Theophrastus: or the
Manners of the Age (1702)." Edited by W. Earl Britton. John
Gay, The Present State of Wit (1711), edited by Donald F. Bond.
Series I, Essays on Wit, 3. Ann Arbor: Augustan Reprint
Society, May, 1947.
Facsimile selections from The English Theophrastus deal
with play-house scenes and give epitomes of the modern players
and dramatists.

Boyle, Roger

works

587 Boyle, Roger, Earl of Orrery. The Dramatic Works. Ed. William
S. Clark, II. 2 vols. Cambridge: Harvard University Press,
1937. xv, 965 pp.
A definitive edition of the ten plays, carefully edited and
fully annotated. The volumes include critical and historical
introductions and an extensive bibliography.

single texts

588 Payne, F.W. "The Dramtic Works of Roger Boyle, Earl of Orrey,
     with Special Reference to the Rise of the Heroic Tragedy, In-
     cluding an Annotated Text of the Unprinted Zoroastres." M.A.
     University of London, 1923.

bibliography and criticism

589 Dames, G. Roger Boyle's "Henry V," besonders vergleichen mit
     dem gleichnamigen Stücke von Shakespeare. Berlin: Mayer &
     Müller, 1904. 84 pp.
          Recounts plot of Boyle's play, first staged in 1664 in the
     Duke of York's Theatre. Based chiefly on Holinshed's chronicles,
     pre-shakespearean English drama, and Corneille's Le Cid
     (1636), Henry V owes very little directly to Shakespeare's play
     of the same name. This conclusion is documented with com-
     parisons of Boyle's and Shakespeare's plays.
590 Seigert, Eduard. Roger Boyle, Earl of Orrery Und Seine Dramen.
     Zur Geschicte des Heroischen dramas in England. Vienna,
     1906. 75 pp.
          A general discussion of Orrery's life and studies of "The
     History of Henry the Fifth," "Mustapha, the Son of Solyman the
     Magnificent," "The Black Prince," "Tryphon," "Herod the Great,
     and "Altemira."
591 Summers, Montague. "Orrery's 'The Tragedy of Zoroastres.'"
     The Modern Language Review, XII (January, 1917), 24-32.
          Summarizes the plot of this heroic drama. Orrery's last
     play, because it was never printed and probably never per-
     formed, is practically unknown, and is in some ways repre-
     sentative of the type.
592 "Roger Boyle, Earl of Orrery." Times Literary Supplement, April
     28, 1921, p. 274.
          A general discussion of Boyle's plays with emphasis on the
     heroic tragedies.
593 Flood, W. H. Grattan. "Orrery's Black Prince." Review of Eng-
     lish Studies, I (July, 1925), 341-342.
          Prints an Orrery letter, July 17, 1666, referring to a pro-
     duction of The Black Prince.
594 Payne, F. W. [The Black Prince]. Review of English Studies,
     I (July, 1925), 342-343.
          Replies to Flood, Review of English Studies, I (July,
     1925), 341-342, on Orrery's play.
595 -----. "The Question of Precedence between Dryden and the
     Earl of Orrery with Regard to the English Heroic Plays."

Review of English Studies, I (April, 1925), 173-181.
    Orrery had written plays in rhymed couplets long before
the appearance of Dryden's first.

596 Clark, William S. "The Earl of Orrery's Play The Generall."
    Review of English Studies, II (October, 1926), 459-460.
    Orrery's first dramatic effort was The Generall, first
performed Sept. 14, 1664, previously performed as Altamira
in Dublin.

597 -----. "Further Light upon the Heroic Plays of Roger Boyle, Earl
    of Orrery." Review of English Studies, II (April, 1926), 206-
211.
    Concerned with the chronology of some of Orrery's plays:
the first written and acted was The General; The Black Prince
first appeared Oct. 19, 1667.

598 -----. "The Published but Unacted 'Heroic Plays' of Roger Boyle,
    Earl of Orrery." Review of English Studies, II (July, 1926),
280-283.
    Herod the Great was not performed because of the burning
of the Theatre Royal in Bridges Street, Jan. 2, 1671/2, and
because Samuel Pordage came out with his own Herod at Dorset
Gardens. Clark attributes the anonymous Tragedy of King Saul
to Orrery.

599 Wagner, Bernard M. "Restoration Heroic Drama." London Times
    Literary Supplement, September 2, 1926, p. 580.
    A letter in one of the Sloane mss. establishes Orrery's
precedence over Dryden in the production of the heroic play.

600 Clark, William S. "The Early Stage History of the First Heroic
    Play." Modern Language Notes, XLII (June, 1927), 381-383.
    The maiden performance of Orrery's Altamira (The General)
occurred at Smock Alley by November, 1662, at least "and thus
came to be the first play by a Restoration author acted at the
Dublin theatre."

601 -----. "The Manuscript of The Generall." Times Literary Sup-
    plement, September 20, 1928, p. 667.
    The ms. used in the Halliwell-Phillipps edition of the play
(1853) has vanished.

602 Summers, Alphonsus Joseph. "Orrery's 'The Tragedy of Zoroast-
    res.'" Essays in Petto. (London: Fortune Press, 1928), 133-145.

603 Clark, William S. "Notes on Two Orrery Manuscripts." Modern
    Language Notes, XLIV (January, 1929), 1-6.
    There is no ms. of The Generall at Plymouth as Nicoll had
stated. In a second note Clark speculates that Zoroastres was
meant to be produced at Dorset Garden.

604 Lynch, Kathleen M. "Conventions of Platonic Drama in the Heroic
    Plays of Orrery and Dryden." Publications of the Modern Language

Association, XLIV (June, 1929), 456-471.

The platonic motives apparent in the dramas of Carlell, Suckling, Killigrew, Cartwright, and the young Davenant were taken over and refashioned by Orrery and Dryden when the theatres reopened in 1660.

605　Clark, William S. "The Relation of Shirley's Prologue to Orrery's The Generall." Review of English Studies, VI (1930), 191-193.

Gives evidence to show that there is no relation between the play for which Shirley's prologue was written and the play by Orrery of the same name. Thus refutes the position taken by Allardyce Nicoll in A History of Restoration Drama.

606　-----. "Roger Boyle, Earl of Orrery and His Successors in the English Heroic Play." Unpublished Ph.D. dissertation, Harvard University, 1926. Harvard University Summaries of Theses, 1926. (Cambridge: Published by the University, 1930), 168-170.

A discussion of the nature of the heroic play, its career on the Restoration stage, and the development of the heroic play by Roger Boyle, Earl of Orrery, and John Dryden.

607　-----. "Lost Stage Directions in Orrery's Plays." Modern Language Notes, XLVII (April, 1932), 240-243.

608　Mills, L. J. "The Friendship Theme in Orrery's Plays." Publications of the Modern Language Association, LIII (1938), 795-806.

In many of Boyle's plays, the traditional theme of friendship is modified in accord with the playwright's interest in the monarchy and in the conflict of love and honor. The Generall, Henry the Fifth, Mustapha, and The Tragedy of King Saul demonstrate how Orrery worked within the older tradition while modifying it to suit his own purposes.

609　Valency, Maurice J. The Tragedies of Herod and Mariamne. New York: Columbia University Press, 1940. 304 pp.

Includes discussion of the plays by Pordage, Orrery, and Fenton.

610　Miller, C. William. "A Source Note on Boyle's The Generall." Modern Language Quarterly, VIII (June, 1947), 146-150.

Parallels for Roger Boyle's play found in his Parthenissa and in Romeo and Juliet.

611　-----. "A Bibliographical Study of Parthenissa, by Roger Boyle Earl of Orrery." Papers of the Bibliographical Society of the University of Virginia, II (1949), 115-137.

A study of the different editions of the dramatist's prose romance.

612　Bogorad, Samuel N. "A Note on Orrery's 'Henry the Fifth.'" Notes and Queries, CXCV (1950), 117-118.

Orrery probably used in part the chroniclers mentioned
in Langbaine (An Account of the English Dramatick Poets,
1691) as sources for the play.

613 Lynch, Kathleen M. Roger Boyle, First Earl of Orrery. Knoxville: University of Tennessee Press, 1965. 308 pp.
A full-length biography of Boyle, tracing his career as
soldier, politician, pamphleteer, and dramatist. Orrery's
heroic plays "offer a valuable sidelight" on his character
and his relationship with the Crown.

614 Biddle, Evelyn Q. "A Critical Study of the Influence of the Classical and Christian Traditions Upon the Character of the Hero
as Revealed Through Concepts of 'Love' and 'Honor" in Three
Restoration Heroic Tragedies." Ph.D. University of Southern
California, 1967. (Order No. 67-6491).
Considers Orrery's Henry V, Dryden's Conquest of Granada,
and Settle's The Empress of Morocco.

Bracegirdle, Anne

615 Spencer. Hazelton. "Downes' Tribute to Mrs. Bracegirdle." Modern Language Notes, XLIV (June, 1929), 375.
Downes' reference is a carefully worded tribute to the actress' skill.

616 Noyes, Robert G. "Mrs. Bracegirdle's Acting in John Crowne's
'Justice Busy.'" Modern Language Notes, XLIII (February,
1938), 390-391.

617 Hook, Lucyle. "Mrs. Elizabeth Barry and Mrs. Anne Bracegirdle, Actresses, Their Careers from 1672 to 1695, A Study
in Influences." Ph.D. New York University, 1945.

618 -----. Mrs. Elizabeth Barry and Mrs. Anne Bracegirdle Actresses,
Their Careers from 1672 to 1695: A Study in Influences. New
York: New York University Press, 1950. 13 pp.
This is an abstract of an earlier thesis (1945).

619 -----. "Anne Bracegirdle's First Appearance." Theatre Notebook, XIII (1959), 133-136.
As a child in Otway's The Orphan, 1685.

620 -----. "Portraits of Elizabeth Barry and Anne Bracegirdle."
Theatre Notebook, XV (Summer, 1961), 129-137.
The two actresses, identified as Britannia and Flora in
Kneller's large Equestrian Picture of William III, now in
Hampton Court. Traces source of engravings in The Biographi-
cal Mirrour.

621 Howarth, R. G. "Congreve and Anne Bracegirdle." English
Studies in Africa, IV (1961), 159-161.
Criticism of John Hodges' account of the relationship. No

evidence that Bracegirdle was Congreve's mistress.

Brereton, William

622 Green-Armytage, R. N. "William Brereton." Notes and Queries,
     CLXXXIX (September 8, 1945), 107-108.
        Biographical notes on the actor, in answer to the query by P.
     W. Montague-Smith (11 August).
623 Montague-Smith, P. W. "William Brereton." Notes and Queries,
     CLXXXVIII (August 11, 1945), 61.
        Requests information about the actor.
624 Wood, Frederick Thomas. "William Brereton." Notes and Queries,
     CLXXXVIII (September 22, 1945), 131.
        Additional biographical information.

Brewer, Anthony

625 Greg, W. W. "The Perjur'd Nun." Times Literary Supplement,
     August 10, 1946, p. 379.
        Asks for information about a supposed 1680 edition of Anthony
     Brewer's play.

Bridges, James

626 Hook, Lucyle. "James Bridges Drops in at the Theatre." Hunting-
     ton Library Quarterly, VIII (1945), 306-311.
        The diary of the future Duke of Chandos gives information
     about performances, especially at Lincolns Inn Fields, 1697 to
     1702.
627 Baker, Charles H. Collins, and Muriel I. Baker. The Life and
     Circumstances of James Brydges, First Duke of Chandos:
     Patron of the Liberal Arts. Oxford: The University Press (in
     cooperation with the Henry Huntington Library), 1949. xix,
     493 pp.
        A sumptuous biography of the great patron, which includes
     a comment on his playgoing and a discussion of his theatrical
     ventures with Rich in Covent Garden in 1732.

Brietzcke, Charles

628 Hailey, Elma, ed. "Charles Brietzcke's Diary (June, July, 1761)."
     Notes and Queries, CCI (1956), 172-174, 311-314.
        Selections from the Diary.
629 -----. "Charles Brietzcke's Diary (1762)." Notes and Queries,
     VI (1959), 94-97, 136-137, 178-181, 228-231, 281-284, 311-

313, 373-375, 412-413.
Selections.

630 -----. "Charles Brietzcke's Diary. (1764)." Notes and Queries,
New Ser., VIII (January, 1961), 9-14; (February, 1961), 61-63;
(March, 1961), 83-86; (April, 1961), 144-147; (May, 1961),
191-193; (June, 1961), 210-214; (July, 1961), 258-262; (August,
1961), 302-307, 320; (September, 1961), 335-339; (October, 1961),
391-395; (November, 1961), 433-434, 437; (December, 1961),
452-461.
Lists the various theatrical functions which he attended.

Brighton

631 Odell, Mary Theresa. Mr. Trotter of Worthing and the Brighton
Theatre, 1814-1819. Worthing: Aldridge Bros., 1945.
A study of Brighton theatre in the early nineteenth century,
with references to provincial performances in the late eighteenth
century.
632 Rosenfeld, Sybil. "Duke Street Theatre, Brighton, 1790-1806."
Theatre Notebook, VIII (1953-1954), 60-61.
This article describes (and illustrates with three plates)
the theatre.

Bristol

633 Watts, Guy Tracey. Theatrical Bristol. Bristol: Holloway and
Son, Ltd., 1915. 131 pp.
Traces the history of theatre in Bristol from 1532 to 1915.
Chapters two through five pertain to Restoration and 18th
century. Two companies performed for eight years from 1691
on. Theatrical activities were suppressed for twenty years
by work of Rev. Arthur Bedford. In 1729 the Jacob's Well
Theatre was opened. Theatre Royal was opened in 1766.
634 Powell, George Rennie. The Bristol Stage, Its Story. Bristol:
Bristol Printing and Publishing Co., Ltd., 1919. 204 pp.
Chapters one and two deal with the years from 1586 to 1800.
They describe the playhouses, the plays, and the players of
Bristol's "pioneer" theatre years.
635 Board, M. E. The Story of the Bristol Stage, 1490-1925. London:
The Fountain Press [1926]. vi, 57 pp.
A year by year account of performances, performers and
events at Bristol theatres.
636 Rosenfeld, Sybil. "Actors in Bristol, 1741-1748." Times Literary
Supplement, August 29, 1936, p. 700.
A detailed account of the state of acting in Bristol taken

from a manuscript account book of the Jacob's Well Theatre.

637 Ross, James. "An Eighteenth Century Playhouse. The Theatre-
Royal, Bristol." Essays by Divers Hands, XXII (1945), 61-85.
A survey of the history of this theatre, with an architectural
description.

638 Barker, Kathleen. The Theatre Royal, Bristol: The First Seventy
Years. Historical Association, Bristol Branch, Local History
Pamphlets, 3. c/o Bristol University: Historical Association,
1961. 19 pp. 4 plates.
Concerns the period 1766-1833.

639 -----. "The First Night of the Theatre Royal, Bristol." Notes
and Queries, XIV (1967), 419-421.
A playbill for the opening of the Theatre Royal in Bristol
on May 30, 1766 shows the farce accompanying Steele's
The Conscious Lovers that night to have been Murphy's
The Citizen.

Brome, Alexander

640 Brooks, John Lee. "Alexander Brome: His Life and Works." Ph.D.
Harvard University, 1933.

Brome, Richard

641 Meyerstein, E. H. W. "Burns and 'The Merry Beggars.'" Times
Literary Supplement, December 13, 1923, p. 876.
A discussion of Richard Brome's 1641 play, A Joviall Crewe;
or The Merry Beggars and Robert Burns' adaptation of a song
from it.

642 Fried, Harvey. "A Critical Edition of Brome's The Northern
Lasse." Ph.D. New York University, 1959.
Cites relations to Restoration comedies.

Brooke, Frances

643 Needham Gwendolyn B. "Mrs. Frances Brooke: Dramatic Critic."
Theatre Notebook, XV (1961), 47-55.
Her criticism in The Old Maid, 1755 and 1756.

Brooke, Henry

644 Palser, E. M. "Henry Brooke, 1703-1783." M.A. London University (University College), 1907.

645 Wright, Herbert. "Henry Brooke's 'Gustavus Vasa.'" Modern
Language Review, XIV (1919), 173-182.

A justification of the prohibition of Brooke's play by the
Licensing Act of 1737 (the first case), a history of its popularity as a book play, and an evaluation of it (chief merit--poetic
style).

646 de Ternant, André. "Plays on Queen Elizabeth and Essex in Spain."
Times Literary Supplement, October 21, 1920, p. 684.
Two 18th-century adaptations of Thomas Corneill's Comte
d'Essex are discussed--Henry Jones' version (1753) and Henry
Brooke's version (1761).

647 Wright, H. G. "Henry Brooke's 'Gustavus Vasa': a Correction."
Modern Language Review, XV (1920), 304.
Correction of errors in a previous article in reference to
the first Dublin production of the play.

648 Scurr, Helèn Margaret. "Henry Brooke." Ph.D. University of
Minnesota, 1922.

649 C[hapman], R. W. "Brooke's Gustavus Vasa." Review of English
Studies, I (October, 1925), 460-461.
Notices some of the subscribers to the printed play, in-
cluding Jonathan Swift and Samuel Johnson.

650 -----. "Brooke's Gustavus Vasa." Review of English Studies, II
(January, 1926), 99.
Notes an announcement by Brooke of a piracy of his play.

651 Rawson, C. J. "Some Aspects of Mid-Eighteenth-Century 'Sensibility' with Special Reference to Henry Brooke's Fool of Quality."
B. Litt. Oxford University (Magdalen), 1958.

652 Pullin, F. M. B. "A Critical Study of the Works of Henry Brooke."
M.A. London University (University College), 1965.

Brown, Thomas

653 Wiley, Autrey Nell. "The Poussin Doctor." Modern Language
Notes, L (1935), 506-508.
The "Poussin Doctor" named in the prologue to Brown's
comedy is Charles Davenant, and Miss Wiley explains how
he came to be known by this name.

Browne, Edward

654 Ward, Sir Adolphus William. "The Female Rebellion." Collected
Papers, Vol. IV (Cambridge: at the University Press, 1921),
434-436.
A discussion of the references in this play to the politics of
the period of Shaftesbury's rebellion; also consideration of the
question of authorship of the play; advances the possibility that
Dr. Edward Browne, son of Sir Thomas Browne, wrote it.

Brunton, Anne

655 Doty, Gresdna. "Anne Brunton in Bath and London." Theatre Sur-
     vey, VIII (May, 1967), 53-65.
         Examines Anne Brunton's English provincial background,
     her London debut (as Horatia in The Roman Father at Covent
     Garden on October 17, 1785), and her successful reception in
     America.

Brydges, James

See, Bridges, James

Buck, Timothy

656 R., G. O. "Timothy Buck, Comedian." Notes and Queries, CLI
     (December 25, 1926), 461.
         Asks for information about him (d. Oct., 1741).

Buckingham, Duke of

657 Villiers, George, 2nd Duke of Buckingham. The Rehearsal, First
     Acted 7 December 1671; Published 1672; Mit Einleitung heraug-
     egeben von Felix Lindner. Heidelberg: Carl Winter, 1904. iv,
     110 pp.
         The introduction discusses many heroic plays and their
     authors; followed by the text of the play with extensive notes,
     especially to the allusions to heroic plays.
658 Charlton, H. B. "Buckingham's Adaptation of 'Julius Caesar' and a
     Note in the 'Spectator.'" Modern Language Review, XVI (1921),
     171-172.
         Identifies a quotation in Spectator 300 as being from the
     prologue to Buckingham's Marcus Brutus, and raises the ques-
     tion of the date of Buckingham's adaptation.
659 Crawford, Bartholonew W. "The Dance of the Kings." Philological
     Quarterly, II (1923), 151-153.
         A description from Eunomus of the dance parodied by Buck-
     ingham in the dance of the Brentford Kings in The Rehearsal.
660 Coffin, Robert Peter Tristram. The Dukes of Buckingham; Play-
     boys of the Stuart World. New York: Brentano's, 1931. 358 pp.
         This work examines the characters and times of the dukes
     of Buckingham, father and son, the "noble mountebanks of
     literature," whose reckless revelries in a Puritan world suggeste
     that "laughter can become a virtue when sobriety has become a

vice." Provides abundant source material for the student of
Restoration drama.

661 MacLaine, Allan H. "Robert Fergusson's 'The Sow of Feeling'
and Buckingham's The Rehearsal." Notes and Queries, CCII
(1957), 485-486.
Buckingham's satire of Dryden in The Rehearsal gave Fergusson the idea to satirize Mackenzie in The Sow of Feeling.

Burgoyne, John

662 Hudleston, F. J. Gentleman Johnny Burgoyne. Garden City, New
York: Garden City Publishing Co., Inc., [1927]. 367 pp.
Burgoyne's life and military career; a survey of his dramatic
efforts in an appendix.

Burlesque

663 Bennett, H. R. "Literary Parody and Burlesque in the Seventeenth
and Eighteenth Centuries." M.A. London University, 1914.

664 Clinton-Baddeley, V.C. The Burlesque Tradition in the English
Theatre after 1660. London: Methuen, 1952. 152 pp.
Pages 29 to 79 deal with Restoration and eighteenth-century
burlesque dramatists (Davenant, Buckingham, Duffett, Gay,
Fielding, Carey, and Sheridan).

665 Kreissman, Bernard. Pamela-Shamela: A Study of the Burlesques,
Parodies and Adaptations of Richardson's Pamela. Lincoln:
University of Nebraska Press, 1960. 98 pp. (New Series No. 22).
Including an extensive bibliography and an index, this study
examines the English Pamela literature as it seems to illustrate
a particular facet of the character of Richardson or of Pamela.
There are several dramatic versions discussed, including those
by Giffard, Dance, and Edge.

666 Wells, Stanley. "Shakespearian Burlesques." Shakespeare Quarter-
ly, XVI (1965), 49-61.
Although the article deals mainly with the burlesques of John
Poole, introductory remarks refer briefly to burlesques by
Thomas Duffett and to the burlesque instinct surrounding Buck-
ingham's The Rehearsal, Fielding's Tom Thumb, and Sheridan's
The Critic.

Burlesque Poetry

667 Bond, Richmond P. English Burlesque Poetry, 1700-1750. Cambridge:
Harvard University Press, 1932. xiv, 483 pp.

Burletta

668 Byrnes, Edward T. "The English Burletta, 1750-1800." Ph.D.
New York University, 1967. (Order No. 68-6046).
The English burletta existed only temporarily, from 1764
to 1780, as a definable genre. After 1779 the term was ex-
tended to include hybrid forms. Special attention is given to
Kane O'Hara's Midas and The Golden Pippin.

Burnaby, William

669 Burnaby, William. The Dramatic Works of William Burnaby. Edited
by F. E. Budd. London: Eric Partridge, At The Scholartis Press,
1931. 469 pp.
The first time that the little read playwright Burnaby's
comedies have been edited. A biography, discussion of the
plays, the text, with notes, and a commentary are included.
The plays are: The Reform'd Wife (1700); The Ladies Visiting-
Day (1701); The Modish Husband (1702); and Love Betray'd
(1703). Bibliography of editions.
670 Kies, Paul P. "Lessing and Burnaby." Modern Language Notes, L
(1935), 225-230.
Finds the source of Lessing's fragmentary scenario, Die
aufgebrachte Tugend in The Modish Husband (1702) by William
Burnaby.

Burnett, Thomas

671 Burnett, Thomas. The Letters of Thomas Burnett to George Duckett,
1712-1722. Edited by David Nichol Smith. Oxford: Printed for
Members of the Roxburghe Club, 1914. 325 pp.
Letters with notes by editor, identifying and explaining allusions to contemporary events, people, plays and playwrights,
e.g., Cato, Rowe, "Rag" Smith. Contains first draft of Burnett's
prologue for Mrs. Centlivre's The Wonder.

Burney, Charles

672 Kidson, Frank. "James Oswald, Dr. Burney, and 'The Temple
of Apollo.'" The Musical Antiquary, II (October, 1910), 34-41.
On the "clubs" of professional and amateur musicians and
some of the musico-dramatic works published under their aegis,
including masques and pantomimes.
673 Loewenberg, Alfred. "Midsummer Night's Dream Music in 1763."

Theatre Notebook, I (April, 1946), 23-26.
    On Dr. Burney's music.

674 Scholes, Percy A. The Great Dr. Burney: his Life, his Travels,
     his Works, his Family, and his Friends. 2 Vols. Oxford: Uni-
     versity Press, 1948.
        A large, important and closely documented study, with
     numerous references to Burney's relationship with actors and
     the stage. The Garricks, Sheridan, Murphy and Mrs. Cibber
     are mentioned passim. Especially relevant are Chapter III,
     "The London Début" (I, 21-34), Chapter XXXVI, "The Garricks
     and the Burneys" (I, 363-371), and Chapter LVII, "London
     Music making towards the End of the Eighteenth Century" (II,
     164-183).

675 Hemlow, Joyce. A Catalogue of the Burney Family Correspondence,
     1749-1878. New York Public Library and McGill University
     Press, 1967.
        A catalogue of the correspondence of Dr. Charles Burney
     and daughter Fanny Burney with prominent persons includes
     letters to and replies from David Garrick, Horace Walpole,
     James Boswell, and Samuel Johnson.

Burney, Fanny

text

676 Burney, Fanny. Edwy and Elgiva. Edited by Miriam J. Benkovitz.
     Hamden, Conn.: Shoe String Press, 1957.

biography and criticism

677 Goodge, Elizabeth. "Fanny Burney: A Play in Four Acts." Three
     Plays. (London: Duckworth, 1939), 221-318.

678 Hemlow, Joyce. "Fanny Burney: Playwright." University of Toronto
     Quarterly, XIX (1950), 170-189.
        Fanny Burney, better known for her novels, also wrote
     several comedies and tragedies, none of which has been re-
     printed. These plays show much about her personality and
     methods of writing.

679 Morrison, Marjorie Lee. "Fanny Burney and the Theatre." Ph.D.
     University of Texas, 1957.
        Influence of theatre seen in Fanny Burney's diaries, novels,
     and nine holograph plays.

680 Hemlow, Joyce. The History of Fanny Burney. Oxford: Clarendon
     Press, 1958. xvi, 528 pp.
        A critical biography of Fanny Burney which discusses her

novels and plays as literary works as well as products of her
life and milieu. Includes an appendix, "The Burney Manuscripts:
A Tentative Summary."

Burney Collection

681 Rosenfeld, Sybil. "The Restoration Stage in Newspapers and Journal
1660-1700." Modern Language Review, XXX (1935), 445-459.
Prints news and notices about the Restoration theatre from the
Burney Collection of newspapers and from Peter Motteux's periodical, The Gentleman's Journal.

682 -----. "Dramatic Advertisements in the Burney Newspapers, 1660-
1700." Publications of the Modern Language Association, LI
(1936), 123-152.
A list of advertisements, quoted in full, from the Burney Collection of newspapers in the British Museum. These provide
factual information about the performance and publication of
certain plays appearing between 1660 and 1700. To verify their
accuracy, the advertisements are collated with bibliographical
data from other contemporary sources and from the Term Catalogues.

Calderon, P.

683 Oppenheimer, Max, Jr. "Supplementary Data on the French and
English Adaptations of Calderón's El Astrologo Fingido." Revue
de Littérature Comparée, XXIV (1948), 547-560.
Studies The Feign'd Astrologer (1668) and Dryden's The
Mock Astrologer.

Canning, George

684 Wonderley, Wayne. "An English Goethe Parody." Monatshefte,
XLVIII (1956), 88-93.
The Rovers, 1798, possibly by Canning.

Canning, Mary

685 Gale, Fred R. "Canning's Mother and the Stage." Notes and Queries
CLXVII (September 14, 1929), 183-185; (September 21, 1929),
201-204.
Actress Mary Ann Canning ("Mrs. Reddish")--a sketch of
her career, largely at Drury Lane and Exeter Theatre (1773
to about 1791).

Capell, Edward

686 Taylor, George C. "The Date of Edward Capell's Notes and Various Readings to Shakespeare, Volume II." Review of English Studies, V (July, 1929), 317-319.
Dates the work as February 21, 1780.

687 Walker, Alice. Edward Capell and His Edition of Shakespeare. Annual Shakespeare Lecture of the British Academy, 1960. Reprinted from the Proceedings of the British Academy, XLVI (London: Oxford University Press, [1960]), [131]-145.
Discusses Capell's edition which was going through the press at the same time as Johnson and compares Capell and Johnson as editors.

Capon, William

688 Rosenfeld, Sybil. "Scene Designs of William Capon." Theatre Notebook, X (1956), 118-122.
Late 18th Century.

Carey, Henry

poems

689 Carey, Henry. The Poems of Henry Carey. Edited by F. T. Wood. London: Constable, 1930. 261 pp.
Includes The Dragon of Wantley, a burlesque opera.

biography and criticism

690 Wood, F.T. [The Disappointment]. Review of English Studies, V (1929), 66-69.
Presents evidence to place The Disappointment in the list of plays by Henry Carey.

691 -----. "Henry Carey, Poet, Dramatist, Satirist." Ph.D. London University (External), 1930.

692 -----. "Henry Carey and an Eighteenth Century Satire on Matrimony." Notes and Queries, CLXV (1933), 363-368.
Henry Carey could not have written Cupid and Hymen, A Voyage to the Isles of Love and Matrimony (1748), although he likely wrote the appendices to it and perhaps falsified a pamphlet "war" about them.

693 -----. "Henry Carey's Betty." Review of English Studies, IX (1933), 64-66.
Wood thinks that the lost play, Betty, or the Country Bumpkins,

was a reworked version of the earlier Hanging and Marriage.
694 Trevithick, Jack. "The Dramatic Work of Henry Carey." Ph.D.
     Yale University, 1939.
695 "'Sally in Our Alley,' Plays of Henry Carey." Times Literary
     Supplement, October 9, 1943, p. 490.
         The genius of the Carey family line; reference to Henry's
     plays.
696 Scholes, Percy A. "'Sally in Our Alley.'" Times Literary Supplement
     October 16, 1943, p. 499.
         Corrects TLS, October 9, 1943, noting that the "'Sally in Our
     Alley" popularly sung is really the traditional tune to "What though
     I am a country lass," which supplanted Carey's song.
697 Hughes, Leo, and Arthur H. Scouten. "The First Season of The
     Honest Yorkshireman." Modern Language Review, XL (January,
     1945), 8-11.
         The stage and printing history of Henry Carey's play, 1735.
698 Sands, Mollie. "The Problem of Teraminta." Music and Letters,
     XXXIII (1952), 217-222.
         The identity of the composer of the music of Teraminta,
     for which Henry Carey wrote the libretto, is still in doubt.
699 Dane, Henry James. "The Life and Works of Henry Carey."
     Ph.D. University of Pennsylvania, 1967. (Order No. 67-12,
     739).
         Emphasizes the central role music played in Carey's life
     (1687-1743). Carey's best works were two dramatic burlesques,
     Chrononhotonthologos (1734), and The Dragon of Wantley.

Carlell, Lodowick

700 Gray, Charles H. "Lodowick Carlell." Ph.D. University of Chicago,
     1904.
701 Ewton, Gene. "A Critical Edition of The Passionate Lover by
     Lodowick Carlell." Ph.D. Rice University, 1963.

Cartwright, William

702 Evans, Gwynne Blakemore. "The Life and Works of William Cart-
     wright." Ph.D. Harvard University, 1940.
         Includes a discussion of Cartwright's influence on Shadwell,
     Otway, Southerne, and Congreve.

Caryll, John

703 Bowers, Fredson Thayer. "Bibliographical Evidence from a Re-
     setting of Caryll's Sir Salomon (1691)." The Library, Fifth

Ser., III (September, 1948), 134-137.

Demonstrates that the book was printed on two presses each using two skeletons.

704 Cameron, Kenneth M. "Strolling with Coysh." Theatre Notebook, XVII (Autumn, 1962), 12-16.

Copy of John Caryll's Sir Salomon, or The Cautious Cox-Comb (London, 1671) at the University of Chicago, contains annotations made by a member of the audience to its cast of characters.

Cavalier Drama

705 Harbage, Alfred. Cavalier Drama. New York: Modern Language Association, 1936. x, 302 pp.

From an analysis of Caroline plays and other materials, Harbage defines the Cavalier mode in drama, traces it through the Commonwealth period, and shows its relation to the Restoration heroic drama. Considered among the last of the Cavalier dramatists are William Killigrew, Robert Boyle, and Robert Howard.

Cavendish, Margaret

706 Gagen, Jean. "Honor and Fame in the Works of the Duchess of Newcastle." Studies in Philology, LVI (1959), 519-538.

Suggests that "Margaret Cavendish alone of all the women writers of her day espoused writing as a career with the avowed intent of winning fame in accordance with the ideals of Renaissance humanism." Studies the treatment of Renaissance ideals of fame and honor in the Duchess' works.

Censorship

707 G., G. M. The Stage Censor, an Historical Sketch: 1544-1907. London: 1908.

708 Palmer, John. The Censor and the Theatres. London: T. Fisher Unwin, 1912. 307 pp.

The history of censorship in the English theater from the Elizabethan age to the twentieth century; the effect of Walpole's Act on eighteenth century theatre.

709 Pollock, John. "The Censorship." The Fortnightly Review, New Ser., XCI (June, 1912), 880-894.

A short history of dramatic censorship in England, with emphasis upon the working of it and its abuses, particularly under Walpole.

710   Fowell, Frank, and Frank Palmer. Censorship in England. Lon-
         don: Frank Palmer, 1913. xii, 390, [2] pp.
              The history of theatrical censorship in England from the
         fifteenth century to 1912. Chapters V, VI, and VII are con-
         cerned with the Restoration and 18th century, with emphasis
         upon the policies and the abuses of power of the censors,
         examiners, and Lords Chamberlain; and some of the plays
         censored with reasons why. In the appendix the author prints
         the text of the Theatres Act of 1737.
711   Summers, Montague. "Stage Censorship under Charles II." Times
         Literary Supplement, April 29, 1920, p. 272.
              This article calls attention to the existence of an MS. of John
         Wilson's Belphegor; or, The Marriage of the Devil and also
         discusses editorial questions relating to Restoration plays.
712   -----. "The Censorship of Restoration Plays." The Drama, New
         Ser., No. 8 (June, 1921), 57-59.
              A report on instances of censorship during the Restoration
         period to show that there was censorship and surveillance of
         the stage during the reign of Charles II and his successors.
713   Krutch, Joseph Wood. "Governmental Attempts to Regulate the Stage
         after the Jeremy Collier Controversy." Publications of the Modern
         Language Association, XXXVIII (1923), 153-174.
              A discussion of the legal aspect of Collier's influence on the
         growth of sentimental comedy from the beginning of the 18th
         century through the Licensing Act.
714   White, Arthur P. "The Office of Revels and Dramatic Censorship
         During the Restoration Period." Western Reserve Bulletin, New
         Ser., XXXIV (September 15, 1931), 5-45.
              Discusses the nature, extent, and effectiveness of censor-
         ship under Charles II.
715   Meadley, Thomas D. "Attack on the Theatre (circa 1580-1680)."
         London Quarterly and Holborn Review, (January, 1953), 36-41.
              Traces the issue of censorship in English drama from
         Elizabeth through Charles II. Approximately three pages are
         devoted to the Restoration, but there is no reference to Collier.
716   -----. "The Second Attack on the English Stage, Preliminary
         Skirmishes." London Quarterly and Holborn Review, (October,
         1953), 279-283.
              Meadley examines the events preceding Collier's attack on
         the Restoration stage.
717   St. John-Stevas. Obscenity and the Law. London: Secker and War-
         burg, 1956. xxii, 289 pp.
              From early 18th century.

Centlivre, Susannah

plays

718 Centlivre, Susanna. The Busie Body (1709). Edited by Jess Byrd. The Augustan Reprint Society, Publication No. 19. Los Angeles: The William Andrews Clark Memorial Library, 1949.
Facsimile text of the play, with an introduction noting sources and briefly outlining the stage history.

719 Stathas, Thalia. "A Critical Edition of Three Plays by Susanna Centlivre." Ph.D. Stanford University, 1965. (Order No. 66-2621).
Modern editions of The Busie Body (1709), The Wonder (1714), and A Bold Stroke for a Wife (1718). Includes textual commentary and notes.

biography and criticism

720 Grober, Fritz. Das Verhältnis von Susannah Centlivre's Lustspiel "The Gamester" zu Regnard's Lustspiel "Le Joueur." Halle: Hofbuchdruckerei von C. A. Kaemmerer & Co., 1900. 45, [1] pp.
This dissertation, divided into three chapters, describes the relationship of the two plays. Grober first deals with the matter of plot organization; then of similarities in characterization. Lastly, he enumerates the remaining significant differences.

721 Hobohm, Maximilian. Das Verhältnis Susannah Centlivre's "Love at a Venture" zu Thomas Corneille's "Le Galant Double." Halle: Heinrich Sohn, 1900. 52 pp.
A comparison and contrast of the two plays in scene arrangement, main characters, and use of language.

722 Ohnsorg, Richard. John Lacy's Dumb Lady, Mrs. Susannah Centlivre's Love's Contrivance und Henry Fielding's Mock Doctor in ihrem Verhältnis zu einander und zu ihrer gemeinschaftlichen Quellen. Hamburg: Bargsted und Ruhland, 1900. 60 pp.
All the writers used Moliere; all made changes independent of Moliere and of each other.

723 Strube, Hans Daniel. Centlivre's Lustspiel "The Stolen Heiress" und sein Verhältnis zu "The Heir" von Thomas May. Nebst Anhang May und Shakespeare. Halle a.S.: C. A. Kaemmerer & Co., 1900. 51, [1] pp.

724 Weidler, Wilhelm. Das Verhältnis von Mrs. Centlivre's "The Busy Body" zu Molière's "L'Etourdi" und Ben Jonson's "The Divell Is an Asse." Halle: Buchdruckerei von Heinrich John, 1900. 45 pp.

After providing a brief sketch of Mrs. Centlivre's early years, Weidler discusses the relationship of The Busy Body to Molière's and Jonson's plays in regard to plot, language, and characterization.

725 Wüllenweber, Albert. Mrs. Centlivre's Lustspiel "Love's Contrivance" und seine Quellen. Halle: Heinrich Sohn, 1900. 43 pp.

Love's Contrivance gives brilliant proof of Mrs. Centlivre's dramatic ability. Even though Molière is the source, the foreign element is not perceived as such, and the most beautiful and liveliest scenes are her own.

726 Hohrmann, Friedrich. "Das Verhältnis Susanna Centlivre's zu Molière und Regnard." Zeitschrift für vergleichende Litteraturgeschichte, XIV (1901), 42-75, 401-429.

Part I: Centlivre's life and works; Part II: Centlivre's relation to Molière and her borrowings in various plays. Part III: Centlivre and Regnard's influence on The Gamester, The Basset-Table, The Platonick Lady, The Man's Bewitch'd. Line comparisons made at times.

727 Poelchau, Karl. Susannah Centlivre's Tragödie "The Cruel Gift" in ihren Verhältnis zur Quelle Boccaccios "Decameron" IV. Halle: C. A. Kaemmerer &Co., 1905. 122 pp.

Although Boccaccio is the source, the treatment is very free: the dramatic action is strongly expanded, the dramatis personae are augmented; and the characterizations, partly described by Boccaccio, are varied.

728 Seibt, Robert. "Die Komödien der Mrs. Centlivre." Anglia, XXXII (1909), 434-480; XXXIII (1910), 77-119.

729 -----. Die Komödien der Mrs. Centlivre. Halle a.S.: E. Karras, 1909. [6], 4-58, [2] pp.

Treats the plays, in terms of incident and character, in roughly chronological order.

730 -----. Mrs. Centlivre und ihre Quelle Hauteroche. Inaugural Dissertation. Kiel, 1909.

731 Evardsen, Hans. Mrs. Centlivre's Drama "The Cruel Gift und seine Quellen. Kiel, H. Fiencke, 1912. 76 pp.

732 Wilson, Mona. These Were Muses. London: Sidgwick and Jackson, Ltd., 1924. 246 pp.

See "An Intriguing Dramatist (Susannah Centlivre)," which is a brief sketch of Mrs. Centlivre's career, with some consideration of her plays.

733 Bowyer, John W. "Susanna Freeman Centlivre." Modern Language Notes, XLIII (February, 1928), 78-80.

Probably born in Ireland during the exile of her father. Adds to the bibliography of her works in the Cambridge History.

734 -----. "Susanna Freeman Centlivre; Life, Works, and Stage His-

tory." 2 vols. Ph.D. Harvard University, 1928.

    A biography of Mrs. Centlivre and a study of her nineteen plays with special attention to the sources, followed by a stage history of the plays and a discussion of Mrs. Centlivre's dramatic theory. The five appendices include a list of the performances of the dramas from 1700 to 1800, with casts and the programme.

735 Schulz, Freda. "Dramas of Mrs. Centlivre." M.A. Ohio State University, 1928.

736 Jerrold, Water and Clare Jerrold. Five Queer Women. New York: London: Brentano, 1929. xii, 356 pp.

    Aphra Behn, Mary Manley, Susanna Centlivre, Eliza Haywood, and Letitia Pilkington.

737 Bowyer, J. W. "Quakers on the English Stage." Publications of the Modern Language Association, XLV (1930), 957-958.

    Referring to Maxfield's "The Quakers in English Stage Plays before 1800," Bowyer points out that the earlier article overlooks an additional eighteenth-century play, A Bold Stroke for a Wife (1718).

738 Wood, Frederick T. "The Celebrated Mrs. Centlivre." Neophilologus, XVI (1931), 268-278.

739 Anderson, Paul Bunyan. "Innocence and Artifice, or Mrs. Centlivre and The Female Tatler." Philological Quarterly, XVI (1937), 358-375.

    Mrs. Centlivre probably wrote about half the periodical, Dr. Bernard Mandeville the other half. The articles can help explain Mrs. Centlivre's interest in (1) dreams, visions, or apparitions, and (2) Quakers. Quotes reviews and discusses actresses and the daily life of the stage and the critic.

740 Boys, Richard C. "A New Poem by Mrs. Centlivre." Modern Language Notes, LVII (May, 1942), 361-362.

    Quotes a poem printed in the periodical-miscellany Caribbeana in 1732.

741 Sutherland, James R. "The Progress of Error: Mrs. Centlivre and the Biographers." Review of English Studies, XVIII (April, 1942), 167-182.

    Examines some contemporary accounts of Mrs. Centlivre's life and points out errors; attempts to solve some problems associated with her biography. Concludes that she has been "unusually unfortunate" in her biographers.

742 Hume, Charles Vernard. "Producing Director's Study of Susanna Centlivre's A Bold Stroke for a Wife." M.A. State University of Iowa, 1947.

743 Bowyer, John Wilson. The Celebrated Mrs. Centlivre. Durham: Duke University Press, 1952. 267 pp.

Bowyer attempts "to make a complete study of her life, writings, stage history, and literary relations . . . and to remove her from the realms of impressions and rumor."

744 Mackenzie, John H. "Susan Centlivre," Notes and Queries, CXCVIII (1953), 386-390.

Mackenzie provides additional information about Mrs. Centlivre and attempts to clear up certain biographical problems.

745 Norton, J. E. "Some Uncollected Authors, XIV: Susanna Centlivre." Book Collector, VI (1957), 172-178, 280-285.

Bibliographical descriptions, including plays.

746 McKillop, Alan D. "Mrs. Centlivre's The Wonder: A Variant Imprint." Book Collector, VII (1958), 79-80.

Rice Library has a variant imprint with only Edmund Curll's name, evidently earlier than imprints also having Bettesworth's name.

747 ten Hoor, Henry. "A Re-Examination of Susanna Centlivre as a Comic Dramatist." Ph.D. The University of Michigan, 1963.

An investigation of seven comedies reveals that the basis of Mrs. Centlivre's comedy is man's inability to distinguish appearance from reality.

748 Strozier, Robert. "A Short View of Some of Mrs. Centlivre's Celebrat'd Plays, Including a Close Accounting of the Plots, Subplots, Asides, Soliloquies, Etcetera, Contain'd Therein." Discourse, VII (Winter, 1964), 62-80.

The development of Mrs. Centlivre's talent in The Perjur'd Husband, The Beaux's Duel, The Man's Bewitch'd, The Perplex'd Lovers, The Stolen Heiress, The Busy Body, and The Wonder.

Cervantes, Miguel

749 Flores, Angel and M. J. Bernardete, eds. Cervantes Across the Centuries A Quadricentennial Volume. New York: The Dryden Press, 1947.

Includes the articles, "Musical Settings to Cervantes' Texts," by Charles Haywood (pp. 254-263) discussing versions by D'Urfey-Purcell-Eccles, Fielding, Ackeroyd and Arnold, and "Cervantes and English Literature," by Edwin B. Knowles (pp. 267-293) describing dramatic versions by D'Urfey, Fielding and others.

Chapman, George

750 Barber, C. L. "TheAmbivalence of Bussy D'Ambois." A Review of English Literature, II (October, 1961), 38-44.

Discusses the reasons for the popularity of the play on the
Restoration stage.

Character Names

751 Withington, Robert. "Notes on Dramatic Nomenclature." Notes
      and Queries, CXLIX (December 5, 1925), 399-401.
         Discusses the significance of characters' names, including
      some from the Restoration and 18th century.

Characterization

752 Bayley, A. R. and William Jaggard. "Helena in All's Well That
      Ends Well." Notes and Queries, CLXXXI (1941), 122.
         A number of actresses have taken the part of Helena in
      All's Well That Ends Well, which became known as an unlucky
      play to act after a 1742 performance attended by sickness and
      death.

Characters

753 Baldwin, Edward Chauncey. "The Character in Restoration Com-
      edy." Publications of the Modern Language Association, XXX
      (1915), 64-78.
         The form of "character" found in Restoration is French,
      not English, and were modeled essentially after Molière, not
      Jonson.
754 Williams, Basil. "'Artificial' Comedy." London Times Literary
      Supplement, January 12, 1928, p. 28.
         Argues, in reply to G. M. Trevelyan (Times Literary Sup-
      plement, January 5, 1928), that characters in Restoration
      comedy are poorly motivated.
755 Walbridge, Earle F. Literary Characters Drawn from Life:
      "Romans à Clef"; "Drames à Clef," Real People in Poetry,
      with Some Other Literary Diversions. New York: H. W.
      Wilson, 1936. 192 pp.
         A catalogue of literary works which contain characters
      drawn from life; classified by genre, alphabetically arranged.
      Each entry consists of the author, title, and description of the
      relationship between the literary character and the actual per-
      son with whom it was drawn. Includes Restoration and 18th
      century plays.
756 Magill, Thomas N. "Character in the Drama." Ph.D. Cornell
      University, 1941.
757 Walbridge, Earle F. "Drames à Clef: A List of Plays with Char-

acters Based on Real People," Bulletin of the New York Public
Library, LX (1956), 159-174, 235-247, 289-297.
1660-1800, pp. 166-169.

758 Sewall, Arthur. "The Concept of Character in the Eighteenth Cen-
tury." Litera, IV (1957), 1-21.
Eighteenth century critics of Shakespeare, e.g., Rowe,
Dryden, Lord Kames, Dr. Johnson, William Richardson, Joseph
Warton, Richard Whately, Maurice Morgann. In the 17th century,
Margaret Cavendish, Duchess of Newcastle.

759 Barron, Leon Oser. "The Quest for the Good Society; Friends and
Families in Restoration Comedy." Ph.D. Harvard University,
1960.

Charke, Charlotte

760 McPharlin, Paul. "Charlotte Clarke's [sic] Marionette Theatre."
Notes and Queries, CLIV (May 5, 1928), 316.
Asks if Cibber wrote marionette drama for his daughter.

761 Wingrave, Wyatt. "Charlotte Charke's Marionette Theatre." Notes
and Queries, CLIV (June 2, 1928), 394.
Her autobiography makes no mention of any Cibber plays
written for her.

762 Charke, Charlotte Cibber. A Narrative of the Life of Mrs. Char-
lotte Charke (Youngest Daughter of Colley Cibber, Esq.).
London: Constable's Miscellany, 1929. 223 pp.
A reprint, no editor named.

763 McPharlin, Paul. "Charlotte Charke's Puppets in New York."
Theatre Notebook, I (July, 1947), 111-113.
Discusses the possibility that her equipment was used in
New York in 1749.

764 Speaight, George. "Charlotte Charke: An Unpublished Letter."
Theatre Notebook, XII (1957), 33-34.
Request for benefit at the Haymarket, 1759.

Charles II

765 Nicoll, Allardyce. "Charles II at the Theatre." Times Literary
Supplement, September 14, 1922, p. 584; September 21, 1922,
pp. 600-601; October 5, 1922, pp. 631-632.
Presentation of the contents of several playbills describing
performances at several theatres--Dorset Garden, Lincoln's
Inn Fields, Drury Lane--during the years 1666-1677.

CHART   101

Chart

766 Rowe, A. E. Synopsis of English Literature, 1688-1760 A.D.
     London: University Examination Postal Institution [1900].
     Chart.
         A large chronological chart, with a column devoted to each
     of the following: poetry, drama, fiction, prose, and Philosophy
     (History, Theology, etc.). For students.

Chatterton, Thomas

767 De Vigny, Alfred. Chatterton. Los Angeles: Lyman-house, 1939.
     82 pp.
768 Meyerstein, E. H. W. "Chatterton's 'Bristowe Tragedie.'" Times
     Literary Supplement, August 5, 1939, p. 467.
         Argues that an anonymous book of anecdotes was Chatterton's
     source for the central situation of the play.
769 -----. "The Forged Letter from Peele to Marlowe." Times Literary
     Supplement, June 29, 1940, p. 315.
         Demonstrates the spuriousness of an "Anecdote of Shakespeare
     . . ." printed in the Annual Register of 1770.
770 -----. "Chatterton's Last Days." Times Literary Supplement,
     June 28, 1941, p. 316.
771 White, Eric Walter. "Chatterton and the English Burletta." Re-
     view of English Studies, IX (1958), 43-48.
         Involves Kane, O'Hara's Midas and Chatterton's Amphitryon
     and The Revenge.

Chaucer, Geoffrey

772 Graves, Thornton S. "Some Chaucer Allusions (1561-1700)."
     Studies in Philology, XX (1923), 469-478.
         A listing of allusions to Chaucer, including four in Resto-
     ration dramas.

Chesterfield, Lord

773 Allen, B. Sprague. "Chesterfield's Objection to Laughter."
     Modern Language Notes, XXXVIII (1923), 279-287.
         Discusses Chesterfield's disapproval of laughter as a
     violation of decorum; also points out references to Chesterfield
     in other 18th century works.

Chinese Influence

774 Fan, Tsen-Chung. "Chinese Culture in England from Sir William
   Temple to Oliver Goldsmith." Ph.D. Harvard University, 1931.
      Chapter 5 discusses pictures of Chinese life in English
   drama and adaptations of Chinese drama.

Chorus

775 Griffin, Ernest E. "The Dramatic Chorus in English Literary
   Theory and Practice." Ph.D. Columbia University, 1959.
      Chapters III and IV cover the period 1666-1800.

Christ in Drama

776 Eastman, Fred. Christ in the Drama, a Study of the Influence of
   Christ in the Drama of England and America. New York: Macmillan, 1947. xv, 174 pp.
      Containing a brief, primarily negative comment on the
   period in Chapter III, "From Shakespeare to Shaw," 40-41.

Churchill, Charles

777 Churchill, Charles. The Poetical Works of Charles Churchill.
   Edited by Douglas Grant. Oxford: Clarendon Press, 1956.
   xxii, 587 pp.
      Annotated and indexed.
778 Sawyer, Paul. "A New Charles Churchill Letter." Notes and
   Queries, New Ser., V (1958), 61-63.
      About Garrick and Joseph Reed's Dido, 1767.
779 Ball, Albert. "Byron and Churchill: Further Parallels." Notes
   and Queries, New Ser., VII (1960), 105-107.
      Verbal reminiscences, structural devices and satiric
   treatment in Byron's English Bards clearly reveal the influence
   of Charles Churchill (1731-1764).
780 Rutherford, Andrew. "Byron and Churchill." Notes and Queries,
   New Ser., VII (1960), 315-316.
      Responds to Albert Ball's comment on Churchill's influence
   on Byron (Notes and Queries, VII, 105) by pointing out that
   the poet whom Byron claimed to be imitating here was not
   in fact Churchill, but Wordsworth.

Cibber, Caius

781 Faber, Harold. Caius Gabriel Cibber, 1630-1700: His Life and

Work. Oxford University Press, 1926. xvi, 80 pp.
The life of Colley Cibber's father, the sculptor.

Cibber, Colley

782 texts

Cibber, Colley. An Apology for the Life of Colley Cibber. 2 vols.
Waltham Saint Lawrence: Golden Cockerel Press, 1925.
A reprint from the 1756 Didsley edition, with some modern-
izations.

783 -----. An Apology for His Life by Colley Cibber. With an Historical View of the Stage During His Own Time. London: J. M. Dent
and Company; New York: E. P. Dutton & Co. [1914]. 302 pp.
The text is preceded by "An Appreciation" by William
Hazlitt which attempts to defend Cibber against Pope's charge
that he was dull and by a bibliography of Cibber's works. The
text, which is not annotated, follows. There is no indication of
the source of the text.

784 -----. An Apology for His Life. Everyman's Library. London: J.
M. Dent & Sons, Ltd., [192--?]. 302 pp.
An unedited printing of the text. Includes "An Appreciation"
by William Hazlitt which discusses the many aspects of Cibber's
career and concludes that he was a "gentleman and scholar."

785 -----. The Rival Queens, with the Humours of Alexander the
Great. Edited by William M. Peterson. Lake Erie College
Studies, 5. Painesville, Ohio, 1965. xxii, 55 pp.
Photographic reprint of the Huntington Library text. The
introduction is devoted to a discussion of Cibber's plays as a
parody on Lee's The Rival Queens.

786 Evans, John Maurice. "A Critical Edition of An Apology for the
Life of Mr. Colley Cibber, Comedian." Ph.D. Yale University,
1966. (Order No. 66-14, 974).
Includes introduction, notes, appendices and a facsimile
edition of 1760 with the author's notes.

787 Cibber, Colley. The Careless Husband. Edited by William W.
Appleton. [Regents Restoration Drama Series]. Lincoln: Uni-
versity of Nebraska Press, 1966.
Includes critical introduction and notes.

788 Fone, Byrne Reginald Spencer. "Colley Cibber's Love's Last Shift.
Edited with an Introduction and Textual Notes." Ph.D. New
York University, 1966. (Order No. 67-4815).
Introduction includes commentary on Cibber's life to 1696
and material discussing the play's contemporary reception,

sources, and its importance as a sentimental comedy.

biography and criticism

789 Koppe, K. Das Verhältnis von Cibber's "Papal Tyranny in the
     Reign of King John" zu Shakespeare's "King John." Inaugural
     Dissertation. Halle, 1902. 100 pp.
790 Besser, Richard. Colley Cibber's "The Double Gallant" und seine
     Quellen. Halle: C. A. Kaemmerer und Co., 1903. 105 pp.
     Sources are Calderon's Hombre Pobre Todo ez Tragos,
     Corneille's Le Galant Double, Burnaby's The Ladies Visiting
     Day, and Centlivre's Love at a Venture, but Cibber has not
     mechanically or slavishly followed them. Rather, he has im-
     proved and surpassed them, particularly Burnaby.
791 Schneider, Wilhelm. Das Verhältnis von Colley Cibber's Lust-
     spiel "The Non-Juror" zu Moliere's "Tartuffe." Halle: C. A.
     Kaemmerer & Co., 1903. 56 pp.
792 Irving, H. B. "Colley Cibber's Apology." The 19th Century, LVI
     (1904), 451-468.
     Concludes that the Apology is a "shrewd reply of the practi-
     cal man of the world to the pedants and theorists who, sitting
     in their studies, would fain conduct from their desks the
     business of the theatre.
793 -----. Occasional Papers, Dramatic and Historical. London:
     Bickers and Son, 1906. v, 251 pp.
     Several essays by Sir Henry Irving's son concern the stage,
     e.g., "The English Stage in the Eighteenth Century," pp. 1-
     63; "Colley Cibber's 'Apology, '" pp. 91-121.
794 Herrmann, Adolf. Colley Cibber's Tragicömedie, Ximena or the
     Heroic Daughter, und ihr verhältnis zu Corneille's Cid. Ph.D.
     University of Kiel, 1908. 116 pp.
     Contains an act and scene analysis of each play. Also shows
     parallels between the two plays by means of printing extracts
     from the text in parallel columns.
795 Michels, Ernst. Quellenstudien zu Colley Cibber's Lustspiel
     "The Careless Husband." Inaugural Dissertation, 1908. 79 pp.
     A short discussion of Cibber's The Careless Husband, show-
     ing that the sources are Van Brugh's The Provoked Husband,
     and Steele's The Tender Husband.
796 Tönse, Ludwig. "Colley Cibber's Comedy The Refusal, or The
     Ladies Philosophy in ihrem verhältnis zu Molieres Les Femmes
     Savantes." Inaugural Dissertation. Kiel, 1910. 76 pp.
797 Bensley, Edward. "Cibber's Apology." Notes and Queries, 11th
     Ser., IV (December 9, 1911), 475.
     Prints letter from Giles Earle to Mrs. Howard which has

information corresponding with Cibber's description in The
Apology of one of the masters of raillery.

798 Croissant, Dewitt C. "The Life and Works of Colley Cibber."
Ph.D. Princeton University, 1911.

799 Hipwell, Daniel. "Colley Cibber's Marriage." Notes and Queries,
11th Ser., IV (November 4, 1911), 366.

Cibber married Cathrine Shore, 6 May, 1693, according to
the Parish Register of St. James, Duke's Place, Aldgate.

800 Nicholson, Watson. "Colley Cibber's Apology." Notes and Queries,
11th Ser., III (April 8, 1911), 266.

Prints copy of a receipt given by Cibber for the amount paid
him by Dodsley for rights to the Apology.

801 Prideaux, W. F. "Cibber's Apology." Notes and Queries, 11th
Ser., IV (March 11, 1911), 381-382.

On information contained in marginalia of Prideaux's copy
of Bellchamber's edition that the Apology may be dedicated to
Bubb Doddington and that Giles (Tom) Earle was one of the two
masters of raillery mentioned by Cibber.

802 Croissant, Dewitt W. H. Studies in the Work of Colley Cibber.
Lawrence: Reprinted from the Bulletin of the University of
Kansas, Humanistic Studies, I, No. 1, 1912. 69 pp.

Part I concerned with notes on Cibber's farces, operas,
tragedies, and comedies. Part II emphasizes Cibber, not
Steele, as the most important figure in the early development
of sentimental comedy.

803 Koop, Theodor. Das Verhältnis von Colley Cibbers Lustspiel
"The Rival Fools" zu Beaumont and Fletchers "Wit At Several
Weapons." Inaugural Dissertation. Greifswald, 1913. 86 pp.

The Rival Fools is indebted to Beaumont and Fletcher,
particularly in Cibber's moralizing tendency and also in the
manner of construction, composition, character and style.

804 Lawrence, W. J. "The Delights of Chorussing." Musical Quarterly, I (1915), 52-56.

The French and Italian practice of inviting the audience to
sing along with the actors the popular airs in plays and ballad
operas was tried at Colley Cibber's Love in a Riddle, but the
experiment ended in "the devil of a row."

805 Miles, Dudley Howe. "The Original of The Non-Juror." Publications of the Modern Language Association, XXX (1915),
195-214.

Miles insists that Cibber's source for The Non-Juror was
not the original of Molière's Tartuffe but Melbourne's English
translation of 1670.

806 -----. "The Political Satire of The Non-Juror." Modern Philology,
XIII (1915), 281-304.

807 -----. "A Forgotten Hit: The Non-Juror." Studies in Philology,
     XVI (1919), 67-77.
808 Glicksman, Harry. "The Stage History of Colley Cibber's The
     Careless Husband." Publications of the Modern Language
     Association, XXXVI (1921), 245-50.
          A history of productions of the play from its premiere (Dec-
     ember 4, 1704) through approximately 1764.
809 Croissant, DeWitt C. "A Note on The Egoist, or Colley upon
     Cibber." Philological Quarterly, III (1924), 76-77.
          An argument that Cibber himself was undoubtedly the author
     of this 1743 play.
810 Eaton, Walter Prichard. "Colley Cibber as Critic." The Actor's
     Heritage; Scenes from the Theatre of Yesterday and the Day
     Before. (Boston: The Atlantic Monthly Press [1924]), 155-198.
          A discussion of Cibber's Apology, described by Eaton as
     "one of the best books on acting ever written."
811 Bateson, F. W. "The Double Gallant of Colley Cibber." Review
     of English Studies, I (July, 1925), 343-346.
          A study of the sources, Mrs. Centlivre's Love at a Venture
     and two comedies by Charles Burnaby.
812 Sprague, Arthur C. "A New Scene in Colley Cibber's Richard III."
     Modern Language Notes, XLII (January, 1927), 29-32.
          Reprints the scene, later omitted by Cibber, from the first
     edition (1700).
813 Groesbeck, Katharine. "Colley Cibber." Notes and Queries, CLV
     (December 8, 1928), 406.
          A petition by Cibber to the Earl of Sunderland for release
     from prison.
814 Habbema, D. M. E. An Appreciation of Colley Cibber, Actor and
     Dramatist, together with a Reprint of his play "The Careless
     Husband." Amsterdam: H. J. Paris, 1928. iv, 190 pp.
          A scholarly but dull study of Cibber's dramatic and theatrical
     career, with appendices on the theatre during the Commonwealth,
     Cibber's attitude toward Collier's Short View, and Cibber and
     Pope. Little that is new.
815 Montgomery, Franz Jackson. "The Songs in the Plays of Colley
     Cibber. A Study of Dramatic History and Technique." M.A.
     Indiana University, 1928.
          Includes a Foreward, "The Songs in English Drama before
     the Eighteenth Century," by John Robert Moore. Biographical
     sketch of Cibber's life, his use of the songs of his predecessors,
     a reprinting of every song in Cibber's plays, with notes, and
     a tracing of the development of the use of songs and music in
     Cibber's work. His work demonstrates a development of techni-
     que as regards the use of song, moving toward an integration of
     song with plot and motivation.

816 Senior, F. Dorothy. The Life and Times of Colley Cibber. London:
     Constable, 1928. xvi, 286 pp.
         The account of the quarrel with Pope is of some value, al-
     though Pope comes off rather badly, but most of the rest makes
     no improvement upon Cibber's own Apology. Includes portraits,
     appendices reprinting "The Careless Husband" and one of the
     Birthday Odes.

817 Wilkinson, Clennell. "Biography and Memoirs." London Mercury,
     XVIII (September, 1928), 546-547.
         Reviews D. Senior, The Life and Times of Colley Cibber
     (1928). Argues that Cibber's contemporaries despised him.

818 Pinto, Vivian de Sola. [Review]. Review of English Studies, V
     (April, 1929), 229-232.
         Reviews D. M. E. Habbema, An Appreciation of Colley Cib-
     ber (1928). Objects that the old English system of punctuation
     in the dramas was based on rhetorical rather than grammatical
     principles.

819 Forbes, Frances L. "Colley Cibber's Theories of Dramatic Pro-
     duction." M.A. Cornell University, 1930.

820 MacMillan, Dougald. "The Text of Love's Last Shift." Modern
     Language Notes, XLVI (1931), 518-519.
         The text was changed from its original form of 1696 when
     it was included in the collected plays of 1721. The changes--
     omission of lines and changes of words--indicate a growing
     delicacy on the part of the public.

821 Griffith, John Maynard. "The Elements of Sentimentalism in the
     Dramatic Work of Colley Cibber." M.A. Northwestern Uni-
     versity, 1933.

822 Griffith, R. H. "A 'Wildfrau Story' in a Cibber Play." Philologi-
     cal Quarterly, XII (1933), 298-302.

823 Telfer, William A. "Colley Cibber's Moral Theory and Practice."
     Ph.D. Cornell University, 1933.

824 Vincent, Howard P. "Two Letters of Colley Cibber." Notes and
     Queries, CLXVIII (January 5, 1935), 3-4.
         Prints two holograph letters dated May and July, 1742, which
     are primarily of biographical interest.

825 Smith, Rebecca. "Colley Cibber's Dramatic Theory and Practice."
     M.A. Duke University, 1938.

826 Avery, Emmett L. "The Craftsman of July 2, 1737, and Colley
     Cibber." Research Studies of the State College of Washington,
     VII (1939), 91-103.
         Reprints and analyzes a letter to The Craftsman which
     argues in favor of the Licensing Act. Though the letter is
     signed with Cibber's initials, Avery believes that his author-
     ship is unlikely.

827 Barker, Richard Hindry. Mr. Cibber of Drury Lane. Columbia
     University Studies in English and Comparative Literature, No.
     143. New York: Columbia University Press, 1939. 278 pp.
          An authoritative biography of the actor-playwright; the stage
     history, but no critical analyses, of the plays; and abundant in-
     formation about the theatre during Cibber's career.
828 Tupper, Fred S. "Colley and Caius Cibber." Modern Language
     Notes, LV (May, 1940), 393-396.
          "New evidence from chancery records, establishing among
     other things the fact that Cibber's son James was blind and
     throwing light thus on the singular pathos of his poem, 'The
     Blind Boy.'"
829 White, Frederic C. "Pre-Malaprop Malapropisms." Notes and
     Queries, CLXXIX (1940), 443-444.
          Cibber put malaprops in the mouth of Mawworm in The Non-
     Juror in 1718 long before Sheridan's Mrs. Malaprop began
     speaking.
830 Klie, Harry K. "Colley Cibber's The Non-Juror." M.A. Univer-
     sity of Illinois, 1941.
831 Wood, Frederick Thomas. "A Letter of Cibber." Notes and Queries
     CXCI (July 13, 1946), 15.
          Comments on a letter from the actor to his daughter Char-
     lotte, c. 1730.
832 Lehner, Francis Charles. "The Literary Views of Colley Cib-
     ber." Ph.D. University of Wisconsin, 1955.
833 Ashley, Leonard R. N. "The Theatre-Royal in Drury Lane, 1711-
     1716, under Colley Cibber, Barton Booth, and Robert Wilks."
     Ph.D. Princeton University, 1956.
          Based on a study of two scrapbooks of bills and accounts
     signed by the managers.
834 "A Cibber 'Puff.'" Notes and Queries, New Ser., III (1956), 388-
     391.
          In The Gentleman's Magazine, February, 1745.
835 Peterson, William M. "Cibber's She Wou'd, and She Wou'd Not
     and Vanbrugh's Aesop." Philological Quarterly, XXXV (1956),
     429-435.
          Cibber borrowed and expanded.
836 -----. "The Text of Cibber's She Wou'd, and She Wou'd Not."
     Modern Language Notes, LXXI (1956), 258-262.
          Finds Cibber's revisions governed by decorum and economy.
837 Parnell, Paul E. "An Incorrectly Attributed Speech-Prefix in
     Love's Last Shift." Notes and Queries, New Ser., VI (1959),
     212-213.
          Two of Young Worthy's speeches given to Elder Worthy,
     III, ii.

838 Peterson, William M. "Cibber's The Rival Queens." Notes and
     Queries, New Ser., VI (1959), 164-168.
         History and sources; burlesque of Lee.
839 Tucker, Susie. "A Note on Colley Cibber's Name." Notes and
     Queries, New Ser., VI (1959), 400.
         "Kibber," that is.
840 Parnell, Paul E. "Equivocation in Cibber's Love's Last Shift."
     Studies in Philology, LVII (1960), 519-534.
         An attempt to "adequately explicate Cibber's motives in
     writing Love's Last Shift," which, says Parnell, is neither
     "Restoration Comedy" nor "Sentimental Comedy" but "comedy
     of equivocation": a type intended to appeal to both antipathetic
     audience groups.
841 McAleer, John J. "Colley Cibber--Shakespeare's Adapter."
     Shakespeare Newsletter, XI (December, 1961), 42.
         Brief biography.
842 Morley, Malcolm. "No Apology for Colley Cibber." New Rambler
     (Johnson Society, London), January, 1962, pp. 25-29.
843 Kalson, Albert E. "The Chronicles in Cibber's Richard III."
     Studies in English Literature, 1500-1900, III (1963), 253-267.
         The indebtedness of Cibber's alteration of Shakespeare's
     Richard III to the histories of Holinshed, Stow, Speed and
     Baker.
844 Peavy, Charles D. "Cibber's Crown of Dulness: A Re-examination
     of the Pope-Cibber Controversy." Ph.D. Tulane University,
     1963.
         Pope's enthronement of Cibber stems from "the basic anta-
     gonism of aesthetic and moral values that underlies the entire
     Pope-Cibber controversy."
845 Prosser, Eleanor. "Colley Cibber at San Diego." Shakespeare
     Quarterly, XIV (1963), 253-261.
         Modern adaptation of Shakespeare's Henry IV, Part 2 at
     San Diego was more in keeping with Shakespeare's intention
     than the "pure" Shakespearean production at Ashland. Com-
     parison of Director Ball to Colley Cibber.
846 Peavy, Charles D. "The Pope-Cibber Controversy: A Bibliography."
     Restoration and 18th Century Theatre Research, III (November,
     1964), 51-55.
         34 primary sources, annotated and in chronological order.
847 Ashley, Leonard R. N. Colley Cibber. New York: Twayne Pub-
     lishers, Inc., 1965.
         Biographical and critical study of Cibber's works. Of parti-
     cular note are Chapter II, "The Actor"; Chapter III, "The Play-
     wright"; Chapter IV, "Drury Lane"; Chapter V, "The Manage-

ment"; and Chapter VI, "The Theatre and the Company." Includes selected bibliography.

848 Gilmore, Thomas B., Jr. "Colley Cibber's Good Nature and His
Reaction to Pope's Satire." Papers on Language and Literature,
II (1966), 361-371.
    Contrary to popular belief, Cibber did not respond with good
nature to Pope's attacks; slowly but perceptibly he became more
scurrilous and abusive.

849 Peavy, Charles D. "Pope, Cibber & the Crown of Dulness." The
South Central Bulletin, XXVI (1966), 17-27.

850 Rogal, Samuel J. "Pope's Treatment of Colley Cibber." Lock
Haven Review, No. 8 (1966), 25-30.

851 Ashley, L. R. "Colley Cibber: A Bibliography." Restoration and
18th Century Theatre Research, VI (May, 1957), 51-57.
    The most modern and complete listing of Cibber's works.
The list of books and articles about Cibber and his period is
selective.

852 Habbema, D. A Appreciation of Colley Cibber, Actor and Dramatist Together with a Reprint of His Play, The Careless Husband.
New York: Haskell House, 1967. 190 pp.
    A reprint of the 1928 edition, the first part of the work is
given to a biography of Cibber as actor, theatre manager and
playwright, the second to a critical introduction for and text of
Cibber's play.

Cibber, Susannah

853 Rogers, Francis. "Handel and the Five Prima Donnas." Musical
Quarterly, XXIX (April, 1943), 214-224.
    In addition to Margherita Durastanti, Anastasia Robinson,
Francesca Cuzzoni, and Faustina Bordoni, the article traces
the career of Susannah Cibber, wife of Theophilus Cibber and
sister of Thomas Arne, for whom Handel wrote the role of
Galatea. Brief mention of her portrayal of Polly in The Beggar's Opera and of her relationship with Garrick.

Cibber, Theophilus

854 [Folland, Harold Freeze.] "Theophilus Cibber; an Essay in Biography." Bowdoin Prize, Harvard University, 1929. 60 pp.
    A biography, stressing Cibber's career as an actor and his
turbulent personal life.

855 Scouten, A. H. "Theophilus Cibber's The Humourists." Notes and
Queries, CC (1955), 114-115.
    Identifies this play as an adaptation of Shakespeare, performe

at Drury Lane, which has not been mentioned in standard works.

Circus

856 Coxe, Antony Hippisley. "The Lesser-Known Circuses of London."
Theatre Notebook, XIII (1959), 89-100.
  Includes 18th century.

Classicism

857 Harvey-Jellie, W. Le Théâtre Classique en Anglettere dans l'Age
de John Dryden. Montreal: Librairie Beauchemin [1932]. 109 pp.
  The author admires Restoration drama not only for the number and talent of its creators but also for the great variety of
works produced during the period. His book, which acknowledges
Dryden as the beacon of the age, contains chapters dealing with
romanticism and classicism, verse drama, the precursors of
Dryden, Dryden's work, Dryden's relationship with French
drama, and the dramaturgy of decadence.
858 Gallaway, Francis. Reason, Rule, and Revolt in English Classicism. New York: Charles Scribner's Sons, 1940. 371 pp.
  Thinks the views of the greater men in the century more
important than the minor ones. "Synthetic presentation of the
artistic outlook of the age." Treats of tragedy in general,
catharsis, and the unities.

Cleopatra

859 Everett, William. "Six Cleopatras." Atlantic Monthly, XCV (1905),
252-263.
  Discussion of Shakespeare's "Antony and Cleopatra,"
Beaumont and Fletcher's "The False One," Corneille's "Mort de
Pompée," Dryden's "All for Love, or the World Well Lost,"
Marmontel's "Cléopatre," and de Giradin's "Cléopatre."

Clive, Kitty

860 Crean, P. J. "A Study of the Life and Times of Kitty Clive." Ph.D.
London University (External), 1933.
861 -----. "Kitty Clive." Notes and Queries, CLXXIV (1938), 309-310.
  Commentary upon a letter written by Kitty Clive in 1767 to
either Garrick or Colman.

Clubs

862 Nevill, Ralph. London Clubs. London: Chatto and Windus, 1911.
316 pp.
The histories and the treasures owned by London clubs.

863 Jones, Louis C. The Clubs of the Georgian Rakes. New York:
Columbia University Press; London: Oxford University Press,
1942. 260 pp.

Cobb, Samuel

864 Cobb, Samuel. "Discourse on Criticism and of Poetry." Poems on
Several Occasions (1707). Edited by Louis I. Bredvold. Ann
Arbor: The Augustan Reprint Society, July, 1946.
A facsimile reproduction. "Of Poetry" is a progress poem
making conventional critical comment on major Elizabethan
and Restoration playwrights.

Cokain, Aston

865 Spaemann, Hermann. "Aston Cokain's Dramen, ihre Beziehungen
zur englischen und romanischen Literatur, insbesondere zur
Commedia dell Arte." Münster Dissertation, 1923.
Inaugural Dissertation. Münster, 1923.

866 Raychaudhuri, D. "The Life and Works of Sir Aston Cokain." M.A.
London University (University College), 1933.

867 Scouten, Arthur Hawley. "Aston Cokain and His Adapter Nahum
Tate." Ph.D. Louisiana State University, 1941.

868 Mathews, Ernest G. "Cokain's The Obstinate Lady and 'Araucana.'"
Modern Language Notes, LVII (January, 1942), 57-58.
". . . traces a borrowing of Cokain's from Zuniga's epic
of the struggle for Chile."

869 Cokain, Sir Aston. The Dramatic Works of Aston Cokain. Edited
by James Maidment and W. H. Logan. New York: Benjamin
Blom, 1967. 319 pp.
A reprint of the 1874 edition contains the dramatic works
of Cokain (1608-1684) including The Tragedy of Ovid (1662).

Colchester

870 R[ickword], G. O. "An Autumn Night's Adventure: an Echo of the
Colchester Stage in 1679." Essex Review, LIV (1945), 59-60.
Colchester public records reveal the presence of a company
of players on 16 October, 1679.

871 ----. "The Theatre Royal, Colchester: 1812-1918." Essex Review,

LIV (1945), 21-29.

Includes notes on the eighteenth century, "when Colchester formed part of the circuit worked by the Norwich Company of Comedians."

Coleridge, Samuel

872 Bowles, W. L. A Wiltshire Parson and his Friends: The Correspondence of W. L. Bowles. Edited by Garland Cheever. London: Constable, 1926. xv, 207 pp.

Includes two letters by Coleridge, one of them throwing important light on the genesis of Osorio.

873 Morrill, D. I. "Coleridge's Theory of Dramatic Illusion." Modern Language Notes, XLII (November, 1927), 436-444.

A state between the extremes of perfect delusion and "the absolute denial of deception as maintained by Johnson."

874 Brinkley, Roberta Florence, ed. Coleridge on the Seventeenth Century. With an introduction by Louis I. Bredvold. [Durham, N.C.]: Duke University Press, 1955. xxxvii, 704 pp.

Reprints excerpts from published and unpublished writings of Coleridge on the subjects of philosophy, the old divines, science, literary prose, poetry, and drama, with an introduction to each section. Special attention to Ben Jonson, Beaumont and Fletcher, Dryden, Etherege, Congreve, and Farquhar.

Collections

875 Modern English Drama: Dryden, Sheridan, Goldsmith, Shelley, Browning, Byron, with Introductions and Illustrations. New York: P. F. Collier & Son [c. 1909]. 444 pp. (The Harvard Classics. Edited by C. W. Eliot.)

Contains All for Love, with Dryden's dedication and preface; The School for Scandal, with "A Portrait"; She Stoops to Conquer, with Goldsmith's inscription to Johnson. The very brief introductions give biographical information.

876 Tupper, Frederick, Ed. Representative English Dramas from Dryden to Sheridan. New York: Oxford University Press, 1914. 461 pp.

877 Tatlock, John Strong Perry, and Robert G. Martin, Eds. Representative English Plays from the Middle Ages to the End of the Nineteenth Century. New York: The Century Co., 1916. 838 pp. [Second edition, 1938].

878 Stevens, David Harrison. Types of English Drama, 1660-1780. Edited from the Original Editions with Notes, Biographical Sketches, and Airs of "The Beggar's Opera." Boston, New

York [etc.]: Ginn and Company [c. 1923]. 920 pp.

Contains The Rehearsal (The Duke of Buckingham), The Man of Mode (Etherege), Aureng-Zebe (Dryden), All for Love (Dryden), Venice Preserved (Otway), Bury Fair (Shadwell), Way Of the World (Congreve), Love for Love (Congreve), Beaux Stratagem (Farquhar), Cato (Addison), Jane Shore (Rowe), The Conscious Lovers (Steele), The Beggar's Opera (Gay), The Tragedy of Tragedies (Fielding), The London Merchant (Lillo), Douglas (Home), The Good Natured Man (Goldsmith), She Stoops to Conquer (Goldsmith), The Rivals (Sheridan), School for Scandal (Sheridan), The Critic (Sheridan).

879 Matthews, Brander, and Paul Robert Lieder, eds. British Dramatis excluding Shakespeare; Twenty-Five Plays from the Middle of the Fifteenth Century to the End of the Nineteenth . . . Boston, New York [etc.]: Houghton Mifflin Co. [c. 1924]. xviii, 1084 pp.

From Restoration and 18th century, contains The Plain Dealer (Wycherley), All for Love (Dryden), Venice Preserved (Otway), The Provoked Wife (Vanbrugh), The Way of the World (Congreve) Beaux Stratagem (Farquhar), She Stoops to Conquer (Goldsmith), School for Scandal (Sheridan).

880 Gosse, Edmund. Restoration Plays from Dryden to Farquhar. London: Dent, 1925. (Everyman)

Reprints the 1912 edition.

881 Stauffer, Ruth M., ed. The Progress of Drama through the Centuries. New York: Macmillan, 1927. 696 pp. (Reprinted May, 1928.)

Contains Goldsmith's She Stoops to Conquer and Sheridan's The School for Scandal; bibliography.

882 Dobrée, Bonamy, ed. Five Restoration Tragedies. Oxford University Press, 1928. xviii, 450 pp. (World's Classics)

Dryden's All for Love, Otway's Venice Preserv'd, Southerne' Oroonoko, Rowe's The Fair Penitent, Addison's Cato. Introduction stresses the admiration and love which dominate serious Restoration drama.

883 Rubinstein, H. F., ed. Great English Plays. Twenty-three Masterpieces from the Mysteries to Sheridan. London: Gollancz, 1928. 1136 pp.

Includes Otway's Venice Preserved, Vanbrugh's The Provoked Wife, Congreve's The Way of the World, Farquhar's The Recruiting Officer, Goldsmith's She Stoops to Conquer, and Sheridan's The School for Scandal.

884 Smith, Robert Metcalf, ed. Types of Social Comedy. New York: Prentice Hall, 1928. 759 pp. (World Drama Series).

Congreve's Way of the World; Goldsmith's She Stoops to Conquer: Sheridan's The School for Scandal. Each play is

preceded by a very brief historical-critical introduction.
885 Hampden, John, ed. Eighteenth Century Plays. London: Dent,
1929. xxviii, 408 pp. (Everyman).

Addison's Cato, Rowe's Jane Shore, Lillo's George Barnwell, Colman and Garrick's The Clandestine Marriage, Cumberland's The West Indian, Gay's The Beggar's Opera, and
Fielding's Tom Thumb. Each play prefaced by a brief account
of the author.
886 Lieder, Paul R., Robert M. Lovett and Robert K. Root, eds.
British Drama. Ten plays from the middle of the fourteenth
century to the end of the nineteenth. Boston: Houghton Mifflin,
1929. v, 374 pp.

Includes Dryden's All for Love, Congreve's The Way of the
World, and Sheridan's The School for Scandal.
887 Moore, John Robert. Representative English Dramas. Boston:
Ginn and Co., 1929. 487 pp.

Includes Dryden's All for Love and Sheridan's The School
for Scandal.
888 Moses, Montrose J., ed. British Plays from the Restoration
to 1820. Boston: Little, Brown, 1929. xvi, 921 pp.

Buckingham's The Rehearsal, Dryden's The Spanish Fryar,
Etherege's The Man of Mode, Wycherley's The Plain Dealer,
Congreve's The Way of the World, Vanbrugh's The Provok'd
Wife, Otway's Venice Preserved, Cibber's The Careless Hus-
band, Steele's The Conscious Lovers, Rowe's Jane Shore,
Farquhar's The Beaux' Stratagem, Gay's The Beggar's Opera,
Home's Douglas, Goldsmith's She Stoops to Conquer, Cumber-
land's The Fashionable Lover, Colman and Garrick's The
Clandestine Marriage, Sheridan's The School for Scandal.
889 Taylor, W. D., ed. Eighteenth Century Comedy. Oxford Uni-
versity Press, 1929. xxviii, 414 pp. (World's Classics)

A succinct and adequate introduction. Includes Farquhar's
The Beaux' Stratagem, Steele's The Conscious Lovers, Gay's
The Beggar's Opera, Fielding's Tom Thumb, and Goldsmith's
She Stoops to Conquer.
890 Uhler, John Earle, ed. The Best Eighteenth-Century Comedies
with Comments on the Drama and Dramatists of the Period.
New York: Knopf, 1929. viii, 480 pp.

Gives a brief account of the main currents of dramatic
literature in the 18th century. Includes the texts of Farquhar's
The Beaux' Stratagem, Gay's The Beggar's Opera, Goldsmith's
She Stoops to Conquer, Sheridan's The Rivals, and The School
for Scandal.
891 Moore, Cecil A. Twelve Famous Plays of the Restoration and
Eighteenth Century. Introduction by Professor Cecil A. Moore.

New York: B. A. Cerf, D. S. Klopfer, The Modern Library
[c. 1933]. 952 pp.

This anthology, preceded by a brief essay describing the
trends, themes, and history of Restoration and 18th-century
drama contains: The Country Wife, All for Love, Venice Preserv'd, Love for Love, The Provok'd Wife, The Way of the
World, The Beaux' Stratagem, The Beggar's Opera, The
Clandestine Marriage, She Stoops to Conquer, The Rivals and
The School for Scandal.

892 Morgan, E. A., ed. English Plays, 1660-1820. New York & London: Harper & Bros., 1935. x, 1167 pp.

A collection of twenty-three play texts, most of them taken
from the first printed editions. In addition to the more familiar
titles, the volume includes many plays that are seldom reprinted:
Shadwell, Bury Fair; Hoadley, The Suspicious Husband; Home,
Douglas; Townley, High Life Below Stairs; and Morton, Speed the
Plough, among others.

893 Gayley, Charles Mills, and Alwin Thaler, eds. Representative
English Comedies. Vol. IV. Dryden and His Contemporaries:
Cowley to Farquhar. New York: Macmillan, 1936. xii, 777 pp.

This last volume of a series is an authoritative anthology
containing texts of Cowley, Cutter of Coleman Street; Dryden,
The Spanish Fryar; Wycherley, Plain Dealer; Vanbrugh, Provok'd Wife; Congreve, Way of the World; and Farquhar, Recruiting Officer. Individual scholars edited each text and included an introductory critical essay and explanatory notes.
Also in the volume is a monograph by A. W. Ward, "John
Crowne, His Place in Restoration Comedy."

894 Kronenberger, Louis, ed. An Eighteenth Century Miscellany.
New York: G. P. Putnam's Sons, 1936. 578 pp.

"A mirror of the age" anthology intended for a general audience. The volume includes undocumented texts of The Beggar's
Opera and The School for Scandal.

895 Nettleton, George H., and Arthur E. Case, eds. British Dramatists from Dryden to Sheridan. Boston: Houghton Mifflin Co.,
1939. vii, 957 pp.

A varied and representative collection of the most important
plays of the period. The texts are authoritative; the documentation is reliable; and the supplemental material completes an
adequate presentation of dramatic history.

896 Feasey, Lynette. And So to the Playhouse. London: Harrap, 1951.
192 pp.

This book contains excerpts from Venice Preserv'd and The
Way of the World. There are also introductions to the Restoration theatre and to the individual plays.

897 Quintana, Ricardo (ed.). Eighteenth-Century Plays. New York:
Modern Library, 1952. 484 pp.
    Included are : Addison, Cato; Rowe, Jane Shore; Steele, The
Conscious Lovers; Gay, The Beggar's Opera; Lillo, The London
Merchant; Goldsmith, She Stoops to Conquer; and Sheridan, The
Rivals.
898 Dean, Leonard F., ed. Nine Great Plays from Aeschylus to Eliot.
Revised ed. New York: Harcourt, Brace and World, Inc., 1956.
[1950].
    Includes The Way of the World, pp. 317-397, annotated.
899 Wilson, John Harold, ed. Six Restoration Plays. Boston: Houghton
Mifflin Co., 1959. (Riverside Editions, B 38.) xiv, 463 pp.
    The Country Wife, The Man of Mode, All for Love, Venice
Preserved, The Way of the World, The Beaux' Stratagem.
900 Dobrée, Bonamy, ed. Five Heroic Plays. (The World's Classics,
No. 576). London, New York: Oxford University Press, 1960.
xiii, 417 pp.
    Boyle, Mustapha; Settle, Empress of Morocco; Lee, Sopho-
nisba; Dryden, Aureng-Zebe; Crowne, Destruction of Jerusalem,
Part 2.
901 Mandel, Oscar. The Theatre of Don Juan: A Collection of Plays and
Views, 1630-1963. Edited with a Commentary. Lincoln: Uni-
versity of Nebraska Press, 1963. 731 pp.
902 Wilson, John Harold, editor. Six Eighteenth-Century Plays. With
and Introduction. Boston: Houghton Mifflin, 1963. 374 pp.
(Riverside Eds., B 85).
    Includes The Fair Penitent, The Conscious Lovers, The
Beggar's Opera, The London Merchant, She Stoops to Conquer,
The School for Scandal.
903 Falle, G. G., editor. Three Restoration Comedies. New York: St.
Martin's Press, 1964. 342 pp.
    Student edition with notes and bibliography of The Country
Wife, The Way of the World, and The Rehearsal.
904 Downer, Alan S., and Arthur C. Kirsch, eds. Restoration. (The
Laurel Masterpieces of World Literature). New York: Dell
Publishing Company, 1965. 512 pp.
    A paperback anthology. Includes Rymer's Othello, Dryden's
An Essay of Dramatic Poesy, and verse from several Restoration
dramas.
905 Spencer, Christopher, Editor. Five Restoration Adaptations of
Shakespeare. Urbana: University of Illinois Press, 1965. 475 pp.
    Includes Tate's King Lear (1681), Cibber's Richard III (1700),
the operatic Tempest (1674), Davenant's Macbeth (1674), and
Granville's Jew of Venice (1701).
906 Inchbald, Elizabeth, ed. The Modern Theatre. 10 vols. New York:

Benjamin Blom, 1967.

A reprint of the 1809 edition includes fifty plays by twenty-three playwrights of the late eighteenth century.

Collier, Jeremy

907 Maclean, Mary E. "The Jeremy Collier Controversy." Ph.D. Yale University, 1905.

908 Ballein, Johannes. Jeremy Collier's Angriff auf die englische Bühne. Marburg: R. Friedrich, 1909. ix, 107 pp.

Discusses Collier controversy, "The Societies for the Reformation of Manners," and Sir Richard Blackmore.

909 Ballein, Johannes. Jeremy Collier's Angriff auf die englische Bühne. Marburg: Elwert, 1910. x, 251, [1] pp.

910 Broxap, Henry. "Jeremy Collier's Two Marriages." Notes and Queries, CXLIX (August 29, 1925), 151.

No record of the marriages.

911 Bradley, L. J. H. "Jeremy Collier's 'Marcus Aurelius.'" Times Literary Supplement, January 19, 1928, p. 44.

Discusses editions of Collier's translation of Marcus Aureliu (first published 1701).

912 Holland, Michael. "Jeremy Collier's 'Marcus Aurelius.'" London Times Literary Supplement, January 26, 1928, p. 62.

A contribution to L. J. H. Bradley (Times Literary Supplement, January 19, 1928), noting a 1702 edition.

913 Cox, James E. "Jeremy Collier's Short View." Ph.D. University of Michigan, 1929.

914 Ressler, Kathleen. "Essays of Jeremy Collier." Ph.D. University of Cincinnati, 1935.

915 Anthony, Sister Rose. The Jeremy Collier Stage Controversy, 1698-1726. Milwaukee: Marquette University Press, 1937. xv, 328 pp.

An exhaustive analysis of Collier's Short View along with a chronological survey of various documents published during the ensuring controversy. A general bibliography of the episode is included.

916 Ressler, Kathleen. "Jeremy Collier's Essays." Seventeenth Century Studies, Second Series. Edited by Robert Shafer. (Princeton Princeton University Press for the University of Cincinnati, 1937), 179-285.

Seeking to rescue Collier from the contempt with which he was regarded by many of his contemporaries, this essay analyze and defends the intrinsic merits of his divinity, psychology, and ethics.

917 Hooker, Helene Maxwell. "Father John Constable on Jeremy Collie

Philological Quarterly, XXIII (1944), 375-378.

A discussion of a pamphlet, Reflections Upon Accuracy of Style, in which the Jesuit John Constable attacks the prose style of Collier whom he calls "Callicrates." The pamphlet was written in 1703 but published many years later.

918   Wimsatt, William K., Jr. "Father John Constable on Collier." Philological Quarterly, XXIV (April, 1945), 119-122.

A reply to the article by Helene M. Hooker, P.Q., XXIII (1944).

919   A Letter to A. H. Esq. Concerning the Stage. The Occasional Paper No. IX (1698). Edited by H. T. Swedenberg, Jr. Los Angeles: The Augustan Reprint Society, September, 1946. (Series III, Essays on the Stage, 1).

The Letter, possibly by Charles Hopkins, is a rejoinder to Collier. The Occasional Paper, possibly by Richard Willis, supports Collier. They are presented in facsimile.

920   Representations of the Impiety and Immorality of the English Stage (1704), Some Thoughts Concerning the Stage. Introduction by Emmett L. Avery and a Bibliographical Note. The Augustan Reprint Society. Los Angeles: William Andrews Clark Memorial Library, 1947.

Avery's introduction sets these two works, both of which support Jeremy Collier's position, in the context of the Collier controversy.

921   Lamb, G. F. "A Short View of Jeremy Collier." English, VII (1949), 270-275.

A review of the controversy.

922   Ewan, E. A. "A Study of the Works of Jeremy Collier." Ph.D. Oxford University (Merton College), 1961.

923   Mattauch, Hans. "A Propos du Premier Jugement Sur Shakespeare en France." Modern Language Notes, LXXVIII (1963), 288-300.

The influence of Jeremy Collier's A Short View of the Profaneness and Immorality of the British Stage (1698) on eighteenth century French criticism of Shakespeare.

924   Rothstein, Eric. "Farquhar's Twin Rivals and the Reform of Comedy." Publications of the Modern Language Association, LXXIX (1964), 33-41.

Farquhar intended to present the kind of moral comedy Collier and other abolitionists claimed to favor. The failure of the play indicated that the New Comedy would not be structured on Collier's principles.

925   Anthony, Sister Rose. The Jeremy Collier Stage Controversy, 1698-1726. New York: Benjamin Blom, 1966. 343 pp.

A reprint of the 1937 edition. Examines all the Collier pamphlets and studies reactions to them.

Collier, John

926 Spencer, Hazelton. "The Forger at Work: A New Case Against
    Collier." Philological Quarterly, VI (January, 1927), 32-38.
       John Payne Collier's unsigned ms. history of the London
    stage from 1660 to 1723 (in the Harvard theatre collection) in-
    cludes notes on plays and players and a number of forgeries.

Colman, Francis

927 Babcock, Robert W. "Francis Colman's Register of Operas, 1712-
    1734." Music and Letters, XXIV (1943), 155-159.
       Corrects errors and omissions in the reprint of this work
    in The Mask, XXX (July, 1926), 110-112; XIII (January, 1927),
    18-23.

Colman, George, Elder

texts

928 Colman, George. The Jealous Wife. Edited by Allardyce Nicoll.
    Oxford: University Press, 1925. 119 pp.
       Reprints the 1777 edition, with a brief survey of Colman's
    career.
929 Traylor, Eugene. "Production and Production Book of Colman's
    Clandestine Marriage." M.F.A. University of Texas, 1963.

biography and criticism

930 Thom, Karl W. George Colman the Elder's Komödie The Man of
    Business und die farce The Deuce is in Him. Kiel Dissertation,
    1908. 66 pp.
931 G. E. P. A. [Letter]. The Musical Antiquary, III (October, 1911-
    July, 1912), 236.
       Letter, from G. E. P.A.'s collection, never before printed,
    from Thomas Linley to George Colman, about terms upon which
    he will permit his daughter to sing and act with Colman or
    Garrick.
932 Beatty, Joseph M., Jr. "Garrick, Colman and The Clandestine
    Marriage." Modern Language Notes, XXXVI (1921), 129-141.
       Examines evidence, both internal and external, to determine
    the "indebtedness of the play to each of its authors," and con-
    cludes that the concept as a whole and the characters are Col-
    man's and Act V and the love scene in Act II are Garrick's.
933 Lund, S. M. "The Life and Works of George Colman the Elder."
    M.A. London University (Royal Holloway), 1928.

934 Baird, Theodore. "The Life and Works of George Colman the
     Elder." Ph.D. Harvard University, 1929.
          Detailed study of Colman's life with critical and historical
     treatment of his thirty-four plays and alterations; emphasizes
     Colman as a man of the theatre, "measuring success and
     failure by box office receipts."
935 Lynch, Kathleen M. "Pamela Nubile, L'Ecossaise, and The Eng-
     lish Merchant." Modern Language Notes, XLVII (February,
     1932), 94-96.
          Goldoni's Pamela Nubile (1750), called "the best of the
     dramatic adaptations of Richardson's Pamela," purportedly sup-
     plied certain details of the plot of Voltaire's l'Ecossaise. George
     Colman the Elder "adapted Voltaire's play in The English Mer-
     chant (1767), but it seems that Colman was also directly in-
     fluenced by Goldoni's play, too."
936 Knochen, Helmut. Der Dramatiker George Colman. Ph.D. Uni-
     versity of Göttingen, 1935. 83 pp.
          An inept melding of biography and criticism that accords
     brief treatment to each of the plays and emphasizes sources
     and stage history.
937 Page, Eugene R. George Colman the Elder, Essayist, Dramatist,
     and Theatrical Manager, 1732-1794. (Columbia University
     Studies in English and Comparative Literature, No. 120). New
     York: Columbia University Press, 1935. xii, 334 pp.
          A biography of Colman that emphasizes his role as play-
     wright-manager in the theatrical milieu of the late 18th century.
     The stage history of the plays is presented, and some attempt is
     made to provide a general history of the theatres from 1769 to
     1790. Included are a bibliography of Colman's plays and a list
     of pertinent sources on late 18th century theatre.
938 Stone, George Winchester, Jr. "A Midsummer Night's Dream in
     the Hands of Garrick and Colman." Publications of the Modern
     Language Association, LIV (1939), 467-482.
          An analysis of Garrick's The Fairies (1755), Colman's Mid-
     summer Night's Dream and Fairy Tale (1763), and Garrick's
     acting copy of Midsummer Night's Dream (1763), to illustrate
     the history of the alterations and to determine each playwrights'
     share in the compositions.
939 Hess, Darthea Marion. "George Colman the Elder, Theatre Man-
     ager." M.A. Brown University, 1942.
940 Vincent, Howard P. "Christopher George Colman, 'Lunatick.'"
     Review of English Studies, XVIII (January, 1942), 38-48.
          "New light on the closing years drawn from documents in
     the P.R.O."
941 Halsband, Robert. "A Parody of Thomas Gray." Philological

Quarterly, XXII (July, 1943), 255-266.

"A full study of the reception and effects of the parodies of Robert Lloyd and George Colman the Elder."

942 Parsons, Coleman O. "Francis and Mary Colman--Biographical Glimpses, 1691-1767." Notes and Queries, CXCII (July 12, 1947), 288-293; (July 26, 1947), 310-314.

Biographical sketch of the parents of George Colman the elder, with notes on Francis Colman's connections with opera.

943 Bergmann, Frederick L. "David Garrick and The Clandestine Marriage." Publications of the Modern Language Association, LXVII (1952), 148-162.

The Clandestine Marriage shows the influence of eighteenth-century acting traditions upon the playwright and his art.

944 Gerber, Helmut E. "The Clandestine Marriage and Its Hogarthian Associations." Modern Language Notes, LXXII (1957), 267-271.

945 Gordan, John D. "New in the Berg Collection." Bulletin of the New York Public Library, LXI (1957), 303-311, 353-363.

Letters of Garrick and Colman.

946 Preston, Thomas R. "Smollett and the Benevolent Misanthrope Type." Publications of the Modern Language Association, LXXIX (1964), 51-57.

Brief comparison of Matt Bramble with the hero of George Colman's The English Merchant.

947 Isles, Duncan E. "Other Letters in the Lennox Collection." Times Literary Supplement, August 5, 1965, p. 685.

Includes letters by Garrick and Colman to Mrs. Charlotte Lennox.

948 Dobson, Austin. Third Series: Eighteenth Century Vignettes. New York: Benjamin Blom, 1967. 376 pp.

A reprint of the 1896 edition includes essays on the last performances of Garrick and of Colman.

Colman, George, Younger

949 Steinwender, Walther. Colman the Younger als Dramatiker. Ein Beitrag zum englischen Literaturgeschichte am Ausgange des 18. Jahrhunderts. Königsberg: Karg und Manneck, 1913. 145 pp.

Summaries of Colman's comedies in the historical introduction. Colman's talent for comic portraiture partly redeems his plays, which are otherwise marred by a sentimental, moralizing outlook and by the growing sentimentalism common to late 18th century English plays.

950 Vincent, Howard Paton. "The Life and Writings of George Colman the Younger." Ph.D. Harvard University, 1933.

A biography of Colman with special attention to his role as manager of the Haymarket Theatre and his plays as examples of catering to the audience's taste.

951 Vincent, Howard P. "George Colman the Younger: 'Adopted Son.'" Philological Quarterly, XV (1936), 219-220.
    Cites evidence to show that the younger Colman was probably born out of wedlock.

952 A., H. "Phrases from Colman's Heir-at-Law." Notes and Queries, CLXXXI (1941), 218.
    Indicates that some popular expressions found in Colman's Heir-at-Law appear there for the first time in literature.

953 Jaggard, William. "Phrases from Colman's Heir-at-Large." Notes and Queries, CLXXXIII (1942), 238.
    The phrase "You can't make a slik purse out of a sow's ear" existed in variants long before its use in Colman's Heir-at-Large.

954 Bagster-Collins, Jeremy F. "George Colman the Younger." Ph.D. Columbia University, 1943.

955 Heffner, Hubert C. "The Haymarket Theatre under Coleman the Younger, 1789-1805." Speech Monographs, X (1943), 23-29.

956 Bagster-Collins, Jeremy F. George Colman the Younger, 1762-1836. New York: King's Crown Press, 1946. viii, 367 pp.
    A detailed biography, including a valuable study of the genres of popular slapstick and melodrama in which Colman achieved his most significant successes.

Comedy

957 Palmer, John Leslie. The Comedy of Manners. London: G. Bell & Sons, Ltd., 1913. 308 pp.
    An historical view of the rise and fall of the comic dramatists of the Restoration with the specific purpose of reforming the point of view. Contains pictures and notes on a number of London theatres.

958 Courtney, W. L. "The Idea of Comedy." The Fortnightly Review, New Ser., XCV (May 1, 1914), 842-858; (June 1, 1914), 1063-1080.
    Part II (Pages 1063-1076) covers the Comedy of Manners of Wycherley and Congreve. Reflected the life of the times, did not criticize it.

959 Palmer, John. Comedy. London: M. Secker, 1914. 63 pp.
    An essay on the comic spirit and the English attempt at comedy. Finds that only Shakespeare, Chapman, Congreve, and Goldsmith are really successful.

960 Miles, Dudley. "Morals of the Restoration." Sewanee Review,

XXIV (January, 1916), 105-114.

Singles out wit as most important element of Restoration comedy. Traces it to foreign influences. Argues that through wit the playwrights indirectly support traditional moral standard

961 Hazlitt, William. Lectures on the English Comic Writers. London: J. M. Dent & Sons, Ltd.; New York: E. P. Dutton & Co., 1920. xii, 340 pp.

Contains two essays on the comedy of Restoration and 18th century theatre: "On Wycherley, Congreve, Vanbrugh, and Farquhar," and "On the Comic Writers of the Last Century."

962 Mathewson, Louise. Bergson's Theory of the Comic in the Light of English Comedy. Lincoln, Nebraska: University of Nebraska Press, 1920. 28 pp. (University of Nebraska Studies in Language, Literature and Criticism.)

Section III (pp. 15-22) is primarily concerned with Restoratio and 18th-century comedy in terms of Bergson's theories of the nature of the comic and comic characters.

963 Loiseau, J. "The Middle Classes in the Comedy of the Restoration (1660-1670)." M.S. University of Paris (Sorbonne), 1922.

964 Heldt, W. "A Chronological and Critical Review of the Appreciation and Condemnation of the Comic Dramatists of the Restoration and Orange Periods." Neophilologus, VIII (1923), 39-59; 109-128; 197-204.

A discussion of the social and political background of the period, followed by a history of the criticism of Restoration comedy from Jeremy Collier through Nettleton.

965 Matthews, J. Brander. Playwrights on Playmaking and Other Studies of the Stage. New York and London: Charles Scribner's Sons, 1923. 328 pp.

In a discussion of "The Old Comedies," Matthews considers the theatrical conditions which resulted in the disappearance of the Old Comedy (comedy written before 1870) from the stage.

966 Moore, John B. "The Comic and the Realistic in English Drama." Ph.D. University of Wisconsin, 1923.

967 Nicoll, Allardyce. Introduction to Dramatic Theory. London: George G. Harrap & Co., 1923. 217 pp.

An introduction to the study of drama, beginning with the Greeks. Pages 186-197 treat "The Comedy of Manners," "The Genteel Comedy," and "The Comedy of Intrigue."

968 Dobrée, Bonamy. Restoration Comedy, 1660-1720. Oxford: The Clarendon Press, 1924. 182 pp.

A study of Restoration comedy, its values and its background with separate chapters on Etherege, Wycherley, Dryden and Shadwell, Congreve, Vanbrugh and Farquhar, and including a short bibliography.

969 Krutch, Joseph Wood. Comedy and Conscience After the Restoration. New York: Columbia University Press, 1924. 270 pp.
Traces "the various influences which led to the decline of
the Restoration comedy and the rise of the sentimental comedy
by considering the general social and literary history of the
times.

970 Lynch, Kathleen M. "English Sources of Restoration Comedy of
Manners." Ph.D. University of Michigan, 1924.

971 Stoll, E. E. "Literature No 'Document.'" Modern Language Review, XIX (1924), 141-157.
An attack on the use of literature as social documents in
which Stoll discusses Restoration comedy of manners and
various critical appraisals of the relationship of that comedy
to Restoration moral codes.

972 "Continuity in English Drama." Times Literary Supplement,
October 29, 1925, pp. 705-706.
English Restoration comedy learned all it could from
Molière without imitating.

973 Isaacs, J. "The Tragic Comedians." Spectator, May 9, 1925,
p. 756.
Reviews B. Dobrée, Restoration Comedy (1660-1720).
Finds the seriousness of Restoration "artificial" comedy to lie
in sex-antagonism.

974 Perry, Henry Ten Eyck. The Comic Spirit in Restoration Drama.
New Haven: Yale University Press, 1925. xii, 148 pp.
A useful and sound study of the debt owed by Restoration
comedy to Molière, and of the sources not supplied by Molière.
The chapter on laughter is weak; that on Vanbrugh is the most
important.

975 Spencer, Hazelton. "Laughter Again." Saturday Review of Literature, II (August 15, 1925), 48.
Reviews H. T. E. Perry, The Comic Spirit in Restoration
Drama (1925). Perry's conclusion fails to take into account a
vigorous survival of the comedy of humors.

976 Woolf, Virginia. "Restoration Comedy." New Republic, XLI
(February 11, 1925), 315-316.
Reviews B. Dobrée, Restoration Comedy (1924) and E.
Gosse, The Life of William Congreve (1924). Disagrees with
Dobrée's statement that Restoration comedy expressed "not
licentiousness, but a deep curiosity, and a desire to try new
ways of living." Woolf says, "We doubt, indeed, whether in
the matter of indecency there is much to choose between the
Elizabethan and Restoration comedy; save that Elizabethan
indecency is put away from us and disguised by the poetry . . . "

977 Lynch, Kathleen M. The Social Mode of Restoration Comedy.
New York: Macmillan, 1926. (University of Michigan Publications in Language and Literature, Vol. III). xi, 242 pp.
Studies late Elizabethan comedy, court comedy under Charles
I, and the comedy of the Commonwealth as explaining the gradual
formation of the social attitude characteristic of Restoration
comedy.

978 Nettleton, George H. "The Restoration Theatre." Yale Review,
XV (January, 1926), 396-398.
Reviews B. Dobrée, Restoration Comedy (1924). Notes that
Vanbrugh's The Relapse "has this year had a zestful revival
by a college fraternity." Reviews H. T. E. Perry, The Comic
Spirit in Restoration Drama (1925). Notes that E. Gosse was
the first to add Etherege to the canon of great Restoration
comedy.

979 Nicoll, Allardyce. Modern Language Review, XXI (April, 1926),
213-214.
Reviews H. T. E. Perry, The Comic Spirit in Restoration
Drama (1925). "It is probably because new standards of social
life were being eagerly sought after in the Restoration and
because the study of the Restoration comic writers admits of
so much intellectual subtlety and research that we in our days
have turned once more to Congreve and his peers."

980 Nicoll, Allardyce, Editor. Lesser Comedies of the Eighteenth
Century. London: Oxford University Press, 1927. xvii, 537 pp.
A brief introduction traces the influence of Congreve in the
lesser dramatists. Includes Murphy's The Way to Keep Him,
Colman's The Jealous Wife, Inchbald's Every One Has His
Fault, Morton's Speed the Plough, and Reynolds' The Dramatist.

981 Stoll, Elmer E. Shakespeare Studies, Historical and Comparative
in Method. New York: Macmillan, 1927. xi, 502 pp.
One chapter deals with Restoration comedy: The philosophy
of conduct in Etherege and Congreve is not that of the period,
but a reflection of the taste for entertainment of the time.

982 Buck, Howard. "A Roderick Random Play, 1748." Modern Language
Notes, XLIII (February, 1928), 111-112.
A comic interlude acquired by the Yale Library, with a
tragedy, The Northern Heroes.

983 Hillhouse, James T. "The Man of Taste." Modern Language Notes,
XLIII (March, 1928), 174-176.
On two comedies, the satiric Mister Taste, The Poetical Fop
(anon.), and James Miller's Man of Taste, a comedy of manners.

984 Lacey, T. A. "'Artificial' Comedy." Times Literary Supplement,
March 15, 1928, p. 188.
Replies to Stoll (TLS, March 1, 1928) that church marriage

carried with it the right of dower.

985 Stoll, Elmer E. "'Artificial' Comedy." London Times Literary
Supplement, March 1, 1928, p. 150.
Restoration drama does not reflect the age but an extremely
small portion of the populace. Comedy in England had always
been indecent.

986 Thorndike, Ashley H. English Comedy. New York: Macmillan,
1928. vi, 635 pp.
A very useful source of reference and of plot outlines. Six
chapters survey the 1660-1800 period.

987 Trevelyan, G. M. "'Artificial' Comedy." London Times Literary
Supplement, January 5, 1928, p. 12.
Offers historical verification for plots in Restoration com-
edy hinging on marriage fraud.

988 Bateson, F. W. English Comic Drama 1700-1750. Oxford: Oxford
University Press, 1929. 160 pp.
Bateson sees the two most important influences on the decline
of Restoration comedy to be the moral responsibility of an author
to his public and the taste for "sentimentalism." Selects six
dramatists to examine (Cibber, Steele, Centlivre, Gay, Carey,
and Fielding), and concludes that the normal development of the
comic drama of the 18th century, through sentimentalism to
realism, was delayed by the obsolete "machinery" of the
theatres.

989 Crawford, Bartholomew V. "High Comedy in Terms of Restoration
Practice." Philological Quarterly, VIII (October, 1929), 339-347.
Tries to determine the contemporary definition. Nine con-
clusions about the characteristics of high comedy.

990 Maclean, Malcolm S. "Eighteenth-Century Theories of the Comic."
Ph.D. University of Minnesota, 1929.

991 Montgomery, Guy. "The Challenge of Restoration Comedy," in
Essays in Criticism, by Members of the English Department,
University of California, Vol. I. (Berkeley: University of Cal-
ifornia Press, 1929), 133-151.
Discusses Restoration comedy as a reflection of the society
which produced it.

992 Nicoll, Allardyce. Modern Language Review, XXIV (October,
1929), 477-478.
Reviews F. W. Bateson, English Comic Drama 1700-1750
(1929). Corrects Bateson, saying that in the Restoration it was
not true that satire expressed personal hostility rather than
criticizing a man for failing to conform to a social norm.

993 Sawyer, Newell W. "The Comedy of Manners from Sheridan to
Maugham, The Study of the Type As a Dramatic Form and As
a Social Document." Ph.D. University of Pennsylvania, 1930.

994 Smith, Willard. The Nature of Comedy. Boston: R. G. Badger
     [1930]. 191 pp.
          Dealing with comedy from the points of view of psychology,
     history, and ethics, this work contains a chapter entitled, "The
     Evolution of the Comic Form on the English Stage." Restoration
     comedy, exemplified through plays of Wycherley and Congreve,
     is seen as a development of the realistic Elizabethan comedy of
     manners modified especially by Molière's French comedies.

995 Nettleton, George Henry. Sheridan et la Comédie de Moeurs.
     Paris: C. Laurent, 1931. 15 pp. (James Hazen Hyde Lecture
     at the Sorbonne).

996 Sawyer, Newell W. The Comedy of Manners from Sheridan to
     Maugham. Philadelphia: University of Pennsylvania Press, 1931
     vi, 275 pp.
          Studies the conventions in the genre and the influence of
     earlier comedies upon the later ones.

997 Fuchs, M. and P. "Comédiens francais à Londres, 1738-1755."
     Revue de Litterature Comparée, XIII (1933), 43-72.
          This essay provides dates and places of performances of
     French comedies in London.

998 Lund, Serena M. "The Comedy of Manners, 1700-1780." Ph.D.
     London University (Queen Mary College), 1933.

999 Jansen, Hildegarde. Die soziologische Selbstcharakteristik des
     Adels in der Restaurationskomödie. Würzburg: Richard Mayr,
     1934. 75 pp.

1000 Stoll, Elmer Edgar. "The Beau Monde at the Restoration." Modern
     Language Notes, XLIX (1934), 425-432.
          States that "the spirit of innovation" in the playwrights and
     not their desire to reflect the social mores of the beau monde
     was responsible for the major characteristics of the Restoration
     comedy of manners.

1001 Johnson, Frank L. "The Conventions of Restoration Comedy."
     Ph.D. University of Wisconsin, 1935.

1002 Mason, John E. Gentlefolk in the Making. Philadelphia: University
     of Pennsylvania Press, 1935. xiv, 393 pp.
          Though not directly concerned with drama, this study of
     courtesy literature and conduct books from 1531 to 1774 defines
     and clarifies the social modes predominating in comedy of the
     Restoration and 18th century.

1003 Wright, Louis B. Middle Class Culture in Elizabethan England.
     Chapel Hill: University of North Carolina Press, 1935. xiv,
     733 pp.
          Although the main emphasis is upon the Elizabethan period,
     the study defines tendencies that continue throughout the 17th
     and 18th centuries. Thus it provides an essential part of the

background for such dramatists as Cibber, Steele, and Lillo.

1004 Perkinson, Richard H. "Aspects of English Realistic Comedy in the Seventeenth Century." Ph.D. Johns Hopkins University, 1936.

1005 -----. "Topographical Comedy in the Seventeenth Century." English Literary History, III (1936), 270-290.

An analysis of the dramatic genre in which locale or setting has a pronounced effect upon plot, characters, and the treatment of manners. Among the plays studied are Etherege's She Would If She Could, Wycherley's Love in a Wood, and Shadwell's Epsom Wells, Squire of Alsatia, and Bury Fair.

1006 Knights, L. C. "Restoration Comedy: the Reality and the Myth." Scrutiny, VI (1937), 122-143.

A study of the comedy as an evocation of the culture it represents. Language, manners, and sexual relationships are the major points of emphasis.

1007 Draper, John W. "The Theory of the Comic in Eighteenth-Century England." Journal of English and Germanic Philology, XXXVII (1938), 207-223.

Based upon commentary published during the period, this history of the theory of comic drama shows how the decay of theory coincided with the qualitative decay of comedy.

1008 Jackson, Alfred. "The Stage and the Authorities, 1700-1714 (As Revealed in the Newspapers)." Review of English Studies, XIV (1938), 53-62.

An account of the various actions taken by the authorities to restrict and censor performances of the kind of comedy popular during the Restoration.

1009 Perry, Henry Ten Eyck. Masters of Dramatic Comedy and Their Social Themes. Cambridge, Mass.: Harvard University Press, 1939. 428 pp.

While this book contains no chapters specifically devoted to Restoration and 18th-century drama, there are numerous references to several of the playwrights. This work attempts to view social history through the eyes of the writer of comedy.

1010 Bigelow, Leslie P. "The Style and the Wit of the Restoration Comedy of Manners." Ph.D. Ohio State University, 1940.

1011 Alleman, Gellert S. Matrimonial Law and the Materials of Restoration Comedy. Wallingford, Pa. [n.p.], 1942. 155 pp.

An "analysis of the manner in which Restoration comedy uses material from matrimonial law to provide dramatic situation to characterization." Treats "the nature of spousals," clandestine marriages, deceptive marriages, and dissolution of marriages.

1012 Eaton, Julia. "Classic and Popular Elements in English Comedy of

the Eighteenth Century and Nineteenth Century." Ph.D. Cornell
University, 1942.

1013 Houghton, Walter E., Jr. "Lamb's Criticism of Restoration Comedy." English Literary History, X (March, 1943), 61-72.
"An excellent analysis and defence of Lamb's views."

1014 Mignon, Elizabeth L. "Old Men and Women in the Restoration
Comedy of Manners." Ph.D. Bryn Mawr University, 1943.

1015 Knights, L. C. Explorations: Essays in Criticism, Mainly Literature of the Seventeenth Century. London: Chatto and Windus,
1945. xii, 198 pp.
Includes the celebrated essay, "Restoration Comedy: the
Reality and the Myth," originally appearing in Scrutiny, VI
(1937).

1016 Symons, Julian. "Restoration Comedy." Kenyon Review, VII
(Spring, 1945), 185-197.
A modern critical approach to Restoration comedy, stress-
ing its social background and its quality of moral insight.

1017 Krapp, Robert Martin. "Class Analysis of a Literary Controversy
Wit and Sense in Seventeenth Century English Literature."
Science and Society, X (Winter, 1946), 80-92.
Blackmore's attack on "wit-writing" and the surrounding
controversy discussed, with frequent reference to the comic
drama.

1018 Mandach, A. de. Molière et la Comédie de Moeurs en Angleterre,
1660-1668: Essai de Littérature Comparée. Neuchâtel: Baconnièr
1946. 128 pp.
The standard study, both of the general influence of Molière's
comic style and of specific characters and plots borrowed from
him.

1019 Mignon, Elizabeth. Crabbed Age and Youth, the Old Men and Women in Restoration Comedy of Manners. Durham: Duke University Press, 1946. ix, 194 pp.
Primarily description and summary of those plays by the
principal dramatists in which elderly characters appear.

1020 Baker, Roberta Hardy. "Producing Restoration and Eighteenth
Century Comedies." M.A. University of Wisconsin, 1948.

1021 Merrin, James T., Jr. "Theory of Comedy in the Restoration."
Ph.D. Chicago University, 1948.

1022 Thackeray, William Makepeace. The English Humourists of the
Eighteenth Century. With an introduction by Derek Stanford.
London: Grey Walls Press, 1949. 208 pp.
A new edition of Thackeray's classic study of the Augustan
comic writers.

1023 Tave, S. M. "Comic Theory and Criticism from Steele to Hazlitt."
Ph.D. Oxford University (Oriel College), 1950.

1024 Bateson, F. W. "Contributions to a Dictionary of Critical Terms: 1.
Comedy of Manners." Essays in Criticism, I (1951), 89-93.
Definition of the term by historical context (e.g., Aristotle,
Dryden, Dennis, Addison). Brief contrasts in connotations of
each critic's treatment of this genre. The term "comedy of
manners" was first used by Charles Lamb in 1822; the eighteenth-
century critics used the term "genteel comedy."

1025 Leech, Clifford. "Restoration Comedy: The Earlier Phase." Essays
in Criticism, I (1951), 165-184.
The survey shows "that the majority of Restoration comedies
were more or less haphazard assemblies of diverting or striking
situations, facile jests, and contradictory stock sentiments."

1026 Kronenberger, Louis. The Thread of Laughter; Chapters on English Stage Comedy from Jonson to Maugham. New York: Knopf,
1952. 298, vi pp.
These classroom lectures survey the English stage for some
300 years by examining, among others, the works of such Restoration and 18th-century playwrights as Etherege, Wycherley,
Dryden, Shadwell, Behn, Congreve, Cibber, Vanbrugh, Farquhar,
Goldsmith, and Sheridan.

1027 McCulley, Cecil M. "A Study of Dramatic Comedy." Ph.D. Columbia University, 1952.

1028 Goodman, Oscar B. "English New Comedy." Ph.D. Columbia
University, 1953. 284 pp. (Publication No. 6625).
The Restoration comic playwrights were strongly influenced
by the Greek New Comedy.

1029 Prideaux, Tom. World Theatre in Pictures from Ancient Times
to Modern Broadway. New York: Greenberg [1953]. 253 pp.
A section entitled "The English Comic Genius" includes
pictorial representations of modern performances of such
Restoration and 18th-century plays as Love for Love, The
Rivals, and School for Scandal.

1030 Howling, Robert T. "Moral Aspects of Restoration Comedy." Ph.D.
Pennsylvania State University, 1954.

1031 Jahn, R. "The Relationship Between the Manners Comedies and
Their Society." M.A. Bristol University, 1954.

1032 McDowell, Margaret B. "Moral Purpose in Restoration Comedy."
Ph.D. University of Iowa, 1954. 438 pp. (Publication No. 9589).
The moral purpose of Restoration comedy may be seen in the
playwright's realistic and objective testing of every ethical code
against the needs of human nature.

1033 Barnhart, William J. "High Comedy and Low Comedy in England,
1660-1676, a Study in the Development of the Comedy of Manners." Ph.D. University of North Carolina, 1955.

1034 Berkeley, David S. "Préciosité and the Restoration Comedy of
      Manners." Huntington Library Quarterly, XVIII (1955), 109-
      128.
          By understanding préciosité (in Berkeley's terms, "a form
      of ceremonious social intercourse which derived its attitudes,
      postures and special vocabulary from the belief that beautiful
      and virtuous ladies have a semi-divine status") we can better
      understand Restoration drama on its own terms.

1035 Loftis, John. "The Social Milieu of Early-Eighteenth-Century
      Comedy." Modern Philology, LIII (November, 1955), 100-
      112.
          Influences of society on drama and distinctions between
      stage life and social life. John Dennis, Defoe, Lillo, Cibber,
      Massinger and others are mentioned. Particular attention is
      paid to the merchant in various plays.

1036 Mudrick, Marvin. "Restoration Comedy." English Stage Comedy.
      Edited with an introduction by William Kurtz Wimsatt. (New
      York: Columbia University Press, 1955), 98-125. (English In-
      stitute Essays, 1954).
          Suggests that the Restoration comic dramatists "had the
      advantage of the last English audience for whom manners were
      graces, and wit an exercise of the mind upon things in the
      world." The essay provides a brief survey and synthesis of
      critical theory as it pertains to Restoration and 18th-century
      comedy.

1037 Van der Weele, Steven J. "The Critical Reputation of Restoration
      Comedy in Modern Times." Ph.D. University of Wisconsin,
      1956.

1038 Bateson, F. W. "Second Thoughts: II. L. C. Knights and Resto-
      ration Comedy." Essays in Criticism, VII (1957), 56-67.
          L. C. Knights' essay "Restoration Comedy: The Reality
      and the Myth" (Reprinted in Exploration, 1947, pp. 131-149),
      misses the essential critical point about Restoration comedy,
      "namely its seriousness, in the paradoxical modes of serious-
      ness appropriate to comedy. Written in response to John Wain's
      "Restoration Comedy and Its Modern Criticis." Essays in
      Criticism, VI (1956), 367-385.

1039 Brookbank, Charles David. "A Realistic Approach to Restoration
      Comedy of Manners." M.A. University of Southern Illinois,
      1957.

1040 Collins, P. A. W. "Restoration Comedy." From Dryden to
      Johnson. The Pelican Guide to English Literature, Vol. IV.
      (Baltimore: Penguin Books, 1957), 156-172.
          Brief criticl survey of major playwrights and plays. Select
      bibliography for each playwright at end of volume.

1041 Empson, William, and Norman H. Holland. "Restoration Comedy
         Again." Essays in Criticism, VII (1957), 318-322.
            Comments on John Wain, "Restoration Comedy and Its
         Modern Critics."
1042 Hazard, Benjamin M. "The Theory of Comedy in the Restoration
         and Early Eighteenth Century." Ph.D. Northwestern University,
         1957.
1043 Ohara, David M. "The Restoration Comedy Perspective: A Study
         of the Comedy of Manners." Ph.D. University of Pennsylvania,
         1957.
            Studies major and some lesser comedies, 1663-1707.
1044 Wain, John. "Restoration Comedy and Its Modern Critics." Pre-
         liminary Essays (London: Macmillan, 1957), 1-35.
            Reprinted from Essays in Criticism, VI (1956), 367-385.
         Wain feels that Restoration comedy generally will not hold up
         against modern criteria. Feels that the one critic who took
         his subject matter seriously was Etherege in The Man of Mode.
1045 Corder, Jimmie Wayne. "The Restoration Way of the World: A
         Study of Restoration Comedy." Ph.D. University of Oklahoma,
         1958.
            Argues that the best comedies emphasize "order being im-
         posed upon disorder."
1046 Cecil, C. D. "Libertine and Precieux Elements in Restoration
         Comedy." Essays in Criticism, IX (1959), 239-253.
            Calls for a knowledge of manners and attitudes of les pre-
         cieuses from Mme. Rambouillet to Mme. Lambert and main-
         tains that the best Restoration comedies attempted an ideal
         hero who synthesized libertinism and self-control and who
         achieved a balance of internal harmony reflected in "indes-
         cribably elegant deportment."
1047 Loftis, John. Comedy and Society from Congreve to Fielding.
         Stanford: Stanford University Press, 1959. xiii, 154 pp.
            Changes in society reflected in comedies to 1737.
1048 Chellis, Barbara A. "Sex Or Sentiment, a Study of Comedy in
         the Period between 1696 and 1707." Ph.D. Brandeis University,
         1960.
1049 Tave, Stuart M. The Amiable Humorist: A Study in the Comic
         Theory and Criticism of the Eighteenth and Early Nineteenth
         Centuries. Chicago: University of Chicago Press, 1960. xi,
         304 pp.
            In his preface, Mr. Tave suggests that "the history of the
         idea of humor . . . can be read as part of the larger histories
         of aesthetics, of nature and human nature." This work appears
         to be required reading for the student of 18th century comic

theory and criticism. Considers the theories of Addison, Steele, Shaftesbury.

1050 Sharma, R. C. "Convention of Speech in the Restoration Comedy of Manners." Indian Journal of English Studies, II (1961), 23-38.

1051 Tatum, Nancy R. "Attitudes Toward the Country in the Restoration Comedy, 1660-1728." Ph.D. Bryn Mawr, 1961. 134 pp.

Stresses that the charges leveled at the country in Restoration comedy are related to its unchanged pattern of life and isolation. Country education, business, diversions, clothing, speech and manners are thoroughly criticized in the comedy.

1052 MacMillan, Dougald. "TheRise of Social Comedy in the Eighteenth Century." Philological Quarterly, XLI (1962), 330-338.

The decline of tragedy and rise of comedy which presented contemporary life and social problems of the century. The place of social comedy in the history of English drama.

1053 Shapiro, Frances E. "Theories of Comedy, an Attempt at Synthesis." Ph.D. Indiana University, 1962.

1054 Bateson, F. W. English Comic Drama 1700-1750. London: Russell & Russell, 1963. 158 pp.

A reprint of the 1929 edition.

1055 Nevo, Ruth. "Toward a Theory of Comedy." Journal of Aesthetics and Art Criticism, XXI (1963), 327-332.

Slight references to Dryden and Restoration theories of comedy.

1056 Simon, Irene. "Restoration Comedy and the Critics." Revue des langues vivantes, XXIX (1963), 397-430.

1057 Bennett, Robert A. "Time for Comedy." The English Journal, LIII (1964), 248-255.

Alludes to Johnson's definition of comedy, Restoration bawdey, and eighteenth century sentimental drama.

1058 Blistein, Elmer M. Comedy in Action. Durham, North Carolina: Duke University Press, 1964. 146 pp.

Author suggests that his book might adequately be described in eighteenth-century style as "A Modest Inquiry into the Nature of the Comic and the Laughable, with Some Animadversions on the Pretensions of the Comic Theorists, and Some Appreciation for the Creators and Actors of Comedy." Although devoted to no particular period, the work includes references to Congreve, Dryden, Fielding, Sheridan, and Wycherley.

1059 Drake, Robert. "Manners Anyone? Or Who Killed the Butler?" South Atlantic Quarterly, LXIII (1964), 75-84.

Restoration and Twentieth century comedy of manners are both animated by the contrast between the sophisticated, aristocratic world and the pseudo-sophisticated, pseudo-aristocratic

one. Restoration lewdness and bawdey are acceptable because
they serve an artistic function.

1060 Hoy, Cyrus. The Hyacinth Room: An Investigation into the Nature
of Comedy, Tragedy, and Tragi-comedy. New York: Alfred A.
Knopf, 1964.

Chapter Six deals with Restoration comedy.

1061 Morrissey, LeRoy John. "The Erotic Pursuit: Changing Fashions
in Eroticism in Early Eighteenth Century English Comic
Drama." Ph.D. University of Pennsylvania, 1964. (Order No.
64-10,409).

The early writers of "sentimental" comedy not only abandoned
the erotic patterns popularized at the beginning of the century,
but found substitutes for them. "Mere titillation or sentimental
erotic expectation or weeping woman eroticism replaced the
erotic pursuit."

1062 Bevis, Richard Wade. "The Comic Tradition on the London Stage,
1737-1777." Ph.D. University of California, 1965. (Order No.
65-13444).

In light of the acting copies preserved in the Larpent Collection of the Huntington Library, which "augment by one-half
the previously known comedy" of the period 1737-1777, sentimental comedy can only be regarded as a "minor feature" of
the century's theatrical history.

1063 Bridges-Adams, W. "Period, Style and Scale." Drama, No. 77
(Summer, 1965), 28-31.

The plays of Wycherley, Congreve, Vanbrugh, and Etherege
are essential to an understanding of their time. In them are
manifested effectively the Restoration virtues of height, style,
and masculinity.

1064 Foxon, David. Libertine Literature in England, 1660-1745. New
Hyde Park, New York: University Books, 1965. 70 pp.

Concerned primarily with a bibliographical description of
pornographic novels, the work makes only occasional references to Restoration comedy.

1065 Sharma, Ram Chandra. Themes and Conventions in the Comedy of
Manners. New York: Asia Publishing House, 1965. xii, 354 pp.

Studies the plays and playwrights against the background of
the age, particularly the fashionable world around the court of
Charles II. Treats the work of Etherege, Wycherley, Congreve,
Vanbrugh, and Farquhar.

1066 Suckling, Norman. "Molière and English Restoration Comedy."
Restoration Theatre. Edited by John Russell Brown and Bernard
Harris. (Stratford-Upon-Avon Studies, 6). (London: Edward
Arnold, 1965; New York: St. Martin's Press, 1965), 93-107.

A reassessment of Molière's contribution that emphasizes
the differences between his comedy and the Restoration comedy
of England.

1067 Taylor, Charlene Mae. "Aspects of Social Criticism in Restoratio
Comedy." Ph.D. University of Illinois, 1965. (Order No. 66-
4308).

Changes in the characterization of the "social climber" from
Dryden to Farquhar would suggest that Restoration comedy con
sciously reflected the social, political, and economic pressure
of the age.

1068 Bateson, F. W. "L. C. Knights and Restoration Comedy." Restoration Drama: Modern Essays in Criticism. Edited by John Lof
A Galaxy Book. (New York: Oxford University Press, 1966), 22
31.

Reprinted from Essays in Criticism, VII (1957), 56-57. Ans
wers L. C. Knights' attack in "Restoration Comedy: The Realit
and the Myth."

1069 Knights, L. C. "Restoration Comedy: The Reality and the Myth."
Restoration Drama: Modern Essays in Criticism. (A Galaxy
Book.) Edited by John Loftis. (New York: Oxford University
Press, 1966), 3-21.

Reprinted from Explorations: Essays in Criticism Mainly
on the Literature of the Seventeenth Century. (London: Chatto
and Windus, 1946), 131-149. Contends that "the criticism
that defenders of Restoration comedy need to answer is not that
the comedies are 'immoral,' but that they are trivial, gross
and dull."

1070 Legouis, P., et al. "Les voies de la critique récente: Comment e
étudie la comédie de la restauration." Etudes Anglaises, XIX
(1966), 412-423.

1071 Macey, Samuel Lawson. "Theatrical Satire as a Reflection of
Changing Tastes." Ph.D. University of Washington, 1966.
(Order No. 67-2179).

Theatrical satire is a valuable tool for gauging the changes
of taste and standards that derive from the middle-class as-
cendancy which came to dominate literature and life. The stud
is chiefly concerned with the works of Buckingham, Duffet, Ga
Carey, Fielding, Foote, Murphy, Goldsmith, and Sheridan.

1072 McLaughlin, John Joseph. "Cruelty in the Comic: A Study of Aggression in Drama." Ph.D. University of California, Los
Angeles, 1966. (Order No. 66-9318).

The Freudian theory of comedy serves to explain the presence of aggression, hostility, and cruelty in comedy. Congreve's The Way of the World and Wycherley's The Country Wi
are used to study comedy in which the aggressive urge is cente
on sex.

1073 Mohanty, Harendra Prasad. "Restoration Comedy: A Revaluation."
      Literary Criterion, VII, ii (1966), 21-27.
         Restoration comedy has little intellectual quality; its wit is
      only verbal.
1074 Montgomery, Guy. "The Challenge of Restoration Comedy."
      Restoration Drama: Modern Essays in Criticism. (A Galaxy
      Book). Edited by John Loftis. (New York: Oxford University
      Press, 1966), 32-43.
         Reprinted from University of California Publications in Eng-
      lish, I (University of California Press, 1929), 133-151. Dis-
      cusses the contemporary system of ideas that illuminates the
      background of Restoration comedy.
1075 Scouten, A. H. "Notes Toward a History of Restoration Comedy."
      Philological Quarterly, XLV (1966), 62-70.
         A history of Restoration Comedy should take into account
      more than a few plays of the best dramatists. The Restoration
      volume of The London Stage shows that the comedy of manners
      appeared in two distinct and separate periods, that it was not
      the only type of current drama, and that it was not the first
      new type to appear at the restoration.
1076 Birdsall, Virginia Ogden. "The English Comic Spirit on the Resto-
      ration Stage." Ph.D. Brown University, 1967. (Order No. 68-
      1439).
         The immorality and libertinism of comic protagonists are
      an essential part of their nature and relate them to an English
      comic tradition that always takes sides with the individual
      against the group. The study concentrates on Etherege,
      Wycherley, and Congreve.
1077 Detisch, Robert John. "High Georgian Comedy: English Stage
      Comedy from 1760 to 1777." Ph.D. University of Wisconsin,
      1967. (Order No. 67-12,115).
         Putting aside the conventional labels of laughing and senti-
      mental comedy, the study attempts to demonstrate that there
      is a high proportion of genuine comedy, naturalness, vitality,
      and satire in most of the full-length comedies written between
      1760 and 1777, a span that encompasses the significant work
      of Murphy, Colman, Cumberland, Kelly, Mrs. Sheridan, Mrs.
      Griffith, Whitehead, and Kenrick.
1078 Hines, Samuel Philip, Jr. "English Translations of Aristophanes'
      Comedies, 1655-1742." Ph.D. University of North Carolina,
      1967. (Order No. 68-2196).
         Studies Thomas Stanley's Clouds (1655), Henry Burnell's
      Plutus (1659), Lewis Theobald's Plutus and Clouds (1715),
      and Henry Fielding and William Young's Plutus (1742).

1079 Lott, James David. "Restoration Comedy: The Critical View,
      1913-1965." Ph.D. University of Wisconsin, 1967. (Order No.
      67-10,639).
          Summarizes 20th century critical works, catagorizes the
      various critical approaches, and comments on the effective-
      ness of each approach.

Command Performance

1080 Northcott, Richard, compiler. Royal Performances in London
      Theatres. London: P. Lindley [1912]. 38 pp.
          This illustrated list of Royal, or command, performances
      includes entertainments for the sovereign and subjects. It
      describes two 1736 performances of Handel's Atlanta, a 1795
      performance of O'Keefe's Life's Vagaries, and others in the
      19th and 20th centuries.
1081 Mitchell, Louis Thomas D. "The Aesthetic and Financial Impact
      of 'Command Performances' on the London Stage in the First
      Quarter of the Eighteenth Century." Ph.D. New York University,
      1967. (Order No. 68-6087).
          The study considers those factors pertinent to a command
      production: text, actors and acting, entr'act performers, the
      play's position in the regular repertory, dramatic theory, and
      the economic advantages gained.

Commedia Dell'Arte

1082 Bader, Arno L. "The Modena Troupe in England." Modern Lan-
      guage Notes, L (1935), 367-369.
          Presents additional information about the Modena troupe and
      its performances of commedia dell' arte plays in England during
      1678-1679.
1083 Cautero, Gerard Salvatore. "Studies in the Influence of the Commec
      dell'arte on English Drama: 1650-1800." Ph.D. University of
      Southern California, 1962. (Order No. 62-6045).
          The influence of the Commedia on the bourgeois comedy of
      Jephson, Garrick and Colman.

Comparative Drama

1084 Simmons, Robert W., Jr. "Comparative Drama in the 17th Cen-
      tury." Restoration and 18th Century Theatre Research, II,
      i (May, 1963), 13-18.
          Reasons for the dearth of scholarship on Russian, Polish,
      and German dramas written before 1800. Suggests areas of

comparative study for the student of English literature.

Congreve, William

letters

1085   Hodges, John C., editor. William Congreve: Letters and Docu-
       ments. New York: Harcourt, Brace, and World, 1964. 295 pp.
            157 letters and documents illuminate Congreve's personal
       life, business, and literary career. Includes his correspondence
       with Joseph Keally, Dryden, Tonson, Dennis, Addison, and
       Pope. Subject index.

complete works

1086   Congreve. William. The Complete Works of William Congreve.
       Edited by Montague Summers. 4 vols. London: Nonesuch Press,
       1923.
            The Introduction consists of a biography of Congreve, fol-
       lowed by a treatment of the plays, including a discussion of
       sources and of early performances.

complete plays

1087   -----. William Congreve. Edited by Alex Charles Ewald. The
       Mermaid Series. London: T. Fisher Unwin, [1903]. xli, 486 pp.
            The complete plays annotated with introductions, and an es-
       say, "William Congreve," from Macaulay's The Comic Drama-
       tists of the Restoration. Reissued in 1947 by E. Benn, London.
1088   -----. William Congreve. With an introduction by William Archer.
       New York, Cincinnati: American Book Company [1912]. v, 466 pp.
            Contains The Double Dealer, Love for Love, The Way of the
       World, The Mourning Bride; also notes and a glossary. Archer's
       introduction provides a brief biographical and critical sketch.
1089   -----. Complete Plays. Edited by Alexander Charles Ewald. New
       York: Hill and Wang, 1956. 438 pp.
            The texts of Congreve's plays--The Old Bachelor, The Double
       Dealer, Love for Love, The Way of the World, The Mourning
       Bride. Each play is preceeded by a very brief introduction; the
       volume includes an introduction focussing on Congreve's bio-
       graphy. Reissued by Hill and Wang (New York), in 1961.
1090   -----. The Complete Plays of William Congreve. Edited by Herbert
       Davis. Chicago: University of Chicago Press, 1967. 503 pp.
            The text is based on the first printed quartos of the single
       plays. A general introduction concerns Congreve's work as a

dramatist and his life before 1700. A short account of the composition and sources, the first performances and subsequent
reputation of each play precedes the text.

comedies

1091 -----. Comedies by William Congreve. Edited by Bonamy Dobrée.
London: Milford, 1925. 472 pp.
    A reprint of the collected edition of 1710, with an essay on
Congreve's style and Restoration comedy in general, finding it
to be essentially of English growth, with little influence of
Molière.

1092 -----. The Comedies of William Congreve. Edited by Joseph Wood
Krutch. New York: Macmillan, 1927. xv, 392 pp.
    The four comedies with an approving introductory sketch of
Congreve's career.

1093 -----. "The Way of the World" and "Love for Love." Two Comedies
by William Congreve. With Illustrations and Decorations by John
Kettelwell. New York: Dodd, Mead and Co.; London: The Bodley
Head, Ltd., 1929. 222 pp.
    Reprints both texts without any apparatus; the sources of the
texts are not indicated.

1094 -----. The Comedies. Edited, with an Introduction by Norman
Marshall. London: John Lehmann, 1948. 416 pp.
    The volume in the "Chiltern Library" series, with an an-
notated text and commentary on the plays in the theatre.

1095 -----. Comedies. Edited, with Introduction and Notes, by Bonamy
Dobrée. World's Classics, No. 276. London: Oxford University
Press [1959]. xxviii, 441 pp.
    Includes a letter from Congreve to Dennis, "Concerning Humor
in Comedy," and the texts of The Old Batchelor, The Double-
Dealer, Love for Love and The Way of the World, from the 1710
edition.

miscellaneous works

1096 -----. The Mourning Bride, Poems, and Miscellanies. Edited by
Bonamy Dobrée. World's Classics. Oxford: Oxford University
Press, 1928. xxxviii, 540 pp.
    Includes also Incognita, Semele, The Judgment of Paris,
Tatler papers, Preface to Dryden. Dobree's introduction is
chiefly biographical.

individual plays

1097 -----. "Love for Love." A Book of Dramas, an Anthology of
       Nineteen Plays. Compiled by Bruce Carpenter. (New York:
       Prentice Hall, 1929), 323-399.
           An unedited reprint of the play.

1098 -----. Love for Love; the play by William Congreve, produced
       in New York, June 3 to 8, 1940, by the Players under the direc-
       tion of Robert Edmond Jones. With an introduction by Franklin
       P. Adams. New York: C. Scribner's Sons [C1940]. 85 pp.
           The "Foreword" by Adams is a humorous poem; the text of
       the play is preceeded by a letter from Congreve, "To the Right
       Honourable Charles, Earl of Dorset and Middlesex, Lord
       Chamberlain of His Majesty's Household."

1099 -----. Love for Love. Edited by Emmett L. Avery. Regents
       Restoration Drama Series. Lincoln: University of Nebraska
       Press, 1966.
           Includes introduction, notes and chronology.

1100 -----. Love for Love. Edited by A. Norman Jeffares. London:
       Macmillan; New York: St. Martin's Press, 1967.
           Includes general introduction, notes, critical extracts, and
       select bibliography.

1101 -----. The Way of the World; an unexpurgated edition, including
       original signed etching by A. R. Middleton Todd and a fore-
       word by M. C. Salaman. London: The Haymarket Press, 1928.
       xxi, 79 pp.
           The "Foreword" contains an appreciation of the play, con-
       centrating on the characters. The text contains, in addition to
       the play, prologue and epilogue, Congreve's dedicatory epistle
       and Steele's "To Mr. Congreve, Occasioned by his Comedy
       called 'The Way of the World.'"

1102 -----. The Way of the World; the acting edition of the Repertory
       Theatre of Boston, Management the Jewett Repertory Theatre
       Fund, Inc. Boston: W. H. Baker Co. [C1928]. ix, 94 pp.
           The unedited text of the play preceeded by a statement about
       the Repertory Theatre of Boston.

1103 -----. The Way of the World. Edited, with an Introduction and
       Explanatory Notes by W. P. Barrett. London: J. M. Dent &
       Sons, Ltd. Aldine House, 1933. xii, 145 pp. (The Temple
       Dramatists).
           The text is based on the Works (1710), which follows the
       1706 quarto edition. The spelling and stage directions are
       modernized, and the division of the scenes is that used in the
       quartos. Notes are kept to a minimum.

1104 -----. "The Way of the World." A Treasury of the Theatre: an

Anthology of Great Plays from Aeschylus to Hebbel. Revised
and adapted for colleges by Philo M. Buck, Jr., John Gassner
and H. S. Alberson. (New York: Simon and Schuster [C1935],
1015-1066.

A one-page introduction by John Gassner precedes the unannotated text of the play.

1105 -----. "The Way of the World," Types of English Drama. Edited
by John William Ashton. (New York: The Macmillan Co., 1940),
385-469.

The text of the play is preceeded by a brief introduction to
Congreve as writer of the comedy of manners. Notes to the
text are fairly meagre; most are glosses.

1106 -----. "The Way of the World." Understanding Drama. Edited by
Cleanth Brooks. (New York: Henry Holt & Co., [1948], 389-441

This college anthology contains introductory essays on the
problems of reading drama. The play is embellished with an
introduction, explanatory footnotes, and a valuable segment of
critical notes and questions, dealing with the play's plot, characterization, themes and irony.

1107 -----. "The Way of the World." Nine Great Plays from Aeschylus
to Eliot. (New York: Harcourt Brace [1950]), 274-354.

A very brief introduction, followed by the text of the play.
Notes, primarily glosses.

1108 -----. The Way of the World. Edited by Henry T. E. Perry. New
York: Appleton-Century-Crofts, 1951. 105 pp.

A critical Introduction and a selected bibliography is provided.

1109 -----. The Way of the World. Edited by Vincent E. Hopper and
Gerald B. Lahey. Great Neck: Barron's Educational Series,
1958.

1110 -----. The Way of the World; Comedy in Five Acts. With Illustrations by T. M. Cleland and an Introduction by Louis Kronenberger. New York: Limited Editions Club, 1959. xxiii, 108 pp.

In the Introduction Kronenberger discusses the areas in
which Congreve is at one with Restoration dramatists and those
in which he is unique.

1111 Banhatti, G. S. William Congreve (With a Detailed Study and Text
of The Way of the World). Masters of English Literature Series
No. 4. Allahabad and Calcutta: Kitab Mahal Pvt. Ltd., 1962.

1112 Barraclough, Elmer D. "A Production Study and Text of William
Congreve's The Way of the World as Presented at Catholic University." M.F.A. Catholic University of America, 1964.

1113 Congreve, William. The Way of the World. Edited by Kathleen M.
Lynch. Regents Restoration Drama Series. Lincoln: University
of Nebraska Press, 1965.

Includes critical Introduction, notes, and bibliography.
1114 -----. Incognita and The Way of the World. Edited by Norman
Jeffares. Arnold's English Texts. London: Edward Arnold,
1966.
Includes Introduction, notes, and bibliography.
1115 -----. The Way of the World. Edited by Gerald Weales. San
Francisco: Chandler Publishing Co., 1966.

translations

1116 -----. Le Train du Monde. Préface et traduction par Aurélien
Digeon. Paris: Aubier, 1943. 313 pp.
1117 Aury, Dominique, et Auguste Desclos. Ainsi Va Le Monde. Comédie satirique de William Congreve. Créé par la Comédie de
Provence (Centre dramatique du Sud-Est), cette pièce a été
représenté pour la première fois à Paris le 5 juin 1955 au
théâtre Hébertot, dans une mise en scène, des décors et costumes de Douking. Paris: France Illustration. Le Monde Illustré [1955]. 31, [1] pp. [Supplement to No. 425, France-Il-
lustration-Le Monde Illustré.]
French text of The Way of the World.

biography and criticism

1118 Crawford, J. P. Wickersham. "On the Relations of Congreve's
Mourning Bride to Racine's Bajazet." Modern Language Notes,
XIX (1904), 193-194.
Argues that Congreve must have known Racine's Bajazet
very well, took its heroic plot of the relations between Bajazet,
Roxane, and Atalide, added two scenes at the beginning of the
play and changed the conclusion to a happy one.
1119 Walkley, Arthur Bingham. "Way of the World." Drama and Life.
(London: Methuen; New York: Brentano's, 1908), 304-308.
Essay from the column of the drama critic, London Times.
1120 Congreve, William. "Concerning Humour in Comedy." Critical
Essays of the Seventeenth Century. Vol. III. Edited by J. E.
Spingarn. (Oxford: Clarendon Press, 1909), 242-252.
The volume also contains material by Gerard Langbaine
and Jeremy Collier.
1121 Archer, William. "The Comedies of Congreve." The Forum,
XLIII (March, 1910), 276-282; (April, 1910), 343-346.
Part I: The Scant success of The Double Dealer and The Way
of the World compared to popularity of The Old Bachelor and
Love for Love due to difficulties in structure. Part II: Congreve
regards life "from a standpoint of complete ethical indifference."

1122 Stuart, Donald Clive. "The Source of Gresset's Méchant." Modern
      Language Notes, XXVII (February, 1912), 42-45.
          Principal characters, their motivation, the main plot and
      double dealing of the two villains in Le Méchant so similar to
      those of The Double Dealer Gresset must have consciously
      used Congreve's play.

1123 Armstrong, Cecil Ferard. Shakespeare to Shaw. London: Mills
      and Boon, 1913. 330 pp.
          Short biographies and criticism of six playwrights, including
      Congreve and Sheridan. Congreve a follower rather than a
      leader but never surpassed in his Hogarthian pictures of the
      times in wit, and epigram; Sheridan improved upon the Resto-
      ration dramatists in nomenclature, their methods and their
      style.

1124 Canby, Henry Seidel. "William Congreve As a Dramatist." The
      Sewanee Review, XXI (October, 1913), 421-427.
          A middling playwright (elusive plot, loose structure, literary
      dialogue) but a great dramatist on account of his dramatic treat-
      ment with imaginative truth of an important phase of civilization,
      the libertine society of his day. Places Congreve as a dramatic
      artist between Shakespeare and Browning.

1125 Heuss, Alfred. "Das Semele-Problem bei Congreve und Händel."
      Sammelbande der Internationalen Musikgesellschaft, XV (1913-
      1914), 143-156.
          Semele, in order to possess Zeus as man and god, must
      transcend the limits of the nature of woman. In the Congreve-
      Händel Semele, an ordinary love story with intrigues, the pro-
      tagonist cannot accomplish this convincingly because of her
      superficial, shallow nature.

1126 Canby, Henry Seidel. "Congreve As a Romanticist." Publications
      of the Modern Language Association, XXXI (1916), 1-23.
          A defense of Congreve by following Lamb's idea of "Utopia
      of Gallantry." Congreve idealized or romanticized the Stuart
      gallantry.

1127 Ball, F. Elrington. "Congreve As a Ballad-Writer." Notes and
      Queries. 12th Ser., VIII (1921), 301-303.
          Attributes six topical ballads (two of which Scott attributed
      to Swift) to Congreve.

1128 Gosse, Edmund. "Note on Congreve." London Mercury, III (1921),
      638-643.
          An essay deploring the failure of scholars to explore Con-
      greve's biography; Gosse also mentions a few items pertaining
      to Congreve's biography that he has discovered since 1888.

1129 ----- . Aspects and Impressions. New York: Charles Scribner's
      Sons, 1922. 299 pp.

"A Note on Congreve" discusses the attribution to Congreve of "An Impossible Thing"--a 1720 poetic tale based on La Fontaine.

1130 Morse, Charles. "Congreve: a Great Comic Dramatist." Dalhousie Review, II (1922), 335-348.
A consideration of Congreve's life and literary achievement as a reflection of the spirit of his age.

1131 -----. "The Plays of William Congreve." The Canadian Magazine, LVIII (April, 1922), 473-480.
A discussion of Congreve's plays which treats each of his major plays in a detailed, critical summary.

1132 Protopopesco, D. "Congreve." Times Literary Supplement, November 8, 1923, p. 751.
A discussion of omissions in Montague Summers' edition of Congreve's works and a reprint of "A Satire Against Love," a short poem by Congreve.

1133 "William Congreve." Times Literary Supplement, October 4, 1923, pp. 641-642.
An article lamenting the fact that Congreve has become a dramatist of the library rather than the stage; the article also reviews Montague Summers' ed. of Congreve's works and provides an analysis of The Way of the World.

1134 Gosse, Edmund. A Life of William Congreve. New York: Charles Scribner's Sons, 1924. 192 pp.
A revision of the 1888 edition. A critical biography of Congreve which focuses primarily on his literary works, especially his novel and four plays.

1135 Krohne, Wilhelm. "Congreves Novelle Incognita." Inaugural Dissertation. Münster, 1924.

1136 Arundell, Dennis. "The Gordian Knot Untied." Times Literary Supplement, June 4, 1925, p. 384; June 18, 1925, p. 416.
First article attempts to identify Squire Trelooby (by Walsh, Congreve, Vanbrugh) with The Gordian Knot Untied. Second article replies to W. J. Lawrence (TLS, June 11, 1925), repeating the evidence for identifying the two plays.

1137 "Congreve's Love for Love." Theatre Arts Monthly, IX (June, 1925), 358-359.
Two designs of costume and setting.

1138 Dukes, Ashley. "Congreve as a Modernist." Theatre Arts Monthly, IX (January, 1925), 53-59.
Congreve's "patient, thoughtful creation of character" links his spirit with our own.

1139 J.[ennings], R.[ichard]. "Ibsen and Congreve." Spectator, CXXXV (November 28, 1925), 967,
Reviews the New Scala Theatre production of The Mourning Bride, a "drama of rant."

1140 Dobrée, Bonamy. "Young Voltaire; a Conversation between William Congreve and Alexander Pope, Twickenham, Sept., 1726. Nation and Athenaeum, XL (November 6, 1926), 179-180.
    An imaginary conversation.

1141 Lawrence, W. J. "A Congreve Holograph." Review of English Studies, II (July, 1926), 345.
    Evidence that Congreve was a holder of South Sea stock.

1142 "Robert Edmond Jones Directing Love for Love." Theatre Arts Monthly, X (October, 1926), 692.
    Set, costumes, lighting.

1143 Isaacs, J. "Congreve and America." Review of English Studies, III (January, 1927), 79.
    On the chariot accident to Congreve at Bath, as recorded in the Daily Post for October 1, 1728.

1144 [Congreve]. Notes and Queries, CLV (October 6, 1928), 236.
    Reprints selections from The Daily Post (October 5, 1728), noticing performances of the Mourning Bride and the Beggar's Opera.

1145 ------. Notes and Queries, CLVI (January, 1929), 56.
    Reprints the notice from the Flying-Post (January 25, 1728/9) of Congreve's death.

1146 Dale, Harrison. "The Comedies of William Congreve." Fortnightly Review, CXXXI (January, 1929), 55-64.
    Reviews Congreve's life and career on the occasion of his bi-centenary. His two greatest comedies are Love for Love and The Way of the World.

1147 Dobrée, Bonamy. William Congreve. A Conversation between Swift and Gay. Seattle: University of Washington Book Store, 1929. 24 pp.
    An imaginary dialogue characterizing Congreve.

1148 Hodges, John C. "William Congreve in the Government Service." Modern Philology, XXVII (November, 1929), 183-192.
    Documents in the Public Records Office reveal Congreve's government offices from 1695 to 1728 and his income during this period.

1149 "William Congreve." London Times Literary Supplement, January 17, 1929, pp. 33-34.
    A perceptive biographical and critical estimate, suggesting that Congreve was motivated in part to leave the theatre because he portrayed on stage the kind of friendship and partnership between man and woman for which his age was not ready.

1150 Taylor, D. Crane. William Congreve. Oxford: University Press, 1931. x, 252 pp.
    A study of Congreve as the master of the artificial comedy of manners.

1151 De Beer, E. S. "Congreve's Incognita: the Source of Its Setting, with a Note on Wilson's Belphegor." Review of English Studies, VIII (1932), 74-77.
A discussion of setting in this early long short story or short novel.

1152 Dobrée, Bonamy. As Their Friends Saw Them: Biographical Conversations. London: Jonathan Cape, 1933. 154 pp.
"A Conversation between Sir George Etherege and Mr. Fitzjames, on John Wilmot, Earl of Rochester," pp. 33-62; "A Conversation between Jonathan Swift and John Gay, on William Congreve," pp. 75-95.

1153 Hodges, John C. "The Ballad of Congreve's Love for Love." Publications of the Modern Language Association, XLVIII (1933), 953-954.

1154 Haraszti, Zoltán. "Early Editions of Congreve's Plays." More Books, IX (March, 1934), 81-95.
Biographical.

1155 Norris, Edward T. "A Possible Source of Congreve's Sailor Ben." Modern Language Notes, XLIX (1934), 334-335.
Argues that the character Durzo in Ravenscroft's King Edgar and Alfrida (1677) was the probable source for Sailor Ben in Love for Love and not Porpuss in Thomas D'Urfey's Sir Barnaby Whigg as Montague Summers suggested.

1156 Hodges, John C. "On the Date of Congreve's Birth." Modern Philology, XXXIII (1935), 83-85.
Clarifies the confusion about Congreve's date of birth by showing it to be 1672.

1157 Swaen, A. E. H. "The Authorship of 'A Soldier and a Sailor.'" Archiv für das Studium der Neuren Sprachen und Literaturen, CLXVIII (1935), 237-240.
A comparison of the song in Love for Love (III, iv) with broadside and other versions indicates that Congreve wrote the original lyric, which is the one appearing in the comedy.

1158 Hodges, John C. "Congreve's Will and Personal Papers." Notes and Queries, CLXXI (1936), 117.
An explanation of the problem and a request for more information about Congreve's original will.

1159 -----. "The Dating of Congreve's Letters." Publications of the Modern Language Association, LI (1936), 153-164.
Prints data pertinent to the sixty-eight extant letters of Congreve and utilizes evidence from various sources to arrange them in proper chronological order.

1160 -----. "William Congreve: Confused Signatures." Times Literary Supplement, August 15, 1936, p. 664.

To alleviate the confusion about signatures created by the existence in 1700 of five persons named William Congreve, Hodges describes how the dramatist's signature is unique.

1161 Howarth, R. G. "The Date of 'The Old Bachelor.'" Times Literary Supplement, June 13, 1936, p. 500.
Congreve wrote the play early in 1689.

1162 Miller, Marvel Garnant. "A Director's Study and Designs for William Congreve's The Way of the World." M.A. University of Iowa, 1936.

1163 Noyes, George Rapall. "William Congreve: Way of the World." Representative English Comedies. Vol. IV: Dryden and His Contemporaries: Cowley to Farquhar. Edited by Charles Mills Gayley and Alwin Thaler. (New York: The Macmillan Company, 1936), 534-560.
An essay treating Congreve's life, the development of the English comedy of manners, and Congreve's comic spirit. The essay is followed by an edition of Way of the World edited by Noyes.

1164 "Congreve's Comedies: Speed, Stillness and Meaning." Times Literary Supplement, September 25, 1937, pp. 681-682.
An explanation and a defense of the artistic quality of the plays.

1165 Snider, Rose. Satire in the Comedies of Congreve, Sheridan, Wilde, and Coward. University of Maine Studies, Second Series, No. 42. Orono, Maine, 1937. x, 135 pp.
This volume includes chronologically oriented analysis of the satiric element in The Old Batchelour, The Double Dealer, Love for Love, The Way of the World, The Rivals, The Critic, and The School for Scandal.

1166 Wilson, J. Dover. "Shakespeare, Milton and Congreve." Times Literary Supplement, January 16, 1937, p. 44.
A passage from Samson Agonistes, believed to have been drawn from Shakespeare, also appears in The Way of the World.

1167 Lynch, Kathleen M. "Congreve's Irish Friend, Joseph Keally." Publications of the Modern Language Association, LIII (1938), 1076-1087.
A concise biography of Joseph Keally which includes a detailed analysis of his relations with Congreve between 1700 and 1710.

1168 Poole, E. Millicent. "A Possible Source of 'The Way of the World.'" Modern Language Review, XXXIII (1938), 258-260.
Finds the source for Act IV, scene i, in Nolant de Fatouville's Arlequin Jason ou Le Toison d'or (1684).

1169 Hodges, John C. "Fresh Manuscript Sources for a Life of William Congreve." Publications of the Modern Language Association, LIV (1939), 432-438.

An analysis of diverse materials bearing on the life of Congreve.

1170 Isaacs, J. "Congreve's Library." Library, XX (1939), 41-42.

Makes a contribution toward a catalogue of the dramatist's library by printing a list of eleven books signed by Congreve and located in the library of the Duke of Leeds.

1171 Jaggard, William. "'The Way of the World': Stage History." Notes and Queries, CLXXVII (1939), 122.

A brief, generalized account of the play's stage history.

1172 Hayman, Leroy W. "William Congreve and Restoration Comedy: A Study in Themes and Conventions." M.A. University of Illinois, 1940.

1173 Avery, Emmett L. "The Popularity of The Mourning Bride in the London Theaters in the Eighteenth Century." Research Studies of the State College of Washington, IX (1941), 115-116.

Cites figures showing that the play was performed 205 times between 1702 and 1776, less often than seven other non-Shakespearean tragedies.

1174 Hodges, John C. William Congreve the Man: A Biography from New Sources. New York: Modern Language Association; London: Oxford University Press, 1941. 151 pp. (The Modern Language Association General Series, XI).

A biography which emphasizes Congreve as boy and man; much information about the circumstances surrounding production and printing of the plays. Contains an index to manuscript sources.

1175 Lann, E. "Forgotten English Comedies: On the English Comedy of the 17th - 18th Centuries and Its Fitness for Modern Repertoire." The Theatre (U.S.S.R.), II (1941), 121-131.

1176 Porter, E. Keith. "A Director's Study and Prompt Book of William Congreve's The Old Bachelor." M.A. University of Iowa, 1941.

1177 Avery, Emmett L. "The Première of The Mourning Bride." Modern Language Notes, LVII (1942), 55-57.

States that the first performance was held on Saturday, February 20, 1696/7.

1178 M., M. "Congreve's Aristophanes." More Books, XVII (1942), 437-438.

"A note on Congreve's copy of Comédies grecques d'Aristophanes (Paris, 1692), now in the Boston Public Library."

1179 Gielgud, John. "Staging 'Love for Love.'" Theatre Arts Monthly, XXVII (November, 1943), 662-668.

A brief essay on Gielgud's approach to the play, treating especially the mise en scène and the dramatic style.

1180 Hodges, John C. "TheComposition of Congreve's First Play." Publications of the Modern Language Association, LVIII (December, 1943), 971-976.

"Congreve wrote the first draft of The Old Bachelor at Stretton, in the spring of 1689 and was still reviving the play as late as August, 1692."

1181 Potter, Elmer B. "The Paradox of Congreve's Mourning Bride." Publications of the Modern Language Association, LVIII (December, 1943), 977-1001.

"Explains the critical disapproval of the play and its effectiveness and long popularity on the stage."

1182 Bhushan, V. N. The Hawk Over Heron. Notes on Comedy and the Comedy Form with Two Special Chapters on Congreve's Way of the World and Barrie's Admirable Crichton. Bombay: Padma Publications, Ltd., 1944. [4], 155 pp.

Congreve's Way of the World is analyzed according to plot, character, theme, and language.

1183 Dukes, Ashley. "Repertory at Last! The English Scene." Theatre Arts, XXIX (January, 1945), 22-31.

Discusses the production of Love for Love in John Gielgud's repertory company season.

1184 Gielgud, John. "The Haymarket and the New London Flocks to Repertory." Theatre Arts, XXIX (March, 1945), 166-171.

Describes the success of his repertory production of Love for Love.

1185 Howarth, R. G. "Addendum to J. C. Hodges' 'The Composition of Congreve's First Play,' PMLA, LVIII, 1943." Publications of the Modern Language Association, LXI (June, 1946), 596-597.

Howarth's earlier note (Times Literary Supplement, 13 June, 1936), suggesting the date 1689 for The Old Bachelor, has been ignored by Hodges.

1186 Smith, John Harrington. "Thomas Corneille to Betterton to Congreve." Journal of English and Germanic Philology, XLV (April 1946), 209-213.

Le Baron d'Albikrac was the source for The Amorous Widow which in turn influenced The Way of the World.

1187 Clancy, James Harvey. "The Humorists: an Elizabethan Method of Characterisation as Modified by Etherege and Congreve." Ph.D Stanford University, 1947.

1188 Dent, Alan. "John Gielgud: Actor." Theatre Arts, (February, 1947), 27-29.

The actor's technique is surveyed, with particular reference to his performance of Valentine in Love for Love.

1189 Kochman, Andrew J. "The Way of the World: a Production Study." M.A. Northwestern University, 1947.

1190 Nickson, Joseph Richard. "Congreve's Theory and Practice of Comedy." M.A. University of North Carolina, 1947.

1191 Bowers, Fredson Thayer. "The Cancel Leaf in Congreve's Double

Dealer, 1694." Papers of the Bibliographical Society of America, XLIII (1949), 78-82.

    A bibliographical study.

1192 Hodges, John C. "Congreve's Letters." Times Literary Supplement, April 9, 1949, p. 233.

    Requests information on the location of letters.

1193 -----. "Congreve's Library." Times Literary Supplement, August 12, 1949, p. 521.

    Describes the collection and its history, and requests information about the present location of items.

1194 Isaacs, J. "Congreve's Library." Times Literary Supplement, September 2, 1949, p. 569.

    Replies to J. C. Hodges query (9 April, 1949), suggesting subscribers' lists and books dedicated to Congreve as useful sources of titles.

1195 Muir, Kenneth. "William Congreve, Local Worthy." University of Leeds Review (December 1, 1949), 274-282.

    Discusses his family background in Bardsey, Yorkshire.

1196 Robson, W. W. "Hopkins and Congreve." Times Literary Supplement, February 24, 1950, p. 121.

    The "blue-bleak embers" in Hopkins's The Windhover echoes a passage in Congreve's Way of the World, V, i.

1197 Avery, Emmett L. Congreve's Plays on the Eighteenth-Century Stage. New York: Modern Language Association, 1951. viii, [4], 226 pp.

    Avery traces the course of Congreve's reputation and the stage-history of his plays during the period.

1198 Feltham, Frederik G. "The Quality of the Wit in Comedies of Etherege, Wycherley, Congreve, and Shadwell." Ph.D. University of Chicago, 1951.

1199 Lynch, Kathleen M. A Congreve Gallery. Cambridge: Harvard University Press, 1951. 196 pp.

    Miss Lynch's essays explore various aspects of Congreve's personality, background, and times, with emphasis upon the friends of his youth.

1200 -----. "References to William Congreve in the Evelyn MSS." Philological Quarterly, XXXII (1953), 337-340.

    Two letters in the manuscript shed additional light on Congreve's relationship with Lady Henrietta Godolphin.

1201 Nolan, Paul T. "William Congreve: His Artistic Milieu." Tulane University Bulletin, Series 54, No. 13 (1953), 39-43.

    Congreve's plays reflect the intellectual and aesthetic values of the late seventeenth century.

1202 Connors, Helen. "A History of the Productions of William Congreve's Way of the World from the First Presentation of the Play to the

Present." M.A. Catholic University of America, 1954.

1203 Cooke, Arthur L. "Two Parallels between Dryden's Wild Gallant
and Congreve's Love for Love." Notes and Queries, CXCIX
(1954), 27-28.

Dryden and Congreve use trick marriages and pretended
illnesses as plot devices in the two plays.

1204 Hodges, John C. "The Library of William Congreve." Bulletin of
the New York Public Library, LVIII (1954), 367-385, 436-454,
478-488, 535-550, 579-591; LIX (1955), 16-34, 92-97.

Hodges lists, describes, and indexes 659 books owned by
Congreve.

1205 Cecil, C. D. "Restoration Comic Diction: Modes of Speech in
Etherege, Wycherley, and Congreve." B. Litt. Oxford University (Wadham), 1955-1956.

1206 Chapman, R. W. "The Congreve Manuscripts." Bodleian Library
Record, V (1955), 118.

Deposit by Major John Congreve of some 18th century manuscripts at the Bodleian, among which are three letters to
Richard Congreve.

1207 Griffin, Alice. "Experiment in Style: Congreve's The Way of the
World at Bennington College." Theatre Arts, XXXIX (1955), 12.

1208 Dalldorff, Horst. "Die Welt der Restaurationskomödie. Ein Querschnitt durch die Lustspiele Hauptsaechlich von Etherege,
Wycherley und Congreve zur Erfassung ihrer Stofflichen Wesenszüge." Kiel Dissertation, 1956.

1209 Holland, Norman Norwood, Jr. "A Critical Reading of the Comedies of Etherege, Wycherley, and Congreve." Ph.D. Harvard
University, 1956.

1210 Brown, T. J. "English Literary Autographs XXI: William Congreve,
1670-1729." Book Collector, VI (1957), 61.

Reprints photostat copy of a New Year's Day letter from Congreve to Edward Porter. The probable date of the letter is 1709.

1211 Harper, Robert Thomas. "The Way of the World by William Congreve, Essay and Production Book." M.F.A. State University
of Iowa, 1957.

1212 Van Voris, W. H. "William Congreve as a Dramatist." Ph.D.
Trinity College, Dublin, 1957.

1213 Chinol, Elio, ed. La Commedia della Restaurazione: Etherege,
Wycherley, Congreve. Collona di Letterature moderne, 3.
Napoli: Edizioni scientifiche italiane [1958]. 534 pp.

A long introduction making stylistic remarks on Dryden,
Vanbrugh and Farquhar as well as the three dramatists named
in the title; includes English texts of Etherege's Man of Mode,
Wycherley's Plain Dealer, and Congreve's Way of the World,
with notes primarily glossing the text.

1214 Estes, Maxie C. "William Congreve's Comedy of Manners The
       Way of the World." M.S. Florida State University, 1958.
1215 Mueschke, Paul and Miriam. A New View of Congreve's Way of
       the World. University of Michigan Contributions in Modern
       Philology, No. 23. Ann Arbor: University of Michigan Press,
       1958. 85 pp.
           Thorough analysis. Stresses influence of Jonson.
1216 Rodenbeck, John von Behren, Jr. "The Planetary Pursuit; Four
       Phases in the Mansion of Marriage. A Study of the Marriage
       Theme in Congreve's Comedies." Honors Thesis. Harvard
       University, 1958. 39 pp.
           Sees Congreve's three early comedies as representing three
       different treatments of the marriage theme: 1) marriage as a
       contract between two individuals (The Old Bachelor); 2) marriage
       as an institution representative of all civilized institutions (The
       Double Dealer); 3) marriage as a reward for the hero (Love
       for Love).
1217 Turner, Darwin T. "The Servant in the Comedies of William Con-
       greve." College Language Association Journal, I (1958), 68-74.
           Congreve's servants are used as confidants, arch-deceivers
       and wits.
1218 Van Voris, William. "Congreve's Gilded Carousel." Educational
       Theatre Journal, X (1958), 211-217.
           The Way of the World.
1219 Holland, Norman N. The First Modern Comedies, The Significance
       of Etherege, Wycherley, and Congreve. Cambridge: Harvard
       University Press, 1959. iv, 274 pp.
           The comedies are about the difference between appearance
       and reality.
1220 Nolan, Paul T. "The Way of the World: Congreve's Moment of
       Truth." Southern Speech Journal, XXV (1959), 75-95.
           A discussion of the background and context of Congreve's
       writing and play, focusing on the values of the play and the
       character Mirabell. Contends that writing the play was an im-
       portant experience for Congreve and that he used solutions he
       would have used in real life.
1221 O'Regan, M. J. "Two Notes on French Reminiscences in Resto-
       ration Comedy." Hermathena, XCIII (1959), 63-70.
           Molière in Dryden's The Mock Astrologer, and Corneille
       in Congreve's The Way of the World.
1222 Bartel, Roland. "Suicide in Eighteenth-Century England: The Myth
       of a Reputation." Huntington Library Quarterly, XXIII (1960),
       145-158.
           Congreve cited as contributing to myth of English tendency
       to suicide.

1223 Monk, Samuel H. "A Note in Montague Summer's Edition of The
      Way of the World, Corrected." Notes and Queries, New Ser.,
      VII (1960), 70.
          The allusion in Act I, sc. v more likely refers to Caliban
      than Sycorax, as Summers has suggested.
1224 Noyes, Robert Gale. "Congreve and His Comedies in the Eighteent
      Century Novel." Philological Quarterly, XXXIX (October, 1960)
      464-480.
          This studies 18th-century novelists' reception of Congreve's
      four comedies and his tragedy. They greatly admired his plots,
      his imitation of nature, his fine ladies, his "agreeably wicked"
      characters, his fools, and even his low characters.
1225 Sharp, William L. "A Play: Scenario or Poem." Tulane Drama
      Review, V (1960), 73-84.
          Cites Congreve, The Double-Dealer.
1226 Howarth, R. G. "Congreve and Anne Bracegirdle." English
      Studies in Africa, IV (1961), 159-161.
          Criticism of John C. Hodges' account of the relationship.
      No evidence that Bracegirdle was Congreve's mistress.
1227 Fujiki, Hakuho. "The Use of Conjunctions in Congreve's Works."
      Anglica (Osaka), V, i (1962), 63-97. Article in Japanese. See
      pp. 93-97 for a summary in English.
1228 Gosse, Anthony Cabot. "Dramatic Theory and Practice in the
      Comedies of William Congreve." Ph.D. Columbia University,
      1962. (Order No. 62-4232).
          The hitherto ignored technical skill of Congreve. Thematic
      and logical unity evident in most of his plays.
1229 Leech, Clifford. "Congreve and the Century's End." Philological
      Quarterly, XLI (1962), 275-293.
          Congreve's important place in Restoration drama. "Con-
      greve brings the diverse and often conflicting elements of
      Restoration comedy into a unity."
1230 Nolan, Paul T. "Congreve's Lovers: Art and the Critic." Drama
      Survey, I (Winter, 1962), 330-339.
          Concept of morality in The Old Bachelor, The Mourning Brid
      and The Way of the World.
1231 Sinko, Grzegorz. Angielska komedia Restauracji: G. Etherege,
      W. Wycherley, W. Congreve. Przelozyl i opracowal. Wroclaw:
      Zaklad Narodowy Im. Ossolinskich [1962]. lxiii, 559 pp. (Biblio
      teka narodowa. Ser. II, 133).
          Introduction, giving historical background, Polish translation
      of Etherege's She Would, If She Could, Wycherley's The Countr
      Wife, and Congreve's The Way of the World.
1232 "An Early Theatre Ticket." Theatre Notebook, XVIII (Winter, 196
      4), 42.

Notes on ticket to Congreve's The Old Batchelour. Includes illustration.

1233 Dobrée, Bonamy. William Congreve. New York: Longman's, Green and Company (for the British Council and the National Book League), 1963. 35 pp.

Brief account of Congreve's life and art with special emphasis on his comedies and the comedy of manners as a literary type.

1234 Germer, Erich. Sentimentale Züge in den Lustspielgestalten Ether-eges, Wycherleys, Congreves, Vanbrughs und Farquhars. In-augural Dissertation. Münster, 1963. 164 pp.

Appearance and treatments of types of sentimentalism in Restoration comedy.

1235 Gosse, Anthony. "The Omitted Scene in Congreve's Love for Love." Modern Philology, LXI (1963), 40-42.

Congreve omitted scene ii of Act III of Love for Love as un-necessary to the characterization of Foresight.

1236 Juengel, Joyce. J. "A Project in Design and Construction of Cos-tumes for a Production of The Way of the World by William Con-greve." M.A. Indiana University, 1963.

1237 Lincoln, Stoddard. "Eccles and Congreve: Music and Drama on the Restoration Stage." Theatre Notebook, XVIII (Autumn, 1963), 7-18.

The importance of Eccles' music for the interpretation and appreciation of Congreve's The Way of the World, The Judgment of Paris, The Ode for St. Cecilia's Day, and Semele.

1238 ------. "The First Setting of Congreve's Semele." Music and Let-ters, XLIV (1963), 103-117.

The collaboration of John Eccles and Congreve in the com-position of Semele (1707). Eccles' attempt was the first by an English composer to produce a completely sung opera in English during this time.

1239 Taylor, D. C. William Congreve. New York: Russell and Russell, 1963.

1240 Barnard, John. "Did Congreve Write A Satyr Against Love?" Bul-letin of the New York Public Library, LXVIII (1964), 308-322.

Takes issue with the view that the satire was "an expression of feelings experienced by Congreve when Anne Bracegirdle rejected him." Outlines the internal evidence against Congreve's authorship of the piece.

1241 Beatty, Max. "A Project in Design and Execution of a Stage Setting for a Production of William Congreve's The Way of the World." M.A. Indiana University, 1964.

1242 Gagen, Jean [Elizabeth]. "Congreve's Mirabell and the Ideal of the Gentleman." Publications of the Modern Language Association, LXXIX (1964), 422-427.

Common misinterpretations of Mirabell's character result
from the failure to distinguish between the gentleman and rake
or libertine of the Restoration period. The hero of The Way of
the World represents the ideal of the gentleman current in Congreve's time.

1243 Lyons, Charles R. "Congreve's Miracle of Love." Criticism, VI
(1964), 331-348.
In Love for Love, Congreve's attitude toward love is neither
insouciant nor morally ambiguous. In the actions of Valentine
and Angelica, Congreve affirms the value of an honest and faithful relationship in marriage.

1244 Bernard, J. M. "'Regularity' in Congreve's Comedies, 1693-1700."
B. Litt. Oxford University (Wadham), 1965.

1245 De Ment, Joseph Willis, Jr. "The Ironic Image: Metaphoric Structure and Texture in the Comedies of William Congreve." Ph.D.
Indiana University, 1965. (Order No. 65-10815).
The metaphorical image patterns and lines of action in Congreve's comedies underscore the conflict between the age's
theoretical Christian outlook and its practical Machiavellian
ethics.

1246 Muir, Kenneth. "The Comedies of William Congreve." Restoration
Theatre. Edited by John Russell Brown and Bernard Harris.
(Stratford-Upon-Avon Studies, 6). (London: Edward Arnold;
New York: St. Martin's Press, 1965), 221-237.
Congreve's success with the matter and form of the comedy
of manners makes him "the best writer of comedy between
Shakespeare and Shaw."

1247 Van Voris, W. H. The Cultivated Stance: The Designs of Congreve's Plays. Dublin: Dolmen Press; London: Oxford University
Press, 1965. 186 pp.
Examines Congreve's assumptions in the structures of his
four comedies and his tragedy. The last chapter studies the
dialogue of the plays.

1248 Dobrée, Bonamy. "Congreve." Restoration Drama: Modern Essays
in Criticism. (A Galaxy Book). Edited by John Loftis. (New York:
Oxford University Press, 1966), 97-121.
Reprinted from Restoration Comedy (Oxford: Oxford Universi
Press, 1924), pp. 121-150. A survey of Congreve's development
and accomplishments as a dramatist.

1249 Downer, Alan S. "Mr. Congreve Comes to Judgment." Humanities
Association Bulletin, XVII (1966), 5-12.

1250 Fujimura, Thomas H. "Congreve's Last Play." Restoration Drama
tists: A Collection of Critical Essays. (Twentieth Century Views
Edited by Earl Miner. (Englewood Cliffs, N.J.: Prentice-Hall,
Inc., 1966), 165-174.

Reprinted from The Restoration Comedy of Wit (Princeton: Princeton University Press, 1952). The Way of the World is not as good a comedy of wit as The Man of Mode or Love for Love because "it lacks not only a strong naturalistic substratum but sceptical and sexual wit, comic wit that is easily grasped, and a consistent attitude toward life."

1251 Holland, Norman N. "Love for Love." Restoration Dramatists: A Collection of Critical Essays. (Twentieth Century Views). Edited by Earl Miner. (Englewood Cliffs, N.J.: Prentice-Hall, Inc., 1966), 151-164.

Reprinted from The First Modern Comedies. (Cambridge, Mass.: Harvard University Press, 1959). Congreve's third comedy concerns three different kinds of knowledge, three different ways of life: "presocial, social, suprasocial."

1252 Klaus, Carl Hanna. "The Scenic Art of William Congreve: An Approach to Restoration Comedy." Ph.D. Cornell University, 1966. (Order No. 66-10,272).

A study of Congreve's plays that focuses on the substance, construction, and disposition of scenes, particularly in The Old Batchelor, The Double Dealer, Love for Love, and The Way of the World.

1253 Leech, Clifford. "Congreve and the Century's End." Restoration Drama: Modern Essays in Criticism. (A Galaxy Book). Edited by John Loftis. (New York: Oxford University Press, 1966), 122-143.

Reprinted from Philological Quarterly, XLI (1962), 275-293. With his work at the end of the century, "Congreve brings the diverse and often conflicting elements of Restoration comedy into a unity."

1254 Birdsall, Virginia Ogden. "The English Comic Spirit on the Restoration Stage." Ph.D. Brown University, 1967. (Order No. 68-1439).

The immorality and libertinism of comic protagonists are an essential part of their nature and relate them to an English comic tradition that always takes sides with the individual against the group. The study concentrates on Etherege, Wycherley, and Congreve.

1255 Dobrée, Bonamy. Variety of Ways: Discussions on Six Authors. Freeport, New York: Books for Libraries Press, 1967. 118 pp.

A reprint of the 1932 edition includes discussions of Congreve, Dryden and Steele.

1256 Lynch, Kathleen M. A Congreve Gallery. New York: Octagon Books, 1967. 196 pp.

A reprint of the 1951 edition. A study of Congreve's personality, background and times with emphasis on the friends of his youth.

1257 Maurocordato, Alexandre. Ainsi Va le Monde: Etude sur la Structure d'une "Comedy of Manners." Paris: Lettres Modernes, 1967. 55 pp.
    Examines the structure of The Way of the World.
1258 Weales, Gerald. "The Shadow of Congreve's Surface." Educational Theatre Journal, XIX (1967), 30-32.
    Analyzes Vainlove's unconventional attitudes toward sex in The Old Bachelor.

Connoisseur

1259 Lams, Victor J., Jr. "A Study of the Connoisseur (1754-56)." Ph.D. Northwestern University, 1965. (Order No. 65-12,119).
    A description and analysis of the essay journal written chiefly by George Colman the elder and Bonnell Thornton. The journal treated manners and morals as well as language, literature, and the arts.

Continental Criticism

1260 Bouchard, Marcel. "Un Précurseur de la Bruyère: les 'Réflexions sur l'Eloquence' du P. Rapin et le'Chapitre de la Chaire.'" Revue d'Histoire Littéraire de la France, XXXVIII (1931), 355-366.
    Personality of the Jesuit P. Rapin and his influence on Bruyerè.

Cooke, George

1261 Trewin, John Courtenay. "The Old Complaint." The Night Has Been Unruly. (London: Robert Hale, Ltd. [1957]), 67-87.
    A sketch of the career of George Frederick Cooke, actor.

Cooke, Henry

1262 Bridge, Joseph C. "A Great English Choir-Trainer: Captain Henry Cooke." The Musical Antiquary, II (January, 1911), 61-79.
    Sections devoted to discussion of Cooke as choir-master, singer, actor, and composer with a list of his compositions.

Copyright Laws

1263 Draper, John W. "Queen Anne's Act: A Note on English Copyrights." Modern Language Notes, XXXVI (1921), 146-154.
    A history of controversies over the copyright in the early 18th century, which includes a discussion of dramatists.

Corneille, Pierre

1264 Mulert, Alfred. Pierre Corneille auf der Englischen Bühne und in
      der Englischen Übersetzungs-Literatur des siebzehnten Jahr-
      hunderts. Erlangen & Leipzig: A. Deichert, 1900. xiv, 61 pp.
         The influence and translations of Le Cid, Polyeucte and
      Horace, on J. Rutter, W. Popple, J. Ozell, and W. Lower.
      The influences on L. Carlell (Heraclius), and on J. Dancer
      (Nicomede) are also considered.
1265 Voisine, J. "Corneille et Racine en Angleterre au dix-huitième
      siècle." Revue de Littérature Comparée, XXII (1948), 161-
      175.
         A general survey of their influence and of plays in English
      based on their plots.
1266 Hartnoll, Phyllis. "Corneille in England." Theatre Research, I,
      No. 2 (1958), 14-16.
1267 French, A. L. "Some Tragedies of Corneille and Racine As Trans-
      lated into English, 1660-1676." M. Litt. Cambridge University
      (Jesus), 1961.

Costume

1268 Campbell, Lily Bess. "History of Costuming on the English Stage
      Between 1660 and 1823." University of Wisconsin Studies in
      Language and Literature, II (1918), 187-223.
         Costuming from 1660 to the early 18th century disregarded
      history and art. Early pioneers in accurate, artistic costumes
      were Aaron Hill, Charles Macklin, Sir John Hill, de Louther-
      bourg, and the antiquaries, but it was the Kembles and Frances
      Douce that really brought such costuming about in the 19th century.
1269 von Boehm, Max. Das Beuhenkosteum in Ulterum Mittelalter und
      Neuzeit. Berlin: Bruno Cassirer, 1921.
         A history of theatrical costume, beginning with the Greeks.
      "Das historiche Kostum" (pp. 376-441) has materials and il-
      lustrations concerning 18th century English drama, especially
      Garrick and Mrs. Siddons.
1270 Mackintosh, D. T. "'New Dress'd, in the Habits of the Times.'"
      Times Literary Supplement, August 25, 1927, p. 575.
         Mackintosh states that the true starting point in the matter
      of the historic dressing of plays is the winter season of 1762-
      63, and that probably George Colman is the father of the firm
      establishment of historic dressing on the English stage.
1271 Barton, Lucy. Historic Costume for the Stage. Boston: Walter H.
      Baker, 1935. viii, 605 pp.
         A thorough history of stage dress that ranges from the early

Egyptian to the Edwardian eras. For any given period, the
author provides detailed descriptions of representative costume
and an abundance of illustrations.

1272 Rule, Margaret Brady. "Details and Accessories of Historical
Costume from the 14th through the 18th Centuries; A Reference
Book for Designers of Theatrical Costumes." M.A. University
of Iowa, 1935.

1273 Falconer, J. P. E. "Coronation Clothes Used on the Stage." Notes
and Queries, CXCIII (August 21, 1948), 363.
Robes from the coronation of George II (1727) used in a
Drury Lane performance of Henry VIII.

1274 Malton, Vera Ellen. "Costume in England, France and America
from 1700-1840." M.A. Cornell University, 1948.

1275 Rosenfeld, Sybil. "The Wardrobes of Lincoln's Inn Fields and
Covent Garden." Theatre Notebook, V (1950-1951), 15-19.
Four documents at the back of a volume of Covent Garden
press cuttings from 1760 to 1789 (now in the British Museum)
and in the Latreille manuscript (Brit. Mus. Add. Ms. 32, 251
f. 299) throw additional light on eighteenth-century wardrobing.

1276 Langham, Norma Eleanor. "Seventeenth Century Costume from
1625-1689, Cavalier, Commonwealth, and Restoration: Its
Development and Modern Stage Representation." M.A. Stanford
University, 1956.

1277 Edwards, Charlene. "The Tradition for Britches in the Three Centuries that the Professional Actresses Have Played Male Roles
on the English-Speaking Stage." Ph.D. Denver University, 1957

1278 Brooke, Iris. Dress and Undress. The Restoration and Eighteenth
Century. London: Methuen & Co., Ltd., 1958. xi, 161 pp.
Another work by the author of numerous books on costume
through the ages. The book is aimed at stage designers, and attempts to show, in chronological order, from 1660-1800, the
groups of garments of one period worn together or individually.

1279 Jones, Sereta Taylor. "The Effect of the Customs and Manners in
England on the Costumes of the Day during the Reigns of Anne
and the Three Georges." M.S. University of Utah, 1960.

1280 Ferrar, Eleanor Barbara. "The Costuming of Harlequin in British
Satirical Prints, 1740-1820." M.A. Ohio State University, 1961
Attempts to trace the evolution of the Harlequin costume,
from 1740-1820, to discover how much effect contemporary
fashions had upon the costume.

1281 Omary, Jeanne Kay. "An Historical Analysis of Eighteenth Century
Costume." M.S. University of Wisconsin, 1963.

1282 Stephenson, Mary Amanda. "The Costume of the Hero of Restoration Tragedy." M.A. University of Florida, 1963.

1283 Pentzell, Raymond Joseph. "New Dress'd in the Ancient Manner:

The Rise of Historical Realism in Costuming the Serious Drama of England and France in the Eighteenth Century." Ph.D. Yale University, 1967. (Order No. 67-8407).

Traces the revolution in stage costuming from operatic fantasy and conventionality to the acceptance of archeological verisimilitude.

Court Platonism

1284 Harrison, J. B. "The Influence of Court Platonism on Caroline Drama." Ph.D. Ohio State University, 1939.

Court Stage

1285 Boswell, Eleanore. "The Court Stage, 1660-1702." Ph.D. London University, 1930.

Covent Garden

1286 Humphreys, A. L. "Covent Garden: Eccentric Characters of the Past." Notes and Queries, CLXXXII (May 9, 1942), 254-256.
1287 Highfill, Philip H., Jr. "Some Covent Garden Scenes." Theatre Notebook, XV (Spring, 1961), 88.

Gives a transcript of BM Add 33, 218, which contains a list by the principal Covent Garden painter Nicholas Thomas Dall, of divers "scenes and pieces of painting" which Colman has caused to be made since 9 September, 1768.

1288 -----. "Rich's 1744 Inventory of Covent Garden Properties." Restoration and 18th Century Theatre Research, V (May, 1966), 7-17; V (November, 1966), 17-26.

Lists of costumes, scenery and other properties at Covent Garden in 1744 are reproduced from the British Museum manuscript (BM Add. MSS. 12,201).

Cowley, Abraham

1289 Nethercot, A. H. "The Reputation of Abraham Cowley." Publications of the Modern Language Association, XXXVIII (1923), 588-641.

Cowley's plays are dealt with in a single paragraph; Nethercot concludes that they had little effect on Cowley's reputation.

1290 -----. "Abraham Cowley's Discourse Concerning Style." Review of English Studies, II (October, 1926), 385-404.

A synthesis of Cowley's numerous incidental utterances about literature, including drama.

1291 -----. "Abraham Cowley as Dramatist." Review of English
        Studies, IV (January, 1928), 1-24.
            Discusses the indebtedness of Love's Riddle (1638) to Ran-
        dolph's The Jealous Lovers and other dramas.
1292 Beers, Henry A. "Abraham Cowley: Cutter of Coleman Street."
        Representative English Comedies. Vol. IV: Dryden and His
        Contemporaries: Cowley to Farquhar. Edited by Charles Mills
        Gayley and Alwin Thaler. (New York: The Macmillan Company,
        1936), 1-12.
            An essay covering Cowley's life, followed by an introduction
        to The Cutter of Coleman Street, its dramatic construction and
        comparing it to The Guardian, the first version of the play. The
        text of the play, edited by Beers, follows.
1293 Hinman, Robert B. Abraham Cowley's World of Order. Cambridge,
        Mass: Harvard University Press, 1960. ix, 373 pp.
            The plays barely mentioned.

Cowley, Hannah

1294 Bleackley, Horace. "Kitty Fisher and The Belle's Stratagem."
        Notes and Queries, 11th Ser., II (July-December, 1910), 346.
            Refutes the Dictionary of National Biography's statement
        that the character of Kitty Willis was taken from Kitty Fisher.
1295 Rhodes, R. Crompton. "The Belle's Stratagem." Review of English
        Studies, V (April, 1929), 129-142.
            Examines Hannah Cowley's popular comedy of the late eigh-
        teenth century.
1296 Norton, J. E "Some Uncollected Authors, XVI: Hannah Cowley,
        1743-1809." Book Collector, VII (1958), 68-76.
            Bibliography.
1297 Todd, William B. "Hannah Cowley: Re-Impressions, Not Reissues."
        Book Collector, VII (1958), 301.
            Emends J. E. Norton's article.

Cox, Robert

1298 Mahoney, John L. "Robert Cox and the Seventeenth-Century Drolls."
        Drama Critique, II (1959), 68-71.
            Summarizes the few known facts about Cox, principal author
        and actor of drolls, the comic scenes presented during the Com-
        monwealth period (1649-1659). His secret productions are
        credited with keeping the theatre alive during the period of the
        closing of the theatres.

Coysh, John

1299 Cameron, Kenneth M. "The Monmouth and Portsmouth Troupes."
      Theatre Notebook, XVII (Spring, 1963), 89-94.
          The importance of John Coysh for the history of these com-
      panies and for an understanding of the nature of provincial
      Restoration companies.

Cradock, Joseph

1300 Dobson, Austin. "Mr. Cradock of Gumley." Old Kensington Palace
      and Other Papers. (London: Chatto and Windus, 1910), 53-81.
          Short sketch of Joseph Cradock's life based on his Memoirs
      with emphasis upon his theatrical reminiscences.

Craven, Lady

1301 Ley, H. Die litterarische Tatigkeit der Lady Craven. Inaugural
      Dissertation. Erlangen, 1904.

Crawfurd, David

1302 Macaree, David. "David Crawfurd (1665-1708?): His Works and
      their Relation to Restoration Literature." Ph.D. University of
      Washington, 1966. (Order No. 66-12,023).
          A study of Crawfurd's contribution to the literature of his
      time in short prose fiction, comedy, and Ovidian verse epistles.
      Crawfurd's comedies, Courtship-a-la-Mode (1700) and Love at
      First Sight (1704), are set in the traditions of Jonsonian com-
      edy of humours as carried on by Shadwell rather than in that
      of Restoration comedy of wit.

Crisp, S.

1303 Macnaughton, Angus I. Family Roundabout. Edinburgh: Oliver &
      Boyd, 1955. xiii, 124 pp.

Critic

1304 Howell, Elmo H. "The Role of the Critic in the Restoration and
      Early Eighteenth Century." Ph.D. University of Florida, 1955.

Criticism

1305 Montgomery, Beatrice. "Distinctions between Tragedy and Comedy
      Made by English Critics from Ben Jonson to Samuel Johnson."
      M.A. Stanford University, 1905.
1306 Spingarn, Joel Elias, ed. Critical Essays of the Seventeenth Cen-
      tury. 3 Vols. Oxford, 1908-09.
          Contains most of the texts of English critical writing publish
          during the seventeenth century. Omits Dryden's essays, begins
          where Gregory Smith's Elizabethan Critical Essays ended. Shov
          development with annotations and comment. Vol. 2 (iv, 362 pp.
          contains Davenant, Richard Flecknoe, and Samuel Butler. Vol.
          (376 pp.) contains Gerard Langbaine, Congreve, and Jeremy
          Collier. Bibliography, Vol. 3, pp. 342-356.
1307 Dutton, George B. "Dramatic Fashions Illustrated in Six Old Plays
      Journal of English and Germanic Philology, XIII (1914), 398-
      417.
          All six plays use legend of the love of King Edgard for Al-
          freda or Elfrid, A Knack to Know A Knave; Ravenscroft's King
          Edgar and Alfreda; Thomas Rymer's Edgar; Aaaron Hill's
          Elfrid; Aaaron Hill's Athelwold; and William Mason's Elfrida.
          Comparison of the plays, with a discussion of the technique,
          form, and neoclassical influences.
1308 Durham, Willard Higley. Critical Essays of the Eighteenth Cen-
      tury, 1700-1725. New Haven: Yale University Press, 1915.
      445 pp.
          Anthology of criticism to clear up misunderstanding of
          theories about literature held by 18th century Englishmen. In-
          cludes works by Gildon, Hughes, Dennis, Farquhar, Steele,
          Addison, Pope, Welstead, Ramsay. Introduction points out
          that these men belong neither to classicism nor any other -ism
          They are individualists.
1309 Routh, James Edward. The Rise of Classical English Criticism.
      A History of the Canons of English Literary Taste and Rhetoric.
      Doctrine, from the Beginning of English Criticism to the Death
      of Dryden. New Orleans: Tulane University Press, 1915. 101 p
          Some matter on tragedy scattered throughout the chapters.
1310 Dutton, George B. "Theory and Practice in English Tragedy, 1650-
      1700." Englische Studien. XLIX (1916), 190-219.
          Uses word "tragedy" to cover "serious drama" as opposed
          to comedy, farce, etc. Says writers were conscious of demands
          of neo-classicism, and tended to accede to them. Influenced by
          criticism, Davenant, Earl of Orrery, Dryden, Settle, Crowne,
          Otway, Lee, Southerne, Congreve.

1311 Clark, Barrett H., ed. European Theories of the Drama: An
      Anthology of Dramatic Theory and Criticism from Aristotle
      to the Present Day, in a Series of Selected Texts, with Com-
      mentaries, Biographies, and Bibliographies. New York: D.
      Appleton and Company, 1918. 503 pp.
          "An attempt to set before the reader the development of the
      theory of dramatic technique in Europe from Aristotle to the
      present time." This anthology contains works by Dryden, Milton,
      Rymer, Congreve, Farquhar, Addison, Johnson, Goldsmith.
      Revised editions, 1929, 1947.

1312 Gott, Charles. "The English Stage (1698-1750) in Controversial
      and Critical Literature." Ph.D. Harvard University, 1919.
      465 pp.
          The thesis is divided into two parts: 1) a discussion of the
      Collier controversy and its ramifications; 2) a discussion of
      periodical criticisms of the stage. While the Collier controversy
      is treated chronologically, the treatment of the periodical criti-
      cism is arranged by subject matter--e.g., Expressions of
      Dramatic Theory, General Discussions of Contemporary Drama.

1313 Saintsbury, George. A History of English Criticism: Being the
      English Chapters of "A History of Criticism and Literary Taste
      in Europe," Revised, adapted, and supplemented. London: Black-
      wood, 1922. 551 pp.
          Chapters III (Dryden and His Contemporaries, pp. 105-146)
      and IV (from Addison to Johnson, pp. 159-234) contain some
      material on dramatic theory and some material on attitudes to
      Shakespeare.

1314 Cline, Thomas Lucian. Critical Opinion in the Eighteenth Century;
      English Personal Letter. Ann Arbor, Michigan: Mimeographed
      and printed by Edwards Brothers, 1926.
          142 numbered leaves.

1315 Ross, Julian Lenhart. "Studies in English Dramatic Criticism,
      1700-1750." Ph.D. Harvard University, 1927.
          An attempt to analyze the opinions concerning drama ex-
      pressed by the playwrights of the early 18th century, centered
      on such topics as theories of comedy, theories of tragedy, attitude
      toward the neo-classic rules.

1316 Bosker, A. Literary Criticism in the Age of Johnson. Groningen:
      J. B. Wolters, 1930. ix, 294 pp.
          The announced subject of the book is the conflict between
      "rationalism" and the doctrines that undermined its sway. Ex-
      amples are taken from non-dramatic sources primarily, but
      there is some discussion of the drama.

1317 Gray, Charles Harold. Theatrical Criticism in London to 1795.
      New York: Columbia University Press, 1931. 333 pp.

By making a distinction between the dramatic critic (scholarly and theoretical) and the theatrical critic, Gray limits his work
to a survey of all periodic writing on current affairs in the London theatre from 1694 to 1795. It contains all comments on the
"living" theatre during that period, from information on current
productions (of both old and new plays), to discussions of acting,
finances, and personal affairs.

1318 Thomas, P. G. Aspects of Literary Theory and Practice, 1550-
1870. London: Heath Cranton, 1931. 210 pp.
Includes discussions of both Restoration and eighteenth-
century dramatic theory and practice.

1319 Chapman, E. F. "The Development of Critical Theories in England
from 1660-1711." Ph.D. University of London, 1935.

1320 Millett, Fred B., and Gerald E. Bentley. The Art of the Drama.
New York: D. Appleton-Century Co., 1935. viii, 253 pp.
This study of dramatic modes and forms is primarily an
essay in definition and classification. Restoration tragedy,
and Restoration and 18th century comedy, are considered chiefly

1321 Ross, Malcolm M. "The Theatre and Social Confusion." University
of Toronto Quarterly, V (1936), 197-215.
Includes a brief discussion of bourgeois drama in the eighteen
century. Lillo and Charles Johnson are cited.

1322 Sper, Felix. "Periodical Criticism of the Drama in London." Ph.D.
New York University, 1936.

1323 White, Irving Hamilton. "Studies in English Dramatic Criticism,
1750-1800." Ph.D. Harvard University, 1936.
A companion study to Ross. An analysis of the opinions on
drama expressed by playwrights of the last half of the 18th
century; focusses on theories of tragedy, theories of comedy
opinions of ancient drama and the classical rules.

1324 Gebauer, Emanuel L. "The Theatrical Criticism of William Archer
Quarterly Journal of Speech, XXIV (1938), 181-192.
An analysis of the principles of a critic who disliked Resto-
ration drama.

1325 Kimmelman, George. "The Concept of Tragedy in Modern Criticism." Journal of Aesthetics and Art Criticism, IV (1945), 141-
160.
Shows how recent criticism returns to Renaissance concepts
and rejects Restoration and eighteenth century critical thinking,
which is categorized as oversimplified and perverse.

1326 Ward, A. C., ed. Specimens of English Dramatic Criticism,
Seventeenth--Twentieth Centuries. Oxford: University Press,
1945. 355 pp.
A general anthology, with the best-known pieces from the
period included.

1327 Coffin, Robert P. T. and Alexander M. Witherspoon, eds. Seven-
      teenth-century Poetry and Prose. New York: Harcourt, Brace,
      1946. xiii, 804pp., viii, 310 pp.
          The second edition of a well-known college anthology which
      includes annotated selections from Dryden's dramatic criticism
      and some songs from the Restoration stage.
1328 Oakes, Frances E. "Neo-classic Literary Theory as an Outgrowth
      of the Eighteenth Century Climate of Opinion." Florida State
      University Studies, VI (1952), 11-22.
1329 Lancaster, H. Carrington. "Observations on French, Spanish,
      and English Theatres in D'Argens's Lettres Juives and Lettres
      Cabalistiques." Modern Language Notes, LXIX (1954), 231-
      237.
          D'Argens' impressions of the English theatre are second-
      hand but nevertheless important in confirming his continental
      readers in their classical prejudices.
1330 Marks, Emerson R. Relativist and Absolutist. The Early Neo-
      Classical Debate in England. New Brunswick, New Jersey:
      Rutgers University Press, 1955. xi, 171 pp.
          An historical and analytical study of the seventeenth and
      eighteenth century beginnings of relativism in criticism. Em-
      phasis on Dryden and Dennis.
1331 Van der Weele, Steven John. "The Critical Reputation of Resto-
      ration Comedy in Modern Times." Ph.D. University of Wis-
      consin, 1955.
1332 Wellek, Rene. A History of Modern Criticism, 1750-1950. Vol.
      I: The Later 18th Century. New Haven: Yale University Press,
      1955. ix, 358 pp.
          The disintegration of neo-classicism and emergence of ro-
      manticism in French, British, Italian, and German criticism;
      employs a "history of ideas" method modified by description
      and evaluation of individual thinkers.
1333 Daiches, David. Critical Approaches to Literature. Englewood
      Cliffs, N.J.: Prentice-Hall, 1956. xi, 404 pp.
          Discussions of dramatic criticism indexed.
1334 Knights, L. C. "The Grounds of Literary Criticism." Neophilologus,
      XL (1956), 207-215.
1335 Spingarn, J. E., ed. Critical Essays of the Seventeenth Century.
      3 vols. Bloomington, Ind.: Indiana University Press, 1957. [Re-
      issue of the 1908 edition.]
          Volumes II and III contain critical writings from 1650 to
      1700. One of the best known collections of critical essays, this
      work contains many items of interest--e.g., essays by Shadwell,
      Dryden, Flecknoe, Rymer, Sir Robert Howard, etc. Useful notes,
      which are placed at the end of each volume.

1336 Davies, Hugh Sykes, ed. The Poets and Their Critics. Vol. I:
       Chaucer to Collins. London: Hutchinson, 1960. 240 pp. [First
       published in 1943 by Penguin.]
            The chapters in Milton and Dryden--in which syntheses of
       various critical opinions relating to these authors are provided
       --ought to prove of interest to the student of Restoration theatre

1337 Monk, Samuel H. The Sublime; a Study of Critical Theories in
       XVIII-Century England. Ann Arbor: University of Michigan Pre
       1960. iv, 250 pp.
            This is a revised version of Monk's 1935 study of "The Sub-
       lime," a history of 18th-century aesthetic and critical specula
       tion in Great Britain. Primarily concerned with the aesthetic
       theories with regard to painting and architecture, it nonetheles
       deals also with 18th-century literary theories.

1338 Hynes, Samuel, editor. English Literary Criticism: Restoration
       and 18th Century. (Goldentree Books). New York: Appleton-
       Century-Crofts, 1963. 322 pp.
            An anthology. Includes essays on drama by Dryden, Collier
       Congreve, Vanbrugh, Steele, Hume and Goldsmith. Brief notes
       and bibliography precede each selection.

1339 Gray, Charles Harold. Theatrical Criticism in London to 1795.
       New York: Benjamin Bloom, 1964. 333 pp.
            Reprint of Gray's 1931 compendium of contemporary reacti
       to plays and players between 1730 and 1795. Arranged chronol
       gically.

Cross, Richard

1340 Pedicord, Harry William. "Rylands English MS. 1111: An Early
       Diary of Richard Cross (d. 1760), Prompter to the Theatres."
       Bulletin of the John Rylands Library, XXXVII (1955), 503-527.
            A description of the manuscript, discussion of proof of its
       being by Cross, the implications of the manuscript, the role
       of the prompter as understudy. Mentions plays Cross would
       have filled in for. Comments on plays and actors of Drury Lan
       1741-1742.

1341 -----. "Course of Plays, 1740-2: An Early Diary of Richard Cros
       Prompter to the Theatres." Bulletin of the John Rylands Librar
       XL (1958), 1-46.
            Covent Garden, 1740-1741; Drury Lane, 1741-1742.

Crowne, John

dramatic works

1342 Hoeberli, E. The Comedies of John Crowne. Berne: Stoempli,
      1905. 69 pp.
           Sketchy summaries of plots and major characters with some
      mention of sources and production data.
1343 Crowne, John. The Dramatic Works of John Crowne. Edited by J.
      Maidment and W. H. Logan. 4 vols. New York: Benjamin Blom,
      1967.
           Reprint of the 1874 edition.

individual plays

1344 -----. City Politiques. Edited by John Harold Wilson. (Regent
      Restoration Drama Series). Lincoln: University of Nebraska
      Press, 1967.
           Includes introduction, notes, and chronology.
1345 Hughes, Charlotte B. "John Crowne's Sir Courtly Nice, a Critical
      Edition." Ph.D. Brown University, 1960.
1346 Crowne, John. Sir Courtly Nice. Edited by Charlotte Bradford
      Hughes. The Hague: Mouton and Co., 1966.
           Includes biography of Crowne, the stage history of the play,
      notes and bibliography.

biography and criticism

1347 Grosse, Wilhelm. John Crownes Komödien und burleske Dichtung.
      Lucka S.A.: Druck von R. Berger, 1903. [4], 116, [3] pp.
           After a brief outline of Crowne's life, the writer devotes the
      main body of the work to an analysis of the five comedies, con-
      sidering purpose, staging, characterization, and aesthetic pro-
      perties.
1348 Jacob, Franz. Die Fabel von Atreus und Thyestes in den wicktig-
      sten Tragödien der englischen, französischen und italienischen
      Literature. Inaugural Dissertation. Munich, 1906. 37 pp.
           Includes a comparison of Crowne's Thyestes with that by
      Seneca.
1349 Koberg, Werner. Quellenstudien zu John Crowne's "Darius."
      Hamburg: Hermann Kampen, 1918. 143 pp.
           For his Darius, Crowne relied to some extent on the ro-
      mances of Alexander and historical sources, but, particularly,
      he made use of Alexander Hardy's La Morte de Daire for the
      suggestion of his theme.

1350 White, A. F. "John Crowne and America." Publications of the
      Modern Language Association, XXXV (1920), 447-463.
           A brief biography of Crowne, who spent three years at Har-
      vard and then returned to England to be a playwright.

1351 ------. John Crowne, His Life and Dramatic Works. Cleveland:
      Western Reserve University Press, 1922. 211 pp.
           A detailed study of Crowne's life and of his plays in the
      order in which they were written. His true importance to the
      drama lies in the fact that his work illustrates all the various
      types of drama in vogue in his time.

1352 Winship, George Parker. The First Harvard Playwright: A Biblio-
      graphy of the Restoration Dramatist John Crowne; with Extracts
      from his Prefaces and the Earlier Version of the Epilogue to Sir
      Courtly Nice, 1685. Cambridge: Harvard University Press,
      1922. 21 pp.
           An annotated, descriptive bibliography of Crowne's works.

1353 Ward, A. W. "Crowne's Place in Restoration Comedy." Representa
      tive English Comedies. Vol. IV: Dryden and His Contemporaries
      Cowley to Farquhar. Edited by Charles Mills Gayley and Alwin
      Thaler. (New York: The Macmillan Company, 1936), 241-255.
           Crowne's life and plays, particulary as the plays relate to
      the politics and social life of the period.

1354 Noyes, Robert G. "Mrs. Bracegirdle's Acting in John Crowne's
      'Justice Busy.'" Modern Language Notes, XLIII (February,
      1938), 390-391.

1355 Gardner, William B. "Dryden and the Authorship of the Epilogue
      to Crowne's Calisto." Texas Studies in English, XXVII (1948),
      234-238.
           Arguing for Crowne's authorship.

1356 Peterson, William M. "Sentiment in Crowne's 'The Married Beau.'
      Notes and Queries, CXCVIII (1953), 483-485.
           The Married Beau contains elements of sentiment which may
      have influenced Cibber in his writing of sentimental comedy.

1357 Berkeley, David S. "Sentiment in Crowne's 'The Married Beau.'"
      Notes and Queries, CXCIX (1954), 179.
           Berkeley questions W. M. Peterson's identification (Notes
      and Queries, CXCVIII, 483) of Christianity with sentimentality
      in The Married Beau.

1358 Capwell, Richard Leonard. "A Biographical and Critical Study of
      John Crowne." Ph.D. Duke University, 1964. (Order No. 64-
      11,204).
           A chronological examination of Crowne's development as a
      dramatist. Each play is studied in relation to its sources, to
      contemporary events, to the drama of the age, and as a popular
      stage production.

Cultural Background

1359 Turberville, A. S., ed. Johnson's England. 2 vols. Oxford:
      Clarendon Press, 1933.
          An account of the life and manners of his age.

Cumberland, Richard

1360 Smith, G. Barnett. "The English Terence." The Fortnightly Re-
      view, LXVII (1900), 243-257.
          A life of Cumberland, with a brief discussion of each of
      Cumberland's works, including his plays.
1361 'Paston, George' [E. M. Symonds]. "Richard Cumberland." Little
      Memoirs of the Eighteenth Century. (New York: E. P. Dutton
      and Co.; London: Grant Richards, 1901), 57-119.
          Biographical essay. The plays are mentioned as events in
      his career.
1362 Baker, George M. "An Echo of Schiller's Räuber in England."
      Modern Language Notes, XXVI (June, 1911), 171-172.
          In addition to the influence of Schiller's Räuber on Holman's
      Red Cross Knights (1799), and Gandy's Lorenzo (1823), pointed
      out by Rea, Richard Cumberland's Don Pedro (1796) "though
      not a professed imitation" is an "offspring" of Die Räuber.
1363 Fehler, Kurst. Richard Cumberlands Leben und dramatische Werke,
      ein Beitrag zur Geschichte des Englischen Dramas im 18 Jahr-
      hundert. Inaugural Dissertation. Kiel, 1911. 124 pp.
1364 Williams, Stanley T. Richard Cumberland: His Life and Dramatic
      Works. New Haven: Yale University Press; London: Humphrey
      Milford; Oxford University Press, 1917.
          A biography which suggests that interest in the subject lies
      less in the plays than in Cumberland's personality. There is, of
      course, information about his plays, as well as discussion of his
      relationships with Garrick, Goldsmith, Johnson, etc.
1365 Newman, Louis Israel. Richard Cumberland, Critic and Friend of
      the Jews . . . With an Edition of "The Jew" Abridged by Ernestine
      P. Franklin. New York: Bloch Publishing Co., 1919. xv, 124 pp.
          Investigates Cumberland's personal relationships with Jews
      and surveys the Jewish characters in his plays to show how they
      related to Cumberland's ambivalent feelings. The version of the
      play is adapted for presentation by high school groups.
1366 Williams, Stanley T. "Richard Cumberland's West Indian." Modern
      Language Notes, XXXV (1920), 413-417.
          A presentation of some 18th-century opinions about the role
      of Belcour and a discussion of the performers who played the
      major roles.

1367 -----. "The Dramas of Richard Cumberland, 1779-1785." Modern
Language Notes, XXXVI (1921), 403-408.
This consideration of Cumberland's plays from 1779 to 1785
is a continuation of Williams' article, "The Early Sentimental
Dramas of Richard Cumberland."

1368 -----. "The Early Sentimental Dramas of Richard Cumberland."
Modern Language Notes, XXXVI (1921), 160-165.
A chronological discussion of Cumberland's ten plays produced from 1761 through 1778; for some of the plays a stage
history is given.

1369 Birrell, Augustine. "Richard Cumberland." Collected Essays and
Addresses, 1880-1920. Vol. I. (London and Toronto: J. M. Dent
& Sons, 1922), 272-277.
An anecdotal account of Cumberland, primarily as a novelist,
with a brief discussion of Coker's assertion that Cumberland was
the original of Sir Fretful Plagiary.

1370 Landa, M. J. "The Grandfather of Melodrama." Cornhill Magazine,
New Ser., LIX (October, 1925), 476-484.
Proposes Richard Cumberland (1732-1811) as the chief pre-
cursor of English melodrama.

1371 Caskey, J. Homer. "Richard Cumberland's Mission in Spain."
Philological Quarterly, IX (1930), 82-86.
A series of letters published in 1904 clarify most of the
mystery about Cumberland's deserting literature for politics
when he served as ambassador to Spain. Among the material
he cites are letters which tell of the production of The Carmelite

1372 Fletcher, Ifan Kyrle. "Cumberland's The Princess of Parma."
Times Literary Supplement, March 15, 1934, p. 187.
Offers evidence that the play was produced at Kelmarsh,
probably in 1774; summary of plot and description of characters.

1373 Van Lennep, William. "The Princess of Parma." Times Literary
Supplement, October 24, 1936, p. 863.
Cites evidence to show that Cumberland's tragedy was first
performed in 1774.

1374 Sypher, Feltus Wylie. "The Anti-Slavery Movement to 1800 in
English Literature Exclusive of the Periodical." Ph.D. Harvard
University, 1937.
Isaac Bickerstaffe's Love in the City, and Cumberland's
West Indian are included in this study of the slavery controversy.

1375 Rosenfeld, Sybil. "Princess of Parma." Times Literary Supplement,
April 26, 1938, p. 264.
Provides evidence to show that Cumberland's play was per-
formed in 1774.

1376 Todd, William B. "Press Figures and Book Reviews as Determin-
ants of Priority: A Study of Home's Douglas (1757) and Cumber-

land's The Brothers (1770)." Papers of the Bibliographical
Society of America, XLV (1951), 72-76.
> Press figures and periodical citations may be used as com-
> plementary methods in studying variants, as these plays by
> Home and Douglas illustrate.

1377 Lyons, J. H. "Bourgeois Sentimentalism; a Critical Study of the
Life and Dramatic Works of Richard Cumberland." M.A. University of Liverpool, 1964.

Cunningham, John

1378 Dodds, M. H. "English Provincial Theatres, XVIII Century."
Notes and Queries, CLXIII (1932), 115.
> A list of poems by John Cunningham, who acted in northern
> stock companies, written between 1760 and 1771 for presenta-
> tion in plays.

Curll, Edmund

1379 Straus, Ralph. The Unspeakable Curll, Being Some Account of
Edmund Curll, Bookseller; To Which Is Added a Full List of
His Books. London: Chapman & Hall, Ltd., 1927. xi, [1], 322 pp.
> "A Handlist (1706-1746)" of books, pp. 199-314. Curll printed
> many plays, and some biographies of dramatists and theatrical
> figures, e.g., on Gay, Robert Wilks, Congreve. A study of his
> life has value for the historian of the period.

1380 Hill, Peter Murray. Two Augustan Booksellers: John Dunton and
Edmund Curll. Lawrence: University of Kansas Libraries, 1958.
30 pp. (University of Kansas Publications. Library Series, 3.)

Dance

1381 Sheehan, J. J. A Guide to Irish Dancing. London, Dublin, and
New York: John Denvir, 1902. 48 pp.
> Contains descriptions of thirteen reels and jigs.

1382 Holt, Ardern. How to Dance the Revived Ancient Dances. London:
Horace Cox, 1907. 158 pp.
> The first chapter deals lightly with 18th-century methods of
> stenochoreography; Chapter II describes some steps used in
> the revived ancient dances; Chapter III has interesting historical
> notes on masques; Chapter IV contains descriptions with musical
> examples of the Pavanne, Gaillarde, Courante, Passepied, Cha-
> conne, Allemande and Sarabande.

1383 Letainturier-Fradin, Gabriel. La Camargo, 1710-1770. Paris:
Ernest Framarion [1908]. 384 pp.
> "An account of the life of this celebrated dancer in the form

of an historical novel. On page 340 is a useful list of the different parts created by her."

1384 Sharp, Cecil James. The Country Dance Book. London: Novello
and Company, Ltd., 1909-1922. Six parts in four volumes.
Part I. Description of 176 country dances: steps, figures,
notations and notes on the sources. Part II. Thirty dances from
the English Dancing Master published by Playford. Beaumont's
bibliography lists dances in each volume.

1385 Pulver, Jeffrey. "The Ancient Dance Forms." Proceedings of the
Musical Association, XXIX (1912-13), 1-25.
". . . a few facts relating to the history of the [dance] forms
made up the Partita--up to, and excluding, the Gique." Includes
of those actually danced during the Restoration and 18th century
the Branle or Brawl, the Gaillarde, the Allemande, the Couran
and the Sarabande.

1386 D'Albert, Charles, Compiler. Technical Encyclopedia of the Theo
and Practice of the Art of Dancing. London: Imperial Society of
Dance Teachers, 1913. 166 pp.
A revised edition appeared in 1921. "A dictionary of technical terms, figures and dances, both ancient and modern."

1387 Pulver, Jeffrey. "The Ancient Dance Forms. Second Paper, The
Gigue." Proceedings of the Musical Association, XL (1913-14),
73-92.
Thorough discussion of the Jig (Gig, Gigue): source of the
name, the Jig as dance, its history (the Italian and English
forms), its rhythms, the Irish Jig so-called, the change in the
in the 17th century.

1388 Kinney, Troy and Margaret W. The Dance, Its Place in Art and
Life. London: William Heineman, 1914. 334 pp.
Chapters three and five are concerned with the dances of
the 17th and 18th centuries and with the style of dancing and
innovations of Sallé, Camargo, and Noverre.

1389 Beaumont, Cyril W. A Bibliography of Dancing. London: The
Dancing Times, Ltd., 1920. 228 pp.
Reprinted in 1963 by Benjamin Blom. An annotated bibliography of selected books in the British Museum on every phase
of dancing, including technical books, scenarii and libretti of
ballets, biographies of dancers, and books on stenochoreograph

1390 Avery, Emmett L. "Dancing and Pantomime on the English Stage,
1700-1737." Studies in Philology, XXI (1934), 417-452. Reprinted: [Chapel Hill, N.C., 1934], 35 pp.
Deals with the emergence and development of dancing and
pantomime as entertainments supplementing the dramatic
presentations of the eighteenth century.

1391 Perugini, Mark Edward. A Pageant of the Dance and Ballet.

London: Jarrolds, Ltd., 1935. 318 pp.

A popular history of the dance, concentrating on ballet. There is a chapter on "Mime, Italian Comedy and English Pantomime" and one on "Ballet in 18th-Century London." An appendix gives a chronology of the dance and ballet.

1392 Vince, Stanley W. E. "Camargo in London, 1750-1754." Theatre Notebook, XII (1958), 117-126; XIII (1958), 26-27.

1393 Cohen, Selma Jeanne. "Theory and Practice of Theatrical Dancing in England in the Restoration and Early Eighteenth Century as Seen in the Lives and Works of Josias Priest, John Weaver, and Hester Santlow." Bulletin of the New York Public Library, LXIII (1959), 541-554; XLIV (1960), 41-54; XLIV (1960), 95-104.

Accounts of the careers of three important figures in 18th-century dance; these three people illustrate different aspects of the development of dance during the century.

1394 Fletcher, Ifan Kyrle. "The History of Ballet in England, 1660-1740." Bulletin of the New York Public Library, LXIII (1959), 275-291. (The Woodward Lecture, delivered at Yale University Library, March 9, 1959).

A history, which includes treatment of dancers in plays, told primarily through the careers of the important figures relating to dance.

1395 Fletcher, Ifan Kyrle, Selma Jeanne Cohen, and Roger Lonsdale. Famed for Dance: Essays on the Theory and Practice of Theatrical Dancing in England, 1660-1740. New York: The New York Public Library, 1960. 64 pp.

Reprints Fletcher's "The History of Ballet in England, 1660-1740," Bulletin of the New York Public Library, LXIII (1959), 275-291; Cohen, "Theory and Practice of Theatrical Dancing in England in the Restoration and Early Eighteenth Century as seen in the Lives and Works of Josias Priest, John Weaver, and Hester Santlaw, Part I, Bull. N.Y.P.L., LXIII (1959), 541-544; Part II, Bull. N.Y.P.L. LXIV (1960), 41-54, 95, 104; and pre-prints Lonsdale, "Dr. Burney, John Weaver, and the Spectator." Bull. N.Y.P.L. LXIV (1960), 286-288. Indexed.

Dance, James

1396 Sale, William M. "The First Dramatic Version of Pamela." Yale University Library Gazette, IX (1935), 83-88.

An analysis of recently discovered texts reveals that Pamela; Or, Virtue Triumphant is the first published play based on Richardson's novel. Sale attributes the play to the actor, James Dance. The version first acted at Goodman's Fields in November, 1741, was published as Pamela with a 1742 imprint. It is almost certainly the work of Henry Giffard.

Dartford

1397   Rosenfeld, Sybil. "Private Theatricals at Bowman's Lodge,
          Dartford." Theatre Notebook, XVI (Summer, 1962), 125-126.
              Theatrical activities of the Society of Kentish Bowmen, 1785-
          1802.

Dating

1398   Spencer, Hazelton. "Theatrics of the Augustans." University of
          California Chronicle, XXVIII (January, 1926), 114-117.
              Reviews A. Nicoll, A History of Early Eighteenth Century
          Drama (1925). Disagrees with Nicoll's categories, preferring
          to end the Restoration period in 1710.
1399   Ryan, M. J. "The Long 'S' and Ye." London Times Literary Sup-
          plement, May 17, 1928, p. 379.
              Offers further evidence for using these two forms in dating
          texts and manuscripts.
1400   Wilson, John Harold. "The Duke's Theatre in March, 1680."
          Notes and Queries, New Ser., IX (1962), 385-386.
              Evidence that King Charles did not attend plays listed in the
          Lord Chamberlain's list, particularly Otway's Souldier's For-
          tune, and Dryden's Spanish Friar. Dates of plays presented by
          the Duke of York's Company.
1401   Wilson, James. "A Note on the Dating of Restoration Plays." 17th
          and 18th Century Theatre Research, I (May, 1962), 18-19.
              Problems to be considered in establishing dates of publication
          and performance.
1402   Wilson, John Harold. "Six Restoration Play Dates." Notes and
          Queries, New Ser., IX (1962), 221-223.
              Dryden's (?) The Mistaken Husband, Chamberlayne's Wits
          Led by the Nose, Dryden and Lee's Oedipus, Crowne's Thyestes,
          and Henry the Sixth, The First Part, and Banks' The Unhappy
          Favourite. Dates are established for their production.
1403   Langhans, Edward A. "Theatrical References in the Greenwich
          Hospital Newsletters." Notes and Queries, New Ser., XI (1964),
          338.
              Information helps date four play performances in January,
          1682: The Tempest (probably Shadwell's version), Crowne's
          Destruction of Jerusalem, Otway's Caius Marius, and Davenant's
          Circe.

Davenant, Charles

1404   Davies, Godfrey, and Marjorie Scofield. "Letters of Charles

Davenant." Huntington Library Quarterly, IV (April, 1941),
309-342.
　　"Prints the text of letters, now in the Huntington Library,
written by the son of the poet."
1405 Waddell, David. "The Writings of Charles Davenant (1656-1714)."
Library, XI (1956), 206-212.
　　Complete list of Davenant's published and unpublished writings,
dated with the help of contemporary newspaper advertisements.
Includes Circe (1677), a tragedy.
1406 -----. "Charles Davenant (1656-1714)--A Biographical Sketch."
Economic History Review, XI (1958), 279-299.

Davenant, William

works

1407 D'Avenant, William. The Works of Sir William D'Avenant. 2 vols.
New York: Benjamin Blom, 1967.
　　A reprint of the 1673 edition which contains all of the plays
as well as selections of prose and poetry.

plays

1408 -----. Love and Honour; and The Seige of Rhodes. Edited by James
W. Tupper (Belles-lettres Series). New York: D. C. Heath, 1909.
410 pp.
　　The text of the first play is that of the 1649 quarto; the text of
the second play is from the 1663 quarto.
1409 Knowland, A. S., editor. Six Caroline Plays. London: Oxford Uni-
versity Press, 1962. 432 pp. (The World's Classics).
　　The introduction discusses four major Caroline dramatists.
Prints the texts of The Wits by Davenant (1636) and The Parson's
Wedding by Thomas Killigrew (1663).

poems

1410 Davenant, Sir William. Select Poems of Sir William Davenant.
With a Prefatory Note by Douglas Bush. Cambridge, Massachusetts:
Willow Press, 1943. 43 pp.

individual plays

1411 Steible, Daniel J. "A Critical Edition of Sir William Davenant's The
Temple of Love and The Platonic Lovers." Ph.D. University of
Cincinnati, 1939.

1412 Spencer, Christopher. Davenant's Macbeth from the Yale Manu-
     script: An Edition, with a Discussion of the Relation of Daven-
     ant's Text to Shakespeare's. New Haven: Yale University Press,
     1961. 226 pp. (Yale Studies in English, Vol. 146).
         Presents a text of Davenant's play, which has been reproduced
     only twice since 1710. Improves on previous editions by the ad-
     dition of line numbers and by the inclusion of the Yale MS, which
     seems to have been used in preparing the promptbook.

     biography and criticism

1413 Illies, Georg. "Das Verhältnis von Davenant's The Law Against
     Lovers zu Shakespeare's Measure for Measure und Much Ado
     About Nothing." Inaugural Dissertation, Halle, 1900.
1414 Campbell, Killis. "The Source of Davenant's Albovine." Journal
     of English and Germanic Philology, IV (1902), 20-24.
         Dryden found immediate source of Albovine in all probability
     in the De Gestis Longobardarum of Paulus Diaconus, and not in
     literary versions of the Albovine story.
1415 -----. "Notes on Davenant's Life." Modern Language Notes,
     XVIII (1903), 236-239.
         A working out of Davenant's pedigree, with geneological
     chart, with comments on Davenant's early military career,
     his projected voyage to Maryland and his imprisonment during
     the commonwealth.
1416 Firth, C. H. "Sir William Davenant and the Revival of the Drama
     during the Protectorate." English Historical Review, XVIII
     (1903), 319-321.
         Identifies as Davenant's a document (quoted in full), "Some
     observations concerning the people of this nation (1656-7)" on
     the desirability of public recreations.
1417 Weber, Gustav. Davenant's "Macbeth" im Verhältnis zu Shakes-
     peare's gleichnamiger Tragödie." Rostock: Carl Boldt, 1903.
     76 pp.
         Discusses Davenant's production of "Macbeth. A Tragedy
     with all the Alterations, Amendments, Additions and New
     Songs" at the Duke's Theater in 1674. Discusses the unfortunate
     effects of Davenant's attempts to augment and "modernize"
     Shakespeare.
1418 Child, C. G. "The Rise of the Heroic Play." Modern Language
     Notes, XIX (1904), 167-173.
         A consideration of Davenant's contribution to the Heroic
     play. A specific study of "Siege of Rhodes" . . . Child com-
     ments upon Holzhausen's sketch of the rise and the develop-
     ment of the heroic play. Child makes the point that Davenant

antidates Dryden in use and development of the heroic play.

1419 Williams, John David Ellis. Sir William Davenant's Relation to
      Shakespeare. With an Analysis of the Chief Characters of
      Davenant's Plays. [Strassburg, 1905]. 120 pp.
          Discusses Shakespeare's influence on Davenant's original
      dramas. Influence of Shakespeare on Davenant's creation of
      tragic, comic, and heroic characters.

1420 Gronauer, Georg. Sir William Davenants "Gondibert." Eine
      literarhistorische Untersuchung. Inaugural Dissertation.
      Munich, 1911.

1421 Morgenroth, Hugo. Quellenstudien zu William Davenants Albovine.
      Borna-Leipzig: R. Noske, 1911. 29 pp.
          Discusses Davenant's Albovine in terms of possible sources
      and parallels to earlier authors.

1422 Ehrle, Karl. "Studien zu Sir William Davenant's Tragödien und
      Tragikomödien." Inaugural Dissertation. Munich, 1922.

1423 Hotson, Leslie. "Sir William Davenant and the Commonwealth
      Stage." Ph.D. Harvard University, 1923.
          A biography of Davenant is followed by a discussion of the
      Commonwealth stage as an "active transition period and finally
      an account of George Jolly and the plot by Davenant and Killigrew
      to cheat him."

1424 Thaler, Alwin. "Thomas Heywood, D'Avenant, and The Siege of
      Rhodes." Publications of the Modern Language Association,
      XXXIX (1924), 624-641.
          A discussion of Heywood's Fair Maid of the West as a pos-
      sible source of D'Avenant's play.

1425 Nicoll, Allardyce. "The Rights of Beeston and D'Avenant in Eliz-
      abethan Plays." Review of English Studies, I (January, 1925),
      84-91.
          Davenant's actors, descendants of William Beeston's com-
      pany, considered themselves as inheritors of certain prompt
      copies of Shakespeare's plays in Beeston's possession.

1426 Spencer, Hazelton. "D'Avenant's Macbeth and Shakespeare's."
      Publications of the Modern Language Association, XL (Sept-
      ember, 1925), 619-644.
          On changes made by Davenant in the 1672-73 revival, most
      of them to clear up obscure readings.

1427 [Davenant]. Notes and Queries, CL (March 6, 1926), 163.
          The date of baptism of Sir William Davenant (March 3,
      1606).

1428 de Beer, E. S. "A Statement of Sir William D'Avenant." Notes
      and Queries, CLIII (November 5, 1927), 327.
          Dated 25 April 1664, involves activities in the Civil War.

1429 Stroup, T. B. "Type-Characters in the Serious Drama of the
      Restoration with Special Attention to the Plays of Davenant,
      Dryden, Lee, and Otway." Ph.D. University of North Carolina,
      1933.
1430 Dowlin, Cornell M. Sir William Davenant's 'Gondibert,' Its Pre-
      face, and Hobbes's Answer. Philadelphia: University of Penn-
      sylvania Press, 1934. 127 pp.
          This volume, derived from Mrs. Dowlin's Ph.D. disserta-
      tion, is designed as "an introduction to a text of Gondibert based
      on the quarto and octavo editions of 1651 and the folio of Daven-
      ant's Works, published in 1673." Chapters cover "continental in
      fluences," "English influences," "heroic virtue and heroic play.
1431 Laig, Friederich Wilhelm. Englische und französische Elemente
      in Sir William Davenants dramatischer Kunst. Emsdatten: Heinr
      & J. Lechte, 1934. vi, 133 pp.
          Section five treats of Davenant's Restoration pieces, such
      as The Play-House To Be Let, Law Against Lovers, Rivals,
      Macbeth, and The Tempest, as well as The Man's The Master.
      Shows French and English influence on his work.
1432 Richardson, W. R. "Sir William Davenant as American Colonizer.
      English Literary History, I (1934), 61-62.
          Discusses Jean Chevalier's account of the capture of Daven-
      ant in 1650 as he was setting out from the island of Jersey for
      the New World.
1433 Berry, E. G. "Sir William Davenant and the 17th Century Theatre.
      M.A. McGill University, 1935.
1434 Harbage, Alfred. Sir William Davenant, Poet Venturer, 1606-1668
      Philadelphia: University of Pennsylvania Press, 1935. viii, 317 p
          A biography and a critical analysis of the plays, this study
      stresses the role of Davenant as the link between Caroline and
      Restoration drama.
1435 Nethercot, Arthur H. Sir William D'Avenant, Poet Laureate and
      Playwright-Manager. Chicago: University of Chicago Press,
      1938. vii, 488 pp.
          Omitting any extended analysis of the poems and plays, this
      volume presents a detailed biography of Davenant that emphasize
      his role as a guiding force in the early Restoration theatre.
1436 Cawley, Robert Ralston. "Characteristic Uses of the Voyagers:
      Davenant." Unpathed Waters: Studies in the Influence of the
      Voyagers on Elizabethan Literature. (Princeton: Princeton Uni-
      versity Press, 1940), 249-253.
          Discusses Davenant's use of voyaging material and his knowl
      edge of geography, especially in the Cruelty of the Spaniards in
      Peru and Sir Francis Drake. Mentions some of Davenant's post-
      Restoration plays.

1437 Lewis, Arthur O., Jr. "Sir William Davenant's Macbeth in Rela-
      tion to Shakespeare's Macbeth." Honors Thesis. Harvard Uni-
      versity, 1940.
1438 McManaway, James G. "The 'Lost' Canto of Gondibert." Modern
      Language Quarterly, I (March, 1940), 63-78.
1439 Stamm, Rudolf. "Sir William Davenant and Shakespeare's Imagery."
      English Studies (Amsterdam), XXIV (1942), 65-79, 97-116.
          This article discusses Davenant, his use of imagery in his
      own plays: Albovine, The Unfortunate Lovers, and The Siege of
      Rhodes; and his use of imagery in his adaptations of Shakespeare,
      The Law Against Lovers (Measure for Measure) and Macbeth.
1440 Rundle, James U. "D'Avenant's The Mans the Master and the
      Spanish Source." Modern Language Notes, LXV (1950), 194-196.
          Rundle points out previously unnoticed parallels between
      Davenant's play and Zorilla's Donde hay agravios no hay celos.
1441 Johnston, Albert S. "The Wits and the Platonic Lovers, by Sir Wil-
      liam D'Avenant." Ph.D. University of Florida, 1951.
1442 Mandach, André de. "The First Translator of Molière: Sir William
      Davenant or Colonel Henry Howard?" Modern Language Notes,
      LXVI (1951), 513-518.
          Howard, rather than Davenant, is the author of A Playhouse
      to be Let and thus the first translator of Molière.
1443 Riewald, J. G. "Laureates in Elysium: Sir William Davenant and
      Robert Southey." English Studies, XXXVII (1956), 133-140.
          Prose satire of Davenant by Richard Flecknoe is compared
      with Byron's Vision of Judgment and similarities are found.
1444 Cope, Jackson I. "Rhetorical Genres in Davenant's First Day's
      Entertainment at Rutland House." Quarterly Journal of Speech,
      XLV (1959), 191-194.
          Treats Davenant's use of oration and rhetoric in the Enter-
      tainment and suggests that he was writing in the tradition of the
      "character," that genre which has allied conceits, sharply
      pointed antitheses, and satire as its hallmark.
1445 Collins, Howard S. "The Comedy of Sir William Davenant." Ph.D.
      Brown University, 1960.
1446 Feil, J. P. "Davenant Exonerated." Modern Language Review,
      LVIII (1963), 335-342.
          There is evidence that Davenant the playwright was not in-
      volved in the murder of Thomas Warren in 1633, that a second
      William Davenant, a resident of Essex, was responsible for
      Warren's death.
1447 Hönninghausen, Lothar. "Der Stilwandel im dramatischen Werk
      Sir William Davenants." Inaugural Dissertation. Bonn, 1963.
1448 Palmer, Paulina. "Carew: An Unnoticed Allusion to Davenant's Il-
      legitimacy." Notes and Queries, New Ser., X (1963), 61-62.

A reference to bastardy in Carew's "To Will. Davenant My
Friend," recalls Davenant's insistence that he was Shakespeare's
illegitimate son.

1449 Squier, Charles Le Barge. "The Comic Spirit of Sir William Davenant: A Critical Study of His Caroline Comedies." Ph.D. University
of Michigan, 1963. (Order No. 63-6958).

A study of The Just Italian, News From Plymouth, The Wits,
The Platonic Lovers.

1450 Parsons, P. E. "The Siege of Rhodes and Restoration Tragedy: an
Interpretation of Some Formal Developments in the Serious
Drama of the Restoration." Ph.D. Cambridge University (Christ's)
1964.

1451 Freehafer, John. "The Formation of the London Patent Companies
in 1660." Theatre Notebook, XX (Autumn, 1965), 6-30.

Studies the struggle of Killigrew and Davenant to establish
their authority over the actors and to bring their companies to
the stage during the period, July 9 to October 8, 1660, following
the granting of patents by Charles II. Includes also corrections
to previous accounts of the London acting companies of 1659 and
1660.

1452 Hoennighausen, Lothar. Der Stilwandel im dramatischen Werk Sir
William Davenants. Köln: Böhlan Verlag, 1965. 252 pp. (Anglistische Studien, 3.)

A broad consideration of Davenant's work--his adaptations
of Shakespeare, his major themes, his intrigue drama, his languag
and the melo-dramatic and sentimental elements in his work.

1453 Quier, Charles L. "Davenant's Comic Assault on Preciosité: The
Platonic Lovers." University of Colorado Studies (Series in
Language and Literature, 10). Edited by J. K. Emery. (Boulder:
University of Colorado Press, 1966), 57-72.

1454 Bartholomeusz, Dennis. "The Davenant-Betterton Macbeth." Komos,
I (1967), 41-48.

1455 Nethercot, Arthur H. Sir William D'Avenant: Poet Laureate and
Playwright-Manager. New York: Russell and Russell, 1967.
488 pp.

A reissue of the 1938 edition with additional notes.

1456 Spencer, T. B. J., Stanley Wells, et al., editors. A Book of Masques: In Honour of Allardyce Nicoll. Cambridge: Cambridge
University Press, 1967. 448 pp.

Fourteen masques, each edited with an introduction, textual
essay and commentary by a different scholar. Includes Davenant's Salmacida Spolia (1640) edited by T. J. B. Spencer.

Davenport, Elizabeth

1457 D'Aulnoy, Baronne Marie Catherine. Memoirs of the Court in
England in 1675. Translated from the Original French by Mrs.
William Henry Arthur; edited and revised with annotations by
George David Gilbert. London: John Lane, 1913. 445 pp.
        Includes a detailed account of Lord Oxford and his "Misse,"
the actress "Roxolana," allegedly based on first hand informa-
tion of the Baroness as confidante of both. In Appendix C, "The
Earl of Oxford and the Actress," Gilbert provides support for
Roxolana's being Elizabeth Davenport.

Davenport, Robert

1458 Bullen, Arthur H. A Collection of Old English Plays. 4 vols. New
York: Benjamin Blom, Inc., [1964].
        Volume IV contains the first collected edition of the works
of Robert Davenport; the plays included are from the years
1639-1661. A brief introduction contains some critical commentary and primarily summaries of the plays.

Davis, Mary

1459 Flood, W. H. Grattan. [On the Paisables.] The Musical Antiquary,
III (October, 1911--July, 1912), 118.
        Note on James Paisable and his wife Mary "Moll" Davis
licensed to return to England from France, January 31, 1697/8
(House of Lords MSS, Historical Manuscripts Commission, V,
203-206).

Dawson, Nancy

1460 Burnim, Kalman A. "'Here We Go Round the Mulberry Bush'--
With Dr. Arne and Nancy Dawson." Restoration and Eighteenth
Century Theatre Research, IV (November, 1965), 39-48.
        Conjectures that Nancy Dawson's song, now the famous
nursery rhyme, was composed by Dr. Arne sometime after
her initial summer success at Sadler's Wells.
1461 -----. "Nancy Dawson's Tombstone." Restoration and 18th Century Theatre Research, V (May, 1966), 59.
        A note on the author's article, "'Here We Go Round the Mul-
berry Bush'--With Dr. Arne and Nancy Dawson." Restoration
and 18th Century Theatre Research, IV (November, 1965), 39-
48. Discusses a problem of the epitaph on the actress's tombstone in St. George's Gardens, Bloomsbury.

De Wilde, Samuel

1462 Mander, Raymond and Joe Mitchenson. "The Village Lawyer by
      Samuel De Wilde. Some Information on the Paintings." Theatre
      Notebook, XX (Autumn, 1965), 33-34.
         De Wilde's paintings of the characters from William Mac-
      ready's play, performed at the Theatre Royal, Haymarket,
      August 28, 1787. 6 plates.

Death on Stage

1463 Graves, Thornton S. "The Comedy of Stage Death." South Atlantic
      Quarterly, XXI (1922), 109-126.
         An essay attempting to prove that death--especially violent
      death--on stage has always been an object of mirth. Extensive
      consideration of Restoration and 18th-century English drama.

Defoe, Daniel

1464 Fletcher, E. G. "Defoe and the Theatre." Philological Quarterly,
      XIII (1934), 382-389.
         Surveys Defoe's relation to the theatre.

Dennis, John

critical works

1465 Dennis, John. The Critical Works of John Dennis. Edited by
      Edward Niles Hooker. 2 Vols. Baltimore: Johns Hopkins Uni-
      versity Press, 1939, 1943.
         All Dennis' dramatic criticism.

biography and criticism

1466 Bryce, Mrs. George. "A Rare Find in the Canadian Archives,
      Being a Tragedy Entitled Liberty Asserted by John Dennis Dedi-
      cated to Antony Henley." Royal Society of Canada Proceedings
      and Transactions, III (1910), 3-25.
         A detailed summary of the tragedy, which has the wars
      between the English-Iroquois and French-Hurons as setting
      for the theme of the right of the people to a voice in their govern-
      ment. Play produced at the New Theatre, Little Lincoln's Inn
      Fields in 1704, with Betterton, Booth, Mrs. Barry, and Mrs.
      Bracegirdle.

1467 Paul, H. G. John Dennis: His Life and Criticism. Columbia Uni-

versity Studies in English. New York: Lemcke and Buchner,
1911. 229 pp.

An analysis and evaluation of Dennis' criticism, its relationship to various schools of criticism of his time, and its
influence upon subsequent criticism.

1468 Lenz, Hermann. John Dennis. Sein Leben und seine Werke. Ein
Beitrag zur Geschichte der englischen Literatur im Zeitalter
der Königin Anna. Halle a. S.: Verlag von Max Niemeyer,
1913. 140 pp.

Studies his tragedies (Rinaldo and Armida, Iphigenia, Liberty
Asserted, Appius and Virginia). Critical works examined also.
Footnotes.

1469 Hooker, Edward Niles. "An Unpublished Autograph Manuscript of
John Dennis." English Literary History, I (1934), 156-162.

This provides a brief account of the history and contents
of a hitherto "unknown" essay by Dennis, "The Causes of the
Decay and Defects of Dramatick Poetry, and of the Degeneracy
of the Publick Tast [sic]." The text is at the Folger Shakespeare
Library.

1470 Sai-Sai-Zui. "A Study of John Dennis' Criticism." Studies in English Literature (Tokyo), XV (1935), 68-90.

1471 Tupper, F. S. "Notes on the Life of John Dennis." English Literary
History, V (1938), 211-217.

Disclosures afforded by a chancery suit and another litigation
recorded in the Public Record Office reveal new aspects concerning Dennis' life.

1472 H., N. B.J. "John Dennis." Caian, XLVII (1939), 58-67.

1473 De Clark, William Everett. "The Earlier Critical Theories of
John Dennis." M.A. University of Illinois, 1940.

1474 Hooker, Edward N. "Pope and Dennis." English Literary History,
VII (September, 1940), 188-198.

"Dennis' attacks on Pope were not gratuitous but provoked
by previous acts of Pope and his friends."

1475 Graham, C. B. "The Jonsonian Tradition in the Comedies of John
Dennis." Modern Language Notes, LVI (May, 1941), 370-372.

Examines Dennis' three comedies to show that "Dennis approved of Jonson's theories and in two of his three comedies
the Jonsonian tradition survives."

1476 Dias, Mary. "A Satire on John Dennis, 1711." Review of English
Studies, XIX (April, 1943), 213-214.

The satire occurs in The Generous Husband, by Charles
Johnson.

1477 Hand, James. "The Criticism of John Dennis." M.A. Columbia
University, 1949.

1478 Wilkins, Arthur N. "An Essay on John Dennis's Theory and Prac-

tice of the Art of Tragedy together with the Text of Appius and
Virginia." Ph.D. Washington University, 1953. 275 pp. (Publication No. 8249).

   Although a poor play, Appius and Virginia exemplifies
   Dennis's theory of tragedy.

1479 Haun, Eugene. "John Dennis's 'Rinaldo and Armida' Confused
      with Handel's 'Rinaldo.'" Notes and Queries, CXCIX (1954),
      249-250.

      Addison's discussion in the Spectator (March 6, 1711) deals
      with Handel's opera rather than Dennis's.

1480 Hardy, Gene B. "John Dennis As Comic Dramatist." Ph.D. Uni-
      versity of Illinois, 1955.

1481 Wilkins, A. N. "A Prologue by John Dennis." Notes and Queries,
      CC (1955), 525-526.

      Summarizes and comments on Dennis' prologue to Charles
      Gildon's The Patriot, or The Italian Conspiracy.

1482 -----. "John Dennis' Stolen Thunder." Notes and Queries, CCI
      (1956), 425-428.

      Pope probably invented the famous anecdote in which John
      Dennis denounced the managers of Drury Lane for stealing
      his method of making thunder in a play.

1483 -----. "John Dennis and Poetic Justice." Notes and Queries, CCII
      (1957), 421-424.

      Among his other rules for tragedy, John Dennis insisted
      upon poetic justice most strongly, but he violated this standard
      in his own play, Appius and Virginia.

1484 -----. "John Dennis on Love As a 'Tragical Passion.'" Notes and
      Queries, CCIII (September, 1958), 369-398; (October, 1958),
      417-419.

      Dennis's criticism and his practice, especially in Iphigenia,
      1700.

1485 -----. "Tragedy and 'The True Politicks.'" Notes and Queries,
      New Ser., VI (1959), 390-394.

      John Dennis's plays.

1486 -----. "Pope and 'Appius.'" Notes and Queries, New Ser., VII
      (1960), 292-294.

      Pope's mention of Appius in his Essay on Criticism clearly
      refers to the author of Appius and Virginia, John Dennis, since
      the character appropriately illustrates Pope's view of the play-
      wright.

1487 Bishay, Z. S. "The Dramatic Criticism of John Dennis." M.A.
      University of Manchester, 1962.

1488 Richeson, Edward, Jr. "John Dennis as a Psychological Critic."
      Ph.D. Boston University, 1962. (Order No. 62-5537).

      Analysis of Dennis criticism concerning the aesthetic creatio

the art object, and the effect dependent upon the emotions of
poet and audience.

1489 Dickens, Louis George. "The Story of Appius and Virginia in
English Literature." Ph.D. University of Rochester, 1963.
(Order No. 63-7762).

Includes a discussion of the dramatic versions of Betteron
and Dennis.

Denouement

1490 Griebling, E. T. "Forms of Denouement in Eighteenth Century
Drama." M.A. Ohio State University, 1928.

Derrick, Samuel

1491 Lawrence, W. J. "Derrick and Wilkes." Times Literary Supplement,
August 9, 1923, p. 533.

A correction of the erroneous belief that Derrick published
in 1759, under the name Thomas Wilkes, A General View of the
Stage; Derrick and Wilkes were not the same person.

Devil

1492 Graves, Thornton S. "The Devil in the Playhouse." South Atlantic
Quarterly, XIX (1920), 131-140.

A history of appearances of Satan as a visitor in the theatre
(primarily the English theatre). Restoration and 18th-century
theatre referred to passim.

Diaries

1493 Hervey, John, Lord. Some Materials towards Memoirs of the
Reign of King George II. Edited by Romney Sedgwick. 3 vols.
London: Eyre and Spottiswoode, 1931.

The complete text printed from a copy of the original MS.
in the Royal Archives at Windsor Castle, and from the original
MS. at Ickworth.

Dibdin, Charles

1494 Dibdin, E. R. A Charles Dibdin Bibliography. Liverpool: Privately Printed, 1937. [8], 146, [17] pp.

A reprint, with additions, from earlier volumes of Notes
and Queries. Musical works predominate. The writer says that
he has verified each item. When more than one edition appears

of a work, he notes the ones which he feels are important.
Numerous annotations. Only thirty copies printed.

1495 Partington, Wilfred. Charles Dibdin, the Man Whose Songs Helped
to Win the Battle of Trafalgar. London: Alan Keen, Ltd., 1944.
A dissertation of a "remarkable cache of manuscripts, unpublished material, holograph letters, rare printings, et cetera,
from the pen of Charles Dibdin."

1496 "Charles Dibdin." Times Literary Supplement, March 3, 1945,
p. 103.
A bicentenary editorial, noting particularly the sailor
characters and Dibdin's skill in writing patriotic ballads.

1497 Dibdin, L. G. "Charles Dibdin." Times Literary Supplement,
March 24, 1945, p. 139.
Further comment on Dibdin's birth-date.

1498 Low, D. M. "Charles Dibdin." Times Literary Supplement, April
7, 1945, p. 163.
Further comment on Dibdin's birth-date.

1499 Sear, H. G. "Charles Dibdin, 1745-1814." Music and Letters,
XXVI (1945), 61-65.
Discusses his ballad-operas.

1500 Windebank, W. "Charles Dibdin." Times Literary Supplement,
March 17, 1945, p. 127.
Notes discrepancies in the evidence of Dibdin's birth-
date.

1501 Oster, Harry. "A Study of the Songs of Thomas D'Urfey, John
Gay, Charles Dibdin, and Thomas Moore." Ph.D. Cornell
University, 1953.

1502 Speaight, George, ed. Professional and Literary Memoirs of
Charles Dibdin the Younger: Dramatist and Upward of Thirty
Years Manager of Minor Theatres. London: Society for Theatre
Research, 1956. x, 175 pp.
From 1797 to May 7, 1830. Selected passages from Dibdin's
memoirs pertaining to his playwrighting and his experiences
in the small theatres. Edited from the original manuscript.
Dibdin was resident manager at Astley's, Sadler's Wells,
and the Surrey.

Dictionary

1503 Adams, William Davenport. A Dictionary of the Drama; a guide
to the plays, playwrights, players and playhouses of the United
Kingdom and America, from the earliest times to the present
. . . Vol. I. London: Chatto and Windus, 1904--. 625 pp.
Summaries of plays, biographies and career descriptions--
some extensive--of performers and playwrights and theatrical
histories of various cities.

1504 Granville, Wilfred. The Theater Dictionary; British and American
        Terms in the Drama, Opera, and Ballet. New York: Philosophical
        Library [1952]. 227 pp.
            Very brief (i.e., two or three lines) definitions of critical
        terms and theatrical slang.

1505 Sobel, Bernard, ed. The New Theatre Handbook and Digest of
        Plays. Preface by George Freedley. 8th ed., revised. New
        York: Crown Publishers, 1959. 748 pp.
            Presents biographical sketches of playwrights, critics, per-
        formers, summaries of many plays and a glossary of theatrical
        terms. Arranged alphabetically.

1506 Bowman, Robert P., and Robert Hamilton Ball. Theatre Language:
        A Dictionary of Terms in English of the Drama and Stage from
        Medieval to Modern Times. New York: Theatre Arts Books,
        1961.

1507 Hartnoll, Phyllis, ed. The Oxford Companion to the Theatre. 3rd
        edition. London: Oxford University Press, 1967. 1088 pp.
            This is really a one-volume encyclopaedia which attempts
        to "provide information on every aspect of the theatre at least
        up to the end of 1964." The emphasis is on the theatrical,
        rather than the literary, aspects of theatre. Originally pub-
        lished in 1951.

Diderot, Denis

1508 Diderot, Denis. Writings on the Theatre. Edited by F. C. Green.
        Cambridge: University Press, 1936. vii, 317 pp.
            A collection of Diderot's criticism which includes "Observa-
        tions sur Garrick ou les Acteurs Anglais."

Digby, George

1509 Cordasco, Francesco. "Spanish Influence on Restoration Drama:
        George Digby's Elvira (1663?)." Revue de Littérature Com-
        parée, XXVII (1953), 93-98.
            Elvira is not a translation or adaptation of any particular
        Spanish play.

Disguises

1510 Grieben, Ernst. Das Pagenmotiv im englischen Drama. Inaugural
        Dissertation. Rostock, 1906. 70 pp.
            Discussion of women disguised as men to catch their beloveds
        in Flecknoe's Erminia, Wycherley's The Plain Dealer, Behn's
        The Younger Brother, and Farquhar's Love and A Bottle.

Documents

1511 Greg, W. W. Dramatic Documents from the Elizabethan Play-
     houses. 2 vols. Oxford: University Press, 1931.
         A study of Elizabethan "lengths" (folio sheets of foolscap
     containing about 42 lines).
1512 Hampden, John, Compiler. An Eighteenth-Century Journal, Being
     a Record of the Years 1774-1776. London: Macmillan, 1940.
     406 pp.
1513 McAnear, Beverly. "An American in London, 1735-1736." Penn-
     sylvania Magazine of History and Biography, LXIV (1940), 164-
     217, 356-406.
1514 Lewis, Wilmarth Sheldon. Three Tours Through London in the
     Years 1748, 1776, 1797. New Haven: Yale University Press;
     London: Humphrey Milford, 1941. xii, 135 pp.
         Social history. A tour of the sights of London over a half
     century, observes changes; contains materials concerning the
     theatres and entertainment.
1515 Beloff, Max. "A London Apprentice's Notebook, 1702-1705."
     History, XXVII (1942), 38-45.
         "Miscellaneous information about the paper trade in the
     early years of Anne's reign."
1516 Read, Stanley E., ed. Documents of Eighteenth-Century English
     Taste. Chicago, Illinois: De Paul University Bookstore, 1942.
     32 pp.
1517 Thomson, Gladys Scott, ed. Letters of a Grandmother, Being the
     Correspondence of Sarah, Duchess of Marlborough, with Her
     Granddaughter Diana, Duchess of Bedford. London: Cape, 1943.
     184 pp.
1518 Yates, Frances A. "An Italian in Restoration England." Journal
     of the Warburg and Courtauld Institute, VI (1943).
         An Italian grammar written out of necessity after the Great
     Fire provides varied and interesting information about con-
     temporary English life.
1519 Rosenfeld, Sybil. "Unpublished Stage Documents." Theatre Note-
     book, XI (1957), 92-96.
         One is a list of players, 1695.
1520 McCollum, John I., Jr. The Restoration Stage. Boston: Houghton,
     Mifflin Company, 1961. x, 236 pp.
         Provides excerpts from twenty-seven documents for the
     teaching of research method. Excerpts are from critical and
     theoretical writings, prologues, epilogues, diaries, memoirs,
     essays, apologies, defences, epistles, and short views.

Dodd, William

1521 Fairchild, A. H. R. "A Shakespearean Who Was Hanged." Western
      Humanities Review, VII (1953), 313-321.
            The Rev. William Dodd (1729-1777) forged Chesterfield's
      name to a bond for £4200; he was tried, found guilty, and
      hanged. Dodd's The Beauties of Shakespeare was first printed
      in 1752.
1522 Willoughby, Edwin Eliott. "A Deadly Edition of Shakespeare."
      Shakespeare Quarterly, V (1954), 351-357.
            The Rev. William Dodd's forgery of Chesterfield's name
      on a bond for 4200 pounds was motivated by his desperation
      in trying to finance his projected edition of Shakespeare. He
      was found guilty and hanged on June 27, 1777.

Dodsley, Robert

1523 Straus, Ralph. Robert Dodsley. Poet, Publisher and Playwright.
      London: John Lane, 1910. 407 pp.
            Chapters three and ten deal with his work in the theatre,
      the latter particularly with the production of Cleone and the
      conflict with Garrick.
1524 Lundeberg, Olav K. "The True Sources of Robert Dodsley's The
      King and the Miller of Mansfield." Modern Language Notes,
      XXXIX (1924), 394-397.
            A statement that the sources of this play were: 1) the ballad
      of the same name first printed in 1624; 2) two stories from
      Painter's Palace of Pleasure. Also an argument that the sources
      assigned by Goldoni in his memoirs are incorrect.
1525 Hill, Charles J. "Applause for Dodsley's Cleone." Philological
      Quarterly, XIV (1935), 181-184.
            Unpublished letters of Richard Graves give a picture of
      the friendship between Robert Dodsley and Graves. The cor-
      respondence particularly relates to Graves' reaction to Cleone.
1526 Schick, G. B. "Dodsley's Contribution." Notes and Queries, VI
      (1959), 279-280.
            Later citations of Dodsley's preface, 1744.

Doggett, Thomas

1527 Cook, Theodore Andres. Thomas Doggett, Deceased. A Famous
      Comedian. London: Archibald Constable, 1908. xiii, 156 pp.
            A biography of the famous comedian.
1528 Hughes, Leo. "Doggett Dancing the Cheshire Round?" Theatre
      Notebook, VII (1952-1953), 12-15.

The famous portrait of Doggett "dancing the Cheshire
round" is not connected with Doggett at all; it was "fabricated"
over a century after his death by George Daniel.

Domestic Drama

1529 Morgan, Arthur Esutace. "English Domestic Drama." Royal
Society of Literature of the United Kingdom, London. Essays
by Divers Hands, being the Transactions. Second Ser., XXXI
(1912), 175-207.
Morgan discusses essential characteristics and specific
examples of domestic tragedy--a drama whose purpose it is
to appeal to an audience as really like life and whose actions
involve events that might befall ordinary people. 17th and
18th-century examples include works by Otway, Rowe, and
Lillo. Morgan argues the 16th-, 17th-, and 18th-century
domestic tragedies differ in degree, not kind, from modern
tragedies.

Domestic Influence

1530 Hoy, Cyrus. "The Effect of the Restoration on Drama." Tennessee Studies in Literature, VI (1961), 85-91.
A brief study of Restoration drama as affected by tendencies present in English drama from the early seventeenth
century, as well as the influences of Tudor and Stuart comedy
and tragedy.

Domestic Tragedy

1531 Warren, Bernice Sue. "A Critical Investigation of Eighteenth
Century Domestic Tragedy." Ph.D. University of Missouri,
1967. (Order No. 68-281).
Studies the beginnings, climax, and decline of 18th century
domestic tragedy, the relationship of the genre to current
moral and religious concepts as well as to current literary
modes and techniques, and evaluates its significance in both
literary and theatrical history.

Don Juan

1532 Weinstein, Leo. The Metamorphoses of Don Juan. Stanford:
Stanford University Press, 1959. xi, 223 pp.
A history of treatments of Don Juan, including the dramatic;
briefly mentions Shadwell's The Libertine and Sir Aston Cock-

ayne's The Tragedy of Ovid as two 17th-century English plays using elements of the legend.

Doncaster

1533 "Doncaster Old Theatre." South Yorkshire Notes and Queries, II (1901), 85-87.

Doors

1534 Lawrence, W. J. "Proscenium Doors; an Elizabethan Heritage." The Elizabethan Playhouse and Other Studies, First Series. (Stratford-on-Avon: Shakespeare Head Press, 1912), 159-189.
   Proscenium doors, the only permanent doors in early picture frame stage, used through first quarter of the 19th century. Also considers use of curtain, placement of musicians, and seating of spectators; and use of guard at proscenium doors in London theatres and Smock Alley, Dublin.

1535 -----. "Doors and Curtains in Restoration Theatres." Modern Language Review, XV (1920), 414-420.
   A reply to Nicoll's article in MLR (q.v.). Lawrence: 1) disagrees with Nicoll about the date when two doors were placed behind the curtain, two in front; 2) argues that the curtain was let down before the end in only six plays in forty years; 3) contends that the curtain fell after the epilogue.

Downes, John

1536 Downes, John. Roscius Anglicanus. Edited by Montague Summers. London: Fortune Press, 1929. xiii, 286 pp.
   A work of prime value for the study of the Restoration stage (1661-1706); previous reprints are rare. Summers provides detailed comments on all the actors and plays mentioned by Downes, bookkeeper for Davenant's company.

1537 Ham, Roswell G. "Roscius Anglicanus." London Times Literary Supplement, August 22, 1929, p. 652.
   Corrects a quotation in Montague Summers' edition of Roscius Anglicanus.

Drake, James

1538 Williams, Edwin E. "Dr. James Drake and the Restoration Theory of Comedy." Review of English Studies, XV (1939), 180-191.
   An analysis of Drake's The Antient and Modern Stages Survey'd (1699) reveals his belief in the moral function of comedy, in the

necessity for comic realism, in general but not personal satire, and in the intellectual rather than the emotional appeal of comedy.

Dramatic Conventions

1539 Praz, M. "Restoration Drama." English Studies, XV (February, 1933), 1-14.
      A study of types and conventions.

Dramatic Form

1540 Otten, Terry Ralph. "The Empty Stage: A Comment on the Search for Dramatic Form in the Early Nineteenth Century." Ph.D. Ohio University, 1966. (Order No. 66-11,898).
      Although the study concentrates on the efforts of Shelley, Byron, Tennyson, and Browning, some references are made to the 18th-century concepts and dramatic forms rejected by these poets.

Dramatic Interest

1541 Harley, M. J. "The Eighteenth-Century Interest in English Drama Before 1640 Outside Shakespeare." M.A. University of Birmingham, 1964.

Dramatic Speech

1542 Nicoll, Allardyce. Readings from British Drama. New York: Thomas Y. Crowell, 1929. 446 pp.
      An attempt to exhibit the growth of drama and its qualities by compiling illustrative passages, many of them from obscure and inferior plays. Also illustrates the growth and variation of a dramatic speech. Thirty-five examples are drawn from Restoration and 18th century drama.

Dramatic Theory

1543 Nicoll, Allardyce. The Theory of Drama. New York: T. Y. Crowell 1931. 262 pp.
      A revision of An Introduction to Dramatic Theory (1923) plus sections on the theory of drama and tragi-comedy. The book is intended as "an introduction to the subject." Many references to Restoration and 18th-century authors, works, and types.

1544   Singh, Sarup. The Theory of Drama in the Restoration Period.
       Calcutta: Orient Longmans, 1963. 299 pp.
           Analyzes Restoration drama from the viewpoint of dedi-
       cations, prefaces, prologues, and epilogues.
1545   Maurocordato, Alexandre. La Critique Classique en Angleterre
       de la Restauration à la Mort de Joseph Addison. Paris: M. Didier,
       1964. 728 pp.
           An essay comparing French and English critical doctrine
       between 1660 and 1719. Intended to show the indebtedness of
       English critics to their French counterparts, the study focuses
       on theories of tragedy, comedy, satire, and ballad and related
       critical concepts.
1546   Simon, Irene. "Critical Terms in Restoration Translation from
       the French." Revue Belge de Philologie et d'Histoire, XLII
       (1964), 852-879.

Dreams

1547   Struve, Jurgen. "Das Traummotiv im englischen Drama des XVII
       Jahrhunderts." Inaugural Dissertation. Heidelberg, 1913.
       105 pp.
           An analysis of the use of folk dream lore--dreams of mis-
       fortune, good luck, revelation and visions of gods, men,
       animals--in the 17th-century drama.

Drolleries

1548   Smith, Courtney Craig. "The Seventeenth-Century Drolleries."
       Harvard Library Bulletin, VI (1952), 40-51.
           Smith defines the genre, classifies certain seventeenth-
       century publications into it, and lists the Harvard holdings.
1549   Whitesell, J. Edwin. "The Wits Drolls: Were They Meant to
       be Acted?" Tennessee Studies in Literature, IV (1959),
       73-82.

Drury-Lane Theatre

1550   [Drury Lane]. Notes and Queries, CLIII (September 24, 1927),
       218.
           Reprints selections from The British Journal (September
       23, 1727), announcing four new plays at Drury-Lane.
1551   -----. Notes and Queries, CLIII (November 12, 1927), 344.
           Reprints selections from The Weekly Journal (November
       11, 1727) concerning the King's attendance at Drury-Lane;
       also the new opera King Richard.

Dryden, John

bibliography

1552 Grollier Club, New York. Exhibition of First and Other Editions
of the Works of John Dryden (1631-1700), Together with a
Few Engraved Portraits and Two Oil Paintings--Commerative
of the Two Hundredth Anniversary of His Death, Exhibited at
the Grolier Club, Twenty-Nine East Thirty-Second Street,
New York, March 8th to 24th, 1900. [New York: De Vinne
Press, 1900]. 88 pp.
   Chronological listings in three sections: original works,
plays, and contributed and translated works; each entry indicates the form of the title-page and description of the item;
some include historical comment.
1553 S. C., Compiler. "A Check List of Dryden's Plays." The Biblio-
grapher, I (1902), 374-378.
   A chronological checklist of editions to 1736, compiled on
the basis of John Payne Collier's interleaved copy of Biographia
Dramatica. Believed by the compiler to be the first printed
checklist. Twenty-seven plays listed, including ones written
with Howard, Devanant, and Lee.
1554 Dobell, Percy John, Compiler. The Literature of the Restoration,
Being a Collection of the Poetical and Dramatic Literature
Produced between the Years 1660 and 1700, with Particular
Reference to the Writings of John Dryden. Described and annotated by Percy John Dobell. [London: P. J., and A. E. Dobell]
1918. vi, [2], 101 pp.
   An annotated alphabetical listing of the names of the writers
and the titles of their productions, together with stipend and
other available publication facts.
1555 -----. John Dryden. Bibliographical Memoranda. London, 1922.
1556 "Dryden First Editions." Times Literary Supplement, April 7,
1927, p. 256.
1557 Wise, Thomas James. A Dryden Library, a Catalogue of Printed
Books, Manuscripts and Autograph Letters by John Dryden.
London: Printed for Private Circulation Only, 1930. xxiv, 89,
[2] pp.
1558 Nicholls, Norah. "Some Early Editions of John Dryden." Bookman, LXXX (1931), 266-267.
1559 Haraszti, Zoltan. "Dryden's Adaptations and Operas." More
Books, VIII (March, 1933), 89-99.
   A survey of the adaptations Dryden made in Elizabethan
and foreign material, with notes on editions of Dryden's plays
and the difficulties of establishing his exact borrowings in opera

1560 -----. "A List of Dryden's Plays in the Boston Public Library."
      More Books, VIII (1933), 100.
1561 -----. "The Plays of John Dryden." More Books, VIII (January,
      1933), 1-13; (February, 1933), 45-59.
      Considers the plays in terms of what Dryden thought of
      them, and the editions which are available at the Boston Public
      Library.
1562 Macdonald, Hugh. John Dryden: A Bibliography of Early Editions
      and of Drydeniana. Oxford: Clarendon Press, 1939. x, 358 pp.
      An authoritative primary bibliography of Dryden's works,
      including the drama. Macdonald provides complete bibliograph-
      ical descriptions of the extant editions of all plays published
      during the Restoration and early 18th century.
1563 Dobell, Percy J., and A. E. Dobell. A Catalogue of the Works of
      John Dryden and Drydeniana. London, 1940.
1564 Bredvold, L. I., and H. Macdonald. "John Dryden (1631-1700)."
      The Cambridge Bibliography of English Literature, Vol. II.
      (Cambridge, 1941), pp. 262-275.
      A bibliography of all of Dryden's works and their editions,
      as well as a listing of selected studies and criticisms of Dryden.
      This is the most complete attempt at a bibliography to 1941.
1565 Osborn, James M. "Macdonald's Bibliography of Dryden: an An-
      notated Check List of Select American Libraries." Modern
      Philology, XXXIX (August, 1941), 69-98; (November, 1941),
      197-212.
      A list of the holdings of the American libraries, with ad-
      ditions and corrections of Macdonald's list.
1566 Woodward, Gertrude L., and James G. McManaway. "Dryden,
      John." A Check List of English Plays, 1641-1700. (Chicago,
      1945), pp. 42-54.
      See Nos. 370-489, for editions of the Works and individual
      plays, and their various editions, to 1700.
1567 Pettit, Henry. "Dryden's Works in Dryden, New York." Bulletin
      of Bibliography, XVIII (1946), 198.
1568 Monk, Samuel Holt. "Dryden Studies: a Survey, 1920 - 45."
      English Literary History, XIV (March, 1947), 46-63.
      Includes criticism of the plays.
1569 Bowers, Fredson Thayer. "Variants in Early Editions of Dryden's
      Plays." Harvard Library Bulletin, III (Spring, 1949), 278-288.
      Supplements the bibliographical materials of Macdonald
      and others.
1570 Steck, James S. "Dryden's Indian Emperor: the Early Editions
      and their Relation to the Text." Studies in Bibliography, II
      (1949), 139-152. (Papers of the Bibliographical Society of the
      University of Virginia).

Gives additions to the material in Macdonald's bibliography. Thirteen editions between 1667 and 1701.

1571 Monk, Samuel H. John Dryden: A List of Critical Studies Published from 1895 to 1948. Minneapolis: University of Minnesota Press, 1950. 52 pp.

Monk lists 768 numbered items, many of them dealing with Dryden's dramatic activity. The entries are not annotated.

1572 Keast, W. R. "Dryden Studies, 1895-1948." Modern Philology, XLVIII (1951), 205-210.

Keast's listing supplements Samuel Monk's John Dryden: A List of Critical Studies Published from 1895 to 1948. (Minneapolis: University of Minnesota Press, 1950).

1573 Hamilton, Marion H. "The Early Editions of Dryden's State of Innocence." Studies in Bibliography, V (1952-1953), 163-166.

Hamilton describes nine editions before the 1701 folio of Dryden's Works.

1574 Kinsley, James. "John Dryden (1631-1700)." The Cambridge Bibliography of English Literature, Vol. V. (Cambridge, 1957), pp. 404-407.

A continuation of the bibliography begun in Vol. 2 of The Cambridge Bibliography of English Literature, listing material published to 1955.

1575 Cameron, W. J. John Dryden in New Zealand: An Account of Early Editions of the Writings of John Dryden (1631-1700) Found in Various Libraries Throughout New Zealand. Wellington: Wellington Library School, 1960. 32 pp.

1576 Nicoll, Allardyce. "Dryden, John." A History of English Drama 1660-1900. Vol. I. Restoration Drama, 1660-1700. (Cambridge, 1961), pp. 403-407.

The titles of each of Dryden's plays, together with a list of editions and dates of performance. Some thirty plays are indicated.

1577 Stratman, Carl J., C.S.V. "John Dryden's All for Love: Unrecorded Editions." The Papers of the Bibliographical Society of America, LVII (1963), 77-79.

The purpose is to give publishing details for the fifteen editions--published between 1710 and 1792--which Jaggard omits in his Shakespeare Bibliography, and to supply additional bibliographical details for four other editions.

1578 Gatto, Louis C. "An Annotated Bibliography of Critical Thought Concerning Dryden's Essay of Dramatic Poesy." Restoration and 18th Century Theatre Research, V (May, 1966), 18-29.

Includes 80 entries: 10 for standard editions, 70 for criticism of the Essay.

1579 MacDonald, Hugh. John Dryden: A Bibliography of Early Editions

and of Drydeniana. London: Dawsons of Pall Mall, 1966. 358
pp.
 Facsimile reprint of the 1939 edition.
1580 Stratman, Carl J., C.S.V. "Dryden, John." Bibliography of English Printed Tragedy, 1565-1900. (Carbondale, 1966), pp.
165-186.
 See Nos. 1520-1709, which list the various editions of
Dryden's Works, Plays, and individual dramas.

concordance

1581 Montgomery, Guy, Compiler. Concordance to the Poetical Works
of John Dryden. New York: Russell and Russell, 1967. 722 pp.
 A reprint of the 1957 edition.

dictionary

1582 Aden, John M., ed. The Critical Opinions of John Dryden: A
Dictionary. Nashville, Tennessee: Vanderbilt University Press,
1963. 290 pp.
 Arranged alphabetically by subject, with quotations from
Dryden's essays, dedications, prefaces, headnotes, notes and
observations, biographies and letters. Includes index and
chronological list of sources.

letters

1583 Ward, Charles E., ed. The Letters of John Dryden, with Letters
Addressed to Him. Durham: Duke University Press, 1942.
196 pp.

works

1584 Dryden, John. Dryden: Poetry, Prose and Plays. Selected by D.
Grant. Cambridge, Massachusetts: Harvard University Press,
1952. 896 pp. (The Reynard Library).
1585 -----. The Works of John Dryden. Vol. I, "Poems 1649-1680."
Edward Niles Hooker, H. T. Swedenberg, Jr. Berkeley and
Los Angeles: University of California Press, 1956. xviii, 414
pp.
 Includes prologues and epilogues.
1586 -----. The Works of John Dryden. General Editor: H. T. Swedenberg, Jr. Textual editor: Vinton A. Dearing. Vol. III: Plays:
The Wild Gallant, The Rival Ladies, the Indian Queen. Editors:

John Harrington Smith, Dougald MacMillan, and Vinton A. Dearing, in association with Samuel H. Monk and Earl Miner. Berkeley and Los Angeles: University of California Press, 1962. 376 pp.

Excellent editions of the three early plays. Includes textual variations, commentary and notes for each play, sections on staging and actors.

1587 -----. The Works of John Dryden. General Editor: H. T. Sweden berg, Jr. Associate General Editor: Earl Miner. Textual Edito Vinton A. Dearing. Vol. IX: Plays: The Indian Emperour, Secr Love, Sir Martin Mar-All. Editors: John Loftis and Vinton A. Dearing. Berkeley and Los Angeles: University of California Press, 1966. 451 pp.

Includes textual variations, commentaries, and notes for each play.

selected works

1588 Dryden, John. Selected Dramas of John Dryden with "The Rehears Edited, with an Introduction, "Dryden As Dramatist," by Georg R. Noyes. Chicago: Scott Foresman, 1910. 504 pp.

Collated, annotated texts of The Conquest of Granada (both parts), Marriage à la Mode, All for Love, and The Spanish Friar. Also included are the essays "Of Heroic Plays," "Defense of the Epilogue," and the "Preface" to All for Love.

1589 -----. All for Love, and The Spanish Friar. Edited by W. Strunk Boston, 1911. xlv, 340 pp.

This edition includes a short biographical sketch of Dryden's life, a chronological list of the plays, and a critique of the two plays.

1590 -----. John Dryden. Edited with an Introduction and Notes by Geo rge Saintsbury. 2 vols. London: T. F. Unwin, Ltd. [192-]. (The Mermaid Series).

Contains the following plays: Almanzor & Almahide, Marriage à la Mode, Aureng-Zebe, The Spanish Friar, Albion & Albanius, and Don Sebastian.

1591 -----. Dryden: Poetry and Prose. Edited by D. Nichol Smith. Oxford: Clarendon Press, 1925. xvi, 204 pp.

Selections from The Conquest of Granada, Aurenge-zebe, A for Love, Of Dramatic Poesy, with Congreve's "Character of Dryden."

1592 -----. The Dramatic Works. Edited by Montague Summers. 6 vols. London: Nonesuch Press, 1931-1932.

See the Times Literary Supplement, February 4, 1932, p. 73, for a severe criticism of the text.

1593 -----. Plays. Vol. I. Edited by George Saintsbury. London:
      Benn, 1949. 439 pp.
         A reprint of the Mermaid text of 1904, including in Vol. I
      Almanzor and Almahide, Marriage à la Mode, and Aurengzebe.
1594 -----. Dryden: Poetry, Prose and Plays. Selected by D. Grant.
      Cambridge: Harvard University Press, 1952; London: Rupert
      Hart-Davis, 1952. 892 pp.
         Contains four plays--Aureng-Zebe, All for Love, The
      Spanish Fryar, Don Sebastian--and two essays--An Essay of
      Dramatick Poesie, and A Defence of an Essay of Dramatique
      [sic] Poesie. No notes.
1595 -----. John Dryden (Three Plays), ed. George Saintsbury. (Mer-
      maid Dramabook, MD 7). New York: Hill and Wang [1957].
      xxv, 355 pp.
         Reprint of Vol. I of Dryden's plays in Mermaid Series.
      London: Ernest Benn Limited, 1949. The Conquest of Granada,
      Parts I and II; Marriage à la Mode; Aureng-Zebe.
1596 -----. Four Comedies. Edited by L. A. Beaurline and Fredson
      Bowers. Chicago: University of Chicago Press, 1967.
         Includes a general introduction as well as notes and brief
      introductory comments on each play: Secret Love, Sir Martin
      Mar-All, An Evening's Love, and Marriage-à-la Mode.
1597 -----. Four Tragedies. Edited by L. A. Beaurline and Fredson
      Bowers. Chicago: University of Chicago Press, 1967.
         Includes a general introduction as well as notes and brief
      introductory comments for each play: The Indian Emperour,
      Aureng-Zebe, All for Love, and Don Sebastian.
1598 Zesmer, David. Dryden: Poems, Plays and Essays. (Bantam
      Classics). New York: Bantam Books, 1967. 529 pp.
         Includes prologues, epilogues and songs by Dryden as
      well as All for Love and An Essay of Dramatic Poesy.

      individual plays

1599 Dryden, John. Anthony [sic] and Cleopatra. (The Text of the
      Folio of 1623, with That of "All for Love, or The World Well
      Lost.") As Done by John Dryden in 1678, with an Introduction
      Touching the Environment of the Restoration Drama, Where-
      by Shakespeare Was Perpetuated Through the Restoration
      Period, by Francis A. Smith. New York: The Shakespeare
      Society of New York, 1908. v-xv, 385 pp.
         Facsimile reprint. Introduction discusses the practice of
      Shakespeare "restoration" by D'Avenant and Dryden.
1600 -----. All for Love: or, The World Well Lost; A Tragedy. San
      Francisco: J. H. Nash, 1929. xxix, 97 pp.
         [Edited by William A. Clark, Jr.]

1601 -----. All for Love. [Photograph facsimile reprint of the Bridge-
      water copy, 4to, 1678. Printed for William Andrews Clark,
      Junior, foolscap folio. 1929.]
1602 -----. "All For Love." The Malvern Festival Plays, MCMXXXIII,
      Arranged for Production by H. K. Ayliff. With an introduction
      by Hugh Walpole, and a preface by Sir Barry Jackson. London:
      Heath Cranton, Ltd., 1933. viii, 343 pp.
          Reprint of the text used in the festival production with
      neither notes nor commentary.
1603 -----. All for Love. Edited by Arthur Sale. London: University
      Tutorial Press, 1938. xxiii, 223 pp.
          An edition of the play with introduction, complete text, and
      ample documentation.
1604 Griffith, Benjamin W., Jr., ed. All for Love, or, The World Well
      Lost. Illustrated by Tom Keough. Great Neck, New York:
      Barron's Educational Series, 1961.
1605 Brossman, Sidney W. "A Critical Edition of Dryden's Cleomenes,
      the Spartan Heroe." Ph.D. University of Southern California,
      1955.
1606 [Dryden, John]. The Indian Queen and [Shadwell, Thomas] The
      Tempest. Edited by Edward J. Dent. London: Novell & Co.,
      Ltd., 1912. xxxii, 17, 187 pp.
1607 -----. King Arthur or The British Worthy: A Dramatick Opera
      by John Dryden. As Performed at the New Theatre Cambridge
      14-18 February 1928 with The Alterations Adopted by Henry
      Purcell. Edited by Dennis Arundell. Cambridge University
      Press, 1928. 14, 80 pp.
          The introductory essay outlines the history of composition
      of the work, its stage history, and the fate of Purcell's music.
1608 -----. Marriage à la Mode. Edited, with an Introduction, Notes,
      and Glossary by J. R. Sutherland. London: J. M. Dent & Sons,
      Ltd., 1934. xiv, 153 pp. (The Temple Dramatists).
          The text used is that of the first quarto of 1673, collated
      with the folio of 1701. The spelling is modernized, but original
      punctuation is generally preserved. There are notes and a
      glossary.
1609 Ward, A. W. "John Dryden: The Spanish Fryar." Representative
      English Comedies. Vol. IV: Dryden and His Contemporaries:
      Cowley to Farquhar. Edited by Charles Mills
      Thaler. (New York: The Macmillan Company, 1936), 103-113.
          Dryden's life and his place in English comedy as well as
      a critical discussion of the play. The text of the play, edited
      by Ward, follows.
1610 Morgan, Appleton (editor). The Bankside-Restoration Shakespeare
      The Tempest: New York: The Shakespeare Society of New York
      1908.

The text of the Folio of 1623 with that as revised finally by
John Dryden in his Second Edition of 1676. Texts printed on
facing pages. Introduction by Frederick W. Kilbourne.

essays

1611 Dryden, John. Essays of John Dryden. Selected and Edited by
      William Paton Ker. 2 vols. Oxford: Clarendon Press, 1900.
         A collection of Dryden's principal essays, prefaces, pro-
      logues, epilogues, and epistles dedicatory on literary subjects,
      with an introduction to explain Dryden's position as a critic.
      The work was also published by Russell & Russell in 1961.
1612 -----. Essay of Dramatic Poesy. Edited by D. Nichol Smith.
      London: Blackie and Son, 1900.
         Text based on edition of 1693. Notes and introduction in-
      tended to show Dryden's indebtedness to earlier writers and
      the place of the Essay in the history of literary criticism.
      Index.
1613 -----. Defence of an Essay of Dramatic Poesy. With an Intro-
      duction by Allen Mawer. London: W. B. Clive [1901].
      26, [1] pp. (University Tutorial Series).
         The Introduction is a summary of the essay. There is no
      mention of the text followed. There are no notes or glossary.
1614 -----. Preface to the Fables. With an Introduction by Allen
      Mawer. London: W. B. Clive [1902]. 30, [1] pp. (University
      Tutorial Press).
         A brief Introduction of four pages, in which the editor
      looks at the work from the polemical and critical points of
      view. There are no notes, although a page is devoted to the
      translation of Latin and Italian quotations.
1615 -----. Essay of Dramatic Poesie. Edited by W. H. Hudson.
      London: Published by J. M. Dent & Co. [1903]. xvi, 140 pp.
      (Dent's Temple Series of English Texts).
         The Introduction gives a brief life, background of the work,
      and an analysis of the Essay. The notes are kept to a minimum.
1616 ----. Dramatic Essays by John Dryden. Introduction by William
      Henry Hudson. London & Toronto: J. M. Dent & Sons, Ltd.;
      New York: E. P. Dutton and Co., 1912. 299 pp. (Everyman's
      Library).
         "An Essay of Dramatic Poesy," 5-59; "A Defence of An Es-
      say of Dramatic Poesy," 60-76; "On Comedy, Farce, and
      Tragedy," the Preface to "An Evening's Love; or The Mock
      Astrologer," 77-86; "Antony and Cleopatra and The Art of
      Tragedy," Preface to "All for Love; or, The World Well Lost,"
      118-125; "The Grounds of Criticism in Tragedy," Preface to
      "Troilus and Cressida," 126-145.

1617 -----. Of Dramatick Poesie An Essay 1668 by Iohn [sic] Dryden.
Introduction by T. S. Eliot. London: F. Etchells and H. Macdonald, 1928. xxvi, 83 pp.
Introduction is unsatisfactory because it is deliberately off-
handed and wandering, though it is epigrammatically witty.

1618 -----. Dryden and Howard 1664-1668: The Text of "An Essay of
Dramatic Poesy," "The Indian Emperor," and "The Duke of
Lerma." With other controversial matter. Edited by D. D.
Arundell. Cambridge: Cambridge University Press, 1929. xiv,
288 pp.
Includes prefatory material by Dryden and Howard to some
of their plays and poetry, most of it related to their contro-
versy over rhyme as opposed to blank verse in drama.

1619 -----. Epilogue Spoken to the King March the Nineteenth 1681.
Oxford: At the Clarendon Press, 1932. 8 pp.
Facsimile reprint of the hitherto unknown edition discovered
in Christ Church Library. The title given is: "The Epilogue
Spoken to the King at the Opening of the Play-House at Oxford
on Saturday last. Being March the Nineteenth 1681. History of
the text given by W. G. Hiscock.

1620 Wesley, Samuel. Epistle to a Friend concerning Poetry (1700).
Essay on Heroic Poetry (second edition, 1697). Edited by
Edward Niles Hooker. Ann Arbor: The Augustan Reprint Society
January, 1947. (Series II, Essays on Poetry, 2).
The Essay, reproduced in facsimile, contains praise of Dry-
den's dramas.

1621 Gardner, William B. (ed.). The Prologues and Epilogues of John
Dryden; a Critical Edition. New York: Columbia University
Press, 1951. 361 pp. Index.
Gardner provides an introduction and explanatory notes, as
well as two appendices dealing with the question of Dryden's
authorship of several other pieces.

1622 Hamilton, Marion H. "Dryden's The State of Innocence: An Old-
Spelling Edition with a Critical Study of the Early Printed Texts
and Manuscripts." Ph.D. University of Virginia, 1952. 371 pp.
A critical edition of the play with textual analysis.

1623 Dryden, John. Essays. Selected and edited by W. P. Ker. 2 vols.
Oxford: The Clarendon Press, 1926; New York: Russell & Russell, 1961.
The contents include many pertinent essays and prefaces to
individual plays. In the introduction, Ker comments on Dryden
and Corneille, the ancients and the moderns, and--very exten-
sively--on Dryden's dramatic criticism.

1624 -----. Of Dramatic Poesy and Other Critical Essays. Edited with
an Introduction by George Watson. (Everyman's Library, Nos.

568, 569). London: Dent; New York: Dutton, 1962. 2 vols.
Includes notes and select bibliography.

1625 -----. Of Dramatick Poesie, an Essay. With Sir Robert Howard's
Preface to The Great Favourite and Dryden's Defence of an
Essay. Edited, with an Introduction and Notes by James T.
Boulton. [London]: Oxford University Press, 1964. 190 pp.
The texts indicated in the title are reprinted and extensively
annotated. The introduction considers the place of these three
works in the history of literary criticism.

1626 -----. An Essay of Dramatic Poesy, A Defence of an Essay of
Dramatic Poesy, Preface to the Fables. Edited by John L.
Mahoney. (Library of Liberal Arts). Indianapolis, Indiana:
Bobbs-Merrill, 1965. 119 pp.
Includes introduction, notes, and selected bibliography.

1627 -----. Literary Criticism of John Dryden. Edited by Arthur C.
Kirsch. (Regents Critics Series). Lincoln: University of
Nebraska Press, 1966.
An edition of Dryden's major works of criticism. Includes
introduction, notes, and selected bibliography.

1628 Elloway, D. R., ed. Dryden's Satire. London: Macmillan; New
York: St. Martin's Press, 1966. 181 pp.
An edition of MacFlecknoe, Absalom and Achitophel, and
The Medal with satiric selections from Dryden's other works,
including the Epilogue to Tyrannic Love and the Prologue to
All for Love. Includes introduction, notes, and select biblio-
graphy.

songs

1629 Dryden, John. The Songs of John Dryden. Edited by Cyrus L. Day.
Cambridge: Harvard University Press, 1932. xvi, 199 pp.
Contains 92 songs, arranged chronologically, many from
Dryden's plays; some 25 songs are presented in facsimile.
Extensive notes, both textual and general. The introduction
treats Dryden's relationship to Purcell in detail.

1630 Day, Cyrus Lawrence, ed. The Songs of John Dryden. New York:
Russell and Russell, 1967. 199 pp.
A reissue of the 1932 edition which includes songs written
by Dryden for the plays.

biography and criticism

1631 Noyes, George R. "Dryden As Critic." The Nation, LXXI (1900),
231-233.

This review of Ker's Essays of John Dryden and Sherwood's
Dryden's Dramatic Theory and Practice considers the Essay of
Dramatic Poesy as a valuable index to the alteration of spirit
that was taking place in English literature.

1632 Scott, Mrs. Anna Miller. Ueber das Verhältnis von Dryden's
"State of Innocence" zu Milton's "Paradise Lost." Halle-Witten
berg: Friedrichs Universität, 1900. 67 pp.

Examines Dryden's 1674 opera, State of Innocence and the
Fall of Man, a rhymed dramatization of Paradise Lost. A comparison of the two works in detail shows how Dryden, though
keeping most of Milton's original language, makes changes in
Milton's poem that sacrifice the poem's spiritual depth to Dryd
bid for popularity.

1633 Garnett, R[ichard]. The Age of Dryden. London: G. Bell and Sons
1901. 292 pp.

Chapters IV through VI provide a brief history of the drama
of the period, told through short biographies of the individual
playwrights.

1634 Krüger, Wilhelm. Das Verhältnis von Colley Cibber's Lustspiel
"The Comical Lovers" zu John Dryden's "Marriage à la Mode"
und "Secret Love; or, The Maiden Queen." Halle-Wittenberg:
Wischan & Wettengel, 1902. 56 pp.

Uses textual comparison to show that Cibber's play consists
of adaptations, with only slight variations, of comic scenes
from the two highly successful plays by Dryden; that is, Cibber
play was a pot-boiler and it shows the same artistic failings as
Dryden's two plays, primarily a lack of dramatic unity.

1635 Castleman, Josiah Hamilton. "Dryden's Dramatic Technique."
M.A. University of Indiana, 1903.

1636 Hannmann, Friedrich. Dryden's Tragodie "All for Love or The
World Well Lost" und ihr Verhältnis zu Shakespeare's
"Antony and Cleopatra." Rostock: Carl Bolt'sche Hof-Buch-
druckerei, 1903. 82 pp.

A general discussion of Dryden's dramatic theory and
practice, followed by a detailed textual comparison of the two
plays. Hannmann contrasts the "mechanical" construction of
Dryden's play with the "organic" construction of Shakespeare's

1637 "Little Bayes." The Academy and Literature, LXIV (January 10,
1903), 34-36.

A discussion of the caricature of Dryden and parody of the
heroic play in The Rehearsal, with attention to Dryden's dress,
manner, habitual expressions.

1638 Zenke, Hermann. Dryden's "Troilus und Cressida" im Verhältnis
zu Shakespeare's Drama und die ubrigen Bearbeitungen des

Stoffes in England. Rostock: Carl Bolt'sche Hofbuchdruckerei,
1904. 47 pp.

Uses textual comparison to show that Dryden's play, first
staged in 1679, is a free adaptation of the First Folio version of
Shakespeare's Troilus and Cressida. There is a scene by scene
summary and analysis of Dryden's play. Sees a decline in English
drama from Shakespeare to Dryden.

1639 Everett, William. "Six Cleopatras." Atlantic Monthly, XCV (1905),
252-263.

Treats Dryden's All for Love.

1640 Schroder, Edwin. "Dryden's letztes Drama, Love Triumphant, or
Nature Will Prevail." Inaugural Dissertation. Rostock, 1905.

1641 Albrecht, L. "Dryden's Sir Martin Mar-All in Bezug auf seine
Quellen." Inaugural Dissertation. Rostock, 1906. 101 pp.

Shows relationship between Quinault's L'Amant Indiscret ou,
Le Maistre Estourdi, Molière's L'Estourdy ou Les Contretemps,
and Dryden's Sir Martin Mar-All.

1642 Bohn, William E. "The Development of John Dryden's Critical
Theory." Ph.D. University of Michigan, 1906.

1643 Churchill, George B. "The Relation of Dryden's State of Innocence
to Milton's Paradise Lost and Wycherley's Plain Dealer, an
Inquiry into Dates." Modern Philology, IV (1906), 381-388.

1644 Clarke, Sir Enrest. "The Tempest As an Opera." Athenaeum, No.
4113 (August 25, 1906), 222-223.

1645 Myers, Clara L. "Opera in England from 1656 to 1728." Western
Reserve University Bulletin, IX (1906), 129-156.

1646 Saintsbury, George Edward Bateman. Dryden. (Half-title: English
men of letters, ed. by John Morley) London and New York:
Macmillan, 1906. vi, 196 pp.

Brief life of Dryden, evaluation of his early writings, his
dramatic output, his later dramas and translations.

1647 Bohn, William E. "The Development of John Dryden's Literary
Criticism." Publications of the Modern Language Association,
XXII (1907), 56-139.

Reviews divergent opinions concerning Dryden's critical
essays. Divides Dryden's critical writing into five periods,
shows that he used four methods of criticism: the romantic;
the French rationalistic or neoclassic; the English rationalistic;
and the historical.

1648 Frye, Prosser H. "Dryden and the Critical Canons of the Eighteenth
Century." University of Nebraska Studies, VII (1907), 1-39.

Reprinted in Literary Reviews and Criticisms, New York and
London, 1908. Dryden's spirit was essentially a prose spirit,
marked by common sense or intelligence rather than fancy or
imagination.

1649 Root, Robert K. "Dryden's Conversion to the Roman Catholic
Faith." Publications of the Modern Language Association, XXII
(1907), 298-308.
The Spanish Friar and The Assignation, or Love in a Nunner
find much of their humour in an expose of corruption in the
monastic orders. But they are not serious attacks on Catholicis
they have no traces of the moral indignation of the reformer.
The hypocrisy of unworthy ecclesiastics afforded a source of
comic effect that appealed to audience of English protestants.

1650 Frye, Prosser Hall. "Dryden and the Critical Canons of the 18th
Century." Literary Reviews and Criticisms. (New York and
London: G. P. Putnam's Sons, 1908), 130-189.

1651 Eichler, Albert. "Christian Wernickes Hans Sachs und sein Dryder
sches Vorbild." Zeitschrift für vergleichende Litteraturgeschichte, XVII (1909), 208-224.
Dryden's foreign reputation and influence.

1652 Hutsinpillar, Jessie. "Aristotle in Dryden's Dramatic Criticism."
M.A. Ohio State University, 1909.

1653 Wheatley, Henry B. "Dryden's Publishers." Transactions of the
Bibliographical Society, XI (October, 1909--March, 1911),
17-38.
Dryden's business association mainly with Henry Herringma
and Jacob Tonson.

1654 Baas, David. Drydens heroische Tragodie; eine ästhetische Untersuchung. Freiberg: C. A. Wagner, 1911. 78 pp.
Studies Dryden's heroic tragedy in terms of the verse, the
ethics, etc., and in the context of the works of such other
writers as Shakespeare, Schiller, and Corneille.

1655 Bailey, John. "Dryden and Shakespeare." Poets and Poetry. (Oxford: At the Clarendon Press, 1911), 72-79.
In art and handling Dryden showed the sounder judgment.
Finds greater unity in All for Love as well as many "glorious
lines."

1656 Friedland, Louis S. "Dramatic Unities in England." Journal of
English and Germanic Philology, X (1911), 183-196.

1657 Heigl, Franz. Die dramatischen Einheiten bei Dryden; ein Beitrag
zur Geschichte der drei Einheiten in England. München: M.
Hueber, 1912. 89 pp.

1658 Baumgartner, Milton D. "Dryden's Relation to Germany." University of Nebraska Studies, XIV (1914), 289-375.

1659 -----. On Dryden's Relation to Germany in the Eighteenth Cen-
tury. Lancaster, Pennsylvania: Press of the New Era Printing
Company, 1914. 87 pp.
Chapter III of this reprinted dissertation deals with The
Spanish Friar, The State of Innocence, Oedipus and All for Love

the four of Dryden's plays which were translated in Germany
by undistinguished poets. All for Love won the greatest
recognition in Germany.

1660 Houston, Percy H. "The Inconsistency of John Dryden." The Sewanee
Review, XXII (1914), 469-482.
Born between two epochs, Dryden argued both sides, unable
really to accept either. Instead of leading his age, he followed
after contemporary thought.

1661 Mundy, P. D. "Portrait of Dryden." Notes and Queries, 11th Ser.,
X (1914), 28.
A query as to the whereabouts of a portrait, said in Brayley's
Survey to have been at West Horsley Place, which was a head in
an oval surrounded by Latin mottoes.

1662 Verrall, Arthur W. Lectures on Dryden. Cambridge: The University
Press, 1914. 271 pp.
A series of nine lectures on Dryden's poetry, criticism, and
drama, made from Verrall's notes and published posthumously.
Treats All for Love, and The State of Innocence at some length.

1663 Wallace, Leonard Delong. "A New Date for the Conquest of Granada."
Modern Philology, XVI (1919), 271-272.
Through letters of Lady Mary Bertie, fixes the dates of first
performances of Conquest of Granada II as January 9, 1671,
and Part I as between December 20, 1670, and January 9, 1671.

1664 "John Dryden." Times Literary Supplement, June 9, 1921, pp. 361-
362.
This is basically an introduction to Dryden's poetry, occas-
sioned by Van Doren's book, but there is a brief discussion of
the poetry in the plays.

1665 Nicoll, Allardyce. "Dryden, Howard, and Rochester." Times
Literary Supplement, January 13, 1921, p. 27.
A discussion of an MS. copy of Howard's The Conquest of
China and the possible roles of Dryden and Rochester in the
composition and revision of the play.
Note: In the January 27th corr., Montague Summers refutes
Nicoll by stating that Rochester's Valentinian could not have
been acted before 1684. In the February 3rd corr., Nicoll
presented his rebuttal and insisted that he was accurate in as-
signing dates.

1666 Boase, T. S. R. "The Danger of Unity." The New Statesman,
XVIII (February 11, 1922), 531.
On Dryden's All for Love.

1667 Nicoll, Allardyce. Dryden as an Adapter of Shakespeare. London:
Published for Shakespeare Association by Humphrey Milford,
Oxford University Press, 1922. 34 pp. (Shakespeare Association
Lecture, 1921).

A detailed consideration of The Tempest; or, The Enchanted Island, All for Love, and Troilus and Cressida in
terms of Nicoll's eight categories of changes made by adapters
Concludes with a brief bibliography of the chief adaptations of
Shakespeare between 1660 and 1700.

1668 Noble, Richard. "Shakespeare Adaptations." Times Literary Supplement, March 23, 1922, p. 196.
A statement that All for Love is not strictly an adaptation
of Antony and Cleopatra.

1669 Strachen, L. R. M. "Reputed Song by Dryden." Notes and Queries
Ser. 12, XI (October, 1922), 341-342.
A consideration of the possibility of Dryden's authorship of
the song, "What shall I do to show how much I love her," espec
ially in relation to the 1690 version of The Prophetess, "a Trag
cal History."

1670 Wood, Ethel Muriel. "Dryden's Views on Tragedy in Relation to
Contemporary Standards." M.A. University of Chicago, 1922.
Although concerned primarily with Dryden's criticism, the
work does consider his views on such questions as the unities,
stage decorum, blank verse, love and honor as proper subjects
for tragedy.

1671 Meyerstein, E. H. W. "Dryden and 'The Soldier.'" Times Liter-
ary Supplement, March 8, 1923, p. 160.
A report on allusions to Dryden's Don Sebastian, King of
Portugal.

1672 Noyes, G. R. "Crites in Dryden's Essay of Dramatic Poesy."
Modern Language Notes, XXXVIII (1923), 333-337.
An argument that Malone's identification of Crites as Sir
Robert Howard is incorrect.

1673 Pendlebury, Bevin John. Dryden's Heroic Plays: A Study of the
Origins. London: Selwyn, 1923. 141 pp.
A discussion of the heroic tradition before Dryden, Dryden's
dramatic theory, the development of the English heroic play
(Davenant and Dryden), and an evaluation of Dryden's dramatic
achievement.

1674 Wollstein, Rose H. English Opinions of French Poetry, 1660-1750
New York: Columbia University Press, 1923. 114 pp.
Chapter 1 (pp. 1-38) treats Dryden's appreciation of the
French Classic theatre and considers both his critical works
and his plays. There are other references to drama and criti-
cism passim.

1675 Mark, Jeffrey. "Dryden and the Beginnings of Opera in England."
Music and Letters, V (1924), 247-252.

1676 McCutcheon, R. P. "Dryden's Prologue to The Prophetess."
Modern Language Notes, XXXIX (1924), 123-124.

A statement that Dryden's prologue to Fletcher's play was written for the 1690 revival of the play but not printed until January, 1707, because Thomas Shadwell had the prologue suppressed.

1677　Bondurant, Alexander L. "The Amphitruo of Plautus, Molière's Amphitryon, and the Amphitryon of Dryden." Sewanee Review, XXXIII (October, 1925), 455-468.

Notes points of difference and similarity, concluding that Plautus' play is the best.

1678　Ellis, Amanda M. "Horace's Influence on Dryden." Philological Quarterly, IV (January, 1925), 39-60.

A detailed examination of Dryden's general indebtedness to Horace's poems, especially in dramatic criticism.

1679　"First Collation of an Interesting Dryden Item." Bookman's Journal, XII (1925), 163-164.

1680　Jaeger, Herman. Dryden og hans tid. Oslo: J. W. Cappelen, 1925. 152 pp.

A discussion of Dryden's career, with little about his literary milieux or about the relationships of Greek and French drama to the English.

1681　Ker, W. P. Collected Essays. Edited with an Introduction by Charles Whibley. 2 vols. London: Macmillan and Co., Limited, 1925.

See, "Dryden," pp. 10-71, where he discusses the "Essay of Dramatic Poesy," the "Defence," "Of Heroic Plays," Prefaces to "The Mock Astrologer," "All for Love," "Albion and Albanius," "The Grounds of Criticism in Tragedy," and Dedication to "The Spanish Friar."

1682　Low, D. M. "An Error in Dryden." London Times Literary Supplement, April 30, 1925, p. 300.

Notes an error of Chassis for Chiassis in "Theodore and Honoria."

1683　Lubbock, Alan. The Character of John Dryden. London: Hogarth Press, 1925. 31 pp.

Dryden was a classicist in spite of a wide appreciation of literature.

1684　Lynch, Kathleen M. "D'Urfé's ·L'Astrée and the 'Proviso" Scenes in Dryden's Comedy." Philological Quarterly, IV (October, 1925), 302-308.

These "proviso" scenes, which constitute Dryden's most marked contribution to English comedy, are imitated from the courtship of Hylas and Stelle in D'Urfé's romance.

1685　Payne, F. W. "The Question of Precedence between Dryden and the Earl of Orrery with regard to the English Heroic Plays."

Review of English Studies, I (April, 1925), 173-181.
Orrery had written plays in rhymed couplets long before the
appearance of Dryden's first.

1686 Smith, John Harrington. "Dryden's Critical Temper." Washington
University Studies, Humanistic Series, XII (April, 1925), 201-
220.
Attempts to resolve the apparent confusion and contradictions
in Dryden's critical essays: "I believe that Dryden merely make
verbal compromises with his circumstances--and so universally
that by far the greater bulk of his opinion must be thoroughly
discredited."

1687 Sweeney, John Joseph. "Dryden and the Tenets of Contemporary
Dramatic Criticism." M.A. Columbia University, 1925.

1688 Thorn-Drury, G. "Some Notes on Dryden." Review of English
Studies, I (July, 1925), 79-83; (April, 1925), 187-197; (Jan-
uary, 1925), 324-330.
Among them, Dryden's use in All for Love of Daniel's
Cleopatra; Buckingham's ridicule of a bull in Dryden; Dryden
and Shadwell; Dryden prologues and epilogues; Dryden's The
Tempest.

1689 Spencer, Hazelton. "Improving Shakespeare." Publications of
the Modern Language Association, XLI (1926), 727-746.

1690 Warmington, E. L. "A Dryden Misprint." London Mercury,
XIV (1926), 188.
On Dryden's All for Love.

1691 Clark, William S. "Dryden's Relations with Howard and Orrery."
Modern Language Notes, XLII (March, 1927), 16-20.
Clark uses an unpublished letter, which shows Dryden
living with Sir Robert Howard in 1663, to argue that through
Howard, Dryden was introduced to the Earl of Orrery, and
that the association of the three and the example of Orrery's
plays influenced the writing of The Indian Queen in rimed
verse.

1692 Harrison, T. P., Jr. "Othello As a Model for Dryden in All for
Love." Studies in English, No. 7 (November 15, 1927), 136-
143.
Alexas was inspired by Iago, and in many points of language
and situation the play is reminiscent of Othello.

1693 Hughes, Merritt Y. "Dryden as a Statist." Philological Quarterly,
VI (October, 1927), 335-350.
The key to his political thought is his belief that "the correct position on every question is an independent and realistic
attitude, guided by respect for the law."

1694 Nolde, Johanna. Die Bühnenanweisungen in John Dryden's Dramen.
Münster, 1927. 52 pp.

1695 Bredvold, Louis I. "Dryden, Hobbes, and the Royal Society."
Modern Philology, XXV (May, 1928), 417-438.
An analysis of the monarchical absolutism in Dryden's plays
and of the frequent references to the problem of free-will and
necessity. Dryden's attitude was one of skepticism, approaching
that of the Society.

1696 [Dobrée, Bonamy]. "Cleopatra and 'that Criticall warr.'" Times
Literary Supplement, October 11, 1928, pp. 717-718.
An appreciation of All for Love, with a comparison of the
Antony-Cleopatra story as treated by Shakespeare, Dryden, and
Daniel.

1697 H. "A British Worthy." Saturday Review, CXLV (February 25, 1928),
219-220.
Reviews the Cambridge University performance of Dryden's
and Henry Purcell's King Arthur, or The British Worthy, a Dramatick Opera.

1698 Ham, Roswell G. "Dryden versus Settle." Modern Philology, XXV
(May, 1928), 409-416.
Attributes to Settle the Tryal of the Poets, Azaria and Hushai,
and The Medal Revers'd, and accounts for Dryden's bitterness
accordingly. From 1673 Settle was Dryden's most formidable
enemy.

1699 -----. "Uncollected Verse by John Dryden." Times Literary Supplement, December 27, 1928, p. 1025.
A copy (dated 13 Feb. 1681/2) of the prologue and epilogue
of Lee's Mithridates in the Huntington Library contains ms.
notes by Narcissus Luttrell which assign them to Dryden. Lists
as well four other uncollected prologues and epilogues.

1700 Havens, Raymond D. "An Adaptation of One of Dryden's Plays."
Review of English Studies, IV (January, 1928), 88.
Quotes an advertisement from Spectator for February 15,
1712, showing that the opera The State of Innocence presented
with puppets at Punch's theatre was probably an adaptation of
Dryden's dramatization of Paradise Lost.

1701 Nolde, Johanna. "Die Bühnenanweisungen in John Dryden's Dramen."
Inaugural Dissertation. Münster, 1928.

1702 Starnes, D. T. "More about Dryden as an Adapter of Shakespeare."
(University of Texas) Studies in English, No. 8 (July 8, 1928),
100-106.
Reminiscences of Julius Caesar, As You Like It, Hamlet,
and Macbeth in All for Love.

1703 Walmsley, D. M. "The Influence of Foreign Opera on English
Operatic Plays of the Restoration Period." Anglia, LII (1928),
37-50.

1704 Wild, B. J. Dryden und die römische Kirche. Leipzig: Robert
      Noske, 1928.
          An analysis of Dryden's religious opinions and an explan-
      ation of his final conversion to Catholicism.

1705 [Dobrée, Bonamy]. "Dryden and Artificial Tragedy." Times
      Literary Supplement, August 15, 1929, pp. 629-630.
          Restoration comedy is close to everyday life, but Resto-
      ration tragedy can be classified as "artificial." Dryden, the
      most accomplished tragic craftsman of the period, was con-
      cerned not with presenting life but with pointing out the dis-
      tinction between life and art.

1706 [Dryden]. Notes and Queries, CLVII (November 23, 1929), 362.
          Reprints a notice from the Universal Spectator (November
      22, 1729) of Royal attendance at Dryden's play Aureng-Zebe
      at Drury-Lane.

1707 Fletcher, Harris F. "Nathaniel Lee and Milton." Modern Lan-
      guage Notes, XLIV (March, 1929), 173-175.
          On verses contributed by Lee to Dryden's The State of
      Innocence.

1708 Lynch, Kathleen M. "Conventions of Platonic Drama in the Heroic
      Plays of Orrery and Dryden." Publications of the Modern Lan-
      guage Association, XLIV (June, 1929), 456-471.
          The Platonic motives apparent in the dramas of Carlell,
      Suckling, Killigrew, Cartwright, and the young Davenant were
      taken over and refashioned by Orrery and Dryden when the
      theatres reopened in 1660.

1709 M., P. D. "Portraits of Dryden." Notes and Queries, CLVI (March
      2, 1929), 155.
          Asks the location of 12 portraits.

1710 Rear, Thelma Mary Jane. "The Classicism of John Dryden as
      Manifested in His Critical Theory." M.A. University of Southern
      California, 1929.

1711 White, H. O. "Dryden and Descartes." Times Literary Supple-
      ment, December 19, 1929, p. 1081.
          Adam's soliloquy in Act I has no original in Paradise Lost
      and is based rather on Descartes' philosophy.

1712 Williamson, George. "Dryden As Critic." University of California
      Chronicle, XXXII (1930), 71-76.

1713 Granville-Barker, Harley. "Wycherley and Dryden." On Dramatic
      Method. (London: Sidgwick and Johnson, Ltd. [1931], 113-155.
          Wycherley is the most skillful of the flatterers, as seen in
      an analysis of The Plain Dealer, and Dryden, the most "in-
      teresting" of the heroic play writers, as seen in a study of
      Aureng-Zebe.

1714 Ham, Roswell G. "An Addition to the Works of Dryden." Times
Literary Supplement, October 8, 1931, p. 778.
A dedication written for Henry Purcell to The Vocal and
Instrumental Musick of the Prophetess (1691).

1715 Hiscock, W. G. "A Dryden Epilogue." Times Literary Supplement,
March 5, 1931, p. 178.
Notes the discovery in Christ Church Library of a printed
broadside, "The Epilogue spoken to the King . . .," apparently printed some time before the London edition.

1716 Lawrence, W. J. "Dryden's Abortive Opera." Times Literary
Supplement, August 6, 1931, p. 606.
Argues, contrary to general opinion, that The State of In-
nocence was in fact written for production.

1717 Legouis, Pierre. "Quinault et Dryden: une source de The Spanish
Friar." Revue de Littérature Comparée, XI (1931), 398-415.
Suggests that Dryden drew heavily on Quinault for his The
Spanish Friar.

1718 Riske, Ella Theodora, Louis I. Bredvold, Thomas B. Stroup,
and Claude Lloyd. "Dryden and Waller as Members of the
Royal Society." Publications of the Modern Language Association, XLVI (1931), 951-962.
Traces the participation of Dryden and Waller and their
concern for the improvement of English prose.

1719 Bredvold, Louis I. "Political Aspects of Dryden's Amboyna and
The Spanish Fryar." University of Michigan Studies in Language and Literature, VIII (1932), 119-132.
In place of the low, mercenary motive attributed to Dryden
in these plays, the author attempts to show Dryden as a firm-
ly loyal Tory throughout this period.

1720 de Beer, E. S. "Mr. Montague Summers and Dryden's Essay of
Dramatic Poesy." Review of English Studies, VIII (1932),
453-456.
An analysis of Summers' methods.

1721 Eliot, T. S. John Dryden. The Poet, the Dramatist, the Critic.
New York: Terence and Elsa Holliday, 1932. 68 pp.

1722 Fornelli, Guido. La restaurazione inglese nell'opera di John
Dryden. Firenzi: "La nuova Italia," 1932. 55 pp.
Chapter III, pp. 31-48, deals with Dryden's plays, parti-
cularly the heroic plays.

1723 Hiscock, W. G. "Oxford History." Times Literary Supplement,
October 13, 1932, p. 734.
Dryden's epilogue spoken at Oxford, March 19, 1681, was
for the performance of Tamerlane the Great, by C. Saunders.

1724 Jünemann, Wolfgang. Drydens Fabeln und ihre Quellen. Hamburg:
Friederichsen, de Gruyter & Co., 1932. 103 pp.

Theorizes that Dryden's modifications of his sources are illustrations of Baroque art.

1725 Legouis, Pierre. "La Religion dans l'Oeuvre de Dryden avant 1682." Revue Anglo-Americaine, IX (1932), 383-392, 525-536.

1726 Mann, Wolfgang. Drydens heroische Tragödien als Ausdruck höfischer Barockkultur in England. Schramberg (Württemberg): Gratzer & Hahn, 1932. iv, 72 pp.

An analysis of Dryden's heroic plays and their influence upon his time, together with a study of the character of the hero.

1727 Ward, Charles E. "A Biographical Note on John Dryden." Modern Language Review, XXVII (1932), 206-210.

Discusses John Dryden's financial condition during "the tense years," 1679-1685.

1728 Whiting, G. W. "The Ellesmere MS. of The State of Innocence." Times Literary Supplement, January 14, 1932, p. 28.

Whiting reports on two MSS. of Dryden's opera in the Huntington Library. He confirms Dryden's statement that many copies of the opera were dispensed before its printing.

1729 Brockmeier, Lena Louise. "Principles of Criticism Discussed by Dryden." M.A. University of Southern California, 1933.

1730 Burrows, Dorothy. "The Relation of Dryden's Serious Plays and Dramatic Criticism to Contemporary French Literature." Ph.D. University of Illinois, 1933.

1731 Fletcher, C. R. L. "A Dryden Allusion." Times Literary Supplement, February 9, 1933, p. 92.

Mr. Fletcher, seeking the reasons for butchers being exempted from jury duty, quotes from the "Prologue" to Secret Love; or, The Maiden Queen: "And the same law shall yield him [the dramatist] from their [critics] fury,/ As hath excluded butchers from a jury."

1732 Hollis, Christopher. Dryden. London: Duckworth, 1933. 224 pp.

This biography contains errors and omissions, but it does contain much material on Dryden's dramatic career.

1733 Marquart, Fern Isabel. "Dryden's Conformity to Aristotle in Practice and Analysis of Dramatic Technique." M.A. University of Southern California, 1933.

1734 Mundy, P. D. "Portraits of John Dryden." Notes and Queries, CLXIV (1933), 423; CLXV (1933), 194.

Lists printers, owners and locations of portraits of John Dryden.

1735 Stroup, T. B. "Type-Characters in the Serious Drama of the Restoration with Special Attention to the Plays of Davenant, Dryden, Lee, and Otway." Ph.D. University of North Carolina, 1933.

1736 Thorp, Willard. "A New Manuscript Version of Dryden's Epilogue to Sir Fopling Flutter." Review of English Studies, IX (1933), 198-199.

Sloane MS. 1458 at the British Museum contains a version of Dryden's epilogue which seems nearer to what Dryden originally intended than the version in the Haward MS.

1737 Bredvold, Louis I. The Intellectual Milieu of John Dryden: Studies in Some Aspects of Seventeenth-Century Thought. University of Michigan Publications. Language and Literature, Vol. XII. Ann Arbor: University of Michigan Press, 1934. viii, 189 pp.

An investigation of the relationship of Dryden's characteristic thought and its background in the seventeenth century. The plays are cited passim.

1738 Noyes, Robert G. "Contemporary Musical Settings of the Songs in Restoration Drama." English Literary History, I (1934), 325-344.

1739 Richter, Walter. Der Hiatus in englischen Klassizismus. Schramberg: Gatzer & Hahn, 1934. 139 pp.

The book is specifically concerned with Milton, Dryden, and Pope. Sections deal with Dryden's dramas.

1740 Seaton, Ethel. "Two Restoration Plays." Times Literary Supplement, October 18, 1934, p. 715.

Treats of Dryden's The Rival Ladies.

1741 Ward, Charles E. "Dryden's Drama, 1662-1677: A Study in the Native Tradition." Ph.D. Duke University, 1934.

1742 Allen, Ned Bliss. The Sources of John Dryden's Comedies. University of Michigan Publications, Language and Literature, Vol. XVI. Ann Arbor: University of Michigan Press, 1935. xviii, 298 pp.

A study of Dryden's comedies and tragicomedies in relation to their possible sources in English and continental literature. It is revealed that Dryden's sensitivity to the changing tastes of his audience produced comedies eclectic in source and notable for their lack of allegiance to any specific comic tradition.

1743 Brooks, Harold. "Some Notes on Dryden, Cowley, and Shadwell." Notes and Queries, CLXVIII (1935), 94-95.

Reprints quotations from volumes dated 1673 and 1674 which contain some contemporary lay criticism of the drama, Marriage à la Mode.

1744 Fletcher, Edward G. "A Dryden Anecdote." Modern Language Notes, L (1935), 366.

Prints an anecdote from Defoe's Review concerning an alleged altercation between Dryden and the Duke of Buckingham.

1745 Ham, Roswell G. "Dryden's Dedication for The Music of the
     Prophetesse, 1691." Publication of the Modern Language
     Association, L (1935), 1065-1075.
          From a study of the MSS., Ham presents evidence that
     Dryden wrote the Dedication of Henry Purcell's opera, al-
     though Purcell's signature appears at the end. He also sug-
     gests that Dryden might have assisted in the revisions of the
     play.
1746 Hartsock, Mildred E. "The Ideas Reflected in the Plays of John
     Dryden." Ph.D. University of Cincinnati, 1935.
1747 Havens, P. S. "Dryden's 'Tagged' Version of Paradise Lost."
     Essays in Dramatic Literature: The Parrott Presentation Vol-
     ume. Edited by Hardin Craig. (Princeton: Princeton University
     Press, 1935), 383-397.
          Havens analyzes The State of Innocence and Fall of Man
     (1677) to show why and how Dryden wrote the play, and to
     demonstrate that Dryden was experimenting with techniques
     which he hoped would culminate in his own great epic.
1748 Nettleton, George H. "Author's Changes in Dryden's Conquest of
     Granada, Part I." Modern Language Notes, L (1935), 360-364.
          A collation of five quartos of the play reveals its textual
     history and shows a series of changes that must be attributed
     to the author.
1749 Perkinson, Richard H. "Lady du Lake." Notes and Queries,
     CLXVIII (1935), 260-261.
          Treats The Wild Gallant.
1750 Ward, Charles E. "Massinger and Dryden." English Literary
     History, II (1935), 263-266.
          A study of the relationships in plot, character, and theme
     between Massinger's The Virgin Martyr and Dryden's Tyrannic
     Love; Or, The Royal Martyr. Ward argues that Dryden's debt
     to Massinger was considerable.
1751 Eidson, John Olin. "Dryden's Criticism of Shakespeare." Studies
     in Philology, XXXIII (1936), 273-280.
          Dryden's attitudes toward Shakespeare are displayed in a
     series of quotations from various works.
1752 Leavis, F. R. "'Antony and Cleopatra' and 'All for Love.'"
     Scrutiny, V (1936), 158-169.
          On the basis of some impressions about various poetic
     qualities, Mr. Leavis attempts to prove that Shakespeare's
     play is superior to Dryden's.
1753 Noyes, Robert G. "Songs from Restoration Drama in Contempor-
     ary and Eighteenth-Century Poetical Miscellanies." English
     Literary History, III (1936), 291-316.
1754 Pulver, Jeffrey. "Purcell and Dryden." Musical Opinion and

Musical Trade Review, LIX (1936), 589-590.
1755 Walcott, Fred G. "John Dryden's Answer to Thomas Rymer's
      The Tragedies of the Last Age." Philological Quarterly, XV
      (August, 1936), 194-214.
          By interpreting the Prefaces to Dryden's All for Love and
      Troilus and Cressida, and his proposed "Heads for an Answer
      to Rymer's Remarks on the Tragedies of the Last Age," Wal-
      cott shows how Dryden sought to refute Rymer's attack upon
      the Elizabethan dramatists.
1756 Ward, Charles E. "The Dates of Two Dryden Plays." Publications
      of the Modern Language Association, LI (1936), 786-792.
          Ward argues that Marriage à la Mode was first performed
      "before the end of 1671," and Amboyna prior to June, 1672.
1757 Ham, Roswell G. "Dryden's Epilogue to The Rival Ladies, 1664."
      Review of English Studies, XIII (1937), 76-80.
          Argues that an anonymous MS. in the Bodleian Library con-
      tains the epilogue intended for Dryden's play.
1758 Hartsock, Mildred E. "Dryden's Plays: A Study in Ideas." Seven-
      teenth Century Studies, Second Series. Edited by Robert Shafer.
      (Princeton: Princeton University Press for the University of
      Cincinnati, 1937), 71-176.
          A study of various thematic problems manifest in Dryden's
      comedies and heroic dramas. After suggesting the intellectual
      milieu in which Dryden lived, Miss Hartsock analyzes the plays
      to show how they reveal the ideas of Montaigne and Hobbes.
1759 Noyes, Robert G., and Roy Lamson, Jr. "Broadside-Ballad Ver-
      sions of the Songs in Restoration Drama." Harvard Studies
      and Notes in Philology and Literature, XIX (1937), 199-218.
1760 Osborn, James M. "Edmond Malone and the Dryden Almanac
      Story." Philological Quarterly, XVI (1937), 412-414; XVII
      (1938), 84-86.
1761 Stroup, Thomas B. "Scenery for The Indian Queen." Modern
      Language Notes, LII (1937), 408-409.
          Old, well worn scenery was used for the play's performances.
1762 Treadway, Thomas J. "The Critical Opinions of John Dryden."
      Ph.D. St. Louis University, 1937-1938.
1763 Ward, C. E. "Some Notes on Dryden." Review of English Studies,
      XIII (1937), 297-306.
          Miscellaneous biographical and historical facts about the
      poet's finances, plays, and poems.
1764 Clark, William S. "Correspondence." Review of English Studies,
      XIV (1938), 330-332.
          Clarifies the meaning of a Dryden letter (Sloane MS. 813, f.
      71, 1663).
1765 Gesner, E. C. "Dryden As a Critic." M.A. University of Dal-
      housie, 1938.

1766 Knipp, George W. "The Stage History of John Dryden's Plays."
      Ph.D. Johns Hopkins University, 1938.
1767 Legouis, Pierre. "Corneille and Dryden as Dramatic Critics."
      Seventeenth Century Studies Presented to Sir Herbert Grierson.
      (Oxford: Clarendon Press, 1938), 269-291.
          A comparative analysis of Corneille's criticism of the
      drama for the purpose of demonstrating Dryden's "essential
      originality" in dramatic criticism. Professor Legouis con-
      cludes that Dryden owes "his unquestionable superiority large-
      ly to his manner" (p. 291).
1768 Maillet, Albert. "Dryden et Voltaire." Revue de literature comparé
      XVIII (April, 1938), 272-286.
          Study of Dryden's influence on Voltaire in the three fields
      of drama, criticism, and deistic thought, particularly the
      Indian Emperour's influence on Alzire.
1769 Muir, Kenneth. "The Imagery of All for Love." Proceedings of
      the Leeds Philosophical and Literary Society, V (1938-1943),
      140-149.
1770 Noyes, Robert G. "Contemporary Musical Settings of the Songs
      in Restoration Dramatic Operas." Harvard Studies and Notes
      in Philology and Literature, XX (1938), 99-121.
1771 Rosecke, Imgo. "Drydens Prologe und Epiloge." Inaugural Dis-
      sertation. Hamburg, 1938.
1772 Ball, Alice D. "An Emendation of Dryden's Conquest of Granada,
      Part One." English Literary History, VI (1939), 217-218.
          In the first edition, the attribution of the speech at 1. 151
      to Zulema is incorrect; the rightful speaker is Selin.
1773 Huntley, Frank L. "Dryden, Rochester, and the Eighth Satire of
      Juvenal." Philological Quarterly, XVIII (1939), 269-284.
          Provides causes for the feud between Rochester and Dryden,
      and shows how Dryden drew upon Juvenal for his censure of
      Rochester in the Preface to All for Love.
1774 Schweitzer, Jerome W. "Dryden's Use of Scudéry's Almahide."
      Modern Language Notes, LIV (1939), 190-192.
          Although Montague Summers claims that Dryden used an
      English translation of Almahide as a source for The Conquest
      of Granada, Schweitzer argues that Dryden drew upon the
      original version of the romance.
1775 Ward, Charles E. "Dryden's 'Spanish Friar' and a Provincial
      Touring Company." Notes and Queries, CLXXVI (1939), 96-
      97.
          A brief history of a small company touring Wales in the
      early summer of 1741.
1776 Wilson, J. Harold. "Rochester, Dryden, and The Rose Street
      Affair." Review of English Studies, XV (1939), 294-301.

Presents evidence to show that Rochester was not responsible for the cudgelling of Dryden in 1679.

1777 Boys, Richard C. "Some Problems of Dryden's Miscellany."
English Literary History, VII (June, 1940), 130-143.
A reassessment of the influence of Dryden's Miscellany
which he considers overestimated.

1778 Brower, Reuben Arthur. "Dryden's Epic Manner and Virgil."
Publications of the Modern Language Association, LV (March,
1940), 119-138.
Discusses the important extent to which Dryden's epic style
is directly indebted to Virgil. Most of the article is devoted to
a study of the heroic plays.

1779 De Beer, E. S. "Dryden: Date of a Prologue, 'Gallants, A Bashful
Poet.'" Notes and Queries, CLXXIX (1940), 440-441.
Dryden's prologue beginning "Gallants, a Bashful Poet" was
more likely composed between 1689 and 1693 than in 1681.

1780 -----. "Dryden: 'The Kind Keeper.' 'The Poet of Scandalous Memory.'" Notes and Queries, CLXXIX (1940), 128-129.
The deceased poet "of scandalous memory" to whom Dryden
alludes in his dedication to The Kind Keeper may not be Flecknoe
but Andrew Marvell.

1781 -----. "Dryden's Anti-Clericalism." Notes and Queries, CLXXIX
(October 12, 1940), 254-257.
Attitude rare before 1677.

1782 Gaupp, Charles John. "John Dryden: His Theory and Practice of
the Drama." M.A. Cornell University, 1940.

1783 Harbage, Alfred. "Elizabethan-Restoration Palimpsest." Modern
Language Review, XXXV (1940), 287-379.
Treats the Wild Gallant.

1784 Jefferson, D. W. "The Significance of Dryden's Heroic Plays."
Proceedings of the Leeds Philosophical and Literary Society,
V (1940), 125-139.

1785 Muir, Kenneth. "The Imagery of 'All for Love.'" Proceedings
of the Leeds Philosophical and Literary Society, V (1940),
140-147.

1786 Osborn, James M. John Dryden: Some Biographical Facts and
Problems. New York: Columbia University Press; London:
Humphrey Milford, 1940. 295 pp.

1787 Pinto, V. de Sola. "Rochester, Dryden, and the Duchess of
Portsmouth." Review of English Studies, XVI (April, 1940),
177-178.

1788 Bald, R. C. "Shakespeare on the Stage in Restoration Dublin."
Publications of the Modern Language Association, LVI
(June, 1941), 369-378.

Discusses annotations in prompt-books for eight of Shakespeare's plays, performed in Dublin before 1700. Concludes
that several of Shakespeare's plays were performed regularly
in Dublin, not merely three, as had been previously thought.

1789 Gomme, G. J. L. "Elizabeth Dryden and Dr. Busby." Times
Literary Supplement, May 10, 1941, p. 227.

1790 Long, Ralph B. "Dryden's Importance As a Spokesman of the
Tories." University of Texas Studies in English (1941), 79-99.
"Argues against attributed importance."

1791 Mundy, P. D. "The Cumberland Ancestry of John Dryden." Notes
and Queries, CLXXX (1941), 290-291; CLXXX (1941), 409.
Records of the Dryden family in Northamptonshire date back
to 1548 before they moved there from Cumberland.

1792 -----. "Recent Work on Dryden." Notes and Queries, CLXXXI
(September 6, 1941), 131-132.
". . . suggests that the Grolier Club portrait reproduced
in Osborn's Dryden: Facts and Problems, is not the poet but,
in all probability, Otway."

1793 Smith, Russell J. "Dryden and Shadwell: A Study in Literary Con-
troversy." Ph.D. Cornell University, 1941.
Feels that Shadwell must receive "considerable credit for
Dryden's position as a critic."

1794 Smith, R. Jack. "Drydeniana." Times Literary Supplement,
December 27, 1941, p. 655.
Notes a translation of essays of Saint-Evremond, overlooked
by MacDonald's bibliography, which praises Dryden generously
in the Preface.

1795 Aldridge, Alfred Owen. "Dryden Song and Wesley Hymn." Saturday Review of Literature, XXV (May 30, 1942), 15.
Argues that the "Song of Venus in Dryden's King Arthur, or
some version of that song, must have influenced Wesley's
"Love Divine." Prints two stanzas of Wesley's song and two
stanzas of a version of Dryden's song.

1796 Dykema, Karl W. "Samuel Sewall Reads John Dryden." American
Literature, XIV (May, 1942), 157-158.
A journal of Sewall's mentions Dryden.

1797 Evans, G. Blakemore. "Dryden's State of Innocence." Times
Literary Supplement, March 21, 1942, p. 144.
An account of the Harvard manuscript of the work.

1798 Huntley, Frank Livingstone. "The Unity of John Dryden's Dramatic
Criticism, 1664-1681." Ph.D. University of Chicago, 1942.
Published later under another title.

1799 Scott, Florence R. "Lady Honoria Howard." Review of English
Studies, XX (April, 1942), 158-159.
"Reason for believing that Dryden did not choose the name

The Rival Ladies because of Honoria Englefield, later the
wife of Sir Robert Howard."

1800 Stallman, Robert W. "Dryden in Modern Poetry and Criticism."
Ph.D. University of Wisconsin, 1942.

1801 Hathaway, Baxter. "John Dryden and the Function of Tragedy."
Publications of the Modern Language Association, LVIII (1943),
665-673.
An attempt to explain Dryden's views on purgation and the
function of tragedy, and to relate them to what he takes to be
the two prevailing conceptions of tragedy in Augustan criticism:
the Neo-Stoic, and the sentimental. Feels Dryden veering away
from Neo-Stoic.

1802 Hooker, Helene Maxwell. "Dryden's and Shadwell's 'Tempest.'"
Huntington Library Quarterly, VI (February, 1943), 224-228.
Variant readings in Huntington Library MS. of Dryden's
"Prologue Spoken at the Opening of the Theatre Royal" support
the belief that in the obscure last line of the Prologue Dryden was
sneering at the operatic Tempest credited to Shadwell.

1803 Loane, George C. "Notes on the Globe Dryden." Notes and Queries,
CLXXXV (1943), 272-281.
A list of biblical references in Dryden not contained in
Christie's edition.

1804 Mundy, P. D. "The Baptism of John Dryden." Notes and Queries,
CLXXXIV (1943), 286.
New evidence indicates that Dryden may have been baptized
August 14, 1631.

1805 Trowbridge, Hoyt. "Dryden's Essay on the Dramatic Poetry of
the Last Age." Philological Quarterly, XXII (1943), 240-250.
Argues that Dryden is criticizing only certain features of
the older drama and that the essay is not a contradiction of the
Essay of Dramatic Poesy.

1806 Wallerstein, Ruth C. "Dryden and the Analysis of Shakespeare's
Techniques." Review of English Studies, XIX (April, 1943),
165-185.
Through an analysis of "All for Love," Wallerstein studies
Dryden's imitation of Shakespeare. Though personally too
shallow to succeed, Dryden sought to improve on Shakespeare
in point of the unities, poetic justice, character type, and
decorum.

1807 Cubbage, Virginia Cox. "The Reputation of John Dryden, 1700-
1799." Ph.D. Northwestern University, 1944.

1808 M., P. D. "John Dryden's Character." Notes and Queries, CLXXX-
VII (July 15, 1944), 34.
Contrary to what Graham Greene says, John Dryden was not
"unlovable."

1809 Smith, R. Jack. "Shadwell's Impact upon John Dryden." Review
      of English Studies, XX (January, 1944), 29-44.
           Argues that Shadwell was the most important of Dryden's
      literary adversaries; their arguments over the merits of comedy
      of repartee vs. comedy of humours, the right of an author to
      borrow from ancient and modern authors, and the rationale of
      heroic tragedy stirred Dryden to consider important aspects of
      his craft.

1810 Burke, Margaret J., Sr. "Dryden and Eliot--a Study in Literary
      Criticism." Ph.D. Niagara University, 1945.

1811 Casey, Rev. Lucian T. "The Biographies and Biographers of
      John Dryden." Ph.D. Niagara University, 1945.

1812 Chapman, R. W. "Cancels in Malone's Dryden." Library,
      4th Ser., XXIII (September-December, 1945), 131.
           A complete list of the cancels in Malone's Critical and
      Miscellaneous Prose. Works of John Dryden (1800).

1813 Sherwood, John Collingwood. "The Sources of John Dryden's
      Critical Essays." Ph.D. Yale University, 1945.

1814 Banks, Margaret Jean. "John Dryden as a Critic of Shakespeare."
      M.A. University of Illinois, 1946.

1815 Milton, William M. "Tempest in a Teapot." English Literary
      History, XIV (1946), 207-218.

1816 Ribner, Irving. "Dryden's Shakespearian Criticism and the
      Neo-Classical Paradox." Shakespeare Association Bulletin,
      XXI (October, 1946), 168-171.
           Dryden sees Shakespeare as a great dramatic artist in
      spite of his neglect of neo-classical rules.

1817 Russell, Trustan Wheeler. Voltaire, Dryden and Heroic Tragedy.
      New York: Columbia University Press, 1946. viii, 178 pp.
           Analyses the main trends in Anglo-French dramatic criti-
      cism from 1650 to 1750, with particular attention to neo-
      classical theories of tragedy.

1818 Trowbridge, Hoyt. "The Place of Rules in Dryden's Criticism."
      Modern Philology, XLIV (1946), 84-96.
           Shows that Dryden thinks of literary evaluation as a rational
      process for which, therefore, rules and principles are valid
      and necessary. This is examined in the light of his views of
      the drama.

1819 Van Doren, Mark. John Dryden: A Study of His Poetry. New York:
      Holt, 1946. x, 298 pp.
           A new edition of the classic work which first appeared in
      1920.

1820 Ward, Charles E. "The Tempest: A Restoration Opera Problem."
      English Literary History, XIII (1946), 119-130.

1821 Williamson, George. "The Occasion of An Essay of Dramatic

Poesy." Modern Philology, XLIV (August, 1946), 1-9.
> The Essay develops from the Sorbière-Sprat controversy
> on English plays.

1822 Gilbert, Allan H., and Henry L. Snuggs. "On the Relation of
>   Horace to Aristotle in Literary Criticism." Journal of English
>   and Germanic Philology, XLVI (1947), 233-247.
>> Includes comment on Dryden and Dennis.

1823 Hanzo, Thomas Andrew. "The Theory of Imitation in the Literary
>   Criticism of John Dryden." M.A. University of Colorado, 1947.

1824 Huntley, Frank Livingstone. "Dryden's Discovery of Boileau."
>   Modern Philology, XLV (1947), 112-117.
>> Huntley attempts to disprove A. F. B. Clark's assertion
>> that Dryden's "Apology" goes counter to the tenets of Boileau.
>> He maintains that the "Longin" inspired the soul, and the "Art
>> Poetique" the brain of Dryden.

1825 Leigh, Richard. Poems, 1675. Edited by Hugh Macdonald. Ox-
>   ford: Blackwell, 1947. xvi, 80 pp.
>> Includes comment on Leigh's "The Censure of the Rota on
>> Mr. Dryden's Conquest of Granada."

1826 Rundle, James Urvin. "The Source of Dryden's 'Comic Plot' in
>   The Assignation." Modern Philology, XLV (1947), 104-111.
>> The source is Caldéron's Con quien vengo vengo.

1827 Schweitzer, Jerome W. "Another Note on Dryden's Use of Georges
>   de Scudéry's Almahide." Modern Language Notes, LXII (April,
>   1947), 262-263.
>> Parallel passages reinforce his earlier theory (M.L.N.,
>> 1939) that Scudéry's play was the main source for Conquest of
>> Granada, I.

1828 Stokes, William Henry. "The Reputation of John Dryden as a
>   Dramatist." M. A. University of Pittsburgh, 1947.

1829 Tyler, Henry. "Milton and Dryden." Times Literary Supplement,
>   April 12, 1947, p. 171.
>> Treats of The State of Innocence.

1830 Albaugh, Ralph M. "Dryden's Literary Relationships, 1689-
>   1700." Ph.D. Ohio State University, 1948.

1831 Gohn, Ernest S. "Seventeenth-Century Theories of the Passions
>   and the Plays of John Dryden." Ph.D. Johns Hopkins University,
>   1948.

1832 Huntley, Frank Livingstone. "On the Persons in An Essay of
>   Dramatic Poesy." Modern Language Notes, LXIII (February,
>   1948), 88-95.
>> Questions the Malone identifications and stresses that the
>> piece is to be considered a dialogue rather than a roman à
>> clef.

1833 Russell, Trustan Wheeler. "Dryden, inspirateur de Voltaire."

Revue de Littérature Comparée, XXII (1948), 321-329.
Studies the influence of Dryden's theories of drama on
Voltaire.

1834 Winterbottom, John A. "Patterns of Piety: Studies in the Intellectual Background of Dryden's Tragedies." Ph.D. Yale University, 1948.

1835 Dunkin, Paul S. "The Dryden Troilus and Cressida Imprint: Another Theory." Papers of the Bibliographical Society of the University of Virginia, II (1949), 185-189.
Supplements the article by Fredson T. Bowers, "Variants
in Early Editions of Dryden's Plays," Harvard Library Bulletin,
1949.

1836 Evans, G. Blakemore. "Edward Ecclestone: His Relationship to
Dryden and Milton." Modern Language Review, XLIV (October,
1949), 550-552.
Noah's Flood (1679), a sequel to State of Innocence (1677),
shows Ecclestone to be a follower of Milton's ideas and Dryden's
techniques.

1837 Kaplan, Charles. "Dryden's An Essay of Dramatic Poesy." Expli-
cator, VIII (1949-1950), Item 36.
In spite of its ending, the essay is not an inconclusive one.
The vindication of English writers parallels the victory of the
English fleet.

1838 MacMillan, Dougald. "The Sources of Dryden's The Indian Emperour." Huntington Library Quarterly, XIII (1949-1950), 355-
370.
Dryden probably derived his suggestion for the play from
Davenant's The Cruelty of the Spaniards in Peru and found his
historical materials in Purchas His Pilgrimes (1625).

1839 -----. "The William Andrews Clark Edition of Dryden--the Plays."
South Atlantic Bulletin (May, 1949), 10-11.
Outlines the plans for the projected edition.

1840 Zesmer, David M. "Rymer and John Dryden: a Study in 17th Century Critical Thought." M.A. Columbia University, 1949.

1841 Aden, John. "The Question of Influence in Dryden's Use of Major
French Critics." Ph.D. University of North Carolina, 1950.

1842 Bowers, Fredson. "Current Theories of Copy-text, with an Illustration from Dryden." Modern Philology, XLVIII (1950),
12-20.
Three early editions of The Indian Emperour illustrate the
dangers involved in choosing the latest revised edition of a
literary work as a copy-text.

1843 -----. "The First Edition of Dryden's Wild Gallant." Library,
5th Ser., (1950), 51-54.
The "Theatre" edition, rather than the "Theater" copy, is
the first edition of The Wild Gallant.

1844 Horsman, E. A. "Dryden's French Borrowings." Review of Eng-
       lish Studies, New Ser., I (1950), 346-351.
          The writer attributes some forty French borrowings to
       Dryden as the first to use them in print.

1845 Kaplan, Charles. "Dryden's An Essay of Dramatic Poesy."
       Explicator, VIII (1950), Item 36.
          Kaplan argues that the Essay is not inconclusive, that, in
       reality, the English achieved two victories that day of the
       dialogue--a naval victory and a victory for English national
       literature.

1846 Kossman, H. "A Note on Dryden's 'All for Love,' v. 165ff."
       English Studies, XXXI (1950), 99-100.
          The lines can be interpreted in the light of the traditional
       view of the human soul.

1847 Prior, Moody E. "Poetic Drama: an Analysis and a Suggestion."
       English Institute Essays 1949. Edited by Alan S. Downer.
       (New York: Columbia University Press, 1950), 3-32.
          Comments briefly on the period, mainly on Dryden's verse
       plays.

1848 Russell, Doris A. "Dryden's Relations with His Critics." Ph.D.
       Columbia University, 1950. 244 pp. (Publication No. 2125).
          Dryden's responses to criticism "suggest a sensitivity
       to criticism, springing from a need for approval." Abstracted
       in Microfilm Abstracts, XI, no. 1 (1951), 117-118.

1849 Sherwood, John C. "Dryden and the Rules: the Preface to 'Troilus
       and Cressida.'" Comparative Literature, II (Winter, 1950),
       73-83.
          Dryden applies French neoclassical principles to Shakespeare
       and comes up with a very favorable judgment. He reconciles
       Shakespeare and the French "rules." To be sure, his plots are
       condemned as defective, and his style as obsolete, but the en-
       thusiastic praise of "natural" thought, distinguished characters,
       and the inciting of terror and pity far outweight the criticism.

1850 Simpson, French, Jr. "The Relationship between Character and
       Action in Neo-Classical Tragedy, with Special Reference to
       Some Tragedies by John Dryden." Ph.D. Stanford University,
       1950. 559 pp.
          Simpson's purpose is "to present the grounds for classifying
       neo-classical tragedy as tragedy of character."

1851 Adams, Henry R. "A Prompt Copy of Dryden's Tyrannic Love."
       Studies in Bibliography, IV (1951-1952), 170-174.
          The prompt copy of 1672 sheds light on the theatrical
       practices of the King's Company.

1852 Albert, Francis L. "Dryden's Debt to Milton." M.A. University
       of North Carolina, 1951.

1853 Bowers, Fredson. "The 1665 Manuscript of Dryden's Indian
      Emperour." Studies in Philology, XLVIII (1951), 738-760.
          The Trinity College manuscript (R. 111.10) is probably
      a copy of the 1665 Herringman manuscript.
1854 Cooke, Arthur L. "Did Dryden Hear the Guns?" Notes and
      Queries, CXCVI (1951), 204-205.
          Although Dryden, Pepys, and others claimed to have heard
      the gunfire from the battle of June 3, 1665, there is strong
      evidence to suggest that they did not hear it; the battle took
      place about 120 miles from London.
1855 Davie, Donald A. "Dramatic Poetry: Dryden's Conversation
      Piece." Cambridge Journal, V (1951-1952), 553-561.
          Dryden's Essay of Dramatic Poesy is more important as
      a conversation piece than as criticism.
1856 Frost, William. "Dryden's Prologue and Epilogue to All for Love.'
      Explicator, X (1951-1952), Note 1.
          The concluding passages of the epilogue and prologue (lines
      33-40; 20-31) may be a deliberate contrast between Elizabethan
      and early Jacobean drama.
1857 Huntley, Frank L. On Dryden's Essay of Dramatic Poesy. Ann
      Arbor: University of Michigan Press, 1951. 71 pp.
          Huntley's study is a close analysis of the structure and
      themes of Dryden's essays.
1858 Tillyard, E. M. W. "A Note on Dryden's Criticism." The Seven-
      teenth Century: Studies in the History of English Thought and
      Literature from Bacon to Pope. (Stanford, California: Stanford
      University Press, 1951), 330-338.
          A brief but comprehensive survey.
1859 Bowers, Fredson. "The Pirated Quarto of Dryden's State of In-
      nocence." Studies in Bibliography, V (1952-1953), 166-169.
          The latter part of Q9 was set from an uncollated copy of
      Q8.
1860 Feder, Lillian. "John Dryden's Interpretation and Use of Latin
      Poetry and Rhetoric." Ph.D. University of Minnesota, 1952.
1861 Suckling, Norman. "Dryden in Egypt: Reflexions on All for Love."
      Durham University Journal, New Ser., XIV (1952), 2-7.
          All for Love represents the classical tragedy, "spoken
      opera" comparable to the works of Racine and Corneille.
1862 Aden, John M. "Dryden and Boileau: the Question of Critical
      Influence." Studies in Philology, L (1953), 491-509.
          The author offers some original studies on this question to
      supplement A. F. B. Clark's, "Boileau and the French Classi-
      cal Critics in England," a standard reference since 1925. He
      finds Boileau's influence overrated.
1863 Bowers, Fredson. "Dryden as Laureate: The Cancel Leaf in King

Arthur." Times Literary Supplement, April 10, 1953, p. 244.
The cancel leaf contains a reference by Dryden to the loss
of his laureateship.

1864 Freedman, Morris. "Milton and Dryden." Ph.D. Columbia University, 1953. 207 pp. (Publication No. 6617).
The author analyzes the literary interrelations of Dryden
and Milton; Part III, "Fellow Dramatists," considers their
dramatic work.

1865 Hamilton, Marion H. "The Manuscripts of Dryden's The State of
Innocence and the Relation of the Harvard MS to the First
Quarto." Studies in Bibliography, VI (1953), 237-246.
Q9 was printed in 1695 or later and was probably a piracy.

1866 Jones, H. W. "Some Further Pope-Dryden Indebtedness?" Notes
and Queries, CXCVIII (1953), 199-200.
Lines 203 and 325 of Pope's Epistle to Arbuthnot echo
phrases in Dryden's An Essay of Dramatic Poesy.

1867 Moore, Frank H. "Dryden's Theory and Practice of Comedy."
Ph.D. University of North Carolina, 1953.

1868 Sherwood, John C. "Dryden and the Rules: the Preface to the
Fables." Journal of English and Germanic Philology, LII (January, 1953), 13-26.
Concludes that "the judgments in the Preface are consistent
with the rules, and that many of them have precedents in other
writers."

1869 Sherwood, John C. "Dryden's Prologue and Epilogue to Mithridates
Revived." Publications of the Modern Language Association,
LXVIII (March, 1953), 251-267.

1870 Smith, John Harrington. "Dryden's Prologue and Epilogue to
Mithridates, Revived." Publications of the Modern Language
Association, LXVIII (1953), 251-267.
The case for Dryden's authorship is strengthened in light
of parallels in his other works.

1871 Winterbottom, John. "The Development of the Hero in Dryden's
Tragedies." Journal of English and Germanic Philology, LII
(1953), 161-173.
In the heroic temperament Dryden sees both potential good
and destructiveness; through education or discipline the former
might be developed and the latter tempered.

1872 Cooke, Arthur L. "Two Parallels between Dryden's 'Wild Gal-
lant' and Congreve's 'Love for Love.'" Notes and Queries,
CXCIX (1954), 27-28.
Dryden and Congreve use trick marriages and pretended
illnesses as plot devices in The Wild Gallant and Love for
Love.

1873 Feder, Lillian. "John Dryden's Use of Classical Rhetoric." Publications of the Modern Language Association, LXIX (1954), 1258-1278.

Dryden's critical writings and his theory of literature were strongly influenced by the principles of classical rhetoric.

1874 Kinsley, James. "A Dryden Play at Edinburgh." Scottish Historical Review, XXXIII (1954), 129-132.

The Indian Emperour was probably staged at Edinburgh in 1681.

1875 Lill, James V. "Dryden's Adaptations from Milton, Shakespeare, and Chaucer." Ph.D. University of Minnesota, 1954. 284 pp. (Publication No. 8462).

Dryden's attempts to apply Restoration rules to his adaptations destroyed the very qualities he most admired in the original works.

1876 Moore, Frank Harper. "Dr. Pelling, Dr. Pell, and Dryden's Lord Nonsuch." Modern Language Review, XLIX (1954), 349-351.

Lord Nonsuch in The Wild Gallant, who is convinced he is pregnant, is perhaps Dr. John Pell rather than Dr. Edward Pelling.

1877 -----. "Heroic Comedy: A New Interpretation of Dryden's Assignation." Studies in Philology, LI (1954), 585-598.

In The Assignation Dryden sought to mingle high comedy with heroic comedy.

1878 Sellers, William Howard. "Literary Controversies among Restoration Dramatists, 1660-1685." Ph.D. Ohio State University, 1954.

Dryden, Shadwell, and the Wits.

1879 Smith, John Harrington. "Dryden and Buckingham: The Beginnings of the Feud." Modern Language Notes, LXIX (1954), 242-245.

The feud had its origin in 1667, when Buckingham attacked Dryden in the epilogue to his adaptation of Fletcher's The Chances.

1880 -----. "Dryden and Flecknow: A Conjecture." Philological Quarterly, XXXIII (1954), 338-341.

Dryden's choice of Flecknoe as retiring ruler of Nonsense was perhaps motivated by Flecknoe's prologue to Emilia (1672).

1881 -----. "The Dryden-Howard Collaboration." Studies in Philology, LI (1954), 54-74.

Acts I and II, as well as II, i, of The Indian Queen can be assigned to Dryden; the rest is Howard's.

1882 Young, Kenneth. John Dryden: A Critical Biography. London: Sylvan Press, 1954. 240 pp.

Young attempts to "give full weight to what Dryden allows us to know of himself."

1883 Aden, John M. "Dryden, Corneille, and the Essay of Dramatic
     Poesy." Review of English Studies, New Ser., VI (1955),
     147-156.
          Argues that Corneille only furnished Dryden with the tradi-
     tion of the unities; Dryden worked out his own philosophy of
     their use. The character of Neander is seen to express Dryden's
     views.
1884 Emerson, Everett H., Harold E. Davis, and Ira Johnson. "In-
     tention and Achievement in All for Love." College English,
     XVII (1955), 84-87.
          According to Dryden's own standards, All for Love lacks
     the inevitability of tragedy since the lovers are not forced
     into their actions. Though Dryden tried to conform to neo-
     classical standards, these and other intentions are not real-
     ized in the play.
1885 Freedman, Morris. "Dryden's 'Memorable Visit' to Milton."
     Huntington Library Quarterly, XVIII (1955), 88-108.
          An account of the supposed visit of Dryden to Milton as
     recorded by John Aubrey; most of the article is devoted to a
     discussion of whether or not the visit occurred. Includes com-
     ments on Dryden's preference for rhymed verse.
1886 Ker, W. P. On Modern Literature: Lectures and Addresses.
     Edited by Terence Spencer and James Sutherland. Oxford:
     Clarendon Press, 1955. xviii, 282 pp.
          The essay, "John Dryden," is an appreciation of Dryden,
     discussing his plays and operas.
1887 Ramsey, Paul. "Dryden's Essay of Dramatic Poesy." Explicator,
     XIII (1955), Item 46.
          A one-page commentary on the opening scene as being one
     of the best passages of prose in the language in that its inter-
     play with the dialogue is as profound as its atmosphere, in-
     voking a range of relations between the great and the small, the
     permanent and the transient.
1888 Stallman, R. W. "The Scholar's Net: Literary Sources." College
     English, XVII (1955), 20-27.
          Mentions All for Love and Antony and Cleopatra to demon-
     strate the difference between a literary source that is a
     parallelism and one that is not. We must see Dryden's play
     as it is in itself, not solely as a derivative of Shakespeare.
1889 Beauchamp, Virginia Walcott. "Dramatic Treatment of 'Antony
     and Cleopatra' in the Sixteenth and Seventeenth Centuries:
     Variations in Dramatic Form upon a Single Theme." Ph.D.
     University of Chicago, 1956.
1890 Biggins, D. "Source Notes for Dryden, Wycherley and Otway."
     Notes and Queries, CCI (1956), 298-301.

Suggests sources for scenes and plot machinery in Dryden,
Wycherley and Otway.

1891 Brossman, S.W. "Dryden's Cassandra and Congreve's Zara."
Notes and Queries, New Ser., III (1956), 102-103.
Dryden's influence.

1892 Cross, Gustav. "Ovid Metamorphosed: Marston, Webster, and
Nathaniel Lee." Notes and Queries, New Ser., III (1956),
244-245, 508-509.
Dryden-Lee Oedipus indebted to Golding's translation of
Ovid.

1893 Dearing, Bruce. "Some Views of a Beast." Modern Language
Notes, LXXI (1956), 326-329.
Dryden's Secular Masque.

1894 Dobree, Bonamy. John Dryden. London: Longmans Green &
Company, for the British Council and the National Book
League, 1956. 48 pp.
A brief, but detailed, overview of Dryden's works; the play,
the poetry, and the criticism are considered separately. Includes select bibliographies of Dryden's works and of criticism
of his work.

1895 Deleted.

1896 Freedman, Morris. "All for Love and Samson Agonistes."
Notes and Queries, New Ser., III (1956), 514-517.
Finds similarities in the plays.

1897 Griffith, Richard Randolph. "Science and Pseudo-Science in the
Imagery of John Dryden." Ph.D. Ohio State University, 1956.
Especially alchemy and astrology; related to the writing
of An Evening's Love: or, The Mock Astrologer.

1898 Manuel, M. "The Seventeenth-Century Critics and Biographers
of Milton." Ph.D. University of Wisconsin, 1956.
Includes discussion of Dryden's The State of Innocence.

1899 McCollum, John I., Jr. "Dryden's 'Adaptations': The Tragedies."
Ph.D. Duke University, 1956.

1900 Padgett, Lawrence E. "Dryden's Edition of Corneille." Modern
Language Notes, LXXI (1956), 173-174.
Trois Discours, 1660, used in An Essay of Dramatic Poesy

1901 Ramsey, Paul, Jr. "The Image of Nature in John Dryden." Ph.D.
University of Minnesota, 1956.
Built upon the definition of a play in An Essay of Dramatic
Poesy.

1902 Allen, Ned Bliss. "The Sources of Dryden's The Mock Astrologer."
Philological Quarterly, XXXVI (1957), 453-464.
Discusses Molière, Quinault, Scudery, and Thomas Corn-
eille as possible sources of Dryden's play.

1903 Arnold, Claude. "Reflections of Political Issues in the Plays,

Prologues and Epilogues of John Dryden." Ph.D. Western
Reserve University, 1957.

1904 Brooks, Harold. "Dryden and Cowley." Times Literary Supplement, April 19, 1957, p. 245.

1905 Brossman, S. W. "Dryden's 'Cleomenes' and Fletcher's 'Bon-
duca.'" Notes and Queries, New Ser., IV (1957), 66-68.
Dryden borrowed both characterization and expression.

1906 Coshow, Betty Gay. "Dryden's Zambra Dance." Explicator,
XVI (1957), Item 16.
Analysis of the song in The Conquest of Granada, Part I.

1907 Crinò, Anna Maria. John Dryden. Florence: Olschki, 1957.
407 pp.
Biography and survey of Dryden's works; in Italian.

1908 Fall, George G. "Dryden: Professional Man of Letters."
University of Toronto Quarterly, XXVI (1957), 443-455.
A rather general and--with the exception of one reference
to the Essay--undocumented analysis of Dryden's critical
career, which is envisioned as an open challenge to Locke's
disparagement of literature in general and of poetry in particular as a source of public enlightenment.

1909 Goodison, J. W. "Cambridge Portraits II: Later Seventeenth
and Early Eighteenth Centuries." Connoisseur, CXL (1957),
231-236.
Includes portrait of Dryden.

1910 Grace, John William. "Theory and Practice in the Comedy of
John Dryden." Ph.D. University of Michigan, 1957.
Describes, classifies, and relates to other comedies.

1911 Hitchman, Percy J. "King Arthur at Nottingham: A Notable Revival." Theatre Notebook, XI (1957), 121-128.
Dryden's 1691; revived 1956.

1912 Kermode, Frank. "Dryden: A 'Poet's Poet.'" Listener, LVII
(1957), 877-878.
Discusses Dryden's relationship with his audience with
reference to various genres. Dryden's Restoration plays indicate his strong sympathy with contemporary taste, particularly the taste for naturalism regarding sex, which permeated even
his heroic tragedy--specifically, The Conquest of Granada.

1913 Lees, F. N. "John Dryden." The Pelican Guide to English Literature, Vol. IV, From Dryden to Johnson. Edited by Boris
Ford. (Baltimore: Penguin Books, 1957), 97-113.
Brief critical survey includes plays and criticism. Select
bibliography, pp. 474-475.

1914 Perkins, Merle L. "Dryden's The Indian Emperour and Voltaire's
Alzire." Comparative Literature, IX (1957), 229-237.
Attempts to show, by a comparison of the two plays, that

Voltaire was employing an experimental form, that he sub-
ordinates action to thought and strives for historical authenticity, and that Dryden's play was a vital contribution to Alzire.

1915 Romagosa, Sister Edward, O.Carm. "A Compendium of the
Opinions of John Dryden." Ph.D. Tulane University, 1957.
A dictionary. Includes opinions on theatre and drama.

1916 Smith, John Harrington. "Some Sources of Dryden's Toryism,
1682-1684." Huntington Library Quarterly, XX (1957), 233-
243.
Cites especially The Duke of Guise.

1917 Wallace, A. E. "Dryden and Pyrrhonism." Notes and Queries,
CCII (1957), 251-252.
A reply to Bredvold and Trowbridge.

1918 Bleuler, Werner. Das heroische Drama John Drydens als Experiment dekorativer Formkunst. Bern: Francke, 1958. 118
pp. (Swiss Studies in English, 45).
A discussion of ideas of the heroic during the late 17th
century and how Dryden used such ideas in his plays.

1919 Howarth, R. G. "Dryden's Letters." English Studies in Africa,
I (1958), 184-194.

1920 Kane, Sister Mary Franzita. "John Dryden's Doctrine of Wit as
Propriety: A Study of the Terms and Relations Involved in the
Definition of 1677." Ph.D. University of Notre Dame, 1958.
Study of the essays, involving dramatic theory.

1921 Le Comte, Edward S. "Samson Agonistes and Aureng-Zebe."
Etudes Anglaises, XI (1958), 18-22.
Milton a major source for Dryden's play.

1922 Maurer, Wallace. "From Renaissance to Neo-Classic." Notes
and Queries, V (1958), 287.
A short speech in Dryden's Troilus and Cressida compared
to Shakespeare's version.

1923 Moore, John Robert. "Political Allusions in Dryden's Later Plays
Publications of the Modern Language Association, LXXIII (1958
36-42.
Despite danger and some censorship, Dryden expressed
Jacobite sentiments as much as he could.

1924 Morton, Richard. "'By No Strong Passion Swayed': A Note on
John Dryden's Aureng-Zebe." English Studies in Africa, I
(1958), 59-68.

1925 Osborn, Scott C. "Heroical Love in Dryden's Heroic Drama."
Publications of the Modern Language Association, LXXIII
(1958), 480-490.
Opposed to "Platonic love" and to reason and virtue.

1926 Winterbottom, John A. "The Place of Hobbesian Ideas in Dryden's
Tragedies." Journal of English and Germanic Philology, LVII

(1958), 665-683.

Dryden does not approve the ideas expressed by some of the characters.

1927 Aden, John M. "Dryden and the Imagination: The First Phase." Publications of the Modern Language Association, LXXIV (1959), 28-40.

Dryden's use of the related terms to 1672.

1928 Alssid, Michael William. "Dryden's Rhymed Heroic Tragedies: A Critical Study of the Plays and of Their Place in Dryden's Poetry." Ph.D. University of Syracuse, 1959.

The Indian Emperor, Tyranic Love, The Conquest of Granada, and Aureng-Zebe are evaluated on the basis of Dryden's essays.

1929 Benson, Donald R. "John Dryden and the Church of England: The Conversion and the Problem of Authority in the Seventeenth Century." Ph.D. University of Kansas, 1959. (Order No. 60-896).

Refers to Dryden's plays and criticism.

1930 Bevan, Allan. "Poetry and Politics in Restoration England." Dalhousie Review, XXXIX (1959), 314-325.

Discusses Dryden, Shadwell, Settle, and Rochester.

1931 Dearing, Vinton A. A Manual of Textual Analysis. Berkeley and Los Angeles: University of California Press, 1959. xi, 108 pp.

Discusses Dryden's epilogue to The Man of Mode.

1932 King, Bruce. "Dryden's 'Zambra Dance.'" Explicator, XVIII (1959), Item 18.

The theme of fancy in the poem. Dryden was making direct use of the psychology of Thomas Hobbes. The poem acts as a satiric reflector on the play.

1933 Lowens, Irving. "St. Evremond, Dryden, and the Theory of Opera." Criticism, I (1959), 226-248.

Comparisons of essays.

1934 Maurer, Wallace. "Dryden's Knowledge of Historians, Ancient and Modern." Notes and Queries, New Ser., VI (1959), 264-266.

Plays and other works.

1935 McArthur, Herbert. "Romeo's Loquacious Friend." Shakespeare Quarterly, X (1959), 35-44.

Dryden's and Johnson's criticisms.

1936 Moore, John Robert. "Dryden and Rupert Brooke." Modern Language Review, LIV (1959), 226.

Don Sebastian.

1937 Nänny, Max. John Drydens rhetorische Poetik: Versuch eines Aufbaus aus seinem kritischen Schaffen. Bern: Francke, 1959. xvii, 101 pp.

1938 O'Regan, M. J. "Two Notes on French Reminiscences in Resto-
     ration Comedy." Hermathena, XCIII (1959), 63-70.
          Molière in Dryden's The Mock Astrologer and Corneille in
     Congreve's The Way of the World.
1939 Regan, Arthur Edwin. "On Dryden's Don Sebastian." Honors
     Thesis. Harvard University, 1959. 43 pp.
          An examination of the language of Dryden's Don Sebastian
     and how Dryden employed imagery to depict the moral dilem-
     ma of the hero.
1940 Strang, Barbara. "Dryden's Innovation in Critical Vocabulary."
     Durham University Journal, LI (1959), 114-123.
          The study defines Dryden's contribution to the English
     critical vocabulary.
1941 "Three Shakespeare Adaptations." Proceedings of the Leeds Philo-
     sophical and Literary Society, Literary and Historical Section,
     VIII (1959), 233-240.
          Dryden's Troilus, Tate's Lear, Theobald's Richard II.
1942 Brown, Richard P. "Antony and Cleopatra and All for Love: a
     Comparison of Two Dramatic Methods." M.A. Indiana Uni-
     versity, 1960.
1943 Cameron, William James. John Dryden in New Zealand: An Ac-
     count of Early Editions of the Writing of John Dryden (1631-
     1700) Found in Various Libraries Throughout New Zealand.
     Wellington Library School, 1960. 32 pp.
          A pamphlet designed to illustrate methods of publicising
     library holdings of rate books.
1944 Fujimura, Thomas H. "The Appeal of Dryden's Heroic Plays."
     Publications of the Modern Language Association, LXXV (1960),
     37-45.
          After criticizing several critics' "unsatisfactory" judgments
     on the appeal of Dryden's heroic plays, Fujimura discusses
     love, honour, cultural primitivism and their harmony with
     Restoration Comedy.
1945 Gallagher, Mary T. "John Dryden's Use of the Classics in His
     Literary Criticism." Ph.D. Northwestern University, 1960.
1946 Hoffman, Arthur W. "Dryden's To Mr. Congreve." Modern Lan-
     guage Notes, LXXV (November, 1960), 553-556.
          Hoffman suggests that Dryden's complimentary epistle
     (1694) to Congreve contains an architectural metaphor that
     refers to the rebuilding of St. Paul's Cathedral.
1947 Hughes, R. E. "Dryden's All for Love: The Sensual Dilemma."
     Drama Critique, III (1960), 68-74.
          Urges a reinvestigation of Restoration tragedy and examines
     All for Love as an example of his theory that Restoration
     tragedy indicted the influence of skepticism on the age by the

use of dilemma. "The crucial scenes of Restoration tragedy are concerned with the inability of the protagonist to choose-- and this inability is the result of skepticism." Also comments briefly on Venice Preserv'd.

1948 King, B. A. "Dryden's Treatment of Ideas and Themes in His Dramatic Works, with Some References to the Intellectual Movements of His Time." Ph.D. University of Leeds, 1960.

1949 Prince, F. T. "Dryden Redivivus." Review of English Literature, I (1960), 71-79.

Reactions to and criticisms of Dryden by T. S. Eliot, Mark Van Doren, and C. S. Lewis are discussed; concludes with a general evaluation of Dryden.

1950 Van Doren, Mark. John Dryden: A Study of His Poetry. Bloom- ington: Indiana University Press, 1960. x, 298 pp.

1951 Wedgewood, C. V. Poetry and Politics under the Stuarts. Cam- bridge: Cambridge University Press, 1960. 220 pp.

Although primarily concerned with pre-Restoration times, these essays provide helpful background readings on the re- lationship between Stuart politics and English poetry. There is extensive coverage of Dryden.

1952 Williamson, George. "The Occasion of An Essay of Dramatic Poesy." Seventeenth-Century Contexts. (London: Faber and Faber, 1960), 272-288.

Attempts to explain the motivation of the Essay "and even its concern with dramatic principles." Deals with specific plays by various authors as well as dramatic principles.

1953 Young, Donald Leroy. "The Reputation of John Dryden, 1895- 1956." Ph.D. Boston University, 1960.

1954 Kirsch, Arthur C. "Dryden's Theory and Practice of the Rhymed Heroic Play." Ph.D. Princeton University, 1961. 248 pp. (Order No. 61-4797).

The first three chapters deal with Dryden's theory; the last two chapters are concerned principally with his practice. Influences upon his theory and practice.

1955 Lavine, Anne Rabiner. "The Bow of Ulysses: Shakespeare's Troilus and Cressida and Its Imitation by Dryden." Ph.D. Bryn Mawr, 1961. 415 pp. (Order No. 62-1).

A study of Dryden's imitation in all its aspects, with spec- ial emphasis on style. Also a study of Dryden's criticism in order to determine some causes for the Restoration practice of adaptation.

1956 Leeman, Richard Kendall. "Corneille and Dryden: Their Theories of Dramatic Poetry." Ph.D. University of Wisconsin, 1961. 445 pp. (Order No. 61-3131).

An examination of their theories shows that they were re-

markably alike in their independence of major neo-Aristotelia
dogmas, especially those concerning dramatic imitation,
dramatic function, and dramatic production.

1957 Mc Fadden, George. "Dryden's 'Most Barren Period' - and Milto
The Huntington Library Quarterly, XXIV (August, 1961), 283-
296.

Deals with the period of adjustment in Dryden's career afte
1674. An examination of Aureng-Zebe discovers the Miltonic
and Vergilian influence Dryden demonstrates in works after
this period.

1958 Singh, Sarup. "Dryden and the Unities." Indian Journal of Englisl
Studies, II (1961), 78-90.

1959 Ward, Charles E. The Life of John Dryden. Raleigh, North
Carolina: University of North Carolina Press, 1961. ix, 380 p
Scholarly work. Each of Dryden's plays receives consider-
ation, as do his theories of drama.

1960 Alssid, Michael W. "The Perfect Conquest: a Study of Theme,
Structure and Characters in Dryden's The Indian Emperor."
Studies in Philology, LIX (1962), 539-559.

Discusses elements which contribute to the play's success
and artistic unity.

1961 Forker, Charles R. "Romeo and Juliet and the 'Cyndus' Speech i
Dryden's All for Love." Notes and Queries, New Ser., IX
(1962), 382-383.

Discussion of similarities between the characters of Cleopatra (Dryden) and Juliet, as well as other parallels between t
two works.

1962 Gagen, Jean [Elizabeth]. "Love and Honor in Dryden's Heroic
Plays." Publications of the Modern Language Association,
LXXVII (1962), 208-220.

A review of the Renaissance humanist's concept of honor a
the concept of Platonic love to show how these affect Dryden's
ideas in The Indian Queen, Aureng-Zebe, Tyrannick Love, Th
Conquest of Granada, The Spanish Fryar, and The Indian
Emperour.

1963 Gibb, Carson. "Figurative Structure in Restoration Comedy."
Ph.D. University of Pennsylvania, 1962. (Order No. 63-4153)
Figurative structure results from the juxtaposition of apparently unrelated actions in selected plays of Dryden, Ethere
and Wycherley.

1964 Hoffman, Arthur W. John Dryden's Imagery. Gainesville: University of Florida Press, 1962. 172 pp.

Considers Dryden's use of the couplet, his use of certain
analogies, and his pattern of monarch images on prologues
and epilogues.

1965 Irie, Keitaro. "The Auxiliary 'Do' in John Dryden's Plays."
       Anglica (Osaka), V (1962), 1-19.

1966 Jeune, Simon. "Hamlet d'Otway, Macbeth de Dryden; ou Shake-
       speare en France en 1714." Revue de littérature comparée,
       XXXVI (1962), 560-564.

1967 King, Bruce. "Don Sebastian: Dryden's Moral Fable." Sewanee
       Review, LXX (1962), 651-670.
            The play is indicative of Dryden's growth toward a fuller
       dramatic form. Discusses the influence of mid-century French
       neo-classical critics in providing Dryden with a moral purpose
       and "thematic organizing principle."

1968 King, Bruce. "Heroic and Mock-Heroic Plays." Sewanee Review,
       LXX (1962), 514-517.
            Dryden's dramatic satire, its implied morality, and attack
       upon Hobbes' theory of natural man.

1969 Kirsch, Arthur C. "Dryden, Corneille, and the Heroic Play."
       Modern Philology, LIX (1962), 248-264.
            A definition of the heroic code of behavior which demonstrates
       a relationship between Dryden and Corneille.

1970 -----. "The Significance of Dryden's Aureng-Zebe." Journal of
       English Literary History, XXIX (1962), 160-174.
            The increased use of sentimental heroes and domestic situa-
       tions and the absence of rhyme in Aureng-Zebe are indicative
       of general changes in serious drama during second decade of
       the Restoration.

1971 Mace, Dean T. "Dryden's Dialogue on Drama." Journal of the
       Warburg and Courtald Institutes, XXV (1962), 87-112.
            On the Essay of Dramatic Poesy. The dispute between two
       aesthetic principles: 1 poetry should be founded on historical
       truth; 2 poetry should ignore the history of things and con-
       centrate on emotional and imaginative effectiveness.

1972 Maxwell, J.C. "Dryden's Epilogue to Oedipus, 11, 5-6."
       Notes and Queries, New Ser., IX (1962), 384-385.
            Line 6 shows an indebtedness to Horace's Ars Poetica,
       lines 38-40.

1973 Reichert, John. "A Note on Buckingham and Dryden." Notes and
       Queries, New Ser., IX (1962), 220.
            Dryden's careless use of letters in Marriage á la Mode led
       Buckingham to satirize the play in The Rehearsal.

1974 van der Welle, J. A. Dryden and Holland. Groningen: J. B.
       Walters, 1962. 153 pp.

1975 Waith, Eugene M. The Herculean Hero in Marlowe, Shakespeare,
       and Dryden. London: Chatto and Windus; New York: Columbia
       University Press, 1962. 224 pp.
            Includes chapters on Conquest of Granada, Aureng-Zebe, and
       All for Love.

1976 Watson, George. The Literary Critics: A Study of English
     Descriptive Criticism. (Pelican Books, A553). Harmonds-
     worth and Baltimore: Penguin Books, 1962. 249 pp.
         Evaluates the critical principles of Dryden and Johnson.
1977 Winterbottom, John A. "Stoicism in Dryden's Tragedies." Journal
     of English and Germanic Philology, LXI (1962), 868-883.
         Dryden's application of the stoic philosophy tempered by
     Christianity in his plays.
1978 Barnard, John. "The Dates of Six Dryden Letters." Philological
     Quarterly, XLII (1963), 396-403.
         Dryden's references to the delayed production of his son's
     play, The Husband his own Cuckhold aid in dating several
     letters to Tonson.
1979 Beckson, Karl, ed. Great Theories in Literary Criticism. (Noon-
     day Paperback 241). New York: Farrar, Straus, 1963. 317 pp.
         Anthology of literary criticism from Aristotle to Arnold.
     Dryden's Essay of Dramatic Poesy included in Chapter 2.
1980 Budick, Sanford Michael. "The Way to Aureng-Zebe: a Study in
     the Development of Form in Dryden's Heroic Plays." Honors
     thesis, Harvard University, 1963. vi, 38 pp.
         Stresses Dryden's originality in imitating the form of the
     heroic play. Asserts that Dryden developed from slavish use
     of the code of honor to the character of Aureng-Zebe, in whom
     individual will and individual consciousness are fused.
1981 Davies, H. Neville. "Dryden, Hobbes, and the Nimble Spaniel."
     Notes and Queries, New Ser., X (1963), 349-350.
         In a reply to George Watson's note (pp. 230-231), Davies
     cites a passage from All for Love to prove that the source of
     Dryden's spaniel images was Hobbes' Leviathan.
1982 Goggin, L. P. "This Bow of Ulysses." Essays and Studies in
     Language and Literature, XXII (1963), 49-86.
         An examination of All for Love as an original work developed
     upon principles expressed in the Essay.
1983 Heise, Howard Sherman. "A Comparative Study of Shakespeare's
     Anthony and Cleopatra and Dryden's All for Love." M.A. Uni-
     versity of South Dakota, 1963.
1984 Illo, John. "Dryden, Sylvester, and the Correspondence of Melan-
     choly Winter and Cold Age." English Language Notes, I (1963),
     101-104.
         Discusses a passage on metaphor from the Dedication of
     The Spanish Friar (1681).
1985 King, Bruce. "Dryden's Intent in All for Love." College English,
     XXIV (1963), 267-271.
         Crucial documents by Dryden before 1678 qualify his state-
     ment in the preface to All for Love that he wrote the play

"for the excellency of the moral."

1986 Klima, S. "Some Unrecorded Borrowings from Shakespeare in
      Dryden's All for Love." Notes and Queries, New Ser., X
      (1963), 415-418.
          Lists borrowings from plays other than Antony and Cleo-
      patra.
1987 Larson, Richard Leslie. "Studies in Dryden's Dramatic Techni-
      que: The Use of Scenes Depicting Persuasion and Accusation."
      Ph.D. Harvard University, 1963.
1988 Moore, Frank Harper. The Nobler Pleasure: Dryden's Comedy
      in Theory and Practice. Chapel Hill: University of North
      Carolina Press, 1963. 264 pp.
          Chronological study of Dryden's comic theory, comedies
      and tragicomedies, and career as a comic writer. Includes
      bibliography and notes.
1989 Nazareth, Peter. "All for Love: Dryden's Hybrid Play." English
      Studies in Africa, VI (1963), 154-163.
1990 Ringler, Richard N. "Two Sources for Dryden's The Indian
      Emperour." Philological Quarterly, XLII (1963), 423-429.
          Evidence of borrowings from Donne's First Anniversarie
      and Spencer's The Fairie Queene suggest the breadth of
      Dryden's literary imagination.
1991 Røstvig, Maren-Sofie, and others. The Hidden Sense and Other
      Essays. (Norwegian Studies in English, No. 9). Oslo: Univer-
      sitetsverlaget; New York: Humanities Press, 1963. 226 pp.
          Contains an essay on Dryden's All for Love by Otto Reinert.
1992 Schilling, Bernard, ed. Dryden: A Collection of Critical Essays.
      Englewood Cliffs, N.J.: Prentice-Hall, 1963. 186 pp.
          Reprints various and significant essays on Dryden scholar-
      ship in the twentieth century. For Dryden's drama, R. J.
      Kaufmann's "On the Poetics of Terminal Tragedy: Dryden's
      All for Love," and Moody E. Prior's "Tragedy and the Heroic
      Play."
1993 Schulz, Max F. "Coleridge's 'Debt' to Dryden and Johnson."
      Notes and Queries, New Ser., X (1963), 189-191.
          Discusses the relationship of Coleridge's Biographia Liter-
      aria to Dryden's An Essay of Dramatic Poesy.
1994 Scott, Sir Walter. The Life of John Dryden. Edited with an Intro-
      duction by Bernard Kreissman. Lincoln, Nebraska: University
      of Nebraska Press, 1963. 471 pp.
          Reproduction of the 1834 edition. Includes notes.
1995 Simon, Irene. "Dryden's Revision of the Essay of Dramatic Poesy."
      Review of English Studies, XIV (1963), 132-141.
          Comparison of the revised Essay with the earlier edition.
      Dryden's alterations make the work more formal and polished

than the first version.

1996 Towers, Tom H. "The Lineage of Shadwell: An Approach to
      MacFlecknoe." Studies in English Literature, 1500-1900,
      III (1963), 323-334.
        Examines the poem as a theatrical document in terms of
      dramatic allusions and structure.

1997 Verrall, A.W. Lectures on Dryden. New York: Russell and
      Russell, 1963.

1998 Waith, Eugene M. "The Voice of Mr. Bayes." Studies in English
      Literature, 1500-1900, III (1963), 335-343.
        Investigates Dryden's attitude toward his protagonists,
      patrons and audience. The voice of Bayes in The Rehearsal is
      a part of Dryden's rhetorical strategy.

1999 Watson, George. "Dryden's First Answer to Rymer." Review of
      English Studies, XIV (1963), 17-23.
        One of Dryden's most "rewarding" statements on drama.
      Tonson's text of the "Heads of an Answer to Rymer" is "the
      one critical document in English between the Restoration and
      Johnson's Shakespeare in which the Poetics of Aristotle are
      attacked frontally and without qualification."

2000 Zebouni, Selma Assir. "The Hero in Dryden's Heroic Tragedy:
      A Revaluation." Ph.D. Louisiana State University, 1963.
      (Order No. 64-169).
        A definition of Dryden's heroes in relation to the contem-
      porary intellectual and historical milieu and to Dryden's own
      psychological evolution demonstrates that heroic tragedy is
      not outside the main course of English literature, but rather
      an important link in the evolution of English drama.

2001 Bately, Janet M. "Dryden's Revisions in the Essay of Dramatic
      Poesy: The Preposition at the End of the Sentence and the Ex-
      pression of the Relative." The Review of English Studies, XV
      (1964), 268-282.
        Corrections made by Dryden for the edition of 1684 evidence
      his consciousness of "correct" language.

2002 Caracciolo, Peter. "Some Unrecorded Variants in the First Edition
      of Dryden's All for Love, 1678." Book Collector, XIII (1964),
      498-500.
        Notes variant readings in the extant copies of the first quarto
      of the play.

2003 Cooke, M. G. "The Restoration Ethos of Byron's Classical Plays."
      Publications of the Modern Language Association, LXXIX (1964),
      569-578.
        Byron's classicism is the classicism of the Restoration.
      His theories and practice of drama are dependent especially
      on Dryden. Includes extensive comparison of Byron's Sardanapa

with Dryden's All for Love, and illustrates some of Byron's
borrowings from Otway's Venice Preserv'd for his Marino
Faliero.

2004   King, Bruce. "The Significance of Dryden's State of Innocence."
Studies in English Literature, 1500-1900, IV (1964), 371-
391.

Examines The State of Innocence as a philosophical work
concerned with "the moral disobedience which results from
the nature of man's appetite, pride, and unrest."

2005   Kirsch, Arthur C. "An Essay on Dramatick Poetry (1681)."
Huntington Library Quarterly, XXVIII (1964), 89-91.

Quotes a brief essay affixed to a translation of Madeleine
de Scudéry which praises Dryden as the leading dramatist
of the age.

2006   Legouis, Pierre. "Ouvrages recents sur Dryden." Etudes
Anglaises, XVII (1964), 148-158.

Reviews six scholarly studies which affirm the vitality of
Dryden's art.

2007   Loftis, John. "The Hispanic Element in Dryden." Emory University Quarterly, XX (1964), 90-100.

The influence of Lope de Vega, Camoens, and especially
of Calderon on Dryden's comedies and heroic plays. Reviews
previous scholarship on the question of Hispanic influence.

2008   McFadden, George. "Dryden and the Numbers of His Native
Tongue." Essays and Studies in Language and Literature.
Edited by Herbert H. Petit. (Pittsburgh: Duquesne Press,
1964), 87-109.

On sound patterns in Dryden's dramatic speeches and songs.

2009   McNamara, Peter Lance. "John Dryden's Contribution to the English Comic Tradition of Witty Love-Play." Ph.D. Tulane University, 1964. (Order No. 65-2517).

Examines Dryden's comedies and subsequent reputation as
a playwright in light of his interest in Fletcher and other
comedians in the love-play tradition.

2010   Monk, Samuel Holt. "Dryden and the Beginnings of Shakespeare
Criticism in the Augustan Age." The Persistence of Shakespeare Idolatry: Essays in Honor of Robert W. Babcock.
Edited by Herbert M. Schueller. (Detroit: Wayne State University Press, 1964), 47-75.

A reexamination of Dryden's criticism of Shakespeare.
"Dryden's generous praise of Shakespeare and his honest confronting of what seemed the faults of the father of the English
stage set the pattern of Shakespeare criticism for subsequent
generations."

2011   Price, Martin. To the Palace of Wisdom: Studies in Order and

Energy from Dryden to Blake. Garden City, New York: Doubleday anc Company, 1964. 465 pp.

Chapter II, "Dryden and Dialectic," concerns Dryden's use
of the heroic couplet and his concept of order in the heroic
plays.

2012 Starnes, D. T. "Imitation of Shakespeare in Dryden's All For Love
Texas Studies in Literature and Language, VI (1964), 39-46.

Contends that Dryden's imitation is not restricted solely to
Antony and Cleopatra. Passages in All For Love may be traced
to The Merchant of Venice, Julius Caesar, As You Like It, and
Macbeth. Moreover, some of the play's imagery is derived from
Othello, and its scene iii is a lengthy imitation of Coriolanus,
V, iii.

2013 Sutherland, James R. "The Date of James Howard's All Mistaken,
or, The Mad Couple." Notes and Queries, New Ser., XI (1964),
339-340.

Fixes the date of Howard's comedy at 1665 and posits the
theory that Dryden's Secret Love; or, The Maiden Queen was
substantially derived from it.

2014 Wasserman, George R. John Dryden. New York: Twayne Publishers
Inc., 1964.

Biographical and critical study of Dryden's life and works.
Chapter III, "Essays on Dramatic and Heroic Poetry," and
Chapter IV, "Comedy and Tragedy," are of special interest.
Includes selected bibliography.

2015 Alssid, Michael W. "The Design of Dryden's Aureng-Zebe."
Journal of English and Germanic Philology, LXIV (1965), 452-
469.

Examines the structural design, thematic unity, characterization, patterns of imagery and metaphor, and Dryden's develop
ment of epic materials in the play.

2016 Archer, Stanley Louis. "John Dryden and the Earl of Dorset."
Ph.D. The University of Mississippi, 1965. (Order No. 65-
6872).

Analyzes the relationship between Dryden and his patron.
Attention is directed to Dryden's reasons for dedicating the
Essay of Dramatic Poesy (1668) to the Earl.

2017 Bacon, David Lee. "Matter and Body-Soul Imagery in Dryden
and Rochester." Honors Thesis. Harvard University, 1965.
43 pp.

Studies aspects of order which Dryden and Rochester
discover in man and in the universe and which they express
through the use of matter and body-soul imagery. Although
primarily concerned with poems, Dryden's plays are discussed
passim.

2018 Bately, Janet M. "Dryden and Branded Words." Notes and
      Queries, New Ser., XII (1965), 134-139.
           Explains vocabulary discrepancies between the first and
      second editions of the Essay of Dramatic Poesy.
2019 Bradbrook, M. C. English Dramatic Form: A History of its
      Development. London: Chatto and Windus, 1965. 205 pp.
           Chapter VI, "Prisoners and Politics: The Social Image
      from Shakespeare to Dryden," contains a discussion of Dry-
      den's heroic plays.
2020 Coleman, Mark Carney. "Structure and Characterization in Dry-
      den's Shakespearean Tragedy: a Confict of Traditions." Honors
      Thesis. Harvard University, 1965. vi, 44 pp.
           Studies The Tempest, All for Love, and Troilus and Cressida
      to show how Dryden's experience as a dramatist and his know-
      ledge of critical theory were both strong and often conflicting
      influences in the reshaping of the Shakespearean material.
2021 Davies, H. Neville. "Dryden's All For Love and Thomas May's
      The Tragedie of Cleopatra Queen of Aegypt." Notes and
      Queries, New Ser., XII (1965), 139-144.
           A review of Dryden's sources for All For Love and a study
      of his indebtedness to May's play (acted 1626, published 1639
      and 1654) for his first act and perhaps also for his conclusion.
2022 Davies, H. N. "Dryden's Libretti in the Light of 17th-Century
      Ideas About Words and Music." M.A. University of Liverpool,
      1965.
2023 Jackson, Wallace. "Dryden's Emperor and Lillo's Merchant: the
      Relevant Bases of Action." Modern Language Quarterly, XXVI
      (1965), 536-544.
           Desires a more closely unified approach to the drama of the
      late seventeenth and early eighteenth centuries. A fundamental-
      ly similar set of assumptions concerning the primacy of social
      contract governs the actions and characters of Dryden's All
      for Love and Lillo's The London Merchant.
2024 Jefferson, D. W. "'All, all of a piece throughout': Thoughts on
      Dryden's Dramatic Poetry." Restoration Theatre. Edited by
      John Russell Brown and Bernard Harris. (Stratford-Upon-
      Avon Studies, 6). (London: Edward Arnold, 1965; New York:
      St. Martin's Press, 1965), 159-176.
           The repetition of words, images, and themes demonstrates
      the interrelationships of Dryden's heroic plays.
2025 King, Bruce. "Absalom and Dryden's Earlier Praise of Monmouth."
      English Studies, XLVI (1965), 332-333.
           Notes an ironic contrast between the dedication of Tyrannic
      Love to Monmouth in 1670 and Dryden's allusion to it in Absalom
      and Achitophel eleven years later.

2026 -----. "Anti-Whig Satire in The Duke of Guise." English Language
    Notes, II (1965), 190-193.
        Offers three possible sources for the Whig propaganda in the
    play: The anonymous A Letter from a Person of Quality to his
    Friend Concerning His Majesties late Declaration, Shadwell's
    Epistle to the Tories, and Filmer's Patriarchia.

2027 -----. "Dryden, Tillotson, and Tyrannic Love." Review of Eng-
    lish Studies, XVI (1965), 364-377.
        Parallels between St. Catherine's speeches in Tyrannic
    Love and Tillotson's early sermons, especially The Excellency
    of the Christian Religion suggest that, at the time of the play,
    Dryden was a Latitudinarian Anglican and influenced by Tillot-
    son's attempt to give faith a logical basis.

2028 -----. "Dryden's Marriage à la Mode." Drama Survey, IV (1965),
    28-37.
        The brilliance of the play derives from "an extended com-
    parison between fashionable Restoration society and Thomas
    Hobbes' theory that man in his natural state is permanently at
    war to conquer the property of others."

2029 Kirsch, Arthur C. Dryden's Heroic Drama. Princeton: Princeton
    University Press, 1965. 157 pp.
        The perennial interest in Dryden's plays rests in their
    fluidity. Dryden's theory of the heroic play, his concept of the
    hero, and his stage practice were modified frequently to meet
    the demands of a transitional society.

2030 Martin Clare, M. F. "Studies in Dryden's Criticism, with Parti-
    cular Reference to His Critical Terminology and to Certain
    Aspects of His Dramatic Theory and Practice." B.Litt. Oxford
    University (Lady Margaret Hall), 1965.

2031 Osborn, James M. John Dryden: Some Biographical Facts and
    Problems. Revised Edition. Gainesville: University of Florida
    Press, 1965. 316 pp.
        A revised edition of the 1940 biography of Dryden. Chapter
    VII surveys Dryden scholarship during the past twenty-five
    years, with particular attention to the work of Kinsley, Mac-
    donald, Ward, Noyes, and Young.

2032 Palmer, Roderick. "Treatments of Antony and Cleopatra."
    CEA Critic, XXVII (1965), iv, 8-9.

2033 Roper, Alan. Dryden's Poetic Kingdoms. New York: Barnes and
    Noble, Inc., 1965.
        Fundamentally a study of Absalom and Achitophel, one
    chapter, "The Kingdom of Letters," refers to Dryden's drama
    and to his correspondence with fellow playwrights.

2034 Weinbrot, Howard D. "Robert Gould: Some Borrowings from
    Dryden." English Language Notes, III (1965), 36-40.

Cites passages in Gould's 'The Playhouse' which manifest
an indebtedness to Dryden's All for Love, The Conquest of
Granada, and Essay of Dramatick Poesy.

2035 West, Michael Davidson. "Dryden's Attitude Toward the Hero."
Ph.D. Harvard University, 1965.

2036 Williamson, George. "Dryden's View of Milton." Milton and
Others (London, 1965), 103-121.

A compilation of Dryden's statements on the limitations
of the Miltonic epic form; its inferiority to the heroic play
in certain dramatic respects.

2037 Zebouni, Selma Assir. Dryden: A Study in Heroic Characterization. Baton Rouge: Louisiana State University Press, 1965.
111 pp.

The protagonist of a Dryden heroic tragedy is not, as has
been previously thought, an egotist possessing superhuman
courage and an all-consuming desire for power. He is rather
an archetypal figure embodying "common sense and order."
A product of the cultural milieu and Dryden's own psychological development, he shares certain characteristics with the
Cornelian hero.

2038 Archer, Stanley. "The Persons in An Essay of Dramatic Poesy."
Papers on Language and Literature, II (1966), 305-314.

Dryden intended the person to represent coherent critical
positions, but the characters do more nearly correspond to
the originals suggested by Malone than recent critics and
editors acknowledge.

2039 Bredvold, Louis I. "Dryden, Hobbes, and the Royal Society."
Essential Articles for the Study of John Dryden. The Essential
Articles Series. Edited by H.T. Swedenberg, Jr. (Hamden,
Connecticut: Archon Books, 1966), 314-340.

Reprinted from Modern Philology, XXV (1928), 417-438.
Dryden's sympathetic interest in the Royal Society and the
new science. Includes references to The Rival Ladies and
The Conquest of Granada.

2040 -----. "Political Aspects of Dryden's Amboyna and The Spanish
Fryar." Essential Articles for the Study of John Dryden. The
Essential Articles Series. Edited by H. T. Swedenberg, Jr.
(Hamden, Connecticut: Archon Books, 1966), 300-313.

Reprinted from University of Michigan Publications, Language
and Literature, VIII (1932), 119-132. A revaluation of his supposed
political activities and changes during the time in which he wrote
these plays reveals that Dryden was a firm, consistent, and
loyal Tory.

2041 Brower, Reuben Arthur. "Dryden's Epic Manner and Virgil."
Essential Articles for the Study of John Dryden. The Essential

Articles Series. Edited by H. T. Swedenberg, Jr. (Hamden,
Connecticut: Archon Books, 1966), 466-492.

    Reprinted from PMLA, LV (1940), 119-138. The influence
of Virgil's epic style on Dryden's works. Includes a discussion
of the epic tone in The Conquest of Granada and Aureng-Zebe.

2042 Doyle, Anne. "Dryden's Authorship of Notes and Observations on
The Empress of Morocco (1674)." Studies in English Literature,
1500-1900, VI (1966), 421-445.

    Reviews the dispute over the authorship of the attack on
Elkanah Settle's play, and contends that only the Preface and
Postscript can be ascribed to Dryden with certainty.

2043 Emery, John P. "Restoration Dualism of the Court Writers."
Révue des Langues Vivantes, XXXII, iii (1966), 238-265.

    Includes study of the plays of Buckingham, Rochester,
Etherege, and Wycherley, among others.

2044 Feder, Lillian. "John Dryden's Use of Classical Rhetoric." Es-
sential Articles for the Study of John Dryden. The Essential
Articles Series. Edited by H. T. Swedenberg, Jr. (Hamden,
Connecticut: Archon Books, 1966), 493-518.

    Reprinted from PMLA, LXIX (1954), 1258-1278. In his
criticism and poetry Dryden adopted principles of classical
rhetoric to the needs of his own time and to his talents.

2045 Golden, Samuel A. "Dryden's 'Cleomenes' and Theophilus Parsons.'
Notes and Queries, New Ser., XIII (1966), 380.

    Theophilus Parsons, author of the prefatory poem to Dry-
den's Cleomenes (1693) was a first cousin of Nahum Tate.

2046 Hemphill, George. "Dryden's Heroic Line." Essential Articles
for the Study of John Dryden. The Essential Articles Series.
Edited by H. T. Swedenberg, Jr. (Hamden, Connecticut: Archon
Books, 1966), 519-540.

    Reprinted from PMLA, LXXII (1957), 863-879. A study of
Dryden's prosody includes occasional references to his statements in the Essay on Dramatic Poesy and to his plays.

2047 Huntley, Frank Livingstone. "Dryden, Rochester, and the Eighth
Satire of Juvenal." Essential Articles for the Study of John
Dryden. The Essential Articles Series. Edited by H. T. Sweden-
berg, Jr. (Hamden, Connecticut: Archon Books, 1966), 91-111.

    Reprinted from Philological Quarterly, XVIII (1939), 269-
284. The Preface to All for Love is "a piece of epideictic
rhetoric devoted to a censure of Rochester" and is more significant as rhetoric than as criticism.

2048 -----. "On the Persons in Dryden's Essay of Dramatic Poesy."
Essential Articles for the Study of John Dryden. The Essential
Articles Series. Edited by H. T. Swedenberg, Jr. (Hamden,
Connecticut: Archon Books, 1966), 83-90.

Reprinted from Modern Language Notes, LXIII (1948),
88-95. Criticizes Malone's identification of Dryden's four
speakers and discusses them as embodiments of attitude
necessitated by the argument.

2049 Jefferson, D. W. "The Significance of Dryden's Heroic Plays."
Restoration Drama: Modern Essays in Criticism. (A Galaxy
Book). Edited by John Loftis. (New York: Oxford University
Press, 1966), 161-179.

Reprinted from Proceedings of The Leeds Philosophical
and Literary Society, V (1940), 125-139. Dryden's "comic"
purpose in the heroic plays helped to develop the qualities
which later made him a superb satirist.

2050 -----. "The Significance of Dryden's Heroic Plays." Restoration
Dramatists. A Collection of Critical Essays. Edited by Earl
Miner. (Englewood Cliffs, New Jersey: Prentice-Hall, Inc.,
1966), 19-35.

This essay appeared in Proceedings of the Leeds Philosophical and Literary Society, V (1940), 125-139.

2051 Jensen, Harvey James. "A Glossary of John Dryden's Critical
Terms." Ph.D. Cornell University, 1966. (Order No. 67-1471).

Definitions of critical terms drawn from George Watson's
Of Dramatic Poesy and Other Critical Essays and the Scott-
Saintsbury edition of Dryden's Works.

2052 Kallich, Martin. "Oedipus: from Man to Archetype." Comparative
Literature Studies, III (1966), 33-46.

Studies the several meanings of the Oedipus myth from
Sophocles to Cocteau and discusses the unusual sentimental
interpretation by Dryden and Lee in Oedipus (1678).

2053 King, Bruce. Dryden's Major Plays. Edinburgh and London:
Oliver and Boyd, 1966. 215 pp.

An interpretation of the individual plays that attempts to
demonstrate "how the same intelligence that worked through
wit and humour in the heroic plays was striving to express
itself in a more serious manner in the later moral fables."
Also traces the intellectual background of Dryden's themes and
his approach to the literary fashions of his day.

2054 Kirsch, Arthur C. "The Significance of Dryden's Aureng-Zebe."
Restoration Drama: Modern Essays in Criticism. (A Galaxy
Book). Edited by John Loftis. (New York: Oxford University
Press, 1966), 180-194.

Reprinted from A Journal of English Literary History, XXIX
(1962), 160-175. The increased use of sentimental heroes and
domestic situations and the absence of rhyme in Aureng-Zebe
are indicative of general changes in serious drama during the
second decade of the Restoration.

2055 -----. "The Significance of Dryden's Aureng-Zebe." Resto-
     ration Dramatists. A Collection of Critical Essays. Edited
     by Earl Miner. (Englewood Cliffs, New Jersey: Prentice-Hall,
     Inc., 1966), 37-49.
          Taken from English Literary History, XXIX (1962), 160-
     175.
2056 Krupp, Kathleen McCoy. "John Dryden on the Function of Drama."
     Ph.D. Florida State University, 1966. (Order No. 67-298).
          While Dryden accepted the "utile" and "dulci" ideas of
     Horace, his critical discussions of comedy, tragedy, and the
     heroic play reveal that he was most interested in the pleasur-
     able emotional effects of plays.
2057 Loftis, John. "Exploration and Enlightenment: Dryden's The Indian
     Emperour and its Backgrounds." Philological Quarterly, XLV
     (1966), 71-84.
          The intellectual dimensions of exploration presented in the
     play include a dramatic elucidation of 17th-century ideas on
     primitivism, religion, and political theory, and enable Dryden
     to expose irrationalities of European beliefs.
2058 Novarr, David. "Swift's Relation with Dryden and Gulliver's
     Annus Mirabilis." English Studies, XLVII (1966), 341-354.
          Concerned primarily with the relationship between Gulliver's
     Travels and Annus Mirabilis, the article makes occasional
     references to Swift's regard for Dryden's playwriting.
2059 Novak, Maximillian E. "The Demonology of Dryden's Tyrannick
     Love and 'Anti-Scot.'" English Language Notes, IV (1966),
     95-98.
          The demonic lovers, Nakar and Damilcar, of Dryden's
     play are traced to A Discourse Concerning the Nature and
     Substance of Devils and Spirits in Reginald Scot's Discovery
     of Witchcraft (1665).
2060 Shergold, N. D., and Peter Ure. "Dryden and Calderon: A New
     Spanish Source for The Indian Emperor." Modern Language
     Review, LXI (1966), 369-383.
          The influence of Calderon's El principe constante on the
     plot, dialogue, and heroic themes of Dryden's play.
2061 Sherwood, John C. "Dryden and the Critical Theories of Tasso."
     Comparative Literature, XVIII (1966), 351-359.
          Dryden was influenced by Tasso for his conception of the
     heroic play and for his approach to the problem of reconciling
     native and classical traditions in drama.
2062 Sherwood, Margaret. Dryden's Dramatic Theory and Practice.
     New York: Russell and Russell, 1966. 110 pp.
          A reissue of the work first published in 1898. One chapter
     discusses Dryden's theories; three succeeding chapters then

apply the theories to his comedies, heroic plays, and tragedies.
2063 Smith, David Nichol. John Dryden. Hamden, Connecticut: Archon
Books, 1966. 93 pp.
A reprint of the original edition of 1950, the book contains
four lectures on Dryden's work delivered at Cambridge in 1948.
Chapter Two deals with Dryden's plays.
2064 Teeter, Louis. "The Dramatic Use of Hobbes's Political Ideas."
Essential Articles for the Study of John Dryden. Edited by H.
T. Swedenberg, Jr. (Hamden, Connecticut: Archon Books, 1966),
341-373.
Reprinted from English Literary History, III (1936), 140-169.
The influence of Hobbes' political ideas on the Restoration drama
was, like Machiavelli's on the Elizabethan, almost completely
theatrical.
2065 Thale, Mary. "Dryden's Critical Vocabulary: The Imitation of
Nature." Papers on Language and Literature, II (1966), 315-326.
Examines the phrase's origin, significations, functions, and
frequency of occurrence to illuminate Dryden's argumentative
techniques and critical ideas. The concept is the principal means
by which Dryden achieves the reconciliation of ancient and modern,
foreign and domestic, poetry and painting, art and science.
2066 -----. "Dryden's Dramatic Criticism: Polestar of the Ancients."
Comparative Literature, XVIII (1966), 36-54.
In his approach to the Ancients for his criticism of modern
dramatic theory and practice Dryden supplemented and reinterpreted classical dramatic theory, appealed to classical non-
dramatic sources, and emphasized a concept of the imitation of
nature.
2067 Trowbridge, Hoyt. "The Place of Rules in Dryden's Criticism."
Essential Articles for the Study of John Dryden. Edited by H. T.
Swedenberg, Jr. (Hamden, Connecticut: Archon Books, 1966),
112-134.
Reprinted from Modern Philology, XLIV (1946), 84-96.
2068 Waith, Eugene M. "All for Love." Restoration Dramatists: A
Collection of Critical Essays. Edited by Earl Miner. (Engle-
wood Cliffs, New Jersey: Prentice Hall, Inc., 1966), 51-62.
From The Herculean Hero (New York: Columbia University
Press, 1962). The resemblances that bind All for Love to its
predecessors, The Conquest of Granada and Aureng-Zebe, are
very strong.
2069 Wallerstein, Ruth. "Dryden and the Analysis of Shakespeare's
Techniques." Essential Articles for the Study of John Dryden.
The Essential Articles Series. Edited by H. T. Swendenberg, Jr.
(Hamden, Connecticut: Archon Books, 1966), 551-575.
Reprinted from Review of English Studies, XIX (1943), 165-

185. Analyzes Dryden's conception of poetry as it is defined
in his "imitation" of Shakespeare in All for Love.

2070 Williamson, George. "The Occasion of An Essay of Dramatic
Poesy." Essential Articles for the Study of John Dryden. Edited
by H. T. Swedenberg, Jr. (Hamden, Connecticut: Archon Books,
1966), 65-82.

Reprinted from Modern Philology, XLIV (1946), 1-9. Studies
the relationship of Samuel Sorbère and Thomas Sprat to Dryden
Essay.

2071 Winterbottom, John A. "The Place of Hobbesian Ideas in Dryden's
Tragedies." Essential Articles for the Studies of John Dryden.
Edited by H. T. Swedenberg, Jr. (Hamden, Connecticut: Archor
Books, 1966), 374-394.

Reprinted from Journal of English and Germanic Philology,
LVII (1958), 665-683. Although Hobbesian ideas are present in
the tragedies, they are not espoused by Dryden himself; other
lines of thought provide a more plausible philosophical basis
for the plays.

2072 Allen, Ned Bliss. The Sources of John Dryden's Comedies. New
York: Gordian Press, 1967. 298 pp.

A reprint of the 1935 edition, chapters discuss The Wild
Gallant, The Rival Ladies, the tragi-comedies, and Dryden's
adaptations of Molière.

2073 Alssid, Michael W. "Shadwell's MacFlecknoe." Studies in English Literature, 1500-1900, VII (1967), 387-402.

In MacFlecknoe Dryden subverted Shadwell's critical ideas
and dramatic practice and "deliberately and ironically metamorphosed Shadwell into a humors character to show us a fool
who, like the humors of his plays, persistently incriminates
himself."

2074 Archer, Stanley. "Dryden's MacFlecknoe." The Explicator, XXVI
(December, 1967), Item No. 37.

"Aston Hall" in line 48 may refer to Santon Hall, Shadwell's
birthplace near Norwich.

2075 Banks, Landrum. "The Imagery of Dryden's Rhymed Heroic Dram
Ph.D. University of Tennessee, 1967. (Order No. 68-9790).

Analyzes the special imagery Dryden created for this specia
genre. Although classical analogies and comparisons are occasionally used to elevate the style, Dryden relies heavily on
traditional associations from the common experiences and the
everyday world of the ordinary man.

2076 Biddle, Evelyn Q. "A Critical Study of the Influence of the Classical and Christian Traditions Upon the Character of the Hero
as Revealed Through Concepts of 'Love' and 'Honor' in Three
Restoration Heroic Tragedies." Ph.D. University of Southern

California, 1967. (Order No. 67-6491).

Considers Orrery's Henry V, Dryden's The Conquest of Granada, and Settle's The Empress of Morocco.

2077 Blackwell, Herbert Robinson. "Some Formulary Characteristics of John Dryden's Comedies." Ph.D. University of Virginia, 1967. (Order No. 67-17,589).

Studies Dryden's use of farce, stage conventions, stock characters, and rhetoric in the comedies.

2078 Davies, H. Neville. "Dryden's All for Love and Sedley's Antony and Cleopatra." Notes and Queries, XIV (1967), 221-227.

Dryden's borrowings from Sedley's work show not only that Dryden is the more skillful dramatist but also that he was consciously "working up" promising material from Sedley's 1677 play.

2079 Dobrée, Bonamy. Variety of Ways: Discussions on Six Authors. Freeport, New York: Books for Libraries Press, 1967. 118 pp.

A reprint of the 1932 edition includes discussions of Congreve, Dryden and Steele.

2080 Falle, George. "Sir Walter Scott as Editor of Dryden and Swift." University of Toronto Quarterly, XXXVI (1967), 161-180.

Discusses Scott's editorial limitations and virtues and analyzes the editions to show why the Dryden is to be preferred to the Swift.

2081 "Dryden's Ark: The Influence of Filmer" Studies in English Literature, 1500-1900, VII (1967), 403-414.

Dryden probably found his favorite image for the Restoration, Noah's ark, in the political theories of Sir Robert Filmer. Reference to Filmer's theories may be found in several plays: The Unhappy Favorite, Oedipus, Don Sebastian, and The Spanish Friar.

2082 Martin, Leslie Howard, Jr. "Conventions of the French Romances in the Drama of John Dryden." Ph.D. Stanford University, 1967. (Order No. 67-11, 953).

Examines parallels in epic theory, theme, and conventions of action and characterization in Dryden's plays and Madeleine de Scudery's Ibrahim, Almahide, and Grand Cyrus.

2083 Miner, Earl. Dryden's Poetry. Bloomington: Indiana University Press, 1967. 354 pp.

A study of Dryden's major poetry that combines scholarly and critical approaches. Chapter II treats All for Love.

2084 Moore, F. H. "The Composition of Sir Martin Mar-All." Essays in English Literature of the Classical Period Presented to Dougald MacMillan. Edited by Daniel W. Patterson and Albrecht

B. Strauss. Studies in Philology, (Extra Series, January, 1967), pp. 27-38.

Discusses the peculiarities of the play and how these may be accounted for as traces of an imperfectly coordinated collaboration between Dryden and the Duke of Newcastle.

2085 Mullin, Joseph Eugene. "The Occasion, Form, Structure, and Design of John Dryden's MacFlecknoe: A Varronian Satire." Ph.D. Ohio State University, 1967. (Order No. 68-3036).

Studies Dryden's use of Varronian satire which centers on some single-mindedness, enthusiastic about its own learning, hypnotized by its own know-how, excited by its own ambitions and lurid fantasies, and crazed by its own hopes for glory.

2086 Nicoll, Allardyce. Dryden and His Poetry. New York: Russell and Russell, 1967. 152 pp.

A reissue of the 1923 edition. Includes commentary on prologues, songs, and epilogues from Dryden's plays.

2087 Pendlebury, Bevin John. Dryden's Heroic Plays: A Study of the Origins. New York: Russell and Russell, 1967. 138 pp.

A reissue of the 1923 edition which examines the heroic tradition before Dryden, his dramatic theory, and the development of the English heroic play.

2088 Staves, Sarah Susan. "Studies in the Comedy of John Dryden." Ph.D. University of Virginia, 1967. (Order No. 67-17,624).

A doubleness of mind is reflected in the structure of the comedies: Dryden affirms traditional values but is too interested in the new science and new philosophy to let scepticism alone.

2089 Swedenberg, H. T., Jr. "Dryden's Obsessive Concern With the Heroic." Essays in English Literature of the Classical Period Presented to Dougald MacMillan. Edited by Daniel W. Patterson and Albrecht B. Strauss. Studies in Philology, (Extra Series, January, 1967), pp. 12-26.

An analysis of Dryden's interest in the heroic begins with a study of An Essay of Dramatic Poesy.

2090 Taylor, Aline Mackenzie. "Dryden's 'Enchanted Isle' and Shadwell's 'Dominion.'" Essays in English Literature of the Classical Period Presented to Dougald MacMillan. Edited by Daniel W. Patterson and Albrecht B. Strauss. Studies in Philology, (Extra Series, January, 1967), 39-53.

Explains Dryden's reference to Barbados in 1.140 of Mac-Flecknoe as part of his angry reaction to Shadwell's successful operatic revision of The Tempest.

2091 Ward, Charles E. and H. T. Swedenberg. John Dryden: Papers Read at a Clark Library Seminar, February 25, 1967. Introduction by John Loftis. Los Angeles: Clark Memorial Library, 1967.

Charles E. Ward discusses "Challenges to Dryden's Biographer"; H. T. Swedenberg, "Challenges to Dryden's Editor."

2092 Weinbrot, Howard D. "Alexas in All for Love: His Genealogy and Function." Studies in Philology, LXIV (1967), 625-639.

Dryden borrowed the eunuch from several earlier plays and Roman histories, but only in All for Love does the character contribute to a vividly felt contest of good and evil and demonstrate the greater nobility of the protagonists.

Dublin

2093 Stockwell, La Tourette. "The Dublin Theatre, 1637-1820." Ph.D. Radcliff College, 1936.

Duelling

2094 Graves, Thornton S. "The Stage Sword and Daggers." South Atlantic Quarterly, XX (1921), 201-212.

An anecdotal history of duels and hand-to-hand struggles on the stage. Primarily concerned with Restoration and 18th-century English drama.

2095 Aylward, J. D. "Duelling in the XVIII Century." Notes and Queries, CLXXXVIII (August 11, 1945), 46-48.

Recounts the Garrick-Baddeley duel in 1700 and the Sheridan-Matthews duel of 1772, and refers to the duels in the drama of the period.

Duffet, Thomas

2096 Haywood, Charles. "The Songs and Masques in the New Tempest: An Incident in the Battle of the Two Theaters, 1674." Huntington Library Quarterly, XIX (1955), 39-56.

Prints the text of The Songs and Masques in the New Tempest and discusses the two versions, one at the Huntington, one at the Folger. Haywood compares them and attempts to illuminate the struggle between the Duke's and King's players. The King's Company used Thomas Duffett to burlesque Shadwell's Songs and Masques . . .

2097 Cameron, Kenneth M. "Duffett's New Poems and Vacation Plays." Theatre Survey, V (1964), 64-70.

Thomas Duffett's New Poems, Songs, Prologues and Epilogues (London, 1676) not only provides a record of the so-called Duchess of Portsmouth's company, but also gives information

on the vacation performances by the hirelings of the Theatre
Royal.

2098 Lewis, Peter Elvet. "The Three Dramatic Burlesques of Thomas
        Duffett." Durham University Journal, LVIII (1966), 149-156.
            Duffett's plays were "burlesques of specific dramatic pro-
        ductions rather than satires of a particular mode of writing.

Dumb Show

2099 Gibbs, Lloyd G. "A History of the Development of the Dumb Show
        As a Dramatic Convention." Ph.D. University of South Carolina
        1959.

D'Urfey, Thomas

songs

2100 D'Urfey, Thomas. Songs, Selected and Edited by Cyrus Lawrence
        Day. Cambridge: Harvard University Press, 1933. x, 168 pp.
            The introduction (pp. 3-44) covers D'Urfey's life and
        writings; it is followed by 36 songs (some with facsimiles of
        music) and textual and explanatory notes.

essay

2101 -----. Preface to "The Campaigners, 1698. Edited, with Preface
        to the Translation of Bossuet's "Maxims and Reflections upon
        Plays, 1699," by Joseph Wood Krutch. Ann Arbor: The Augusta
        Reprint Society, 1948.
            A facsimile text. D'Urfey's Preface is a response to Col-
        lier's attack. The Preface to Bossuet argues that efforts to
        reform the stage are doomed: the theatre must be completely
        outlawed.

individual plays

2102 Vaughan, Jack Alfred. "Thomas D'Urfey's A Fond Husband: An
        Edition and Critical Study." Ph.D. University of Denver,
        1964. (Order No. 64-13, 176).
            Critical commentary on 32 other dramatic works of D'Urfey
        supplement the general introduction to The Fond Husband.

2103 D'Urfey, Thomas. A Fool's Preferment or, the Three Dukes of
        Dunstable. London: Printed for J. Knight and F. Saunders,
        1688. Forsythe, R. A. A Study of the Plays of Thomas D'Urfey
        Part 2. 1917.

Reprinted, Cleveland, Ohio, Western Reserve University
Press, 1917. Text based on the 1688 quarto; except for long
s's and minor typographical irregularities, an exact reproduction, with errors noted but not corrected.

2104 Sanville, Donald W. "Thomas D'Urfey's Love for Money, or, the
Boarding School; An Edition, with Introduction and Notes."
Ph.D. University of Pennsylvania, 1950. 193 pp. (Publication
No. 1913).

This is a critical edition of D'Urfey's play (1691), collated
with the second edition of 1696.

2105 Biswanger, Raymond A., Jr. "Thomas D'Urfey's The Richmond
Heiress or, A Woman Once in the Right: An Edition with Introduction and Notes." Ph.D. University of Pennsylvania, 1951.
287 pp. (Publication No. 2699).

This is a critical edition based on the first edition of 1693
and collated with the second of 1718.

2106 Carpenter, William E., Jr. An Edition of Thomas D'Urfey's The
Virtuous Wife." Ph.D. University of Kansas, 1967. (Order
No. 68-571).

The Virtuous Wife, first produced in 1679, is one of D'Urfey's
better plays and provides a lively presentation of his themes and
techniques.

2107 D'Urfey, Thomas. Wonders in the Sun; or, The Kingdom of the
Birds (1706). With an Introduction by William W. Appleton.
Los Angeles: Clark Memorial Library, University of California,
Los Angeles, 1964. 71 pp.

A facsimile reproduction of the Tonson edition of the comic
opera. (No. 104 in the Augustan Reprint series).

biography and criticism

2108 Hutchinson, William G. "Tom D'Urfey." Macmillan's Magazine,
LXXXV (November, 1901), 61-69.

A short summary of D'Urfey's life and works, in a popular
vein, with concentration more on his works as a poet than as
a dramatist. Stresses how D'Urfey amused his generation.

2109 Forsythe, Robert Stanley. A Study of the Plays of Thomas D'Urfey
with a Reprint of A Fool's Preferment. 2 vols. Cleveland:
Western Reserve University Press, 1916-1917.

Volume I is "an account of the numerous but now forgotten
dramatic works of the Restoration writer, Thomas D'Urfey."
Concerned with sources, stage history, summaries. D'Urfey
is important because he is an early writer of sentimental
comedy and a borrower from Elizabethans. Volume II is an
edition of A Fool's Preferment, first D'Urfey play printed

since 1729. Typical D'Urfey and accessible.

2110 Summers, Montague. "Thomas D'Urfey." The Bookman, LXIII
(1923), 272-274.

A brief analysis of the life and works, stressing how closely
D'Urfey reflects his period in his plays, and attempting to
understand why he is not more studied by modern writers.

2111 "Tom D'Urfey." Times Literary Supplement, February 22, 1923,
p. 121.

A brief essay, commemorating the 200th anniversary of
D'Urfey's death; emphasis is on his songs rather than his plays.

2112 Baring-Gould, S. Devonshire Characters and Strange Events.
First Series. London: John Lane, The Bodley Head, Ltd. 1926.
xiv, 420 pp.

Devotes a chapter to D'Urfey, emphasizing his family background and his songs.

2113 Day, C. L. "The Life and Non-Dramatic Writings of Thomas
D'Urfey." Ph.D. Harvard University, 1930.

While the critical portion of this thesis pertains to D'Urfey's
non-dramatic writings, the biography contains information
relative to D'Urfey as a playwright.

2114 Lynch, Kathleen M. "Thomas D'Urfey's Contribution to Sentimental
Comedy." Philological Quarterly, IX (1930), 249-259.

The sentimental heroine appears in D'Urfey's plays before
Colley Cibber's Loves Last Shift, or, The Fool in Fashion.
The heroines of The Virtuous Wife, or, Good Luck at Last,
Love for Money, The Richmond Heiress, and The Campaigners,
are discussed in particular.

2115 Day, O. L. "Pills to Purge Melancholy." Review of English Studies,
VIII (1932), 177-184.

This casts new insights into the history and content of the
songs and ballads (some drawn from theatre-songs) which com-
prise the six-volume, 18th century poetical miscellany (1698-
1720). "Though D'Urfey was the most voluminous single contributor to all the volumes from 1698 to 1714, he did not himself edit any of them until 1719."

2116 -----. "A Lost Play by D'Urfey." Modern Language Notes, XLIX
(1934), 332-334.

Day expands on W. Barclay Squire's discovery (DNB) that
D'Urfey wrote the lost play, "A Wife for Any Man." It was
probably written between December, 1695, and September,
1697.

2117 Ustick, W. Lee. "Tom D'Urfey and the Graveyard." Modern
Philology, XXXVI (1939), 303-306.

2118 Graham, C.B. "The Jonsonian Tradition in the Comedies of Thomas
D'Urfey." Modern Language Quarterly, VIII (1947), 47-52.

A study of the techniques of "humours" satire in D'Urfey.

2119 A., H. "Thomas D'Urfey." Notes and Queries, CXCIV (April
16, 1949), 173.

Queries source of a quotation in Love for Money.

2120 Bowers, Fredson Thayer. "The Comical History of Don Quixote,
1694." Papers of the Bibliographical Society of America,
XLIII (1949), 191-195.

A bibliographical analysis.

2121 Day, Cyrus L. Dates and Performances of Thomas D'Urfey's
Plays. Charlottesville: Bibliographical Society of the University
of Virginia, 1950. 24 pp.

This work confirms, supplements, and corrects information
in Nicoll and Genest.

2122 Sanville, Donald W. "Thomas D'Urfey's 'Love for Money,' a
Bibliographical Study." University of Pennsylvania Library
Chronicle, XVII (1950), 71-77.

An examination of the six 1691 editions of Love for Money
and an attempt to place them in their chronological order, with
some attention to later editions of 1696, 1724, and 1726.

2123 Bowers, Fredson. "The Two Issues of D'Urfey's Cynthia and
Endymion (1697)." Princeton University Library Chronicle,
XIII (1951), 32-34.

In Woodward and McManaway's Check List of English Plays
1641-1700, D'Urfey's Cynthia and Endymion is listed as No.
526 with a second edition as No. 527. Bowers shows that 527
is a mixture of original and reimpressed sheets.

2124 Biswanger, Raymond A., Jr. "Thomas D'Urfey's Richmond
Heiress (1693): A Bibliographical Study." Studies in Bibliography,
V (1952-1953), 169-178.

This article analyzes the bibliographical problems concerning the play.

2125 -----. "The Date of Thomas D'Urfey's 'The Richmond Heiress.'"
Notes and Queries, CXCVIII (1953), 105-106.

A letter from Dryden to William Walsh (May 9, 1693) indicates
that the play was probably produced in late April 1693.

2126 Oster, Harry. "A Study of the Songs of Thomas D'Urfey, John Gay,
Charles Dibdin, and Thomas Moore." Ph.D. Cornell University,
1953.

2127 Biswanger, Raymond A., Jr. "Several Words First Employed in
D'Urfey's The Richmond Heiress." Modern Language Notes,
LXX (1955), 577-578.

The New English Dictionary lists as first illustrations of
the use of a word several words which are used in Richmond
Heiress earlier than those illustrations in NED. There are also
two words in Richmond Heiress that are not defined in NED.

2128 Ellis, William D., Jr. "Thomas D'Urfey, the Pope-Philips Quar-
      rel, and The Shepherd's Week." Publications of the Modern
      Language Association, LXXIV (1959), 203-212.
          Several references to plays of D'Urfey and of Gay.

2129 Vaughan, Jack A. "A D'Urfey Play Dated." Modern Philology,
      LXIV (1967), 322-323.
          A Fond Husband was first printed in the summer of 1677,
      shortly after its premier performance at Dorset Gardens in
      May of that year.

2130 -----. "'Persevering, Unexhausted Bard': Tom D'Urfey." Quarter
      ly Journal of Speech, LIII (1967), 342-348.
          Reviews the life and works of D'Urfey whose plays exhibit a
      frenetic theatricality and vitality and reveal the tastes of the
      Restoration audience.

Eccles, J.

2131 Jackson, Allan S. "The Frontispiece to Eccles's Theater Musick,
      1699." Theatre Notebook, XIX (Winter, 1964/5), 47-49.
          Offers explanations for several errors in the print used to
      illustrate Eccles's three volume work.

Ecclestone, Edward

2132 Baird, J. R. "Milton and Edward Ecclestone's 'Noah's Flood.'"
      Modern Language Notes, LV (March, 1940), 183-187.
          Ecclestone's debt is rather to Paradise Lost than to Dryden'
      operatic version.

2133 Evans, G. Blakemore. "Edward Ecclestone: His Relationship to
      Dryden and Milton." Modern Language Review, XLIV (October,
      1949), 550-552.
          Noah's Flood (1679), a sequel to State of Innocence (1677),
      shows Ecclestone to be a follower of Milton's ideas and Dryden'
      techniques.

Echo-Device

2134 Colby, Elbridge. The Echo-Device in Literature. New York: The
      New York Public Library, 1921. 61 pp.
          Covers the introduction of the device from French and Italia
      poetry, its development in the English Renaissance, and its
      occasional further use in Restoration and 18th century poems
      and plays.

Eclogue

2135 Jones, Richard F. "Eclogue Types in English Poetry of the
          Eighteenth Century." Journal of English and Germanic Philo-
          logy, XXIV (January, 1925), 33-60.
               The distinguishing characteristic of the eclogue is its
          dramatic form whereas the term "pastoral" refers only to
          content.

Edinburgh

2136 Cameron, Kenneth M. "The Edinburgh Theatre, 1668-1682."
          Theatre Notebook, XVIII (Autumn, 1963), 18-25.
               An historical account reveals the activities of the Edinburgh
          Theatre which was especially vigorous from 1668 to 1673.

Editing

2137 Spencer, Hazelton. "A Caveat on Restoration Play Quartos."
          Review of English Studies, VI (1930), 315-316.
               Points out discrepancies between title pages and the rest
          of the edition.

Edition

2138 Chapman, R. W. "Numbering of Editions." Review of English
          Studies, VII (1931), 213-215.
               Discusses the general principle of numbering editions in
          the eighteenth and early nineteenth centuries and mentions
          exceptions. Does not profess to come to a conclusion.

Edkins, Michael

2139 Barker, Kathleen. "Michael Edkins, Painter." Theatre Notebook,
          XVI (Winter, 1961-62), 39-55.
               Edkins' work for the Theatre Royal, Bristol. Entries from
          Edkins' ledger for 1768 to 1783.

Edwards, Thomas

2140 Dobson, Austin. "Edwards' 'Canons of Criticism.'" Later Essays,
          1917-20. (London, New York [etc.]: H. Milford, Oxford Uni-
          versity Press, 1921), 1-24.
               An essay on Thomas Edwards' "burlesque code of Canons,
          deduced directly from Warburton's notes [to his edition of

Shakespeare] with illustrations drawn from that writer's
emendations."

Elizabethan Drama

2141 Frohberg, Georg. "Das Fortleben des Elisabethanischen Drama
      im Zeitalter der Restauration." Münster Dissertation, 1925.
2142 Harbeson, William P. "The Elizabethan Influence on the Tragedy
      of the Late Eighteenth and Early Nineteenth Centuries." Ph.D.
      University of Pennsylvania, 1926.
2143 Baxter, F. C. "Criticism and Appreciation of the Elizabethan
      Drama: Dryden to Swinburne." Ph.D. Cambridge University
      (Trinity), 1933.
2144 Williams, Robert D. "Antiquarian Interest in Elizabethan Drama
      before Lamb." Publications of the Modern Language Association,
      LIII (1938), 434-444.
           By citing a number of 18th century histories and collected
      editions, Williams shows that scholarly interest in the Elizabeth
      and Jacobean drama was widespread long before the appearance
      of Lamb's Specimens.
2145 Weisinger, Herbert. "The Seventeenth-Century Reputation of the
      Elizabethans." Modern Language Quarterly, VI (1945), 13-21.
           Quotes and analyses the views of the Elizabethan dramatists
      held by Dryden, Rymer and Drake.
2146 Hoctor, M. A. "The Recovery of the Literary Reputation of Cer-
      tain Elizabethan Dramatists (Including Shakespeare) in the
      Early Nineteenth Century, 1790-1833." B. Litt. Oxford Uni-
      versity (St. Anne's), 1966.

Elizabethan Revival

2147 Wasserman, Earl R. "The Elizabethan Revival: Its Background
      and Beginning." Ph.D. Johns Hopkins University, 1937.
2148 -----. "The Scholarly Origin of the Elizabethan Revival." Eng-
      lish Literary History, IV (1937), 213-243.
           A study of the increasing interest in Elizabethan literature
      revealed in the works of scholars from Theobald to Warton.
      The revival of appreciation for the drama is a major consider-
      ation.
2149 -----. "Henry Headley and the Elizabethan Revival." Studies in
      Philology, XXXVI (1939), 491-502.
           A history of the revival of interest in Elizabethan literature
      in the later 18th century, particularly as it was influenced by
      Henry Headley's Select Beauties of Ancient English Poetry
      (1787).

Encyclopedia

2150 Enciclopedia dello spettacolo. 9 vols. Roma: Casa Editrice Le
        Maschere [1954-1962].
            Covers theatrical entertainment in all its forms (drama,
        opera, dance, cinema, TV, the circus, etc.). About thirty
        thousand entries, in alphabetical order. For playwrights' entries
        includes bibliography.

Engravings

2151 Nicoll, Allardyce. "In Search of the Theatre-Material for the
        Yale Collection." Theatre Arts Monthly, XVIII (1934), 860-869.
            Engravings are seen as an important source of information
        regarding the history of the art of the theatre.

Entertainments

2152 Avery, Emmett. "Entertainments on the English Stage, 1700-
        1737." Ph.D. University of Chicago, 1933.
2153 Rulfs, Donald J. "Entr'acte Entertainment at Drury Lane and
        Covent Garden, 1750-1770." Theatre Annual, XII (1954), 17-27.
            Rulfs surveys the various types of entertainment offered
        the London audiences in Garrick's time.

Epigrams

2154 "English Epigrams." Times Literary Supplement, March 8, 1934,
        pp. 149-150.
2155 "French Epigrams." Times Literary Supplement, August 2, 1934,
        pp. 533-534.
2156 Sieber, Sally Meredith. "The Epigram in the Restoration Comedy
        of Manners." M.A. University of North Carolina, 1944.

Epsom

2157 Rosenfeld, Sybil. "Players in Epsom." Theatre Notebook, VII
        (1953), 47-48.
            Dramatic performances were held in Epsom in 1708 and
        1724.

Etherege, George

letter-book

2158 Etherege, George. The Letter-book of Sir George Etherege.
Edited by Sybil Rosenfeld. Oxford University Press, 1928;
London: H. Milford, 1928. 441 pp.
An excellent introduction summarizes the main facts of
Etherege's life and the European situation in 1685-89 when
E. was in Ratisbon. Illuminates Restoration society and its
expression in the theatre. Prints all other letters and writings
omitted in Verity's Works.

poems

2159 -----. The Poems of Sir George Etherege. Edited by James
Thorpe. Princeton: Princeton University Press, 1963. 149 pp.
Includes the principal songs from the plays with textual
and explanatory notes.

dramatic works

2160 -----. The Dramatic Works of Sir George Etherege. Edited by
H. F. B. Brett-Smith. 2 vols. (The Percy Reprints, No. 6).
Oxford: Blackwell, 1927.
Replaces Verity (1888) as the standard edition. Based on th
original quartos of the three plays. A sound introduction to
Etherege's career and a bibliography of the plays.

individual plays

2161 Chinol, Elio, ed. La Comedia della Restaurazione; Etherege,
Wycherley, Congreve. Collona di Letterature moderne, 3.
Napoli: Edizioni scientifiche italiane [1958]. 534 pp.
A long introduction making stylistic remarks on Dryden,
Vanbrugh and Farquhar as well as the three dramatists
of the title; includes English texts of Etherege's Man of Mode,
Wycherley's Plain Dealer, and Congreve's Way of the World,
with notes primarily glossing the text.
2162 Etherege, George. The Man of Mode. Edited by W. B. Carnochan
(Regents Restoration Drama Series). Lincoln: University of
Nebraska Press, 1966.
Includes introduction, notes, and chronology.

translation

2163 Sinko, Grzegorz. Angielska komedia Restauracji: G. Etherege,
W. Wycherley, W. Congreve. Przelozyl i opracowal. Wroclaw
Zaklad Narodowy Im. Ossolinskich [1962]. lxiii, 559 pp.

(Biblioteka narodowa. Ser. II, 133).

Introduction, giving historical background. Polish translations of Etherege's She Would, If She Could, Wycherley's The
Country Wife, and Congreve's The Way of the World.

biography and criticism

2164 Wurzbach-Tannenberg, Alfred Ritter von, Jr. George Etheredge.
      Leipzig: O. R. Reisland, 1900.

      Etherege, the first characteristically Restoration drama-
      tist, prepared the way for the more able playwrights, Wycher-
      ley, Congreve, and Farquhar. Part I is biographical; Part II
      contains a discussion of: The Comical Revenge, or Love in
      a Tub (1663), and its individual characters; She Would If She
      Could (1668), The Man of Mode, or Sir Fopling Flutter (1676).

2165 Wurzbach, Wolfgang von. "George Etheredge." Englische Studien,
      XXVII (1900), 234-252.

      Part one is devoted to a brief review of the known facts of
      Etherege's life, and part two to an analysis of his plays, with
      especial reference to Sir Fopling Flutter.

2166 Meindl, Vincenz. Sir George Etheredge, sein Leben, seine Zeit
      und seine Dramen. Leipzig. Wilhelm Braumüller, 1901. 278 pp.

      Includes a general chapter on Restoration theater, the
      historical background, and a plot summary and analysis of
      each of Etheredge's three comedies: "The Comical Revenge"
      (1664), "She Would, If She Could" (1668), and "The Man of
      Mode, or Sir Fopling Flutter" (1676). Though these plays were
      enormously successful in their day, Meindl believes they've
      been deservedly forgotten.

2167 Isaacs, J. "Sir George Etherege at Constantinople." Times Liter-
      ary Supplement, November 10, 1921, p. 723; November 17,
      1921, p. 752; November 24, 1921, p. 771; December, 1921,
      pp. 788-789.

      Discussion of various letters of Etherege written while he
      was in Turkey.

2168 Foster, D. "Concerning the Grandfather and Father of Sir George
      Etherege." Notes and Queries, 12th Series, X (1922), 341-344;
      362-365; 414.

      A discussion of the economic affairs of Etherege's grand-
      father in the Virginia Company; the author concludes that the
      investigation proves the respectability of the Etherege family.

2169 Foster, Miss D. "Sir George Etherege I." Times Literary Sup-
      plement, February 16, 1922, p. 108.

      Records of a law suit in the family.

2170 -----. "Sir George Etherege II." Times Literary Supplement,

February 23, 1922, p. 124.

Family records, with letters reprinted from the Letter Book.

2171 Dobrée, Bonamy. Essays in Biography, 1680-1726. Oxford University Press, 1925. xii, 362 pp.

Covers the period 1680-1726. Sympathetic sketches of Etherege and Vanbrugh (primarily as architect); and a generally unfavorable account of Addison.

2172 -----. Rochester. A Conversation between Sir George Etherege and Mr. Fitzjames. London: Hogarth Press, 1926. 50 pp.

An imaginary conversation at Ratisbon, summer of 1686.

2173 Wainewright, John B. "Sir George Etherege." Notes and Queries, CL (April 10, 1926), 260.

Etherege left his library of political and historical books to the monastery of St. James; the Abbot says he became a Catholic before his death in Paris.

2174 Foster, Dorothy. "Sir George Etherege: Collections." Notes and Queries, CLIII (December 10, 1927), 417-419; (December 17, 1927), 435-440; (December 24, 1927), 454-459; (December 31, 1927), 472-476.

Notes on his ancestry, a 1656 lawsuit involving Etherege, his sister's will, a lawsuit of his nephew, date of Etherege's death (10 May, 1692).

2175 Hewins, Elizabeth L. "Etherege and Cowley." London Times Literary Supplement, October 13, 1927, p. 715.

Cowley as the source of two lines in Etherege's Man of Mode.

2176 Williamson, George. "Sir George Etherege and His Gilded Butterflies." University of California Chronicle, XXIX (January, 1927), 44-51.

A sketch of his character and career.

2177 [Etherege]. Notes and Queries, CLV (December 29, 1928), 467-468.

Reviews S. Rosenfeld, The Letter-book of Sir George Etherege (1928). Corrects numerous errors in copying.

2178 Foster, Dorothy. "Sir George Etherege." London Times Literary Supplement, May 31, 1928, p. 412.

Biographical data concerning Etherege's family and early life in Maidenhead, Berks.

2179 -----. "Sir George Etherege Collections: Addenda." Notes and Queries, CLIV (January 14, 1928), 28.

A description of his house at Ratisbon and an Etherege pedigree.

2180 "Sir George Etherege." London Times Literary Supplement, March 1, 1928, pp. 137-138.

An interesting and perceptive sketch of his life and career.
Without models Etherege "introduced a new way of writing plays
which was thenceforth to serve as a model for English social
comedy," replacing humours comedy.

2181 Brett-Smith, H. F. B. "The Works of Etherege." Review of English Studies, V (January, 1929), 77-78.
    Comments on readings in The Comical Revenge.

2182 Boswell, Eleanore. "Sir George Etherege." Review of English
Studies, VII (1931), 207-209.
    Miss Boswell pursues other records in the chancery pro-
ceedings of Etherege vs. Etherege (studied by Miss D. Forbes,
Times Literary Supplement, February 16, 1922) to further illustrate the dramatist.

2183 Foster, Dorothy. "Sir George Etherege." Review of English
Studies, VIII (1932), 458-459.
    Miss Foster here answers Eleanor Boswell's comments
("Sir George Etherege," R.E.S., VII [1931]) with regard to
the Chancery case of Etherege vs. Etherege.

2184 Rosenfeld, Sybil. "Sir George Etherege in Ratisbon." Review of
English Studies, X (1934), 177-189.
    Based upon "recently acquired" papers of the Earl of Mid-
dleton, containing some 230 of Etherege's letters from Ratisbon,
this article reveals the playwright as loyal and devoted to his
king, shrewd and comical, but irresponsible and tactless.

2185 Hadsell, John D. "The Relationship of the Plays of Sir George
Etherege to Seventeenth Century Drama." M.A. University of
Colorado, 1940.

2186 Howarth, R. G. "Untraced Quotations in Etherege." Notes and
Queries, CLXXXVIII (June 30, 1945), 281.
    The quotations show Restoration familiarity with Elizabethan
and Jacobean tags.

2187 Clancy, James Harvey. "The Humorists: an Elizabethan Method
of Characterization As Modified by Etherege and Congreve."
Ph.D. Stanford University, 1947.

2188 Wilson, John Harold. "Etherege's Julia." Modern Language Notes,
LXII (January, 1947), 40-42.
    Rejects the theory that Julia was the name of Etherege's
Bavarian actress friend.

2189 Nichol, John W. "Dame Mary Etherege." Modern Language Notes,
LXIV (June, 1949), 419-422.
    A biographical note.

2190 Sherbo, Arthur. "A Note on The Man of Mode." Modern Language
Notes, LXIV (May, 1949), 343-344.
    Notes a parallel in Les Précieuses Ridicules.

2191 -----. "Sir Fopling Flutter and Beau Hewitt." Notes and Queries,

CXCIV (July 9, 1949), 296-303.

Disputes the traditional belief that the portrait of Sir Fopling was based on Hewitt.

2192 Feltham, Frederik G. "The Quality of the Wit in Comedies of Etherege, Wycherley, Congreve, and Shadwell." Ph.D. University of Chicago, 1951.

2193 Rosenfeld, Sybil. "The Second Letterbook of Sir George Etherege." Review of English Studies, New Ser., III (1952), 19-27.

This manuscript, now in the Harvard Library Theatre Collection, covers the "last ten months of Etherege's envoyship up to the time of his flight to Paris."

2194 Underwood, Dale S. "The Comic Art of Etherege." Ph.D. Yale University, 1952.

2195 Pinto, Vivian de Sola. Restoration Carnival; Five Courtier Poets: Rochester, Dorset, Sedley, Etherege and Sheffield. London: Folio Society, 1954. 253 pp.

Biography and poems. Four of the poems are songs from plays.

2196 Cecil, C. D. "Restoration Comic Diction: Modes of Speech in Etherege, Wycherley, and Congreve." B. Litt. Oxford University (Wadham), 1955-1956.

2197 Dalldorff, Hprst. Die Welt der Restaurationskomödie. Ein Querschnitt durch die Lustspiele Hauptsaechlich von Etherege, Wycherley und Congreve zur Erfassung ihrer Stofflichen Wesenszüge. Inaugural Dissertation. Kiel, 1956.

2198 Fujimura, Thomas H. "Etherege at Constantinople." Publications of the Modern Language Association, LXXI (1956), 465-481.

Secretary to Ambassador, 1668-1671. Perhaps gained experience and maturity which made his last play the best.

2199 Holland, Norman Norwood, Jr. "A Critical Reading of the Comedies of Etherege, Wycherley, and Congreve." Ph.D. Harvard University, 1956.

2200 Smyth, Charles. "John Evelyn and His Diary." Church Quarterly Review, CLVII (1956), 262-270.

A brief survey of Evelyn scholarship, and an analysis of E. S. de Beer's six volume edition of the Diary.

2201 Underwood, Dale. Etherege and the Seventeenth-Century Comedy of Manners. Yale Studies in English, 135. New Haven: Yale University Press: London: Oxford University Press, 1957. ix, 165 pp.

Stresses irony in the plays as more important than wit or manners.

2202 Cross, Gustav. "Another Donne Allusion." Notes and Queries, New Ser., V (1958), 532-533.

In Etherege, The Comical Revenge.

2203 Vieth, David M. "Etherege's 'Man of Mode' and Rochester's
      'Artemisa to Cloe.'" Notes and Queries, New Ser., V (1958),
      473-474.
          Resemblance of ideas.
2204 Holland, Norman N. The First Modern Comedies: The Significance
      of Etherege, Wycherley, and Congreve. Cambridge: Harvard
      University Press, 1959. iv, 274 pp.
          The comedies are about the difference between appearance
      and reality.
2205 Aiken, W. Ralph, Jr. "Nature to Advantage Dress'd: A Study of
      Sir George Etherege As Playwright." Ph.D. Duke University,
      1962. (Order No. 63-859).
          A study of Etherege's development from The Comical
      Revenge; or, Love in a Tub, and She Wou'd If She Could, to
      The Man of Mode; or, Sir Fopling Flutter.
2206 Gibb, Carson. "Figurative Structure in Restoration Comedy."
      Ph.D. University of Pennsylvania, 1962. (Order No. 63-4153).
          Figurative structure results from the juxtaposition of ap-
      parently unrelated actions in selected plays of Dryden, Etherege,
      and Wycherley.
2207 Germer, Erich. Sentimentale Züge in den Lustspielgestalten
      Ethereges, Wycherleys, Congreves, Vanbrughs und Farquhars.
      Inaugural Dissertation. Münster, 1963. 164 pp.
          Appearance and treatments of types of sentimentalism in
      Restoration comedy.
2208 Hymas, Scott Simpson. "The Satiric Attitude: Rejection in the
      Comedies of Wycherley and Etherege." Ph.D. Western Re-
      serve University, 1964. (Order No. 65-2325).
          Seeks to discover that the drama of Wycherley and Ether-
      ege are "more expressive of the rejection of the satiric at-
      titude than the acceptance of the comic."
2209 Wilkinson, D. R. M. The Comedy of Habit: An Essay on the Use
      of Courtesy Literature in a Study of Restoration Comic Drama.
      (Leidse Germanistische en Anglistiche Reehs von de Ryksuniver-
      siteit Leiden, 4). The Hague: Martinus Nijhoff, 1964. 190 pp.
          Uses Francis Osborne's Advice to a Son (1656-1658) and
      other contemporary courtesy literature to examine the wit
      and characterization of the gallant, particularly in the plays
      of Etherege and Wycherley.
2210 Powell, Jocelyn. "George Etherege and the Form of a Comedy."
      Restoration Theatre. Edited by John Russell Brown and Bernard
      Harris. (Stratford-Upon-Avon Studies, 6). (London: Edward
      Arnold, 1965; New York: St. Martin's Press, 1965), 43-69.
          Love in a Tub, She Wou'd if She Cou'd, and The Man of
      Mode show an increasing economy of dramatic means and an

increasing dissatisfaction with comic conventions. Gradually,
Etherege moves from the "comedy of judgment" to the "comedy of experience."

2211 Auffret, J. M. "The Man of Mode and The Plain Dealer: Common
Origin and Parallels." Etudes Anglais, XIX (1966), 209-222.

2212 Boyette, Purvis E. "The Songs of George Etherege." Studies in
English Literature, 1500-1900, VI (1966), 409-419.

Etherege surpassed his fellow playwrights in the composition of songs for his plays, and believed in the architectonic
relationship of lyrics to the structure of the play.

2213 Brett-Smith, H. F. B. "Sir George Etherege." Restoration Drama
Modern Essays in Criticism. (A Galaxy Book). Edited by John
Loftis. (New York: Oxford University Press, 1966), 44-56.

Reprinted from the Introduction to The Works of Sir George
Etherege (Oxford: Basil Blackwell, 1927). Etherege's contributions to later Restoration comedy.

2214 Underwood, Dale. "The Comic Values - The Man of Mode."
Restoration Drama: Modern Essays in Criticism. (A Galaxy
Book). Edited by John Loftis. (New York: Oxford University
Press, 1966), 57-81.

Reprinted from Etherege and The Seventeenth-Century
Comedy of Manners (New Haven: Yale University Press,
1957), pp. 72-93. The play gives a comprehensive definition
to those questions of reality and value which constitute the
essential interest of Restoration comedy of manners.

2215 -----. "The Comic Language." Restoration Dramatists: A Collection of Critical Essays. (Twentieth Century Views). Edited
by Earl Miner. (Englewood Cliffs, New Jersey: Prentice-Hall,
Inc., 1966), 87-103.

Reprinted from Etherege and the Seventeenth-Century
Comedy of Manners (New Haven: Yale University Press, 1957)
The language of the Restoration comedy of manners may be
divided into two distinct sets of literary characteristics, the
metaphoric and the non-metaphoric, which have distinct
rhetorical characters and complicate the logical surfaces of
the language in somewhat different ways.

2216 Birdsall, Virginia Ogden. "The English Comic Spirit on the
Restoration Stage." Ph.D. Brown University, 1967. (Order
No. 68-1439).

The immorality and libertinism of comic protagonists are
an essential part of their nature and relate them to an English
comic tradition that always takes sides with the individual
against the group. The study concentrates on Etherege, Wyche
ley, and Congreve.

2217 Bracher, Frederick. "The Letterbooks of Sir George Etherege."

Harvard Library Bulletin, XV (1967), 238-245.

Three letterbooks, (BM Add Mss 11513), edited as The Letterbook of Sir George Etherege by Sybil Rosenfeld in 1927, and Harvard Library's fMS Thr. 11 and FMS Thr. 11.1 shed considerable light on Etherege's three-year residence at Ratisbon.

2218 Bracher, Frederick. "Sir George Etherege and His Secretary." Harvard Library Bulletin, XV (1967), 331-344.

Etherege's secretary, Hugo Hughes, plotted to discredit and replace him as English envoy at Ratisbon.

2219 Dobrée, Bonamy. Essays in Biography, 1680-1726. Freeport, New York: Books for Libraries Press, 1967. 362 pp.

A reprint of the 1925 edition contains biographes of Etherege, Vanbrugh and Addison.

Euripides

2220 Lucas, Frank L. Euripides and His Influence... Boston: George G. Harrap & Co., [1923]. 188 pp. (Our Debt to Greece and Rome Series).

A brief account (pp. 133-141) of Euripides in 18th-century England--the adaptations of his plays and critical opinion of his plays.

Evelyn, John

text

2221 Evelyn, John. The Diary of John Evelyn. Now first Printed in Full from the Manuscripts Belonging to Mr. John Evelyn and Edited by E. S. de Beer. 6 vols. Oxford: The Clarendon Press, 1955.

The complete text, fully annotated with description of the manuscripts, including a volume of introduction and of index. The Diary contains much information about plays and operas and their productions as well as about contemporary actors and actresses.

2222 -----. The Diary of John Evelyn. Edited by E. S. de Beer. London, New York, Toronto: Oxford University Press, 1959. xii, 1307 pp. Index.

This edition contains the whole of the principal MS. of the Diary, with omissions of such things as Evelyn's reports of the contents of sermons which he heard between May 29, 1660, and the end of 1705.

biography and criticism

2223 Craig, Edward Gordon. "John Evelyn and the Theatre in England,
France and Italy." The Mask: A Journal of the Art of the Theatre,
X (1924), 97-115; 143-160.
    An essay summarizing Evelyn's comments on the theatre
of England, France and Italy which makes extensive use of
quotations from Evelyn's diary.
2224 Lawrence, W. J. "A Restoration Opera Problem." London Times
Literary Supplement, September 26, 1929, p. 737.
    John Evelyn's "Italian Opera" of January 5, 1673/74 was
the French Ariane, probably performed at Court.
2225 Esdaile, Arundell. "Evelyn's Diaries." Quarterly Review,
CCXCIV (January, 1956), 224-231.
    Basically to be a review of E. S. de Beer's six-volume edi-
tion of the Diary (1955), but really a discussion of Evelyn himself.
2226 Hill, Christopher. "The Diary of John Evelyn." History, XLII
(1957), 12-18.
    Hill, reviewing The Diary of John Evelyn edited by E. S.
de Beer, denies Evelyn's importance and feels that de Beer's
work was a careful, scholarly waste of time. Some discussion
of the events of the latter half of the 17th century and indications of Evelyn's inadequate handling of them. The article is
most valuable in its treatment of the political atmosphere of
the time.

Family Relations

2227 Hofstad, Lois Valborg. "The Comic Use of Family Relationships,
1760-1779." Ph.D. Case Western Reserve University, 1967.
(Order No. 68-3312).
    Comic playwrights from 1760 to 1779 were generally unable
to produce authentic comedies because they were unable to
create a vigorous family conflict. Examines sixty-three
comedies, eighty-five percent of which were acted for the first
time from 1760 to 1779 at the Drury Lane, Covent Garden,
and Haymarket Theatres.

Farce

2228 Hughes, Leo. "English Farce in the Restoration." Ph.D. University of Illinois, 1938. ix, 362 pp.
    A decade by decade history of the form which includes
chapters on medieval origins and the reputation of the genre

during the period. The study combines structural analysis
with detailed stage history.

2229 Hughes, Leo. "Attitudes of Some Restoration Dramatists toward
Farce." Philological Quarterly, XIX (1940), 268-287.
"The attitude of various groups ranging from determined
opposition to tacit acceptance and even open defence." Such
people as Lacy and Aphra Behn favored it, Dryden, Edward
Howard and Shadwell opposed it on aesthetic and patriotic
grounds.

2230 Hughes, Leo. "The Early Career of Farce in the Theatrical
Vocabulary." University of Texas Studies in English, 1940,
pp. 82-95.

2231 Hughes, Leo and Arthur H. Scouten, eds. Ten English Farces.
Austin: University of Texas Press, 1948. xiv, 286 pp.
Includes text, with introductions, of the following: Tate's
A Duke and No Duke, Mrs. Behn's The Emperor of the Moon,
Ravenscroft's The Anatomist, Doggett's Hob, Johnson's The
Cobler of Preston, Jevon's The Devil to Pay, Bullock's The
Bilker Bilk'd, T. Sheridan's The Brave Irishman, Mrs. Inch-
bald's Appearance Is Against Him, and Hoare's No Song No
Supper.

2232 Hughes, Leo. A Century of English Farce. Princeton: Princeton
University Press, 1956. viii, 307 pp. Bibliography.
1660-1750.

2233 Golden, Samuel A. "An Early Defense of Farce." Studies in
Honor of John Wilcox. Edited by A. Dayle Wallace and Wood-
burn O. Ross. Detroit: Wayne State University Press, 1958.

2234 Kohl, Ernst. Der Begriff "Farce" im Spiegel des allgemeinen
Sprachgebrauchs und der literarischen Kritik in England.
Bonn: Printed by the University, 1958.
A history of the genre up to the 20th century, using primarily an etymological approach. Farce, introduced to England
from France during the Restoration, was originally a largely
improvised interlude, such as the jig or comic sketch, with
the emphasis on situation and character-sketches rather than
on plot and construction. Throughout the Restoration and 18th
century it was rated lower than comedy proper.

2235 Schutz, Walter Stanley. "The Nature of Farce: Definition and
Devices." Ph.D. Michigan State University, 1967. (Order No.
68-4211).
A definition and analysis of the form includes an examination
of Nahum Tate's preface to A Duke and No Duke (1693) and
other Restoration plays.

Farquhar, George

works

2236 Farquhar, George. The Complete Works of George Farquhar.
       Edited by Charles Stonehill. 2 vols. Bloomsbury: The Nonesuch
       Press, 1930.
            The text of all of the plays, with the exception of The Stage-
       Coach, is that of the first edition. This edition includes a
       number of items, viz., The Adventures of Covent Garden, which
       have not been printed in any edition of Farquhar's Works. The
       Introduction gives a life. Theatrical history of each play is
       given, as well as textual and explanatory notes.
2237 -----. The Complete Works. Edited by Charles Stonehill. 2 vols.
       New York: Gordian Press, 1967.
            Reprint of the 1930 edition.

       plays

2238 -----. Plays. Edited by William Archer. London: Ernest Benn,
       1949. 455 pp.
            A reprint of the Mermaid Edition of 1906, containing The
       Constant Couple, The Twin-Rivals, The Recruiting Officer
       and The Beaux Stratagem.
2239 -----. A Discourse upon Comedy, the Recruiting Officer and The
       Beaux Stratagem. Edited by Louis A. Strauss. Boston: D. C.
       Heath and Co., 1914. 358 pp.

       individual texts

2240 -----. The Beaux-Stratagem; a Comedy. Edited with a Preface
       and Notes by H. Macauley Fitzgibbon. London and Toronto:
       J. M. Dent and Sons, Ltd., 1928. 142 pp. (The Temple Drama-
       tists).
            The Preface presents the circumstances in which Farquhar
       wrote Beaux-Stratagem, its stage history, and a criticism of
       the work. The text of the play is followed by eleven pages of
       notes.
2241 -----. The Beaux' Stratagem. A Comedy. Introduction by Bonamy
       Dobrée. Bristol: Douglas Cleverdon, 1929. xxviii, 128 pp.
            The Introduction notes that Farquhar's primary purpose was
       not to satirize or moralize but to entertain.
2242 Gnau, Margaret Strauss. "A Production of The Beaux Stratagem
       by George Farquhar." M.F.A. Yale University, 1940.
2243 Farquhar, George. The Beaux' Stratagem. Edited by Vincent F.

·Hopper and Gerald B. Lahey. With a Note on the Staging by
George L. Hersey. (Theatre Classics for the Modern Reader).
Great Neck, New York: Barron's Educational Series, 1963.
182 pp.
    Includes biographical sketch, critical introduction, notes
on staging, and brief bibliography.

2244 -----. La Ruse des Galants/ /The Beaux' Stratagem. Edited by
J. Hamard. Paris: Aubier, 1966. 382 pp.
    The introduction is a study of Farquhar's career and plays.

2245 -----. The Beaux' Stratagem. Edited by Eric Rothstein. New
York: Appleton-Century Crofts, 1967.
    Includes introduction, notes, and select bibliography.

2246 -----. The Recruiting Officer. Edited by Michael Shugrue.
(Regents Restoration Drama Series). Lincoln: University
of Nebraska Press, 1965.
    Includes critical introduction, notes, bibliography, and an
appendix on variant passages.

2247 -----. The Recruiting Officer. Edited by Kenneth Tynan. London: Hart-Davis, 1965. 144 pp.

2248 -----. The Recruiting Officer. Edited by Michael Shugrue.
(Regents Restoration Drama Series). London: Edward Arnold,
1966.
    Includes critical introduction, notes, bibliography, and
an appendix on variant passages.

biography and criticism

2249 Lawrence, W. J. "Foigard in 'The Beaux' Stratagem.'" Notes
and Queries, 9th Ser., XI (January 17, 1903), 46-47.
    Suggests that the prototype of Foigard is Father Fogourdy
described in Pepys, February 6, 1663/4.

2250 Schmid, D. "George Farquhar, sein Leben und seine Original-
Dramen." Wiener Beiträge zur Englischen Philologie, XVIII
(1904), 1-372.
    Contains chapters on Farquhar in Ireland, on Robert Wilks
and Anne Oldfield, and individual chapters on the plays.

2251 Robertson, J. G. "Lessing and Farquhar." Modern Language Review,
II (1907), 56-59.
    "Lessing owes to Farquhar those elements in his ripest
comedy which appeal to us today as national, humane, and
modern."

2252 Beach, Joseph Warren. "The King's Shilling." The Nation, XC
(1910), 287.
    Dénouement of Holberg's comedy Erasmus Montanus
brought about by a trick for enlising a soldier, a trick used

by Sergeant Kite in Farquhar's Recruiting Officer, which was
presented during Holberg's stay in England.

2253 Campbell, Oscar J. "Holberg and The Recruiting Officer." The
Nation, XC (April 14, 1910), 374.
  Calls attention to Holberg's note to a line in Peder Paars
recommending Farquhar's play to soldiers desiring to learn
tricks of recruiting.

2254 Larson, Martin A. "The Influence of Milton's Divorce Tracts on
Farquhar's Beaux' Stratagem." Publications of the Modern
Language Association, XXXIX (1924), 174-178.
  An argument that many of the remarks on divorce in
Farquhar's play are derived from Milton's Doctrine and
Discipline of Divorce.

2255 Birrell, Francis. "Farquhar at Cambridge." Nation and Athenaeum
XXXVII (June 20, 1925), 368.
  Reviews the Cambridge performance, with a sketch of Far-
quhar's characters.

2256 Brown, Ivor. "Sweet Sullen." Saturday Review, CXLIII (January
29, 1927), 153-154.
  Reviews Nigel Playfair's Lyric Theatre production of Farquhar's The Beaux' Stratagem. Farquhar at his best aims at a
"reality of human doubt and distress instead of complacently
manipulating the lecherous puppets of the dramatist's routine."

2257 Horsnell, Horace. "A Notable Revival." Outlook (London), LIX
(January 29, 1927), 106.
  Reviews the Lyric Theatre (Hammersmith) production,
directed by Nigel Playfair.

2258 Maine, Basil. "Crooks and Stratagists." Spectator, CXXXVIII
(January 29, 1927), 147.
  Reviews the Lyric Theatre production of the play.

2259 "A Scene from Farquhar's The Beaux' Stratagem." Theatre Arts
Monthly, XI (September, 1927), 698.
  A photo of the scene, as produced by the Dramatic Asso-
ciation of Smith College, directed by Sam Eliot, Jr.

2260 Shipp, Horace. "Artificial Comedy." English Review, XLIV
(March, 1927), 379-381.
  Reviews the Lyric Theatre performance of Farquhar's play.

2261 Sydenham, John. "Farquhar at Hammersmith." New Statesman,
XXVIII (March 5, 1927), 634.
  On excisions in the Beaux' Stratagem produced by Nigel
Playfair.

2262 Lawrence, W. J. "The Mystery of 'The Stage Coach.'" Modern
Language Notes, XXVII (1932), 392-397.
  This is an intricate study which seeks to correct the None-
such edition's stage history of the play. Apparently Wilkes

actually printed "the book of the ballad opera, in all good faith,
as the literal text of the original farce. Beyond the insertion of
fifteen new songs to old ballad airs, no alteration is to be noted."
Lawrence feels that the text was derived from a Dublin prompt-
book. Thus, the prologue and epilogue associated with it refer
not to Farquhar but, perhaps, to William Rufus Chetwood, writer
of the added songs.

2263 Whiting, G. W. "The Date of the Second Edition of The Constant
      Couple." Modern Language Notes, XLVII (1932), 147-148.
          A discussion of the play produced first in 1700 and as a
      sequel in 1701.

2264 Brooke, Tucker. "George Farquhar: The Recruiting Officer."
      Representative English Comedies. Vol. IV: Dryden and His
      Contemporaries: Cowley to Farquhar. Edited by Charles Mills
      Gayley and Alwin Thaler. (New York: The Macmillan Company,
      1936), 667-680.
          Treats Farquhar's life and his position in the history of
      English comedy.

2265 Sutherland, J. R. "New Light on George Farquhar." Times Liter-
      ary Supplement, March 6, 1937, p. 171.
          Two petitions of Margaret Farquhar to Queen Anne and three
      appended certificates from the dukes of Ormondy, Bolton, and
      Orrery--dated 1709--provide further biographical data about
      the playwright.

2266 Pottorff, La Rue E. "George Farquhar." M.A. University of
      Michigan, 1942.

2267 Kies, Paul P. "Lessing's Intention in Der Dorfjunker." Research
      Studies of the State College of Washington, XI (1943), 257-263.
          "Contends that Farquhar's The Beaux' Stratagem and Van-
      brugh's The Relapse were sources of Lessing's play."

2268 Kavanagh, Peter. "Farquhar." Times Literary Supplement, Feb-
      ruary 10, 1945, p. 72.
          Refutes traditional biographical information by a scrutiny
      of the records of Trinity College, Dublin.

2269 Connely, Willard. "George Farquhar." Times Literary Supplement,
      August 16, 1947, p. 415.
          A brief notice of his forthcoming life.

2270 -----. Young George Farquhar: the Restoration Drama at Twilight.
      London: Cassell, 1949. 349 pp.
          A detailed critical biography.

2271 Guardia, Charles Edward. "Studies in the Dramatic Technique of
      George Farquhar." Ph.D. Harvard University, 1953.

2272 Hough, Robert L. "An Error in 'The Recruiting Officer.'" Notes
      and Queries, CXCVIII (1953), 340-341.
          A plot error in Act IV, scene II indicates that Farquhar wrote

the play in a relatively short time.

2273 -----. "Farquhar: 'The Recruiting Officer.'" Notes and Queries,
CXCIX (1954), 474.

Confusion in the use of names indicates that the play was
hastily written.

2274 Morton, Richard, and William M. Peterson. "The Jubilee of 1700
and Farquhar's 'The Constant Couple.'" Notes and Queries, CC
(1955), 521-525.

Reprints comments which describe the Jubilee and the public
reactions to it, in order to provide background for allusions to
the Jubilee by Farquhar and other dramatists.

2275 Loomis, Ralph A. "George Farquhar As Dramatic Theorist." Ph.D.
Northwestern University, 1956.

2276 Schrader, Klaus-Dietrich. "Die Stellung Sir John Vanbrughs und
George Farquhars in der Geschichte der englischen Komödie."
Inaugural Dissertation. Berlin, 1956.

2277 Spinner, Kaspar. George Farquhar als Dramatiker. Bern: Franke,
1956. 119 pp. (Schweitzer Anglistische Arbeiten, 40).

A somewhat detailed analysis of Farquhar's technique through
his use of comedy, conflict, sentiment and blank verse. One
brief chapter is devoted to Farquhar's "Discourse upon Comedy
Stonehill's edition (1930), is used for the text.

2278 James, Eugene Nelson. "The Development of George Farquhar as
a Comic Dramatist." Ph.D. State University of Iowa, 1958.

Reviews all plays.

2279 Pyle, Fitzroy. "George Farquhar (1677-1707)." Hermathena,
XCII (1958), 3-30.

Life and works in brief.

2280 Peterson, William M. "Sense and Sentiment in 'The Beaux'
Stratagem." Nota Bene, III (1960), 33-40.

2281 Germer, Erich. Sentimentale Züge in den Lustspielgestalten
Ethereges, Wycherleys, Congreves, Vanbrughs und Farquhars.
Inaugural Dissertation. Münster, 1963. 164 pp.

Appearance and treatment of types of sentimentalism in
Restoration comedy.

2282 Rosenfeld, Sybil. "Notes on The Recruiting Officer." Theatre
Notebook, XVIII (Winter, 1963/4), 47-48.

Farquhar had definite actors in mind when he composed the
play which was an immediate success at its first performance
on April 8, 1706. A new edition is needed.

2283 Rothstein, Eric. "Farquhar's Twin Rivals and the Reform of
Comedy." Publications of the Modern Language Association,
LXXIX (1964), 33-41.

Farquhar intended to present the kind of moral comedy Collier and other abolitionists claimed to favor. The failure of the

play indicated that the New Comedy would not be structured on Collier's principles.

2284 Berman, Ronald. "The Comedy of Reason." Texas Studies in Literature and Language, VII (1965), 161-168.

An analysis of The Beaux' Stratagem demonstrates that "the fundamental verity in the play is money; the fundamental metaphor involves commerce; the fundamental axiom is that poverty is nonexistence."

2285 James, Eugene Nelson. "The Burlesque of Restoration Comedy in Love and a Bottle." Studies in English Literature, 1500--1900, V (1965), 469-490.

The play intentionally satirizes and imitates exaggeratedly the hero of Restoration comedy, its intrigues, moral, form, wit, humor, characters, and comic situations.

2286 Nelson, David Arthur. "The Laughing Comedy of the Eighteenth Century." Ph.D. Cornell University, 1965. (Order No. 65-14711).

The comic technique and situations of Vanbrugh, Farquhar, Goldsmith, and Sheridan are evaluated in terms of their ability to create and maintain aesthetic distance between playgoer and character.

2287 Farmer, A. J. George Farquhar. London and New York: Longman, Green and Co., 1966. 40 pp.

A brief survey of the playwright's life and works. Includes select bibliography.

2288 Hutton, Virgil R. "The Aesthetic Development of George Farquhar in His Early Plays." Ph.D. University of Michigan, 1966. (Order No. 67-8280).

Analyzes Love and a Bottle, The Constant Couple, Sir Harry Wildair, The Inconstant, and The Twin-Rivals. Also examines Farquhar's critical theories, the moral stance of the plays, and the relation of the plays to earlier Restoration comic tradition and to the growing sentimental tradition.

2289 Rothstein, Eric. George Farquhar. New York: Twayne Publishers, Inc., 1967. 206 pp.

Biographical and critical study of Farquhar. Separate chapters are given to discussions of The Recruiting Officer and The Beaux' Stratagem. Includes selected bibliography.

Faust

2290 Igo, John. "A Calendar of Fausts." Bulletin of the New York Public Library, LXXI (1967), 5-24.

A list of most of the Fausts created in the last four hundred and fifty years includes nineteen titles of plays, pantomimes,

operas, prose works, and engravings published in England
between 1664 and 1798.

Female Tatler

2291 Anderson, Paul Bunyan. "The History and Authorship of Mrs.
      Crackenthorpe's Female Tatler." Modern Philology, XXVIII
      (1931), 354-360.
          The Female Tatler, "the feminine counterpart of its
      masculine contemporary," was written by a Mrs. Cracken-
      thorpe, who, hitherto has never been identified. She was Mrs.
      Mary Manley.

Female Wits

2292 Hook, Lucyle, ed. The Female Wits (Anonymous) (1704). (ARS
      Publication, 124). Los Angeles: Clark Memorial Library,
      U.C.L.A., 1967.
          First played around October 1696 at the Theatre Royal in
      Drury Lane. "A devastating satire in the manner of Bucking-
      ham's The Rehearsal, it attacks all plays by women playwrights
      but Mary de la Riviere Manley's blood and thunder female
      tragedy, The Royal Mischief (1696), in particular."

Fenton, Elijah

2293 Harlan, Earl. Elijah Fenton, 1683-1730. Philadelphia, 1937. 205
      pp.
2294 Valency, Maurice J. The Tragedies of Herod and Mariamne.
      New York: Columbia University Press, 1940. 304 pp.
          Includes discussion of the plays by Pordage, Orrery, and
      Fenton.

Fenton, Lavinia

2295 "Lavinia Fenton." Bookman, XLIV (August, 1913), 217.
          A portrait, with a short sketch.

Fielding, Henry

bibliography

2296 Cordasco, Francesco. Henry Fielding: a List of Critical Studies
      Published from 1895 to 1946. Eighteenth Century Bibliographical

Pamphlets, No. 5. Brooklyn: Long Island University Press,
1948. 17 pp.
   An annotated check-list, including items on Fielding's plays.
2297 Masengill, Jeanne A. "Variant Forms of Fielding's Coffeehouse
   Politician." Studies in Bibliography, V (1952), 178-183.
      This article discusses the problems posed by the three
   variant issues of the satiric play.

works

2298 Fielding, Henry. The Complete Works of Henry Fielding, Esq.
   With an Essay on the Life, Genius and Achievement of the Author
   by William Ernest Henley. 16 vols. London: W. Heinemann:
   New York: Printed by Croscup and Sterling, 1903.
2299 -----. Works. With the Author's Preface, and an Introduction by
   G. H. Maynadier. University edition. 12 vols. in 6. New York:
   Sully and Kleinteich [190?]. [Also issued in 1905 in 12 vols and
   in 1907.]
2300 -----. The Complete Works of Henry Fielding, Esq. With an Essay on the Life, Genius and Achievement of the Author by William Ernest Henley. 16 vols. New York: Barnes and Noble,
   1967.
      A reprint of the 1902-03 edition with Fielding's plays and
   poems contained in five volumes.

plays

2301 Brown, Jack Richard. "Four Plays by Henry Fielding. A Critical
   Edition of The Grub Street Opera, Pasquin, The Historical
   Register for 1736, and Eurydice Hiss'd." Ph.D. Northwestern
   University, 1937.
2302 Roberts, Edgar Verne. "The Ballad Operas of Henry Fielding,
   1730-32: A Critical Edition. (The Author's Farce, The Grub-
   Street Opera, The Lottery, The Mock Doctor). Volumes I and
   II. Ph.D. University of Minnesota, 1960. 1007 pp.
      Volume one moves from a general study of English ballad
   operas to specific ballad operas of Fielding. Volume two contains the complete texts (with notes) of the titles listed above.

individual works

2303 Fielding, Henry. The Author's Farce (Original Version). Edited
   by Charles B. Woods. (Regents Restoration Drama Series).
   Lincoln: University of Nebraska Press, 1966.
      Includes introduction, notes, bibliography, and appendices

concerning the revision of the play, the individual represented, and the tunes of the play.

2304 -----. The Life and Death of Tom Thumb the Great and Some Miscellaneous Writings. London: J. M. Dent & Co., 1902. 242 pp. (The Temple Fielding).

2305 -----. The Tragedy of Tragedies or the Life and Death of Tom Thumb the Great with Annotations of H. Scriblerus Secundus. Edited by James T. Hillhouse. New Haven: Yale University Press, 1918. 223 pp.

    Scholarly edition. In the Introduction, Notes, and Appendices, Hillhouse refutes the idea that young Fielding was a careless writer. The Tragedy, in originals or adaptations, held the stage for about 45 years. The Tragedy burlesques 42 plays, 14 of which (mostly heroic plays) receive most of the ridicule. Fielding's notes to The Tragedy satirize the critics, especially Dryden and Dennis.

2306 -----. Tom Thumb the Great. Edited by John Hampden. London: Wells, Gardner and Darton, 1925. xxxviii, 50 pp. (The Garrick Playbooks edition).

    One of a series of old plays designed for modern amateur production, with shortened scenes and amplified stage directions

other works

2307 Jensen, Gerard E. "The Covent-Garden Journal, by Sir Alexander Drawcansir, Knt. Censor of Great Britain Henry Fielding. Edited with Introduction and Notes." Ph.D. Yale University, 191

2308 Fielding, Henry. The Covent-Garden Journal, by Sir Alexander Drawcansir, Knt. Censor of Great Briatain (Henry Fielding). Edited by Gerard Edward Jensen. 2 vols. New Haven: Yale University Press; London: H. Milford, Oxford University Press, 1915.

2309 Davies, E. O. "A Critical Edition of Pasquin and the Historical Register by Henry Fielding." B. Litt. Oxford University (Jesus), 1948.

2310 Fielding, Henry. The Female Husband and Other Writings. Edited by Claude E. Jones. Liverpool: Liverpool University Press, 1960. xi, 54 pp.

    Includes four epilogues.

2311 Paulson, Ronald, ed. Fielding: A Collection of Critical Essays. Englewood Cliffs, New Jersey: Prentice-Hall, 1962. 186 pp.

    Contains thirteen essays dealing mainly with his fiction, but "Fielding's Early Aesthetic and Technique," by Winsfield H. Rogers (pp. 25-44), deals with the plays, pointing out the patience with which Fielding shaped them artistically, the way

in which he developed a symbolic use of words, and the way he
used allegory to interpret life.

2312   Jensen, Gerard Edward, ed. The Covent-Garden Journal. 2 vols.
New York: Russell and Russell, 1964. 368, 293 pp.
       A scholarly edition of Fielding's contributions to his Covent-
Garden Journal. The origin of the periodical, its format, general
character, program of reform, and theatrical criticism are
discussed in detail in the Introduction. Includes Notes and Index.

2313   Fielding, Henry. The Historical Register for the Year 1736 and
Eurydice Hissed. Edited by William A. Appleton. (Regents
Restoration Drama Series). Lincoln: University of Nebraska
Press, 1967.
       Includes introduction, notes, and chronology.

biography and criticism

2314   Homann, Wilhelm. "Henry Fielding als Humorist." Inaugural Dissertation. Marburg, 1900.

2315   Ohnsorg, Richard. John Lacy's Dumb Lady, Mrs. Susannah
Centlivre's Love's Contrivance und Henry Fielding's Mock
Doctor in ihrem Verhältnis zu einander und zu ihrer gemeinschaftlichen Quellen. Hamburg: Bargsted und Ruhland, 1900.
60 pp.
       All the writers used Molière; all made changes independent
of Molière and of each other.

2316   Elwin, Whitwell. Some XVIII Century Men of Letters; Biographical
Essays by the Rev. Whitwell Elwin. Edited by his son Warwick
Elwin. 2 vols. London: John Murray, 1902.
       The brief biography of Fielding in volume two treats his
theatrical involvement, with only brief critical comments on
each work.

2317   McSpadden, Joseph Walker. Henry Fielding. New York: Croscup
and Sterling Co. [1902]. 32 pp.
       Very brief treatments of Fielding as man, as playwright,
and as novelist.

2318   Oschinsky, H. Gesellschaftliche zustände Englands während der
ersten hälfte des 18. Jahrhunderts im Spiegel Fieldingscher
Komödien. Wissenschaftliche beilage zum jahresbericht des
Friedrichs-real gymnasiums zu Berlin. Berlin: R. Gaertners
Verlagsbuchhandlung, 1902. 19 pp.

2319   Waldsschmidt, Karl. Die Dramatisierungen von Fielding's
"Tom Jones." Inaugural Dissertation, Rostock, 1906. 104 pp.

2320   Keightley, Thomas. The Life and Writings of Henry Fielding,
Esq. Taken from the Pages of Fraser's Magazine; and Edited

by Frederick Stoever Dickson. Clveland: The Rowfant Club,
1907. [11]-162 pp.

Biography of Keightley, followed by text of Keightley's
biography of Fielding, whose object is "to vindicate the character of Fielding."

2321 Godden, G. M. Henry Fielding. London: Sampson Low, Marston
and Company, 1910. 325 pp.

Chapters II, IV and V are devoted to a discussion of Fielding's comedies, farces, and political plays, as well as his
management of The Little Theatre in the Haymarket and production of Lillo's plays.

2322 Gorham, Maud Bassett. "The Traditions of Restoration Comedy
in the Works of Richardson, Fielding and Smollett." M.A.
Radcliffe College, 1910. 2 vols.

2323 Metcalf, John Calvin. "Henry Fielding, Critic." The Sewanee
Review, XIX (1911), 138-154.

On Fielding's dramatic criticism of traditions of the theatre,
of the heroic drama, of adaptations of Shakespeare, and of
Italian and French importations, Fielding brought criticism
back to nature and common sense.

2324 Wells, John Edwin. "Some New Facts Concerning Fielding's
Tumble-Down Dick and Pasquin." Modern Language Notes,
XXXVIII (May, 1913), 137-142.

On the performance and publication dates.

2325 Cross, Wilbur. The History of Henry Fielding. 2 vols. New Haven:
Yale University Press, 1918.

Chapters III-IX, Volume I, cover the dramatic career of
Fielding, 1730-1737. Summaries of each play are given, along
with accounts of stage history of each. Also accounts of theatrical companies and the background of the Licensing Act of 1737.
Cross's assessment of Fielding as dramatist: "Fielding and
Garrick, working together, would have given the British theatre
a fame unequalled since the days of Shakespeare."

2326 Nichols, Charles W. "An Edition of Fielding's Satirical Plays of
1736 and 1737." Ph.D. Yale University, 1918.

2327 Hamilton, Guy. "Fielding and the 'Motions.'" Times Literary
Supplement, March 11, 1920, p. 172.

Fielding's description of a puppet show in Book XII, chapter
5 of Tom Jones.

2328 Squire, John Collings. "Tom Thumb." Life and Letters: Essays
by J. C. Squire. (London: Hoddel and Staughton, Ltd. [1920].),
114-120.

An appreciation of Fielding's play, based on the Hillhouse edition, which calls for more discussion of eighteenth-century
plays.

2329 Henley, William Earnest. "Henry Fielding." Essays. (London:
      Macmillan & Co., Ltd., 1921), 1-46.
         A brief biography of Fielding prompted by the obscurity of
      the "real" Fielding; while the essay does treat the plays, they
      are deprecated.

2330 Nichols, Charles W. "The Date of 'Tumble-Down Dick.'" Modern
      Language Notes, XXXVI (1921), 312-313.
         An item establishing the correct date of this play as 1736.

2331 Hughes, Helen S. "A Dialogue--possibly by Henry Fielding."
      Philological Quarterly, I (1922), 49-55.
         A discussion of the authorship of "A Dialogue between a
      Beau's Head and his Heels..." a 1731 work by a Mr. Fielding;
      after considering the claims of Henry Fielding and Timothy
      Fielding (a comedian at Drury Lane), the writer concludes
      that Henry Fielding was almost certainly the author.

2332 -----. "Fielding's Indebtedness to James Ralph." Modern Philology,
      XX (1922), 19-34.
         A discussion of James Ralph's probable influence on The
      Author's Farce and Tom Thumb.

2333 Nichols, Charles W. "Fielding and the Cibbers." Philological
      Quarterly, I (1922), 278-279.
         An essay covering Fielding's satire on Colley and
      Theophilus Cibber in Pasquin and The Historical Register.

2334 -----. "Fielding's Tumble-Down Dick." Modern Language Notes,
      XXXVIII (1923), 410-416.
         A presentation of parallel passages from Fielding's Tumble-
      Down Dick and the work it satirizes, Pritchard's The Fall of
      Phaeton, in order to illuminate Fielding's particular type of
      humor.

2335 -----. "A New Note on Fielding's Historical Register." Modern
      Language Notes, XXXVIII (1923), 507-508.
         A discussion of an advertisement which appeared in the St.
      James' Evening-Post and the London Evening-Post, March 8-
      10, 1737, announcing the forthcoming production of The His-
      torical Register.

2336 -----. "Social Satire in Fielding's Pasquin and The Historical
      Register." Philological Quarterly, III (1924), 309-317.
         A consideration of these two plays as mirrors of social
      follies and vices of Fielding's times, especially the period's
      love for Italian opera.

2337 Stonehill, Charles. "Fielding's The Miser." London Times Liter-
      ary Supplement, October 22, 1925, p. 698.
         Comments on an edition of the play which appears to be
      earlier than 1733.

2338 Blanchard, Frederic T. Fielding the Novelist: A Study of Historical

Criticism. New Haven: Yale University Press, 1926. xiv,
655 pp.
Concentrates upon Fielding as novelist, with a history of
critical attitudes toward his work. Only occasional references
to the plays, especially Pasquin and Tom Thumb. Full bibliography.

2339 Radtke, Bruno. Henry Fielding als Kritiker. Leipzig: Mayer and
Müller, 1926.
A painstaking German dissertation, organizing citations
from Fielding on the principle of a dictionary rather than of a
systematic exposition of ideas.

2340 Parfitt, G. E. L'Influence francaise dans les oeuvres de Fielding
et dans le théâtre anglais contemporain de ses comédies.
Paris: Les Presses Modernes, 1928. 158 pp.
The first effort to trace the French influence on Fielding's
plays, novels, critical theory, and satire. Fielding was steeped
in modern French literature, and its influence is considerable,
especially in his drama. Includes a list of French books in
Fielding's library.

2341 Banerji, H. K. Henry Fielding, Playwright, Journalist and Master
of the Art of Fiction: His Life and Works. Oxford: Blackwell,
1929. viii, 342 pp.
A useful introduction to the works of Fielding rather than a
biography. The chief value is for its detailed account of Fielding's minor writing as journalist and playwright.

2342 Horn, Robert D. "The Farce Technique in the Dramatic Work of
Henry Fielding and Samuel Foote and Its Influence on the
Märchensatiren of Ludwig Lieck." Ph.D. University of Michigan,
1930.

2343 Glenn, Sidney Erwin. "Some French Influences on Henry Fielding."
Ph.D. University of Illinois, 1931.
Concerned with Fielding's French literary background in
his formative years--up to the publication of Joseph Andrews.
Glenn recounts Fielding's particular debt to Molière and
Regnard with regard to the drama.

2344 Nichols, Charles Washburn. "Fielding's Satire on Pantomime."
Publications of the Modern Language Association, XLVI (1931),
1107-1112.
Considers Fielding's objections to and attacks on pantomime,
as seen in Pasquin and, especially, in Tumble-Down Dick.

2345 Read, Stanley E. "Fielding's Miser." Huntington Library Bulletin,
No. 1 (May, 1931), 211-213.
This article shows that the folio edition of the play was a
"somewhat careless reprint from the octavo."

2346 Taylor, Houghton W. "Fielding upon Cibber." Modern Philology,

XXIX (1931), 73-90.
> Surveys Fielding's satirical, often cutting, reviews on Cibber in both his novels and plays.

2347 Voorde, F. P. van der. Henry Fielding: Critic and Satirist. Gravenhage: Westerbaan, 1931. 230 pp.

2348 Graham, Walter. "The Date of the Champion." Times Literary Supplement, February 4, 1932, p. 76; and Notes and Queries, CLXIII (1932), 150-151.

2349 Joesten, Maria. Die Philosophie Fieldings. (Kölner Anglistische Arbeiten, Vol. XV). Leipzig: Bernard Tachnitz, 1932. 107 pp.
> The author suggests that Fielding's work may be interpreted in terms of stoicism.

2350 Avery, Emmett L. "An Early Performance of Fielding's Historical Register." Modern Language Notes, XLIX (1934), 407.
> To prove that The Historical Register was being performed over a week before the end of March, 1737, Avery refers to the diary of Viscount Percival who wrote that he attended a performance of the play on March 22, 1737.

2351 -----. "Some Notes on Fielding's Plays." Research Studies of the State College of Washington, III (1935), 48-50.
> Data about performances of The Historical Register (1737), Don Quixote in England (1734), and the Covent Garden Tragedy, with additional facts about other plays.

2352 Woods, Charles B. "Studies in the Dramatic Works of Henry Fielding." Ph.D. Harvard University, 1935.
> Designed as a supplement to Cross's History of Henry Fielding, this dissertation provides "a partial substitute for an annotated edition of [Fielding's] dramatic works." The study is confined to the twenty-four plays that appeared before the Licensing Act of 1737.

2353 Gill, W. W. "Early Fielding Documents." Notes and Queries, CLXXI (1936), 242.
> Notes an incident in 1725 involving Fielding's attemped abduction of an heiress.

2354 Hessler, Mabel Dorothy. "The Literary Opposition to Sir Robert Walpole, 1721-1742; Fielding's Attacks on Walpole." Chicago: Private edition, distributed by the University of Chicago libraries. Part of a dissertation at the University of Chicago, 1936, pp. 124-150.
> Treatment of Fielding's satires on Walpole from Tom Thumb to the Licensing Act and in the selections in the Miscellanies.

2355 Woods, Charles B. "Notes on Three of Fielding's Plays." Publications of the Modern Language Association, LII (1937), 359-373.
> Woods argues that The Letter Writers (1731) was inspired

by contemporary attempts at extortion by mail; that The Modern
Husband (1732) was based upon a contemporary episode illustrating 'criminal conversation'; and that Eurydice Hiss'd (1737)
is a "double allegory" based on an analogy between Fielding's
struggles as a playwright and his opposition to Walpole's Excise
Bill.

2356 Avery, Emmett L. "Fielding's Universal Gallant." Research Studies
of the State College of Washington, VI (1938), 46.
Speculations about why Fielding's play, probably completed
by December, 1733, was not performed until February 10,
1735.

2357 -----. "Fielding's Last Season with the Haymarket Theatre."
Modern Philology, XXXVI (1939), 283-292.
An examination of advertisements by the New Theatre in
the Haymarket in The Daily Advertiser reveals many new facts
about Fielding's relations with this theatre from January to May,
1737.

2358 Brown, Jack Richard. "From Aaron Hill to Henry Fielding?"
Philological Quarterly, XVIII (1939), 85-88.
Prints a letter of Hill's and provides evidence to show that
it was written to Fielding.

2359 Fowler, A. Murray. "Comparative Study of Humours: Characters
in Ben Johson and Henry Fielding." Eugene, Oregon: Oregon
State System, 1939. 22 pp. (Mimeographed).

2360 S., E. "Fielding as a Dramatist." More Books, XIV (June, 1939),
260.
Brief notice of the acquisition by the Boston Public Library
of a first edition of Pasquin (1736).

2361 Bayley, A. R. "A Portrait of Fielding." Notes and Queries,
CLXXVIII (1940), 124.
The only authentic portrait of Fielding is from a pen-and-
ink sketch by Hogarth from memory or, perhaps, from a
paper profile.

2362 C., O. "A Portrait of Fielding." Notes and Queries, CLXXVIII
(1940), 63-64.
Is there any truth in the story that Garrick made up on the
deceased Fielding, "appeared" to Hogarth and demanded that
Fielding's portrait be painted?

2363 De Castro, J. Paul. "Fielding Manuscripts." Times Literary
Supplement, June 1, 1940, p. 267.

2364 -----. "Revivals of Fielding's Plays." Notes and Queries, CLXXIX
(1940), 461.
Three of Fielding's plays were revived in the early twentieth-
century.

2365 Marx, George Edwards. "Henry Fielding and His Place in the

Theatre." M.A. Cornell University, 1940.

2366 N., A. E. "Revivals of Fielding's Plays." Notes and Queries,
       CLXXIX (December 14, 1940), 423.

2367 Rogers, Winfield H. "The Significance of Fielding's Temple
       Beau." Publications of the Modern Language Association, LV
       (June, 1940), 440-444.
       "An interpretation of the play in the light of Addison's
       discussion of pedants here noted as an important source."

2368 Wallace, Robert M. "Fielding Manuscripts." London Times
       Literary Supplement, May 18, 1940, p. 243.
       Argues, contrary to Wilbur Cross, that Fielding did leave
       important Mss. unpublished, some of which survive.

2369 Bayley, A. R. and Jaggard, William. "Revivals of Fielding's
       Plays." Notes and Queries, CLXXX (1941), 15.
       Tom Thumb was recently revived. A comic opera of Tom
       Jones written by Joseph Reed in 1769 was revived in 1907.

2370 Hammond, Geraldine Elizabeth. Evidences of the Dramatist's
       Technique in Henry Fielding's Novels. Wichita, Kansas: The
       University [1941]. 27 pp. (Wichita, Kansas Municipal Univer-
       sity Bulletin, Vol. 16, Oct., 1941, No. 10).
       Aside from the many direct references to the theater,
       dramatic lessons are evident in the use of dialogue, character-
       ization by form of speech, type of satire against authorities,
       the use of "humour" names, and the use of parenthetic "stage
       directions."

2371 Irwin, William Robert. "An Attack on John Fielding." Modern
       Language Notes, LVI (November, 1941), 523-525.

2372 Jaggard, William. "Revivals of Fielding's Plays." Notes and
       Queries, CLXXX (1941), 15.

2373 Vincent, Howard P. "Henry Fielding in Prison." Modern Language
       Review, XXXVI (October, 1941), 499-500.
       "A rare pamphlet of 1740 records an occasion on which Sir
       Robert Walpole secured Fielding's release from prison, some
       time before 1728."

2374 Avery, Emmett L. "Proposals for a New London Theatre in 1737."
       Notes and Queries, CLXXXII (1942), 286-287.
       Reprints an advertisement from The Daily Advertiser
       (February 4) inviting builders to submit plans and connects the
       project which came to nothing, with Fielding.

2375 Heilman, Robert B. "Fielding and 'The First Gothic Revival.'"
       Modern Language Notes, LVII (December, 1942), 671-673.
       "Comment upon reflections in Fielding's writing of the
       vogue for Gothic architecture."

2376 Heller, M. "TheSignificance of Henry Fielding's Dramatic Work."
       M.A. McGill University, 1942.

2377 Price, Lawrence M. "The Works of Fielding on the German
    Stage, 1762-1801." Journal of English and German?c Philology,
    XLI (July, 1942), 257-278.
       Treats content and stage histories of translations of Field-
    ing's plays and German dramatizations of Tom Jones (which
    were very popular) from the earliest translations in 1759
    through approximately 1801.

2378 Rogers, Winfield H. "Fielding's Early Aesthetic and Technique."
    Studies in Philology, XL (1943), 529-551.
       Examines four ideas important to Fielding's novels which
    were developed in the plays: (1) his impatience with the restric-
    tions of comedy and his consequent developing of farce as a
    satiric and moral medium for a criticism of life; (2) adapting
    of the commonplace 'humour' as a basis for the study and
    analysis of the springs of human action; (3) his developing
    words as symbols which often carry allegorical meaning;
    (4) his development of a genuinely comprehensive allegorical
    method of interpreting life.

2379 Hughes, Leo. "The Influence of Fielding's Milieu upon His Humour."
    University of Texas Studies in English, 1944.

2380 Swaen, A. E. H. "Fielding's The Intriguing Chambermaid."
    Neophilologus, XXIX (April, 1944), 117-120.
       Examines Fielding's debt to Plautus's Mostellaria.

2381 Hughes, Leo. "The Influence of Fielding's Milieu upon his Humor."
    Studies in English, Department of English, The University of
    Texas, 1944. (Austin: University of Texas Press, 1945), 269-
    297.
       Discusses Fielding's plays, relating them to his work as
    a naturalistic comic novelist.

2382 Sherburn, George. "The Dunciad, Book IV." Studies in English,
    Department of English, the University of Texas, 1944. (Austin:
    University of Texas Press, 1945), 174-190.
       Compares the structure of the imagery in Pope's poem with
    that in The Author's Farce and Pasquin.

2383 Irwin, W. R. "Satire and Comedy in the Works of Henry Fielding."
    English Literary History, XIII (1946), 168-188.
       In his plays and early satirical writings Fielding evolves
    the theory of comedy which is the basis for his novels.

2384 Jenkins, Elizabeth. Henry Fielding. London: Home and Van Thal,
    1947. 102 pp.
       A general critical study, mainly on the novels but including
    mention of the dramatic works.

2385 Weide, Erwin. Henry Fieldings Komödien und die Restaurations-
    Komödien. Hamburg: Hansischer Gildenverlag, 1947. 140 pp.
    (Dichtung, Wort, und Sprache, X).

Fielding recognizes the emotional nature of man, and in
his plays rejects the mechanical and rationalist theories
which were accepted by Restoration writers.

2386 Willcocks, M. P. A True-Born Englishman: being a Life of Henry
Fielding. London: Allen and Unwin, 1947. vii, 288 pp.
A popular general biography, dealing with the plays, and
theatrical affairs in the earlier chapters.

2387 Woods, Charles B. "Fielding's Epilogue for Theobald." Philological Quarterly, XXVIII (July, 1949), 419-424.
A hitherto unnoticed epilogue to Orestes is described.

2388 Baker, Sheridan. "Henry Fielding's Comic Romances." Papers
of the Michigan Academy of Science, Arts, and Letters, XLV
(1950), 411-419.
Cites The Author's Farce.

2389 Baker, Sheridan W., Jr. "Setting, Character, and Situation in
the Plays and Novels of Henry Fielding." Ph.D. University
of California, 1950.

2390 Goggin, Leo P. "The Development of Fielding's Technique As a
Writer of Comedies." Ph.D. Chicago University, 1950.

2391 Peterson, William. "Satire in Fielding's An Interlude between
Jupiter, Juno, Apollo, and Mercury." Modern Language Notes,
LXV (1950), 200-202.
Fielding's brief dramatic sketch satirizes the influence
of Queen Caroline and Walpole's mistresses upon his govern-
ment.

2392 Willy, Margaret. "Portrait of a Man: Henry Fielding." Life Was
Their Cry. (London: Evans Brothers, Ltd., 1950), 98-152.
An "appreciation" of Fielding as a humanitarian, especially
in his novels and his career as magistrate. Treats his theatrical work as a training ground for novel writing.

2393 Goggin, L. P. "Development of Techniques in Fielding's Comedies."
Publications of the Modern Language Association, LXVII (1952),
769-781.
Fielding's comedies show a development of technique which
later emerges in his novels.

2394 -----. "Fielding and the Select Comedies of Mr. de Molière."
Philological Quarterly, XXXI (1952), 344-350.
Fielding probably translated none of the works in the Select
Comedies, but may have consulted the book for at least one
adaptation from Molière.

2395 Sergienko, Alexander Edward. "Characterization in Fielding's
Novels and Plays." Honors Thesis. Harvard University, 1952.
35, iii pp.
A comparison of Parson Adams to Don Quixote in Don
Quixote in England and a discussion of some of Fielding's

techniques of characterization.

2396 Kahrl, Stanley Jadwin. "Development of Moral Attitudes in
Fielding's Comedies." Honors Thesis. Harvard University,
1953. 45 pp.
  Examines four of Fielding's comedies in terms of two types
  of characters: the "humor" types, illustrating qualities Fielding
  feels are harmful but not dangerous; and, the straight parts,
  illustrating complex moral problems.

2397 Todd, William B. "Three Notes on Fielding." Papers of the Bibliographical Society of America, XLVII (1953), 70-75.
  Todd makes bibliographical comments on An Apology for
  the Life of Mr. T[heophilus]. C[ibber]. (1740) and two other
  works by Fielding.

2398 Butt, John. Fielding. Writers and Their Work, No. 57. London:
Longmans, Green & Co., [1954]. 35 pp.
  Treats the influence of Fielding's theatrical experiences
  upon his novels as well as some aspects of theory, technique,
  and form in the novels.

2399 Coley, William B., II. "Fielding's Theory of Comedy." Ph.D.
Yale University, 1954.

2400 Brown, Jack Richard. "Henry Fielding's Grub-Street Opera."
Modern Language Quarterly, XVI (1955), 32-41.
  Concludes that Fielding's first attempt at political satire
  is "lighthearted" and "nonpartisan," since Fielding's political
  views were not yet fully developed. Also attempts to trace the
  stage history of the play and to examine critically the three
  printed versions of the play.

2401 Kreutz, Irving William. "A Study of Henry Fielding's Plays."
Ph.D. University of Wisconsin, 1956.
  24 plays analyzed and classified.

2402 Murry, John Middleton. "In Defence of Fielding." Unprofessional
Essays. (London: Cape, 1956), 11-52.

2403 Parker, A. A. "Fielding and the Structure of Don Quixote." Bulletin of Hispanic Studies, XXXIII (1956), 1-16.
  The contrast between two approaches of constructing a
  novel is discussed through a consideration of the differences
  in technique between Fielding and Cervantes. Most of the
  discussion is about Don Quixote, but the author feels that the
  structure of Tom Jones is superior.

2404 Ramondt, Marie. "Between Laughter and Humour in the Eighteenth
Century." Neophilologus, XL (1956), 128-138.
  Includes Fielding's theories.

2405 Dyson, A. E. "Satiric and Comic Theory in Relation to Fielding."
Modern Language Quarterly, XVIII (1957), 225-237.

2406 Goggin, L. P. "Fielding's The Masquerade." Philological Quarterly,

XXXVI (1957), 475-487.

Cites Fielding's plays.

2407 Humphreys, A. R. "Fielding and Smollett." The Pelican Guide
to English Literature, Vol. IV. From Dryden to Johnson,
edited by Boris Ford. (Baltimore: Penguin Books, 1957), 313-
332.

Fielding's playwriting mentioned. Select Bibliographies
at end of the volume.

2408 Ryan, Marjorie. "The Tom Jones Hero in Plays and Novels,
1750-1800: A Study of Fielding's Influence." Ph.D. University
of Minnesota, 1957.

2409 Cohen, M. A. "The Plays of Henry Fielding." M.A. University
of Leeds, 1958-1959.

2410 Baker, Sheridan. "Henry Fielding and the Cliché." Criticism, I
(1959), 354-361.

Cites Fielding's plays and Cibber's.

2411 -----. "Henry Fielding's The Female Husband: Fact and Fiction."
Publications of the Modern Language Association, LXXIV (1959),
213-224.

Cites Congreve's and Fielding's plays.

2412 Carroll, John J. "Henry Fielding and the 'Trunk-Maker.'" Notes
and Queries, VI (1959), 213.

Theatrical allusion in Tom Jones (IV, 6) from Spectator
235.

2413 Coley, William B. "The Background of Fielding's Laughter."
Journal of English Literary History, XXVI (1959), 229-252.

Fielding's literary treatment is neither serious nor low, but
a mixed mode, a peculiar synthesis, called "witty seriousness."
Traces the history of this comic mode from Lucian, emphasizing Shaftesbury and illustrating the idea with quotations from
Convent Garden Journal 18.

2414 Loftis, John, ed. Essays on the Theatre from Eighteenth-Century
Periodicals. Los Angeles: Clark Memorial Library, 1960.
57 pp.

This deals with Fielding's political burlesques. Eleven essays, 1722-1737.

2415 Wright, Kenneth Daulton. "Henry Fielding and the London Stage,
1730-1737." Ph.D. Ohio State University, 1960.

"Concerned with all aspects of Fielding's life in the theatre."

2416 Roberts, Edgar V. "Eighteenth-Century Ballad Opera: The Contribution of Henry Fielding." Drama Survey, I (1961), 77-85.

2417 Baker, Sheridan. "Political Allusion in Fielding's Author's Farce,
Mock Doctor, and Tumble-Down Dick." Publications of the
Modern Language Association, LXXVII (1962), 221-231.

Baker illustrates Fielding's anti-Walpole satire in three
plays composed between 1730-1736, and demonstrates also how
the satire is leveled at Cibber, Dr. John Misaubin, and John
Rich respectively, so that Fielding simultaneously supported
the Opposition as well as good theatre in his attacks.

2418 Coley, William B. "Fielding and the Two Covent-Garden Journals."
Modern Language Review, LVII (1962), 386-387.
His relation to the journals of 1749 and 1752.

2419 Combs, William Wesley. "Man and Society in Fielding's Works."
Ph.D. Harvard University, 1962.

2420 Kaiser, John I. "A Study of the Plays of Henry Fielding as a Commentary on the Early Eighteenth-Century Theatre." Ph.D.
St. John's University, Brooklyn, 1962.

2421 Roberts, Edgar V. "Henry Fielding's Lost Play, Deborah; or,
A Wife For You All (1733): Consisting Partly of Facts and
Partly of Observations Upon Them." Bulletin of the New York
Public Library, LXVI (1962), 576-588.
Discussion of existing facts concerning the lost play. Con-
cludes that Deborah "was a brief entertainment based upon a
farcial trial scene handled in his usual way" and contained a
condemnation of the English judicial structure.

2422 -----. "Possible Additions to Airs 6 and 7 of Henry Fielding's
Ballad Opera, The Lottery." Notes and Queries, New Ser.,
IX (1962), 455-456.
There is evidence that stanzas of Airs 6 and 7 of The Lottery
may have been written by Fielding, that they were suppressed
when the play was performed and published.

2423 Woods, Charles B. "The 'Miss Lucy' Plays of Fielding and Gar-
rick." Philological Quarterly, XLI (1962), 294-310.
The relationship of Fielding's The Virgin Unmask'd and
Miss Lucy in Town to Garrick's Lethe.

2424 Chaudbury, Awadhesh. "Henry Fielding: His Attitude Towards
the Contemporary Stage." Ph.D. The University of Michigan,
1963. (Order No. 64-6664).
A detailed study of Fielding's novels and prefaces reveals
his desire to expose and correct the decadent taste of 18th
century playwrights, actors, and spectators.

2425 Roberts, Edgar V. "Fielding's Ballad Opera The Lottery (1732)
and the English State Lottery of 1731." Huntington Library
Quarterly, XXVII (November, 1963), 39-52.
Supplies pertinent information about lotteries prior to 1732
as a background for an understanding of Fielding's play.

2426 -----. "Henry Fielding and Richard Leveridge: Authorship of 'The
Roast Beef of Old England.'" Huntington Library Quarterly,
XXVII (1964), 175-181.

Concerns the authorship of 'The Mighty Roast Beef' in
Fielding's The Grub-Street Opera (1731) and Don Quixote in
England (1734). Evidence from songbooks and miscellany collections of the period proves that Fielding's version anticipated
that of Leveridge.

2427 Woods, Charles B. "The Folio Text of Fielding's The Miser."
Huntington Library Quarterly, XXVIII (1964), 59-61.
The folio Miser was probably published in 1734 as a sup-
plement to the fifth number of Cotes's Weekly Journal, or,
The English Stage-Player.

2428 Wright, Kenneth D. "Henry Fielding and the Theatres Act of
1737." Quarterly Journal of Speech, L (1964), 252-256.
Studies the actual passing of the Licensing Act through
Parliament and Fielding's participation in events leading to
its passage. Testimony by Fielding's contemporaries, especially Colley Cibber and Benjamin Victor, confirms his responsibility for passage of the Act.

2429 Levine, George R. "Henry Fielding's 'Defense' of the Stage
Licensing Act." English Language Notes, II (1965), 193-196.
In The Champion of December 10, 1739-40, Fielding
assumes a persona which typifies the elements of society held
accountable for the Licensing Act.

2430 Smith, J. Oates. "Masquerade and Marriage: Fielding's Comedies
of Identity." Ball State University Forum, VI (1965), 10-21.
Studies the development of the masquerade motif in Fielding's dramas and novels. Fielding skillfully treats the struggle
of the individual for virtue and self-identity in a hypocritical
world.

2431 Woods, Charles. "Cibber in Fielding's Author's Farce: Three
Notes." Philological Quarterly, XLIV (1965), 145-151.
Fielding's satirical representation of Cibber as Mr. Keyber,
Marplay, and Sir Farcical Comic.

2432 -----. "Theobald and Fielding's Don Tragedio." English Language
Notes, II (1965), 266-271.
Identifies Lewis Theobald as the source of Fielding's satirical
characterization of Don Tragedio.

2433 Wright, Andrew. Henry Fielding: Mask and Feast. London: Chatto
and Windus, 1965. 214 pp.
The comic structure, characterization, and dramatic
tableaux of Tom Jones, Joseph Andrews, and Amelia offer
ample proof that Fielding's dramatic career was responsible
for many of the artistic devices employed in his novels.

2434 Battestin, Martin C. "Fielding and 'Master Punch' in Panton
Street." Philological Quarterly, XLV (1966), 191-208.
For one season in 1748 Fielding owned and operated his own

puppet theatre in Panton Street under the name of "Madame de
la Nash."

2435 Coley, W. B. "Henry Fielding and the Two Walpoles." Philological
Quarterly, XLV (1966), 157-178.

The writings of Horace Walpole give valuable information on
the relationship of Fielding to Robert Walpole and on Fielding's
political disillusionment.

2436 Dircks, Richard J. "The Perils of Heartfree: A Sociological Review
of Fielding's Adaptation of Dramatic Convention." Texas Studies
in Literature and Language, VII (1966), 5-13.

For purposes of social criticism in Jonathan Wild Fielding
reflects, directly and by contrast, ideas found in the drama of
sensibility and adopts the techniques of the sentimental dramatis
in his characterization and manipulation of plot.

2437 • Dudden, Frederick Homes. Henry Fielding: His Life, Works, and
Times. Hamden, Connecticut: Archon Books, 1966. 582 pp.

A reissue of the work first published in 1952. Chapters I-
VIII deal with Fielding's career as a playwright.

2438 Amory, Hugh. "Henry Fielding's Epistles to Walpole: A Reexamination." Philological Quarterly, XLVI (1967), 236-247.

Studies the relationship of the Epistles to Fielding's attacks
on Walpole and includes references to Tom Thumb and The
Grub-Street Opera.

2439 Hatfield, Glenn W. "Quacks, Pettyfoggers, and Parsons: Fielding's
Case Against the Learned Professions." Texas Studies in Literature and Language, IX (1967), 69-83.

Examines Fielding's "responsible" satire in the plays and
novels. Fielding had a clear conception of the ideal standard
of these professions and a respect for them.

2440 -----. "The Serpent and the Dove: Fielding's Irony and the
Prudence Theme in Tom Jones." Modern Philology, LXV (1967),
17-32.

Studies Fielding's interest in the clear meaning of words.
Fielding exhibits this interest not only in his fiction but also in
The Covent Garden Journal, in his comedies which can be read
as dramatic definitions of abstract social and moral virtues,
and in his theatrical burlesques and satires that include attacks on debasers of language.

2441 Irwin, Michael. Henry Fielding: The Tentative Realist. Oxford:
Clarendon Press, 1967. 147 pp.

Emphasizes Fielding's didactic intentions in the novels but
also considers the plays as vehicles for Fielding's didacticism.

2442 Kinder, Marsha. "Henry Fielding's Dramatic Experimentation: A
Preface to His Fiction." Ph.D. University of California, Los An
1967. (Order No. 67-9652).

Examines the general decline of the drama and the rise of
the novel in the eighteenth century by studying the relationships
between Fielding's plays and novels. Emphasis is given to the
most experimental plays: The Author's Farce, The Tragedy
of Tragedies, Pasquin, and The Historical Register.

Finances

2443 Beljame, A. Men of Letters and the English Public in the Eigh-
      teenth Century, 1660-1744: Dryden, Addison, Pope. Translated
      by E. O. Lorimer with an Introduction by Bonamy Dobrée.
      London: Kegan Paul, 1948. 492 pp.
          A translation of the classic Le Public et les Hommes de
      Lettres en Angleterre au dix-huitième Siècle (1881), which
      studies patronage and theatrical finances during the period.

Finch, Anne

2444 Finch, Anne, Countess of Winchilsea. Poems, 1661-1720. Edited
      by John Middleton Murry. London: Jonathan Cape, 1928. 112
      pp.
          Among the poems is the Prologue to Aristomenes and the
      Epilogue to Jane Shore. An introductory sketch of her career.

Fishbourne, Christopher

2445 Baine, Rodney M. "Rochester or Fishbourne: a Question of Author-
      ship." Review of English Studies, XXII (July, 1946), 201-206.
          The infamous Sodom was probably written by Christopher
      Fishbourne.

Flecknoe, Richard

texts

2446 Flecknoe, R. A Short Discourse of the English Stage, 1664. In
      Spingarn, J. E., editor. Critical Essays of the Seventeenth
      Century, Vol. 2. (Oxford, 1908), 91-96.
2447 -----. Of One that Zany's the Good Companion. Edited by Ernest
      Niles Hooker. Ann Arbor: The Augustan Reprint Society, Nov-
      ember 1946. (Series I, Essays on Wit, 2).
          Includes "Of a Bold Abusive Wit" (1665), "Essay on Wit"
      (1748) with remarks on Cato, Otway and Shakespeare, Joseph
      Warton's The Adventurer, numbers 127, 133 (1754) on Molière,
      Jonson and Congreve, and "Of Wit" (Weekly Register, 1732).

biography and criticism

2448 Lohr, Anton. Richard Flecknoe. Eine literarhistorische Unter-
      suchung. Leipzig: A. Deichert, 1905. xii, 114 pp.
          The fullest treatment to date of Richard Flecknoe, con-
      sidering the plays, Ermina, Love's Dominion, The Damoiselles
      à la Mode, Love's Kingdom.
2449 Doney, Paul H. "The Life and Works of Richard Flecknoe." Ph.D.
      Harvard University, 1928.
2450 Davies, P. C. "The Life and Works of Richard Flecknoe." B.
      Litt. Oxford University (Jesus), 1963.

Fleming, Daniel

2451 Blair, Frederick G. "Restoration Plays." Times Literary Sup-
      plement, March 29, 1923, 217 pp.
          Quotes excerpts from the correspondence of Sir Daniel
      Fleming referring to dramas from 1661-1668.

Fletcher, John

2452 Nicoll, Allardyce. "Restoration Plays." Times Literary Supplemen
      April 5, 1923, p. 233.
          A correction of Frederick Blair's reference to The Tanner
      Tanned in Blair's March 29th letter (q.v.). Nicoll corrects
      this to Fletcher's The Tamer Tamed.
2453 Price, Cecil. "A Playbill c. 1686." Notes and Queries, CXCIV
      (November 26, 1949), 519.
          A bill for a performance of A King and No King preserved
      in the Public Record Office.

Foote, Samuel

2454 Fyvie, John. Wits, Beaux, and Beauties of the Georgian Era.
      London: Lane, 1909.
          Eight essays concerned with social England in the eighteenth
      century. Biographical sketches with emphasis on social life.
      Introductory essay on Samuel Foote defends actor-dramatist
      and discusses world that Foote satirized on London stage.
2455 Fitzgerald, Percy. Samuel Foote. A Biography. London: Chatto
      & Windus, 1910. vii, [1], 382 pp.
          A somewhat detailed study of Foote's life, relations with
      other dramatists and writers, as well as two chapters devoted
      to a study and evaluation of his comedies.
2456 Belden, Mary M. "The Dramatic Works of Samuel Foote." Ph.D.

Yale University, 1919.
2457 Balch, Marston. "The Theatre Reforms the Pulpit." Theatre Arts
Monthly, XII (October, 1928), 753-762.
On Samuel Foote's satire on Methodist preaching in The
Minor (1760), with a Reynolds portrait of Foote.
2458 Belden, Mary Megie. The Dramatic Work of Samuel Foote. Yale
Studies in English, LXXX. New Haven: Yale University Press,
1929. viii, 224 pp.
Except for Percy Fitzgerald's life, the first 20th-century
examination. Criticism and history of the plays, and notes on
stage productions. Bibliography and index.
2459 Horn, Robert D. "The Farce Technique in the Dramatic Work of
Henry Fielding and Samuel Foote and Its Influence on the
Märchensatiren of Ludwig Lieck." Ph.D. University of Michigan,
1930.
2460 Wimsatt, W. W., Jr. "Foote and a Friend of Boswell's: A Note
on The Nabob." Modern Language Notes, LVII (May, 1942),
325-335.
"A consideration of the prototypes of Sir Matthew Mite,
hero of the play, and an account of the 'nabob' George Gray,
whom Foote met through Boswell."
2461 Weatherly, Edward H. "Foote's Revenge on Churchill and Lloyd."
Huntington Library Quarterly, IX (November, 1945), 49-60.
The revision of Foote's Taste, 1761, a satire on Churchill and Lloyd, is in response to The Rosciad and The Actor.
2462 Sinko, Gregory. Samuel Foote: The Satirist of Rising Capitalism.
Breslau, 1950. 72 pp.
Sinko analyzes Foote's personality and works and classifies
him as a satirist who was a spokesman for a "bourgeois type
of civilization."
2463 "Gainsborough's Portrait of Samuel Foote." Connoisseur, CXXVIII
(1951), 215-216.
This short essay retells a number of interesting anecdotes
about Foote. Gainsborough's portrait is reproduced in black
and white on page 214.
2464 Corner, Betsy C. "Dr. Melchisedek Broadbrim and the Playwright." Journal of the History of Medicine, VII (1952), 122-
135.
The play becomes much clearer in light of later eighteenth-
century medicine and doctors.
2465 Scouten, Arthur H. "On the Origin of Foote's Matinees." Theatre
Notebook, VII (1952-1953), 28-31.
Evidence from the London Daily Advertiser indicates that
Foote adopted the practice of matinee performances from
entertainers already using it.

2466 Wharton, Robert V. "Satire and Panegyric in the Plays of Samuel
      Foote." Ph.D. Columbia University, 1954. 266 pp. (Publication
      No. 8861).
           Foote's work is closely related to the tradition of Tory
      satire as exemplified earlier in Pope and Swift.

2467 Sinko, Grzegorz. Anglieski dramat mieszczanski XVIII wieku;
      G. Lillo, E. Moore, S. Foote. Przelozyl i opracowal G.
      Sinko. Wroclaw: Zaklad im. Ossolinskich Wydawnictwo [1955].
      cxl, 367 pp. (Biblioteka narodowa, Ser. 2, 95).
           Introduction, giving historical background. Polish translation
      of Lillo's The London Merchant, Moore's The Gamester, and
      Foote's The Nabob.

2468 Price, Cecil. "Hymen and Hirco: A Vision." London Times Literary
      Supplement, July 11, 1958, p. 396.
           Cites Foote, The Maid of Bath.

2469 Byrnes, Joseph Alfred. "Four Plays of Samuel Foote: The Knights,
      The Minor, The Lyar, The Mayor of Garratt; An Edition with
      Commentary." Ph.D. New York University, 1963. (Order No.
      63-7210).
           General introduction places Foote in the theatrical history
      of the eighteenth century; introductions to individual plays
      provide information about the targets of Foote's satire.

2470 Berveiller, Michel. "Anglais et Francais de comédie chez Louis
      de Boissy et Samuel Foote." Comparative Literature Studies,
      II (1965), 259-269.
           A comparison of the comic techniques of Louis de Boissy
      and Samuel Foote, especially in their treatment of displaced
      persons.

2471 Wharton, Robert V. "The Divided Sensibility of Samuel Foote."
      Educational Theatre Journal, XVII (1965), 31-37.
           A strange mingling of sentimentalism and satire pervades
      the comedies of Samuel Foote. It stems from Foote's in-
      ability to reconcile his Hobbesian temperament with the per-
      iod's Shaftesburyean climate.

2472 Bogorad, Samuel N. "Samuel Foote: the Prospects for a Life and
      Works." Restoration and Eighteenth Century Theatre Research,
      VI (May, 1967), 11-13.
           Reviews the most important scholarly work on Foote's life
      and plays and explains the need for a documented biography
      and critical edition of the works. Suggests available resources.

2473 Trefman, Simon. "Sam. Foote, Comedian, 1720-1777." Ph.D.
      New York University, 1967. (Order No. 68-10,099).
           Foote's comedies, despite their topicality, are a sure and
      lively guide to the temper of mid-eighteenth century life.

Ford, John

2474 Leech, Clifford. "A Projected Restoration Performance of Ford's
      The Lover's Melancholy." Modern Language Review, LVI
      (July, 1961), 378-381.
            A study of a copy of the Quarto of Ford's The Lover's
      Melancholy (1629), at the Folger Library, which has been ex-
      tensively worked for abridgement, to determine if this is done
      for a projected Restoration performance.
2475 Anderson, Donald K., Jr. "The Date and Handwriting of a Manu-
      script Copy of Ford's Perkin Warbeck." Notes and Queries,
      New Ser., X (1963), 340-341.
            There is evidence that a manuscript of Ford's play was
      written in 1745 for the December 19 production at Goodman's
      Fields.

Foreign Actors

2476 Avery, Emmett L. "Foreign Performers in the London Theaters
      in the Early Eighteenth Century." Philological Quarterly, XVI
      (1937), 105-123.
            An historical record of visiting troupes of repertory actors,
      mainly French and Italian, along with a review of English
      critical reactions to their performances.

Foreign Influence

2477 Becker, Gustav. Die Aufnahme des Don Quixote in die englische
      Literatur (1605-c.1770). Berlin: Mayer und Müller, 1906.
      246 pp. (Palaestra, XIII).
            The influence of Don Quixote and the pseudo-Don Quixote
      of the novels on English authors, particularly on Fielding
      and Davenant, in humor, episodes, and characters.
2478 Harvey-Jellie, Wallace R. Les Sources du Théâtre anglais à
      l'époque de la Restauration. Paris, 1906. 167 pp.
            Indicates the influences upon the Restoration stage in England.
2479 Kerby, William Moseley. Molière and the Restoration Comedy in
      England. London. [n.p.], 1907. vii, 121 pp.
            Influence of the French comic drama upon those dramatists
      who shared in the foundation of a classic or regular drama in
      England (Davenant, Dryden, Etherege, Shadwell, and Sedley)
      as well as later dramatists such as Wycherley, Otway, Mrs.
      Behn, Crown, Congreve, Cibber, Vanbrugh, and Farquhar.
      Insists upon "vast superiority" of Molière over the English
      writers from the point of view of construction.

2480 Hill, Herbert Wynford. La Calprenède's Romances and the Resto
      ration Drama. Chicago: The University of Chicago Press
      [1912]. 158 pp. [Reprinted from the University of Nebraska
      Studies, II, No. 3 (1910) and III, No. 2 (1911)].
         The influence of La Calprenède's romances Cassandra
      and Cleopatra on the heroic plays of Dryden, Pordage, Lee,
      Banks, Filmer, Cooke, Horden, and Aphra Behn in incidents,
      situation, and characters.

2481 Jourdain, Eleanor Frances. The Drama in Europe; in Theory and
      Practice. New York: Henry Holt and Company, 1924.
         A discussion of European drama and theatre, including
      English; chapters IV through VI treat drama and theatre from
      the Renaissance through the 18th century.

2482 Pfitzner, Käthe. "Die Ausländertypen im englischen Drama der
      Restorationszeit." Inaugural Dissertation. Breslau, 1931. 99 ᵖ

2483 Kinne, Willard Austin. Revivals and Importations of French
      Comedies in England, 1749-1800. New York: Columbia Uni-
      versity Press, 1939. xv, 310 pp.
         A detailed historical study of the use of French drama by
      English playwrights. By examining both new plays and revivals
      Kinne attempts to define the nature and extent of the borrow-
      ings. A bibliography of plays and secondary sources is include

2484 Harvey-Jellie, Wallace. L'entente littéraire; etude de litterature
      comparée. Montreal: [Lib. Beauchemin, Ltd.], 1940.
         The influence of the French and Spanish drama on the Eng-
      lish drama of John Dryden's time.

2485 Kaufman, Paul. "Spanish Players at Tangier: A New Chapter in
      Stage History." Comparative Literature, XII (1960), 125-132.
         This commentary of John Luke's Journal has reference to
      Anglo/Spanish literary relations during the Restoration period

France

2486 Gaiffe, F. Le Drame en France au XVIIIe siecle. Paris: A. Colin
      1910. 600 pp.
         A thorough discussion of the "drame" and its growth out of
      "la comédie larmoyante." Pages 46-59 are devoted to the in-
      fluence of English dramatists, Shakespeare, Otway, Steele,
      Garrick, Colman, Sheridan, and particularly George Lillo,
      and Edward Moore.

2487 Wray, Edith. "English Adaptations of French Drama Between
      1780 and 1815." Modern Language Notes, XLIII (February,
      1928), 87-90.
         Lists French plays on stage and the translator's name.

2488 Wood, Kathryn L. "The French Theatre in the XVIIIth Century

According to Some Contemporary English Travelers." Revue de Litterature Comparée, XII (1932), 601-618.

There are comparatively few references to the 18th-century French theatre in the journals, letters, and diaries of contemporary cultivated English travelers to France. Miss Wood here surveys the meagre scraps to be found in writings of Gray, Chesterfield, Gibbon, Sterne, Garrick, Mrs. Pye, and others.

2489 Saer, H. A. "English Contributions to Experiments in French Drama in the Eighteenth Century." Ph.D. London University, 1934.

2490 Lancaster, Henry Carrington. A History of French Dramatic Literature in the Seventeenth Century. Part V: Recapitulation, 1610-1700. Baltimore: Johns Hopkins Press; London: Humphrey Milford, Oxford University Press; Paris: Les Belles-Lettres, 1942.

Freemasons

2491 Pedicord, Harry William. "White Gloves at Five: Fraternal Patronage of London Theatres in the Eighteenth Century." Philological Quarterly, XLV, (1966), 270-288.

Freemasons attended performances as a group, encouraged the arts, and supported actors, and reflected in their behavior Augustan ideals of decency, decorum, and sentiment.

French Actors

2492 Lawrence, W. J. "Early French Players in England." The Elizabethan Playhouse and Other Studies. First Series. (Stratford-on-Avon: Shakespeare Head Press, 1912), 125-156.

Includes a short history of French actors in England, their plays, operas, and dancing, from 1661-1769, and of the growing antagonism against them and other foreign players.

2493 Horn-Monval, M. "French Troupes in England during the Restoration." Theatre Notebook, VII (1952-1953), 81-82.

Madame Horn-Monval's notes provide additional information and conjectures about French comedians in England.

French Influence

2494 Canfield, Dorothy Fisher. Corneille and Racine in England. New York: Columbia University Press, 1904. 277 pp.

A study of the English translations of the two Corneilles and Racine (through the first quarter of the 19th century) with especial reference to their presentation on the stage.

2495 Charlanne, L. L'influence en Angleterre au XVIIe siècle: Le
Théâtre et la critique. Etudes sur les relations littéraires
de la France et de l'Angleterre surtout dans la seconde moitié
du XVIIe siècle. Paris, Société Francaise d'imprimerie et de
Librairie, 1906. 374 pp.

2496 Greg, Walter W. Pastoral Poetry and Pastoral Drama. A Literary
Inquiry, with special reference to the Pre-Restoration Stage in
England. London: A. H. Bullen, 1906. ix, 464 pp.
　　Bulk of the work devoted to treatment of the pastoral drama
in Elizabethan literature, but the French influence imported in
1660 is also treated.

2497 Goggin, S. E. "A General View of the Influence of the French
Drama on That of England between 1660 and 1714." M.A. London University (External), 1908.

2498 Cucuel, Georges. Les Créateurs De L'Opéra-Comique Francais.
Avec une planche hors texte et citations musicales dans le texte.
Paris: Librairie Félix Alcan, 1914. 243 pp.
　　Influences of Italian opera, and the French writers. Francois
André Danican Philidor's Tom Jones.

2499 Clark, A. F. B. Boileau and the French Classical Critics in England (1660-1830). Paris: Champion, 1925. 18, 534 pp.
　　Boileau's influence was especially great upon Dryden, primarily in the effort to make society conscious of the dignity of literature.

2500 Macaulay, T. C. "French and English Drama in the Seventeenth
Century: Some Contrasts and Parallels." Essays and Studies by
Members of the English Association, XX (1935), 45-74.
　　This essay points out random similarities between French
and English drama with emphasis upon the French. Only slight
attention is given to Restoration drama.

2501 Smith, John Harrington. "French Sources for Six English Comedies
1660-1750." Journal of English and Germanic Philology, XLVII
(1948), 390-394.
　　Discusses Shadwell's The Woman-Captain, Granville's The
She-Gallants, Mrs. Pix's The Beau Defeated, Molloy's The
Coquet, Hewitt's A Tutor for the Beaus and the anonymous
Injured Love.

2502 Cecil, C. D. "'Une espèce d'éloquence abrégée: 'The Idealized
Speech of Restoration Comedy." Etudes Anglaises, XIX (1966),
15-25.
　　Studies the influence of the classics and especially the French
on Restoration writers' attempts to achieve elegant expression.
Examines Dancourt, Etherege, Requard, and Congreve.

French Opera

2503 Lawrence, W. J. "The French Opera in London: A Riddle of
1686." Times Literary Supplement, March 28, 1936, p. 268.
Demonstrates that the opera performed in 1686 was Lully's
Cadmus et Hermione.

French Revolution

2504 Grieder, Theodore Godfrey, Jr. "The French Revolution in the
British Drama: A Study in British Popular Literature of the
Decade of Revolution." Ph.D. Stanford University, 1958.

French Translations

2505 Tucker, Joseph E. "Wing's Short-Title Catalogue and Translations
from the French, 1641-1700." Papers of the Bibliographical
Society of America, XLIX (1955), 37-67.
Proposes corrections for S.T.C. in translations from the
French. As the S.T.C. is now, it sometimes is inconsistent
in translations and attributions. Includes 25 pages of corrections.

Friendship

2506 Kornbluth, Martin Leonard. "Friendship in Fashion: The Dramatic
Treatment of Friendship in the Restoration and Eighteenth
Century." Ph.D. Pennsylvania State University, 1956.

Frodsham, Bridge

2507 Boynton, John. "On a Certain Provincial Player." London Mercury,
VII (1922), 158-163.
A biographical sketch of Bridge Frodsham, "the York Gar-
rick," (1734-1768) centering on his two calls on David Garrick.

Fuller, Thomas

2508 Wood, James O. "Thomas Fuller's Oxford Interlude." Huntington Library Quarterly, XVII (1954), 185-208.
Fuller may be the author of Andronicus: A Tragedy (1661).

Fuseli, Henry

2509 Allentuck, Marcia E. "Henry Fuseli." Notes and Queries, CCII
(1957), 252.

Blake and Hayden were close friends of the Swiss painter
Fuseli, who died April 16, 1825.

2510 Hammelmann, H. A. "Eighteenth-Century English Illustrators.
Henry Fuseli." Book Collector, VI (1957), 350-360.

Fuseli's favorite subjects were from Shakespeare and
Milton. Includes a handlist of books illustrated by Fuseli as
well as reproductions of his work.

Gaelic

2511 Bartley, J. O. "The Gaelic Language in English Plays." Journal
of the Royal Society of Antiquaries of Ireland, LXXX (1950),
29-35.

Gaelic phrases frequently appear in Restoration and eighteen
century drama.

Gardner, Sarah

2512 Greene, Godfrey. "Mrs. Sarah Gardner: A Further Note." Theatr
Notebook, VIII (1953-1954), 6-10.

Greene reprints press notices for Mrs. Gardner's The Advertisement; or, A Bold Stroke for a Husband.

2513 Grice, F., and A. Clarke. "Mrs. Sarah Gardner." Theatre Notebook, VII (1953), 76-81.

Mrs. Gardner's manuscript book sheds additional light on
stage practices and persons in the 1770's.

Garrick, David

letters

2514 Baker, George Pierce, ed. Some Unpublished Correspondence of
David Garrick. Boston: Houghton, Mifflin & Company, 1907.
xiv, 140 pp.

Also contains plates, portraits, and facsimilies.

2515 Garrick, David. Pineapples of Finest Flavor, or A Selection of
Sundry Unpublished Letters of the English Roscius, David
Garrick. Edited with an Introduction and Notes by David Mason
Little. Cambridge: Harvard University Press, 1930. xx, 101 pp
Many of the letters discuss dramatic and managerial proble
faced by Garrick.

2516 -----. Letters of David Garrick and Georgiana Countess Spencer
1759-1779. Edited by Earl Spencer and Christopher Dobson.
Cambridge: Printed for Presentation to Members of The Roxburghe Club, 1960. xvii, [1], 174, 1 pp. Index.

72 letters, written between June 13, 1759, and January 20, 1800. Explanatory notes for each letter. The letters are preserved at Althorp. With the exception of Nos. 2 and 10, they have not been published before.

2517 -----. Letters. Edited by David M. Little and George M. Kahrl. Associate Editor, Phoebe de K. Wilson. 3 vols. Cambridge, Massachusetts: Belknap Press of Harvard University Press, 1963.

Of the 1360 letters here assembled, more than half are here published for the first time. Volume one includes sources of the manuscripts, short titles and abbreviations, a chronology of Garrick's life, and 334 of the letters; volume two continues the letters; volume three completes the letters and includes the appendices. All three volumes are illustrated.

2518 Little, David Mason. Pineapples of Finest Flavour or A Selection of Sundry Unpublished Letters of the English Roscius, David Garrick. New York: Russell and Russell, 1967. 101 pp.

A reissue of the 1930 edition contains 44 letters by Garrick to friends, colleagues and members of his family.

journals

2519 Garrick, David. The Diary of David Garrick, Being a Record of His Memorable Trip to Paris in 1751. Edited by Ryllis Clair Alexander. New York: Oxford University Press, 1928. x, 117 pp.

A brief journal, copiously annotated by the editor, notable especially for Garrick's reactions to French plays. There are several errors in transcription.

2520 -----. The Journal of David Garrick Describing His Visit to France and Italy in 1763. Edited by George Winchester Stone, Jr. New York: Modern Language Association, 1939. xvi, 74 pp.

Primarily of biographical interest, this volume contains no overt comment about the theatre.

plays

2521 -----. Three Farces by David Garrick. Edited by Louise Brown Osborn. New Haven: Yale University Press, 1925. xi, 135 pp.

The Lying Valet, A Peep Behind the Curtain, Bon Ton. With a brief sketch of his career.

2522 -----. Three Plays by David Garrick. Printed from Hitherto Unpublished Mss. with Introductions and Notes by Elizabeth P. Stein, Ph.D. New York: William Edwin Rudge, 1926. xii, 451 pp.

Contains the text of three plays: Harlequin's Invasion (1759);
The Jubilee (1769); The Meeting of the Company or Bayes's Art
of Acting (1774). Each play is preceded by a brief introduction
which sets it in the theatrical context of the period, and each
play is followed by notes.

2523 -----. Miss in Her Teens, or The Medley of Lovers; a Farce in
Two Acts Arranged for the Chiddingfold Players by W.G.
Robertson. London and Edinburgh: T. Nelson and Sons, Ltd.
[1930]. 59 pp. [Nelson Playbooks, ed. John Hampden; No. 119].
Robertson takes the same freedom with Garrick's text that
Garrick had taken with others. This version contains all of
Garrick's text, with the addition of two characters used by
Garrick in an earlier, unavailable script, and with additions
from other contemporary plays and from the editor's own
imagination.

2524 Stein, Elizabeth P., ed. Three Plays by David Garrick. New York:
Benjamin Blom, 1967.
A reprint of the 1926 edition includes texts, introductions
and notes for Harlequin's Invasion, The Jubilee, and The Meeting of the Company.

biography and criticism

2525 Roberts, W. "Garrick and Drury Lane." Athenaeum, II (July 7,
1900), 35.
An announcement and brief illustration of 13 Mss. diaries,
1747-1776, which record pieces produced during Garrick's
management.

2526 Weber, Fritz. Lacy's "Saucy the Scot" and Garrick's "Catharine
and Petruchio" im Verhältnis zu ihren Quellen. Rostock: Carl
Hinstoffs Buchdruckerei, 1901. 85 pp.
Compares these two adaptations of Shakespeare's "Taming
of the Shrew" (Lacy's 1698, Garrick's 1756), with the original
play. Lacy keeps the plot structure of Shakespeare's play but
shifts the scene to contemporary England. Garrick simplifies
Shakespeare's play by eliminating the secondary plots and
compressing five acts into three. Other adaptations of "Taming
of the Shrew" from this period are also listed.

2527 Goerner, Wilhelm. Das Verhältnis von Garricks's "The Fairies"
zu Shakespeare's "A Midsummer Night's Dream." Halle:
Druck von Wischan & Wettengei, 1902. 50 pp.
Discusses Garrick's popular opera, "altered from Shakespeare" and set to music by Mr. Smith, presented in Drury
Lane in 1755, with children playing most of the roles. Argues
that Garrick relied mostly on Hanmer's 1744 edition of Shake-

speare. Discusses why and how Garrick reworked the fantas-
tic element of Shakespeare's play into operetta form.

2528   Schnaus, C. Über das Verhältnis von David Garricks "Catharine
and Petruchio" zu Shakespeares "The Taming of the Shrew."
Inaugural Dissertation. Halle, 1902. 46 pp.

2529   Schneider, Walter. Über das Verhältnis von David Garricks
Florizel and Perdita zu Shakespeare's "Winter's Tale." Halle-
Wittenberg: Hofbuchdruckerei von C. A. Kaemmerer & Co.,
1902. 112 pp.

Uses scene-by-scene comparison of Garrick's Florizel and
Perdita with Shakespeare The Winter's Tale, to prove that
Garrick's purpose was to reintroduce Shakespeare gradually
to the English stage.

2530   Kraemer, F. Das Verhältnis von David Garricks "Every Man in
His Humour" zu dem gleichnamigen Lustspiel Ben Jonsons.
Inaugural Dissertation. Halle, 1903. 102 pp.

2531   Maass, Heinr. Ben Jonson's Lustspiel "Every Man in His Humour"
und die gleichnamige Bearbeitung durch David Garrick. Rostock:
Carl Boldt'sche Hof-Buchdruckerei, 1903. 50 pp.

Detailed textual comparison of the Folio edition (1616) of
Jonson's play with Garrick's production of 1751. Examines
changes Garrick made in Jonson's text because of changing
taste and technical progress (e.g., scene changes made possible by introduction of a stage curtain.)

2532   Fitzgerald, Percy H. The Garrick Club. London: Elliot Stock,
1904. xviii, 252 pp.

A description of the club--its rooms, traditions, and mem-
bers--with references to several eighteenth-century actors
and dramatists who attended there and portraits of some of
them.

2533   Gaehde, Christian. David Garrick also Shakespeare-Darsteller
und seine Bedeutung für die heutige Schauspielkunst. Berlin:
Georg Reimer, 1904. x, [2], 198 pp.

A somewhat detailed study of Garrick's work with Shakespeare,
as adapter and actor, with the various roles played by Garrick.
The material is drawn from a good amount of contemporary
sources.

2534   Martin, Sir T. Monographs: Garrick, Macready, Rachel and
Baron Stockmar. London: Murray; New York: Dutton, 1906.
ix, 341 pp.

Sketches of the life and career of each of the persons
selected. Illustrated.

2535   Garrick Club Catalogue of the Pictures and Miniatures in the
Possession of the Garrick Club. Revised edition. London:

Eyre and Spattiswoode, Ltd., 1909.
2536 Norman, William. "Garrick's Version of Romeo and Juliet."
      Notes and Queries, 11th Ser., II (July 30, 1910), 95.
            On the "additional scene" and the "advertisement" as
      found in "an odd volume of old plays."
2537 Hedgcock, F. A. Un Acteur Cosmopolite; David Garrick et ses
      Amis Francais. Paris: Librairie Hachette et Cie., 1911.
      283 pp.
2538 Cribble, Francis. Romances of the French Theatre. London:
      Chapman and Hall, Ltd., 1912. 288 pp.
            Includes information on Garrick's relationship with some
      of the actors.
2539 Hedgcock, F. A. A Cosmopolitan Actor, David Garrick and His
      French Friends. New York: Duffield, 1912. 442 pp.
            Emphasis upon visits to Paris in 1751 and 1763-1765 and
      on Garrick's correspondence with French playwrights, theatre
      managers, actors, and literary men. Also includes an account
      of the visit of Jean Monnet and the French actors to London,
      1749.
2540 Lawrence, W. S. "Garrick's First Appearance As Hamlet." The
      Elizabethan Playhouse and Other Studies. Second Studies.
      (Stratford-on-Avon: Shakespeare Head Press, 1913), 229-234.
            At Smock Alley, Dublin, August 12, 1742. Includes parts
      of anonymous letter to Garrick praising performance and
      regretting some pronunciations, omissions, and inclusions.
2541 Clarke, Sir Ernest. "David Garrick and Junius." Nineteenth
      Century, LXXV (January, 1914), 180-185.
            On the attack made by Junius on Garrick and Garrick's
      retort. Prints correspondence between Woodfall and Garrick
      relative to the attack.
2542 Marston, R. B. "David Garrick as Angler and Golfer." Times
      Literary Supplement, February 19, 1920, pp. 124-125.
            A discussion of Garrick as a fisherman and golfer, espec-
      ially concerned with his possession of the necessary equipment
2543 Millar, J. H. "Garrick as Golfer." Times Literary Supplement,
      February 26, 1920, p. 140.
            A statement that Garrick owned at least one golf club
      (article also includes a statement as to how he acquired the
      club).
2544 Beatty, Joseph M., Jr. "Garrick, Colman and The Clandestine
      Marriage." Modern Language Notes, XXXVI (1921), 129-141.
            Examines evidence, both internal and external, to determine
      the "indebtedness of the play to each of its authors," and con-
      cludes that the concept as a whole and the characters are Col-
      man's and Act V and the levee scene in Act II are Garrick's.

2545 Stein, Elizabeth P. "David Garrick, Dramatist." Ph.D. New
York University, 1921.

2546 -----. "The Manuscript Diary of David Garrick's Trip to Paris
in 1751." Colonnade, XIV (1922), 149-174.
A description of the diary, with sample entries. Concludes
that the diary is probably genuine but that its authenticity has
not been proven.

2547 Williams, I. A. [Garrick's Epitaph in William Hogarth]. London
Mercury, VI (1922), 80.
A note on this item to be included in the sale of the Burdett
Coutts Library, to take place at Sotheby's on May 15, 16 and
17, 1922.

2548 Clark, Ruth. "D'Holbach et Garrick." Revue de littérature comparée, V (1925), 671-672.
D'Holbach's gifts to Garrick of an umbrella and a collection
of Voltaire's writings (1765).

2549 "David Garrick, 1717-1779." Theatre Arts Monthly, IX (July,
1925), p. 422.
From G. P. Baker's Unpublished Letters of David Garrick.

2550 "Mr. Garrick as Sir John Brute." Theatre Arts Monthly, IX
(December, 1925), 814.
In Vanbrugh's The Provok'd Wife.

2551 "Some Typical Shakespearean Costumes." Theatre Arts Monthly,
X (July, 1926), 470.
As Lear, Macbeth, Richard III, and Hamlet.

2552 Alexander, Ryllis Clair. "Garrick Goes to the Play in Paris."
Yale Review, XVII (October, 1927), 206-208.
Announces the forthcoming Oxford University Press edition.
The diary is especially valuable for the light shed on the state
of French theatre in the mid-18th century.

2553 Freund, Frank E. W. "'Mrs. Garrick' by Thomas Gainsborough."
International Studio, LXXXVIII (December, 1927), 53-55.
History of Gainsborough's painting of Violetta, with a color
reproduction and a Hogarth black-and-white.

2554 Nicoll, Allardyce. "Garrick's Lost 'Jubilee.' First Stratford
Celebration. A Manuscript Copy." London Times, June 25,
1927, pp. 13-14.
Reports the discovery of a manuscript of Garrick's Drury
Lane skit (1769), honoring Shakespeare, and reprints some
of the scenes.

2555 Reynolds, Joshua. Johnson & Garrick: Two Dialogues. Edited by
R. Brimley Johnson. Kensington: Cayme Press, 1927. 31 pp.
Reprints, with explanations of their history, the two
imaginary conversations by Reynolds, one between R. and
Johnson concerning Garrick and one between Johnson and Gibbon
on the same.

2556 Chapman, R. W. "Garrick's Hotel." Times Literary Supplement,
      July 26, 1928, p. 552.
          Comments on the review of R. C. Alexander's edition of
      Garrick's Diary (TLS, July 19, 1928), noting that the trans-
      cription should be "Hotel d'Entragues."
2557 "The Garrick Jubilee of 1769 at Stratford-upon-Avon." Theatre
      Arts Monthly, XII (November, 1928), 794.
          A print of the theatre of 1769.
2558 Klercker, Elda. David Garrick och hans medspelare i livet och
      på scenen. Kulturskildringar och porträtter från Englands
      1700. Stockholm: Hugo Geber, 1928. 371 pp.
          A biography in Swedish.
2559 "Two Garrick Collections." London Times Literary Supplement,
      June 7, 1928, p. 436; June 28, 1928, p. 492.
          First announces Sotheby's sale of two Garrick collections
      and briefly traces their history. Second announces total,
      £6,622, and regrets scattering of the collection.
2560 Dean, Richard. "Garrick Posed for Fielding's Portrait." Mentor,
      XVII (February, 1929), 30-31.
          Repeats the story crediting Garrick with posing for Hogarth's
      portrait of Fielding. Includes reproduction of Hogarth's
      Fielding, and one of R. E. Pine's Garrick.
2561 Wecter, D. "The Family Correspondence of David Garrick." B.
      Litt. Oxford University, 1929.
2562 Williams, Charles Riddell. "Letters of David Garrick." Cornhill
      Magazine, LXVI (March, 1929), 289-297.
          Previously unpublished, property of the Garrick Club.
      Written from Paris in January and March of 1765 to Thomas
      Love, a member of the Drury Lane company.
2563 Lees, Charles Lowell. "The French Influence upon Garrick's
      Staging Methods." M.A. Northwestern University, 1932.
2564 Babler, Otto F. "Two Letters of David Garrick." Notes and
      Queries, CLXVI (1934), 367.
          The text of two letters written by David Garrick to the
      Danish ambassador, Baron D. Vede, referring to the presenta-
      tion of Macbeth before Christian VII, King of Denmark, in
      London in 1768.
2565 MacMillan, Dougald. "David Garrick As Critic." Studies in
      Philology, XXXI (1934), 69-83.
          Garrick's critical standards and his application of them
      as manager.
2566 Stone, George Winchester. "Garrick's Long Lost Alteration of
      Hamlet." Publications of the Modern Language Association,
      XLIX (1934), 890-921.
          Garrick's emended version of Hamlet.

2567 Dukes, Ashley. "The Garrick Club Collection." Theatre Arts
      Monthly, XIX (1935), 601-616.
         Commentary and reprints of portraits from the collection
      of the Garrick Club. Paintings of King, Bannister, and of the
      screen scene in the 1777 performance of The School for Scandal
      are included.
2568 Diderot, Denis. Writings on the Theatre. Edited by F. C. Green.
      Cambridge: University Press, 1936. vii, 317 pp.
         A collection of Diderot's criticism which includes "Observa-
      tions sur Garrick ou les Acteurs Anglais."
2569 Stone, George Winchester, Jr. "Garrick's Presentation of Antony
      and Cleopatra." Review of English Studies, XIII (1937), 20-38.
         A history of the events leading up to Garrick's production,
      along with an analysis and evaluation of the changes in the
      original.
2570 Stein, Elizabeth P. David Garrick, Dramatist. (Revolving Fund
      Series, VII). New York: Modern Language Association, 1938.
      xx, 315 pp.
         A study of Garrick's plays which concentrates upon the
      sources, dramatic structure, and theatrical history. Garrick's
      life is a minor consideration. The volume includes a bibliography
      of various 18th century individual and collected editions.
2571 Angus, William. "An Appraisal of David Garrick: Based Mainly upon
      Contemporary Sources." Quarterly Journal of Speech, XXV
      (1939), 30-42.
         An analysis of Garrick's "naturalistic" style of acting and
      of its influence upon his career.
2572 C., T. C. "Garrick's 'Christmas Tale.'" Notes and Queries,
      CLXXVII (1939), 477.
         Brief comment on performances of Garrick's play in 1774
      and early 1775.
2573 Fischer, Walther. "Ein unbekannter Brief David Garricks an
      Samuel Richardson." Anglia, LXIII (1939), 436-444.
         Besides printing a letter dated September 4, 1753, in which
      Garrick comments on Sir Charles Grandison, Fischer provides
      an elaborately detailed commentary on the historical milieu
      and the occasion of the letter.
2574 Stone, George Winchester, Jr. "Garrick and an Unknown Operatic
      Version of Love's Labour's Lost." Review of English Studies,
      XV (1939), 323-328.
         A comparative analysis of the alteration produced by Edward
      Thompson at the request of Garrick in 1773. The play was
      never performed.
2575 -----. "A Midsummer Night's Dream in the Hands of Garrick
      and Colman." Publications of the Modern Language Association,

LIV (1939), 467-482.

An analysis of Garrick's The Fairies (1755), Colman's Midsummer Night's Dream and Fairy Tale (1763), and Garrick's acting copy of Midsummer Night's Dream (1763), to illustrate the history of the alterations and to determine each playwright's share in the compositions.

2576 Wecter, Dixon. "David Garrick and the Burkes." Philological Quarterly, XVIII (1939), 367-380.

Prints several letters exchanged by Garrick and Edmund Burke and analyzes them so as to clarify the history of the relationship.

2577 "Garrick the Author." Times Literary Supplement, October 18, 1941, p. 519.

Reviews summarily Garrick's letters, satires, plays, and revisions of Shakespeare.

2578 Rosenfeld, Sybil. "David Garrick and Private Theatricals." Notes and Queries, CLXXX (October 25, 1941), 230-231.

"... expresses the belief that Garrick never acted on amateur boards and rarely could be persuaded to attend a performance."

2579 Stone, George Winchester, Jr. "Garrick's Handling of Macbeth." Studies in Philology, XXXVIII (October, 1941), 609-628.

"Compares Garrick's prompt-book (1744) with the Davenant version which it displaced and analyzes Garrick's text."

2580 Clutter, Fairy Harsh. "The Influence of David Garrick in the Theatre." M.A. University of Pittsburgh, 1942.

2581 De Castro, J. Paul. "David Garrick and Private Theatricals." Notes and Queries, CLXXXII (April 25, 1942), 234.

Suggests that Garrick appeared with amateurs at least once.

2582 Knapp, Mary E. "The Poetry of David Garrick." Ph.D. Yale University, 1942.

2583 Martz, Louis L. and Edwine M. "Notes on Some Manuscripts Relating to David Garrick." Review of English Studies, XIX (April, 1943), 186-200.

Several small bits of verse, some unpublished, some with biographical value, printed with commentary. The Mss. are in the Yale University library.

2584 Motter, T. H. Vail. "Garrick and the Private Theatres. With a List of Amateur Performances in the Eighteenth Century." English Literary History, XI (March, 1944), 63-75.

"An 'Attempt ... to relate Garrick to the aristocratic private actors, to the drama in the schools, and to his amateur playwright friend, James Townley.'" Also lists supplementary records to the ones printed in his School Drama in England (1929

2585 Knapp, Lewis M. "Smollett and Garrick." Elizabethan Studies
     in Honor of G. F. Reynolds. (Boulder: University of Colorado
     Press, 1945), 233-243.
         Although their relationship seemed cordial, Smollett and
     Garrick never forgot their enmity of 1746-1749.
2586 Pedicord, Harry William. "Mr. and Mrs. Garrick: Some Unpub-
     lished Correspondence." Publications of the Modern Language
     Association, LX (September, 1945), 775-783.
         Six letters are reprinted, from the originals in the posses-
     sion of the Historical Society of Pennsylvania.
2587 Brooks, Cleanth, ed. The Percy Letters II. The Correspondence
     of Thomas Percy and Richard Farmer. Baton Rouge: Louisiana
     State University Press, 1946. xviii, 218 pp.
         Covers the years 1762-1778, with numerous references to
     Garrick's performances and other theatrical events.
2588 Weatherly, Edward H. "The Personal and Literary Relationship
     of Charles Churchill and David Garrick." Studies in Honor of
     A. H. R. Fairchild. Edited by Charles T. Prouty. (Columbia:
     University of Missouri Press, 1946), 151-160. (University of
     Missouri Studies, XXI, i).
         Discusses the background and implications of The Rosciad
     and Apology and studies the correspondence between Churchill
     and Garrick.
2589 Bodtke, Richard A. "Garrick's Revisions of Shakespeare." M.A.
     Columbia University, 1947.
2590 Barton, Margaret. David Garrick. London: Faber and Faber,
     1948. 324 pp.
         A detailed biography, with commentary on the theatre of
     the period, illustrations and a full bibliography.
2591 -----. "Greatest of Actors." Times Literary Supplement, June
     19, 1948, p. 345.
         Garrick's great role of Drugger is in Jonson's The Alchemist,
     not Francis Gentleman's The Tobacconist (1771).
2592 Boas, Guy. The Garrick Club, 1831-1947. London: Published by
     the Club, 1948. 128 pp.
         Devoted to the founding of the club, the original members,
     later members, pictures, the library, other possessions,
     and the centenary dinner.
2593 Guthrie, David Leslie Robin. "On the Destruction by Fire of
     Gainsborough's Portrait of David Garrick." Shakespeare
     Association Bulletin, XXIII (October, 1948), 143.
         The portrait, destroyed 5 December, 1946, is reproduced
     and commemorated in a sonnet.
2594 Lancaster, H. Carrington. "Garrick at the Comédie Francais,
     June 9, 1751." Modern Language Notes, LXIII (April, 1948),
     265.

He saw performances of Rodogune and Le Usurier Gentil-
homme.

2595 Little, David M. and George M, Kahrl. "Garrick's Letters."
Times Literary Supplement, October 2, 1948, p. 555.
Requests information for their forthcoming edition.

2596 MacMillan, Dougald. "David Garrick, Manager: Notes on the
Theatre as a Cultural Institution in England in the Eighteenth
Century." Studies in Philology, XLV (October, 1948), 630-646.
An important study, showing how Drury Lane reflected the
popular taste of the time by combining the traditional classic
plays with the sensational and the trivial output of contemporary
writers. Manuscript evidence used to illustrate Garrick's
business dealings.

2597 Stone, George Winchester, Jr. "Garrick's Production of King
Lear: a Study in the Temper of the Eighteenth-Century Mind."
Studies in Philology, XLV (January, 1948), 89-103.
His interpretation of Lear is in tune with the tastes and
interests of his audience.

2598 -----. "The God of his Idolatry: Garrick's Theory of Acting and
Dramatic Composition with Especial Reference to Shakespeare."
J. Q. Adams Memorial Studies, edited by James G. McMana-
way, Giles E. Dawson and Edwin E. Willoughby. (Washington:
The Folger Shakespeare Library, 1948), 115-128.
A brilliant study of Garrick at work, particular attention
being paid to his effect as a moulder of the public taste.

2599 Knapp, Mary E. "Garrick's Last Command Performance." The
Age of Johnson: Essays Presented to Chauncey Brewster Tinker.
(New Haven: Yale University Press, 1949), 61-71.
An analysis of the concluding stages of Garrick's career,
and a description of his performance of Lethe before the
Court in 1777.

2600 Pedicord, Harry William. "Garrick's Audiences." Ph.D. University of Pennsylvania, 1949.

2601 R., V. "Christmas Notices: In Fact and Fancy." Notes and
Queries, CXCIV (December 24, 1949), 552-553.
Includes a comment on Garrick's winter entertainment,
A Christmas Tale, given at Drury Lane in 1774.

2602 Knapp, Mary E. "Garrick's Verses to the Marquis of Rockingham." Philological Quarterly, XXIX (1950), 78-81.
The verses express thanks to Rockingham for obtaining
a royal pardon for Benjamin Robert Turbott, son of Robert
Turbott, Garrick's early acting associate at the Drury Lane.

2603 Mann, Isabel R. "The Garrick Jubilee at Stratford-upon-Avon."
Shakespeare Quarterly, I (1950), 129-134.
Summary of the major events in Garrick's Shakespeare
jubilee festival.

2604 Stone, George Winchester, Jr. "David Garrick's Significance in
the History of Shakespearean Criticism: A Study of the Impact upon the Change of Critical Focus during the Eighteenth
Century." Publications of the Modern Language Association,
LXV (1950), 183-197.
    Eighteenth-century editors and critics, as well as the
theatrical public in general, were strongly influenced by Garrick's treatment of Shakespeare.

2605 Bergmann, Frederick L. "David Garrick and The Clandestine
Marriage." Publications of the Modern Language Association,
LXVII (1952), 148-162.
    The Clandestine Marriage shows the influence of eighteenth-
century acting traditions upon the playwright and his art.

2606 Price, Cecil. "David Garrick and Evan Lloyd." Review of English
Studies, New Ser., III (1952), 28-38.
    Evan Lloyd, a curate at Rotherhithe, was one of Garrick's
intimate acquaintances after 1765.

2607 Greene, Godfrey. "Notes on an Unpublished Garrick Letter and
on Messink." Theatre Notebook, VIII (1953-1954), 4-6.
    Greene provides information about Garrick's letter on
costuming Macbeth and about Messink, who drew the sketches.

2608 Price, Cecil. "Chesterfield and Garrick." Times Literary Supplement, October 23, 1953, p. 677.
    Dobrée's edition of Chesterfield's letters omits several
letters to Garrick.

2609 Bergmann, Frederick L. "A Study of Garrick's Alterations of
Non-Shakespearean Plays." Ph.D. George Washington University, 1954.

2610 Martin, W. B. "David Garrick's Attitude toward, and Influence
upon, 18th Century Sentimental Comedy." Ph.D. University
of Edinburgh, 1954.

2611 Pedicord, Harry W. The Theatrical Public in the Time of Garrick. New York: King's Crown Press, 1954. 267 pp.
    Pedicord deals with such problems as audience size, the
economics of the companies, quality of the audience, and
repertoire.

2612 Malnick, B. "David Garrick and the Russian Theatre." Modern
Language Review, L (1955), 173-175.
    Garrick knew Dmitrevskoy and Le Kain in Paris. Discusses
and attempts to define cross-influences in style, technique,
stagecraft, temperament, and admirers.

2613 Price, Cecil. "Some Garrick Letters." Notes and Queries, CC
(1955), 209-211.
    Letters by or to David Garrick printed first in Victorian
publications not now accessible. Price feels "the correspondence

reveals interesting sides of the great actor-manager's character."

2614 Beck, Martha Ryan. "A Comparative Study of Prompt Copies of Hamlet Used by Garrick, Booth, and Irving (Volumes I and II)." Ph.D. University of Michigan, 1956.

Garrick's book of 1747 with changed ending.

2615 Boswell, James. Boswell in Search of a Wife, 1766-1769. Edited by Frank Brady and Frederick A. Pottle. New York: McGraw-Hill Book Company, Inc., 1956. xxviii, 390 pp.

This volume of the Yale edition of Boswell's private papers contains his comments on the Stratford Jubilee and observations on Gay's, Goldsmith's, and John Home's drama.

2616 "David Garrick and The London Cuckolds." Notes and Queries, CCC (1956), 263-264.

After David Garrick revived the bawdy comedy The London Cuckolds at Drury Lane in 1748, he abandoned it in 1750 because public outcry against its obscenity hurt box office receipts.

2617 England, Martha Winburn. "Garrick's Stratford Jubilee: Reactions in France and Germany." Shakespeare Survey, IX (1956), 90-100.

Reactions to Garrick's Shakespeare Jubilee held at Stratford-upon-Avon in 1769 showed the varied courses romanticism would follow. In France, Voltaire and Le Tourneur; in Germany, George Christoph Lictenberg, and Johann Wilhelm von Archenholz.

2618 McGlone, James P. "Production Methods of Garrick's Drury Lane Theatre and Their Effect on His Acting Technique as Illustrated in Three Major Shakespearian Roles: Hamlet, King Lear, and Richard III." M.A. Catholic University of America, 1956.

2619 Sawyer, Paul. "David Garrick and The London Cuckolds." Notes and Queries, New Ser., III (1956), 263-264.

2620 Scouten, Arthur H. "The Increase in Popularity of Shakespeare's Plays in the Eighteenth Century: A Caveat for Interpretors of Stage History." Shakespeare Quarterly, VII (1956), 189-202.

Argues that Shakespeare was a popular playwright and a dominant force in 18th-century theatre before Garrick; thus, Garrick was not the chief factor in Shakespeare's rising popularity in the 18th century.

2621 Stone, George Winchester, Jr. "Shakespeare's Tempest at Drury Lane during Garrick's Management." Shakespeare Quarterly, VII (1956), 1-7.

Versions of the play--both dramatic and operatic--which Garrick produced, ending with his 1757 production of Shakespeare's own text.

2622 Gallagher, Robert Emmett. "John Hawkesworth: A Study toward

a Literary Biography." Ph.D. Northwestern University, 1957.
Editor and essayist, he altered two plays for Garrick.

2623 Gerber, Helmut E. "The Clandestine Marriage and Its Hogarthian
Associations." Modern Language Notes, LXXII (1957), 267-271.

2624 Gordan, John D. "New in the Berg Collection." Bulletin of the New
York Public Library, LXI (1957), 303-311, 353-363.
Letters of Garrick and Colman.

2625 Burnim, Kalman. "David Garrick: Director." Ph.D. Yale University,
1958.

2626 -----. "Garrick's Quarrel with Lacy in 1745." Yale University
Library Gazette, XXXIII (1958), 29-34.
Defense of Garrick by Somerset Draper.

2627 -----. "TheSignificance of Garrick's Letters to Hayman." Shakespeare Quarterly, IX (1958), 149-152.
Discusses King Lear and Othello.

2628 Mander, Raymond, and Joe Mitchenson. "The Derby Figure of
David Garrick." Theatre Notebook, XIII (1958), 36.

2629 Oman, Lenanton Carola. David Garrick. London: Hodder and
Stoughton [1958]. xx, 427 pp.
A detailed critical biography of Garrick concentrates on his
activities as actor and theater manager.

2630 Shipley, John B. "David Garrick and James Ralph: Remarks on a
Correspondence." Notes and Queries, (1958), 403-408.
Prints five letters, 1754, 1757.

2631 Bergmann, Fred L. "Garrick's Zara." Publications of the Modern
Language Association, LXXIV (1959), 225-232.
Discusses Garrick's revisions of Hill's play.

2632 Burnim, Kalman A. "Garrick as Director of Shakespeare's Plays."
Shakespeare Newsletter, IX (1959), 13.
Manager of Drury Lane, 1747-1776.

2633 England, Martha Winburn. "The Grass Roots of Bardolatry." Bulletin of the New York Public Library, LXIII (1959), 117-133.
Garrick's Stratford Jubilee, 1769.

2634 Evans, G. Blakemore. "Garrick's The Fairies (1755): Two Editions."
Notes and Queries, New Ser., VI (1959), 410-441.
Disputes W. Jaggard. Editions, not issues.

2635 Mander, Raymond, and Joe Mitchenson. "The Derby Figure of
David Garrick." Theatre Notebook, XIII (1959), 112.
Discusses variations.

2636 Sackett, S. J. "To Write like an Angel." Western Folklore, XVIII
(1959), 250-251.

2637 Haywood, Charles. "William Boyce's 'Solemn Dirge' in Garrick's
Romeo and Juliet Production of 1750." Shakespeare Quarterly,
XI (1960), 175-187.
This article discusses John Rich's gala spectacular, The

Solemn Dirge of Juliet's funeral procession, which he devised
to lure David Garrick's audience to his Covent Garden productic
Haywood seeks to prove that Francis Hopkinson's rendition of
the dirge is really the long-sought score of Dr. Boyce.

2638 Sawyer, Paul. "The Garrick-Mrs. Cibber Relationship." Notes
and Queries, VII (1960), 303-305.

An unpublished manuscript, "Theatrical Duplicity," sur-
prisingly reveals that Garrick and Mrs. Cibber were jealous
of each other's reputations.

2639 Burnim, Kalman. David Garrick: Director. Pittsburgh: University
of Pittsburgh Press, 1961. 234 pp.

A detailed study of the actor's work as manager of the Drury
Lane Theatre, with a close analysis of four Garrick promptbooks of Shakespearean tragedies and a Vanbrugh comedy.
Most complete treatment of mid-eighteenth century production
techniques that has appeared.

2640 Deelman, Christian. "Garrick at Edial." Johnsonian News Letter,
XXI (September, 1961), 12.

Discusses Garrick's Lethe and the question of Garrick's
debt to Lucian.

2641 Loose, Dorothy Loretta. "The Theatrical Opinions and Policies
of David Garrick as Expressed in His Private Correspondence,
1747-1779." M.A. University of Nebraska, 1961.

2642 Boulton, James T. "David Garrick (1717-1779)." Burke Newsletter,
IV (1962), 171-174.

Burke's correspondence reveals Garrick as generous, kind
and affable.

2643 England, Martha Winburn. "Garrick and Stratford." Bulletin of
the New York Public Library, LXVI (1962), 73-92, 178-204,
261-272.

Garrick's Shakespeare jubilee in 1769. "The combination
of Garrick and Stratford formed a catalyst that precipitated
the concepts of romanticism."

2644 England, Martha Winburn. Garrick and Stratford. New York:
The New York Public Library, 1962. 72 pp.

Garrick's Shakespeare Jubilee in 1769. A reprint with ad-
ditions and illustrations of Miss England's "Garrick and
Stratford" in the Bulletin of the New York Public Library,
LXVI (1962), 73-92; 178-204; 261-272.

2645 Highfill, Philip H. "A Real 'Bill of Mortality.'" Theatre Notebook,
XVI (Spring, 1962), 107-108.

Copy of a Drury Lane Bill for January 19, 1779, at Huntington Library. Bill contains note by William Hopkins, Drury Lane
prompter, which refers to cancellation of performance due to
Garrick's death.

2646 McNamara, Brooks. "The Stratford Jubilee: Dram to Garrick's
      Vanity." Educational Theatre Journal, XIV (1962), 135-140.
         Story of Garrick's Stratford Jubilee of 1769. The three-day
      festival, though a failure to Garrick himself, was indicative
      of Shakespeare idolatry in the later Eighteenth Century.

2647 Price, Joseph G. "From Farce to Romance: All's Well That Ends
      Well, 1756-1811." Shakespeare Jahrbuch, XCIX (1963), 57-71.
         A study of the 18th Century adaptations of Garrick, Pilon,
      and Kemble. "The freedom and exuberance of the theatre in
      the first half of the century were curbed by the drift toward
      Romantic sentimentality and Victorian prudery at the end of the
      century; that drift is recorded in the increasing modifications
      of the original Shakespearean text which led finally to the ex-
      purgated version of John Kemble."

2648 Deelman, Christian. The Great Shakespeare Jubilee. New York:
      The Viking Press, 1964. 326 pp.
         Full-length study of the Jubilee of 1769, beginning with a
      review of Shakespeare's reputation to 1741. Examines the
      elaborate and confused preparations, progress, close, and
      aftermath of the festival with which "Garrick chose to stage
      the worship of his god." Includes illustrations, notes, biblio-
      graphy and index.

2649 England, Martha Winburn. Garrick's Jubilee. Columbus: Ohio
      State University Press, 1964. 273 pp.
         A more extensive study of the Jubilee by the author of Gar-
      rick and Stratford (New York Public Library, 1962). Includes
      two appendices containing a list of some persons who attended
      the Jubilee and Garrick's Ode to Shakespeare.

2650 Jennings, John. "David Garrick and Nicholas Nipclose." Educational
      Theatre Journal, XVI (1964), 270-275.
         A reexamination of those portions of Nipclose's The Theatres;
      a Poetical Dissection which are directed at Garrick. Includes
      critical response to the piece.

2651 McAleer, John J. "Garrick--'High-Priest of Avon's Oracle.'"
      The Shakespeare Newsletter, XIV (1964), 6.
         Brief review of Garrick's productions of Shakespeare.

2652 Pritchett, V. S. "Unfrogged Frenchman." New Statesman, LXVII
      (January 31, 1964), 167-168.
         The popular allegation that Garrick owed his acting genius
      to his French blood is denied by Garrick in his letters. Com-
      ments also on Garrick's personality and dramatic ability as
      revealed in his formal and informal correspondence.

2653 Stockholm, Johanne M. Garrick's Folly: The Shakespeare Jubilee
      of 1769 at Stratford and Drury Lane. London: Methuen, 1964.
      178 pp.

A study of the Jubilee's failure at Stratford, its success at Drury Lane, and its influence on the literary and theatrical world.

2654 Wolfit, Donald. "Little Davy." Drama, No. 72 (Spring, 1964), 37-39.

Review of Little and Kahrl's edition of David Garrick's letters. The "vivid picture (which the letters) give of the life of the theatre spanning the middle of the 18th century from Quin to Sheridan" makes them unique in English literature.

2655 Burnim, Kalman A. "David Garrick's Early Will." Theatre Research, VII (1965), 26-44.

Publishes the text of a will discovered in the Harvard Theatre Collection which was drawn up by Garrick on March 23, 1767.

2656 -----. "The Theatrical Career of Guiseppe Galli-Bibiena." Theatre Survey, VI (1965), 32-53.

Includes brief reference to Garrick's use of transparent back scenes at Drury Lane for a production of Harlequin's Invasion, 1759.

2657 Isles, Duncan E. "Other Letters in the Lennox Collection." Times Literary Supplement, August 5, 1965, p. 685.

Includes letters by Garrick and Colman to Mrs. Charlotte Lennox.

2658 Knight, Donald. "The Technique of Nature in the Age of Garrick." M.F.A. Yale University, 1965.

2659 Lloyd-Evans, Gareth. "Garrick and the 18th-Century Theatre." Transactions of the Johnson Society (December, 1965), 17-27.

David Garrick influenced the whole of 18th century theatre by his "naturalistic" acting, use of contemporary material, unique staging techniques, and magnetic personality.

2660 Kahrl, George M. "Garrick, Johnson, and Lichfield." New Rambler Serial No. C.I. (June, 1966), 15-28.

Describes the social and economic disparities that separated the Johnson and Garrick families in Lichfield and discusses the relationship of the two men there and in London.

2661 Lehnert, Martin. "Arthur Murphy's Hamlet-Parodie (1772) auf David Garrick." Shakespeare Jahrbuch, CII (1966), 97-167.

Studies the history of Murphy's parody and includes the full text of his play.

2662 Stone, George Winchester, Jr. "Garrick and Othello." Philological Quarterly, XLV (1966), 304-320.

A history of Garrick's experience with Othello in which he played Iago twice as many times as he played the hero. Considers contemporary comment on his performances, the probable text used by Garrick, and the impact of the play on Garrick personally.

2663 Dobson, Austin. Third Series: Eighteenth Century Vignettes.
       New York: Benjamin Blom, 1967. 376 pp.
       A reprint of the 1896 edition includes essays on the last
       performances of Garrick and on Colman.
2664 Gottesman, Lillian. "Garrick's Institution of the Garter." Re-
       storation and Eighteenth Century Theatre Research, VI (Nov-
       ember, 1967), 37-43.
       A discussion of Garrick's play produced at Drury Lane for
       at least twenty-six performances. "Its historical value lies
       in that it is the only obtainable dramatic work on the subject
       of this supposed Arthurian society, that it is a patriotic inter-
       pretation and glorification of a theme associated with Arthurian
       tradition, and that it embodies the Elizabethan concept of the
       divine guidance of monarchs."
2665 Hafter, Ronald. "Garrick and Tristram Shandy." Studies in Eng-
       lish Literature, 1500-1900, VII (1967), 475-489.
       Sterne's adaptation of Garrick's stage technique to the pur-
       pose of prose fiction gives Tristram Shandy much of its unique
       coloration.
2666 Sawyer, Paul. "Garrick, Joseph Reed, and Dido." Restoration
       and Eighteenth Century Theatre Research, VI (November,
       1967), 44-50.
       Studies the tireless efforts of Joseph Reed (1723-1787) to
       persuade Garrick to produce Dido at Drury Lane.
2667 Stein, Elizabeth. David Garrick, Dramatist. (MLA Revolving
       Fund Ser. 7.) New York: Benjamin Blom, 1967. 315 pp.
       A reprint of the 1938 edition, the book examines Garrick's
       plays to determine their merit, to assess Garrick's con-
       tribution to the dramatic literature of the period, and to dis-
       cover Garrick's own position in the history of drama.

Gay, John

letters

2668 Burgess, C. F., ed. The Letters of John Gay. Oxford: Clarendon
       Press, 1966. 142 pp.
       Edition of 81 letters written by Gay from 1705 to 1732. In-
       cludes introduction, notes, and index.

collected works

2669 Gay, John. The Poetical Works of John Gay. Edited by G. C. Faber.
       London: Oxford University Press, 1926. 700 pp.
       A scholarly and accurate edition, the first serious attempt

to disentangle spurious from genuine poems. Includes Polly,
The Beggar's Opera, and selections.

collected poems

2670 -----. The Poetical Works of John Gay with a Memoir. 2 vols.
      Boston: Houghton Mifflin & Co. [1904?].
          Reprints Johnson's "Life of John Gay." Volume two contains
      the text of Acis and Galatea and "Prologue. Designed for the
      Pastoral Tragedy of Dione."

collected plays

2671 -----. The Plays of John Gay... Ornamented by Martin Travers.
      2 vols. London: Chapman and Dodd [1923]. (The Abbey Classics
          The text of Gay's plays, without notes, preceded by Samuel
      Johnson's "Life of John Gay."
2672 -----. The Beggar's Opera and Other Works. Edited by Horst Hohⁱ
      Halle: Niemeyer, 1959. 327 pp.
          English text, German notes.
2673 Fuller, J. L. "An Edition with Notes and Critical Introduction of
      Select Plays by John Gay, viz. The Mohocks, The Wife of Bath,
      The What D'Ye Call It, Three Hours After Marriage, The
      Distress'd Wife and The Rehearsal at Goatham." B. Litt. Ox-
      ford University (New College), 1965.
2674 Gay, John. The Beggar's Opera and Companion Pieces. Edited by
      C. F. Burgess. (Crofts Classics). New York: Appleton-Century
      Crofts, 1966.
          Besides introduction, notes, and bibliography, the edition als
      provides related materials such as "Newgate's Garland" and
      selections from Trivia and Gay's letters.

individual plays

2675 [-----]. Words of Acis and Galatea, a Serenata Composed in the
      Year 1720 by G. F. Handel. London: J. Curwen & Sons, Ltd.
      [1905?]. 10 pp.
          A one page introduction (unsigned) recounts the legend of
      Acis and Galatea; the words to the thirty airs follow.
2676 -----. The Beggar's Opera. [Edited by G. H. Macleod.] London:
      Alexander Moring, Ltd., De la More Press, 1905. viii, 110
      pp. (The King's Library.)
          Contains a life of Gay and a brief discussion of the reception
      of the play, the text of the play, and notes and bibliography.

2677 -----. The Beggar's Opera. London: M. Secker, 1920.
       The text has been inlaid and is extra-illustrated by the ad-
       dition of signed portraits of the manager and the original cast
       of the production at the Lyric theatre, Hammersmith, 1920.
2678 -----. The Beggar's Opera. Written by Mr. Gay. To Which is
       Prefixed the Musick to Each Song... London: William Heine-
       mann, 1921. vii-xiv, 93 pp.
       The text is preceded by a "Note on the Scene and Costumes
       at the Lyric Theatre, Hammersmith" by Claud Lovat Fraser,
       designer of the scenery and costumes for the Lyric Theatre's
       revival of The Beggar's Opera, in which he discusses his
       reasons for abandoning the attempt to render costumes in
       historically authentic detail. Contains plates illustrating the
       costumes.
2679 -----. The Beggar's Opera. With an introduction by Oswald
       Doughty. London: D. O'Connor, 1922, 99 pp.
       Introduction gives history of play's success, and notes on
       date of writing. The few explanatory notes are drawn entirely
       from Gay's contemporaries. No note on the text used.
2680 -----. The Beggar's Opera. Written by Mr. Gay. New York: W.
       Huebsch, Inc., 1922. 83 pp.
       A copy of the text, without notes, based on the 1765 edition.
2681 -----. The Beggar's Opera. London: Martin Secker, 1928. 83,
       [1] pp. (The New Adelphia Library, Vol. 42).
       The text follows that of the edition of 1765, which has been
       collated with the first. The first publication of this edition
       was in 1920. No introduction, notes, or glossary.
2682 -----. The Beggar's Opera. Edited with an Introduction, Notes,
       and Glossary by F. W. Bateson. London: J. M. Dent & Sons,
       Ltd., 1934. xvii, [1], 123 pp.
       The text used is that of the third edition of 1729, which the
       editor says appears to be the last one revised by Gay. Minor
       misprints are corrected, spelling, punctuation, use of capital
       letters and italics are modernized.
2683 -----. The Beggar's Opera. Preface by A. P. Herbert. (Paris:
       Printed for members of Limited Editions Club by G. Govone,
       1937), 27-121.
       An elaborate and costly edition complete with large print,
       rag paper, and abundant lithographs. This books was meant
       to be displayed, not read.
2684 -----. "The Beggar's Opera." Types of English Drama. Edited
       by John William Ashton. (New York: The Macmillan Co.,
       1940), 470-532.
       The text of the play is preceeded by a brief introduction to
       Gay's life and to The Beggar's Opera as an example of "song

drama." Notes to the text are fairly meagre; most are
glosses.

2685 -----. The Beggar's Opera, a Ballad Opera by John Gay, in a
New Musical Version Realised from the Original Airs. Vocal
Score by Arthur Oldham. London, New York [1949], 192 pp.

2686 -----. The Beggar's Opera. The Overture Composed and the
Songs Arranged by John Christopher Pepusch. Edited by
Edward J. Dent. London: Oxford University Press [1954].

2687 Handley-Taylor, Geoffrey, and Frank Granville Barker. Ninth
Music Book Containing "John Gay and the Ballad Opera (The
Beggar's Opera." London and New York: Hinrichsen, 1956.
30 plates.

2688 Gay, John. The Beggar's Opera. A Faithful Reproduction of the
1729 Edition, Which Includes the Words and Music of All the
Airs, As Well as the Score for the Overture. With Commentaries by Louis Kronenberger and Max Goberman on the Literary
and Musical Background and with the Original Words of All the
Airs that John Gay Adapted for this Work. Larchmont, New
York: Arganaut Books, 1961. viii, 60 pp. (text facsimile);
46 pp. (music facsimile); xxv-liv pp.

2689 Noble, Yvonne. "John Gay, The Beggar's Opera: A Critical Edition.
Ph.D. Yale University, 1966. (Order No. 66-13, 922).
        Provides a text for both dialogue and music, examines in a
critical introduction pertinent historical phenomena, and supplies the sources of airs in this work and in its sequel, Polly.

2690 Gay, John. Polly; an Opera. Being the Second Part of The Beggar's
Opera. Written by Mr. Gay. The Foreword by Oswald Doughty.
London: Daniel O'Connor, 1922. xxiv, 117 pp.
        Contains the text of Polly, preceded by Gay's Preface, and
a foreword in which Oswald Doughty discusses the political
elements in Polly, its "reception," and its relationship to
The Beggar's Opera.

2691 -----. Polly; An Opera by Mr. Gay. Being the Sequel to The Beggar's Opera. Now Freely Adapted by Clifford Bax. London:
Chapman & Hall, Ltd., 1923. 64 pp.
        Bax's adaptation modernizes much of Gay's language.

2692 -----. Polly. An Opera. Being the Sequel to "The Beggar's Opera."
Now Freely Adapted by Clifford Bax. London: Chapman & Hall,
1923. 64 pp.
        Much of the language is modernized.

2693 -----. Polly; an Opera by Mr. Gay, Being the Sequel to "The Beggar's Opera." Now Freely Adapted by Clifford Bax. New York:
Moffat, Yard & Co., 1923. 64 pp.

2694 -----. Polly: an Opera, Being the Second Part of the Beggar's
Opera. London: Gowans and Gray, 1927. 140 pp.
        A cheap edition.

2695 -----, Alexander Pope, and John Arbuthnot. Three Hours After
Marriage. Edited by Richard Morton and William M. Peterson. Painesville, Ohio, 1961. xvi, 111 pp. (Lake Erie College
Studies, Vol. I).
Prints the 1717 edition, noting it in both corrected and un-
corrected state. Also gives substantive variants in all editions
of any authority later.

2696 -----. Three Hours After Marriage. Edited, with an Introduction
by John Harrington Smith. Los Angeles: Clark Memorial
Library, University of California, 1961. 14, [vi], 139-222 pp.
(Augustan Reprint Society. Publication Nos. 91-92).
Uses as a text the second edition of the Dublin Supplement
to the Works of Alexander Pope (1758).

biography and criticism

2697 Delany, Mrs. (Mary Granville). A Memoir, 1700-1788. Compiled
by George Pastow. New York: E. P. Dutton and Company, 1900.
310 pp.
An abridgment of Lady Llanover's six volume edition of
1861-1862 to which have been added some unpublished letters
of Mrs. Delany's. Scattered throughout are allusions to Italian
operas, singers, and a few plays. Included is an account of the
disgrace of the Duchess of Queensberry for her championship
of Gay's Polly and a copy of the impertinent letter her grace
wrote to George II.

2698 Shaw, Martin. Souvenir [of] Acis and Galatea [and the] Masque of
Love as produced at the Great Queen Street Theatre, March
10th, 1902 by Martin Shaw and Gordon Craig. [London, 1902.]
Contains: 1) a foreword describing the Purcell Operatic
Society; 2) drawings for sets and costumes of Acis and Galatea,
followed by the libretto; 3) W. Barclay Squire's account of the
early stage history of Acis and Galatea; 4) drawings of costumes and scenery for Purcell's Masque of Love; 5) Christopher
St. John's description of the action of Masque of Love.

2699 Swift, Jonathan. The Correspondence of Jonathan Swift, D.D.
Edited by F. Elrington Ball, with an Introduction by the Very
Reverend J. H. Bernard, D.D. 6 vols. London: G. Bell &
Sons, Ltd., 1910-1914.
A complete edition of Swift's letters, which also contains
many letters to Swift and some letters about Swift. Naturally,
the letters to and from John Gay will be of greatest interest
to the student of drama.

2700 Paull, H. M. "John Gay." The Fortnightly Review, New Ser.,
XCI (May, 1912), 1095-1111.

". . . if Gay has claim to be a classic, it is on account of his songs . . ."

2701 Pearce. C. E. Polly Peachum and The Beggar's Opera. London: Stanley Paul and Company, 1913. 245 pp.

A complete history of Gay's Beggar's Opera, its inception, first night, cast, particularly Lavinia Fenton, together with chapters on Hogarth and on ballad singing in the 18th century; also the story of Polly and its censorship.

2702 -----. "Polly Peachum," Being the Story of Lavinia Fenton (Duche of Bolton) and "The Beggar's Opera." London: Stanley Paul & C [1913]. xvi, 376 pp.

The theatrical history of The Beggar's Opera land Lavinia Fenton, its famed leading lady; literary background of the play the circumstances of its production, the effect of "Polly Peachu on London society, and criticism of the play. Appendix listing actresses who played Polly, 1728-1879.

2703 -----. "Polly Peachum": Being the Story of Lavinia Fenton (Duche of Bolton), and "The Beggar's Opera." New York: Brentano's, xvi, 382 pp.

2704 Swaen, A.E. H. "The Airs and Tunes of John Gay's Beggar's Opera." Anglia, XLIII (1919), 152-190.

Attempts to trace the history of all the airs and tunes of The Beggar's Opera because "a full appreciation of the opera is only possible if we understand the references to the then popular tunes."

2705 Williams, I.A. "The Author of The Beggar's Opera." London Mercury, III (December, 1920), 166-179.

A biography of Gay which makes liberal use of his plays but treats them primarily as "events" in Gay's life.

2706 Herbert, A. P. "The London of 'The Beggar's Opera,' Court Reports of 1733." The London Mercury, V (December, 1921), 156-171.

A discussion of the treatment of criminals in 18th-century London which uses the characters of The Beggar's Opera as points of comparison to their counterparts in criminal society.

2707 Mais, S. P. B. "Such a Book as The Beggar's Opera." Why We Should Read. (London: Grant Richards, Ltd., 1921), 58-62.

This essay is really a summary of the play with a view to stirring up interest in this and other "old" plays.

2708 Melville, Lewis, pseud. [Lewis Saul Benjamin]. Life and Letters of John Gay (1685-1732), Author of "The Beggars Opera." London: Daniel O'Connor, 1921. xii, 167 pp.

A biography which is only incidentally concerned with Gay's works.

2709 Reynolds, Myra. "The Beggar's Opera." The Drama, XI (April,

1921), 227-231.

An essay which presents the circumstances of composition of Gay's play, provides a brief stage history and a brief discussion of the satire.

2710 Birrell, Augustine. "John Gay." Collected Essays and Addresses, 1880-1920. Vol. I. (London and Toronto: J. M. Dent & Sons, 1922), 100-106.

An essay arguing that Gay's fame is undeserved and that The Beggar's Opera is "wholly without sincerity."

2711 Doughty, Oswald. "Foreword" to Polly: An Opera. Being the Second Part of 'The Beggar's Opera.' By John Gay. Foreward by Oswald Doughty. London: Daniel O'Connor, 1922.

A brief discussion (pp. vii-xxiv) of The Beggar's Opera and Polly, which considers the close alliance of politics and the theatre.

2712 Duff, D. G. "Art and Crime." Mercury, V (1922), 413-414.

A quotation from a letter of Horace Walpole to Horace Mann (Nov. 4, 1773), which mentions The Beggar's Opera.

2713 Evans, Powys. The Beggar's Opera; Caricatures. London: C. Palmer [cop. 1922].

A one-page introduction on the life of Gay followed by a series of caricatures of the cast of the 1922 production.

2714 Hewlett, Maurice Henry. "Ballad-touch." Extemporary Essays. (London, Oxford: H. Milford, Oxford University Press, 1922), 47-51.

Argues that Gay's songs lack the "heart" that Shakespeare's and Burns' have.

2715 Kidson, Frank. The Beggar's Opera; Its Predecessors and Successors. Cambridge: The University Press, 1922. [8], 109 pp.

A "handbook" on The Beggar's Opera, which treats the background--the Italian opera, earlier English ballad operas--and the various aspects of The Beggar's Opera--the music, the plot and characters--and Gay's sequel, Polly, and other later ballad operas.

2716 Colville, Kenneth Newton. "John Gay." Fame's Twilight; Studies of Nine Men of Letters. (London: P. Allan & Co., 1923), 213-235.

A biographical essay on Gay which considers his works, though not in detail.

2717 Compton-Rhodes, P. "The Beggar's Opera in Birmingham." Times Literary Supplement, December 23, 1923, p. 896.

A list of revivals of The Beggar's Opera in Birmingham from 1752 through 1883.

2718 Pearce, Charles E. "Polly Peachum: The Story of Polly" and "The Beggar's Opera." London: S. Paul and Co. [1923]. 245 pp.

A history of the play, from Gay's first idea and his writing,

through its 18th century performances, with details on the
actresses who played Polly.

2719 Schultz, William Eben. Gay's Beggar's Opera: Its Content, History
and Influence. New Haven: Yale University Press, 1923. 420 pp.
A complete and detailed consideration of The Beggar's Opera
in terms of stage history, background, musical aspects, satirical elements, morality.

2720 Stevens, David Harrison. "Some Immediate Effects of The Beggar's Opera." Manly Anniversary Studies in Language and Liter
ature. Chicago: University of Chicago Press, 1923.
A discussion of the political ramifications of the play, covering the period 1728 to 1731.

2721 Colville, Kenneth Newton. Fame's Twilight; Studies of Nine Men
of Letters. Boston: Small, Maynard & Co. [1924]. vii, 263 pp.

2722 Melville, Lewis [Lewis Saul Benjamin]. Lady Suffolk and Her
Circle. Boston and New York: Houghton Mifflin, 1924. 306 pp.
A biography of George II's mistress which incidentally
touches on Gay, Addison, Swift and other literary figures.

2723 Baring-Gould, S. Devonshire Characters and Strange Events.
Second Series. London: John Lane, The Bodley Head, Ltd.
[1926]. xiv, 420 pp.
A chapter on Gay discusses The Beggar's Opera.

2724 Craig, Edward Gordon. [Illustration of a design for a production
of The Beggars' [sic] Opera, Act. I.] Mask, XII (January,
1926), opposite p. 1.

2725 Sherburn, George. "The Fortunes and Misfortunes of Three
Hours after Marriage." Modern Philology, XXIV (August,
1926), 91-109.
A discussion of the farce by Pope, Gay, and Arbuthnot,
assembling much contemporary evidence and correcting
several misconceptions.

2726 [Gay]. Notes and Queries, CLV (September 8, 1928), 164.
Reprints selections from the Country Journal (September
7, 1728), noticing performances of Gay's play at the Smith-
field and Southwark fairs.

2727 Irving, William H. John Gay's London Illustrated from the Poetry
of the Time. Cambridge, Massachusetts: Harvard University
Press, 1928. xviii, 460 pp.
A pleasant book, depicting the life of London in Gay's time.

2728 Wood, Ruth Kedzie. "A Play That Has Run for Two Centuries."
Mentor, XV (January, 1928), 48-51.
A second centennial appreciation, with a brief account of
the opera's performances in America. An illustration of
Lavinia Fenton as Polly Peachum, after Hogarth's illustration in
the National Gallery, London.

2729 [Gay]. Notes and Queries, CLVI (April 13, 1929), 256.
      Reprints selections from the Universal Spectator and
      Weekly Journal (April 12, 1729), noting spurious editions
      of Gay's Beggar's Opera, a trip to Bath by Booth, and Timon
      of Athens at Drury-Lane.

2730 -----. Notes and Queries, CLVI (June 15, 1929), 418.
      Reprints a notice from the Universal Spectator (June 14,
      1729) of a judgment favoring Gay, involving a pirated edition
      of Polly.

2731 -----. Notes and Queries, CLVII (August 24, 1929), 128.
      Reprints selections from the Daily Post (August 25, 1729),
      noting performances at Bartholomew-Fair, including the
      Beggar's Opera.

2732 -----. Notes and Queries, CLVII (December 21, 1929), 434.
      Reprints a notice from the Universal Spectator (December
      20, 1729) of Gay's play, The Wife of Bath Alter'd, in rehearsal
      and a Scotch opera by Mitchel.

2733 Goulding, Sybil. "Eighteenth-Century French Taste and 'The Beg-
      gar's Opera.'" Modern Language Review, XXIV (July, 1929),
      276-293.
      Discusses differences between English and French standards
      of taste during the period and examines French translations of
      the play.

2734 Heynen, Walter. "The Beggar's Opera." Masken, Jahrgang 23
      (1929), 21-27.

2735 Sherwin, Oscar. Mr. Gay. Being a Picture of the Life and Times
      of the Author of the Beggar's Opera. New York: John Day,
      1929. 184 pp.
      A journalistic sketch of Gay's career, of little value.

2736 Whiting, George W. "To Miss Polly Peachum." Times Literary
      Supplement, June 16, 1932, p. 447.
      Brings to light a hitherto unmentioned enthusiastic commen-
      dation of Polly Peachum, printed in the second edition of Bul-
      lock's "Woman's Revenge."

2737 Wood, Frederick T. "John Gay of The Beggar's Opera." Bookman
      (London), LXXXIII (1932), 162-164.

2738 Loiseau, J. "John Gay et le Beggar's Opera." Revue Anglo-Amer-
      icain, XII (1934), 3-19.
      Gay's important theatrical contribution is seen to lie in
      his fusion of the particular and the universal without which
      "no theatre can be durable."

2739 Tolksdorf, Cäcilie. John Gays "Beggar's Opera" und Bert Brechts
      "Dreigroschenoper." Rheinberg, Rhl. Sattler & Koss, 1934.
      80 pp.
      This German dissertation first analyzes Gay's play, then

Brecht's. The author then provides a study of the similarities
between the works and the extent to which Brecht was dependent
on Gay.

2740 Sutherland, James R. "The Beggar's Opera." Times Literary
Supplement, April 25, 1935, p. 272.
Cites an anecdote from The Flying Post, January 11, 1728/
29, about the origin of the play.

2741 Swift, Jonathan. The Letters of Jonathan Swift to Charles Ford.
Edited by David Nichol Smith. Oxford: Clarendon Press, 1935.
Includes letters to Ford from Gay, Pope, Parnell, Boling-
broke, and the Duchess of Ormond.

2742 Berger, A. V. "The Beggar's Opera, the Burlesque, and Italian
Opera." Music and Letters, XVII (1936), 93-105.
Compares the traditional operatic burlesque with Gay's
opera to show how Gay used devices from the burlesque to
satirize Italian opera.

2743 Swaen, A. E. H. "The Airs and Tunes of John Gay's Polly."
Anglia, LX (1936), 403-422.
Identifies the airs and tunes by author and title, and cites
sources which reprint them.

2744 Gaye, Phoebe Fenwick. John Gay: His Place in the Eighteenth
Century. London: Collins, 1938. 496 pp.
A popular biography of Gay, factually detailed but without
documentation.

2745 Kern, Jean B. "A Note on The Beggar's Opera." Philological
Quarterly, XVII (1938), 411-413.
The quarrel between Peachum and Lockit (II, x) is not based
upon an actual quarrel between Sir Robert Walpole and Lord
Townsend.

2746 Hamilton, Edwrrd W. "The Life of John Gay." Ph.D. University
of Minnesota, 1940.

2747 Irving, William H. John Gay, Favorite of the Wits. Durham,
North Carolina: Duke University Press, 1940. 334 pp.

2748 Lowenstein, Irma. "The Beggar's Opera by John Gay." M.A. Yale
University, 1940.

2749 "Notes of the Day: 'The Beggar's Opera.'" Monthly Musical Record, LXX (1940), 73-76.
The Beggar's Opera is a period piece. Its music and satire
could not have been written and are not applicable in the twentiet
century. It is appreciated for its quality only.

2750 Van Arsdale, Ronald Albert. "A Producing Director's Study of John
Gay's Beggar's Opera." M.A. University of Iowa, 1940.

2751 Bronson, Bertrand H. "The Beggar's Opera." University of California Publications in English, VIII (1941), 197-231.
Attempts to account for the sensational success of the piece,

emphasizing its parodies of popular songs and of Italian operas
and the devastating irony of its view of life.

2752 -----. "The Beggar's Opera." Studies in the Comic. (Berkeley and
Los Angeles: University of California Press, 1941), 155-298.

2753 Ryniker, Harriet E. "The Early Literary Career of John Gay."
M.A. University of Illinois, 1941.

2754 Wright, Harriett Cleveland. "The Development of a Costuming
Project for a University." M.A. University of Wisconsin,
1941.

2755 Sutherland, James R. "'Polly' among the Pirates." Modern Language
Review, XXXVII (July, 1942), 291-303.
Traces the history of pirated editions of Polly from its cen-
sorship to the granting of a court injunction in 1737.

2756 Trowbridge, Hoyt. "Pope, Gay, and 'The Shepherd's Week.'"
Modern Language Quarterly, V (March, 1944), 79-88.
Argues that Gay's poem was designed as a burlesque of
Ambrose Philips' Pastorals and that this intention determined
content, form, manner and diction. Some references to theatre.

2757 Jaggard, William. "The Beggar's Opera." Notes and Queries,
CLXXXVIII (June 2, 1945), 241.
Correcting the erroneous belief that Thomas Linley com-
posed the music.

2758 Loewenberg, Alfred. "The Beggar's Opera." Notes and Queries,
CLXXXVIII (June 16, 1945), 260.
Thomas Linley orchestrated the play for a 1777 revival.

2759 Stroup, Thomas B. "Gay's Mohocks and Milton." Journal of English and Germanic Philology, XLVI (April, 1947), 165-167.
Traces echoes of Milton in the play.

2760 Winters, Earle William. "The Beggar's Opera: a New Production
Script." M.A. Denver University, 1947.

2761 Herbert, Alan Patrick. Mr. Gay's London with Extracts from
the Proceedings at the Sessions of the Peace for the City of
London and the County of Middlesex in the Years 1732 and
1733. London: E. Benn, 1948. 136 pp.
Demonstrating the verisimilitude of The Beggar's Opera
by a study of records of criminal cases similar to those
portrayed in the play.

2762 Hussey, D. "Opera zebracza J. Gay'a. Wczoraj i dziś." Glos
Anglii (Cracow), LI (1948).
A study of The Beggar's Opera.

2763 Knotts, Walter E. "Press Numbers As a Bibliographical Tool: A
Study of Gay's The Beggar's Opera, 1728." Harvard Library
Bulletin, III (Spring, 1949), 198-212.
Using the frequently disregarded press numbers, four
impressions of the first edition are distinguished. See attack

on this piece by William B. Todd, in Philological Quarterly,
XXIX (1950), 238-240.

2764 Sutherland, James. "John Gay." Pope and his Contemporaries:
Essays presented to George Sherburn, edited by James L.
Clifford and Louis A. Landa. (Oxford: University Press, 1949),
201-214.

Mainly a study of the poetry, but making allusion to The
Beggar's Opera.

2765 Armens, Sven Magnus. "John Gay as Pastoral Poet; a Study of
His Views on Social Responsibility." Ph.D. Harvard University
1951.

2766 Loftis, John. "The Eighteenth-Century Beginnings of Modern Dram
Emory University Quarterly, VII (1951), 225-236.

Many aspects of modern theatrical practice first appeared in
the plays of Gay, Lillo, and Steele.

2767 Bronson, Bertrand. "The Beggar's Opera." Studies in the Literatur
of the Augustan Age: Essays Collected in Honor of Arthur Ellicc
Case. Edited by Richard C. Boys. (Ann Arbor: George Wahr,
1952), 14-19.

Bronson discusses the play, its technique, and its relationship to the period.

2768 Sherburn, George. "The Duchess Replies to the King." Harvard
Library Bulletin, VI (1952), 118-121.

The Duchess of Queensberry replied rather strongly to
George II after he had forbidden her the court for seeking sub-
scriptions for the printing of Gay's Polly.

2769 Gilbert, Vedder M. "Unrecorded Comments on John Gay, Henry
Travers, and Others." Notes and Queries, CXCVIII (1953),
337-339.

In a letter of February 21, 1727, Thomas Edwards expresse:
his enthusiastic approval of The Beggar's Opera.

2770 Hunting, Robert S. "How Much is a Cowcumber Worth?" Notes
and Queries, CXCVIII (1953), 28-29.

Gay's reference to the value of a cucumber (Beggar's Opera,
Air VII) is ambiguous.

2771 Oster, Harry. "A Study of the Songs of Thomas D'Urfey, John
Gay, Charles Dibdin, and Thomas Moore." Ph.D. Cornell
University, 1953.

2772 White, Eric W. "Beggar's Opera Note." Theatre Notebook, VIII
(1953), 24.

A copy of the fifth edition in the Atheneum Library at Barn-
staple, England, has a short manuscript addition at the end of
Act 3, Scene 6.

2773 Armens, Sven. John Gay, Social Critic. New York: King's Crown
Press, 1954. viii, 262 pp. Bibliography pp. [253]-255.

Although primarily a pastoral poet, Gay was nevertheless
a serious critic of the society in which he lived. Chapter II
concerns Gay's social criticism in The Beggar's Opera.

2774 Bentley, E. R. "Sir Laurence Machealth." The Dramatic Event.
(New York: Horizon Press, 1954), 140-143.

2775 Harris, Harold Joel. "Neo-Classical Satire: The Conservative
Muse." Ph.D. Ohio State University, 1954.
Cites The Beggar's Opera prominently.

2776 "The Beggar's Opera." Theatre Arts Monthly, XLI (May, 1957),
21.

2777 Kenffel, Kenneth William. "The 'Great Man' in English Satire,
1710-1743." Ph.D. University of Pennsylvania, 1959.
Includes The Beggar's Opera.

2778 Sherwin, Judith Johnson. "The World is Mean and Man Uncouth."
Virginia Quarterly Review, XXXV (1959), 258-270.
Treats The Beggar's Opera.

2779 Smith, Robert. "The 'Great Man' Motif in Jonathan Wild and The
Beggar's Opera." College English Association Journal, II
(1959), 183-184.
Contrasts the techniques of Fielding and Gay.

2780 Williams, E. E. "A Critical Study of the Works of John Gay, with
Special Reference to Invention and Craftsmanship." M.A.
Westfield College, London University, 1959-60.

2781 Höhne, Horst. "John Gay's Bühnenwerke in Ihrem Verhältnis zum
zeitgenössischen Dramenschaffen." Inaugural Dissertation.
Berlin, 1960.

2782 Thompson, Keith Maybin. "Honest John Gay, A Re-Estimate of
the Man and His Work." Ph.D. New York University, 1961.
(Order No. 62-3337).
A reexamination of the crosscurrents in his writings, with
a view to the re-evaluation of the author as, probably, belonging in the continuum of British "romantic" tradition, rather than
to the school of his great contemporaries, Pope, Swift, Arbuthnot,
and Addison. Examines the songs in The Beggar's Opera.

2783 Burgess, C. F. "The Genesis of The Beggar's Opera." Cithara, II
(1962), 6-12.
Gay was concerned with the subject matter of The Beggar's
Opera before Swift's suggestion for a "Newgate pastoral."

2784 Fuller, John. "Cibber, The Rehearsal at Goatham and the Suppression of Polly." Review of English Studies, XIII (1962), 125-
134.
The Rehearsal at Goatham hints that Gay believed Cibber to
have been influential in the suppression of Polly.

2785 Griffith, Benjamin W., Jr., ed. The Beggar's Opera. Great Neck,
New York: Barron's, 1962.
Includes music.

2786 Höhne, Horst. "John Gay's Bühneneverke in Verhältnis zum
zeitgenössischen Dramenschaffen." Wissenschaftliche Zeitschrift der Humboldt-Universität zu Berlin, XI (1962), 150.

2787 Burgess, C. F. "John Gay's 'Happy Vein': the Ambivalent Point
of View." Ph.D. University of Notre Dame, 1962. (Order No.
62-4405).
Gay's "happy vein" consists in the union of satiric and sympathetic attitudes demonstrated in The Shepherd's Week, The
What D' Ye Call It, Trivia, and The Beggar's Opera.

2788 Siegmund-Schultze, Dorothea. "Betrachtungen zur satirisch-
polemischen Tendenz in John Gays Beggar's Opera." Wissenschaftliche Zeitschrift der Martin-Luther Universitat Halle-
Wittenberg. Gesellschaftsund Sprachwissenschaftliche Reihe,
XII (1963), 1001-1014.

2789 Forsgren, Adina. John Gay, Poet "of a Lower Order": Comments
on His Rural Poems and Other Early Writings. Stockholm:
Natur och kultur, 1964. 249 pp.
A critical and historical study of Gay's early writings as
typical of his mature work. Includes references to Gay's
plays and ballad operas.

2790 Warner, Oliver. John Gay. New York: Longman's, Green and
Company (for the British Council and the National Book League),
1964. 40 pp.
Short introduction to Gay as a man of letters. Significant
sections on The Beggar's Opera, Polly, and Achilles.

2791 Bronson, Bertrand H. "The True Proportions of Gay's Acis and
Galatea." Publications of the Modern Language Association,
LXXX (1965), 325-331.
Critics have slighted the achievement of Gay and Handel in
Acis and Galatea, a supreme masterpiece in its genre. "It
can only be truly apprehended as a pastoral opera, words and
music inseparably united."

2792 Burgess, C. F. "Political Satire: John Gay's The Beggar's Opera."
The Midwest Quarterly, VI (1965), 265-276.
The motives, nature, and the immediate impact of Gay's
satire on Walpole, Gay, and the Tory party.

2793 Höhne, Horst. "John Gay's Beggar's Opera und Polly, Teil I."
Zeitschrift fur Anglestik und Amerikanistik, XIII (1965), 232-
260.
A philological and aesthetic analysis of The Beggar's Opera
and Polly reveal them to be a reliable key to the age's Weltan-
schauung.

2794 -----. "John Gay's Beggar's Opera und Polly, Teil II." Zeitschrift
fur Anglistik und Amerikanistik, XIII (1965), 341-359.
Gay's use of irony, wit, satire, and humor in his two masterpieces.

2795 Hogarth, William. The Beggar's Opera. A portfolio compiled by
      Wilmarth Sheldon Lewis and Philip Hafer. Cambridge, Harvard
      University Press; New Haven, Yale University Press, 1965.
          11 plates reproduce Hogarth and Blake's illustrations of
      Gay's ballad opera.
2796 Spacks, Patricia Meyer. John Gay. New York: Twayne Publishers,
      Inc., 1965.
          Biographical and critical study of Gay's life and works.
      Chapter V, "The Poet's Plays" and Chapter VI, "The Beggar's
      Triumph," are of special interest. Includes selected biblio-
      graphy.
2797 Armens, Sven M. John Gay, Social Critic. New York: Octagon
      Books, 1966. 262 pp.
          A reprint of the book first published in 1954.
2798 Bronson, Bertrand H. "The Beggar's Opera." Restoration Drama:
      Modern Essays in Criticism. A Galaxy Book. Edited by John
      Loftis. (New York: Oxford University Press, 1966), 298-327.
          Reprinted from Studies in the Comic (Berkeley: University
      of California Press, 1941), pp. 197-231. An analysis of the
      ballad opera explains its popularity at its original production
      and even today.
2799 Fuller, John. "A New Epilogue by Pope?" Review of English
      Studies, XVII (1966), 409-413.
          The epilogue to Gay's The Wife of Bath (1713).
2800 Preston, John. "The Ironic Mode: A Comparison of Jonathan
      Wild and The Beggar's Opera." Essays in Criticism, XVI
      (1966), 268-280.
          Studies the rhetorical and structural function of irony in
      the two works. For Fielding irony is a stylistic device, for
      Gay a means of articulating and organizing his knowledge of
      life.
2801 Rees, John O., Jr. "'A Great Man in Distress': Macheath as
      Hercules." University of Colorado Studies. Edited by J. K.
      Emery. (Boulder: University of Colorado Press, 1966), 73-
      77.
2802 Lewis, Peter Elvet. "Gay's Burlesque Method in The What D'Ye
      Call It." Durham University Journal, LX (1967), 13-25.
          The play attacks the mixed forms that were being produced
      at the time. "Although Gay's satire is directed against several
      dramatic and poetic modes as the title indicates, his principal
      targets are undoubtedly the main tragedians of the previous
      forty years, Otway, Lee, Dennis, Rowe, Philips, and Addison."
2803 Parlakian, Nishan. "The Image of Sir Robert Walpole in English
      Drama, 1728-1742." Ph.D. Columbia University, 1967. (Order
      No. 67-14,076).

The image of Walpole can be found in the plot, character, dianoia, and diction of more than fifty plays written during the period. Special attention is given to Gay's The Beggar's Opera.

2804 Schultz, William Eben. Gay's Beggar's Opera: Its Content, History and Influence. New York: Russell and Russell, 1967. 407 pp.
A reissue of the 1923 edition.

General History

2805 Hastings, Charles. Le Théatre Francais et Anglais. Ses origines Grecques et Latines. Paris: Firmin-Didot et Cie. 1900. 377 pp.
Contains chapters on Renaissance plays which were carried over into the Restoration and 18th Century and a brief history of the English stage, 1640-1900, which lists most popular plays of principal playwrights.

2806 Broadbent, R. J. Stage Whispers. London: Simpkin, Marshall, Hamilton, Kent, and Co., Ltd., 1901. 181 pp.
A general history of the English theatre from the mystery play to 18th century court amusements, containing chapters on the first English actresses, Players' benefits in the Restoration, and the history of playbills, theatrical costume, and theatrical scenery.

2807 Millar, J. H. The Mid-Eighteenth Century. New York: Charles Scribner's Sons, 1902. xii, 387 pp. (Periods of European Literature).
Chapter VI discusses the bourgeois tragedy of Lillo and Moore, compares French and English comedy, and shows how the sentimental Comedy of Cumberland and Kelly precipitated the revolt of Goldsmith and Sheridan.

2808 -----. The Mid-Eighteenth Century. Edinburgh: William Blackwood & Sons, 1902. 379 pp.

2809 Bates, Alfred; Boyd, James P.; and Lamberton, John P. British Drama. London: Smart and Stanley, 1903. 336 pp.
Chapter XIV, Section III, covers Restoration Drama; Section IV, The Later Restoration Drama. Gives history of drama, specific comments on dramatists, actors, actresses, plays, on plays' success, style, composition, influence. Also, contains the complete text of Home's Douglas, Colman and Garrick's The Clandestine Marriage, Mrs. Hannah Cowley's The Belle's Stratagem and The Provoked Husband.

2810 Hazlitt, William. "A View of the English Stage." Vol. 8. Collected Works of William Hazlitt, edited by A. R. Waller and Arnold Glover, with Introduction by William Ernest Henley.

(London: J. M. Dent & Co., 1903), 170-379.

2811 Mantzius, Karl. History of Theatrical Art in Ancient and Modern
      Times. Authorized translation by Louise von Cossel. Intro-
      duction by William Archer. 6 vols. New York: Lippincott,
      1903-1921.
          Volume VI "Classicism and Romanticism" was published
      in 1921. It contains a section dealing with Goldsmith and Sheri-
      dan, the Kembles and Edmund Kean. 1937 edition, New York:
      Peter Smith. Reprint.

2812 Matthews, Brander. The Development of the Drama. New York:
      Charles Scribner's Sons, 1903. 351 pp.
          Chapter 8 covers the drama in the 18th century.

2813 Lintilhac, Eugene Francis. Histoire Générale du Théâtre en
      France. 5 vols. Paris: E. Flammarion, 1904-1911.
          Vol. III covers the comedy of the 17th century and vol. IV
      covers the comedy of the 18th century.

2814 Matthews, Brander. The Development of the Drama. New York:
      Charles Scribner's Sons, 1904. vii, 351 pp.
          A survey of drama from the classical age of Greece through
      the 19th century in Europe. Touches briefly on the Restoration
      comedy of manners and the 18th-century sentimental comedy
      and bourgeois tragedy.

2815 Taine, H. A. History of English Literature. Translated by H. Van
      Laun. 4 vols. London: Chatto and Windus, 1907.
          Vol. II contains discussion of the Restoration theatre, pp.
      350-370, influence of Molière on restoration drama, pp. 399-
      409, drama of Wycherley, Congreve, Vanbrugh, and Farquhar,
      pp. 407-432, Sheridan and the degeneration of comedy, pp.
      432-447. Vol. III contains a discussion of Dryden's life and
      works, pp. 1-72.

2816 Moore, Frank Frankfort. A Georgian Pageant. London: Hutchinson
      and Co., 1908. 346 pp.
          Character sketches and anecdotes from the Johnson circle
      and other literary figures of the reign of George III.

2817 McNeill, William E. "A History of the English Drama from 1788
      to 1832 with Special Reference to Theatrical Conditions." Ph.D.
      Harvard University, 1909. 484 pp.
          An attempt to relate the drama and other types of enter-
      tainment to the conditions that produced it. The study, divided
      into six-year periods, discusses audiences, theatrical manage-
      ment, the drama of terror, and the relationship of the Romantic
      movement to drama.

2818 Sharp, R.F. A Short History of the English Stage from Its Begin-
      nings to the Summer of the Year 1908. London, New York
      [etc.]: The Walter Scott Publishing Co., Ltd., 1909. 355 pp.

A history of the English theatre, without footnotes or bibliography, concentrating on performers and productions. Some
50 pages devoted to Restoration and 18th-century theatre.

2819 Bartholomew, A. T. "The Restoration Drama, III." Cambridge
History of English Literature. Vol. VIII. (Cambridge: Cambridge University Press, 1912), 178-197.
Concerned with "characteristics of lesser Restoration
tragedy," the heroic play, the influence of Racine and Corneille,
the works of Otway, Lee, Crowne, and other playwrights.

2820 Elton, Oliver. A Survey of English Literature, 1780-1830. 2 vols.
London: E. Arnold, 1912.
The author calls his work a series of judgments on works of
art. Though largely concerned with the Romantics, Chapter I,
entitled "Anticipations," deals with backgrounds--philosophical,
literary, social; references to Restoration and 18th-century
dramatists are found throughout the work.

2821 Oliver, D. E. The English Stage, its Origins and Modern Development. London: John Ouseley, Ltd. [1912]. 151 pp.
Chapter II treats theatre from the Restoration to the death
of Kean.

2822 Schelling, Felix. "The Restoration Drama, I." Cambridge History
of English Literature. Vol. VIII. (Cambridge: Cambridge University Press, 1912), 115-145.
Begins with a discussion of plays and players after the closing
of the theatres, tells of various influences upon the English stage
and ends with a commentary on Wycherley's The Plain Dealer.

2823 Whibley, Charles. "The Restoration Drama, II." Cambridge History
of English Literature. Vol. VIII. (Cambridge: Cambridge University Press, 1912), 146-177.
Deals with Congreve, Vanbrugh, Rymer, Collier, Farquhar,
Dryden, D'Urfey, Dennis, Shadwell, and Cibber.

2824 Nettleton, George. "The Drama and the Stage." Cambridge History
of English Literature. (Cambridge, [England]: Cambridge University Press, 1913), Vol. X, pp. 67-92.
This historical sketch defines "Eighteenth Century English
Drama" and then illustrates the principal dramatists, dramatic
schools, sources and influences of the period. The essay ends
with a discussion of the reaction against sentimental comedy.

2825 -----. English Drama of the Restoration and Eighteenth Century.
New York: The MacMillan Company, 1914. 366 pp.
From 1642-1780. Emphasis on English elements, the relationship of each period to the preceding. Denies strong French
influence.

2826 Routh, H. V. "The Georgian Drama." Cambridge History of English

Literature. Vol. XI. Cambridge: Cambridge University Press, 1914.

Dealing with later 18th-century drama (See George Nettleton, "The Drama and the Stage"), Routh discusses the emergence of the actor, 18th-century audiences and the works of such authors as Goldsmith, Sheridan, Inchbald, Morton and others. The chapter ends with a treatise on "realism" and the drama.

2827 Schelling, Felix E. English Drama. London: J. M. Dent & Sons, Ltd., 1914. 341 pp. (The Channels of English Literature).

The story of English drama from the beginnings in the miracle and morality plays to the production of Sheridan's Critic in 1779. A final chapter outlines drama since Sheridan's time.

2828 Beers, Henry A. "Retrospects and Prospects of the English Drama." Connecticut Wits and Other Essays. (New Haven: Yale University Press, 1920), 115-157.

A discussion of English drama since 1700 which uses 18th century drama primarily as a point of comparison for contemporary drama.

2829 Elton, Oliver. A Survey of English Literature, 1780-1880. New York: Macmillan & Company, 1920.

In Chapter XXI, Part IV, (Vol. II, pp. 304-311), Elton surveys the drama at the end of the 18th century briefly, primarily with a view to showing its low quality.

2830 Poel, William. What is Wrong with the Stage; Some Notes on the English Theatre from the Earliest Times to the Present Day. London: G. Allen and Unwin, Ltd., 1920. 38 pp.

Sketchy history.

2831 Brawley, Benjamin. A Short History of the English Drama. New York: Harcourt Brace & Company, 1921. 269 pp.

Chapters VII-X (pp. 127-192) constitute a history of English drama from Dryden through Goldsmith and Sheridan.

2832 Rollins, Hyder E. "A Contribution to the History of English Commonwealth Drama." Studies in Philology, XVIII (1921), 267-333.

A history of the Interregnum drama based on the collection of newsbooks, pamphlets, etc., in the Thomasen Collection at the British Museum.

2833 Strong, Archibald T. A Short History of English Literature. London: Humphrey Milford, 1921. 415 pp.

A general literary history. Chapter XVIII (pp. 193-210) treats Dryden and the poetry and drama of the Restoration, Chapter XXIII (pp. 245-251) covers eighteenth-century drama.

2834 Summers, Montague. "Introduction." (pp. xiii-xlvi) Restoration

Comedies, edited by Montague Summers. (London: Jonathan
Cape, 1921), 446 pp.
　　　A brief, general history of Restoration drama.
2835　Archer, William. The Old Drama and the New: An Essay in Re-
　　　evaluation. Boston: Small, Maynard & Company, 1923. 404 pp.
　　　　　Lectures VI through IX (pp. 141-227) are concerned with
　　　Restoration and 18th century drama--examined mainly in
　　　terms of the reasons for the decline of drama in these periods.
2836　Nicoll, Allardyce. A History of Restoration Drama, 1660-1700.
　　　Cambridge: Cambridge University Press, 1923. 403 pp.
　　　　　A history, "covering not only the history of comedy and
　　　tragedy in the Restoration period but the history of the theatres
　　　and stage conditions as well." Contains three appendices: A.
　　　History of the Playhouses, 1660-1700; B. Select Documents
　　　Illustrating the History of the Stage; C. Hand-List of Restoration
　　　Plays.
2837　Rollins, Hyder E. "The Commonwealth Drama: Miscellaneous
　　　Notes." Studies in Philology, XX (1923), 52-69.
　　　　　A collection of miscellaneous notes on dramatic or theatrical
　　　activity, grouped under "The London Theatre" and "The Pro-
　　　vinces."
2838　Routh, H. V. "The [Eighteenth-Century] Drama." A History of
　　　English Literature. Edited by John Buchan. (London: T. Nelson
　　　& Sons, Ltd., 1923), 372-378.
　　　　　A brief summary of 18th-century drama, as part of a history
　　　of English literature.
2839　Summers, Montague. "The Restoration Drama." A History of
　　　English Literature. Edited by John Buchan. (London: T. Nelson
　　　& Sons, Ltd., 1923), 256-268.
　　　　　A brief summary of the drama of the Restoration, as part
　　　of a history of English literature.
2840　Cazamian, Louis. Histoire de la littérature anglaise. Paris:
　　　Librairie Hatchette, 1924. 276 pp.
　　　　　Book VI, Chapitre IV, "Le Theatre," is a survey history of
　　　Restoration drama. Book VIII, Chapitre VI, "Le Theatre," deal
　　　with the drama of the mid- through late eighteenth century,
　　　ending with Sheridan.
2841　Miller, Nellie. The Living Drama; Historical Development and
　　　Modern Movements Visualized, A Drama of the Drama. New
　　　York and London: The Century Co. [1924]. 447 pp.
　　　　　Pages 136 through 148 contain a discussion of Restoration
　　　and 18th-century drama. This appears to be a textbook.
2842　Nicoll, Allardyce. British Drama: An Historical Survey from the
　　　Beginnings to the Present Time. London: Harrap, 1925. 498 pp.
　　　　　Nicoll's thesis is that the development of English drama has

been continuous rather than interrupted.

2843 -----. A History of Early Eighteenth Century Drama, 1700-1750.
Cambridge University Press, 1925. xii, 431 pp.

Nicoll's thesis is that the first half of the 18th century was a
period of decay and disintegration, when critics laid down rules
which audiences would not accept. But it was also a period of
lively experimentation. Heroic plays had an important influence
on the early 18th century; masques, burlesques, and pantomimes
came to be powerful rivals to standard plays. The vogue of sentimental drama, however, was more limited than has been supposed. The hand-list of plays in the appendix is very valuable.

2844 Watson, Ernest Bradlee. Sheridan to Robertson: A Study of the
Nineteenth Century London Stage. Cambridge: Harvard University Press, 1926. xix, 485 pp.

An occasional 18th-century reference.

2845 Crump, Geoffrey H. Selections from English Dramatists; with a
Running Commentary Showing the Development of the Drama
in England. London: G. C. Harrap & Co., Ltd. [1927]. (Also:
London: Dennis Dobson, Ltd., 1950.)

Chapter V, "Restoration Drama," discusses social conditions, acting conditions, tragedy and comedy. Chapter VI,
"Drama of the Eighteenth and Early Nineteenth Centuries,"
treats sentimental drama, classical tragedy and Goldsmith
and Sheridan. Includes selections from Otway, Vanbrugh, Congreve, Lillo, Goldsmith, Sheridan.

2846 Eaton, Walter Prichard. A Study of English Drama on the Stage.
Chicago: American Library Association, 1927. 32 pp.

This short study "comprises a brief survey of the subject
and a guide to a few outstanding plays and books about the
drama."

2847 Nicoll, Allardyce. The Development of the Theatre. London:
Harrap, 1927. 246 pp.

One chapter is devoted to the commedia dell' arte influence
in the 16th and 17th centuries. Nicoll believes that Puritanism
in various ways impoverished the history of the English theatre.
Much new illustrative material.

2848 -----. A History of Late Eighteenth Century Drama, 1750-1800.
Cambridge University Press, 1927. x, 387 pp.

One chapter discusses contemporary stage conditions, and
three chapters give a comprehensive survey of the entire
dramatic production of the period. Goldsmith and Sheridan are
treated as only two among a great many successful playwrights.
An excellent discussion of 18th century farce and a valuable
hand-list of plays in the appendix.

2849 Elton, Oliver. Survey of English Literature 1730-1780. 2 vols.

London: Arnold, 1928.

Chapters on Goldsmith, Johnson, Fielding; two on comedy, one on tragedy. There were three kinds of comedy--pantomimic trifles, satiric comedy, and sentimental comedy. Tragedy was either too cold or too bombastic.

2850 George, M. Dorothy. England in Johnson's Day. London: Methuen, 1928. xvi, 239 pp.

Includes a section devoted to the theatre.

2851 Hughes, Glenn. The Story of the Theatre; a Short History of Theatrical Art from its Beginnings to the Present Day. New York: S. French; London: S. French, Ltd., 1928. ix, 422 pp.

This survey purports to be the "first attempt in English to summarize in one volume the main events in theatrical history from the earliest times to the present." Treats both Restoration and 18th-century drama.

2852 Lynch, James J. "Drama in the Theatre During the Mid-Eighteenth Century." M.A. University of Alabama, 1928.

2853 Nicoll, Allardyce. A History of Restoration Drama, 1660-1700. 2nd ed. Cambridge University Press, 1928. ix, 410 pp.

Several errors have been corrected and new evidence has necessitated a number of revisions: D'Urfey's Cinthia and Endimion should be dated April and not September 1697; Motteux' The Loves of Mars and Venus and Ravenscroft's The Antagonist ought to be dated November 1696 and not March 1697; Vanbrugh's The Relapse appeared in November and not December 1696.

2854 Cazamian, Louis. A History of English Literature. Translated by W. D. MacInnes and Louis Cazamian. Rev. ed. New York: Macmillan, 1929.

"Part II, Modern Times (1660-1914)" includes brief chapters on Dryden, the Restoration theatre, and eighteenth-century theatre.

2855 Cheney, Sheldon. The Theatre; Three Thousand Years of Drama, Acting and Stagecraft. With 204 illustrations. London: Longmans, Green & Co., 1929. ix, 558 pp.

Chapters XIII ("The Puritans and the Chapel of Satan"), XIV ("Kings, Courtesans, and Dramatists of France") and XV ("Opera, Picturing and Acting") are relevent for the student of Restoration and eighteenth-century drama.

2856 Dubech, Lucien. Histoire Générale Illustrée du Théâtre... 5 vols. Paris: Librairie de France [1931-1934].

Part III (pp. 215-296) of Volume 4 of this illustrated history of the theatre deals with Restoration and 18th-century drama. See also "Le Théâtre Romantique" (1790-1830) in Vol. 5.

2857   Eaton, Walter Prichard. The Drama in English. London: C.
       Scribner Sons, 1931. xiv, 365 pp.
           This book intends to give a general outline of English
       dramatic history; to sketch the physical playhouse, the tone
       and temper of the audience and the spirit of the times; and to
       analyze typical plays of each period from the point of view of
       the stage craftsman. Chapters 17 through 23 deal with the
       Restoration and 18th century.
2858   Mayorga, Margaret Gardner. A Short History of the American
       Drama, Commentaries on Plays Prior to 1920...with Illustra-
       tions and Bibliographies. New York: Dodd, Mead & Co., 1932.
       xxi, 493 pp.
           This history naturally includes references to British in-
       fluences upon American drama. It begins with earliest drama
       and the Revolutionary War.
2859   Ellehauge, Martin. English Restoration Drama. Its Relations to
       Past English and Past and Contemporary French Drama.
       From Jonson via Molière to Congreve. Copenhagen: Levin &
       Munksgaard, 1933. 322 pp.
           Concentration on the evolutionistic significance of Resto-
       ration drama, with the influence of Italy, Spain and France.
       Many Restoration motifs are traced back to Italians.
2860   Smith, Preserved. A History of Modern Culture. Vol. II: The
       Enlightenment, 1687-1776. London: Routledge; New York:
       Henry Holt, 1934. vii, 703 pp.
           Chapter X of volume two deals specifically with poetry and
       drama of the Enlightenment. The portion on Restoration drama
       is necessarily brief but interesting as a reflection of the
       philosophy and sociology of the period.
2861   Summers, Montague. The Restoration Theatre. London: Kegan
       Paul, 1934. xxi, 352 pp.
           Study of the conventions, physical aspects, companies and
       audiences of the Restoration theatre.
2862   Baesecke, Anna. Das Schauspiel der englischen Komödianten in
       Deutschland; seine dramatische Form und seine Entwicklung.
       Halle (Saale): M. Niemeyer, 1935. 154 pp.
           Pages 113-152 only are specifically on Restoration and 18th
       century. Describes the traveling English troupes of Green &
       Reinhold, Robert Brown, Roes, Joliphus, and the influence of
       their productions on the form and language of English comedy.
2863   Summers, Montague. The Playhouse of Pepys. London: Kegan
       Paul, 1935. xvi, 485 pp.
           Designed as the second part of the study begun with his
       Restoration Theatre, Summers presents in this volume a
       history of the drama from 1660 to 1682, excluding the rhymed

heroic play. He concentrates upon the biographies of dramatists
and the stage histories of their plays.

2864　Otis, William B., and Morriss H. Needleman. An Outline-History
of English Literature. New York: Barnes and Noble, Inc., 1936.
xiv, 326 pp.

A skeletal history of Restoration and 18th century drama is
included.

2865　Stevens, Thomas Wood. The Theatre from Athens to Broadway;
a Brief History. New York: D. Appleton-Century Company,
1936. 264 pp.

This illustrated history of the theatre emphasizes the often
"crossing and confusing" waves of dramatic and theatrical,
creative and technical, playwright and actor through the ages.
A popular study, Stevens' book includes sketchy chapters on
the Restoration period and "Garrick and the Age of Giants."

2866　Morrill, Allen Conrad. "Restoration Leisure: The Background of
English Drama, Prose and Poetry between 1660 and 1688."
(Cambridge, Massachusetts: Harvard University Press, 1938),
276-282.

A study of the cultural milieu which includes some historical
commentary upon university drama, touring dramatic companies
and the relations of the court with the theatre.

2867　Ernst, Earle. "Cycles in the Development of the Dramatic Arts."
Ph.D. Cornell University, 1940.

2868　Gassner, John. Masters of the Drama. New York: Random House
[1940]. xvii, 804 pp.

Chapter XVI, which focuses on Molière, briefly treats
Restoration and 18th-century comedy.

2869　Djivelegov, A. K., and G. B. Boyardjiev. The History of the
European Theatre from its Origins to 1789. Moscow and
Leningrad: Iskusstvo, 1941. 616 pp.

2870　Freedley, George. A History of the Theatre, with Hundreds of
Illustrations from Photographs, Playbills, Contemporary Prints,
etc. New York: Crown Publishers [c. 1941]. xvi, 688 pp.

This profusely illustrated volume is an attempt to set down
the main events in the history of theatre since the drama's
beginnings in Egypt. Chapters eleven and nineteen deal with
the Restoration and eighteenth century.

2871　Greene, Graham. British Dramatists. With eight plates in colour
and twenty-six illustrations in black and white. London: W.
Collins, 1942. 46 pp.

Mr. Greene's essay traces the development of English drama
from the mysteries and moralities through the early twentieth
century.

2872　Bridges-Adams, William. The British Theatre. London, New York,

Toronto: Published for the British Council by Longmans
Green & Co., 1944. 51 pp. 16 photographs.

Pages 18-27 give a very brief discussion of Restoration
and 18th-century drama, with an analysis of the trends in the
theatre.

2873 Brook, Donald. The Romance of the English Theatre. London:
Rockliff, 1945. 160 pp.

A popular survey of English theatrical history, containing
comment on the Restoration and eighteenth century dramas.

2874 Rapp, Franz. "Notes on Little-Known Materials for the History
of the Theatre." Theatre Annual for 1944 (1945), 60-78.

A variety of evidences and sources cited.

2875 Boas, Frederick S. An Introduction to Stuart Drama. London:
Oxford University Press, 1946. viii, 443 pp.

No discussion of drama after 1660 as such but the last
section (pp. 416-433) covers the early career of William
Davenant.

2876 Cleaver, James. The Theatre through the Ages. London: Harrap,
1946. 146 pp.

A general historical survey, including brief comment on
the period.

2877 Mavor, Osborne Henry [James Bridie]. The British Drama.
Glasgow: Craig and Wilson, 1946. 40 pp.

British Way Pamphlet, 12, surveying the theatre arts in
Britain and the relationship of stage and society, and making
some references to the period.

2878 Pierpont Morgan Library, New York. English Drama from the
mid-Sixteenth to the Later Eighteenth Century. Catalogue of
an Exhibition. October 22, 1945--March 2, 1946. New York,
1946. 95 pp.

Depicts and discusses the drama exhibition and includes a
succinct introductory essay on the development of English
drama by Samuel C. Chew. Contains references to Restoration
and 18th-century dramatists.

2879 Saintsbury, George. The Peace of the Augustans: A Survey of
Eighteenth Century Literature as a Place of Rest and Refresh-
ment. With an introduction by Herbert Grierson. Oxford: University Press, 1946. xiii, 408 pp. (World's Classics series).

A new edition of the celebrated study first published in
1916.

2880 Bachler, Karl, and Paul Zimmermann. Das Englische Drama von
den Anfängen bis zur Gegenwart. Gelsenkirchen-Buer: Post,
1947. 63 pp.

A brief survey, tightly packed with persons, plays and
dates. The period from Dryden to the end of the eighteenth

century is covered on pages 17-27.
2881 Baugh, A. C., ed. A Literary History of England. New York:
Appleton Century Crofts, 1948. 1613 pp.
Includes the admirable general survey, "The Restoration
and Eighteenth Century, 1660-1789," by George Sherburn
(pp. 697-1108).
2882 Evans, B. Ifor. A Short History of English Drama. Harmondsworth
Penguin Books, 1948. 172 pp.
A rapid general survey, with comment on the period.
2883 Lynch, James J. "Drama in the Theatre During the Mid Eighteenth
Century, 1737-1777." Ph.D. University of California at Berkeley, 1948.
2884 Marriott, James W. The Theatre. New edition, revised. London:
G. G. Harrap & Co. [1948]. 224 pp.
Intended for the amateur theatregoer, this deals primarily
with contemporary drama, but there are chapters dealing with
the history of English drama, including two sketchy chapters
entitled "Restoration Drama" and "The Eighteenth Century."
2885 McKillop, Alan D. English Literature from Dryden to Burns.
New York: Appleton Century Crofts, 1948. xii, 445 pp.
A general survey of the literature of the period, including
drama.
2886 Miles, Bernard. The British Theatre. London: Collins, 1948. 48
pp.
An historical sketch by the eminent actor, concentrating
on the actor and his relationship with the audience and including
a survey of acting techniques during the period.
2887 Trewin, J. C. The English Theatre. London: Elek, 1948. 122 pp.
Essentially a study of modern drama, but including an
historical sketch covering the plays of the Restoration and
eighteenth century.
2888 Gibbs, Henry. Theatre Tapestry. London, New York: Jarrolds
[1949]?. 263 pp.
A largely anecdotal history of British theatre.
2889 Krutch, Joseph Wood. Comedy and Conscience after the Restoration. New York: Columbia University Press, 1949. xii,
300 pp.
A second printing of the 1924 classic, with a new preface,
a bibliography by G. S. Alleman and an index
2890 Schirmer, Walter F. Kurze Geschichte der Englischen Literatur
von den Anfangen bis zur Gegenwart. Tübingen: Neomarius
Verlag, 1949. 322 pp.
A brief historical sketch, noting the major aspects of the
drama.
2891 Downer, Alan S. The British Drama, a Handbook and Brief Chronic

New York: Appleton-Century-Crofts [1950]. x, 397 pp.

An elementary history emphasizing "the development of the drama as a form of communication and artistic expression"; extensive treatment of early periods, briefer discussion of developments after 1700. Includes lists of suggested readings on topics and authors.

2892 Stamm, Rudolf. Geschichte des Englischen Theaters. Bern: A. Francke, 1951. 483 pp.

Stamm's history of the English theatre analyzes the close relationship between the drama and the milieu which produces it.

2893 Nagler, A. M. Sources of Theatrical History. New York: Theatre Annual, 1952. 611 pp.

Chapter VII and X provide source materials for the study of Restoration and eighteenth-century drama.

2894 Boas, Frederick S. An Introduction to Eighteenth-Century Drama, 1700-1780. Oxford: Clarendon Press, 1953. 365 pp.

Boas surveys the drama of the period largely by plot summary.

2895 Clunes, Alec. British Theatre History. Cambridge: Published for The National Book League at the University Press, 1955. 27 pp. (Reader's Guide. Second Series III).

Pages 11-25 are a "Reading List" intended for the "ordinary reader," and covers works on the history of the theatre in general as well as on individual theatres, biography, and criticism; also included are a few basic reference works.

2896 Coggin, Philip A. The Uses of Drama: A Historical Survey of Drama and Education from Ancient Greece to the Present Day. New York: George Braziller, 1956. 327 pp.

An historical survey of drama and education with special emphasis on how various philosophers and thinkers have viewed drama's role in education; less concern with the playwright's view of drama's function. Chapter XVIII treats English drama of the 18th century.

2897 Stamm, Rudolf, ed. Die Kunstformen des Barockzeitalters: Vierzehn Vorträge . . . Bern: Francke, 1956. 447 pp.

Includes Stamm's lecture on Renaissance and Restoration drama.

2898 Tomkins, A. R. "The Elizabethan Revival: A Study of the Contribution to Elizabethan Drama to the Romantic Movement." Ph.D. Kings College, Cambridge, 1956-1957.

2899 Hazlitt, William. Hazlitt on Theatre. Edited by William Archer and Robert Lowe. New York: Hill and Wang, 1957.

2900 Burton, K. M. P. Restoration Literature. London: Hutchinson University Library, 1958. 240 pp.

Some 30 pages of the section entitled "The Entertainers,"

are devoted to Restoration drama and a brief consideration
of the major writers. The author concludes that the drama
as a whole is of little literary value, and "does not merit the
lengthy critical works that have been devoted to it."

2901 D'Amico, Silvio. Storia del teatro drammatico. II. L'Europa dal
rinascimento al romanticismo. Milan: Garzanti, 1958. 390 pp.
England, pp. 278-286.

2902 Clifford, James L., ed. Eighteenth-Century English Literature:
Modern Essays in Criticism. Galaxy Book 23. New York: Oxford
University Press, 1959. xi, 364 pp.
References to drama and theatre in reprinted essays in-
cluded.

2903 Boulton, Marjorie. The Anatomy of Drama. London: Routledge
and K. Paul, 1960. 212 pp.
Containing references to many facets of drama, this avowed
popularization about "literature that walks" is intended "to help
the person with . . . rare access . . . towards a clearer notion
of the function and nature of drama and a greater enjoyment of
plays." Contains a section on heroic drama and on comedy of
manners.

2904 Burton, E. J. The British Theatre: Its Repertory and Practice
1100-1900 A.D. London: Herbert Jenkins, 1960. 271 pp.
Three chapters are of particular interest with reference
to the Restoration and 18th century: "Restoration Theatre,"
"Eighteenth Century, 1700-50: Formal Theatre," and "The
Later Eighteenth Century." This work is intended "to assist
producers and designers of setting, . . . to give necessary
basic information concerning the plays . . . and to indicate
the wide variety of material available."

2905 Daiches, David. A Critical History of English Literature. 2 vols.
New York: Ronald Press, 1960.
Volume II of this work of "description, explanation and
critical interpretation," intended not to be "looked up but to be
read," deals with English literature from the Restoration to
modern times. There are chapters entitled "The Restoration"
and "Drama from the beginning of the Eighteenth Century."

2906 Morrah, Patrick. 1660: The Year of Restoration. London: Chatto
& Windus, 1960. 237 pp.

2907 Watson, John Steven. The Reign of George III, 1760-1815. Oxford:
The Clarendon Press, 1960. xviii, 637 pp.
Aside from providing historical and sociological background,
this work contains some passing references to 18th-century
dramatists as in Chapter XIII in the sections entitled "literature"
and "playwrights."

2908 Khan, B. A. The English Poetic Drama. Aligarh, India: Muslim

University [1962]. xiv, 79 pp.

2909 Knight, G. Wilson. The Golden Labyrinth: A Study of British Drama.
      London: Phoenix House; New York: Norton Press, 1962. xiv, 402
      pp.
            Historical and critical survey. Chapter VII, "Restoration,"
      pp. 130-170. Chapter VIII, "Augustan," pp. 171-200.

2910 Burton, Ernest James. The Student's Guide to British Theatre
      and Drama. London: Herbert Jenkins, [1963]. 191 pp.
            A basic history of British theatre, treated by literary per-
      iods. Chapters VIII through X treat Restoration and eighteenth-
      century theatre. Each chapter begins with a discussion of social
      background, followed by comments on methods of staging during
      the period; finally, the major playwrights are commented on
      individually.

2911 Nicoll, Allardyce. British Drama: An Historical Survey from the
      Beginnings to the Present Time. 5th edition. New York: Barnes
      & Noble, Inc., 1963. 365 pp.
            A survey of British drama from the medieval period through
      the mid-20th century. Some 70 pages are devoted to Restoration
      and 18th-century drama, with emphasis on the different types
      of drama written in each period.

2912 Whitfield, G. J. An Introduction to Drama. London: H. Milford,
      Oxford University Press [1939]. 188 pp. 2nd ed. London: Ox-
      ford University Press, 1963. 206 pp.
            Discusses Way of the World as an example of the comedy
      of manners and The London Merchant as an example of the
      play of sentiment. Contains excerpts from scenes from each
      play.

2913 Clunes, Alec. The British Theatre. London: Cassell, 1964.
            Slight text accompanies this popular pictorial treatment
      of Restoration and eighteenth-century dramatists, characters,
      types, and players.

2914 Schmid, Hans. The Dramatic Criticism of William Archer. Bern:
      Francke Verlag [1964]. 111 pp.
            Archer's attitude toward Restoration and 18th-century drama
      is treated briefly.

2915 Rankin, Hugh F. The Theatre in Colonial America. Chapel Hill:
      University of North Carolina Press [1965]. xiii, 239 pp.
            Starting with the first theatre in America, that at William-
      sburg, the author traces the development of American drama
      in the 18th century. He naturally includes references to Amer-
      ican performances of such popular British playwrights as Dryden,
      Otway, Congreve, Farquhar, Rowe, and Gay.

2916 Wilson, John Harold. A Preface to Restoration Drama. (Riverside
      Studies in Literature). Boston: Houghton Mifflin Company, 1965.
      208 pp.

Intended as an introduction to Restoration drama for students, includes chapters on the nature of Restoration theatre,
tragedy, comedy, and a selected bibliography.

2917 Sorelius, Gunnar. "The Giant Race Before the Flood": Pre-Restoration Drama on the Stage and in the Criticism of the Restoration
(Acta Universitatis Upsaliensis, Studia Anglistica Upsaliensia
4.) Uppsala: Almqvist and Wiksells, 1966. 227 pp.

Concerned with the repertory of old plays that was the background of the Restoration stage. Discusses the changing conditions of the theatre, repertories and companies from 1660 to
1700 and transitions that occurred in comedy and tragedy.

Gentleman, Francis

2918 Highfill, Philip Henry, Jr. "Francis Gentleman, Critic." M.A.
University of North Carolina, 1948.

2919 -----. "A Study of Francis Gentleman's The Dramatic Censor,
1770." Ph.D. University of North Carolina, 1950.

German Drama

2920 Baker, Louis Charles. The German Drama in English on the New
York Stage to 1830. American Panorama, No. 31. [Philadelphia]:
University of Pennsylvania, 1917. 168 pp.

The avowed purpose of this work is to study German influence
on the New York Stage and to show the importance of this influence. This history, beginning with 1732, also reveals early
instances of British dramatic performances in New York.

2921 Brede, Charles Frederic. The German Drama in English on the
Philadelphia Stage from 1794 to 1830, Preceded by a General
Account of the Theatre in Philadelphia from 1749-1796. Philadelphia: Americana Germanica Press, 1918. 295 pp. (Americana Germanica, No. 34).

Until the Revolution, Philadelphia was the "most important
theatrical center in the colonies." This work begins with a
description of the theatre there in the late 18th century and
discusses not only German, but for comparative analysis,
English and French influences on the Philadelphia stage to
1830.

2922 Kelly, John A. England and Englishmen in German Literature of
the 18th Century. New York: Columbia University Press, 1921.

A section of Chapter IV--a general discussion of English
culture--considers English literature; drama is considered in
terms of its effects on German drama and dramatic criticism.

German Influence

2923 Oppel, Horst. Der Einfluss der englischen Literatur auf die
      Deutsche. Berlin: Bielefeld; Munich: Erich Schmidt [1954].
      98 pp.
2924 Grieder, Theodore. "The German Drama in England, 1790-
      1800." Restoration and 18th Century Theatre Research, III
      (November, 1964), 39-50.
          Studies the popularity of German drama in England from
      Holcroft's The German Hotel (1790). The low quality of the
      English plays and the emotionalism of the times accounted
      for its popularity; weak translations, English nationalism,
      and charges of social and political immorality contributed to
      its decline.
2925 Milburn, Douglas Lafayette. "German Drama in England: 1750-
      1850, With a List of German Plays Published and Performed."
      Ph.D. Rice University, 1964. (Order No. 64-10,185).
          The changing attitudes toward German drama in Great
      Britain between the middle of the 18th century and the middle
      of the 19th century can be attributed to political and historical
      considerations rather than to objective criticism of the works
      translated.

German Visitors

2926 Kelly, John Alexander. German Visitors to English Theaters in
      the Eighteenth Century. Princeton: Princeton University Press,
      1936. 178 pp.
          A study of commentary about the English theatre written by
      German playwrights, critics, and producers who visited Eng-
      land during the period 1696-1800. The volume includes bio-
      graphical information about the visitors and a bibliography of
      sources.

Germany

2927 Beam, Jacob Newton. Die ersten deutschen übersetzungen eng-
      lische lustspiele in achtzehnten jahrhundert. Hamburg and
      Leipzig: L. Voss, 1906. x, 95 pp.
          Published also as the author's inaugural dissertation, Jena,
      1904. Concerns 18th Century English drama and its transla-
      tions into German.
2928 Price, Lawrence Marsden. The Reception of English Literature
      in Germany. Berkeley: University of California Press, 1932.
      vii, 596 pp.

This study attempts to prove nothing, for the author is
cautious in attributing influence of author upon author or nation
upon nation. Chapter VII treats of "moralizing drama" and
discusses Addison's Cato, The London Merchant, The Rehearsal, The Beaux' Stratagem and other examples of the drama
of the period.

Gibbon, Edward

2929 Low, D. M., ed. Edward Gibbon's Journal. London, New York:
      Chatto and Windus, 1929. cxvii, 261 pp.
      Includes entries to January 28, 1763.

Giffard, H.

2930 McKillop, Alan D. "Giffard's Pamela. A Comedy." Book Collec-
      tor, IX (1960), 455-456.
      A short note describing a pirated edition in the library of
      Rice University.

Gifford, William

2931 Baring-Gould, S. Devonshire Characters and Strange Events.
      Second Series. London: John Lane, The Bodley Head, Ltd.
      [1926]. xiv, 420 pp.
      The chapter on William Gifford emphasizes his biography.
2932 Clark, Roy Benjamin. William Gifford, Tory Satirist, Critic,
      and Editor. New York: Columbia University Press, 1930. 294
      pp.
      A critical biography emphasizing Gifford's satirical writings,
      translation of Juvenal and editions of the dramatists Massinger,
      Ben Jonson, Ford, and Shirley, and his editorship of The Quar-
      terly Review.
2933 Tunnicliffe, S. "William Gifford, 1756-1826: His Early Life,
      Literary Friendships, and Editing of Massinger and Other
      Jacobean Dramatists." M.A. London University (Queen Mary),
      1965.

Gilbert-Cooper, John

2934 Guest, Alan D. "Charles Adams and John Gilbert-Cooper."
      Theatre Notebook, XI (1957), 135-141.
      Actor and playwright, ca. 1762.

Gildon, Charles

text

2935 Gildon, Charles, supposed author. A Comparison between the
      Two Stages; a Late Restoration Book of the Theatre. Edited,
      with an introduction and notes, by Staring B. Wells. Princeton:
      Princeton University Press, 1942. 206 pp. Bibliography, pp.
      [191]-200.

biography and criticism

2936 T.[horn]-D.[rury], G. "A Comparison Between the Two Stages."
      Review of English Studies, I (January, 1925), 96.
            Not by Gildon, on the basis of internal evidence.
2937 Wells, Staring B. "A Comparison between the Two Stages."
      Ph.D. Princeton University, 1935.
2938 -----. "An Eighteenth Century Attribution." Journal of English
      and Germanic Philology, XXXVIII (1939), 233-246.
            Argues that Charles Gildon did not write A Comparison
      Between the Two Stages and that "the ascription of the book
      to him was based on deceptive evidence."
2939 Anderson, George L. "Charles Gildon's A New Rehearsal, or
      Bays the Younger: Edited with an Introduction and Notes." Ph.
      D. University of Pennsylvania, 1953. 434 pp. (Publication No.
      4911).
            Gildon's dialogue is important as evidence in the Pope-
      Addison quarrel, the emergence of Whig and Tory literary
      camps, and the recognition of a new kind of neo-classicism.
      Gildon had much to say about Rowe's tragedies.
2940 Anderson, George L. "Lord Halifax in Gildon's New Rehearsal."
      Philological Quarterly, XXXIII (1954), 423-426.
            Argues that Sir Indolent Easie is probably Charles Montague.
2941 -----. "Charles Gildon's Total Academy." Journal of the History
      of Ideas, XVI (1955), 247-251.
            Short historical background on Gildon's desire for a literary
      academy in England to regulate all phases of literature, in-
      cluding language, content and form. A detailed description of
      Gildon's dream, including his proposal to reorganize the
      theatres. Includes discussion of Phaeton, The Patriot, and
      other works to indicate Gildon's standards of dramatic criticism.
2942 Wright, H. Bunker. "Prior and Gildon." Notes and Queries, CCI
      (1956), 18-20.
            This is a comment on a note by G. L. Anderson: "Gildon
      vs. Prior," Notes and Queries, CXCIX, 51-58. Wright dis-

cusses the letters between Gildon and Prior.

2943 Anderson, G. L. "The Authorship of 'Cato Examin'd' (1713)."
      Publications of the Bibliographical Society of America, LI
      (1957), 84-90.
          Attributes authorship to Charles Gildon.

2944 Goldstein, Malcolm. "Gildon's New Rehearsal Again." Philolo-
      gical Quarterly, XXXVI (1957), 511-512.
          Identifies characters in the pamphlet of 1714 criticizing
      Rowe's plays as Addison and Steele.

2945 Anderson, G. L. "'A Little Civil Correction': Langbaine Re-
      vised." Notes and Queries, New Ser., V (1958), 266-269.
          A discussion of Charles Gildon's 1698 revision.

2946 Howell, Wilbur Samuel. "Sources of the Elocutionary Movement
      in England: 1700-1748." Quarterly Journal of Speech, XLV
      (1959), 1-18.
          Cites Gildon's life of Betterton.

Glasgow

2947 Colby, Elbridge. "Melodrama at Glasgow." Notes and Queries,
      13th Series, I (1923), 364-367.
          Discussion of plays the public enjoyed, based on playbills
      from 1831-1837. Predominant are revivals of seventeenth and
      eighteenth-century successes, dramatizations of Walter Scott,
      and melodramas. Gives lists of plays performed in Glasgow
      and neighboring cities.

Gloucestershire

2948 Hannam-Clark, Theodore. Drama in Gloucestershire. Gloucester:
      Minchin and Gibbs, 1928. 240 pp.
          A popular account with occasional references to 18th century
      theatre: the anti-theatre activities of revivalist George White-
      field, an account of actor John Kemble and wife Sarah Siddons.
      Reproduces the birth registration of her daughter Sarah Martha
      at Gloucester, November 30, 1775.

Glover, Richard

2949 Schaaf, Johannes (Gustav). Richard Glover. Leben und Werke.
      Leipzig, 1900. 70, (2) pp.

2950 Briggs, Fletcher. "Notes on Glover's Influence on Klopstock."
      Philological Quarterly, I (1922), 290-300.

Goethe

2951 Carré, Jean-Marie. Bibliographie de "Goethe en Angleterre."
      Paris: Plon-Nourrit & Cie, 1920. 184 pp.
      A companion to the same author's Goethe en Angleterre,
      this volume provides a bibliography of translations of Goethe's
      plays, criticisms in the English press. As with the major
      volume, the first two sections deal with the years 1780 to
      1800.
2952 -----. Goethe en Angleterre. Paris: Plon-Nourrit & Cie, 1920.
      318 pp.
      Chapters 1 and 2 deal with the years 1780 to 1800. Chapter
      1 discusses Frederic Reynolds' adaptation of Werther (1785),
      and Chapter 2 discusses the reaction to Goethe's early plays
      and Henry Mackenzie's discussions of German drama to the
      Royal Society of Edinburgh.
2953 Hill, Charles J. "The First English Translation of Werther."
      Modern Language Notes, XLVII (January, 1932), 8-12.
      The Reverend Richard Graves, hitherto considered the
      first English translator of Werther, was indeed only the trans-
      lator's agent. The name of the translator remains a mystery.
2954 Willoughby, L. A. "Goethe Looks at the English." Modern Lan-
      guage Review, L (1955), 464-484.
      Goethe's favorable prejudice toward the English is examined
      in the light of those Englishmen he knew, particularly his friend
      Harry Lupton. Brief references to Lillo, Edward Young, and
      Goldsmith.

Goldsmith, Oliver

bibliography

2955 Balderston, Katharine C. A Census of the Manuscripts of Oliver
      Goldsmith. New York: The Brick Row Book Shop, 1926. xii,
      73 pp.
      A list of all extant manuscripts, every signature and letter,
      with brief descriptions and ownership.
2956 Dix, E. R. McClintock. "The Works of Oliver Goldsmith: A
      Hand-List of Dublin Editions before 1801." Publications of
      the Bibliographical Society of Ireland, III (1928), 93-101.
2957 Scott, Temple. Oliver Goldsmith, Bibliographically and Biograph-
      ically Considered, based on the collection of materials in
      the library of W. M. Elkins, Esq. Introduction by A. Edward
      Newton. New York: Bowling Green Press, 1928. xix, 368 pp.
      The most nearly complete bibliography to date, including a
      life of Goldsmith.

2958 Yale University Library. An Exhibition in the Yale University
      Library of the Works of Oliver Goldsmith in Connection with
      the Bicentenary of His Birth. New Haven: Printed for the Yale
      University Library, 1928. 2 pp.
          A descriptive bibliography of 56 items, including Goldsmith'
      plays and plays of others for which he wrote prologue or epilog

letters

2959 The Collected Letters of Oliver Goldsmith. Edited by Katharine
      C. Balderston. Cambridge: Cambridge University Press, 1928.
      LI, 190 pp.
          The introduction discusses the production of She Stoops to
      Conquer. The text includes letters to David Garrick, George
      Colman, Joseph Cradock and others relating to Goldsmith's
      dramatic career.

collected works

2960 Goldsmith, Oliver. The Collected Works of Oliver Goldsmith.
      Edited by Arthur Friedman. 5 vols. Oxford: Clarendon Press,
      1966.
          Volume V includes the plays with introductions and notes.

plays

2961 -----. The Plays of Oliver Goldsmith. London: J. M. Dent and
      Co., 1901. [4], 265 pp.
          Contains The Good Natur'd Man, which is a reprint of the
      fifth edition, 1768; She Stoops to Conquer, a reprint from the
      fourth edition, 1773; scene from The Grumbler, printed by Pri
      in the Miscellaneous Works, 1837. The notes are based on
      those in the edition of the Poems and Plays in "The Temple
      Library," 1889.

individual texts

2962 -----. The Good-Natur'd Man. Edited with Introduction and Notes
      by G. G. Whiskard. Oxford: The Clarendon Press, 1912. 95 pp
          The text, followed by ten pages of notes, is preceded by a
      discussion of the circumstances surrounding the first produc-
      tion of the play.
2963 -----. Goldsmith. The Good-Natured Man. Edited by A. S.
      Collins. London: University Pictorial Press, Ld. [sic.]
      [1936]. xix, [1], 102 pp.

Edition which gives a life, the production of the play,
general criticism, and characters of the play. The notes
aim at giving information about life in Goldsmith's day.

2964 -----. She Stoops to Conquer. New York and Boston: H. M.
Caldwell Co. [1900]. vi, 178 pp.
Contains Goldsmith's dedicatory epistole to Dr. Johnson,
Garrick's "Prologue," and the unannotated text of the play.

2965 -----. She Stoops to Conquer; or, The Mistakes of a Night: A
Comedy. Edited by J. M. Dent. London: Dent, 1900. 147 pp.
Short preface deals with first performance and publication
of the play, its sources, characters and ideas. Notes explain
obscure references in the text.

2966 -----. She Stoops to Conquer; a Comedy. Philadelphia: H. Altemus
[190--]. 202 pp.
The Introduction discusses the plays of Goldsmith in relation to theatrical conditions of the period and the relationship
of the plays to English comic tradition.

2967 -----. Goldsmith. She Stoops to Conquer. Edited with Introduction
and Notes by G. A. F. M. Chatwin. Oxford: At the Clarendon
Press, 1912. xiv, 100 pp.
The text of the play, except for a "few slight alterations,"
is that of C. E. Doble, prepared for the Oxford edition of The
Plays and The Vicar of Wakefield. Editor does not tell the
necessity for introducing consistency into Goldsmith's spelling
and punctuation. Since so many of the notes are borrowed from
other editions it is not quite clear what is the purpose of this
particular edition, and how it agrees or disagrees with earlier
ones.

2968 -----. She Stoops to Conquer. Edited by John Hampton. London:
J. M. Dent, 1927. (King's Treasuries of Literature). 192 pp.
Student's edition.

2969 -----. "She Stoops to Conquer." Famous Plays in Miniature.
Edited by Roger Wheeler. (Boston: W. H. Baker, 1935), 53-69.
A version abridged and condensed into three acts so as to
form "a complete entertainment . . . in thirty minutes of
playing time."

2970 -----. She Stoops to Conquer. Telescoped from the original
play by N. Ratcliff. London: Nelson, 1936. 66 pp.

2971 -----. She Stoops to Conquer. Retold by David Fullerton. London: Oxford University Press, 1938. v, 85 pp.

2972 -----. She Stoops to Conquer, or the Mistakes of a Night. Edited
by Katherine C. Balderston. New York: Appleton-Century-
Crofts, 1951. 73 pp.
The introduction deals briefly with the history, sources,
and significance of the play.

2973   -----. She Stoops to Conquer. Edited by H. A. Kresner. Sydney,
       Australia: Horwitz, 1963.

2974   -----. She Stoops to Conquer. Edited with an Introduction by A.
       Norman Jeffares. London: Macmillan, 1965. 100 pp.

selected works

2975   -----. The Good Natur'd Man and She Stoops to Conquer. The
       Introduction and Biographical and Critical Material by Austin
       Dobson . . . the Text Collated by George P. Baker, A. B.
       Boston and London: D. C. Heath and Company [1903]. xxix,
       285 pp. (Belles Lettres Series.)
           In addition to the two plays, this volume contains "Registry
       of Scotch Marriages," and "Essay on the Theatre. . ." The
       introduction contains a biography of Goldsmith and information
       on the theatrical and cultural background of the plays.

2976   -----. The Good-Natured Man. She Stoops to Conquer. Edited,
       with introduction and notes by Thomas H. Dickinson. Boston:
       Houghton Mifflin Co. [cop. 1908.] xxi, 105 pp. (The Riverside
       Literature Series.)
           The introduction treats Goldsmith's life and writings, his
       theory of dramatic art, the plays and their sources, and gen-
       eral conditions of 18th-century drama.

2977   -----. She Stoops to Conquer and The Good-Natured Man. Lon-
       don: Cassell and Co., Ltd., 1909. 191 pp.
           The unannotated text is preceded by an unsigned introduction
       which recounts the circumstances of the first production of
       each play.

2978   -----. Poems and Plays. Everyman Edition. Introduction by Austi
       Dobson. New York: E. P. Dutton [1910?]. 317 pp.
           Contains the Good-Natured Man, She Stoops to Conquer, pro
       logues, epilogues, a scene from The Grumbler, and, in an ap-
       pendix, the "Essay on the Theatre, or A Comparison Between
       Laughing and Sentimental Comedy." The Introduction calls The
       Good-Natured Man a substantial gain to humorous drama and
       emphasizes She Stoops to Conquer's fidelity to nature.

2979   -----. Essays, Poems, Letters and Plays. Edited by Padraic Coli
       Dublin: Talbot Press, 1928. 364 pp.
           With an appreciation and bibliography.

2980   -----. Selections from Oliver Goldsmith. Edited by John Earn-
       shaw. London: Methuen and Co., 1929. 220 pp.
           Includes She Stoops to Conquer.

2981   -----. The Good Natured Man and She Stoops to Conquer. Edited
       by A. S. Collins. London: University Tutorial Press, 1936.
       [Unpaged.]

2982 -----. "She Stoops to Conquer." The Vicar of Wakefield and
Other Writings. Edited, with an Introduction and Notes, by
Frederick W. Hills. New York: Random House, 1955. xxv,
580 pp. (The Modern Library).
2983 -----. The Vicar of Wakefield and She Stoops to Conquer. With
an Introduction by R. H.W.Dillard. (Harper Perennial Classics).
New York: Harper and Row Publishers, 1965. 265 pp.
Includes biographical notes, bibliography and Goldsmith's
"On the Theatre."
2984 -----. She Stoops to Conquer. Sheridan, Richard Brinsley. The
School for Scandal. New York: Bantam Books, Inc., 1966.
(Bantam Pathfinder Editions).
With brief introduction and notes.

translations

2985 -----. Ŝi klinigâs por venki; komedio en kvin aktoj. Tradukis A.
Motteau. Londono, Eldonata de "The Esperantist," [1903?].
79 pp.
Esperanto translation of She Stoops to Conquer.
2986 -----. Íslíû chun buadha .i. "She Stoops to Conquer" te Oliver
Goldsmith. Piaras Béaslaí. Baile Atha Cliath, Oifig an tSola-
thair [not after 1940]. 101 pp.
A Welsh translation, first staged in 1929, with Piaras
Beaslai playing the role of Sir Searlus. Brief Introduction.

biography and criticism

2987 B., E. A. "Comedy or Farce." The Academy and Literature,
LVIII (February 3, 1900), 109.
Argues that She Stoops to Conquer is a farce, not a comedy,
since rules of probability and character drawing are set aside.
2988 Wedmore, Frederick. "Notes on Players and Old Plays." The 19th
Century, XLVIII (1900), 249-255.
A comparison of the dramatic art of Goldsmith and Sheridan,
specifically She Stoops to Conquer and School for Scandal.
2989 Black, William. Goldsmith. English Men of Lⁿtters Series. Edited
by John Morley. London: Harper & Bros., 1901. 152 pp.
The events of Goldsmith's life simply related, interspersed
with appreciations and accounts of his major works. No documentation or index.
2990 Forster, John. The Life and Times of Oliver Goldsmith. Edited
by Roger Engpen. New York: F. A. Stokes Co., 1903. (Originally published, 1877.)
A standard work praised by Dickens and Macauley. A de-

tailed account of Goldsmith's life, documented by his own
papers and letters. A chronology is appended, apparently
Forster's. The editor has not indicated abridgements but has
appended a biographical note on Forster and notes correcting
and adding to Forster's information.

2991 Irving, Washington. Oliver Goldsmith; A Biography. The author's
revised edition, with introduction and notes by Willis Boughton.
Boston, New York [etc.]: Houghton Mifflin and Co. [1903]. xv,
382 pp. (The Riverside Literature Series).

First published in 1840.

2992 Jenks, Tudor. In the Days of Goldsmith. New York: A. S. Barnes
and Co., 1907. vii, 275 pp. (Lives of Great Writers).

Stresses public events and literary history of the period. See
Chapter 11, "Vicar" and the first play; and Chapter 14, "Poet
and Playwright." Appendix, Bibliography, pp. 267-268.

2993 Leichsering, A. S. C. Uber das verhältnis von Goldsmith's
"She Stoops to Conquer" zu Farquhar's "The Beaux Stratagem."
Cruxhaven, 1909. 82 pp.

Inaugural dissertation. An analysis by act and scene of the
two plays. Shows parallels between the two plays by means
of printing the texts in double columns.

2994 King, Richard Ashe. Oliver Goldsmith. London: Methuen and
Company, Ltd., 1910. 295 pp.

A biography, being a refutation by an Irishman of the idea
of Goldsmith's English contemporaries and biographers that
Goldsmith was "Poor Poll" and an "Inspired Idiot."

2995 Moore, F. Frankfort. The Life of Oliver Goldsmith. London:
Constable and Company, 1910. 492 pp.

A life of Goldsmith with emphasis upon the idea that his
impractical unworldliness, which he shared with other members of his family, accounts for his lack of material success.

2996 Mendt, Arthur. Goldsmith als Dramatiker. Leipzig: Dr. Seele
& Co., 1911. vi, 116 pp.

Discusses the background of 18th-century comedy and
treats Goldsmith's plays as they relate to the other comic
drama of the 18th century.

2997 Thompson, Hugh. Goldsmith's "She Stoops to Conquer." New
York: Doran, 1912.

Contains a series of pen and ink drawings for the beginning
of each act representing the situation at the rise of the curtain.
Also some illustrations within scenes, most in color.

2998 Colum, Padraic. Oliver Goldsmith. Chicago: F. G. Browne & Co.,
1913. xx, 345 pp.

Contains She Stoops to Conquer and two scenes from The
Good-Natured Man. Colum's introduction is an appreciation
of Goldsmith's works.

2999 Goldsmith, Oliver. Comic Iambics, Translation from "She
     Stoops to Conquer, Act II" by Reuben Cohen. [Recited in the
     Divinity School, June 23, 1915.] Oxford: B. H. Blackwell,
     1915.

3000 Hudson, William Henry. Johnson and Goldsmith and Their Poetry.
     London: G. G. Harrap & Co., Ltd., 1918. 175 pp.
        Attempts to associate the poetry of Johnson and Goldsmith
     with their characters and careers. Treats Johnson's Drury
     Lane Prologue (1747).

3001 Strahan, J. A. "Oliver Goldsmith." Blackwood's Magazine, CCX
     (August, 1921), 221-223.
        A biographical sketch of Goldsmith.

3002 Dobson, Austin. "Goldsmith." Modern English Essays. Edited by
     E. Rhys. Vol. II. (London: Dutton, 1922), 193-214.
        This article is an introductory essay to Goldsmith's works;
     the emphasis is historical--at what point in Goldsmith's life the
     plays were written, and especially their success (or lack of it).

3003 Pitman, James Hall. Goldsmith's Animated Nature; A Study of
     Goldsmith. New Haven: Yale University Press; London: Hump-
     hrey Milford, Oxford University Press, 1924. [4], 159 pp.
     (Yale Studies in English, LXVI.)
        The concentration of emphasis is on Goldsmith rather than
     on the book. The drama is touched upon, but briefly.

3004 Sells, Arthur Lytton. Les Sources francaises de Goldsmith.
     Paris: Librairie Ancienne Edouard Champion, 1924. 241 pp.
        Chapter five of Part III (pp. 155-168) deals with Goldsmith
     as a dramatist--his debt to Molière, Voltaire, and especially
     Marivaux.

3005 Tupper, Caroline F. "Essays Erroneously Attributed to Gold-
     smith." Publications of the Modern Language Association,
     XXXIX (1924), 325-342.
        An argument that Goldsmith was not the author of the Belles
     Lettres series of essays, one of which--"On Hyperbole"--
     concerns Shakespeare.

3006 Williams, Iolo A. "Oliver Goldsmith." Seven 18th Century Biblio-
     graphies. (London: Dulau & Co., 1924), 118-177.
        An annotated, descriptive bibliography of first editions of
     Goldsmith's works, arranged chronologically.

3007 McKerrow, R. R. and I. A. Williams. "Notes on Sheets L and M
     of the First Edition of Goldsmith's She Stoops to Conquer."
     London Mercury, XI (January, 1925), 302-303.
        Comments on an earlier discussion by editor J. C. Squire
     on the two sections of the first edition of the play.

3008 Balderston, Katharine C. The History and Sources of Percy's
     Memoir of Goldsmith. Cambridge: Cambridge University Press,
     1926. 61 pp.

Percy's memoir prefixed to the 1801 edition of Goldsmith's Works was the first considerable authentic biography of Goldsmith. This work traces the "history of the Memoir's genesis and publication, and . . . the sources of Percy's information."

3009 "Harmatopegos." "Olivers Goldsmith." Notes and Queries, CLI (December 4, 1926), 404.

Goldsmith took his medical degree at Dublin.

3010 "A Blundering Genius." Mentor, XV (May, 1927), 16-17.

The story of the first night of She Stoops to Conquer.

3011 Goldsmith, Oliver. "Better to Bite." Saturday Review of Literature, IV (December 3, 1927), 386.

Reprints an anonymous letter (by Goldsmith) to the Public Ledger, August 19, 1761, offering to supply literary news to the paper.

3012 "Oliver Goldsmith, 1728(?)-1774." London Times Literary Supplement, November 8, 1928, pp. 813-814.

A judicious character sketch and leading article. Reviews K. C. Balderston's Collected Letters of Oliver Goldsmith (1928) and R. S. Crane's New Essays. By Oliver Goldsmith (1928).

3013 Shipp, Horace. "First Fruits of the Autumn Season." English Review, XLVII (October, 1928), 484-485.

Reviews Nigel Playfair's Lyric Theatre production of the play.

3014 Walsh, Thomas. "Oliver Goldsmith, the Irishman." North American Review, CCXXVI (September, 1928), 352-355.

Biographical sketch, emphasizing Goldsmith's Irish background.

3015 Welsh, Martin G. "Goldy." Quarterly Review, CCLI (October, 1928), 270-280.

An essay honoring the second centenary of Goldsmith's birth. His greatest works are essentially autobiographical.

3016 Balderston, Katharine C. "The Birth of Goldsmith." Times Literary Supplement, March 7, 1929, pp. 185-186.

Urges inconclusively that "there is more weight for 1730 as the correct birth year than for any other."

3017 Colum, Padraic. "Young Goldsmith." Scribner's Magazine, LXXXVI (November, 1929), 555-563.

A biographical sketch of Goldsmith from 1749 to 1752.

3018 Ingalls, Gertrude Van Arsdale. "Some Sources of Goldsmith's She Stoops to Conquer." Publications of the Modern Language Association, XLIV (June, 1929), 565-568.

Suggests Spectators 289 and 427 as sources for incidents in the plot.

3019 Leslie, James B. "The Birth of Goldsmith." London Times Literary Supplement, March 14, 1929, p. 207.
    Replies to K. C. Balderston (TLS, March 7, 1929) that the
matriculation record of Trinity College, Dublin, is not reliable.
3020 "Prologue Written by Goldsmith." Morning Post (London), October 22, 1929, p. 9.
    On the ms. of the Prologue to Cradock's Zobeide.
3021 Windle, Bertram C. A. "Gold." Catholic World, CXXIX (July,
1929), 396-403.
    A character sketch of Goldsmith.
3022 Balderston, K.C. "A Manuscript Version of She Stoops to Conquer." Modern Language Notes, XLV (1930), 84-85.
    Notes on the licenser's manuscript copy belonging to the
Larpent Collection in the Huntington Library.
3023 Baudin, Maurice. "Une Source de She Stoops to Conquer." Publications of the Modern Language Association, XLV (1930), 614.
    Discusses parallels, which could easily be mere coincidences,
with the Galant Courer of Marc Antoine Le Grand (1722).
3024 Gallaway, W.F. "The Sentimentalism of Goldsmith." Publications
of the Modern Language Association, XLVIII (1933), 1167-1181.
    An article which traces the vogue of sentiment in She Stoops
to Conquer and The Vicar of Wakefield.
3025 Kent, Elizabeth Eaton. Goldsmith and His Booksellers. Ithaca,
New York: Cornell University Press, 1933.
    An examination of Goldsmith's observations on booksellers
and of his relationships with Ralph Griffiths, Robert and James
Dodsley, John Newberry, Thomas Davies and William Griffin.
3026 Schorer, Mark. "She Stoops to Conquer: A Parallel." Modern
Language Notes, XLVIII (1933), 91-94.
    The author advances Mrs. Centlivre's The Man's Bewitched
as a "remarkable coincidence" in its similarity to Goldsmith's
play.
3027 Gwynn, Stephen. Oliver Goldsmith. London: Butterworth, 1935.
x, 326 pp.
    A reliable biography on the whole, though without documen-
tation. Chapter X presents a brief stage history of The Good
Natur'd Man; Chapter XII, a more detailed treatment of She
Stoops to Conquer.
3028 Emery, John P. "An Unpublished Letter from Arthur Murphy to
Oliver Goldsmith Concerning She Stoops to Conquer." Philological Quarterly, XVII (1938), 88-90.
    Prints a letter dated March 2, 1773, in which Murphy sug-
gests a plan for an epilogue to Goldsmith's play.
3029 Reynolds, W. Vaughan. "Goldsmith's Critical Outlook." Review
of English Studies, XIV (1938), 155-172.

Stating that Goldsmith's views about the drama "might well
form the subject of a separate study," Reynolds notes briefly
that his opposition to sentimentality derives from an Aristotelia
concept of the distinction between tragedy and comedy; he was
equally opposed to genteel affection and excessive moralizing.

3030 Heilman, Robert B. "The Sentimentalism of Goldsmith's Good-
Natured Man." Studies for William A. Read. Edited by Nathanie
M. Coffee and Thomas A. Kirby. (Baton Rouge, La.: Louisiana
State University Press, 1940), 237-253.

3031 Stice, Cora Evelyn. "Producing Director's Study of Goldsmith's
Good-Natured Man." M.A. University of Iowa, 1940.

3032 Larrabee, Stephen A. "The 'Closet' and the 'Stage' in 1759."
Modern Language Notes, LVI (April, 1941), 282-284.
Calls attention to discussion of closet-drama in Edward
Young's Conjectures on Original Composition and Goldsmith's
An Enquiry into the Present State of Polite Learning.

3033 Sells, A. Lytton. "Oliver Goldsmith's Influence on the French
Stage." Durham University Journal, New Ser., II (March,
1941), 88-101.
Covers Goldsmith's borrowings from French drama, French
imitations of his plays and She Stoops to Conquer, and French
editions and opinions of the play.

3034 Parsons, Coleman O. "Textual Variations in a Manuscript of She
Stoops to Conquer." Modern Philology, XL (August, 1942),
57-69.
Traces the evolution of the title and lists 91 textual variants
between the Larpent MS. and the edition of 1773, some of them
author's revisions.

3035 Moore, John Robert. "Goldsmith's Degenerate Song-Birds: An
Eighteenth-Century Fallacy in Ornithology." Isis, XXXIV
(1943), 324-327.
Birds in North America were generally felt to be inferior
to British birds. The article is primarily a discussion of the
reasons for this belief with references to Goldsmith and Sherida

3036 Murphy, Elisabeth A. "Goldsmith's Intellectual Background." Ph.D
University of Wisconsin, 1943.

3037 Smith, John Harrington. "Tony Lumpkin and the Country Booby
Type in Antecedent English Comedy." Publications of the Moder
Language Association, LVIII (1943), 1038-1049.
On prototypes of Tony in earlier plays.

3038 MacDermot, H.E. "Goldsmith as a Talker." Queen's Quarterly,
LI (Summer, 1944), 184-193.
Attempts to show, mainly through conversations of Samuel
Johnson and Reynolds, that Goldsmith was not a good talker.
Some of Goldsmith's own phrases and sentences are used.

3039 Price, Lawrence Marsden. "The Works of Oliver Goldsmith on
the German Stage, 1776-1795." Modern Language Quarterly,
V (December, 1944), 481-486.
Stage history of Goldsmith's two plays and of German
dramatizations of Vicar of Wakefield; discusses the alterations
necessary to make Goldsmith--or any other English playwright
--acceptable to the German audience.

3040 [Starkey, James.] "Goldsmith and 'The Bee.'" Essays and Recol-
lections, by Seumas O'Sullivan. (Dublin and Cork: Talbot Press,
1944), 24-28.

3041 -----. "Goldsmith's Birthplace." Essays and Reflections, by
Seumas O'Sullivan. (Dublin and Cork: Talbot Press, 1944),
29-37.
Evidence that Goldsmith's birthplace was Ardnagow, not
Elphin.

3042 Tobin, Patricia Eleanor. "A Production Prompt Book for She
Stoops to Conquer, by Oliver Goldsmith." M.A. University
of Michigan, 1944.

3043 Behringer, Clara M. "A Production Prompt Book for She Stoops
to Conquer." M.A. University of Michigan, 1945.

3044 Hammer, Carl, Jr. "Goethe's Estimate of Oliver Goldsmith."
Journal of English and Germanic Philology, XLIV (1945), 131-
138.
A presentation of Goethe's views, including those on the
plays.

3045 Neveu, Raymond. "Oliver Goldsmith, romancier, poète et médecin." Mémoires de la Société d'Histoire de la Médecine, II
(1946), 3-9.
A survey of Goldsmith's achievements, mainly in the non-
dramatic fields.

3046 Knaack, Louis. "Designing of Costumes for She Stoops to Conquer." M.F.A. Carnegie Institute of Technology, 1949.

3047 Popovich, Maxim. "She Stoops to Conquer: a Production Book."
M.F.A. Yale University, 1949.

3048 Freeman, William. Oliver Goldsmith. London: Jenkins [1951].
286 pp.
A biography which provides detailed information about the
circumstances surrounding the early productions of Goldsmith's plays--particularly the critics' reception of them--
but there is no criticism of the plays.

3049 Jackson, Robert Wyse. Oliver Goldsmith. Essays Toward an
Interpretation. [Dublin: A.P.C.K., 1951]. 47 pp.
Goldsmith's personality is frequently revealed in his
characters.

3050 Murphy, Sister Miriam Joseph, S.C. "A Revaluation of the Works of Oliver Goldsmith." Ph.D. University of Wisconsin, 1952. 230 pp.

Included in Sister Miriam's discussion is a revaluation of Goldsmith's dramatic works.

3051 Eichenberger, Karl. Oliver Goldsmith: Das Komische in den Werken seiner Reifeperiode. Bern: A.Francke, 1954. 126 pp.

Eichenberger analyzes the comic technique in Goldsmith's major works, including the comedies.

3052 Hennig, John. "The Auerbachs Keller Scene and She Stoops to Conquer." Comparative Literature, VII (1955), 193-202.

Discusses apparent echoes of Goldsmith's play in Goethe's Faust.

3053 Neal, Minnie Mills. Oliver Goldsmith. New York: Pageant Press, 1955. [8], 86 pp.

The work concentrates on how Goldsmith wrote, his inspirations, incentives and motives. A tendency to moralize. There are no footnotes or critical apparatus. The writer's feelings intervene.

3054 Menon, K. R. A Guide to Oliver Goldsmith's "She Stoops to Conquer." Singapore: India Publishing House, 1957. [2], 76 pp.

Merely a student guide, giving an outline of Goldsmith's life, the story and plot, the characters, and a summary and notes for each act.

3055 Wardle, Ralph M. Oliver Goldsmith. Lawrence: University of Kansas Press, 1957. 330 pp.

Scholarly biography. References to plays and theatrical relations indexed.

3056 Todd, William B. "The First Editions of The Good Natur'd Man and She Stoops to Conquer." Studies in Bibliography, XI (1958), 133-142.

Attempts to distinguish the several variants of Goldsmith's two plays. Within a year of its publication, The Good Natur'd Man "ran through five impressions, two or which are unlabelled two called a 'New Edition,' and one described as a Fifth Edition. Within a year of its publication in 1773, She Stoops to Conquer ran through six impressions, two of which are unlabelled, the next called either the "Second" or "Third," the only following termed the "Fourth Edition," and the fifth and sixth both described as a "Fifth Edition."

3057 Fallon, Gabriel. "Dublin International Theatre Festival, 1959." Threshold, III (1959), 63-75.

Goldsmith, The Good-Natured Man.

3058 Jeffares, A. Norman. Oliver Goldsmith. (Writers and Their Work, No. 107). London: Longmans for the British Council and the National Book League, 1959. 44 pp.

3059 Snider, Patricia Wilson. "Production Book of She Stoops to Con-
         quer." M.F.A. University of Oklahoma, 1959.
3060 Gassman, Byron. "French Sources of Goldsmith's The Good
         Natur'd Man." Philological Quarterly, XXXIX (January, 1960),
         56-65.
         A 1768 review of Goldsmith's play in The London Magazine
         asserted that Goldsmith used six French plays as sources for
         The Good-Natur'd Man. Gassman finds that Goldsmith was
         clearly indebted to only two of the French plays: Le Philanthrope
         by Marc Antoine Le Grand and L'Important by David Augustin de
         Brueys.
3061 Montague, John. "Tragic Picaresque: Oliver Goldsmith; the Bio-
         graphical Aspect." Studies (Irish Quarterly Review), XLIX
         (Spring, 1960), 45-53.
         Montague laments the fact that, until recently, biographical
         portraits of Goldsmith have been irrelevant and distorted and
         have, therefore, hindered a true picture of his achievement.
         Works by men like Sells, Seitz, Friedman and Crane may create
         a truer picture of Oliver Goldsmith.
3062 Sherwin, Oscar. Goldy: The Life and Times of Oliver Goldsmith.
         New York: Twayne Publishers, 1961. 367 pp.
         Popular life, "based on fact . . . and . . . artisitic imagina-
         tion." Goldsmith's relations to the theatre are mentioned. Some
         contemporary documents used.
3063 Reed, Duane E. "A Project in Design and Execution of Costumes
         for a Production of Goldsmith's She Stoops to Conquer." M.A.
         Indiana University, 1962.
3064 Butzier, Kenneth G. "An Evaluation of Technical Problems En-
         countered in a Period Revival at State College High School,
         Cedar Falls, Iowa, of Oliver Goldsmith's She Stoops to Con-
         quer." M.S. University of Wisconsin, 1963.
3065 Garrod, H. W. The Study of Good Letters. Edited by John Jones.
         Oxford: Clarendon Press, 1963. 211 pp.
         An essay on Goldsmith's achievement (originally published
         in 1924 as part of the Nelson's Poets series) stresses the hu-
         manistic value of The Good-Natured Man, and She Stoops to
         Conquer.
3066 Coulter, John Knox, Jr. "Oliver Goldsmith's Literary Reputation,
         1757-1801." Ph.D. Indiana University, 1965. (Order No. 65-
         10,814).
         Considers the reaction of contemporary critics to Gold-
         smith's works and suggests that both The Good-Natured Man
         and She Stoops to Conquer represent an attack upon sentimental
         comedy and the author's attempt to revive a comic tradition
         unhindered by false illusions about man's goodness.

3067 De Haas, Jeanne Marie. "The Design and Execution of Costumes
for Oliver Goldsmith's She Stoops to Conquer." M.F.A. Ohio
University, 1965.

3068 Ferguson, Oliver W. "The Materials of History: Goldsmith's Life
of Nash." Publications of the Modern Language Association,
LXXX (1965), 372-386.
Information about Goldsmith's success, particularly from
George Scott, for his The Life of Richard Nash, Esq.

3069 Griffin, Robert Julian. "Goldsmith's Augustanism: A Study of
his Literary Works." Ph.D. University of California, Berkeley, 1965. (Order No. 65-13497).
Considers The Good Natur'd Man and She Stoops to Conquer
as efforts to correct the age's onesided "sentimental" view.

3070 Nelson, David Arthur. "The Laughing Comedy of the Eighteenth
Century." Ph.D. Cornell University, 1965. (Order No. 65-
14711).
The comic technique and situations of Vanbrugh, Farquhar,
Goldsmith, and Sheridan are evaluated in terms of their ability
to create and maintain aesthetic distance between playgoer and
character.

3071 Quintana, Ricardo. "Goldsmith's Achievement as Dramatist."
University of Toronto Quarterly, XXXIV (1965), 159-177.
Occupies itself with such questions as the relationship
between Goldsmith's earlier works and his dramas, the influence of Georgian comedy upon his dramatic career, and the
nature of his comic disposition.

3072 Quintana, Ricardo. "Oliver Goldsmith as a Critic of the Drama."
Studies in English Literature, 1500-1900, V (1965), 435-454.
Goldsmith's criticism of his own plays, of comedy, and of
contemporary dramatists reveal "a truly sophisticated poetic
of the drama."

3073 Schenk, William Murrel. "A Development of the Scenic Designs for
the Ohio State University Production of She Stoops to Conquer."
M.A. Ohio State University, 1965.

3074 Jeffares, A. Norman. A Critical Commentary on Goldsmith's
'She Stoops to Conquer.' (Macmillan Critical Commentaries).
London: Macmillan, 1966. 40 pp.
Besides an analysis of the play's plot, characters, and
significance, the work provides a brief biography, a description
of the contemporary stage, and a selected bibliography.

3075 Rodway, Allan. "Goldsmith and Sheridan: Satirists of Sentiment."
Renaissance and Modern Essays. Edited by G. R. Hibbard.
(London: Routledge and Kegan Paul, 1966), 65-72.
The anti-sentimental plays of Goldsmith and Sheridan are
themselves affected by the "usurping Genteel of Sentimental

Mode they purported to attack."

3076 Baer, Joel H. "Revival of the Comic Spirit: Goldsmith's
She Stoops to Conquer." Setting the Stage. Minnesota Theatre
Company Publication, 1967.

3077 Ferguson, Oliver W. "Goldsmith." South Atlantic Quarterly,
LXIV (1967), 465-472.
A general review of Goldsmith's achievements and character.

3078 Gutting, John D. "Humour Humbled and Exalted: Oliver Goldsmith
and the Theatre of Comedy." M.A. Xavier University, 1967.

3079 Joel, Helmuth Wulf, Jr. "The Theme of Education in the Works of
Oliver Goldsmith." Ph.D. University of Pennsylvania, 1967.
(Order No. 67-12,761).
Studies Goldsmith's approach to the problems attendant upon
bringing up the young to survive in a hostile world. Includes
discussion of The Good Natur'd Man and She Stoops to Conquer.

3080 Kirk, Clara M. Oliver Goldsmith. New York: Twayne Publishers,
1967. 202 pp.
Biographical and critical study of Goldsmith's major works.
Chapter IV, "Two Laughing Comedies," is of particular note.
Includes selected bibliography.

3081 Quintana, Ricardo. Oliver Goldsmith: A Georgian Study. (Masters of
World Literature Series). New York: Macmillan Co., 1967.
213 pp.
A biographical and critical study of Goldsmith's works.
Chapter VIII, "Comedy for the Theatre," is of special interest.

Goodman

3082 Wilson, John Harold. Mr. Goodman the Player. Pittsburgh: University of Pittsburgh Press, 1964. 153 pp.
Studies Goodman's colorful career particularly in his association with the King's Company of Comedians from 1673 to
1682.

Gothic

3083 Haferkorn, Reinhard. Gotik und ruine in der englischen dichtung
des achtzehnten Jahrhunderts. Leipzig: B. Tauchnitz, 1924.
204 pp.

3084 McClamroch, R. P. "The Gothic Drama, a Study of That Part of
English Drama between the Years 1780 and 1820 Which Owed Its
Existence to the Gothic Novel." Ph.D. University of North
Carolina, 1927.

3085 Thorp, Willard. "The Stage Adventures of Some Gothic Novels."
Publications of the Modern Language Association, XLIII (June,

1928), 476-486.

Analyzes seven plays produced 1781-1798 to discover the
extent to which themes and effects of Gothic romances were
carried over to English stage before 1800. Authors of the seven
minimized the horrors of the original romances rather than ex-
ploiting them.

3086   Hanawalt, Leslis L. "The Rise of the Gothic Drama, 1765-1800."
Ph.D. University of Michigan, 1929.

3087   Evans, Richard B. "Dramatic Participation in the Gothic Revival."
Ph.D. University of California, 1942.

3088   Evans, Bertrand. Gothic Drama from Walpole to Shelley. Berkeley:
University of Califonria Press, 1947. viii, 257 pp. (University
of California Publications in English, XVIII).

Based on the Larpent MS collection in the Huntington Library.
A study of the form from 1768, showing how the Byronic hero
derives from the stage villain of the early melodrama.

Gould, Robert

3089   Sloane, Eugene Hulse. Robert Gould, Seventeenth-Century Satirist.
Philadelphia: University of Pennsylvania Press; Oxford: Oxford
University Press, 1940. 126 pp.

Attributes Gould's obscurity to his venemous attacks on the
nobility and the stage.

3090   Weinbrot, Howard D. "Robert Gould: Some Borrowings from Dryden." English Language Notes, III (1965), 36-40.

Cites passages in Gould's "The Playhouse" which manifest
an indebtedness to Dryden's All for Love, The Conquest of
Granada, and Essay of Dramatick Poesy.

Granville, George

3091   Cashmore, H. M. "Lord Lansdowne's Comedies." Notes and
Queries, CLV (December 29, 1928), 464.

A brief bibliography of works dealing with his plays.

3092   [Granville]. Notes and Queries, CLV (September 22, 1928), 200.

Reprints selections from the Weekly Journal (September
21, 1728), noticing rope-dancing at Southwark Fair and a new
comedy by Lord Lansdowne.

3093   Handasyde, Elizabeth. Granville the Polite. The Life of George
Granville, Lord Lansdowne, 1666-1735. London: Humphrey
Milford, Oxford University Press, 1933. ix, [3], 287 pp.

Detailed study, based primarily on contemporary documents.
The four plays are discussed in some detail showing that
Granville had no real dramatic impulse.

3094 Wilson, J. H. "Granville's 'Stock-Jobbing Jew.'" Philological
      Quarterly, XIII (1934), 1-15.
          Through a study of his Shylock, Wilson depicts Granville
      as an honest craftsman, if not a great playwright, who intended
      the Jew to be a comic character while, at the same time, "re-
      moving all the Shakespearean motivation, and heightening the
      quality of unreasoning malice."

Graves, Richard

3095 Hook, R. "Richard Graves, 1715-1804." M.A. London University
      (Birkbeck), 1935.

Gray, Thomas

3096 Gray, Thomas. Letters of Thomas Gray. Edited by John Beres-
          ford. London: Oxford University Press, 1925. xxii, 395 pp.
      (World's Classics).
          A few dramatic references in these selected letters.
3097 -----. The Correspondence of Thomas Gray. Edited by Paget
      Toynbee and Leonard Whibley. Oxford: Oxford University
      Press, 1935.
          Contains some matter of importance to the student of drama.

Greek Tragedies

3098 Heinemann, Karl. Die tragischen Gestalten der Griechen in der
          Weltliteratur. Leipzig: Dietrich, 1920.
          A study of the major Greek tragedies and their influence on
      or treatment by subsequent dramatists. Includes references to
      the plays of the Restoration and 19th-century passim.

Greenwich

3099 Rosenfeld, Sybil. "Penkethman's Greenwich Theatre." Notes and
          Queries, CLXIX (1935), 434-437.
          Prints data about the repertory and players at the Green-
      wich Fair, 1709-12.

Griffin, Benjamin

3100 Peterson, William M. "Performances of Benjamin Griffin's Whig
          and Tory." Notes and Queries, New Ser., IV (1957), 17-19.
          Twenty-one performances, 1720-31.

Griffith, Elizabeth

3101 Eshleman, Dorothy H. "Elizabeth Griffith." Times Literary Supplement, June 9, 1945, p. 271.
        Request for information about Elizabeth Griffith (1720?-
1793), Shakespearean and collaborator with Garrick.

Grub Street Journal

3102 Hillhouse, James T. The Grub-Street Journal. Durham, North
Carolina: Duke University Press, 1928. x, 354 pp.
        Summarizes a mass of literary and dramatic material in the
Journal.

Guns

3103 Morton, Richard and William M. Peterson. "Guns on the Restoration Stage." Notes and Queries, VI (1959), 267-272, 307-311.
        Extends into 18th century.

Gwynn, Nell

3104 Price, F. G. Hinton. "Nell Gwyn, Gwynn, or Gwynne." Notes
and Queries, 9th Ser., VI (November 3, 1900), 350-351.
        Though "Gwyn" was the usual form of spelling the name of
the actress, Price finds at least six variants.
3105 Hazelton, George Cochrane, Jr. Mistress Nell; a Merry Time
(Twixt Fact and Fancy). New York: S. Scribner's Sons, 1901.
viii, 311 pp.
        A fictional account of Nell Gwyn's career, adapted from a
play by the same author ("Let not poor Nelly starve").
3106 Marshall, Julian. "Royal Tennis Court and Nell Gwyn." Notes and
Queries, 9th Ser., IX (February 15, 1902), 136.
        States that there never was a Royal tennis court in the Hay-
market, only a court in James St., Haymarket, but questions
that Nell Gwyn visited it.
3107 Prideaux, W. F. "Royal Tennis Court and Nell Gwyn." Notes and
Queries, 9th Ser., IX (February 15, 1902), 136.
        Asserts that there was a Royal tennis court on the south side
of James St., Haymarket, a favorite resort of Charles II and
very probably visited by Nell Gwyn.
3108 Cunningham, Peter. Story of Nell Gwyn. Edited by Gordon Goodwin
Edinburgh: J. Grant, 1908. xii, 236 pp.
        Later edition of Cunningham's Story of Nell Gwyn (London,
1852), a popular biography which portrays a profligate English
court and society of the Restoration period.
3109 Orr, Lyndon. "Famous Affinities of History." Munsey Magazine,

XLIV (October, 1910), 73-80.

Includes a short sketch of the "affinity" of Charles II for Nell Gwynn.

3110 Williams, Hugh Noel. Rival Sultanas: Nell Gwyn, Louise de Keroualle, and Hortense Mancini. London: Hutchinson & Co., 1915. 376 pp.

A popular account of loves and social wars profusely illustrated from paintings and engravings.

3111 Melville, Lewis [Lewis Saul Benjamin]. Nell Gwyn, the Story of Her Life. [2nd ed.] London: Hutchinson &Co. [1923]. 326 pp.

A very thorough account of Nell's personal life and loves based on sources described in a bibliographical appendix; however, there is little comment on her performance as an actress, except as it affected her lovers. Contains text of Nell's will.

3112 Pierpoint, Robert. "Chelsea Hospital, Nell Gwyn, Sir Stephen Fox." Notes and Queries, Ser. 13, I (December, 1923), 423-425.

A discussion of Nell Gwynne's role in the founding of the Chelsea Hospital.

3113 Dasent, Arthur Irwin. Nell Gwynne, 1650-1687: Her Life Story from St. Giles's to St. James's. With Some Account of Whitehall and Windsor in the Reign of Charles the Second. London: Macmillan & Co., 1924. 333 pp.

A biography of Nell Gwynne which explores the social life and social conditions at Court and which attempts to give a more complete record of Nell's stage history than had been offered before. Appendix I is a chronological list of plays acted at Drury Lane in which Nell Gwynne appeared.

3114 B., G. F.R. "Nell Gwyn." Notes and Queries, CXLVIII (May 16, 1925), 358.

Her mirror in the Public Museum, Brighton.

3115 C., C. S. "Nell Gwyn." Notes and Queries, CXLVIII (April 11, 1925), 213.

Notes a knife (dated 1680) and a mirror once hers.

3116 Segrè, Carlo. "Una della prime comiche inglesi." Nuova Antologia, CCXLII (August, 1925), 294-325.

A sketch of Nell Gwynn's career.

3117 Gwyn, Nell. [A portrait by Sir Peter Lely, now in the Metropolitan Museum of Art, N.Y.] Reprinted in Connoisseur, LXXVI (September, 1926), 31.

3118 Bax, Clifford. Pretty Witty Nell; an Account of Nell Gwyn and Her Environment. London: Chapman and Hall, Ltd. [1932]. 261 pp.

A rather digressive account, carefully following the chronology of Nell's life. Illustrated with portraits, and including Nell's will and the Drury Lane Patent, with brief bibliography.

3119 Fea, Allan. "Portraits of Nell Gwynn, Moll Davis and Others."
       Connoisseur, CXI (1943), 29-33.
              Discusses problems of identifying these paintings.

3120 Wilson, John Harold. "Nell Gwyn as an Angel." Notes and Queries,
       CXCIII (February 21, 1948), 71-72.
              She played Angelo in The Virgin Martyr, May, 1668.

3121 -----. "Nell Gwyn's House in Pall Mall." Notes and Queries, CXCIV
       (April 2, 1949), 143-144.
              Reveals new biographical details.

3122 Van Lennep, William. "Nell Gwyn's Playgoing at the King's Expense
       Harvard Library Bulletin, IV (1950), 405-408.
              Charles II paid for Nell's playgoing at Dorset Garden; an ex-
       tant bill for 35 pounds 19 shillings is for plays seen by her and
       her friends during 1674-1675, 1675-1676, and part of 1676-1677.

3123 Wilson, John Harold. Nell Gwyn: Royal Mistress. London: Fre-
       derick Muller; New York: Pelligrini and Cudahy, 1952. 309 pp.
              Wilson treats in great detail the personal life and profession-
       al career of the actress.

3124 Todd, William B. "An Unidentified Portrait of Charles II, the
       Duchess of Cleveland, and Nell Gwyn." Notes and Queries,
       CXCIX (1954), 114.
              The portrait is by Lely.

3125 Cohen, Selma Jeanne. "Mr. Pepys Goes to the Theatre." Dance
       Magazine (July, 1956), 36-37, 60-61, 66.
              Comments on the dances and the dancers he saw, especially
       Nell Gwynn.

3126 Wilson, John Harold. "Nell Gwyn: Two Portraits." Notes and
       Queries, CCI (1956), 204-206.
              There are two nude portraits of Nell Gwyn which can be
       authenticated by contemporary vouchers.

3127 Moncada, Ernest J. "The Source of an Epigraph Attributed to
       Rochester." Notes and Queries, New Ser., XI (1964), 95-96.
              Ascribes to James Howell the authorship of an obscene
       poem written under the portrait of Nell Gwynn in Curll's The
       Works of the Earl of Rochester, Roscommon, and Dorset
       (1718).

Haines, Jo.

3128 Biswanger, Raymond A., Jr. "Jo. Haines as a Fortune-Teller."
       Notes and Queries, CCI (1956), 253-254.
              There are at least four contemporary literary references
       to Jo. Haines' fortune telling.

Halifax

3129 Gaunt, J. ["Halifax Theatre."] Yorkshire Notes and Queries, I
      (1904), 167.
          A very brief history--of a few lines--of the recently demol-
      ished Theatre Royal at Halifax, from 1791-1904.

Hammon, Anthony

3130 [Hammon, Anthony]. A Letter to A. H., Esq; Concerning the
      Stage (1698) and The Occasional Paper: No. IX (1698). With an
      Introduction by H. T. Swedenberg, Jr. [Ann Arbor, Michigan]
      1946. (Augustan Reprint Society. Series Three: Essays on the
      Stage. No. 1.)

Handbook

3131 Elwin, Malcolm. The Playgoer's Handbook to Restoration Drama.
      London: Cape, 1928. 260 pp.
          General coverage of the subjects, but numerous errors.
      Inadequate bibliography.
3132 Barnhart, Clarence, ed., with assistance of William D. Halsey.
      The New Century Handbook of English Literature. New York:
      Appleton-Century-Crofts, 1956. viii, 1167 pp.
          Arranged in dictionary fashion, this work lists and gives
      information about English writers, works of literature, char-
      acters from works of literature, and other related matters.

Handel, George

3133 Crowest, F. J. "Handel and English Music." Social England.
      Edited by H. D. Trail and J.S. Mann. (London: Casell and Co.,
      Ltd., 1909), 118-130.
          A discussion of Handel's operas, his oratorios, his methods,
      and his influence.
3134 Streatfield, R. A. Handel. New York: John Lane, 1909. 366 pp.
          Handel against the background of the first half of the 18th
      century with description and explanation of the operatic feuds
      in which he took part. Based on court memoirs, correspondence,
      and diaries. Also published in London, 1910.
3135 -----. "The Granville Collection of Handel MSS." The Musical
      Antiquary, II (October, 1910--July, 1911), 213-216.
          On the differences between the two versions of Scipione and
      the third in the Granville Collection and on the discrepancies
      between scores and libretti.

3136 Leichentritt, Hugo. Handel. Stuttgart-Berlin: Deutsche Verlags-
Anstatt, 1924. 871 pp.
A biography.

3137 Dent, Edward Joseph. Händel in England. (Hallische Universität-
sreden 68). Halle: Niemeyer, 1936. 17 pp.
A brief, undocumented account of Handel's experiences in
the English theatre during the early 18th century. The critical
comment is mainly adulatory.

3138 Weinstock, Herbert. Handel. New York: Alfred A. Knopf, 1946.
xvi, 326 pp.
A biography concentrating on the political and social background to Händel's career, but including some comment on
the eighteenth century operatic theatre.

3139 Flower, Newman. George Frideric Handel: His Personality and
His Times. London: Cassell, 1947. 399 pp.
A revised edition of Sir Newman's classic study of 1923,
with frequent reference to the drama and opera of the period.

3140 Myers, Robert Manson. Anna Seward: an Eighteenth-Century
Handelian. Williamsburg: Manson Park Press, 1947. 25 pp.
Anna Seward's sympathetic and acute criticism of Händel's
operas and oratorios is demonstrated and shown to typify the
best in contemporary taste.

3141 -----. Early Moral Criticism of Handelian Oratorio. Williamsburg: Manson Park Press, 1947. 39 pp.
Contemporary response is seen to vary from high praise to
denunciation of his work as "religious farce."

3142 Paumgartner, Bernhard, ed. John Mainwaring, G. F. Händel.
Nach Johann Matthesons deutscher Ausgabe von 1761 mit and-
eren Dokumenten herausgegeben. Zürich, 1947.
An edition of John Mainwaring's standard Memoirs, with
additional material.

3143 Dent, Edward J. Handel. London: Duckworth, 1948. 140 pp. (Great
Lives Series).
A popular study, with material on the operas, oratorios and
their background in eighteenth century London.

3144 Cherbuliez, Antoine-E. Georg Friedrich Händel. Leben und Werk.
Olten, 1949.

3145 Mueller von Asow, Hedwig and E. H. Georg Friedrich Händel,
Biographie von Mainwaring. Briefe und Schriften. Lindau and
Vienna: Herausgegeben im Auftrage des Internationalen Musiker
Brief-Archivs, 1949.
Reprints John Mainwaring's Memoirs (1760), in Johann
Mattheson's translation (1761), which provide intimate con-
temporary information about Händel's theatrical connections.

3146 Myers, Robert Manson. Händel's Messiah: A Touchstone of Taste.

London: Macmillan, 1949. xxii, 338 pp.
An account of its early performances and reception.

3147 Smith, William C. Concerning Handel: His Life and Works. London: Cassell, 1949. 299 pp.
References to the theatre are found throughout, especially in the essay, "Acis and Galatea in the Eighteenth Century."

3148 Young, Percy M. The Oratorios of Handel. London: Dobson, 1949. 244 pp.
A detailed analysis, concentrating on the biblical oratorios, and discussing the Italian sources of English opera and oratorio in the eighteenth century.

3149 Seranky, Walter. Georg Friedrich Händel: Sein Leben--sein Werk. Vol. III. "Von Händels innerer Neuorientierung bis zum Abschluss des 'Samson' (1738-1743)." Cassel and Basel: Bärenreiter-Verlag, 1956. 948 pp.

3150 Dean, Winton. "Handel's Dramatic Music on Records." Music and Letters, XXXIX (1958), 57-65.
A review of several recordings of Handel as regards especially the interpretation of the works. He criticizes Sir Thomas Beecham's "Solomon" and Sir Malcolm Sargent's "Israel in Egypt" while praising several recordings of Professor Anthony Lewis who "brings us into direct contact with Handel."

3151 -----. Handel's Dramatic Oratorios and Masques. London: Oxford University Press, 1959. xiii, 694 pp.
Handel's dramatic music and its backgrounds.

3152 -----. "Two Aspects of Handel." Listener, LXI (1959), 528.
Discusses the opera Alcina.

3153 Hall, James S. "Handel among the Carmelites." Dublin Review, CCXXXIII (1959), 121-131.
Handel in Rome, 1707; sources of his later work.

3154 Knapp, J. Merrill. "Handel, the Royal Academy of Music, and Its First Opera Season in London (1720)." Musical Quarterly, XLV (1959), 145-167.

Hanmer, Thomas

3155 Thorpe, Clarence D. "Thomas Hanmer and the Anonymous Essay on Hamlet." Modern Language Notes, XLIX (1934), 493-498.
Presents evidence that Hanmer could not have been the author of this essay.

Harlequin

3156 Sand, Maurice. The History of the Harlequinade. 2 vols. London: M. Secker [1915].

Deals with the Commedianti dell'Arte, "the impromptu
comedy begotten of Atellanae," disclosing their history and
tracing their types with the aid of drawings.

3157 Smith, Winifred. "Harlequin Dances." Theatre Arts Monthly,
XII (August, 1928), 551-553.

On the popularity of harlequin's dancing in England in the
early 18th century, and translations of works on dancing by
R. A. Feuillet.

3158 Fletcher, Ifan Kyrle. "Harlequinades." Theatre Notebook, I
(July, 1946), 46-48.

Lists rare "Turn-Ups" issued by Sayer and others, 1750
to 1820.

3159 Niklaus, Thelma. Harlequin Phoenix, or The Rise and Fall of a
Bergamask Rogue. London: The Bodley Head, 1956. 259 pp.

In France, Italy, and England.

3160 Ferrar, Eleanor Barbara. "The Costuming of Harlequin in British
Satirical Prints, 1740-1820." M.A. Ohio State University,
1961.

Attempts to trace the evolution of the Harlequin costume,
from 1740-1820, to discover how much effect contemporary
fashions had upon the costume.

3161 Beaumont, Cyril W. The History of Harlequin; With a Preface by
Sacheverell Sitwell. London: C. W. Beaumont, 1926; New York:
Benjamin Blom, 1965. 156 pp.

From Mr. Beaumont's summary of the contents in his Bibliography of Dancing: "A study of the derivation and development
of Harlequin as actor and dancer, tracing his career in Italy
and France down to his virtual last appearance in English
pantomime, with notes on the qualities of Harlequin and some
celebrated players of the characters."

Harris, Henry

3162 Van Lennep, William. "Henry Harris, Actor, Friend of Pepys."
Studies in English Theatre History in Honor of Gabrielle
Enthoven, O.B.E. Edited by M. St. C. Byrne (London: Society
for Theatre Research, 1952), 9-23.

This article traces the acting career of Harris and his
friendship with Pepys.

Harris, Joseph

3163 Harris, Joseph. The City Bride (1696). Edited, with an Introduction by Vinton A. Dearing. Los Angeles: Clark Memorial
Library, University of California, 1952. (Augustan Reprint

Society, Publication No. 36.)
A facsimile reprint.

Hats

3164 F., J. T. "Hats." Notes and Queries, 11th Ser., II (December
      24, 1910), 518.
         Calls attention to Anstey's "A Row in the Pit; or The Ob-
      structive Hat" in Voces Populi, Second Series, on the nuisance
      of women's hats in the theatre.
3165 Robbins, Alfred F. "Ladies Hats in Theatres." Notes and Queries,
      11th Ser., II (December 10, 1910), 477.
         Quotes from advertisement in The Public Advertiser, 27
      March 1788, by the manager of The King's Theatre about the
      nuisance of "enormous Caps and Bonnets."

Hatton, Ann

3166 Salmon, David. "Ann of Swansea's Will." Notes and Queries,
      11th Ser., I (May 28, 1910), 422-423.
         Reprints the will of Ann Hatton, Mrs. Siddons' "scapegrace
      sister."

Hawkesworth, John

3167 Gallagher, Robert Emmett. "John Hawkesworth: A Study toward a
      Literary Biography." Ph.D. Northwestern University, 1957.
         Editor and essayist, he altered two plays for Garrick.
3168 Eddy, Donald O. "John Hawkesworth: Book Reviewer in the Gen-
      tleman's Magazine." Philological Quarterly, XLIII (1964),
      223-238.
         Contemporary reviews of plays by Hawkesworth in the
      Monthly Review and Gentleman's Magazine. Table of entries
      includes reviews of Wit's Last Stand by T. King; Fatal Dis-
      covery by J. Home; The Sister by Mrs. C. Lennox; The West
      Indian by R. Cumberland; Almida by D. Celisia and D. Gar-
      rick; A Word to the Wise by H. Kelly; and 'Tis Well It's No
      Worse by I. Bickerstaffe.

Haydn

3169 Geiringer, Karl. "Haydn as an Opera Composer." Proceedings
      of the Musical Association, Sixty-Fifth Session, LXVI (1939-
      1940), 23-32.
         Haydn wrote his opera L'anima del filosofo (later entitled

Orfeo Ed Euridice), for the newly-opened King's Theatre. It, however, was refused "the permission of the King for its performance." His Cantata, Ariana a Naxos was composed in 1782, and produced in London in 1791.

3170 Hughes, Rosemary S. M. "Haydn at Oxford; 1773-1791." Music and Letters, XX (July, 1940), 242-249.

Traces the rise of his career through his association with Oxford, from his first recorded performance there till the conferring of an honorary Doctor of Music degree.

3171 Shepard, Brooks, Jr. "A Haydn Opera at Yale." Yale University Library Gazette, XXXVI (1962), 184-187.

A copy of Philemon and Baucis under the title of "Die Feuerbrunst" at Yale.

Hayley, William

3172 Stoner, Oliver. Blake's Hayley. The Life, Works, and Friendship of William Hayley, by Evelyn Marcard Bishop [pseud.] London: Gollancz, 1951. 372 pp.

Haywood, Eliza

3173 Whicher, George Frisbie. The Life and Romances of Mrs. Eliza Haywood. New York: Columbia University Press, 1915. 210 pp.

In Chapter I is a brief account of Mrs. Haywood's plays: "The Fair Captive" (1721), "A Wife to be Lett: A Comedy" (1723), "Frederick, Duke of Brunswick-Lunenburgh" (1729), and "Operas of Operas" (with William Hatchett--adaptation of Tom Thumb, 1733). She acted in Smock Alley (Orange Street), Dublin (1715) and in "A Wife" (1723), and in William Hatchett's "Rival Father" (1730).

3174 Jerrold, Walter and Clare Jerrold. Five Queer Women. New York, London: Brentano, 1929. xii, 356 pp.

Aphra Behn, Mary Manley, Susanna Centlivre, Eliza Haywood, and Letitia Pilkington.

3175 Fletcher, E. G. "The Date of Eliza Haywood's Death." Notes and Queries, CLXVI (1934), 385.

Viscount Percival, the first Earl of Egmont, in recording the death of Eliza Haywood on December 10, 1743, was probably confusing her with another Mrs. Haywood.

3176 Walmsley, D. M. "Eliza Haywood: a Bicentenary." Times Literary Supplement, February 24, 1956, p. 117.

Indicates that the date of her death is established as February 25, 1756, by an obituary in the Whitehall Evening Post.

3177 Elwood, John R. "The Stage Career of Eliza Haywood." Theatre

Survey, V (1964), 107-116.
Biographical notes on the novelist-playwright-actress
whose stage career extended at least from 1715 to 1737.

Henderson, J.

3178 Sinclair, G. A. "A Successor of David Garrick." Scottish Historical Review, I (1904), 306-313.
A biographical sketch of Henderson as Shakespearean actor
and as popularizer of comic readings.

Herbert, Henry

3179 Adams, Joseph Quincy, ed. The Dramatic Records of Sir Henry
Herbert, Master of the Revels, 1623-1673. (Cornell Studies in
English, Vol. III.) New Haven: Yale University Press, 1917.
xiii, 155 pp.
This work consists of Herbert's Office Book (1622-1642),
several documents relating to this period, and other documents
dealing with the management of the office after the Restoration
(1660-1670).

Hero

3180 Smith, John H. "Heroes and Heroines in English Comedy, 1660-
1750." Ph.D. Harvard University, 1946.

Herod

3181 Fletcher, J. B. "Herod in the Drama." Studies in Philology, XIX
(1922), 292-316.
A history of the Herod story in post-Elizabethan drama,
which mentions Roger Boyle's and Elijah Fenton's versions.

Herod and Mariamne

3182 Grack, W. Studien über die dramatische Behandlung der Geschichte
von Herodes und Mariamne in der englischen und deutschen
Literatur. Inaugural Dissertation. Königsberg, 1901.

Heroic Drama

3183 Chase, Lewis N. The English Heroic Play. New York: Columbia
University Press, 1903. 250 pp.
A description of the Restoration heroic play which discusses

plot, character, and sentiment as distinguishing characteristics
of the genre. Appendix D lists plays written partly or wholly in
heroic verse (1656-1703).

3184 Child, C. G. "The Rise of the Heroic Play." Modern Language Not
XIX (1904), 167-173.

A consideration of Davenant's contribution to the Heroic play
A specific study of the Siege of Rhodes. Child comments upon
Holzhausen's sketch of the rise and development of the heroic
play. Child makes the point that Davenant antidates Dryden in
use and development of the heroic play.

3185 Tupper, James W. "The Relation of the Heroic Play to the Romance
of Beaumont and Fletcher." Publications of the Modern Language
Association, XX (1905), 584-621.

Certain scenes in Beaumont and Fletcher's and Shakespeare's
plays may be readily considered as the model for corresponding
scenes in the heroic plays.

3186 Bohn, William E. "The Decline of the English Heroic Drama."
Modern Language Notes, XXIV (1909), 49-54.

Refutes Tupper's article, "The Relation of the Heroic Play
to the Romances of Beaumont and Fletcher." Argues that to assign a date as late as 1720 to the decline of the heroic drama is
"to rob that type of its social and artistic significance."

3187 Grübner, Willy. Der Einfluss des Reims auf den Satzbau der englischen "Heroic Plays." Königsbergs i Pr.: Karg & Manneck,
1912. 68 pp.

Studies the works of John Dryden, Nathaniel Lee, Thomas
Otway, and John Crowne.

3188 Nicoll, Allardyce. "An Early Heroic Tragedy." Notes and Queries
12th Ser., VI (1920), 181-182.

A discussion of The Heroick Lover: or, The Infanta of Spain
by George Cartwright, printed in 1661.

3189 -----. "The Origin and Types of the Heroic Tragedy." Anglia,
XLIV (1920), 325-336.

A discussion of Elizabethan and French influences on the
heroic drama and the two "schools" of heroic plays which
developed from the works of Dryden and Orrery. To disprove th
idea that because a play is written in couplets it is "heroic
drama."

3190 -----. "A Correction." Anglia, XLV (1921), 200.

A correction of errors in dates in "The Origin and Types
of Heroic Tragedy."

3191 Poston, Mervyn L. "The Origin of the English Heroic Play."
Modern Language Review, XVI (1921), 18-22.

A consideration of French influence on early writers of the
rhymed plays.

3192   Clark, William S. "The Sources of the Restoration Heroic Play."
         Review of English Studies, IV (January, 1928), 49-63.
             Opposes the interpretation of the heroic play as a develop-
         ment of pre-Restoration romantic drama and emphasizes in-
         stead the debt to contemporary French heroic romances.

3193   Carey, J. D. "The Influence of Elizabethan Drama on Heroic
         Tragedy." M.A. London University (University College), 1929.

3194   Deane, C. V. "Dramatic Theory and the Rhymed Heroic Play."
         Ph.D. Cambridge University (Emmanuel), 1929.

3195   Stumberg, Frances Helene. "The Origins of the Heroic Play: a
         History of the Question." M.A. University of Chicago, 1929.

3196   Clark, William S., and Lynch, Kathleen M. "The Platonic Ele-
         ment in the Restoration Heroic Play." Publications of the Modern
         Language Association, XLV (1930), 623-626.
             Suggests that both Plato's theory of ideas and the relation-
         ship of virtue to those ideas are basic to heroic drama.

3197   Deane, Cecil V. Dramatic Theory and the Rhymed Heroic Play.
         London: H. Milford, 1931. vii, 235 pp.
             The purpose is to see how far the heroic plays observed the
         neoclassic "Rules" as expounded by the French theorists, and
         adapted by English critics. The heroic play is an offspring of
         incoming neoclassicism. Corneille and Dryden are considered
         at length.

3198   Prinsen, J. Het Drama in de 18^e Eeuw in West-Europa. Zutphen:
         W. J. Thieme & Cie, 1931. viii, 591 pp.
             Analysis of the development of drama in the 18th century.
         Considers: 1) Heroic Plays--Dryden, Otway, Rowe, Addison;
         2) Restoration Comedy--Shadwell, Etherege, Wycherley, Con-
         greve, Cibber; 3) Tearful Comedy--Lillo, Edward Moore,
         Kelly; 4) Regular Comedy--Gay, Fielding, Goldsmith, Sheridan.

3199   Clark, William S. "The Definition of the 'Heroic Play' in the
         Restoration Period." Review of English Studies, VIII (1932),
         437-444.
             Examines contexts in which "heroic" was used between 1656
         and 1678. Concludes that "heroic play" to the people of that time
         could be described as "a wholly serious play, composed in
         rimed verse, with a tone befitting heroic poetry, and concerned
         with the lofty sentiments of persons in high station." Mentions
         D'Avenent, Flecknoe, Dryden, Otway, Rymer.

3200   Hall, Katherine. "The Heroic Drama of the Seventeenth Century."
         M.A. University of Wisconsin, 1934.

3201   Ziegler, Hans S. "Über den Begriff des heroischen Dramas."
         Wende und Weg, Kulturpolitische Reden und Aufsatze. Weimar:
         F. Fink, 1937. viii, 106 pp.

3202   Parsons, A. E. "The English Heroic Play." Modern Language

Review, XXXIII (December, 1938), 1-14.

Rules formulated during the Renaissance for the heroic
poem and heroic prose romance were applied to the drama
to produce the heroic play. The theory known well by Davenant
was also used by Dryden.

3203 Ryan, Rev. Harold, S.J. "Heroic Play Elements in Earlier English Drama." Ph.D. St. Louis University, 1944.

3204 Russell, Trustan Wheeler. Voltaire, Dryden and Heroic Tragedy.
New York: Columbia University Press, 1946. viii, 178 pp.

Analyses the main trends in Anglo-French dramatic criticism from 1650 to 1750, with particular attention to neo-
classical theories of tragedy.

3205 McLaughlin, Charles A. "A History of the English Heroic Play."
Ph.D. Chicago University, 1957.

3206 Spingarn, Edward. "The Restoration Heroic Play." Ph.D. Columbia
University, 1959. 308 pp.

Sources, parallels, analogues, characterization, style and
themes are investigated, especially in the works of Orrery and
Dryden.

3207 Newman, Robert Stanley. "The Tragedy of Wit: the Development
of Heroic Drama from Dryden to Addison." Ph.D. University
of California, Los Angeles, 1964. (Order No. 65-2556).

Argues that "heroic artifice was not a reflection of literary
history but rather of political and psychological malaise, and
that its idealizing quality was always associated with a skeptical
and satiric wit identical in attitude to that of Restoration comedy

3208 Righter, Anne. "Heroic Tragedy." Restoration Theatre. Edited by
John Russell Brown and Bernard Harris. (Stratford-Upon-Avon
Studies, 6). (London: Edward Arnold, 1965; New York: St.
Martin's Press, 1965), 135-157.

Studies the opposition of Restoration comedy and tragedy in
their subject matter, language, setting, manner of presentation,
acting style, and effects on the audience.

3209 Rasco, Kay Frances Dilworth. "Supernaturalism in the Heroic
Play." Ph.D. Northwestern University, 1966. (Order No. 67-
4261).

Studies Restoration attitudes toward the appropriateness
and function of supernatural elements in drama, evaluates
their function particularly in the heroic play, and considers
the relevance of supernatural elements to serious Restoration
drama. Concerned especially with the works of Davenant,
Dryden, Orrery, Otway, and Lee.

3210 Biddle, Evelyn Q. "A Critical Study of the Influence of the Classical
and Christian Traditions Upon the Character of the Hero as Revealed Through Concepts of 'Love' and 'Honor' in Three Restor-

ation Heroic Tragedies." Ph.D. University of Southern California, 1967. (Order No. 67-6491).

Considers Orrery's Henry V, Dryden's The Conquest of Granada, and Settle's The Empress of Morocco.

Herringman, Henry

3211 Miller, C. William. Henry Herringman. Charlottesville: Bibliographical Society of the University of Virginia, 1948.

A mimeographed text of the lecture delivered on February 13, 1948.

3212 -----. "Henry Herringman, Restoration-Bookseller-Publisher." Papers of the Bibliographical Society of America, XLII (1948), 292-306.

Survey of the work of the Restoration playbook publisher.

Hertford

3213 Hughes, Helen Sard. The Gentle Hertford: Her Life and Letters. New York: Macmillan, 1940. 506 pp. (Wellesley College Series).

Heywood, Thomas

3214 Wright, Louis B. "Notes on Thomas Heywood's Later Reputation." Review of English Studies, IV (April, 1928), 135-144.

An account of Heywood performances, adaptations, borrowings, and criticism in the Restoration and 18th century.

Hill, Aaron

texts

3215 Hill, Aaron. "The Preface to The Creation (1720)." Anon., "Of Genius (The Occasional Paper, Vol. II, no. 10, 1719)." Edited by Gretchen G. Pahl. Los Angeles: The Augustan Reprint Society, 1949. (Series IV, no. 2).

Facsimile reprints with a critical introduction.

3216 Hill, Aaron and William Popple. The Prompter: A Theatrical Paper (1734-1736). Edited by William A. Appleton and Kalmin A. Burnim. New York: Benjamin Blom, 1965.

Contemporary reviews of plays and essays on the art of acting.

biography and criticism

3217 Ludwig, Hans. The Life and Works of Aaron Hill. A Complementa
      Study to the Era of Pope. Inaugural Dissertation. Berne. Lon-
      don [1911]. iv, 176 pp.
3218 Brewster, Dorothy. Aaron Hill, the Poet, Dramatist, Projector.
      New York: Columbia University Press, 1913. 301 pp. (Columbi
      University Studies in English and Comparative Literature.)
          Hill's life; his experiences with the stage, 1709-1749; and
      his relations with Pope and Richardson.
3219 Dobson, Austin. "Aaron Hill." The National Review, LXIII (May,
      1914), 443-460.
          A short sketch of Hill's life as projector, producer of plays
      and operas, playwright, adapter of Voltaire, and critic.
3220 -----. Rosalba's Journal and Other Papers. London: Chatto and
      Windus, 1915. 304 pp.
          Life of Aaron Hill (pp. 229-262), which touches on his
      theatrical activities as manager (Drury Lane 1709-1710 and
      Haymarket 1710), playwright (Elfrid, Trick upon Trick, The
      Walking Statue, Rinaldo, The Fatal Vision, The Fatal Extra-
      vagance, Henry V, Zara, Alzira, and Merope), and critic
      ("The Prompter"). In "A New Dialogue of the Dead" Fielding
      corrects mistakes of his biographer Murphy--the date of Love
      in Several Masques and the date when Fielding left the theatre.
3221 [Pratt, John M.] "Aaron Hill-Disciple and Defender of Shakes-
      peare." (Jacques B. Nym [pseud.]). [For the Winthrop Sargent
      Prize, Harvard University, 1932]. 49 pp.
          A discussion of "Hill's tragedies, the depth, extent, and
      various types of Shakespearean influence on them and Hill's
      defense of Shakespeare against Voltaire."
3222 Brown, Jack Richard. "From Aaron Hill to Henry Fielding?"
      Philological Quarterly, XVIII (1939), 85-88.
          Prints a letter of Hill's and provides evidence to show that
      it was written to Fielding.
3223 Horsley, Phyllis M. "Aaron Hill: An English Translator of
      Meropé." Comparative Literature Studies, XII (1944), 17-23.
3224 Hughes, Leo. "'The Actor's Epitome.'" Review of English Studies
      XX (1944), 306-307.
          Concerning Hill's versified treatment of the art of acting.
3225 Dunkin, Paul S. "The Authorship of The Fatal Extravagance."
      Modern Language Notes, LX (May, 1945), 328-330.
          The play is a possible collaboration between Aaron Hill
      and Joseph Mitchell.
3226 Kies, Paul Philemon. "The Authorship of The Fatal Extravagance.
      Washington State College Research Studies, XII (1945),

155-158; XIV (1946), 88.
>   Concludes that Joseph Mitchell collaborated with Hill.
3227 Kies, Paul Philemon. "Notes on Millay's The King's Henchman."
>   Washington State College Research Studies, XIV (1946), 247-
>   248.
>   Does Edna St. Vincent Millay's celebrated play of 1927 owe
>   a debt to Aaron Hill's Elfrid?
3228 Russell, Fielding Dillard. "Six Tragedies by Aaron Hill." Ph.D.
>   George Washington University, 1947.
3229 Sutherland, W. O. S., Jr. "A Study of the Prompter (1734-1736)."
>   Ph.D. University of North Carolina, 1950. 320 pp.
>   Sutherland analyzes the history, content, and significance
>   of the periodical with some attention to its relationship to
>   Hill's career in the theatre.
3230 -----. "Polonius, Hamlet, and Lear in Aaron Hill's Prompter."
>   Studies in Philology, XLIX (1952), 605-618.
>   The essays on three Shakespearean characters in the Prompter
>   in 1735 anticipate the critics of the second half of the century
>   in both method and subject.
3231 Burnim, Kalman A. "Some Notes on Aaron Hill and Stage Scenery."
>   Theatre Notebook, XII (1957), 29-33.
3232 -----. "Aaron Hill's The Prompter: An Eighteenth-Century The-
>   atrical Paper." Educational Theatre Journal, XIII (May, 1961),
>   73-81.
>   An analysis of The Prompter, and Hill's purposes. The
>   Prompter is valuable for reconstructing acting styles.
3233 Bergman, Gosta M. "Aaron Hill: Ein englischer Regisseur des
>   18. Jahrhunderts." Maske und Kothurn (Graz-Wein), VIII
>   (1962), 295-340.
3234 Burns, Landon C. "Three Views of King Henry V." Drama Sur-
>   vey, I (Winter, 1962), 278-300.
>   Includes a discussion of Aaron Hill's adaptation of Henry V,
>   written in 1723.
3235 Eddison, Robert. "Topless in Jerusalem." Theatre Notebook,
>   XXII (Autumn, 1967), 24-27.
>   Discusses the success of Hill's Zara, produced at Drury
>   Lane in 1736 and a drawing depicting Susannah Cibber in the
>   title role.

Hill, Abraham

3236 Adams, Joseph Quincy. "Hill's List of Early Plays in Manuscript."
>   Library, XX (1939), 71-99.
>   Prints a list of play MSS taken from the notebooks of Abraham

Hill (1635-1721) and provides extensive analysis of the
bibliographical problems. Most of the fifty-one plays were
apparently written prior to 1660.

Hill, John

3237   Angus, William. The Actor: A Treatise on the Art of Playing.
       (Abstract of thesis). Ithaca, New York: Cornell University
       Press, 1935. 6 pp.
            A thesis consisting of the text of the first edition of John
       Hill's treatise, The Actor (1750), along with an introduction
       and notes.
3238   Emery, John Pike. "Murphy's Authorship of the Notes of Smart's
       Hilliad." Modern Language Notes, LXI (March, 1946), 162-
       165.
            Outlines the continuing feud between Murphy and John Hill
       in the drama of the 1750's.

Historical Annotations

3239   Friedman, Arthur. "Principles of Historical Annotation in
       Critical Editions of Modern Texts." English Institute Annual
       (1941), 115-128.
            The illustrations are drawn from 18th-century literature
       and from modern editions of 18th-century works.

Historical Drama

3240   Purcell, Sister Margaret John. "English Historical Plays of the
       Early Eighteenth Century." Ph.D. University of Missouri,
       1949. 246 pp. (Publication No. 1478).
            From 1714 to 1754 English dramatists produced over fifty
       plays on historical subjects, about half of them dealing with
       English history.

History

3241   Bastian, J. M. "The Treatment in the Drama of 1660-1750 of
       British History to the Time of the Restoration." M.A. Uni-
       versity College, London, 1957-58.
3242   Boswell, Eleanore. The Restoration Court Stage. London: George
       Allen and Unwin, 1966. 370 pp.
            A reprint of the work originally published in 1932. Part I
       concerns the court theatres, Part II problems of maintenance
       and production, and Part III the masque Calisto (1675).

History Play

3243 Bogorad, Samuel N. "The English History Play in Restoration
     Drama." Ph.D. Northwestern University, 1947.

Hobbes

3244 Teeter, Louis. "The Dramatic Use of Hobbes's Political Ideas."
     English Literary History, III (1936), 140-169.
          Hobbes's theories about the rights of kings and the nature of
     monarchial politics are shown to underlie many of the concepts
     voiced in the heroic drama, in particular, Dryden's Indian
     Emperor, Indian Queen, Conquest of Granada, and Tyrannic Love,
     Dryden and Lee's The Duke of Guise, Lord Orrery's Tryphon,
     and Crowne's Calisto.
3245 Weiss, Samuel A. "Hobbism and Restoration Comedy." Ph.D.
     Columbia University, 1953. 240 pp. (Publication No. 6735).
          The Hobbesian psychological, ethical, and critical principles
     appearing in Restoration comedy are antithetical to those under-
     lying sentimental comedy.
3246 Nigh, Douglas J. "Hobbes' Relevance to Dramatic Theory." Xavier
     University Studies, V (1966), 153-163.

Hogarth, William

3247 Reiter, Hildegard. William Hogarth und die Literatur seiner Zeit;
     ein Vergleich zwischen malerischer und dichterischer Gestaltung.
     Breslau und Oppeln: Priebatsch's Buchhandlung, 1930. 105 pp.
          In his paintings, Hogarth attempted to convey dramatic situ-
     ations through the expressions, dress, and gestures of his
     characters in the manner of a playwright. Specific comparison
     with technique and characters of plays by Lillo, Farquhar,
     Cibber, Burnaby, Mrs. Centlivre, Congreve, Fielding.
3248 Moore, Robert Etheridge. Hogarth's Literary Relationships.
     Minneapolis: University of Minnesota Press, 1948. 202 pp.
          Eighteenth century drama referred to constantly in a study
     of Hogarth's influence on the writers of his day.
3249 Gerber, Helmut E. "The Clandestine Marriage and Its Hogarthian
     Associations." Modern Language Notes, LXXII (1957), 267-271.
          Argues that the connection between The Clandestine Marriage
     and Hogarth's Marriage-a-la-Mode is more indirect than Robert
     Moore suggests in his book on Hogarth.

Holcroft, Thomas

3250 Colby, Elbridge. "A Bibliography of Thomas Holcroft." Notes
and Queries, 11th Ser., X (1914), 1-3; 43-46; 83-85; 122-125;
163-165; 205-207; 244-247; 284-286; 323-325; 362-365; 403-
405; 442-444; 484-486.

A tentative bibliography with comments of Holcroft's works
arranged chronologically by first editions, other editions being
listed along with the first.

3251 -----. "Was the Countess de Marsac one of Thomas Holcroft's
Four Wives?" Notes and Queries, 11th Ser., X (November 14,
1914), 386.

Some information connecting Holcroft with the Countess de
Marsac together with information about her descendants.

3252 -----. "A Bibliography of Thomas Holcroft." Ph.D. Columbia
University, 1922.

3253 -----. "A Bibliography of Thomas Holcroft." Bulletin of the New
York Public Library, XXVI (1922), 455-492; 664-686; 775-787

An annotated bibliography of Holcroft's works, arranged
chronologically. The first part (pp. 455-482) contains an introduction.

3254 -----. "Bibliography as an Aid to Biography." Papers of the
Bibliographical Society of America, XVII (1923), 1-11.

A report on Colby's investigation into Thomas Holcroft's
knowledge of foreign languages.

3255 -----. "Thomas Holcroft--Man of Letters." South Atlantic
Quarterly, XXII (1923), 53-71.

A discussion of Holcroft's works to "see something of what
the English public were actually reading and so naturally of
what they were thinking" around the time of the French Revolu
tion.

3256 Kitchen, Paul C. "Dickens, David Copperfield & Thomas Holcroft
Schelling Anniversary Papers by His Former Students. (New
York: The Century Co., 1923), 181-188.

An indication that some of the material in David Copperfield
is borrowed from the memoirs of Thomas Holcroft.

3257 Colby, Elbridge. "Financial Accounts of Holcroft's Plays." Notes
and Queries, 12th Ser., VI (January 19, 1924), 42-43; (January
26, 1924), 60-63.

A record of the receipts for seven of Holcroft's plays from
performances in the late 18th and early 19th centuries.

3258 -----. "Thomas Holcroft, Translator of Plays." Philological
Quarterly, III (1924), 228-236.

A consideration of Holcroft's translations and adaptations as
an indication of the interdependence of French and English dra

3259 Eaton, Walter Prichard. "An 18th-Century Strolling Player: Pages
from the Life of Thomas Holcroft." The Actor's Heritage;
Scenes from the Theatre of Yesterday and the Day Before.
(Boston: The Atlantic Monthly Press [1924]), 12-44.
A brief biography of Thomas Holcroft.

3260 Benn, T. Vincent. "Holcroft en France." Revue de Litterature
Comparée, VI (1926), 331-337.
Holcroft made three visits to France. His activities and
relationships are described. Mention of Mme. de Staël,
Hazlitt, Lamb, James Kenney.

3261 Stallbaumer, Virgil R. "Thomas Holcroft, Radical and Man of
Letters." Ph.D. Johns Hopkins University, 1934.

3262 Aughterson, W. V. "The Influence of Radical Doctrine and the
French Revolution on English Drama in the Time of Thomas
Holcroft 1776-1806." Ph.D. London University (Kings), 1936.

3263 Stallbaumer, Virgil R. "Thomas Holcroft: A Satirist in the Stream
of Sentimentalism." A Journal of English Literary History,
III (March, 1936), 31-62.
Holcroft is seen as having a natural inclination to satire
unsuited to a sentimental style, as a writer wishing to use
the stage for teaching lessons of morality, yet one much at-
tuned to the public taste and determined to be popular.

3264 Stallbaumer, Virgil R. "Holcroft's German." Times Literary
Supplement, January 23, 1937, p. 60.
Stallbaumer argues that Holcroft was capable of translating
directly from a German text. Teichman ["Correspondence" by
Oskar Teichman, February 6, 1937, p. 92] disagrees.

3265 Stallbaumer, Virgil R. "Translations by Holcroft." Notes and
Queries, CLXXIII (December 4, 1937), 402-405.
Argues against Holcroft as the translator of Brandes' Der
Gasthof, which was performed at Covent Garden in 1790 as
The German Hotel.

3266 Park, Bruce Robertson. "Thomas Holcroft and Elizabeth Inchbald: Studies in the Eighteenth-century Drama of Ideas." Ph.D.
Columbia University, 1952. 333 pp. (Publication No. 3911).
Holcroft and Mrs. Inchbald are representative of the intellectual milieu of the late eighteenth century.

3267 Eva, John. "Mrs. Inchbald and Thomas Holcroft in Canterbury."
Notes and Queries, CXCIX (1954), 173-174.
The Kentish Gazette advertises their appearances on the
Canterbury stage in 1777.

3268 Wilkinson, Alfred Oliver. "Thomas Holcroft: Perfectibility's
Playwright." Ph.D. Stanford University, 1956.
Ideas of social reform in plays.

3269 Morgan, Stewart S. "The Damning of Holcroft's Knave or Not?

and O'Keefe's She's Eloped." Huntington Library Quarterly,
XXII (1958), 51-62.
Political Censorship, 1798.

3270 Renwick, W. L. English Literature: 1789-1815. (Oxford History
of English Literature. Edited by F. P. Wilson and Bonamy
Dobree, Vol. IX). Oxford: Clarendon Press, 1963. 293 pp.
Chapter on drama outlines briefly the dramatic careers of
Mrs. Inchbald and Thomas Holcroft.

3271 Ter-Abramova, V. G. "Roman Tomasa Xolkrofta Anna Sent-Iv."
Filologiceskie Nauki, VII (1964), iv, 93-108.

Home, John

text

3272 Parker, Gerald Douglas. "Edition of John Home's Douglas: A
Tragedy (1757)." Ph.D. University of Toronto, 1967.
Includes discussion of the editorial controversy surrounding
the two "first" editions and an account of the play's stage histor

biography and criticism

3273 Wölbe, Eugen. Quellenstudien zu John Home's Douglas. Berlin:
Mayer & Müller, 1901. 48 pp.
Home's Douglas (1756) and his earlier play Agis represent
his ambition to become "the Scottish Shakespeare." Wölbe
compares the play in detail to the history of the Douglas family,
to Merope by Scipione Maffei (1714; first English translation
1731), and to similar scenes in Shakespeare, Addison, and
other playwrights.

3274 Katz, Samuel. "John Home." Ph.D. New York University, 1909.

3275 Weber, Kathryn Annette. "The Plays of John Home." M.A. University of Chicago, 1912.

3276 Gipson, Alice Edna. John Home: A Study of His Life and Works
with Special Reference to His Tragedy of Douglas and the
Controversies Which Followed Its First Representations.
Caldwell, Idaho: The Caxton Printers, 1917. viii, [2], 213 pp.
"This dissertation aims to give a complete account of the
life of John Home and of his dramatic works, with special
emphasis on his tragedy, Douglas."

3277 Tunney, Hubert J. "A Critical Edition of Home's Douglas." M.A.
University of Kansas, 1924. 206 pp.

3278 -----. Home's Douglas. Bulletin of the University of Kansas.
Humanistic Studies, Vol. III, No. 3., 1924.
The introduction covers the life of John Home, the plays

of Home (excluding Douglas), the relation of Douglas to the
romantic movement, and the stage history of Douglas.

3279 MacMillan, Dougald. "The First Edition of Home's Douglas."
Studies in Philology, XXVI (1929), 401-409.
MacMillan cites differences between the first two editions
of John Home's Douglas, the Edinburgh edition, which is "more
nearly authoritative," and the London edition. Some lines were
dropped from the London edition to speed up the production and
to avoid offense.

3280 [Byerley, Thomas]. "John Home on Burns." Burns Chronicle and
Club Directory. 2nd Ser., XV (1940), 116.
A seven line quotation from Relics of Literature, by Stephen
Collect [i.e., Thomas Byerley], 1823, by John Home on Robert
Burns as a poet.

3281 Mossner, Ernest C. "Hume and the Scottish Shakespeare."
Huntington Library Quarterly, III (July, 1940), 419-441.
Sets forth the far-reaching literary results both in England
and Scotland of Hume's dedication of John Home's Douglas, a
Tragedy.

3282 Forse, Edward J. G. "'Norval.'" Notes and Queries, CLXXXI
(August 23, 1941), 106-107.
See: M. St. Vincent Troubridge and William Jaggard, Notes
and Queries, CLXXXI (September 13, 1941), 148-149; L. R.
M. Strachan, Notes and Queries, CLXXXI (September 20, 1941),
163; Hibernicus, Notes and Queries, CLXXXI (September 27,
1941), 181. On the reception and literary merit of Home's
Douglas.

3283 Carswell, Catherine. "Walpole, Hume, and Home." Times Literary Supplement, April 25, 1942, p. 211.
Notes that it is John Home, not David Hume, to whom Walpole refers in his letter of January 18, 1759, to William Robertson.

3284 Boas, F. S. "John Home's First Two Plays." Fortnightly, CLVIII
(1950), 331-336.
The old Scottish ballad "Child Maurice" was in part the
source of Douglas. Boas also discusses this play's relationship to Home's earlier tragedy, Agis.

3285 Todd, William B. "Press Figures and Book Reviews as Deter-
minants of Priority: A Study of Home's Douglas (1757) and
Cumberland's The Brothers (1770)." Papers of the Biographical
Society of America, XLV (1951), 72-76.
Press figures and periodical citations may be used as com-
plementary methods in studying variants, as these plays by
Home and Douglas illustrate.

3286 Thomas, R. George. "Lord Bute, John Home and Ossian: Two

Letters." Modern Language Review, LI (1956), 73-75.
   Two letters printed with little commentary--from Home
to Lord Bute, "offered as an interesting commentary on the
relationship between patron and man of letters." Thomas
believes them of value to the student of poetry and poetic
theory in the latter half of the 18th century.

3287 Stratman, Carl J., C.S.V. "John Home: A Check List Continued."
      The Bibliotheck, III (1962), 222-226.
         Some sixty-six additions are made to Jean M. Lefevre's
      check list of the editions of the works of John Home. Of these
      fifty-six are devoted to his play, Douglas. Library locations
      are indicated.

3288 Emslie, MacDonald. "Home's Douglas and Wully Shakespeare."
      Studies in Scottish Literature, II (1964), 128-129.

Honour

3289 Barber, C. L. The Idea of Honour in the English Drama, 1591-
      1700. Goteborg: Elanders Boktryckeri; Stockholm: Almqvist
      and Wiksell, 1957. 368 pp.
         Cultural history based on plays.

Hook, Theodore

3290 St. Cyres, Viscount. "Theodore Hook." Cornhill Magazine,
      LXXXIX (1904), 77-92.
         A biographical sketch using anecdotes to justify Hook's
      fame as joke-maker.

Hoole, John

3291 Sägesser, Arthur. John Hoole, His Life and His Tragedies. Bern:
      Buchdruckerei J. Fischer-Lehmann [1922]. 61 pp.
         This work, a dissertation, is in English. After a short sum-
      mary of Hoole's life, based largely on Boswell's Life of Johnson,
      Sägesser analyses Hoole's tragedies as adapted from Metastasio.

Hopkins, Charles

3292 Maxwell, Baldwin. "Notes on Charles Hopkins' Boadicea." Re-
      view of English Studies, IV (January, 1928), 79-83.
         Hopkins is an imitator of Shakespeare's style; Boadicea
      (1697) owes much in addition to the Powell recasting of Fletcher's
      Bonduca.

3293 Jones, Alice E. "A Note on Charles Hopkins (c. 1671-1700)."

Modern Language Notes, LV (March, 1940), 191-194.
　　Biographical information on Hopkins, a playwright and a
friend of both Dryden and Congreve.

Houghton Library

3294　An Exhibition To Honor William B. Van Lennep, Curator of the
　　　Harvard Theatre Collection from 1940 to 1960. Cambridge:
　　　The Houghton Library, Spring, 1963. 32 pp.
　　　　Pamphlet in honor of one of the authors of The London Stage,
　　　1660-1800 describes some of the holdings of the Houghton
　　　Theatre Collection.

Howard, Edward

text

3295　Howard, Edward. The Change of Crowns a Tragi-Comedy. Edited
　　　by Frederick S. Boas. Oxford: University Press, 1949. viii,
　　　99 pp. (Published for the Royal Society of Literature).
　　　　The first printing of this play, edited from the MS prompt
　　　copy, with a full critical apparatus.

biography and criticism

3296　Boas, Frederick S. "A Lost Restoration Play Restored." Times
　　　Literary Supplement, September 28, 1946, p. 468.
　　　　Discusses the discovery of a prompt-copy of The Change
　　　of Crowns.
3297　-----. "Edward Howard's Lyrics and Essays." Contemporary
　　　Review, CLXXIV (1948), 107-111.
　　　　Analyses Howard's critical views on Shakespeare, Jonson
　　　and the Elizabethan dramatists.

Howard, James

3298　Seaton, Ethel. "Two Restoration Plays." Times Literary Sup-
　　　plement, October 18, 1934, p. 715.
　　　　The article states that James Howard's The English Monsieur
　　　was played as early as July 30, 1663, before Dryden's Royal
　　　Ladies, to which it is supposed to be indebted.
3299　Sutherland, James R. "The Date of James Howard's All Mistaken,
　　　or, The Mad Couple." Notes and Queries, New Ser., XI (1964),
　　　339-340.
　　　　Fixes the date of Howard's comedy at 1665 and posits the

theory that Dryden's Secret Love, or, The Maiden Queen was
substantially derived from it.

Howard, Robert

3300 Tellenbach, Alfred. "Robert Howard's Comedy The Committee
and Teague, an Irish Stage-Type." Dissertation. Zurich,
1913. 62 pp.
    A discussion of the plot and characters of The Committee
as a satire against the Cromwellites, together with a comparison of Howard's footman Teague with the Teagues of Shadwell
and Farquhar, only Howard's deserving "our sympathy."

3301 Thurber, Carryl Nelson. "Introduction." Sir Robert Howard's
"The Committee." Edited by Carryl Nelson Thurber. [Urbana:]
The University of Illinois, 1921. 138 pp.
    The "Introduction" presents a brief biography of Howard,
a consideration of his literary works, and a detailed analysis
of The Committee and of one of its characters, Teague.

3302 Mooney, J. J. "Robert Howard, Dramatist and Critic." M.A.
University of California, 1932.

3303 Scott, Florence R. "Sir Robert Howard as Financier." Publication
of the Modern Language Association, LII (1937), 1094-1100.
    Presents new information about the life and financial affairs
of the playwright and director of the King's Theatre.

3304 -----. "The Marriage of Sir Robert Howard." Modern Language
Notes, LV (June, 1940), 410-415.
    Attempts to give accurate dates for Howard's four marriages.
References to Howard and the theatre, especially to his rela-
tionship with Susanna Uphill, an actress.

3305 de Beer, E. S. "The Dramatist Sons of Thomas, Earl of Berkshire."
Notes and Queries, CLXXXVII (1944), 19.
    "Sir Robert Howard's third wife . . . was perhaps Mary
Uphill. . . ."

3306 -----. "The Dramatist Sons of Thomas, Earl of Berkshire."
Notes and Queries, CLXXXVII (1944), 214-215.
    Although reliable information is lacking, several points
seem worth discussion in connection with Sir Robert Howard's
third marriage.

3307 H., H. S. "The Dramatist Sons of Thomas, Earl of Berkshire."
Notes and Queries, CLXXXVII (1944), 281-283.
    Provides some details of the lineage of the Uphill and Howard
families.

3308 M., P. D. "The Dramatist Sons of Thomas, Earl of Berkshire."
Notes and Queries, CLXXXVII (1944), 248.
    Thomas, First Earl of Berkshire, fathered Sir Robert Howard

James Howard, and Edward Howard, for all of whom very little biographical information is known.

3309 Seton-Anderson, James. "The Dramatist Sons of Thomas, Earl
of Berkshire." Notes and Queries, CLXXXVII (1944), 85.
Sir Robert Howard's obstinacy and pride gained him many
enemies, some of whom attempted to ridicule him in plays.

3310 M., P. D. "The Dramatist Sons of Thomas, Earl of Berkshire."
Notes and Queries, CLXXXVIII (February 24, 1945), 81.
Questions the burial place of Lady Elizabeth Dryden.

3311 W., L. M. "The Dramatist Sons of Thomas, Earl of Berkshire."
Notes and Queries, CLXXXVIII (February 10, 1945), 61-62.
Notes on the Uphill family.

3312 Ward, Charles E. "An Unpublished Letter of Sir Robert Howard."
Modern Language Notes, LX (February, 1945), 119-121.
The letter manifests the same inflated style as the heroic
dramas of Sir Robert.

3313 Scott, Florence R. The Life and Works of Sir Robert Howard.
New York: New York University Press, 1946. 21 pp.
Praises Howard's comic style and describes the sources
and reception of his plays, especially The Duke of Lerma.

3314 de Beer, E. S. "The Third Wife of Sir Robert Howard." Notes
and Queries, CXCII (October 18, 1947), 447.
Replies to Florence R. Scott's article (July 26, 1947), by
showing that Howard was not associated with the actress
Susanna Uphill, who was not the sister of his wife, Mary Uphill.

3315 Scott, Florence R. "The Dramatist Sons of Thomas, Earl of
Berkshire." Notes and Queries, CXCII (January 11, 1947), 17-
18.
Discusses the evidence of the Church Oakley registers.

3316 -----. "The Third Wife of Sir Robert Howard." Notes and Queries,
CXCII (July 26, 1947), 314-316.
Shows that Howard was associated with the actress, Susanna
Uphill, sister of his wife, Mary Uphill of Dagenham.

3317 Smith, John Harrington. "The Dryden-Howard Collaboration."
Studies in Philology, LI (1954), 54-74.
Acts I and II, as well as II, i, of The Indian Queen can be
assigned to Dryden; the rest is Howard's.

3318 Oliver, H. J. Sir Robert Howard (1626-1698): A Critical Biography.
Durham, North Carolina: Duke University Press, 1963. 346 pp.
Treats extensively Howard's literary relationship with Dry-
den. Important discussion on the authorship of The Indian Queen.

Hughes, John

3319 Knapp, J. Merrill. "A Forgotten Chapter in English Eighteenth-

Century Opera." Music and Letters, XLII (1961), 1-16.
An account of John Hughes' Calypso and Telemachus produced 1712, with music by John Ernest Galliard.

3320 Moore, John Robert. "Hughes's Source for The Siege of Damas-
cus." Huntington Library Quarterly, XXI (1958), 362-366.
Ockley's The History of the Saracens, 1708.

Hughes, Margaret

3321 Wilson, John Harold. "Pepys and Peg Hughes." Notes and Queries,
CCI (1956), 428-429.
The "Pegg" whom Samuel Pepys reportedly kissed backstage at
the King's Theatre on May 7, 1668, was probably the actress
Margaret Hughes.

Huguenots

3322 Fäche, E. Charles. "Huguenots and the Stage." Proceedings of
the Huguenot Society of London, XV, iv (1937), 597-611.
A public address which presents brief biographies of Garrick,
Tom D'Urfey, John Genest, and others, showing that they all
had Huguenot ancestors.

Hull

3323 Sheppard, Thomas. Evolution of the Drama in Hull and District.
Hull, London [etc.]: A. Brown & Sons, Limited, 1927. 254 pp.
This illustrated history begins with a commentary on the
15th-century miracle plays performed in Hull, and--drawing
upon a rich collection of histories, playbills, books, pamphlets
and anecdotes--continues the history of the drama, playhouses
and actors who performed there through modern times.

Hume, David

text

3324 Hume, David. "Of Tragedy." Criticism: The Major Texts. Edited
by Walter Jackson Bate. (New York: Harcourt, Brace and Company, 1952), 193-197.

3325 -----. "Of Tragedy." Dramatic Essays of the Neoclassic Age.
Edited by Henry Hitch Adams, and Baxter Hathaway. (New
York: Columbia University Press, 1950), 341-348.

Criticism

3326 Doering, J. Frederick. "Hume and the Theory of Tragedy." Publi-

cations of the Modern Language Association, LII (1937), 1130-
1134.
 Compares and contrasts Hume's concept of tragedy with
the theories of Aristotle, Corneille, and Dryden on imitation.

3327 Brunins, T. David Hume on Criticism. Stockholm: Almqvist,
1952. 137 pp.

3328 Hipple, Walter J., Jr. "The Logic of Hume's Essay 'Of Tragedy.'"
Philosophical Quarterly, VI (1956), 43-52.

3329 Cohen, Ralph. "The Transformation of Passion: a Study of Hume's
Theories of Tragedy." Philological Quarterly, XLI (1962), 450-
464.
 A comparison of Hume's theory of sympathy in the Treatise
of Human Nature and his later Four Dissertations.

Humfrey, Pelham

3330 Bridge, Sir Frederick. "Pelham Humfrey, 1647-1674." Twelve
Good Musicians: from John Bull to Henry Purcell. (London:
Kegan Paul, Trench, Trubner & Co., Ltd., 1920), 95-107.
 A biographical sketch of the man who composed several
songs for the plays and operas of D'Avenant and Dryden.

Humor

3331 Cazamian, Louis. The Development of English Humor. Parts I
and II. Durham, North Carolina: Duke University Press,
1952. viii, 421 pp.
 Discusses humor in literary genres and major writers from
the Old English period through the English Renaissance. Treats
in conclusion the growing self-consciousness of humor in
Restoration and 18th-century writers, e.g., Dryden, Congreve,
Steele and Addison.

Humours

3332 Snuggs, Henry L. "The Comic Humours: a new Interpretation."
Publications of the Modern Language Association, LXII (March,
1947), 114-122.
 Describes the use of a Jonsonian conception of "humours" in
plays by Dryden, Shadwell and Congreve.

Hurdis, James

3333 Hurdis, James. Letters of the Rev. James Hurdis, Vicar of Bishop-
stone, Sussex, to William Cowper, 1791-1794. Edited by J. F.

Tattersall. 1927. 36 pp.

A minor poet and playwright of late 18th and early 19th century, author of the tragedy Sir Thomas More. The letters are mere chit-chat.

Illustrations

3334 Burnim, Kalman A. "Eighteenth-Century Theatrical Illustrations in the Light of Contemporary Developments." Theatre Notebook, XIV (1959-1960), 45-55.

Treats of the large supply of eighteenth-century illustrations of theatrical subjects which can be helpful for "the reconstruction of staging practices and as pictorial records of specific moments in specific productions."

Impersonation

3335 Sharpe, Robert Boies. Irony in the Drama: an Essay on Impersonation, Shock, and Catharsis. Chapel Hill: University of North Carolina Press [1959]. 222 pp.

This work is concerned with the matter of impersonation in Western drama, "its relation to drama in its essence . . . and to irony." It contains specific references to Restoration and 18th-century English drama in chapters 7, 8, and 9.

Inchbald, Elizabeth

3336 Tobler, Clara. Mrs. Elizabeth Inchbald, eine vergessene englische Bühnendichterin und Romanschriftstellerin des 18 Jahrhunderts. Zurich: Dieterichs Universitäts-Buchdruckerei; Berlin: Mayer & Müller, 1910. [6], 119 pp.

Short summaries of the plots with date and place of first production, and excerpts from contemporary criticism and reviews in newspapers and journals.

3337 Littlewood, Samuel Robinson. Elizabeth Inchbald and Her Circle, The Life Story of a Charming Woman (1753-1821). London: Daniel O'Connor, 1921. 142 pp.

This is a "personal" biography of Elizabeth Inchbald, in which only passing attention is paid to her plays; much attention is paid, however, to her romantic involvements and to her relationship with the members of the Kemble family.

3338 [Nicoll, Allardyce]. "Elizabeth Inchbald." Times Literary Supplement, August 4, 1921, p. 498.

An article on the occasion of the 100th anniversary of Mrs. Inchbald's death, which discusses her primarily as a writer

representative of her period.
3339 Colby, Elbridge. "The Inchbalds Strolling into Glasgow." Notes and Queries, 13th Ser., I (November, 1923), 343-344.
Records (primarily from the Glasgow press) of the Inchbalds in Glasgow, 1770-1774.
3340 Joughin, George Louis. "The Life and Work of Elizabeth Inchbald." Ph.D. Harvard University, 1932.
A biography and a study of Elizabeth Inchbald's plays, novels and literary criticism. Appendices include bibliographies of: 1) the 223 printings of her works; 2) the unpublished and ascribed writings; 3) the letters and mss.; 4) those books she is known to have read. Also includes a transcription of All on a Summer's Day, her single, unpublished, original, dramatic piece. Three appendices furnish indexes to The British Theatre.
3341 Reitzel, William. "Mansfield Park and Lovers' Vows." Review of English Studies, IX (1933), 451-456.
This article discusses Jane Austen's satiric intent in having the characters in her Mansfield Park enact the "politically and socially dangerous" Lovers' Vows.
3342 Joughin, George Louis. "An Inchbald Bibliography." Texas University Studies in Literature and Language, XIV (July, 1934), 59-74.
A listing of the writings of Mrs. Inchbald.
3343 Park, Bruce Robertson. "Thomas Holcroft and Elizabeth Inchbald: Studies in the Eighteenth-Century Drama of Ideas." Ph.D. Columbia University, 1952. 333 pp. (Publication No. 3911).
Holcroft and Mrs. Inchbald are representative of the intellectual milieu of the late eighteenth century.
3344 Stebbins, Lucy Poate. London Ladies: True Tales of the Eighteenth Century. New York: Columbia University Press, 1952. 208 pp.
Mrs. Inchbald is the subject of Chapter II, pp. 29-58.
3345 Eva, John. "Mrs. Inchbald and Thomas Holcroft in Canterbury." Notes and Queries, CXCIX (1954), 173-174.
The Kentish Gazette advertises their appearances on the Canterbury stage in 1777.
3346 De Beer, E. S. "Lovers' Vows: 'The Dangerous Insignificance of the Butler." Notes and Queries, New Ser., IX (1962), 421-422.
By altering the part of the butler, Mrs. Inchbald has averted the theatrical dangers of the character in Kotzebue's Das Kind der Liebe.
3347 Renwick, W. L. English Literature: 1789-1815. (Oxford History of English Literature. Edited by F. P. Wilson and Bonamy Dobree, Vol. IX). Oxford: Clarendon Press, 1963. 293 pp.
Chapter on drama outlines briefly the dramatic careers of Mrs. Inchbald and Thomas Holcroft.

Indian

3348 Bissell, Benjamin. "The Indian in Drama." The American Indian
      in English Literature of the Eighteenth Century. Yale Studies
      in English, LXVIII. (New Haven: Yale University Press, 1925),
      118-162.
          Traces Indians in drama from their first stage appearance in
      Davenant's opera The Cruelty of the Spaniards in Peru (1658) to
      Sheridan's Pizarro (1799).

Influence

3349 Matthews, Brander. "The Drama in the Eighteenth Century." The
      Sewanee Review, XI (January, 1903), 1-20.
          An historical essay on the drama of the Restoration and 18th
      century, concentrating on the influence of the neo-classical
      rules and on the influence of Molière on later comic writers.
3350 Hoole, William Stanley. The Ante-Bellum Charleston Theatre.
      [University, Alabama]: University of Alabama Press, 1946.
      230 pp.
          This work presents a complete list of the productions upon
      the Charleston Stage, together with an historical account of the
      city's cultural development. It includes indices of plays, of
      players and of playwrights from 1800-1861.
3351 Malone, Mary Elizabeth. "Four Influences on the English Theatre
      from 1660 to 1737." M.A. Louisiana State University, 1949.

Intrigue Drama

3352 Maurer, David W. "The Spanish Intrigue Play on the Restoration
      Stage." Ph.D. Ohio State University, 1936.
          A literary history of the intrigue play, this study traces
      the type from its sources in the Spanish cape and sword play,
      the Spanish romance, and native tradition to its various mani-
      festations on the Restoration stage, especially during the
      period 1660-1675.

Ipswich

3353 Lingwood, H. R. Ipswich Playhouses: Chapters of Local Theatrical
      History. Ipswich: "East Anglian Daily Times," 1936. 40 pp.
          This brief history of playhouses at Ipswich not only lists the
      various theatres there but discusses, occasionally through play-
      bills and other sources, the major plays that were performed
      there from Renaissance times to "the present."

3354 Rosenfeld, Sybil. "An Ipswich Theatre Book." Theatre Notebook,
     XIII (1959), 129-133.
          18th and 19th centuries.

Ireland, William

3355 Nichols, Nelson. "An Early Newspaper of Alexandria, Va." Bul-
     letin of the New York Public Library, XXV (1921), 663-669.
          A listing of interesting items from an early American news-
     paper, two of which are pertinent to drama (an advertisement for
     Ireland forgeries of Shakespeare and proposals for publishing
     the plays of Charles M'Grath.)
3356 Hodgson, Mrs. Willoughby. "A Shakespearian Forgery." Apollo,
     XXXVII (1943), 12-13.
          Relates the story of William Henry Ireland and his forgeries
     of Shakespeare's plays.
3357 Hyde, Mary Crapo. "Shakespeare, Jr." To Doctor R: Essays Here
     Collected and Published in Honor of the Seventieth Birthday of
     Dr. A. S. W. Rosenbach. (Philadelphia: Privately printed,
     1946), 85-96.
          A study of Ireland's Vortigern, 1796.
3358 de la Torre, Lillian. The Detections of Dr. Sam: Johnson. New
     York: Davis, 1947.
          Contains a fiction, "The Missing Shakespeare Manuscript,"
     based on the events surrounding the first production of Vortigern
     in 1796.
3359 S., F.W. "Fair Rosamond in Literature." Notes and Queries,
     CXCIII (February 21, 1948), 69-70.
          Gives some additions to V. B. Heltzel's book, noting Ire-
     land's play of 1799.
3360 Trewin, John Courtenay. "Solemn Mockery." The Night Has Been
     Unruly. (London: Robert Hale, Ltd., [1957]), 31-46.
          A discussion of Vortigern by William Ireland, the attempt
     to pass it off as a play by Shakespeare, and its production at
     Drury Lane, 1796.
3361 Grebanier, Bernard. The Great Shakespeare Forgery. New York:
     W. W. Norton, 1965. 308 pp.
          Deals with the forgeries of Shakespeare plays and material
     perpetrated by William Henry Ireland, 1794-1796. 12 chapters
     and bibliography.

Irish Drama

3362 Lawrence, W. J. "Irish-Printed Plays." Notes and Queries, 10th
     Ser., I (January 30, 1904), 84-85.

Notes on finding copies of several plays in Dublin, notably
a copy of a ballad opera "Calista" in Dublin by "Mr. Gay, "
James Miller's "The Mother-in-Law, or, The Doctor The
Disease" (1734) ascribed to Fielding.

3363 -----. "Tommaso Giordani, An Italian Composer in Ireland."
The Musical Antiquary, II (October, 1910--July, 1911),
99-107.

Mossop of Smock Alley brought the Giordani family, including La Spiletta, to Smock Alley in November, 1764, for a
burletta. Describes Giordani's career at Smock Alley, Capel
Street, and Crow Street theatres.

3364 Brown, Stephen James Meredith, S.J. A Guide to Books on Ireland. Pt. I: Prose Literature, Poetry, Music and Plays. Dublin:
Hodges, Figgis and Co., Ltd., 1912. 388 pp.

Section V, entitled "Irish Plays" is a list of plays Irish in
subject. The parts entitled "Before 1700" and "The Eighteenth
Century" are germane here. There is also a bibliography of
books dealing with various aspects of the theatre in Ireland,
including Restoration and 18th century theatre.

3365 Lawrence, W. J. "Ireland's First Theatrical Manager." The
Weekly Freeman, St. Patrick's Day Number, March 11, 1916.

3366 -----. "Early Irish Ballad Opera and Comic Opera." Musical
Quarterly, VIII (1922), 397-412.

Discusses many ballad operas presented in Dublin between
1728 and 1774, after making the point that the distinction between ballad opera and comic opera is not so much one of form
as one of method.

3367 Malone, Andrew E. The Irish Drama. London: Constable, 1929.
351 pp.

Gives the briefest of mentions to playwrights having some
Irish connection: Congreve, Farquhar, Goldsmith, and Sheridan

3368 Cooper, M. "The Irish Theatre, Its History and Its Dramatists."
M.A. University of Manitoba, 1931.

3369 Stockwell, La Tourette. "The Dublin Theatre, 1637-1820." Ph.D.
Radcliffe College, 1936

3370 -----. "The Dublin Pirates and the English Laws of Copyright,
1710-1801." Dublin Magazine, XII (1937), 30-40.

A history of the piratical publishers in Dublin and of the
attempts to control their activities.

3371 -----. Dublin Theatres and Theatre Customs (1637-1820). Kingston, Tennessee: Kingston Press, 1938. xvii, 406 pp.

A history of the Dublin theatres which includes comment
on plays performed, conditions of performance, and data
about actors and actresses. A full account of the late 18th
century rivalry between the theatres is also presented.

3372 Bald, R. C. "Shakespeare on the Stage in Restoration Dublin."
Publications of the Modern Language Association, LVI (1941),
369-378.

3373 Spencer, Hazelton. "Shakespearean Cuts in Restoration Dublin."
Publications of the Modern Language Association, LVII (June,
1942), 575-576.
   Comments on R. C. Bald's article, PMLA, LVI (1941),
369-378.

3374 Stevenson, Allan H. "James Shirley and the Actors at the First
Irish Theater." Modern Philology, XL (November, 1942), 149-
160.
   Suggests that the nucleus of the Dublin company was four
members of the dissolved Queen's company; considers also
the evidence for assigning several other London actors to the
roster.

3375 McDowell, R. B. Irish Public Opinion, 1750-1800. London: Faber,
1944. 306 pp.

3376 Kavanagh, Peter. The Irish Theatre, Being a History of the Drama
in Ireland from the Earliest Period Up to the Present Day. Tralee:
The Kerryman, Ltd., 1946. xiii, 489 pp.
   A general history, with full treatment of the touring players
and the Dublin theatre during the period.

3377 Van Lennep, William. "The Smock Alley Players of Dublin."
English Literary History, XIII (September, 1946), 216-222.
   A Harvard MS collection of prologues and epilogues il-
lustrates the history of the players in Dublin.

3378 Stewart, John Hall. "The Fall of the Bastille on the Dublin Stage."
Journal of the Royal Society of Antiquaries of Ireland, LXXXIV
(1954), 78-91.
   Theatrical productions recreating the fall of the Bastille
were played at two Dublin theatres on November 13 and 26,
1789, less than five months after the historical event.

3379 Avery, Emmett L. "The Dublin Stage, 1736-1737." Notes and
Queries, CC (1955), 61-65.
   A chronological list of plays advertised in Dublin for the
season 1736-1737.

3380 Clark, William Smith. The Early Irish Stage: The Beginnings to
1720. Oxford: Clarendon Press, 1955. x, 227 pp.
   History of the Irish theatre and the activity surrounding it
through the death of Joseph Ashbury. Lists of plays performed
and actors and actresses at the Dublin theatres, 1637-1720.

3381 Murphy, F. J. "Some Irish Dramatists of the Eighteenth Century
Against the Background of Their Time." M.A. National University of Ireland, 1957-1958.

3382 Murphy, D. J. "The Irish Contribution to English Comedy in the

18th Century." M.A. National University of Ireland, 1961.

3383 Stewart, John Hall. "The French Revolution on the Dublin Stage, 1790-1794." Journal of the Royal Society of Antiquaries of Ireland, XC (1961), 183-192.

The Revolution depicted in plays produced by Philip and John Astley of London. Reflections of the Revolution and these performances in the Dublin Press.

3384 Clark, William Smith. The Irish Stage in the County Towns: 1720-1800. Oxford: Clarendon Press, 1965. 405 pp.

A "tour" of nine county seats, interspersed with social and political history of the era, provides a significant account of the theatrical activities during the 18th century. Considerable attention is devoted to biographical data on English actors and actresses who performed in Ireland during the period. Two appendixes list Plays and Actors in Ireland outside Dublin, 1720-1800. A comprehensive bibliography of maps, manuscripts, playbills, newspapers, books and articles completes the text.

Islington

3385 Bulloch, J. M. "Islington as a Circus Centre." Notes and Queries, CLVI (January 19, 1929), 43.

Briefly traces the history of the circus from mid-eighteenth century to the present.

Italian Actors

3386 de Ternant, Andrew [sic]. "Italian Actor in England in the 17th Century." Notes and Queries, 12th Ser., XII (January, 1923), 75; (March, 1923), 218.

Biographical information about Tiberio Fiurelli, who appeared before King Charles in 1675.

3387 Smith, H. Maynard. "Italian Actor in England in the 17th Century." Notes and Queries, 12th Ser., XII (January, 1923), 75.

Biographical information regarding Tiberio Fiurelli, an actor mentioned by Evelyn who appeared before King Charles in 1675.

3388 Fletcher, Ifan Kyrle. "Italian Comedians in England in the Seventeenth Century." Theatre Notebook, VIII (1953-1954), 86-91.

Fletcher describes the activities of Italian actors in England from about 1630 to 1687.

Italian Drama

3389 Smith, Winifred. The Commedia dell'Arte. A Study in Italian
Popular Comedy. New York: Columbia University Press,
1912. 290 pp.
Appendix B is on the relationship between English and Italian
drama in the 16th, 17th, and 18th centuries.
3390 Bader, Arno L. "The Italian Commedia dell'Arte in England, 1660-
1700." Ph.D. University of Michigan, 1933.
3391 Cautero, Gerard S. "Studies in the Influence of the Commedia dell'
Arte on English Drama, 1650-1800." Ph.D. University of Southern
California, 1962.

Italian Opera

3392 Henderson, William James. Some Forerunners of Italian Opera.
London: J. Murray, 1911.
3393 Laurencie, Lionel de la. Lully. Paris: Felix Alcan, 1911. 242
pp. (Les Maîtres de la Musique).
A study of the life and works of Lully.
3394 Fassini, Sesto. Il Melodramma Italiano a Londra nella Prima
Meta del Settecento. Torino: Fratelli Bocca, 1914. 191 pp.
The story of the Italian opera in the first half of the 18th century
in London: its rise and decline; its composers, librettists, singers,
patronage, financial difficulties; Handel's controversies; and
famous feuds of the divas. In an appendix is the complete libretto
of Fernando.
3395 Nicoll, Allardyce. "The Italian Opera in England. The First Five
Years." Anglia, XLVI (1922), 257-281.
A history of Italian opera in England, 1705-1710.
3396 Lawrence, W. J. "Foreign Singers and Musicians at the Court of
Charles II." Musical Quarterly, IX (1923), 217-225.
A discussion of early attempts to establish the Italian opera
in England.
3397 Montgomery, Franz. "Early Criticism of Italian Opera in England."
Musical Quarterly, XV (July, 1929), 415-425.
A survey of early 18th century criticism of Italian opera during its first flourishing, 1705-1729, prefaced with a brief history
of 17th century English opera.
3398 West, Dorothy I. "Italian Opera in England, 1660-1740, and Some
of Its Relationships to English Literature." Ph.D. University
of Illinois, 1938.
3399 Smith, William C. The Italian Opera and Contemporary Ballet in
London, 1789-1820. London: The Society for Theatre Research
[1955]. xviii, 191 pp.

A chronicle of opera and ballet productions providing the title, description, date, and number of performances of each work. Information about the theaters and companies precedes the listings for each season of performances.

Ivory, Abraham

3400 Hotson, Leslie. "Abraham Ivory." Times Literary Supplement, May 24, 1928, p. 396.
      Agrees with W. J. Lawrence's identification (TLS, April 26, 1928) of the Abraham arrested in 1649 as Abraham Ivory, mentioned in The Rehearsal (1671).

3401 Lawrence, W. J. "Abraham Ivory the Player." Times Literary Supplement, April 26, 1928, p. 314.
      The Abraham whom Leslie Hotson found arrested in 1649 is Abraham Ivory, the actor mentioned later in The Rehearsal (1671).

Jamaica

3402 Wright, Richardson Little. Revels in Jamaica, 1682-1838; Plays and Players of a Century, Tumblers and Conjurors, Musical Refugees and Solitary Showmen, Dinners, Balls and Cockfights, Dark Mummers and Other Memories of High Times and Merry Hearts. New York: Dodd, Mead &Co., 1937. 378 pp.
      A history, told anecdotally, of entertainment in Jamaica up to the freeing of the slaves. Includes considerable commentary on the appearances of English entertainers there (e.g., Tony Ashton, Hallam).

Jansenism

3403 Young, Johnny L. "Jansenist Opposition to the Theatre, 1657-1715." Ph.D. University of North Carolina, 1959.

Jeffreys, George

3404 Oliver, Thomas Edward. The "Mérope" of George Jeffreys as a Source of Voltaire's "Mérope." (University of Illinois Studies in Language and Literature. Vol. XII, No. 4. November, 1927.) Urbana: University of Illinois Press, 1927. 111 pp.
      An edition of the play. Oliver's conclusion that Voltaire had read and had made use of Jeffrey's play is not convincing.

Jephson, Robert

3405 Lätt, Arnold. Robert Jephson and His Tragedies. Inaugural Dis-
      sertation. Zurich, 1913. 90 pp.
3406 Peterson, Martin Severin. Robert Jephson (1736-1803): A Study
      of His Life and Works. Lincoln: University of Nebraska Press,
      1930. 45 pp. (University of Nebraska Studies in Language and
      Literature and Criticism, No. 11.)
        This treatise deals, in two sections, with the life and the
      works of Robert Jephson, Irish dramatist (1736-1803). The
      second section discusses the individual plays and observes
      the dramatist at work. Includes a bibliography of Jephson's works.
3407 Parrott, T. M. "Two Late Dramatic Versions of the Slandered
      Bride Theme." J. Q. Adams Memorial Studies. Edited by James
      G. McManaway, Giles E. Dawson, and Edwin E. Willoughby.
      (Washington, D.C.: The Folger Shakespeare Library, 1948),
      537-551.
        Includes a discussion of Robert Jephson's The Law of
      Lombardy (1779).

Jerningham, Edward

3408 Bettany, Lewis, ed. Edward Jerningham and His Friends: A Series
      of Eighteenth Century Letters. London: Chatto and Windus,
      1919. 388 pp.
        Correspondence of Edward Jerningham, poet, dramatist
      ("The Welsh Heiress," "Duke of Anjou," and "The Siege of
      Berwick"), man of fashion, and friend to Garrick and Sheridan.

Jesuits

3409 Greg, W. W. "A Correction." Library, XII (1957), 203.
        The Jesuites Comedie.

Jevon, Thomas

3410 Scouten, Arthur H. and Leo Hughes. "The Devil to Pay, a Pre-
      liminary Check List." University of Pennsylvania Library
      Chronicle, XVI (1948), 15-24.
        A bibliographical history of this popular stage piece.
3411 Waller, Frederick O. "Notes on Restoration Plays: (3) Three
      1695 Editions of Jevon's Devil of a Wife." Studies in Bibliography,
      III (1950-1951), 255.
        Waller comments on bibliographical peculiarities of the
      three editions.

3412 Bowers, Fredson. "Another Early Edition of Thomas Jevon's
      'Devil of a Wife.'" Publications of the Bibliographical Society
      of America, XLIX (1955), 253-254.
          Detailed history of editions and texts; special consideration
      of the four texts of 1695.

Jewish Prototypes

3413 Coleman, Edward Davidson. "Jewish Prototypes in American and
      English romans and drames a clef." Publications of the America
      Jewish Historical Society, No. 35 (1939), 227-280.
          Lists dramas and novels published in English between 1634
      and 1936 which either contain a character or mention a characte
      of fictional name whose historical prototype was Jewish. Ten
      Restoration and eighteenth-century plays are included.

Jigs

3414 Baskervill, Charles R. The Elizabethan Jig and Related Song
      Drama. Chicago: University of Chicago Press, 1929. x, 642 pp.
          Although he deals primarily with pre-Restoration material,
      Baskervill speculates that satiric ballads of the Restoration
      period may have been performed in the jig tradition. There
      was much satire after the Restoration on "the passion for
      song and dance . . . on the stage."

Johnson, Charles

3415 [C. Johnson.] Notes and Queries, CLVI (March 2, 1929), 146.
          Reprints from the Flying-Post (March 1, 1728/9) an account
      of a riot at the performance of the play at Drury-Lane.
3416 Boys, R. C. "Rural Setting in the Drama: an Early Example."
      Notes and Queries, CLXX (1936), 207.
          Notes the "realistic" rural setting in Charles Johnson's
      Country Lasses (1714) as one of the first of its kind.
3417 Hooker, Edward N. "Charles Johnson's The Force of Friendship
      and Love in a Chest: A Note on Tragi-Comedy and Licensing
      in 1710." Studies in Philology, XXXIV (1937), 407-411.
          Hooker demonstrates that The Force of Friendship was
      originally a tragicomedy containing the incidents of Love in a
      Chest, and he shows how the Master of the Revels censored the
      play.
3418 Shudofsky, Maurice M. "The Plays of Charles Johnson." Ph.D.
      Johns Hopkins University, 1939.
3419 Dias, Mary. "A Satire on John Dennis, 1711." Review of English

Studies, XIX (April, 1943), 213-214.
    The satire occurs in The Generous Husband, by Charles
Johnson.

3420 Shudofsky, M. Maurice. "Charles Johnson and 18th-Century
        Drama." English Literary History, X (June, 1943), 131-158.
            On aspects of 18th-century drama as reflected in the work
        of a prolific minor playwright.

3421 -----. "A Dunce Objects to Pope's Dictatorship." Huntington
        Library Quarterly, XIV (1950-1951), 203-207.
            In his prologue to The Sultaness Johnson ridiculed Three
        Hours after Marriage, and thus became the object of Pope's
        satire. Later, in his 1731 preface to Medea, Johnson again at-
        tacked Pope.

Johnson, James

3422 Kenwood, Sydney H. "Lessing in England." Modern Language
        Review, IX (1914), 197-212.
            On the English translations and adaptations of some of
        Lessing's plays. Minna was adapted by Major James Johnson
        and produced in 1786 at the Haymarket and at York with the
        title, The Disbanded Officer.

Johnson, Samuel

bibliography

3423 Grolier Club, New York. Catalogue of an Exhibition Commemor-
        ative of the Bicentenary of the Birth of Samuel Johnson (1709-
        1909); Consisting of Original Editions of His Published Works,
        Special Presentation Copies, and Several of His Original Manu-
        scripts; Together with a Large Number of Engraved Portraits.
        Held at the Grolier Club New York, from November 11 until
        December 11, 1909. [New York: De Vinne Press, 1909]. viii,
        106 pp.
            Collection of first editions lacks only two titles. Chronolo-
        gical listing of works with historical comments and biblio-
        graphical description; list of portraits with descriptions.

3424 Yale University Library. List of Books and Articles Relating to
        Samuel Johnson, 1709-1784, Compiled on the Occasion of the
        Exhibition Held at the Yale University Library. November 1-6,
        1909. [New Haven, 1909.] 24 pp.
            Books and articles arranged chronologically---1755--1909.

3425 -----. Catalogue of an Exhibition of Manuscripts, First Editions,
        Early Engravings and Various Literature Relating to Samuel

Johnson, 1709-1784, Arranged by Chauncey Brewster Tinker, Assistant Professor of English in Yale College. Yale University Library, November 1-6, 1909. [New Haven, 1909.] 12 pp.

The exhibition contained a copy of Irene and several items relating to the edition of Shakespeare.

3426 Adam, Robert B. Catalogue of the Johnsonian Collection of R. B. Adam. Introduction by Dr. Charles Grosvenor Osgood. Buffalo, New York: Privately printed, 1921. 437 pp.

Letters and manuscripts of Johnson and Boswell separately catalogued chronologically and excerpted; lives, letters, and editions listed in section of Johnsoniana and Boswelliana; alphabetical listing of autograph letters in the collection, some excerpted. Illustrated with portraits, facsimile pages and prints showing handwriting samples.

3427 Courtney, William Prideaux, and David Nichol Smith. A Bibliography of Samuel Johnson: A Reissue of the Edition of 1915. Illustrated with Facsimiles. Oxford: The Clarendon Press, 1925. viii, 186 pp.

A record of the publication of the writings and compositions of Johnson, arranged chronologically. The 1925 edition adds thirty-eight facsimiles.

3428 Mathews, Elkin, Ltd., firm, booksellers, London. A Catalogue of Books by or relating to Dr. Johnson and Members of his Circle Offered for Sale by Elkin Mathews, Ltd. With an introduction by John Drinkwater. London: E. Mathews, Ltd., 1925. vi, 110 pp.

Includes 616 items, alphabetically arranged. Full title-page information is given, and several items have notes describing Johnson's relationship to the volume. Many items are related to Foote, Garrick, Goldsmith, and other dramatists. The introduction is an appreciation of Johnson and of book collecting.

3429 Adam, Robert B. The R. B. Adam Library Relating to Dr. Samuel Johnson. 3 vols. Buffalo, New York: Printed for the author by Oxford University Press, 1929. Not consistently paged.

Vol. I, letters of Johnson, Boswell, etc.; Vol. II, facsimile of Johnson's "Prologue" at the 1747 opening of Drury-Lane, etc.; Vol. III, numerous facsimile portraits.

3430 Yale University Library. A Catalogue of an Exhibition of First Editions of the Works of Samuel Johnson in the Library of Yale University, 8 November to 30 December, 1935, by Allen T. Hazen and Edward L. McAdam, Jr. New Haven, 1935. 32 pp.

Arranged chronologically. For each item, provides full bibliographical information plus an annotation describing contents.

3431 Chapman, Robert William, with the collaboration of Hazen, Allen
      T. "Johnsonian Bibliography; a Supplement to Courtney." Ox-
      ford Bibliographical Society, Proceedings and Papers, V, Part
      III (1938), 117-166.
          A chronological listing of items lacking in Courtney (espec-
      ially prefaces and dedications). Expands wherever possible the
      bibliographical description of the items in Courtney.
3432 Liebert, Herman W. "Additions to the Bibliography of Samuel
      Johnson." Papers of the Bibliographical Society of America,
      XLI (1947), 231-238.
          On Johnson's revisions of Henry Lucas's tragedy, The Earl
      of Somerset.
3433 Clifford, James L. Johnsonian Studies, 1887-1950, Survey and
      Bibliography. Minneapolis: Minnesota University Press [1951].
      ix, 140 pp.
          2018 items arranged alphabetically under subject headings.
      Includes a "Bibliography of Individual Works," subdivided into
      editions and criticism of each work.
3434 Eddy, Donald D. "Samuel Johnson's Editions of Shakespeare
      (1765)." Papers of the Bibliographical Society of America,
      LVI (1962), 428-444.
          Presents variations of all the editions of Johnson's Shake-
      speare published in 1765.

      letters

3435 Chapman, R. W., ed. The Letters of Samuel Johnson with Mrs.
      Thrale's Genuine Letters to Him. 3 vols. Oxford: The Claren-
      don Press, 1952.
          The most complete edition of Johnson's letters to date,
      based, with few exceptions, on the original texts or photographs
      thereof. Annotated with appendices and indexes. Comments on
      actors, plays, and playwrights and references to Johnson's own
      theatre-going.

      lives of the poets

3436 Johnson, Samuel. Lives of the English Poets. Edited by G. B.
      Hill. Oxford: The Clarendon Press, 1905.
3437 -----. Lives of the English Poets. Edited by George Birkbeck Hill.
      3 vols. New York: Octagon Books, 1967.
          A reprint of the 1905 edition. Volume I includes Milton,
      Dryden, and Otway; Volume II Rowe, Addison, Congreve and
      Gay.

selections

3438 Chapman, R. W., ed. Selections from Samuel Johnson. 1709-1784.
London, New York, Toronto: Oxford University Press, Geoffrey
Cumberlege, 1955. xv, [1], 446 pp.
　　　The arrangement is chronological. Extracts from The Pre-
face, on Shakespeare, on Shakespeare and Congreve, Dryden's
dramatic work, Congreve, and Gay.

3439 Johnson, Samuel. Samuel Johnson on Shakespeare. Edited by W. K.
Wimsatt, Jr. New York: Hill and Wang, 1960. xxxviii, 115 pp.
(Dramabooks, 22).

3440 Davies, R. T., editor. Samuel Johnson: Selected Writings. London
Faber and Faber, 1965. 398 pp.
　　　This anthology includes the Preface to Shakespeare and Notes
from the Edition of Shakespeare.

miscellaneous texts

3441 Johnson, [Samuel]. Johnson's Proposals for His Edition of Shakespeare, 1756. Printed in type-facsimile. London: H. Milford,
1923. 8 pp.
　　　A facsimile reprinted plus a note on the original printing of
the text.

3442 -----. The Drury-Lane Prologue, by Samuel Johnson, and the
Epilogue by David Garrick, 1747. Reproduced in type-facsimile
from the edition printed by W. Webb. London: Oxford University
Press, H. Milford, 1924. v pp.
　　　A quarto edition of two leaves only, printed in smaller type
than the edition offered by Rosenbach in 1902.

3443 -----. Prologue Written by Samuel Johnson and Spoken by David
Garrick at a Benefit-Performance of "Comus," April 1750.
Oxford University Press, 1925. 4 pp.
　　　Reproduced in type facsimile.

3444 -----. The Critical Opinions of Samuel Johnson. Edited by John
Epes Brown. Princeton: Princeton University Press, 1926.
lxxvi, 551 pp.
　　　Arranged in dictionary form, with many entries under drama
and under the name of individual playwrights.

3445 Hazen, Allen T. Samuel Johnson's Prefaces and Dedications. New
Haven: Yale University Press, 1937. xxiii, 257 pp.
　　　See pp. 60-62, "Dr. Johnson and John Hoole," for Hoole's
tragedy Cyrus.

3446 Knapp, Mary E. "Prologue by Johnson." Times Literary Supplement, January 4, 1947, p. 9.
　　　Prints the prologue by Johnson to Lethe, 1740, from the MS
in the Folger Library.

3447 Johnson, Samuel. Notes to Shakespeare. Vol. I. Comedies.
      Edited by Arthur Sherbo. Augustan Reprint Society, Publi-
      cation Nos. 59-60. Los Angeles: William Andrews Clark Memor-
      ial Library, University of California, 1956.
      Notes to 14 plays.

3448 -----. Notes to Shakespeare. Edited by Arthur Sherbo. Vol. III:
      Tragedies. Augustan Reprint Society, Publications Nos. 71-73.
      Los Angeles: William Andrews Clark Memorial Library, Uni-
      versity of California, 1958.
      Notes to 12 plays.

3449 -----. Notes to Shakespeare. Edited by Arthur Sherbo. Vol. II:
      Histories. Augustan Reprint Society, Publication Nos. 65-66.
      Los Angeles: William Andrews Clark Memorial Library, Uni-
      versity of California, 1957.
      Notes to 10 plays.

3450 -----. Preface to Shakespeare, with Proposals for Printing the
      Dramatic Works of William Shakespeare. London: Oxford Uni-
      versity Press, 1957. [4], 63 pp.

3451 -----. Samuel Johnson: Preface to Shakespeare e altri scritti.
      Edited by Agostino Lombardo. Bari: Adriatica Editrice, 1960.
      Includes notes, prologues, Rambler 168, and the Proposals.

3452 Wimsatt, W. K., Jr., ed. Samuel Johnson on Shakespeare with
      an Introduction. Dramabook D22. New York: Hill and Wang,
      1960. xxxviii, 115 pp.
      This handy volume is a compendium of Johnson's notes on
      the plays of Shakespeare including "Proposals for Printing the
      Dramatick Works of William Shakespeare" and "Preface to
      Shakespeare."

3453 Sherbo, Arthur, ed. Johnson on Shakespeare. Introduction by
      Bertrand Bronson. (The Yale Edition of the Works of Samuel
      Johnson, Vols. VII and VIII). New Haven: Yale University Press,
      1967.
      Includes the notes of Johnson's first and revised edition of
      Shakespeare, the Preface and General Observations, the Mis-
      cellaneous Observations on the Tragedy of Macbeth, the
      Preface to Mrs. Lennox's Shakespeare Illustrated and the
      Proposals for an edition.

biography and criticism

3454 Evans, H. A. "A Shakespearian Controversy of the Eighteenth
      Century." Anglia, XXVIII (1905), 457-476.
      Concerned with eighteenth century criticism of Shakespeare
      (Theobald, Pope, Johnson).

3455 Raleigh, Walter. Johnson on Shakespeare. London: Oxford University Press, 1908.

Contains most of what Johnson wrote on Shakespeare.

3456 Houston, Percy H. "Dr. Johnson As a Literary Critic." Ph.D. Harvard University, 1910.

3457 Walkley, Arthur B. "Johnson and the Theatre." Johnson Club Papers, by Various Hands. Second Series. Edited by George Whale and John Sargeaunt. (London: T. Fischer, Unwin, 1920), 199-217.

A discussion of Johnson's attendance at the theatre and his reactions to the plays he saw, as well as a consideration of Irene.

3458 Houston, Percy Hazen. Doctor Johnson; a Study of 18th-Century Humanism. Cambridge: Harvard University Press, 1923. 286 pp.

A study of Johnson's intellectual life, placing him in the tradition of conservatism. One chapter is devoted to the Preface to Shakespeare, another to Johnson's criticism of the drama.

3459 Spittal, John Ker, ed. Contemporary Criticisms of Dr. Johnson, His Works and His Biographies. London: John Murray, 1923. 412 pp.

A collection of essays from The Monthly Review published in the late eighteenth century; contains material on Johnson's Shakespeare and an article on the Lives of the Poets which discusses Congreve and Collier.

3460 Beatty, Joseph M., Jr. "Dr. Johnson and 'Mur.'" Modern Language Notes, XXXIX (February, 1924), 82-88.

A history of the friendship of Samuel Johnson and Arthur Murphy.

3461 Brown, John Epes. "The Critical Opinions of Samuel Johnson." M.A. Princeton University, 1925.

3462 Mason, Eugene. "Dr. Samuel Johnson and the Shakespearean Drama. Considered Writers Old and New. (London: Methuen and Co., 1925), 1-26.

An appreciation of Shakespeare, with reference to Johnson's Preface as the most important criticism of the plays and to Johnson's inability to appreciate acted drama.

3463 Young, Karl. Samuel Johnson on Shakespeare; One Aspect. [Madison, Wisconsin, 192-]. Reprinted from University of Wisconsin Studies in Language and Literature, Number 18 (1925?), [147]-247

A discussion of Johnson's failure to present, as he had promised he would in the "Proposals," a detailed treatment of Shakespeare's use of his sources. Johnson never presents anything close to a thorough comparison of source to play and suggests no new sources.

3464 Cuming, A. "A Copy of Shakespeare's Works Which Formerly
Belonged to Dr. Johnson." Review of English Studies, III (April,
1927), 208-212.
   The Pope-Warburton eight-volume edition of 1747, used by
Johnson in preparing the dictionary.

3465 Small, Miriam R. "The Source of a Note in Johnson's Edition of
Macbeth." Modern Language Notes, XLIII (January, 1928), 34-
35.
   An instance of Johnson's indebtedness to Mrs. Charlotte
Lennox's Shakespeare Illustrated.

3466 Callicot, M. G. "Doctor Samuel Johnson on Plays and Players."
M.A. University of Missouri, 1929.

3467 Smith, D. Nichol. "Johnson's Irene." Essays and Studies by Members of the English Association, XIV (1929), 35-53.
   Presents all known facts about the tragedy, sources and
analogues, composition and performance.

3468 Sutherland, Jr R. [On Johnson's Irene.] Essays and Studies by
Members of the English Association, XIV (1929), 35-53.

3469 Struble, Mildred C. A Johnson Handbook. New York: Crofts, 1933.
xi, 353 pp.
   This work is intended to provide "a compendium of the
salient data concerning the life, the character, and the principal works" of Samuel Johnson. An appropriately scant number
of paragraphs refers to Irene.

3470 Wohlers, Heinz. "Der persönliche Gehalt in den Shakespeare-
Noten Samuel Johnsons." Inaugural Dissertation. Hamburg,
1934.

3471 Klein, J. "The History of Johnson's Preface to Shakespeare,
1765-1934." M.A. McGill University, 1936.

3472 Chapman, Robert William. Johnson's Letters. London: Sidgwick
& Jackson, Ltd., [1937]. 38 pp. (Reprinted from Review of
English Studies, XIII [1937], 1-38.)
   Primarily devoted to a chronological listing of Johnson's
letters, 1731-1784. For each letter, provides date, place of
composition, recipient, and source or owner.

3473 Hart, C. W. "Dr. Johnson's 1745 Shakespeare Proposals." Modern
Language Notes, LIII (1938), 367-368.
   No part of the text of Johnson's edition had been set up at the
the Proposals were printed.

3474 Hazen, A. T. "Johnson's Shakespeare: A Study in Cancellation."
Times Literary Supplement, December 24, 1938, p. 820.
   A study of those cancels which show how Johnson modified
his remarks about Bishop Warburton's conjectures.

3475 Sato, Kiyoshi. "Samuel Johnson's Criticism of Milton and Shakespeare." Studies in English Literature by the English Literary

Society of Japan, XIX (1939), 339-350.

A discussion in Japanese of Johnson's critical theory and recent commentary upon it. The author is principally concerned with Johnson's view of Paradise Lost; the comment on Shakespea is limited to a consideration of Johnson's ideas about tragi-come

3476 Orlovich, Robert B. "Samuel Johnson's Political Ideas and Their Influence on His Works." Ph.D. University of Illinois, 1941.

3477 Bacot, Gladys Riats. "The Dramatic Criticism of Samuel Johnson." M.A. Louisiana State University, 1942.

3478 Lass, Robert N. "A Brief History of the Criticism of Dr. Johnson.' Ph.D. University of Iowa, 1942.

3479 Loane, George G. "Time, Johnson, and Shakespeare." Notes and Queries, CLXXXIV (1943), 184.

Discusses the meaning of a couplet in a prologue on Shakespeare written by Johnson for Garrick.

3480 Bronson, Bertrand H. Johnson Agonistes and Other Essays. Cambridge: The University Press, 1946. 156 pp.

An English edition of the University of California Press 1944 volume, containing an important essay on Irene.

3481 Eastman, Arthur M. "Johnson's Edition of Shakespeare, 1765." Ph.D. Yale University, 1947.

3482 -----. "Johnson's Shakespearean Labours in 1765." Modern Langu: Notes, LXIII (December, 1948), 512-515.

An account of the composition of Johnson's edition.

3483 Evans, G. Blakemore. "The Text of Johnson's Shakespeare (1765). Philological Quarterly, XXVIII (1949), 425-428.

Johnson's use of Theobald's Shakespeare (1757).

3484 Hagstrum, Jean H. "Johnson on the Beautiful, Pathetic, and Sublime." Publications of the Modern Language Association, LXIV (1949), 124-157.

Includes comment on the "pathetic" in Otway and Rowe.

3485 Eastman, Arthur M. "Johnson's Shakespeare and the Laity: A Textual Study." Publications of the Modern Language Associatio LXV (1950), 1112-1121.

Johnson designed his text to make Shakespeare readable for the untrained reader.

3486 -----. "The Texts from Which Johnson Printed His Shakespeare." Journal of English and Germanic Philology, XLIX (1950), 182-191.

Johnson, like most eighteenth-century editors of Shakespeare based his texts on those of earlier editors, particularly Warburton's (1747).

3487 Metzdorf, Robert F. "A Newly Recovered Criticism of Johnson's Irene." Harvard Library Bulletin, IV (1950), 265-268.

The anonymous "Criticism of Mahomet and Irene" in the

General Advertiser for February 21, 1749, severely censures
Johnson's characterization and style.

3488 Sherbo, Arthur. "Dr. Johnson on Macbeth: 1745 and 1765." Review
of English Studies, New Ser., II (1951), 40-47.

Differences between Johnson's comments on Macbeth in
1745 and 1765 show "little evidence of heightened aesthetic or
critical insight in Johnson."

3489 Greene, D. J. "Was Johnson Theatrical Critic of the Gentleman's
Magazine?" Review of English Studies, New Ser., III (1952),
158-161.

Several dramatic reviews in the Gentleman's Magazine may
be Johnson's.

3490 Hagstrum, Jean H. Samuel Johnson's Literary Criticism. Minneapolis: University of Minnesota Press, 1952. 212 pp.

Hagstrum seeks to describe and analyze Johnson's criticism
with unprecedented accuracy and depth. Interspersed throughout his book are comments on Johnson's criticism of the drama
in general.

3491 Sherbo, Arthur. "The Proof-Sheets of Dr. Johnson's Preface to
Shakespeare." Bulletin of the John Rylands Library, XXXV
(1952), 206-210.

A discussion of the corrections Johnson made in the Preface.
Many more alterations appear in the published text than are
indicated on the proofs.

3492 Monaghan, T. J. "Johnson's Additions to His Shakespeare for the
Edition of 1773." Review of English Studies, New Ser., IV (1953),
234-248.

Contrary to popular belief, Johnson contributed a large number
of new textual and explanatory notes to his edition of 1773.

3493 Liebert, Herman W. "Proposals for 'Shakespeare,' 1756." Times
Literary Supplement, May 6, 1955, p. 237.

A letter which points out that there are five copies of Johnson's
Proposals for Shakespeare besides the two in the Rothchild Library.

3494 Bartel, Roland, ed. Johnson's London: Selected Source Materials for
Freshman Research Papers. New York: Heath, 1956. 118 pp.

References to theater.

3495 Moran, Berna. "The Irene Story and Dr. Johnson's Sources."
Modern Language Notes, LXXI (1956), 87-91.

3496 Sherbo, Arthur. Samuel Johnson, Editor of Shakespeare. With
an Essay on The Adventurer. Urbana: University of Illinois
Press, 1956. xi, 181 pp.

Analyzes notes; considers Johnson's debt to earlier editors.

3497 Tucker, Susie. "Johnson and Lady Macbeth." Notes and Queries,
New Ser., III (1956), 210-211.

The Rambler, No. 168.

3498 Eastman, Arthur M. "In Defense of Dr. Johnson." Shakespeare Quarterly, VIII (1957), 493-500.

Probably Johnson did not plagiarize in his notes to Shakespeare.

3499 Maxwell, J. C. "Othello and Johnson's Irene." Notes and Queries, IV (1957), 148.

Images from Othello in Irene removed before publication.

3500 Graham, W. H. "Dr. Johnson and Opera." Times Literary Supplement, April 4, 1958, p. 183.

3501 Lucas, F. L. The Search for Good Sense: Four Eighteenth-Century Characters: Johnson, Chesterfield, Boswell, Goldsmith. London: Cassell; New York: Macmillan, 1958. xiii, 354 pp.

References to plays indexed.

3502 Sherbo, Arthur. "Sanguine Expectations: Dr. Johnson's Shakespeare." Shakespeare Quarterly, IX (1958), 426-428.

Emendations before 1756.

3503 White, Eric W. "Dr. Johnson and Opera." Times Literary Supplement, March 28, 1958, p. 169.

Refutes misconception that Johnson defined opera as "the exotic and irrational entertainment."

3504 Kolb, Gwin J. "Johnson Echoes Dryden." Modern Language Notes, LXXIV (1959), 212-213.

The State of Innocence.

3505 McArthur, Herbert. "Romeo's Loquacious Friend." Shakespeare Quarterly, X (1959), 35-44.

Dryden's and Johnson's criticisms.

3506 Metzdorf, Robert F. "Johnson at Drury Lane." New Light on Dr. Johnson: Essays on the Occasion of His 250th Birthday. Edited by Frederick W. Hilles. (New Haven: Yale University Press, 1959), 57-64.

A "history" of Irene from Johnson's writing of the play in 1736 through its production in 1749 and the critical reaction to the production.

3507 Adler, Jacob H. "Johnson's 'He that Imagines This.'" Shakespeare Quarterly, XI (1960), 225-228.

Adler clarifies the meaning of Johnson's famous critical remark by suggesting that his attack is a rationalistic one and that "'he who imagines this may imagine more' is not a mental process that Johnson would endorse at all." Thus, Johnson is said nearly to abolish illusion as an element in stagecraft.

3508 Davis, Bertram H. Johnson before Boswell: A Study of Sir John Hawkins' "Life of Samuel Johnson." New Haven: Yale University Press, 1960. xi, 222 pp.

References to theatrical matters indexed.

3509 Gray, James. "Dr. Johnson and the 'Intellectual Gladiators.'"
       Dalhousie Review, XL (1960), 350-359.
          Johnson on Restoration comedy.
3510 Scholes, Robert E. "Dr. Johnson and the Bibliographical Criti-
       cism of Shakespeare." Shakespeare Quarterly, XI (1960),
       163-171.
          Scholes directs this study to the fact that Johnson's "Theore-
       tical criticism had a considerable influence on later editors."
       Johnson's study of Elizabethan handwriting, his establishing
       the First Folio as the only authoritarian Folio, his indication
       that the best text was the most Shakespearean--these and
       other considerations affirm Johnson's role as a bibliographical
       scholar.
3511 Griffin, Robert J. "Dr. Johnson and the Drama." Discourse, V
       (Winter, 1961-62), 95-101.
          Discussion of Johnson's idea of the function of drama and
       its relation to nature.
3512 Hardy, John. "The Unities Again: Dr. Johnson and Delusion."
       Notes and Queries, New Ser., IX (1962), 350-351.
          Suggests that R. K. Kaul's article on the unities can be sub-
       stantiated further by common allusions to Alexander the Great
       in both Farquhar's and Johnson's writings. Additional remarks
       on Johnson's idea of illusion.
3513 Kaul, R. K. "The Unities Again: Dr. Johnson and Delusion." Notes
       and Queries, New Ser., IX (1962), 261-264.
          Johnson supports the position of Farquhar rather than Lord
       Kames in his defense of English drama's failing to adhere to
       the unities.
3514 Maxwell, J. C. "Prescriptive." Notes and Queries, New Ser.,
       IX (1962), 268.
          The use of "prescriptive" in Johnson's Preface to Shakespeare
       antedates the first quotations for it in the OED and in Blackstone.
3515 Sorelius, Gunnar. "The Unities Again: Dr. Johnson and Delusion."
       Notes and Queries, New Ser., IX (1962), 466-467.
          Stresses similarities between passages from Dryden's
       Epistle Dedicatory to Love Triumphant and Johnson's Preface
       to Shakespeare.
3516 Kaul, R. K. "Dr. Johnson on the Emotional Effect of Tragedy."
       Cairo Studies in English (1963-1966), 203-211.
          Collects Johnson's statements on the effects of tragedy and
       discusses their relationship to Aristotelian catharsis.
3517 Barnes, G. "Johnson's Edition of Shakespeare." Johnson Society
       Transactions, 1964, 16-39.
          Although Johnson's Preface is a work of merit and distinction,

the actual edition of Shakespeare's plays falls short of Johnson' abilities and intentions.

3518 Kazin, Alfred. "The Imagination of a Man of Letters." The American Scholar, XXXIV (1964/5), 19-27.

Maintains that Johnson's commentary on Shakespeare is the beginning of a tradition of criticism by men of letters with imagination.

3519 McAdam, E. L. and George Milne, editors. A Johnson Reader. New York: Pantheon Books, 1964. 464 pp.

Popular anthology of Johnson's writings. "Preface to Shakespeare," reprinted with notes.

3520 Misenheimer, James Buford. "Samuel Johnson and the Didactic Aesthetic." Ph.D. University of Colorado, 1964. (Order No. 65-4261).

Johnson's ideas on specific literary genres, e.g., drama, are founded on his belief in a "didactic aesthetic" which demanded a truthful portrayal of human nature, moral edification and spiritual enrichment.

3521 Sullivan, Gerald Joseph. "Politics and Literature of Samuel Johnson." Ph.D. The University of Oklahoma, 1964. (Order No. 64-10,505).

The action of Irene "corresponds to Johnson's belief that government can function successfully and preserve the peace and order necessary to happiness only if it has the authority to insure the proper subordination of its members."

3522 Wolper, Roy S. "Samuel Johnson and the Drama." Ph.D. University of Pittsburgh, 1964. (Order No. 65-7950).

This inquiry into Johnson's activities in the theatre and his relation to 18th century drama stresses his friendship with Garrick, his attendance at theatrical productions, and his familiarity with world drama.

3523 Findlay, Robert R. "Samuel Johnson: A Transitional View of Mixing Tragedy and Comedy." Ohio Speech Journal, III (1965), 29-33.

3524 Gardner, Helen. "Johnson on Shakespeare." New Rambler, No. B. XVII (1965), 2-12.

An appreciation of Johnson's Shakespeare criticism based on his qualities as a serious editor, professional writer, and Christian moralist.

3525 Hardy, J. P. "Dr. Johnson As a Critic of the English Poets, Including Shakespeare." D. Phil. Oxford University (Magdalen), 1965.

3526 Sachs, Arieh. "Generality and Particularity in Johnson's Thought." Studies in English Literature, 1500-1900, V (1965), 491-511.

Johnson's statements on particularity and generality in poetr

are related to his moral and religious thought. Includes references to Johnson's Shakespeare criticism.

3527 Sherbo, Arthur. "Johnson as Editor of Shakespeare: The Notes."
Samuel Johnson: A Collection of Critical Essays. Edited by
Donald J. Greene. (Englewood Cliffs, New Jersey: Prentice-
Hall, 1965), 124-137.

An abridgment of an earlier article from Samuel Johnson,
Editor of Shakespeare, with an Essay on the Adventurer, published in 1956. Examines Johnson's critical principles as revealed in his textual commentary on Shakespeare.

3528 Waingrow, Marshall. "The Mighty Moral of Irene." From Sensibility
to Romanticism: Essays Presented to Frederick A. Pottle. Edited
by W. Hilles and Harold Bloom. (New York: Oxford University
Press, 1965), 79-92.

Argues against the traditional interpretation that the play's
simple moral is a reflection of poetic justice and of Johnson's
subscription to "the absolute imperatives of the Christian religion." Irene is the play's heroine who, in Johnson's words, is "in
a kind of equipoise between good and ill."

3529 Dobson, Austin. Second Series: Eighteenth Century Vignettes. New
York: Benjamin Blom, 1967. 312 pp.

A reprint of the 1894 edition includes essays on Richardson,
Johnson, and Swift.

3530 Fleischmann, Wolfgang Bernard. "Shakespeare, Johnson, and the
Dramatic 'Unities of Time and Place.'" Essays in English Literature of the Classical Period Presented to Dougald MacMillan.
Edited by Daniel W. Patterson and Albrecht B. Strauss. Studies
in Philology (Extra Series, January, 1967), pp. 128-134.

Explores Johnson's view of Shakespeare's disregard of the
rules and relates Johnson's reflections on Shakespeare and the
unities to a larger intellectual framework concerned with concepts of time in literature.

3531 Hagstrum, Jean H. Samuel Johnson's Literary Criticism. Chicago:
University of Chicago Press, 1967. 212 pp.

A reissue of the 1952 edition with a new preface by the author
and a bibliography of studies of Johnson's literary criticism since
1952, this study attempts to define the principles underlying
Johnson's criticism of particular works.

3532 Hamilton, Harlan W. "Samuel Johnson's Appeal to Nature."
Western Humanities Review, XXI (1967), 339-345.

Examines Johnson's "consuming interest in closely ascer-
tained details" in selected works, including the Preface to
Shakespeare.

3533 Hardy, John. "The 'Poet of Nature' and Self-Knowledge: One Aspect
of Johnson's Moral Reading of Shakespeare." University of Toronto

Quarterly, XXXVI (1967), 141-160.

Although Johnson felt that Shakespeare was "so much more careful to please than to instruct," his "just representations of general nature" were nevertheless able to provide a picture of human nature from which all men could learn something about themselves.

3534 Isles, Duncan E. "Johnson and Charlotte Lennox." The New Rambler, Serial No. C. III (June, 1967), 34-48.

A discussion of the financial and literary assistance given to Mrs. Lennox by Johnson includes mention of her three dramas and her Shakespeare Illustrated, a work on the sources of the plays.

3535 McAleer, John J. "Samuel Johnson and 'The Sovereign of the Drama' Shakespeare Newsletter, XVII (1967), 28.

Relates the circumstances leading to Johnson's edition of Shakespeare and discusses the quality of his criticism.

3536 Misenheimer, James B., Jr. "Dr. Johnson's Concept of Literary Fiction." Modern Language Review, LXII (1967), 598-605.

The phrases "irregular combination of fanciful invention" and "the stability of truth" in Johnson's Preface to Shakespeare point to the two kinds of literary fiction Johnson recognized.

3537 Stock, Robert Douglas. "The Intellectual Background of Dr. Johnson's Preface to Shakespeare." Ph.D. Princeton University, 1967. (Order No. 68-2522).

Uses an investigation of dramatic critical theory from 1730 to 1770 to approach the Preface with something of an eighteenth-century perspective.

Jolly, George

3538 Hotson, J. Leslie. "George Jolly, Actor-Manager. New Light on the Restoration Stage." Studies in Philology, XX (1923), 422-443.

A history of Jolly's activity as a stroller on the continent and as an actor in England after the Restoration.

3539 Wagner, Bernard M. "George Jolly at Norwich." Review of English Studies, VI (1930), 449-452.

From references in account books, notes and journals, it seems that Jolly's troupe was at Norwich in 1663 and 1664. Wagner attempts to define the length of their stay. He includes information on the life-style of acting troupes.

Jones, Henry

3540 de Ternant, André. "Plays on Queen Elizabeth and Essex in

Spain." Times Literary Supplement, October 21, 1920,
p. 684.
    Two 18th-century adaptations of Thomas Corneille's
Comte d'Essex are discussed--Henry Jones' version (1753)
and Henry Brooke's version (1761).

Jones, William

3541 Cannon, Garland H. "Sir William Jones and the Sakuntala."
      Journal of the American Oriental Society, LXXIII (1953),
      198-202.
          A series of thirty-three diary letters to Earl Spencer,
      indicating Jones' enthusiasm for the East and his task of
      reading the Sakuntala. A brief history of the popularity of
      the Sakuntala is given. Three of the letters are printed.

Jonson, Ben

3542 Briggs, W. D. "The Influence of Jonson's Tragedy in the Seven-
      teenth Century." Anglia, XXXV (1911-1912), 277-337.
          Considers the influence of Jonson on The Unfortunate
      Usurper (1663) and Andronicus Commenius (1663).
3543 Noyes, Robert Gale. "Ben Jonson on the English Stage, 1660-
      1776." Ph.D. Harvard University, 1921.
          A detailed history of the six of Jonson's plays acted from
      the opening of the theatres in 1660 to the retirement of Gar-
      rick in 1776 and the subsequent lapse of the comedies on the
      stage. Appendices: 1) a chronology of performances for each
      play, cross-indexed by years with all important material on
      each performance; 2) an essay tracing the history of the word
      Volpone in the political satires of the Queen Anne era; 3) the
      main events in the history of the major London theatres; 4) a
      handlist of all actors and actresses who performed in Jonson's
      play, 1660-1776.
3544 Bradley, J. F., and J. Q. Adams. The Jonson Allusion Book. A
      Collection of Allusions to Ben Jonson from 1597 to 1700. (Cor-
      nell Studies in English.) New Haven: Yale University Press,
      1922. vi, 466 pp.
          Pages 320-451 are devoted to post-1660 allusions to Jon-
      son in verse, dramatic criticism, plays, playbills, etc. Ar-
      ranged chronologically.
3545 Noyes, Robert Gale. Ben Jonson on the English Stage, 1660-
      1776. (Harvard Studies in English, Vol. XVII). Cambridge,
      Massachusetts: Harvard University Press, 1935. viii, 350 pp.
          A short analysis of Jonson criticism for the period 1660-

1760, followed by chapters presenting the stage histories of
seven plays. Production details, theatrical conditions, and
actors and actresses receive the main emphasis.

3546 Graham, Cary B. "The Influence of Ben Jonson on Restoration
Comedy." Ph.D. Ohio State University, 1936

3547 Noyes, Robert G. "Ben Jonson's Masques in the Eighteenth Century." Studies in Philology, XXXIII (1936), 427-436.
Theatrical and critical history of two versions of masques
by Jonson: Colman's The Fairy Prince (1771) and Henry Woodward's The Druids (1774).

3548 Avery, Emmett L. "Ben Jonson in the Provinces." Notes and
Queries, CLXXIII (1937), 238.
A list of plays by Jonson performed in the provinces between
1746 and 1754. Data was taken from advertisements in the Daily
Advertiser.

3549 Noyes, Robert Gale. "A Manuscript Restoration Prologue for Volpone." Modern Language Notes, LII (1937), 198-200.
Prints a recently discovered unpublished prologue of unknown
authorship which was probably delivered at the command performance of Volpone in 1676.

3550 Graham, C.B. "Jonson Allusions in Restoration Comedy." Review
of English Studies, XV (1939), 200-204.
Graham points out sixteen unnoticed allusions to Jonson appearing in the texts of various Restoration comedies.

3551 Bentley, Gerald E. "Seventeenth Century Allusions to Ben Jonson."
Huntington Library Quarterly, V (October, 1941), 65-113.
Some 23 pages are devoted to allusions to Jonson or his works
1662-1699; many allusions are from plays or works of dramatic
criticism.

3552 -----. Shakespeare and Jonson: Their Reputations in the Seventeenth
Century Compared. 2 vols. Chicago: University of Chicago
Press, 1945.
A meticulous collection and analysis of allusions.

3553 Barish, Jonas A. Ben Jonson and the Language of Prose Comedy.
Cambridge: Harvard University Press, 1960. [xii], 335 pp.
Several comedies 1660-1800 cited and indexed.

3554 Sprague, Arthur Colby. "The Alchemist on the Stage." Theatre
Notebook, XVII (Winter, 1962-63), 46-47.
Includes information on the play's popularity from 1721 until
the retirement of Garrick in 1776.

3555 Tiedje, Egon. Die Tradition Ben Jonsons in der Restaurationskomodi
(Britannica et Americana, Band 11). Hamburg: Cram, de Gruyste
and Company, 1963. 168 pp.
An examination of comedy written after 1660 reveals the influe
of Jonson on Restoration theory and practice. Several chapters

are concerned principally with similarities in technique, theme, characterization, satire, and realism.

Jordan, Dorothy

3556 Lawrence, W. J. "Mrs. Jordan in Dublin." Notes and Queries, 9th Ser., VII (March 23, 1901), 221-222.
     Argues that Mrs. Jordan's debut was not earlier than 1779.

3557 -----. "Mrs. Jordan in Dublin." Notes and Queries, 9th Ser., XII (October 10, 1903), 285.
     Discusses Miss Francis' debut at Crow Street as Phoebe in As You Like It, November, 1779.

3558 -----. "The Portraits of Mrs. Jordan." Connoisseur, XXVI (January-April, 1910), 143-150.
     Sketch of her life as an actress with emphasis on the various portraits of drawings, eight of which are reproduced.

3559 Sergeant, Philip Walsingham. Mrs. Jordan, Child of Nature. London: Hutchinson & Co., 1913. 356 pp.
     A popular biography well documented from contemporary sources.

3560 M., P. D. "Dorothy Jordan, Actress, 1762-1816." Notes and Queries, CLXXXII (1942), 232.
     The parentage of Dorothy Jordan is confused, but her father's name seems to have been Bland.

3561 Fothergill, Brian. Mrs. Jordan: Portrait of an Actress. London: Faber and Faber [1965]. 333 pp.
     A readable biography of the comic actress emphasizing events in her personal life rather than stage history; includes a list of characters played by Mrs. Jordan and a brief bibliography.

Jordan, Thomas

3562 T.[horn]-D.[rury], G. "Jordan's Money Is an Asse. 1668." Review of English Studies, I (April, 1925), 219-220.
     Notices a copy of Tho. Jordan's play with a new title, Wealth Out-witted.

Kames, Lord

3563 Randall, Helen Whitcomb. "The Critical Theory of Lord Kames." Smith College Studies in Language and Literature, XXII (1940-1941), 1-4.

3564 McKenzie, Gordon. "Lord Kames and the Mechanist Tradition." Essays and Studies. By Members of the Department of English, University of California. (Berkeley: University of California Press, 1943), 93-122.

3565 Randall, Helen Whitcomb. The Critical Theory of Lord Kames.
      Northampton, Mass.: Smith College, 1944. 147 pp. (Smith Col-
      lege Studies in Modern Languages, Vol. XXXII, No. 1-4).
          A biography and an analysis of Kames' criticism to show "ho⬤
      Kames shaped a critical position according to methods adapted
      from contemporary moral philosophy, and how he helped to tur⬤
      the stream of criticism into new channels."

Kelly, Hugh

3566 Schorer, Mark. "Hugh Kelly: His Place in the Sentimental School.'
      Philological Quarterly, XII (1933), 389-401.
          A study of sentiment in the work of the Irish playwright whos⬤
      plays were produced by Garrick.
3567 Watt, William W. "Hugh Kelly and the Sentimental Drama." Ph.D.
      Yale University, 1935.
3568 Rawson, C. J. "Some Remarks in Eighteenth Century 'Delicacy, '
      with a Note on Hugh Kelly's False Delicacy (1768). Journal of
      English and Germanic Philology, LXI (1962), 1-13.
          Definition of "delicacy." Its spiritual and physical attributes
3569 O'Leary, Thomas Kenneth. "Hugh Kelly: Contributions Toward a
      Critical Biography." Ph.D. Fordham University, 1965. (Order
      No. 65-920).
          The life and writings of dramatist Hugh Kelly provide an ex-
      cellent guide to the taste and goals of the 18th century.

Kelly, Michael

3570 Agate, James. "Scissors and Paste." White Horse and Red Lion:
      Essays in Gusto. (London: W. Collins & Sons & Co., 1924),
      253-273.
          A biographical sketch of Michael Kelly, for thirty years
      stage manager of the Old King's Theatre in the Haymarket.
      Much use of material from Kelly's memoirs.
3571 Ellis, S. M. The Life of Michael Kelly. London: V. Gollancz, 193(
      400 pp.
          Of particular interest in this study of Kelly are Chapters V
      ("The Stage at the Close of the Eighteenth Century"), VI ("With
      Sheridan at Drury Lane"), and VII ("The Opera"). The author
      goes beyond a biographical study, indicating that his object is
      to make his·study the basis of a survey of the theatrical life of
      Kelly's period (1762-1826).

Kemble, John

3572 Agate, James. "An Old Actor." White Horse and Red Lion: Essays
     in Gusto. (London: W. Collins & Sons & Co., 1924), 73-84.
         A biographical sketch of John Philip Kemble.
3573 Child, Harold. The Shakespearian Productions of John Philip Kemble.
     London: Published for the Shakespeare Association by Humphrey
     Milford, Oxford University Press, 1935. 22 pp.
         Stresses the changes which Kemble introduced into the plays,
     and especially the careless attention to Shakespeare's poetry.
     Coriolanus is treated at some length.
3574 Baker, Herschel Clay. "John Philip Kemble." Unpublished Ph.D.
     Harvard University, 1939.
         A critical biography which seeks to explain Kemble's re-
     action to and influence on the London stage of his day.
3575 -----. John Philip Kemble: The Actor in His Theatre. Cambridge,
     Massachusetts: Harvard University Press, 1942. 414 pp.
         A very detailed biography of the actor; especially interesting
     are the materials on Kemble's approach to Shakespeare and his
     opinions (quoted) of the works of other actors and managers.
3576 Holmes, Martin. "Portrait of a Celebrity." Theatre Notebook, XI
     (1957), 53-55.
         Kemble, not Garrick, as Richard III.
3577 Donohue, Joseph W., Jr. "Kemble's Production of Macbeth (1794)."
     Theatre Notebook, XXI (Winter, 1966/7), 63-74.
         Discusses the specific contributions of individual painters,
     the scenic effects and costumes of the production at the new
     Drury Lane on April 21, 1794.
3578 -----. "Kemble and Mrs. Siddons in Macbeth: The Romantic Ap-
     proach to Tragic Character." Theatre Notebook, XXII (Winter,
     1967/8), 65-86.
         Examines the Kembles' approach to their roles in several
     performances to determine how "theatrical performance faith-
     fully mirrors an age."
3579 McAleer, John J. "John Kemble-Shakespeare's First Great Pro-
     ducer." Shakespeare Newsletter, XVII (1967), 17.
         A brief biography that concentrates on Kemble's relationship
     to Sheridan and his Shakespeare revivals, twenty-five produc-
     tions between 1788 and 1817.

Kemble, Roger

3580 Grice, F. "Roger Kemble's Company at Worcester." Theatre
     Notebook, IX (1955), 73-75.
         The years discussed are 1768-1780. Gives description of the

theatre and the company's popularity. Mentions plays performed and particular actors in the cast.

Kenrick, W.

3581 McKusker, Honor. "Doctor Kenrick of Grub Street." More Books, XIV (1939), 3-10.
       Drawing on materials in the Boston Public Library, the author presents a concise account of the literary career of Kenrick (1730-1779), including commentary about his plays.

Killigrew, Thomas

plays

3582 Killigrew, Thomas. Comedies and Tragedies Written by Thomas Killigrew. New York: Benjamin Blom, 1967. 656 pp.
       Reprint of the 1664 edition.
3583 Flecknoe, Richard. The Life of Tomaso the Wanderer: an attack upon Thomas Killigrew by Richard Flecknoe. Reprinted from the original of 1667. Edited by G. Thorn-Drury. London: P. J. and A. E. Dobell, 1925. vii, 11 pp.
       A libellous prose abuse of Killigrew with a brief prefatory note by the editor.
3584 Lesch, Edward C. A. "Thomas Killigrew, Courtier, Playwright, Manager." Ph.D. Princeton University, 1928.
3585 Harbage, Alfred. Thomas Killigrew, Cavalier Dramatist, 1612-1683. Philadelphia: University of Pennsylvania Press; London: H. Milford, Oxford University Press, 1930. ix, 247 pp.
       A biography of Killigrew which treats his career as actor, manager, and playwright.
3586 Borgman, Albert S. "The Killigrews and Mrs. Corey." Times Literary Supplement, December 27, 1934, p. 921.
       A document in the Record Office bearing on Restoration theatrical history.
3587 Boas, F. S. "Killigrew's 'Claracilla.'" Times Literary Supplement, March 18, 1944, p. 144.
       Account of a manuscript found in the Castle Howard Library.
3588 Van Lennep, William. "Thomas Killigrew Prepares His Plays for Production." J. Q. Adams Memorial Studies, edited by James G. McManaway, Giles E. Dawson and Edwin E. Willoughby. (Washington: The Folger Shakespeare Library, 1948), 803-811.
       On the marginal notes in a copy of the 1664 edition in Worcester College Library.
3589 Keast, William Rea. "Some Seventeenth Century Allusions to

Shakespeare and Jonson." Notes and Queries, CXCIV (October 29, 1949), 468-469.

Refers to passages in Killigrew's The Parson's Wedding and Thomaso.

3590 -----. "Killigrew's Use of Donne in 'The Parson's Wedding.'" Modern Language Review, XLV (1950), 512-515.

Some of the wit in The Parson's Wedding derives from Donne's poems, especially A Lecture upon the Shadow, Break of Day, and Love's Alchemy.

3591 Reich, William T. "Claracilla, by Thomas Killigrew." Ph.D. University of Pennsylvania, 1953. 243 pp. (Publication No. 5614).

This is a critical edition of the play based upon the 1664 folio edition.

3592 Freehafer, John. "The Formation of the London Patent Companies in 1660." Theatre Notebook, XX (Autumn, 1965), 6-30.

Studies the struggle of Killigrew and Davenant to establish their authority over the actors and to bring their companies to the stage during the period, July 9 to October 8, 1660, following the granting of patents by Charles II. Includes also corrections to previous accounts of the London acting companies of 1659 and 1660.

3593 Harbage, Alfred. Thomas Killigrew, Cavalier Dramatist 1612-83. New York: Benjamin Blom, 1967. 256 pp.

A reprint of the 1930 biography.

Killigrew, William

text

3594 Killigrew, Sir William. The Siege of Urbin. Edited by Ivan E. Taylor. Philadelphia: University of Pennsylvania Press, 1946. xxiv, 53 pp.

A full critical edition.

criticism

3595 Lawrence, W. J. "Sir William Killigrew's 'The Siege of Urbin.'" Times Literary Supplement, October 18, 1928, p. 755.

A manuscript of Sir William Killigrew's play is preserved in the Bodleian; it contains an actor-list proving that the play was arranged for performance at the Theatre Royal in 1665.

3596 Wagner, Bernard M. "The Siege of Urbin." Times Literary Supplement, November 1, 1928, p. 806.

The handwriting of the manuscript of Sir William Killigrew's play is Killigrew's.

3597 McCabe, William H. "The Imperial Tragedy." Philological Quarterly,

XV (1936), 311-314.

Compares this play with its "parent," Joseph Simeon's
Zeno, and finds evidence which strengthens the ascription
of the English adaptation of Sir William Killigrew.

King's Lynn

3598 Rosenfeld, Sybil. "St. George's Hall, King's Lynn." Theatre
Notebook, III (January, 1949), 24-27.
Surveys the theatrical activity of King's Lynn during the
eighteenth century.

Kirkman, Francis

3599 Greg, W. W. "Authorship Attributions in the Early Play-Lists
1656-1671." Edinburgh Bibliographical Transactions, II,
Part 4 (1946), 305-329.
An authoritative study of the three play catalogues by Rogers
and Ley (1656), Edward Archer (1656), and Francis Kirkman
(1661, and 1671), to show the trustworthiness, or lack thereof.
3600 Hamlyn, Hilda M. "Eighteenth Century Circulating Libraries."
The Library, Fifth Series, I (March, 1947), 197-222.
Comments on Francis Kirkman's dramatic lending library.
3601 Bowers, Fredson Thayer. "The First Series of Plays Published by
Francis Kirkman in 1661." The Library, Fifth Series, II
(March, 1948), 289-291.
They were A Cure for a Cuckold and The Thracian Wonder
by Webster and Rowley, Gammer Gurton's Needle and J. C.'s
A Pleasant Comedy of Two Merry Milkmaids.
3602 Gibson, Strickland. "Francis Kirkman." Times Literary Supple-
ment, June 24, 1948, p. 359.
Requests information for his bibliography.
3603 -----. A Bibliography of Francis Kirkman with his Prefaces,
Dedications and Commendations (1652-1680). (Oxford: Uni-
versity Press, 1949), 47-152. (Oxford Bibliographical Society
Publications New Series I, ii, for 1947).
The introduction gives information about the book trade at
the Restoration. Includes a study of The Wits by Fredson T.
Bowers.
3604 Cameron, W. J. "Francis Kirkman's 'The Wits,' 1672-1673."
Notes and Queries, CCII (1957), 106-108.
Conjectures on J. J. Elson's bibliographical process in
preparing his 1932 edition of The Wits.
3605 -----. "Francis Kirkman's The Wits, 1672-73; Further Notes."
Notes and Queries, CCIII (1958), 147-150.

Draws further conclusions about the bibliographical history
of Kirkman's The Wits 1672-1673.
3606 Gerritsen, Johan. "The Dramatic Piracies of 1661: A Comparative
      Analysis." Studies in Bibliography, XI (1958), 117-131.
      Francis Kirkman.

Kit-Cat Club

3607 Allen, Robert J. "The Kit-cat Club and the Theatre." Review of
      English Studies, VII (1931), 56-61.
      Relationship between the theatre and the members of Jacob
      Tonson's famous Whig club.

Knyveton, John

3608 de Castro, J. Paul. "'John Knyveton.'" Notes and Queries, CLXXX
      (February, 1941), 76-77.
      Questions the authenticity of certain parts of The Diary of a
      Surgeon in the Year 1751-52 by John Knyveton.

Kotzebue, A.

3609 Sellier, Walter. Kotzebue in England. Ein Beitrag zur Geschichte
      der englischen Buhne und der Beziehungen der deutschen Liter-
      atur zur englischen. Leipzig: Oswald Schmidt, 1901. 95, [1] pp.
      Traces the influence of Kotzebue's works on various writers
      in England, and on the English stage in general, showing how
      widespread this influence was. Based on contemporary works.
3610 Thompson, L. F. Kotzebue: A Survey of His Progress in France
      and England. Paris, 1928. 174 pp.
      The 53-page essay on Kotzebue in England is largely con-
      cerned with the vogue of German literature in England at the
      turn of the 18th century. Thompson includes a list of Kotzebue's
      36 plays translated into English.
3611 Butler, E. M. "Mansfield Park and Kotzebue's Lovers' Vows."
      Modern Language Review, XXVIII (1933), 326-337.
      Butler writes that "Mansfield Park is nothing more nor less
      than Lovers' Vows translated into terms of real life with the
      moral standard subverted by Kotzebue neatly re-inverted."
      Butler concludes, however, after a detailed comparison of the
      two plots, that Austen regretted her ferocity in Mansfield Park
      and her "unholy alliance" with Kotzebue.
3612 Gosch, Marcella. "'Translators' of Kotzebue in England." Monat-
      shefte für deutschen Unterricht, XXXI (1939), 175-183.
      A study of changes in the originals made by English trans-

lators of Kotzebue's Plays: Anne Plumptre's version of Die
Spanier in Peru adapted by Sheridan as Pizarro; Menschenhass
und Reue as Thompson's Stranger; and Das Kind der Liebe as
Mrs. Inchbald's Lovers' Vows.

La Roche, Sophie

3613 Robertson, J. G. "Sophie von La Roche's Visit to England in 1786.
Modern Language Review, XXVII (1932), 196-203.
The author records Sophie von La Roche's impressions of
England, including her reactions to The Disbanded Officer, the
English version of Lessing's Minna von Barnhelm.

Lacy, John

works

3614 Lacy, John. The Dramatic Works of John Lacy, Comedian. Edited
by James Maidment and W. H. Logan. New York: Benjamin
Blom, 1967. 416 pp.
A reprint of the 1874 edition includes five plays by Lacy.

criticism

3615 Ohnsorg, Richard. John Lacy's "Dumb Lady," Mrs. Susanna Centlivre's "Love's Contrivance," und Henry Fielding's "Mock Doctor" in ihrem verhältnis zu einander und zu ihrer gemeinschaftlichen Quellen." Hamburg: Bargsted und Ruhland, 1900. 60, [2]
pp.
3616 Weber, Fritz. Lacy's "Sauny the Scot" and Garrick's "Catharine
and Petruchio" im Verhältnis zu ihren Quellen. Rostock: Carl
Hinstoffs Buckdruckever, 1901. 85 pp.
Compares these two adaptations of Shakespeare's "Taming
of the Shrew" (Lacy's 1698, Garrick's 1756) with the original
play. Lacy keeps the plot structure of Shakespeare's play but
shifts the scene to contemporary England. Garrick simplifies
Shakespeare's play by eliminating the secondary plots and
compressing its five acts into three. Other adaptations of
"Taming of the Shrew" from this period are also listed.
3617 Mossman, E. John Lacy's "Sauny the Scot." Eine Bearbeitung von
Shakespeare's "The Taming of the Shrew" aus der Restauration
szeit. Inaugural Dissertation. Halle, 1902. 70 pp.
3618 Wernicke, Arthur. Das Verhältnis von John Lacy's "The Dumb
Lady, or The Farrier Made Physician," zu Molière's "Le Méde

malgré lui" und "L'amour Médecin." Halle a. S.: Druck von
Wischan & Wettengel, 1903. 114 pp.

3619 Cooper, Charles W. "John Lacy, the Comedian, a Study in the
Early Restoration Theatrical Tradition." Ph.D. University of
California, 1931.

3620 Spring, Joseph E. "Two Restoration Adaptations of Shakespeare's
Plays--Sauny the Scot, or The Taming of the Shrew by John
Lacy and The History and Fall of Caius Marius, Thomas Otway's
Appropriation of Romeo and Juliet. Ph.D. University of Denver,
1952. 417 pp.
    This study documents, by means of textual analysis, "the al-
ready existing contributions toward Shakespeare's plays and the
ways of adapting them."

Lamb, Charles

3621 Houghton, Walter E., Jr. "Lamb's Criticism of Restoration Comedy." English Literary History, X (March, 1943), 61-72.
    "An excellent analysis and defence of Lamb's views."

3622 Schwarz, John Henry, Jr. "Charles Lamb on the Drama." Ph.D.
Duke University, 1967. (Order No. 68-5244).
    Chapter IV considers Lamb's critical judgments of Restora-
tion and 18th century playwrights and studies his "On the Artificial Comedy of the Last Century."

Langbaine, Gerard

3623 Watkin-Jones, A. "Langbaine's Account of the English Dramatick
Poets (1691)." Essays and Studies by Members of the English
Association, XXI (1936), 75-85.
    A history and bibliographical analysis of the various editions
of Langbaine's work based upon a study of extant copies in the
British Museum.

3624 Greg, W. W. "Gerard Langbaine the Younger and Nicholas Cox."
Library, 4th Series (June-September, 1944), 67-70.
    Uncovers evidence in Langbaine's An Account of the English
Dramatick Poets (1691) which suggests that the anonymous An
Exact Catalogue (of printed dramas--1680), printed by Nicholas
Cox, rather than Momus Triumphans (1688) was Langbaine's
first work in dramatic bibliography,

3625 Macdonald, Hugh. "Gerard Langbaine the Younger and Nicholas
Cox." The Library, 4th Series, XXV (December, 1944--
March, 1945), 186.
    Additional evidence to support W. W. Greg's conclusions in
The Library (June--September, 1944), 67-70, that the Exact
Catalogue is Langbaine's.

3626 McCall, John Joseph. "Gerard Langbaine's An Account of the English Dramatick Poets, 1691." Ph.D. Florida State University,
1957.

Language

3627 Skeat, Walter W. A Glossary of Tudor and Stuart Words, Especially from the Dramatists. Edited with additions by A. L. Mayhew.
Oxford: The Clarendon Press, 1914. xviii, 461 pp.
      Alphabetical listing of rare words with their meanings,
literary sources, and, frequently, etymologies. Includes usages
of several playwrights of the Restoration and 18th century.
3628 Weiss, Adolf. Die Mundart im englischen Drama von 1642-1800.
University of Giessen: The English Seminar, 1924.
      A study of the speech characteristics, dialectical and gram-
matical peculiarities of several plays.
3629 Dunlop, A. R. "'Vicious' Pronunciations in Eighteenth-Century
English." American Speech, XV (December, 1940), 364-367.
      Two paragraphs in the Massachusetts Gazette in 1769 indicate
the concern of one writer about change in pronunciation of such
words as "nature," "creature," "immediate," etc.
3630 Noyes, Gertrude E. "The Development of Cant Lexicography in
England, 1566-1785." Studies in Philology, XXXVIII (July, 1941)
462-479.
      Traces the beginnings of the "cant" dictionary from Harman,
Greene, and Dekker to the publication of Grose's dictionary in
1785.
3631 Soderlind, Johannes. Verb Syntax in John Dryden's Prose. Uppsala:
A. B. Lundequistska Bokhandeln; Coppenhagen: Ejnar Munksgaar
Cambridge: Harvard University Press, 1951. xxii, 261 pp. (Ess
and Studies on English Language and Literature, X).
      Examines the dedications and prefaces to the plays, the Essa
of Dramatick Poesie, and A Defence of an Essay of Dramatic
Poesy. A very technical study on construction, voice, concord,
tense, aspect, mood, and the use of "shall and will," "can and
may," and "do."
3632 Feddern, Gert-Detleff. "Der Parallelismus als Heimisches Stilele-
ment in der Prosadiktion und Komposition der Englischen Restaurationskomödie." Berlin Dissertation (Frei), 1954.
3633 Clinton-Baddeley, V.C. "A Speculation on Stars." Theatre Noteboo
IX (1955), 78-79.
      Citations from Cibber and Fanny Burney to indicate early
usage of "blazing star" in referring to a good actor. Cibber's
example is four years earlier than that of the O.E.D.
3634 Minor, Charles B. "An Analytical Study of Grammatical Uses and

Tendencies in Some Restoration Playwrights of Comedies with
Comparisons to Present-Day Usages and Tendencies." Ph.D.
University of Denver, 1957.

3635 Lewis, C. S. Studies in Words. Cambridge: The Cambridge University Press, 1960. vii, 240 pp.
A historical and lexical study of several words pertaining to
basic literary ideas, e.g., "wit," "nature," "sense"; cites usages
by critics, historians, and literary artists. Passing references
to drama.

3636 Roberts, Edgar V. "An Unrecorded Meaning of 'Joke' (or 'Joak') in
England." American Speech, XXXVII (1962), 137-140.
A bawdy meaning of "joke" which would have been familiar to
Eighteenth Century Englishmen. References to this meaning
found in Charles Coffey's The Beggar's Wedding, and Fielding's
Tumble Down Dick, and The Letter Writers.

3637 Troubridge, St. Vincent. "OED Antedatings from Play Titles,
1660-1900--I." Notes and Queries, New Ser., X (1963), 104-
106.
Notes 4 play titles from the period 1660-1800 containing
phrases which antedate the citations in OED.

3638 -----. "OED Antedatings from Play Titles 1660-1900--II." Notes
and Queries, New Ser., X (1963), 136-138.
Part II of Troubridge's study lists 2 play titles between 1660
and 1800.

3639 Harris, Bernard. "The Dialect of Those Fanatic Times." Restoration Theatre. Edited by John Russell Brown and Bernard Harris. (Stratford-Upon-Avon Studies, 6). (London: Edward
Arnold, 1965; New York: St. Martin's Press, 1965), 11-40.
Traces the language of comedy from Etherege to Vanbrugh.
Comic language had for its object "not so much clarity of
analysis as substantial human mimicry."

3640 Kearful, Frank Jerome. "The Rhetoric of Augustan Tragedy."
Ph.D. University of Wisconsin, 1966. (Order No. 66-9154).
Studies the linguistic devices and patterns used to affect the
appeals of Augustan tragedy. Special attention is given to Rowe,
Addison, Dennis, and Lillo.

Laroche, Jemmy

3641 Firth, C. H. "Jemmy Laroche." Times Literary Supplement,
May 31, 1928, p. 412.
Concerning the portrait of the boy singer on the ballad "The
Raree Show."

3642 Lawrence, W. J. "Jemmy Laroche, the Boy-singer." Times Literary Supplement, May 17, 1928, p. 379.

Biographical data about Laroche, who appeared in masques in 1696 and 1697.

Larpent Collection

3643 Nicoll, Allardyce. "Twenty-Three Thousand." Theatre Arts Monthly, XIII (April, 1929), 279-289.
   Includes a discussion of the value of the Larpent collection of MS. plays, 1800 of them from 1737 to 1824, amassed at the Lord Chamberlain's office and now at the Huntington Library.

Latin Plays

3644 Harbage, Alfred. "A Census of Anglo-Latin Plays." Publications of the Modern Language Association, LIII (1938), 624-629.
   A finding list of over 150 MSS. of plays written in Latin during the sixteenth and seventeenth centuries. Several plays dating from the Restoration are included.

Law

3645 Isaacs, Sidney C. The Law Relating to Theatres, Music-Halls, and Other Public Entertainments, and to the Performers Therein, including the Law of Musical and Dramatic Copyright. London: Stevens and Sons, Ltd., 1927. 448 pp.

Law, William

3646 Wormhoudt, Arthur. "A Note on William Law's The Absolute Unlawfulness of the Stage Entertainment." Modern Language Notes LXIV (1949), 180-181.
   An attempt to date the pamphlet.

Lawes, Henry

3647 Evans, Willa McClung. Henry Lawes: Musician and Friend of Poets. New York: Modern Language Association, 1941. 250 pp.

Le Blanc, Abbé

3648 Havens, George R. "The Abbé Le Blanc and English Literature." Modern Philology, XVIII (1920), 423-441.
   A discussion of the Abbe's reactions to English literature, including several plays--Cato, All for Love, The Beggar's Opera.

Le Texier, M.

3649 Roberts, W. "M. Le Texier: Reader of Plays." Times Literary
  Supplement, September 19, 1936, p. 752.
  Points out the unique nature of the works of Le Texier, a
  specialist in dramatic readings.

Lediard, Thomas

3650 Fletcher, Ifan Kyrle. "The Discovery of Thomas Lediard."
  Theatre Notebook, II (May, 1948), 42-45.
  Notes on the stage designer.
3651 Rosenfeld, Sybil. "The Career of Thomas Lediard." Theatre Note-
  book, II (May, 1948), 46-48.
  Additional notes.
3652 Southern, Richard. "Lediard and Early 18th Century Scene Design."
  Theatre Notebook, II (April, 1948), 54.
  A brief comment on Thomas Lediard's work.
3653 -----. "Lediard and Early 18th Century Scene Design." Theatre
  Notebook, II (May, 1948), 49-57.
  Additional notes.

Lee, Nathaniel

works

3654 Lee, Nathaniel. Works. Edited with Introduction and Notes by
  Thomas B. Stroup and Arthur L. Cooke. 2 vols. New Brunswick,
  New Jersey: Scarecrow Press, 1954-1955.
  The entire edition is preceded by a general introduction to
  Lee's life, and each play is preceded by an introduction dealing
  with dates and stage history of the play, sources, criticism, and
  text. Textual notes are with the body of the play; explanatory
  notes at the end of each volume.

individual texts

3655 -----. Constantine the Great. Kritisch Herausgegeben und mit
  einer Einleitung verseben von Walter Hafele. Heidelberg: C.
  Winter, 1933. 166 pp. (Englische Textbibliothek, XX).
3656 -----. Lucius Junius Brutus. Edited by John Loftis. (Regents
  Restoration Drama Series). Lincoln: University of Nebraska
  Press, 1967.
  Includes introduction, notes and chronology.
3657 -----. The Tragedy of Nero, Emperor of Rome. Nach dem Ori-

ginalquarto von 1675 und handschriftlichen verbesserungen des
Dichters hrsg. und mit einleitung, Anmerkungen und den Vari-
ationem späterer ausgaben versehen von Rich. Horstmann.
Heidelberg: Carl Winters, 1914. 76 pp.
Based on the original quarto of 1675.

3658 -----. Sophonisba, or Hannibal's Overthrow. Edited by F. Holthausen. Kiel: Lipsius and Tischer, 1913. 60 pp.
Based on the quarto of 1681.

translation

3659 von Lohenstein, Daniel Casper. Afrikanische Trauerspiele:
Cleopatra, Sophonisbe, ed. Klaus Gunther Just. Stuttgart:
Anton Hiersemann, 1957.

biography and criticism

3660 Sanders, H. M. "The Plays of Nathaniel Lee, Gentleman." Temple Bar, CXXIV (1901), 497-508.
3661 Dencker, Hermann. "Über du Quellen von Nathaniel Lee's Alexander the Great." Halle-Wittenberg: Hofbuchdruckerei von C. A.
Kaemmerer & Co., 1903. 74 pp.
Uses textual comparisons to show that de la Capreuedes'
novel Cassandre was the source of several scenes in Alexander
the Great and exerted a greater influence on Lee's play than
has previously been recognized. Also examines Lee's use of
other sources.
3662 Auer, Otto. Über einige Dramen National Lees, mit besonderer
Berücksichtigung seiner Beziehung zum französischen heroisch-
galenten Roman. Berlin: E. Ebering, 1904. 103 pp.
Examines Lee's use of Clelie for his Lucius Junius Brutus.
3663 Resa, Fritz. Nathaniel Lee's Trauerspiel Theodosius, Or, The
Force of Love. Berlin und Leipzig: E. Felber, 1904. 219 pp.
3664 Geiersbach, Walter. Nathaniel Lees Zeittragödien und ihre Vor-
läufer im Drama Englands. Bernau: E. Gruner, 1907. 63 pp.
An attempt to show the relationship between Marlow's and
Lee's Massacre of Paris. An inaugural dissertation, Rostock.
3665 Mehr, Otto. Neue Beiträge zur Leekunde und Kritik, insbesondere
zum "Caesar Borgia" und zur "Sophonisba." Literarhistorische
Forschungen, XXXVII. Berlin: E. Felber, 1909. 154 pp.
A general study of Lee's dramatic career. Particular emphasis is given to "Sophonisba" and "Caesar Borgia," analysis
and influence.
3666 Bentzien, Werner. Studien zu Drydens "Oedipus." Rostock: Carl
Boldt, 1910. 101 pp.

A comparison of Dryden's tragedy with those of Sophocles, Seneca, and Corneille with the conclusion that although Dryden and Lee have retained Sophocles' tragic theme, their changes, additions, and emphasis upon externals and upon ugliness and violence have blurred the clarity of the dramatic action.

3667 Mühlback, Egon. Die englischen Nerodramen des XVII. Jahrhunderts Insonderheit Lees Nero. Weida in Thur: Thomas & Hubert, 1910. 105 pp.

A detailed study of Lee's Nero.

3668 Saintsbury, George. "Nathaniel Lee's 'Sophonisba.'" Englische Studien, XLVII (1913-1914), 96-97.

3669 Haupt, Richard Wilhelm. Quellenstudien zu Lee's "Mithridates, King of Pontus." Kiel: Schmidt und Klaunig, 1916.

A study of Lee's sources--La Calprenède, Racine, Shakespeare, and classical sources.

3670 Bensley, Edward. "'The Tragedy of Nero' and 'Piso's Conspiracy.'" Notes and Queries, Ser. 12, V (1919), 323.

3671 Newall, George. "'The Tragedy of Nero' and 'Piso's Conspiracy.'" Notes and Queries, 12th Ser., IV (1919), 299-300.

3672 Nicoll, Allardyce. "'The Tragedy of Nero' and 'Piso's Conspiracy.'" Notes and Queries, 12th Ser., V (October, 1919), 254-257.

The Tragedy of Nero (Nathaniel Lee, 1675) and Piso's Conspiracy (1676) have been mistaken for one another by historians. They are two different plays--both in style and content. Piso's Conspiracy is by an anonymous playwright.

3673 Beers, Douglas Stowe. "The Life and Works of Nathaniel Lee." Ph.D. Yale University, 1925.

3674 White, Felix. "The Gordian Knot Untied." Times Literary Supplement, June 11, 1925, p. 400.

Replies to D. Arundell (TLS, June 4, 1925), noting a second instance of marriage as a Gordian Knot (in Lee's play Theodosius, 1680).

3675 Ham, R. G. "The Prologue to 'Mithridates.'" Times Literary Supplement, December 27, 1928, p. 1025.

3676 Fletcher, Harris F. "Nathaniel Lee and Milton." Modern Language Notes, XLIV (March, 1929), 173-175.

On verses contributed by Lee to Dryden's The State of Innocence.

3677 Ghosh, J. C. "Prologue and Epilogue to Lee's 'Constantine the Great.'" Times Literary Supplement, March 14, 1929, p. 207.

While both the prologue and epilogue to Lee's play were printed anonymously in 1683, the epilogue was given to Dryden in 1684 and the prologue to Otway in 1712.

3678 Kies, Paul P. "Lessing's Das befreite Rom and Lee's Lucius Junius

Brutus." Journal of English and Germanic Philology, XXVIII
(July, 1929), 402-409.

Kies traces Lessing's knowledge of Nathaniel Lee and the
influence of the Englishman upon the German playwright.

3679 Saupe, Gerhard. Die Sophonisbe-tragodien der englischen Literatur des 17. und 18. Jahrunderts. Inaugural dissertation. Halle-
Wittenberg: Osterwieck am Harz, A. W. Zickfeldt, 1929. 78 pp.

Discusses four treatments of the Sophonisba story: Marston,
The Wonder of Women (1606); Thomas Nabbes, Hannibal and
Scipio (1635); Lee, Sophonisba (1676); Thomson, Sophonisba
(1730). Presents detailed comparisons of the treatments of
various elements in the plays and of the major characters.

3680 Ham, Roswell Gray. Otway and Lee: Biography from a Baroque
Age. New Haven: Yale University Press, 1931. vii, 250 pp.
Index.

Analysis of the works of each stresses the fact that Otway
worked according to the public mind. Comparison of their
works. Feels that these two reveal salient features of Restoration tragedy.

3681 Otwell, Ruth Holmes. "History of Alexander the Great by Nathaniel Lee." M.A. University of Chicago, 1932.

3682 Hafele, W. "Constantine the Great." Kritisch herausg. und mit
eine Einleitung versehen. Heidelberg: Winter, 1933. 166 pp.

3683 Stroup, T. B. "Type-Characters in the Serious Drama of the
Restoration with Special Attention to the Plays of Davenant,
Dryden, Lee, and Otway." Ph.D. University of North Carolina,
1933.

3684 Wülker, Anton. Shakespeares Einfluss auf die dramatische Kunst
von Nathaniel Lee. Inaugural dissertation. Emsdetten: H. & J.
Lechte, 1933.

After a discussion of Lee's biography and of Shakespeare's
tragedies in the Restoration, Wülker treats Shakespeare's influence on Lee's tragedies.

3685 Van Lennep, William Bird. "Nathaniel Lee: A Study of His Life
and Works." Ph.D. Harvard University, 1934.

A study of Lee's plays, the influences on his work and the
use he made of his sources. Concludes that his early plays
are in the mold of heroic tragedy but that the later plays show
the pernicious influence of the romance.

3686 Greene, Graham. "Rochester and Lee." Times Literary Supplement, November 2, 1935, p. 697. [Cf. correspondence by W.
J. Lawrence, November 9, 1935, p. 722.]

Provides further evidence for identifying Duke Nemours in
Lee's Princess of Cleve with the Earl of Rochester. Lawrence
adds clarifying bibliographical data.

3687 Stroup, Thomas B. "The Princess of Cleve and Sentimental Comedy." Review of English Studies, XI (1935), 200-203.
 Argues that Lee's play is the first example of sentimental drama.

3688 Hasan, M. "The Life and Works of Nathaniel Lee." Ph.D. Oxford University (St. John), 1938.
 An exhaustive biographical and critical account of Lee and his works with the purpose of establishing Lee "next to Dryden" among the Restoration dramatists.

3689 Barbour, Frances. "The Unconventional Heroic Plays of Nathaniel Lee." University of Texas Studies in English, XX (1940), 109-116.
 Lee's early plays (before 1679) contrast with the usual sympathy for the doctrine of the divine right of kings.

3690 Trueax, Mary Clive. "The Influence of William Shakespeare on Nathaniel Lee." M.A. George Washington University, 1941.

3691 Leary, Lewis. "St. George Tucker Attends the Theatre." William and Mary Quarterly, 3rd Ser., V (1948), 396-398.
 A performance of Lee's Alexander the Great in New York in 1786.

3692 Evans, G. Blakemore. "Milton and Lee's The Rival Queens, 1677." Modern Language Notes, LXIV (December, 1949), 527-528.
 A Milton source for Cassandra's soliloquy in Act IV.

3693 Stroup, Thomas B. and A. L. Cooke. "Nathaniel Lee." Times Literary Supplement, October 7, 1949, p. 649.
 Requests information for their forthcoming edition of the works.

3694 Bowers, Fredson. "A Crux in the Text of Lee's Princess of Cleve." Harvard Library Bulletin, IV (Autumn, 1950), 409-411.
 The omission of Marguerite's speech on sig. C4 recto is an unauthoritative alteration.

3695 -----. "Nathaniel Lee: Three Probable Seventeenth-Century Piracies." Papers of the Bibliographical Society of America, XLIV (1950), 62-66.
 Bibliographical evidence suggests pirated editions of The Rival Queens, The Tragedy of Nero, and Sophonisba.

3696 -----. "The Prologue to Nathaniel Lee's Mithridates, 1678." Papers of the Bibliographical Society of America, XLIV (1950), 172-175.
 A variant form in the prologue of the Princeton University and Huntington Library copies does not suggest that Lee did not write the prologue.

3697 Cooke, Arthur L., and Thomas B. Stroup. "The Political Implications in Lee's Constantine the Great." Journal of English and

Germanic Philology, XLIX (1950), 506-515.

Lee's last play (1683) is essentially a political one which reflects the Popish Plot and its aftermath more accurately and adequately than other plays of the period.

3698 McLeod, A. L. "Nathaniel Lee's Portrait." Notes and Queries, CXCVIII (1953), 103-105.

A portrait attributed to William Dobson is unflattering to Lee, but it is also artistically better than the one in the Monthly Mirror (1812).

3699 Smith, John Harrington. "Dryden's Prologue and Epilogue to Mithridates, Revived." Publications of the Modern Language Association, LXVIII (1953), 251-267.

The case for Dryden's authorship is strengthened in light of parallels in his other works.

3700 McLeod, A. L. "Nathaniel Lee's Birth Date." Modern Language Notes, LXIX (1954), 167-170.

McLeod suggests 1651.

3701 Stroup, Thomas B. "The Authorship of the Prologue to Lee's 'Constantine the Great.'" Notes and Queries, CXCIX (September, 1954), 387-388.

Lee, rather than Otway, wrote the prologue.

3702 Axelrad, A. José. Le Thème de Sophonisbe dans les principales tragédies de la littérature occidentale (France, Angleterre, Allemagne). Etude suivie de la Sophonisbe inédite de la Grange Chancel représentée à la Comédie francaise le 10 Novembre 1716. Travaux et Mémoires de l'Université de Lille. Nouv. Ser., Droit et Lettres, No. 28. Lille: Bibliothèque Universitaire, 1956. 188 pp.

Traces the theme chronologically from 1500-1913 through French, German, and English plays, including Nathaniel Lee's Sophonisbe, or Hannibal's Overthrow, and James Thomson's The Tragedy of Sophonisba.

3703 Cross, Gustav. "Ovid Metamorphosed.: Marston, Webster, and Nathaniel Lee." Notes and Queries, New Ser., III (1956), 244-245, 508-509.

Dryden-Lee Oedipus indebed to Golding's translation of Ovid.

3704 Barbour, Frances M. "William Gilmore Simms and The Brutus Legend." Midwest Folklore, VII (1957), 159-162.

Includes discussion of Nathaniel Lee's Lucius Junius Brutus.

3705 Lewis, Nancy Eloise. "Nathaniel Lee's The Rival Queens: A Study of Dramatic Taste and Technique in the Restoration." Ph.D. Ohio State University, 1957.

The milieu--social and theatrical--and the play's success and influence.

3706 Knight, G. Wilson. "The Plays of Nathaniel Lee." Venture, I

(1960), 186-196.

3707 McLeod, A. L. "The Douai MS. of Lee's 'Mithridates.'" Notes
      and Queries, New Ser., VII (1960), 69-70.
          Establishes that the MS. copy of Mithridates in the Biblio-
      thèque Publique at Douai is not, as Wing's Short Title Catalogue
      indicates, a Lee holograph.

3708 Birley, Robert. Sunk without Trace; Some Forgotten Masterpieces
      Reconsidered. The Clark Lectures, 1960-61. London: Rupert
      Hart-Davis, 1962. 208 pp.
          Includes a chapter on Nathaniel Lee's The Rival Queens,
      discussing the theory of tragedy the play exemplifies and analyz-
      ing the sources and text of the play itself.

3709 McLeod, A. L. "A Nathaniel Lee Bibliography, 1670-1960." 17th
      and 18th Century Theatre Research, I (November, 1962), 27-39.
          Includes listings of Lee's collected works, individual plays,
      occasional poems, and books and articles concerning Lee.

3710 Tucker, Yvonne Yaw. "The Villains and Heroes of Nathaniel Lee:
      a Study in Dramatic Characterization." Ph.D. Harvard Uni-
      versity, 1965.

Leisure

3711 Morrill, Allen C. "Restoration Leisure, the Background of Eng-
      lish Drama, Prose, and Poetry between 1660 and 1688." Ph.D.
      Harvard University, 1937.

Lennox, Charlotte

3712 "The Centenary of a Blue-Stocking." The Academy and Lit., LXVI
      (January 23, 1904), 102.
          Biographical sketch of Mrs. Lennox, emphasizing particular-
      ly her connection with Dr. Johnson, her success with the novel,
      the failure of "The Sisters," which, with Epilogue by Goldsmith,
      was produced by Colman; It fell flat at Covent Garden but was
      plagarized by General Burgoyne in his "Heiress" to an extent at
      once shameful and complimentary.

3713 Small, Miriam R. "Letters of Dr. Johnson and Mrs. Charlotte
      Lennox." Notes and Queries, CXLVIII (January 24, 1925), 62.
          Asks about letters by dramatist Lennox.

3714 Small, Miriam Rossiter. Charlotte Ramsay Lennox, An Eighteenth-
      Century Lady of Letters. (Yale Studies in English, Vol. LXXXV).
      New Haven: Yale University Press, 1935. viii, 268 pp.
          A scholarly biography of the novelist who was also a play-
      wright. Chapter VI contains an analysis of her dramatic works.

3715 Isles, Duncan E. "Johnson and Charlotte Lennox." The New Rambler,

Serial No. C. III (June, 1967), 34-48.

A discussion of the financial and literary assistance given
to Mrs. Lennox by Johnson includes mention of her three dramas
and her Shakespeare Illustrated, a work on the sources of the
plays.

Lessing, G.

3716 Todt, Wilhelm. Lessing in England, 1767-1850. Heidelberg: Carl
     Winter's Universitätsbuchhandlung, 1912. [6], 67 pp. (Anglistiche
     Arbeiten).
         A brief resumé of Lessing's Nathan der Weise, Minna von
     Barnhelm, Emilia Galotti, in the 18th century. The criticisms
     of the works are drawn from the English periodicals of the day,
     e.g., Monthly Review, Critical Review, New Review.
3717 Kenwood, Sydney H. "Lessing in England." Modern Language Re-
     view, IX (1914), 197-212.
         On translations and adaptations of Lessing's dramas and the
     production of some on the late 18th-century London and York
     stages.
3718 Kies, Paul P. "The Sources and Basic Model of Lessing's Miss
     Sara Sampson." Modern Philology, XXIV (August, 1926), 65-90.
         Based primarily upon Shadwell's The Squire of Alsatia but
     with borrowings from other English plays.
3719 -----. "Lessing's Early Study of English Drama." Journal of Eng-
     lish and Germanic Philology, XXVIII (January, 1929), 16-34.
         Lessing "studied Restoration comedy of manners extensively
     from 1747 to 1749 and borrowed from it much material."
3720 Nolte, Fred O. "Lessing and the Bourgeois Drama." Journal of
     English and Germanic Philology, XXXI (1932), 66-83.
         Lessing's letter of November, 1756, to Nicolai and his Vor-
     rede to a 1756 translation of Thomson's tragedies allegedly ac-
     count for Lessing's attraction to bourgeois tragedy, an attitude
     based more on Shaftesbury's social philosophy than on The
     Poetics.
3721 Walzel, Oskar. Das Prometheus-symbol von Shaftesbury zu Goethe.
     [Second revised edition.] Munich: Max Hueber, 1932. 110 pp.
         This study contains references to such English writers as
     Milton, Pope, Otway and their development of the Prometheus
     symbol, though it is primarily concerned with German writers,
     particularly Goethe.

Lewis, John

3722 Lawrence, W. J. "John Lewis, Portrait Painter and Scenic Artist."

Notes and Queries, 10th Ser., I (January 30, 1904), 87.
Discusses the mid 18th-century scenic artist of Smock Alley
Theatre, Dublin.

Lewis, M.

3723 Guthke, Karl S. "M. G. Lewis' The Twins." Huntington Library
Quarterly, XXV (1962), 189-223.
"The only hitherto unpublished manuscript known to be by
Lewis." Includes criticism, possible sources, and complete
text of play.

3724 -----. "F. L. Schröder, J. F. Regnard, and M. G. Lewis."
Huntington Library Quarterly, XXVII (November, 1963), 79-
82.
Detailed comparison of Lewis's The Twins with its source,
F. L. Schröder's adaptation of J. F. Regnard's Les Ménechmes,
ou les Jumeaux.

Licensing Act

3725 B[aldensperger], F. Un incident théâtral franco-anglais au xviii[e]
siècle d'après un témoignage diplomatique." Revue de littérature comparée, IX (July-September, 1929), 573-578.
The effect of the 1737 Licensing Act on a French company
in London.

3726 Crean, P. J. "The Stage Licensing Act of 1737." Modern Philology,
XXXV (1938), 239-255.
An account of certain events between 1729 and 1737 which
contributed to passage of the Licensing Act. Among other causes
for opposition to the stage were the repeated attempts to build
new playhouses, and the dramatic satires on the Walpole minis-
try, such as those by Hen ry Fielding.

Lichtenberg, Georg

3727 Betz, Gottlieb. "Lichtenberg as a Critic of the English Stage."
Journal of English and Germanic Philology, XXIII (1924), 270-
288.
Reports Lichtenberg's observations on the London theatre
during his 1774-75 visit to England with emphasis on his evaluations of performers--particularly Garrick.

3728 Lichtenberg, Georg Christoph. Lichtenberg's Visits to England
as Described in His Letters and Diaries. Translated and annotated by Margaret L. Mare and W. H. Quarrell. Oxford: The
Clarendon Press, 1938. 130 pp.

The letters reveal Lichtenberg's impressions of England during his two journeys there; for everything English, Lichtenberg had an innate sympathy--especially for Shakespeare (and Garrick as his interpreter), Pope, Swift, Fielding, and Sterne.

Lighting

3729 Lawrence, W. J. "Stage and Theatre Lighting (1580-1800)." The Stage Year Book (London, 1927), 9-22.
      Discusses the efforts of Elizabethan theatre to utilize natural light, and argues against the notion that private theatres used artificial light exclusively. Treats the changes in lighting technique in Restoration theatre, Wren's design for Old Drury, and Garrick's introduction of wing lights.

3730 Kiefer, E. B. "The Development of Stage Lighting in England and America." M.A. McGill University, 1929.

Lillo, George

texts

3731 Lillo, George. Fatal Curiosity. Edited by William H. McBurney. Lincoln: University of Nebraska Press, 1966. (Regents Restoration Drama Series).
      Includes introduction, notes, and appendices for variant and additional passages and for the source of the play.

3732 -----. "The London Merchant or The History of George Barnwell" and "Fatal Curiosity." Edited by A. W. Ward. Boston: D. C. Heath and Company, 1906. lix, 247 pp. (Belles Lettres Series).

3733 -----. The London Merchant. Edited by Bonamy Dobrée. London: Harvill, 1948. xxvi, 122 pp.
      A reprint with general critical introduction and commentary on the stage history.

3734 -----. The London Merchant. Edited by William H. McBurney. (Regents Restoration Drama Series). Lincoln: University of Nebraska Press, 1965.
      Includes critical introduction, notes, bibliography, and appendices with Lillo's advertisement and "The Ballad of George Barnwell."

3735 -----. When Crummles Played, being the Full Original Text of Lillo's Tragedy of the London Merchant or George Barnwell . . . Introduction by F. J. Harvey Darton. London: Chapman and Hall, 1927. 6, 136 pp.
      Directed by Sir Nigel Playfair with Vincent Crummle's company at the Lyric Theatre, Hammersmith.

translation

3736 -----. Le marchand de Londres. Ed. critique traduction, preface
      et notes de J. Hammard. Paris: Les belles lettres, 1962. 158 pp.
      (Annales litteraires de l'université de Besancon [ser. 2] vol.
      51).
          Text collated from the first six editions authorized by the
      author. English text and French translation on facing pages,
      with notes on collation and variants in English. Bibliography of
      editions of the play.

biography and criticism

3737 Rautner, Hans. George Lillos The Christian Hero und dessen
      Rival Plays. Eine Studie zur vergleichenden Literaturgeschichte
      . . . München: Kastner & Lossen, 1900. 39 pp.
          Includes a discussion of Thomas Whincop's play Scanderbeg;
      or, Love and Liberty and William Havard's Scanderbeg.
3738 Halthausen, F. "Rhythmische Prosa in Lillos The London Merchant."
      Archiv fur das Studium Der Neuren Sprachen und Literaturen,
      CXIII (1904), 307-314.
          Except for an introduction of eleven lines, and a conclusion
      of eight lines, the article reprints lines from the play to illustrate
      the idea of rhythmical prose.
3739 Walz, John A. "Goethe's 'Götz von Berlichingen' and Lillo's 'His-
      tory of George Barnwell.'" Modern Philology, III (1906), 493-505.
          Although Goethe acknowledged his indebtedness only to "Miss
      Sara Sampson" and "Antony and Cleopatra," many passages in
      "Götz von Berlichingen" parallel those in Lillo's play, particular-
      ly characters and some of the scenes.
3740 Kunze, Albert. Lillos Einfluss auf die englische und die deutsche
      Literatur. Magdeburg: Oxtern, 1911. 18 pp.
          Lillo's influence on Hogarth, Edward Moore, Cumberland
      and on Lessing, Pfeil, Breithaupt, Brandes, and other German
      playwrights.
3741 Hudson, William Henry. A Quiet Corner in a Library. Chicago:
      Rand McNally & Company, 1915. 238 pp.
          The essay "George Lillo and 'The London Merchant'" (pages
      93-162) criticizes the play as a bad one aesthetically but praises
      it as the first domestic tragedy (historically) and for its inter-
      est in the middle class (socially).
3742 Ward, Sir Adolphus William. "Introduction to Lillo's London
      Merchant and Fatal Curiosity." Collected Papers, Vol. IV.
      (Cambridge: at the University Press, 1921), 243-289.
          An introduction to the two plays, which presents historical

background, sources, information on early productions, followed by a critical analysis of each play.

3743 Benham, Allen R. "Notes on Plays." Modern Language Notes,
      XXXVIII (1923), 252.
          Mentions an eighth edition (1743) of Lillo's Fatal Curiosity
      before the collected edition of 1750; a note on Otway's Venice
      Preserv'd indicates that Jaffeir is related to the hero caught
      between love and honor in the heroic drama.

3744 Sandbach, F. E. "Karl Philip Moritz's Blunt and Lillo's Fatal
      Curiosity." Modern Language Review, XVIII (1923), 449-457.
          A refutation of J. Minor's thesis that Lillo did not directly
      influence Moritz.

3745 Benn, T. Vincent. "Notes sur la fortune du George Barnwell de
      Lillo en France." Revue de Littérature Comparée, VI (1926),
      682-687.
          Comments on 18th-century French translations and trans-
      lators' reactions to the play.

3746 Jennings, Richard. "When Crummles Played." Spectator, CXXXVII
      (June 18, 1927), 1061-1062.
          Reviews Nigel Playfair's Lyric Theatre production of George
      Lillo's London Merchant.

3747 Wynn, Earl Raymond. "An Authentic Reproduction of George
      Lillo's The London Merchant." M.S. Northwestern University,
      1934.

3748 Griffith, R. H. "Early Editions of Lillo's 'London Merchant.'"
      University of Texas Studies in English, XV (1935), 23-27.
          To the lists published by A. W. Ward and Allardyce Nicoll,
      Griffith adds a pirated fifth edition (1733), a sixth edition
      (1735), and a pirated eighth edition (1737).

3749 Lossack, Gerhard. George Lillo und Seine Bedeutung für die
      Geschichte des englischen dramas. Göttingen: Druck der
      Dieterischen Universitäts-Buchdruckerei, 1939. 86 pp.
          A study of The London Merchant, Fatal Curiosity, and The
      Christian Hero. There is a review of recent scholarship.
      Somewhat pedantic in approach and treatment.

3750 Pallette, Drew B. "Notes for a Biography of George Lillo." Philolo
      gical Quarterly, XIX (July, 1940), 261-267.
          Plausibly identifies Lillo's parents and possibly his own
      baptism in the register of the Dutch Reformed Church, The
      Austin Friars.

3751 Thorndike, Oliver. "The London Merchant, by George Lillo."
      Master's production-thesis. M.A. Yale University, 1940.

3752 Pendell, W. D. "The London Merchant and Le Mierre's Barnevelt.
      Modern Language Notes, LVI (June, 1941), 432-433.
          Argues that the French play is not an adaptation of the Eng-
      lish.

3753 Price, Lawrence M. "George Barnwell on the German Stage."
      Monatshefte für den deutschen Unterricht, XXXV (1943), 205-
      214.

3754 -----. "The Bassewitz Translation of The London Merchant,
      1752." Journal of English and Germanic Philology, XLIII (1944),
      354-357.
          An account of the earliest German translation of Lillo's
      tragedy.

3755 Havens, Raymond Dexter. "Sentimentality in The London Merchant."
      English Literary History, XII (September, 1945), 183-187.
          Replies to George Bush Rodman's article (March, 1945, 45-
      61).

3756 Rodman, George Bush. "Sentimentality in The London Merchant."
      English Literary History, XII (March, 1945), 45-61.
          The accepted definitions of "sentimentality" do not apply to
      Lillo's play.

3757 Sklare, Arnold Beryl. "George Lillo: a Biographical and Critical
      Study." M.A. University of Illinois, 1947.

3758 Kazanoff, Theodore. "The World of George Lillo in Relation to his
      Play, The London Merchant." M.A. Smith College, 1948.

3759 Price, Lawrence Marsden. "George Barnwell Abroad." Comparative
      Literature, II (1950), 126-156.
          The London Merchant was very popular and influential in
      France, Germany, and America during the latter half of the
      eighteenth century.

3760 Loftis, John. "The Eighteenth-Century Beginnings of Modern Drama."
      Emory University Quarterly, VII (1951), 225-236.
          Many aspects of modern theatrical practice first appeared in
      the plays of Gay, Lillo, and Steele.

3761 Sinko, Grzegorz. Anglieski dramat mieszczanski XVIII wieku; G.
      Lillo, E. Moore, S. Foote. Przelozyl i opracowal G. Sinko.
      Wroclaw: Zaklad im. Ossolinskich-Wydawnictwo [1955]. cxl,
      367 pp. (Biblioteka narodowa, Ser. 2, 95).
          Introduction, giving historical background. Polish transla-
      tions of Lillo's The London Merchant, Moore's The Gamester,
      and Foote's The Nabob.

3762 Daunicht, Richard. "Die ersten Aufführungen des 'Kaufmanns von
      London' in Deutschland." Zeitschrift für Anglistik und Ameri-
      kanistik, IV (1956), 243-247.
          A brief summary of Lillo's The London Merchant in Germany
      from 1752-1769.

3763 Bremmer, G. "Millwood, Lady Milford and Maria Stuart." German
      Life and Letters, XI (1957), 41-48.
          Cites Lillo's Merchant of London.

3764 Virtanen, Reino. "Camus' Le Malentendu and Some Analogues."

Comparative Literature, X (1958), 232-240.
Includes Lillo's Fatal Curiosity.

3765 Carson, Herbert L. "The Play That Would Not Die: George Lillo's
The London Merchant." Quarterly Journal of Speech, XLIX
(1963), 287-294.
Conditions which favored the composition of the play; its
weaknesses and influence on subsequent drama.

3766 Daunicht, Richard. Die Entstehung des Bürgerlichen Trauerspiels
in Deutschland. (Quellen und Forschungen zur Sprach-und-
Kulturgeschichte der germanischen Völker. Neue Folge, herausgegeben von Hermann Kunisch, 8). Berlin: Walter de Gruyte:
and Company, 1963. 309 pp.
Several chapters of this critical treatise are devoted to the
influence of English drama on German bourgeoise tragedy.
Chapter V contains a history of the first printings and performances of The London Merchant in Germany.

3767 De Boer, Fredrik Eugene. "George Lillo." Ph.D. University of
Wisconsin, 1965. (Order No. 65-9232).
A descriptive history of the life, writings, and reputation
of Lillo. Lillo's dramatic endeavors are seen as "direct attempts to turn the theatre to the service of a specifically Cal-
vinistic morality." A bibliography lists all the published editior
of Lillo's works.

3768 Jackson, Wallace. "Dryden's Emperor and Lillo's Merchant: the
Relevant Bases of Action." Modern Language Quarterly, XXVI
(1965), 536-544.
Desires a more closely unified approach to the drama of the
late seventeenth and early eighteenth centuries. A fundamentall
similar set of assumptions concerning the primacy of social
contract governs the actions and characters of Dryden's All for
Love and Lillo's The London Merchant.

3769 McBurney, William H. "What George Lillo Read: A Speculation."
Huntington Library Quarterly, XXIX (1966), 275-286.
A partially annotated list of books probably owned by Lillo
and sold at auction by the bookseller John Oswald in 1739.

3770 Burgess, C. F. "Further Notes for a Biography of George Lillo."
Philological Quarterly, XLVI (1967), 424-428.
Two recently discovered documents, one an entry in the Ap-
prentice Register in Goldsmith's Hall, London, and the other
in the Lambeth Palace Library respectively reveal that George
Lillo's brother James was an apprenticed goldsmith and that
Lillo's religious orientation was not Puritan but Anglican.

Lincoln's Inn Fields

3771 Fairbrother, E. H. "Rope-Dancing in Lincoln's Inn Fields."
       Notes and Queries, CXLIX (November 14, 1925), 349.
          An entry in the Lord Chamberlain's Books prohibiting rope-
       dancing, puppet plays, and dumb shows in the Fields.

Linley, E. A.

3772 Black, Clementina. The Linleys of Bath. With an introduction by
       G. Saintsbury. London: Secker, 1926. 316 pp.
          First issued in 1911. A popular family biography, focussing
       upon Elizabeth Ann Linley, wife of Richard Brinsley Sheridan.

Literary History

3773 Kirk, Rudolph and C. F. Main, eds. Essays in Literary History
       Presented to J. Milton French. New Brunswick, New Jersey:
       Rutgers University Press, 1960. 270 pp.
          This miscellany contains two essays of particular interest:
       "The Right Vein of Rochester's Satyr" (categorized as an
       Augustan formal verse satire, England's first) and "The
       Frailty of Gulliver," which reveals Swift's "quick sympathetic
       humanity."
3774 Thrall, William Flint, and Addison Hibbard. A Handbook to Liter-
       ature, Revised and enlarged by C. Hugh Holman. New York:
       Odyssey Press, 1960. viii, 598 pp.
          A useful volume providing definitions of literary terms and
       including an outline history of English and American literature.

Liverpool

3775 Broadbent, R. J. Annals of the Liverpool Stage, from the Earliest
       Period to the Present Time; Together with Some Account of the
       Theatres and Music Halls in Bootle and Birkenhead. Liverpool:
       E. H. Howell, 1908. ix, 393 pp.
          Includes records of various theatres, actors and their per-
       formances, concert halls and variety stage in Liverpool.
       Numerous illustrations of playhouses and players.
3776 Wardle, Arthur C. "Liverpool's First Theatre Royal." Transactions
       of the Historic Society of Lancashire and Cheshire for the Year
       1938, XC (1939), 207-209.
          Liverpool's Drury Lane Theatre, originally opened in 1750,
       became the city's first Theatre Royal in 1771 under the patent
       granted to William Gibson.

Lloyd, Robert

3777 Dobson, Austin. "Robert Lloyd." At Prior Park and Other Papers.
     (New York: Frederick A. Stokes Company, 1912), 210-242.
          Sketch of the life and works of Robert Lloyd--magazine
     editor, poet ("The Actor"), writer of prologues and epilogues
     and of one comic opera, The Capricious Lovers.

Locke, Matthew

3778 Lawrence, W. J. "Lock'e Music for 'Macbeth.'" Notes and Queries
     10th Ser., II (August 20, 1904), 142.
          Corrects the date for the first performance of Davenant's al-
     teration of Macbeth in 1672, by showing that the play had been
     produced earlier with dancing and music in 1666-67, when Mat-
     thew Locke wrote the music.
3779 Cummings, W. H. "Matthew Locke, Composer for the Church and
     Theatre." Sammelbande der Internationalen Musikgesellschaft,
     XIII (1911-1912), 120-126.
          Locke's musical career with emphasis upon his dramatic
     music for The Siege of Rhodes at Rutland House, for Macbeth,
     The Tempest, and Shadwell's Psyche.
3780 Bridge, Sir Frederick. "Matthew Locke, 1630 [?]-1677." Twelve
     Good Musicians: from John Bull to Henry Purcell. (London:
     Kegan Paul, Trench, Trubner &Co., Ltd., 1920), 84-94.
          The biographical sketch of the man Bridge identifies as the
     "Father of English Opera," on the basis of Locke's having
     composed the music for Shadwell's Psyche (1673).

London Fairs

3781 Rosenfeld, Sybil M. The Theatre of the London Fairs in the
     Eighteenth Century. Cambridge: Cambridge University Press,
     1960. xii, 194 pp.
          A study, primarily of dramatic entertainments at 18th-
     century London Fairs, whose traditionalism "preserves ele-
     ments from older times and folk lore from immemorial ones."

London Journal

3782 Joshi, K. L. "The London Journal, 1719-1738." Journal of the
     University of Bombay, IX (1940), 33-66.

Lounsbury, Thomas

3783 Lounsbury, Thomas R. Text of Shakespeare, Its history from the
      publication of the quartos and folios down to and including the
      publication of the editions of Pope and Theobald. Vol. III. New
      York: Scribner, 1906. xxii, 579 pp.
          An elaborate account of eighteenth century criticism over the
      text of Shakespeare.

Loutherbourg, Philip

3784 Dobson, Austin. "Exhibitions of the Eidophusikon." At Prior Park
      and Other Papers. (London: Chatto and Windus, 1912), 277-281.
          An account of De Loutherbourg's production of "Moving
      Pictures" with musical accompaniment composed by Arne and by
      Burney and with singing by Mrs. Sophia Baddeley.
3785 -----. "Loutherbourg, R. A." At Prior Park and Other Papers.
      (London: Chatto and Windus, 1912), 94-127.
          Sketch of De Loutherbourg's life with some account of the
      artist's stage work for Drury Lane and Covent Garden.
3786 Preston, Lillian Elvira. "Philippe Jacques de Loutherbourg: Eight-
      eenth Century Romantic Artist and Scene Designer." Ph.D. Uni-
      versity of Florida, 1957.
          Designer for Drury Lane under Garrick from about 1771.
3787 Allen, Ralph G. "De Loutherbourg and Captain Cook." Theatre
      Research, IV (1962), 195-211.
          The staging of Omai with settings by De Loutherbourg in
      1785. ". . . undoubtedly the most spectacular and costly
      entertainment ever produced in London up to that time."
3788 Gage, John. "Loutherbourg: Mystagogue of the Sublime." History
      Today, XIII (1963), 332-339.
          A brief history of the theatrical Eidophusikon. De Loutherbourg's
      association with Garrick.
3789 Rosenfeld, Sybil. "The Eidophusikon Illustrated." Theatre Notebook,
      XVIII (Winter, 1963/4), 52-54.
          An explanation and reprinted illustration of Philip James de
      Loutherbourg's "Eidophusikon; or, Various Imitations of Natural
      Phenomena, Represented by Moving Pictures," recently acquired
      by the British Museum.
3790 Allen, Ralph G. "Topical Scenes for Pantomime." Educational
      Theatre Journal, XVII (1965), 289-300.
          An examination of five "topical spectacles" prepared by
      P. J. De Loutherbourg during his stay at Drury Lane for Gar-
      rick and Sheridan.
3791 Oliver, Anthony, and John Saunders. "De Loutherbourg and Pizarro,

1799." Theatre Notebook, XX (Autumn, 1965), 30-32.
De Loutherbourg's relationship to the scenery for Pizarro,
the translated and adapted version of Kotzebue's Die Spanier in
Peru, first performed at Drury Lane on May 24, 1799.

3792 Preston, Lillian E. "The Noble Savage: Omai; or, A Trip Round
the World." Drama Critique, VIII (1965), 130-132.
An account of Loutherbourg's realistic designs for the
musical pantomime of 1785-1786.

3793 -----. "Loutherbourg's Letters to Garrick." Drama Critique, IX
(1966), 42-44.
Reprints two letters from the Forster Collection at the Victoria and Albert Museum that illuminate some of Loutherbourg'
early plans for the Drury Lane stage.

Love

3794 Berkeley, David S. "The Art of 'Whining' Love [in Restoration
Comedy]." Studies in Philology, LII (1955), 478-496.
A chief characteristic of Restoration and later drama is
sentimental love-making; the woman is ideal, the love constant,
and the language complimentary. Numerous illustrations from
plays.

Lupton, Arthur

3795 Wilkie, John R. "Goethe's English Friend Lupton." German Life
and Letters, IX (1955), 29-39.
Supported by letters that Arthur Lupton was a friend of
Goethe's; the reconstructed figure Harry Lupton can be replace
with the real Arthur.

Mackenzie, Henry

text

3796 Mackenzie, Henry. The Anecdotes and Egotisms of Henry Macken
zie, 1745-1831. Edited by Harold William Thompson. Oxford
University Press, 1927. xxxiv, 303 pp.
First publication. Accounts of poets, actors, artists, etc.,
and a description of the genesis of The Man of Feeling. The
introduction gives the main facts of Mackenzie's life. Some
of the anecdotes seemed to Thompson not worth publishing.
The material is arranged by the editor into chapters; that on
the stage (XIII) gives anecdotes of Garrick and his contemporaries, Sheridan, his own plays.

criticism

3797 Kluge, Johannes. "Henry MacKenzie sein Leben und seine Werke."
Anglia, XXXIV (1911), 1-112.
Pages 105-108 are devoted to a short discussion of MacKenzie's
dramatic works--The Prince of Tunis, The Spanish Father, and
False Shame or The White Hypocrite. Kluge concludes that it is
proper that nobody speaks of MacKenzie as a dramatist.
3798 Schwärtz, Hans. Henry MacKenzie. Zürich, 1911.
3799 Mackenzie, Harold William. "Henry Mackenzie: His Life and His
Works." Ph.D. Harvard University, 1915.
3800 Richmond, Helen M. "Mackenzie's Translations from the German."
Modern Language Review, XVII (1922), 412.
A report on the publication circumstances of Henry Mackenzie's
translation of The Set of Horses, a dramatic work incorrectly attributed to Lessing.
3801 Thompson, Harold William. A Scottish Man of Feeling; Some Account of Henry Mackenzie of Edinburgh, and of the Golden Age
of Burns and Scott. London, New York: Oxford University Press,
1931.
Covers Mackenzie's plays and his criticism of German drama.
3802 Rouch, John S. "Henry Mackenzie: A Re-examination." Ph.D. University of Cincinnati, 1961. 271 pp. (Order No. 61-5231).
The analysis given of three of his plays, The Prince of Tunis
(1773), The Spanish Father (1773), and False Shame (1789),
shows his moral dualism functioning in both tragedy and comedy.
3803 Quaintance, Richard E., Jr. "Henry Mackenzie's Sole Comedy."
Huntington Library Quarterly, XXVI (1962), 249-251.
Substantiates from manuscript of the play that False Shame;
or, The White Hypocrite is merely another title for The Force
of Fashion (1789).
3804 Lindsay, David W. "Henry Mackenzie, Alexander Thomson and
Dramatic Pieces from the German." Studies in Scottish Literature, III (1966), 253-255.
Thomson, not Mackenzie, is the translator of the work published in Edinburgh in 1792.

Macklin, Charles

texts

3805 Macklin, Charles. Covent Garden Theatre. With an Introduction
by Jean B. Kern. Los Angeles: Clark Memorial Library, University of California, Los Angeles, 1965. vi, 73 pp.
A facsimile reproduction for the Augustan Reprint Society.

The introduction treats Macklin's life and discusses this farce afterpiece, especially in relation to his other works.

3806 -----. The Man of the World (1792). With an Introduction by Dougald MacMillan. (Augustan Reprint Society, Publication No. 26). Los Angeles: William Andrews Clark Memorial Library, University of California, 1951. iv, 68 pp.

Text, printed in modern type. The introduction discusses the play in relation to Macklin's career, especially as the main character relates to the types of roles Macklin played.

biography and criticism

3807 Lawrence, W. J. "Mackliniana." Notes and Queries, 10th Ser., I (June 25, 1904), 506.

A discussion of Macklin's profits during a Smock Alley engagement, 1763-64.

3808 Barnard, F. P. "Names of Authors Wanted." Notes and Queries, 12th Ser., XI (October, 1922), 337.

Identifies Charles Macklin as author of The Man of the World, a 1764 comedy.

3809 Eaton, Walter Prichard. "The Jew That Shakespeare Drew." The Actor's Heritage; Scenes from the Theatre of Yesterday and the Day Before. (Boston: The Atlantic Monthly Press [1924]), 45-58.

A history of the role of Shylock with emphasis on Charles Macklin's 1741 portrayal of that part.

3810 Bensley, Edward. "'The Glorious Uncertainty of the Law': Sterne and Macklin." Notes and Queries, CLVII (October 26, 1929), 294-295.

A similar phrase in Charles Macklin's Love à la Mode (1759) and Lawrence Sterne's Political Romance (1759).

3811 Matthews, W. "The Piracies of Macklin's Love à-la-Mode." Review of English Studies, X (1934), 311-318.

Studies the piracies of the play by Garrick's actor-writer.

3812 MacMillan, Dougald. "The Censorship in the Case of Macklin's The Man of the World." Huntington Library Bulletin, No. 10 (1936), 79-102.

A textual history of Macklin's play showing how it was altered to satisfy the demands of the Examiner of Plays.

3813 Raushenbush, Esther M. "Charles Macklin's Lost Play about Henry Fielding." Modern Language Notes, LI (1936), 505-514.

The Larpent MS. of Macklin's The Covent-Garden Theatre;

Or, Pasquin Turn'd Drawcansir (1752) reveals that instead of
being an attack upon Fielding, the play actually presents "a
thoroughly sympathetic portrait" of the playwright-novelist.

3814 Barrow, Bernard E. "Macklin's Costume and Property Notes for
the Character of Lovegold: Some Traditional Elements in
Eighteenth Century Low-Comedy Acting." Theatre Notebook,
XIII (1958), 66-67.
Macklin as a character in Fielding's The Miser.

3815 Appleton, William W. Charles Macklin. Cambridge" Harvard University Press, 1960. 280 pp.
This new biographical study supersedes four previous, out-
of-print studies in illustrating Macklin's contributions to later
laws of literary property, improving the actor's status and contributing to the evolution of the modern stage director.

3816 Findlay, Robert Raymond. "A Critical Study of the Extant Plays
of Charles Macklin." Ph.D. State University of Iowa, 1964.
(Order No. 64-7917).
Examines ten dramatic works of Macklin as vehicles of
satire written to "display his acting talents."

3817 -----. "Macklin's Legitimate Acting Version of Love à la Mode."
Philological Quarterly, XLV (1966), 749-760.
Disputes W. Matthews' conclusion in "The Piracies of
Macklin's Love à-la-Mode" in Review of English Studies, X
(1934), and contends that Macklin used in performance the
text he authorized for publication in 1793.

3818 Maloney, Timothy. "Charles Mackon and 'The Art and Duty of an
Actor.'" M.A. University of Delaware, 1966.

3819 Bartley, J. O. "Charles Macklin: Appearances Outside London."
Theatre Notebook, XXII (Autumn, 1967), 4-5.
An alphabetical list of 18 plays in which Macklin acted.
Each item includes the author and title of the play, the char-
acter played by Macklin, and the places and dates of perform-
ances.

3820 Findlay, Robert R. "Charles Macklin and the Problem of Natural
Acting." Educational Theatre Journal, XIX (1967), 33-40.
Examines all of Macklin's roles to discover a distinct pattern among them that does not demand or even suggest "natural"
acting.

Macready, William

3821 Bassett, Abraham Joseph. "The Actor-Manager Career of William
Charles Macready." Ph.D. Ohio State University, 1962.
The managerial career of Macready is studied in respect to
the staging of the plays and popular reaction to them.

3822 Wolfit, Donald. "The Actor's Life Today and Yesterday." <u>Drama,</u>
      No. 69 (Summer, 1963), 26-29.
          The life of the actor from Elizabethan times to the present.
      Some references to William Macready.

3823 Downer, Alan S. <u>The Eminent Tragedian: William Charles Mac-</u>
      <u>ready</u>. Cambridge: Harvard University Press, 1966. 392 pp.
          This biography of Macready includes comments on his con-
      tribution to stagecraft during the transitional period between
      the late 18th century and the later reform of Craig, Appia, and
      others.

Malapropism

3824 Stallmann, Heinz. <u>Malapropismen im englischen Drama von den</u>
      <u>Anfangen bis 1800</u>. Bottrop i. W.: W. Postberg, 1938.
          A history of the use of malapropism in English drama from
      the middle ages. Of the chapter devoted to Restoration and 18th-
      century drama, half is a discussion of <u>The Rivals</u>. There is an
      index of malapropisms.

Mallet, David

3825 Little, David Mason. "The Letters of David Mallet." Ph.D. Harvard
      University, 1935.
          A dissertation consisting of the collated texts of 109 letters
      from Mallet to various 18th century figures, including Thomson,
      Hill, and Pope.

3826 Starr, Herbert W. "Notes on David Mallet." <u>Notes and Queries,</u>
      CLXXVIII (April 20, 1940), 277-278.

3827 -----. "Sources of David Mallet's 'Mustapha, a Tragedy.'" <u>Notes</u>
      <u>and Queries</u>, CLXXXI (November 22, 1941), 285-287.
          Some influence of earlier dramatic versions, but the main
      sources was Knolles's <u>Generall Historie of the Turkes</u>.

3828 Boswell, James, Andrew Erskine, and Georg Dempster. <u>Critical</u>
      <u>Strictures on the New Tragedy of Elvira, Written by Mr. David</u>
      <u>Malloch. (1763)</u>. With an Introduction by Frederick A. Pottle.
      Los Angeles, William Andrews Clark Memorial Library, Uni-
      versity of California, 1952. (24) pp.
          Play is essentially an adaptation or translation of Lamotte-
      Houdar's French tragedy "Inès de Castro." Condemnation of
      the play.

Malone, Edmund

3829 Horne, Colin J. "Malone and Steevens." Notes and Queries, CXCV (1950), 56.
    Steevens' resentment at Boswell's praise of Malone in the Advertisement to the Life of Johnson is reflected in his retort in the St. James's Chronicle for May 19, 1791.
3830 Wilson, J. Dover. "Malone and the Upstart Crow." Shakespeare Survey (Cambridge: Cambridge University Press, 1951), 56-68.
    Malone's theory of the authorship of the three parts of Henry VI is still valid.
3831 McAleer, John J. "Malone and Ritson." Shakespeare Newsletter, XIII (1963), 12.
    Clears Malone of the charge that he bought 3 volumes of Ritson's manuscripts for the latter's proposed edition of Shakespeare in order to destroy them.
3832 Walton, J. K. "Edmund Malone: an Irish Shakespeare Scholar." Hermathena, XCIX (1964), 5-26.
    Supplies biographical facts about Malone's Irish origin and education. Briefly indicates the textual achievements of his 1790 edition of Shakespeare's works.

Manchester Theatre

3833 Hodgkinson, J. L., and Rex Pogson. The Early Manchester Theatre. London: Anthony Blond for the Society for Theatre Research, 1960. xii, 189 pp.
    This work is intended to give as reliable an account as possible of the two theatres--The Marsden Street Theatre (1750-1775) and the First Theatre Royal (1775-1807)--which operated in Manchester during the 18th century.

Manley, Mary

3834 Carter, Herbert. "Three Women Dramatists of the Restoration." Bookman's Journal, XIII (December, 1925), 91-97.
    Sketches the careers of Mrs. Mary Manley, Mrs. Mary Pix, Mrs. Catharine Trotter, and discusses the position of women generally.
3835 Jerrold, Walter and Clare Jerrold. Five Queen Women. New York: Brentano, 1929. xii, 356 pp.
    Aphra Behn, Mary Manley, Susanna Centlivre, Eliza Haywood, and Letitita Pilkington.
3836 Anderson, Paul Bunyan. "Mary de la Riviere Manley, a Cavalier's Daughter in Grub Street." Ph.D. Harvard University, 1931.

A detailed discussion of Mrs. Manley's life and projects; the emphasis is on her personal and literary relationships in the years after 1709.

3837 -----. "Mistress Delariviere Manley's Biography." Modern Philology, XXXIII (1936), 261-278.

Discusses her life, character, and publications; contains references to her tragedy Almyna, other plays, essays, and memoirs.

3838 Needham, Gwendolyn B. "Mary de la Rivière Manley, Tory Defender." Huntington Library Quarterly, XII (1949), 253-288.

A biographical article, concerned mainly with Mrs. Manley's political writings, but including a comment on the plays.

Manuscripts

3839 Batchelor, G. E. "A Study of the Manuscripts of Theatrical and Dramatic Interest Preserved in the British Museum (1660-1720). M.A. London University (King's), 1929.

3840 -----. "A Study of the Manuscripts of Theatrical and Dramatic Interest Preserved in the British Museum, 1660-1720." Bulletin of the Institute of Historical Research, VIII (1930), 37-38.

3841 Wagner, Bernard M. "Manuscript Plays of the Seventeenth Century." Times Literary Supplement, October 4, 1934, p. 675.

Description and location of several manuscript plays.

3842 Wright, C. E. "Archives of a Printing House." British Museum Quarterly, XX (1956), 30-31.

Indication of the types of holding of the Department of Manuscripts in the area of printing and publishing. Particular attention is given to indicating the scope and types of papers of the William Strahan (printer; 1715-1785) collection.

Maps

3843 Merden, R.. and P. Lea. London Etc., Actually Survey'd, 1682.

Reproduced by the London Typographical Society, 1904.

3844 Moore, J. "Map of London, Westminster, and Southwark." Reproduced by the London Typographical Society, 1912.

Drawn in 1662.

3845 [Craig, Edward Gordon]. "Plan of the Cities of London and Westminster." Mask, XII (April, 1926), 52-65; (July, 1926), 100-103.

Reprints in 16 plates, R. Horwood's 1794 map of London with individual houses; includes numerous detailed comments on people connected with the theatre.

Margate

3846 Bleackley, Horace. "Theatricals in Margate." Notes and Queries,
      11th Ser., I (March 25, 1910), 256.
          A description of the New Theatre in Margate taken from
      Hall's New Margate and Ramsgate Guide for 1790.
3847 Fynmore, R. J. "Theatricals in the Country." Notes and Queries,
      11th Ser., I (January 22, 1910), 65.
          Mr. Mate mentioned in Kentish Tales as being a comedian
      at Theatre Royal in Margate.
3848 M., W. J. "Theatricals in Margate." Notes and Queries, 11th
      Ser., I (February 26, 1910), 167.
          Notes on companies, plays, and theatres (Old Theatre,
      New Theatre, Theatre Royal) at Margate 1730-1787.
3849 Morley, Malcolm. Margate and its Theatres, 1730-1965. London:
      Museum Press, 1966. 176 pp.
          A history of the Theatre Royal; includes illustrations and an
      index of plays.

Marlowe, Christopher

3850 Perkinson, Richard H. "A Restoration 'Improvement' of Doctor
      Faustus." A Journal of English Literary History, I (1934), 305-
      324.
          Shows that Faustus was treated much as some of Shakespeare's
      plays.
3851 Perkinson, Richard Henry. Topographical Comedy in the Seven-
      teenth Century and A Restoration Improvement of "Doctor Faustus,"
      A Portion of Aspects of English Realistic Comedy in the Seven-
      teenth Century. Baltimore: Johns Hopkins University Press,
      1937. 43 pp.
          A selection of characters characteristic of Restoration
      comedy and life found in the realistic comedy of Jacobean and
      Caroline theatres are traced through the drama from Jonson to
      Congreve to demonstrate that comic realism was idealized or
      heightened and therefore cannot be used as documentary evi-
      dence of Restoration life.
3852 Pitcher, Seymour M. "Some observations on the 1663 Edition of
      of Faustus." Modern Language Notes, LVI (December, 1941),
      588-594.
          Argues that the 1663 edition of Faustus gives us the play as
      George Jolly's 'Licensed Players' had staged it, and that Jolly
      prepared the text in deference to the terms of his Grant from
      the King.

Marriage

3853 Vernon, P. F. "The Treatment of Marriage in the Drama, 1660-
      1700." M.A. University College, London, 1958-59.
3854 -----. "Marriage of Convenience and Moral Code of Restoration
      Comedy." Essays in Criticism, XII (1962), 370-387.
      In opposition to former criticism, contends that "Restora-
      tion comedy presupposes a wholly consistent moral standpoint."

Mason, William

3855 Draper, John W. "The Life and Works of William Mason." Ph.D.
      Harvard University, 1920.
3856 -----. William Mason: a Study in Eighteenth-Century Culture.
      New York: New York University Press, 1924. 413 pp.
      William Mason, author of two tragedies modelled on the
      Greek--Elfrida and Caractacus--and an associate of Johnson
      and Reynolds was fairly representative of the "commonplace
      of his period and social class."
3857 Whibley, Leonard, editor. The Correspondence of Richard Hurd
      and William Mason and Letters of Richard Hurd to Thomas
      Gray. With an introduction and notes by the late Ernest Harold
      Pearce. Edited with additional notes. Cambridge: University
      Press, 1932. xxxi, 179 pp.
      This was intended to be part of a "life" of Richard Hurd.
      The letters, including many literary (and dramatic) references,
      are arranged in two basic groups: those of Hurd to Mason and
      to Gray (1747-1775) and those of Hurd to Mason and Mason to
      Hurd (1788-1797). Appendices include letters written after
      Mason's death and "Manuscripts of Poems by Gray and Mason."
3858 Gaskell, Philip. The First Editions of William Mason. Cambridge:
      Bowes & Bowes, 1951. xiv, 41 pp. (Cambridge Bibliographical
      Society. Monograph No. 1).
3859 Lewis, W. S., Grover Cronin, Jr., and Charles H. Bennett,
      editors. Horace Walpole's Correspondence with William Mason.
      2 vols. New Haven: Yale University Press, 1955. (The Yale
      Edition of Horace Walpole's Correspondence, edited by W. S.
      Lewis, vols. 28 and 29).
      The complete correspondence, thoroughly annotated, print-
      ing five of Mason's letters and one of Walpole's for the first
      time. Contains criticism of several contemporary plays,
      discussion of Greek drama, of Shakespeare, of the state of
      contemporary theatre, and comments on numerous dramatists.

Massinger, Philip

3860 McManaway, James G. "Philip Massinger and the Restoration
      Drama." A Journal of English Literary History, I (1934), 276-
      304.

3861 -----. The Plays of Philip Massinger; Stage History and Adapta-
      tions, 1660-1722. Baltimore, 1934. 28 pp. (Reprinted from
      A Journal of English Literary History, I, No. 3 [December,
      1934]).
          Covers the stage history of Massinger's plays and of alter-
      ations and adaptations of his works. Appendix I contains a
      comparison of readings in the four quartos of The Virgin Martyr
      to show that the quarto of 1661 was printed from that of 1651.
      Appendix II covers misplaced speech tags in The Canterbury
      Guests.

3862 Ball, Robert Hamilton. The Amazing Career of Sir Giles Over-
      reach. Princeton: Princeton University Press, 1939. xiv,
      467 pp.
          Organized as a biography of the leading character in Mas-
      singer's A New Way to Pay Old Debts, this book traces the
      stage history of the play in England and America from its
      original performance into the twentieth century. In Chapters II
      and III, the author analyzes English performances during the
      Restoration and 18th century.

3863 Kermode, J. Frank. "A Note on the History of Massinger's The
      Fatal Dowry in the Eighteenth Century." Notes and Queries,
      CXCII (May 3, 1947), 186-187.
          The quality of Massinger's verse survives the revision of
      Hill in The Insolvent.

Mellon, Harriot

3864 Pearce, Charles E. The Jolly Duchess: Harriot Mellon, After-
      wards Mrs. Coults and the Duchess of St. Albans. London:
      Stanley Paul and Co. [1915]. xx, 332 pp.
          The acting career of Harriot Mellon; many details concern-
      ing the Drury Lane Theatre and the London theatrical world.

Melodrama

3865 Thompson, Alan Reynolds. "A Study of Melodrama as a Dramatic
      Genre." Ph.D. Harvard University, 1926.
          An investigation of the nature and development of melodrama
      in France and England; includes a discussion of the role of the
      heroic drama and sentimental drama in the development of the
      genre.

3866 Mandeville, G. E. "The Origins and Early Development of Melodrama on the London Stage, 1790-1840." M.A. Columbia University, 1946.

3867 Disher, Maurice Willson. Blood and Thunder. Mid-Victorian Melodrama and its Origins. London: Muller, 1949. 280 pp.
Mainly a study of the nineteenth century genre, but making constant allusion to the eighteenth century Gothic mode.

3868 Mandeville, Gloria E. "A Century of Melodrama on the London Stage, 1790-1890." Ph.D. Columbia University, 1954.

3869 Kahan, Stanley. "Pre-Victorian Romantic Melodrama." Ph.D. University of Wisconsin, 1959.

3870 Booth, Michael R. English Melodrama. London: Herbert Jenkins, 1965. 223 pp.
Concentrating on the period 1790-1900, the work discusses melodrama's relationship to previous drama and its social and theatrical background. Includes index and bibliography.

Merry, Robert

3871 Adams, M. Ray. "A Newly Discovered Play of Robert Merry, Written in America." Manuscripts, XII (1961), 20-26.
Manuscripts description, plot summary, and short criticism of Merry's The Tuscan Tournament, a blank verse tragedy, completed on January 2, 1798. In the Manuscript Division of the Library of Congress.

Methodism

3872 Shepherd, T. B. Methodism and the Literature of the Eighteenth Century. London: The Epworth Press [1940]. 286 pp.
A study of the thought and writings of the Wesleys as they influenced the 18th century literary world. Chapter VIII treats Rev. Whitefield's and the Wesleys' attacks on theatre, the counter-attacks by Mrs. Bellamy and Tate Wilkinson, and anti-Methodist references in the theatre itself.

Mickle, William

3873 Taylor, Sister Eustace. William Julius Mickle (1734-1788), a critical study. Washington, D.C., The Catholic University of America, 1937. xi, 242 pp.

Microprint

3874 Hartnoll, Phyllis. "Three Centuries of Drama." Theatre Notebook

XIII (1959), 137.
Describes microprint collection.

Middle Class Drama

3875 Nolte, Fred O. Early Middle Class Drama, 1696-1774. (N.Y.U.
Ottendorfer Memorial Series of Germanic Monographs, XIX).
Lancaster, Pa.: Lancaster Press, 1935. vi, 213 pp.
After establishing a workable definition of the "middle class"
as a social group, Nolte examines plays appearing in England,
France, and Germany to show the nature and critical value of
bourgeois influence upon the drama.

Middle Class Philosophy

3876 Wade, Ira O. "Middle Class Philosophies, Middle-class Philosophy,
in the Drama of the Eighteenth Century." Modern Philology,
XXVI (1928), 215-219.

Middleton, Thomas

3877 Balch, Marston Stevens. "The Dramatic Legacy of Thomas Middleton: a Study of the Use of His Plays from 1627 to 1800." Ph.D.
Harvard University, 1931.
Analyzes adaptations and alterations of Middleton's plays.
The adaptations of each play are discussed separately and
chronologically. Extensive discussion of Restoration and eighteenth-century plays and playwrights.

Mildmay

3878 Ralph, Philip L. "References to the Drama in the Mildmay Diary."
Modern Language Notes, LV (December, 1940), 589-591.

Miller, James

3879 Nichols, Charles W. "A Reverend Alterer of Shakespeare." Modern
Language Notes, XLIV (January, 1929), 30-32.
An attack on Rev. James Miller's 1737 adaptation.
3880 Stewart, Powell. "An Eighteenth-Century Adaptation of Shakespeare."
University of Texas Studies in English, No. 12 (1932), 98-117.
The Universal Passion, based on Much Ado, by the Rev. James
Miller was performed at Drury Lane, Feb. 28, 1737.
3881 Stewart, Walter P. "The Dramatic Career of James Miller." Ph.D.
University of Texas, 1939.

3882 Stewart, Powell. "A Bibliographical Contribution to Biography:
         James Miller's Seasonable Reproof." The Library, 5th series,
         III (March, 1949), 295-298.
              Describes the Rev. James Miller's response (1735) to Bishop
         Gibson's remonstration against him for writing plays.

Miller, Joe

3883 Esar, Evan. "The Legend of Joe Miller." American Book Collector,
         XIII (October, 1962), 11-26.
              Short history of Joe Miller (1684-1738), a comic actor who
         performed at Drury Lane for almost thirty years. The use of
         his name in subsequent jestbooks.

Mills, William

3884 Ferguson, Oliver W. "Partridge's Vile Encomium: Fielding and
         Honest Billy Mills." Philological Quarterly, XLIII (1964), 73-78.
              In Book XVI, Chapter V of Tom Jones, Partridge's praise
         for the actor playing Claudius to Garrick's Hamlet is a refer-
         ence to William Mills, the Claudius at Drury Lane.

Milton, John

bibliography

3885 Thomson, E. N.S. John Milton: A Topical Bibliography. New
         Haven: Yale University Press, 1916.
3886 Carlton, W.N.C. "The First Edition of Milton's Comus, 1637."
         American Collector, V (1927), 107-113.
              Reprints the title-page, and attempts to record all available
         copies (21 in number).
3887 Stevens, David Harrison. Reference Guide to Milton From 1800 to
         The Present Day. Chicago, Illinois: The University of Illinois
         Press, 1930. x, 302 pp.
              2850 numbered entries, which list bibliographies, collected
         works, poetical works, and individual works, as well as
         criticism. A section is devoted to Samson Agonistes. Each
         section is arranged in chronological order. Brief annotations.
3888 Fletcher, Harris Francis. Contributions to A Milton Bibliography
         1800-1930. Being A List of Addenda to Stevens's Reference
         Guide to Milton. [Urbana:] The University of Illinois, 1931.
         166 pp.
              A compilation, in chronological order, of material not found
         in Stevens's work. Only two or three entries which touch on

Samson Agonistes. Annotated.
3889 Stevens, D. H. "Milton, John." The Cambridge Bibliography of
English Literature. Edited by F. W. Bateson. Vol. I. (Cambridge:
Cambridge University Press; New York: Macmillan, 1941), 463-
473.
The 1957 Supplement volume has the Milton bibliography pre-
pared by W. Arthur Turner, Alberta T. Turner, and W. Edson
Richmond, pp. 225-237.
3890 Huckabay, Calvin. John Milton: A Bibliographical Supplement, 1929-
1957. (Duquesne Studies, Philological Series). Pittsburgh: Duquesne
University Press; Louvain: Editions P. Nauwelaerts, 1960. xi, [1],
211 pp.
This bibliography provides a supplement to D. H. Stevens'
Reference Guide to Milton, 1800-1928 and H. F. Fletcher's
Contributions to a Milton Bibliography, 1800-1930.
3891 Stratman, Carl J., C.S.V. "Milton's Samson Agonistes: A Check-
list of Criticism." Restoration and 18th Century Theatre Research, IV (1965), 2-10.
141 entries, arranged in chronological order, from 1751-1964,
of articles, theses, dissertations, and books.
3892 Hanford, James Holly, and Charles W. Crupi. Milton. (Goldentree
Bibliographies). New York: Appleton-Century-Crofts, 1966.
63 pp.
A selective bibliography of primary and secondary materials
for the study of Milton.
3893 Low, Anthony. "Milton Bibliography." Seventeenth Century News,
XXV (1967), 2.
Contributes four items, including essays by Johnson and
Richard Cumberland, as addenda to Carl J. Stratman, C.S.V.,
"Milton's Samson Agonistes: A Checklist of Criticism." Restoration and Eighteenth Century Theatre Research, IV (1965),
2-10.

complete works

3894 Milton, John. The Works of John Milton. General Editor, Frank
Allen Patterson. 18 vols in 21. New York: Columbia University
Press, 1931-1938.

poetical works

3895 -----. The Poetical Works of John Milton. Edited from the Original Texts by the Rev. H. C. Beeching. Oxford: The Clarendon
Press, 1900. xiii, [3], 554 pp.
3896 -----. The Poetical Works of John Milton, With a Memoir and

Critical Remarks on His Genius and Writings by James Montgomery. With an Index to Paradise Lost, Todd's Verbal Index
to All the Poems and a Variorum Selection of Explanatory
Notes by Henry G. Bohn. London: G. Bell & Sons, 1900.

3897 -----. The Complete Poetical Works of John Milton from the Edition of the Rev. H. C. Beeching. London, New York: H. Frowde
1900. vii, [1], 1082 pp.

3898 -----. Poetical Works. Reprinted from the Best Editions, with
Biographical Notice, etc. New York: Hurst & Company [c. 1900]
562 pp.

3899 -----. The Poems of John Milton. London: George Newnes, Ltd.,
1901. [8], 526 pp.

3900 -----. The Poetical Works of John Milton. With Introductions by
David Masson. London: Macmillan and Co., Ltd.; New York:
The Macmillan Company, 1901. xi, 625 [1] pp. (Globe Edition)

3901 -----. English Poems by John Milton. Edited, with Life, Introduction, and Selected Notes by R. C. Browne. New Edition,
with Etymological Notes Revised by Henry Bradley. 2 vols.
Oxford: Clarendon Press, 1901-1902.

3902 -----. The Poetical Works of John Milton. Edited with Critical
Notes by William Addis Wright, M.A. Cambridge: At the University Press, 1903. xxiv, [2], 607 pp.

3903 -----. The Poetical Works of John Milton. Edited, with Memoir,
Introductions, Notes, and an Essay on Milton's English Versi-
fication, by David Masson. 3 vols. London: Macmillan and Co.,
Ltd.; New York: The Macmillan Company, 1903.

3904 -----. The Poetical Works of John Milton. 2 vols. London: Macmillan and Co., Ltd.; New York: The Macmillan Company, 190
Edited by A. W. Pllard, with slight changes, from the text
of David Masson.

3905 -----. The Poetical Works of John Milton. Etchings Mezzotints an
Copper Engravings by William Hyde. [London]: The Astolat Pre
1904. [10], 194 pp.
Follows the Oxford text by Rev. Canon Beeching.

3906 -----. The Poetical Works of John Milton. Edited from the Origina
Texts by the Rev. H. C. Beeching, M. A. London, Edinburgh,
Glasgow, New York, and Toronto: Henry Frowde, 1904. [16],
554 pp. (Oxford Complete Edition).

3907 -----. The Complete Poetical Works of John Milton, from the
Edition of the Rev. H. C. Beeching. London, New York: H.
Frowde, Oxford University Press Warehouse, 1904. 1054 pp.
(The Oxford Miniature Edition).

3908 -----. [Poems of Milton]. With a Critical and Biographical Introduction by Brander Matthews, and a Frontispiece in Color by E
J. Cross. New York and London: The Co-operative Publications

Society [c. 1905]. v, 3, [xxiii]-xxv, [2], 514 pp.

3909 -----. English Poems, by John Milton. Edited, with Life, Introduction, and Selected Notes, by R. C. Browne. New Edition,
with the Etymological Notes Revised by Henry Bradley. 2
vols. Oxford: The Clarendon Press, 1906, '02.

3910 -----. The Poetical Works of John Milton, with Biographical
Introduction and Notes by Arthur Waugh. The "Edina" Edition.
London, Edinburgh: Eyre and Spottiswoode [c. 1906]. x, 596 pp.

3911 -----. The Poetical Works of John Milton. With Introductions by
David Masson. London: Macmillan and Co., Ltd., 1907. xi,
625, [1] pp.
First edition printed, May, 1877.

3912 -----. The Poetical Works of John Milton, with a Life of the
Author and Illustrations. 4 vols. Boston: R. H. Hinkley Com-
pany [c. 1908].
"The Life of Milton," by John Mitford.

3913 -----. The Poetical Works of John Milton. Edited after the
Original Texts by the Rev. H. C. Beeching. London, New York:
H. Frowde, Oxford University Press, 1908. xiii, 554 pp.

3914 -----. The Complete Poems of John Milton, Written in Eng-
lish. With Introduction, Notes, and Illustrations. New York:
P. F. Collier & Son [c. 1909]. [2], 463 pp. (The Harvard
Classics).

3915 -----. The Poetical Works of John Milton, with a Memoir by
James Montgomery and One Hundred and Twenty Engravings
by John Thompson, S. and T. Williams, O. Smith, J. Linton,
etc., from Drawings by William Harvey. 2 vols. London: G.
Bell & Sons, 1910-1912. (Bohn's Standard Library)

3916 -----. The Complete Poetical Works of John Milton, Edited after
the Original Texts by the Rev. H. C. Beeching. London: H.
Frowde, Oxford University Press, 1911. xiii, [3], 554, [2] pp.

3917 -----. The Poetical Works of John Milton. With Introductions by
David Masson. London: Macmillan and Co., 1911. xi, 625, [1] pp.
(Globe edition)

3918 -----. The Poetical Works of John Milton, Edited after the Original
Texts by the Rev. H. C. Beeching, M.A. London, New York:
H. Frowde, Oxford University Press, 1912. xiii, [3], 554 pp.
(Oxford edition)

3919 -----. The Poetical Works of John Milton. London: J. M. Dent &
Sons, Ltd.; New York: E. P. Dutton & Co. [1919]. xvi, 554 pp.
(Everyman)
First issue of this edition, 1909.

3920 -----. The Complete Poetical Works of John Milton, Edited after
the Original Texts by H. C. Beeching, D.D. London, Edinburgh:
H. Milford, Oxford University Press, 1921. xiii, [3], 554, [1] pp.

3921 -----. Poetical Works. With an Introduction by David Masson.
        London: Macmillan, 1922. xi, 625 pp. (Globe edition)
3922 -----. English Poems by John Milton, Edited with Life, Intro-
        duction, and Selected Notes by R. C. Browne. New Edition
        with the Etymological Notes Revised by Henry Bradley. 2 vols.
        Oxford: Clarendon Press [1923].
        First edition, 1870.
3923 -----. The Poems of John Milton. Edited by H. J. C. Grierson.
        2 vols. London: Florence Press, 1925.
3924 -----. Poems in English, with Illustrations by William Blake.
        2 vols. London: The Nonesuch Press, 1926.
3925 -----. The Poetical Works of John Milton. London: J. M. Dent
        & Co.; New York: E. P. Dutton & Co. [1929]. xvi, 554 pp.
        (Everyman)
3926 -----. The Poetical Works. Edited by H. C. Beeching. Oxford:
        University Press, 1938.
3927 -----. The English Poems of John Milton. With an Introduction by
        Charles Williams, and a Reader's Guide to Milton Compiled by
        Walter Skeat. (World's Classic Series.) Oxford: Oxford Uni-
        versity Press; London: Milford, 1940. xxii, 545 pp.
3928 -----. Complete Poetical Works. A New Text Edited with Intro-
        duction and Notes by Harris Francis Fletcher. Cambridge:
        Houghton Mifflin [c. 1941]. x, [3], 574 pp.
        "The new Cambridge edition; a revision of the Cambridge
        edition edited by William Vaughn Moody."
3929 -----. John Milton's Complete Poetical Works, Reproduced in
        Photographic Facsimile. A Critical Text Edition, Compiled and
        Edited by Harris Francis Fletcher. 4 vols. Urbana: The Uni-
        versity of Illinois Press, 1943-1948.
3930 -----. Poems of Mr. John Milton: the 1645 Edition with Essays
        in Analysis. Edited by Cleanth Brooks, and John E. Hardy.
        New York: Harcourt, Brace, 1951.
3931 -----. The Poetical Works of John Milton. Edited by Helen Darb-
        ishire. 2 vols. Oxford: Clarendon Press, 1952-1955.
3932 -----. The Poetical Works of John Milton; with Introductions by
        David Masson. London, New York: Macmillan, 1954. xi, 625,
        [1] pp.
        First edition printed May, 1877. Reprinted June, 1877, etc.
        The Globe edition.
3933 -----. John Milton. Poems. Edited by B. A. Wright. (Everyman's
        Library) London: Dent; New York: Dutton, 1956.
3934 -----. The Complete English Poetry of John Milton (Excluding
        His Translations of Psalms 80-88). New York: New York Uni-
        versity Press, 1963.
3935 -----. The Complete Poetical Works of John Milton. Edited by

Douglas Bush. Boston: Houghton Mifflin, 1965. (Cambridge
Edition)

poetry and prose

3936 -----. The Student's Milton. Being the Complete Poems of John
      Milton, with the Greater Part of His Prose Works, Now Printed
      in One Volume, Together with New Translations into English of
      His Italian, Latin, and Greek Poems, Edited by Frank Allen
      Patterson. New York: Printed for F. S. Crofts &Co., 1930.
      ix, 1090, 41 pp.

3937 -----. The Student's Milton, Being the Complete Poems of John
      Milton, with the Greater Part of His Prose Works, Now Printed
      in One Volume, Together with New Translations into English of
      His Italian, Latin and Greek Poems. Revised Edition. Edited by
      Frank Allen Patterson. New York: Crofts, 1933.
          First published in 1930.

3938 -----. Milton. Complete Poetry & Selected Prose, with English
      Metrical Translations of the Latin, Greek, and Italian Poems.
      Edited by E. H. Vesiak with a Foreword by Sir Arnold Wilson.
      [London]: The Nonesuch Press [c. 1938]. xxvii, 860 pp.

3939 -----. The Student's Milton; Being the Complete Poems of John
      Milton with the Greater Part of His Prose Works, Now Printed
      in One Volume, Together with New Translations into English
      of His Italian, Latin, and Greek Poems, Edited by Frank Allen
      Patterson. Revised Edition. New York: Printed for F. S. Crofts,
      1947. liv, 1176, 119 pp.

3940 -----. Complete Poetry and Selected Prose; with English Metrical
      Translations of the Latin, Greek and Italian Poems, Edited by
      E. H. Visiak; with a Foreword by Sir Arnold Wilson, M.P.
      [London]: The Nonesuch Press, 1948. xxxii, 860 pp.

3941 -----. Complete Poetry and Selected Prose of John Milton. New
      York: The Modern Library [1948]. vi, 756 pp.

3942 -----. The Student's Milton; Being the Complete Poems of John
      Milton with the Greater Part of His Prose Works, Now Printed
      in One Volume, Together with New Translations into English
      of His Italian, Latin, and Greek Poems, Edited by Frank Allen
      Patterson. Revised Edition. New York: Appleton-Century Crofts
      [c. 1948]. liv, 1176, 119 pp.

3943 -----. Complete Poetry and Selected Prose. Introduction by
      Cleanth Brooks. New York: Modern Library [c. 1950]. xxiv,
      756 pp.

3944 -----. Complete Poems and Major Prose. Edited by Merritt Y.
      Hughes, with Notes and Introduction. New York: Odyssey Press,
      1957. xix, 1059 pp.

selected works

3945 -----. Samson Agonistes and English Sonnets. Introduction and
Notes by A. M. Percival. Sonnets, edited by W. Bell. New
York: Macmillan, 1931. xlviii, 219 pp.
A reprint of Stevens' No. 1141.

3946 -----. Paradise Regained, the Minor Poems and Samson Agonistes.
Edited by Merritt Y. Hughes. New York: Odyssey Press, 1937.
lxiii, 633 pp.
An authoritative, scholarly edition which includes a fully
annotated text of Samson Agonistes.

3947 -----. Milton's Dramatic Poems. Edited by Geoffrey and Margaret
Bullough. London: Athlone Press, University of London; Fair
Lawn, N. J.: Essential Books, 1958. 224 pp.
Text of "Arcades," "Comus," and "Samson Agonistes,"
based on the 1645 and 1671 editions, with introduction and com-
mentary.

3948 -----. Arcades and Comus. With Preface by Giovanna Foa. Milano:
La goliardica, 1964. 49 pp.

individual texts

3949 -----. Comus: A Mask. With Eight Illustrations by William Blake.
Preface by Darrell Figis. London: Ernest Benn, 1926. xxiv, 35 pp.
Reprints the edition of 1645.

3950 -----. The Masque of Comus. The Poem by John Milton, with a
Preface by Mark Van Doren. The Airs by Henry Lawes. With a
Preface by Hubert Foss. Illustrated with Water-Colors by Edmund
Dulac. Cambridge: Printed for the Members of The Limited Editions Club At the University Press, 1954. [8], 57, [15] pp.
The text is from the definitive one of 1673, the minor poems,
with the spelling modernized. The words of the songs have been
transcribed mainly from the British Museum text, after collation
with the Lawes one. Textual notes on the songs are included.

3951 -----. Samson Agonistes. Edited by E. H. Blakeney. Edinburgh
and London: William Blackwood and Sons, 1902. xxxiv, 129 pp.
The text is that of Masson's collated with Beeching's Oxford
Milton. A student's edition.

3952 -----. "Samson Agonistes" by John Milton. With Introduction,
Notes, and Glossary. Edited by A. J. Grieve. London: Dent &
Co., [1904]. xiv, 90 pp.

3953 -----. Samson Agonistes. With Introduction, Notes, Glossary
and Indexes by A. W. Verity. Third Reprint of the First Edition of 1892. Cambridge: At the University Press, 1910. 168 pp.
The text is "that of the first edition (1671), compared with

the second edition (1680)." An appendix "Milton and Vondel"
answers Ed. Munden's charge that Milton was under great
obligations to four works by Vondel.

3954 -----. "Samson Agonistes. Types of Philosophic Drama. Edited
by Robert Metcalf Smith. (New York: Prentice Hall, Inc.,
1928), [227]-283.

A brief introduction discussing Samson Agonistes as a
philosophical drama precedes an unedited reprint of the text.

3955 samson agonistes a dramatic poem the author john milton.
florence: stamperia del santuccio, 1930/31. 76 pp.

Printed in semi-uncial characters without capitals.

3956 Milton, John. Samson Agonistes: A Dramatic Poem. With wood
engravings by Robert A. Maynard. Harrow Weald: Raven Press,
1931. xi, 63 pp.

3957 -----. Samson Agonistes. Printed under the direction of Victor
Hammer. Florence: Stamperia del Santuccio, 1931.

3958 -----. Milton's Samson Agonistes, with Introduction, Notes,
Glossary and Indexes by A. W. Verity. Cambridge: Cambridge
University Press, 1932.

A reprint of Stevens' No. 1142.

3959 -----. Samson Agonistes. Edited by A. J. Wyatt and A. J. F.
Collins. The Sonnets. Edited by A. R. Weeks. London: University Tutorial Press, 1932. viii, 160 pp.

3960 -----. Samson Agonistes. A Dramatic Poem. The Author John
Milton. Florence: Stamperia del Santuccio, 1933.

3961 -----. Samson Agonistes. Edited by John Churton Collins. Oxford: Clarendon Press, 1935. 94 pp.

A reprint of an edition first published in 1883. The text
was apparently taken from the 1671 edition.

3962 -----. Samson Agonistes. Edited with Introduction and Notes by
John Churton Collins. Oxford: Clarendon Press, 1938. 94 pp.

A reprint of Stevens' No. 1139.

3963 -----. Samson Agonistes. Edited by F. T. Prince, with an Introduction, Notes, and Appendices. London and New York: Oxford University Press, 1957.

3964 -----. John Milton's "Samson Agonistes": The Poem and Materials
for Analysis. Edited by Ralph E. Hone. San Francisco: Changler
Publishing Company, 1966. 284 pp.

Includes the text of the play, previous versions of the Samson story in the Bible, criticism of the play, and an appendix
with suggested topics for study.

prefaces

3965 -----. "Preface to Samson Agonistes." Critical Essays of the

Seventeenth Century. Edited by J. E. Spingarn. Vol. 1. (Oxford: At the Clarendon Press, 1909), 207-209.

3966 -----. "The Preface to Samson Agonistes." Literary Criticism, Plato to Dryden. Edited by Allan H. Gilbert. (New York: American Book Company, 1940), 592-594.

3967 -----. From the "Preface to Samson Agonistes." The Art of Literary Criticism. Edited by Paul Robert Lieder, and Robert Withington. (New York and London: D. Appleton-Century Company, 1941), 167-168.

3968 -----. "Samson Agonistes. Preface." Dramatic Essays of the Neoclassic Age. Edited by Henry Hitch Adams, and Baxter Hathaway. (New York: Columbia University Press, 1950), 118-120.

3969 -----. "Preface to Samson Agonistes." Criticism: The Major Texts. Edited by Walter Jackson Bate. (New York: Harcourt, Brace and Company, 1952), 121.

translations

3970 -----. L'Allegro, il Penseroso et Samson Agonistes. Tr. avec une introd. par Floris Delattre. Paris: Aubier, 1937. xcii, 151 pp.
Has a critical and historical essay on Samson. Reprinted, 1945.

3971 -----. Liriche e drammi. Trans. and ed. by Alberto Castelli. Milan: Montuoro, 1941. 228 pp.
Includes Samson Agonistes.

3972 -----. Samsone agonista, Sonetti. Versione col testo a fronte, introduzuone e nota a cura di Carlo Izzo. Florence: G. C. Sansoni, 1948. xli, 272 pp.

3973 -----. Samson. Trans. by Tihamer Dybas. Budapest: Uj Magyar Kiado, 1955. 111 pp.

biography and criticism

3974 Beerbohm, Max. "Samson Agonistes and Zaza." Saturday-Review (London), LXXXIX (April, 1900), 489.

3975 Fränkel, Ludwig. "Klassisches (Shakespeare, Milton) auf der heutigen Londoner Bühne." Englische Studien, XXVIII (1900), 479-480.

3976 "Puritan Drama." Academy, LVIII (1900), 317-318.
Treats Samson Agonistes.

3977 Ross, H. V. "Samson Agonistes: Its Autobiographical Character and Its Relation to Greek Drama." Ph.D. Cornell University, 1900.

3978 "Samson Agonistes and Zaza." The Saturday Review, LXXXIX (April 21, 1900), 489.

A comparison of Milton's Samson Agonistes and Belasco's
Zaza which charges that both are failures. Milton's play has
no dramatic quality, no organic life, no progress, "all is static,
marmoreal."

3979 Garnett, R. [An emendation by M. W. Sampson of Samson Agonistes,
1. 218]. Athenaeum, December 28, 1901. p. 878.
3980 Sampson, George. "Emendation in Milton's Samson." Athenaeum,
January 11, 1902, p. 50.
3981 Bridges, Robert. "Extraordinary." Athenaeum, July 18, 1903, pp.
93-94.
Treats Samson Agonistes.
3982 Dupuy, Ernest. "Les origines littéraires d'Alfred de Vigny."
Revue d'histoire littéraire de la France, X (1903), 373-412.
Has a discussion of Samson Agonistes.
3983 Brown, John Macmillan. The "Samson Agonistes" of Milton. London: Whitcombe and Tombs Limited [1905]. 135 pp.
3984 Strengers, Jeanne. "Le Samson de Milton et de Vondel." Revue
de l'université de Bruxelles, X (1905), 261-284.
3985 Van Steenderen, F. C. L. "Vondel's Place As a Tragic Poet."
Publications of the Modern Language Association, XX (1905),
546-566.
Treats Samson Agonistes.
3986 Cook, Albert S. Samson Agonistes, 11. 1665-66. Modern
Language Notes, XXI (1906), 78.
3987 Jebb, Sir Richard Claverhouse. "Samson Agonistes and the
Hellenic Drama." Proceedings of the British Academy, III
(1908), 341-348.
3988 Moore Smith, G. C. "Milton's Samson Agonistes." Modern Language Review, III (1908), 74.
3989 Rible, Blanch. "Euripidean Influences in Samson Agonistes."
M.A. Stanford University, 1910.
3990 Bense, J. F. "The Conduct of 'The Attendant Spirit' in Comus."
Englische Studien, XLVI (1912-1913), 333-335.
Defends conduct of The Attendant Spirit after the Lady has
fallen into the hands of Comus.
3991 Cook, Albert Stanburrough. "Milton's View of the Apocalypse as
a Tragedy." Archiv für das Studium der neueren Sprachen und
Literaturen, CXXIX (1912), 74-80.
Treats of Samson Agonistes.
3992 Condell, Kathleen. "Samson Agonistes and Prometheus Bound:
A Comparison." M.A. McMaster University, 1913. 65 pp.
3993 Gilbert, Allan H. "Samson Agonistes, 1096." Modern Language
Notes, XXIX (June, 1914), 161-162.
Defends reading "with other arms" of the earliest printed
edition, instead of "wish other arms" of some editions.

3994 Epps, P. H. "Two Notes on English Classicism." Studies in
     Philology, XIII (1916), 190-196.
       Treats Samson Agonistes.
3995 Thompson, Edward J. "Samson Agonistes: Criticism." London
     Quarterly Review, CXXV (1916), 244-254.
3996 Gilbert, Allan H. "Milton on the Position of Woman." Modern
     Language Review, XV (1920), 7-27, 240-264.
       Part I (pp. 7-27) treats Milton's prose works; Part II (pp.
       240-264) his poetry. The first section of Part II (pp. 240-244)
       discusses the character of Dalila in Samson Agonistes.
3997 Himes, John A. "Some Interpretations of Milton." Modern Lan-
     guage Notes, XXXV (1920), 441-442.
       Himes disagrees with accepted interpretations of words and
       passages in Lycidas, Comus, and "On the Death of a Fair In-
       fant."
3998 Thaler, Alwin. "Milton in the Theatre." Studies in Philology, XVII
     (1920), 269-308.
       A discussion of Miltonic adaptations in the theatre from the
       early 18th through mid-19th centuries: the article focusses on
       the methods of adaptation.
3999 Tupper, James Waddell. "The Dramatic Structure of Samson
     Agonistes." Publications of the Modern Language Association,
     XXXV (1920), 375-389.
       An article in support of Samuel Johnson's criticism that
       Samson Agonistes' plot lacks a "middle."
4000 Baum, Paull Franklin. "Samson Agonistes Again." Publications of
     the Modern Language Association, XXXVI (September, 1921),
     354-371.
       A discussion of Samson Agonistes in terms of Aristotle's
       statements on plot in response to Johnson's criticism that the
       play is not a dramatic whole in the Aristotelian sense.
4001 Draper, J. W. "Aristotelian Mimesis in Eighteenth-Century
     England." Publications of the Modern Language Association,
     XXXVI (1921), 372-400.
       Believing "mimesis" to mean "creating according to a true
       idea," Draper points out that in the first half of the 18th century,
       English writers interpeted the term as mere "imitation."
4002 Hanford, James Holly. "Milton and Ochino." Modern Language Notes,
     XXXVI (1921), 121-122.
       Milton probably did not know Ochino and therefore was not
       indebted to him at all for his concept of the Trinity.
4003 Himes, John A. "Further Interpretations of Milton." Modern
     Language Notes, XXXVI (1921), 414-419.
       Interpretations of lines and words in Milton, with general
       evaluations as well.

4004 Thompson, Elbert N. S. "Milton's Part in Theatrum Poetarum."
Modern Language Notes, XXXVI (1921), 18-21.
A discussion of the influence of Milton's first published work
on Edward Philip's (Milton's nephew) statements in Theatrum
Poetarum Anglicanorum, with the conclusion that Warton exag-
gerated Milton's influence.

4005 Emerson, Oliver Farrar. "Milton's Comus, 93-94." Modern
Language Notes, XXXVII (1922), 118-120.
An interpretation. See the articles in Modern Language Notes,
by John H. Hines (XXXV, 1930, p. 441), (XXXVI, 1921, p. 414),
and James Holly Hanford (XXXVI, 1921, pp. 121-122).

4006 Havens, Raymond Dexter. The Influence of Milton on English Poetry.
Cambridge: Harvard University Press, 1922. 734 pp.
Only five pages are devoted to the influence of Comus and
Samson Agonistes; Havens concludes that neither was very in-
fluential on other writers.

4007 Knowlton, Edgar Colby. "Causality in Samson Agonistes." Modern
Language Notes, XXXVII (June, 1922), 333-339.
An attempt to refute Baums's view (q.v.) that Samson Agonistes lacks conflict which is the essence of tragic action; the
author, asserting that the value of tragedy depends on causality,
discusses the operation of causal relations in Samson Agonistes.

4008 Ker, William Paton. "Samson Agonistes" in The Art of Poetry:
Seven Lectures, 1920-1922. Oxford: at the Clarendon Press,
1923. 160 pp.
A discussion of the form of Milton's play, which concentrates
on the character of Samson.

4009 Visiak, Edward Harold. Milton Agonistes, A Metaphysical Criticism. London: A. M. Philpot, Ltd. [1923]. 104 pp.

4010 Curry, Walter Clyde. "Samson Agonistes Yet Again." Sewanee
Review, XXXII (July, 1924), 336-352.

4011 Kilgo, J. W. "Hebrew Samson and Milton's Samson." Methodist
Quarterly Review, LXXIII (1924), 312-316.

4012 Langdon, Ida. Milton's Theory of Poetry and Fine Art. An Essay;
with a Collection of Illustrative Passages from His Works. New
Haven: Yale University Press, 1924. 342 pp.
Chapter IV, "Milton and the Drama," (pp. 83-123) is primarily concerned with Milton's attitudes toward dramatic theory (the
Unities, the Tragic Form); illustrations from Samson Agonistes
are used. Also considers allusions to drama in Milton's work.

4013 Saurat, Denis. Milton: Man and Thinker. London: Jonathan Cape,
1924. 363 pp.
Samson Agonistes is treated as part of the consideration of
Milton's Great Poems. Saurat contends that Samson is a three-
fold picture of life--man's life in general, the history of England,

and Milton's own life.

4014 Brie, F. "Das Märchen von Childe Rowland und sein Nachleben." Palaestra, CXLVIII (1925), 118-143.

Relationship to Comus.

4015 Hanford, James H. "Samson Agonistes and Milton in Old Age." Studies in Shakespeare, Milton, and Donne, By Members of the English Department of the University Of Michigan. (New York: Macmillan, 1925), 167-189.

Dates Samson 1665-1671, and sees it as Milton's most autobiographical work.

4016 Thaler, Alwin. "The Shakesperian Element in Milton." Publications of the Modern Language Association, XL (September, 1925), 645-691.

Lists parallel passages from Shakespeare's plays and Milton's, including Comus and a few from Samson Agonistes, many of them unconvincing.

4017 Chapman, R. W. "Misprints in Comus." Times Literary Supplement, April 8, 1926, p. 264.

Replies to TLS, April 1, 1926, that misprints in the "Julian" Comus are the silent corrections intended.

4018 Hanford, James H. A Milton Handbook. New York: Appleton-Century-Crofts, 1926. 304 pp.

A section devoted to Samson Agonistes and Paradise Regained.

4019 "The Julian Comus." Times Literary Supplement, April 1, 1926, p. 246.

Reviews Milton's Comus, Preface by Darrell Figis (1926). Points out misprints and other editorial errors.

4020 Kreipe, Christian E. Milton's Samson Agonistes. Halle: Niemeyer, 1926. ix, 70 pp.

Argues that the play reflects Milton's own life, character, and feelings. Little new material.

4021 Powell, Chilton L. "Milton Agonistes." Sewanee Review, XXXIV (April-June, 1926), 169-183.

A treatment of Samson Agonistes.

4022 Taylor, George Coffin. "Shakespeare and Milton Again." Studies in Philology, XXIII (April, 1926), 189-199.

Discusses Shakespearean influences in Comus and Samson Agonistes.

4023 Brewer, Wilmon. "Two Athenian Models for Samson Agonistes." Publications of the Modern Language Association, XLII (December, 1927), 910-920.

Notes striking structural parallels between Samson Agonistes and Prometheus Bound and the Oedipus at Colonus.

4024 Clark, Evert M. "Milton's Earlier Samson." University of Texas

Studies in English, No. 7 (November 15, 1927), 144-154.
Milton tells the story to illustrate a point in The Reason of
Church Government; Samson is the King, seduced by "the
strumpet flatteries of prelates."

4025 Fletcher, Harris F. "Milton's Use of Biblical Quotations." Journal
of English and Germanic Philology, XXVI (1927), 145-165.
Considers Samson Agonistes.

4026 Fretz, Grace Faulks. "Samson Agonistes: An Appreciation."
Methodist Review, CX (January-February, 1927), 103-108.
Samson Agonistes was written entirely from inner prompt-
ings, to oppose the immorality of the Restoration plays being
staged.

4027 Stevens, David Harrison. "The Bridgewater Manuscript of Comus."
Modern Philology, XXIV (February, 1927), 315-320.
Reflects Henry Lawes' alterations for staging; the Trinity
College draft remains of higher authority.

4028 Welsford, Enid. The Court Masque. Cambridge: Cambridge University Press, 1927.
Treats Comus.

4029 Clark, Evert M. "Milton's Conception of Samson." University of
Texas Studies in English, No. 8 (July 8, 1928), 88-99.
Milton sees Samson as beginning and ending his career as
"the approved and irresistible champion of God."

4030 Morgan, Tess. "The Relation of Samson Agonistes to Greek
Drama." M.A. State University of Iowa, 1928.

4031 Saltzman, Katherine Eleanor. "The Influence of the Dramatic
Theory and Practice of the Greeks on Milton's Samson Agonistes." M.A. State University of Iowa, 1928.

4032 Thaler, Alwin. Shakespeare's Silences. Cambridge: Harvard University Press, 1929.
Includes two essays on Milton, "The Shakespearean Element
in Milton," (pp. 139-208): "Milton in the Theatre," (pp. 209-
256).

4033 Collins, E. J. "The Biographical Influence on Paradise Lost,
Paradise Regained, and Samson Agonistes." M.A. Ohio State
University, 1930.

4034 Grierson, H. J. C. "A Note upon the Samson Agonistes of John
Milton and Sampson of Heilige Wraeck by Joost van den Vondel."
Mélanges d'histoire littéraire générale... offerts à Fernand
Baldensperger. (Paris, Champion, 1930), 332-339.
Reprinted in Essays and Addresses. London: Chatto and
Windus, 1940. pp. 55-64.

4035 Shapcott, G. M. "A Study of the Workings of Milton's Imagination
As Revealed in the Portrayal of the Chief Characters in Paradise
Lost, Paradise Regained and Samson Agonistes." M.A. London

University (Bedford), 1930.

4036 Jones, Nita Robinson. "The Influence of Greek Tragedy on Milton's Samson Agonistes." M.A. University of Illinois, 1931.

4037 Kaler, Frank Henri. "Milton's Samson Agonistes and the Greek Drama." M.A. University of Illinois, 1931.

4038 Fowler, Louis Heath. "Samson Agonistes." M.A. McMaster University, 1932. 27 pp.

4039 Hall, Alfreda Carlotta Natalie. "I. The Biblical Elements in Milton's Paradise Regained. II. The Classical Features in Milton's Samson Agonistes. III. A Summary of Milton's Second Defence of the People of England." M.A. McMaster University, 1933.

4040 Legett, Elva. "The Dramatic Poems of John Milton." M.A. Louisiana State University, 1933.

4041 Parker, W. R. "A Critical Study of Milton's Samson Agonistes." B. Litt. Oxford University, 1934.

4042 -----. "The Greek Spirit in Milton's Samson Agonistes." Essays and Studies, XX (1934), 21-44.
Defines "Greek spirit" as a combination of two tones: one resulting from "artistic principles" and technique, the other arising from ideas expressed. Such a tonal analysis applied to Samson leads to a definition of the essential "Greekness" of the play and to commentary on its philosophy, theology, and theme.

4043 Belloc, Hilaire. Milton. London: Cassell, 1935. 313 pp.
Includes a brief, superficial comparative analysis of Samson Agonistes and Greek tragedy.

4044 Deleted.

4045 Parker, William Riley. "The 'Kommos' of Milton's Samson Agonistes." Studies in Philology, XXXII (1935), 240-244.

4046 -----. "Symmetry in Milton's Samson Agonistes." Modern Language Notes, L (1935), 355-360.

4047 -----. "Trinity Manuscript and Milton's Plans for a Tragedy." Journal of English and Germanic Philology, XXXIV (1935), 225-232.
Treats Samson Agonistes.

4048 Timberlake, P. W. "Milton and Euripides." Parrott Presentation Volume. (Princeton, New Jersey: Princeton University Press, 1935), 315-340.
Treats Samson Agonistes.

4049 Galland, René. "Milton et Buchanan." Revue Anglo-Americaine, XIII (1936), 326-333.
Gives parallels between Samson Agonistes and Buchanan's Baptistes, sive Calumnia.

4050 Gilbert, K. W. "Aesthetic Imitation and Imitators in Aristotle."

Philosophical Review, LXV (1936), 558-573.
Treats Samson Agonistes.
4051 Jones, Nita Robinson. "The Influence of Greek Tragedy on Milton's
Samson Agonistes." M.A. University of Oklahoma, 1936.
4052 Kirkpatrick, Olive Ann. "Samson Agonistes in Relation to Its
Historical Background." M.A. University of Illinois, 1936.
4053 Summers, S. E. "A Study of Milton's Dramatic Works." M.A.
University of Missouri, 1936.
4054 Adler, E. N. "Milton's Harapha." Times Literary Supplement,
January 16, 1937, p. 44.
4055 Chan, ShanWing. "Nineteenth-Century Literary Criticism of
Paradise Lost, Paradise Regained, and Samson Agonistes."
Ph.D. Stanford University, 1937.
4056 Leveen, Jacob. "Milton's Harapha." Times Literary Supplement,
January 23, 1937, p. 60.
4057 Loane, George G. "Shakespeare, Milton and Pope." Times Literary Supplement, January 23, 1937, p. 60.
4058 Loewe, H. "Milton's Harapha." Times Literary Supplement,
January 23, 1937, p. 60.
4059 McManaway, James G. "Milton and Harrington." Times Literary
Supplement, February 20, 1937, p. 131.
Touches on Samson Agonistes.
4060 Parker, William Riley. Milton's Debt to Greek Tragedy in "Samson
Agonistes." Baltimore: Johns Hopkins Press, 1937. xvi, 260 pp.
A detailed and probing study of the relation between Samson
and Greek tragedy in terms of the play's general conformity to
the classical pattern and its specific "debts" to particular plays.
The author concludes that the influence of Sophocles predominates,
and that the play is actually a re-creation of Greek art.
4061 -----. "Milton's Harapha." Times Literary Supplement, January
2, 1937, p. 12.
4062 -----. "'Misogyny' in Milton's Samson Agonistes." Philological
Quarterly, XVI (1937), 139-144.
Argues that expressions of misogyny in the play do not
necessarily reflect Milton's own attitudes; instead, such at-
tidues are essential to those aspects of the drama where they
appear.
4063 -----. "Tragic Irony in Milton's Samson Agonistes." Etudes
Anglaises, I (1937), 314-320.
Professor Parker distinguishes the two kinds of irony used
by Sophocles, which he calls conscious and unconscious,
and then he cites passages to reveal the same kind of irony
in Milton's play.
4064 Wilson, J. Dover. "Shakespeare, Milton and Congreve." Times
Literary Supplement, January 16, 1937, p. 44.

A passage in Samson Agonistes, believed to have been drawn
from Shakespeare, also appears in The Way of the World.

4065 Young, G. M. "Milton and Harrington." Times Literary Suppleme
January 9, 1937, p. 28.
The ship-woman image in Milton and Harrington--Samson
Agonistes.

4066 Stephenson, Andrew. "Samson Agonistes." Theatre Arts Monthly,
XXII (1938), 914-916.

4067 Tillyard, E. M. W. The Miltonic Setting: Past and Present. Cambridge: Cambridge University Press, 1938. xi, 208 pp.
An eclectic critical study of the poetry and its milieu with
some commentary on Samson Agonistes.

4068 Bonk, Sister Eleonore, C. S. C. "Milton's Debt to Aristotle's
Poetics in Samson Agonistes." M.A. De Paul University, 1939.

4069 Dodds, M. H. "Chaucer: Spenser: Milton in Drama and Fiction."
Notes and Queries, CLXXVI (1939), 69.

4070 McColley, Grant. "Milton's Lost Tragedy." Philological Quarterly
XVIII (1939), 78-83.
Feels that Milton drafted a tragedy that is different from the
drafts in the Trinity manuscripts.

4071 Morand, Paul P. De Comus à Satan: L'oeuvre poétique de John
Milton expliquée par sa vie. Paris: Didier, 1939.

4072 Parkinson, Mabel Bobin. "Milton: the Drama and the Theatre."
M.A. University of Alabama, 1939.
Considers Samson Agonistes.

4073 Finney, Gretchen Ludke. "Comus, Drama per Musica." Studies
in Philology, XXXVII (1940), 482-500.

4074 Grierson, Sir Herbert John Clifford. Essays and Addresses. London: Chatto and Windus, 1940. 274 pp.
A consideration is devoted to Samson Agonistes.

4075 Woodhouse, A. S. P. "The Argument of Milton's Comus." University of Toronto Quarterly, XI (1941), 46-71.

4076 Le Comte, Edward. "New Light on the Haemony Passage in Comus
Philological Quarterly, XXI (1942), 283-298.

4077 Sams, Alma F. "Samson Agonistes: Its Date and Fallacies in the
Autobiographical Interpretation." M.A. Duke University, 1942.

4078 Finney, Gretchen L. "Chorus in Samson Agonistes." Publications
of the Modern Language Association, LVIII (1943), 649-664.
Samson Agonistes and Italian dramatic background.

4079 Boughner, Daniel C. "Milton's Harapha and Renaissance Comedy."
English Literary History, XI (1944), 297-306.
Treats Samson Agonistes.

4080 Sensabaugh, George F. "The Milieu of Comus." Studies in Philolo
XLI (1944), 238-249.

4081 Ellis-Fermor, Una. "Samson Agonistes and Religious Drama."

The Frontiers of Drama. (London: Methuen, 1945), 17-33.

4082 Womack, Lucille. "A General Commentary on Samson Agonistes."
M.A. Emory University, 1945.

4083 Ellis-Fermor, Una. "Samson Agonistes and Religious Drama."
The Frontiers of Drama. (New York: Oxford University Press,
1946), 17-33.
Makes a distinction between religious drama, wherein she
places Milton's play and tragedy.

4084 Little, Marguerite. "Some Italian Elements in the Choral Practice
of Samson Agonistes." Ph.D. University of Illinois, 1946.

4085 Bruser, Fredelle. "Comus and the Rose Song." Studies in Philology,
XLIV (October, 1947), 625-644.
Discusses the tradition of carpe diem and notes Milton's
partial reconciliation of the thorny path and the "roses along
the way."

4086 Little, Arthur. The Nature of Art or the Shield of Passas. London:
Longmans, 1947. x, 264 pp.
Includes comments on Samson Agonistes in its thesis that
the essence of the artistic process is contemplation of the soul.

4087 Burke, Kenneth. "The Imagery of Killing." Hudson Review, I
(1948), 151-167.
Milton brings together, in Samson Agonistes, images of the
suicide and of warlike death.

4088 Farnham-Flower, F. E. "Samson Agonistes and Milton." Times
Literary Supplement, August 21, 1948, p. 471.
Comment on R. Flatter's theory, which appeared in the
Times Literary Supplement for August 7, 1948.

4089 Flatter, R. "Samson Agonistes and Milton." Times Literary Sup-
plement, August 7, 1948, p.443; September 4, 1948, p. 499.
Samson's destruction of the temple is an oblique allusion to
Milton's intended publication of De Doctrina Christiana.

4090 Kelley, Maurice. "Samson Agonistes and Milton." Times Literary
Supplement, August 21, 1948, p. 471.
Lines 1423-1426 in the play.

4091 Maxwell, J. C. "The Pseudo-Problem of Comus." Cambridge
Journal, I (1948), 376-380.

4092 Williams, Arnold. "A Note on Samson Agonistes, 90 - 4." Modern
Language Notes, LXIII (December, 1948), 537.
Illustrates the passage by reference to Christian views on
the location of the soul.

4093 Allen, Don Cameron. "Milton's Comus as a Failure in Artistic
Compromise." English Literary History, XVI (1949), 104-119.
Milton's stated theme of chastity is not as crucial as the
theme of temptation--the conflict between the moral purpose
and the dramatic intensity is not resolved.

4094 French, J. Milton, ed. The Life Records of John Milton. 5 vols. New Brunswick, New Jersey: Rutgers University Press, 1949-1958.

4095 Gilbert, Allan H. "Is Samson Agonistes Unfinished?" Philological Quarterly, XXVIII (1949), 98-106.
Argues that Samson Agonistes is an early work of Milton's which did not receive his final revisions. Uses Milton's "Argument" for the play as evidence.

4096 Kirkconnell, Watson. "Six Sixteenth-Century Forerunners of Milton's Samson Agonistes." Transactions of the Royal Society of Canada, 3rd Series, XLIII (1949), 73-85.
Gives the analogues.

4097 Krouse, F. Michael. Milton's Samson and the Christian Tradition. Princeton: Princeton University Press, 1949. viii, 159 pp.
A detailed analysis of the theological background to Samson Agonistes, showing the way in which Milton develops his idea of a Christian Hero.

4098 Mathies, Maria Dorner. "Untersuchungen zu Milton's Samson Agonistes." Inaugural Dissertation. Hamburg, 1949. 271 pp.

4099 McCall, Lois G. "Imagery and Symbolism in Samson Agonistes." M.A. Mt. Holyoke College, 1949.

4100 Parker, William Riley. "The Date of Samson Agonistes." Philological Quarterly, XXVIII (1949), 145-166.
Originally written in the 1640's and revised about 1653.

4101 Woodhouse, A. S. P. "Samson Agonistes and Milton's Experience." Transactions of the Royal Society of Canada, 3rd Series, XLIII, Sec. 2 (1949), 157-175.
Suggests a late date for the writing of the play.

4102 Ure, Peter. "A Simile in Samson Agonistes." Notes and Queries, CXC (1950), 298.
Parallels are given to the woman-ship figure (lines 710-718) are taken from Jonson's The Devill is an Asse, and The Staple of News.

4103 Woodhouse, A. S. P. "Comus Once More." University of Toronto Quarterly, XIX (1950), 218-223.

4104 Albert, Francis L. "Dryden's Debt to Milton." M.A. University of North Carolina, 1951.

4105 Durling, Dwight. "Coghill's Samson Agonistes at Oxford." Seventeenth Century News, XI (1951), 63.
A presentation at Oxford, July, 1951.

4106 Spencer, Terence. "Samson Agonistes in London." Seventeenth Century News, IX (1951), 35.
A performance of the play in the Church of St. Martin's-in-the Fields, May, 1951.

4107 Spencer, Terence, and James Willis. "Milton and Arnobius."

Notes and Queries, CXCVI (1951), 387.
　　Lists parallels between Samson Agonistes and Arnobius'
　　Libri Septem Adversus Gentes.
4108　Tillyard, E. M. W. "The Action of Comus." Studies in Milton.
　　(London: Chatto &Windus; New York: Macmillan, 1951), 82-99.
4109　Whiting, George W. "Samson Agonistes and the Geneva Bible."
　　Rice Institute Pamphlet, XXXVIII (1951), 18-35.
　　Hebraic material in Milton's play.
4110　Zanco, Aurelio. Milton: Samson Agonistes e Paradise Regained.
　　Dalle lezioni svolte nell' Anno Accademico 1950-51 e raccolte
　　a cura di Grazia Caliumi. Milano: "La Goliarica" [1951?]. 113 pp.
4111　Buchanan, Edith. "The Italian Neo-Senecan Background of Samson
　　Agonistes." Ph.D. Duke University, 1952.
4112　Johnston, Robert De Sales. "A Study of Milton's Samson Agonistes."
　　M.A. University of Missouri, 1952.
4113　Maxwell, J. C. "Milton's Knowledge of Aeschylus: the Argument
　　from Parallel Passages." Review of English Studies, New Ser.,
　　III (1952), 366-371.
　　Considers Samson Agonistes.
4114　Scott-Craig, T.S.K. "Concerning Milton's Samson." Renaissance
　　News, V (1952), 45-53.
　　Sees the play as a lustration, a Protestant equivalent of the
　　Mass.
4115　Adams, Robert M. "Reading Comus." Modern Philology, LI (1953),
　　18-32.
4116　Beerborhn, Sir Max. "Agonising Samson." Around Theatres.
　　(London: British Book Centre, 1953), pp. 527-531.
4117　Fell, Kenneth. "From Myth to Martyrdom: Towards a View of
　　Milton's Samson Agonistes." English Studies, XXXIV (1953),
　　145-155.
　　Martyrdom in Samson Agonistes and in Eliot's Murder in
　　the Cathedral.
4118　Freedman, Morris. "Milton and Dryden." Ph.D. Columbia Uni-
　　versity, 1953. 207 pp. (Publication No. 6617).
　　The author analyzes the literary interrelations of Dryden
　　and Milton; Part III, "Fellow Dramatists," considers their
　　dramatic work.
4119　Kermode, Frank. "Samson Agonistes and Hebrew Prosody." Dur-
　　ham University Journal, XIV (1953), 59-63.
　　Milton's imitation of Hebrew lyric measures and rhymes.
4120　Allen, Don Cameron. "The Idea as Pattern: Despair and Samson
　　Agonistes." The Harmonious Vision: Studies in Milton's
　　Poetry. (Baltimore, Maryland: Johns Hopkins Press, 1954),
　　71-94.
4121　Arthos, John. On "A Mask Presented at Ludlow-Castle." Ann

Arbor: University of Michigan Press, 1954.
Treats Comus.
4122 Haun, Eugene. "An Inquiry into the Genre of Comus." Essays in
Honor of W. C. Curry. (Nashville, Tennessee: Vanderbilt University Press, 1954), 221-239.
The masque as a transitional genre between drama and opera
4123 Maxwell, J. C. "Milton's Samson and Sophocles' Heracles."
Philological Quarterly, XXXIII (1954), 90-91.
4124 McDavid, Raven I., Jr. "Samson Agonistes 1096: a Re-examinatic
Philological Quarterly, XXXIII (1954), 86-89.
Inclines to the word "wish" instead of "with."
4125 Bowra, Sir Cecil Maurice. "Samson Agonistes." Inspiration and
Poetry. (London: Macmillan, 1955), 112-129.
"In Samson Milton has rediscovered his taste for action and
abandoned the quietism of Paradise Regained."
4126 Dyson, A.E. "The Interpretation of Comus." Essays and Studies,
New Ser., VIII (1955), 89-114.
4127 Finnegan, Mary Frances. "A Comparison of Milton's Samson
Agonistes to Dryden's Absalom and Achitophel." M.A. University of Colorado, 1955.
4128 Grenander, M. E. "Samson's Middle: Aristotle and Dr. Johnson."
University of Toronto Quarterly, XXIV (July, 1955), 377-389.
While Johnson maintained that Samson Agonistes had no
middle, Aristotle indicated in the Poetics that action could take
place outside the play. In Samson incidents before the opening
of the play are a part of the beginning and middle.
4129 Tinker, Chauncey B. "Samson Agonistes." Tragic Themes in
Western Literature. Edited by Cleanth Brooks. (New Haven:
Yale University Press, 1955), 59-76.
The Bible account as it is transferred to a drama.
4130 Freedman, Morris. "All for Love and Samson Agonistes." Notes
and Queries, New Ser., III (1956), 514-517.
Finds similarities in the plays.
4131 Lynch, James J. "Evil Communcations." Notes and Queries, New
Ser., III (1956), 477.
Indicates that neither Milton (in his preface to Samson) or
Fielding attributes the phrase to the original author who was
Menander.
4132 Daiches, David. Milton. London: Hutchinson University Library,
1957. 254 pp.
A discussion of Comus and Samson Agonistes which sees
Samson as a remarkable play, but not a great tragedy. In a
sense, the play is not even a tragedy.
4133 Gossman, Ann Mary. "The Synthesis of Hebraism and Hellenism
in Milton's Samson Agonistes." Ph.D. Rice Institute, 1957.

4134 Marilla, E. L. "Samson Agonistes: An Interpretation." Studia
      Neophilologica, XXIX (1957), 67-76.
           Argues that "Milton is concerned not primarily with the
      individual or with a specific nation . . . but with mankind as a
      whole. . . . Milton seeks in this work . . . to demonstrate the
      basic forces of evil that persistently menace man's efforts to-
      ward establishing a society compatible with his spiritual needs."

4135 Price, E. R. "The Chorus in Samson Agonistes." B. Litt. Merton
      College, Oxford, 1957-58.

4136 Stein, Arnold. Heroic Knowledge: An Interpretation of Paradise
      Regained and Samson Agonistes. Minneapolis: University of
      Minnesota Press, 1957. xi, 237 pp.

4137 Tuve, Rosemond. "Image, Form and Theme in A Mask." Images
      and Themes in Five Poems by Milton. (Cambridge, Massachusetts:
      Harvard University Press, 1957), 113-161.
           Treats Comus.

4138 Hughes, Merritt Y. "The Seventeenth Century." Contemporary
      Literary Scholarship. Edited by Lewis Leary. (New York:
      Appleton-Century-Crofts, 1958), 67-82.
           Samson Agonistes is the only Restoration play mentioned.

4139 Le Comte, Edward S. "Samson Agonistes and Aureng-Zebe."
      Etudes Anglaises, XI (1958), 18-22.
           Sees Milton as a major source for Dryden's play.

4140 Nash, Ralph. "Chivalric Themes in Samson Agonistes." Studies
      in Honor of John Wilcox, by Members of the English Department,
      Wayne State University. Edited by A. Dayle Wallace and Wood-
      burn O. Ross. (Detroit: Wayne State University Press, 1958),
      23-38.

4141 Parker, William Riley. "The Date of Samson Agonistes: A Post-
      script." Notes and Queries, V (1958), 201-202.
           Supplements argument (PQ, XXVIII [1949], 145-166) that
      "the inception of Samson Agonistes should be dated 'as early
      as 1646-48.'"

4142 Sanders, Franklin David. "Samson Agonistes and the Critics."
      M.A. University of North Carolina, 1958.

4143 Cook, Albert. "Milton's Abstract Music." University of Toronto
      Quarterly, XXXIX (1959-60), 370-385.
           This is a study of Milton's personal rhythms in several
      poems, including Samson Agonistes. "For several accentual
      patterns to be present at once, and to be felt as coiling ahead
      and backwards, is Milton's achievement in Samson."

4144 Fisch, Harold. The Dual Image: A Study of the Figure of the Jew
      in English Literature. London: Published for the World Jewish
      Congress, British Section, by Lincolns-Prager (Publishers)
      Ltd., 1959. 86, [1] pp.

Chapter five devotes a section to Milton and the new Hebraic temper, as revealed in Samson Agonistes. The writer stresses Milton's self-identification with heroes of the Old Testament.

4145 Fox, Robert C. "Vida and Samson Agonistes." Notes and Queries, CCIV (1959), 370-372.

A possible source for the entrance of Dalila in Samson Agonistes can be traced to the Renaissance humanist Marco Girolamo Vida.

4146 Jayne, Sears. "The Subject of Milton's Ludlow Mask." Publication of the Modern Language Association, LXXIV (1959), 533-543.

Treats Comus.

4147 Lewalski, Barbara Kiefer. "The Ship-Tempest Imagery in Samson Agonistes." Notes and Queries, CCIV (1959), 372-373.

Milton has carefully integrated his ship simile of Dalila into the total pattern of ship and tempest imagery in Samson Agonistes

4148 Major, John M. "Comus and The Tempest." Shakespeare Quarterly, X (1959), 177-183.

4149 Samarin, R. "John Milton: Various Opinions on His Life and Work (To the 350th birthday of Milton)." Voprosi Literaturi, No. 1 (January, 1959), 155-172.

Discusses Samson Agonistes particularly.

4150 Whiting, George W. "Dalton's 'Comus' Again." Notes and Queries, VI (1959), 220-221.

Prevalent in 18th century.

4151 Woodhouse, A. S. P. "Tragic Effect in Samson Agonistes." University of Toronto Quarterly, XXVIII (1959), 205-222.

4152 Collins, Dan Stead. "Rhetoric and Logic in Milton's English Poems." Ph.D. University of North Carolina, 1960. 241 pp.

This dissertation analyzes Milton's interest in disputation and oratory upon his poetry. Comus, like several other works, contains a "temptation pattern" in which self-temptation leads to a debate.

4153 Empson, William. "A Defense of Delilah." Sewanee Review, LXVIII (April-June, 1960), 240-255.

An original "defense" of Milton's villainess, Delilah. To understand Samson's unintellectual character, one must realize that Milton purposely pitched Delilah's temptations "staggeringly high" in Samson Agonistes.

4154 Gossman, Ann. "Ransom in Samson Agonistes." Renaissance News, XIII (Spring, 1960), 11-15.

Manoa's attempt to ransom his son is analogous not only to Christ's redemption of mankind, but to Crito's attempt to ransom Socrates and Priam's attempt to rescue Hector.

4155 Gossman, Ann, and George W. Whiting. "Comus, Once More, 1761." Review of English Studies, XI (1960), 56-60.

This deals with a confusion of the text in Comus with that
of a stage rendition by Dalton (1738).

4156 Lloyd, Michael. "Comus and Plutarch's Daemons." Notes and
Queries, VII (1960), 421-423.

The Trinity Manuscript indicates that Comus' Attendant
Spirit was a "Guardian spirit, or Daemon." This reflects
Plutarch's statement that the souls of the virtuous may become
guardian daemons, the same which Christians call Angels.

4157 Muldrow, George McMurry. "The Theme of Man's Restoration in
Milton's Later Poetry." Ph.D. Stanford University, 1960. 391
pp.

This dissertation examines the theme of man's restoration
to God's grace in Paradise Lost, Paradise Regained and Samson
Agonistes. Samson Agonistes is seen as the dramatic struggle
in which fallen man regains God's favor.

4158 Rans, Geoffrey. "Mr. Wilkinson on Comus." Essays in Criticism,
X (July, 1960), 364-369.

In a reply to Mr. Wilkinson's "The Escape from Pollution:
A Comment on Comus," Mr. Rans insists that "not to attend
to the moral basis of (Milton's) poem is to court incompre-
hension."

4159 Shawcross, John T. "Certain Relationships of the Manuscripts of
Comus." Papers of the Bibliographical Society of America,
LIV (1960), 38-56.

This studies relationships between the texts of Comus found
in the Trinity MS and in the Bridgewater MS; it includes a table
for comparative study.

4160 Steadman, John M. "The Samson-Nisus Parallel: Some Renaissance
Examples." Notes and Queries, New Ser., VII (1960), 450-451.

Although Milton no doubt knew the Nisus myth, which is mentioned in several Renaissance works, for him to have compared
Samson with Nisus in Samson Agonistes would have seemed an
anachronism, since the Nisus myth was regarded as an imitation
of the story of Samson.

4161 Waggoner, George R. "The Challenge to Single Combat in Samson
Agonistes." Philological Quarterly, XXXIX (January, 1960), 82-
92.

A study of Milton's interest in the duel and his knowledge of
it; Milton utilized this device "to provide a motive and a symbol
for Samson's revived will to act."

4162 Wilkinson, David. "The Escape from Pollution: A Comment on
Comus." Essays in Criticism, Oxford, X (January, 1960),
32-43.

Dealing with the masque's dramatic and poetic aspects, Wilkinson's article suggests that Milton's emphasis lies in "the

private significance and personal relevance of what was
enacted, " not on a moral interpretation. The author intended
to compliment the Egerton family.

4163 Wright, E. "Samson as the Fallen Champion in Samson Agonistes.'
Notes and Queries, New Ser., VII (1960), 222-224.

Points to passages in Samson Agonistes which indicates that,
while Milton held rigidly to subject and form, he had also in
mind a romantic conception of the law as knightly champion.

4164 Arthos, John. "The Realms of Being in the Epilogue of Comus."
Modern Language Notes, LXXVI (1961), 321-324.

4165 Broadbent, J. B. Milton: Comus and Samson Agonistes. Studies in
English Literature Series. Edited by David Daiches. London:
Edward Arnold, Ltd., 1961. 63 pp.

Critical analyses and evaluations intended for university
students. Includes biographical and historical materials,
select bibliography.

4166 Cox, Lee Sheridan. "The 'Ev'ning Dragon' in Samson Agonistes:
A Reappraisal." Modern Language Notes, LXXVI (November,
1961), 577-584.

Line 1692--Interpretation of the phrase.

4167 Ebbs, John Dale. "Milton's Treatment of Poetic Justice in Samson
Agonistes." Modern Language Quarterly, XXII (December,
1961), 377-389.

Includes a brief review of past criticism and scholarship
for purposes of explication. Attempts to clarify Milton's
treatment of poetic justice, the most significant means by
which Milton presents the lesson of the poem.

4168 Parker, William Riley. "Notes on the Text of Samson Agonistes."
Journal of English and Germanic Philology, LX (1961), 688-
698.

A discussion and illustration of problems of spelling and
punctuation in modern editions of Milton's text.

4169 Sellin, Paul R. "Sources of Milton's Catharsis: A Reconsideration."
Journal of English and Germanic Philology, LX (1961), 712-
730.

Treats Samson Agonistes.

4170 Steadman, John M. "Milton's Harapha and Goliath." Journal of
English and Germanic Philology, LX (1961), 786-795.

Treats Samson Agonistes.

4171 Beum, Robert. "The Rhyme in Samson Agonistes." Texas Studies
in Literature and Language, IV (1962), 177-182.

A distinct pattern of rhyme is discernible in the work.
Milton's use of rhyme enforces climaxes and the role of the
chorus.

4172 Cox, Lee Sheridan. "Structural and Thematic Imagery in Samson

Agonistes and Paradise Regained." Ph.D. Indiana University,
1962. (Order No. 63-3812).

The contribution of imagery to the framework of thought, to
structure, motive, and theme. Reveals Milton's relationship
to Elizabethan dramatists and to the Metaphysicals.

4173 Fox, Robert C. "A Source for Milton's Comus." Notes and Queries,
New Ser., IX (1962), 52-53.

A figure in Jonson's Poetaster (1601) as a possible source
for the character of Comus.

4174 Gohn, Ernest S. "The Christian Ethic of Paradise Lost and Samson
Agonistes." Studia Neophilologica, XXXIV (1962), 243-268.

Considers the didactic aim and ethics of Milton's works in
relation to Renaissance ethical theory.

4175 Gossman, Ann. "Milton's Samson as the Tragic Hero Purified by
Trial." Journal of English and Germanic Philology, LXI (1962),
528-541.

Discusses Samson as a combination of the classical and
Christian concepts of the hero.

4176 Haller, William. "The Tragedy of God's Englishman." Reason
and the Imagination: Studies in the History of Ideas, 1600-1800.
Edited by J. A. Mazzeo. (New York: Columbia University Press;
London: Routledge & Kegan Paul, 1962), 201-211.

Treats Samson Agonistes.

4177 Kranidas, Thomas. "Milton's Concept of Decorum." Ph.D. University of Washington, 1962. (Order No. 63-3123).

Decorum as a concept which contributes to "unity" as well as
to consistency in the parts of discourse. Discusses Samson's
moving toward "wholeness" in Samson Agonistes.

4178 Landy, Marcia K. "Of Highest Wisdom: a Study of John Milton's
Samson Agonistes as a Dramatization of Christian Conversion."
Ph.D. The University of Rochester, 1962. (Order No. 62-6668).

Samson experiences conversion before regeneration. He
undergoes the steps of conversion as outlined by Christian
writers of the Renaissance and Seventeenth Century.

4179 Radzinowicz, Mary Ann Nevins. "Eve and Dalila: Renovation and
the Hardening of the Heart." Reason and the Imagination. Edited
by J. A. Mazzeo. (New York: Columbia University Press, 1962),
155-181.

Treats Samson Agonistes.

4180 Riley, Sister Mary Geraldine, R.S.M. "Infinite Variety in Milton:
A Study of John Milton's Concept of Woman as Shown in His
Works." Ph.D. Rutgers University, 1962. (Order No. 62-5316).

Milton's attitude toward women is typical of a seventeenth-
century gentleman. Considers Comus and Samson Agonistes.

4181 Steadman, John M. "Milton's Haemony: Etymology and Allegory."

Publications of the Modern Language Association, LXXVII
(1962), 200-207.
Treats Comus.

4182 -----. "Notes: Dalila, the Ulysses Myth, and Renaissance Al-
legorical Tradition." Modern Language Review, LVII (1962),
560-565.
In rejecting Dalila, Samson uses terms and figures from
classical mythology.

4183 Stroup, Thomas B. "The Cestus: Manuscript of an Anonymous
Eighteenth Century Imitation of Comus." Studies in English
Literature, 1500-1900, II (1962), 47-55.
Contends that the play has considerable literary merit and
suggests likely candidates for authorship. Shows influence of
Milton.

4184 Tung, Mason. "The Search for Perfection in John Milton." Ph.D.
Stanford University, 1962. (Order No. 62-5521).
The search for perfection in Milton's life and works as a
"secure principle" with which much Milton scholarship can
be coordinated.

4185 Woodman, Ross. "Literature and Life." Queen's Quarterly,
LXVIII (Winter, 1962), 621-631.
Uses Samson Agonistes, along with the work of Shakespeare
and Keats to show that literature is more comprehensible, and
therefore, in some respects, greater than life.

4186 Chambers, A. B. "Wisdom and Fortitude in Samson Agonistes."
Publications of the Modern Language Association, LXXVIII
(1963), 315-320.

4187 Daniells, Roy. Milton, Mannerism and Baroque. Toronto: University of Toronto Press, 1963. 229 pp.
An analysis of Comus reveals that "the dislocations are such
as to provoke an aesthetic response" in the reader, that the
techniques employed are a translation of 17th Century art
theories into appropriate literary practice.

4188 Freedman, Morris. "Milton's 'On Shakespeare' and Henry Lawes."
Shakespeare Quarterly, XIV (1963), 279-281.
Brief account of Milton's relationship with Lawes through
Comus.

4189 Goldberg, S. L. "The World, the Flesh, and Comus." Melbourne
Critical Review, VI (1963), 56-68.
In Comus the diction and imagery fail to provide sufficient
support for the philosophical ideas. The Lady's view of Comus
is not convincing.

4190 Grewe, Eugene Francis. "A History of the Criticism of John
Milton's Comus, 1637-1941." Ph.D. The University of Michigan
1963.

Surveys English and American criticism of Comus from
the comments in the first edition to the present day. Three appendices scrutinize the annotations in the editions of Newton,
Warton, and Todd. A fourth appendix lists editions of Comus
from 1637 to 1941.

4191 Harris, William O. "Despair and 'Patience as the Truest Fortitude'
in Samson Agonistes." Journal of English Literary History, XXX
(1963), 107-120.
Examines the structural and thematic importance of two
choral passages (11. 652-666 and 11. 1268-1296) in Samson
Agonistes in light of Milton's statements on patience and fortitude.

4192 Hill, R. F. "Samson Agonistes." Time and Tide, XLIV (April 4-
10, 1963), 28.

4193 Krouse, F. M. Milton's Samson and the Christian Tradition.
Hamden, Connecticut: The Shoe String Press, 1963.

4194 Nicolson, Marjorie Hope. John Milton: A Reader's Guide to His
Poetry. New York: Farrar, Straus and Company, 1963. 385 pp.
Survey of Milton's writings for undergraduates. Includes a
discussion of Milton's dramatic pieces.

4195 Parker, W.R. Milton's Debt to Greek Tragedy in Samson Agonistes.
Hamden, Connecticut: The Shoe String Press, 1963.

4196 Ricks, Christopher. Milton's Grand Style. Oxford: Clarendon
Press, 1963. 154 pp.
Milton's style is not only powerful and grand, it is also
delicate and subtle. Chapter II includes a study of metaphors
in Samson Agonistes.

4197 Samuels, Charles T. "Milton's Samson Agonistes and Rational
Christianity." Dalhousie Review, XLIII (1963), 495-506.
In Samson Agonistes Milton departs from his lifelong com-
mitment to make God seem "humanly, rationally correct."

4198 Van Kluyve, Robert A. "'Out, Out Hyaena!'" American Notes and
Queries, I (1963), 99-101.
Deals with the encounter of Samson and Dalila.

4199 Wilkes, G. A. "The Interpretation of Samson Agonistes." Huntington Library Quarterly, XXVI (August, 1963), 363-379.
Samson Agonistes is the story not only of Samson but also
of the Chorus, Manoah, and other characters who arrive
gradually at an understanding of the power of providence.

4200 Barker, Arthur E. "Structural and Doctrinal Patterns in Milton's
Later Poems." Essays in English Literature from the Renais-
sance to the Victorian Age Presented to A. S. P. Woodhouse,
1964. Edited by Millar MacLure and F. W. Watts. (Toronto:
University of Toronto Press, 1964), 168-194.
Samson Agonistes, like Paradise Regained, depends upon

"the contrast and relation between the Law and the Prophets"
for its content and development.

4201 Blondel, Jacques. Le 'Comus' de John Milton, masque neptunien.
Publs. de la Faculté des Lettres et Sciences Humaines de
l'Université de Clermont-Ferrand, 2me Série, fasc. XX.
Paris: Presses Universitaires de France, 1964.

4202 Bush, Douglas. John Milton. New York: Macmillan Company,
1964. 224 pp.
Critical and biographical introduction for students. Eluci-
dates the main problems in Comus and Samson Agonistes.

4203 Daniels, Edgar F. "Samson in 'Areopagitica.'" Notes and Queries,
New Ser., XI (1964), 92-93.
Interprets the allusion to Samson's restored strength in
Areopagitica which pictures England as "a noble and puissant
Nation rousing herself like a strong man after sleep, and
shaking her invincible locks."

4204 Dawson, S. W., and A. J. Smith. "Two Points of View: Samson
Agonistes." The Anglo-Welsh Review, XIV (1964/5), 92-101.
The merits and shortcomings of Samson Agonistes are juxta-
posed to provide a good introduction to the work.

4205 Demaray, John G. "Comus as a Masque." Ph.D. Columbia University, 1964. (Order No. 67-10,367).
An attempt to recreate what the first performance of Comus
was like as a staged presentation. Includes a brief review of
the history of the masque and a study of recent Comus criticism.

4206 Emma, Ronald David. Milton's Grammar. (Studies in English
Literature, Volume II). The Hague: Mouton and Company, 1964.
164 pp.
A study of Milton's grammar, its relationship to the English
of his own time and to modern English. Includes references to
Comus and Samson Agonistes.

4207 Fixler, Michael. Milton and the Kingdoms of God. Evanston,
Illinois: Northwestern University Press, 1964. 293 pp.
Milton's approach through poetry, prophecy, and politics
to the establishment of God's truth and the visionary ideal of
Puritanism. Includes references to Comus and Samson
Agonistes.

4208 Gossman, Ann. "Samson, Job, and 'The Exercise of Saints!'"
English Studies, XLV (1964), 212-224.
The Book of Job as part of the tradition behind Samson
Agonistes.

4209 Greene, Donald. "The Sin of Pride: A Sketch for a Literary Exploration." New Mexico Quarterly, XXXIV (Spring, 1964), 8-30.
Uses Samson Agonistes as an example of self-psychoanalysis
in literature.

4210 Kirkconnell, Watson. That Invincible Samson: The Theme of
      Samson Agonistes in World Literature With Translations of
      the Major Analogues. Toronto: University of Toronto Press,
      1964. 218 pp.
         Notes 107 versions of Samson Agonistes from the 12th cen-
      tury B.C. to 1944.
4211 Klein, Joan Larsen. "Some Spencerian Influences on Milton's
      Comus." Annuale Mediaevale, V (1964), 27-47.
4212 Miriam Clare, Sister. Samson Agonistes: A Study in Contrast.
      New York: Pageant Press, 1964. 153 pp.
         Investigates the use of the classical figures of contrast,
      particularly Antithesis, in the characterization, action, key
      concepts, and grammar of the play.
4213 Mueller, Martin E. "Pathos and Katharsis in Samson Agonistes."
      Journal of English Literary History, XXXI (1964), 156-174.
         Samson differs from Greek tragedy in that "the catastrophe
      has no immediate bearing on any human relationship but is
      only meaningful as the final event in the relationship of Samson
      and God."
4214 Rajan, B. "Milton Seen Anew." Canadian Literature, No. 21
      (1964), 55-58.
         Review article of Roy Daniells' Milton, Mannerism, and
      Baroque (Toronto: University of Toronto Press, 1963). Com-
      ments on Daniells' interpretation of Comus and Samson Agonistes.
4215 Riese, Teut Andreas. "Die Theatralik der Tugend in Milton Comus."
      Festschrift für Walter Hubner. Edited by Dieter Riesner, and
      Helmut Gneuss. (Berlin: Schmidt, 1964), 192-202.
         On the artistic unity of Comus.
4216 Saillens, Emile. John Milton: Man, Poet, Polemicist. New York:
      Barnes and Noble, 1964. 371 pp.
         First published in 1959 as John Milton, poète combattant,
      and intended as a popular biography.
4217 Sellin, Paul R. "Milton's Epithet Agonistes." Studies in English
      Literature, 1500-1900, IV (1964), 137-162.
         Agonistes may mean "dissembling," "assuming a mask,"
      "playing a part," and "acting." These meanings are relevant to
      the structure of the play and especially important for the theme
      expressed by the chorus in its final ode.
4218 Sensabaugh, George F. Milton in Early America. Princeton:
      Princeton University Press, 1964. 320 pp.
         Studies American interest in Milton during the colonial period.
      Includes occasional references to Samson Agonistes.
4219 Shawcross, John T. "Henry Lawes's Settings of Songs for Milton's
      Comus." Journal of the Rutgers University Library, XXVIII

(1964), 22-28.

An examination of the manuscripts shows that there is uncerta[ ]
ty regarding modern conclusions about the original form of the w[ ]
Revisions in the songs of Comus are pointed up by a collation
of the British Museum MS with the Lawes MS.

4220 Wilkenfield, Roger B. "Act and Emblem: A Study of Narrative
and Dramatic Patterns in Three Poems of John Milton." Ph.D.
The University of Rochester, 1964. (Order No. 64-12,453).

The "dramatic" in Comus and Samson Agonistes derives from
a complex system of ironic and verbal motifs. Their power
rests in the expansive emblems of the Paralyzed Lady and the
Rising Phoenix.

4221 Ades, John I. "The Pattern of Temptation in Comus." Papers on
English Language and Literature, I (1965), 265-271.

Comus might justifiably be regarded as Milton's first major
work on the theme of redemption. Here, as in Paradise Regained, Milton employs a three-part structure to symbolize
the temptations of the world, the flesh, and the Devil.

4222 Arai, A. "Milton in Comus." Studies in English Literature (The
English Literary Society of Japan), XLII (1965), 19-31.

4223 Barber, C. L. "A Mask Presented at Ludlow Castle: The Masque
as a Masque." The Lyric and Dramatic Milton. Selected Papers
from the English Institute. Edited with a Foreword by Joseph
H. Summers. (New York and London: Columbia University
Press, 1965), 35-63.

Attempts to answer two questions: (1) How does Milton succeed "in making a happy work which centers, seemingly, on
the denial of impulse, when typically in the Renaissance such
works involve, in some fashion or other, release from
restraint?" and (2) How does the form of the piece relate to
Renaissance comedy and allied traditions?

4224 Diekhoff, John S., ed. Milton on Himself: Milton's Utterances
upon Himself and His Works. London: Cohen and West, 1965.
307 pp.

The second edition with a new preface. Extracts from
Milton's statements grouped by subject and arranged within
the groups in order of composition.

4225 Empson, William. Milton's God. London: Chatto and Windus,
1965. 320 pp.

A revised edition of Empson's 1961 work. Chapter VI
concerns Dalilah's role in Samson Agonistes.

4226 Ghosh, Prabodh Chandra. Poetry and Religion as Drama.
Calcutta: TheWorld Press, Private Ltd., 1965. xii, 211 pp.

Chapter IV treats Samson Agonistes as "a testament of
faith" and compares Milton's treatment of the story to the Old
Testament version.

4227 Jayne, Sears. "The Subject of Milton's Ludlow Mask." Milton:
       Modern Essays in Criticism. Edited by Arthur E. Barker.
       (New York: Oxford University Press, 1965), 88-111.
           A revised article that appeared in PMLA, LXXIV (1959),
       533-543. Proposes that Milton's Platonism in the works is the
       Renaissance Platonism of Ficino.
4228 Landy, Marcia. "Character Portrayal in Samson Agonistes."
       Texas Studies in Literature and Language, VII (1965), 239-
       253.
           Milton's characters are less allegorizations than individuals
       realized with human depth and complexity.
4229 Lemay, J. A. Leo. "Jonson and Milton: Two Influences in Oakes's
       Elegie." The New England Quarterly, XXXVIII (1965), 90-92.
           The influence of Samson Agonistes on American poet, Urian
       Oakes's An Elegie upon the Death of the Reverend Mr. Thomas
       Shepard (1677).
4230 Madsen, William G. "From Shadowy Types to Truth." The Lyric
       and Dramatic Milton. Selected Papers from the English Institute.
       Edited with a Foreword by Joseph H. Summers. (New York and
       London: Columbia University Press, 1965), 95-114.
           A typological interpretation of Samson Agonistes suggests
       that it is both non-Christian and Christian in much the same
       way as the Old Testament may be considered non-Christian and
       Christian, and that the play may be regarded as a companion
       piece to Paradise Regained.
4231 Merchant, W. Moelwyn. Creed and Drama: An Essay in Religious
       Drama. London: S.P.C.K., 1965. 119 pp.
           Includes a discussion of Samson Agonistes.
4232 Mitchell, Charles. "Dalila's Return: The Importance of Pardon."
       College English, XXVI (1965), 614-620.
           Samson does not become conscious of God's pardon until
       after the appearance of Dalila who, in contrast to the hero,
       seeks pardon without having earned it through penance.
4233 Moss, Leonard. "The Rhetorical Style of Samson Agonistes."
       Modern Philology, LXII (1965), 296-301.
           Milton's use of classical rhetoric, particularly the device of
       synonymia, for the crucial arguments of Samson Agonistes.
4234 Radzinowicz, M. A. N. "Samson Agonistes and Milton the Politician
       in Defeat." Philological Quarterly, XLIV (1965), 454-471.
           An "epic of defeat," Samson Agonistes represents Milton's
       attempt to justify God's ways in the fall of the Commonwealth.
4235 Rosenberg, Donald M. "Milton and the Laughter of God." Ph.D.
       Wayne State University, 1965.
           Specific comic elements can be recognized in the point of
       view, tone, structure, characterization, and style of Comus,

Paradise Lost, Paradise Regained, and Samson Agonistes to
show that Milton is sensitive to contradictions fundamental to
man's condition.

4236 San Juan, E., Jr. "The Natural Context of Spiritual Renewal in
Samson Agonistes." Ball State University Forum, VI (1965),
55-60.

Studies Samson's human nature as it "undergoes its regeneration when it begins to participate in the organic processes
of nature subsumed within a Divine Order of things."

4237 Steadman, John M. "'Faithful Champion': The Theological Basis
of Milton's Hero of Faith," Milton: Modern Essays in Criticism
(A Galaxy Book). Edited by Arthur E. Barker. (New York: Oxford University Press, 1965), 467-483.

Reprinted from Anglia, LXXVII (1959), 12-28. Contends tha
the dominant motif of the tragedy is the hero's spiritual rebirtl
or sanctification so that Milton's primary emphasis falls on
what happens in the hero's soul.

4238 Summers, Joseph H. "The Movements of the Drama." The Lyric
Dramatic Milton. Selected Papers from the English Institute.
Edited with a Foreword by Joseph H. Summers. (New York anc
London: Columbia University Press, 1965), 153-175.

The dramatic movements of Samson Agonistes are often
ironical or paradoxical and cannot be simply reduced to a
formula of "degradation and suffering to triumph."

4239 Sundell, Roger Henry. "Internal Commentary in the Major Poems
of John Milton." Ph.D. Washington University, 1965. (Order
No. 66-1626).

Within his major poems Milton consciously included "interpretative commentary" to insure that the works would be pro-
perly understood. The Attendant Spirit in Comus and the Chort
in Samson Agonistes prepare and guide the audience's sym-
pathies while highlighting the dramatic action.

4240 Weismiller, Edward. "The 'Dry' and 'Rugged' Verse." The Lyric
and Dramatic Milton. Selected Papers from the English Institu
Edited with a foreword by Joseph H. Summers. (New York and
London: Columbia University Press, 1965), 115-152.

A prosodic study of Samson Agonistes, particularly of the
choral odes which may be written "in that ultimate form of
seventeenth-century English irregular verse, the blank or
near-blank Italianate Pindaric."

4241 Wilkenfield, Roger B. "Act and Emblem: The Conclusion of Samson Agonistes." Journal of English Literary History, XXXII (1
160-168.

Discusses the relationship between the phoenix symbol and
the motifs of freedom and transformation.

4242 Williamson, George. "The Context of Comus." Milton and Others.
      (London, 1965), 26-41.
           Interprets Comus in the light of Milton's elegiac utterances
      and his unrealized play on the fall of Sodom, Cupids Funeral
      Pile.
4243 ------. "Tension in Samson Agonistes." Milton and Others. (Lon-
      don, 1965), 85-102.
           In Samson Agonistes Milton gives vent to his own personal
      anxiety and frustrations. He utilizes a theory of tragedy based
      on the Paracelsian principle of similia similibus.
4244 Woodhouse, A. S. P. "Tragic Effect in Samson Agonistes." Milton:
      Modern Essays in Criticism. (A Galaxy Book). Edited by Arthur
      E. Barker. (New York: Oxford University Press, 1965), 447-
      466.
           Reprinted from the University of Toronto Quarterly, XXVIII
      (1958-59), 205-222. Interprets Samson Agonistes as a classical
      tragedy with a Christian theme and outlook.
4245 Allain, Mathé. "The Humanist's Dilemma: Milton, God, and Rea-
      son." College English, XXVII (1966), 379-384.
           Traces the conflict of humanism and Christianity in Milton's
      major works. The peace of Samson Agonistes results from a
      resolution: "man whose essence is rational cannot conflict with
      God who is Reason."
4246 Blondel, Jacques. "The Function of Mythology in Comus." Durham
      University Journal, LVII (1966), 63-66.
           The mythology in Comus has ethical significance; it also
      serves to magnify the players and to define the contrast between
      reason and self-indulgence.
4247 Carrithers, Gale H., Jr. "Milton's Ludlow Mask: From Chaos to
      Community." Journal of English Literary History, XXXIII
      (1966), 23-42.
           The work is animated by an ideal of community: man finds
      fulfillment in a loving, God-seeking society.
4248 Demaray, John G. "Milton's Comus: The Sequel to a Masque of
      Circe." Huntington Library Quarterly, XXIX (1966), 245-254.
           Henry Lawes's masquing career and his contribution to
      Comus.
4249 Frank, Joseph. "The Unharmonious Vision: Milton as a Baroque
      Artist." Comparative Literature Studies, III (1966), 95-108.
           Milton's poetry generally becomes more Baroque and his
      theology becomes less assured. Includes discussion of Comus
      and Samson Agonistes.
4250 Hanford, James Holly. John Milton: Poet and Humanist. Foreword
      by John S. Diekhoff. Cleveland: The Press of Western Reserve
      University, 1966. 286 pp.

Reprints eight essays written by Professor Hanford between 1910 and 1925. "Samson Agonistes and Milton in Old Age," pp. 264-286, is reprinted from Studies in Shakespeare, Milton and Donne. New York: Macmillan, 1925.

4251 Huntley, John. "A Revaluation of the Chorus' Role in Milton's Samson Agonistes." Modern Philology, LXIV (1966), 132-145.

The chorus participates in Samson's regeneration as they gradually experience "a change from vanity covered with platitud to knowledge posed for action."

4252 Hyman, Lawrence W. "Milton's Samson and the Modern Reader." College English, XXVIII (1966), 39-43.

Not the justification of God's ways but Samson's courage in confronting a God whose ways are dark to our understanding gives the poem a special interest for the modern reader.

4253 Kranidas, Thomas. "Dalila's Role in Samson Agonistes." Studies in English Literature, 1500-1900, VI (1966), 125-137.

A study of Dalila's speeches that attempts to test the validity of her arguments and to justify Samson's outraged responses.

4254 Mueller, Martin. "Sixteenth-Century Italian Criticism and Milton's Theory of Catharsis." Studies in English Literature, 1500-1900, VI (1966), 139-150.

Milton was indebted to Italian theories of catharsis current in the 16th century. His chief debt was to Florence and to the scholarly tradition represented by men like Pietro Bettori and Lorenzo Giacomini.

4255 Tillyard, E. M. Milton. Rev. ed. With a Preface by Phyllis B. Tillyard. London: Chatto and Windus, 1966. 390 pp.

The biographical and critical study originally published in 1930. Part I, Chapter VI treats Comus; Part III, Chapters XI-XIV treats Samson Agonistes, its origin, quality, the dramatic motive, and its relation to Milton's experience and thought.

4256 Wilkenfeld, Roger B. "The Seat at the Center. An Interpretation of Comus." Journal of English Literary History, XXXIII (1966), 170-197.

The center or "hinge" in the structure of Comus is an emblem "the concrete, visual, dramatically viable emblem of the Lady paralyzed in the seat of Comus."

4257 Carey, John. "Sea, Snake, Flower, and Flame in Samson Agonistes Modern Language Review, LXII (1967), 395-399.

The imagery does not merely reinforce the drama's upward arc. "On the contrary, it contributes meaning which threaten to invert this arc and bring the weak-minded, vengeful hero to the level of Dalila and the Philistines."

4258 Fraser, Russell. "On Milton's Poetry." Yale Review, LVI (1967), 172-196.

A study of Milton's attempt to make the language of poetry convey the truth with absolute reality and precision includes a discussion of Samson Agonistes.

4259 Gabrieli, Vittorio. "Milton agonista." Cultura, V (1967), 316-334.

4260 Hall, James Martin. "Milton's Rhetoric in Prose and Poetry." Ph.D. Yale University, 1967. (Order No. 67-7019).

Examines the controversial rhetorical techniques in Milton's prose to show how they elucidate certain problems of form, character, and action in the major poetry. Includes discussion of Comus and Samson Agonistes.

4261 Long, Anne Bowers. "The Relation Between Classical and Biblical Allusions in Milton's Later Poems." Ph.D. University of Illinois, 1967. (Order No. 68-8151).

Examines Samson Agonistes as well as Paradise Lost and Paradise Regained.

4262 Major, John M. "Milton's View of Rhetoric." Studies in Philology, LXIV (1967), 685-711.

Studies the relationship between Milton's attitudes toward rhetoric and his training and beliefs. Discusses the debate between the Lady and Comus in Comus and the character of Dalila as sophistorator in Samson Agonistes.

4263 Mish, Charles C. "Comus and Bryce Blair's Vision of Theodorus Verax." Milton Newsletter, I (1967), 39-40.

Blair also used Milton's source, the Comus of Erycius Puteanus, for his version of the story.

4264 Neuse, Richard. "Metamorphosis and Symbolic Action in Comus." Journal of English Literary History, XXXIV (1967), 49-64.

The Lady's enchantment and release are not a mere concluding flourish to her refusal of the cup. The Lady's paralysis and liberation by Sabrina present a genuine complication and resolution initiated by the original clash between the Lady and Comus.

4265 Raleigh, Sir Walter. Milton. New York: Benjamin Blom, 1967. 286 pp.

A reissue of the 1900 edition in which Raleigh presents a brief biography and discusses the major works, their themes, characters, style and influence.

4266 Rudrum, Alan. A Critical Commentary on Milton's Comus and Shorter Poems. (Macmillan Critical Commentaries). London: Macmillan Co., 1967. 113 pp.

A line by line analysis of the play's plot, characters and theme.

4267 Sadler, Mary Lynn Veach. "Samson Agonistes and the Theme of Consolation." Ph.D. University of Illinois, 1967. (Order No. 68-8210).

For Milton, consolation is regeneration. The theme also
brings together two foci of Milton criticism: his reading of
the ways of God in historical dispensations and of the psycholog
of religious experience.

4268 Deleted.

4269 Shawcross, John T. "A Metaphoric Approach to Reading Milton."
Ball State University Forum, VIII (1967), 17-22.

A metaphoric reading of specific words suggests somewhat different or deeper interpretations of lines and passages
in which they appear, and it echoes motives found elsewhere
in the work. Includes a discussion of lines from Samson
Agonistes.

4270 Smith, Logan Pearsall. Milton and His Modern Critics. Hamden,
Conn.: Archon Books, 1967. 87 pp.

A reprint of the 1941 edition.

4271 Steadman, John M. Milton and the Renaissance Hero. New York:
Oxford University Press, 1967.

The first six chapters analyze Milton's treatment of the mos
important formulae for an epic hero: another chapter relates
his heroic image to the Biblical archetypes and classical prototypes.

4272 -----. "The Tragic Glass: Milton, Minturno, and the Condition
Humaine." Th' Upright Heart and Pure: Essays of John Milton
Commemorating the Tercentenary of the Publication of Paradise
Lost. Edited by Amadeus P. Fiore, O.F.M. (Pittsburgh: Duque
University Press, 1967), pp. 101-115.

Takes issue with critics who see Milton's later work only as
an expression of subjective feeling. In Minturno's L'Arte Poetic
Milton could have found ideas and images that led to the conception of Samson as an emblem of humanity.

4273 Teunissen, John James. "Of Patience and Heroic Martyrdom: The
Book of Job and Milton's Conception of Patient Suffering in
'Paradise Regained' and 'Samson Agonistes.'" Ph.D. University
of Rochester, 1967. (Order No. 67-13,652).

A large part of Samson's suffering stems from his very
ignorance of the fact that he is being afflicted not because of
past sins but because, as in the case of Job, God wishes to
expose him to a period of probation.

4274 Thorpe, James. "On the Pronunciation of Names in Samson
Agonistes." Huntington Library Quarterly, XXXI (1967), 65-
74.

Scansion of Milton's lines shows that he intended the names
of Dalila, Manoa, and Harapha to be accented on the first sylla

4275 Tyson, John Patrick. "The Elements of Aristotelian Tragedy in
      Paradise Lost." Ph.D. Tulane University, 1967. (Order No.
      68-4071).
          Aristotle's plot, character, thought, diction, spectacle,
      and song from the Poetics serves as the basis for analysis.
4276 Wilkenfeld, Roger B. "Theoretics or Polemics? Milton Criticism
      and the 'Dramatic Axiom.'" Publications of the Modern Language
      Association, LXXXII (1967), 505-515.
          Because Milton critics do not make an effort to separate the
      "vocal" and "modal" definitions of the dramatic, it is impossible
      to say whether they are defining a technique, the results of a
      technique, or an aspect of personality. Includes references to
      Comus and Samson Agonistes.

Miscellaneous

4277 Matthews, Brander. "The Dramatist and the Theater." The Century
      Magazine, LXXXIX (November, 1909), 3-19.
          A brief essay on the relationship of the playhouse to the
      presentation of a play (e.g., how theatrical conditions affect
      the play). Mentions the theatre of the Restoration and 18th
      century.
4278 Scott, W. "Restoration Plays." Notes and Queries, 11th Ser., I
      (January 15, 1910), 56.
          Assigns publication date of 1660 for Troaydes, a Tragedy
      by Samuel Pordage; and of 1661 for A Cure for a Cuckold, The
      Presbyterian Lash (supposed by Malone to be by Francis Kirkman),
      and The Merry Conceited Humours of Bottom the Weaver by
      Robert Cox.
4279 Flögel, Karl Friedrich. Geschichte des Grotesk-Komischen. Ein
      beitrag zur Geschichte der Menschheit. 2 vols. München:
      Georg Muller, 1914.
          This illustrated work deals with such theatrical types as
      puppet shows and burlesques and studies their history in various
      countries, including England.
4280 A Catalogue of Old English Plays and Poetry, in which is included
      a selection of rare theatrical books and prose works by drama-
      tists and poets offered for sale by Pickering and Chatto. Lon-
      don [circa 1918]. 327 pp.
          Arranged alphabetically by author with full bibliographical
      description and often with detailed, descriptive annotations.
4281 Robertson, William George. Neglected English Classics. Aber-
      deen: D. Wylie and Sons, 1920. 303 pp.
          Section II (pp. 75-164) deals with favorite plays with eight-
      eenth-century playgoers, Otway's Venice Preserved, Farquhar's

Beaux' Stratagem, Addison's Cato, and Gay's Beggar's Opera.
This volume is intended primarily for students; the method is a
summary of the contents of the play, comments on sources,
followed by a critical commentary on the play.

4282 Colby, Elbridge. "Two Slices of Literature." Modern Language
Notes, XXXVIII (1923), 473-480.
Focus of the article is the mood and general opinions of the
eighteenth century as expressed by literature. Mentions Edwar
Young, Congreve, and other literary figures of the time.

4283 Jakobowitz, Israel. "Inkle und Jarico, eine stoffgeschichtliche
Untersuchung." Inaugural Dissertation. Heidelberg, 1924.

4284 Weiss, Adolf. "Die Mundart im Englischchen Drama von 1642-
1800." Giessen Dissertation, 1924.

4285 Johnson, R. Brimley, ed. Mrs. Delaney at Court and among the
Wits. London: Stanley Paul, 1926. xliv, 292 pp.
A condensation from the six-volume edition of the life and
correspondence of Mrs. Delaney, Mary (Granville) Pendarves,
published 1861 and 1862. Several references to 18th-century
plays, players, and playwrights.

4286 Turberville, A. S. English Men and Manners in the Eighteenth
Century: an Illustrated Narrative. Oxford: Clarendon Press,
1926. xxiii, 531 pp.
Includes a chapter on writers, artists, actors, and musiciar

4287 Voltaire, Francois Marie Arouet de. Letters Concerning the English Nation. Introduction by Charles Whibley. London: P. Davie
1926. 197 pp.
Includes remarks on English drama.

4288 "The Drama in Decline." Times Literary Supplement, March 17,
1927, p. 182.
Reviews A. Nicoll's A History of Late Eighteenth Century
Drama (1927). Objects to Nicoll's assertion that Goldsmith
and Sheridan occupy an "over-exalted position."

4289 Isaacs, J. "English Men of Letters at Padua in the Seventeenth
Century." Review of English Studies, III (January, 1927), 75.
The list includes John Evelyn, Edmund Waller, Kenelm
Digby, Thomas Killigrew, Thomas Vaughan, Bolingbroke,
and Addison.

4290 Murray, Grace A. Personalities of the Eighteenth Century. London: Heath, Cranton, 1927. 3, 9-230 pp.
A collection of anecdotes, arranged without plan, graced
with illustrations of play-bills and theatre tickets.

4291 Purdie, Edna. The Story of Judith in German and English Literature. Paris: H. Champion, 1927. vi, 161 pp.
Section one is a bibliography listing instances of versions
of the story, as, in 1663, a puppet play performed at Lincoln's

Inn Fields; Siege of Bethalia (1732), performed at Bartholomew's Fair; and Judith (1761), performed at Drury Lane. Part II deals with various treatments of the Judith story.

4292 Summers, Montague, ed. Covent Garden Drollery. London: Fortune Press, 1927. vii, 124 pp.

Reprint of the first edition, containing miscellaneous Restoration prologues, epilogues, and songs from plays; numerous printing errors.

4293 Hotson, Leslie. The Commonwealth and Restoration Stage. Cambridge University Press, 1928. ix, 424 pp.

A universally praised set of essays--on Davenant's "opera" from 1655-1660, on various nurseries for young actors, on patent companies and Chancery suits in which they were interested. Valuable appendix of nearly 100 pp.--(1) a list of all the Chancery Bills and Answers found, (2) selection of the more important texts of these, (3) miscellaneous documents. Research in the Public Records Office has made available 120 important documents.

4294 Neighbors, Julia. "English Drama of the Eighteenth Century." M.A. University of Alabama, 1928.

4295 Summers, Alphonsus Joseph M.[ontague]. Essays in Petto. London: Fortune Press, 1928. ix, 183 pp.

Essays include "A Restoration Prompt-Book," "Pepys' 'Doll Common,' Mrs. Corey," "Orrery's 'The Tragedy of Zoroastres,'" and "The Source of Southerne's 'The Fatal Marriage.'"

4296 Thorn-Drury, G., ed. Covent Garden Drollery. A Miscellany of 1672. London: Dobell, 1928. xxi, 154 pp.

A careful reprint of the second edition, containing a large number of miscellaneous theatrical pieces--prologues, epilogues, songs from plays; perhaps compiled by Aphra Behn.

4297 Grierson, Sir Herbert J. C. Cross Currents in 17th Century English Literature. London: Chatto and Windus, 1929. xvi, 345 pp.

Chapters on Milton, Restoration literature, and Dryden.

4298 Boswell, Eleanore. "Footnotes to Seventeenth-Century Biographies." Modern Language Review, XXVI (1931), 176, 341.

The first article deals with Povey's suit against Pepys and William Hewer; the second discusses Inigo Jones' work as Surveyor-General, Charles Sedley's support of William III and a government loan, the existence of another "Thomas Shadwell," Og's contemporary, and some documents signed by William Wycherley.

4299 Bryant, Arthur. King Charles II. London: Longmans, 1931. 215 pp.

A biography which contains some amusing material on the drama and its background.

4300 Bain, M. Les Voyageurs francais en Ecosse (1770-1830) et leur

curiosités intellectuelles. Paris: Honore Champion, 1932.
Author makes no claim to presenting a complete list of
travels and travelers, but he does attempt to trace the travels
made by the French to Scotland between 1770-1830 and also attempts to show an amicable political relationship between the
two countries.

4301 Dobrée, Bonamy. Variety of Ways. Oxford: University Press,
1932. 306 pp.
Essays on literary figures of the eighteenth century; some
material on drama and dramatists included.

4302 Engel, C. E. "Echo de la Revocation dans les théâtres anglais."
Bulletin de la Société de l'histoire de Protestantisme francais,
LXXXI (1932), 278-285.

4303 Stoll, Elmer Edgar. "Literature and Life Again." Publications of
the Modern Language Association, XLVII (1932), 283-302.
Stoll utilizes modern art and, to some extent, Restoration
drama, to show the divergence between life and art but he also
indicates to what extent they "may be considered to coincide."

4304 Brett-James, Norman. The Growth of Stuart London. London:
Allen, 1935. 556 pp.

4305 A Journal From Parnassus. Now Printed From a Manuscript
"circa" 1688. With an Introduction by Hugh Macdonald. London: Printed for P. J. Dobell, 1937. xiv, 67 pp.
Account of the "Sessions" held on Parnassus so that Apollo
might decide who deserved the laurel. It mentions Behn, Betterton, Crown, Dryden, D'Urfey, Etherege, Settle, Shadwell,
Tate, and Wycherley. In the tradition of Suckling's "Session
of the Poets" (1637?).

4306 Withington, Robert. Excursions in English Drama. New York;
London: D. Appleton-Century Co., Inc. [c. 1937]. xvii,
264 pp.
This study in the continuity of dramatic development studies
the four agencies to which drama owes its existence: the playwright, the playhouse, the player, and the public. Touches on
18th-century drama.

4307 Mendenhall, John C., ed. English Literature, 1650-1800. Philadelphia: Lippincott, 1940. 1166 pp.

4308 Shudofsky, M. Maurice. "The Gentleman-Cully." Modern
Language Notes, LV (May, 1940), 396-399.
Argues that Nicoll has overlooked the unique quality of
this anonymous 1701 comedy--"its spirit of reaction against
Restoration comedy."

4309 Monk, Samuel Holt. "From Jacobean to Augustan." Southern
Review, VII (Autumn, 1941), 366-384.
Contends that simplification is what characterizes the change

in poetry from Donne to Dryden; attacks Robert Lathrop
Sharp's From Donne to Dryden. Also discusses Clarence De
Witt Thorpe's The Aesthetic Theory of Thomas Hobbes which
necessitates revision of the usual picture of Hobbes. Hobbes
was really interested in the works of the imagination.

4310 Wilson, John Harold, ed. The Rochester-Savile Letters. Columbus:
Ohio State University Press, 1941. 127 pp.
Thirty-three letters are printed with extensive annotations.
Many references to theatrical figures, including Killigrew,
Mrs. Barry, Dryden, and Nell Gwyn.

4311 Kronenberger, Louis. Kings and Desperate Men: Life in Eighteenth-
Century England. New York: Knopf, 1942. 323 pp.

4312 Sypher, Wylie. Guinea's Captive Kings: British Anti-Slavery Literature of the XVIII Century. Chapel Hill: University of North
Carolina Press, 1942. 340 pp.
After establishing the cultural milieu and 18th-century currents of opinion, Sypher considers the literary expression of
anti-slavery. One chapter, devoted to anti-slavery drama,
treats types of Negroes in drama, Thomas Bellamy's The Benevolent Planters, translations of Bernardin St. Pierre's Paul et
Virginie, and George Colman's Africans.

4313 Hartnoll, Phyllis. "Juvenile Drama: A Birmingham Bequest."
Times Literary Supplement, October 7, 1944, p. 492; October
14, 1944, p. 504.
"Concerned in part with eighteenth-century plays."

4314 Barbetti, Emilio. "Note Storiche sul Teatro Inglese 'La Claque.'"
Anglica, I (April-June, 1946), 96-99.
Traces the history of the London claques during the period.

4315 Van Tieghem, Paul. Histoire Littéraire de l'Europe et de l'Amér-
ique de la Renaissance à nos jours. Paris: Librairie Armand
Colin, 1946. vi, 426 pp.
Second edition. Book II, chapters two and three, survey
classical tragedy and comedy in Italy, Spain, England, and
France.

4316 Rose, Kenneth. Georgiana. London: Muller, 1948. 48 pp.
Plays about distinguished Georgians, including "Perdita"
Robinson and Mrs. Siddons, written for schools.

4317 Hughes, Leo. "Trick upon Trick; or, Methodism Display'd."
Studies in English (University of Texas), XXIX (1950), 151-161.
This article tells about a polemical version of the old vintner
theme from Marston and about a losing battle an Edinburgh
troupe fought with Wesley's followers at Newcastle.

4318 Sherburn, George. "A Theatre Party of 1729." Harvard Library
Bulletin, IV (1950), 111-114.
Two letters (January 9, 1728/9, and April 24, 1729), by the

fifth Earl of Cork and Orrery give a partially fictional account
of an excursion to the theatre.

4319 Dietrich, Margaret. Europäische Dramaturgie: Der Wandel ihre
Menschenbilds von der Antike bis zur Goethezeit. Wien-Meisen-
heim: Verlag A. Sexl, 1952. 404 pp.

A discussion of treatments of man in literature from Plato.
Chapter IV, "Des Menschenbild in der englischen Dramaturgie
des 17. Jahrhunderts. (Das Porträts) "treats Sidney, Jonson,
Congreve, and Dryden (individually)."

4320 Theatre Miscellany; Six Pieces Connected with the 17th-Century
Stage. Oxford: B. Blackwell, 1953. v, 129 pp. (Luttrell Society
Reprints. No. 14.)

These original texts, reprinted without modernization, include the following post-1660 items: 1) William Davenant's
Voyage to the Other World, by Richard Flecknoe (1688); 2) Songs
and Masques in The Tempest (c. 1674); 3) Musical Entertainments in Rinaldo and Armida, by John Dennis (1694).

4321 Clinton-Baddeley, V.C. All Right on the Night. London: Putnam,
1954. 243 pp.

Contains brief references to the Restoration and eighteenth-
century theatre.

4322 Leech, Clifford. "Art and the Concept of Will." Durham University
Journal, XLVIII (December, 1955), 1-7.

Sees the Restoration play as mirroring man's attempt to
impose order on our responses to the human situation, suggesting a dichotomy between man and his environment.

4323 Avery, Emmett L. "A Royal Wedding Royally Confounded."
Western Humanities Review, X (1956), 153-164.

Problems and postponements of the marriage of Anne,
daughter of King George II, to William Charles Henry, Prince
of Orange, during the winter of 1733-34. Considers effects
of the event on London and the theatre.

4324 Crinò, Anna Maria. I Letterati della Restaurazione nella rela-
zione magalottiana del 1668. Florence: Sansini, 1956.

4325 Peacock, Ronald. The Art of Drama. London: Routledge and
Kegan Paul, 1957. vi, 263 pp.

Discusses aesthetics; only scattered references to Restoration and 18th-century dramatists.

4326 Pitou, Spire. "A Forgotten Play: La Roche-Guilhen's Rare en
Tout (1677)." Modern Language Notes, LXXII (1957), 357-359.
Written and performed in England.

4327 Agate, James E., ed. English Drama Critics: An Anthology, 1660-
1932. London: A Barker, Ltd. [1932]; New York: Hill and Wang
[1958]. 370 pp. (A Dramabook).

No notes. Contains selections by Richard Flecknoe, Addison,

Steele, Goldsmith, Boswell, Francis Gentleman, Henry Bate, Thomas Holcroft, as well as reviews reprinted from The London Chronicle and The Theatrical Review.

4328 Borinski, Ludwig. "Ideale der Restaurationzeit." Festschrift für Walther Fischer. (Heidelberg: Carl Winter, 1959), 49-64.

4329 Langner, Lawrence. The Play's The Thing. New York: Putnam, 1960. 258 pp.

This work, though providing a review of various aspects of the theatre--writing methods, play construction, adaptations, etc.--is of interest to the student of 18th-century theatre primarily in terms of its brief references to such writers as Sheridan.

4330 Miner, Earl. "1660 and All That." Hudson Review, XIII (1960), 612-617.

Miner pleads for a true understanding of the period and provides a review of seven works dealing with the Restoration theatre.

4331 Peake, C. H. and Lillian F. Haddakin. "The Eighteenth Century." Year's Work in English Studies, XXXIX (1960), 201-228.

A review of important 18th-century literary materials published in 1958.

4332 Pearson, Hesketh. Charles II: His Life and Likeness. London: Heinemann, 1960. 274 pp.

Still another account of the life and times of Charles II, this book's 16th chapter--"Literature, Scandal and Politics" --contains references to Etherege, Wycherley, Dryden, Buckingham and the like.

4333 Schönberger, Arno and Halldor Soehner, with collaboration of Theodor Müller. The Age of Rococo: Art and Civilization of the 18th Century. Translated by Daphne Woodward. London: Thames & Hudson; New York: McGraw-Hill, 1960. 392 pp.

4334 Shumaker, Wayne. Literature and the Irrational: A Study in Anthropological Background (Prentice-Hall, 1960), 275 pp.

Relating to 18th century drama only in the broadest sense, this work is a study in the anthropological backgrounds of literature. Section six, of particular interest to the student of drama, is entitled "The Major Literary Types: Tragedy and Comedy."

4335 "Statues, Busts, Monuments and Wax Portraits of Theatrical Interest." Theatre Notebook, XIV (1960), 123-126.

Extracted from Rupert Gannis, Dictionary of British Sculptors, 1660-1851.

4336 Ternois, Rene. "Les Francais en Angleterre au temp de Charles II, 1660-1676," Révue de Littérature comparée, XXXIV (1960), 196-211.

Cites reactions to theatres and performances.

4337 Williamson, George. Seventeenth Century Contexts. London:
Faber and Faber [1960]. 291 pp.

A collection of essays on seventeenth century literary sub-
jects including an analysis of neo-classical wit in terms of
Latin rhetoric and a discussion of the occasional aspects of "An
Essay on Dramatic Poesy."

4338 Camden, Carroll, ed. Restoration and Eighteenth-Century Literature: Essays in Honor of Alan Dugald McKillop. Chicago: University of Chicago Press for William Marsh Rice University,
1963. 435 pp.

Includes papers on Dryden, Blake, Johnson, Stevens, and
Steele.

4339 Schless, Howard H. "The Yale Edition of Poems on Affairs of
State." Restoration and Eighteenth Century Theatre Research,
IV (May, 1965), 17-19.

An explanation of items in the edition that are of special interest to scholars in Restoration and Eighteenth-Century Theatre:
political verse by Restoration dramatists, prologues, and ballad
materials.

4340 Zielske, Harald. "Handlungsort und Bühnenbild im 17. Jahrhundert.
Untersuchungen zur Raumdarstellung in europaischen Barock-
theater." Ph.D. Frei Universität Berlin, 1965.

4341 Hilles, Frederick W. "Recent Studies in the Restoration and
Eighteenth Century." Studies in English Literature, 1500-
1900, VI (1966), 599-628.

A review article of major critical works published in 1965-
1966 contains information on studies of Gay, Fielding, and
Goldsmith.

4342 Langhans, Edward A. "Restoration Manuscript Notes in Seventeenth
Century Plays." Restoration and Eighteenth Century Theatre Research, V (May, 1966), 30-39; (November, 1966), 3-17.

A list of 252 manuscript notes in printed and manuscript
plays, prologues and epilogues that provide information on
performances and publication dates, casts and cast changes,
and staging practices. Includes a bibliography of recent books
and articles that cite or discuss many of the items.

4343 Loftis, John. Restoration Drama: Modern Essays in Criticism.
New York: Oxford University Press, 1966. xi, 376 pp.

4344 Miner, Earl. "Introduction." Restoration Dramatists: A Collection
of Critical Essays. (Twentieth Century Views). Edited by Earl
Miner. (Englewood Cliffs, New Jersey: Prentice Hall, Inc.,
1966), 1-18.

A survey of the subjects, forms, and styles that characterize
Restoration drama.

Mitchell, Joseph

4345 Kies, Paul Philemon. "The Authorship of The Fatal Extravagance."
     Washington State College Research Studies, XII (1945), 155-158;
     XIV (1946), 88.
        Concludes that Joseph Mitchell collaborated with Hill.

Mohocks

4346 Graves, Thornton S. "Some Pre-Mohock Clansmen." Studies in
     Philology, XX (1923), 395-421.
        An account of gangs like the Mohocks in the 17th century;
     while the article is primarily social history, there is mention
     of a few post-Restoration plays to indicate how such gangs were
     presented on the stage.

Molière

4347 Miles, Dudley Howe. The Influence of Molière on Restoration
     Comedy. Columbia University Studies in English and Compara-
     tive Literature. New York: The Columbia University Press,
     1910. 272 pp.
        Rather than to Jonson and Fletcher, Restoration comedy
     owed its beginning and development in plots, situations, and
     types of characters, to Molière. The Appendix lists "important
     direct borrowings" in ninety-two Restoration plays.
4348 Besing, M. Molières Einfluss auf das englische Lustspiel bis
     1700. Inaugural Dissertation. Leipzig, 1913.
4349 Gillet, J. E. Molière en Angleterre, 1660-1700. Paris: Champion,
     1913. 240 pp.
        The nineteen adaptations of Molière's plays show three
     schools developing under his influence: (1) the school of action,
     with emphasis upon intrigue and external action; (2) the school
     of manner, introducing the spirit of Molière; and (3) the school
     of characters, the most vigorous of the three. Considers the
     adaptations of Davenant, Etherege, Dryden, Shadwell, Flecknoe,
     Sedley, Lacy, Caryll, Medbourne, and Betterton.
4350 Wilcox, John. The Relation of Molière to Restoration Comedy.
     New York: Columbia University Press, 1938. ix, 240 pp.
        A carefully controlled and documented study of the use of
     Molière's plays by various Restoration playwrights, such as
     Congreve, Dryden, Etherege, Farquhar, Shadwell, Vanbrugh,
     and Wycherley.
4351 Kerby, W. M. "Some Thoughts Concerning Molière and the
     Restoration Drama." Modern Language Notes, XXIII (1942), 120-
     131.

4352 Saintonge, Paul, and Robert Wilson Christ. Fifty Years of Molière
Studies: A Bibliography, 1892-1941. Baltimore: Johns Hopkins
Press; London: Humphrey Milford, Oxford University Press;
Paris: Société d'éditions Les Belles Lettres, 1942. (The Johns
Hopkins Studies in Romance Literatures and Languages, Extra
Vol. XIX).
The works are listed under subject subdivisions of four
large sections: I. Biography; II. Criticism; III. Critical Works c
Specific Plays; IV. Miscellanea. The sections on "The Idea of
Comedy and Dramatic Technique" (53 items) and "Relation
to England" (53 items) are of particular interest.

4353 Tucker, Joseph E. "The Eighteenth Century English Translations o
Molière." Modern Language Quarterly, III (March, 1942), 83-1(
A bibliographical account of the translation of Molière's play
from 1693 through the 18th century (most of the translations are
pre-1740). Concludes that Ozell's translation of Molière's work
was the best.

4354 Saintonge, Paul and Christ, R.W. "Omissions and Additions to
Fifty Years of Molière Studies." Modern Language Notes, LIX
(April, 1944), 282-285.
Adds 42 items to bring their earlier bibliography--which
had terminated with 1941--up to date.

4355 "Molière in England." Times Literary Supplement, April 20, 1946
p. 187.
An editorial survey of Molière's influence and popularity
during the Restoration and eighteenth century, inspired by A.
de Mandach's study.

4356 Loiselet, J. L. "L'apport de Molière au théâtre anglais du début
de la Restauration au milieu du XVIII siècle." La revue francaise, VI (1954), 52, 53, 54.

4357 Mitra, D. "Adaptations of the Plays of Molière for the English
Stage, 1660-1700." M.A. London University (Bedford), 1956-
1957.

4358 Jones, Claude E. "Molière in England to 1775: A Checklist." Note:
and Queries, IV (1957), 383-389.
Translations, adaptations, and borrowings.

4359 Copley, J. "On Translating Molière into English." Durham Uni-
versity Journal, LII (June, 1960), 116-124.
Copley describes the difficulty of reproducing Molière in
English. Prints sample translations from Shadwell, Dryden,
Fielding and Miles Malleson and evaluates them.

4360 Wilcox, John. The Relation of Molière to the Restoration Comedy.
New York: Benjamin Bloom, 1964. 240 pp.
Reprint of Wilcox's 1940 text.

Montagu, Elizabeth

4361 Boulton, James T. "Mrs. Elizabeth Montagu (1720-1800)." Burke
Newsletter, III (Winter-Spring, 1961-62), 96-98.
The personality and talent of Mrs. Elizabeth Montagu. Friend-
ships with Burke, Johnson, Sterne, and Reynolds.

4362 "Simplicity." Johnsonian Newsletter, XXVII (1967), 2.
A brief discussion of Lady Mary Wortley Montagu's Simplicity
(c. 1735) adapted from Marivaux's Le Jeu de l'amour et du
hasard (1730).

Moore, Edward

4363 Miller, Mary Noreene. "Edward Moore's The Gamester." M.A.
University of Illinois, 1924.

4364 Van Bellen, E. C. "Trois Jouers." Neophilologus, IX (1924),
161-172.
The purpose of the article is to analyze three French plays
to illustrate the changing treatment of the gambler in drama.
The second play selected, Beverley by Saurin (1768) is an
adaptation of Edward Moore's The Gamester; Moore's play is
treated at some length, as is Saurin's method of adaptation.

4365 Caskey, John Homer. The Life and Works of Edward Moore. New
Haven: Yale University Press, 1927. vii, 202 pp.
Examines Moore's work as dramatist, essayist, and fabulist.
The Gamester is his best, a tragedy with much greater influence
on the Continent than in England. Moore is almost negligible from
a literary point of view.

4366 Collins, Ralph L. "Moore's The Foundling--An Intermediary."
Philological Quarterly, XVII (1938), 139-143.
Argues that several aspects of the play were determined by
Richardson's Clarissa and that the play influenced Fielding in
the composition of Tom Jones.

4367 Moore, Edward. The Gamester (1753). Edited by Charles H.
Peake, with a bibliographical note by Philip R. Wikelund. Ann
Arbor: The Augustan Reprint Society, July, 1948. (Series V,
no. 1).
A facsimile of the celebrated middle-class acting vehicle,
with an introduction stressing the moral attitudes of eighteenth
century comedy.

4368 Sinko, Grzegorz. Anglieski dramat mieszczanski XVIII wieki; G.
Lillo, E. Moore, S. Foote. Przelozyl i opracowal G. Sinko.
Wroclaw: Zaklad im. Ossolinskich Wydawnictwo [1955]. cxl,
367 pp. (Biblioteka narodowa, Ser. 2, 95).

Introduction, giving historical background. Polish translations
of Lillo's The London Merchant, Moore's The Gamester, and
Foote's The Nabob.

Moores

4369 Turner, Frederic. "The Moores of Milton Place, Surrey." Notes
      and Queries, Ser. 12, VI (1920), 118.
      An identification of this Moore family with that of the play-
      wright who died in 1735.

Moral Revolution

4370 Bahlman, Dudley W. R. The Moral Revolution of 1688. Yale Histor-
      ical Publications. The Wallace Noteseen Essays, No. 2. New
      Haven: Yale University Press, 1957. 112 pp.
      The failures and successes of individuals and societies for
      the reformation of manners who saw moral improvement as a
      necessary companion of political improvement.

More, Hannah

4371 Terhune, Mrs. M. V. (H). Hannah More. New York, 1900. 14,
      [1], 238 pp.
4372 Meaken, Annette M. B. Hannah More, A Biographical Study. Lon-
      don: John Murray, 1911. xxxi, 415 pp.
      Hannah More's life based mostly on her letters with em-
      phasis upon her friendships with the well-known people of her
      time, particularly with the Garricks. Several chapters devoted
      to the success of her plays.
4373 Bracey, Robert, O.P. "Hannah More and Joseph Berington."
      Eighteenth-Century Studies and Other Papers. With a Fore-
      ward by the Bishop of Clifton. Oxford: Basil Blackwell, 1925.
      142 pp.
      A paper on Hannah More, treating her religious conversion
      and rebuke by Joseph Berington.
4374 Forster, E. M. "Mrs. Hannah More." New Republic, XLV (Dec-
      ember 16, 1925), 106-109.
      Includes a mention of her successful five-act tragedy Percy.
      (A reprint from the Nation and Athenaeum, XXXVIII (January
      2, 1926), 493-494).
4375 More, Hannah. The Letters of Hannah More. Selected by R.
      Brimley Johnson. London: John Lane, 1925. ix, 212 pp.
      An effusive introduction. More was a friend of Johnson and
      Horace Walpole, and was encouraged by Garrick to write plays.

Gossippy letters about her friends, about Garrick's acting.

4376 Forster, E. M. "Mrs. Hannah More." Nation and Athenaeum,
XXXVIII (January 2, 1926), 493-494.

Biographical sketch, and a mention of her successful five-
act tragedy Percy.

4377 Knox, E. V. "'Percy' (the Tale of a Dramatic Success)." London
Mercury, XIII (March, 1926), 509-515.

On Hannah More's successful blank verse tragedy (1777).

4378 Sparke, Archibald. "Author Wanted." Notes and Queries, CLV
(July 21, 1928), 52-53.

Gives details of performances of Hannah More's play.

4379 Woods, R. "Hannah More: Her Life and Works." M.A. University
of Colorado, 1928.

4380 Child, Philip. "Portrait of a Woman of Affairs--Old Style." University of Toronto Quarterly, III (1933), 87-102.

Sketches the life and actions of Hannah More, friend of
Garrick and Johnson.

4381 Malim, M. C. "Hannah More: 1745-1833." Contemporary Review,
CXLIV (1933), 329-336.

Provides a short biographical sketch of Hannah More and
her efforts to reorganize education for women.

4382 Snodgrass, A.E. "Dr. Johnson's Petted Lady." Cornhill Magazine,
CXLVIII (1933), 336-342.

This article seeks to uncover reasons for the favor which
Miss More found in Dr. Johnson's eye. After providing a brief
biographical sketch, Snodgrass concludes that she was efficient,
industrious and had an unshakeable common sense. "If she
never had a brilliant thought, [she] never wrote a bad one."

4383 Hopkins, Mary Alden. Hannah More and Her Circle, 1745-1833.
New York: Longmans, Green and Co., 1947. 274 pp.

A biography with critical comments on the plays and notice
of her friendships with Garrick and Johnson.

4384 Shaver, Chester L. "The Publication of Hannah More's First Play,
A Search after Happiness." Modern Language Notes, LXII
(May, 1947), 343.

The play was published on May 10, 1773.

4385 Jones, Mary Gwladys. Hannah More. Cambridge (England): University Press, 1952. 284 pp.

4386 Spector, Robert D. "William Roberts' 'Memoirs of the Life and
Letters of Hannah More.'" Notes and Queries, CXCVII (1952),
140-141.

The first edition of the Memoirs was a four-volume octavo.
Spector also provides other bibliographical information about
the work.

Morgann, Maurice

4387 Morgann, Maurice. Morgann's Essay on the Dramatic Character
      of Sir John Falstaff. Edited by William Arthur Gill. London:
      Henry Frowde, 1912. xvi, [4], 185, [1] pp.
        A reprint, which follows the original edition of 1777, ex-
      cept for correcting a few obvious misprints. The final page
      lists "errata." This is really the fourth edition, the others
      being 1777, 1820, and 1825.
4388 Tave, Stuart M. "Notes on the Influence of Morgann's Essay on
      Falstaff." Review of English Studies, New Ser., III (1952),
      371-375.
        Morgann's essay, ultimately very influential, had an initially
      small but devoted audience.

Morris, Corbyn

4389 Morris, Corbyn. An Essay towards Fixing the True Standards of
      Wit, Humor, Raillery, Satire, and Ridicule (1744). Edited by
      James L. Clifford. Ann Arbor: The Augustan Reprint Society,
      November, 1947. (Series I: Essays on Wit, no. 4).
        A facsimile text of the essay which includes comment on
      Shakespeare and Jonson, especially Falstaff and Abel Drugger
      as comic roles.
4390 Tave, Stuart M. "Corbyn Morris: Falstaff, Humor, and Comic
      Theory in the Eighteenth Century." Modern Philology, L (1952),
      102-115.
        In his essay of 1744, Morris explores the nature of humor
      and uses Falstaff as one of several examples of its operation.

Morris, Thomas

4391 Cooper, C. B. "The Ideas of Captain Thomas Morris." Manly Anni-
      versary Studies in Language and Literature. (Chicago: Univer-
      sity of Chicago Press, 1923), 197-203.
        A discussion of Morris' view of dramatic art, especially
      his preference for the French over the English style of acting.

Morris Dance

4392 Sharp, Cecil James, and Herbert C. Macilwaine. The Morris
      Book. London: Novello and Company, Ltd., 1907-1913. Five
      Parts.
        "A description of fifty-six Morris dances and fourteen
      Morris jigs, giving the costume, music, steps, figure and

notation for each, together with notes on the origin and development of the dances."

Morton, Thomas

4393 Mortvedet, Robert A. L. "Thomas Morton, His Life and Works." Ph.D. Harvard University, 1934.

Motteux, Peter

4394 Charlanne, Louis. "Un Francais écrivain anglais au XVII siècle, Pierre-Antoine Motteux." Revue Bleue, August 26, 1911, pp. 282-286; September 2, 1911, pp. 300-306.
    The works of Motteux in England, his criticism, journalism, translations, comedies, tragedies, farces, librettos.

4395 Nicoll, Allardyce. "'Farewell Folly' and 'The Amorous Miser.'" Notes and Queries, 12th Ser., V (December, 1929), 310-312.
    Tries to clear up the mystery around two plays "Farewell Folly" (1707) and "The Amorous Miser" (1705), which have been mistaken for one another. "Farewell Folly" he believes to be Motteux's because of its topical allusions. "The Amorous Miser" is by some other hand because of insult to L'Epine in epilogue.

4396 Bateson, F.W. "Motteux and The Amorous Miser." Review of English Studies, III (1927), 340-342.
    Attempts to clarify the confusion between Amorous Miser: or, The Younger the Wiser (1705) and Farewell Folly: or, The Younger the Wiser (1707).

4397 Cunningham, Robert Newton. "A Bibliography of the Writings of of Peter Anthony Motteux." Proceedings and Papers of the Oxford Bibliographical Society, Vol. III, Part III (1933), 317-337.
    Author tries to give a complete list of first editions as found in the Bodleian, British Museum, Library of Congress, Harvard, Huntington, and Yale libraries. Bibliography divided into three sections, each arranged chronologically: (1) works of which Motteux was author or part author; (2) shorter writings which Motteux contributed to undertakings of others; (3) doubtful works.

4398 ------. Peter Anthony Motteux, 1663-1718; a Biographical and Critical Study. Oxford: B. Blackwell, 1933. x, 217 pp.

4399 Bowers, Fredson. "Motteux's Love's a Jest (1696): a Running-Title and Presswork Problem." Papers of the Bibliographical Society of America, XLVIII (1954), 268-273.
    Motteux's play illustrates the problems arising from the use of running-titles as bibliographical evidence.

Mountfort, William

4400 Borgman, Albert S. The Life and Death of William Mountford.
      Harvard Studies in English, Vol. XV. Cambridge: Harvard
      University Press, 1935. vi, 221 pp.
         An authoritative biography of the Restoration actor with a
      detailed account of his career on the stage and of his relations
      with Dryden, Shadwell, Southerne, and others.
4401 Hughes, Leo. "The Date of Mountfort's Faustus." Notes and
      Queries, CXCII (August 23, 1947), 358-359.
         Probably October or November, 1688.
4402 Cadwalader, John, ed. King Edward the Third, with the Fall of
      Mortimer Earl of March. 1691. Philadelphia: University of
      Pennsylvania Press, 1949. v, 88 pp.
         A detailed critical edition of the play published by Mountford
      and sometimes attributed to Thomas Bancroft.

Moving Pictures

4403 Jones, Tom. "Moving Pictures to Cinematographs." Notes and
      Queries, 11th Ser., II (December 24, 1910), 502-504.
         Includes brief descriptions of Villette's mirrored images
      of 1679, the magic picture of Van Loo 1759, the Eidophusikon,
      and the Panorama.
4404 Rhodes, A. "'Moving Pictures' in Fleet Street." Notes and Queries,
      11th Ser., II (December 3, 1910), 457.
         Mechanical toy made by Jacobus Morian. Prints advertise-
      ment in The Daily Courant, May 9, 1709, and description in a
      handbill.
4405 Robbins, A. F. "Moving Pictures in Fleet Street in 1709." Notes
      and Queries, 11th Ser., II (November 19, 1910), 403.
         Prints advertisement in The Post Boy, March 10-12, 1709,
      for "the most curious original moving picture" at the Duke of
      Marlborough's Head in Fleet Street.
4406 Jones, Tom. "Moving Pictures to Cinematographs." Notes and
      Queries, 11th Ser., III (March 11, 1911), 194.
         Panorama of London circa 1794 by Thomas Girton, a painter.
      Descriptions of other panoramas to 1834.
4407 Scouten, Arthur H. "Swift at the Moving Pictures." Notes and
      Queries, CLXXXVIII (January 27, 1945), 38-39.
         An early moving-picture device, referred to in the Journal
      to Stella, is described from newspaper accounts.

Mummer's Play

4408 Rhodes, R. Crompton. "The Mummer's Play." Times Literary
       Supplement, January 25, 1934, p. 60.

Munford, Robert

4409 Baine, Rodney M. Robert Munford: America's First Comic Drama-
       tist. Athens, Georgia: University of Georgia Press, 1967. 132
       pp.
           A critical biography of the 18th century American playwright
       includes references to Restoration and 18th century English
       drama.

Murphy, Arthur

texts

4410 Murphy, Arthur. New Essays by Arthur Murphy. Edited with an
       Introduction by Arthur Sherbo. East Lansing: Michigan State
       University Press, 1963. 217 pp.
           Theatrical criticism attributed to Murphy, chiefly from
       dramatic periodicals of the period. Approximately 35 essays.
4411 -----. The Way to Keep Him. Edited by Allardyce Nicoll. London:
       Oxford University Press, 1925. (English Comedies of the 18th
       Century Series). viii, 131 pp.
           Reprints the edition of 1786, with a brief introduction.
4412 -----. The Way to Keep Him and Five Other Plays by Arthur
       Murphy. Edited by John Pike Emery. New York: New York
       University Press, 1956. x, 434 pp.
           Annotated.

biography and criticism

4413 Beatty, Joseph M., Jr. "Dr. Johnson and 'Mur.'" Modern Language
       Notes, XXXIX (February, 1924), 82-88.
           A history of the friendship of Johnson and Arthur Murphy.
4414 Dunbar, H. H. "Plays of Arthur Murphy." Times Literary Sup-
       plement, September 13, 1928, p. 648.
           Requests information on 12 plays and fragments.
4415 Caskey, J. Homer. "Arthur Murphy and the War on Sentimental
       Comedy." Journal of English and Germanic Philology, XXX
       (1931), 563-577.
           Thinks that this playwright of Garrick's era drew on Molière
       in his attack on the conventions of sentimental comedy.

4416 Cockcroft, Ethel. "A Study of the Life and Dramatic Works of Arthur Murphy." Ph.D. London University (External), 1931.

4417 Caskey, J. Homer. "The First Edition of Arthur Murphy's Sallust." Philological Quarterly, XIII (1934), 404-408.

First published under the pseudonym of "George Frederic Sydney" in 1795.

4418 Emery, John Pike. "The Life and Works of Arthur Murphy." Ph.D. Harvard University, 1936.

Arguing that Murphy's plays "enable him to rival even Sheridan as a comic dramatist," Emery tries to present every known fact about the playwright's life and writings, including detailed analyses of twenty plays.

4419 White, Milton C. "Arthur Murphy. His Life and Work with Especial Reference to the Contemporary Stage." Ph.D. University of Wisconsin, 1936.

A biography of Murphy with equal emphasis on his life and writings.

4420 Emery, John P. "An Unpublished Letter from Arthur Murphy to Oliver Goldsmith Concerning She Stoops to Conquer." Philological Quarterly, XVII (1938), 88-90.

Prints a letter dated March 2, 1773, in which Murphy suggests a plan for an epilogue to Goldsmith's play.

4421 Bradford, Curtis B. "Arthur Murphy's Meeting with Johnson." Philological Quarterly, XVIII (1939), 318-320.

Verifies and elaborates Mrs. Piozzi's account of the meeting.

4422 Emery, John P. "Murph's Criticisms in the London Chronicle." Publications of the Modern Language Association, LIV (1939), 1099-1104.

Argues that Murphy is the author of the column called "The Theatre" which appeared in the London Chronicle during 1757 and 1758.

4423 Caskey, J. Homer. "Arthur Murphy's Commonplace-Book." Studies in Philology, XXXVII (1940), 598-609.

An account of a portion of a commonplace-book preserved in manuscript; the portion contains notes on "The Constituent Parts of the Drama."

4424 Lewis, Louise S. "Arthur Murphy, Dramatist." M.A. University of Texas, 1941.

4425 Dunbar, Howard. "Arthur Murphy." Ph.D. Columbia University, 1942.

4426 Botting, Roland B. "Bolingbroke and Murphy's Aboulcasem." Modern Language Quarterly, V (1944), 89-91.

Believes that Arthur Murphy's Oriental tale of Aboulcasem, which appeared in the Gray's Inn Journal, June 8, 1754, is a direct indictment of Bolingbroke.

4427 -----. "Christopher Smart's Association with Arthur Murphy."
Journal of English and Germanic Philology, XLIII (1944), 49-
56.
Suggests that Murphy admired Smart and aided him in his
quarrel with Hill--in fact, their mutual dislike of Hill brought
them together. References to other figures associated with
theatre.

4428 Brown, John J. "Samuel Johnson 'Making Aether.'" Modern Language
Notes, LIX (April, 1944), 286.
Throws light on Arthur Murphy's account of Johnson's attempts
to make ether.

4429 Dunbar, Howard Hunter. The Dramatic Career of Arthur Murphy.
New York: The Modern Language Association, 1946. ix, 339
pp. (Modern Language Association Revolving Fund Series, XIV).
A full critical biography.

4430 Emery, John Pike. Arthur Murphy, an Eminent English Dramatist
of the Eighteenth Century. Philadelphia: University of Pennsylvania
Press, 1946. 224 pp. (Temple University Publications).
A detailed biographical and critical study.

4431 -----. "Murphy's Authorship of the Notes of Smart's Hilliad."
Modern Language Notes, LXI (March, 1946), 162-165.
Murphy and Smart worked together on the production of The
Hilliad, 1753. Outlines the continuing feud between Murphy and
John Hill in the drama of the 1750's.

4432 -----. "Arthur Murphy." Times Literary Supplement, December
23, 1949, p. 841.
A request for information about Sir Joshua Reynolds' portrait
of Murphy.

4433 Aycock, Roy E. "A Study of Arthur Murphy's Gray's Inn Journal,
1752-1754." Ph.D. University of North Carolina, 1960.

4434 Miller, Henry Knight. "Internal Evidence: Professor Sherbo and the
Case of Arthur Murphy." Bulletin of the New York Public Library, LXIX (1965), 459-470.
Contends that Sherbo's evidence is not scientific or weighty
enough to attribute The Entertainer and several other theatrical
writings to Arthur Murphy.

4435 Sherbo, Arthur. "Imitation or Concealment: Who Wrote the Entertainer Essays?" Bulletin of the New York Public Library, LXIX
(1965), 471-486.
Strengthens his original arguments for Murphy's authorship
of The Entertainer with statistics on diction and vocabulary.

4436 Lehnert, Martin. "Arthur Murphy's Hamlet-Parodie (1772) auf
David Garrick." Shakespeare Jahrbuch, CII (1966), 97-167.
Studies the history of Murphy's parody and includes the full
text of his play.

4437 Trefman, Simon. "Arthur Murphy's Long Lost Englishman From
     Paris: A Manuscript Discovered." Theatre Notebook, XX (Sum-
     mer, 1966), 137-141.
          Comments on the manuscript at the Newberry Library,
     Chicago, and on the play's production on April 3, 1756 at Drury
     Lane, particularly its competition with Samuel Foote's English-
     man Returned from Paris.

Music

4438 Flood, Wm. H. Grattan. A History of Irish Music. Dublin: Browne
     and Nolan, Limited, 1905. xiii, [1], 357, [1] pp.
          Some eight chapters are devoted to Irish music, from 1650-
     1800. Running references to the theatre, with some treatment
     of Arne and Handel in Ireland.
4439 "Index to the Songs and Musical Allusions in The Gentleman's
     Journal, 1692-1694." The Musical Antiquary, II (July, 1911),
     225-234.
          List of songs and music under names of composers alpha-
     betically arranged, together with an index to allusions to operas
     and plays for which Purcell is known to have written songs and
     music.
4440 Lavignac, Albert, and Lionel de la Laurencie. Encyclopedie de la
     Musique et Dictionnaire du Conservatoire. 11 vols. Paris:
     Delagrave, 1913-1931.
          Part I, Vols. 1-5, presents the history of music by country,
     incorporating into the continuous text a wealth of definitions
     and illustrations, biographical data on composers, and analyses
     of specific works.
4441 Flood, W. H. Grattan. "Notes on the Irish Jig." Musical Opinion
     and Music Trade Review, February, 1914, p. 361.
          Traces the origin of the jig, not to Italy but to Ireland. Gives
     some titles popular in the Restoration and the eighteenth century
4442 Lawrence, W. J. "Music and Song in the Eighteenth Century Theatre
     The Musical Quarterly, II (1916), 67-75.
          Discusses four musical customs of 18th century theatre: first,
     second, third music; composition of new act tunes for new
     plays; the speaking of lines of a song before singing them; and
     the encore.
4443 Bridge, Sir Frederick. Shakespearean Music in the Plays and Early
     Operas. London and Toronto: J. M. Dent & Sons, Ltd., 1923.
     94 pp.
          In addition to discussion of the music in Shakespeare's plays,
     Bridge considers the Restoration operatic versions of Shakespear
     especially the Davenant-Dryden version of The Tempest (a play),

Shadwell's The Tempest (opera), Purcell's operas, and the
setting to music of Hamlet's soliloquy, "To be or not to be."

4444 Pulver, Jeffrey. A Biographical Dictionary of Old English Music.
London: Kegan Paul, Trench, Trübner and Company, Ltd.,
1927. 537 pp.
  ". . . the biographies and bibliographies of the more important musicians to the death of Purcell."

4445 Gladding, Bessie A. "Music as a Social Force During the English
Commonwealth and Restoration (1649-1700)." Musical Quarterly,
XV (October, 1929), 506-521.
  On music in masques, plays, and dramatic-musical entertainments, its importance in the revival of drama under the Pro-
tectorate, the rise of opera, and the love of music along all English classes. Includes a facsimile of the title page of The Banquet
of Musick (1688), a Collection of the newest and best Songs sung
at Court, and at Publick Theatres.

4446 Draper, J. W. "Poetry and Music in Eighteenth-Century Aesthetics."
Englische Studien, LXVII (1932), 70-85.

4447 Noyes, R. G. "Contemporary Musical Settings of the Songs in
Restoration Drama." English Literary History, I (1934), 325-
344.
  A catalog of songs used in Restoration dramas from contemporary music books. Excludes songs of Dryden and D'Urfey.

4448 "Peregrinus." "A Year's Drama and Music." Notes and Queries,
CLXVII (1934), 219-222, 237-238.
  Based on the diary of the first earl of Egmont for the year
1734.

4449 Burney, Charles. A General History of Music. Revised Edition,
with Critical and Historical Notes, by Frank Mercer. 2 vols.
London: Foulis, 1935.
  Burney's contemporary account brought up to date in a
critical edition.

4450 Noyes, Robert Gale. "Songs from Restoration Drama in Contemporary and Eighteenth-Century Poetical Miscellanies." English
Literary History, III (1936), 291-316.
  An alphabetical list of songs from Restoration drama along
with citations showing where they appear in Restoration and
eighteenth century collections.

4451 Noyes, Robert Gale, and Roy Lamson, Jr. "Broadside-Ballad
Versions of the Songs in Restoration Drama." Harvard Studies
and Notes in Philology and Literature, XIX (1937), 199-218.
  A census of about 1,000 songs in some 500 plays and broad-
side ballads in the major collections of England and the United
States.

4452 Noyes, Robert Gale. "Conventions of Song in Restoration Tragedy."

Publications of the Modern Language Association, LIII (1938),
162-188.

An analysis of the special conventions governing the function
of song in Restoration tragedy. Although made to serve a variety
of purposes, the songs are almost always an integral part of the
dramatic structure.

4453 Sands, Mollie. "English Song-writers of the Eighteenth Century."
Monthly Musical Record, LXIX (1939), 228-233.

Traces influences, trends, types of songs--ballads, love
songs, topical songs--and lesser known song writers of the
period--William Boyce, James Hook, Stephen Storace, and
Thomas Linley.

4454 -----. "English Singers of the Eighteenth Century." Monthly
Musical Record, LXX (1940), 56-60, 76-80.

Part II of a two-part article deals mostly with female singers.
It includes an analysis of the influence of The Beggar's Opera
on English singers and singing. Brief discussion of Susanna
Cibber, Cecilia Arne and Kitty Cline.

4455 Scott, Marion M. "Playthings Come Alive." Monthly Musical
Record, LXX (1940), 12-15.

4456 Scholes, Percy A. "A New Inquiry into the Life and Work of Dr.
Burney." Proceedings of the Musical Association, LXVII
(1941), 1-30.

4457 Sands, Mollie. "The Singing-Master in Eighteenth-Century England." Music and Letters, XXIII (1942), 69-80.

Analysis of the role of the singing master with reference
to contemporary documents, the careers of various foreign
and native teachers, and to technique. The eighteenth century
singing master aimed at perfection in the use of the instrument
over interpretation.

4458 Scholes, Percy A. "George the Third as Music Lover." Musical
Quarterly, XXVIII (January, 1942), 79-92.

Examines George III's relationship with Charles Burney,
Fanny's father, who was a member of the king's private
orchestra. Includes excerpts from Fanny's diary and the dedication "To the King" written by Dr. Johnson for Burney's Handel
book.

4459 Farmer, Henry George. A History of Music in Scotland. London:
Hinrichsen, 1948. 557 pp.

Discusses the 18th century theatre, pp. 300-308.

4460 Simonds, Bruce. "Music in Johnson's London." In The Age of
Johnson, Essays Presented to Chauncey Brewster Tinker. (New
Haven: Yale University Press, 1949), 411-420.

Comments on the opera and music in public performance
generally.

4461 Manifold, J. S. The Music in English Drama from Shakespeare
      to Purcell. London: Rockliff, [1956]. ix, 208 pp.
          A study of the musical conventions and instruments employed
      in the theaters of Shakespeare and Purcell, with a discussion of
      the music in modern productions of six seventeenth century plays.
4462 Sadie, Stanley. "Eighteenth-Century Byways on the Gramaphone."
      Music and Letters, XXXVIII (1957), 378-387.
          Recordings of 18th century music.
4463 Cudworth, Charles. "Laying Handel's Ghost." Listener, LIX (1958),
      297.
          There was other music in the eighteenth century besides
      mere imitations of Handel and Mendelssohn.
4464 Ohl, John F. "Recent Additions to the Music Collection." The New-
      berry Library Bulletin, IV (1958), 302-308.
          Ballad operas, 1728-31.
4465 Matthews, Betty. "Unpublished Letters concerning Handel." Music
      and Letters, XL (1959), 261-268.
          5 letters.
4466 "Purcell and Handel Exhibition." Times Literary Supplement, May
      15, 1959, p. 296.
          Review of a commemorative exhibition at Kings Library of
      the British Museum.
4467 Shaw, Watkins. "A Collection of Musical Manuscripts in the Auto-
      graph of Henry Purcell and Other English Composers, c. 1665-
      1685." Library, XIV (1959), 126-131.
          Barber MS. 5001 in the Music Library of the Barber Institute
      of Fine Arts, University of Birmingham, contains helograph
      copies of works by Blow, Purcell, Cooke, and probably Humfrey
      and Turner. Gives description and index.
4468 Duncan-Jones, E. E. "Marvell and the Song 'In Guilty Night.'"
      Times Literary Supplement, September 9, 1960, p. 577.
4469 Routley, Erik. Music, Sacred and Profane: Occasional Writings
      on Music, 1950-58. London: Independent Press, 1960. 192 pp.
4470 Sadie, Stanley. "The Chamber Music of Boyce and Arne." Musical
      Quarterly, XLVI (October, 1960), 425-436.
          Although Thomas Arne is remembered primarily for his
      songs and music for the 18th century stage, and William Boyce,
      for his symphonies and sacred music, Sadie cites them for
      their contribution "to the chamber music repertory in the form
      of a set of trio sonatas."
4471 -----. "Two British Worthies." Listener, LXIII (1960), 241.
          This discusses "musical careers of William Boyce and
      Thomas Arne."
4472 Schueller, Herbert M. "The Quarrel of the Ancients and the
      Moderns." Music and Letters, XLI (1960), 313-330.

This analyzes the traditional quarrel between classical
economies versus dynamic as it pertains to 18th century music

4473 Avery, Emmett L. "The London Stage." 17th and 18th Century
Theatre Research, I (May, 1962), 12.
Suggestions for further study of the music, dancing, and
periodicals related to Restoration and Eighteenth Century theatre

4474 Mellers, Wilfrid. Harmonious Meeting: A Study of the Relation-
ship Between English Music, Poetry and Theatre, c. 1600-1900.
London: Denis Dobson, 1965. 318 pp.
Deals with the union of poetry and music from the time of
Elizabethan composers to the end of the Romantic Movement.
Although the work concentrates heavily on the seventeenth
century, some chapters consider Purcell, Handel, Gay and
Pepusch.

Musical Drama

4475 Albright, H. Darkes. "The Theory and Staging of Musical Drama."
Ph.D. Cornell University, 1936. 326 pp.
A history of musical drama in Western Europe with emphasis upon the masque, Ballet de Cour, opera, and Wagnerian
music-drama. One chapter treats the masques and first operas
in England. Comic opera is omitted.

4476 Winesanker, Michael. "The Record of English Musical Drama,
1750-1800." Ph.D. Cornell University, 1944.

4477 Henigan, Robert Hamilton. "English Dramma Per Musica: A Study
of Musical Drama in England from The Siege of Rhodes to the
Opening of the Haymarket Theatre." Ph.D. University of Mis-
souri, 1961. 417 pp. (Order No. 61-4068).
Stresses the importance of "Dramma per Musica" in the
Restoration, and demonstrates how typical it is of the period.

Musicians

4478 Stokes, E. "Lists of the King's Musicians from the Audit Office
Declared Accounts." The Musical Antiquary, I (1909-1910);
II (1910-1911); III (1911-1912); IV (1912-1913).

Names

4479 Malone, Kemp. "Meaningful Fictive Names in English Literature."
Names, V (1957), 1-13.
In plays and elsewhere.

Near East

4480 Brown, Wallace Cable. "The Near East in English Drama, 1775-
      1825." Journal of English and Germanic Philology, XLVI (1947),
      63-69.
          The exotic Near East was thoroughly suitable as a setting
      for the Romantic melodrama of the age. Plays on oriental sub-
      jects mirror the English audience's taste for the strange and
      mysterious.

Negro

4481 Dykes, Eva Beatrice. The Negro in English Romantic Thought Or
      A Study of Sympathy for the Oppressed. Washington, D.C.:
      Associated Publishers, Inc., 1942. 197 pp.
          Traces the sympathetic attitude found in poetry and prose
      of the 18th and 19th centuries and finds the Negro and the ame-
      lioration of his condition vital factors in the "main stream of
      romanticism." The anticipations of this attitude in 17th- and
      18th-century authors are also discussed.

Neo-Classicism

4482 Wood, Paul S. "The Opposition to Neo-Classicism in England
      between 1660 and 1700." Publications of the Modern Language
      Association, XLIII (March, 1928), 182-197.
          Discusses a number of obstacles that interferred with "the
      complete dominance of the neo-classical movement after
      1600," especially individualism of the English people, "the
      prestige of Elizabethan literature," and the tendency to object
      to strict Aristotelian rules.
4483 Draper, J. W. "The Rise of English Neo-Classicism." Revue
      Anglo-Americain, X (1933), 399-409.
          Draper defines neo-classical literature as being imitative
      of the classics and based on the principle of symmetrical
      repetition; it is social in theme, unemotional and didactic.
      Neoclassicism "chronicles a moment of pause in the conflict
      of society."
4484 Védier, Georges. Origine et évolution de la dramaturgie néo-
      classique. Paris: Presses Universitaires de France, 1955.
      215 pp.
          The role of the curtain and staging in the neo-classical
      dramaturgy of France and Italy; the relationship between the
      three unities and the plastic arts in the theatre.

New Woman

4485 Gagen, Jean Elizabeth. "Foreshadowings of the New Woman
in English Drama of the Seventeenth and Early Eighteenth
Century." Ph.D. Columbia University, 1950. 311 pp.
(Publication No. 1851).
The modern woman who has achieved equality with man
is foreshadowed in English drama of the seventeenth and
early eighteenth centuries.

Newcastle

4486 Newcastle, Marquis of, William Cavendish. The Phanseys of
William Cavendish Marquis of Newcastle addressed to
Margaret Lucas and Her Letters in Reply. Edited by
Douglas Grant. London: Nonesuch Press, 1956.

Newcastle, Margaret

4487 Turner, James. The Dolphin's Skin: Six Studies in Eccentri-
city. London: Cassell, 1956. xxii, 218 pp.
Includes Duchess of Newcastle.
4488 Grant, Douglas. Margaret the First: A Biography of Margaret Canendish, Duchess of Newcastle, 1623-1673. London: Rupert Hart-Davis, 1957. 253 pp.
A biography discussing her works including her plays
and mentioning drama and dramatists passim.

Newdigate

4489 Wilson, John Harold. "Theatre Notes from the Newdigate Newsletters." Theatre Notebook, XV (Spring, 1961), 79-84.
Newsletters from 1674 through 1715. The collection, total-
ling 3,950 letters are at the Folger Shakespeare Library.
Professor Wilson has culled the theatre news from them, and
prints the entries in chronological order, from March 21,
1673/4, to May 10, 1715.
4490 -----. "More Theatre Notes from the Newdigate Newsletters."
Theatre Notebook, XVI (Winter, 1961/2), 59.
A continuation of material in Theatre Notebook XV (Spring,
1961). From Feb. 4, 1681/2, to Jan. 11, 1693/4/.
4491 -----. "More Theatre Notes from the Newdigate Newsletters."
Theatre Notebook, XVI (Winter, 1962), 59.
Supplement to those already published in Theatre Notebook,
XVI (1961), 79.

Newspapers

4492 Early Newspapers from 1625 to 1850. Offered for sale by Birrell
      & Garnett. Catalogue No. 26. London: Birrell & Garnett, Ltd.
      [1927?-33]. 3 Nos. in 1 Vol.
         Catalogue of a collection which was acquired by Duke Uni-
      versity.
4493 Jackson, A. "Drama and Stage During Anne, Especially As Re-
      flected in the Newspapers." Ph.D. London University (External),
      1936.

Nokes, Robert

4494 Wiley, Autrey Nell. "A Comment upon Nokes." Times Literary
      Supplement, November 9, 1933.

Non-Conformist

4495 Scott, Virgil Joseph.'Topical Satire of the Non-Conformist in
      Restoration Comedy, 1660-1685." Ph.D. Ohio State University,
      1946.

North Shields

4496 King, Robert. North Shields Theatres. A History of the Theatres
      at North Shields and the adjoining village of Tynemouth from
      1765, including an account of the travelling booths, with il-
      lustrations from play-bills, etc. Gateshead on Tyne: Northum-
      berland Press Limited, 1948. 164 pp.
         The first three chapters are devoted to the 18th century
      theatres. Much of the material is drawn from contemporary
      newspaper accounts, particularly the Newcastle Chronicle.

Norwich

4497 Rosenfeld, Sybil. "The Players in Norwich, 1669-1709." Review
      of English Studies, XII (1936), 129-138.
         A history of strolling players visiting Norwich based on
      the Court Books for the period, 1669-1709.
4498 -----. "The Players in Norwich, 1710-1750." Review of English
      Studies, XII (1936), 285-304.
         A history of actors, plays, and theatrical conditions based
      on the Norwich Gazettes for the period, 1710-1750.

Nossiter, Maria

4499 Hogan, Charles B. "A Note on Miss Nossiter." Shakespeare
       Quarterly, III (1952), 284-285.
          Maria Nossiter, actress and mistress of Spranger Barry,
       was born about 1735 and died in 1759. Her first performance
       was in the role of Juliet on October 10, 1753.
4500 Stone, George Winchester, Jr. "The Authorship of A Letter to
       Miss Nossiter (London, 1753)." Shakespeare Quarterly, III
       (1952), 69-70.
          A pamphlet of fifty-six pages (October 30, 1753), strongly
       praising Maria Nossiter for her portrayal of Juliet, was written
       by MacNamara Morgan, an Irish lawyer.

Nurseries

4501 Lawrence, W. J. "Restoration Stage Nurseries." Archiv fur das
       Studium der Neuren Sprachen und Literaturen, CXXXII, New
       Ser., XXXII (1914), 301-315.
          Existed under management of Killigrew and Davenant from
       1667-c.1682 in Hatton Garden, then Vere Street Theatre, then
       on the site of the Old Fortune Theatre; all were failures.

Odell, Thomas

4502 Green-Armytage, R. N. "The Smugglers." Notes and Queries,
       CLXXXVI (1944), 168.
          T. Odell's farce The Smugglers was produced at the Little
       Theatre in the Haymarket in 1729.

Ogilby, J.

4503 Bowers, Fredson. "Ogilby's Coronation Entertainment (1661-
       1689)." Papers of the Bibliographical Society of America,
       XLVII (1953), 339-355.
          Bowers distinguishes the various editions and issues of
       Ogilby's narration of the coronation festivities for Charles II.

O'Hara, Kane

4504 Maxwell, Margaret F. "Olympus at Billingsgate: The Burlettas
       of Kane O'Hara." Educational Theatre Journal, XV (1963),
       130-135.

O'Keefe, John

4505 Huse, William A. "A Noble Savage on the Stage." Modern Philology,
      XXXIII (1936), 303-316.
          A study of the composition and performance of John O'Keefe's
      pantomime, Omai (1785), which analyzes the causes for its
      popularity and demonstrates its importance to the history of
      realism in theatrical costume and scenery.

O'Keeffe, Adelaide

4506 Babcock, R. W. "Adelaide O'Keeffe." Times Literary Supplement,
      January 9, 1937, p. 28.
          Corrects DNB regarding the location of a letter from Adelaide
      O'Keeffe to Henry Colburn of the New Monthly Magazine. Col-
      burn was publishing sections of O'Keeffe's recollections. Con-
      tains selections from the letter.

Oldfield, Anne

4507 Gore-Brown, Robert. Gay was the Pit: The Life and Times of Anne
      Oldfield, Actress (1683-1730). London: Max Reinhardt, 1957.
      192 pp.
          Emphasis on the "Times."

Oldham, John

4508 Brooks, H. F. "The Complete Works of John Oldham (1653-83):
      Edited with an Introduction, Biographical and Critical, Textual
      Apparatus, and Explanatory Notes." Ph.D. Oxford University,
      1940.
4509 Dale, Donald. "John Oldham as a Satirist." Notes and Queries,
      CLXXIX (1940), 42-44.
          John Oldham's verse was considered too rugged by Pope
      and Dryden, but he defended metrical harshness and breaking
      of other rules, on the grounds that his satirical meaning was
      most important.
4510 -----. "The Life of John Oldham." Notes and Queries, CLXXVIII
      (1940), 452-455.
          A brief biography and characterization of John Oldham.
4511 -----. "The Likenesses of John Oldham." Notes and Queries,
      CLXXX (1941), 97-98.
          A portrait of John Oldham is in the possession of a family
      descendant, Mr. William Iles Hillier.
4512 Williams, Weldon M. "The Genesis of John Oldham's Satyrs upon

the Jesuits." Publications of the Modern Language Association, LVIII (1943), 958-970.

> Discusses the various false starts made by Oldham before he took Jonson's Catiline as his model.

4513 -----. "The Influence of Ben Jonson's Catiline upon John Oldham's Satyrs upon the Jesuits." English Literary History, XI (March, 1944), 38-62.

> Finds Oldham's debt greater than he acknowledged.

Opera

4514 Myers, Clara L. "Opera in England from 1656 to 1728." Western Reserve University Bulletin, IX, No. 3 (1906), 129-156.

4515 Krehbiel, Henry Edward, Collector. Voices from the Golden Age of Bel Canto. Edited by Max Spicker. New York: G. Schirmer [c. 1910].

> A collection of 26 opera songs of the 17th and 18th centuries from rare manuscripts and early prints.

4516 Towers, John. Dictionary-Catalogue of Operas and Operettas Which Have Been Performed on the Public Stage. Morgantown, West Virginia: Acme Publishing Company [c. 1910]. 1045 pp.

> Contents: Part I--Dictionary of Opera and Operettas; Part II--Composers and their Operas; Part III--Libretti with the Number of Times They Have Been Set to Music for the Public Lyric Stage.

4517 Cummings, W. H. "Muzio Scevola." Musical Times, LII (1911), 18-19.

> Evidence supports Pipo (Fillipo Mattei) as the composer of Act I, not Ariosti as usually claimed.

4518 Forsyth, Cecil. Music and Nationalism, A Study of English Opera. London: MacMillan and Company, 1911. vii, [3], 359 pp.

> A study of the relationship of nationalism and music. Chapter IV, "The Eighteenth Century and After" (pp. 91-123), discusses the three trends of development after Purcell: (1) Italian opera; (2) English opera, the application of Italian methods to English drama; and (3) the ballad opera. Chapter VI, "Opera Books," discusses librettos, making the point that, excepting Dryden and Gray, they have been written by "literary mongrels."

4519 Goddard, Joseph. The Rise and Development of Opera. Embracing A Comparative View of The Art in Italy, Germany, France and England--Showing the Cause of the Falling Back of the English School in the Modern Period and the Conversation Which That Falling Back Involved. Numerous Musical Examples. Portraits and Facsimiles. London: Wm. Reeves, 1911. vii, [1], 210 pp. Index.

In the fourth section six chapters are devoted to English
opera, more in the nature of a summary than a study of any
specific details.

4520 Prunières, Henri. L'Opéra Italien en France Avant Lulli. Paris:
Edouard Champi on, 1913. 431 pp.

Chapter VII is on the influence of Italian opera on the French
theatre and French music.

4521 Cummings, W. H. "The Lord Chamberlain and Opera in London,
1700-1740." Proceedings of the Musical Association, XL (January 20, 1914), 37-71.

A description of the content of documents--letters, agree-
ments, lists of salaries, receipts for performances, autographs
of notable people--connected with the establishment of Italian
Opera in London at Drury Lane, the Haymarket, and Covent
Garden--originally in the possession of Vice-Chamberlain Coke.

4522 Sonneck, O. G. The Early Opera in America. New York: G.
Schirmer [1915?]. 230 pp.

The history to 1800.

4523 Armstrong, A. Joseph. Operatic Performances in England before
Handel. Waco, Texas: Baylor University, 1918. 74 pp.

A history of "the rise and progress of English opera from
1656...until the introduction of Italian librettos by Handel and
his co-workers." An examination of forty-two operas by Motteux, Davenant, Dryden, Durfet, Duffet, Durfey, Settle,
MacSwiney, Shadwell, Addison, Congreve, Dennis, and Granville.

4524 Landormy, Paul C. R. A History of Music. Translated, with a
supplementary chapter on American music, by Frederick H.
Martens. New York: Charles Scribner's Sons, 1923.

Chapter IV, "Opera in the 17th Century," includes a two
page treatment of Henry Purcell and English opera.

4525 Colman, Francis. "Opera Register, 1712-34." Mask, XII (July,
1926), 110-112.

Reprints the register, with an illustration of the Haymarket
Opera House in 1790.

4526 -----. "Opera Register, 1712-1734." The Mask, XIII (1927), 18-
23.

Part Two of a two-part article, this reprints Colman's
Opera Register for January 9, 1713-14 to April 18, 1734. The
problem is that Colman died in 1733. (Part One is in The Mask,
XII [1926], 110-112).

4527 Dent, Edward J. Foundations of English Opera: A Study of Musical Drama in England during the Seventeenth Century. Cambridge University Press, 1928. xi, 242 pp.

A survey of English opera from 1656 to 1700, with plot sum-

meries, a study of pre-Restoration masques, and an examination of the efforts of Davenant, Dryden, and Shadwell, who
worked with Purcell and other musicians.

4528 "Eighteenth Century Italian Opera." Etude, XLVI (October, 1928),
735.

On the rigid laws governing operatic composition.

4529 [Opera]. Notes and Queries, CLV (August 11, 1928), 106.

Reviews E. Dent, Foundations of English Opera (1928). Asserts that Dent has neglected the importance of the tradition of
English spoken drama in causing the failure of opera.

4530 Predeek, Albert. "Handel in London." Living Age, CCCXXXIV
(March 1, 1928), 438-441. (Reprinted from Neue Zürcher
Zeitung, December 28, 29, 1927.)

Reprints three 1728 letters describing operatic performances
including the Beggar's Opera.

4531 Walmsley, D. M. "The Influence of Foreign Opera on English Oper
atic Plays of the Restoration Period." Anglia, LII (1928), 37-50.

An effort to follow the court masque element through the
Restoration age, focussing upon structure and showing the indebtedness of late English opera to the masque form.

4532 Babcock, R.W. "Eighteenth Century Comic Opera Manuscripts."
Publications of the Modern Language Association, LII (1937),
907-908.

A brief examination of twelve late eighteenth century comic
opera MSS listed in British Museum Catalogue 91 of Drama
Manuscripts.

4533 Noyes, Robert Gale. "Contemporary Musical Settings of the Songs
in Restoration Dramatic Operas." Harvard Studies and Notes
in Philology and Literature, XX (1938), 99-121.

A list of songs and of the sources containing the music to
which they were set.

4534 West, Dorothy Irene. Italian Opera in England (1660-1740), and
Some of Its Relationships to English Literature. Abstract of
doc. diss. Urbana: University of Illinois Press, 1938. 24 pp.

An extended criticism of opera with emphasis upon its
relation to neoclassical literary standards, to romanticism,
and to contemporary musical theory. A survey of the critical
opinion of the form during the period is included.

4535 Dewes, Simon. Mrs. Delony. London: Rich & Cowan, Ltd. [1940].
xii, [13]-320 pp.

The story of Mary Granville, niece of Lord Lansdowne,
and her acquaintance with Handel is treated, together with a
picture of the society and theatre of the time, particularly
opera.

4536 Brockway, Wallace, and Weinstock, Herbert. The Opera, a History

of Its Creation and Performance: 1660-1941. New York: Simon
& Schuster [c 1941]. viii, 603 pp.

A survey of opera in England, France, Germany, Italy,
Russia and the United States. Special attention to Purcell and
Handel in England; also comment on Gay's Beggar's Opera.

4537 Loewenberg, Alfred. Annals of Opera, 1597-1940. Cambridge:
Heffer and Sons, 1943. 879 pp.

4538 Betz, Siegmund A. E. "The Operatic Criticism of The Tatler and
The Spectator." Musical Quarterly, XXXI (1945), 318-330.

Locates and studies those passages in the periodicals dealing
with opera.

4539 Grout, D. A Short History of Opera. Oxford: University Press,
1947. xiii, 711 pp.

A general survey, with very full bibliography. Includes
"Opera in England," "The Operas of Handel," and "Eighteenth-
Century Comic Opera."

4540 Schueller, Herbert M. "Literature and Music as Sister Arts: An
Aspect of Aesthetic Theory in Eighteenth Century Britain."
Philological Quarterly, XXVI (1947), 193-205.

Considers theories of opera in the eighteenth century, particularly the view that the words, the music and the acting produced an organic unit.

4541 Haun, Eugene. "The Libretti of the Restoration Opera in English:
A Study in Theatrical Genres." Ph.D. University of Pennsylvania,
1954. 330 pp. (Publication No. 8551).

The dramatic opera, which reached its peak about 1690, had
its origin in the "dramatic masque." Davenant, Dryden, Flecknoe,
and Tate worked with this type of opera.

4542 Gaydon, A. H. "The Comic Character in English Opera before 1776."
M.A. Bristol University, 1955-56.

4543 Loewenberg, Alfred. Annals of Opera, 1597-1940. Compiled from
the Original Sources. With an Introduction by Edward J. Dent.
2nd edition. Revised and Corrected [by Frank Walker]. 2 vols.
Genève: Societas Bibliographica [1955]. xxvi, 1756 columns.

A catalogue of opera performances and history. Entries arranged chronologically in order of first performance, and consist of composer/librettist, title as it first appeared on playbills or libretto, date and town of first performance, literary
source of libretto (if any), and notes on subsequent history of
the work. Indexes: operas, composers, librettists, general.

4544 Heriot, Angus. The Castrati in Opera. London: Secker & Warburg,
1956. 243 pp.

Special attention to 18th century England.

4545 Kerman, Joseph. Opera as Drama. London: Oxford University
Press, 1957. 269 pp.

References to 18th century works indexed.

4546 Ingram, R. W. "Operatic Tendencies in Stuart Drama." <u>Musical</u>
      <u>Quarterly,</u> XLIV (1958), 489-502.
      Pre-Davenant.

4547 Rosenthal, Harold. <u>Two</u> <u>Centuries</u> <u>of</u> <u>Opera</u> at <u>Covent</u> <u>Garden</u>.
      With a Foreword by the Earl of Harewood. London: Putnam,
      1958. xiv, 849 pp.
      A history of the Covent Garden Theatre, its founding and
      management, and the performances of opera there through
      1957. Detailed information concerning composers, librettists,
      musicians, actors, and opera companies associated with the
      theatre. Numerous illustrations and portraits.

4548 White, Eric Walter. "The Rehearsal of an Opera." <u>Theatre</u> <u>Note-</u>
      <u>book,</u> XIV (1960), 79-90.
      Discusses the authorship and subject of paintings traced to
      Walpole's Strawberry Hill Collection, one of which is "The
      Rehearsal of an Opera."

4549 McManaway, James G. "Entertainment for the Grand Duke of
      Tuscany." <u>Theatre</u> <u>Notebook,</u> XVI (Autumn, 1961), 20-21.
      Reproduces the passage recording a performance of an
      opera and ballet based on the story of Psyche, performed be-
      fore Cosimo the Third Grand Duke of Tuscany, at Drury Lane,
      June 3, 1669.

4550 Rosenfeld, Sybil. "An Opera House Account Book." <u>Theatre</u> <u>Note-</u>
      <u>book,</u> XVI (Spring, 1962), 83-88.
      Account Book for the 1716-17 season of the King's Theatre,
      Haymarket, from a manuscript in the Hampshire Record Office
      in Winchester.

4551 Shepperson, Wilbur S., and John G. Folkes. "Biographical Notes
      on Sir John Oldmixon." <u>Notes</u> <u>and</u> <u>Queries,</u> New Ser., IX
      (1962), 4-5.
      Discussion and a correction of erroneous statements con-
      cerning the biography of Sir John Oldmixon published in <u>Notes</u>
      <u>and</u> <u>Queries</u> in 1867, and in other periodicals.

4552 Krummel, Donald W. "'Viva tutti': the Musical Journeys of an
      Eighteenth-Century Part-Song." <u>Bulletin</u> <u>of</u> <u>the</u> <u>New</u> <u>York</u> <u>Public</u>
      <u>Library,</u> LXVII (1963), 57-64.
      The use of "Viva tutti" in 18th century London comic opera.

4553 Temperley, Nicholas. "The English Romantic Opera." <u>Victorian</u>
      <u>Studies,</u> IX (1966), 293-301.
      A study of 19th-century English opera which includes brief
      references to the English opera of the 18th century.

4554 White, Eric Walter. "English Opera Research, the Immediate
      Past and the Future: A Personal Viewpoint." <u>Theatre</u> <u>Note-</u>
      <u>book,</u> XXI (Autumn, 1966), 32-37.

Comments on English opera research during the last fifteen
years. Includes references to English versions of 17th-century
Italian operas, to works by Purcell and Handel, and to 18th-
century ballad operas, pasticcio operas, burlettas, and comic
operas.

4555 Fenner, Theodore Lincoln. "Leigh Hunt on Opera: The Examiner
Years." Ph.D. Columbia University, 1967. (Order No. 68-
8578).

Chapter I discusses the traditions of Italian Opera and "English opera" and describes the complex cultural attitudes and
conditions that affected the state of opera during the Examiner
years (1808-1822).

Orchestra

4556 Lawrence, W. J. "The English Theatre Orchestra; Its Rise and
Early Characteristics." Musical Quarterly, III (1917), 9-27.

The theatre orchestra began in the Restoration period. Its
origins were with opera. Numerous references to plays,
operas and theatres, with plates of stages and theatres.

Orient

4557 Clark, Thomas B. "The Orient in England As Reflected in Eighteenth-
Century Drama." Ph.D. Vanderbilt University, 1937.

Oriental Influence

4558 Wann, Louis. "The Oriental in Restoration Drama." University
of Wisconsin Studies in Language and Literature, No. 2 (September, 1918), 163-186.

Forty-five plays of the Restoration are Oriental in setting
or character. These plays are mostly heroic plays and tragedies, are based mostly on history, travel, French dramas
and romances, use sources loosely, distort character, but
do contain many details on Oriental customs.

4559 Clarke, Blake. "The Orient in England as Reflected in Eighteenth
Century Drama." Ph.D. Vanderbilt University, 1937.

This essay in cultural history is a study of the relation
between the growing interest in the Orient and the dramatic
representation of Eastern ideas and institutions. It seeks to
define the prevalent English attitudes toward the Orient.

4560 Clark, T[homas] Blake. Oriental England: A Study of Oriental
Influences in Eighteenth-Century England as Reflected in the
Drama. Shanghai: Kelly & Walsh, 1939. 200 pp.

An extended discussion of the historical background of
Oriental influence in England; covers heroic drama, fantasy
plays, the Nabob or very rich Indian, and plays concerned with
real presentation of the institutions and customs of the Orient.

Otway, Thomas

works

4561 Otway, Thomas. The Complete Works of Thomas Otway. Edited
by Montague Summers. 3 vols. London: Nonesuch Press, 1926.
The complete and definitive edition. The prefatory note ob-
serves that the tragedies of Otway often satirize the Popish Plot.
Introduction presents a full examination of Otway's career.
Copiously annotated.

4562 -----. "An Edition of the Works of Thomas Otway, with Biography
and Commentary." Edited by J. C. Ghosh. Ph.D. Oxford University, 1929.
Several new facts are introduced: the date of death of Otway's
father (Feb. 1671), a new record of Otway's birth at Winchester
College, and records of his attendance at Christ Church.

4563 -----. The Works of Thomas Otway. Plays, Poems and Love-Let-
ters. Edited by J. C. Ghosh. 2 vols. Oxford: Clarendon Press,
1932.
This edition of Otway's works contains critical essays on the
life and works of Otway as well as a bibliography. With a minor
exception, the present text is based on the first edition of every
work.

individual texts

4564 -----. The Orphan and Venice Preserved. Edited by C. F.
McClumpha. Boston and London: D. C. Heath & Co., 1908.
xl, 351 pp.
This edition includes a brief life of Otway as well as a critical
essay on the restoration in general, Otway's literary contributions in particular. The edition is a reprint of the 17th-century
spelling and "recovers the text of the quartos from oversights
and unnecesary emendations of former editors."

biography and criticism

4565 Johnson, Alfred. Lafosse, Otway, St. Réal: Origines et Trans-
formations d'un Thème Tragique. Paris: Librairie Hachette et
Cie., 1901. 449 pp. (Thèse présentée pour le doctorat de

l'universite de Paris [lettres].)

    Analyzes Otway's Venice Preserved and discusses its rela-
tion to works of St. Réal and Lafosse. Appendix: "Notes et documents sur Otway et ses oeuvres."

4566 Luick, Karl. "Uber Otway's Venice Preserved." Inaugural Dis-
      sertation. Wien, 1902.

4567 Gerould, Gordon Hall. "The Sources of Venice Preserved." Journal
      of English and Germanic Philology, V (1903), 58-61.

    Argues that Otway borrowed the character of Belvidera, the
circumstance of her being held as surety, and the buffoon character of Antonio from the characters Bellamira and Ascanio in
Lee's Caesar Borgia.

4568 Falke, Johannes. Die deutschen Bearbeitungen des "geretteten
      Venedig" von Otway, 1682. Rostock Dissertation, 1906. 62 pp.

    Treats adaptations--primarily German, with some French--
of Otway's Venice Preserv'd from Lafosse's Manlius Capitolinus
(1698), to Hofmannsthal's Das gerettete Venedig (1905).

4569 Ashwell, K. E. "Otway: His Indebtedness in Tragedy to French
      Drama and to the Nouvelles de Saint-Réal." M.A. London Uni-
      versity (External), 1908.

4570 Sperlin, Otis Bedney. "The Relation of Otway's Tragedies to the
      Heroic Play." Ph.D. University of Chicago, 1908. 63 pp.

    Discusses Alcibiades (1675), Don Carlos (1676), The Orphan
(1680), and Venice Preserved (1682). Otway's first tragedy
was entirely under the heroic influence, his second was a compromise, his third almost wholly a translation, and his last
three tragedies early attempts in that field. Otway's desertion
of the Heroic Play was complete, not partial, as was Lee's.

4571 Wenther, Fritz. Das gerettete Venedig, eine vergleichende Studie.
      Berkeley: University of California Press, 1914. 160 pp.

4572 Hagemann, Gustav. Shakespeare's Einfluss auf Otway's künstler-
      ische Entwiklung. Münster: Westfälischen Vereindruckerei,
      1917. 71 pp.

    An analysis of Alcibiades and Don Carlos shows increasing
Shakespearian influence in use of themes, ghosts, and phrase-
ology and reveals that Otway learned the real essence of tragedy
from Shakespeare.

4573 Dulong, Gustave. L'Abbé de Saint-Real: Étude sur Les Rapports
      de l'Histoire et du Roman au XVIIe Siècle. 2 vols. Paris:
      Libraire Ancienne Honoré Champion. 1921.

    A consideration, in Vol. II, of Otway's adaptation of Dom
Carlos. In addition, throughout the section on "Les Adaptations
Dramatiques de Dom Carlos," there are many references to
Otway.

4574 Benham, Allen R. "Notes on Plays." Modern Language Notes,

XXXVIII (1923), 252.

Mentions an eighth edition (1743) of Lillo's <u>Fatal Curiosity</u> before the collected edition of 1750; a note on Otway's <u>Venice Preserv'd</u> indicates that Jaffeir is related to the hero caught between love and honor in the heroic drama.

4575 Ghosh, J. C. "Thomas Otway and Mrs. Barry." <u>Notes and Queries</u>, 12th Ser., XII (February, 1923), 103-105.

A discussion of the tradition of Otway's unhappy love for Mrs. Barry, with the conclusion that there is no basis in fact for such legends.

4576 -----. "New Light on Some Episodes in the Life of Thomas Otway." <u>Notes and Queries</u>, 13th Ser., I (1924), 421-424; 439-442; 459-463.

A discussion of various episodes in Otway's life, including consideration of his relationships with Mrs. Behn, Dryden, Rochester, Nell Gwynne, Thomas Shadwell.

4577 Schumacher, Edgar. <u>Thomas Otway</u>. Bern, N. Dürrenmatt-Egger, 1924. 175 pp.

Study of the life and works. Extended analysis of "Venice Preserved."

4578 Ham, Roswell G. "The Life and Writings of Thomas Otway." Ph.D. Yale University, 1925.

4579 -----. "The Portraits of Thomas Otway." <u>Notes and Queries</u>, CXLIX (August 15, 1925), 111-113.

Discusses the seven extant portraits.

4580 -----. "Thomas Otway, Rochester, and Mrs. Barry." <u>Notes and Queries</u>, CXLIX (September 5, 1925), 165-167.

Discusses references to Barry's career and relations with Otway and Rochester.

4581 McCarthy, Desmond. "<u>The Orphan</u>." <u>New Statesman</u>, XXV (May 16, 1925), 134-135.

A confused comment on Elizabethan acting and a review of the Phoenix production of Otway's play.

4582 Royde-Smith, N. G. "Murder and Orphans." <u>Outlook</u> (London), LV (May 16, 1925), 329.

Reviews the Phoenix Society production.

4583 Ham, Roswell G. "Additional Material for a Life of Thomas Otway." <u>Notes and Queries</u>, CL (January 30, 1926), 75-77.

His ancestry; Humphrey Otway, his father; Elizabeth Otway, his mother; at Cambridge; rival plays; a Whiggish criticism of <u>Venice Preserved</u>.

4584 -----. "New Facts about Otway." <u>Times Literary Supplement</u>, January 14, 1926, p. 28.

Discusses Otway's playhouse brawl with John Churchill and promises new facts on Otway's death.

4585 ------. "Otway's Duels with Churchill and Settle." Modern Lan-
        guage Notes, XLI (February, 1926), 73-80.
            Reports the discovery of a duel between Otway and Church-
        ill, and reinterprets the quarrel between Otway and Settle.
4586 [Dobrée, Bonamy]. "Thomas Otway." Times Literary Supplement,
        March 3, 1927, pp. 133-134.
            An essay on the nature of heroic tragedy and Otway's con-
        tribution to it. (A lead article, reviewing M. Summers' edition
        of the Complete Works of Thomas Otway [1926].)
4587 Fayle, C. Ernest. "An Otway Play." Times Literary Supplement,
        August 23, 1928, p. 605.
            A lost play by Otway is sought by Thomas Betterton in the
        Gazette for 25-29 November 1686.
4588 Leader, Dorothy Estella. "Shakespeare's Influence on Otway."
        M.A. University of Minnesota, 1928. 93 pp.
            Sees the Restoration as a time of battle between French order
        and English lawlessness in drama, and finds Otway's powers of
        moving the passions to be derived from Shakespeare; finds simi-
        larities of plot, character, dialogue, and dramatic technique.
4589 Moore, John Robert. "Contemporary Satire in Otway's Venice
        Preserved." Publications of the Modern Language Association,
        XLIII (March, 1928), 166-181.
            A detailed study of the satire directed at Shaftesbury and
        his supporters.
4590 Summers, Montague. "An Otway Play." Times Literary Supplement,
        August 30, 1928.
            Observes that the "lost play" of C. E. Fayle (TLS, August
        23, 1928) has long been known to students.
4591 Ham, Roswell Gray. Otway and Lee: Biography from a Baroque
        Age. New Haven: Yale University Press, 1931. vii, 250 pp.
        Index.
            Analysis of the works of each. Stresses fact that Otway
        worked according to the public mind. Comparison of their
        works. Feels these two reveal salient features of Restoration
        tragedy.
4592 Babcock, R.W. "The Reverend Montague Summers as Editor of
        Otway." Publications of the Modern Language Association,
        XLVIII (1933), 948-952.
4593 Stroup, T. B. "Type-Characters in the Serious Drama of the
        Restoration with Special Attention to the Plays of Davenant,
        Dryden, Lee, and Otway." Ph.D. University of North Carolina,
        1933.
4594 Riva, S. "Otway, Saint Réal e la 'Venezia Salvata.'" Dante, Revue
        de Culture Latine, June, 1936, pp. 278-282.
            Riva argues that Otway knew the novels and historical writings

of Cesare Vichard, Abbe of Saint Réal, and that these writings
had some influence on the content of <u>Don Carlos</u> and on the
setting and plot of <u>Venice Preserv'd</u>.

4595 Eich, Louis M. "A Previous Adaptation of <u>Romeo and Juliet</u>."
      <u>Quarterly Journal of Speech</u>, XXIII (1937), 589-594.
         An analysis of Otway's <u>The History and Fall of Caius Marius</u>
      (1680) with speculation about the reasons for Otway's changes
      in the Shakespearean text.

4596 Mackenzie, Aline F. "Otway and the History of His Plays on the
      London Stage, A Study of Taste." Ph.D. Bryn Mawr University,
      1943.

4597 -----. "A Note on the Date of <u>The Orphan</u>." <u>English Literary</u>
      <u>History</u>, XII (December, 1945), 316-326.
         It was composed 1676-1678, and revised in 1679.

4598 -----. "A Note on Pierre's White Hat." <u>Notes and Queries</u>,
      CXCII (March 8, 1947), 90-93.
         A Stuart emblem worn on stage by actors Mills and Quin in
      the early eighteenth century.

4599 -----. "<u>Venice Preserved</u> Reconsidered." <u>Tulane Studies in Eng-</u>
      <u>lish</u>, I (1949), 81-118.
         The play was composed during two different periods, and
      so shows an ambiguity of political reference.

4600 Goldberg, Homer. "Notes on Restoration Plays: (2) The Two 1692
      Editions of Otway's <u>Caius Marius</u>." <u>Studies in Bibliography</u>,"
      III (1950-1951), 253-254.
         Goldberg analyzes the bibliographical problems raised by
      the two editions.

4601 -----. "The Two 1692 Editions of Otway's 'Caius Marius.'"
      <u>Studies in Bibliography</u>, III (1950-1951), 253-254.
         The author states that Woodward and McManaway entry No.
      882, as an issue, is in error and that No. 882 is, in reality,
      another edition.

4602 Taylor, Aline M. <u>Next to Shakespeare: Otway's Venice Preserv'd</u>
      <u>and The Orphan and Their History on the London Stage</u>. Dur-
      ham: Duke University Press, 1950. 328 pp.
         This study is (1) a critical analysis of the two plays, (2) a
      detailed history of their fortunes on the London stage, and (3)
      a survey of Otway's reputation.

4603 Meyerstein, E. H. W. "The Dagger in <u>Venice Preserv'd</u>." Times
      <u>Literary Supplement</u>, September 7, 1951, p. 565.
         In Act V (lines 475-477 of Ghosh's edition) Jaffeir's command
      "bear this in safety to her" refers to the dagger.

4604 Spring, Joseph E. "Two Restoration Adaptations of Shakespeare's
      Plays--<u>Sauny the Scot</u>, or <u>The Taming of the Shrew</u> by John
      Lacy and <u>The History and Fall of Caius Marius</u>, Thomas Otway's

Appropriation of Romeo and Juliet." Ph.D. University of Denver, 1952. 417 pp.

This study documents, by means of textual analysis, "the already existing contributions toward Shakespeare's plays and the ways of adapting them."

4605 Gregor, Joseph. Der Schauspielfürer. 8 vols. Stuttgart: Hiersemann, 1953-[1965].

Vol. 3 (Das englische Drama) includes material on Otway's Venice Preserved, 1682. Vol. 6 includes Sheridan's School for Scandal. Entries consist of scene-by-scene summary of the play, general information including dates of first performance and printing. Indexes according to genre, author, title, year of first printing.

4606 Kiendler, Grete. Konvertierte Formen in den Dramen Otways und Lees: Ein Vergleich mit der Sprache Shakespeares. Graz, 1953. 207 pp.

4607 Challen, W. H. "Thomas Otway." Notes and Queries, New Ser., I (July 1, 1954), 316-317.

4608 Batzer, Hazel Margaret. "Heroic and Sentimental Elements in Thomas Otway's Tragedies." Ph.D. University of Michigan, 1956.

Regards Otway as a transitional dramatist.

4609 Martin, Jay Herbert. "An Essay on Venice Preserved." M.A. Ohio State University, 1957.

4610 Blakiston, Noel. "Otway's Friend." Times Literary Supplement, August 15, 1958, p. 459.

Discusses Otway's relationship with Milton.

4611 Hauser, David R. "Otway Preserved: Theme and Form in Venice Preserv'd." Studies in Philology, LV (1958), 481-493.

A discussion of the ways in which Otway overcomes the heroic conventions to write a "sound tragedy"; the most important way is his ordering of language as revealed in a study of the relationship between imagery and plot.

4612 Hughes, R. E. "'Comic Relief' in Otway's 'Venice Preserv'd.'" Notes and Queries, CCIII (February, 1958), 65-66.

Defense of Antonio-Aguilina scenes.

4613 McBurney, William H. "Otway's Tragic Muse Debauched: Sensuality in Venice Preserv'd." Journal of English and Germanic Philology, LVIII (1959), 380-399.

Suggests that sensuality has an element of pivotal importance in the total impact of the play has been overlooked. Argues that Otway used types of characters and erotic imagery as it was often found in Restoration comic drama.

4614 Lefèvre, André. "Racine en Angleterre au XVIIe siècle: Titus and Berenice de Thomas Otway." Revue de littérature comparée,

XXXIV (1960), 251-257.

Parallel passages.

4615 Cole, David Stuart. "Venice Preserv'd: Morality, Structure and Dramatic Uses of Language." Honors Thesis. Harvard University, 1963. 33, v pp.

Discusses the play in terms of three major themes: 1) the love and honor theme as it has been melded with the assignment of moral responsibility; 2) the parallel scenes as a device of dramatic structure; 3) the language of the play.

4616 Cooke, M. G. "The Restoration Ethos of Byron's Classical Plays." Publications of the Modern Language Association, LXXIX (1964) 569-578.

Byron's classicism is the classicism of the Restoration. His theories and practice of drama are dependent especially on Dryden. Includes extensive comparison of Byron's Sardanapalus with Dryden's All for Love, and illustrates some of Byron's borrowings from Otway's Venice Preserv'd for his Marino Faliero.

4617 Fried, Gisela. Gestalt und Funktion der Bilder im Drama Thomas Otways. Göttingen: Vandenhoeck und Ruprecht, 1965. 154 pp. (Palaestra: Untersuchungen aus der deutschen und englischen Philologie und Literaturgeschichte, Bd. 239).

Treats the plays in chronological order.

4618 Summers, Montague. "A Note on Otway." Times Literary Supplement, June 7, 1965, p. 275.

4619 Gillespie, Gerald. "The Rebel in Seventeenth Century Tragedy." Comparative Literature, XVIII (1966), 324-336.

A comparative study of Savinien Cyrano de Bergerac's La Mort d'Agrippine (1633), Daniel Casper von Lohenstein's Epicharis (1665), and Otway's Venice Preserv'd (1682) outlines the development of the 17th century rebel from satanic antagonist to sentimental villain.

4620 Hauser, David R. "Otway Preserved: Theme and Form in Venice Preserv'd." Restoration Dramatists: A Collection of Critical Essays. (Twentieth Century Views). Edited by Earl Miner. (Englewood Cliffs, N.J.: Prentice-Hall, Inc., 1966), 139-149.

Reprinted from Studies in Philology, LV (1958), 481-493. Purposes to demonstrate "how Otway partially overcomes the obstructions of the heroic conventions to reanimate the dramatic mechanism of his age," and "to explore means by which the play may be viewed as more organic and more highly wrought artistically than has previously been allowed."

4621 Taylor, Aline Mackenzie. "Venice Preserv'd." Restoration Drama: Modern Essays in Criticism. (A Galaxy Book). Edited by John Loftis. (New York: Oxford University Press, 1966), 195-228.

Reprinted from Next to Shakespeare: Otway's Venice
Preserv'd and The Orphan (Durham: Duke University Press,
1950), 39-72. An analysis of the plot, characterization and
theme of the play which attempts to explain the play's early
popularity and the conflicting impressions modern readers derive
from the text.

4622 Kleineberger, H. R. "Otway's 'Venice Preserv'd' and Hofmannsthal's 'Das Gerettete Venedig.'" Modern Language Review, LXII
(1967), 292-297.
Discusses Hofmannsthal's 1903-04 adaptation of Otway's
play and notes particularly the changes the author made in the
relationship of Pierre and Jaffier to reflect his own relationship with his fellow poet, Stefan George.

4623 Stroup, Thomas B. "Otway's Bitter Pessimism." Essays in English
Literature of the Classical Period Presented to Dougald Mac-
Millan. Edited by Daniel W. Patterson and Albrecht B. Strauss.
Studies in Philology, (Extra Series, January, 1967), pp. 54-75.
Studies the outgrowth of Otway's pessimism as it finds ex-
pression in dramatic devices and contrivances, in the elements
of structure, and in the quality and meaning of the plays, espec-
ially the tragedies.

4624 Williams, Gordon. "The Sex-Death Motive in Otway's Venice
Preserv'd." Trivium, II (1967), 59-70.

Oxford

4625 Lawrence, W. J. "The King's Players at Oxford, 1661-1712."
Times Literary Supplement, February 28, 1929, p. 163.
Adds to the evidence of R. C. Rhodes (TLS, February 21,
1929) that plays were performed at Oxford.

4626 Rosenfeld, Sybil. "Some Notes on the Players in Oxford, 1661-
1713." Review of English Studies, XIX (October, 1943), 366-
375.
A chronologically arranged account of the companies which
played in Oxford, 1661-1713--treats the plays they performed
and other relevant material.

Ozell, John

4627 Hodges, John C. "The Authorship of Squire Trelooby." Review of
English Studies, IV (October, 1928), 404-413.
Ascribes the printed play of 1704 to John Ozell and notes it as
reprinted in Ozell's translated works of Molière (1714). John
Downes ascribed the earlier acted version to Congreve, Vanbrugh,
and Walsh. James Ralph published what he said was Vanbrugh's
play in 1734.

Pageants

4628 Bunt, Cyril G. E. "The Art of the Pageant as Illustrated in Prints."
      Connoisseur, CXV (1945), 71-78, 111.
          Pageants during the reigns of William III and Anne are dis-
      cussed and illustrated.

Paintings

4629 Mander, Raymond, and Joe Mitchenson. The Artist and the Theatre
      The Story of the Paintings Collected and Presented to the Nation-
      al Theatre by W. Somerset Maugham. Melbourne, London,
      Toronto: William Heinemann, Ltd., 1955. xxii, 280 pp.
          Some forty-two sets of paintings, most of which are 18th-
      century works, or depictions from 18th-century plays, by such
      artists as John Zoffany, Samuel de Wilde, Robert William Buss,
      Francis Hayman, J. B. Van Loo, John Boaden. A large number
      of pictures are devoted to Garrick. The background of each
      work is discussed.

Paisible, James

4630 Lawrence, W. J. "Rare en Tout; and James Paisible." The Musi-
      cal Antiquary, II (October, 1910), 57-58.
          A comedy in three acts and prologue "Melée de Musique et
      de Balets," the third act changing to a "feste pastoralle,"
      produced by the authoress, Mme. Le Roche-Guillren, and
      James Paisible at Whitehall in 1677 and published the same year.

Palimpsest

4631 Harbage, Albert. "Elizabethan-Restoration Palimpsest." Modern
      Language Review, XXXV (1940), 287-319.
          "Certain playwrights after 1660 secured, in manuscript, un-
      printed plays written before 1642, modernized them, and had
      them produced and published as their own." Suggests identificati
      of several lost originals.

Palmer, John

4632 Knight, Joseph. "John Palmer." Mask, XIV (1928), 133.
          Extracts from Knight's DNB biography of the actor, with a
      silhouette by Daniel Nicholas Chodowiecki.
4633 Spencer, David G. "Gentleman John and Jack Plausible." Notes
      and Queries, New Ser., VIII (February, 1961), 60-61.

Clarifies the confusion between the two John Palmers who
appeared as leading actors at Drury Lane in the eighteenth
century.

Pantomime

4634 Broadbent, R. J. A History of Pantomime. London: Simpkin,
Marshall, Hamilton, Kent & Co., Ltd., 1901. 226 pp.
This history contains chapters on pantomimes and drolls
during the Commonwealth, the introduction of pantomime to
the English stage by John Weaver and John Rich, and on Joseph
Grimaldi, reputed to be the unrivaled clown in pantomime.
4635 Park, William. "Some Unfilmed Movies of Our Forefathers."
The Drama, X (January, 1920), 145-147.
An article on pantomime which discusses at length Julia of
Louvain (1797) and The Child of Mystery (1800).
4636 Disher, M. W. Clowns and Pantomimes. London: Constable and
Co., 1925. xx, 344 pp.
This is an illustrated study of clowns and pantomimes, including an essay on laughter and emotion, ranging from the
comic figures of Menander and beyond to Charles Chaplin.
Generous sections are devoted to 18th century English Literature.
4637 Avery, Emmett L. "Dancing and Pantomime on the English Stage,
1700-1737." Studies in Philology, XXI (1934), 417-452.
Deals with the emergence and development of dancing and
pantomime as entertainments supplementing the dramatic
presentations of the eighteenth century.
4638 "Christmas Pantomime." Times Literary Supplement, November
22, 1934, pp. 803-804.
4639 Wells, Mitchell P. "Some Notes on the Early Eighteenth Century
Pantomime." Studies in Philology, XXXII (1935), 598-607.
Further corrective commentary upon E. L. Avery, "Dancing
and Pantomime on the English Stage, 1700-1737," SP, XXXI
(1934), 417-452. Wells distinguishes the native pantomime from
the commedia dell' arte and adds some notes about the popularity of the form after 1723.
4640 Wilson, A. E. King Panto, The Story of Pantomime. (London
edition title: Christmas Pantomime, The Story of an English
Institution). New York: E. P. Dutton, 1935. 262 pp.
A superficial, careless, and distorted history of pantomime
with negative value as scholarship.
4641 Avery, Emmett L. "The Defense and Criticism of Pantomimic
Entertainments in the Early Eighteenth Century." English
Literary History, V (1938), 127-145.

A history of the critical controversy surrounding the theatrical performance of pantomime during the first forty years
of the century. Although the form was belittled and satirized,
its economic success made it increasingly popular in the theatre

4642 Wells, Mitchell. "Spectacular Scenic Effects of the Eighteenth-
Century Pantomime." Philological Quarterly, XVII (1938), 67-81
An historical account illustrating the range and variety of unusual, often extravagant, scenic devices which were a prominent
feature in the performances of pantomimes.

4643 Wilson, Albert Edward. Pantomime Pageant; a Procession of Harle
quins, Clowns... London: S. Paul & Co., [1946]. 136 pp.
Describes the producers, managers, writers, and artists
associated with pantomime since it became a recognized
"Christmas institution." Pantomime is depicted through the
eyes of contemporary critics and playgoers. Many references
to 17th- and 18th-century pantomime, especially in chapters
1-3.

4644 Miesle, Frank L. "The Staging of Pantomime Entertainment on
the London Stage: 1715-1808." Ph.D. Ohio State University,
1955.
The study describes pantomime programming, literary aspects of pantomime, performers and their styles, scenes,
scene-changing, mechanical tricks, and grand finales.

Parody

4645 Kitchin, George. A Survey of Burlesque and Parody in English.
Edinburgh and London: Oliver and Boyd, 1931. xxiv, 388 pp.
Chapters III-VII deal with the Restoration and 18th century.

Partridge, John

4646 Eddy, William A. "Tom Brown and Partridge the Astrologer."
Modern Philology, XXVIII (1930), 163-168.
Indicates that Brown was the earliest as well as the most
persistent of Partridge's tormenters and compares the character of Brown's parody with those of Swift and Steele. No
references to drama.

4647 -----. "The Wits vs. John Partridge, Astrologer." Studies in
Philology, XXIX (1932), 29-40.
This essay, including a bibliography of satires written
against him, recounts Partridge's career, his "literary output," and his notoriety.

Pastoral Drama

4648 Laidler, Josephine. "A History of Pastoral Drama in England until 1700." Englische Studien, XXXV (1905), 193-259.

 Traces the history of the type from early court comedies and Sidney's Lady of the May (1578) down to the close of the seventeenth century. Discussions of Lower's Noble Ingratitude (1661) and Enchanted Lovers (1658), pp. 249-250; Flecknoe's Love's Kingdom (1664), pp. 251-252; Tutchin's Unfortunate Shepherd (1685), pp. 253-256; Oldmixon's Thyrsis (1697), pp. 256-257.

4649 Marks, Jeanette Augustus. English Pastoral Drama from the Restoration to the Date of the Publication of the "Lyrical Ballads." London: Methuen, 1908. xii, 228 pp.

 Study of origin, development, and production of eighteenth century "pastoral drama." Contains summaries of some 50 plays. Extensive bibliography pp. 135-219.

Payne, Henry

4650 Payne, Henry Nevil. The Fatal Jealousie (1673). Edited by Willard Thorp. Los Angeles: The Augustan Reprint Society, November, 1948. (Series V, no. 2).

 A facsimile text, with a biographical note and comment on Payne's use of Shakespeare, and a survey of Payne's career as a dramatist.

Peep Show

4651 Weitenkampf, Frank. "Peep Show Prints." Bulletin of the New York Public Library, XXV (1921), 359-366.

 A history of the peep show or "raree show."

4652 -----. "The Peep Show Again." Bulletin of the New York Public Library, XXVIII (1924), 6.

 An addition to the author's 1921 article (q.v.) which adds information on the apparatus used.

Pepusch, John

4653 Hughes, Charles W. "John Christopher Pepusch." Musical Quarterly, XXXI (1945), 54-70.

 A critical study of the work of the arranger of The Beggar's Opera.

Pepys, Samuel

texts

4654 Pepys, Samuel. Private Correspondence and Miscellaneous Papers
      of Samuel Pepys, 1679-1703 in the Possession of J. Pepys Cock-
      erell. Edited by J. R. Tanner. 2 vols. London: G. Bell and Sons,
      1926.
          Documents in the collection date from April 14, 1679 to 1703.
      A few literary references, including references to Dryden's
      death and burial.

4655 -----. The Diary of Samuel Pepys. Edited by Henry B. Wheatley.
      3 vols. London: Bell, 1928.
          A cheaper edition of an earlier work.

4656 -----. The Diary of Samuel Pepys. Edited by John D. Jump. New
      York: Washington Square Press, 1964. 336 pp.

biography and criticism

4657 Yardley, E. "Marlborough and Shakespeare." Notes and Queries,
      10th Ser., I (April 9, 1904), 292.
          Uses Papys' responses to plays to show that Jonson was held
      in higher esteem during the Restoration than Shakespeare.

4658 Lee, Sidney. "Pepys and Shakespeare." Shakespeare and the
      Modern Stage, with Other Essays... (New York: C. Scribner's
      Sons, 1906), 82-110.
          Considers several topics--Pepys as the microcosm of the
      average playgoer, the London theatres of Pepys's Diary, the
      Restoration versions of Shakespeare, and Betterton's inter-
      pretations of Shakespeare.

4659 McAfee, Helen. Pepys on the Restoration Stage. New Haven: Yale
      University Press, 1916. 353 pp.

4660 Warshaw, J. "Pepys as a Dramatic Critic." The Drama, X (March-
      April, 1920), 209-213.
          A defense of Pepys as a dramatic critic; Warshaw presents
      Pepys' qualifications, his views on Shakespeare, and his general
      conception of drama.

4661 Ponsonby, Arthur. Samuel Pepys. London: Macmillan and Co.,
      1928. (English Men of Letters Series, Gen. ed. J. C. Squire).
      xiii, 160 pp.
          Chapter VII--Music, Art, and Letters--gives brief treatment
      to Pepys' play attendance.

4662 Shand, John. "To Theatre with Pepys." Theatre Arts Monthly,
      XIII (June, 1929), 445-452.
          On descriptions of playgoing, including Papys'.

4663 Drinkwater, John. Pepys, His Life and Character. London: Heine-
      mann: Garden City; Doubleday, Doran and Co. [1930]. viii, 380 pp

Public and domestic life of Pepys; samplings from letters
and Diary. Scattered references to Pepys' opinions on plays
and his delight in the theatre.

4664 Pendleton, Louis. "Pepys as a Dramatic Critic." South Atlantic
Quarterly, XXXV (1936), 411-419.
Pepys's attitudes toward the theatre are shown by extensive
quotation from the Diary.

4665 Spencer, Hazelton. "Mr. Pepys Is Not Amused." English Literary
History, VII (September, 1940), 163-176.
Shows how often the diarist's judgments were colored by
external events.

4666 Esdaile, Katharine A. "Pepys's Plaisterer." Times Literary Supplement, October 2, 1943, p. 480.
Three of the "plaisterer's" known sitters were Pepys, Monck,
and James II.

4667 Emslie, MacDonald. "Three Early Settings of Jonson." Notes and
Queries, CXCVIII (1953), 466-468.
In 1666 Pepys composed a song based on a speech in Jonson's
Catiline (I.i.73ff).

4668 Cohen, Selma Jeanne. "Mr. Pepys Goes to the Theatre." Dance
Magazine (July, 1956), 36-37; 60-61; 66.
Comments on the dances and the dancers he saw, espec-
ially Nelly Gwyn.

4669 Abernethy, Cecil. Mr. Pepys of Seething Lane. New York: McGraw-
Hill, 1957. ix, 385 pp.
This falls somewhere between a biography and a novel. The
author says that he wants to elucidate the mind of Pepys as he
interprets it. Many events from the diary are described, among
them several visits to and comments on the theatre.

4670 Piper, David. "The Passion for Faces." Listener, LVII (February
14, 1957), 261-262.
Written for the centenary of the National Portrait Gallery,
this is primarily a discussion of the significance of portraiture,
not as art but as records. Discusses a portrait of Samuel
Pepys; through x-rays some of the changes Pepys forced in the
picture can be identified.

4671 Quinlan, John. "Mrs. Pepys." Contemporary Review, CXLII
(July, 1957), 31-34.
A character study of Elizabeth St. Michael Pepys and
the story of her marital problems--finances and Samuel's
affection for women.

4672 Weiss, David G. Samuel Pepys, Curioso. Pittsburgh: University
of Pittsburgh Press, 1957. xii, 122 pp.
Pepys and music.

4673 Hunt, Percival. Samuel Pepys in the Diary. Pittsburgh: University of Pittsburgh Press, 1958. [xii], 178 pp.

4674 McAfee, Helen. Pepys on the Restoration Stage. New York: Benjamin Bloom, 1963. 353 pp.

Reprints of the 1916 edition of passages selected from
Pepys's Diary relating to the theatre and drama. An elaborate
introduction deals with Pepys as a dramatic historian, his relationship with the Restoration theatre, and his reputation as
a drama critic. References in Pepys's Diary to the theatre are
arranged by subject. Includes bibliography, notes, and illustrations.

Performances

4675 Scouten, Arthur H. and Leo Hughes. "A Calendar of Performances
of I Henry IV and 2 Henry IV during the first half of the Eighteenth Century." Journal of English and Germanic Philology,
XLIII (1944), 23-41, XLIV (1945), 89-90.

Listing of performances. Corrects earlier studies by Avery.

4676 Avery, Emmett L. "A Tentative Calendar of Daily Theatrical Performances, 1660-1700." Research Studies of the State College o
Washington, XIII (1945), 225-283.

A daily listing of known performances.

4677 Reed, Isaace. Diaries, 1762-1804. Edited by Claude E. Jones.
Berkeley and Los Angeles: University of California Press, 1946.
xiv, 334 pp. (University of California Publications in English,
X).

Numerous visits to the theatre are noticed throughout and
recorded by the editor in a "Table of Theatres and Performances

4678 Avery, Emmett L. and Arthur H. Scouten. "A Tentative Calendar
of Daily Theatrical Performances in London, 1700-1701 to 1704-
1705." Publications of the Modern Language Association,
LXIII (March, 1948), 114-180.

A listing in calendar form of known productions.

4679 MacMillan, Dougald. "A Tentative Calendar of Daily Theatrical
Performances in London, 1700-1701 to 1704-1705." Philological
Quarterly, XXVIII (1949), 366-367.

A detailed analysis of the calendar compiled by Emmett L.
Avery and Arthur H. Scouten, PMLA, LXIII (March, 1948).

Periodicals

4680 Turkin-Lerch, Eugenie. Die forderungen an das Drama und die
bühne Englands im "Tatler," "Spectator," und "Guardian."
Zurich: Frauenfeld, Huber & Co., 1918. 65 pp.

4681 Graham, Walter. The Beginning of the English Literary Periodicals

A Study of Periodical Literature, 1665-1715. New York: Oxford Press, 1926. 91 pp.

Among others, includes a brief account of the Weekly Comedy (1669), which announced dramatis personae and included such material in dialogue; a similar periodical, The Humours of a Coffee-House (1707); The Observator, and others which commented on the theatre.

4682 Crane, Ronald S., and F. B. Kaye, with M. E. Prior. A Census of British Newspapers and Periodicals, 1620-1800. Chapel Hill: University of North Carolina Press, 1927. 205 pp. (Reprinted from Studies in Philology, XXIV [1927], 1-205.)

A twofold bibliography: (1) a finding-list of the precise holdings of the leading American libraries and a list of British periodicals not found in these libraries (altogether 2426 periodicals are considered). All recognized types of periodicals are included from 1620 to 1800--Scotch, Irish, and Welsh as well as English publications. (2) Two indexes: one chronological, the other geographical.

4683 Graham, Walter. English Literary Periodicals. New York: Thomas Nelson & Sons, 1930. 424 pp.

Basic reference work and history of periodicals.

4684 Gabler, Anthony J. "Check List of English Newspapers and Periodicals ... before 1800 in the Huntington Library." Huntington Library Bulletin, No. 2 (1931), 1-66.

4685 Thatcher, John H. "Dramatic Criticism in the Magazines from 1750-1780." M.A.Columbia University, 1933.

4686 Milford, R. T., and D. M. Sutherland. A Catalogue of English Newspapers and Periodicals in the Bodleian Library 1622-1800. Oxford: Bibliographical Society, 1936. 184 pp.

Also appeared in the Oxford Bibliographical Society Proceedings and Papers, IV, 2 (1935), 163-346.

4687 "Sir John Falstaffe." The Theatre (1720). Edited by John Loftis. Ann Arbor: The Augustan Reprint Society, May, 1948. (Series IV, number 1).

The pseudonymous Falstaffe's continuation of his The Anti-Theatre (rival to Steele's The Theatre), after Steele ended his series in April, 1720.

4688 Loftis, John. "Sir John Falstaffe's Theatre." Journal of English and Germanic Philology, XLVIII (April, 1949), 252-258.

"Falstaffe" continued his journal for eleven numbers after the end of the Steele controversy.

4689 Stewart, Powell. British Newspapers and Periodicals 1632-1800. A Descriptive Catalogue of a Collection at the University of Texas. Austin: University of Texas, 1950. 172 pp.

4690 Cranfield, Geoffrey A. A Handlist of English Provincial News-

papers and Periodicals 1700-1760. Cambridge: Bowes and
Bowes, 1952. viii, 31 pp.

Supplements in Transactions of the Cambridge Bibliographica
Society, II, 3 (1956), 269-274, II, 5 (1959), 385-389.

4691 Ward, Wm. S. Index and Finding List of Serials Published in the
British Isles 1789-1832. Lexington: University of Kentucky
Press, 1953. xv, 180 pp.

4692 Loftis, John. "Sir John Falstaffe's Theatre, a Correction."
Journal of English and Germanic Philology, LIII (1954), 141.

Loftis's discovery of an anonymous continuation of Steele's
Theatre was anticipated by H. Lavers-Smith in 1900. Lavers-
Smith's collection of the continuation is now at the Folger
Shakespeare Library.

4693 Rondy, Joseph J., Jr. "Some Aethetic Developments Reflected in
English Periodicals, 1770-1798." Ph.D. University of Illinois,
1955.

4694 Jones, Claude E. "The Critical Review's First Thirty Years
(1756-1685)." Notes and Queries, CCI (1956), 78-80.

In spite of some romantic leanings, The Critical Review's
approach to literature was essentially conservative and re-
actionary, especially with reference to critical rules. Brief
mention of drama.

4695 Bond, Richmond P., ed. Studies in the Early English Periodical.
Chapel Hill: University of North Carolina Press, 1957. 206 pp.

Six studies covering 1700-1760.

4696 Rosenberg, Albert. "Defoe's Pacificator Reconsidered." Philological Quarterly, XXXVII (1958), 433-439.

Poem, 1700, satirizing literary wars, including attacks on
the stage.

4697 Dandridge, Edmund P., Jr. "Literary Criticism in British Periodicals to the Mid-Eighteenth Century." Ph.D. University of
Virginia, 1959.

Includes dramatic criticism.

4698 Jones, Claude E. "Dramatic Criticism in the Critical Review,
1756-1785." Modern Language Quarterly, XX (1959), 18-26,
133-144.

Emphasis upon "common sense."

4699 Haig, Robert L. "The Gazetteer," 1735-1797: A Study in the
Eighteenth-Century English Newspaper. Carbondale: Southern
Illinois University Press, 1960. xi, 335 pp.

Touches upon theatrical news and advertising.

4700 Loftis, John, ed. Richard Steele's The Theatre, 1720. Oxford:
Clarendon Press, 1962.

First edition of the work since the Eighteenth Century. Contains Steele's views on theatre, politics, economics, morals,

manners, and personalities. With introduction and explanatory
notes.

4701 Stratman, Carl J., C.S.V. A Bibliography of British Dramatic
Periodicals, 1720-1960. New York: New York Public Library,
1962. 58 pp.

A list of 674 dramatic periodicals published in England,
Scotland, and Ireland. Gives complete titles, title changes,
editors, place of publication, number of volumes and issues,
dates of first and last issues, frequency of issue, libraries
where periodical may be found.

4702 -----. "Cotes' Weekly Journal; or, The English Stage Player."
Papers of the Bibliographical Society of America, LVI (1962),
104-106.

The earliest theatrical paper published in England from May
11 to July 16, 1734, in nine issues.

4703 -----. "Preparing a Bibliography of British Dramatic Periodicals,
1720-1960." Bulletin of the New York Public Library, LXVI
(1962), 405-408.

Contains a brief consideration of the general plan and scope
of the bibliography.

4704 [Stratman, Carl J., C.S.V.] "Microfilm of British Dramatic Periodicals." Restoration and 18th Century Theatre Research, II
(May, 1963), 20-31.

Lists 160 British dramatic periodicals which are available on
microfilm at Loyola University Library, Chicago, Illinois.

4705 Stratman, Carl J., C.S.V. "Scotland's First Dramatic Periodical:
The Edinburgh Theatrical Censor." Theatre Notebook, XVII
(Spring, 1963), 83-86.

An analysis of the Censor's format, type of drama criticism,
remarks on theatrical conditions and acting. Includes a discussion of the periodical's criticism of the following plays: Douglas
by John Home; Hear Both Sides by Thomas Holcroft; The Inconstant and The Beaux Stratagem by George Farquhar; Pizarro by
R. B. Sheridan; A Bold Stroke for a Wife by Susanna Centlivre;
John Bull and The Heir at Law by George Colman; The Way to
Keep Him by Arthur Murphy; and The Marriage Promise by J.
T. Allingham.

4706 McVeagh, J. "Dramatic Criticism in the Periodicals, 1775-1795."
M.A. University of Birmingham, 1965.

4707 White, Robert Benjamin, Jr. "A Study of the Female Tatler (1709-
1710)." Ph.D. The University of North Carolina, 1966. (Order No.
67-1065).

Studies the backgrounds and development of the periodical,
the later issues of which have been attributed to Susanna Centlivre.
The contents of the periodical include dramatic criticism.

Perspective

4708   Stadler, Edmund. "Die Raumgestaltung im barocken Theater."
       Die Kunstformen des Barockzeitalters: Vierzehn Vortrage...
       Edited by Rudolf Stamm. (Sammlung Dolp, Band LXXII.) Bern:
       Francke, 1956. 447 pp.
           Traces the development of perspective, and, in general, of
       illusionism in the theatrical architecture of the time.

Philips, Ambrose

4709   Wellhausen, K. Ambrose Philips as a Dramatist: a Contribution
           to the History of English Literature in the Eighteenth Century.
       Leipzig: Borna, 1915. 82 pp.
4710   Bryan, Adolphus Jerome. "The Life and Works of Ambrose Philips."
       Ph.D. Harvard University, 1936.
4711   Fogle, S. T. "Notes on Ambrose Philips." Modern Language Notes,
       LIV (1939), 354-359.
           Corrects two errors and an omission in the biographical
       introduction to The Poems of Ambrose Philips (Oxford, 1937).
4712   Bryan, Adolphus J. "Humphrey, Duke of Gloucester: A Study in
       Eighteenth-Century Adaptation." Studies for William A. Read.
       Edited by Nathaniel M. Coffee and Thomas A. Kirby. (Baton
       Rouge: Louisiana State University Press, 1940), 221-236.
4713   McCue, Lillian Bueno. "The Canon of Philips: Some Observations
           on Criteria." Philological Quarterly, XIX (1940), 313-316.
           Attacks Mary Segar's inclusion of "The Death of the Just"
       in her edition of Philips' poems.Some of Miss McCue's reasons
       for denying Philips' authorship are based on the verse of his
       plays.
4714   Bateson, F.W. "Ambrose Philips." Times Literary Supplement,
       February 22, 1941, p. 91.
           Comments on Mary Segar's first article, infra.
4715   Segar, Mary G. "Ambrose Philips." Times Literary Supplement,
       February 1, 1941, p. 60.
           Miss Segar disclaims responsibility for revising the Philips
       entry in CBEL, I, 324. Corrects birth date and adds twelve
       poems to the listing in CBEL.
4716   -----. "Ambrose Philips." Times Literary Supplement, March 8,
       1941, p. 117.
           In answer to Mr. Bateson and the revision of the Ambrose
       Philips bibliography in Vol. 2 of the Cambridge Bibliography
       of English Literature.
4717   Mander, Gerald P. "Ambrose Philips' English Background."
       Times Literary Supplement, October 10, 1942, p. 504.

Prints letters concerning the epitaph Philips wrote for his
cousin Penelope Vernon, and discusses his friendship with
Captain William Congreve.

4718 Segar, Mary. "Ambrose Philips." Times Literary Supplement,
December 26, 1942, p. 631.
A letter in answer to Gerald P. Mander's article "Ambrose
Philip's English Background." Times Literary Supplement,
October 10, 1942, p. 504, and Philips' relations with the Con-
greves.

4719 Wheatley, Katherine E. "Andromaque as the 'Distrest Mother.'"
Romanic Review, XXXIX (1948), 3-21.
A comparison between Phillips's The Distrest Mother and
Racine's Andromaque.

4720 Parnell, Paul E. "The Distrest Mother, Ambrose Philips' Morality Play."Comparative Literature, XI (1959), 111-123.
Changes from Racine.

Philips, Katherine

4721 Souers, Philip Webster. The Matchless Orinda. Cambridge, Mass.:
Harvard University Press, 1931. viii, 326 pp.
A biography of the woman whose London literary salon was
famous during her brief life; her translation of Corneille's
Pompée was a great success.

Phillips, Edward

4722 Nichols, Charles. "A Note on The Stage Mutineers." Modern Language Notes, XXXV (1920), 225-277.
A suggestion that Edward Phillips was the author of this play,
that this play inspired two scenes in Fielding's Historical
Register, and that this play burlesqued the revolt of the players
from Drury Lane in 1733.

Phillips, Stephen

4723 Phelps, George Baldwin. "A Production of Stephen Phillips's [sic]
Paolo and Francesca." M.F.A. Northwestern University, 1940.

Phoenix Society

4724 Dukes, Ashley. "The London Phoenix Society." Theatre Arts
Monthly, VIII (1924), 763-768.
A discussion of a society devoted to the revival of old plays,
especially Restoration dramas; includes a list of the plays revived.

Physical Theatre

4725 Lawrence, W. J. The Elizabethan Playhouse and Other Studies.
First Series. Stratford-on-Avon: Shakespeare Head Press,
1912; New York: J. B. Lippincott, 1912; New York: Russell
and Russell, 1963.

4726 -----. The Elizabethan Playhouse and Other Studies. Second Series. Stratford-on-Avon: Shakespeare Head Press, 1913; New
York: J. B. Lippincott, 1913; New York: Russell and Russell,
1963.

Picaresque Drama

4727 Pabisch, Marie. Picaresque Dramas of the 17th and 18th Centuries.
Berlin: Mayer and Muller, 1910. 110 pp.
In the Restoration, picaresque dramas were built on French
models, especially Molière's Fouberies de Scapin; in the 18th
century, there was a shift from jolly rogues to criminals. Influence on Otway.

Picture-Stage

4728 Lawrence, W. J. "The Origin of the English Picture-Stage." The
Elizabethan Playhouse and Other Studies. Second Series.
(Stratford-on-Avon: Shakespeare Head Press, 1913), 121-147.
Picture-stage era began with the revival of The Siege of
Rhodes at the opening of the new Duke's Theatre in Lincoln's
Inn Fields, June, 1661.

Piety

4729 Clarke, W. K. Lowther. Eighteenth Century Piety. London:
S.P.C.K., 1944. 160 pp.

Pilkington, Letitia

4730 Jerrold, Walter and Clare Jerrold. Five Queer Women. New York:
London: Brentano, 1929, xii, 356 pp.
Aphra Behn, Mary Manley, Susanna Centlivre, Eliza Haywood
and Letitia Pilkington.

Pirate Printing

4731 Wood, Frederick T. "Pirate Printing in the XVIII Century." Notes
and Queries, CLIX (1930), 381-384, 400-403.

> Gives background material on methods of getting a manuscript
> published, types of piracy, copyright laws, and representative
> particular cases.

4732 Gerritsen, John. "The Dramatic Piracies of 1661: A Comparative
      Analysis." Studies in Bibliography, XI (1958), 117-132.
> Primarily devoted to an account of Francis Kirkman, one of
> the most notorious of the printers who engaged in theatrical
> piracy.

Pit

4733 Lawrence, W. J. "Pit of a Theatre." Notes and Queries, 10th Ser.,
      I (April 9, 1904), 286-287.
> This discussion of the origin of the word "pit" in a strictly
> theatrical sense connects it with "bear pit" or "cockpit" his-
> torically.

Pity

4734 Aldridge, A. O. "The Pleasures of Pity." English Literary History,
      XVI (1949), 76-87.
> 18th century theories (on why pleasure from painful scenes)
> were based on pity: five types of theories: 1) Enjoy exercise of
> all the passions; 2) we recognize the fictitious nature of the
> representation in tragedy; 3) we appreciate talent and skill of
> artist; 4) pity is a form of self love; 5) pity is a natural affection.
> Source of pity: benevolence or self love? Discusses in detail
> views of various 18th century thinkers on these problems.

Pix, Mary

4735 Carter, Herbert. "Three Women Dramatists of the Restoration."
      Bookman's Journal, XIII (1925), 91-97.
> Sketches the careers of Mrs. Mary Manley, Mrs. Mary Pix,
> Mrs. Catharine Trotter.

4736 Edmunds, J. M. "An Example of Early Sentimentalism." Modern
      Language Notes, XLVIII (1933), 94-97.
> Sentimental touches are seen in The Spanish Wives, by Mary
> Griffith Pix (1696).

4737 Avery, Emmett L. "Lincoln's Inn Fields, 1704-1705." Theatre
      Notebook, V (1950-1951), 13-15.
> The news columns of the weekly Diverting Post in 1704-1705
> contain information about Zalmayna (by Mrs. Pix?) and Rowe's
> The Biter.

4738 Bowers, Fredson. "Underprinting in Mary Pix, The Spanish Wives

(1696)." Library, 5th Ser., IX (1954), 248-254.

The Spanish Wives illustrates how the order of presswork
may be determined by bibliographical analysis of running-titles.

Play Lists

4739 De Beer, Esmond. "Late XVIIth Century Play Lists." Times Liter-
      ary Supplement, March 28, 1923, p. 160.
          Identifies The Politician, a play mentioned by Nicoll.
4740 Nicoll, Allardyce. "Late 17th-Century Play Lists." Times Liter-
      ary Supplement, January 4, 1923, p. 12.
          This list of plays performed at Court or in public theatres
      before royalty, 1677-1693 completes the listing begun in
      "Charles II at the Theatre."
4741 -----. "Late 17th-Century Play Lists." Times Literary Supple-
      ment, February 22, 1923, p. 124.
          A discussion of the turbulent fortunes of the Theatre Royal
      from 1673 to 1682; includes a list of plays acted before royalty
      by the united companies in Dorset Garden and Drury Lane,
      November, 1677 to January, 1684-85.
4742 Baskervill, Charles R. "Play-Lists and Afterpieces of the Mid-
      Eighteenth Century." Modern Philology, XXIII (May, 1926),
      445-464.
          Calls attention to the importance of the lists of current plays
      contained in the periodical publications such as the Gentleman's
      Magazine, especially for the information they give in regard to
      afterpieces.
4743 Stratman, Carl J., C.S.V. "Dramatic Play Lists: 1591-1963."
      Bulletin of the New York Public Library, LXX (1966), 71-85.
          A chronological arrangement of play lists that gives full
      title of each list, indicates the scope and relative merits of
      each as a reference work. Includes information on subsequent
      editions, additions, changes, and scholarly studies of particular
      lists. Part I of the collection contains 34 entries; 31 entries
      published during the Restoration and 18th century.

Play Notices

4744 Jackson, Alfred. "Play Notices from the Burney Newspapers,
      1700-1703." Publications of the Modern Language Association,
      XLVIII (1933), 815-849.
          Presents, in chronological order, all references to plays
      found in the 27 different newspapers which comprise the Burney
      collection for the years 1701-1703.

Play Within a Play

4745 Hewitt, Barnard. "Some Uses of the 'Frame' in Playwriting."
      Quarterly Journal of Speech, XXXII (1946), 480-484.
          Brief notice of the "play within a play" structure of The
      Rehearsal and The Critic.

Playbills

4746 Lawrence, W. J. "The Oldest Known English Playbills." The
      Elizabethan Playhouse and Other Studies. Second Series.
      (Stratford-on-Avon: Shakespeare Head Press, 1913), 240-241.
          Four playbills in the Verney Papers from Drury Lane and the
      Queen's in Dorset Gardens: Henry the Second King of England,
      The Indian Emperor, All for Love, and Theodosius. Corrects
      inaccurate description assigning plays to one bill which occurs
      in the calendaring of the Verney Papers in Historical Manuscripts
      Commission Report of 1879.
4747 -----. "The Origin of the Theatre Programme." The Elizabethan
      Playhouse and Other Studies. Second Series. (Stratford-on-Avon:
      Shakespeare Head Press, 1913), 57-91.
          Custom of selling playbills with name of play, characters,
      and entr' acte entertainment began about 1714.
4748 Oxberry, John. "A Play Bill of April, 1786, which Relates to a
      Performance to be Given at the Theatre in the Big Market for
      the Benefit of Mr. Platt." Proceedings of the Society of Anti-
      quaries of Newcastle-upon-Tyne, 4th Ser., I (1923-1924), 48-
      50.
4749 [Enthoven Collection]. Notes and Queries, CXLIV (November 28,
      1925), 379-380.
          Notices the acquisition by the Victoria and Albert Museum
      of the Enthoven Collection of playbills, the earliest 1738 (Comus
      at Drury Lane).
4750 Boswell, Eleanore. "A Playbill of 1687." Library, 4th Ser., XI
      (1931), 499-502.
          Description and reproduction of a playbill of the type men-
      tioned by Pepys as having been hung "upon the posts." In the
      collection of State Papers Domestic, the bill advertises the
      February 22, 1687 production of A King and No King at the
      Theatre Royal.
4751 Andrews, H. C. "A Census of Extant Collections of English Pro-
      vincial Playbills of the Eighteenth Century." Notes and Queries,
      CXCI (August 10, 1946), 65.
          Describes the Hertford collection.
4752 Cashmore, H. M. "A Census of Extant Collections of English Pro-

vincial Playbills of the Eighteenth Century." Notes and Queries,
CXCI (July 13, 1946), 20.
  Describes the Birmingham collection.
4753 Cooper, Francis J. "A Census of Extant Collections of English Pro-
      vincial Playbills of the Eighteenth Century." Notes and Queries,
      CXC (June 29, 1946), 282.
        Further details on holdings in Lincoln.
4754 Piper, A. Cecil. "A Census of Extant Collections of English Pro-
      vincial Playbills of the Eighteenth Century." Notes and Queries,
      CXCI (August 10, 1946), 65.
        Describes the Richmond collection.
4755 Rees, Edmund J. "A Census of Extant Collections of English Pro-
      vincial Playbills of the Eighteenth Century." Notes and Queries,
      CXC (June 29, 1946), 283.
        Playbills in Monmouth, Tenby and Wynnstay noted.
4756 Wood, Frederick Thomas. "A Census of Extant Collections of Eng-
      lish Provincial Playbills of the Eighteenth Century." Notes and
      Queries, CXC (June 1, 1946), 222-226; CXCI (August 24, 1946),
      195.
        Collections are listed in Bath, Birmingham, Brighton, Bristol,
      Cheltenham, Farmington, Gloucester, Harvand, Lancaster,
      Lincoln, Liverpool, London, Manchester, Margate, New York,
      Norwich, Nottingham, Plymouth, Salisbury, Sheffield, Spalding,
      Warrington, Washington, D.C., Whitby, Yale and York. The
      additional note lists the Derby collection.
4757 Van Lennep, William. "The Earliest Known English Playbill."
      Harvard Library Bulletin, I (1947), 382-385.
        Describes and reproduces a playbill of about 1655.
4758 H., A. J. "Provincial Playbills of the Eighteenth Century." Notes
      and Queries, CXCIII (March 6, 1948), 108.
        Playbills in the public libraries of Wigan and Liverpool.
4759 Avery, Emmett L. "Two Early London Playbills." Notes and
      Queries, CXCV (1950), 99.
        Playbills in the British Museum advertise performances of
      The Pilgrim (1708) and Volpone (1703).
4760 Macleod, Joseph. "The Earliest Amateur Playbill." Theatre Note-
      book, IX (1954), 11-14.
        A Latin playbill of 1681 announces two performances of
      Terence's Eunuchus, possibly at the University of Edinburgh.
4761 Van Lennep, William. "Some Early English Playbills." Harvard
      Library Bulletin, VIII (1954), 235-241.
        Van Lennep reproduces and discusses two playbills from
      the late seventeenth century and one from the early eighteenth.
4762 Bunch, Antonia. "Playbills and Programmes in Guildhall Library."
      Theatre Notebook, XIV (1959-60), 66-67.

The Guildhall Library collection of playbills and programmes is not confined to the purely theatrical but embraces entertainment in its various forms. It includes "a collection of acting editions of various 18th- and 19th-century plays"; playbills and programmes cover the years 1760-1924.

4763   Nash, George W. "An Early London Playbill." Theatre Notebook, XIV (1959-60), 55.

This depicts and describes a Playbill of 1718 in the Gabrielle Enthoven Theatre Collection.

4764   Fletcher, Ifan Kyrle. "British Playbills Before 1718." Theatre Notebook, XVII (Winter, 1962-63), 48-50.

List of eight illustrations of the earliest British playbills.

4765   Kilfoil, Thomas F. "The Brander Matthews Dramatic Museum." Restoration and Eighteenth Century Theatre Research, IV (May, 1965), 10-12.

This theatre collection at Columbia University contains models of stages (Lisle's Tennis-Court Theatre and Drury Lane), playbills (dating from 1753 for Drury Lane, from 1774 for the Haymarket, from 1790 for Covent Garden, eighteenth-century engravings and theatre tokens.

4766   Rachow, Louis A. "The Players--The Walter Hampden Memorial Library." Restoration and Eighteenth Century Theatre Research, IV (May, 1965), 15-16.

The library contains the William Henderson Collection of English Playbills--forty albums containing 4,000 bills and dating from 1750 to 1888.

Players' Petition

4767   Lawrence, W. J. "The Players' Petition to Charles II." Athenaeum, I (April 18, 1903), 508.

Corrects entry in CSPD, Charles II, Vol. CLXXXIII, No. 72, dated 1666, noting that players' petition for money to pay debts incurred from rebuilding of Theatre Royal in Drury Lane should be dated c. 1673.

Play-House Journal

4768   "Dublin's First Dramatic Periodical." Restoration and 18th Century Theatre Research, II (May, 1963), 32-36.

A reproduction of The Play-House Journal published in Dublin on January 18, 1749-50.

Playwrights

4769 Johnson, Samuel. Lives of the English Poets. Introduction by L.
      Archer-Hind. 2 vols. London: J. M. Dent, 1925. (Everyman)

Poet Laureate

4770 Hopkins, Kenneth. The Poets Laureate. London: John Lane, 1954.
      295 pp.
          Chapters on Shadwell, Tate, Rowe, and Cibber, discuss their
      plays as well as their poetry.

Poetic Justice

4771 Quinlan, Michael A. Poetic Justice in the Drama: The History of
      an Ethical Principle in Literary Criticism. Notre Dame, Ind.:
      University of Notre Dame Press, 1912. 238 pp.
          Discussion of the idea, of Greek origin, from Sidney through
      the 18th century with emphasis upon the dramatic criticism of
      Addison, Rymer, Dennis, Dryden, Gildon.
4772 Magill, L. M. "Poetic Justice: The Dilemma of the Early Creators
      of Sentimental Tragedy." Research Studies of the State College
      of Washington. XXV (March, 1957), 24-32.
4773 Tyre, Richard H. "Versions of Poetic Justice in the Early Eighteen
      Century." Studies in Philology. LIV. No. 1 (1957), 29-44.
          A multiple connotation in the term as used in the 18th century
      Both Addison and Dennis came to see poetic justice as a neces-
      sary literary recognition of the divine order controlling men's
      destinies.
4774 Ebbs, John Dale. "The Principle of Poetic Justice Illustrated in
      Restoration Tragedy." Ph.D., University of North Carolina,
      1958.
          1656-1700.
4775 Singh, A. "The Concept of Poetic Justice in Neo-Classical Dramatic
      Theory." Ph.D., London University, 1959-60.
4776 -----. "The Argument of Poetic Justice. (Addison versus Dennis)."
      Indian Journal of English Studies, III (1962), 61-77.

Poetic Style

4777 Ridland, John Murray. "Poetic Style in Augustan Tragedy (1700-
      1750)." Ph.D. Claremont Graduate School and University Cen-
      ter, 1964. (Order No. 66-3348).
          The central reason for the failure of English tragedy in the
      first half of the 18th century is the poets' incapacity to write a

poetically valid style which was also dramatically effective.

Poland

4778 Tumasz, Sister M. Florence, C.S.F.N. "Eighteenth Century Eng-
      lish Literature and the Polish Enlightenment." Ph.D. Fordham
      University, 1963. (Order No. 64-2411).
         Descriptive study of the influence of English letters in Poland
      between 1764 and 1822. Chapter V is devoted to the reception of
      18th century playwrights, especially Moore, Addison, and Sher-
      idan.

Political Drama

4779 Wright, Mrs. Rose. "The Political Plays of the Restoration." Ph.D.
      Yale University, 1914.
4780 Wright, Rose Abel. The Political Play of the Restoration. Montesano
      (Washington), 1916. 197 pp.
         This thesis traces the evolution of the political play from
      Elizabethan times and the Commonwealth through the Restoration
      (to about 1688). The author notes five kinds of political drama in
      the Restoration: 1. old plays revived, 2. new plays directly
      bearing on politics, 3. new plays alluding to politics, 4. political
      prologues and epilogues, 5. masques and operas. Plays dealt
      chiefly with Puritans (1658-1668), Whigs (1680-1682), and
      Catholics (1680-1688). One-tenth of the dramas of the time were
      directly political and have "little value as literature."
4781 Nicoll, Allardyce. "Political Plays of the Restoration." Modern
      Language Review, XVI (1921), 224-242.
         A history of the political drama of the period divided into
      three parts: 1) c. 1660-65--plays about the fall of the Common-
      wealth and the restoration of the monarchy; 2) 1679-85--plays
      about the Catholic-Protestant struggle; 3) 1689-- plays about
      the defeat of James and the triumph of William.

Political Propaganda

4782 Eyler, Clement M. "Techniques of Political Propaganda in English
      Drama, 1700-1750." Ph.D. George Peabody University, 1946.

Political Satire

4783 Whiting, George W. "Political Satire on the London Stage, 1675-90."
      Ph.D. University of Chicago, 1926.
         Names plays with political implications; most of them date

from 1679 to 1683, few from 1685 to 1689.

4784 Whiting, George W. "Political Satire in London Stage Plays, 1680-
83." Modern Philology, XXVIII (1930), 29-43.

Gives a survey of the political situation and of the stage as
a political force. Numerous references to particular plays and
to dramatists, including Dryden, Lee, Settle, Otway, Crowne,
Tate, D'Urfey, Mrs. Behn, Shadwell.

Politics

4785 Ramsland, Clement. "Britons Never Will be Slaves, a Study in
Whig Political Propaganda in the British Theatre, 1700-1742."
Quarterly Journal of Speech, XXVIII (December, 1942), 393-
399.

Sees "British love of liberty and its counterpart, hatred of
slavery"--both ideas which Ramsland associates with the Whigs
--as the most popular themes in 18th-century British drama.

4786 Clancy, James H. "Preliminaries to Restoration Comedy." Speech
Monographs, XV (1948), 85-98.

Considers social and political forces behind the civil war
and the relationship of the stage to the political scene. Particula
playwrights discussed are Congreve, Wycherley, Jonson,
D'Avenant, Etherege.

4787 Loftis, John. "The London Theaters in Early Eighteenth-Century
Politics." Huntington Library Quarterly, XVIII (1955), 365-393.

Political propaganda was an inseparable part of much of early
18th-century drama. Includes discussion of Drury Lane, Lincol
Inn Fields, Doggett, Cibber, Dennis, and others. Among the
plays mentioned are Cato, The Perplex'd Lovers, Cobbler of
Preston, and The Non-Juror.

4788 Pattison, E. "Politics and Literature, 1700-1750." M.A. Universit
of Southampton, 1955.

4789 Loftis, John. The Politics of Drama in Augustan England. Oxford:
Oxford University Press, 1963. 173 pp.

A thorough examination of the political background of early
18th century drama. Discusses litigation affecting the theatres,
political affiliations of playwrights and actors, as well as
specific plays on topical subjects.

4790 -----. "The Political Strain in Augustan Drama." Restoration
Drama: Modern Essays in Criticism. (A Galaxy Book). Edited
by John Loftis. (New York: Oxford University Press, 1966),
229-235.

Reprinted from The Politics of Drama in Augustan England
(Oxford: Oxford University Press, 1963), pp. 154-161. Studies
the shortcoming of the period's political drama, "a political

drama that is clever rather than profound."

Pope, Alexander

texts

4791 Wise, Thomas James. A Pope Library, A Catalogue of Plays,
Poems, and Prose Writings. London: Printed for Private Circulation Only, 1931. xxiv, 112, [4] pp.
4792 Pope, Alexander. The Dunciad Variorum with the Prolegomena of
Scriblerus, reproduced in facsimile from the first issue of the
original edition of 1729, with an Introductory Essay by Robert
Kilburn Root. Princeton University Press, 1929. 42, 16, 30,
124 pp.
Pope's notes contain many references to players and playwrights.

criticism

4793 Evans, H. A. "A Shakespearian Controversy of the Eighteenth
Century." Anglia, XXVIII (1905), 457-476.
Concerned with 18th-century criticism of Shakespeare
(Theobald, Pope, Johnson).
4794 Schmidt, Hans. Die Shakespeare-Ausgabe von Pope. Darmstadt:
K. F. Bender, 1912.
An analysis of Pope's edition of Shakespeare which points
up Pope's shortcomings as editor: his faulty method of setting
up a text which was based on inadequate sources; and his
changes in diction, syntax, verse form, and style.
4795 Johnson, John R. L. "Alexander Pope and the Theatre." M.A.
University of Chicago, 1921.
An analysis of Pope's attitude toward the theatre, a discussion of Pope's relationships with the playwrights of his age, and
a report on the influence of Pope on the dramatic productions of
his contemporaries.
4796 Sherburn, George. "Notes on the Canon of Pope's Works, 1714-
20." The Manly Anniversary Studies in Language and Literature.
Chicago: University of Chicago Press, 1923.
Section V of this article discusses Pope as the probable
author of a pamphlet The Plot Discover'd; or, a Clue to the
Comedy of the Non-Juror, an attack on Cibber's play. Refutes
the theory that Pope wrote A Compleat Key to the Non-Juror.
4797 -----. "The Fortunes and Misfortunes of Three Hours after Marriage." Modern Philology, XXIV (August, 1926), 91-109.
A discussion of the farce by Pope, Gay, and Arbuthnot, as-

sembling much contemporary evidence and correcting several misconceptions.

4798 Warren, Austin. Alexander Pope as Critic and Humanist. Princeton University Press, 1929. viii, 289 pp. (Princeton Studies in English, No. 1).

Chapters devoted to the Essay on Criticism, the edition of Shakespeare, and the Dunciad, and to a survey of Pope's reading Pope ranks third among critics of the classical period, behind Dryden and Johnson.

4799 -----. "Pope's Index to Beaumont and Fletcher." Modern Language Notes, XLVI (1931), 515-517.

Describes a MS. in the British Museum containing three shee of an incomplete index to the 1679 folio of Beaumont and Fletche1 by Pope. Describes some of Pope's annotations and concludes th Pope at one time entertained the idea of editing Shakespeare's contemporaries.

4800 Ault, Norman. "Pope's Lost Prologue." Times Literary Supplemen September 19, 1936, p. 742.

Argues that a supernumerary prologue to the 1715 edition of Rowe's Tragedy of Lady Jane Gray was written by Pope.

4801 Butt, John. Pope's Taste in Shakespeare. Oxford: University Press the Shakespeare Association, 1936. 21 pp.

Defining taste as affection, Butt analyzes Pope's emendations in his edition of Shakespeare so as to reveal his likes and dislik

4802 Tobin, James Edward. Alexander Pope: A List of Critical Studies Published from 1895 to 1944. New York: Cosmopolitan and Art Service Company, 1945. 30 pp.

A check-list containing items relevant to the theatre of Pope' day.

4803 -----. "Alexander Pope and Classical Tradition." Bulletin of the Polish Institute of Arts and Sciences in America. III (1945), 343-354.

4804 Johnston, Doris Irene. "The Relationship of Alexander Pope to Drama." M.A. Wayne State University, 1948.

4805 Ault, Norman. New Light on Pope with Some Additions to His Poetr Hitherto Unknown. London: Methuen, 1949. viii, 379 pp.

The new biographical material includes passim comments on Pope's relationship with the stage, particularly through John Gay

4806 Goldstein, Malcolm. "Pope, Sheffield, and Shakespeare's Julius Caesar." Modern Language Notes, LXXI (1956), 8-10.

Pope borrowed from adaptation for his edition.

4807 -----. Pope and the Augustan Stage. Stanford: Stanford University Press, 1958. xii, 139 pp.

4808 Rawson, C. J. "Some Unpublished Letters of Pope and Gay; and Some Manuscript Source s of Goldsmith's Life of Thomas Parnell

Review of English Studies, X (1959), 371-387.
   10 letters, Pope and Gay to Parnell, 1714-1716.
4809 Jones, W. Powell, ed. Sawney and Colley (1742) and Other Pope
   Pamphlets. Augustan Reprint Society Publication No. 83.
   Los Angeles: William Andrews Clark Memorial Library,
   University of California, 1960.
      Several allusions to dramatic works and to other theatrical
   Cibbers.
4810 Williams, George W. "Shakespeare's Antony and Cleopatra III,
   xiii, 26." Explicator, XX (1962), Item 79.
      Discussion of Pope's emendation of "gay comparisons" to
   "gay caparisons."
4811 Huseboe, Arthur Robert. "Alexander Pope's Dramatic Imagination."
   Ph.D. Indiana University, 1963. (Order No. 64-476).
      Pope's relation to drama and the theatre; its effect on his life
   and work.
4812 Creeth, Ned H., editor. "The Preface of the Editor--Alexander
   Pope." Shakespeare Newsletter, XVI (1966), 25.
      A reprint of Pope's preface to his 1725 edition of Shakespeare's
   works.
4813 Fuller, John. "A New Epilogue by Pope?" Review of English Studies,
   XVII (1966), 409-413.
      The epilogue to Gay's The Wife of Bath (1713).
4814 Rogal, Samuel J. "Pope's Treatment of Colley Cibber." Lock Haven
   Review, No. 8 (1966), 25-30.

Popish Plot

4815 Whiting, George W. "The Condition of the London Theaters, 1679-
   83: A Reflection of the Political Situation." Modern Philology, XXV
   (November, 1927), 195-206.
      The Popish Plot reflected in prologues, dedications, and the
   like; and political unrest seen in the banning of Whig plays.

Popple, William

4816 A., H. "William Popple (1701-1764)." Notes and Queries, CXCIII
   (July 24, 1948), 323.
      A request for information about this minor dramatist.
4817 Brockwell, Maurice W. "William Popple (1701-1764)." Notes and
   Queries, CXCIII (September 4, 1948), 394.
      A reply to the query of H.A. (q.v.), giving references for
   source material on the Popple family.

Pordage, S.

4818 Clark, William S. "Pordage's Herod and Mariamne." Review of
English Studies, V (1929), 61-64.
The play was produced at Dorset Garden rather than at
Lincoln's Inn Fields.

4819 Valency, Maurice J. The Tragedies of Herod and Mariamne.
New York: Columbia University Press, 1940. 304 pp. (Columbia
University Studies in English and Comparative Literature, No.
145.)
Includes discussion of the plays by Pordage, Orrery, and
Fenton.

Portraits

4820 A.L.A. Portrait Index: Index to Portraits Contained in Printed Books
and Periodicals. Edited by William Coolidge Lane and Nina E.
Browne. Washington: U. S. Government Printing Office, 1906.
1600 pp.

4821 Salaman, Malcolm C. The Old Engravers of England in Their
Relation to Contemporary Life and Art (1540-1800). Philadelphia: J. B. Lippincott, 1907. 224 pp.
Scattered throughout are pieces of information about Restoration and 18th century managers, actors, dancers, and
singers whose portraits were engraved.

4822 O'Donoghue, Freeman. British Museum Catalogue; Catalogue of
Engraved British Portraits Preserved in the Department of
Prints and Drawings in the British Museum. 6 vols. London:
The British Museum, 1908-1925.

4823 Historical Portraits, Richard II to Henry Wriothesley, 1400-
1600. Historical Portraits, 1600-1700. Edited by C. R. L.
Fletcher. 2 vols. Oxford: At the Clarendon Press, 1909-1911.

4824 Johnson, Charles. English Painting. London: Bell, 1932. xvi,
350 pp.

4825 Wind, Edward. "Humanitätsidee und heroisiertes Porträt in der
Englischen Kultur des 18. Jahrhunderts." England und die
Antike. (Leipzig, Berlin: B. G. Teubner, 1932), 156-229.
Portrait painting. Treatment of 18th century people such
as Garrick, in both comedy and tragedy. Garrick and Gains-
borough, Mrs. Siddons as the tragic muse.

4826 "Actor Prints of the Nineteenth Century." Theatre Arts, XXIX
(December, 1945), 731-732.
Notice of the City of New York Museum's exhibition. "Tin-
sel Pin Ups of the Nineteenth Century," with examples of the
theatrical prints. Alludes to eighteenth century beginnings of

theatrical portraits.

4827 Isaacs, Edith J. R. "A New Way to Pay Old Debts: The Artist as
      Drama Critic." Theatre Arts, XXXI (May, 1947), 38-43.
          Illustrations by Rowlandson and Cruikshank are reproduced,
      to show the cartoonists as satirists of the theatre and theatrical
      taste.

4828 Reynolds, Graham. "Painters of the British Stage: Francis Hayman
      and John Zoffany." New England Review, New Ser., I (1948),
      90-96.
          Uses the Garrick Club collection to illustrate the work of the
      two distinguished painters. Portraits of Garrick, Mrs. Cibber,
      Mrs. Pritchard, Spranger Barry and others are reproduced and
      analyzed.

4829 Fink, Frances Sharf. Heads across the Sea: An Album of Eighteenth-
      Century English Literary Portraits in America. lviii, 251 pp.
      Charlottesville: Bibliographical Society of the University of Vir-
      ginia, 1959.
          Includes playwrights. Bibliography.

4830 "Statues, Busts, Monuments and Wax Portraits of Theatrical In-
      terest." Theatre Notebook, XIV (1960), 123-126.
          Includes a selection from Rupert Gunnis' Dictionary of Bri-
      tish Sculptors, 1660-1851, which is of interest to students of
      Restoration and 18th-century drama inasmuch as it includes
      busts and monuments of such men as Congreve, Garrick, Gay,
      Oldfield and others.

4831 Kerslake, J. F., ed. Catalogue of Theatrical Portraits in London
      Public Collections. London: Society for Theatre Research, 1961.
      xi, 63 pp.
          A handlist of portraits, other than engravings, of performers
      in the theatre, which can be located in public collections in Lon-
      don. Includes portraits of professional performers, individually
      and in groups, in drama, opera, music hall, variety, the cir-
      cus, and ballet, both British and foreign. (Modelled on the Har-
      vard Catalogue of Theatrical Portraits.)

Pottinger, Israel

4832 Nicholson, Watson. "The Methodist." Notes and Queries, 11th Ser.,
      II (December 31, 1910), 526.
          Punctuation on the title page suggests that Foote is the author,
      but Pottinger wrote the play.

Powell, John

4833 Stone, George Winchester, Jr. "The Authorship of Tit for Tat: A

Manuscript Source for 18th-Century Theatrical History."
Theatre Notebook, X (1955), 22-28.
  Describes the excitement of the 1748-49 theatre season and
gives selections from the pamphlet, after presenting the situation which inspired it. Concludes that the author of the pamphlet
is John Powell.

Pratt, Samuel

4834 Jason, Philip K. "Samuel Johnson Pratt's Unpublished Comedy of
       Joseph Andrews." Notes and Queries, XIV (1967), 416-418.
         Pratt successfully dramatizes some of the major incidents
       in the first and fourth books of Fielding's novel in this play
       which was presented as an afterpiece at Drury Lane on April
       20, 1778.

Prévost, Abbé

4835 Havens, George R. The Abbé Prévost and English Literature.
       Princeton, N.J.: Princeton University Press; Paris: Librairie
       Edouard Champion, 1921. ix, 135 pp. (Elliott Monographs)
         A study of Prévost's criticism in Pour et Contre of England's
       major literary figures of the 17th and early 18th centuries; in-
       cludes dramatists Dryden, Gay, and Lillo.
4836 Anderson, Paul Bunyan. "English Drama Transferred to Prévost's
       Fiction." Modern Language Notes, XLIX (1934), 178-180.
         Argues that Prévost appropriated Steele's Conscious Lovers
       and Otway's The Orphan for use in his fiction.
4837 Roddier, Henri. L'Abbé Prévost, l'Homme et l'Oeuvre. Paris:
       Hatier-Boivin, 1955. 200 pp. (Connaissance des Lettres.)
         His first and second sojourn in England are treated, and the
       possible influence of English plays on him--e.g., Way of the
       World, Constant Couple, Provoked Husband.
4838 Rutherford, Marie-Rose. "The Abbé Prévost and the English
       Theatre, 1730-1740." Theatre Notebook, IX (1955), 111-118.
         Prévost took great critical interest in the English stage,
       often contrasting it with the French drama. The article covers
       the following: general background of the place of the theatre in
       London at that time; comments by Dennis on taste; actors at
       Drury Lane and Covent Garden; Handel; Italian opera; the
       character of English audiences.

Priest, Josias

4839 Cohen, Selma Jeanne. "Theory and Practice of Theatrical Dancing

in England in the Restoration and Early Eighteenth Century as
Seen in the Lives and Works of Josias Priest, John Weaver, and
Hester Santlow. Part I." Bulletin of the New York Public Lib-
rary, LXIII (1959), 541-554.

    This item treats the career of Josias Priest, "a choreographer
in the great 17th-century tradition, but with a sensitivity and a
feeling for dramatic values that raised that tradition to a higher
level."

Printing

4840 English Literature and Printing from the 15th to the 18th Century.
     London: Maggs Brothers, Catalogues 461 and 462. [1925]
     272 pp.
     A descriptive, annotated catalogue alphabetically arranged.
    Includes all books in the field of English literature and printing
    from the 15th-18th centuries available in the original through
    Maggs Brothers, Ltd.

4841 Chapman, R. W. "Eighteenth-century Imprints." Library, 4th Ser.,
     XI (1931), 503-504.
     Examples of various phrasings of printing information as it
    appears on books to distinguish between printers and sellers of
    books. Suggests that more study on the topic is needed.

4842 Vardac, A. Nicholas. "From Garrick to Griffith." Ph.D. Yale Uni-
     versity, 1942.

4843 Bronson, Bertrand H. "Printing as an Index of Taste in Eighteenth
     Century England. Part II." Bulletin of the New York Public
     Library, LXII (1958), 443-462.
     Also printed as a separate pamphlet (New York: New York
    Public Library, 1958) with its own pagination. Concentrates
    primarily on title pages, since the author's wishes are primary
    in deciding whether "it shall be determinative, descriptive, or
    suggestive; whether to include or omit the writer's name;
    whether to add a motto and of what sort." Several references
    to printing of plays.

Prior, Matthew

4844 Prior, Matthew. The Literary Works of Matthew Prior. Edited
     by H. Bunker Wright and Monroe K. Spears. 2 vols. Oxford
     English Text Series. Oxford: Oxford University Press,
     1959.
     Includes (at least) 2 plays.

Private Theatres

4845 Bridge, Joseph C. "Private Theatres in England." Notes and
        Queries, 12th Ser., XI (November, 1922), 373.
            Information about the Wynnstay theatre in the 18th century.
4846 Whitmore, J. B. "Private Theatres in England." Notes and
        Queries, 12th Ser., XI (November, 1922), 373.
            Information about the Wynnstay theatre in the 18th century.
4847 Bridge, Joseph. "Private Theatres in England." Notes and
        Queries, 12th Ser., XII (February, 1923), 112-113.
            Reprints an item from Chester Courant, September, 1775,
        about a private theatre at Weston in Shropshire.

Probability

4848 Berkeley, David S. "Some Notes on Probability in Restoration
        Drama." Notes and Queries, CC (1955), 237-239; 342-344;
        432.
            Suggests reasons for improbability of character, setting,
        language, historical sense; reasons for avoiding satire of
        royalty and nobility. References to numerous plays.

Processions

4849 Sawyer, Paul. "Processions and Coronations on the London Stage,
        1727-1761." Theatre Notebook, XIV (1960), 7-12.
            Includes list of plays to which these spectacles were added.

Production

4850 Lawrence, W. J. "The Persistence of Elizabethan Conventional-
        isms." The Elizabethan Playhouse and Other Studies. Second
        Series. (Stratford-on-Avon: Shakespeare Head Press, 1913),
        151-188.
            Persistence in the Restoration of conventions of the private
        and public Elizabethan theatres in matters of production and
        dramatic structure.
4851 Nicoll, Allardyce. "Late 17th-Century Play Lists." Times Liter-
        ary Supplement, March 15, 1923, pp. 179-180.
            A list of plays acted before royalty by the united companies in
        Dorset Garden and Drury Lane from January 13, 1684/5--Jan-
        uary, 1692/3.

Prologues and Epilogues

4852 Rosenfeld, S. "Prologues and Epilogues of the Restoration Period, 1660-1700, Considered in Relation to the Audience, Theatrical Conditions and Dramatic Productivity of the Age." M.A. London University (King'), 1925.

4853 Hannah, Robert. "The Interpretation of the Prologue and Epilogue." Quarterly Journal of Speech Education, XIII (April, 1927), 123-132.

Largely devoted to discussing the functions of prologue and epilogue during the Restoration and 18th century.

4854 Lawrence, W. J. "Oxford Restoration Prologues." Times Literary Supplement, January 16, 1830, p. 43.

Discusses the prologue, written for performance at Oxford University, to Settle's Cambyses, King of Persia.

4855 Wiley, Autrey Nell. "The English Vogue of Prologues and Epilogues." Modern Language Notes, XLVII (April, 1932), 255-257.

A discussion of the popularity (and the reasons for it) of prologues and epilogues.

4856 -----. "Female Prologues and Epilogues." Publications of the Modern Language Association, XLVIII (December, 1933), 1060-1079.

4857 -----. "The Prologue and Epilogues to the Guardian." Review of English Studies, X (October, 1934), 443-447.

4858 -----. Rare Prologues and Epilogues, 1642-1700. London: George Allen and Unwin, 1940.

An excellent study, careful and detailed, which presents both texts and relevant discussion of theatrical conditions, authorship, and significance. The New York edition was published in 1941.

4859 Knapp, Mary E. Prologues and Epilogues of the Eighteenth Century. New Haven: Yale University Press, 1961. xi, 350 pp. (Yale Studies in English, No. 149).

First real work on the subject. Analysis of the prologues and epilogues. Gives a good picture of the taste of the audiences.

4860 Butt, John, et al., eds. Of Books and Humankind: Essays and Poems Presented to Bonamy Dobree. London: Routledge and Kegan Paul [1964]. x, 232 pp.

Contains an essay by James Sutherland on the use of prologues and epilogues in the Restoration theatre to interest and satirize the various segments of the audience. Lists chronologically books and major essays published by Dobree, 1919-1962.

4861 Avery, Emmett L. "Some New Prologues and Epilogues, 1704-1708." Studies in English Literature, 1500-1900, V (1965), 455-467.

Six Prologues and Epilogues, which appeared between 1704 and 1708 and were preserved by Narcissus Luttrell, are reprint with introductory notes.

Promptbooks

4862 "Catalogue of the Becks Collection of Prompt Books in the New York Public Library." New York Public Library Bulletin, X (1906), 10 148.

This list of promptbooks presented to the Tilden Library by George Becks is arranged alphabetically by titles, followed by ar index of authors, editors, adapters, etc. It includes such Restoration and 18th-century items as a 1775 version of As You Lil It, a 1709 version of Coriolanus, a 19th-century version of Wycherley's The Country Girl, and others.

4863 Summers, Montague. "A Restoration Prompt Book." Times Literary Supplement, June 24, 1920, p. 400.

A discussion of a prompt copy of Shirley's The Sisters which belonged to Killigrew's company, Theatre Royal, Covent Garden; the prompt book was used for a revival which, Summers conjectures, occurred between 1668 and 1671.

4864 Linton, Marion. "Prompt-Books in the Bute Collection of English Plays." Theatre Notebook, XI (1956), 20-23.

18th century. Annotated list.

4865 Kerr, Barlyn B. "A Study of Selected Prompt Books for Productions of Measure for Measure Between 1772 and 1846." M.A. Ohio State University, 1962.

4866 Langhans, Edward A. "Research Opportunities in Early Promptbooks." Educational Theatre Journal, XVIII (March, 1966), 73-76.

4867 -----. "Three Early Eighteenth Century Promptbooks." Theatre Notebook, XX (Summer, 1966), 142-150.

Presents information on promptbooks prepared for Settle's Pastor Fido, c. 1706; Behn's The Rover, c. 1720's; and Otway's The Cheats of Scapin, c. 1730's.

4868 -----. "Three Early Eighteenth-Century Manuscript Promptbooks." Modern Philology, LXV (1967), 114-129.

Provides a transcription of three promptbooks and comments on them. The three manuscripts (Theobald's The Perfidious Brother, Settle's The Lady's Triumph, and Southerne's Money, the Mistress) were probably prepared by John Steed for production during the 1710's and 1720's at Rich's Lincoln's Inn Fields.

Prompt Notes

4869 Clark, William S. "Restoration Prompt Notes and Stage Practices."
      Modern Language Notes, LI (1936), 226-230.
      Prompt notes in a few Restoration dramatic texts reveal
      some of the techniques of play production.

"Prompter"

4870 Booth, M. R. "An Edition of the Theatrical Numbers of The
      Prompter, with Critical Introduction and Notes." Ph.D. Lon-
      don University (External), 1958.
4871 Hummert, Paul A. "The Prompter: An Intimate Mirror of the
      Theatre in 1789." Restoration and 18th Century Theatre Re-
      search, III (May, 1964), 37-46.
      Detailed examination of the contents of The Prompter re-
      veals that the periodical "mirrored typical dramatic opinions
      and customs prevailing in the theatre at this time."

Prose Drama

4872 Alden, Raymond M. "The Development of the Use of Prose in the
      English Drama: 1600-1800." Modern Philology, VII (July, 1909),
      1-22.
      Verse was gradually abandoned in comedy because the roman-
      tic spirit died out from comedy in the interest of a purely des-
      criptive or satiric presentation of human life. A similar effort
      was made to win tragedy for prose, in the interest of the real-
      istic treatment of human suffering, but failed.

Protagonist

4873 MacGibbon, Alexander Duncan. "From Ridicule to Respect: The
      Emergence of the Bourgeois Hero in the Popular Literature of
      Earlier Eighteenth-Century England." Ph.D. University of
      Kansas, 1960. 268 pp.
      This describes the typical Protestant Dissenter of the com-
      mercial middle class and shows "how he rose to respectable
      prominence in English journalism, drama and prose fiction
      before 1731."

Provincial Theatre

4874 Thaler, Alwin. "Strolling Players and Provincial Drama after
      Shakespeare." Publications of the Modern Language Association,

XXXVII (1922), 243-280.

A presentation of the business organizations, methods, repertory, and history of the strolling players in the late 17th and the 18th centuries.

4875 Wood, Frederick T., et al. "Notes on English Provincial Playhouses in the Eighteenth-Century." Notes and Queries, CLX (1931), 147-150, 165-169, 183-187, 209-210, 226-227, 247-248, 253, 267, 283-284, 301, 317-318, 338-339, 356-357, 388; CLXI (1931), 30-31.

Attempts an exhaustive list of provincial playhouses in England and Wales together with available facts and sources of information on each theatre.

4876 Wood, Frederick T. "Some Aspects of Provincial Drama in the Eighteenth Century." English Studies, XIV (1932), 65-74.

Tate Wilkinson, manager of the Theatre-Royal at York during the last quarter of the 18th century, toured the north of England and Yorkshire with his acting company, which included several noted actors and actresses: Mr. and Mrs. Inchbald, Mrs. Siddons, Peg Woffington, Mrs. Dorothy Jordan, John and Stephen Kemble.

4877 Avery, Emmett L. "The Summer Theatrical Seasons at Richmond and Twickenham, 1746-1753." Notes and Queries, CLXXIII (October 23, 1937), 290-294; (October 30, 1937), 312-315; (November 6, 1937), 328-332.

Compiled from advertisements in the Daily Advertiser.

4878 Rosenfeld, Sybil. Strolling Players & Drama in the Provinces, 1660-1765. Cambridge: Cambridge University Press, 1939. ix, 333 pp.

A detailed history of plays, performances, actors, and theatre outside London. Major emphasis is given to companies in Norwich, York, and Bath.

4879 Thaler, Alwin. "Strolling Players and Provincial Drama after Shakespeare." Shakespeare and Democracy. (Knoxville: University of Tennessee Press, 1941), 185-223.

This paper, reprinted with additions, from PMLA, XXXVII (1922), 243-280.

Publishers

4880 Mumby, Frank Arthur. Publishing and Bookselling. A History from the Earliest Times to the Present Day. With a bibliography by W. H. Peet. London: Jonathan Cape, 1930. 480 pp.

Chapters 8 and 9 are devoted to the Restoration and 18th-century printers and publishers, with their products. Jacob Tonson and Robert Dodsley are considered at some length.

4881 Wood, Frederick T. and Ambrose Heal. "Notes on London Book-
       sellers and Publishers, 1700-1750." Notes and Queries, CLXI
       (1931), 39-42, 60-64, 76-82, 93-99, 114-118, 130-133, 150-
       154, 169-173, 185-189, 203-206, 219-221, 240-244, 255-257,
       275-277, 291-293, 313-316, 328-329, 347-351, 363-367, 382-385,
       400-404, 435-439.
          An alphabetical list of names of booksellers and publishers,
       giving information about their specific work. Extensive notes by
       Heal.

Puns

4882 Cecil, C. D. "Delicate and Indelicate Puns in Restoration Com-
       edy." Modern Language Review, LXI (1966), 572-578.
          The attitudes of Dryden, Wycherley, and Etherege toward
       word-play were complex. Congreve was especially impressed
       by the pun as a vehicle for wit.

Puppet Theatre

4883 Rehm, Hermann S. Das Buch der Marionetten. Berlin: E. Frensdorff
       [1905]. 307 pp.
          Chapter XI of this illustrated study of marionettes in various
       lands deals with puppet shows in England from 1642 through the
       18th century.
4884 Thaler, Alwin. "Elizabethan 'Motions.'" Times Literary Supple-
       ment, February 26, 1920, p. 140.
          A presentation of James Ralph's description of a puppet-
       show in The Taste of the Town (1731); the article is primarily
       concerned with the mechanical aspects of puppet shows.
4885 Anderson, Madge. "The Strange History of Mr. Punch." Heroes
       of the Puppet Stage. (New York: Harcourt, 1923), 69-96.
          This study contains some discussion of Punch in the late
       seventeenth and eighteenth centuries (e.g., Addison and Steele's
       comments on Punch).
4886 Lawrence, W. J. "Marionette Operas." Musical Quarterly, X
       (1924), 236-243.
          A history of marionette operas from the beginnings in Flor-
       ence in the late 17th century to England (at the beginning of the
       18th century) through about 1773.
4887 Ronsome, Grace Greenleaf. Puppets and Shadows: A Bibliography.
       Boston: F. W. Faxon Co., 1931. [8], 66 pp.
          There are some few references to English puppet plays in
       the 17th and 18th centuries. See pp. 6-9, on the English puppets.

4888 Stephens, Thelma Ethel. "Bibliography of Puppetry." M.A. University of Washington, 1940.

4889 Steaight, George. "Puppet Theatres in London: II. Restoration to the End of the Eighteenth Century." Theatre Notebook, II (October, 1947), 2-5.
> Lists the known theatres.

4890 -----. "Punch's Opera at Bartholomew Fair." Theatre Notebook, VII (1952-1953), 84-85.
> Punch's Puppet Show (1772?) illustrates, in a series of plates, a puppet performance at a late eighteenth-century fair.

4891 -----. "'Pull Devil, Pull Baker.'" Notes and Queries, CXCVIII (1953), 286-288.
> The origin of the phrase can be found in eighteenth-century puppet shows.

4892 -----. The History of the English Puppet Theatre. New York: J. de Graff [1955]. 350 pp.
> Chapters V through VIII are of particular interest. They treat such topics as "Puppet Theatres in 18th-century London," and "English Punch: The Popular Puppet Show of the 18th Century." Appendices include "Puppet Showmen in England" and "Plays Performed by Puppets in England."

4893 -----. "A Restoration Puppet Show." Theatre Notebook, XII (1958), 69-71.
> Puppets in Lacy's The Old Troop, 1668.

Purcell, Henry

4894 Cummings, William H. "Purcell's Music for 'The Tempest.'" Notes and Queries, 10th Ser., II (October 1, 1904), 270-271.
> The purpose of the article is to show that no part of Purcell's music for The Tempest was published before 1695 [sic] and that to 1680, Purcell had never collaborated with Shadwell.

4895 Squire, William Barclay. "Purcell's Dramatic Music." Sammelbande der internationalen Musikgesellschaft, V (1904), 506-514.

4896 Lawrence, W. J. "Who Wrote the Famous 'Macbeth' Music?" The Elizabethan Playhouse and Other Studies. First Series. (Stratford-on-Avon: Shakespeare Head Press, 1912), 209-224.
> Purcell the composer. The tradition that Locke wrote the famous music due to misinformation of Downes.

4897 Bridge, Sir Frederick. "Henry Lawes, 1595-1662." Twelve Good Musicians: from John Bull to Henry Purcell. (London: Kegan Paul, Trench, Trubner & Co., Ltd., 1920), 71-83.
> A biographical sketch of one of the composers of The Siege of Rhodes.

4898   -----. "Henry Purcell, 1658-1695." Twelve Good Musicians:
       from John Bull to Henry Purcell. (London: Kegan Paul, Trench,
       Trubner & Co., Ltd., 1920), 118-141.
           A biographical sketch of Purcell which treats his operas very
       briefly and his accomplishments as a theoriest in detail.
4899   Kendall, E. D. "Some Notes on Purcell's Dramatic Music: With
       Especial Reference to The Fairy Queen." Music & Letters, I
       (1920), 135-144.
           A consideration of Purcell's method, the poets he worked
       with, and a detailed examination of the songs in The Fairy Queen.
4900   Arundell, Dennis. "The Tragedy of Henry Purcell." London Mer-
       cury, VII (January, 1923), 257-265.
           A brief biographical sketch followed by a discussion of Pur-
       cell's contribution to music; much of this discussion centers
       around his operas. (The "tragedy" mentioned in the title is that
       Purcell is not better known.)
4901   Arundell, Dennis. Henry Purcell. Oxford: Oxford University Press;
       London: Milford, 1927. 136 pp.
           A critical biography, with a chapter on dramatic music
       provided by Purcell for several Restoration plays.
4902   Holland, A. K. Henry Purcell: the English Musical Tradition.
       London: Bell, 1932. 191 pp.
           A biography.
4903   Lamson, Roy, Jr. "Henry Purcell's Dramatic Songs and the Eng-
       lish Broadside Ballad." Publications of the Modern Language
       Association, LIII (1938), 148-161.
           Proof of the popularity of Purcell's music is adduced from
       a number of his dramatic songs that were published, often
       without music, as broadside ballads.
4904   Strangways, A. H. Fox. "The Genius of Purcell." Listener, XXIV
       (November 21, 1940), 749.
           Praises Purcell, primarily for his variety.
4905   Westrup, J. A. "Purcell and His Operatic Style." Listener, XXIV
       (August 22, 1940), 285.
4906   Fellowes, Edmund H. English Cathedral Music from Edward VI
       to Edward VII. London: Methuen & Co., Ltd., 1941. ix, [1],
       268 pp. Index.
           Six chapters are devoted to the Restoration and 18th century
       cathedral music, and the composers. A chapter is devoted to
       Purcell, with an analysis of the charge that his works are
       theatrical.
4907   Westrup, Jack A. Purcell. London: J. M. Dent, 1947. (Master
       Musicians Series).
           A general study, with reference throughout to English opera
       of the period.

4908 Holland, A. K. Henry Purcell: The English Musical Tradition.
      Harmondsworth: Penguin Books, 1948. 191 pp.
          A reprint of the 1932 biographical study, which contains in-
      formation of the theatre of Purcell's age.
4909 Manifold, J. S. The Music in English Drama from Shakespeare to
      Purcell. London: Rockliff, 1956. ix, 208 pp.
4910 White, Eric Walter. "Early Theatrical Perfromances of Purcell's
      Operas, With a Calendar of Recorded Performances, 1690-
      1710." Theatre Notebook, XIII (1958), 43-65.
4911 Holst, Imogen, ed. Henry Purcell, 1659-1695. Essays on His
      Music. London: Oxford University Press, 1959. [8], 136 pp.
4912 Westrup, J. A. "Purcell and Handel." Music and Letters, XL
      (1959), 103-108.
          Handel was not much influenced.
4913 Purcell, Henry. Dido and Aeneas, an Opera. New York: Broude
      Brothers, [195-].
          Libretto by Nahum Tate.
4914 Bicknell, Joan Colleen Patton. "Interdependence of Word and Tone
      in the Dramatic Music of Henry Purcell." Ph.D. Stanford Uni-
      versity, 1961. 273 pp. (Order No. 61-1216).
4915 Moore, Robert Etheridge. Henry Purcell and the Restoration The-
      atre. Foreword by Sir Jack Westrup. London: Heinemann; Cam-
      bridge, Massachusetts: Harvard University Press, 1961. xvi,
      223 pp.
4916 Zimmerman, Franklin B. Henry Purcell, 1659-1695. London:
      Macmillan Co., 1967. 429 pp.
4917 Purcell, Henry. Suite for Strings from "The Double Dealer."
      Edited by Paul Stassevitch. New York: Music Press, Inc.
      [n.d.]

Puritanism

4918 Graves, Thornton S. "Notes on Puritanism and the Stage." Studies
      in Philology, XVIII (1921), 141-169.
          A three-part article: Part 1 concerns attacks on the stage
      before 1642; Part 2 attempts to show that the defenders of the
      stage were not idle during the Interregnum; Part 3 discusses
      Puritan attacks on the stage after the Restoration and before
      Collier.
4919 Whiting, C. E. Studies in English Puritanism from the Restoration
      to the Revolution. London: S.P.C.K., 1931. 584 pp.
          Particularly interesting in its treatment of Puritan views
      about the stage as well as the representation of Puritans on the
      stage.
4920 Gordon, Isabel S. "Satire of the Puritan in the English Drama,

1558-1660 together with an Appendix of Materials for a Similar
Study for the Years 1660-1700." Ph.D. New York University,
1932.

4921 Marlowe, John. The Puritan Tradition in English Life. London:
Cresset Press, 1956. 148 pp.
        A history of Puritanism in England from the Reformation
through the 19th century, traced through politics, social life,
and the fine arts. Passing references to drama.

4922 Morgan, Edmund S. "Puritan Hostility to the Theatre." Proceedings of the American Philosophical Society, CX (1966), 340-
347.
        An analysis of Puritan arguments which attempts to account
for the intensity of hostility against the theatre. Although most
of the article is devoted to events of the late 16th century, there
are many references to the Restoration and 18th century.

Quin, Anne

4923 Wilson, John Harold. "The Marshall Sisters and Anne Quin."
Notes and Queries, CCII (1957), 104-106.
        The various dramatic roles of the two Marshall sisters can
be separated by concluding that after 1665 or 1666 the elder
appeared as Anne Quin while the younger played as Mrs. Marshall.

Quin, James

4924 Taylor, Aline Mackenzie. "The Patrimony of James Quin: The
Legend and the Facts." Tulane Studies in English, VIII (1958),
55-106.

4925 Mander, Raymond and Joe Mitchenson. "The China Statuettes
of Quin as Falstaff." Theatre Notebook, XII (1958), 54-58.
        Ceramic history, illustrated.

Racine, Jean

4926 Eccles, F. Y. Racine in England. Taylorian Lecture, 1921. Oxford: The Clarendon Press, 1922. 30 pp.
        Deals with translations and adaptations of Racine's plays
and their critical reception in England.

4927 Parnell, Paul E. "The Early English Adaptations of Racine's
Tragedies." M.A. New York University, 1947.

4928 Wheatley, Katherine E. Racine and English Classicism. Austin:
University of Texas Press, 1956. xi, 345 pp.
        English adaptations.

4929 French, A. L. "Some Tragedies of Corneile and Racine As Trans-

lated into English, 1660-1676." M. Litt. Cambridge University
(Jesus), 1961.

Raillery

4930 Hayman, John Griffiths. "Raillery during the Restoration Period
and Early Eighteenth Century." Ph.D. Northwestern University,
1964. (Order No. 64-12,288).
   Chapter IV examines "the raillery engaged in by the wits
and the women of Restoration comedy."
4931 Cecil, C. D. "Raillery in Restoration Comedy." Huntington Library Quarterly, XXIX (1966), 147-159.
   Studies the importance of raillery for the energetic manner
of Restoration comedy: "Raillery is the Augustan mode for
clarifying the tenet s and refining the values of conversational
man."

Ralph, James

4932 Hughes, Helen S. "Fielding's Indebtedness to James Ralph."
Modern Philology, XX (1922), 19-34.
   A discussion of James Ralph's probable influence on The
Author's Farce, and Tom Thumb.
4933 Kenny, Robert W. "James Ralph: An Eighteenth Century Philadel-
phian in Grub Street." Pennsylvania Magazine of History and
Biography, LXIV (April, 1940), 218-242.
4934 MacMillan, Dougald. "Some Notes on Eighteenth-Century Essex
Plays." Modern Language Notes, LV (March, 1940), 176-183.
   On plays about Essex by James Ralph, Henry Jones, and
Henry Brooke.
4935 Shipley, John B. "David Garrick and James Ralph: Remarks on a
Correspondence." Notes and Queries, (1958), 403-408.
   Prints five letters, 1754, 1757.
4936 Lowens, Irving. "The Touch Stone (1728): A Neglected View of
London Opera." Musical Quarterly, XLV (1959), 325-342.
   Questions attribution to James Ralph.
4937 Bastian, J. M. "James Ralph's Second Adaptation from John
Banks." Huntington Library Quarterly, XXV (1962), 181-188.
   Ralph's adaptation of Banks' Anna Bullen (1682) into Vertue
Betray'd; or, Anna Bullen (ca. 1735). Grace and strength of
Ralph's poetry makes the adaptation superior to the original.
4938 Shipley, John Burke. "James Ralph: Pretender to Genius." Ph.D.
Columbia University, 1963. (Order No. 63-7433).
   Surveys his theatrical career, his relationship with Gar-
rick and Fielding.

Ramsay, Allan

4939 Martin, Bruno. Allan Ramsay: A Study of His Life and Works.
       Cambridge: Harvard University Press, 1931. vi, 203 pp.
       A biography.
4940 -----. Bibliography of Allan Ramsay. Glasgow: Jackson, Wylie,
       1932. 114 pp.
       Reprinted from Records of the Glasgow Bibliographical
       Society, Vol. X. A bibliography of the works of the author of the
       pastoral drama The Gentle Shepherd.

Ravenscroft, Edward

4941 McManaway, James G. "The Copy for The Careless Lovers."
       Modern Language Notes, XLVI (1931), 406-409.
       Suggests that Ravenscroft was heavily indebted to Molière.
4942 Norris, E. T. "The Original of Ravenscroft's Anatomist."
       Modern Language Review, XLVI (December, 1931), 522-526.
       This identifies the source of The Anatomist as Hauteroche's
       Crispin Médecin, denies that Jemmy Spiller is the actor eulogized
       by Riccoboni, and suggests that "the version of The Anatomist
       which the Italian saw was probably the original and not the altered
       one."
4943 -----. "Titus Andronicus." Times Literary Supplement, May 11,
       1933, p. 331.
4944 -----. "The Italian Source for Ravenscroft's Italian Husband."
       Review of English Studies, X (1934), 202-205.
       Argues that Giacinto Andrea Cicognini's 1664 play Il Tradi-
       mento per l'Honore is the source of Ravenscroft's play--not
       The Glory of God's Revenge as some writers have suggested.
4945 Lancaster, H. C. "Calderon, Boursault, and Ravenscroft."
       Modern Language Notes, LI (1936), 523-528.
       Ravenscroft's Wrangling Lovers (1676) is based directly
       upon Boursault's novel, Ne pas croire ce qu'on void, histoire
       espagnole.
4946 Parshall, Raymond E. "Dramatic Works of Edward Ravenscroft."
       Ph.D. Yale University, 1936.
4947 -----. "The Source of Ravenscroft's The Anatomist." Review of
       English Studies, XII (1936), 328-333.
       Argues that the Crispin Médecin of Noël le Breton is the
       source of Ravenscroft's farce.
4948 Rundle, James U. "More about Calderón, Boursault, and Raven-
       scroft." Modern Language Notes, LXII (June, 1947), 382-384.
       The Wrangling Lovers derives from Boursault, not Calderón.

4949 Lancaster, H. Carrington. "Still More about Calderón, Boursault
      and Ravenscroft." Modern Language Notes, LXII (June, 1947),
      385-389.
           Contests the arguments of James U. Rundle, pp. 382-384,
      concerning The Wrangling Lovers.
4950 Rundle, James U. "Footnote on Calderón, Ravenscroft and Bour-
      sault." Modern Language Notes, LXIII (March, 1948), 217-219.
           Answers the contentions of H. Carrington Lancaster, LXII
      (1947), 385-389.
4951 Zimansky, Curt A. "Edward Ravenscroft's First Play." Philolo-
      gical Quarterly, XXVIII (1949), 516-517.
           Ravenscroft's King Edgar and Alfrida was written--and pro-
      bably performed--about 1667, not 1677 as most historians say.
      Considers Rymer's debt to Ravenscroft in Rymer's Edgar, the
      English Monarch.
4952 Pettersen, N. H. "The Life and Works of Edward Ravenscroft
      (1644-1704)." M.A. University College, London, 1955-56.

Reading

4953 Wright, Louis B. "The Reading of Plays during the Puritan Revolu-
      tion." The Huntington Library Bulletin, No. 6 (1934), 73-108.
           An account of how drama survived in play readings during
      the interregnum.

Reed, Isaac

4954 Metzdorf, Robert F. "Isaac Reed and the Unfortunate Dr. Dodd."
      Harvard Library Bulletin, VI (1952), 393-396.
           Isaac Reed (1742-1807), lawyer and scholar, edited Dodd's
      Thoughts in Prison, wrote an anonymous biography of Dodd,
      and collected at least twenty pamphlets by or about Dodd.
4955 Jones, Claude E. "Isaac Reed's Theatrical Obituary." Notes and
      Queries, IV (1957), 390-392.
4956 McAleer, John J. "Isaac Reed: Editor of the 'First Variorum.'"
      Shakespeare Newsletter, XIII (1963), 26.
           Brief biography of the 18th century Shakespeare scholar.
      Includes excerpts from his Biographica Dramatica (1782) on
      specific Shakespearean plays.

Reed, Joseph

4957 Wilson, Robert H. "Reed and Warton on the Old Wives Tale."
      Publications of the Modern Language Association, LV (1940),
      605-608.

Argues that Thomas Warton "plagiarized" from Joseph Reed
in his comments on the Old Wives Tale in his edition of the
minor poems of Milton (1785).

4958 Sawyer, Paul. "Garrick, Joseph Reed, and Dido." Restoration and
Eighteenth Century Theatre Research, VI (November, 1967),
44-50.
Studies the tireless efforts of Joseph Reed (1723-1787) to
persuade Garrick to produce Dido at Drury Lane.

Rehearsals

4959 Schmidt, Karlernst. Die Bühnenprobe als Lustspieltyp in der englischen
Literatur. Halle (Saale): Max Niemeyer Verlag, 1952. 32 pp.
Discusses use of the rehearsal as the subject matter of 12
plays (11 English, 1 French), including George Villiers' "The
Rehearsal" (1671-2), Fielding's "The Author's Farce" (1729),
"Eurydice" (1735), "Pasquin" (1736), "The Historical Register
for the Year 1736" (1737), "Tumble-down Dick, or Phaeton in the
Suds" (1744), and Sheridan's "The Critic" (1779). The rehearsal
theme is used as a means of parodying current dramatic forms
and expressing criticisms of them through the "actors," "spectators" and "author" of the play within the play.

Renaissance

4960 Walker, E. M. "The Impact of the Renaissance on the English
Drama." M.A. Dalhousie University, 1934.

Repertory

4961 Greg, W. W. "Theatrical Repertories of 1662." Gentleman's
Magazine, XXXI (1906), 69-72.

4962 Macleod, William R. "Stage Repertories of the First Decade of
the Restoration." Ph.D. Fordham University, 1934.

Restoration Scholarship

4963 Langhans, Edward A. "Restoration Theatre Scholarship 1960-66:
A Resume and Suggestions for Future Work." Restoration and
Eighteenth Century Theatre Research, VI (May, 1967), 8-11.
Most of the theatre scholarship of the last six years has
been devoted to performance information, scenery and staging
methods, actors and acting, theatre architecture, costumes,
music, promptbooks and theatre management. One pressing need
is for critical editions or facsimile reprints of existing primary
source material.

Revivals

4964 Child, Harold. "Revivals of English Dramatic Works, 1919-1925."
      Review of English Studies, II (April, 1926), 177-188.
            Includes a list of Restoration and 18th-century plays.
4965 -----. "Revivals of English Dramatic Works, 1901-1918, 1926."
      Review of English Studies, III (April, 1927), 169-185.
            Supplements the earlier list in Review of English Studies,
      including Restoration and 18th-century plays and operas.
4966 Hampden, John. "Eighteenth-Century Plays." Times Literary
      Supplement, November 3, 1927, p. 790.
            Requests information on stage revivals since 1900 of 12 plays.

Reynolds, Frederick

text

4967 Reynolds, Frederic. The Dramatist: or Stop Him Who Can! A Com-
      edy. Edited by Allardyce Nicoll. London: Milford, 1925. (Eng-
      lish Comedies of the 18th Century Series). 90 pp.
            Reprints the edition of 1789 with a brief introduction.

biography and criticism

4968 Collins, M. H. A. "The Life and Works of Frederick Reynolds,
      Dramatist, (1764-1841)." M.A. London University (Royal
      Holloway), 1929.
4969 Rapp, Merton H. "Frederick Reynolds and the English Drama,
      1785-1840." Ph.D. State University of Iowa, 1939.

Rhetoric

4970 Fussell, Paul. The Rhetorical World of Augustan Humanism: Ethics
      and Imagery from Swift to Burke. Oxford: Clarendon Press,
      1965. 314 pp.
            Concentrating on the rhetorical techniques, especially the
      polemic imagery of Swift, Pope, Johnson, Reynolds, Gibbon,
      and Burke, the work makes occasional references to Augustan
      drama.

Rhetorical Jest

4971 Miller, Henry Knight. "The Paradoxical Encomium with Special
      Reference to its Vogue in England, 1600-1800." Modern Philology
      LIII (1956), 145-178.

The paradoxical encomium, which dates from earliest Greek rhetoric, is an independent literary form of "rhetorical jest" through the praise of trivial or unadmirable objects. Discussion of the use of this device includes references to playwrights of the period.

Rhodes, Ebenezer

4972 Wood, Frederick Thomas. "The Authorship of an Eighteenth-Century Play." Notes and Queries, CXCII (April 5, 1947), 149.
On the authority of Joseph Hunter, Alfred, 1789, is attributed to Ebenezer Rhodes.

Rhodes, John

4973 Wagner, Bernard M. "John Rhodes and Ignoramus." Review of English Studies, V (January, 1929), 43-48.
On the actors under Rhodes who performed before the King (November 1, 1662).

Rich, John

4974 Disher, M. Willson. "Pope's 'Angel of Dulness.'" Times Literary Supplement, December 11, 1943, p. 595.
Concerned with the relationship of Rich to the origin of English pantomime.
4975 Hughes, Leo and Arthur H. Scouten. "John Rich and the Holiday Seasons of 1732-3." Review of English Studies, XXI (January, 1945), 46-52.
Additional information about Rich's management.
4976 Bell, R. A. "Rich as Lun." Notes and Queries, CXCII (August 9, 1947), 348.
A postscript to C. A. C. Davis's article (May 31, 1947), noting the reference to "Lun" in Charles Lamb's "My First Play."
4977 Davis, C. A. C. "John Rich as Lun." Notes and Queries, CXCII (May 31, 1947), 222-224.
Rich adopted the stage name of "Lun" for his harlequin performances from the great French mime, Francisque Moylin.
4978 Vincent, Howard P. "John Rich and the First Covent Garden Theatre." Journal of English Literary History, XVII (1950), 296-306.
The building of the first Covent Garden Theatre (opened 1732), in the face of difficulties with architect and builder Edward Sharp, was one of Rich's most illustrious achievements.

4979 Sawyer, Paul S. "John Rich versus Drury Lane, 1714-1761: A Study in Theatrical Rivalry." Ph.D. Columbia University, 1954. 305 pp.

This study traces Rich's career as manager of Lincoln's Inn Fields and Covent Garden.

4980 Francis, Basil. "John Rich's 'Proposals.'" Theatre Notebook, XII (1957), 17-19.

Financing of Covent Garden in 1731.

4981 Sawyer, Paul. "John Rich: A Biographical Sketch." Theatre Annual, XV (1957-58), 55-68.

A biography which studies both Rich's influential "if hardly beneficial" theatrical career and his "taste for noble vices and noble friends."

4982 Green, Elvena M. "John Rich's Art of Pantomime as Seen in his The Necromancer, or Harlequin Doctor Faustus: A Comparison of the Two Faustus Pantomimes at Lincoln's-Inn-Fields and Drury Lane." Restoration and Eighteenth Century Theatre Research, IV (May, 1965), 47-60.

More successful and artistic than the rival Drury Lane production of John Thurmond's Harlequin Doctor Faustus, John Rich's The Necromancer (1723) surpasses its rival not in spectacular effects but in the greater care taken with the selection and arrangement of major sequences and with the development of the protagonist's character.

4983 Highfill, Philip H., Jr. "Rich's 1744 Inventory of Covent Garden Properties, Part 3." Restoration and Eighteenth Century Theatre Research, VI (May, 1967), 27-35.

Lists of costumes, scenery and other properties at Covent Garden in 1744 are reproduced from the British Museum manuscript (BM Add. MSS. 12,201). Concludes the article from Restoration and Eighteenth Century Theatre Research, V (May, 1966), 7-17 and V (November, 1966), 17-26.

Richards, William

4984 Stroup, Thomas B. "'The Christmas Ordinary': Manuscript and Authorship." Papers of the Bibliographical Society of America, L (1956), 184-190.

Ca. 1682; perhaps by William Richards.

Richardson, Samuel

4985 Sale, William M. Samuel Richardson, A Bibliographical Record of His Literary Career with Historical Notes. New Haven: Yale University Press, 1936. xxiv, 141 pp.

Under "works inspired in whole or in part by the publication of Richardson's novels," Sale includes pertinent bibliographical information about the comedies and operas based upon Pamela.

4986 Kreissman, Bernard. Pamela-Shamela: A Study of the Criticisms, Burleques(?), Parodies, and Adaptations of Richardson's "Pamela." University of Nebraska Studies, N.S. 22. Lincoln: University of Nebraska Press, 1960. 98 pp.

Includes dramatizations.

4987 Sherburn, George. "Samuel Richardson's Novels and the Theatre: A Theory Sketched." Philological Quarterly, XLI (1962), 325-329.

The possible indebtedness of Richardson to the theatre for plot-focus, character types, and conversation.

4988 Konigsberg, Ira. "The Tragedy of Clarissa." Modern Language Quarterly, XXVII (1966), 285-298.

Discusses the novel's relationship to a theory of tragedy and to 18th century tragedies.

4989 Dussinger, John A. "Richardson's Tragic Muse." Philological Quarterly, XLVI (1967), 18-33.

Examines Richardson's interest in the drama and its effect on Clarissa, appreciated by his contemporaries as "a work of tragic species." Includes references to Hill, Fielding and Cibber.

Richardson, William

4990 Boulton, M. "A Study of William Richardson with Special Reference to His Shakespearian Criticism." B. Litt. Oxford University, 1948.

4991 Cordasco, Francesco. "William Richardson's Essays on Shakespeare (1784): A Bibliographical Note on the First Edition." Notes and Queries, CXCVI (1951), 148.

The date of the first edition of Richardson's Essays on Shakespeare is 1784 rather than 1783.

Richmond

4992 Dodds, M. H. "XVIII-Century Theatre at Richmond, Yorks." Notes and Queries, CLXXXV (1943), 166.

A theatre built in Richmond, Yorks, in 1788 and used as a warehouse for a century was reopened on August 2, 1943.

4993 Rosenfeld, Sybil. The XVIII Century Theatre at Richmond Yorkshire. York: Georgian Society, 1947. 28 pp. (York Georgian Society Occasional Papers, 3).

A paper read before the York Georgian Society on March 15, 1947, summarizing the materials relating to the Richmond theatre.

4994 Southern, Richard. "Progress at Richmond, Yorkshire." Theatre
        Notebook, IV (October, 1949), 9-12.
        A report, with photographs, of the restoration of the Georgian
        theatre.

4995 -----. "Richmond Redivivus." Drama (Autumn, 1949), 15-17.
        A comment on the restored playhouse at Richmond, opened
        in 1788.

4996 Rosenfeld, Sybil. "Report on Two Georgian Theatres." Theatre
        Notebook, XIV (1960), 100-101.
        Describes progress in the reconstruction of Richmond
        (York's) Theatre and Stockton-on-Tees Theatre.

Riots

4997 Tait, Stephen. "English Theatre Riots." Theatre Arts, XXIV (Feb-
        ruary, 1940), 97-104.
        An anecdotal history of riots in the London theatres, from
        1721 through about 1809.

4998 Troubridge, Sir St. Vincent, Bt. "Theatre Riots in London."
        Studies in English Theatre History, in Memory of Gabrielle
        Enthove, O.B.E., first president of the Society for Theatre
        Research, 1948-1950. (London, 1952), 84-97.
        A general treatment of riots in the London theatres from
        the middle of the 18th century to the 20th century. Detailed
        treatment of the Battle-Conjuror Riots of 1749 and the Chinese
        Festival Riots of 1755.

Robertson, James

4999 Bronson, Bertrand H. "James Robertson, Poet and Playwright."
        Modern Language Notes, XLIX (1934), 509-511.
        Comments on editions of the plays and poems of Robertson
        who was "a bad poet, a bad dramatist, and a doubtless mediocre
        actor-manager."

Robinson, Perdita

5000 Barrington, E. [Mrs. Lily Adams Beck]. The Exquisite Perdita.
        New York: Dodd, Mead and Co., 1926. 377 pp.
        Historical novel about Mrs. Perdita Robinson, her discovery
        by Sheridan and stage training by Garrick.

Romantic Drama

5001 McNeill, William E. "A History of the English Drama from 1788

to 1832, with Special Reference to Theatrical Conditions."
Ph.D. Harvard University, 1909.

5002 Ellison, Lee M. "The Early Romantic Drama at the English
Court." Ph.D. Chicago University, 1916.

5003 Musafar, K. C. "Romantic Drama in England, 1780-1830: an
Examination of Acted and Unacted Plays in the Light of The-
atrical History of the Period." Ph.D. London University
(King's), 1924.

5004 Fletcher, Richard M. "English Romantic Drama, 1795-1843.
A Critical and Historical Study." Ph.D. University of Pennsylvania, 1962.

Romantic Poets

5005 Bair, George E. "The Plays of the Romantic Poets, Their Place
in Dramatic History." Ph.D. University of Pennsylvania,
1951.

Romantic Theory

5006 Robertson, John George. Studies in the Genesis of Romantic
Theory in the Eighteenth Century. Cambridge: At the University Press, 1923. 298 pp.

This is a general discussion of the abandonment of Classicism and the movement to Romanticism, which, in the chapter
on England, discusses Addison's criticism of tragedy and
mentions the drama throughout the chapter.

Rosamond

5007 Heltzel, Virgil B. Fair Rosamond: A Study in the Development of
a Literary Theme. Evanston: Northwestern University Press,
1947. viii, 135 pp. (Northwestern University Studies in the
Humanities).

Includes eighteenth century dramatic treatment of the story,
such as Addison's opera.

Rousseau, Jean

5008 Politzer, Robert L. "Rousseau on the Theatre and the Actors."
Romanic Review, XLVI (1955), 250-257.

Attempts to define Rousseau's aesthetic theory and the
significance of Lettre à d' Alembert in the light of this.
Rousseau confused art and reality. His contribution is not to
theory but lies in the application of theory.

Rowe, Nicholas

texts

5009 Rowe, Nicholas. The Fair Penitent and Jane Shore. Edited by
Sophie Chantal Hart. Boston: D. C. Heath, 1907. li, 255 pp.
Contains brief biography, forty-three page introduction,
appendices, and bibliography.

5010 -----. Some Account of the Life of Mr. William Shakespear
(1709). Edited by Samuel Holt Monk. Ann Arbor: The Augustan
Reprint Society, November, 1948. (Extra series 1).
A facsimile of the original text, usually read in Pope's al-
teration, with an introduction describing the background of
Rowe's edition and noting his significance in the stream of
Shakespearean criticism.

5011 -----. Tamerlane, a Tragedy. Edited by Landon C. Burns, Jr.
Philadelphia: University of Pennsylvania Press, 1966.
With introduction and notes.

5012 -----. Three Plays by Nicholas Rowe. Edited by James R. Sutherland. London: Scholartis Press, 1929. 353 pp.
Tamarlane, The Fair Penitent, Jane Shore, with texts based
on the first quarto of each play. A full bibliography of the several editions of all Rowe's plays published in his lifetime. The
Introduction gives an account of Rowe's life and achievement
but needs fuller annotation.

biography and criticism

5013 Gilde, Alfred. Die dramatische Behandlung der Rückkehr der
Odysseus bei Nicholas Rowe, Robert Bridges und Stephen
Phillips. Inaugural Dissertation. Koenigsberg, 1903. 72 pp.
Contains an extended discussion of Rowe's Ulysses as com-
pared to Homer's.

5014 Behrend, Alfred. Nicholas Rowe als Dramatiker. Leipzig Dissertation, 1907. 66 pp.
Brief, general discussion of Rowe.

5015 Schwarz, Ferdinand H. Nicholas Rowe, "The Fair Penitent." A
Contribution to Literary Analysis with a Side-Reference to
Richard Beer-Hofmann, Der Graf von Charolais. Bern: A.
Francke, 1907. 84 pp.
Mostly a summary of the evaluations of the play by Cumber-
land, Johnson, Ward, and Gosse.

5016 Budig, Willy. Untersuchungen über "Jane Shore." Rostock: Schwerin,
1908. 111 pp.
A study of Jane Shore in English literature of the 16th, 17th,

18th, and 19th centuries and in French literature.

5017 Bünning, Eduard. Nicholas Rowe's "Tamerlane, " 1702. Rostock:
      Schwerin i.M., 1908. 72 pp.
          Analysis of Charles Saunders' Tamerlane the Great and
      Rowe's Tamerlane; treatment of Rowe's sources and discussion
      of parallelisms between Steele's A Christian Hero and Rowe's
      Tamerlane.

5018 Borgwardt, Paul. The Royal Convert von Nicholas Rowe 1707.
      Rostock: Wm. H. Winterberg, 1909. 91 pp.
          A discussion of editions, textual variations and sources of
      The Royal Convert.

5019 Stahl, Ludwig. Nicholas Rowes Drama "The Ambitious Step-
      mother." Inaugural Dissertation. Rostock: Carl Henstorffs,
      1909. 88 pp.
          A study of Rowe's play: a summary of its plot and characters;
      its sources; its production; Charles Gildon's criticism; and a
      general evaluation by the author.

5020 Intze, O[ttokar]. Nicholas Rowe. Leipzig: Fr. Richter [1910]. 268
      pp.
          The second edition of Tamerlane with variant readings from
      the first edition, typography and some spellings modernized, to
      which is added Rowe's poems and his biography of Shakespeare.
      Introductory material includes a short sketch of English drama
      from the time of Henry VII to the death of Queen Anne and a short
      biography of Rowe with shorter critical evaluations of his other
      plays.

5021 Colville, Captain Kenneth N. "Shakespeare's First Critical Editor."
      Nineteenth Century, LXXX (1919), 266-279.

5022 Sutherland, J. R. "Nicholas Rowe." B. Litt. Oxford University,
      1926.

5023 Swindell, Alice Blanche. "Nicholas Rowe As an Exponent of Eight-
      eenth Century Drama." M.A. Columbia University, 1926.

5024 Conley, Irene Grace. "The Influence of Shakespere on the Dramas
      of Nicholas Rowe." M.A. University of Minnesota, 1929. x,
      127 pp.
          Contends that politics and theatre innovations played a greater
      role in bringing about adaptations of Shakespeare than did neo-
      classicism and the imitation of French thought. Chapters on the
      altering of Shakespeare's plays, on Shakespeare's influence on
      Rowe, and on Rowe's plays.

5025 Jackson, A. "Life and Works of Nicholas Rowe." M.A. University
      of London, 1929.

5026 "Nicholas Rowe." Times Literary Supplement, October 10, 1929,
      pp. 773-774.
          Reviews J. R. Sutherland, Three Plays by Nicholas Rowe

(1929). A leading article; sketches Rowe's career.

5027 Jackson, Alfred. "Rowe's Edition of Shakespeare." Library, 4th
Ser., X (1930), 455-473.
Discussion of Rowe's stage directions and his division of the
plays into acts and scenes.

5028 -----. "Rowe's Historical Tragedies." Anglia, LIV (1930), 307-33(
Critical estimates of The Royal Consort, Jane Shore, and
Lady Jane Gray.

5029 Blanchard, Rae. "A Prologue and Epilogue for Nicholas Rowe's
Tamerlane by Richard Steele." Publications of the Modern
Language Association, XLVII (1932), 772-776.
Evidence to prove that the prologue and epilogue to Rowe's
Tamerlane uncovered among the P. A. Taylor papers in the
British Museum are by Richard Steele and that he wrote them,
probably in the early 1720's for use at Dr. Newcome's School
in Clapton, Hackney.

5030 Askew, H. "Private Theatricals in the Eighteenth Century." Notes
and Queries, CLXIV (1933), 430.
On December 29, 1790, The Fair Penitent was performed at
Seaton Delaval Hall in Northumberland. Performers and other
useful information relating to the performance are listed.

5031 McKerrow, R. B. "Rowe's Shakespeare, '1709.'" Times Literary
Supplement, March 8, 1934, p. 168.
Argues that Tonson published another edition of Rowe's
Shakespeare between the well-known 1709 and 1714 eds., pro-
bably in 1710, which was intended to be indistinguishable from
the first edition, but differs in several characteristics.

5032 Whiting, George W. "Rowe's Debt to Paradise Lost." Modern
Philology, XXXII (1935), 271-279.
Internal evidence shows the influence of Paradise Lost upon
Rowe's The Fair Penitent, Jane Shore, Lady Jane Gray, and
especially Tamerlane.

5033 Suling, Karl Heinz. Die Shakespeare-Ausgabe Nicholas Rowes
[1709]. Würzburg: Triltsch, 1939. 111 pp.

5034 Wright, G. W. "Nicholas Rowe." Notes and Queries, CLXXVI
(1939), 51-52.
A protest against the removal of Rowe's memorial from
Poets' Corner, Westminster Abbey.

5035 Schuster, Sister Celine. "Nicholas Rowe and the Whig Movement."
M.A. University of Oregon, 1941.

5036 Williamson, Julie. "Nicholas Rowe's Theory of Tragedy." M.A.
University of Illinois, 1941.

5037 Philbrick, Norman. "Act and Scene Division in the First Edition
of Shakespeare: A Study of Nicholas Rowe's Treatment of the
Problems." M.A. Stanford University, 1942.

5038 Doughty, Howard N. "Nicholas Rowe and the Widow Spann." Mod-
      ern Language Quarterly, IV (December, 1943), 465-472.
         Prints documents showing that in the year 1712 Rowe was
      involved in dubious financial transactions connected with the ef-
      forts to "hasten" a petition of one Elizabeth Spann at the Admiralty
      office.

5039 Hughes, Helen Sard. "Elizabeth Rowe and the Countess of Hert-
      ford." Publications of the Modern Language Association, LIX
      (1944), 726-746.
         New light on the personal and literary relationship between
      the two women, particularly evidence that the gentle Hertford
      contributed some of the letters in Mrs. Rowe's Letters Moral
      and Entertaining.

5040 Clark, Donald Bettice. "Nicholas Rowe: A Study in the Develop-
      ment of the Pathetic Tragedy." Ph.D. George Washington Uni-
      versity, 1947.

5041 Hesse, Alfred W. "Nicholas Rowe's Translation of Lucan's
      Pharsalia 1719. A Study in Literary History." Ph.D. University
      of Pennsylvania, 1948.

5042 Kerns, Ralph. "Direction and Production of The Tragedy of Jane
      Shore." M.F.A. Carnegie Institute of Technology, 1948.

5043 Thorp, Willard. "A Key to Rowe's Tamerlane." Journal of Eng-
      lish and Germanic Philology, XXXIX (January, 1948), 124-127.
         Explains the contemporary political allegory of the play.

5044 Avery, Emmett L. "Lincoln's Inn Fields, 1704-1705." Theatre
      Notebook, V (1950-1951), 13-15.
         The news columns of the weekly Diverting Post in 1704-
      1705 contain information about Zalmayna (by Mrs. Pix ?)
      and Rowe's The Biter.

5045 Clark, Donald B. "The Source and Characterization of Nicholas
      Rowe's Tamerlane." Modern Language Notes, LXV (1950),
      145-152.
         Rowe's source was most likely Richard Knolles's The Gen-
      erall Historie of the Turkes (1603), of which he owned a copy.

5046 Schwarz, Alfred. "The Literary Career of Nicholas Rowe." Ph.D.
      Harvard University, 1951.

5047 Clark, Donald B. "An Eighteenth-Century Adaptation of Massinger."
      Modern Language Quarterly, XIII (1952), 239-252.
         The seventeenth-century shift in tragic theory is illustrated
      by a comparison of Rowe's The Fair Penitent with the play from
      which it was adapted, Massinger and Field's The Fatal Dowry.

5048 Burns, Langdon Crawford, Jr. "The Tragedies of Nicholas Rowe."
      Ph.D. Yale University, 1958.

5049 Schwarz, Alfred. "Thomas Percy at the Duke of York's Private
      Theatre." Bulletin of the New York Public Library, LXIII

(1959), 393-398.

Letter by Percy, 1767; performance of Jane Shore.

5050 -----. "An Example of Eighteenth-Century Pathetic Tragedy:
Rowe's Jane Shore." Modern Language Quarterly, XXII
(1961), 236-247.

A study of Rowe's purpose and success with a pathetic family tragedy, a type well received by the London audience in
spite of its disregard for the outmoded rules dictated by the
neoclassical critics.

5051 Wyman, Lindley A. "The Tradition of the Formal Meditation in
Rowe's The Fair Penitent." Philological Quarterly, XLII
(1963), 412-416.

Rowe's use of the Elizabethan formal meditation accounts
for the melodramatic aspects of the final act.

5052 Ingram, William. "Theobald, Rowe, Jackson: Whose Ajax?" The
Library Chronicle, XXXI (1965), 91-96.

Bibliographical and biographical evidence points to Rowe as
the probable translator of Sophocles' Ajax, published by Lintot
in 1714.

5053 Kearful, Frank J. "The Nature of Tragedy in Rowe's The Fair
Penitent." Papers on Language and Literature, II (1966), 351-
360.

The function of tragedy in The Fair Penitent is not merely
to arouse vicarious suffering: it is also to instruct Rowe's
audience in the kind of moral knowledge requisite to their own
lives.

5054 Rowan, D. F. "Shore's Wife." Studies in English Literature,
1500-1900, VI (1966), 447-464.

Traces the popular and literary treatments of Jane Shore
from her own day to Rowe's Tragedy of Jane Shore (1714).

5055 Kleitz, Philip Rex. "Nicholas Rowe: Developer of the Drama of
Sympathy." Ph.D. University of Minnesota, 1967. (Order No.
68-7342).

Discusses the transition in Rowe's works from the heroic
to sentimental tragedy and his development of language and
the pitiful heroine for the latter form.

5056 McAleer, John J. "Nicholas Rowe--Matrix of Shakespearean
Scholarship." Shakespeare Newsletter, XVII (1967), 6.

A brief biography of Rowe that considers the qualities of
his edition of Shakespeare.

Russia

5057 Morton, Richard, and William M. Peterson. "Peter the Great
and Russia in Restoration and Eighteenth Century Drama."

Notes and Queries, CXCIX (1954), 427-432.
References to Peter the Great, Russians, and Russia may
be found in plays by Cowley, Banks, Dryden, Congreve, Farquhar, Durfey, and others.

Rymer, Thomas

critical works

5058 Rymer, Thomas. The Critical Works of Thomas Rymer. Edited
by Curt A. Zimansky. New Haven: Yale University Press,
1956. li, 299 pp.
Famous dramatic criticism.

biography and criticism

5059 Broadus, Edmund K. "Thomas Rymer as a Critic." M.A. Chicago
University, 1900.
5060 Hofherr, Albert. Thomas Rymers Dramatische Kritik. Heidelberg:
C. Winter, 1908. 165 pp. (Beiträge zur neueren literaturgeschichte, I Band, 1 Heft.)
Rymer's life and general critical principles with special attention to his "Tragedies of the last Age."
5061 Dutton, George Burwell. "Thomas Rymer and Aristotelian For-
malism in English Literary Criticism, 1650-1700." Ph.D.
Harvard University, 1910.
5062 -----. "The French Aristotelian Formalists and Thomas Rymer."
Publications of the Modern Language Association, XXIX (1914),
152-188.
In general critical attitude and in a number of detailed rules,
from phrasal similarities and acknowledgment, it is clear that
Rymer derived the essential features of his critical theory
from members of the French school of rules.
5063 Tedrow, Floyd W. "Thomas Rymer: The Worst Critic That Ever
Lived." M.A. Fordham University, 1933.
5064 Stoll, Elmer Edgar. "Oedipus and Othello: Corneille, Rymer and
Voltaire." Revue Anglo-Américaine, XII (1935), 385-400.
Since the author is concerned principally with French criticism, Rymer's opinions about Othello are given only passing
notice.
5065 Zimansky, Curto Arno. "The Critical Works of Thomas Rymer
with Edgar, an Heroic Tragedy." Ph.D. Princeton University,
1937.
5066 -----. "Thomas Rymer." Times Literary Supplement, December
23, 1939, p. 743.

5067 Howard, Angela Alison. "Thomas Rymer: His Criticisms of
Shakespeare and Their Influence on Drama." M.A. Cornell
University, 1940.

5068 Zesmer, David M. "Rymer and John Dryden: a Study in 17th Century Critical Thought." M.A. Columbia University, 1949.

5069 Leech, Clifford. "Rymer on 'Othello.'" Shakespeare's Tragedies,
and Other Studies in Seventeenth-Century Drama. (London:
Chatto and Windus, 1950), 87-110.
Leech deals with, among other things, Restoration adaptations of Shakespeare and the gulf between Restoration comedy
and Restoration tragedy.

5070 Dollard, Frank D. "French Influence on Thomas Rymer's Dramatic Criticism." Ph.D. University of California, 1953.

5071 Watson, George. "Dryden's First Answer to Rymer." Review of
English Studies, XIV (1963), 17-23.
One of Dryden's most "rewarding" statements on drama.
Tonson's text of the "Heads of an Answer to Rymer" is the
"one critical document in English between the Restoration and
Johnson's Shakespeare in which the Poetics of Aristotle are at-
tacked frontally and without qualification."

5072 Downer, Alan S., and Arthur C. Kirsch, eds. Restoration. (The
Laurel Masterpieces of World Literature). New York: Dell
Publishing Company, 1965. 512 pp.
A paperback anthology. Includes Rymer's Othello, Dryden's
An Essay of Dramatic Poesy, and verse from several Restora-
tion dramas.

S.P.C.K.

5073 Scouten, Arthur H. "The S.P.C.K. and the Stage." Theatre Notebook, XI (1957), 58-62.
From the minutes of the Society for the Promoting of Christi
Knowledge we can get a picture of the types of harrassment the
players in the early 18th century had to endure. Descriptions of
anti-theatre lobbying and pamphleteering.

Sackville, Charles

5074 Harris, Brice. Charles Sackville, Sixth Earl of Dorset. Urbana:
University of Illinois Press, 1940. 269 pp. (Illinois Studies in
Language and Literature, Vol. XXVI, No. 3-4.)
A biography of Sackville, including a study of him as a man
of pleasure, a statesman, and as friend and patron to Dryden,
Congreve, Prior, Shadwell, Lee, Otway, Etherege.

Salle, Marie

5075 Vince, Stanley W. E. "Marie Salle, 1707-56." Theatre Notebook,
        XII (1957), 7-14.
        Dancer.

Santlow, Hester

5076 Cohen, Selma Jeanne. "Theory and Practice of Theatrical Dancing
        in England in the Restoration and Early Eighteenth Century as
        Seen in the Lives and Works of Josias Priest, John Weaver, and
        Hester Santlow, Part III." Bulletin of the New York Public Library,
        XLIV (1960), 95-104.
        An account of the career of Hester Santlow, John Weaver's
        prima ballerina and a "beautiful, gifted and incomparable dancer/
        actress."

Satire

5077 Jones, Virgil Laurens. "English Satire, 1650-1700." Ph.D. Harvard
        University, 1911. 2 vols.
        The thesis explores satire as it appeared in various literary
        modes. Chapter VI, "The Comedy," is a discussion of the satirical
        elements in the comedy of humors, the comedy of intrigue, the
        comedy of manners, the political play, and satire in The Rehear-
        sal and its imitators.
5078 ------. "Methods of Satire in the Political Dramas of the Restoration."
        Journal of English and Germanic Philology, XXI (1922), 662-669.
        A presentation of the four major types of political satire in
        drama: 1) the parallel play (i.e., Dryden's Duke of Guise) with
        basis in real or feigned history; 2) the "typical character";
        3) the use of persons in drama; 4) insertion of remarks about
        political conditions or problems.
5079 Goldsborough, Laird Shields. "Satire in Stage Direction." The
        Drama, XIV (December, 1923), 88, 103.
        An appreciation of the satirical wit in the stage directions
        for The Rehearsal, The Tragedy of Tragedies, and The Critic.
5080 Bordner, Jean. "Satire in the English Drama, 1720-1750." Ph.D.
        University of Wisconsin, 1937.
        A study of social, political, and literary satire which con-
        cludes that the amount of satire is a symptom of both the decad-
        ence and the increasing didacticism of the drama.
5081 Williams, Weldon. "The Early Political Satire of the Restoration."
        Ph.D. University of Washington, 1940.
5082 Randolph, Mary Claire. "'Candour' in XVIII-th Century Satire."

Review of English Studies, XX (1944), 45-62.

The changing career of the word "candour" in its association with Satire is examined because "the decay of the genus Satire is so faithfully mirrored in the deterioration of this single critical term." Many references to plays.

5083 Sutherland, James. English Satire. Cambridge: Cambridge University Press, 1958. 174 pp.

Devotes a chapter to satire in the Elizabethan, Restoration, and 18th-century theatre.

5084 Lyles, Albert M. Methodism Mocked: The Satiric Reaction to Methodism in the Eighteenth Century. London: Epworth Press, 1960. 191 pp.

Discusses satire in the theatre of Methodist doctrine and practice, and especially of Wesley and Whitefield. Also considers Methodist attitudes towards theatre.

5085 Love, H. H. R. "Satire in the Drama of the Restoration." Ph.D. Cambridge University (Pembroke), 1964.

5086 McDonald, Charles O. "Restoration Comedy as Drama of Satire: An Investigation Into Seventeenth-Century Aesthetics." Studies in Philology, LXI (1964), 522-544.

Restoration comedy is the "most complexly and consciously moral comedy, avoiding the sentimental conception of the 'hero' in its presentation of a satiric scale of ridicule in protagonists and antagonists (knaves and fools) and basing its humorus effects on the Hobbesian idea of laughter through superiority to the things ridiculed." Includes references to Collier, Congreve, Dennis, Dryden, Etherege, Farquhar, and Wycherley.

5087 Sharrock, Roger. "Modes of Satire." Restoration Theatre. Edited by John Russell Brown and Bernard Harris. (Stratford-Upon-Avon Studies, 6). (London: Edward Arnold, 1965; New York: St. Martin's Press, 1965), 109-132.

Studies the relationship of non-dramatic satire to Restoration comedy. The business of satire was not only to rail at the permanent vices of mankind and to demolish reputations but also to help define the ethos of a new elite.

Satirical Prints

5088 Thomson, Margaret Hunter. "The Theatrical Value of the English Eighteenth Century Satirical Print." Ph.D. Yale University, 1944.

Savage, Richard

5089 Tracy, Clarence. The Artificial Bastard, A Biography of Richard

Savage. Cambridge: Harvard University Press, 1953. 164 pp.
Chapter III, "The Stage and the Green Room," (pages 38-
53) concentrates on Savage's connections with the theatre.

5090 Savage, Richard. An Author to be Lett (1729). Edited with an introduction by James Sutherland (Augustan Reprint Society, Pub. No.
84). Los Angeles: Clark Memorial Library, 1960. iv, v, 12 pp.
This is a reprint of Savage's picture of a typical Grub Street
author.

5091 Shugrue, Michael. "Richard Savage in the Columns of 'Applebee's
Original Weekly Journal.'" Notes and Queries, New Ser., VIII
(February, 1961), 51-52.
From 1723-1727. One is the reprint of the epilogue written
by Aaron Hill, Esq., and spoken by Mrs. Breet, of Savage's
play, Sir Thomas Overbury, June 22, 1723.

5092 Tracy, Clarence. "Some Uncollected Authors XXXVI: Richard
Savage, 1743." Book Collector, XII (1963), 340-349.
Theatrical writings included in checklist of Savage's separ-
ate printed works.

Scene Painters

5093 Lawrence, W. J. "Louis XIV's Scene Painters." Elizabethan Playhouse and Other Studies. Second Series. (Stratford-on-Avon:
Shakespeare Head Press, 1913), 203-212.
The stories of Gaspare and Carlo Vigarani erroneously fused
into one, whose scenic and mechanical work influenced the trend
in English stage mounting in the post-Restoration period.

5094 Rosenfeld, Sybil, and Edward Croft-Murray. "A Checklist of Scene
Painters Working in Great Britain and Ireland in the 18th Century (3)." Theatre Notebook, XIX (Spring, 1965), 102-113.
The third installment of an index to 18th Century scene
painters begun in Theatre Notebook, XIX (Autumn, 1964). Entries
are arranged alphabetically by artist and include biographical
and bibliographical material. 18 entries, including De Loutherbourg.

5095 -----. "A Checklist of Scene Painters Working in Great Britain
and Ireland in the 18th Century (4)." Theatre Notebook, XIX
(Summer, 1965), 133-145.
Continues list of scene painters begun in Theatre Notebook,
XIX (Autumn, 1964); 38 entries.

5096 -----. "A Checklist of Scene Painters Working in Great Britain
and Ireland in the 18th Century (5)." Theatre Notebook, XX
(Autumn, 1965), 36-44.
The fifth installment of the list of scene painters begun in
Theatre Notebook, XIX (Autumn, 1964). 37 entries.

5097 -----. "A Checklist of Scene Painters Working in Great Britain
      and Ireland in the 18th Century, Additions and Corrections."
      Theatre Notebook, XX (Winter, 1965/6), 69-72.
         11 additions, 14 corrections.
5098 Rosenfeld, Sybil. "Scene Painters at the London Theatres in the
      18th Century." Theatre Notebook, XX (Spring, 1966), 113-
      118.
         An appendix to "A Checklist of Scene Painters" which ap-
      peared in Volumes XIX and XX (1964-1966) of Theatre Notebook.
      The tables enable readers to trace those painters who were
      operating at the London theatres in any particular season.

Scenery

5099 Lawrence, William J. "A Forgotten Stage Conventionality." Anglia,
      XXVI (1903), 447-460.
         Traces the uses and reasons for existence of the proscenium
      doors and balconies from 1661-1822, when the doors began to be
      replaced.
5100 Keith, William Grant. "The Designs for the First Movable Scenery
      on the English Public Stage." Burlington Magazine, XXV
      (1914), 29-33; 85-98.
         Some plans of scenes and stage for The Siege of Rhodes at
      Rutland House prove that Webb brought Inigo Jones' type of stage
      mounting for the court theatres into the public theatres, thus
      refuting the claim of foreign influences on public stage design.
5101 A Catalogue of Models and of Stage-Sets in the Dramatic Museum
      of Columbia University, New York. Introduction by Brander
      Matthews. Printed for the Dramatic Museum of Columbia Uni-
      versity, 1916. 55 pp.
         Lists historical models possessed, ordered and desired by
      the Dramatic Museum of Columbia University. Includes a list of
      articles about the Museum which have appeared in American
      periodicals.
5102 Gamble, William Burt, compiler. The Development of Scenic Art
      and Stage Machinery: a List of References in the New York Pub-
      lic Library. New York: New York Public Library, 1920. 128 pp.
         This bibliographical listing which includes 2471 works owned
      by the library on June 1, 1919, is arranged primarily according
      to country and type. There are sections on "The English Stage"
      and "The Post-Elizabethan Stage" and on "Little Theatres,"
      "Lighting History" and so forth. There are useful indexes of
      authors and subjects.
5103 Nicoll, Allardyce. "Scenery in the Restoration Theatre." Anglia,
      XLIV (1920), 217-225.

A history of the advancement of scenery and machinery in
the Restoration theatre, including a discussion of the relationship of certain plays to the external equipment of the theatre.

5104 Chambers, Isabel M. "Aesthetics in Stage Scenery." Architectural
Association, London, Journal, XXXVII (1921), 42-48, 61-62.
A brief history of scenic art, emphasizing its relation to
architecture.

5105 Haddon, Archibald. "Green Limelight." Living Age, CCCXVIII
(1923), 520-521.
A discussion of "ghostly scenery," two paragraphs of which
discusses 18th-century costumes and scenery.

5106 McGachen, F. "The History and Development of Scenery on the
English Stage from Medieval Times to the Year 1700." M.A.
McGill University, 1931.

5107 Nicoll, Allardyce. "Scenery Between Shakespeare and Dryden."
Times Literary Supplement, August 15, 1936, p. 658.
A stage plan recently discovered in a manuscript of a play
performed in 1640/41 provides additional facts about the
transition from the "bare" Elizabethan platform to the wing-
set stage of Drury Lane and Dorset Garden.

5108 Oenslager, Donald. Scenery Then and Now. New York: W. W.
Norton, 1936. 265 pp.
A highly selective history of scenic conventions which ac-
cords brief space to the Restoration and 18th century: the discussion is limited to problems of staging Venice Preserv'd.

5109 Fulford, G. L. "The History and the Development of Scenery
and Lighting of the English Stage from Medieval Times to the
Year 1700." M.A. McGill University, 1940.

5110 Thomas, Russell. "Contemporary Taste in the Stage Decorations of
London Theaters, 1770-1800." Modern Philology, XLII (November, 1944), 65-78.
Discusses De Loutherbourg as bringing to the theatre an increasing sensitiveness to the possibilities of a better coordinated
mise en scène. Also treats those who followed him and developed
or refined his ideas (e.g., William Capon).

5111 Hamar, Clifford E. "Scenery on the Early American Stage." Theatre
Annual (1948), 84-103.
Includes comment on English stage settings imported to Amer-
ica during the eighteenth century.

5112 Laver, James. Drama: Its Costume and Decor. London: The Studio,
Ltd., 1951. 276 pp.
An historical survey, copiously illustrated, of scenery and
costume since the Greeks. Chapter XI, "English Decor from
Webb to Loutherbourg," covers the Restoration and 18th cen-
tury.

5113 Southern, Richard. Changeable Scenery: Its Origin and Development in the British Theatre. London: Faber and Faber, 1952.
Part Two, pp. 109-245, deals with the theatrical scenery of
the Restoration and eighteenth century.

5114 Croft-Murray, E. John Devoto: A Baroque Scene Painter. London:
Society for Theatre Research, 1953. 16 pp.
Survey of Devoto's life and work for the English theatre,
especially his connections with Drury Lane, Lincoln's Inn
Fields and Goodman's Fields, and his designs for pantomime.
Twelve plates of his designs.

5115 Armstrong, William A. "Changeable Scenery at Plymouth in 1764."
Theatre Notebook, X (1955), 31-32.
A quotation of Tate Wilkinson describes the advantages and
disadvantages of scenery which is moved upward and downward
in a vertical groove.

5116 Burnim, Kalman A. "Oblique Wings." Theatre Notebook, XII
(1958), 105.

5117 Kern, Ronald C. "Two Designs by the Elder Thomas Greenwood in
1777." Theatre Notebook (1960), XV.
Water-color sketches for stage scenery at Covent Garden are
here dealt with.

5118 Peet, Alice Lida. "The History and Development of Simultaneous
Scenery in the West from the Middle Ages to Modern United
States." Ph.D. University of Wisconsin, 1961. 393 pp. (L.C.
Card No. Mic 61-1547).
A study of simultaneous scenery "which is characterized by
its recognizable, representational quality and the use of multi-
ple locales which remain essentially in view of the audience
during the entire performance," from its beginnings in the
Middle Ages to modern United States. Includes a discussion of
the stage sets of the neo-classical drama.

5119 Jackson, Allan Stuart. "The Perspective Landscape Scene in the
English Theatre, 1660-1682." Ph.D. The Ohio State University,
1962. (Order No. 63-4670).
Studies the pictorial appearance of the perspective land-
scapes painted upon theatrical scenery during the Restoration.
Appendices include a list of printed stage directions, and two
catalogues of paintings representative of taste during the
period.

5120 Peterson, William M., and Richard Morton. "Mirrors on the
Restoration Stage." Notes and Queries, New Ser., IX (1962),
10-13, 63-67.
Traditional and new uses of mirrors in drama. ". . . in
general, the Restoration stage used mirrors to insure observance of its elaborate and formal code of decorum."

5121 McManaway, James G. "L'héritage de la Renaissance dans la
  mise en scène en Angleterre (1642-1700)." Le lieu théâtral à
  la Renaissance. Edited by Jean Jacquot, Elie Konigson, and
  Marcel Oddon. (Paris: Eds. du Centre National de la Recherche
  Scientifique, 1964), 459-472.
5122 Mander, Raymond, and Joe Mitchenson. "De Loutherbourg and
  Pizarro, 1799." Theatre Notebook, XX (Summer, 1966), 160.
  Additional information on De Loutherbourg's relationship
  to the scenery for Pizarro, discussed in Theatre Notebook, XX
  (Autumn, 1965), 30-32.

Schiller, Friedrich

5123 Rea, Thomas. Schiller's Dramas and Poems in England. London:
  T. Fisher Unwin, 1906. xi, [1], 155 pp.
  The Appendix lists the English translations and editions of
  Schiller's dramas and poems, with Die Rauber, Die Versch-
  worung des Fiesko Kabale und Liebe, and Don Carlos, falling
  in the 18th century, with perhaps the best known name being
  "Monk" Lewis, and his The Minister, from Kabale und Liebe.
5124 Buyers, G. "The Influence of Schiller in England, 1780-1830."
  Englische Studien, XLVIII (1915), 349-393.
  A history of Schiller's influence on the English stage during
  the period from 1780-1830. Concludes that the influence was
  negligible. It was mostly felt from 1794-1798 and 1813-1817.
5125 Cooke, Margaret W. "Schiller's Robbers in England." Modern
  Language Review, XI (April, 1916), 156-175.
  A survey of the influence of Schiller's play on English
  writers from Henry McKenzie (1788) to Shelly (1819) and English writing from Wordsworth's Borderers through The Cenci.
5126 Willoughby, L. A. "English Translations and Adaptations of
  Schiller's Robbers." Modern Language Review, XVI (1921),
  297-315.
  A history of translations of this play from 1788 to 1889 and
  of adaptations through 1823.
5127 -----. "Schiller's 'Kabale und Liebe' in English Translation."
  Publications of the English Goethe Society, New Ser., Vol. I.
  (London: Published for the Society by Alexander Waring, Ltd.,
  1924), pp. 44-66.
  The first play of Schiller's rendered in English by Dr. Ash,
  in The Spectator for 1790. Consideration is given to the anonymous translation of 1795 (by Timäus), and those by Mathew
  Gregory Lewis (entitled The Minister), Henry George Bohn
  (18th century).
5128 Leurig, Paul Murray. "The Influence of Schiller upon the English

Drama of the Late Eighteenth and Early Nineteenth Centuries."
M.A. University of Illinois, 1925.

5129 Ewen, F. The Prestige of Schiller in England, 1788-1859. New
York: Columbia University Press, 1932. xiii, 287 pp.
Part one of this work deals with the period from 1788-1805.
It includes references to Henry Mackenzie's "Account of the
German Theatre," "the first traceable mention of Schiller in Eng
land," discusses opposition to and defense of Schiller, rendition
and translations of Schiller in England. The book seeks to describe the "successive aspects under which Englishmen came
to view" Schiller.

5130 Waterhouse, G. "Schiller's Raüber in England before 1800." Mod-
ern Language Review, XXX (1935), 355-357.
Quotes a brief account of Schiller's play from the Dublin
Chronicle, November 29, 1788.

Schmid, Christian

5131 Price, Lawrence Marsden. Christian Heinrich Schmid and His
Translations of English Dramas, 1767-1789. Berkeley and Los
Angeles: University of California Press, 1942. 122 pp. (Uni-
versity of California Publications in Modern Philology, Vol.
XXVI, No. 1).
Schmid represents the earliest phase of the infiltration of
English dramatic art into the German theatre of the 18th cen-
tury--the phase of simple translation. He translated plays by
Farquhar, Dryden, Vanbrugh, Congreve, Rowe, Sheridan,
Cibber, Otway, and others.

School Drama

5132 Motter, Thomas Hubbard Vail. The School Drama in England.
London, New York [etc.]: Longmans, Green & Co., 1929.
325 pp.
This history of the origin and development of dramatics in
English schools describes many plays--including representation
of the Restoration and 18th century--performed in selected
British schools from medieval times. Beginning with a history
of boy actors, Motter discusses such matters as 18th-century
play presentation at Eton, "The Happy Nuptials" at Rugby
(1724), and a post-Restoration revival at Merchant Taylors.

5133 Avery, Emmett L. "Private Theatricals in and near London,
1700-1737." Theatre Notebook, XIII (1959), 101-105.
Deals with performances in schools.

Scotland

5134 Lawson, Robb. The Story of the Scots Stage. Paisley: A. Gardner,
      1917. iv, 303 pp.
          An attempt at a history of the Scottish theatre at Aberdeen,
      Edinburgh, Arbroath, Dundee, Glasgow, and Perth from the
      bards to the 19th century. Author complains about the dearth
      of records for history.
5135 Mackenzie, Agnes Mure. An Historical Survey of Scottish Liter-
      ature to 1714. London: Maclehose, 1933. viii, 253 pp.
          Chapter VI, entitled "Drama," speaks of the golden age of
      "Scots drama as the 15th and even quite late 16th century."
      This drama, "a tragic drama relieved by fierce comedy," is
      reminiscent of Middleton and Webster. Some of the 17th- and
      18th-century works mentioned include Tarugo's Wiles or The
      Coffee-House (1668), David Crawfurd's comedies, and Catherine
      Cockburn's plays.
5136 McKenzie, J. "School and University Drama in Scotland, 1650-
      1760." Scottish Historical Review, XXXIV (1955), 102-121.
          Six performances, 1660-1700; forty performances, 1701-
      1760.
5137 -----. "A Study of 18th Century Drama in Scotland, 1660-1760."
      Ph.D. St. Andrew's University, 1956.

Scott, Walter

5138 Falle, George. "Sir Walter Scott as Editor of Dryden and Swift."
      University of Toronto Quarterly, XXXVI (1967), 161-180.
          Discusses Scott's editorial limitations and virtues and
      analyzes the editions to show why the Dryden is to be preferred
      to the Swift.

Sedley, Charles

5139 Prideaux, W. F. "Sir Charles Sedley's Escapade." Notes and
      Queries, 9th Ser., VIII (August 24, 1901), 157-158.
          Argues that Sedley has been a much misunderstood man, and
      that reports of his debauchery have been misleading.
5140 -----. "The Sedley Family." Notes and Queries, 9th Ser., X
      (October 11, 1902), 286-287.
          Notes on the geneology of descendants of Sir Charles Sedley.
5141 Plückhahn, Edmund. Die Bearbeitung auslander stoffe in englischen
      Drama am Ende des 17 Jahrhunderts dargelegt an Sir Charles
      Sedley's The Mulberry Garden and Bellamira or the Mistress.
      Hamburg Dissertation, 1904.

Emphasis is upon Sedley's use of foreign material in his
drama.

5142 Lissner, Max. "Sir Charles Sedley's Leben und Werke." Anglia,
XXVIII (1905), 145-254.
Contains a thirty-seven page biography and lengthy discussion
of The Mulberry Garden; Antony and Cleopatra; Bellamira, or
the Mistress.

5143 de Sola Pinto, V. "Some Notes on Sir Charles Sedley." Times
Literary Supplement, November 2, 1922, pp. 706-707; Nov-
ember 9, 1922, p. 728.
Presentation of certain biographical information regarding
Sedley.

5144 Dobrée, Bonamy. "Dryden's Lisideius." Nation and Athenaeum,
XLII (October 8, 1927), 30.
Reviews V. de S. Pinto's Sir Charles Sedley (1927). What is
most peculiar about Sedley and the poets of his circle (Buckingham
Rochester, Etherege, Killigrew, etc.) "is their disgustingly bad
manners."

5145 Pinto, Vivian de Sola. Sir Charles Sedley, 1639-1701, A Study in the
Life and Literature of the Restoration. London: Constable, 1927
xi, 400 pp.
Divided into life and estimate of the works, with two appendice
of relevant documents and one of Sedley's library. Bibliography
of principal ms. and printed sources.

5146 Sedley, Sir Charles. The Poetical and Dramatic Works. Edited by
Vivian de Sola Pinto. 2 vols. London: Constable, 1928.
A painstaking edition with thorough notes, which establishes
the Sedley canon; omits Pompey the Great, Beauty the Conqueror
and The Tyrant King of Crete.

5147 Pinto, Vivian de Sola. "Sedley and Beau Fielding." Notes and
Queries, CXCII (September 6, 1947), 393.
A comment on James Thorpe's note (June 14, 1947), 251-252.

5148 Thorpe, James. "Sedley and Beau Fielding." Notes and Queries,
CXCII (June 14, 1947), 251-252.
Describes the annotations in a Princeton copy of Sedley's
Works, 1702.

5149 Pinto, Vivian de Sola. Restoration Carnival: Five Courtier Poets:
Rochester, Dorset, Sedley, Etherege and Sheffield. London:
Folio Society, 1954. 253 pp.
Biography, followed by selected poems, some of which are
songs from the plays.

5150 Davies, H. Neville. "Dryden's All for Love and Sedley's Antony
and Cleopatra." Notes and Queries, XIV (1967), 221-227.
Dryden's borrowings from Sedley's work show not only that
Dryden is the more skilful dramatist but also that he was con-

sciously "working up" promising material from Sedley's 1677 play.

Seedo

5151 Roberts, Edgar V. "Mr. Seedo's London Career and His Work with Henry Fielding." Philological Quarterly, XLV (1966), 179-190.
     Uses The London Stage to describe the career of Seedo; theatre music director, composer and organist in London from the mid 1720's until 1736, who collaborated with writers of ballad operas, including Fielding and Charles Coffey.

Sentimental

5152 Bernbaum, Ernest. "Sentimental and Domestic Drama in England and France, Its Nature, Its Origin, and Its History to the Year 1750." Ph.D. Harvard University, 1907.
5153 Waterhouse, O. "The Development of English Sentimental Comedy in the Eighteenth Century." Anglia, XXX (1907), 137-172.
     Divided into two chapters; Ch. I, Literary and social tendencies which influenced 18th century drama, Ch. II, The Development of Sentimental Comedy as seen in "Aesop" and in the plays of Cibber and Steele.
5154 Scheurer, C. M. "An Early Sentimental Comedy." Anglia, XXXVII (1913), 125-218.
     The Town Shifts, or The Suburb Justice by Edward Revet (L.I.F., c. March, 1671) "is not only essentially moral and 'instructive' but meets a surprising number of other sentimental requirements."
5155 Bernbaum, Ernest. The Drama of Sensibility: A Sketch of the History of English Sentimental Comedy and Domestic Tragedy, 1696-1780. Boston: Ginn and Company, 1915. 288 pp.
     The purpose of the book is stated in the subtitle. The drama of sensibility began in 1696. It did not really triumph in England until 1780. Although founded on the benevolist philosophy, this drama in England was impure, unlike the French examples in drama and English examples in poetry, novels, and essays.
5156 Morgan, Arthur Eustace. "Currents of English Drama in the Eighteenth Century." Royal Society of Literature of the United Kingdom, London. Essays by Divers Hands, being the Transactions. Second Ser., XXXV (1917), 125-158.
     The 18th-century comedies of manners were at their best when they did not moralize but, rather, appealed primarily to the intellect. Steele's moralizing sentimentalism sounded the

death knell for Britain's glorious comedies, although, as Morgan points out, the seeds of sentimental drama had been planted in the late 17th century.

5157 Berard, Le Roy Henry. "Sentimental Comedy in the Last Quarter of the Eighteenth Century." M.A. University of Chicago, 1920.

Attempts to show that sentimental comedy continued after Goldsmith and Sheridan by a discussion of social and literary conditions conducive to the survival of the genre and by consideration of the plays themselves and the author's purpose as expressed in prologues, epilogues, prefaces, memoirs, and critical essays.

5158 Bernbaum, Ernest. The Drama of Sensibility: A Sketch of the History of English Sentimental Comedy and Tragedy, 1696-1780. Cambridge: Harvard University Press; London: Humphrey Milford, Oxford University Press, 1925. (Harvard Studies in English, Vol. III).

After a discussion of the new ethics of sentimentalism, Bernbaum examines various approaches to and types of sentimental drama, including the works of Lillo, Goldsmith, Cumberland, and Sheridan.

5159 Williams, Stanley T. "The English Sentimental Drama from Steele to Cumberland." Sewanee Review, XXXIII (October, 1925), 405-426.

Cibber began sentimental drama with Love's Last Shift, a middle-class comedy notable chiefly for its dullness and for faith in the goodness of the human nature of ordinary people. Lillo's George Barnwell established domestic tragedy as a form of sentimental drama. Cumberland epitomized the sentimental playwright.

5160 Cox, James E. The Rise of Sentimental Comedy. Springfield, Missouri: By the Author, Drury College, 1926.

Argues that Cibber, although he contributed to the development of sentimentalism in drama, was still of the old school, and Steele was the true founder of sentimental comedy.

5161 Wood, Frederick T. "The Beginning and Significance of Sentimental Comedy." Anglia, LV (1931), 368-392.

The first tocsins of sentimental comedy are to be found in the morality plays.

5162 Kies, Paul P. "Lessing's Relation to Early English Sentimental Comedy." Publications of the Modern Language Association, XLVII (1932), 807-826.

Suggests Lessing's indebtedness to English comedy.

5163 Allen, B. Sprague. "The Dates of Sentimental and Its Derivatives." Publications of the Modern Language Association, XLVIII (1933), 303-307.

Traces the history of the words dealing with the vogue of
sentiment.

5164 Wood, Frederick T. "Sentimental Comedy in the Eighteenth Century. II." Neophilologus, XVIII (1933), 281-289.
Overview of sentimental comedies from Fielding's The Temple Beau (1730) to Thomas Morton's Speed the Plough (1800).
Continuation of an article in Neophilologus, XVIII (1933), 37-44.

5165 Croissant, DeWitt C. "Early Sentimental Comedy." Essays in
Dramatic Literature: The Parrott Presentation Volume. Edited
by Hardin Craig. (Princeton: Princeton University Press, 1935),
47-71.
Distinguishing between the "debased romanticism" of eighteenth-century sentimental comedy and Caroline "romanticism,"
Croissant uses the distinction to classify a number of Restoration
comedies and concludes that "romanticism and sentimentalism"
became dominant near the end of the period.

5166 Dameron, Louise. Bibliography of Stage Settings, to which is attached
an index to illustrations of stage settings. Baltimore, Md.: Enoch
Pratt Free Library, 1936. 48 pp.
These are annotated alphabetical listings of historical, theoretical and practical aspects of stage setting. An index lists illustrations of stage settings by title and designer, whenever
feasible.

5167 McLeod, F. M. "Sentimental Drama in the 18th Century." M.A.
University of Alberta, 1939.

5168 Garey, Doris Bates. "Eighteenth-Century Sentimentalism: An
Essay toward Definition." Ph.D. University of Wisconsin, 1941.

5169 Coventry, F. "Sentiment and Sensibility in English Literature of
the Eighteenth Century." Ph.D. Cambridge University (Emman-
uel), 1942.

5170 Berkeley, David S. "Origins of Sentimental Comedy." Ph.D. Harvard University, 1949.

5171 Magill, Lewis M., Jr. "Elements of Sentimentalism in English
Tragedy, 1680-1704." Ph.D. University of Illinois, 1949. 278
pp. (Publication No. 1554).
An examination of representative English tragedies between
1680 and 1704 shows that sentimentalism is not easily defined.

5172 Freehafer, John H. "The Emergence of Sentimental Comedy, 1660-
1707." Ph.D. University of Pennsylvania, 1950.

5173 Sherbo, Arthur. "English Sentimental Drama." Ph.D. Columbia
University, 1950. 251 pp. (Publication No. 1899).
Sherbo defines and illustrates the characteristics of senti-
mental comedy.

5174 Reed, Robert R., Jr. "James Shirley and the Sentimental Comedy."
Anglia, LXXIII (1955), 149-170.

Shirley, whose realistic comedies possess elements of
sentimentalism, has not been given the recognition he deserves
as the first conscious advocate of sentimentalism. The Morality,
assumptions, and techniques of the sentimental school are discussed and Shirley's plays measured against them. Also consider
his influence on the Restoration period and the popularity of his
plays.

5175 Sherbo, Arthur. English Sentimental Drama. East Lansing: Michigan
State University Press, 1957. viii, 181 pp.
Defines the genre. Bibliography.

5176 Nicolson, Sir Harold. The Age of Reason (1700-1789). London: Constable, 1960. xxii, 424 pp.
Dealing with the sociological, political and philosophical import of the Age of Reason (1687-1776), this work provides useful
background information and contains references to such men as
Addison, Steele, and Sheridan. Of particular interest is the
chapter on "Sensibility."

5177 Ross, Judy Joy. "Marriage, Morals, and the Muse: The Vindication
of Matrimony on the Eighteenth Century Stage." Ph.D. New York
University, 1962. (Order No. 63-7199).
Examines both Restoration and 18th century views of marriage
and women; analyzes the various types of sentimental drama,
and distinguishes the emotional drama of sensibility from "up-
lift" drama.

5178 Parnell, Paul E. "The Sentimental Mask." Publications of the
Modern Language Association, LXXVIII (1963), 529-535.
A study of the moral ambiguity of sentimentalism. Reviews
previous scholarship on the definition of sentimentalism and
includes references to Cumberland's West Indian (1771), Lillo's
The London Merchant (1731), Steele's The Lying Lover (1703),
and The Conscious Lovers (1722), Cibber's Love's Last Shift
(1722), and The Careless Husband (1704).

5179 -----. "The Sentimental Mask." Restoration Drama: Modern Essays in Criticism. (A Galaxy Book). Edited by John Loftis.
(New York: Oxford University Press, 1966), 285-297.
Reprinted from PMLA, LXXVIII (1963), 529-535. Attempts
to define the basic relationship between sentimentalism and
virtue or morality, and to explain why the term carries a generally unfavorable connotation.

Settle, Elkanah

5180 Brown, F[rank] C[lyde]. Elkanah Settle, His Life and Works.
Chicago: University of Chicago Press [ᶜ1910]. x, 170 pp.
Much of the book is devoted to Settle's life and to the quarrels

and controversies in which he was involved. The section on the
plays--arranged chronologically--contains summaries of the
plots. Also included are a list of Shadwell's occasional poems
and a list of the city pageants for which he wrote.

5181 Steeves, Harrison R. "The Athenian Virtuosi and the Athenian
Society." Modern Language Review, VIII (1912), 358-371.
Often confused, the two societies were distinct and unrelated.
The Athenian Society organized as the Virtuosi had Temple as
patron, Swift as contributor, Defoe as panigyrist, Gildon as
historian and was burlesqued by Settle.

5182 Ham, Roswell G. "Otway's Duels with Churchill and Settle."
Modern Language Notes, XLI (February, 1926), 73-80.
Reports the discovery of a duel between Otway and Churchill,
and reinterprets the quarrel between Otway and Settle.

5183 -----. "Dryden versus Settle." Modern Philology, XXV (May,
1928), 409-416.
Attributes to Settle the Tryal of the Poets, Azaria and Hushai,
and The Medal Revers'd, and accounts for Dryden's bitterness
accordingly. From 1673 Settle was Dryden's most formidable
enemy.

5184 Fletcher, E. G. "Bibliography of Elkanah Settle." Notes and Queries,
CLXIV (February 18, 1933), 114.
Fletcher refers to a copy of Settle's wedding poem "Thalia
Triumphans," to a copy of "Minerva Triumphans," both in the
University of Texas library and to "A Poem to the Charming
Fair One." These are evidently intended as additions to Pro-
fessor Brown's 1910 bibliography of Settle's works.

5185 Ham, Roswell G. "The Authorship of A Session of the Poets
(1677)." Review of English Studies, IX (1933), 319-322.
Mr. Ham answers critic D. M. Walmsey's comments on his
book Otway and Lee. He adds one piece of additional evidence
to substantiate his belief that Elkanah Settle, not the Earl of
Rochester, is the author of A Session of the Poets (1677).

5186 Moss, W. E. "Elkanah Settle: The Armorial Binding Expert."
Bookcollector's Quarterly, XIII (January, 1934), 7-22.
Basically a study of Settle's work in binding of books, with
the dates of his publications bearing specific arms. These
are based on Moss's own photographs or rubbings.

5187 Lawrence, W. J. "The Plates in Settle's The Empress of Morocco."
Times Literary Supplement, July 11, 1935, p. 448.
Illustrations in the original quarto are unreliable as an in-
dication of methods of staging.

5188 Dunkin, Paul S. "Issues of The Fairy Queen, 1692." The Library,
4th Ser., XXVI (March, 1946), 297-304.
Nine issues analyzed.

5189 Settle, Elkanah. The Preface to Ibrahim. Reprinted from the Edition of 1677. [Edited by Hugh Macdonald]. Oxford: Published for the Luttrell Society by Basil Blackwell, 1947. vi, 14 pp.

The text of the Preface reprinted from the 1677 edition with an introduction briefly outlining the quarrel between Settle and Shadwell, Crowne, and Dryden.

5190 Haviland, Thomas P. "Elkanah Settle and the Least Heroic Romance." Modern Language Quarterly, XV (1954), 118-124.

Settle's Ibrahim or the Illustrious Bassa derives from Madeleine de Scudery's Ibrahim.

5191 Doyle, Ann Therese. "The Empress of Morocco: a Critical Edition of the Play and the Controversy Surrounding It." Ph.D. University of Illinois, 1963. (Order No. 63-5089).

Investigates the attack of Dryden, Crowne, and Shadwell on the play and Settle's response.

5192 Zielske, Harald. "Handlungsort und Buhnenbild im 17. Jahrhundert. Untersuchungen zur Raumdarstellung im europäischen Barock-theater." Ph.D. FU Berlin, 1965.

Includes a study of scenery in Settle's The Empress of Morocco.

5193 Barsam, Richard Meran. "A Critical Edition of Elkanah Settle's Cambyses, King of Persia." Ph.D. University of California, 1967. (Order No. 67-13,736).

Provides text with relevant critical and textual apparatus.

5194 Biddle, Evelyn Q. "A Critical Study of the Influence of the Classical and Christian Traditions Upon the Character of the Hero as Revealed Through Concepts of 'Love' and 'Honor' in Three Restoration Heroic Tragedies." Ph.D. University of Southern California, 1967. (Order No. 67-6491).

Considers Orrery's Henry V, Dryden's The Conquest of Granada, and Settle's The Empress of Morocco.

Seward, Anna

5195 Ashmun, Margaret. The Singing Swan: An Account of Anna Seward and Her Acquaintance with Dr. Johnson, Boswell and Others of Their Time. With a preface by Frederick A. Pottle. New Haven: Yale University Press, 1931. xiv, 298 pp.

The life and career of Anna Seward with many biographical details concerning her literary acquaintances.

5196 Laithwaite, P. "Anna Seward and Dr. Johnson." Times Literary Supplement, January 7, 1932, p. 12.

This letter cites two of Miss Seward's anti-Johnsonian marginal annotations in what had once been Mrs. Piozzi's copy of "Letters to and from the late Samuel Johnson."

Sewell, George

5197 Maxwell, J. C. "Classic." Notes and Queries, New Ser., X
         (1963), 220.
            George Sewell's use of the term "classic" in his Preface to
         Pope's Shakespeare, Vol. VII (1725), to refer to literature other
         than Greek or Latin, antedates the earliest quotation in O.E.D.

Shadwell, Thomas

complete works

5198 Shadwell, Thomas. The Complete Works. Edited by Montague
         Summers. 5 vols. London: The Fortune Press, 1927.
            An excellent biographical and critical introduction, and
         full notes to each play.

works

5199 -----. Thomas Shadwell. Edited by George Saintsbury. London:
         T. Fisher Unwin, 1925. (Mermaid Series). xxviii, 459 pp.
            Reprints The Sullen Lovers, A True Widow, The Squire of
         Alsatia, and Bury Fair. The introduction suggests that Shadwell
         rather than Etherege may be the father of 17th- and 18th-century
         comedy of manners.
5200 -----. Epsom Wells, and The Volunteers, or The Stock-Jobbers.
         Edited by D. M. Walmsley. New York: D. C. Heath and Com-
         pany, 1930. lxi, 387 pp.
            Epsom Wells follows the 1673, based on the first edition of the
         British Museum copy. The Volunteers is based on the quarto
         edition of 1693. Obvious misprints are corrected and punctu-
         ation is changed to conform more to modern stanzas. There
         are notes for each play.

single texts

5201 -----. The Virtuoso. Edited by Marjorie Hope Nicolson and
         David Stuart Rodes. Lincoln: University of Nebraska Press,
         1966. (Regents Restoration Drama Series).
            Includes critical introduction and notes.

biography and criticism

5202 Samter, F. Studien zu Ben Jonson mit berucksichtigung von Shad-
         well's Dramen. Inaugural Dissertation. Bern, 1902. 62 pp.

5203 Bayley, A. R. "Shadwell's 'Bury Fair.'" <u>Notes and Queries</u>, 10th
      Ser., I (March 19, 1904), 221-222.
            Examines Oldwit's allusions to Jonson and Fletcher; Dryden
      deriding the would-be wits in defence of the "Epilogue" to <u>Con</u>-
      <u>quest of Granada</u>.

5204 Lawrence, William. "Did Shadwell write an Opera on 'The Tem-
      pest'?" <u>Anglia</u>, XXVII (1904), 205-217.
            Argues that the quarto of 1674 of <u>The Tempest</u> was the out-
      come of a direct commission to Shadwell on the part of the
      Duke's company who were the owners of the rights in the comedy.

5205 -----. "Purcell's Music for 'The Tempest.'" <u>Notes and Queries</u>,
      10th Ser., II (August 27, 1904), 164-165.
            Dates Shadwell's operatic "Tempest" as April, 1674, Dor-
      set Garden theatre and states that Purcell collaborated with
      Matthew Locke in writing the score for the Shadwell opera of
      1674. Argues against Cummings.

5206 -----. "Purcell's Music for 'The Tempest.'" <u>Notes and Queries</u>,
      10th Ser., II (October 22, 1904), 329-330.
            Uses arguments of Professor Cummings to prove that the
      anonymous edition of 1674 <u>Tempest</u> was unquestionably Shad-
      well's.

5207 Reihmann, Oskar. <u>Thomas Shadwells Tragodie "The Libertine,"</u>
      <u>und ihr Verhaltnis zu den vorausgehenden Bearbeitungen der</u>
      <u>Don Juan-Sage</u>. Leipzig: Heinrich John, 1904. 67 pp.
            Shadwell's play and its relationship to various treatments of
      the Don Juan story.

5208 Steiger, August. Thomas Shadwell's "Libertine." A Complemen-
      tary Study to the Don Juan Literature. Bern: Francke, 1904.
      viii, 66 pp.
            Considers <u>The Libertine</u> the chief link of English literature
      with the Don Juan tradition, and describes wherein Shadwell
      departs from the usual tale of Don Juan. Attempts to prove
      that Shadwell relied on Rosimond, not Molière.

5209 Ammann, Ernst. <u>Analysis of Thomas Shadwell's Lancashire</u>
      <u>Witches and Tegue O'Divelly the Irish Priest</u>. Bern: Buch-
      druckerei Gustav Grunau, 1905. 60 pp.
            German doctoral dissertation, written in English, to il-
      lustrate Shadwell's importance as a literary man. The writer
      gives a short biography, a study of the sources, and a detailed
      analysis of the play, with a good amount devoted simply to re-
      telling the story.

5210 Clarke, Sir Ernest. "<u>The Tempest</u> as an Opera." <u>Athenaeum</u>,
      No. 4113 (August 25, 1906), 222-223.
            The anonymous quarto of 1674 presents the text of Shad-
      well's lost musical "perversion" of the play.

5211 Erichsen, Asmus. Thomas Shadwells Komödie "The Sullen
     Lovers" in ihrem Verhältnis zu Molières Komodien "Le Misan-
     thrope" und "Les Facheux." Inaugural Dissertation. Kiel, 1906.
          Nearly all the figures of this play are taken from characters
     of "Les Facheux" and "Le Misanthrothrope," though figure of Sir
     Positive-At-all is original.
5212 Lawrence, W. J. "Shadwell's Opera of 'The Tempest.'" Anglia,
     XXIX (1906), 539-541.
          Letter to editor of Anglia, attacks Sir Ernest Clarke's "The
     Tempest as an Opera," Athenaeum, August 25, 1906, as unori-
     ginal. Revised and republished in The Elizabethan Playhouse
     and Other Studies (Stratford-on-Avon: Shakespeare Head Press,
     1912), 193-206.
5213 Heinemann, Georg. Shadwell-Studien. Kiel: H. Fiencke, 1907.
     vi, 105 pp.
          A study of the origins, contents, sources, structure, and
     characters of Shadwell's The Squire of Alsatia, Psyche, and
     Bury-Fair.
5214 Marti, Paul. Fletcher's Play: The Night-Walker and Shadwell's
     Comedy The Woman Captain. Dissertation. Berne, 1910. 75 pp.
          Can find "no convincing connection" between The Night-Walker
     and The Woman Captain as A. W. Ward had suggested exists.
     May be a connection between Moll in Middleton and Dekker's
     Roaring Girl and Mrs. Gripe, the woman captain.
5215 Lawrence, W. J. "Did Thomas Shadwell Write an Opera on 'The
     Tempest'?" The Elizabethan Playhouse and Other Studies.
     First Series. (Stratford-on-Avon: Shakespeare Head Press,
     1912), 193-206.
          The Tempest, or The Enchanted Island, issued by Herringman
     as Q_2 of the Dryden-D'Avenant Tempest and including the Dryden
     preface, prologue, and epilogue of Q_1, is in truth, as Downes
     said, by Shadwell. From 1674 on, Shadwell's Tempest super-
     ceded the Dryden-D'Avenant version.
5216 Browne, William Hand. "Thomas Shadwell." The Sewanee Review,
     XXI (1913), 251-276.
          Short discussions of Shadwell's plays, most against the back-
     ground of his quarrel with Dryden. Argues that he had inventive
     genius and facility in dialogue, but his characters are eccentric
     and unrealistic and he carried humors characters too far.
5217 Borgman, Albert Stephens. "The Dramatic Works of Thomas Shad-
     well." Ph.D. Harvard University, 1919. 392 pp.
          Discusses sixteen of the seventeen plays contained in the
     1720 edition of Shadwell's works (omits The Rewards of Virtue).
     For each play, Borgman gives facts of production, outlines the
     play's early stage history, and points out similarities to earlier

and contemporary dramas. Three appendices relate to Shadwell's biography, Shadwelliana, and the 1670 edition of The Tempest.

5218 Squire, William Barclay. "The Music of Shadwell's Tempest." The Musical Quarterly, VII (1921), 565-578.

A survey of the Restoration versions of The Tempest, followed by an attempt to reconstruct the musical setting of Shadwell's version.

5219 Bensley, Edward. "Thomas Shadwell: Date and Place of Birth." Notes and Queries, 12th Ser., VI (1924), 195.

Information on Shadwell's date and place of birth.

5220 Guillemard, F. H. H. "Thomas Shadwell: Date and Place of Birth." Notes and Queries, 12th Ser., VI (1924), 217.

Information on Shadwell's date of birth and place of birth.

5221 Summers, Montague. "New Light on Thomas Shadwell." Times Literary Supplement, May 7, 1925, p. 316.

Replies to D. M. Walmsley (TLS, April 16, 1925): besides Shadwell's wife, there was another actress named Ann Gibbs.

5222 -----. "New Light on Thomas Shadwell." Times Literary Supplement, May 21, 1925, p. 352.

Replies to D. M. Walmsley (TLS, May 14, 1925), denying that he has contributed new material.

5223 Walmsley, D. M. "New Light on Thomas Shadwell." Times Literary Supplement, April 16, 1925, p. 268.

A collection of biographical evidence; doubts that actress Ann Gibbs was Shadwell's wife.

5224 Walmsley, D. M. "New Light on Thomas Shadwell." Times Literary Supplement, May 14, 1925, p. 335.

Replies to Montague Summers (TLS, May 7, 1925), denying a second Ann Gibbs.

5225 -----. "Two Songs Ascribed to Thomas Shadwell." Review of English Studies, I (July, 1925), 350-352.

A discussion of two previously unnoticed manuscript songs by Shadwell.

5226 -----. "Shadwell and the Operatic Tempest." Review of English Studies, II (October, 1926), 463-466.

The 1674 Tempest, an operatic version of the Dryden-D'Avenant play, was the work of Shadwell.

5227 Ham, Roswell G. "Shadwell and The Tory Poets." Notes and Queries, CLII (January 1, 1927), 6-8.

The pamphlet was used by Malone but afterwards disappeared It is in the South Kensington Museum and seems best attributed to Shadwell.

5228 Rye, Walter. "The Poet Shadwell." Some Historical Essays Chiefly Relating to Norfolk, Part IV. (Norwich: H. W. Hunt, 1927), 287-292.

Thomas Shadwell was the son of John Shadwell (of Broom-
hill, Norfolk), whose genealogical connections Rye traces.

5229 Thorn-Drury, G. "Shadwell and the Operatic Tempest." Review
of English Studies, III (April, 1927), 204-208.

The Tempest of Dryden and Davenant was capable of being
added to and elaborated upon as performance succeeded performance; hence Shadwell found it already in operatic form.

5230 Walmsley, D. M. "Shadwell and the Operatic Tempest." Review
of English Studies, III (October, 1927), 451-453.

Answers Thorn-Drury (RES, II, April, 1927, 204-208).
Since no edition as such of Dryden's works was published before 1701, the inclusion by Dryden's son in 1701 of the 1670
text of The Tempest indicates it was Dryden's.

5231 Borgman, Albert S. Thomas Shadwell: His Life and Comedies.
New York: New York University Press, 1928. x, 269 pp.

A well-written and documented survey of Shadwell's life
and work, with some new material.

5232 W.[almsley], D. M. "A Song of D'Urfey's Wrongly Ascribed to
Shadwell." Review of English Studies, IV (October, 1928),
431.

The song "Bright was the morning, cool the Air," which
Walmsley discovered in manuscript in 1925 and attributed to
Shadwell, was indeed written by D'Urfey and published above
his name in 1683 and in 1719.

5233 Lloyd, Claude. "Shadwell and the Virtuosi." Publications of the
Modern Language Association, XLIV (June, 1929), 472-494.

An analysis of Shadwell's satire of the Royal Society in his
comedy The Virtuoso, with reference to scientific experiments
actually conducted.

5234 Needham, Francis. "A Letter of Shadwell's." Times Literary
Supplement, October 23, 1930, p. 866.

Prints the letter, which is among the Cavendish papers at
Welbech. The letter is written to Henry Cavendish, son of
William Cavendish, who had been one of Shadwell's earliest
patrons.

5235 McKeithan, D. M. "The Authorship of The Medal of John Bayes."
University of Texas Studies in English, No. 12 (1932), 92-97.

McKeithan assigns The Medal of John Bayes to Shadwell
because it echoes Shadwell's earlier works, and Shadwell's
later works echo The Medal of John Bayes.

5236 Whitehall, Harold. "Thomas Shadwell and the Lancashire Dialect."
Essays and Studies in English and Comparative Literature.
Vol. X (Ann Arbor: University of Michigan Press, 1933), 261-
278.

Among Restoration dramatists only Shadwell, principally in

The Lancashire Witches and The Squire of Alsatia, continued
the pre-Restoration interest in dialect character roles.

5237 Brooks, Harold. "Some Notes on Dryden, Cowley, and Shadwell."
      Notes and Queries, CLXVIII (1935), 94-95.
          Reprints quotations from volumes dated 1673 and 1674 which
      contain some contemporary lay criticism of the drama, Mar-
      riage à la Mode.

5238 Harris, Brice. "The Date of Thomas Shadwell's Birth." Corres-
      pondence in Times Literary Supplement, October 10, 1936,
      p. 815. [Cf. correspondence by D. M. Walmsley, October 17,
      1936, p. 839.]
          Presents evidence that Shadwell was born March 24, 1640/41.
      Walmsley disagrees and argues for more trustworthy evidence.

5239 Appelt, D. "Shadwell's London." M.A. University of Alberta,
      1937.

5240 Iacuzzi, Alfred. "The Naive Theme in The Tempest as Link be-
      tween Thomas Shadwell and Ramón de la Cruz." Modern Lan-
      guage Notes, LII (1937), 252-256.
          Traces some scenes from the French translation by Destouche
      of Shadwell's version of The Tempest to Harni de Guerville's
      opéra-comique, Georget et Georgette, and then to Juanito y
      Juanita, a Spanish sainete by Cruz.

5241 Ward, Charles E. "Shadwell, 1658-68." Times Literary Supple-
      ment, April 3, 1937, p. 256.
          Provides new biographical data for the period noted.

5242 H., N. B. J. "Thomas Shadwell: A Biography." Caian, XLVI (1938),
      93-99.

5243 Stroup, Thomas B. "Shadwell's Use of Hobbes." Studies in Philology
      XXXV (1938), 405-432.
          Contending that Shadwell wanted to capitalize on the popularity
      of Hobbes's philosophy, Stroup shows how Hobbes's ideas per-
      meate certain of Shadwell's plays, particularly those appearing
      in the early 1670's and the 1680's.

5244 Evans, G. Blakemore. "The Source of Shadwell's Character of
      Sir Formal Trifle in The Virtuoso." Modern Language Review,
      XXXV (1940), 211-214.
          The character owes not a little to Sir Solemn Trifle in
      D'Avenant's News from Plymouth.

5245 Hoskwith, Arnold K. "The Squire of Alsatia, by Thomas Shadwell."
      M.F.A. Yale University, 1940.

5246 Smith, Russell J. "Dryden and Shadwell: A Study in Literary Con-
      troversy." Ph.D. Cornell University, 1941.
          Feels that Shadwell must receive "considerable credit for
      Dryden's position as a critic."

5247 Kelly, Mildred. "The Plays of Thomas Shadwell and the Courtesy

Books of the Seventeenth Century." Ph.D. University of Louisiana, 1942.

5248 Hooker, Helen Maxwell. "Dryden's and Shadwell's 'Tempest.'" Huntington Library Quarterly, VI (February, 1943), 224-228.

"Variant readings in Huntington Library MS. of Dryden's 'Prologue Spoken at the Opening of the Theatre Royal,' support the belief that in the obscure last line of the Prologue Dryden was sneering at the operatic Tempest credited to Shadwell."

5249 Scott, Florence R. "News from Plimouth and Sir Positive At-All." Modern Language Review, XXXIX (April, 1944), 183-185.

Opposes the suggestion of Mr. Blackmore Evans that Shadwell derived much, if anything, in the character from D'Avenant's play.

5250 Smith, R. Jack. "Shadwell's Impact upon John Dryden." Review of English Studies, XX (January, 1944), 29-44.

Argues that Shadwell was the most important of Dryden's literary adversaries; their arguments over the merits of comedy of repartee vs. comedy of humours, the right of an author to borrow from ancient and modern authors, and the rationale of heroic tragedy stirred Dryden to consider important aspects of his craft.

5251 Ward, Charles E. "The Tempest: a Restoration Opera Problem." English Literary History, XIII (June, 1946), 119-130.

Produces evidence that Betterton was responsible for the 1674 operatic version.   .

5252 Milton, William M. "Tempest in a Teapot." English Literary History, XIV (September, 1947), 207-218.

Describes the controversy over the attribution of the Restoration The Tempest. Shadwell is responsible for the revisions in the operatic version.

5253 Smith, John Harrington. "Shadwell, the Ladies and the Change in Comedy." Modern Philology, XLVI (August, 1948), 22-33.

The move to sentimentalism is attributed to Shadwell and the women in the audience during the late 1680's.

5254 Humbert, Beate. "Die Lustspiele Wycherleys und Shadwells in ihrer Beziehung zu den Komödien Molières." Inaugural Dissertation. Hamburg, 1950.

5255 Feltham, Frederik G. "The Quality of the Wit in Comedies of Etheredge, Wycherley, Congreve, and Shadwell." Ph.D. University of Chicago, 1951.

5256 Jones, Everett L. "Robert Hooke and The Virtuoso." Modern Language Notes, LXVI (1951), 180-182.

Entries in Hooke's diary indicate that he saw the play and interpreted it as a personal attack.

5257 Sellers, William Howard. "Literary Controversies among Restoration Dramatists, 1660-1685." Ph.D. Ohio State University, 1954.

Dryden, Shadwell, and the Wits.

5258 Pearsall, Ronald. "The Case for Shadwell." Month, New Ser., XXIX (1963), 364-367.

Suggests that Shadwell's reputation might have equaled that of his contemporaries had he not been involved in a series of unhappy events.

5259 Towers, Tom H. "The Lineage of Shadwell: An Approach to Mac-Flecknoe." Studies in English Literature, 1500-1900, III (1963), 323-334.

Examines the poem as a theatrical document in terms of dramatic allusions and structure.

5260 Vernon, P. F. "Social Satire in Shadwell's Timon." Studia Neo-philologica, XXXV (1963), 221-226.

Shadwell's adaptation is a satirical reflection on the evil effects of money on society.

5261 Love, H. H. R. "The Authorship of the Postscript of Notes and Observations on The Empress of Morocco." Notes and Queries, New Ser., XIII (1966), 27-28.

Attributes the postscript to Thomas Shadwell.

5262 See, Earl Edward. "An Examination of Selected Plays of English Restoration Dramatist, Thomas Shadwell." M.A. Central Missouri State College, 1966.

5263 Smith, John Harrington. "Shadwell, the Ladies, and the Change in Comedy." Restoration Drama: Modern Essays in Criticism. (A Galaxy Book). Edited by John Loftis. (New York: Oxford University Press, 1966), 236-252.

Reprinted from Modern Philology, XLVI (1948), 22-33. Differences between Restoration comedy and the comedy of the early 18th century may be attributed to Shadwell's attempt to correct the dubious morality of the plays of his contemporaries and to ladies of the audience who deplored the stage's cynicism and immorality.

5264 Alssid, Michael W. "Shadwell's MacFlecknoe." Studies in English Literature, 1500-1900, VII (1967), 387-402.

In MacFlecknoe Dryden subverted Shadwell's critical ideas and dramatic practice and "deliberately and ironically metamorphosed Shadwell into a humors character to show us a fool who, like the humors of his plays, persistently incriminates himself."

5265 -----. Thomas Shadwell. New York: Twayne Publishers, Inc., 1967. 191 pp.

A biographical and critical study of Shadwell's life and works whose general purpose is to show "how highly conscious an

artist Shadwell was and how intelligently and perceptively he
translated into his plays many of the profound and ironic views
of man, society, and art which he and his age held."

5266 Archer, Stanley. "Dryden's MacFlecknoe." The Explicator, XXVI
(December, 1967), Item No. 37.

      "Aston Hall" in line 48 may refer to Santon Hall, Shadwell's
birthplace near Norwich.

5267 Dearmin, Michael G. "Thomas Shadwell: Playwright." Ph.D. University of Wisconsin, 1967. (Order No. 66-9899).

      Studies Shadwell as the best of the Restoration dramatists of
character and situation and examines his plays in light of his
own theories of drama.

5268 Edmunds, John. "Shadwell and the Anonymous Timon." Notes and
Queries, New Ser., XIV (1967), 218-221.

      Discusses the extent of Shadwell's borrowing from the anony-
mous play for his 1678 adaptation of Shakespeare's Timon of
Athens.

5269 Taylor, Aline Mackenzie. "Dryden's 'Enchanted Isle' and Shadwell's
'Dominion.'" Essays in English Literature of the Classical Period Presented to Dougald MacMillan. Edited by Daniel W. Patterson and Albrecht B. Strauss. Studies in Philology, (Extra
Series, January, 1967), 39-53.

      Explains Dryden's reference to Barbados in 1. 140 of Mac-
Flecknoe as part of his angry reaction to Shadwell's successful
operatic revision of The Tempest.

Shaftesbury

5270 Aldridge, Alfred Owen. "Lord Shaftesbury's Literary Theories."
Philological Quarterly, XXIV (1945), 46-64.

      Briefly discussed in the article is Shaftesbury's ideas on
tragedy.

5271 Tuveson, Ernest. "The Importance of Shaftesbury." Restoration
Drama: Modern Essays in Criticism. (A Glaaxy Book). Edited
by John Loftis. (New York: Oxford University Press, 1966), 253-
284.

      Reprinted from A Journal of English Literary History, XX
(1953), 267-299. Discusses the extent of Shaftesbury's influence
on the 18th century through his theory of the "moral sense" and
his glorification of external nature.

5272 Alderman, William E. "English Editions of Shaftesbury's Characteristics." Papers of the Bibliographical Society of America,
LXI (1967), 315-334.

      Lists 17 "authenticated English editions" between 1711 and
1964. 13 editions were published in the 18th century.

5273 Tuveson, Ernest. "Shaftesbury and the Age of Sensibility." Studies
      in Criticism and Aesthetics, 1660-1800: Essays in Honour of
      Samuel Holt Monk. Edited by Howard Anderson and John S. Shea
      (Minneapolis: University of Minnesota Press, 1967), 73-93.
      Corrects misinterpretations of Shaftesbury's philosophy
      and discusses his influence on his own time and thereafter.

Shakespeare

bibliography

5274 Kilbourne, Frederick W. "Stage Versions of Shakespeare before
      1800." Poet-Lore, XIV (1904), 111-122.
      A catalogue of Restoration and 18th century alterations of
      Shakespeare which regards the plays as literary curiosities,
      as "manifestations of dramatic notions forever and rightfully
      rejected."

5275 Dodd, Mead & Co., firm, Booksellers, New York. The Four Folios
      of Shakespeare's Plays; an Account of the Four Collected Editions
      With a Census of the Known Perfect Copies of the First Folio.
      A description of [a] set offered for sale. New York [1907]. 32
      pp.
      A description of the four folios, followed by a history of the
      first folio, a census of perfect copies in private hands and in
      public libraries in the United States and England (four separate
      lists), and, finally, histories of the other three folios.

5276 [Sherzer, Jane Belle]. "American Editions of Shakespeare: 1753-
      1866." Publications of the Modern Language Association, XXII
      (1907), 633-696.
      A survey with detailed descriptions of the editions and the
      circumstances of their publications; includes comments from
      reviews and critics contemporary with publication. (Made less
      useful by formlessness.)

5277 Jaggard, William. Shakespeare Bibliography. Stratford-on-Avon:
      At the Shakespeare Press, 1911. 729 pp.
      An encyclopedia of Shakespearian information and stage
      history. Includes information on Restoration and 18th century
      theatres, actors, adaptations, jubilees, editors, and publishers.

5278 Bartlett, Henrietta C., and Alfred W. Pollard. A Census of Shake-
      speare Plays in Quarto, 1594-1709. New Haven: Yale Univer-
      sity Press, 1916. 153 pp.
      Plays listed alphabetically, editions arranged chronologi-
      cally under titles; bibliographical description of each edition,
      followed by listing and description of copies, alphabetical by
      location. Also includes a list of unidentified copies, and an

index of owners and binders.

5279 Spencer, Hazelton. "The Restoration Play Lists." Review of English Studies, I (October, 1925), 443-446.

Sources for Restoration versions of Shakespearean adaptations can be readily identified.

5280 A Catalogue of Shakespeareana. With some notes and a preface by Falconer Madan. London [Edinburgh: Turnbull and Spears, Printers] 1927. London: Printed for presentation only.

A sale catalogue of 734 items related to Shakespeare, including letters, later dramatic history. Each item is fully described; often there are explanatory notes. Includes many items from Restoration and 18th century, e.g., an autograph letter of Frances Abington. Seventeen items of Dryden, primarily editions of plays borrowed from or with reference to Shakespeare. Seven Garrick items, his copies of three works, an autograph permit signed by DG. Arranged alphabetically.

5281 Babcock, R. W. "A Preliminary Bibliography of Eighteenth-Century Criticism of Shakespeare." Studies in Philology, Extra Series, No. 1 (May, 1929), 58-76.

A useful check-list of texts and studies.

5282 -----. "A Secondary Bibliography of Shakespeare Criticism in the Eighteenth Century." Studies in Philology, Extra Series, No. 1 (May, 1929), 77-98.

5283 Ford, H[erbert] L. Shakespeare, 1700-1740. A Collation of the Editions and Separate Plays with Some Account of T. Johnson and R. Walker. Oxford: University Press, 1935. 145 pp.

Individual discussions of Rowe's, Pope's, and Theobald's editions, the Tonson-Walker quarrel, and an extensive list of plays and adaptations printed separately, 1700-1740. The list is arranged alphabetically by title of Shakespeare's plays and contains complete publication information, description of the book, and library location.

5284 Black, Matthew W. "Shakespeare's Seventeenth Century Editors." Proceedings of the American Philosophical Society, LXXVI (1936), 707-717.

A study of the folios of 1623, 1632, 1664, and 1684, which reveals a consistent effort on the part of printing house editors to improve and restore the text. Black concludes that the editors performed a creditable service to the cause of textual authenticity.

5285 Black, Matthew W., and Matthias A. Shaaber. Shakespeare's Seventeenth-Century Editors, 1632-1685. New York: Modern Language Association, 1937. xii, 420 pp.

An exhaustive textual analysis of the Second (1632), Third (1664), and Fourth (1685) Folios, which reveals the nature and evolution of editorial practices during the period.

5286 Lefranc, Abel. "La Question Shakespearienne au XVIIIe Siècle."
Revue Bleue, LXXVI (1938), 44-50.

An analysis of a series of works from the late 18th and early
19th centuries which show that the controversy over authorship
of the plays began many years before the date commonly accepted by earlier scholars.

5287 Bartlett, Henrietta, and Alfred W. Pollard. Census of Shakespeare's
Plays in Quarto, 1594-1709. New Haven: Yale University Press,
1939. v, 165 pp.

A finding list with complete bibliographical descriptions of
extant copies of the quartos published within the chronological
limits of the volume.

5288 Steensma, Robert C. "Shakespeare Criticism in Eighteenth-Century England: A Bibliography of Modern Studies." Shakespeare
Newsletter, XI (November, 1961), 39.

A list of 57 books and articles from 1863-1960. Not annotated.

5289 -----. "Shakespeare on the Eighteenth-Century English Stage: A
Bibliography." Shakespeare Newsletter, XI (September, 1961),
29.

A list of forty-four of the more important books and articles.
Not annotated.

5290 Gordan, John D. The Bard and the Book; Editions of Shakespeare
in the Seventeenth Century; an Exhibition by the New York Public Library. New York: Astor Lenox and Tilden Foundations,
1964. 23 pp.

Includes the Third and Fourth Folios and six post-1660
adaptations. For each item, publication information is given,
followed by a paragraph or two on the nature of the work and
its relationship to Shakespeare, the nature of the alterations,
etc.

5291 Milwaukee, Wisconsin. Public Library. William Shakespeare,
His Editors and Editions. A commentary on the major editions
of Shakespeare's works prepared by the Milwaukee Public
Library for the quatracentenary observance of his birth in
1564. [Milwaukee: Public Library System, 1964]. 68 pp.

A brief history of editions of Shakespeare's works, followed
by individual treatments of major editions from Rowe through
Hardin Craig.

biography and criticism

5292 Lounsbury, Thomas R. Shakespeare as a Dramatic Artist. Vol. I.
New York: Charles Scribner's Sons, 1901.

Criticism of Shakespeare including that written in the 17th
and 18th centuries.

5293 Smith, David Nicol, ed. Eighteenth Century Essays on Shakespeare.
      Glasgow: J. MacLehose and Sons, 1903. viii, 358 pp.
          Shakespeare's reputation in the eighteenth century is presented
      through nine major critical essays representing the various
      phases of Shakespeare criticism from the time of Dryden to
      Coleridge. Texts collated with the originals. Notes, index.

5294 Evans, H. A. "A Shakespearian Controversy of the Eighteenth
      Century." Anglia, XXVIII (1905), 457-476.
          Concerned with eighteenth century criticism of Shakespeare
      (Theobald, Pope, Johnson).

5295 Adler, Johannes. "Zur Shakespeare-Kritik des 18. Jahrhunderts.
      Die Shakespeare-Kritik in Gentleman's Magazine." Inaugural
      Dissertation. Königsberg, 1906.

5296 Lee, Sidney. "Perils of Shakespearean Research." Shakespeare
      and the Modern Stage, with Other Essays. (New York: Charles
      Scribner's Sons, 1906), 188-197.
          Discusses George Steevens' 1763 fabrication of a letter
      signed by "G. Peel" regarding the association of Shakespeare
      and Edward Alleyn.

5297 Warner, Beverley. Famous Introductions to Shakespeare's Plays
      by Notable Editors of the Eighteenth Century. New York: Dodd,
      Mead, and Company, 1906.
          Compilation of best known introductions, including those by
      Rowe, Pope, Theobald, Warburton, and Johnson. Edited with
      a critical introduction, biographical and explanatory notes.

5298 Johnson, Charles F. Shakespeare and His Critics. Boston and
      New York: Houghton Mifflin, 1909.
          A history of the criticism of Shakespeare as poet and play-
      wright. Weakest section of volume is the treatment of 18th
      century criticism. Discussion of Samuel Johnson on pp. 113-
      126.

5299 Munro, John. The Shakspere [sic] Allusion-Book: a Collection of
      Allusions to Shakspere from 1591 to 1700. Originally compiled
      by C. M. Ingleby, Miss L. Toulmin Smith, and by Dr. F. J.
      Furnivall, with the assistance of the New Shakspere Society;
      and now re-edited, revised and re-arranged with an introduc-
      tion, by John Munro. 2 vols. London: Chatto and Windus; New
      York: Duffield & Co., 1909.
          Volume II covers the years 1650-1700 and contains 460 pages
      of allusions arranged chronologically. For each allusion,
      complete publication information is provided.

5300 Wood, Alice I. "State History of Shakespeare's Richard III."
      Ph.D. Columbia University, 1909.

5301 Bolland, W. C. "The Morocco Ambassador of 1682." The Anti-
      quary, VI (April, 1910), 124-134, 179-184.

His state visit to London, where, among other arranged
entertainments, he saw early in 1682 The Tempest at the
Duke's Theatre in Dorset Garden. He claimed to be extremely pleased, though he did not understand English.

5302 "Theatre in the 18th Century." Illustrated London News, CXXXVI
(April 16, 1910), 579.

Macbeth played in costumes of 1763.

5303 Winter, William. Shakespeare on the Stage. New York: Moffat,
Yard and Co., 1911. 564 pp.

Descriptions of the production and the manner of performance of the principal actors from Shakespeare's own time to
the 20th century.

5304 -----. "Shakespeare on the Stage: Hamlet." The Century Magazine, LXXXI (February, 1911), 485-500.

Great actors and actresses who have played Hamlet, including Betterton, Garrick, John Philip Kemble, and, in Dublin
and Edinburgh, Mrs. Siddons.

5305 -----. "Shakespeare on the Stage: King Henry VIII." The Century
Magazine, LXXXII (October, 1911), 905-917.

Famous actors as Henry, Wolsey, and Katharine, including
Henry Harris, John Philip Kemble, and Mrs. Siddons.

5306 -----. "Shakespeare on the Stage: Macbeth." The Century Magazine, LXXXI (April, 1911), 923-938.

Acting of Betterton, Garrick and of Spranger Barry, Mossop,
B. Booth, Wilks, Henderson, Macklin and Kemble. Mrs. Siddons and Mrs. Pritchard as Lady Macbeth.

5307 -----. "Shakespeare on the Stage: Othello." The Century Magazine, LXXXII (August, 1911), 502-520.

Roles of Othello, Iago, and Desdemona as played by Mohun,
M. Hughes, Charles Hart, and Betterton.

5308 -----. "Shakespeare on the Stage: Richard the Third." The Century Magazine, LXXXII (May, 1911), 40-55.

Richard III as interpreted by Colley Cibber, Garrick, John
Philip Kemble, George Frederick Cooke and Kean.

5309 Poel, William. Shakespeare in the Theater. London and Toronto:
Sidgwick & Jackson, Ltd., 1913. vii, 247 pp.

This work emphasizes the "interdependence of Shakespeare's
dramatic art with the form of the theatre for which Shakespeare
wrote his plays." It provides a kind of survey of mistakes of the
editors and actors, stage versions of particular plays, and the
National Theatre.

5310 Wheatley, Henry B. "Post-Restoration Quartos of Shakespeare's
Plays." The Library, 3rd Ser., IV (July, 1913), 237-269.

Account of the quarto editions of each play from 1660-1771
"giving due notice of the different adaptations" and the different

ways plays were adapted.

5311 Winter, William. "Twelfth Night: Shakespeare on the Stage." The
      Century Magazine, LXXXVIII (September, 1914), 683-694.
           Emphasis on the acting of Betterton, Harris, and Garrick
      and Mrs. Pritchard, Peg Woffington, Mrs. Yates, and Mrs.
      Barry as Viola.

5312 -----. Shakespeare on the Stage. Second Series. New York: Moffat,
      Yard, and Co., 1915. 663 pp.
           Continuation of the first series, with other plays.

5313 Liddell, Mark Harvey. The Typography of Shakespeare's Mid-
      sommer Nightes Dreame. San Francisco: John Howell, 1920.
           A discussion of some of the typographical peculiarities of
      a pair of quartos of Midsummer Night's Dream issued in 1660.
      One was printed by James Robert with no mention of the publisher;
      the other "Imprinted for Thomas Fisher" with no mention of the
      printer.

5314 Odell, G. C. D. Shakespeare from Betterton to Irving. New York:
      Charles Scribner's Sons, 1920. 2 vols.
           A history of Shakespeare on the London stage, with a con-
      sideration of the theatres, principles of staging, costumes,
      scenery. Vol. I is primarily concerned with Restoration and
      18th-century; Vol. II covers "The Age of Kemble," (1776-
      1817) and the 19th century.

5315 Pink, M. A. "The Influence of Shakespeare on the Eighteenth-
      Century Drama." M.A. London University, 1920.

5316 Sharp, R. F. "Travesties of Shakespeare's Plays." The Library,
      I (1920), 1-20.
           Discusses some 59 travesties of Shakespeare's plays,
      produced between 1792 and 1895; there are several from the
      eighteenth century, but none of them is English.

5317 [Thorn-Drury, George], compiler. Some Seventeenth-Century Al-
      lusions to Shakespeare and His Works, Not Hitherto Collected.
      London: P. J. and A. E. Dobell, 1920. 48 pp.
           Allusions to Shakespeare and/or his works in the literature
      of the 17th century (primarily post-Restoration). Each allusion
      is identified by author, work, date. Arranged chronologically.
      Index by author.

5318 Williams, Stanley T. "Some Versions of Timon of Athens on the
      Stage." Modern Philology, XVIII (1920), 269-285.
           A survey of adaptations of this play in various languages,
      including Thomas Shadwell's (1678), James Love's (1768),
      Richard Cumberland's (1771), and Thomas Hull's (1786).

5319 Clutton-Brock, A. "Shakespeare Treads the Boards." Times Liter-
      ary Supplement, December 1, 1921, p. 788.
           A chronological enumeration of plays, from 1769 on, in

which Shakespeare appeared in propria persona.

5320 Crosse, Gordon. "Shakespearean Mares'-Nests in the Eighteenth Century." London Mercury, IV (1921), 623-632.

A discussion of 18th century criticism of Shakespeare directed toward indicating the idolatry of Shakespeare and the general ridiculousness of the century's critics on Shakespeare.

5321 Spielmann, M. H. "Shakespeare's Ghost." Times Literary Supplement, October 27, 1921, pp. 698-699.

A discussion of appearances of Shakespeare's ghosts in the drama of the 17th and 18th centuries.

5322 Rollins, Hyder E. "Shakespeare Allusions." Notes and Queries, Ser. 12, X (1922), 224-225.

A list of allusions, not noted in any of the allusion books, dated 1621 to 1700 (all but three are from the Restoration period).

5323 Summers, Montague. Shakespeare Adaptations. The Tempest, The Mock Tempest, and King Lear. With an Introduction and Notes. London: Jonathan Cape, 1922. cviii, 282 pp.

Text of the 1670 edition of The Tempest, by Davenant. Text of the 1675 edition of T. Duffett's The Mock-Tempest. Text of N. Tate's edition of King Lear. The long introduction discusses the history of the adaptations of each play, into the 19th century.

5324 Thaler, Alwin. Shakespeare to Sheridan, a Book about the Theatre of Yesterday and Today. Cambridge: Harvard University Press, 1922. 339 pp.

Deals in separate chapters with the playwrights, the players, the managers, the theatres and the court, the playhouses (financing, costumes and properties, etc.). Appendix I covers extracts from the Lord Chamberlain's Books, 1661-1683, concerning allowances to players and managers, and the regulation of the stage.

5325 "Tonson and Walker's Edition of Shakespeare." Times Literary Supplement (Notes on Sales), December 28, 1922, p. 876.

A presentation of Walker's viewpoint in the Tonson-Walker controversy.

5326 "Unrecorded Editions of Shakespeare." Times Literary Supplement, November 30, 1922, p. 788.

A discussion of Tonson's and Walker's editions of 1734/5, concentrating on the advertisement issued by Tonson denouncing Walker.

5327 Boas, F. S. Shakespeare and the Universities. Oxford: B. Blackwell 1923. 272 pp.

Including references to the early years of the Restoration, this work is intended to illustrate "the influence on the presenta-

tion by professional actors of stageplays in the 16th and 17th
centuries of two external bodies--the Universities and the Office
of the Revels."

5328 Eich, Louis M. "Alterations of Shakespeare, 1660-1710, and an
Investigation of the Critical and Dramatic Principles and Theatrical Conventions Which Prompted These Revisions." Ph.D. University of Michigan, 1923.

5329 Maxwell, Baldwin. "Further 17th-Century Allusions to Shakespeare."
Modern Language Notes, XXXVIII (1923), 181-183.
   A report on allusions to Shakespeare in two poems and in
several of Shirley's plays.

5330 Spencer, Hazelton. "Hamlet under the Restoration." Publications
of the Modern Language Association, XXXVIII (1923), 588-641.
   A discussion of Quarto 6 of Hamlet (1637) which indicates
that this version belongs among Shakespeare alterations and
concludes that this version is the work of William D'Avenant.

5331 Neumann, Joshua. "Shakespearean Criticism in the Tatler and
Spectator." Publications of the Modern Language Association,
XXXIX (1924), 612-623.
   A discussion of Shakespearean criticism in the Tatler and
Spectator as it indicates a break from the strict neo-classical
standards and as it looks forward to later romantic criticism.

5332 [Thorn-Drury, George, ed.] More Seventeenth Century Allusions
to Shakespeare and His Works Not Hitherto Collected. [London]:
P.J. and A. E. Dobell, 1924. 52 pp.
   More allusions to Shakespeare and/or his works arranged
chronologically. Each allusion is identified by author, work,
date, page (where appropriate).

5333 Eich, Louis M. "Alterations of Shakespeare in the Theatre of the
Restoration." Quarterly Journal of Speech Education, XI
(June, 1925), 229-236.
   Some changes were made for the sake of poetic justice, to
enlarge the roles of actresses, or to permit Shakespeare to be
produced sumptuously, with full stage paraphernalia.

5334 Nicoll, Allardyce. [Shakespeare]. Review of English Studies, I
(October, 1925), 446.
   Replies to Spencer (RES, I [Oct., 1925], 443-446) that un-
known prompt books must remain as possible sources for
Restoration versions of Shakespeare.

5335 Tolman, Albert H. Falstaff and Other Shakespearean Topics.
New York: Macmillan, 1925. x, 270 pp.
   Includes a discussion of editions and criticism of Shakespeare
in the Restoration and eighteenth century.

5336 Corvesor, D. "Shakespeare Adaptations from Dryden to Garrick."
Ph.D. London University (Birkbeck), 1926.

5337 Spencer, Hazelton. "Improving Shakespeare: Some Bibliographical
      Notes on the Restoration Adaptations." Publications of the
      Modern Language Association, XLI (September, 1926), 727-746.
          Lists bibliographies of Restoration alterations, first editions
      of altered stage versions, with a discussion of five plays some-
      times mistaken for Shakespearean adaptations.

5338 -----. Shakespeare Improved. Cambridge: Harvard University
      Press, 1927. xii, 406 pp.
          Spencer's thesis is that many of the improvements were
      due to the excessive passion for scenery which inspired Daven-
      ant and his fellows. Gives a detailed account of the various
      adaptations and of the London theatres and companies of players.

5339 Raysor, Thomas M. "The Study of Shakespeare's Characters in
      the Eighteenth Century." Modern Language Notes, XLII (Dec-
      ember, 1927), 495-500.
          Adds a number of studies of Shakespeare's characters to the
      list given by Nichol Smith in his Eighteenth-Century Essays on
      Shakespeare.

5340 Rhodes, R. Crompton. "Shakespeare's Ladies." Shakespeare Re-
      view, I (July, 1928), 182-184.
          Supporters of Shakespearean productions in the 18th century.

5341 [Shakespeare]. Notes and Queries, CLV (September 15, 1928), 182.
          Reprints a selection from the Daily Journal (September 14,
      1728), announcing a performance of King Lear at Lincoln's-Inn-
      Fields.

5342 "Shakespeare on the Stage." Times Literary Supplement, July 5,
      1928, pp. 493-494.
          Reviews H. Spenser, Shakespeare Improved (1927); dis-
      agrees with Spenser's assertion that in the Restoration theatre
      the platform of the Elizabethans was eliminated.

5343 Smith, D. Nichol. Shakespeare in the Eighteenth Century. Ox-
      ford University Press, 1928. 91 pp.
          Three lectures describe the general movement of Shakespearean
      acting, scholarship, and criticism from the Restoration to the
      end of the 18th century.

5344 Babcock, Robert Witbeck. "The Genesis of Shakespeare Idolatry."
      Ph.D. University of Chicago, 1929.

5345 -----. "The Attack of the Late Eighteenth Century upon Alter-
      ations of Shakespeare's Plays." Modern Language Notes, XLV
      (1930), 446-451.
          Deals with reaction against "improvements" on Shakespeare's
      plays made earlier in the century.

5346 -----. "The Attitude toward Shakespeare's Learning in the Late
      18th Century." Philological Quarterly, IX (1930), 116-122.
          Traces the gradually changing opinions of Shakespeare's

learning among later writers and critics.

5347 -----. "The Direct Influence of Late Eighteenth-Century Criticism on Hazlitt and Coleridge." Modern Language Notes, XLV (1930), 377-387.

An interesting link between late classical and mature romantic criticism of Shakespeare.

5348 -----. "The English Reaction Against Voltaire's Criticism of Shakespeare." Studies in Philology, XXVII (1930), 609-625.

Various defenses against Voltaire's charge that Shakespeare lacked taste and was ignorant of the rules of classical drama.

5349 Robinson, H. S. "English Shakespearean Criticism in the 18th Century." M. Litt. Cambridge University, 1930.

5350 Babcock, Robert Witbeck. The Genesis of Shakespeare Idolatry, 1766-1799: A Study in English Criticism of the Late Eighteenth Century. Chapel Hill: University of North Carolina Press, 1931. xxviii, 307 pp.

Eighteenth century critical defense of Shakespeare; the development of new emphases on conscious art and moral philosophy.

5351 Black, A. Bruce, and Robert M. Smith. Shakespeare Allusions and Parallels. Bethlehem, Pa.: Lehigh University, 1931. vii, 59 pp.

Hitherto unnoted allusions from the period 1599-1701.

5352 Chambers, Edmund. The Shakspere [sic] Allusion-Book: a Collection of Allusions to Shakspere from 1591 to 1700... Originally compiled by C. M. Ingleby, Miss L. Toulmin Smith, and by Dr. F. J. Furnivall, with the assistance of the New Shakspere society: re-edited, revised and re-arranged, with an introduction by John Munro (1909), and now re-issued with a preface by Sir Edmund Chambers. 2 vols. London: H. Milford, Oxford University Press, 1932.

The preface by Chambers is devoted to presenting several additional allusions; otherwise, this is the same as the 1909 edition (for which see Munro).

5353 Ralli, Augustus. A History of Shakespearian Criticism. 2 vols. Oxford: University Press, 1932.

Includes discussion of both the 18th-century "improvements" and the reaction against them.

5354 Stewart, Powell. "An Eighteenth-Century Adaptation of Shakespeare." University of Texas Studies in English, No. 12 (1932), 98-117.

The Universal Passion, based on Much Ado, by the Rev. James Miller was performed at Drury Lane, February 28, 1737.

5355 Sutherland, J. R. "Shakespeare's Imitators in the Eighteenth Century." Modern Language Review, XXVIII (1933), 21-36.

A discussion of borrowings.

5356 Wood, Frederick T. "The Merchant of Venice in the Eighteenth Century." English Studies, XV (1933), 209-218.
Traces changes in text, interpretation, and performances.

5357 Paul, Henry N. "Mr. Hughs' Edition of Hamlet." Modern Language Notes, XLIX (1934), 438-443.
A study of an emended version.

5358 Ross, M. M. "Shakespeare and Romantic Tragedy: a Study of the Fate of the Shakespearean Influence on Romantic Currents in English Tragedy from Dryden to Keats, with Special Reference to the Decline of Poetic Drama." M.A. University of Toronto, 1934.

5359 Green, Frederick Charles. Minuet: A Critical Survey of French and English Literary Ideas in the Eighteenth Century. London: Dent, 1935. 489 pp.
Divided into three sections, the author treats of the drama, poetry, and the novel. An entire chapter is devoted to Shakespeare and Voltaire, Shakespeare and the French dramatic tradition, among other considerations. Included also is a chapter on contacts in tragedy.

5360 Kahrl, George M. "The Influence of Shakespeare on Smollett." Essays in Dramatic Literature: The Parrott Presentation Volume, Edited by Hardin Craig. (Princeton: Princeton University Press, 1935), 399-420.
A study of various works, but primarily the novels, which endeavors to show the extent to which Smollett was indebted to the plays of Shakespeare for situations and characters, and for his concept of the function of comedy.

5361 Kidd, C. E. "The Stage Performance of King Lear, a Critical Review." M.A. Queen's University, 1935.

5362 Lovett, David. "Shakespeare as a Poet of Realism in the Eighteenth Century." English Literary History, II (1935), 267-289.
An analysis of the critical commentary upon realism or nature in Shakespeare's plays. Critics from Thomas Rymer to William Richardson are included.

5363 -----. Shakespeare's Characters in Eighteenth Century Criticism. Baltimore: Johns Hopkins University Press, 1935. 30 pp.
This study reveals how character gradually replaced the primacy of plot in criticism, and also how the era's climate of opinion appears in its attitudes toward the plays. All the major critics and many of the minor ones are among those considered.

5364 Spriggs, Charles O. "Hamlet on the Eighteenth Century Stage." Quarterly Journal of Speech, XXII (1936), 78-85.
After attributing the alterations in the quarto of 1676 to Betterton, Spriggs comments upon the purpose and effects

of Garrick's version (1772) and upon Garrick's interpretation
of the leading role.

5365 Babcock, R. W. "An Early Eighteenth Century Note on Falstaff."
Philological Quarterly, XVI (1937), 84-85.

Prints a comment from B. M. Sloane MS. 4046f66 (2/26/
1720/21) which stands as an early precursor of the argument
about Falstaff's character.

5366 Crundell, H. W. "'The Taming of the Shrew' on the XVII Century
Stage." Notes and Queries, CLXXIII (1937), 207.

Commentary principally concerned with the use of the
Epilogue in Restoration performances of the play.

5367 Jaggard, William. "Imitations of Shakespeare." Notes and Queries,
CLXXIII (1937), 370-373.

A selective list of imitations, some of which appeared during
the 18th century.

5368 Huang, J. "A Short History of Shakespearean Production." M. Litt.
Cambridge University (King's), 1938.

5369 Summers, Montague. "The First Illustrated Shakespeare." Connoisseur, CII (1938), 305-309.

An illustrated essay on Rowe's editions of Shakespeare with
commentary about the engravings.

5370 Brown, Ivor, and Fearon, George. This Shakespeare Industry,
Amazing Monument. New York and London: Harper, 1939.
xii, 332 pp.

Attempts to explain how "a local loyalty" became a "cosmic
industry" by presenting a brief history of attitudes toward
Shakespeare's plays. Chapters II-IV are concerned with the
Restoration and 18th century.

5371 Castelnuovo-Tedesco, Mario. "Shakespeare and Music." Shakespeare Association Bulletin, XV (July, 1940), 166-174.

5372 Derrick, Leland Eugene. "The Stage History of King Lear."
Ph.D. University of Texas, 1940.

5373 Deutsch, Albert. "Tom O' Bedlam and His Song." Yale Review,
XXIX (June, 1940), 856-861.

Brief picture of the commonness of the wandering insane
and their condition; background of the song and allusions to it
in works, including Hogarth and Shakespeare; the song itself
is printed.

5374 Linton, Calvin Darlington. "Shakespeare Staging in London from
Irving to Gielgud." Ph.D. Johns Hopkins University, 1940.

5375 Seymour, John L. "Drama and Libretto: A Study of Four Libretto
Adaptations of Two of Shakespeare's Plays." Ph.D. University
of California, 1940.

5376 Stone, George Winchester, Jr. "Garrick's Treatment of Shakespeare's Plays and His Influence upon the Changed Attitude of

Shakespearean Criticism during the Eighteenth Century." Ph.D. Harvard University, 1940.

Indicates that Garrick was the most important single figure in the spread of knowledge of Shakespeare. Scholarly study of all phases of Garrick's treatment of Shakespeare.

5377 Toyoda, Minoru. Shakespeare in Japan: An Historical Survey. Tokyo: The Iwanami Shoten, 1940. 139 pp.

Stories and adaptations of Shakespeare's plays.

5378 Bald, R. C. "Shakespeare on the Stage in Restoration Dublin." Publications of the Modern Language Association, LVI (1941), 369-378.

Discusses annotations in prompt-books for eight of Shakespeare's plays performed in Dublin before 1700. It had previously been thought that fewer of Shakespeare's plays had been performed in Dublin before 1700.

5379 Gregor, Joseph. Kulturgeschichte der Oper. Vienna: Gallus Verlag, 1941. 426 pp.

5380 Lowery, Margaret R. "Performances of Shakespearian Plays at Covent Garden and Drury Lane Theaters." Shakespeare Association Bulletin, XVI (April, 1941), 102-103.

A tabular list of performances and dates.

5381 Schmitz, R. Morrell. "Scottish Shakspere." Shakespeare Association Bulletin, XVI (October, 1941), 229-236.

An account of Blair's edition of the works (Edinburgh, 1753).

5382 Alden, Barbara. "The History and Interpretation of Shakespeare's Othello on the American Stage." Ph.D. University of Chicago, 1942.

5383 Travers, Seymour. Catalogue of Nineteenth Century French Theatrical Parodies; A Compilation of the Parodies between 1789 and 1914. New York: King's Crown Press, 1942. 130 pp.

5384 Blair, Elizabeth. "The Costuming of Hamlet from Shakespeare's Time to the Present." M.A. University of North Carolina, 1943.

5385 Davis, Reginald. "Shakespeare's Contribution to Music." M.A. University of Ottawa, 1943.

5386 Wallerstein, Ruth. "Dryden and the Analysis of Shakespeare's Techniques." Review of English Studies, XIX (April, 1943), 165-185.

Reprinted in Essential Articles for the Study of John Dryden. Edited by H. T. Swedenberg, Jr. (Hamden, Conn.: Archon Books, 1966), 551-575. (The Essential Articles Series). Analyzes Dryden's conception of poetry as it is defined in his "imitation" of Shakespeare in All for Love.

5387 Einstein, Alfred. "Mozart und Shakespeares Tempest." Monatshefte für den deutschen Unterricht, XXXVI (1944), 43-48.

5388 Havens, George R. Voltaire and English Critics of Shakespeare.
New York: American Society of the French Legion of Honor,
1944. 12 pp. (Franco-American Pamphlets, 2nd Ser., No. 16).

5389 Lovell, John, Jr. "Shakespeare's American Play." Theatre Arts,
XXVIII (1944), 363-370.

5390 Noyes, Robert Gale. "Shakespeare in the Eighteenth Century Novel."
English Literary History, XI (September, 1944), 213-236.
Having investigated 250 novels from Pamela (1740) to 1780,
the year following Garrick's death, Noyes here selects passages
which illustrate the history of Shakespeare's plays during the
age of Garrick. The general attitude is favorable. The plays
are praised for their adherence to nature, are compared with
those of Jonson, and the alterations of 18th-century editors
are sometimes decried.

5391 Scouten, Arthur H. "Shakespeare's Plays in the Theatrical Repertory when Garrick Came to London." Texas Studies in English, XXIV (1944), 257-268.

5392 Avery, Emmett L. "1 Henry IV and 2 Henry IV during the First
Half of the Eighteenth Century." Journal of English and Germanic
Philology, XLIV (January, 1945), 89-90.
Additional notes on performances of these plays.

5393 Bentley, Gerald Eades. Shakespeare and Jonson: Their Reputations
in the Seventeenth Century Compared. 2 vols. Chicago: University of Chicago Press, 1945.
A meticulous collection and analysis of allusions.

5394 Evans, G. Blakemore. "A Seventeenth-Century Reader of Shakespeare." Review of English Studies, XXI (1945), 271-279.
Extracts from a MS diary of 1688 give contemporary views
on Shakespeare.

5395 Hogan, Charles Beecher. "Shakespeare Performances." Times
Literary Supplement, October 13, 1945, p. 487.
Notice concerning his work-in-progress towards a calendar
of performances during the eighteenth century.

5396 Parker, W. M. "Shakespeare Concordances." Times Literary
Supplement, May 12, 1945, p. 228.
Notes the early concordances, from 1787.

5397 Rosenbach, Abraham Simon Wall. A Description of the Four
Folios of Shakespeare, 1623, 1632, 1663-4, 1685 in the
Original Bindings; the gift of Mr. P. A. B. Widener and Mrs.
Josephine Widener Wichfeld to the Free library of Philadelphia
in memory of their father, Joseph E. Widener. [n.p.] 1945.
18 pp.
Facsimiles of the title-pages, and brief histories of their
printing, with a history of the Widener family's interest in
book collecting.

5398 Scouten, Arthur H. "Shakespeare's Plays in the Theatrical Re-
pertory when Garrick came to London." Studies in English,
Department of English, the University of Texas, 1944. (Austin:
University of Texas Press, 1945), 257-268.

Shakespeare's plays were already popular when Garrick
arrived in London, giving him a firm basis in popular tastes
for him to build on.

5399 Aubin, Robert A. "Black as the Moor of Venice." Times Literary
Supplement, July 13, 1946, p. 331.

A hitherto unnoticed allusion to Othello in 1689.

5400 Dawson, Giles E. "The Copyright of Shakespeare's Dramatic
Works." Studies in Honor of A.H.R. Fairchild. Edited by
Charles T. Prouty. (Columbia, Missouri: University of Missouri
Press, 1946), 9-35.

Traces the ownership of the copyright to 1774.

5401 Dunkin, Paul S. "A Shakespeare Allusion." Notes and Queries,
CXC (January 12, 1946), 15.

In the dedication to Lee's Caesar Borgia, 1680.

5402 Boase, T.S.R. "Illustrations of Shakespeare's Plays in the Seventeenth and Eighteenth Centuries." Journal of the Warburg and
Courtauld Institutes, X (1947), 83-108.

47 illustrations (plates) painted from 1655 to the end of the
18th century, showing the growth of illustrating Shakespeare.
The Shakespeare Gallery and its painters of the 18th century
are studied in some detail.

5403 Conklin, Paul S. A History of Hamlet Criticism, 1601-1821.
New York: King's Crown Press, 1947. viii, 176 pp.

A general survey, including comments on the varying stage
interpretations, and showing how the sentimental-melancholy
image of the hero developed on the eighteenth century stage.

5404 Eastman, Arthur M. "Johnson's Edition of Shakespeare, 1765."
Ph.D. Yale University, 1947.

5405 "Shylocks of Bygone Days." Shakespeare Quarterly, I (Summer,
1947), 18-21.

Includes notes on performances by Macklin and other
eighteenth century actors.

5406 Some Remarks on the Tragedy of Hamlet, Prince of Denmark,
Written by Mr. William Shakespeare (1736). Introduction by
Clarence D. Thorpe and a Bibliographical Note. The Augustan
Reprint Society. Los Angeles: William Andres Clark Memorial
Library, 1947. Publication No. 9.

Thorpe's introduction denies Thomas Hanmer as author and
discusses the views of the work's anonymous author who anticipates some of Johnson's arguments.

5407 Van Tieghem, Paul. Le Préromantisme: Etudes d'Histoire Littér-

aire Européenne. La Découverte de Shakespeare sur le Continent. Paris: Sfelt, 1947. xi, 412 pp.

    A scrupulous and detailed account of Shakespeare on the
Continental stage during the eighteenth century.

5408 Wilson, John Dover and C. B. Young. "The Stage History of
Henry V." In John Dover Wilson, ed. King Henry V. Cambridge:
University Press, 1947. xlviii-lvi.

    The play was not much performed until the later eighteenth
century; performances at Covent Garden and Drury Lane are
noted.

5409 Young, C. B. "The Stage History of Macbeth." In John Dover
Wilson, ed. Macbeth. (Cambridge: University Press, 1947),
lxix-lxxxii.

    Shows that the play was frequently performed, and gives
particular notice to Betterton, Mrs. Betterton, Mrs. Barry,
Garrick and Kemble in the principal roles.

5410 Byrne, Muriel St. Clare. "Bell's Shakespeare." Times Literary
Supplement, January 31, 1948, p. 65.

    On problems of dating in the 1770's.

5411 -----. A History of Shakespearian Production. London: Common
Ground for the Arts Council of Great Britain and the Society
for Cultural Relations with the U.S.S.R., 1948. 36 pp.

    A catalogue of an exhibition, "A History of Shakespearian
Production 1700-1800: Scenes and Characters in the Eighteenth
Century," held in 1948-1949. Included in the volume are portraits of Barry, Macklin, Woffington, Garrick and others,
with illustrations from eighteenth century editions of Shakespeare.

5412 Danks, K. B. "Chetwind's Folios." Times Literary Supplement,
July 17, 1948, p. 401.

    A letter concerning the motives of Chetwind for publishing
his second issue of the Third Folio.

5413 Dawson, Giles E. "Three Shakespeare Piracies in the Eighteenth
Century." Papers of the Bibliographical Society of the University
of Virginia, I (1948-1949), 49-58.

    Hamlet (1723), Othello (1724), and Macbeth (1729), are
duplicated in pirated editions.

5414 Dunkel, W. D. "An Error in Shakespeare Improved Corrected."
College English Association Critic, X (1948), 1-3.

    A note on Hazelton Spencer's work of 1927.

5415 Eastman, Arthur M. "Johnson's Shakespearean Labours in 1765."
Modern Language Notes, LXIII (December, 1948), 512-515.

    An account of the composition of Johnson's edition.

5416 Springer, R. "A History of Falstaff Criticism." Ph.D. Columbia
University, 1948.

5417 Young, C. B. "The Stage History of Titus Andronicus." Titus

Andronicus. Edited by John Dover Wilson. (Cambridge:
University Press, 1948), lxvi-lxxi.

Discusses Thomas Ravenscroft's version and its performances
during the Restoration and 18th century.

5418 Child, Harold. "The Stage History of King Henry IV." The First
Part of the History of Henry IV. Edited by John Dover Wilson.
(Cambridge: Cambridge University Press, 1949), xxix-xlvi.

Deals particularly with Cartwright as Falstaff, Kynaston as
the King, Betterton as Falstaff, Quin as Hotspur and Falstaff,
and Henderson as Falstaff.

5419 Chute, Marchette. "The Bubble, Reputation." Virginia Quarterly
Review, XXV (1949), 575-584.

A survey of Shakespeare's reputation during the Restoration
period.

5420 Dawson, Giles E. "Warburton, Hanmer, and the 1745 Edition of
Shakespeare." Papers of the Bibliographical Society of the University of Virginia, II (1949), 35-48.

The 1745 edition reprints the 1744 text, marking "those
passages in the text altered by Hanmer." Warburton probably
compiled the references.

5421 Evans, G. Blakemore. "The Text of Johnson's Shakespeare
(1765)." Philological Quarterly, XXVIII (1949), 425-428.

Johnson's use of Theobald's Shakespeare (1757).

5422 Mann, Isabel R. "The First Recorded Production of a Shakespearian
Play in Stratford-upon-Avon." Shakespeare Association Bulletin,
XXIV (1949), 203-208.

A performance of Othello was given on September 9, 1746
to raise money for the repair of the Shakespeare Monument in
the Stratford Church.

5423 McManaway, James G. "The Two Earliest Prompt Books of
Hamlet." Papers of the Bibliographical Society of America,
XLIII (1949), 288-320.

Restoration texts with additional stage directions from about
1740.

5424 Palmer, Arnold. "Mistakes cut in Marble." Times Literary Supplement, February 25, 1949, p. 89.

Misquotations on the Westminster Abbey Shakespeare Memorial, erected 1740.

5425 Wagner, Bernard M., ed. The Appreciation of Shakespeare: a
Collection of Criticism--Philosophic, Literary, and Esthetic--
by Great Writers and Scholar-Critics of the Eighteenth, Nineteenth and Twentieth Centuries. Washington: Georgetown University Press, 1949. xiv, 522 pp.

An elaborate collection, with much valuable comment from
the eighteenth century.

5426 Young, C. B. "The Stage History of Julius Caesar." In John Dover
Wilson, ed. Julius Caesar. (Cambridge: University Press, 1949),
xxiv-xlvi.
Comments on Betterton, Booth, Powell and Quin in the major
roles.

5427 Williamson, Claude C. H., compiler. Readings on the Character
of Hamlet: 1661-1947. London: George Allen and Unwin, 1950.
783 pp.
Pages 1-30 contain a chronological sampling of Restoration
and eighteenth-century criticism of Hamlet from John Evelyn
(1661) to Michael Kelly (1799).

5428 Prior, Moody E. "The Elizabethan Audience and the Plays of
Shakespeare." Modern Philology, XLIX (1951), 101-123.
Prior's article deals, in passing, with the neo-classical
notion of Shakespeare's relationship to his audience.

5429 Stone, George Winchester, Jr. "Shakespeare in the Periodicals,
1700-1740." Shakespeare Quarterly, II (1951), 221-231.
Stone surveys Shakespeare's reputation and the knowledge
of his works from 1700 to 1720.

5430 Byrne, M. St. Clare. "The Stage Costuming of Macbeth in the
Eighteenth Century." Studies in English Theatre History, in
Memory of Gabrielle Enthoven, O.B.E., first president of
the Society for Theatre Research, 1948-50. (London, 1952),
52-64.
A study of two aspects of this topic--Charles Macklin and
his possible introduction of the kilt into Macbeth costuming,
and Garrick's interest in historical costume as related in a
letter from Garrick to Luke Gardiner, London, December 13,
1777.

5431 Hogan, Charles B. Shakespeare in the Theatre, 1701-1800. 2 vols.
Oxford: Clarendon Press, 1952-1957.
Hogan's volumes record performances of Shakespeare's
plays in London. The first volume covers the period from
1701 to 1750, the second volume the remainder of the century.

5432 Mander, Raymond, and Joe Mitchenson. Hamlet through the Ages.
A Pictorial Record from 1709. Edited with an Introduction by
Herbert Marshall. London: Rockliff, 1952. xvii, [1], 156 pp.
Pictures and drawings of settings and actors, with notes
explaining each. Sources for each picture are given, as well
as location, when known.

5433 Nichols, J. W. "A Study of William Shakespeare As a Character
in the English Drama." M.A. University of Birmingham, 1952.

5434 Stone, George Winchester, Jr. "Shakespeare in the Periodicals,
1700-1740 (Part II)." Shakespeare Quarterly, III (1952), 313-
328.

This continuation surveys Shakespeare's reputation and the knowledge of his works from 1720 to 1740.

5435 Bowers, R. H. "A New Shakespeare Allusion." Shakespeare Quarterly, IV (1953), 362.

The Merry Loungers, an anonymous farce of the late Restoration or early eighteenth century, misquotes Shakespeare for comic purposes.

5436 Hook, Lucyle. "Shakespeare Improv'd, or a Case for the Affirmative." Shakespeare Quarterly, IV (1953), 289-299.

The revisions of Shakespeare's plays in the Restoration illustrate significant changes in dramatic history: "Paradoxical as it may seem, it is possible that the preservation of Shakespeare even in garbled form . . . made certain his present reputation."

5437 Noyes, Robert Gale. The Thespian Mirror: Shakespeare in the Eighteenth-Century Novel. Providence: Brown University Press, 1953. 200 pp.

Novels from 1740 to 1780 reflect the widespread interest in Shakespeare. Noyes has separate chapters on Shakespeare's comedies, histories, tragedies, and romances.

5438 Rosenberg, Marvin. "The 'Refinement' of Othello in the Eighteenth Century British Theatre." Studies in Philology, LI (1954), 75-94.

By the second half of the century much of the erotic action and language had been "refined" out of the play.

5439 Sprague, Arthur Colby. The Stage Business in Shakespeare's Plays: A Postscript. London: Society for Theatre Research, 1954. 35 pp.

A discussion of specific items of stage business in productions of Shakespeare's plays from the late 17th through the 19th centuries. Based on portraits and newspapers.

5440 Aden, John M. "Shakespeare in Dryden's First Published Poem?" Notes and Queries, CC (1955), 22-23.

Points out four lines which are similar to lines Hamlet speaks; this indicates very early, if faint, influence of Shakespeare on Dryden.

5441 Fiehler, Rudolph. "How Oldcastle Became Falstaff." Modern Language Quarterly, XVI (1955), 16-31.

In the course of presenting the derivation of Falstaff, the author comments on Pope's Dunciad, and on Shakespeare critics of the 18th century.

5442 Schwartzstein, Leonard. "Knight, Ireland, Steevens, and the Shakespeare Testament." Notes and Queries, CC (1955), 76-78.

Accuses Knight of suspecting Steevens in connection with the

Shakespeare Testament without basis in fact. This error was perpetuated and changed as other writers thought Knight was speaking of Ireland as the inventor of the Shakespeare Testament.

5443 Avery, Emmett L. "The Shakespeare Ladies Club." Shakespeare Quarterly, VII (1956), 154-158.
Discusses activities of the club, 1736-1738.

5444 Branam, George C. Eighteenth-Century Adaptations of Shakespearean Tragedy. Berkeley and Los Angeles: University of California Press, 1956. 220 pp.
Treats the eighteenth-century alterations as "a kind of laboratory manual of the diction, dramatic theory, and dramatic practice of the age. Discusses the adaptations in terms of the influence of critical theory, language, character and moral, stage effectiveness. An Appendix contains a checklist of the adaptations of Shakespeare's plays, 1660-1820.

5445 Brock, Elizabeth. "Shakespeare's The Merry Wives of Windsor: A History of the Text from 1623 through 1821." Ph.D. University of Virginia, 1956.
A study of emendations.

5446 McKenzie, Jack. "Shakespeare in Scotland before 1760." Theatre Notebook, XI (1956), 24-26.

5447 Scouten, Arthur H. "The Increase in Popularity of Shakespeare's Plays in the Eighteenth Century: A Caveat for Interpretors of Stage History." Shakespeare Quarterly, VII (1956), 189-202.
Argues that Shakespeare was a popular playwright and a dominant force in 18th-century theatre before Garrick; thus Garrick was not the chief factor in Shakespeare's rising popularity in the 18th century.

5448 Stone, George Winchester, Jr. "Shakespeare's Tempest at Drury Lane during Garrick's Management." Shakespeare Quarterly, VII (1956), 1-7.
Versions of the play--both dramatic and operatic--which Garrick produced, ending with his 1757 production of Shakespeare's own text.

5449 Guthke, Karl S. "Johann Heinrich Füssli und Shakespeare." Neuphilologische Mitteilungen, LVIII (1957), 206-215.

5450 Halliday, F. E. The Cult of Shakespeare. London: Duckworth, 1957. xiii, 218 pp.
Restoration through Victorian era.

5451 Mander, Raymond and Joe Mitchenson. "Further Notes on the Porcelain Statuette of Richard III." Theatre Notebook, XI (1957), 128-130.

5452 Merchant, W. M. "Classical Costume in Shakespearian Productions." Shakespeare Survey, X (1957), 71-76.

17th century. Illustrated.

5453 Schulz, Max F. "King Lear: A Box-Office Maverick among Shake-
spearian Tragedies on the London Stage 1700-01 to 1749-50."
Tulane Studies in English, VII (1957), 83-90.
Less often staged than Hamlet, Macbeth, and Othello.

5454 Trewin, John Courtenay. "Mulberry and Artichoke." The Night
Has Been Unruly. (London: Robert Hale, Ltd. [1957]), 13-30.
A discussion of the Garrick Jubilee at Stratford, 1769.

5455 Evans, G. Blakemore. "The Problem of Brutus: An Eighteenth-
Century Solution." Studies in Honor of T.W. Baldwin. Edited
by Don Cameron Allen. (Urbana: University of Illinois Press,
1958), 229-236.
Letter, probably ca. 1715, from T. Killigrew, suggests
making Shakespeare's Brutus nobler.

5456 Merchant, W. M. "Francis Hayman's Illustrations of Shakespeare."
Shakespeare Quarterly, IX (1958), 141-147.
For Hanmer's edition, 1744.

5457 Dawson, Giles E. "Robert Walker's Editions of Shakespeare."
Studies in the English Renaissance Drama: In Memory of Karl
Julius Holzknecht. Edited by Josephine W. Bennett, Oscar Car-
gill, and Vernon Hall, Jr. (New York: New York University
Press, 1959), 58-81.
An historical treatment of Walker's 1734-35 edition of Shake-
speare's Works, including a very detailed discussion of the
controversy over this edition between Walker and Tonson.

5458 Kroll, Daniel Ronald. "Hamlet from Edwin Booth to Laurence
Olivier: Some Changing Interpretations Reflecting Changes in
Culture and in the Taste of Audiences." Ph.D. Columbia Uni-
versity, 1959.

5459 Merchant, W. Modwyn. Shakespeare and the Artist. Oxford: Oxford University Press, 1959. 254 pp.
Settings, illustrations, paintings.

5460 Starnes, Mary Elizabeth. "Ophelia: A Survey of Interpretation
from the Restoration to the Present." M.F.A. Yale University,
1959.

5461 Brooks, Helen Elphinstone. "Eighteenth Century French Translations and Adaptations of Shakespeare." Ph.D. Northwestern
University, 1960.
This treats of the bowdlerized and often sentimentalized
18th-century French translations of Shakespeare, especially
those of La Place, Ducis and Le Tourneur.

5462 Brown, E. M. "The Reviewing of Shakespearean Productions in
The Times Newspaper, 1788-1860." M.A. University of Wales,
Cardiff, 1960.

5463 Brown, John Russell. "Three Adaptations." Shakespeare News-
      letter, XIII (1960), 137-145.
          Discusses adaptations of The Tempest, All's Well that Ends
      Well, and Midsummer Night's Dream.
5464 Byrne, M. St. Clare. "The Earliest Hamlet Prompt Book in an
      English Library." Theatre Notebook, XV (1960), 21-31.
          This describes the value of an actor's marked copy of a 1785
      Newcastle prompt book, "the earliest Hamlet prompt book in
      this county, though not in the United Kingdom."
5465 Evans, G. Blakemore, ed. Shakespearean Promptbooks of the
      Seventeenth Century. Vol. I, Pt. 1: 39 p. General Introduction.
      Introduction to the Padua Macbeth Collations. Part 2: Text of
      the Padua Macbeth (facsimile). Bibliographical Society of the Uni-
      versity of Virginia, 1960. Two parts in portfolio.
          This is the first in a series of seventeenth-century Shake-
      spearean promptbooks published under the auspices of the Biblio-
      graphical Society of the University of Virginia. These studies
      provide detailed information about the text of Shakespeare's
      plays as they were staged during the last three quarters of the
      17th century.
5466 Johnson, Samuel. Samuel Johnson on Shakespeare. Edited by W. K.
      Wimsatt, Jr. New York: Hill and Wang, 1960. xxxviii, 115 pp.
      (Dramabooks, 22).
5467 M., L. "The Merchant of Vengeance." Shakespeare Newsletter,
      X (1960), 32.
          Performances of Shylock in 18th century and later.
5468 Merchant, W. Moelwyn. "Costume in King Lear." Shakespeare
      Survey, XIII (1960), 72-80.
          Considering the garb of Lear, Cordelia, Edgar, and the
      Fool as reflections of the play's interior tragedy, Merchant
      suggests that the costumes produced through the ages (including
      the 18th century) reflect the distortions as well as offering
      critical insights into their age.
5469 Sacks, Claire and Edgar Whan, eds. Hamlet: Enter Critic. New
      York: Appleton-Century-Crofts, 1960. 298 pp.
          Some excerpts from 18th century comments are included.
5470 Walker, Alice. "Edward Capell and His Edition of Shakespeare."
      Proceedings of the British Academy, XLVI (1960), 131-145.
          Capell's edition (1768) is seen as the first of the "new school"
      of Shakespeare editions, "based on a thorough examination of
      variant readings in early texts and on reasoned deductions about
      their transmission." Feels that Johnson's edition was the last
      of the "old school" of editing.
5471 Knight, G. Wilson. "Timon of Athens and Its Dramatic Descendants."
      A Review of English Literature, II (October, 1961), 9-18.

A brief study of the themes of Timon of Athens and its influence on English drama and dramatists of the eighteenth and nineteenth centuries.

5472 Knight, L. H. "Stage Adaptations of Shakespeare, 1660-1900." Ph.D. University of Wales (Swansea), 1961.

5473 Lelyveld, Toby [Bookholtz]. Shylock on the Stage. Western Reserve University Press, 1960; London: Routledge, 1961. 149 pp.

A careful tracing of the Shylock role from the beginning to the present. Contains references to portrayals by Edmund Kean, William Charles Macready, Edwin Booth, and Charles Macklin.

5474 McManaway, James G. "A 'Hamlet' Reminiscence in 1660." Notes and Queries, CCVI (1961), 388.

In Thomas Jordan's Speech Made to ... the Lord General Monk.

5475 Moore, Robert E. "The Music to Macbeth." Musical Quarterly, XLVII (1961), 22-40.

On the eighteenth century "original musick."

5476 Rosenberg, Marvin. The Masks of Othello; the Search for the Identity of Othello, Iago, and Desdemona by Three Centuries of Actors and Critics. Berkeley: University of California Press, 1961. xii, 313 pp.

Pages 16-54 treat the Restoration and 18th-century interpretations of the play with discussion of Betterton, Quin, Garrick, Spranger Barry. Relies on critics' comments on the actors' interpretations of the roles.

5477 Camden, Carroll. "Songs and Choruses in The Tempest." Philological Quarterly, XLI (1962), 114-122.

Suggests that two songs in a unique copy of Songs and Choruses in the Tempest were written by Sheridan for production in 1777.

5478 Evans, G. Blakemore. "The Douai Manuscript--Six Shakespearean Transcripts (1694-95)." Philological Quarterly, XLI (1962), 158-172

Discusses transcripts of Twelfth Night, As Your Like It, The Comedy of Errors, Romeo and Juliet, Julius Caesar, and Macbeth.

5479 Stone, George Winchester. "The Poet and the Players." Proceedings of the American Philosophical Society, CVI (1962), 412-421.

Interpretations of Shakespeare by various actors, including Garrick.

5480 Banks, Howard Milton. "A Historical Survey of the Mise-en-Scene Employed in Shakespearean Productions from the Elizabethan Period to the Present." Ph.D. University of Southern California, 1963.

Considers what changes occurred in the structure of the stage

between 1660 and 1800, especially the scenic innovations of
Davenant.

5481 Brockbank, J. P. "Shakespeare and the Fashion of These Times."
Shakespeare Survey, XVI (1963), 30-41.
        Considers 18th century interpretations of Cleopatra's suicide
speech opening Act V, Scene ii of Antony and Cleopatra.

5482 Nichols, James W. "Shakespeare as a Character in Drama: 1679-
1899." Educational Theatre Journal, XV (1963), 24-32.

5483 Odell, George C. D. Shakespeare: From Betterton to Irving. New
York: Benjamin Blom, 1963. 2 vols.
        Reprint of Professor Odell's chronological history of Shake-
speare on the London stage from 1660 to 1902, first published
in 1920. Vol. I concentrates on stage production during the
theatrical careers of Betterton, Cibber, and Garrick. Illustrations.

5484 Sen, Sailendra Kumar. "Shakespeare as a Borrower: Kellet and
Eighteenth-Century Critics." Notes and Queries, New Ser., X
(1963), 332-334.
        Kellet's thesis about the gaps in Shakespeare's plays "was
one which seems to have been well understood and well illustrated
in Johnson's time."

5485 Smith, David Nicol, ed. Eighteenth Century Essays on Shakespeare.
Second Edition. Oxford: Clarendon Press, 1963. 340 pp.
        A new edition of an important work originally published by
Professor Smith in 1903. Especially noteworthy is his revised
commentary on Johnson.

5486 Spencer, Hazelton. Shakespeare Improved: the Restoration Versions
in Quarto and on the Stage. New York: Ungar, 1963. 406 pp.
        A new edition of the 1927 study of Shakespeare's plays pro-
duced during the Restoration from 1660 to 1710, the year of
Betterton's death.

5487 Thaler, Alwin. Shakespeare to Sheridan: A Book about the Theatre
of Yesterday and To-Day. New York: Benjamin Blom, 1963.
339 pp.
        Reprint of Thaler's 1922 study of the indebtedness of the
17th and 18th century theatre to that of Shakespeare and his
contemporaries. Points of comparison include players, managers, dramatists, financing, staging, publicity. Illustrations
and 3 appendices.

5488 Bell, M. "A Study of the History of the Criticism of Shakespeare's
Style." Ph.D. University of Birmingham, 1964.

5489 Brennecke, Ernest. Shakespeare in Germany, 1590-1700. Chicago:

The University of Chicago Press, 1964. 301 pp.

A translation of five German versions of Shakespeare's plays. A brief introduction of each work demonstrates the role played by quasi-Shakespearean material in the development of Shakespeare's reputation on the Continent.

5490 Hartnoll, Phyllis, editor. Shakespeare in Music. London: Macmillan and Company, 1964. 333 pp.

Essays on musical achievements which drew their inspiration directly from Shakespeare's plays and poems. In "Song and Part Song Settings of Shakespeare's Lyrics, 1660-1900," pp. 50-87, Charles Cudworth outlines the history of compositions written especially for theatrical productions of Shakespeare. Winton Dean, "Shakespeare and Opera," pp. 89-175, surveys briefly the operatic expressions of Purcell, Leveridge, and Smith. A "Catalogue of Musical Works Based on the Plays and Poetry of Shakespeare" is appended to the work.

5491 Ripley, J. D. "A Stage History of Julius Caesar 1599-1934." Ph.D. University of Birmingham, 1964.

5492 Spencer, T.B.J. "The Course of Shakespeare Criticism." Shakespeare's World. Edited by James Sutherland and Joel Hurtsfield. (London, 1964), 156-173.

Contains a brief survey of Restoration and 18th century Shakespearean scholarship.

5493 -----. "The Great Rival: Shakespeare and the Classical Dramatists." Shakespeare: 1564-1964. Edited by Edward A. Bloom. (Providence: Brown University Press, 1964), 177-193.

An account of critical comparisons between Shakespeare and the Ancients. Alludes to the comments of Johnson, Dryden, Rymer, and Collier.

5494 Brown, Arthur. "The Great Variety of Readers." Shakespeare Survey, XVIII (1965), 11-21.

A critical study of Shakespearean editions. Notes that the 18th century editors of Shakespeare established a tradition of publishing 'modern' texts designed for the general reading public and therefore containing a minimum of scholarly explication.

5495 Brown, F. Andrew. "Shakespeare and English Drama in the German Popular Journals, 1717-1759." Kentucky Foreign Language Quarterly, XII (1965), 13-27.

Presents samples and discussion of German journals that demonstrate an interest in Shakespeare and English drama even before Lessing's Literaturbrief. Includes references to a discussion of Moore's Gamester and Lillo's London Merchant in the Hamburgische Beytrage (1753).

5496 -----. "Shakespeare in Germany: Dryden, Langbaine, and the Acta

Eruditorum." The Germanic Review, XL (1965), 86-95.

Acta Eruditorum, a scholarly journal founded by Otto Mencke in 1682, set the tone of subsequent German studies in Shakespeare and Dryden with its introduction of the controversy regarding "ingenio" and "arte."

5497 Coleman, William S. E. "Shylock from Dogget to Macready." Ph.D. University of Pittsburgh, 1965.

This chronological account of the London productions of The Merchant of Venice reveals a change in attitude among Englishmen towards those of the Jewish race. Interpretations of Shylock rendered by Charles Macklin, Thomas King, John Henderson and John Kemble are analyzed in detail.

5498 Dean, Winton. "Shakespeare in the Opera House." Shakespeare Survey, XVIII (1965), 75-93.

Brief mention of Restoration and 18th century operatic adaptations of Shakespeare. A valuable list of composers, titles, and librettists of known operas based on Shakespeare's dramas concludes the article.

5499 Donohue, Joseph Walter, Jr. "Toward the Romantic Concept of Dramatic Character: Richard III and Macbeth in Criticism and Performance, 1740-1820." Ph.D. Princeton University, 1965. (Order No. 66-4991).

The 18th Century "closet" criticism of Johnson, Montague, and Whately, and the theatrical productions of Garrick and Mrs. Siddons reveal the increasing tendency to interpret Shakespeare's heroes in terms of their "mental processes."

5500 Fried, Gisela. "Das Charakterbild Shakespeares im 17. und 18. Jahrhundert." Deutsche Shakespeare-Gesellschaft West (Jahrbuch, 1965), 161-183.

Concerns 17th and 18th century critical assessments of Shakespeare's personal qualities.

5501 Geckle, George Leo. "A History of the Literary Criticism of Shakespeare's Measure for Measure." Ph.D. University of Virginia, 1965. (Order No. 66-3183).

Sees the eighteenth century criticism of Measure for Measure as primarily an outgrowth of the era's philosophical penchant for order and balance.

5502 Hoffman, D. S. "Some Shakespearian Music, 1660-1900." Shakespeare Survey, XVIII (1965), 94-101.

Traces the musical elements in Shakespeare's plays from Davenant's Macbeth to the late 18th century operatic interpretations of Mrs. Jordan, Michael Kelly, and Mrs. Crouch.

5503 Hyde, Mary. "Shakespeare's Head." Shakespeare Quarterly, XVI (1965), 139-143.

The Shakespeare portrait, discovered by Mr. Jacques Veller-

koop in 1962 and exhibited at the Morgan Library in 1964, probably belonged to Jacob Tonson (1656-1736), publisher, bookseller, and collector. It was probably viewed by Dryden,
Wycherley, Johnson, and many other writers of Tonson's
acquaintance.

5504 Jenkins, Harold. "'Hamlet' Then Till Now." Shakespeare Survey,
    XIII (1965), 34-45.

    An historical view of Hamlet's reputation. Early 18th century
    treatments of Hamlet stressed the virtue, boldness, and manli-
    ness of the hero (e.g. Betterton's portrayal). Those after 1763
    were hymned for their sensitivity in capturing the personality
    of an irresolute, inconsistent, and pathetic young man.

5505 Meldrum, Ronald Murray. "Changing Attitudes Toward Selected
    Characters of Shakespeare." Ph.D. Arizona State University,
    1965. (Order No. 65-10377).

    Interest in Shakespeare's characters during the Restoration
    and eighteenth century was both literary and theatrical. The
    acting style of David Garrick had a significant influence on
    contemporary interpretations of Shakespearian heroes.

5506 Merchant, W. Moelwyn. "Shakespeare 'Made Fit.'" Restoration
    Theatre. Edited by John Russell Brown and Bernard Harris.
    (Stratford-Upon-Avon Studies, 6). (London: Edward Arnold;
    New York: St. Martin's Press, 1965), 195-219.

    Discusses the principles used especially by Tate, Dryden,
    and Shadwell in adapting Shakespeare to the Restoration stage.

5507 Shattuck, Charles H. The Shakespeare Promptbooks: A Descriptive
    Catalogue. Urbana: University of Illinois Press, 1965. 553 pp.

    A catalogue describing all the marked copies of Shakespeare
    used in English-language professional theatre productions from
    the 1620's to 1961 that are available in public collections, in
    the production departments of the late Old Vic and the Festival
    theatres by the three Stratfords. Entries are arranged alpha-
    betically by the title of the play and then chronologically.

5508 Shoemaker. Neille. "The Aesthetic Criticism of Hamlet from
    1692 to 1699." Shakespeare Quarterly, XVI (1965), 99-103.

    The publication of replies to the studies of Thomas Rymer
    and Jeremy Collier made a beginning in the field of aesthetic
    criticism. James Drake, author of The Antient and Modern
    Stages Survey'd, Or, Mr. Collier's View of the Immorality
    and Profaneness of the English Stage Set in a True Light (1699),
    is entitled to rank as the first Hamlet critic.

5509 Weinmann, R. "Shakespeares Publikum und Platformbuhne im
    Spiegel klassizistischer Kritik (bei Rymer, Dryden, u.a.)."
    Bulletin de la Faculte des Lettres de Strasbourg, XLIII (Mai-
    Juin, 1965), 891-1007.

5510 "Acting Characteristics via EDP." Shakespeare Newsletter, XVI
       (1966), 49.
            A review of the Data Processing project of Ben R. Schneider,
       Jr. of Lawrence University whose work on The London Stage may
       lead to evidence for the interpretation of Shakespearean roles
       on the 18th-century English stage.
5511 Cosgrove, B. D. "Eighteenth-Century Attitudes to the Supernatural
       in Shakespeare." B. Litt. Oxford University (Balliol), 1966.
5512 Evans, G. Blakemore, ed. Shakespearean Prompt-books of the
       Seventeenth Century. Vol. LV: Part 1. (Published for the Biblio-
       graphical Society of the University of Virginia). Charlottesville:
       University Press of Virginia, 1966.
            Reproduces the text of the Smock Alley Hamlet (c. 1676-
       1679), the earliest prompt-book of the play now extant. In-
       cludes introduction and collations.
5513 Harbage, Alfred. Conceptions of Shakespeare. Cambridge: Harvard
       University Press, 1966. 164 pp.
            A series of five lectures with three related essays reprinted
       and revised for this edition. While references to the Restoration
       and 18th century are made throughout the book, Chapter 3,
       "These Our Actors," contains matter of special interest con-
       cerning Betterton and Garrick.
5514 Odell, G. C. D. Shakespeare from Betterton to Irving. With a
       new introduction by Robert Hamilton Ball. 2 vols. New York:
       Dover Publications, 1966.
            A paperback edition of the work originally published in 1920.
5515 Saunders, J. G. "Hamlet, a Survey of Its Textual History and of
       Present-day Problems, Illustrated Mainly from Act I." B. Litt.
       Oxford University (Worcester), 1966.
5516 Spencer, Christopher. "'Count Paris's Wife': Romeo and Juliet
       on the Early Restoration Stage." Texas Studies in Literature
       and Language, VII (1966), 309-316.
            Uses John Downes' description of the play's performance
       at Lincoln's Inn Fields in the early 1660's to discuss the
       possibilities of an adaptation before that of James Howard.
5517 Summers, Montague, ed. Shakespeare Adaptations. New York:
       Haskell House, 1966. 282 pp.
            A reprint of the 1922 edition of D'Avenant and Dryden's The
       Tempest (1670), Duffett's The Mock-Tempest (1675), and
       Tate's King Lear (1681). Includes introduction and notes.
5518 Carlisle, Carol J. "Hamlet's 'Cruelty' in the Nunnery Scene:
       The Actors' Views." Shakespeare Quarterly, XVIII (1967),
       129-140.
            A review of Actors' interpretations of the Nunnery scene
       includes references to Garrick, Charles Didbin and William
       Oxberry.

5519 Coleman, William S. E. "Post-Restoration Shylocks Prior to
      Macklin." Theatre Survey, VIII (May, 1967), 17-36.
          Feels that villainy rather than comedy was the role of
      Shylock prior to Macklin.
5520 Grover, P. R. "The Ghost of Dr. Johnson: L. C. Knights and
      D. A. Traversi on Hamlet." Essays in Criticism, XVII (1967),
      143-157.
          The criticism of L. C. Knights in An Approach to Hamlet
      and of D. A. Traversi in An Approach to Shakespeare reflects
      the pre-Romantic and now outdated moral criticism of Johnson.
5521 Gruber, Christian P. "Falstaff on an 18th Century Battlefield."
      Theatre Notebook, XXI (Spring, 1967), 120-121.
          Affirms that the I Henry IV plate from Robert Walker's
      edition of Shakespeare (London, 1734) provides authentic evi-
      dence of current stage practice.
5522 Kujoory, Parvin. "The Development of Shakespeare Biography
      From 1592 Through 1790." Ph.D. Catholic University of Amer-
      ica, 1967. (Order No. 67-15,450).
          Discusses biographers' scholarship, their sources for facts,
      and their opinions and attitudes. Includes a study of Rowe's
      biography and its use by Pope, Johnson, Warburton, and Steevens
5523 Marder, Louis. "Shakespeare Concordances: 1787-1967." Shake-
      speare Newsletter, XVII (1967), 33-34.
          Includes descriptions of concordances by Pope, Andrew
      Beckett, and Samuel Ayscough.
5524 Nilan, Mary Margaret. "The Stage History of The Tempest: A
      Question of Theatricality." Ph.D. Northwestern University,
      1967. (Order No. 67-15,305).
          Discusses how the theatricality of the play has been handled
      in productions over the years and how the various approaches
      have been received by audiences and reviewers. Includes a
      study of adaptations from 1667 to 1837.
5525 Smith, David Nichol. Shakespeare in the Eighteenth Century.
      New York: Oxford University Press, 1967.
          A reprint of the 1928 edition which examines the ways in
      which 18th century critics, scholars, and actors contributed
      to Shakespeare's fame.

Sheffield

5526 Wood, Frederick Thomas. "Sheffield Theatres in the Eighteenth
      Century." Transactions of the Hunter Archaeological Society,
      VI (1947), 98-116.
          A listing of references to known sources of evidence.

Sheridan, Elizabeth

5527 Sheridan, Elizabeth. Betsy Sheridan's Journal: Letters from
    Sheridan's Sister, 1784-1786 and 1788-1790. Edited by Wil-
    liam LeFavre. London: Eyre and Spottiswoode; New Brunswick;
    Rutgers University Press, 1960. xii, 223 pp.
        Correspondence of 6 years.

Sheridan, Frances

5528 Wadlington, Mary E. "Mrs. Frances Sheridan, Her Life and
    Works, Including a Study of Her Influence on Richard Brinsley
    Sheridan's Plays, and an Edition of Her Comedy, The Discovery."
    Ph.D. Yale University, 1914.
5529 Chew, Samuel Peaco, Jr. "The Life and Works of Frances
    Sheridan." Ph.D. Harvard University, 1937.
        A biographical and critical study of special interest to stu-
    dents of the drama because of the extended analysis of the
    sources and stage history of Mrs. Sheridan's three comedies.
5530 -----. "The Dupe: A Study of the 'Low.'" Philological Quarterly,
    XVIII (1939), 196-203.
        A study of audience reactions to The Dupe which shows
    how much public ideals of delicacy and decorum influenced
    the content of plays during this period.

Sheridan, Richard

bibliography

5531 Sichel, W. Sheridan, From New and Original Material; Including
    a Manuscript Diary by Georgiana, Duchess of Devonshire.
    2 vols. London: Constable & Co., Ltd., 1909.
        The bibliography of Sheridan's published and unpublished
    works was the most complete at the time. The work is based
    on much material found in the collection of the Sheridan family
    at Frampton Court. The work adds to, and corrects, material
    in the works by Thomas Moore, and Fraser Rae. Primary
    sources are used whenever possible.
5532 Howes, C. Catalogue of Books Mainly of the 17th and 18th Cen-
    turies from the Library of Richard Brinsley Sheridan, offered
    by C. Howes, St. Leonards-on-Sea, England. [Birmingham:
    F. Juckes, Ltd., 1923?] 36 pp.
        456 items arranged alphabetically; full bibliographical des-
    cription of each work with occasional notes.

5533 Rhodes, R. Crompton. "Sheridan Bibliography." Times Literary
      Supplement, June 17, 1926, p. 414.
          Asks for contributions to a proposed bibliography.
5534 -----. "Sheridan: A Study in Theatrical Bibliography." London
      Mercury, XV (February, 1927), 381-390.
          Reviews I. A. Williams, The Plays of Richard Brinsley
      Sheridan (1926). Recapitulates the printing history of Sheridan's
      plays and notes that Williams has printed the one reliable text.
5535 -----. "Some Aspects of Sheridan Bibliography." Library, Fourth
      Series, IX (December, 1928), 233-261.
          Discusses dramatic piracy in the Sheridan period.
5536 "Notes and News." The Bodleian Library Record, VI (1958), 393-
      400.
          Additions to the Sheridan collection.

letters

5537 Price, Cecil, ed. The Letters of Richard Brinsley Sheridan. 3
      vols. Oxford: The Clarendon Press, 1966.
          A chronological arrangement of 937 letters written by
      Sheridan between 1766 and 1816. Includes introduction and index.

dramatic works

5538 Sheridan, Richard Brinsley. The Dramatic Works of Richard
      Brinsley Sheridan. Edited by G. G. Sigmond. London: George
      Bell and Sons, 1902. 563 pp.
          An edition of the seven plays, without notes. There is a
      "Life of Sheridan" and "Verses to the Memory of Garrick."
5539 -----. Dramatic Works. With a Short Account of His Life by
      G.G.S. 2 vols. London: S. Bagster and Sons, Ltd., 1902.
          The Introduction, in the first volume, contains a biography
      with appreciations of plays.
5540 -----. Sheridan's Plays Now Printed As He Wrote Them. And
      His Mother's Unpublished Comedy, "A Journey to Bath."
      Edited by W. Fraser Rae. With an Introduction by Sheridan's
      Great-Grandson, the Marquess of Dufferin and Ava. London:
      David Nutt, 1902. xl, 318 pp.
          Contains the texts of The Rivals, St. Patrick's Day, The
      Duenna, The School for Scandal, The Critic, A Journey to
      Bath. The author says that he attempts to give Sheridan's own
      words, and supplements from Moore's edition, as printed by
      Murray in 1821.
5541 -----. Plays. The Rivals, St. Patrick's Day, The Duenna, A
      Trip to Scarborough, The School for Scandal, The Critic,

Pizarro. London and New York: Unit Library, Limited, 1903.
v, [3], 499 pp. (The Unit Library, No. 28).

This "issue" is based upon Moore's edition of 1821, with
references to W. Fraser Rae's edition of 1902, and to various
other editions. The editor says that some obvious misprints
have been collected. Some brief notes for each play.

5542 -----. The Plays of Richard Brinsley Sheridan. With Frontispiece
Portrait of the Author. London: Hutchinson & Co., 1906. v,
[3], 499 pp.

The text of the plays (The Rivals, St. Patrick's Day, The
Duenna, A Trip to Scarborough, The School for Scandal, The
Critic, Pizarro) is based on Moore's edition of 1821, with
references made to W. Fraser Rae's Sheridan's Plays (1902),
as well as to other editions. Some notes. No reason is given
for the edition.

5543 -----. The Plays of Richard Brinsley Sheridan. London: J. M.
Dent & Co.; New York: E. P. Dutton & Co. [1906]. viii, [2],
487, [1] pp. (Everyman's Library).

Contains: The Rivals, St. Patrick's Day, The Duenna, A
Trip to Scarborough, The School for Scandal, The Critic,
Pizarro. There is no indication of the editions used in prepar-
ing the present text. There are no notes.

5544 -----. Plays. London: Dent [1908]. 411 pp. (Everyman's Library.
Poetry and Drama).

Contains The Rivals, St. Patrick's Day, The Duenna, A
Trip to Scarborough, The School for Scandal, The Critic, and
Pizarro, with author's prefaces and dedications, and lists of
original cast. Reprinted in [1913], [1915], [1926], and [1928].

5545 -----. Dramatic Works. London, New York, Toronto, Melbourne:
Cassell and Company, Ltd., 1909. 427 pp. (The People's Library).

The texts of the six plays are given. There is no indication
of what editions have been followed, nor are there any notes. A
popular edition.

5546 -----. Plays. With an Introduction by R. Brimley Johnson. London:
Blackie & Son, Ltd. [1910]. xi, [1], 319 pp. (Red Letter Library).

The plays are: The Rivals, The School for Scandal, and The
Critic. Johnson, in his Introduction, gives no information on
why the edition, what edition was followed for the plays, and
no information on his critical apparatus. There are no notes.

5547 -----. Plays. Edited by Clayton M. Hamilton. New York: Macmillan, 1926. xxvi, 339 pp.

Includes The Rivals, St. Patrick's Day, The Duenna, The
School for Scandal, The Critic; with brief notes.

5548 -----. The Plays. Edited by Iolo A. Williams. London: Herbert

Jenkins, 1926. 384 pp.

R. C. Rhodes' discovery of Sheridan's final revised text of The School for Scandal has been here incorporated. The stand-ard text to date, with a concise biographical and critical preface.

5549 -----. The Dramatic Works of Richard Brinsley Sheridan. With Introduction and Notes by Joseph Knight. [London]: Oxford University Press, H. Milford [1927]. xxi, [4], [3]-494 pp.

5550 -----. The Plays and Poems. Edited by R. Crompton Rhodes. 3 vols. Oxford: Blackwell, 1928.

The purpose is to establish the most authentic texts for Sheridan's plays and poems. Valuable introductions and ap-pendices establish the play's proper setting, explain allusions, and note possible sources and analogues. Rhodes has attempted the impossible task of giving, at the same time, the "full and genuine" text of The School for Scandal as it was performed the first night, and "the last complete revision of the comedy ever made by Sheridan."

5551 -----. The Plays. Edited by John Hampden. London, Edinburgh, Paris [etc.]: Thomas Nelson & Sons, Ltd. [1937]. xi, [1], 542 pp.

The Rivals follows "The Third Edition Corrected," of 1776; St. Patrick's Day follows the Dublin edition of 1788, with an alternative ending from Cumberland's edition of 1831; The Duenna follows the Longman, 1794 London edition; A Trip to Scarborough follows the Wilkie 1781 London edition; The School for Scandal follows the Rhodes edition of 1928; The Critic fol-lows the T. Becket, 1781 London edition; Pizarro follows the first edition of 1799.

5552 -----. The Plays of Richard Brinsley Sheridan. London: Oxford University Press [1952]. viii, 536 pp. (The World's Classics).

This edition, in "The World's Classics" series, is sup-posed to be reset from a newly collated text. The Rivals (3rd ed., 1775), St. Patrick's Day (The 1788 edition, together with Cumberland's additions of 1829), The Duenna (1794 edition), School for Scandal (1799 edition, with the Crewe markings, and emendations from Cumberland's edition of 1826), The Critic (1st edition, 1781), A Trip to Scarborough (1st edition, 1781), Pizarro (1st edition, 1799). No notes.

5553 -----. Complete Plays. With an Introduction by Tyrone Guthrie. London and Glasgow: Collins, 1954. 415, [1] pp.

Contains The Rivals, St. Patrick's Day, The Duenna, A Trip to Scarborough, The School for Scandal, The Critic, Pizarro. First published in Collins Pocket Classics, 1930. The editor does not indicate what editions were used in preparing the present edition. There are no notes.

5554 -----. Six Plays. Edited by Louis Kronenberger. (Mermaid Dramabook, MD5). New York: Hill & Wang, 1957.

several plays

5555 -----. The Rivals and The School for Scandal. With an Introduc-tion by Henry Morley. London, Paris, New York, and Mel-bourne: Cassell and Company, Limited, 1904. iv, 5-191 pp. (Cassell's National Library).

The editor does not indicate what editions were used in pre-paring the present text. There are no notes. Morley's two-page introduction sheds no new light on the plays.

5556 -----. The Major Dramas of Richard Brinsley Sheridan. The Rivals, The School for Scandal, The Critic. Edited, with In-troduction and Notes by George Henry Nettleton. Boston [etc.]: Ginn & Co. [1906]. cxvii, [1], 331 pp.

The Rivals is taken from Fraser's Sheridan's Plays (1902), after collating the first three editions at Yale University; The School for Scandal text is taken from Fraser's work, as is The Critic. Various minor changes. Notes.

5557 -----. The Rivals and The School for Scandal. (Both plays slightly abridged). Edited by John Peile. Glasgow and Bombay: Blackie and Son, Limited, 1911. 111 pp. (The Plain-Text Plays).

A brief introduction. There is no indication of the editions used in preparing this edition. Only a few brief notes.

5558 -----. The Rivals and The School for Scandal. Edited with Intro-duction and Notes by Will David Howe. New York, London: The Macmillan Co., 1918. xxxiii, [1], 319 pp.

This edition, published first in 1907, was reprinted in 1910, 1911, 1912, 1913, 1914, 1916, and 1917. Although the editor mentions "some of the best editions," he does not say what editions he bases his texts upon. There are some notes for each play.

5559 -----. The Rivals and The School for Scandal. Edited with intro-duction and notes by Will David Howe. New York [etc.]: The Macmillan Co., 1925.

Very brief biographical introduction; texts of plays, including author's preface, and a few notes glossing the texts.

5560 -----. The Critic, and The Rehearsal, by George Villiers, Duke of Buckingham. Edited by A. G. Barnes. London: Methuen, 1927. [7], 168 pp.

A critical edition showing the relation of these burlesques to the serious drama of the time. The introduction gives brief accounts of the each playwright and of the intervening dramatic literature. Sheridan's The Critic is an attack on contemporary drama as a whole.

5561 -----. Three Plays of Sheridan. The Rivals, The School for Scandal, And The Critic. Edited by Guy Boas. London: Edward Arnold & Co. [1928]. xv, [1], 294 pp.

A student's edition. The editor does not indicate the editions used in preparing the present text. There are notes, essay questions, and specific questions on each play.

5562 -----. Three Plays: The Rivals; School for Scandal; The Critic. Edited by A. J. J. Ratcliff. London and Edinburgh: Thomas Nelson & Sons, Ltd., 1937. 297 pp.

A brief introduction is given for each play. Following each play is a series of questions, seemingly for students to answer. There is no indication what edition is followed. There are no notes.

5563 -----. The Critic and The School for Scandal. Edited by W. H. Low and A. S. Collins. London: University Tutorial Press, 1938 xxiii, 20-205 pp.

5564 -----. The School for Scandal and The Critic. Edited by C. H. Lockitt. London, New York, Toronto: Longmans, Green and Co., 1939. [8], 212 pp. (The Heritage of Literature Series. Section B. No. 16).

Lockitt says that the text of this edition has been carefully collated with Moore's edition of 1821. There are notes. There is a discussion of each play, which takes in general points, plot, and text. Appendices are devoted to dramatic method, style, and audience.

individual plays

5565 -----. The Critic. Edited by Philip Carr. London: Alston Rivers, 1905. 75 pp.

The present text is taken from Fraser Rae's edition of Sheridan's Plays. There are no notes.

5566 -----. The Plays of Sheridan. The Critic. With an Introduction by Edmund Gosse and a Plate Representing King as "Puff." London: William Heinemann, 1905. x, [2], 70 pp. (Favourite Classics).

There is no indication of the edition used in preparing the present text. There are no notes.

5567 -----. The Critic. With an Introduction by Edmund Gosse. New York: E. P. Dutton & Co. [etc., etc.], 1905. xii, 70 pp. (Favourite Classics: The Plays of Sheridan).

A brief introduction pointing out what Sheridan owed to previous burlesques, and wherein he differed. Includes Sheridan dedicatory epistle.

5568 -----. The Critic; or, A Tragedy Rehearsed; a Dramatic Piece in

Two Acts by Richard Brinsley Sheridan. Acting version of the Yale University Dramatic Association, with a preface by William Lyon Phelps...and an introduction by George Henry Nettleton... New Haven: Published under the supervision of A. A. Gammell, 1911. xx, 44 pp.

> The text is a modern acting version, though prepared with reference to manuscript and early printed editions; the preface enumerates activities of the Association; the introduction points out the sentimental and tragic styles that Sheridan effectively burlesqued.

5569 -----. The Critic; or, An Opera Rehearsed. Opera in Two Acts. The text by Richard Brinsley Sheridan, arranged for the opera by L. Cairns James and the Composer. The Music by Charles V. Stanford. London: Boosey & Co. [1915]. 32 pp.

> There is no indication of the edition used in preparing the present text. There are no notes.

5570 -----. The Critic. Edited by W. H. Low, and A. S. Collins. London: W. B. Clive [1927]. 83 pp. (University Tutorial Press).

> There is no indication of the edition used in preparing the text. The notes are placed at the end of the play. The Introduction is a summary of Sheridan's life, and a short analysis of The Critic.

5571 -----. The Critic, Or A Tragedy Rehearsed. A Farcical Comedy In Three Acts. London and Edinburgh: Thomas Nelson and Sons, Ltd. [1931]. 72 pp. (The Nelson Playbooks, No. 105).

> There is no indication of the edition used in preparing this text. The notes are placed at the foot of the page.

5572 -----. The Critic Or A Tragedy Rehearsed. Edited by John Hampden. New York: E. P. Dutton and Co.; London & Toronto: J. M. Dent & Sons, Ltd., 1931. 191 pp.

> A student's edition. No indication of the text used in preparing this edition. Notes are placed at the foot of the page. A Commentary is devoted to The Critic and its forerunners, the first night, Sheridan and his times. There are student exercises, and an extract from The West Indian by Richard Cumberland.

5573 -----. The Critic. Edited by Robert Herring. London: Macmillan, 1935. xxxii, 92 pp.

5574 -----. The Critic; Or, A Tragedy Rehearsed. Edited by R. F. Patterson. London: Blackie & Son, 1935. xxviii, 83 pp.

5575 -----. "The Critic." Three Comedies. Edited by G. P. W. Earle. London: Ginn & Co., 1936. ix, 309 pp.

> Also included in the volume are The Knight of the Burning Pestle and The Importance of Being Earnest.

5576 -----. The Critic. London: James Brodie, 1939. 40 pp.

5577 -----. "The Critic." Types of English Drama. Edited by John
      William Ashton. (New York: The Macmillan Co., 1940), 533-
      580.
           The text of the play is preceeded by an introduction to burles-
      que drama and Sheridan's place in the genre. Notes to the text a:
      meagre; most are glosses.

5578 -----. The Critic, or A Tragedy Rehearsed; edited and introduced
      by J. C. Trewin. London: Falcon Educational Books [1949]. 88
      pp. (The Falcon Plays).
           A brief introduction giving an account of the tone of the play,
      and its relationship to other Sheridan plays, with a note on its
      performance history. No notes; a short chronological table of
      Sheridan's life.

5579 -----. The Critic, or A Tragedy Rehearsed. Edited with an Intro-
      duction, Translation and Notes by Germaine Landre-Augier.
      Paris: Aubier, Editions Montaigne, Collection Bilingue, 1963.
      231 pp.
           English text with French translation on opposite pages. The
      introduction in French reviews current scholarship on the play.

5580 -----. The Duenna; a Comic Opera in Three Acts. London: Martin
      Secker, 1924. 87 pp.
           But for the text of the opera, this edition contains nothing
      but the author's date and the date of the first performance
      (1775).

5581 -----. The Duenna. Edited by Nigel Playfair. London: Constable,
      1925. 27, 105 pp.
           An edition with a preface and reproductions of playbills and
      title pages.

5582 -----. The Rivals; a Comedy. New York: The Century Co., 1902.
      206 pp.
           Introduction reprinted from "Autobiography of Joseph Jef-
      ferson." List of original actors (Covent Garden, 1775). Omits
      author's preface, and has no notes.

5583 -----. The Plays of Sheridan. The Rivals. With an Introduction
      by Edmund Gosse, and a Plate representing Dowton as 'Sir
      Anthony Absolute.' London: William Heinemann, 1905. xiv,
      [2], 102 pp. (Favourite Classics).
           There is no indication of the edition used in preparing this
      text. There are no notes.

5584 ----. The Rivals. Edited with Introduction and Notes by Joseph
      Quincy Adams, Jr. Boston: Houghton Mifflin Company, 1910.
      129 pp. (Riverside Literature Series).
           Reprint of the first edition.

5585 -----. The Rivals. Edited with Introduction and Notes by T.
      Balston. Oxford: At the Clarendon Press, 1913. xi, [1], 110 pp.

The editor says that he is indebted to G. H. Nettleton's edition of The Major Dramas (Boston, 1906), and to W. H. Low's edition of The Rivals. He prints the title page from the 6th London edition, 1798. Introduction and notes.

5586 -----. The Rivals. A Comedy. London: The Holerth Press [1924]. 139 pp. (The Holerth Library).

There is no introduction, or attempt to indicate what edition has been used in preparing the present text. There are no notes.

5587 -----. The Rivals. Edited by John Hampden for Use in Schools. With Introduction and Full Acting Appendix. New York: E. P. Dutton & Company; London & Toronto: J. M. Dent & Sons [1925]. 187 pp.

This edition is designed for performance by amateurs.

5588 -----. The Rivals. Edited by W. H. Low, and A. S. Collins. London: W. B. Clive [1927]. 120 pp. (University Tutorial Press).

The editors do not indicate what text forms the basis of the present edition. The short Introduction is very general. There are notes.

5589 -----. The Rivals. A Comedy. London, Edinburgh: T. Nelson and Sons, Ltd. [1929]. 110 pp. (The Nelson Playbooks. Edited by John Hampden).

The editor follows "The Third Edition Corrected," 1776. Spelling, punctuation, and capitalization have been modernized, and a few phrases omitted. Several notes at the bottom of the page of text.

5590 -----. The Rivals. With Introduction and Notes by Robert Herring. London: Macmillan and Co., Ltd., 1929. xxviii, 131 pp. (English Literature Series, No. 119).

A student's edition, with notes and questions. The editor does not indicate upon what edition he bases the present text.

5591 -----. The Rivals, A Comedy, As It Was First Acted at the Theatre-Royal in Covent Garden... Edited from the Larpent MS. by Richard Little Purdy. Oxford: Clarendon Press, 1935. lii, 122 pp.

The Larpent MS. printed beside the text of the first edition, 1775. The introduction discusses the production of The Rivals and the history and significance of the Larpent MS.

5592 -----. "The Rivals." Famous Plays in Miniature. Edited by Roger Wheeler. (Boston: W. H. Baker, 1935), 101-135.

An abridged acting script in three acts designed to be performed in thirty minutes.

5593 -----. The Rivals, Arranged and Adapted by Kenneth Weston Turner. Chicago: The Dramatic Publishing Company [c. 1941]. xxv, 103 pp.

A 3-act adaptation with simplified staging directions based
on the revised text used for production January 28, 1775, but
including lines from the Larpent MS. prepared January 9,
1775. Extensive production notes.

5594 -----. The Rivals. Edited by Alan S. Downer. New York: Appleton-Century-Crofts, 1953. 99 pp.

This edition contains a critical introduction and a selected
bibliography.

5595 Sheridan, Richard Brinsley. The Rivals. Edited by Vincent F.
Hopper and Gerald B. Lahey. With a note on the staging [by]
George L. Hersey. Illustrated by Fritz Kredel. Great Neck,
N.Y.: Barron's Educational Series [1958]. 176 pp. (Theatre
Classics for the Modern Reader).

Besides a description and diagram of the late 18th-century
stage, the edition contains a brief biography of Sheridan, a
history and analysis of the play, and a very brief bibliography,
with a few notes glossing the text. Although the editors twice
describe Sheridan's revision of the original text of The Rivals,
they do not note exactly which text is here printed.

5596 -----. The Rivals. Edited by A. Norman Jeffares. London: Macmillan; New York: St. Martin's Press, 1967. (English Classics-
New Series).

Includes general introduction, notes, critical extracts, and
selected bibliography.

5597 -----. The School for Scandal; a Comedy in Five Acts. New York
[etc.]: Samuel French, c. 1901. (American Academy of Dramatic
Arts Edition of Standard Plays, 2).

"Remodeled and rearranged by Augustin Daly, with marginal
notes by Fred. Williams." Text of an 1874 American revival;
notes give stage directions.

5598 -----. The Plays of Sheridan. The School for Scandal. With an
Introduction by Edmund Gosse, and a Portrait of Sheridan
after the painting by Gainsborough. London: William Heinemann, 1905. x, [2], 110 pp. (Favourite Classics).

There is no indication of the edition used in preparing the
text. There are no notes.

5599 -----. The School for Scandal. Collated and edited by Hanson
Hart Webster. Boston: Houghton, Mifflin [1917]. liii, 161 pp.
(Riverside College Classics).

5600 -----. The School for Scandal. A Comedy. London: The Holerth
Press [1924]. 106 pp. (The Holerth Library).

There is no indication of the edition used in preparing this
text. There are no notes.

5601 -----. The School for Scandal. With Introduction and Notes by
Robert Herring. London: Macmillan & Co., Limited, 1927.

xv, [1], 133, [1] pp.

A student's edition, with a brief introduction, notes, questions, and a list of subjects for short essays. The editor follows the edition of the plays by Iolo Williams.

5602 -----. Sheridan's School for Scandal. Edited by E. M. Jebb. Oxford: At the Clarendon Press, 1928. 112 pp.

The text of the play is taken, with the permission of Crompton
Rhodes, from that used by Iolo Williams in his edition of the
Plays (1926). Some variants between the 1821 (John Murray)
text, as followed in the Oxford 1906 edition, and the Crewe
Dublin text are recorded in the Notes. Includes early sketches
for the play.

5603 -----. The School for Scandal... Edited by J. A. G. Bruce. London & Toronto: J. M. Dent & Sons, Ltd.; New York: E. P. Dutton and Co. [1928]. 191, [1] pp. (The King's Treasuries of
Literature).

A student's edition with footnotes, a Commentary on the play,
the writer, and "Five Days in Lady Teazle's Diary," as well
as suggested exercises, an acting appendix, and floor plans.
There is no indication of the edition used in preparing this text.

5604 -----. The School for Scandal. Edited, with an Introduction, by
R. Crompton Rhodes. The Decorations by Thomas Lowinsky.
Oxford: Printed at the Shakespeare Head Press, Stratford-upon-
Avon and published for the Press by Basil Blackwell, 1930.
xxvii, 145 pp.

Large paper edition of 475 copies. This edition prepared by
collation of Thomas Moore work on the manuscript sent to Mrs.
Crewe and the 1826 edition. The editor says that he has, however, omitted the minutiae of collation, which are set out in
his edition of Sheridan's Plays and Poems.

5605 -----. The School for Scandal. A Comedy. London and Edinburgh:
Thomas Nelson and Sons, Ltd. [1931]. vii, [1], 9-116 pp. (The
Nelson Playbooks, No. 104).

The editor does not indicate the edition used in preparing
the present text. There are footnotes.

5606 -----. The School for Scandal. London: James Brodie, Ltd. [1932].
64 pp. (The Brodie Books, Number Eighty-Five).

There is no indication of the edition used in preparing this
text. There are no footnotes, introduction, etc. Only the text.

5607 -----. The School for Scandal. Edited by A. S. Collins. London:
University Tutorial Press, 1938. xviii, 84-205 pp.

A separate issue of pp. 84-205 of the edition of The Critic
and The School for Scandal published in one volume in the
same year.

5608 -----. The School for Scandal. The Rivals. The Critic. London:

G. Martin [1947]. 268 pp.

A brief, anonymous, biographical introduction; no notes on the texts; includes Sheridan's preface to The Rivals and dedicatory epistle to The Critic.

5609 -----. The School for Scandal. Introduction by Laurence Olivier. London: Cassell, for the Folio Society, 1949. 120 pp.

A souvenir edition, illustrating the Old Vic production. The introduction describes the problems of producing and acting in the play, and notes particularly the differences between modern and eighteenth century lighting technique.

5610 -----. The School for Scandal. Edited by John Loftis. New York: Appleton-Century-Crofts, 1966. (Crofts Classics).

With introduction, notes, and selected bibliography.

5611 -----. The School for Scandal. Edited by A. Norman Jeffares. London: Macmillan; New York: St. Martin's Press, 1967.

Besides general introduction, notes, critical extracts, and selected bibliography, this edition includes two appendices: one on Sheridan's rewriting of the play taken from Thomas Moore's Memoirs (1825) and the other on details of the play's history from R. Crompton Rhodes' Harlequin Sheridan (1933).

5612 -----. "St. Patrick's Day; or, The Scheming Lieutenant." Golden Book Magazine. VII (March, 1928), 351-360.

Reprints the two-act play.

selections

5613 -----. Selections from Comedies and Speeches; also Verses to the Memory of Garrick and Anecdotes and Witty Sayings. New York and London: Street and Smith, 1902. (Street and Smith Little Classics).

Very brief selections from The Rivals, The School for Scandal, and The Critic, with slightly longer extracts from eleven speeches, and an introduction by Arthur D. Hall.

5614 -----. The Quarrel Scene (Curwen's Editon, 4024). From "The School for Scandal." London: J. Curwen & Sons, Ltd. [1912]. 6 pp.

Simply a reprinting of the scene.

5615 -----. An Ode to Scandal together with a Portrait. Edited by R. Crompton Rhodes. Oxford: Blackwell, 1927. 46 pp.

Reprints, with the two poems, two essays on the correct text of The School for Scandal, and scandal as a theme which continually interested Sheridan.

5616 -----. Puff's Masterpiece. Arranged from Sheridan's The Critic, by Nora Ratcliff. London [etc.]: Thomas Nelson & Sons, Ltd., 1937. 48 pp.

Puff's Masterpiece is adapted from acts two and three of
The Critic, and written as one act. The arranger gives some
advice about the play, as well as hints as to producing it.

translations

5617 -----. Sheridan's "Lasterschule." [Edited and translated by]
V. G. Humbert. Berlin: F. Tontane & Co., 1904. 104 pp.
5618 -----. "School for Scandal, Act IV, Scene 1." Translated into
Greek comic iambics by A. E. F. Spencer. Oxford, 1909. 15
pp. (Gaisford Prize. Greek Verse. English and Greek Texts).
Recited in the Sheldonian Theatre, June 23, 1909.
5619 -----. L'École de la Médisance. Edited and translated by A.
Barbeau. Paris: La Renaissance du Livre, 1925. 170 pp.
French translation of the play, an account of Sheridan's
plays, and two acts of The Critic.

biography and criticism

5620 "Acting Good and Evil." The Saturday Review, LXXXIX (April
7, 1900), 424-425.
A review of a contemporary Haymarket production of The
Rivals with comments of Sheridan's character drawing of Mrs.
Malaprop and Lydia Languish.
5621 Hartmann, Hermann. Sheridan's School for Scandal. Beiträge zur
Quellenfrage. Königsberg i. Pr.: Hartungsche Buchdruckerei
[1900]. 46 pp.
Refutes various speculations on the play's models, especially
the speculations in Thomas Moore's Memoirs of the Life of the
Right Honourable Richard Brinsley Sheridan (2 vols. Philadelphia,
1826). Scene-by-scene summary and analysis of the play and
of Sheridan's two versions of an early satirical sketch, "The
Slanderers."
5622 Street, G. S. "Sheridan and Mr. Shaw." Blackwood's Magazine,
CLXVII (June, 1900), 832-836.
Comparison of Sheridan's The Rivals with Shaw's You Never
Can Tell, and also a comparison of comic characters in Congreve and Sheridan which concludes that Congreve, not Sheridan,
should be regarded as the "great and permanent exemplar" of
witty English comedy.
5623 Wedmore, Frederick. "Notes on Players and Old Plays." The 19th
Century, XLVIII (1900), 249-255.
A comparison of the dramatic art of Goldsmith and Sheridan,
specifically She Stoops to Conquer and School for Scandal.

5624 Oliphant, Mrs. Margaret [Oliphant (Wilson)]. Sheridan. New
      York and London: Harper & Brothers, 1901. 199 pp. (English
      Men of Letters).
          Apparently precisely the same text as that published by
      Fowle, "Makers of Literature" series. No way to determine
      (internally) which came first.

5625 Rhodes, Crompton. "An 'Authentic' Version of Sheridan." Times
      Literary Supplement, July 4, 1902, p. 198.
          A review of Fraser Rae's volume of Sheridan's plays. In-
      cludes comments on the way the plays were originally per-
      formed and produced.

5626 Armes, Prof. W. D. "The Source of Sheridan's Rivals." Trans-
      actions and Proceedings of the American Philological Associa-
      tion, XXXIV (1903), cv-cvii.
          A discussion of the close similarities of plot, important
      characters, and principal incidents between The Rivals and
      Smollett's Humphry Clinker.

5627 Green, Emanuel. Thomas Linley, Richard Brinsley Sheridan,
      and Thomas Mathews: Their Connection with Bath. Bath: At the
      Herald Office, 1903. 81 pp.
          An account of Sheridan's elopement with the granddaughter
      of Bath musician Thomas Linley and Sheridan's subsequent duel
      with Thomas Mathews. Suggests that some of the incidents sur-
      rounding these events inspired School for Scandal.

5628 Adams, J[oseph] Q[uincy]. "The Original Performance of The
      Rivals." The Nation, XC (April, 1910), 374-375.
          Letter to the editor defending the fact that The Rivals was
      produced only once (January 17) before it was withdrawn rather
      than twice as claimed by Fitzgerald, Sichel, B. Matthews,
      Aitken and others.

5629 -----. "The Text of Sheridan's The Rivals." Modern Language
      Notes, XXV (1910), 171-173.
          Considers the various editions of The Rivals to Nettleton's
      and concludes that the only complete and authoritative text is
      that of the first edition.

5630 Bensley, Edward. "R. B. Sheridan and Bishop Hall." Notes and
      Queries, 11th Ser., III (February 11, 1911), 104.
          Finds resemblance between a line in The Rivals, ". . .
      she has a most observing thumb," and the opening words in
      Book VI of Joseph Hall's Virgidemiae, edited by William
      Thompson, 1753.

5631 Black, Clementina. The Linleys of Bath. London: Martin Secker,
      1911. 339 pp.
          A biography of the Linley family with emphasis upon them
      as people of talent and charm and particularly upon Elizabeth,

her career and her courtship and marriage with Richard B. Sheridan.

5632 Green, Emanuel. Sheridan and Mathews at Bath. A Criticism of the Story as Told in the Several Sheridan Biographies. London: Harrison & Sons, 1912. 56 pp.

A somewhat elongated study, attempting to put straight the would-be love affair triangle, with Sheridan, Mathews and a young lady of Bath. Green concentrates on attempting to show that Mr. Walter Sichel's work is not quite correct on the matter. Letters, accusations, etc., are printed.

5633 Milne, James Mathewson. Molière and Sheridan. Glasgow, 1912.

5634 Sadler, Michael Thomas Harvey. The Political Career of Richard Brinsley Sheridan. Followed by some hitherto unpublished letters of Mrs. Sheridan. Oxford: B. H. Blackwell [etc., etc.] 1912. 87 pp. (The Stanhope Essay for 1912).

The facts of Sheridan's political career, especially of his relations with the Prince of Wales, are set forth with documentation. Sheridan's failure as a politician, as well as his changes of conviction, is seen as a result not of insincerity, but of conflicting commitments to patriotism and liberty, or fluent oratory which did not always express his convictions, and of vanity.

5635 Graham, Harry. Splendid Failures. London: E. Arnold, 1913. 268 pp.

5636 Steuber, Fritz. Sheridans "Rivals." Entstehungsgeschichte und Beitrage zu einer deutschen Theatergeschichte des Stuckes. Borna-Leipzig: Robert Noske, 1913. 99 pp.

A short history of The Rivals in England--the causes of its first-night failure and subsequent success in London and the provinces--together with a discussion of the translation of the play in the Hamburg theatre and the Heimeroche adaptation in Stuttgart.

5637 Bayley, A. R. "A Note on Sheridan." Notes and Queries, 11th Ser., X (July-December, 1914), 61-63, 81-83.

Some notes on the insertions found in a first edition (1825) of Moore's life of Sheridan.

5638 Elias, Edith L. In Georgian Times. Boston: Little, Brown and Company, 1914. 272 pp.

5639 Monahan, Michael. Nova Hibernia; Irish Poets and Dramatists of Today and Yesterday. New York: Kennerly, 1914. 274 pp.

Pages 267-274 provide a brief sketch of Sheridan. Failed to produce plays of comparable worth after School for Scandal on account of dissipation, laziness, and feeling that a playwright was out of tune with society.

5640 Beers, Henry A. "Sheridan." Connecticut Wits and Other Essays.
(New Haven: Yale University Press, 1920), 159-178
An appreciation of Sheridan as the great comic playwright
of the late 18th century.

5641 Gosse, Edmund, ed. The School for Scandal by Richard Brinsley
Sheridan. New York: Dutton & Co., 1920. (Heinemann's Favorite
Classics Series).

5642 Hewlett, Maurice Henry. "Sheridan as Maniac." In A Green Shade;
a Country Commentary. (London: G. Bell and Sons, 1920), 105-
118.
Discusses the relationship of Sheridan and Lady Bessbor-
ough, Mother of Lady Caroline Lamb; Sheridan, Hewlett concludes, was either a bad rogue or a madman.

5643 Williams, Iolo A. "Richard Brinsley Sheridan." Seven 18th Century Bibliographies. (London: Dulau & Co., 1924), 210-239.
An annotated, descriptive bibliography of first editions
of Sheridan's works, arranged chronologically (pp. 210-239).

5644 "Barry V. Jackson's Design for The Rivals, Act I, Scene 1."
Theatre Arts Monthly, IX (April, 1925), 253.
An illustration.

5645 Rhodes, R. Crompton. "The Early Editions of Sheridan." Times
Literary Supplement, September 17, 1925, p. 599; September
24, 1925, p. 617.
The undated duodecimo edition of The Dramatic Works (ca.
1797) is "an impoverished paraphrase," undoubtedly pirated;
discusses other early editions, and announces the discovery
of the text of The School for Scandal as revised and approved
by Sheridan, the Dublin 1799 edition.

5646 Roberts, W. "Sheridan's School for Scandal." Times Literary
Supplement, October 15, 1925, p. 675.
Adds a surreptitious Dublin edition of 1786 to those listed
by R. C. Rhodes (TLS, September 17, 24, 1925).

5647 Atkinson, J. B. "Sheridan--Whom the Gods Loved." North American Review, CCXXIII (December/January/February, 1926-
1927), 645-655.
On the contradictions in his character, his quixotic nature,
and his remarkable career.

5648 "The Duenna." Theatre Arts Monthly, X (September, 1926), 645.
The set for Alexander Dean's production of Sheridan's play.

5649 Hoffman, Rudolf Stephan. Die Lästerschule. Komische Oper in
Drei Akten. Dichtung nach Sheridans "School For Scandal."
Musik von Paul von Klenau. Wein, New York: Universal-Edition
A. G., 1926. 62, [1] pp.
Text in German. No introduction, notes, etc.

5650 H.[orsnell], H.[orace]. "Period Farce." Outlook (London), LVIII

(December 18, 1926), 609.

Reviews Sheridan's The Critic, a performance by A. Nicoll's company at the East London College Theatre.

5651 Matthews, Brander. "Old Playwrights and Modern Playbooks." Literary Digest International Book Review, IV (June, 1926), 428-429.

Reviews Nigel Playfair's edition of Sheridan's Duenna (1925) and comments on the play's acting history.

5652 Panter, George W. "Early Editions of Sheridan." Times Literary Supplement, April 15, 1926, p. 283.

Offers an autographed copy of the 1799 Dublin edition of the play as evidence that Sheridan considered it nearest his original ms.

5653 Rhodes, R. Crompton. "Sheridan Apocrypha." Times Literary Supplement, August 26, 1926, p. 564.

"The General Fast: a Lyric Ode: With a Form of Prayer proper to the occasion and a Dedication to the King by the Author of the Duenna" is not by Sheridan.

5654 G.[abriel], G.[ilbert] W. "School for Scandal Is 150 Years Old." Mentor, XV (May, 1927), 8-11.

An appreciation, tracing the background of composition of the comedy, with an illustration of the screen scene in the performance by Augustin Daly's company in 1891, and a 1778 print of the principals in the cast and one of Sheridan.

5655 Sedgwick, W.B. "Two Medieval Parallels to 'The Critic.'" Times Literary Supplement, May 26, 1927, p. 375.

Concerning a jeu d'esprit in The Critic.

5656 Smedley, Constance. "An Undiscovered Heroine." Bookman, LXXII (July, 1927), 210-212.

Julia is the heroine in The Rivals, not Lydia or Mrs. Malaprop.

5657 Chapman, R. W. "Ye for The." Times Literary Supplement, April 26, 1928, p. 314.

Replies to M. J. Ryan (TLS, March 22, 1928), noting that ye as a contraction for the in mss. of The School for Scandal is not unusual for the time.

5658 Gabriel, Miriam and Paul Mueschke. "Two Contemporary Sources of Sheridan's The Rivals." Publications of the Modern Language Association, XLIII (March, 1928), 237-250.

Attempts to trace the main plot to Garrick's Miss in Her Teens and the sub-plot to Colman's Deuce Is in Him.

5659 Lawrence, W. J. "The Text of 'The School for Scandal.'" Times Literary Supplement, April 5, 1928, p. 257.

Replies to M. J. Ryan (TLS, March 22, 1928) that a Drury Lane prompt copy of "The School for Scandal" is extant at Harvard.

5660 Rhodes, R.Crompton. "The Text of 'The School for Scandal.'"
Times Literary Supplement, April 26, 1928, pp. 313-314.
Replies to M. J. Ryan (TLS, March 22, 29, 1928), an-
nouncing his own critical edition of Sheridan's plays.

5661 -----. "The Text of 'The School for Scandal.'" Times Literary
Supplement, May 24, 1928, p. 396.
The Dublin edition of 1780 is the editio princeps of the
"spurious" text.

5662 Ryan, M. J. "The Text of 'The School for Scandal.'" Times Literary Supplement, March 22, 1928, p. 212; March 29, 1928, p.
240.
Iolo A. Williams's Dublin 1799 text of The School for Scandal
in The Plays of Richard Brinsley Sheridan (1926) claims to be
the one reliable text, but in fact includes many silent emendation
Ryan makes numerous corrections and provides a collation of
Williams's text and the Dublin 1799 edition.

5663 -----. "'The School for Scandal' and the Round 'S.'" Times Liter-
ary Supplement, April 19, 1928, p. 290.
Continues his discussion (TLS, March 22, 1928) of the
"Ewling" edition of the play.

5664 -----. "The Text of 'The School for Scandal.'" Times Literary
Supplement, May 10, 1928, p. 358.
Defends his collation as not confined to "trivial points" (R.
C. Rhodes, TLS, April 26, 1928).

5665 -----. "The Text of 'The School for Scandal.'" Times Literary
Supplement, June 7, 1928, p. 430.
Replies to R. C. Rhodes (TLS, May 24, 1928), saying that
he (Ryan) was the first to uncover the 1780 edition as the first.

5666 Bateson, F.W. "The Text of Sheridan." Times Literary Supplement, November 28, 1929, p. 998; December 5, 1929, p. 1029.
Announces the discovery at the Huntington Library of the MS.
of the first acted version of The Rivals and of Sheridan's final
revised edition. Favors the text of The School for Scandal
found in the Works of 1821, printed by John Murray.

5667 MacCarthy, Desmond. "An Old Comedy Very Much Revived."
New Statesman, XXXIV (December 14, 1929), 329-330.
Reviews the Kingsway Theatre performance. The play is a
cross between artificial and sentimental comedy.

5668 Playfair, Nigel. "Faulkland on the Stage." Times Literary Supplement, January 10, 1929, p. 28.
The part of Faulkland can be made funny, as Claude Rains
has shown.

5669 Rhodes, Raymond Crompton. "The School for Scandal." Times
Literary Supplement, December 26, 1929, p. 1097.
Argues against F. W. Bateson (TLS, December 5, 1929) that

the only reliable text is that edited by George Daniel in 1826.

5670 -----. "The Text of Sheridan." Times Literary Supplement, December 19, 1929, pp. 1081-1082.

Replies to F. W. Bateson (TLS, November 28, 1929) that Bateson's "third and final revision" is devoid of authority and that the third edition corrected is the textus receptus.

5671 [Sheridan]. Notes and Queries, CLVI (February 9, 1929), 92.

Notes the acquisition by Gabriel Wells of Sheridan's first draft of The School for Scandal.

5672 "Sheridan's Plays and Poems." Times Literary Supplement, January 3, 1929, pp. 1-2.

Reviews R.C. Rhodes, ed., The Plays and Poems of Richard Brinsley Sheridan (1928). A leading article. Notes that a great many problems still remain to be solved in connection with the Sheridan canon.

5673 White, Newport B. "The Text of Sheridan." Times Literary Supplement, December 5, 1929, p. 1032.

Replies to F.W. Bateson (TLS, November 28, 1929), suggesting that Sheridan corrected The Rivals between 1775 and 1778.

5674 MacMillan, Dougald. "Sheridan's Share in The Stranger." Modern Language Notes, XLV (1930), 85-86.

Discusses Sheridan's role in the English production of the sentimental and technically clever play by August von Kotzebue.

5675 F., R. "The Sheridan Papers." British Museum Quarterly, VII (1932), 38-39.

This describes papers presented by the Duke of Bedford to the Museum. Two main categories include papers relating to the administration of Drury Lane Theatre by Tom Sheridan and papers concerning Tom's three children. A few autographs of R. B. Sheridan are included.

5676 Fijn, van Draat, P. "Sheridan's Rivals and Ben Jonson's Every Man in His Humour." Neophilologus (1932), 44-50.

The suggestion is that Bob Acres "is a compound of Stephen and Bobadil, with a grain of Brainworm, Cob and Matthew thrown in."

5677 Darlington, W. A. Sheridan. London: Duckworth, 1933. 144 pp. (Great Lives).

Biography emphasizing family life and political involvements; brief treatment of his dramatic career.

5678 Rhodes, R.Compton. Harlequin Sheridan, the Man and the Legends. Oxford: Blackwell, 1933. xvii, 305 pp.

A biography of the playwright-politician which attempts to separate fact from myth.

5679 Brown, John. Letters from Greenroom Ghosts. New York: The

Viking Press, 1934. 207 pp.

This work comprises a series of five letters written by dead actors to "living performers," after the fashion of Tom Brown. The fourth, from Richard Brinsley Sheridan to Noel Coward, provides a pseudo-autobiography and an 18th century interpretation of Mr. Coward's accomplishments.

5680 Legouis, Pierre. "Buckingham et Sheridan: ce que le Critique doit à la Répetition." Revue Anglo-Américaine, XI (1934), 423-434.

5681 Nettleton, George H. "The First Edition of The School for Scandal. Times Literary Supplement, October 17, 1934, p. 695. [Corrected by M. J. Ryan, in Times Literary Supplement, October 25, 1934, p. 735.]

Establishes the Dublin edition of 1780 as the first edition of the play.

5682 -----. "The School for Scandal: An Early Edition." Times Literary Supplement, March 28, 1935, p. 200.

Records evidence that the version printed by Robert Bell (Philadelphia, 1782) is the earliest American edition of the Play. [See Bateson, ibid., (January 4, 1936), p. 15.]

5683 -----. "The School for Scandal: First Edition of the Authentic Text. Times Literary Supplement, December 21, 1935, p. 876.

Presents evidence that Hugh Gaines's New York edition of 1786 contains an authentic text, while Mr. Bateson contends that this text is "piratical" and "valueless." [See, ibid., by F. W. Bateson, January 4, 1936, p. 15.]

5684 Vance, Charles. "An Authentic Reproduction of Richard Brinsley Sheridan's 'A School for Scandal.'" M.A. Northwestern University, 1935.

5685 Hammond, J. L. "Gladstone on Sheridan." Times Literary Supplement, July 4, 1936, p. 564.

Calls attention to an article by Gladstone in which Sheridan's public character is commended.

5686 Johnson, Philip, and Howard Agg. The New School for Scandal; An Impertinence in Three Acts. London: H. F. W. Deane, 1936. 70 pp.

5687 "Trailing Richard Brinsley Sheridan." Colophon, I (Spring, 1936), 612.

Reprints an item from the papers of Thomas Townshend, Vicount Sydney (1733-1800), containing facts about a night visitation by Sheridan.

5688 Snider, Rose. Satire in the Comedies of Congreve, Sheridan, Wilde, and Coward. University of Maine Studies, Second Series, No. 42. Orono, Maine, 1937. x, 135 pp.

This volume includes a chronologically oriented analysis

of the satiric element in The Old Batchelour, The Double
Dealer, Love for Love, The Way of the World, The Rivals,
The Critic, and The School for Scandal.

5689 Bates, George. The School for Scandal: A Manuscript. London:
      Offered by George Bates [1938?]. [24] pp.
          Argues the inadequacy of the 1799 text for recovery of the
      Drury Lane version of the play, and offers a manuscript from
      the Frampton Court sale of Sheridan material as the closest
      version to the Drury Lane spoken text.

5690 The School for Scandal: A Manuscript. Catalogue No. 19. London:
      George Bates, 1938. 24 pp.
          An offering for sale of a manuscript claimed to be "the
      earliest and most authentic text of the play." In the argument
      supporting the validity of the text, fallacious propositions and
      special pleading too often substitute for adequate concrete
      evidence.

5691 Foss, Kenelm. Here Lies Richard Brinsley Sheridan. London:
      Richard Press, 1939. 390 pp.
          A popular biography of questionable authenticity. Cursory
      treatment of the plays.

5692 Arnavon, Jacques. "Une 'Ecole de la Médisance' au Théâtre des
      Mathurins." Etudes Anglaises, IV (1940), 43-48.
          Claude Spaak made an adaptation of School for Scandal and
      Arnavon feels he ruined the play, that it would have been better
      to translate the play than tamper with it.

5693 Bateson, F.W. "Notes on the Text of Two Sheridan Plays." Review
      of English Studies, XVI (July, 1940), 312-317.
          Compares the corrupt printed version of The Camp to the
      Larpent MS. Also argues on the basis of three different texts
      of The Critic that the accepted text which was authorized by
      Sheridan himself was not in use on the stage at any time in his
      lifetime.

5694 Frederick, Robert Lee. "A Producing Director's Study of Sheridan's
      School for Scandal." M.A. University of Iowa, 1940.

5695 Glasgow, Alice. Sheridan of Drury Lane, a Biography . . . with
      Illustrations from Old Prints and Portraits. New York: Frederick
      A. Stokes Co., 1940. 310 pp.
          A popular biography with much attention to the social setting
      in which Sheridan lived and rather fanciful descriptions of
      places and characters. Includes a brief chronology of Sheridan's
      life, a short bibliography, and index.

5696 Kemp, Robert. "Chronique théâtrale." Le Temps, February 19,
      1940, p. 4.

5697 Sauble, Elizabeth. "Director's Prompt Book of Richard B. Sheri-
      dan's The Critic, as Produced by the Student Stage of Wayne

University, with an Introductory Study of Sheridan's Life and
Works." M.A. Wayne University, 1940.

5698 Taylor, Garland F. "Richard Brinsley Sheridan's The Duenna."
Ph.D. Yale University, 1940.

5699 Vachell, Horace Annesley. Great Chameleon: A Biographical
Romance. London: Hutchinson and Co., 1940. 287 pp.

5700 Alspach, Russell K. "Making the Green One Red." Shakespeare
Association Bulletin, XVI (1941), 166-168.
Indicates that Thomas Sheridan, independently of Arthur
Murphy, also advocated the accepted reading of Macbeth
II, ii, 64.

5701 Gelfand, M. "Sheridan and the Moscow Art Theatre." The
Theatre (U.S.S.R.), III (1941), 115-123.

5702 Loewenberg, Alfred. "The Songs in 'The Critic.'" Times
Literary Supplement, March 28, 1942, p. 168.
Draws attention to the significance of the folio Favorite
Airs in The Critic (1779).

5703 Hewitt, Barnard. "The Rivals and An Enemy of the People."
High School Thespian, 1943. pp. 8-9.

5704 Loewenberg, Alfred. "An Uncollected Poem of Sheridan." Notes
and Queries, CLXXXVI (1944), 3-4.
The poem, "A Glee," whose traditional author is Elizabeth
Ann Linley, was more likely penned by her husband, Richard
Brinsley Sheridan.

5705 Moore, John R. "Sheridan's 'Little Bronze Pliny.'" Modern
Language Notes, LIX (March, 1944), 164-165.
Name changed to "Shakespeare" in later versions of School
for Scandal.

5706 Rosenfeld, Sybil. "Robinson Crusoe." Times Literary Supplement,
March 4, 1944, p. 120.
Offers, as a footnote to Nettleton, an additional date and
place of performance of the play; cites cast.

5707 Daghlian, Philip B. "Sheridan's Minority Waiters." Modern
Language Quarterly, VI (December, 1945), 421-422.
Explains a passage in The Rivals (II, i) as a reference
to the election in 1774 of Robert Macreth, a waiter at White's.

5708 Houghton, Norris. "Notes on the London Season." Theatre
Arts, XXIX (November, 1945), 614-617.
Reports on The Critic at the Old Vic, and The School for
Scandal and The Constant Couple at the Arts.

5709 Motter, Opal E. "A Production Prompt Book for The Critic."
M.A. University of Michigan, 1945.

5710 Nettleton, George H. "Sheridan's Robinson Crusoe." Times
Literary Supplement, June 23, 1945, p. 300; June 30,
1945, p. 312.

A study of the Newcastle upon Tyne scenario of 1791 and its variants from the London text.

5711 Wenzel, Betty Jane. "A Director's Prompt Book and Designs for a Production of Sheridan's The Rivals." M.A. State University of Iowa, 1945.

5712 Kernodle, George R. "Excruciatingly Funny Or, The 47 Keys of Comedy." Theatre Arts, XXX (December, 1946), 719-722.

A comment on The Critic is included in a general study of comic dramatic structure.

5713 Oliver, Robert Tarbell. Four Who Spoke Out: Burke, Fox, Sheridan, Pitt. Syracuse: Syracuse University Press [1946]. x, 196 pp.

Describes these men's actions during the period 1765-1806, setting up the historical and social background and detailing the methods of dissent. Contains a biographical table and a bibliographical note on types of sources, as well as a selected bibliography.

5714 Stokes, Leslie. "The Revivals." Theatre Arts, XXX (January, 1946), 22-24.

Comments on the productions of The Rivals, The Constant Couple and The School for Scandal in the London season.

5715 Gibbs, Lewis. Richard Brinsley Sheridan: His Life and Theatre. London: Dent, 1947. viii, 280 pp.

A general biography, stressing his activities in theatre management.

5716 Gross, Richard M. "Anti-Sentimentalism in the Drama of Richard Brinsley Sheridan." M.A. University of Oregon, 1947.

5717 James, Sterling W. "The School for Scandal." M.A. Baylor University, 1947.

5718 Purdy, Richard L. "A Gift of Sheridan Manuscripts in Honor of Professor Nettleton." Yale University Library Gazette, XXII (1947), 42-43.

A brief description of a newly acquired collection.

5719 Reid, Loren D. "Sheridan's Speech on Mrs. Fitzherbert." Quarterly Journal of Speech, XXXIII (1947), 15-22.

A rhetorical analysis of Sheridan's speech in Parliament, May 4, 1787.

5720 "Sheridan Manuscripts." Yale University Library Gazette, XXII (1947).

Describes the Yale University Library holdings in Sheridan MSS.

5721 Vincent, Howard P. "An Attempted Piracy of The Duenna." Modern Language Notes, LXII (April, 1947), 268-270.

Describes the case of Sheridan versus Robert Faulkner in Chancery.

5722 Wittop, Freddy. "Two Costume Designs for The School for
      Scandal." Theatre Arts, XXXI (February, 1947), 19.
      Reproduces illustrations of the designs.
5723 Brumbaugh, Thomas B. "An Unpublished Letter of Richard Brinsley
      Sheridan." Emory University Quarterly, IV (March, 1948),
      55-57.
      Probably written in 1809, it refers to the burning of Drury
      Lane Theatre.
5724 Gibbs, Lewis. "Sheridan against Warren Hastings." Quarterly
      Journal of Speech, XXXIV (December, 1948), 464-468.
      Discussing Sheridan's political rhetoric.
5725 Leech, William. "Direction and Production of Sheridan's The
      Mistress of the Inn." M.F.A. Carnegie Institute of Techology,
      1948.
5726 Miller, Tatlock, ed. The Old Vic Theatre Company. A Tour of
      Australia and New Zealand. London: The British Council, 1949.
      60 pp.
      An account of the tour which included a successful produc-
      tion of The School for Scandal in its repertory.
5727 Nettleton, George H. "A Comment on Sheridan against Warren
      Hastings." Quarterly Journal of Speech, XXXV (1949), 71-72.
      A rhetorical analysis of Sheridan's political speeches.
5728 Sinko, Grzegorz. Sheridan and Kotzebue: a Comparative Essay.
      Wroclaw: Sklad Glowny W. Domu Ksiazki, for the Wroclaw
      Society of Science and Letters, 1949. 32 pp. (Series A, no.
      27).
      Comments on Kotzebue's vogue in England and the mutual
      influences of the two dramatists.
5729 Nettleton, George H. "Sheridan's Introduction to the American
      Stage." Publications of the Modern Language Association,
      LXV (1950), 163-182.
      The American Company was "the constant and dominant
      agency" in establishing Sheridan's popularity on the Amer-
      ican stage before 1800.
5730 Williams, George Woods. "A New Source of Evidence for Sheri-
      dan's Authorship of The Camp and The Wonders of Derby-
      shire." Studies in Philology, XLVII (1950), 619-628.
      An examination of the Treasurer's Account Books of Drury
      Lane Theatre, now at the Folger Shakespeare Library, sug-
      gests that the two afterpieces are by Sheridan.
5731 Darlington, W. A. Sheridan, 1751-1816. London: Longmans, 1951.
      29 pp.
      Darlington's essay is an appreciation written for the bi-
      centary of Sheridan's birth. A selected bibliography is appended.

5732 Van Lennep, William. "The Chetwynd Manuscript of The School
    for Scandal." Theatre Notebook, VI (1951-1952), 10-12.
        Van Lennep describes the manuscript of seventy-nine pages
    which was the Licenser's copy of Sheridan's play. It is now
    in the Yale Library.

5733 Yoklavich, J. "Hamlet in Shammy Shoes." Shakespeare Quarterly,
    III (1952), 209-218.
        As critic and actor Sheridan was the first to portray Hamlet
    as "consistent, studious, irresolute."

5734 Gregor, Joseph. Der Schauspielführer. 8 vols. Stuttgart: Hierse-
    mann, 1953-[1965].
        Vol. 3 (Das englische Drama) includes material on Otway's
    Venice Preserved, 1682. Vol. 6 includes Sheridan's School for
    Scandal. Entries consist of scene-by-scene summary of the play,
    general information including dates of first performance and
    printing. Indexes according to genre, author, title, year of
    first printing.

5735 Matlaw, Myron. "English Versions of Die Spanier in Peru."
    Modern Language Quarterly, XVI (1955), 63-67.
        Sheridan's only tragedy Pizarro (1799) was the most popular
    of many English adaptations of Kotzebue's play. Other adapta-
    tions of the play, as well as six literal translations, are
    discussed and compared.

5736 Price, J. B. "Richard Brinsley Sheridan (1751-1816)." Contem-
    porary Review, CXC (1956), 159-163.
        Life and works in brief.

5737 Schiller, Andrew. "The School for Scandal: The Restoration Un-
    restored." Publications of the Modern Language Association,
    LXXI (1956), 694-704.
        A success but not as a "comedy of manners."

5738 Todd, William B. "Sheridan's The Critic." Book Collector, V
    (1956), 172-173.
        Bibliographical note (68) on defective copies of the 1781
    edition.

5739 Matlaw, Myron. "Adultery Analyzed: The History of The
    Stranger." Quarterly Journal of Speech, XLIII (1957), 22-28.
        Sheridan's adaptation from Kotzebue.

5740 -----. "'This is Tragedy !!!'; The History of Pizarro." Quarterly
    Journal of Speech, XLIII (1957), 288-294.
        Sheridan's adaptation from Kotzebue.

5741 Moore, John Robert. "Lydia Languish's Library." Notes and
    Queries, New Ser., IV (1957), 76.
        Parallel in Defoe's Family Instructor.

5742 Chandler, Margaret M. "The Technical Problems Involved in a
    Modern Production of The School for Scandal." M.A. Bowling

Green State University, 1958.

5743 Woehl, Arthur L. "Richard Brinsley Sheridan, Parliamentarian."
The Rhetorical Idiom: Essays in Rhetoric, Oratory, Language
and Drama Presented to August Wichelns, with a Reprinting of
His "Literary Criticism of Oratory" (1925). Ithaca: Cornell
University Press, 1958. x, 334 pp.

An historical discussion of Sheridan's career in parliament,
his positions on some legislation, and contemporary opinions
of his political career. Sheridan's theatrical career is treated
as background and as a political liability.

5744 Lueken, John Harry. "A Project in Scenery Design for the Production of The School for Scandal." M.A. San Diego State College,
1959.

5745 Price, Cecil. "The Text of the First Performance of The Duenna."
Papers of the Bibliographical Society of America, LIII (1959),
268-270.

Review in Morning Chronicle, November 22, 1755.

5746 Buckingham, George, Duke of. The Rehearsal, as Performed at
the Theatre Royal in Drury Lane. To which Is added a Key, or
critical view of the authors, and their writings exposed in this
play, by S. Briscoe, (1704) and Sheridan, Richard Brinsley.
The Critic, or A Tragedy Rehearsed, A Dramatic Piece in
Three Acts as Performed at the Theatre Royal in Drury Lane.
Edited by Cedric Gale. Great Neck, New York: Barron's Educational Series, 1960. 168 pp.

Editor's preface, pp. 5-20, supplements "key" and discusses
background and influences. Paperback edition.

5747 Johnson, Maurice. "Charles Surface and Shaw's Heroines."
Shaw Review, III (May, 1960), 27-28.

Contends that Charles Surface was brought up to date in
the characters of Candida and Anne Whitefield. Offers evidence from Shaw's writing on School for Scandal.

5748 LeFanu, William, ed. Betsy Sheridan's Journal: Letters from
Sheridan's Sister, 1784-1786 and 1788-1790. London: Eyre
and Spottiswoode; Rutgers University Press, 1960. xii, 223
pp.

This represents the first printing of Betsy Sheridan's weekly letters to her elder sister, Alicia LeFanu, from September,
1784 to September, 1786 and from July, 1788 to March, 1790.
The letters throw light on Betsy's playwright brother.

5749 Marshova, Natal'ia Matveena. Richard Brinsli Sheridan, 1751-
1816. Mockba: Iskusstvo, 1960. 122 pp.

A short but documented biography in Russian, with a brief
list of further suggested readings at the end.

5750 Matlaw, Myron. "Menschenhass und Reue in English." Symposium,

XIV (1960), 129-134.

"The study of the English translations of Kotzebue's 1789 Menschenhass und Reue sheds further light on Sheridan's connections with The Stranger (1798) and supplements the history of one of the most popular dramas of the first half of the 19th century."

5751 O'Connell, Richard B. "Gorostiza's Contigo, pan y cepolla and Sheridan's The Rivals." Hispania, XLIII (1960), 384-387.

Influence of Sheridan upon Gorastiza.

5752 Sen, Sailendra Kumar. "Sheridan's Literary Debt: The Rivals and Humphrey Clinker." Modern Language Quarterly, XXI (December, 1960), 291-300.

Disarms critics who accuse Sheridan of plagiarism on the basis of characterization by showing that The Rivals and The School for Scandal are classical comedies (in the tradition of Jonson's comedies of humours) which by their very nature conceive of individuals as types that inevitably repeat themselves. Sen goes on to illustrate similarities of situation in The Rivals and Humphrey Clinker.

5753 Sherwin, Oscar. Uncorking Old Sherry: The Life and Times of Richard Brinsley Sheridan. New York: Twayne Publishers; London: Vision Press, 1960. 352 pp.

5754 Smith, Mary Lou. "A Production Book for The School for Scandal." M.F.A. University of Oklahoma, 1960.

5755 Styan, J. L. TheElements of Drama. Cambridge, England: Cambridge University Press, 1960. 306 pp.

Intended as a guide for playgoers interested in the drama, this book suggests what the student should look for and how to find it, "both in the theatre and in the text of the play." In a section entitled "Tempo and Meaning," Styan analyzes aspects of The School for Scandal.

5756 Trainer, James. "Tieck's Translation of The Rivals." Modern Language Quarterly, XXI (1960), 246-252.

Trainer describes Tieck's last rendition (1850) of The Rivals.

5757 Fiske, Roger. "A Score for 'The Duenna.'" Music and Letters, XLII (April, 1961), 132-141.

The author attempts to discover the original score, or parts of it, that were evidently taken from existing airs. Comment on the popularity of the opera, for which Sheridan provided the libretto.

5758 Jackson, J. R. de J. "The Importance of Witty Dialogue in The School for Scandal." Modern Language Notes, LXXVI (November, 1961), 601-607.

5759 Price, Cecil. "The Columbia Manuscript of The School for Scandal." Columbia Library Columns, XI (1961), 25-29.

5760 Deelman, Christian. "The Original Cast of The School for Scandal." Review of English Studies, XIII (1962), 257-266.

The success of The School for Scandal as a theatrical production can be traced to Sheridan's putting the play together "with a particular cast in view."

5761 Delpech, Jeanine. "Sheridan, le Beaumarchais Anglais." Nouvelles Litteraires, (17 Mai, 1962), p. 3.

5762 Donaldson, Ian. "New Papers of Henry Holland and R. B. Sheridan: (1) Holland's Drury Lane, 1794." Theatre Notebook, XVI (Spring, 1962), 90-96.

Concerns the correspondence between Holland and Sheridan on the rebuilding of Drury Lane in 1794.

5763 -----. "New Papers of Henry Holland and R. B. Sheridan: (II) The Hyde Park Corner Operas and the Dormant Patent." Theatre Notebook, XVI (Summer, 1962), 117-125.

Sheridan's attempts to defend the monopoly rights of Drury Lane and the Covent Garden by proposing a new theatre and two opera houses at Hyde Park Corner which would be under the control of the two major theatres.

5764 Dulck, Jean. Les Comédies de R. B. Sheridan. Paris: Didier, 1962. 611 pp.

Historical, formal, textual, and comparative study of the comedies.

5765 Landfield, Jerome. "Sheridan." Quarterly Journal of Speech, XLVIII (1962), 5-7.

Sheridan's uncertain position in British public address.

5766 Price, Cecil. "Sheridan's 'Doxology.'" Times Literary Supplement, May 4, 1962, p. 309.

Sheridan's signature on the manuscript of The School for Scandal.

5767 Skinner, Quentin. "Sheridan and Whitbread at Drury Lane, 1809-1815." Theatre Notebook, XVII (Winter, 1962-63), 40-46.

Presents problems which seem to have been ignored in the appreciation of Whitbread's works after the fire of 1809.

5768 Nussbaum, R.D. "Poetry and Music in 'The Duenna.'" Westerly, No. 1 (1963), 58-63.

Sheridan's The Duenna, with music by Thomas Linley and son, is considered in "the history of light music drama before Gilbert and Sullivan."

5769 Price, Cecil. "Another Crewe MS. of The School for Scandal?" Papers of the Bibliographical Society of America, LVII (1963), 79-81.

Textual differences between G. H. Nettleton's text, the Yale Ms and the Dublin edition of 1799 suggest that there might have been two Crewe Mss.

5770 Pryce-Jones, Alan. "The School for Scandal." Theatre Arts, XLVII (March, 1963), 57.

The January 24, 1963 production of Sheridan's play at the Majestic Theatre in New York.

5771 Skinner, Quentin. "Sheridan and Whitbread at Drury Lane, 1809-1815, II." Theatre Notebook, XVII (Spring, 1963), 74-79.

Because of Sheridan's contention that Whitbread was "the scoundrel," the latter's positive achievements have been underrated. Part I of this article appeared in Theatre Notebook, XVII (Winter 1962/3), 40-46.

5772 Cichoke, Anthony J. "The Rivals: A Production Book." M.A. St. Louis University, 1964.

5773 Coggin, Frederick Marsh. "The Design of the Setting for The Rivals." M.A. University of Georgia, 1964.

5774 Sprague, Arthur Colby. "In Defense of a Masterpiece; The School for Scandal Re-examined." English Studies Today, 3rd Ser. (1964), 125-135.

Responding to the denigration which followed universal Victorian acclaim for the play, Sprague defends it as an acting play and a play for actors, pointing out its theatrical appropriateness in plot and characterization, and its richness for several generations of actors, who found many interpretations legitimate.

5775 Nelson, David Arthur. "The Laughing Comedy of the Eighteenth Century." Ph.D. Cornell University, 1965. (Order No. 65-14711).

The comic technique and situations of Vanbrugh, Farquhar, Goldsmith, and Sheridan are evaluated in terms of their ability to create and maintain aesthetic distance between playgoer and character.

5776 Price, Cecil. "Nouverre and Sheridan, 1776." Theatre Research, VII (1965), 45-46.

A hitherto unpublished letter of Charles Greville contains details on the attempts of Richard Sheridan to obtain the services of the balletmaster, Jean-Georges Nouverre for Drury Lane.

5777 Tillett, Jeffrey, ed. Shakespeare, Sheridan, Shaw. London: Heinimann Educational Books, 1965.

Sheridan's St. Patrick's Day.

5778 Bryant, Donald C. "London Notes, 1769-1774." Quarterly Journal of Speech, LII (1966), 179-181.

Reprints an advertisement in the July 30, 1774 Middlesex Journal for a performance by the popular mimic George Saville Carey and a comment condemning Sheridan's "Attic Entertainment" in 1769.

5779 Lutaud, Oliver. "Des acharniens d'Aristophanes au critique de Sheridan." Les Langues Modernes, LX (1966), 433-438.

5780 Michael, Keith. "A Scenic and Lighting Design for 'The Rivals.'" M.A. University of Denver, 1966.

5781 Niederauer, Rev. George Hugh. "Wit and Sentiment in Sheridan's Comedies of Manners." Ph.D. University of Southern California, 1966. (Order No. 66-11,579).

Analyzes the plots, characters, and dialogue of The Rivals and School for Scandal to determine the extent to which Sheridan combined conventions of the Restoration and sentimental comic traditions in his two most successful comedies of manners.

5782 Price, Cecil. "The Larpent Manuscript of St. Patrick's Day." Huntington Library Quarterly, XXIX (1966), 183-189.

More than any other copy of the play, the Larpent manuscript shows most clearly Sheridan's personal touch.

5783 -----. "The Completion of The School for Scandal." Times Literary Supplement, December 28, 1967, p. 1265.

Discusses circumstances surrounding the composition of the play. Events and personalities contemporary with Sheridan may explain incidents and characterizations in the play.

5784 -----. "The Second Crewe MS of The School for Scandal." Papers of the Bibliographical Society of America, LXI (1967), 351-356.

A description of the recently discovered Hodgson Ms. reveals that it is not the second Crewe Ms. but that a third Crewe Ms. is or was in existence.

5785 -----. "Sheridan-Linley Documents." Theatre Notebook, XXI (Summer, 1967), 165-167.

Describes the papers of Sheridan and his wife now at the British Museum. The best of them is a copy of their marriage articles.

5786 Rothwell, Kenneth S. "The School for Scandal: The Comic Spirit in Sheridan and Rowlandson." The School for Scandal: Thomas Rowlandson's London. (Lawrence: Kansas University Museum of Art, 1967), 23-45.

Analyzes and compares the comic spirit in Sheridan's play and in Rowlandson's watercolor of Vauxhall Gardens.

5787 Oliphant, Mrs. Margaret [Oliphant (Wilson)]. Sheridan. New York: A. L. Fowle [19--]. 199 pp. (Makers of Literature).

Prefaced by a note on previous biographies, this volume relates Sheridan's life entirely without scholarly apparatus, and treats extensively his role as dramatist; with rather skimpy mention of his civic life. Some critical appraisal of plays.

Sheridan, Thomas

text

5788 Sheridan, Thomas. A Course of Lectures on Elocution: Together
      with Two Dissertations on Language. New York: Benjamin
      Blom, 1967. 392 pp.
          A reprint of the 1798 edition includes Sheridan's remarks
      on the art of speaking in the theatre.

biography and criticism

5789 Flood, W. H. Grattan. "Thomas Sheridan's Brave Irishman."
      Review of English Studies, II (July, 1926), 346-347.
          The date of the first performance February 21, 1736-37.
5790 Hinton, Percival F. "A Sheridan Pamphlet."Times Literary Sup-
      plement, June 28, 1928, p. 486.
          Notices a previously unrecorded pamphlet written by Sheri-
      dan for the Prince of Wales.
5791 Alden, Donald H. "Thomas Sheridan, 1719-1788." Ph.D. Yale
      University, 1933.
5792 Winans, James A. "Whately on Elocution." Quarterly Journal of
      Speech, XXXI (1945), 1-8.
          Bishop Whately's Elements of Rhetoric, 1828, shows the
      influence of the theories and practice of Thomas Sheridan and
      John Walker.
5793 Griffin, Leland M. "Letter to the Press: 1778." Quarterly Journal
      of Speech, XXXIII (1947), 148-150.
          A letter in the Gentleman's Magazine championing the views
      on rhetoric of actor Thomas Sheridan.
5794 Sheldon, Esther K. "Thomas Sheridan: Gentleman or Actor?"
      Theatre Survey, II (1961), 3-14.
          On the Kelly riots, Smock Alley Theatre, Dublin, 1747, to-
      gether with associated pamphlet literature, and Sheridan's
      refusal to appease a faction of the audience.
5795 -----. "Sheridan's Coriolanus: An 18th Century Compromise."
      Shakespeare Quarterly, XIV (1963), 153-161.
          Acts I and II of Sheridan's Coriolanus; or The Roman Matron
      (1752) are from Shakespeare's play; Acts III, IV, and V are
      chiefly from Thomson's Coriolanus.
5796 -----. Thomas Sheridan of Smock-Alley. Princeton: Princeton
      University Press, 1967. 530 pp.
          An account of Sheridan's career as theatre manager based
      on biographies of his contemporaries, on 18th century news-
      papers, pamphlets, playbills, and on letters written to and by

Sheridan. Includes information about Sheridan's relations with Garrick and a Smock-Alley Calendar that gives a daily record of performances and casts.

Shirley, James

5797 Langhans, Edward A. "The Restoration Promptbooks of Shirley's The Sisters." Theatre Annual, XIV (1956), 51-65.
     A study of the most fully annotated Restoration prompt-book extant--that for Shirley's The Sisters; the production for which the prompt-book was prepared probably took place between 1668 and 1671. There is material referring to scene design, scene shifting, editing of speeches, actors' warnings, actors' entrances, etc.

5798 Mumper, Nixon. "A Critical Edition of Love Tricks, or The School of Compliment by James Shirley." Ph.D. University of Pennsylvania, 1959.
     Includes a life and history of production and publication. 3rd ed., 1667.

Siddons, Sarah

5799 Morris, Clara. "Sarah Siddons' Tryst." McClure's Magazine, XIX (1902), 78-83.
     A sentimental account of Sarah Siddons' tryst with her younger self.

5800 Parsons, Florence Mary. The Incomparable Siddons. London: Methuen; New York: Putnam, 1909. xix, 298 pp.
     Account of life, personality, and art of Siddons. Contains comments on the theatre of the period and prominent theatrical contemporaries. Profusely illustrated. Works consulted, pp. xv-xvii.

5801 C., C.S. "Ann of Swansea." Notes and Queries, 12th Ser., VI (1920), 45.
     Identifies Ann of Swansea as Ann Kemble, a sister of Sarah Siddons.

5802 "Mrs. Siddons." Theatre Arts Monthly, IX (July, 1925), 485.
     "From a crayon formerly in her own possession."

5803 Warde, Thomas. "Gainsborough's Original 'Siddons.'" Notes and Queries, CXLVIII (April 11, 1925), 260.
     Seeks Gainsborough's painting of the actress.

5804 Eaton, Walter Prichard. "Professor Is Thrilled." Theatre Arts Monthly, X (July, 1926), 472-478.
     A sketch of the career of Sarah Siddons, with a portrait. Uses Prof. G. J. Bell's description of her acting manner.

5805 Ffrench, Yvonne. Mrs. Siddons, Tragic Actress. London: Cobden
          - Sanderson, 1936. 286 pp.
              A biographical account of Mrs. Siddons's career, this volume
          contains many pertinent details about the theatre between 1755
          and 1831, but its accuracy is often questionable.
5806 McGuire, Lucille Maurine. "The Style of Mrs. Siddons and Her
          Characterisation of Lady Macbeth." M.F.A. Yale University,
          1940.
5807 Van Lennep, William, ed. The Reminiscences of Sarah Kemble
          Siddons 1773-1785. Cambridge: Widener Library, 1942.
              Mrs. Siddons' reminiscences of "meer commonplace matter,
          and events already partly known" recounts her famous meetings
          with Samuel Johnson, her sitting for Reynold's Tragic Muse,
          and many other interesting events in the life of the young actress.
          Written at the age of 75 when the actress was suffering from
          erysipelas, this slim, beautifully printed volume is printed
          from a newly discovered manuscript in her own hand. It covers
          the Drury Lane season of 1784-85.
5808 Swale, Ellis. "Mrs. Siddons's Residence in Paddington." Notes
          and Queries, CLXXXVIII (September 8, 1945), 108.
              Evidence for her residence and movements at the beginning
          of the nineteenth century.
5809 Ffrench, Yvonne. Mrs. Siddons, Tragic Actress. Rev. ed. London:
          Derek Verschoyle, 1954. 256 pp.
5810 Clark, William Smith. "'The Siddons' in Dublin." Theatre Note-
          book, IX (1955), 103-111.
              An account of the first three visits of Sarah Kemble Siddons
          to Dublin, 1783-1785, her reception by the newspaper critics
          and public. Includes comments on characters she played (in-
          cluding Hamlet) and her acting techniques.
5811 Donohue, Joseph W., Jr. "Kemble and Mrs. Siddons in Macbeth:
          The Romantic Approach to Tragic Character." Theatre Note-
          book, XXII (Winter, 1967/8), 65-86.
              Examines the Kembles' approach to their roles in several
          performances to determine how "theatrical performance faith-
          fully mirrors an age."

Sidney, Philip

5812 Andrews, Michael Cameron. "Sidney's Arcadia on the English
          Stage: A Study of the Dramatic Adaptions [sic] of The Countess
          of Pembroke's Arcadia." Ph.D. Duke University, 1966. (Order
          No. 67-6094).
              Studies nine plays that constitute all the English drama known
          to draw upon Sidney's Arcadia as their primary source. One

18th century play, <u>Philoclea</u> (1754), reflects the influence of decadent heroic drama.

Simeon, Joseph

5813 Sandham, G. P. "An English Jesuit Dramatist: Fr. Joseph Simeon, 1593-1671." <u>Month</u>, New Ser., XXIV (1960), 308-313.
      The Jesuits helped awaken interest in the theatre and made many contributions to staging, particularly through pagentry. There are numerous references to stage technique, little criticism of plays.

Smith, Adam

5814 Lothian, John M. "Adam Smith As a Critic of Shakespeare." <u>Papers, Mainly Shakespearean</u>. Edited by G. I. Duthie. (Edinburgh: Oliver and Boyd, 1964), 1-9. (Aberdeen University Studies, 147).

Smith, Edmund

5815 Geffen, Elizabeth M. "The Expulsion from Oxford of Edmund ("Rag") Smith." <u>Notes and Queries</u>, CLXX (1936), 398-401.
      Biographical; discusses the circumstances of Smith's expulsion.
5816 -----. "The Parentage of Edmund ("Rag") Smith." <u>Review of English Studies</u>, XIV (1938), 72-78.
      Finds fault with the treatment of Smith's parentage in the biographical account of Smith by William Oldisworth; the errors are repeated by Johnson, Allibone, and Sidney Lee.
5817 Wheatley, Katherine E. "The Relation of Edmund Smith's <u>Phaedra and Hippolitus</u> to Racine's <u>Phèdre</u> and <u>Bajazet</u>." <u>Romanic Review</u>, XXXVII (1946), 307-328.
      Smith's borrowing ignores the Racinian spirit--he moves from the tragic to the melodramatic, from the dramatic to the static.

Smith, William

5818 Highfill, Philip H., Jr. "Charles Surface in Regency Retirement: Some Letters From Gentleman Smith." <u>Essays in English Literature of the Classical Period Presented to Dougald MacMillan</u>. Edited by Daniel W. Patterson and Albrecht B. Strauss. <u>Studies in Philology</u>. (Extra Series, January, 1967), 135-166.
      Letters in the Folger Shakespeare Library from William

"Gentleman" Smith (1730-1819), Garrick's contemporary and
sometime protege, to banker Thomas Coutts contribute to an
understanding of the changing status of the acting profession.

Smock Alley Players

5819 Lawrence, W. J. "Irish Players at Oxford, 1677." The Elizabethan
      Playhouse and Other Studies. Second Series. (Stratford-on-Avon:
      Shakespeare Head Press, 1913), 192-200.
         The successful visit to Oxford for the Act in 1677 of the
      Smock Alley players under leadership of Ashbury and sponsored
      by the Duke of Ormond, Chancellor of the University and Lord
      Lieutenant of Ireland.

Smollett, Tobias

5820 Ellison, Lee Monroe. "Elizabethan Drama and the Works of
      Smollett." Publications of the Modern Language Association,
      XLIV (September, 1929), 842-862.
         Traces the influence of Shakespeare and Jonson upon Smollett's
      novels.
5821 McKillop, Alan Dugald. "Smollett's First Comedy." Modern Lan-
      guage Notes, XLV (1930), 396-397.
         There is evidence that Smollett wrote a comedy entitled
      The Absent Man between Roderick Random and Peregrine
      Pickle; there is no known copy of the play, so the major part
      of the article is devoted to proof, not comment.
5822 Deutsch, Otto Erich. "Poetry Preserved in Music. Biographical
      Notes on Smollett and Oswald, Handel, and Haydn." Modern
      Language Notes, LXIII (February, 1948), 73-88.
         The lyrics from Smollett's lost tragedy Alceste are pre-
      served in a setting by Handel. Other Smollett songs are simi-
      larly traced.
5823 Knapp, Lewis Mansfield. Tobias Smollett Doctor of Men and Man-
      ners. Princeton: Princeton University Press, 1949. xiii, 362 pp.
         A general biography. Particularly relevant are Chapter
      four, "Friendships and ventures in opera and drama 1747-1750,"
      73-92 (dealing with The Regicide and Alceste), and Chapter
      ten, "Success with The Reprisal," 196-220. Plate V reproduces
      a playbill for The Reprisal.
5824 Jones, Claude E. "Smollett Editions in Eighteenth-Century Britain."
      Notes and Queries, CCII (1957), 252.
         Prints a table of editions of Smollett's books published during
      the 18th century.
5825 -----. "Tobias Smollett (1721-1771)--The Doctor as Man of Letters."

Journal of the History of Medicine, XII (1957), 337-348.
Biographical background, treating Smollett's contributions
to the literature of medicine and the references to medicine
in his literature, especially in Humphrey Clinker. Only minimal
references to drama.

5826 Spector, Robert Donald. "Attacks on the 'Critical Review' in the
'Literary Magazine.'" Notes and Queries, VII (1960), 300-301.
Concern Smollett's The Reprisal, among other works.

Social History

5827 Chancellor, E. Beresford. The Eighteenth Century in London; An
Account of Its Social Life and Arts. London: B. T. Batsford,
[1921]. x, 278 pp.
While only a few pages are devoted to a discussion of theatre,
there is much material about the dramatists of the period--
their clubs, their involvements in the social life of the period,
the coffee houses they frequented, areas of London mentioned
in their plays.

Social Problems

5828 Morgan, Stewart S. "Social Problems in Drama of the Last Quarter
of the Eighteenth Century." Ph.D. Ohio State University, 1933.

Social Purpose

5829 Dasgupta, K. "The Drama of Social Purpose in England, Its Rise
and Decline." Ph.D. London University (Queen Mary), 1958.

Songs

5830 Doughty, Oswald. "Eighteenth-Century Song." English Studies,
VII (1925), 161-169.
Discusses qualities of 17th-century song, transitional
lyrics, and 18th-century songs. Includes examples from Gay,
Shenstone, Henry Carey and comments by Addison, Boswell,
and Fielding.

5831 Reed, Edward Bliss, ed. Songs from the British Drama. New
Haven: Yale University Press, 1925. 386 pp.
Includes some from Restoration and 18th-century drama.

5832 Gladding, Bessie A. "The Song in Restoration Drama, 1660-
1700." Ph.D. New York University, 1926.

5833 Thorp, Willard, ed. Songs from the Restoration Theatre.
Princeton: Princeton University Press, 1934. 138 pp.

Sixty-six pages devoted to songs (with music) from Restoration drama, excluding opera, followed by extensive notes
(48 pages) and an index. Each song is printed separately as a
poem, with a paragraph placing it in context in the play. Then
it is printed with music. The introduction discusses the importance of song to Restoration drama.

5834   Boas, Frederick S., ed. Songs and Lyrics from the English Play-
       books. Illustrated by Hans Tindall. London: Cresset Press,
       1945. xvii, 258 pp.
           A general anthology, containing many songs from the Resto-
       ration and eighteenth century dramas.

5835   Ottieri, Ottiero. "Lirica del Dramma Inglese." Anglica, I (August,
       1946), 154-159.
           A brief historical survey of the use of songs in the plays,
       holding Dryden to be the main influence.

5836   Stead, P. J., ed. Songs of the Restoration Theatre. London:
       Methuen, 1948. xvii, 91 pp.
           An anthology with a critical introduction.

5837   Boas, Frederick S., ed. Songs from the English Masques and
       Light Operas. London: Harrap, 1949. 176 pp.
           A general anthology, which contains several pieces from
       the Restoration and eighteenth century dramas.

5838   Dorlag, Arthur. "Song in English Comedy, 1660 to 1728." Ph.D.
       University of Wisconsin, 1953. 264 pp.
           Examines the use of song in fifty-eight comedies by ten
       dramatists: Baker, Davenant, Duffett, D'Urfey, Etherege, Gay,
       Motteux, Otway, Settle, and Shadwell.

Sophonisbe

5839   Saupe, Gerhard. "Die Sophonisbe-Tragödien in der Englishcen
       Literatur des 17. und 18. Jahrhunderts." Inaugural Disserta-
       tion. Margurg, 1929.

Sources

5840   Hogan, Floriana T. "Notes on Thirty-One English Plays and Their
       Spanish Sources." Restoration and Eighteenth Century Theatre
       Research, VI (May, 1967), 56-59.
           Lists thirty-one Restoration and 18th century plays and
       their actual, erroneous, or questionable Spanish sources. In-
       cludes references to Dryden, Wycherley, Behn, Killigrew,
       Cibber and Centlivre.

Southerne, Thomas

text

5841 Southern, Thomas. The Loyal Brother; or The Persian Prince.
Edited by P. Hamelius. Liege: H. Vaillant-Carmanne, 1911.
131 pp.
Text of 1682 collated with that of 1774. Introduction concerned with source, first performance, and summary. Notes
attempt to clear up "with no final certainty," the personal and
political allusions.

biography and criticism

5842 Nuck, Richard. Über Leben und Werke von Thomas Southerne.
Berlin: Weidmann, 1904. 29 pp.
Brief consideration of each of his plays.
5843 Hamelius, P. "The Source of Southerne's 'Fatal Marriage.'"
Modern Language Review, IV (1909), 352-356.
Concerned with the Spanish sources of the play, particularly Montalvan.
5844 Friedrich, Karl. Thomas Southerne als Dramatiker. Inaugural Dissertation. Nurnberg: R. Stich, 1914. 78 pp.
Argues that Southerne's plays show careful management in dramatic sequence and in revealing character in
action and speech; however, characters and situations
which proved stage-worthy were used again and again
without alteration.
5845 Summers, Montague. "The Source of Southerne's The Fatal
Marriage." The Modern Language Review, XI (April,
1916), 149-155.
Clears up the mystery of the source of "The Fatal Marriage." The source is Mrs. Behn's The Nun: or The Fair
Vow Breaker and not Mrs. Behn's The Nun: or The Per-
jured Beauty.
5846 Summers, Alphonsus Joseph. "The Source of Southerne's 'The
Fatal Marriage.'" Essays in Petto. (London: Fortune Press,
1928), 147-155.
5847 Leach, C.E.J. "The Life and Works of Thomas Southerne."
M.A. University of London, 1932.
5848 Mallery, R.D. "Thomas Southerne." Times Literary Supplement,
December 1, 1932, p. 923.
Mallery corrects D.N.B. on dates of Southerne's birth and
entry into the Middle Temple. Leech further corrects D.N.B.
and C.B.E.L. entries on Southerne. See correction by Clif-

ford Leech, Times Literary Supplement, December 8, 1932,
p. 943.

5849 Dodds, John Wendell. Thomas Southerne, Dramatist. New Haven:
Yale University Press, 1933. viii, 237 pp. (Yale Studies in
English, LXXXI).

An analysis of each play, with emphasis upon tearful pathos,
or pity. Dodds feels that Southerne's fame depends largely upon
The Fatal Marriage and Oroonoko.

5850 Leech, Clifford. "A Cancel in Southerne's The Disappointment,
1684." Library, 4th Ser., XIII (1933), 395-398.

Sheet E of the quarto volume of The Disappointment; or The
Mother in Fashion has only three leaves, which indicates that
E₁ and E₂ are cancels.

5851 -----. "The Political 'Disloyalty' of Thomas Southerne." Modern
Language Review, XXVIII (1933), 421-430.

A study of political implications in Oronooko, The Fatal Marriage and other plays.

5852 -----. "Thomas Southerne and On the Poets and Actors in King
Charles II's Reign." Notes and Queries, CLXIV (1933), 401-
403.

The important but anonymous On the Poets and Actors in King
Charles II's Reign was probably written by Thomas Southerne.

5853 Richardson, William Rittenhouse. "The Life and Works of Thomas
Southerne." Ph.D. Harvard University, 1933.

A discussion of Southerne's life and works, with special attention to the sources of the works. Concludes that Southerne's
tragedies were written in the tradition of the Restoration heroic
play and the Elizabethan romantic drama, and his comedies
show the influences of the comedy of intrigue and the comedy
of manners.

5854 Stroup, T. B. "Philosophy and Drama." Times Literary Supplement,
January 19, 1933, p. 40.

Philosophical ideas in plays by Southerne and Howard.

5855 Hummel, Ray O., Jr. "A Further Note on Southerne's The Disappointment." The Library, Fifth Series, I (June, 1946), 67-69.

A bibliographical study of the first edition, 1684, giving
information additional to that in the study by Clifford Leech
(The Library, Fourth Series, XIII (1933), 395-398).

5856 Leech, Clifford. "Southerne's The Disappointment." The Library,
Fifth Series, II (June, 1947), 64.

Reply to R. O. Hummel, Jr., in I (June, 1946), 67-69.

5857 Bowers, Fredson. "The Supposed Cancel in Southerne's The Disappointment Reconsidered." Library, Fifth Series, V (1950),
140-149.

The irregular three-leaf gathering E is the original gathering rather than a cancellation.

5858 Younghughes, S. K. "An Edition of 'The Fatal Marriage, or A
      Second Lucreatya,' from the Manuscript Egerton 1994 in the
      British Museum." M.A. London University, 1956.

5859 Thornton, Ralph Rees. "The Wives Excuse by Thomas Southerne:
      A Critical Edition." Ph.D. University of Pennsylvania, 1966.
        Includes a study of the play's composition, earlier editions,
      staging, popular success, and its importance in the revival
      of the comedy of manners.

Southey, Robert

5860 Knowlton, E. C. "Southey's Monodramas." Philological Quarterly,
      VIII (October, 1929), 408-410.
        From 1793 to 1802 Southey composed seven blank verse
      monodramas modelled on Dr. Sayers' Oswald.

Soviet Stage

5861 Esenin, Sergei. "Foreign Plays on Soviet Stage." Indian Review,
      LX (1959), 483-484.
        Among others, Sheridan, Fielding, and Goldsmith.

Spain

5862 Mathews, Ernest Garland. "Studies in Anglo-Spanish Cultural
      and Literary Relations, 1598-1700." Ph.D. Harvard University,
      1938.
        Discusses the transitional nature of the relationship of Spain
      to England (a foe becoming a friend), the English knowledge
      of the Spanish language and Spanish writers. Includes a section
      on the portrayal of Spaniards in the plays of the Restoration.

5863 Loftis, John. "Spanish Drama in Neoclassical England." Compara-
      tive Literature, XI (1959), 29-34.
        Adaptations.

Spectacle

5864 Thomas, Russell B. "Spectacle in the Theaters of London from
      1767 to 1802." Ph.D. University of Chicago, 1942.

Spiller, Jemmy

5865 Lawrence, W. J. "A Player-Friend of Hogarth's." The Elizabethan
      Playhouse and Other Studies. Second Series. (Stratford-on-

Avon: Shakespeare Head Press), 216-226.

Jemmy Spiller, Rich's clown at his new theatre in Lincoln's Inn Fields.

Squire Trelooby

5866 Lawrence, W. J. "The Gordian Knot Untied." Times Literary Supplement, June 11, 1925, p. 400.

Replies to Dennis Arundell (TLS, June 4, 1925): sees no reason for identifying The Gordian Knot Untied with Squire Treeloby [sic].

St. Omers

5867 McCabe, William H. "Music and Dance on a 17th Century College Stage." Musical Quarterly, XXIV (1938), 313-322.

A history of music and dance performed at the English College at St. Omers, Pas de Calais.

5868 -----. "Notes on the St. Omers College Theatre." Philological Quarterly, XVII (1938), 225-239.

A description of actors, plays, audiences, and other matters relevant to the theatre in the English Jesuit college of St. Omers, Pas de Calais, from 1592 to 1762.

Stage Design

5869 Nicoll, Allardyce. The English Stage. London: Ernest Benn, 1928. (Benn's Sixpenny Library, No. 32). 80 pp.

Two chapters survey briefly Restoration and 18th-century stage design.

5870 Scholz, Janos, editor. Baroque and Romantic Stage Design. Introduction by A. Hyatt Mayor. New York: Bittner, 1950. xiii, 24 pp.

Covers the period between 1550 and 1730 with black and white drawings for set designs. While each design is identified, it is rarely asociated with a specific play.

Stage Devices

5871 Graves, Thornton S. "The Echo-Device." Modern Language Notes, XXXVI (1921), 120-121.

An essay calling attention to several uses of the echo-device missed by Colby (q.v.), including William Lower's The Enchanted Lovers (1658) and Walter Montague's The Shepherd's Paradise (1659).

5872 Sprague, Arthur Colby. "Off-Stage Sounds." University of Toronto
Quarterly, XV (1945), 70-75.
A general note on a theatrical device.

Stage History

5873 Baker, Henry Barton. History of the London Stage and Its Famous
Players (1576-1903). Rev. Ed. London: Routledge, 1904. 557 pp.
An account of the dramatists and the stage careers of noted
actors, not their biographies. Chronological list of London
theatres from the earliest period to 1904, pp. ix-xix.
5874 "The English Stage in the Eighteenth Century." The [London] Times
February 16, 1906, p. 11.
Review of the first of three lectures given by H. B. Irving
on "The English Stage in the 18th Century" at the Royal Institution (February 15, 1906). "To Cibber, Garrick, and John Kemble
as actor-managers was due the credit of rescuing the theatre
of the 18th century from the dishonesty and incompetence or
extravagance of such worthless managers as Rich, Fleetwood,
or Sheridan."
5875 "The English Stage in the Eighteenth Century." The [London] Times,
February 23, 1906, p. 23.
Review of the second of three lectures given by H. B. Irving
at the Royal Institution (February 22). Deals with the career of
Garrick and the difficulties encountered by the provincial actors.
5876 Nicholson, Watson. Struggle for a Free Stage in London. Boston
and New York: Houghton, 1906. xii, 475 pp.
Traces the long struggle which began with Charles II and
culminated in 1843, when the Theatre Regulations Bill deprived
the two patent theatres, Drury Lane and Covent Garden, of
their century-old monopoly of playing Shakespeare and national
drama. Bibliography, pp. 435-460.
5877 Lawrence, William John. "Title and locality boards on the Restoration stage." Deutsche Shakespeare-Gesellschaft. Jahrbuch,
Jahrg. 45 (1909), 146-170.
5878 Boswell, Eleanore. The Restoration Court Stage. Cambridge:
Harvard University Press, 1932. xviii, 370 pp.
Discusses the physical set-up of the Restoration stage as
well as specific plays performed.
5879 Rulfs, Donald Jacob. "The Lesser Elizabethan Playwrights on the
London Stage from 1776-1833." Ph.D. University of North
Carolina, 1940.
5880 Foster, George Harding. "British History on the London Stage,
1660-1760." Ph.D. University of North Carolina, 1941.
5881 Harbage, Alfred. "A Choice Ternary. Belated Issues of Elizabethan

Plays." Notes and Queries, CLXXXIII (1942), 32-34.
　　　The composition, dates, and authors of the three plays
　　published in A Choice Ternary of English Plays (1662) provide
　　some interesting speculation.
5882　Stoll, Elmer E. "The 'Real Society' in Restoration Comedy:
　　　Hymeneal Pretenses." Modern Language Notes, LVIII (1943),
　　　175-181.
　　　　The author cites additional evidence in support of his view
　　that "art reflected the taste rather than the life of the time."
5883　Woehl, Arthur L. "Some Plays in the Repertories of the Patent
　　　Houses." Studies in Speech and Drama in Honor of Alexander
　　　M. Drummond. Edited by Donald C. Walker, et al. Ithaca,
　　　New York: Cornell University Press; London: Oxford University
　　　Press, 1944, 105-122.
　　　　"On the preponderance of Elizabethan plays in the acting
　　repertories to 1682."
5884　Rulfs, Donald J. "Reception of the Elizabethan Playwrights on the
　　　London Stage, 1776-1833." Studies in Philology, XLVI (1949),
　　　54-69.
　　　　A survey of the performances with assessment of the
　　changing tastes which they mirror.

Stage Manager

5885　Howard, Gordon S. "An Analysis of the Contribution of the English
　　　Stage Manager to the Evolution of the Director." M.S. Uni-
　　　versity of Oregon, 1963.

Stage Properties

5886　Perrigard, E. E. "The Development of Properties in Drama on
　　　the English-speaking Stage." M.A. McGill University, 1936.

Stagecraft

5887　Heil, Liselotte. Die Darstellung der englischen Tragödie zur
　　　Zeit Bettertons. Ph.D. University of Berlin, 1936.
　　　　A technical history concerned with theatre construction,
　　stagecraft, scenery, and theories and modes of acting. Eng-
　　lish theories--Gildon, Cibber, Rymer, Dryden, Southerne.
5888　Clark, William S. "Corpses, Concealments, and Curtains on the
　　　Restoration Stage." Review of English Studies, XIII (1937),
　　　438-448.
　　　　Clark describes the construction and function of the stage
　　traverse in the Restoration theatre and shows how it was

used in various plays of the period.

5889 Nicoll, Allardyce. The Development of the Theatre. Rev. ed.
New York: Harcourt, Brace, 1937.

An elaborate illustrated history of theatre design, stagecraft,
costume, and scenery. The period of the Restoration and 18th
century is treated concisely in two chapters.

5890 -----. The Development of the Theatre. A Study of Theatrical Art
from the Beginnings to the Present Day. London: Harrap, 1948.
318 pp.

A revised and enlarged edition of the 1927 volume.

Staging

5891 Courtney, Arthur W. "Stage Presentation of Plays in the Restoration
Period." Ph.D. New York University, 1917.

5892 Campbell, Lily Bess. Scenes and Machines on the English Stage
During the Renaissance: a Classical Revival. Cambridge: The
University Press, 1923. 312 pp.

An attempt to show that "the classical influence and the
resulting theories and practices of stagecraft found their way
to England before the Restoration for the most part directly
from Italy, but after the Restoration by way of both Italy and
France." Part IV deals with Stage Decoration in England after
the Restoration.

5893 Graves, Thornton S. "The Literal Acceptance of Stage Illusion."
South Atlantic Quarterly, XXIII (1924), 124-141.

An anecdotal history of the "audience accepting as actual
occurrences the incidents which take place on the stage."
Restoration and 18th-century English drama are treated passim.

5894 Payne, F. W. "Staging in the Restoration, with Special Reference
to Stage Directions in the Plays of the Time." Ph.D. London
University (Kings), 1926.

5895 Crean, P. J. "Footlights." Notes and Queries, CLXIV (1933), 61-
62.

The article suggests that footlights were introduced into
theatres in 1765-66.

5896 Lawrence, William J. Old Theatre Days and Ways. London:
Harrap, 1935. 255 pp.

5897 Sprague, Arthur Colby. Shakespeare and the Actors. The Stage
Business in His Plays (1660-1905). Cambridge, Massachusetts:
Harvard University Press, 1944. 440 pp.

5898 McDowell, John H. "Historical Development of the Box Set."
Theatre Annual 1945 (1945), 65-83.

A general survey, going back to the last decade of the
eighteenth century.

5899 Hummel, Ray O., Jr. "The Wonderful Secrets of Stage Tricks,
      1794." Notes and Queries, CXCII (September 6, 1947), 391.
      Describes the book, asking for further information.

5900 Falls, Gregory A. "An Analytical and Historical Investigation
      of the Staging of Restoration Comedy as Related to Modern
      Revivals." Ph.D. Northwestern University, 1953. 273 pp.
      (Publication No. 7029).
      The purpose of this study is to encourage modern revivals
      of Restoration comedies by showing means of successfully
      producing them.

5901 Watters, Don Albert. "The Pictorial in English Theatrical Staging,
      1773-1833." Ph.D. Ohio State University, 1954.

5902 Martin, Lee Jackson. "Action within the Scene on the English
      Restoration Stage." Ph.D. Stanford University, 1956.
      Amount and type of action behind proscenium arch.

5903 Adelsperger, Walter Charles. "Aspects of Staging of Plays of
      the Gothic Revival in England." Ph.D. Ohio State University,
      1959. (Order No. 60-1168).
      A study of scenery, based on material from promptbooks.

5904 Martin, Lee J. "From Forestage to Proscenium: a Study of Resto-
      ration Staging Techniques." Theatre Survey, IV (1963), 3-28.
      From a study of text and stage directions in several plays,
      it is evident that the Restoration stage increased acting space
      by gradually removing it from the forestage to the area behind
      the proscenium arch.

5905 Payne, Rhoda. "Stage Direction during the Restoration." Theatre
      Annual, XX (1963), 41-63.
      Concludes that "although the director's role has grown in
      importance, its germ may certainly be seen in the practices
      of directing during the Restoration." Examines the director-
      ship of Davenant, Betterton, Cibber, Dryden and others. In-
      cludes illustrations.

5906 Langhans, Edward Allen. "Staging Practices in the Restoration
      Theatres 1660-1682." Ph.D. Yale University, 1965. (Order
      No. 65-9469).
      The development of machines, lighting, and other theatrical
      effects to meet the demand of Restoration audiences for
      spectacle was in part responsible for the type of play Dryden
      and his compatriots wrote.

Stallman

5907 Bateson, F. W. "The Discrimination of Literary Sources: Mr.
      Stallman's Muddles." College English, XVII (1955), 131-135.
      Minor references to Pope, Dryden, Sterne--but only as

examples to explain the distinctions between types of sources and Stallman's alleged inner contradictions and "muddles." (Most examples from other periods--Romantic and Modern.)

Stapylton, Robert

5908 Bowers, Fredson. "The First Editions of Sir Robert Stapylton's The Slighted Maid (1663) and The Step-Mother (1664)." Papers of the Bibliographical Society of America, XLV (1951), 143-148.
    Bowers corrects erroneous beliefs about the printing of these two plays.

Stationers' Company

5909 Blagden, Cyprian. The Stationers' Company: A History, 1403-1959. London: Allen & Unwin; Cambridge: Harvard University Press, 1960. 321 pp.
    This is a history of the Stationers' Company, an institution that has had a corporate existence for over 550 years. It seeks to fill in details not hitherto available in print while providing full reference to secondary works covering aspects previously available.

Stedman, John

5910 Doyle, Paul A. "A Rare Copy of John Stedman's Laelius and Hortensia." Publication of the Bibliographical Society of America, LI (1957), 241-244.

Steele, Richard

letters

5911 Steele, Richard. The Letters of Richard Steele. Selected by R. Brimley Johnson. London: John Lane, 1927. xii, 202 pp. (The Quill Library).
    A selection, including about 200 to his wife Prue and the long one to Congreve about Addison.
5912 -----. The Correspondence of Richard Steele. Edited by Rae Blanchard. London: Oxford University Press, H. Milford, 1941. xxviii, 562 pp.
    Contains Steele's general correspondence, his family correspondence and miscellaneous printed letters and papers. Extensively annotated and thoroughly indexed. Considerable material on Steele and the theatre.

works

5913 -----. Richard Steele. With an Introduction and Notes by G. A.
       Aitken. London: T. F. Unwin, 1903. lxxi, 452 pp. (The Mer-
       maid Series).
           Biographical introduction, followed by texts of The Funeral,
       The Lying Lover, The Tender Husband, The Conscious Lovers,
       and two fragments, The School of Action and The Gentleman.
       Notes to the plays include introductory information listing first
       productions and casts, with general history of other presenta-
       tions, and extensive notes on textual variants and explanations of
       references.

essays

5914 -----. Essays of Richard Steele. Selected and Edited by L. E.
       Steele. London: Macmillan, 1907.
           Steele's "Theatrical Essays" contained on pp. 187-217;
       "The Pleasures of the Playhouse," "Betterton the Actor,"
       "The Death of Estcourt," "The Opera and the Puppet Show,"
       "The Scornful Lady," "The Distrest Mother."
5915 -----. Richard Steele's Periodical Journalism, 1714-16. The
       Lover, The Reader, Town-Talk in a Letter to a Lady in the
       Country, Chit-Chat in a Letter to a Lady in the Country.
       Edited by Rae Blanchard. Oxford: Clarendon Press, 1959.
       xxviii, 346 pp.
           Topics include the theatre.

individual texts

5916 -----. The Tender Husband. Edited by Calhoun Winton. (Regents
       Restoration Drama Series). Lincoln: University of Nebraska
       Press, 1967.
           Includes introduction, notes and chronology.

biography and criticism

5917 Wendt, Otto. Steeles litterarische Kritik Über Shakespeare im
       Tatler und Spectator. Rostock: Carl Boldt'sche Hofbuchdruck-
       erei, 1901. 44 pp.
           The actual number of pages devoted to an analysis of Steele's
       treatment of Shakespeare is quite small. Steele is also con-
       sidered as a critic, and a brief discussion of his style is given.
5918 Hare, M. E. "Steele and the Sentimental Comedy." Eighteenth
       Century Literature. An Oxford Miscellany. (Oxford: At the

Clarendon Press, 1909), 5-41.

An analysis of Steele's comedies to show how the sentimental dominates them, and what Steele meant by the term.
Somewhat of a patronizing attitude is adopted toward Steele.

5919 Blume, Paul. "Die Stellung von Addison und Steele zum Theater
in den Moralischen Wochenschriften." Inaugural Dissertation.
Münster, 1920.

5920 Steele, Richard. "Grief a-la-mode, 1702." Theatre Arts Monthly,
IX (May, 1925), 306.

From the Prologue to The Funeral.

5921 Blanchard, Rae. "Richard Steele as a Moralist and Social Reformer." Ph.D. University of Chicago, 1928.

There are indications that Steele's thought is related to that
current of thought which was antithetical to rationalism.

5922 -----. "Richard Steele and the Status of Women." Studies in
Philology, XXVI (July, 1929), 325-355.

In his essays and plays Steele "praises rational courtship
and the dignity of marriage."

5923 "Richard Steele." Times Literary Supplement, August 29, 1929,
pp. 657-658.

A character sketch of Steele and a critical estimate of his
part in the Tatler and Spectator, with only passing reference
to the plays.

5924 Thomas, Gilbert. "Sir Richard Steele." Spectator, CXLIII (August
31, 1929), 268-269.

A sketch of his career.

5925 Waugh, Arthur. "Richard Steele." Fortnightly Review, CXXXII
(September, 1929), 388-396.

Biographical and critical sketch.

5926 Laney, Emma M. "The Theatre by Richard Steele." Ph.D. Yale
University, 1930.

5927 Blanchard, Rae. "A Prologue and Epilogue for Nicholas Rowe's
Tamerlane by Richard Steele." Publications of the Modern
Language Association, XLVII (1932), 772-776.

Evidence to prove that the prologue and epilogue to Rowe's
Tamerlane uncovered among the P. A. Taylor papers in the
British Museum are by Richard Steele, and that he wrote them,
probably in the early 1720's, for use at Dr. Newcome's School
in Clapton, Hackney.

5928 -----. "Some Unpublished Letters of Richard Steele to the Duke
of Newcastle." Modern Language Notes, XLVIII (1933), 232-
246.

Reprints, with commentary, a dozen letters: ten from
Steele to his patron, the Duke of Newcastle and two to Henry
Pelham, Newcastle's brother. Several letters contain refer-

erences to Steele's plays and to his management of Drury Lane.

5929 Connely, Willard. Sir Richard Steele. London: C. Scribner's,
1934. 462 pp.

Connely's extensive, lucid biography includes documents
that have come to light since the publication of Aitken's study.

5930 Eaker, Susan. "Steele and Percy MacKaye: Their Theories and
Practice in the Theatre." M.A. Cornell University, 1940.

5931 Blanchard, Rae. "Additions to The Correspondence of Richard
Steele." Review of English Studies, XVIII (October, 1942),
466-470.

Discusses material from the Steele Papers in the George A.
Aitken Collection at the University of Texas which helps to
complete descriptions of some letters in Rae Blanchard's edition
of Steele's Correspondence.

5932 -----. "Richard Steele's West Indian Plantation." Modern Philology,
XXXIX (February, 1942), 281-285.

Examines new data, chiefly bearing on financial transactions,
from the archives at Bridgetowen, Barbados.

5933 Stratman, Carl Joseph, C.S.V. "An Analysis of Sir Richard Steele's
Principles for Sentimental Comedy As Defined in His Criticism
and Demonstrated in His Plays." M.A. Catholic University of
America, 1945.

5934 Sites, Thelma W. "Sir Richard Steele's Dramatic Criticism along
with His Comments on the Theatre." M.A. Duke University,
1947.

5935 Baine, Rodney M. "The Publication of Steele's Conscious Lovers."
Studies in Bibliography, II (1949-1950), 170-173.

Baines acquits Steele of any wrongdoing in selling the printing
rights to the play. Steele's contractual dealings with the Ton-
sons.

5936 Blanchard, Rae. "The Songs in Steele's Plays." Pope and His Contemporaries: Essays Presented to George Sherburn. Edited by
James L. Clifford and Louis A. Landa. (Oxford: Oxford University Press, 1949), 185-200.

An analysis of the songs and their composition, noting the
extent to which they affect the dramatic mood of the plays.

5937 Loftis, John. "Richard Steele, Drury Lane, and the Tories."
Modern Language Quarterly, X (March, 1949), 72-80.

Was Steele approached with an offer of the governorship
of Drury Lane in 1713?

5938 -----. "Steele and the Drury Lane Patent." Modern Language
Notes, LXIV (January, 1949), 19-21.

Information from an expense account preserved at Blenheim
Castle.

5939 -----. "The Genesis of Steele's 'The Conscious Lovers.'" Essays

Critical and Historical Dedicated to Lily B. Campbell (Berkeley and Los Angeles: University of California Press, 1950), 173-182

The Conscious Lovers dramatizes themes and ideas to which Steele's audience had been previously exposed in The Tatler, The Spectator, and The Guardian.

5940 -----. "Richard Steele's Censorium." Huntington Library Quarterly, XIV (1950-1951), 43-66.

From 1712 to 1722 or 1723 Steele used the Censorium, a private theatre, to incorporate his proposed stage reforms into theatrical practice.

5941 -----. "The Eighteenth-Century Beginnings of Modern Drama." Emory University Quarterly, VII (1951), 225-236.

Many aspects of modern theatrical practice first appeared in the plays of Gay, Lillo, and Steele.

5942 -----. "Richard Steele and the Drury Lane Management." Modern Language Notes, LXVI (1951), 7-11.

Steele's hiring of "Mr. Baxter and his Companion" in 1715-1716 indicates that he occasionally "took an active share in conducting the routine business of the Drury Lane Company."

5943 -----. Steele at Drury Lane. Berkeley and Los Angeles: University of California Press, 1952. 260 pp.

Loftis examines "Steele's theatrical career in the context of early eighteenth-century stage and dramatic history."

5944 Foxon, D. F. "A Piracy of Steele's The Lying Lover." Library, Fifth Series, X (1955), 127-129.

Suggests that William Serle was the pirate, and offers a few other possibilities. Gives his reasons for believing the

5945 copy to be pirated.

5945 Parnell, Paul E. "A New Molière Source for Steele's The Tender Husband." Notes and Queries, CCIV (1959), 218.

The inventory of the marriage portion in Steele's The Tender Husband was modeled on a similar scene in Molière's L'Avare.

5946 -----. "A Source for the Duel Scene in The Conscious Lovers." Notes and Queries, New Ser., IX (1962), 13-15.

Discussion of the relationship between Act IV, Sc. i of The Conscious Lovers, and Colley Cibber's Woman's Wit (1697).

5947 Dobrée, Bonamy. Variety of Ways: Discussions on Six Authors. Freeport, New York: Books for Libraries Press, 1967. 118 pp.

A reprint of the 1932 edition includes discussions of Congreve, Dryden and Steele.

5948 Dobson, Austin. First Series: Eighteenth Century Vignettes. New York: Benjamin Blom, 1967. 264 pp.

A reprint of the 1892 edition includes essays on Goldsmith's library and on Steele.

Sterne, Laurence

5949 Stedmond, J. M. "Uncle Toby's 'Campaigns' and Raree-Shows."
        Notes and Queries, CCI (1956), 28-29.
             Describes this common form of public entertainment in the
        18th century and suggests that Sterne was referring to the
        raree-show in Tristram Shandy.
5950 Anderson, Howard. "A Version of Pastoral: Class and Society in
        Tristram Shandy." Studies in English Literature, 1500-1900,
        VII (1967), 509-529.
             A study of Sterne's use of pastoral to reflect on the contem-
        porary world includes references to Steele's The Conscious
        Lovers and Gay's The Beggar's Opera.

Stevens, George

5951 Thomas, Robert Blaine. "The Life and Works of George Alexander
        Stevens." Ph.D. Louisiana State University, 1961. 241 pp.
        (Order No. 61-5156).
             Minor literary figure of the eighteenth century; writer who
        was an actor, puppeteer, poet, novelist, dramatist, essayist,
        and lecturer. Some plays were never intended for the stage,
        although his farces were.

Strahan, William

5952 Gaskell, Philip. "The Strahan Papers." Times Literary Supple-
        ment, October 5, 1956, p. 592.
             A discussion of the records, accounts and papers of Wil-
        liam Strahan, Master Printer, with brief references to his
        friends, David Hume and Samuel Johnson. Primarily of interest
        to the student of 18th- and 19th-century publishing.

Structure

5953 Berghäuser, Wilhelm. "Die Darstellung des Wahnsinns im englis-
        chen Drama bis zum Ende des 18 Jahrhunderts." Inaugural
        Dissertation. Giessen, 1914.
5954 Hoy, Cyrus. "Renaissance and Restoration Dramatic Plotting."
        Renaissance Drama, IX (1966), 247-264.
             Examines the dramatic plotting in the tragicomedies and
        comedies of the late Jacobean and Caroline periods and in the
        Restoration heroic play. Since plays of both periods are con-
        cerned with erotic passion, they exhibit similarities in theme
        and in the arrangement and movement of the action.

Strutt

5955 Fox, E. Margery. "Moving Pictures and Cinematographs." Notes
      and Queries, 11th Ser., III (February 25, 1911), 155-156.
          Description in Strutt's Sports and Pastimes of moving pic-
      tures in Anne's time as having some likeness to puppets and
      Strutt's own recollection of seeing in 1760 pasteboard figures
      ascending and descending to slow music.

Swift, Jonathan

letters

5956 Swift, Jonathan. The Correspondence of Jonathan Swift, D.D.
      Edited by F. Elrington Ball, with an Introduction by the Very
      Reverend J. H. Bernard, D.D. 6 vols. London: G. Bell & Sons,
      Ltd., 1910-1914.
          A complete edition of Swift's letters, which also contains
      many letters to Swift and some letters about Swift.

biography and criticism

5957 Webster, C. M. "Swift and the English and Irish Theatre." Notes
      and Queries, CLXIII (1932), 452-454.
          Attempts to illuminate Swift's personality by summarizing
      his estimates of 17th- and 18th-century theatrical life and
      thought.
5958 B[ond], D[onald] F. "Swift at the Moving Pictures." Notes and
      Queries, CLXXXVIII (March 24, 1945), 130.
          Adds to A. H. Scouten's references (January 27) passages
      from The Spectator.
5959 Jackson, R. Wyse. Swift and His Circle A Book of Essays. Dublin:
      The Talbot Press, 1945. 124 pp.
          Chapter Three ("The Drapier and the Theatre, 18-21) re-
      counts Swift's support of a play produced for the relief of un-
      employed weavers.
5960 Landa, Louis A. and James Edward Tobin. Jonathan Swift: A List
      of Critical Studies Published from 1895 to 1945. To which is
      added remarks on some Swift Manuscripts in the United States
      by Herbert Davis. New York: Cosmopolitan Science and Art
      Service Co., 1945. 62 pp.
          An annotated bibliography, with items of theatrical interest.
5961 Williams, Harold. "Swift and Shakespeare." Notes and Queries,
      CXCIII (May 1, 1948), 194-195.
          Discusses Swift's knowledge of Shakespeare.

5962 Mayhew, George. "Some Dramatizations of Swift's Polite
        Conversations (1738)." Philological Quarterly, XLIV (1965),
        51-72.
            Productions of Swift's prose work in Dublin theatres shortly
        after its publication in 1738.
5963 Williams, Kathleen. "Restoration Themes in the Major Satires of
        Swift." Review of English Studies, XVI (1965), 258-271.
            Includes brief references to Dryden, Wycherley, and Ether-
        ege. "Like them, he is affected by the view of man as animal
        or automation, and by the moral narrowness and defeatism
        and the intellectual pride of the new age, and in the three
        major satires he can be seen as coming to terms with the
        disturbing views of the later seventeenth century."

Sword Dance

5964 Sharp, Cecil James. The Sword Dances of Northern England,
        Together with the Horn Dance of Abbets Bromley. 3 vols.
        London: Novello and Company, Ltd. [1911-1913].
            A description of eleven long-sword and short-sword dances
        of northern England, giving the costume, music, steps,
        figures and notation for each, together with notes on the origin
        and development of the dances.

Tancred and Gismund

5965 Murray, John. "Tancred and Gismund'; The Tragedy in English
        Drama." Review of English Studies, XIV (1938), 385-395.
            Murray traces the plot of "Tancred and Gismund" in its
        various appearances on the stage from the 1744 Dodsley ver-
        sion to the treatments by Dryden and Wilmot, pointing up
        changes in and additions to the original plot.

Taste

5966 Havens, Raymond B. "Changing Taste in the Eighteenth Century."
        Publications of the Modern Language Association, XLIV (1929),
        501-536.
5967 Brett, R. L. "The Aesthetic Sense and Taste in the Literary
        Criticism of the Early Eighteenth Century." Review of English
        Studies, XX (1944), 199-213.
            A consideration of the conflicts between Reason and Taste
        in 18th-century critical writings. References to dramatic
        criticism.
5968 Bate, Walter Jackson. From Classic to Romantic: Premises of

Taste in Eighteenth-Century England. Cambridge, Mass.:
Harvard University Press; London: Geoffrey Cumberlege,
1946. 197 pp.

5969 Bronson, Bertrand H. "Printing as an Index of Taste in Eighteenth
Century England. Part II." Bulletin of the New York Public
Library, LXII (1958), 443-462.

Also printed as a separate pamphlet (New York: New York
Public Library, 1958) with its own pagination. Concentrates
primarily on title pages, since the author's wishes are primary
in deciding whether "it shall be determinative, descriptive, or
suggestive; whether to include or omit the writer's name;
whether to add a motto and of what sort." Includes references
to printed dramatic works.

Tate, Nahum

texts

5970 Tate, Nahum. Dido and Aeneas. An Opera Perform'd at Mr. Josias
Priest's Boarding-school at Chelsey by Young Gentlemen. The
Words Made by Mr. Nahum Tate. The Music Composed by Mr.
Henry Purcell. London: Humphrey Milford, Oxford University
Press [1926]. 29, [2] pp.

German and English texts on facing pages. Only the text is
given.

5971 -----, and Henry Purcell. Dido and Aeneas. Libretto Facsimile
of the First Edition. London: Boosey and Hankins, 1961. [3],
8 pp.

biography and criticism

5972 Tregaskis, James. "Shakespeare Allusions." Times Literary Supplement, June 5, 1924, p. 356.

Notes on allusion to The Comedy of Errors in Tate's A
Duke and No Duke (1693).

5973 Lea, Kathleen M. "Sir Aston Cokayne and the 'commedia dell'
arte." Modern Language Review, XXIII (January, 1928), 47-
51.

Traces commedia as a source of Cokayne's Trappolin
(printed 1658), and notes Tate's revision in A Duke and No
Duke (1684).

5974 Scott-Thomas, H. F. "The Date of Nahum Tate's Death."
Modern Language Notes, XLIX (March, 1934), 169-171.

Irrespective of the dates suggested by other "confused"
literary historians, Tate is here alleged to have died on
July 30, 1715.

5975   -----. "Nahum Tate and the Seventeenth Century." English Liter-
       ary History, I (1934), 250-275.
             Nahum Tate was behind his times and looks back to the neo-
       classicism of the Renaissance.
5976   Spencer, H. "Tate and The White Devil." English Literary History,
       I (1934), 235-249.
             Tate's adaptation of The White Devil was published in 1707
       as Injur'd Love: or, The Cruell Husband. A Tragedy. Designed
       to be Acted at the Theatre Royal. The copy of the play was a
       corrected quarto (Q3 [1665] or Q4 [1672]). Spencer analyzes the
       revisions of the plot, act by act, and then writes about alter-
       ations of diction.
5977   Scott-Thomas, H. F. "Nahum Tate, Laureate: Two Biographical
       Notes." Modern Language Notes, LVI (1941), 611-612.
             Calls attention to Tate's "weakly constitution from the very
       Cradle" and to the fact that the Earl of Carlisle was his patron.
5978   Scouten, Arthur H. "An Italian Source for Nahum Tate's Defense
       of Farce." Italica, XXVII (1950), 238-240.
             The discourse "concerning farce" prefacing A Duke and No
       Duke is derived largely from the De Personis of Agesilao
       Mariscotti (1577-1618).
5979   Golden, S. A. "Nahum Tate--Poet and Dramatist." Ph.D. Trinity
       College, Dublin, 1954.
5980   -----. "The Three Faithful Teates." Notes and Queries, CC
       (1955), 374-380.
             A biographical note, which attempts to unravel the identity
       of Nahum Tate's father.
5981   -----. "Variations in the Name of Nahum Tate." Notes and
       Queries, New Ser., III (1956), 72.
             Also "Nathaniel."
5982   -----. "The Late Seventeenth-Century Writer and the Laureate-
       ship: Nahum Tate's Tenure." Hermathena, LXXXIX (1957),
       30-38.
             Discusses the finances of Tate, and his attempted use of
       the laureateship for financial help.
5983   "Three Shakespeare Adaptations." Proceedings of the Leeds
       Philosophical and Literary Society, Literary and Historical
       Section, VIII (1959), 233-240.
             Dryden's Troilus, Tate's Lear, Theobald's Richard II.
5984   Spencer, Christopher. "A Word for Tate's King Lear." Studies
       in English Literature, 1500-1900, III (1963), 241-251.
             Suggests that Tate's adaptation of Shakespeare's play is
       in keeping with his own dramatic purposes.
5985   Black, A. J. "A Critical Edition of Nahum Tate's The History of
       King Lear." Ph.D. University of Birmingham, 1965.

5986 McGugan, Ruth Ella. "Nahum Tate and the Coriolanus Tradition
      of English Drama with a Critical Edition of Tate's The In-
      gratitude of a Common-Wealth." Ph.D. University of Illinois,
      1965. (Order No. 66-4234).
          A scholarly Introduction traces the probable sources and
      subsequent influence of Tate's Ingratitude. Tables appended to
      the work compare Tate's version with those of Dennis, Thom-
      son, and Thomas Sheridan.
5987 Morris, Helen. Shakespeare's King Lear. New York: Barnes and
      Noble, 1965. 73 pp.
          See Chapter IV on Tate's version of King Lear.
5988 Hodson, Geoffrey. "The Nahum Tate 'Lear' at Richmond." Drama,
      No. 81 (Summer, 1966), 36-39.
          An account of a modern production of Tate's play under the
      auspices of the Inner London Education Authority.
5989 Williams, T. D. Duncan. "Mr. Nahum Tate's King Lear." Studia
      Neophilologica, XXXVIII (1966), 290-300.
          Examines the validity of charges made against Tate's
      adaptation and discusses the reasons for the play's long popular-
      ity, not the least of which is the age's taste for didactic novels
      and sentimental drama.
5990 Black, James. "An Augustan Stage-History: Nahum Tate's King
      Lear." Restoration and Eighteenth Century Theatre Research,
      VI (May, 1967), 36-54.
          Reviews comprehensively the productions of Tate's play
      from 1680 to the present and gives information on casts,
      scenery, and contemporary criticism. Includes a discussion
      of Garrick's relationship to Tate and the play.
5991 -----. "The Influence of Hobbes on Nahum Tate's King Lear."
      Studies in English Literature, 1500-1900, VII (1967), 377-385.
          Tate possessed more than the popular notion of Hobbes'
      doctrines and saw in Shakespeare's Edmund an adumbration,
      if not an actual type, of the Hobbesian "natural" man.

Tatham, John

5992 Tatham, John. The Dramatic Works of John Tatham. Edited by
      James Maidment and W. H. Logan. New York: Benjamin Blom,
      1967. 320 pp.
          A reprint of the 1874 edition includes five plays by Tatham.
5993 Scott, Virgil Joseph. A Reinterpretation of John Tatham's The
      Rump: or the Mirrour of the Late Times." Philological Quarter-
      ly, XXIV (1945), 114-118.
          The play is not a Royalist piece, but a party satire bidding
      for General Monk's favor.

Tell-Tale

5994 Foakes, R. A. and J. C. Gibson, eds. The Tell-Tale.
       London: Oxford University Press for the Malone Society,
       1960.

Theatre Buildings

5995 Nicoll, Allardyce. "Doors and Curtains in Restoration
       Theatres." Modern Language Review, XV (1920), 137-142.
            An endorsement of Lowe's view that there was a pair of
       doors at each side of the stage (Nicoll suggests that one door
       was in front of the curtain and the other behind). Regarding
       curtains, Nicoll states that in most cases the curtain was
       raised after the Prologue and lowered before the Epilogue.
5996 Summers, Montague. "Doors and Curtains in Restoration
       Theatres." Modern Language Review, XVI (1921), 66-71.
            An attack citing numerous inaccuracies in Allardyce
       Nicoll's article "Doors and Curtains in Restoration Theatres"
       (q.v.); especially concerned with errors in Nicoll's position
       on the use of the curtain.

Theatre Companies

5997 Sorelius, Gunnar. "The Rights of the Restoration Theatrical
       Companies in the Older Drama." Studia Neophilologica,
       XXXVII (1965), 174-189.
            The rights of Davenant's and Killigrew's companies to the
       production of plays written by Elizabethan and Jacobean play-
       wrights. Killigrew's King's Men enjoyed a virtual monopoly.

Theatre Construction

5998 Nicoll, Allardyce. The English Theatre: A Short History. New
       York: Thomas Nelson, 1936. xi, 252 pp.
            A history of theatre construction from the beginnings to
       the present day along with much incidental stage history. Two
       chapters treat the Restoration and 18th Century.

Theatre Tickets

5999 Davis, W. J., and A. W. Waters. Tickets and Passes of Great
       Britain and Ireland Struck or Engraved on Metal, Ivory, etc.
       Leamington Spa: Privately printed at the Courier Press, 1922.
       347 pp.

Section of Dramatic Tickets listed alphabetically by place
of use; entries give date, size and description as complete as
may be determined, as well as known dates of theatres listed.
Complete index.

Theatres

6000 Maude, Cyril. The Haymarket Theatre, Some Records and Re-
      miniscences. Edited by Ralph Monde. London: Grant Richards,
      1903. 235 pp.
6001 'Hood, Eu.' [i.e., Joseph Haslewood]. "Of the London Theatres."
      Gentleman's Magazine, LXXXIII (1813), 121-123, 217-221,
      333-334, 437, 553-563; LXXXIV (1814), 337-339; LXXXIV
      (July, 1814), 9-12. Reprinted Gentleman's Magazine, XV (1904).
          A brief study of the following theatres: Fortune Theatre,
      Whitefriars, Salisbury, Vere Street, Rose, Sadler's Wells,
      The Children of Powles, Dorset Gardens.
6002 Lawrence, W. J. "A Forgotten Restoration Playhouse." Englische
      Studien, XXXV (1905), 279-289.
          Concerned with the Cockpit Theatre in Drury Lane.
6003 Wyndham, Henry Saxe. Annals of Covent Garden Theatre from
      1732 to 1897. London: Chatto and Windus, 1906. 2 vols., xv,
      382; viii, 367 pp.
          Many anecdotes about Covent Garden players, managers,
      and singers. Appendix contains lists of the managers and
      principal events arranged chronologically, and lists of theatri-
      cal properties, scenery, and other items. 45 illustrations.
6004 Brereton, Austin. The Literary History of the Adelphi and Its
      Neighborhood. New York: Duffield, 1909. xi, 294 pp.
          Plates. Map. Mentions Garrick and his contemporaries.
6005 Bell, Hamilton. "Contributions to the History of the English
      Playhouse." Architectural Record, XXXIII (1913), 262-267;
      359-368.
          Part I, pp. 262-267, contains discussion of some plans of
      John Webb's in the Inigo Jones Collection of drawings at
      Worcester College, Oxford. Part II is a discussion and repro-
      duction of three plans of Sir Christopher Wren's at All Souls
      College, Oxford, one, perhaps, being the plan of the Duke's
      Theatre, Dorset Gardens.
6006 Lawrence, W. J. "Amended Chronological List of Elizabethan
      and Quasi-Elizabethan Playhouses (1576-1663)." The Elizabethan
      Playhouse and Other Studies. Second Series. (Stratford-on-Avon:
      Shakespeare Head Press, 1913), 237-239.
          Includes (p. 239) a one-paragraph description and history of
      the Vere Street Theatre to 1809.

6007 Douglas, William. "Correspondence." Notes and Queries, 11th
Ser. (April 4, 1914), 275.
Says Patagonian Theatre did not exist under that name after
1779.

6008 Tipping, H. A. Grinling Gibbons and the Woodwork of His Age.
New York: Charles Scribner's Sons, 1914. 259 pp.
Record of Gibbons' work. Includes description of the carvings
in the Old Duke's Theatre in Dorset Garden.

6009 Lawrence, W. J. "The Old Duke's Theatre in Dorset Garden."
Architectural Review, XLVI (1919), 112-115.
Attempts to set right some errors about Dorset Garden
history and architecture. Dorset Garden was pulled down in
1709. It had only one front--southern aspect to the Thames.
Its stage was illuminated by candlelight and the auditorium by
natural light.

6010 -----. "The Early Years of the First English Opera House."
Musical Quarterly, VII (1921), 104-117.
A discussion of the Old Queen's Theatre in the Haymarket,
built by John Vanbrugh in 1705, covering the appearance of the
theatre and performances through 1711 when the theatre became
a permanent opera house.

6011 Martin, S. "The New Theatre, Hammersmith." Notes and Queries,
Ser. 12, VIII (1921), 409.
A statement of the opinion that this theatre was a room ad-
joining the Windsor Castle Tavern, King Street.

6012 Ellis-Fermor, Una M. "Studies in the 18th-Century Stage."
Philological Quarterly, II (1923), 289-301.
Deals with three minor aspects of 18th-century theatre:
1) touring companies in the middle of the 18th century; 2) minor
theatres of London and its environs during the same period;
3) theatrical booths at the 18th-century London fairs.

6013 "Drury Lane As It Appeared on the Second Night of The School for
Scandal." Theatre Arts Monthly, IX (July, 1925), 453.
Depicts the screen scene.

6014 Forman, W. Courthope. "Sadler's Wells." Notes and Queries,
CXLVIII (April 18, 1925), 273-274.
A historical sketch of the oldest theatre in London (erected
1765).

6015 Sherson, Erroll. London's Lost Theatres of the Nineteenth Century. London: John Lane, 1925. 392 pp.
Includes an occasional reference to earlier drama, to Rich's
pantomime, the founding in 1770 of Astley's Circus theatre,
and 18th-century fair booths.

6016 Southam, Henry. "Theatre Royal, Westminster." Notes and
Queries, CXLIX (October 31, 1925), 313.

Notices a fire there, July 20, 1673.

6017 Chancellor, E. Beresford. "A Manuscript Account Book of Drury
Lane Theatre for 1746-48." Connoisseur, LXXV (August, 1926),
217-221.

A discussion of actors and actresses named in the account
book, and three pages reproduced.

6018 -----. "More Concerning a Manuscript Account Book of Drury
Lane Theatre for 1746-48." Connoisseur, LXXVI (September,
1926), 90-94.

A discussion of the plays performed September 15, 1747--
May 13, 1748, and four pages of the book reproduced.

6019 "The Dorset Gardens Theatre. 1671-1720." Mask, XII (July, 1926),
115.

Reprints a portion of Strype's map (1720), showing the Duke's
Playhouse.

6020 "Ground Plan Showing the Cockpit Theatre." Mask, XII (July, 1926),
117.

A reproduction from Fisher's Plan of Whitehall (c. 1663-
1670).

6021 Spencer, Hazelton. "The Blackfriars Mystery." Modern Philology,
XXIV (November, 1926), 173-180.

Pepys's "Blackfriars" is an error for Whitefriars or Salisbury Court, where Davenant's men were performing.

6022 "View of Whitehall." Mask, XII (July, 1926), facing p. 87.
Shows a portion of the Cockpit Theatre (1670-77).

6023 Burley, T. L. G. Playhouses and Players of East Anglia. Norwich: Jarrold and Sons, 1928. xi, 180 pp.

Records the history of East Anglian theatres from the 18th
century to the present.

6024 [Hay-Market]. Notes and Queries, CLIV (May 5, 1928), 308.
Reprints selections from The Daily Courant (May 4, 1728)
on the opera Ptolemy and rope-dancing at the Hay-Market.

6025 Mackintosh, Donald T. "Restoration Stage." Edinburgh Review,
CCXLVIII (July, 1928), 172-185.

Attempts to correct current misunderstanding about the
stages of Restoration theatres. The apron at Drury Lane
was much smaller than Nicoll believes. Holds that Restoration
stage designers owed little to the Elizabethans.

6026 [Theatre Royal]. Notes and Queries, CLIV (February 25, 1928),
128.

Reprints selections from The Daily Journal (February 26,
1728), concerning plays at the Theatre-Royal and at the Hay-
Market.

6027 Wood, Frederick T. "Goodman's Fields Theatre." Modern Language Review, XXV (1930), 443-456.

History of this unlicensed theatre.

6028 Jackson, Alfred. "London Playhouses, 1700-1705." Review of
English Studies, VIII (1932), 291-302.
A collection of newspaper references to the theatres.

6029 Welby, Alfred, and John Bean King. "Notes on 18th century theatres
in various cities." Lincolnshire Notes and Queries, XXI (Jan-
uary, 1931), 69-70; (July, 1931), 104-107; XXII (April, 1932),
19-20.
Theatres in Lincolnshire, including Alford, Boston, Bourne,
Brigg, Gainsborough, Grantham, Grimsby, Horncastle,
Lincoln, Louth, Market Deeping, Market Rasen, Spalding,
Stamford.

6030 Wood, F. T. "The Account Books of Lincoln's Inn Fields Theater,
1724-1727." Notes and Queries, CLXIV (1933), 220-224, 256-260,
272-274, 294-308.

6031 Loukomski, G.-K. Les Théâtres Anciens et Modernes. Preface
de Louis Hautecoeur. Ouvrage illustré de 88 planches en hélio-
gravure. Paris: Firmin-Didot et Cie, Editeurs [1935]. lxxxviii,
39 pp.
Plates of Drury Lane and Covent Garden.

6032 Avery, Emmett L., and Mildred Avery Deupree. "The New Theatre
in the Haymarket, 1734 and 1737." Notes and Queries, CLXXI
(1936), 41-42.
Supplements Nicoll's History by printing information from
Library of Congress files of the Daily Advertiser about the
history of the Haymarket Theatre for the periods, April-
August, 1734, and March-May, 1737.

6033 Smith, Dane F. Plays About the Theatre in England from 'The
Rehearsal' in 1671 to the Licensing Act in 1737. New York
and London: Oxford University Press, 1936. xxiv, 287 pp.
Concerned with all plays containing explicit comment about
the stage and theatrical conditions, this study is not restricted
to the genre of dramatic burlesque. Rather, it presents a
history of the theatre as it was recorded by practicing playwrights of the period. Includes an extensive bibliography.

6034 Gilder, Rosamond. "TheWorld in the Mirror of the Theatre."
Theatre Arts Monthly, XXI (1937), 599-671.
Drawings, prints, paintings, and narrative commentary
are used to illustrate the history of the theatre. Several
representative items from the Restoration and 18th Century
are included.

6035 Avery, Emmett L. "The Richmond Theatre in 1734 and 1735."
Notes and Queries, CLXXVIII (1940), 262.
Fills in the gap in knowledge about the activities of the
Richmond Hill theatre during 1734 and 1735.

6036 Turner, Vivian. "Our Colonial Theater." Quarterly Journal of Speech, XXVII (December, 1941), 559-573.

Accounts of opposition to the theatre and early dramatic performances (many of which were Restoration and 18th-century plays). Focuses on Charleston, Williamsburg, New York.

6037 Heal, Ambrose. "Old London Theatres and Music Halls." Notes and Queries, CLXXXIII (1942), 383.

Notes that Gordon Craig published a useful list of 18th-century London playhouses in his periodical The Mask during 1926.

6038 Scouten, A. H., and Leo Hughes. "The New Theatre in the Haymarket, 1734 and 1737." Notes and Queries, CLXXXVI (January 15, 1944), 52-53.

Correction to the list of performances given by E. L. Avery, Notes and Queries, CLXXI (1936), 41-42.

6039 "On Listing Theatres." Theatre Notebook, I (October, 1945), 2-5; (January, 1946), 16-17; (April, 1946), 34-35; (July, 1946), 48-50; (October, 1946), 59; I (January, 1947), 75-79; (April, 1947), 97.

A preliminary listing of British playhouses and materials relating to them compiled by the editorial staff of Theatre Notebook.

6040 Rosenfeld, Sybil. "Theatres in Goodman's Fields." Theatre Notebook, I (October, 1945), 50.

Summarizes the evidence extant.

6041 MacQueen-Pope, W. J. Theatre Royal, Drury Lane. London: W. H. Allen, 1946. 350 pp.

A general history, showing the theatre's movement towards preeminence in the eighteenth century. Numerous anecdotes.

6042 Summerson, John. Georgian London. London: Pleiades Books, 1946. xi, 315 pp. (The Georgian Handbooks Series).

A general survey of the architecture and town planning of eighteenth century London, with frequent references to the theatres.

6043 Williams, Charles D. "Some Tyneside Places of Amusement." Notes and Queries, CXC (January 26, 1946), 31-33.

Describes theatres and assembly rooms in the eighteenth century.

6044 Johannes, Irmgard. "Des Königs Schauspieler. Rings um Drury Lane." Athena, I, x (1947), 52-57.

A general survey of the Theatre Royal, Drury Lane, including comment on Garrick, Sheridan and the Kembles.

6045 King, Robert. North Shields Theatres. Gateshead: Northumberland Press, 1948. 164 pp.

A survey of regional theatres from 1765. In part previously

published in the Shields Evening News, 1940-1941.

6046 MacGregor, John E. M. and Richard Southern. "Report of a Survey of St. George's Hall, King's Lynn. 23 March 1945." Unpublished typescript in the possession of the Society for the Protection of Ancient Buildings.

A detailed survey of the building described in Theatre Notebook, III, 1 (October, 1948).

6047 MacQueen-Pope, W. J. Haymarket: Theatre of Perfection. London: W. H. Allen, 1948. xxv, 394 pp.

A general history of the theatre, with especially detailed comments on Samuel Foote.

6048 Southern, Richard. "Concerning a Georgian Proscenium Ceiling." Theatre Notebook, III (October, 1948), 6-12.

The proscenium ceiling at St. George's Hall, King's Lynn is described, with photographs.

6049 -----. The Georgian Playhouse. London: Pleiades Book, 1948. 72 pp. (The Georgian Handbooks Series).

The architectural development of the Georgian theatre is studied in detail with numerous illustrations.

6050 Hogan, Charles Beecher. "The New Wells, Goodman's Fields, 1739-1752." Theatre Notebook, III (July-September, 1949), 67-72.

An illustrated description of the theatre and an account of the Hallam family.

6051 MacQueen-Pope, W. J. "His Majesty's Theatre." Drama, Summer, 1949, 16-19.

An historical sketch, with notes on the theatre's development during the eighteenth century.

6052 Mander, R. P. "The Old-Time Stage. Two Hundred Years of Theatrical History in Bury St. Edmunds." The East Anglian Magazine, IX (November-December, 1949), nos. 3-4.

A survey of the available evidence of provincial performances during the eighteenth century.

6053 O., A. S. "From Guildhall to Theatre. The Restoration of St. George's Hall, King's Lynn." Country Life, CVI (November 18, 1949), 1521-1524.

An account of the Georgian building and its theatrical equipment.

6054 Southern, Richard. "The Theatre Remains at Wisbeck." Theatre Notebook, IV (October, 1949), 21-23.

Gives an account of the 1793 theatre shell.

6055 Avery, Emmett L. "The Capacity of the Queen's Theater in the Haymarket." Philological Quarterly, XXXI (1952), 85-87.

The capacity was at least 700.

6056 Scanlan, Elizabeth G. "Tennis-Court Theatres and the Duke's

Playhouse, 1661-1671." Ph.D. Columbia University, 1952.
409 pp.

The Duke's Playhouse is reconstructed on the basis of documents in Hotson's Commonwealth and Restoration Stage and
extant information on tennis-court theatres.

6057 Hogan, Charles Beecher. "The China Hall Theatre, Rotherhithe."
Theatre Notebook, VIII (1954), 76-80.

This minor theatre operated from 1776 to 1778.

6058 Sawyer, Paul. "The Seating Capacity and Maximum Receipts of
Lincoln's Inn Fields Theatre." Notes and Queries, CXCIX
(1954), 290.

The LIF probably held less than 1,400 people.

6059 Macqueen-Pope, W[alter]. Pillars of Drury Lane. London: Hutchinson, 1955. 267 pp.

65 illustrations. A somewhat rambling story of the theatre
from its beginnings to 1955; with stress laid upon some of the
great names who have figured in its life. There is no attempt at
a chronological approach. The pillars are the people who made
the theatre what it was and is.

6060 Scanlan, Elizabeth G. "Tennis Court Theatres in England and
Scotland." Theatre Notebook, X (1955), 10-15.

The use of tennis courts as theatres was not a widespread
practice in England and Scotland, and it was usually a temporary
measure. Scanlan discusses twelve (from 1653 on) with a short
history of each.

6061 Bordinat, Philip. "A New Site for the Salisbury Court Theatre."
Notes and Queries, CII (1956), 51-52.

The location of the sign indicating the site of the Salisbury
Court Playhouse is incorrect.

6062 Grice, F. "The Thetre Royal at Worcester." Theatre Notebook,
X (1956), 83-86.

6063 Hogan, Charles Beecher. "An Eighteenth-Century Prompter's
Notes." Theatre Notebook, X (1956), 37-44.

6064 Langhans, Edward A. "Notes on the Reconstruction of the Lincoln's
Inn Fields Theatre." Theatre Notebook, X (1956), 112-114.

6065 Scanlan, Elizabeth G. "Reconstruction of the Duke's Playhouse
in Lincoln's Inn Field, 1661-1671." Theatre Notebook, X
(1956), 48-50.

Photographs of a model.

6066 Speaight, George. "Tennis Court Theatres." Theatre Notebook,
X (1956), 64.

James Street, 18th century.

6067 Mander, Raymond, and Joe Mitchenson. A Picture History of the
British Theatre. London: Hulton Press, 1957.

6068 Rosenfeld, Sybil. "Goodman's Fields Theatre." Theatre Notebook,

XII (1957), 38.

Auction of contents, 1738.

6069 Arnott, J. F. "Two Drawings by Alexander Nasmyth." Theatre
Notebook, XIII (1958), 18-20.

Discusses some eighteenth-century theatre drawings.

6070 Quennell, Peter. "Echoes of Two Centuries at Covent Garden."
The Reporter, XIX (July 10, 1958), 31-33.

From 1732.

6071 Steer, Francis W. "Sources of Information on 18th and Early 19th
Century Theatres in Sussex." Theatre Notebook, XII (1958),
58-64.

6072 Kern, Ronald C. "Documents Relating to Company Management,
1705-1711." Theatre Notebook, XIV (1959-1960), 60-65.

Five documents suggest the manner in which the affairs of
the company were then directed at Drury Lane and especially
at the Queen's Theatre in the Haymarket.

6073 Morley, Malcolm. "More about the Royal Kent Theatre." Theatre
Notebook, [Winter], XIV (1959), 43-44.

6074 Dickson, P. G. M. The Sun Insurance Office, 1710-1960. London:
Oxford University Press, 1960. 324 pp.

A little information about the theatres that were insured
and the size of the policies in the 18th century.

6075 Eddison, Robert. "Capon and Goodman's Fields." Theatre Notebook, XIV (1960), 127-132.

This is an attempt to reconstruct the seating arrangements
and stage of Goodman's Fields Theatre as it appeared when
Garrick played there in 1741; the article is based on a plan
drawing by William Capon.

6076 Joseph, Stephen. "Three Hundred Years After . . . ." Encore,
VII (1960), 18-23.

English theatres have changed little since the Restoration.

6077 Rosenfeld, Sybil. "Report on Two Georgian Theatres." Theatre
Notebook, XIV (1960), 100-101.

6078 Smith, Roy. Three Model Theatres: Elizabethan, Eighteenth
Century, Modern. Edinburgh: Thomas Nelson and Sons,
Ltd., 1960. vii, [1], 151 pp.

A book of instructions on how to build model theatres.
One section, pp. 62-108, gives detailed instructions, with
diagrams, of how to build an 18th-century theatre.

6079 Mander, Raymond, and Joe Mitchenson. The Theatres of London.
Illustrated by Timothy Birdsall. London: Rupert Hart-Davis,
1961. 292 pp.

Four-to-eight page histories of 64 London theatres, listed
alphabetically under geographical areas, each entry illustrated
with drawing; includes chronological list of London theatres

and a list of architects of present London theatres.

6080 Joseph, Bertram L. "Famous Theatres: 1 The Theatre Royal, Bristol." Drama Survey, II (1962), 139-145.

6081 Wilson, John Harold. "A Theatre in York House." Theatre Notebook, XVI (Spring, 1962), 75-78.

Evidence for the existence of a theatre at York House from 1672-1674.

6082 Kennedy, James Keith. "The Restoration Theatre: A Study in Period Vision." Ph.D. University of Florida, 1963.

Designed to meet the visual requirements of the day, the Restoration stage combined the best elements of the classical and the baroque theatres.

6083 Kennedy-Skipton, Laetitia. "Notes on a Copy of William Capon's Plan of Goodman's Fields Theatre, 1786 and 1802, and on a Copy of One of the Ceiling Paintings in the Folger Shakespeare Library." Theatre Notebook, XVII (Spring, 1963), 86-89.

Descriptions of James Winston's copy of Capon's plan for Goodman's and the Folger's watercolor copies of the ceiling painting of Apollo and the Muses at this theatre.

6084 Lea, John Kepler. "A Study of the Management of Theatre Royal, Drury Lane, Between 1663 and 1791." M.A. Miami University (Ohio), 1964.

6085 Little, Bryan. The Theatre Royal: The Beginning of a Bicentenary. Bristol: Bristol Building Design Centre, 1964. 12 pp.

Commemorative pamphlet on the foundation of the "Theatre in King Street," 1764. 9 illustrations.

6086 Kallop, Edward L. "Theatre Designs in the Cooper Union Museum." Restoration and Eighteenth Century Theatre Research, IV (May, 1965), 12-15.

Of special interest in this collection are "A Treatise on Theatres" by George Saunders (London, 1790), and views of the rotunda in Ranelagh Gardens (1794), of the Sheldonian Theatre, and of the Pantheon Theatre (1784).

6087 Langhans, Edward A. "The Dorset Garden Theatre in Pictures." Theatre Survey, VI (1965), 134-146.

Twelve new prints of the theatre's exterior discovered in the Harvard Theatre Collection, the Brander Matthews Dramatic Museum and the British Museum.

6088 -----. "A Picture of the Salisbury Court Theatre." Theatre Notebook, XIX (Spring, 1965), 100-101.

The Dorset Garden Theatre pictured on the Lea and Glynne map of London (1706) may actually represent the old Salisbury Court playhouse. 2 plates.

6089 McNamara, Brooks Barry. "The Development of the American
      Playhouse in the Eighteenth Century." Ph.D. Tulane University,
      1965. (Order No. 66-1562).
            American theatres in the 1800's owe their design and con-
      struction to the English playhouses of the 17th and 18th cen-
      turies.

6090 Carter, Rand. "The Architecture of English Theatres: 1760-1860."
      Ph.D. Princeton University, 1966. (Order No. 66-13,298).
            Studies the evolution of theatre architecture in the major and
      minor London theatres of the period.

6091 Hogan, Charles Beecher. "The London Theatres, 1776-1800: A
      Brief Consideration." Theatre Notebook, XXI (Autumn, 1966),
      13-14.
            A brief comment on the importance of the last quarter of
      the 18th century for theatrical developments.

6092 Langhans, Edward A. "Pictorial Material on the Bridges Street
      and Drury Lane Theatres." Theatre Survey, VII (1966), 80-
      100.
            New information about the architectural designs with the
      two theatres. 18 illustrations.

6093 McNamara, Brooks. "The English Playhouse in America." The
      Connoisseur, CLXVI (December, 1967), 262-267.
            The English tradition of stagecraft and theatre architecture
      dominated the 18th century American playhouse. Includes ten
      illustrations.

6094 Mullin, Donald C. "The Queen's Theatre, Haymarket: Vanbrugh's
      Opera House." Theatre Survey, VIII (1967), 84-105.
            Studies the development of the theatre designed by Vanbrugh
      and begun in 1704.

6095 -----. "The Theatre Royal, Bridges Street: A Conjectural Restora-
      tion." Educational Theatre Journal, XIX (1967), 17-29.
            Reviews available evidence concerning the form of the theatre
      before Wren's reconstruction in 1674.

Theatrical Management

6096 Thaler, Alwin. "The 'Free-List' and Theatre Tickets in Shake-
      speare's Time and After." Modern Language Review, XV (1920),
      124-136.
            A history of the "free-list" and of theatre tickets from Shake-
      speare to the days of Garrick and Sheridan.

Theobald, Lewis

6097 Evans, H. A. "A Shakespearian Controversy of the Eighteenth

Century." Anglia, XXVIII (1905), 457-476.

Concerned with 18th-century criticism of Shakespeare (Theobald, Pope, Johnson).

6098 Schevill, Rudolph. "Theobald's Double Falsehood?" Modern Philology, IX (October, 1911), 269-285.

Theobald is the author of Double Falsehood or The Distressed Lovers, a play taken from the novel The Adventures on the Black Mountains as printed by Croxall (1729) and not from Shakespeare or from Shelton's translation of Don Quixote as Theobald claimed.

6099 Jones, Richard Foster. Lewis Theobald: His Contribution to English Scholarship with Some Unpublished Letters. New York: Columbia University Press, 1919. 363 pp.

The biography is sympathetic to Theobald, following Professor Lounsbury's lead, but adding some unpublished letters to Warburton. The thesis: "Basic principles of critical editing were derived directly from method employed by Bentley in the classics." An account of Theobald's career in the theatre is given.

6100 Graham, Walter, ed. Double Falsehood; or, The Distrest Lovers. Written Originally by W. Shakespeare and Now Revised. Western Reserve University Bulletin, New Ser., XXIII (1920), 1-89. (Library Section Supplement).

6101 Paul, Henry N. "Players' Quartos and Duodecimos of Hamlet." Modern Language Notes, XLIX (1934), 369-375.

A description of Theobald's stage edition of 1743, and the Betterton text of 1683.

6102 Whiting, George W. "The Temple of Dullness and Other Interludes." Review of English Studies, X (1934), 206-211.

The Interlude from The Happy Captive, The Temple of Dullness and Capochio and Dorinna are satires from Italian opera for which Theobald, not Cibber, should receive credit.

6103 Castle, Eduard. "Theobalds 'Double Falsehood' and 'The History of Cardenio' von Fletcher und Shakespeare." Archiv für das Studium der Neuren Sprachen und Literaturen, CLXIX (1936), 182-199.

Castle presents the history of the Cardenio play, argues for its authorship by Shakespeare and revision by Fletcher, and tries to establish the identity and transmission of the text to Theobald. The argument is tenuous, prolix, and marred by chauvinism.

6104 Cadwalader, John. "Theobald's Alleged Shakespeare Manuscript." Modern Language Notes, LV (1940), 108-109.

A letter of Theobald's offering to submit the play in manuscript to the Countess of Oxford.

6105 Field, Caroline C. "Textual Comparison of Four Plays in Pope
     and Theobald." M.A. St. Louis University, 1940.

6106 King, H. M. "The Work of Theobald and His Predecessors on
     the Text of Shakespeare." Ph.D. London University (External),
     1940.

6107 Joseph, Bertram L. "Lewis Theobald and Webster." Comparative
     Literature Studies, XVII-XVIII (1945), 29-31.
        The Catalogue of Theobald's library shows his lively interest
     in Elizabethan and Jacobean dramatists.

6108 Woods, Charles B. "Fielding's Epilogue for Theobald." Philological
     Quarterly, XXVIII (July, 1949), 419-424.
        A hitherto unnoticed epilogue to Orestes is described.

6109 Theobald, Lewis. Preface to the Works of Shakespeare (1734).
     Edited, with an Introduction by Hugh G. Dick. Los Angeles:
     Clark Memorial Library, University of California, 1950.
     (Augustan Reprint Society, Publication No. 20).
        A facsimile reprint of the original version, falsely dated
     1733. The preface describes the reputation of Theobald's work,
     and traces the influence at work on his theory of editing.

6110 Hammelmann, H. A. "Shakespeare Illustration: The Earliest Known
     Originals." Connoisseur, CXLI (1958), 144-149.
        Gravelot's for Theobald's second edition, 1740.

6111 Muir, Kenneth. "Cardenio." Etudes anglaises, XI (1958), 201-209.
        Theobald's Double Falsehood, 1728, probably really was based
     on a Shakespeare-Fletcher play.

6112 "Three Shakespeare Adaptations." Proceedings of the Leeds Philoso-
     phical and Literary Society, Literary and Historical Section,
     VIII (1959), 233-240.
        Dryden's Troilus, Tate's Lear, Theobald's Richard II.

6113 Kaul, R. K. "What Theobald Did to Webster." Indian Journal of
     English Studies, II (1961), 138-144.
        Versification of The Fatal Secret compared with that of its
     source, The Duchess of Malfi.

6114 Frazier, Harriet Cornelia. "Shakespeare, Cervantes, and Theo-
     bald: An Investigation into the Cardenio-Double Falsehood
     Problem." Ph.D. Wayne State University, 1967. (Order No. 68-
     2090).
        Presents evidence to assert that the numerous echoes of
     Hamlet, which Theobald edited in 1726, and of other Shakespearean
     plays in the apocryphal work point to its being a deliberate
     forgery on Theobald's part rather than Shakespeare's work or
     that of another Jacobean dramatist.

6115 -----. "Theobald's The Double Falsehood: A Revision of Shake-
     speare's Cardenio?" Comparative Drama, I (1967), 219-233.
        Theobald's play does not have its source in a manuscript by

Shakespeare and Fletcher as Theobald claimed but in Shelton's
Don Quixote (1725).

Theology

6116 Lloyd, Roger. The Borderland: An Exploration of Theology in
      English Literature. London: Allen and Unwin, 1960. 112 pp.

Theory

6117 Cowl, Richard Pape. The Theory of Poetry in England; Its Develop-
      ment in Doctrine and Ideas from the Sixteenth Century to the
      Nineteenth Century. London: Macmillan & Co., 1914. 319 pp.
6118 Partridge, Eric. "The 1762 Efflorescence of Poetics." Studies in
      Philology, XXV (1928), 27-35.
         A study of four books on poetics published in England in
      1762: John Foster's "Essay on the Nature of Accent and Quan-
      tity," John Newbery's "Art of Poetry on a New Plan," James
      Ogden's "Epistle on Poetical Composition" (in verse), and
      Daniel Webb's "Remarks on the Beauties of Poetry." Ogden's
      book has disappeared, but a notice is extant.
6119 Davies, Hugh Sykes. Realism in the Drama. Cambridge: At the
      University Press, 1934. 122 pp.
         Chapters on theory and practice in Greece, Elizabethan,
      Neo-Classic Period, Nineteenth Century. To attain the realistic
      character writers had to escape the critical categories of the
      Greeks.
6120 Klotz, Volker. Geschlossene und offene Form in Drama. Munich:
      Carl Hanser, 1960. 275 pp.

Thomson, James

6121 Case, Arthur E. "Aaron Hill and Thomson's Sophonisba." Modern
      Language Notes, XLII (March, 1927), 175-176.
         Autograph verses by Hill in the first edition of the play.
6122 Williams, George G. "Who Was 'Census' in the Poem To the
      Memory of Mr. Congreve?" Publications of the Modern Lan-
      guage Association, XLIV (June, 1929), 495-500.
         Identifies Census as Joseph Mitchell, an enemy of James
      Thomson, to whom the poem is attributed.
6123 Davenport, Joyce. "A Study of the Plays of James Thomson."
      M.A. Northwestern University, 1932.
6124 Johnson, Walter Gilbert. James Thomson's Influence on Swedish
      Literature in the Eighteenth Century. Urbana, Illinois: Uni-
      versity of Illinois Press, 1936. 202 pp.

This study is concerned primarily with the poetry. Of Thomson's plays, only Agamemnon was translated into Swedish, and it "had no effect on the development of Swedish drama."

6125 Kern, Jean B. "The Fate of James Thomson's Edward and Eleanora." Modern Language Notes, LII (1937), 500-502.

Both external and internal evidence support the belief that Thomson's play was banned by the Licenser because of a feud between his patron, the Prince of Wales, and George II.

6126 Dibdin, Edward Rimbault. "The Bicentenary of 'Rule Brittania.'" Music and Letters, XXI (July, 1940), 275-290.

Gives the circumstances of the composition of the masque "Alfred," and shows the significance of the ode, which closes the play, and traces the history of the masque on the stage. The "Rule Brittania" ode was composed by James Thomson and set to music by Thomas A. Arne.

6127 Holthausen, F. "Die Quellen von Thomsons 'Edward and Eleonora.'" Beiblatt Zur Anglia, LI (1940), 116-118.

A brief resumé of the basic sources of Thomson's play, Edward and Eleonora.

6128 Taylor, Eric S. "James Thomson's Library." Times Literary Supplement, July 5, 1941, p. 323.

6129 Wells, John E. "Thomson's Agamemnon and Edward and Eleonora --First Printings." Review of English Studies, XVIII (October, 1942), 478-486.

Lists and differentiates the printings of these two plays made during Thomson's lifetime.

6130 Todd, William B. "Unauthorized Readings in the First Edition of Thomson's Coriolanus." Papers of the Bibliographical Society of America, XLVII (1952), 62-66.

The first issue of the play exists in two variants which indicate Lord Lyttelton's revisions.

6131 Axelrad, A. José. Le Thème de Sophonisbe dans les principales tragédies de la littérature occidentale (France, Angleterre, Allemagne). Étude suivie de la Sophonisbe inédite de la Grange Chancel representée a la Comédie francaise le 10 Novembre 1716. (Travaux et Mémoires de l'Université de Lille. Nouv. Ser., Droit et Lettres, No. 28.) Lille: Bibliothèque Universitaire, 1956. 188 pp.

Traces the theme chronologically from 1500-1913 through French, German, and English plays, including Nathaniel Lee's Sophonisba, or Hannibal's Overthrow, and James Thomson's The Tragedy of Sophonisba.

6132 Francis, T. R. "S me Dublin Editions of James Thomson's Tancred and Sigismunda." Book Collector, VII (1958), 190.

Describes the first Dublin edition, and three others in the author's collection.

6133 McKillop, Alan D. "Thomson and the Licensers of the Stage."
Philological Quarterly, XXXVII (1958), 448-453.

6134 Foxon, D. F. "Oh! Sophonisba! Sophonisba! Oh!" Studies in Bibliography, XII (1959), 204-213.
An analysis of the 1730 printings of Thomson's Sophonisba.

6135 Francis, T. R. "James Thomson's Tancred and Sigismunda."
Book Collector, VIII (1959), 181-182.
6 editions.

6136 Stratman, Carl J., C.S.V. "Tancred and Sigismunda." Book Collector, IX (Summer, 1960), 188.
Lists eight editions (printed before 1800) of the play not
noted in CBEL, Nicoll, Lowndes, or in T.R. Francis's "Six
Unrecorded Editions of Thomson's Tancred and Sigismunda."

6137 McKillop, Alan D. "Two More Thomson Letters." Modern
Philology, LX (1962), 128-130.
Second letter to an anonymous lady makes reference to her
collection for Tancred and Sigismunda and to Thomson's new
play on "Titus Marcius Coriolanus."

6138 Kern, Jean B. "James Thomson's Revision of Agamemnon."
Philological Quarterly, XLV (1966), 289-303.
Studies the differences in the Huntington Library Larpent
Collection's manuscript version of Thomson's play and the two
printed versions of 1738 and 1752.

Thornton, Bonnell

6139 Gardner, Bellamy. "A Burlesque Band at Ranelagh in 1759."
Connoisseur, CVI (1940), 186-189; 220.
Discusses the instruments and performances of a band which
performed Bonnell Thornton's burlesque of Handel's "Ode on St.
Cecelia's Day" at Ranelagh Gardens in Chelsea.

6140 Brown, Wallace Cable. "A Belated Augustan: Bonnell Thornton,
Esq." Philological Quarterly, XXXIV (1955), 335-348.
Thornton, admired by Johnson and Boswell, has not received
due attention. Brief biography; discussion of his Drury-Lane
Journal and essays and satires; collaboration with Christopher
Smart; Thornton's poetry and translation of Plautus.

Thrale, H.

6141 Piozzi, Mrs. Hester Lynch Thrale. The Letters of Mrs. Thrale.
Edited by R. Brimley Johnson. London: John Lane, 1926. ix,
218 pp.
An occasional dramatic reference.

Tickell, Richard

6142 B., G. F. R. "Richard Tickell, Pamphleteer and Dramatist."
     Notes and Queries, CXLVIII (May 23, 1925), 372.
     Born at Bath in 1751.
6143 Libbis, G. Hilder. "Richard Tickell, Pamphleteer and Dramatist."
     Notes and Queries, CXLVIII (May 30, 1925), 395.
     Married in 1789.
6144 Tickell, R. E., ed. Thomas Tickell and the Eighteenth Century
     Poets (1685-1740). London: Constable, 1931. xv, 256 pp.
     Relations of Tickell to Addison and Pope.

Ticket Collection

6145 Lawrence, W. J. "The Seventeenth Century Theatre Systems of
     Admission." Anglia, XXXV (1912), 526-538.
     Reprinted with some additions in the author's Elizabethan
     Playhouse, Second Series, pp. 96-118, as "Early Systems of
     Admission."
6146 -----. "Early Systems of Admission." The Elizabethan Playhouse
     and Other Studies. Second Series. (Stratford-on-Avon: Shakespeare
     Head Press, 1913), 96-118.
     Various practices in ticket collections in the Elizabethan
     and Restoration theatres and the abuses by the public, door
     keepers, and bookkeepers.

Tofts, Catherine

6147 Sands, Mollie. "Mrs. Tofts, 1685?-1756." Theatre Notebook, XX
     (Spring, 1966), 100-113.
     A biographical study of Catherine Tofts, her life and career
     as an opera singer.

Tonson

6148 Boddy, Margaret. "Tonson's 'Loss of Rowe.'" Notes and Queries,
     New Ser., XIII (1966), 213-214.
     The rivalry of Lintot and Tonson in publishing Rowe's plays
     and translation.

Toy Theatres

6149 H., H. "Toy Theatre Lighting." Notes and Queries, CLXXXVIII
     (February 24, 1945), 86.
     Additions to George Speaight's note (January 13, 1945).

6150 Speaight, George. "Toy Theatre Lighting." Notes and Queries,
      CLXXXVIII (January 13, 1945), 20-21.
            Replies to C. D. Williams' article (CLXXXVII, 212), show-
      ing early use of footlights in 1672 and 1715.

6151 Williams, Charles D. "Toy Theatre Lighting." Notes and Queries,
      CLXXXVIII (February 24, 1945), 86.
            Further additions to George Speaight's note (January 13,
      1945).

6152 Speaight, George. Juvenile Drama: The History of the English Toy
      Theatre. London: Macdonald, 1946.
            Mainly on the nineteenth century, but with comment on the
      earlier periods.

Tragedy

6153 Courtney, William Leonard. Idea of Tragedy in ancient and modern
      drama. With note by A. W. Pinero. London: Constable, 1900.
      132 pp.

6154 Neilson, William Allan. Tragedy (Types of English Literature;
      edited by William A. Neilson). Boston and New York: Houghton,
      1908. vi, 390 pp.
            Author traces course of English tragedy from its beginnings
      to middle of nineteenth century, indicating its part in the history
      of literature and the theatre. Only representative plays are con-
      sidered after 1600. Bibliography at end of each chapter.

6155 Thorndike, Ashley H. Tragedy. Boston and New York: Houghton
      Mifflin Company, 1908. vi, 390 pp. (Types of English Literature
            Chapters VIII and IX constitute a superificial treatment of
      Restoration and 18th-century tragic drama and dramatic
      criticism.

6156 Vaughan, C. E. Types of Tragic Drama. London: Macmillan,
      1908. viii, 275 pp.
            Reproduction of a series of lectures on the classical tragedy
      of the Greeks, Seneca, Racine and Alfieri, and the romantic
      tragedy of Shakespeare, Calderon, Goethe and others. The
      historical movement of the drama toward an increasingly broade
      comprehension and presentation of human experience serves as
      focal point of the series.

6157 Hussey, Bertha. "Classicism in English Tragedy from 1750-1775."
      M.A. University of Chicago, 1910.

6158 Elder, Lucius Walter. A Criticism of Some Attempts to Rationalize
      Tragedy... [Kansas City, Mo.: 1915]. 90 pp.
            This study conceives of tragedy as "an attempt to make men's
      position in the world intelligible"; the tragic situation has three
      factors: "the tragic guilt; the reversal of fortune; and the inevit-
      able conditions."

6159 Whitmore, Charles Edward. The Supernatural in Tragedy. Cam-
      bridge, Massachusetts: Harvard University Press, 1915. viii,
      370 pp.
            Chapters are devoted to Restoration and the Eighteenth Cen-
      tury.
6160 Harbeson, William Page. The Elizabethan Influence on the Tragedy
      of the Late 18th and Early 19th Centuries. Lancaster, Pa.:
      Wickersham Printing Co., 1921. 85 pp.
            Examines tragedy during parts of the 18th and 19th centuries
      for evidence of an Elizabethan revival. Treats Lillo, Cumberland,
      Garrick, etc., and concludes that the search for romanticism in
      this period gives negative results.
6161 Dixon, William Macneile. Tragedy. London: E. Arnold & Co., 1924.
      228 pp.
            The book treats of the enjoyment of tragedy, tragedy as an
      art, the word tragedy, and famous tragedians.
6162 Ashby, Stanley Royal. "The Treatment of the Themes of Classical
      Tragedy in English Tragedy between 1660 and 1738." Ph.D.
      Harvard University, 1927.
            A comparison designed to illuminate differences and similar-
      ities in dramatic technique between the two types of drama.
      Compares the natures of the conflicts, the tragic effects, the
      treatments of poetic justice. Concludes that the classical tra-
      gedies were more concerned with significance, the English with
      emotional effect.
6163 Dobrée, Bonamy. Restoration Tragedy, 1660-1720. Oxford: At the
      Clarendon Press, 1929. 189 pp.
            Attempts to show why Restoration tragedy took the "heroic"
      form; to see the characteristics of its chief proponents--Dryden,
      Lee, Otway, Rowe, Addison; to see what lessons can be learnt
      for the writing of tragedy today.
6164 Russell, Fielding Dillard. "Eighteenth Century Tragedy and Some
      of Its Conventional Types." M.A. University of Georgia, 1930.
6165 [Pratt, John M.] "The Influence of Shakespeare on Early 18th-
      Century Domestic Tragedies." (John A. Dreams [pseud.].
      [For the Winthrop Sargent Prize, Harvard University, 1931].
      40 pp.
            An attempt to explore the influence of Shakespeare on plot,
      character, style, diction, and atmosphere of domestic tragedies
      from the anonymous The Rival Brothers (1704) to Thomas
      Cooke's The Mournful Nuptials (1739). Includes discussion of
      Aaron Hill's and Lillo's works.
6166 Montgomery, Harriet Rose. "English Domestic Tragedy from 1731
      to 1800." M.A. McGill University, Canada, 1933.

6167 Green, Clarence Corleon. The Neo-Classic Theory of Tragedy in
England during the 18th Century. Cambridge: Harvard University
Press, 1934. 245 pp. (Harvard Studies in English, Vol. XI).
Mr. Green's avowed purpose is "to supply the student of the
drama with a unified and reasonably complete history of the
defeat of the neo-classic forces at the hands of the 18th-century
critics."

6168 Hartley, D. L. "Theory of Tragedy in England, 1660-1702." B.
Litt. Oxford University, 1934.

6169 Latimer, Mary E. "English Domestic Tragedy of the Eighteenth
Century." Ph.D. University of Wisconsin, 1936.
An essay in generic definition which emphasizes the traits
common to a selected number of domestic tragedies. Plot,
character, diction, and theme are among the aspects considered.

6170 Teeter, Louis. "I. Political Themes in Restoration Tragedy.
II. The Dramatic Use of Hobbes's Political Ideas. A Chapter
from Political Themes in Restoration Tragedy." Ph.D. Johns
Hopkins University, 1936.

6171 Pratt, John Miller. "The Influence of Shakespeare on Eighteenth
Century Tragedy, 1700-1750." Ph.D. Harvard University, 1938.
A consideration of the influence of Shakespeare on character-
ization, style, atmosphere, and technical and mechanical details
in the plays of Rowe and Hill, and on the heroic, pseudo-classic,
Augustan, and domestic tragedies.

6172 Giovannini, Giovanni. "The Theory of Tragedy As History in
Renaissance and Neo-classical Criticism." Ph.D. University
of Michigan, 1940.

6173 Hathaway, Baxter L. "The Function of Tragedy in Neo-Classic
Criticism." Ph.D. University of Michigan, 1940.

6174 Peake, Charles Howard. "Domestic Tragedy in Relation to Theology
in the First Half of the 18th Century." Ph.D. University of
Michigan, 1941.

6175 Spassky, Y. "Tragedy in the Seventeenth and Eighteenth Centuries."
The Theatre (U.S.S.R.), V (1941), 89-105.

6176 Vinograd, Sherna S. "The Tragic Lament and Related Means of
Achieving Acquiescence in Tragic Drama." Ph.D. Stanford
University, 1941.

6177 Hathaway, Baxter. "The Lucretian 'Return upon Ourselves' in
Eighteenth-Century Theories of Tragedy." Publications of the
Modern Language Association, LXII (1947), 672-689.
Examines the theories that an audience's pleasure is
derived from witnessing distress which it does not itself ex-
perience.

6178 Prior, Moody E. The Language of Tragedy. New York: Columbia
University Press, 1947. ix, 411 pp.

Chapter III (154-212) deals in detail with Aureng-Zebe,
Tate's Lear, Venice Preserv'd and All for Love.

6179 Roditi, Edouard. "The Genesis of Neoclassical Tragedy." South
       Atlantic Quarterly, XLVI (1947), 93-108.
       Sixteenth-century Italian tragedy directly influenced Eliz-
       abethan drama and French neo-classical tragedy. Roditi goes
       back to Plato and Aristotle and focuses on Trissino, discussing
       his plays in terms of methods and structure and compares them
       with Greek tragedy and the works of Racine and Corneille.

6180 Wasserman, Earl R. "The Pleasures of Tragedy." English Literary
       History, XIV (1947), 283-307.
       Shows that eighteenth century theories of tragedy derive from
       Hobbes and Descartes.

6181 Magill, Lewis Malcolm, Jr. "Elements of Sentimentalism in Eng-
       lish Tragedy, 1680-1704." Ph.D. University of Illinois, 1949.
       278 pp.

6182 Leech, Clifford. "Restoration Tragedy: A Reconsideration."
       Durham University Journal, XI (1950), 106-115.
       Leech's article is a re-examination and summary of Resto-
       ration tragedy from a twentieth-century point of view.

6183 Gisi, Othmar. Historische Elemente in der englischen Tragödie
       vor der Romantik. Aarau: Keller, 1953. 118 pp.
       A discussion of the English tragic playwrights' treatments
       of characters, plots, etc., derived from history; covers the
       period from the beginnings of English drama through the end
       of the 18th century.

6184 Steiner, F. G. "Problems in the Relationship between the Rise of
       Romanticism and the State of Tragedy, Cir. 1790-1820." Ph.D.
       Oxford University (Balliol), 1955.

6185 Henn, T. R. The Harvest of Tragedy. London: Methuen, 1956.
       320 pp.

6186 Muller, Herbert J. The Spirit of Tragedy. New York: Knopf, 1956.
       335 pp.
       Includes 17th and 18th centuries.

6187 Magill, Lewis M. "Poetic Justice: The Dilemma of the Early
       Creators of Sentimental Tragedy." Research Studies of the
       State College of Washington, XXV (1957), 24-32.

6188 McCollom, William G. "The Downfall of the Tragic Hero." Col-
       lege English, XIX (1957), 51-56.
       In discussing the connection between a hero's character and
       his fate, McCollom considers Racine's Phèdre.

6189 Noyes, Robert Gale. The Neglected Muse: Restoration and Eighteenth-
       Century Tragedy in the Novel (1740-1780). Providence: Brown
       University Press, 1958. xii, 187 pp.
       Emphasis on the tragedies.

6190 Stratman, Carl J., C.S.V. "Unpublished Dissertations in the
      History and Theory of Tragedy, 1889-1957." Bulletin of Biblio-
      graphy, XXII (September-December, 1958), 161-164; Part II.
      XXII (January-April, 1959), 190-192; Part III. XXII (May-August,
      1959), 214-216; Part IV. XXII (September-December, 1959),
      237-240; Part V. XXIII (January-April, 1960), 15-20.
          Some 859 theses and dissertations are listed for colleges and
      universities in the United States, Canada, England, Ireland,
      Scotland, and South Africa. The 17th and 18th centuries are
      found in Parts III and IV.
6191 Carson, Herbert L. "Modern Tragedy and Its Origins in Domestic
      Tragedy: A Study of Select English and American Domestic
      Tragedies from Elizabethan and Modern Times." Ph.D. Uni-
      versity of Minnesota, 1959.
          Carson divines the distinguishing characteristics of domestic
      tragedy, then its contributions to serious modern drama. Cites
      the influence of the moral sentiment of the 18th century.
6192 Insch, A. "English Blank Verse Tragedy, 1790-1825." Ph.D. Dur-
      ham University, 1959.
6193 Park, Hugh Winston. "Revenge in Restoration Tragedy." Ph.D.
      University of Utah, 1959.
          27 Restoration tragedies related to Elizabethan revenge
      tragedy.
6194 Raphael, David Daiches. The Paradox of Tragedy. Bloomington:
      Indiana University Press, 1960. 112 pp.
          Professor Raphael attempts to answer the paradoxical ques-
      tions about drama: "Why does one receive satisfaction from
      seeing the representation of misery"? "Why should one want
      to see a tragic drama"? Contains references to Sheridan.
6195 Maurocordato, A. "La Critique Anglaise et la Fonction de la
      Tragédie (1660-1720)." Études Anglaises, XIV, January-March,
      1961, 10-24.
6196 Stratman, Carl J., C.S.V. "A Survey of the Huntington Library's
      Holdings in the Field of English Printed Drama." Huntington
      Library Quarterly, XXIV (February, 1961), 171-174.
          Survey of the Huntington Library holdings in English tragedy
      in comparison with the holdings of the British Museum, Folger
      Shakespeare Library, Harvard University, Yale University,
      the New York Public Library, Columbia University, and New-
      berry Library. From 1565 to 1900.
6197 Rothstein, Eric. "English Tragic Theory in the Late Seventeenth
      Century." Journal of English Literary History, XXIX (1962),
      306-323.
          Discusses the parallel between dramatic theory and the
      practice of English tragedians during the late 17th century.

Indicates the critical channels (particularly in Dryden and
Rapin) through which sentimental tragedy came to succeed
heroic tragedy.

6198 -----. "Unrhymed Tragedy, 1660-1702." Ph.D. Princeton University, 1962. (Order No. 62-3638).

The development of sentiment and "natural" speech in tragedy
during Restoration and Orange Periods.

6199 Stratman, Carl J., C.S.V. "Unpublished Dissertations in the History
and Theory of Tragedy, 1889-1957: Addenda." Bulletin of Bibliography, XXIII (January-April, 1962), 162-165.

This and the following entry give some 397 additional items,
and carry the work through 1959. Includes sections on European
nations, in addition to England and the United States.

6200 -----. "Unpublished Dissertations in the History and Theory of
Tragedy, 1899-1957: Addenda." Bulletin of Bibliography, XXIII
(May-August, 1962), 187-192.

6201 Alexander, R. N. "A Study of the English Theory of Tragedy with
Special Reference to Criticism of Sophocles." B. Litt. Oxford
University (Magdalen), 1963.

6202 Kenion, Alonzo Williams. "The Influence of Criticism upon English
Tragedy, 1700-1750." Ph.D. Duke University, 1963. (Order No.
63-4245).

An examination of one hundred and forty tragedies written
between 1700 and 1750 reveals that criticism, "though by no
means a dead force, did not dominate tragedy." Writers "tended
to bow to the demands of popular taste rather than to the injunc-
tions of criticism."

6203 Stephenson, Mary Amanda. "The Costume of the Hero of Restoration
Tragedy." M.A. University of Florida, 1963.

6204 Stratman, Carl J., C.S.V. "A Survey of the Bodleian Library's
Holdings in the Field of English Printed Tragedy." The Bodleian
Library Record, VII (January, 1964), 133-143.

Notes the number of authors and tragedies in both the 17th
and 18th centuries which are at the Bodleian Library, indicating
the great wealth of the library's holdings.

6205 Booth, Michael R., ed. Eighteenth Century Tragedy. World's
Classics. London: Oxford University Press, 1965. 394 pp.

Anthology with introduction. Includes Lillo's The London
Merchant, Johnson's Irene, Moore's The Gamester, Home's
Douglas, and George Colman the Younger's The Iron Chest.

6206 Fletcher, Richard M. English Romantic Drama, 1795-1843: A
Critical History. New York: Exposition Press, 1966. 226 pp.

Purposes to bring poetic tragedy as a genre into sharper
focus, both as it reflected and as it delineated the spirit of its
age. Chapter I, "Romantic Drama and Its Theatre," refers to
18th century theatre.

6207 Ingram, William Henry. "Greek Drama and the Augustan Stage:
      Dennis, Theobald, Thomson." Ph.D. University of Penn-
      sylvania, 1966. (Order No. 66-10,625).
          Studies Augustan theories of translation, particularly
      Dryden's; the state of classical scholarship at the time,
      centering on Richard Bentley; the split between scholarly and
      polite learning, particularly in the Phalaris controversy.
      Separate chapters are then devoted to the Iphigenia (1700) of
      John Dennis, the Orestes (1731) of Lewis Theobald, and the
      Agamemnon (1737) of James Thomson.
6208 Kearful, Frank Jerome. "The Rhetoric of Augustan Tragedy."
      Ph.D. University of Wisconsin, 1966. (Order No. 66-9154).
          Studies the linguistic devices and patterns used to affect
      the appeals of Augustan tragedy. Special attention is given to
      Rowe, Addison, Dennis, and Lillo.
6209 Leech, Clifford. "Restoration Tragedy: A Reconsideration."
      Restoration Drama: Modern Essays in Criticism. (A Galaxy
      Book). Edited by John Loftis. (New York: Oxford University
      Press, 1966), 144-160.
          Reprinted from Durham University Journal, XI (1950),
      106-115. Considers the relationship of Restoration tragedy
      to earlier tragedy and the special problems faced by Resto-
      ration writers of tragedy.
6210 Rothstein, Eric. Restoration Tragedy: Form and the Process
      of Change. Madison: University of Wisconsin Press, 1967.
      194 pp.
          A study of Restoration tragedy, incidentally in terms of
      individual plays, specifically in terms of the developing gentre.
      One chapter discusses tragic theory in the Restoration, others
      are devoted to the repertory tradition, the late heroic play,
      language, and the conventions of structure.

Tragicomedy

6211 Ristine, Frank Humphrey. English Tragicomedy. Its Origin and
      History. New York: Columbia University Press, 1910. 247 pp.
      (Columbia University Studies in English).
          Tragicomedy sprang into full-blown existence in the early
      17th century, grew rapidly in popular favor, reached its hey-
      day by 1610-1642, and by 1700 was a relic of the past. Chapter
      VI is concerned with the causes of its decline which effected
      its replacement by sentimental comedy. An appendix lists
      some 250 tragicomedies, a few not extant, with publication
      dates.
6212 Herrick, Marvin T. Tragicomedy: Its Origin and Development in

Italy, France, and England. Urbana: University of Illinois
Press, 1955. vii, 331 pp. (University of Illinois Studies in
Language and Literature, Vol. 39).

Treats the development of tragic-comedy from its classical
backgrounds through a detailed discussion of Davenant's plays
and brief consideration of some of Dryden's plays.

6213 -----. "The Revolt in Tragicomedy against the Grand Style." The
Rhetorical Idiom: Essays in Rhetoric, Oratory, Language, and
Drama. Edited by Donald C. Bryant. (Ithaca, N.Y.: Cornell
University Press, 1958), 271-280.

6214 Guthke, Karl S. Modern Tragicomedy, An Investigation into the
Nature of the Genre. New York: Random House, 1966.

Contains a chapter on English neoclassicism.

Translations

6215 Haskell, Daniel C. "Foreign Plays in English. A List of Translations in the New York Public Library." Bulletin of the New York
Public Library, XXIV (1920), 61-92; 219-261.

A list of plays arranged alphabetically by language which
includes translation from the late 17th and 18th centuries.

6216 West, Constance B. "La Theorie de la traduction au XVIIIe siècle
par rapport surtout aux traductions franciases d'ouvrages
anglais." Revue de litterature comparée, XII (1932), 330-355.

Discusses methods of translating the true feeling of French
and English literature--the "absolute" vs. the "relative" style.
References to drama.

6217 Tucker, Joseph E. "English Translation from the French, 1650-
1700: Corrections and Additions to the C.B.E.L." Philological
Quarterly, XXI (1942), 391-404.

Criticizes the inaccuracy of C.B.E.L. and presents a list
arranged alphabetically by French author of additions to and
corrections of C.B.E.L.'s section on translation of French
works. Many items pertain to drama.

Trapp, Joseph

6218 Herrick, Marvin T. "Joseph Trapp and the Aristotelian 'Catharsis.'"
Modern Language Notes, XLI (1926), 158-163.

Says that it was Joseph Trapp (1679-1747) the first professor of poetry at Oxford, kept alive the medical interpretation
of catharsis (touched upon by Milton), although he also held
the prevailing moral interpretations. The 19th century sharply
differentiated these two theories.

6219 Evans, Jean. "A Study of Joseph Trapp's Theory of Tragedy."

Ph.D. Catholic University of America, 1941.

6220 Moran, Berna. "The Source of Joseph Trapp's 'Abra-Mule.'"
Modern Language Review, LIII (1958), 81-83.
Novél Abra-Mulè by de Tennelière, translated 1696.

Trotter, Catharine

6221 Carter, Herbert. "Three Women Dramatists of the Restoration."
Bookman's Journal, XIII (1925), 91-97.
Sketches the careers of Mrs. Mary Manley, Mrs. Mary Pix,
Mrs. Catharine Trotter.

Tuke, George

6222 Clark, William S. "George and Samuel Tuke." Times Literary
Supplement, May 3, 1928, p. 334.
John Evelyn, a family friend, twice makes Sir George Tuke
the author of the play; there seems to have been a consistent
confusion between the two brothers, George and Samuel.

Tuke, Samuel

text

6223 Tuke, Sir Samuel. The Adventures of Five Hours. Edited by B.
van Thal. London: Holden, 1927. xxxii, 155 pp.
Reprints the third edition (1671) of the play, an adaptation
of Los Empenos de Seis Horas (author anonymous). Less
scholarly than Swaen's edition.

6224 -----. The Adventures of Five Hours. Edited by A.E.H. Swaen.
Amsterdam: Swets and Zeitlinger, 1927. liv, 261 pp.
An elaborate critical edition, with the text of the Spanish
source and the 1663 folio and 1671 revision of the Tuke play.

biography and criticism

6225 Gaw, Allison. "Tuke's Adventures of Five Hours in Relation to
the 'Spanish Plot' and to John Dryden." Studies in English
Drama. Edited by Allison Gaw. (Baltimore: University of
Pennsylvania, 1917), 1-61.
Early history of play (free translation of Los Empenos de
Seis Horas by Tuke, produced January 8, 1662-3), significance
of the play (first translation of Spanish play, observes unity
of time, early heroic play), and revised version of 1671 (even
more heroic--use of couplets).

6226 Swaen, A.E.H. "George and Samuel Tuke." Times Literary Supplement, May 24, 1928, p. 396.
      Replies to W. S. Clark (TLS, May 3, 1928) that Samuel Tuke must be accepted (rather than his brother George) as the author of the play; Evelyn confused the names of his two cousins.

6227 de Beer, E. S. "Sir Samuel Tuke." Notes and Queries, CLXI (1931), 345-347.
      Discusses his family history; gives a diagrammed pedigree.

Tyler, Royal

6228 Péladeau, Marius B. "Royall Tyler's Other Plays." New England Quarterly, XL (1967), 48-60.
      Studies four manuscript plays, three manuscript fragments, and six other plays, most of which were probably produced during Tyler's lifetime but are now totally lost. One of the lost plays, The Mock Doctor (1795) was based on Molière's Le Medicen Malgre Lui or on Fielding's Mock Doctor.

6229 Tanselle, G. Thomas. "Author and Publisher in 1800: Letters of Royall Tyler and Joseph Nancrede." Harvard Library Bulletin, XV (1967), 129-139.
      Four letters reveal the awkward plight of the gentleman of letters in the early republic and the cultivation, wit, and business acumen of the early American publisher.

6230 -----. Royall Tyler. Cambridge, Mass.: Harvard University Press, 1967. 281 pp.
      A well documented biography of Tyler (1757-1828) that includes information on the playwright's knowledge of the devices and themes of 18th century British drama.

Type Characters

6231 Lawrence, W. J. "Irish Types in Old-Time English Drama." Anglia, XXXV (1912), 347-356.
      The stage Irish in the plays of Jonson, Dekker, Shadwell, Sir Robert Howard, and Cumberland.

6232 Duncan, C. S. "The Scientist as a Comic Type." Modern Philology, XIV (1916), 281-291.
      Refutes idea that the scientist in Restoration comedy was presented as alchemist, astrologer, believer in witchcraft. From time of Shadwell's Virtuoso (1676), he was the comic presentation of the new experimental philosophy of the Royal Society, founded in 1660.

6233 Augsburg, Heinrich. "Der Offizier im Spiegel des englischen Lustspiels von der Zeit der Bügerkriege bis zum Ausgang des

18. Jahrhunderts." Münster Dissertation, 1919.

6234 Lawrence, W. J. "The Coming of Mr. Punch." Times Literary
Supplement, December 23, 1920, p. 874.

A history of the Punch character on the stage in the Restoration and 18th century; the author indicates that Punch was
probably first a character, then a puppet.

6235 Taylor, Daniel Crane. "The Fop in the Comedy of Manners."
M.A. University of Chicago, 1921.

A discussion of the fop in comedy from 1665 to 1721, which
considers the role of the general tendency of the time toward
the conventional in the creation of the type characters of the
period and discusses causes for the prominence of the fop in
society and then in drama.

6236 McIntyre, Clara F. "The Later Career of the Elizabethan Villain-
hero." Publications of the Modern Language Association, XL
(December, 1925), 874-880.

Parallels between "villain-heroes" of Elizabethan romantic
tragedies and typical characters in the romances of Mrs.
Radcliffe and Monk Lewis.

6237 Mills, Joye. "A Study of the Variations of the Types of Comic
Characters Found in Drama from the Greek Period Through
the Eighteenth Century." M.A. Northwestern University,
1928.

6238 Trevelyan, G. M. "'Artificial' Comedy." Times Literary Supplement, March 8, 1928, p. 170.

Replies to Stoll (TLS, March 1, 1928) that Trevelyan's illustrations from history were of real Restoration comedy
types, but not of typical English people.

6239 Maxfield, Ezra Kempton. "The Quakers in English Stage Plays
before 1800." Publications of the Modern Language Association,
XLV (1930), 256-273.

The Puritan was the stock character on the Elizabethan stage;
the Restoration and 18th-century used sects, of which the
Quakers were the most popular. Discusses the treatment of
Quakers by various playwrights, including Wycherley, Van-
brugh, Congreve, Farquhar, D'Urfey, Williamson, Mrs.
Centlivre.

6240 Pfitzner, Käthe. "Die Ausländertypen im englischen Drama
der Restaurationszeit." Inaugural Dissertation. Breslau, 1931.

6241 Watson, Harold Francis. The Sailor in English Fiction and Drama,
1550-1800. New York: Columbia University Press, 1931. 241 pp.

A collection of passages which deal with the characters and
exploits of sailors. There are no general conclusions reached.

6242 Hecht, Ilse. Der heroische Frauentyp in Restaurationsdrama.
Leipzig: A. Edelmann, 1932. 141 pp.
A discussion of the treatment of various types of women
(the mother, the "heroic woman," the pagan woman, the
woman in politics) in the drama of the Restoration.

6243 Smith, Henry E. "Foreigners Represented As National Types in
the English Comedy of the Restoration and the Eighteenth
Century." Ph.D. Boston University, 1932.

6244 Snuggs, Henry L. "The Humourous Character in English Comedy,
1596-1642, with an Outline of a Continuation for the Years 1642-
1700." Ph.D. Duke University, 1934.

6245 Tomlinson, Warren Everett. Der Herodes-Charakter im englischen
Drama. Leipzig: Mayer & Muller, g.m.b.h., 1934. x, 182 pp.
This is a survey of the Herod figure as he appears in English
drama. The work is divided into three sections, (1) Herod in
the mystery plays; (2) Herod in the plays of John the Baptist;
(3) Herod and Mariam tragedies. Includes works by Boyle,
Samuel Pordage, Elija Fenton, Francis Peck, and Stephen
Phillips.

6246 Van der Veen, Harm R. S. Jewish Characters in Eighteenth Century
English Fiction and Drama. Groningen, Batavia: J. B. Wolters,
1935. 308 pp.
Part II of this treatise presents an analysis of Jewish characters and a history of attitudes toward Jews as revealed in a
series of plays, from Dryden's Love Triumphant (1693) to T. J.
Dibdin's farce, The Jew and the Doctor (1798). The Jewish character is invariably used to excite laughter or contempt.

6247 Mau, Hedwig. "Das 'junge Mädchen.' Ein Beitrag zu dem Thema:
Die Frau in der Komödie der Restauration." Britannica, XIII
(1936), 67-89.
This analysis of the stereotype of the young girl uses Harriet
Woodvill in The Man of Mode as a norm from which to generalize
about other similar characters and about Restoration comedy as
a whole.

6248 Silvette, Herbert. "The Doctor and the Stage: Medicine and Medical
Men in Seventeenth Century English Drama." Annals of Medical
History, VIII (1936), 520-540; IX (1937), 62-87, 174-188, 264-
279, 371-394, 482-507.
An extensive analysis of seventeenth century medical practice
and of the manner in which it was reflected on the stage. Besides
defining many terms and allusions, the author presents a coherent
synopsis of the medical theory contemporary with the plays.

6249 Welsford, Enid. The Fool, His Social and Literary History. London:
Faber and Faber, 1935; New York: Farrar and Rinehart, 1936.
xv, 374 pp.

Discusses the English court fool in reality as well as in
literature and on stage.

6250 Duggan, George C. The Stage Irishman. Dublin: Talbot Press,
1937. 331 pp.

A patriotic history in two parts, the first presenting a history
of plays written in English on Irish subjects, the second a
history of Irish characters in British drama. Restoration and
18th century plays and characters are treated in some detail.
The volume contains an index but neither documentation nor
bibliography.

6251 Stroup, Thomas B. "Supernatural Beings in Restoration Drama."
Anglia, LXI (1937), 186-192.

Stroup examines several heroic dramas to show how ghosts
of departed mortals serve an organic function in the plot while
unearthly spirits are used mainly for theatrical effect.

6252 Coleman, Edward D. "The Jew in English Drama. An Annotated
Bibliography." Bulletin of the New York Public Library, XLII
(1938), 827-850, 919-932; XLIII (1939), 45-52, 374-378, 443-
458.

An elaborate list which includes bibliographical works on
the subject, general works, collections, and individual plays.
Covering the period from earliest times to 1837, this is at
once an annotated bibliography and a finding list.

6253 Modder, Montagu F. The Jew in the Literature of England, to
the End of the Nineteenth Century. Philadelphia, Pa.: Jewish
Publication Society of America, 1939. xvi, 435 pp.

An historical survey of Jewish characters for the purpose
of revealing changes in social attitudes. A few plays are included in the chapter on the 18th century.

6254 Sypher, Wylie. "The West Indian as a 'Character' in the Eighteenth
Century." Studies in Philology, XXXVI (1939), 503-520.

After defining the unique traits of the creole character,
Sypher traces its appearances in various works including such
plays as Bickerstaffe's Love in the City (1767), and Cumberland's West Indian (1771).

6255 Horne, Mark Daniel. "The Villain in Restoration Tragedy." Ph.D.
Louisiana State University, 1940.

6256 Clarke, Mary Coffin. "The Sentimental Hero from Steele to
Sheridan." M.A. University of Pittsburgh, 1941.

6257 Bartley, J. O. "The Development of a Stock Character: I. The
Stage Irishman to 1800." Modern Language Review, XXXVII
(October, 1942), 438-447.

A stock character develops in three stages and becomes a
convention only in the last. The article illustrates the development of the Irishman, the "largest and most important group

of nationalized characters in English drama." The second stage
of development is represented in plays 1660-1759, the third
stage in plays 1760-1800.

6258 Boas, Frederick S. "The Soldier in Elizabethan and Later English
Drama." Essays by Divers Hands, Being the Transactions of
the Royal Society of Literature of the United Kingdom, New Ser.,
XIX (1942), 121-156.
Some discussion of the works of Farquhar, Steele, and
Sheridan.

6259 Bartley, J. O. "The Development of a Stock Character. II. The
Stage Scotsman; III. The Stage Welshman (to 1800)." Modern
Language Review, XXXVIII (October, 1943), 279-288.
The Scotsman and the Welshman developed to the stage of
stock characters in three periods. The second period includes
the plays 1660-1749, the third period, 1750-1800.

6260 Scott, Florence R. "Teg - the Stage Irishman." Modern Language
Review, XLII (July, 1947), 314-320.
Adds to J. O. Bartley's study (M.L.R., 1942) some examples;
mainly from pre-Restoration drama, but including Sir Robert
Howard's The Committee, 1662.

6261 Smith, John Harrington. The Gay Couple in Restoration Comedy.
Cambridge: Harvard University Press, 1948. xii, 252 pp.
A detailed scrutiny of the conventional pairs of witty lovers
in seventeenth century comedy.

6262 Berkeley, David S. "The Penitent Rake in Restoration Comedy."
Modern Philology, XLIX (1952), 223-233.
At least twenty-five penitent rakes can be found in Restoration comedy, most of them repenting in the fifth act. As a
stock character the reformed rake was the most popular between 1696 and 1700.

6263 Bartley, J. O. Teague, Shenkin and Sawney: Being an Historical
Study of the Earliest Irish, Welsh, and Scottish Characters
in English Plays. Cork: Cork University Press, 1954. 339 pp.
Chapters VI through XIII deal with the appearance of the stage
Irishman, Welshman and Scotsman (each type is treated individually) in plays from 1660-1800. Chapter XIV discusses
the actors who played such parts.

6264 Jones, Sarah Dowlin. "The Treatment of Religious and National
Types in Late Eighteenth-Century Drama." Ph.D. University
of Pennsylvania, 1954. 241 pp. (Publication No. 7791).
This study deals with character stereotypes of minority
groups and with attempts to modify or break the sterotypes.

6265 Bennett, G. A. "A Study of the English Stage Villain, 1588-
1900." M.A. University of Wales, 1956-57.

6266 Vane, George T. "The Father-Figure in Eighteenth Century English Comedy." Ph.D. University of Minnesota, 1958.

6267 Berkeley, David S. The "Précieuse" or Distressed Heroine in Restoration Comedy. Stillwater: Oklahoma State University, 1959. 21 pp.

6268 Owens, William Henry, Jr. "The Dramaturgical Treatment of Character Types by the Playwrights of Heroic Drama." Ph.D. University of Denver, 1959.

6269 Rapport, James Louis. "A Lean and Slippered Pantaloon; A Historical Examination of the Comic Stock-Type Character, the Old Man." Ph.D. Ohio State University, 1960. 319 pp.

    Traces the evolution of the comic stock-type Old Man from the earliest sources to the present.

6270 Rosenberg, Edgar. From Shylock to Svengali: Jewish Stereotypes in English Fiction. Stanford: Stanford University Press, 1960. 388 pp.

    An historical survey of the ways, both positive and negative, that Jews have been presented. Considers Cumberland's The Jew as the first work to present "the saintly Jew"; also considers Cumberland's treatments of Jews in some detail.

6271 Porte, Michael Sheldon. "The Servant in Restoration Comedy." Ph.D. Northwestern University, 1961.

    Examines the sociological position of the domestic servant in Restoration England, and compares servants in seven Restoration adaptations with their prototypes. Relates these findings to some sixty Restoration comedies.

6272 Norell, Lemuel N. "The Cuckold in Restoration Comedy." Ph.D. The Florida State University, 1962. (Order No. 63-1823).

    The meaning of "cuckold." Various characteristics of cuckolds in Restoration drama.

6273 Wall, Donald Clark. "The Restoration Rake in Life and Comedy." Ph.D. The Florida State University, 1963. (Order No. 64-7588).

    Compares the history and comedies of Charles II's reign in order to determine to what extent Restoration comedy portrayed the attitudes of the Restoration libertine.

6274 Bennett, Gilbert. "Conventions of the Stage Villain." The Anglo-Welsh Review, XIV (1964), 92-102.

    Cites Otway, Congreve, Mrs. Centlivre, Theobald, Moore, and Mrs. Manley to show the increasing tendency in eighteenth century drama to use set patterns of speech and action to characterize the villain.

6275 Somers, Charles Norman. "Offspring of Distress: The Orphan in Eighteenth Century English Drama." Ph.D. University of Maryland, 1964. (Order No. 65-644).

Analyzes the orphan's function as victim, hero, and villain in 50 representative plays.

6276 Williams, E. A. "The Dramatic Origins of the Restoration Comic Hero." M.A. University of Liverpool, 1964.

6277 Potter, L. D. "The Fop and Related Figures in Drama from Jonson to Cibber." Ph.D. Cambridge University (Girton), 1965.

6278 Riddell, James Allen. "The Evolution of the Humours Character in Seventeenth-Century English Comedy." Ph.D. University of Southern California, 1966. (Order No. 66-8796).

Traces the development of the "humours character" from Jonson to Farquhar. The Jonsonian humour character did not appear in Restoration comedy when "humour" took on the meaning of any kind of odd or eccentric behavior. Widely differing attitudes towards humour characterization were held by Etherege, Wycherley, Congreve, Vanbrugh, and Farquhar.

6279 Traugott, John. "The Rake's Progress from Court to Comedy: A Study in Comic Form." Studies in English Literature, 1500-1900, VI (1966), 381-407.

Studies the efforts of Restoration playwrights to find a comic form suitable for the rake as a representative of the society's values and as the center of a legitimate comedy.

6280 Broich, Ulrich. "Libertin und heroischer Held: Das Drama der englischen Restaurationzeit und seine Leitbilder." Anglia, LXXXV (1967), 34-57.

Uffenbach, Conrad

6281 Quarrell, W. H., and Margaret Mare, translators and eds. London in 1710. From the Travels of Zacharias Conrad von Uffenbach. London: Faber, 1934. 194 pp.

Unities

6282 Friedland, Louis Sigmund. "The Dramatic Unities in England." Journal of English and Germanic Philology, X (1911), 56-89; 280-299; 453-467.

An historical study, beginning with Aristotle, through Italian ideas of the Renaissance. Draws much material from actual plays. Through the 18th century. The second paper, after brief consideration of French ideas, discusses Dryden and Dennis and other writers of the period--Rymer, Farquhar, Collier, Milton.

6283 Stuart, Donald Clive. "Stage Decoration and the Unity of Place in France in the Seventeenth Century." Modern Philology, XI (1912), 393-406.

The rule of unity of place was evidently stronger in theory
than in practice judged by various methods of changing scenery.
The single setting appeared in a not overwhelming majority
of plays.

6284 Raysor, Thomas M. "The Downfall of the Three Unities." Modern
Language Notes, XLII (January, 1927), 1-9.
Treats of attacks on the unities between 1755 and 1765, and
the downfall of dogma in English criticism between 1765 and
1800.

6285 Auerbach, Lawrence. "The Uses of Time in Plays of Four Periods
of Drama." Ph.D. University of Wisconsin, 1960. (Order No.
60-3165).
The "unity of time" is invalid.

Unmarried Women

6286 Gorowara, Krishna K. "The Treatment of the Unmarried Woman
in Comedy, 1584-1921." Ph.D. Glasgow University, 1962.

Unrecorded Plays

6287 Budd, F. E. "Four unrecorded Plays." Times Literary Supplement,
June 22, 1933, p. 428.
Refers to four unrecorded eighteenth-century plays probably
never seen outside Portsmouth: Harlequin's Revels at Ports-
down Fair; A Fig for the French; December and May: Or, The
Consequences; and The Enchanted Tavern.

Vanbrugh, John

works

6288 Vanbrugh, Sir John. The Complete Works: The Plays. Edited by
Bonamy Dobrée. The Letters. Edited by Geoffrey Webb. 4 vols.
London: Nonesuch Press, 1927-1928.
The standard edition. Dobrée's Introduction is brief and
admirable. The Letters are almost all about Van's business
affairs as architect.

plays

6289 -----. Sir John Vanbrugh. Edited, with an Introduction and Notes,
by A. E. Swaen. London: T. Fisher Unwin; New York: Charles
Scribner's Sons, 1904. 501 pp. (Mermaid Series. The Best
Plays of the Old Dramatists).

The text of The Relapse is an "exact reprint" of the edition
of 1776; The Provok'd Wife (no indication of the text used); The
Confederacy is an "exact reprint" of the edition of 1735; A
Journey to London is the text of that of 1734. The editor says that
he has corrected obvious mistakes in the plays.

6290 -----. Plays. Edited by A. E. H. Swaen. London: Ernest Benn,
1949. 501 pp.

A reprint of the Mermaid edition of 1896, containing texts of
The Relapse, The Provok'd Wife, The Confederacy and A
Journey to London.

individual texts

6291 "Sir John Vanbrugh: The Provok'd Wife." Representative English
Comedies. Vol. IV: Dryden and His Contemporaries: Cowley
to Farquhar. Edited by Charles Mills Gayley and Alwin Thaler.
(New York: The Macmillan Company, 1936), 407-426.

An essay treating Vanbrugh's life, his career, the play,
and Vanbrugh's place in English comedy. The essay is followed
by the text of The Provok'd Wife, edited by Thaler.

6292 Vanbrugh, Sir John. The Relapse, or Virtue in Danger. With an
introduction by Cyril Ritchard. London: Nevill, 1948. 176 pp.

A new edition, with an introduction in which the noted actor
speaks of his experiences in the role of Foppington.

biography and criticism

6293 Lovegrove, Gilbert H. The Life, Work, and Influence of Sir John
Vanbrugh (1663-1726). Being The Architectual Association
Prize Essay for 1901. London: Reprinted from the "Architectual
Association Notes, " 1902. 38 pp.

The introductory pages discuss his drama, but the bulk of
the essay relates to his architecture. The author sees Vanbrugh's
plays and architecture as a product of his times and, in them
both, surpassing "all his contemporaries in license and extravagance."

6294 Titherington, R. H. "The Architect of Blenheim." Munsey's
Magazine, XXVIII (1902-03), 448-452.

A sketch of Vanbrugh, dramatist and architect, including a
discussion of his long, bitter controversy with Sarah Churchill,
first Duchess of Marlborough.

6295 Birrell, Augustine. "Sir John Vanbrugh." Collected Essays and
Addresses, 1880-1920. Vol. I. (London and Toronto: J. M.
Dent & Sons, 1922), 107-112.

6296 Colville, Kenneth Newton. "Sir John Vanbrugh." Fame's Twilight;

Studies of Nine Men of Letters. (London: P. Allen & Co.,
1923), 185-212.

A brief biography which treats Vanbrugh's works superfi-
cially.

6297 Webb, Geoffrey. "Sir John Vanbrugh." Burlington Magazine, XLVII
(November, 1925), 222-227.

His romantic character led to his experiments in Gothic
architecture.

6298 "Sir John Vanbrugh." Nation and Athenaeum, XXXVIII (March 27,
1926), 893-894.

A sketch of his architectural career.

6299 Hague, René. "Sir John Vanbrugh." London Mercury, XVIII
(August, 1928), 395-402.

Reviews B. Dobrée and G. Webb, The Complete Works of
Sir John Vanbrugh (1927-28). Includes a biographical sketch;
argues that Vanbrugh's plays represent what the average man
preferred as amusement.

6300 Mortimer, Raymond. "Vanbrugh." Nation and Athenaeum, XLIII
(April 14, 1928), 48-49.

Reviews B. Dobrée and G. Webb, eds., The Complete Works
of Sir John Vanbrugh, 2 vols. (1927-1928). Includes a brief
evaluation of Vanbrugh.

6301 Porter, Alan. "Too Much Restoration." Spectator, CXL (March 10,
1928), 375, 377.

Reviews B. Dobrée and G. Webb, The Complete Works of
Sir John Vanbrugh (1927-28). Includes a brief essay on the indecency of Restoration comedy.

6302 Shanks, Edward. "Sir John Vanbrugh." Saturday Review (London),
CXLV (March 3, 1928), 258.

Reviews B. Dobrée and G. Webb, The Works of Sir John
Vanbrugh (1927-28). Vanbrugh's plays "are racy and healthily
vigorous."

6303 "Sir John Vanbrugh." New Statesman, XXXI (June 9, 1928), 298.

Reviews B. Dobrée and G. Webb, eds., The Complete Works
of Sir John Vanbrugh (1927-28). A brief estimate of his
reputation.

6304 "Vanbrugh's Plays and Letters." Times Literary Supplement,
April 19, 1928, p. 287.

Reviews B. Dobrée and G. Webb, The Complete Works of
Sir John Vanbrugh (1927-28). Includes a sketch of his merits
as a dramatist--fluent, witty, but a little trivial.

6305 Vaughan, Herbert S. "Vanbrugh Family." Notes and Queries, CLV
(August 18, 1928), 117.

Notes on his brothers and nephews, with miscellaneous
information about the family.

6306 -----. "Some Vanbrugh Problems." Notes and Queries, CLVII
      (July 27, 1929), 62.
          Notes on Vanbrugh's family.
6307 Mueschke, Paul, and Jeanette Fleisher. "A Re-Evaluation of
      of Vanbrugh." Publications of the Modern Language Association,
      XLIX (1934), 848-889.
          This article indicates the need for a re-study of both the
      critical and the historical aspects of the comedy of manners.
6308 Whistler, Laurence. Sir John Vanbrugh, Architect and Dramatist,
      1664-1726. London: Cobden-Sanderson, 1938. xii, 327 pp.
          Although the emphasis is upon Vanbrugh the architect, this
      biography chronicles the stage history of the plays and includes
      a truncated bibliography.
6309 Botton, Arthur T., and H. Duncan Hendry, eds. The Seventeenth
      Volume of the Wren Society. Oxford: Wren Society, 1940. 86 pp.
6310 Kies, Paul P. "Lessing's Intention in Der Dorfjunker." Research
      Studies of the State College of Washington, XI (1943), 257-263.
          Contends that Farquhar's Beaux' Stratagem and Vanbrugh's
      The Relapse were sources of Lessing's play.
6311 Boys, Richard C. "Sir Joshua Reynolds and the Architect Van Brugh:
      a Footnote to Boswell." Papers of the Michigan Academy of
      Science, Arts and Letters, XXXIII (1949), 323-336.
          A study of Reynold's valuation of Vanbrugh, particularly as
      an architect.
6312 Hinton, Denys. "Vanbrugh's The Provok'd Wife." Drama (Winter,
      1949), 25.
          A description, with photograph, of the stage settings for a
      modern performance of the play.
6313 Hooks, N. C. "Sir John Vanbrugh: A Reevaluation of His Plays."
      M.A. University of Liverpool, 1955-1956.
6314 Schrader, Klaus-Dietrich. "Die Stellung Sir John Vanbrughs und
      George Farquhars in der Geschichte der englischen Komödie."
      Berlin (Frei) Dissertation, 1956.
6315 Rosenberg, Albert. "A New Move for the Censorship of Owen
      Swiney's 'The Quacks.'" Notes and Queries, New Ser., V
      (1958), 393-396.
          Attack on Vanbrugh and the Kit-Cat Club, 1705.
6316 Germer, Erich. Sentimentale Züge in den Lustspielgestalten
      Ethereges, Wycherleys, Congreves, Vanbrughs und Farquhars.
      Inaugural Dissertation. Münster, 1963. 164 pp.
          Appearance and treatment of types of sentimentalism in
      Restoration comedy.
6317 Nelson, David Arthur. "The Laughing Comedy of the Eighteenth
      Century." Ph.D. Cornell University, 1965. (Order No. 65-
      14711).

The comic techniques and situations of Vanbrugh, Farquhar,
Goldsmith, and Sheridan are evaluated in terms of their ability
to create and maintain aesthetic distance between playgoer
and character.

6318 Barnard, John. "Sir John Vanbrugh: Two Unpublished Letters."
Huntington Library Quarterly, XXIX (1966), 347-352.
Reprints and discusses two letters: the first in Vanbrugh's
earliest extant letter (December 28, 1685); the second (May 14,
1708) concerns Vanbrugh's difficulties as an opera impressario
for the season of 1707 and 1708.

6319 Patterson, Frank Morgan. "The Achievement of Sir John Vanbrugh."
Ph.D. University of Iowa, 1966.
Analyzes the structure and themes of Vanbrugh's original
plays, and studies improvements on the five 17th-century French
plays that he translated.

6320 Rosenberg, Albert. "New Light on Vanbrugh." Philological Quarterly, XLV (1966), 603-613.
Eight letters by Vanbrugh. Four letters concern Vanbrugh's
financial interest in the Haymarket Theatre.

6321 Dobrée, Bonamy. Essays in Biography, 1680-1726. Freeport,
New York: Books for Libraries Press, 1967. 362 pp.
A reprint of the 1925 edition contains biographies of Etherege,
Vanbrugh and Addison.

6322 Harris, Bernard. Sir John Vanbrugh. London: Longmans, Green
and Co., 1967. 43 pp.
A brief survey of the playwright's life and works. Includes
select bibliography.

Vanbrugh, Philip

6323 Vaughan, Herbert S. "Captains C. and P. Vanbrugh." Times
Literary Supplement, June 2, 1927, p. 392.
Announces a biography of Charles and Philip, brothers to
Sir John Vanbrugh.

6324 -----. Captain Philip Vanbrugh, R.N." Times Literary Supple-
ment, August 30, 1928, p. 617.
Requests information concering a Reynolds painting of
Philip Vanbrugh (1743-44), brother to Sir John.

Vaudeville

6325 Avery, Emmett L. "Vaudeville on the London Stage, 1700-1737."
Research Studies of the State College of Washington, V (1937),
65-77.
Performance records and descriptions of exhibitions on the

stage of "physical novelties (posturers, strong men, tall men,
imitators)," and "short musical offerings."

Vaughan, Thomas

6326 Macray, W. D. "Sheridan's Critic: Thomas Vaughan." Notes and
       Queries, 11th Ser., IV (July 29, 1911), 95.
       Notice about Vaughan, his two farces and a novel in Dr.
       River's Literary Memoirs of Living Authors, 1798, volume 2.

Vauxhall

6327 Southworth, James Granville. Vauxhall Gardens: A Chapter in the
       Social History of England. New York: Columbia University Press;
       London: Humphrey Milford, 1941. 192 pp.

Verse

6328 Taylor, A.C.R. "English Verse Drama, Its History and Its Place
       in the Twentieth Century." M. Litt. Cambridge University
       (Girton), 1934.
6329 Collins, William. Drafts and Fragments of Verse. Edited by J. S.
       Cunningham. Oxford: Clarendon Press, 1956. xii, 49 pp.
       Includes verses on Restoration drama.

Villains

6330 Danziger, Marlies K. "Heroic Villains in Eighteenth-Century
       Criticism." Comparative Literature, XI (1959), 35-46.
       Examines the "tradition of relating heroic villains to the sub-
       lime in order to explain their appeal" in continental and English
       criticism. References to criticism of tragedy passim.

Vienna

6331 Gunther, R. "Vienna's Popular Theatre." The American German
       Review, XXVIII (August-September, 1962), 12-13.
       Review of contemporary theatre in Vienna. Short references
       to the "Teutsche Komödie" and Parvlatschentheter of the Eight-
       eenth Century in recent seasons and revivals.

Villiers, Barbara

6332 Gilmour, Margaret. The Great Lady: A Biography of Barbara
       Villiers, Mistress of Charles II. New York: Knopf, 1941. 386 pp.

Villiers, Georgie

texts

6333 Villiers, George. The Rehearsal. First Acted 7 December 1671,
      Published 1672. Mit Einleitung herausgegeben von Felix Lindner.
      Heidelberg: Carl Winter, 1904. iv, 110, [1] pp.
           The text of the play based on the 1672 edition. A detailed
      study of the play, sources, and influence.
6334 -----. 2nd Duke of Buckingham. The Rehearsal. Edited by Montague
      Summers. Stratford-upon-Avon: The Shakespeare Head Press,
      1914. xxv, 163 pp.
           The introduction discusses Sir Robert Howard's relationship
      to The Rehearsal, the career of John Lacy, the actor who
      portrayed Bayes, and the stage history of the play. The text
      follows, based on the 1675 quarto (the third edition). Extensive
      notes.
6335 Villiers, George, Duke of Buckingham. The Rehearsal, and The
      Critic, by Richard Brinsley Sheridan. Edited by A. G. Barnes.
      London: Methuen, 1927. 7, 168 pp.
           A critical edition showing the relation of these burlesques to
      the serious drama of the time. The introduction gives an ac-
      count of the heroic play and notes that the formlessness of The
      Rehearsal is not a fair parody of the self-conscious heroic
      drama.
6336 -----. The Rehearsal, as Performed at the Theatre Royal, Drury
      Lane, to Which Is Added a Key, or Critical View of the Authors
      and Their Writings Exposed in This Play, by S. Briscoe, 1704;
      and Richard Brinsley Sheridan, The Critic, or A Tragedy Re-
      hearsed, A Dramatic Piece in Three Acts as Performed at The
      Theatre Royal in Drury Lane. Great Neck, New York: Barron's
      Educational Series, 1960. 168 pp.
           A new paperback edition of the two plays, including a reprint
      of "The Key" to The Rehearsal. Edited by Cedric Gale.

biography and criticism

6337 Gardner, Winifred, Lady Burghclere. George Villiers, Second
      Duke of Buckingham, 1628-1687. A Study in the History of the
      Restoration. London: J. Murray, 1903. 414 pp.
           A carefully documented biography, based largely on pre-
      viously unedited manuscript sources, with running chronology
      at page-tops, and good index. Emphasizes his relationship to
      family and court.
6338 Nicoll, Allardyce. "The Theatre of the Past." Drama (British

Drama League, London), IV (April, 1926), 145.

Mr. E. S. DeBeer has made two discoveries connected with
the satirical Buckingham-Howard play and with The Rehearsal.

6339 Sabatini, Rafael. "His Insolence of Buckingham; George Villiers'
Courtship of Anne of Austria." Golden Book, VIII (July, 1928),
25-32.

Traces Buckingham's early effort (1625) to court the Queen
of France, and sees him as a symbol of the misconduct that
led to Charles I's downfall.

6340 Fairfax-Blakeborough, J. "George Villiers, 2nd Duke of Buckingham, as Master of Hounds." Notes and Queries, CLVI (May
18, 1929), 349.

On the sale of a hunting horn once belonging to Buckingham.

6341 Legouis, Pierre. "Buckingham et Sheridan: ce que le Critique
doit à la Répetition." Revue Anglo-Américaine, XI (1934), 423-
434.

6342 Mizener, Arthur M. "George Villiers, Second Duke of Buckingham,
His Life and a Canon of His Works." Ph.D. Princeton University, 1934.

6343 Avery, Emmett L. "The Stage Popularity of The Rehearsal, 1671-
1777." Research Studies of the State College of Washington,
VII (1939), 201-204.

Complete performance records of Buckingham's play with
commentary upon the actors.

6344 Chapman, Hester W. Great Villiers: a Study of George Villiers,
Second Duke of Buckingham, 1628-1687. London: Secker and
Warburg, 1949. xxiv, 289 pp.

A detailed biography, with copious information on the Duke's
dramatic connections.

6345 Smith, John Harrington. "Dryden and Buckingham: The Beginnings
of the Feud." Modern Language Notes, LXIX (1954), 242-245.

The feud has its origin in 1667, when Buckingham attacked
Dryden in the epilogue to his adaptation of Fletcher's The Chances.

6346 Wilson, John Harold. A Rake and His Times: George Villiers, 2nd
Duke of Buckingham. New York: Farrar, Straus and Young, 1954.
280 pp.

Wilson is concerned mainly with Villiers' private and public
life, and only in passing with his dramatic activity.

Voiture

6347 Mish, Charles C. "Voiture's 'Alcidalis et Zélide' in English."
Notes and Queries, New Ser., IV (1957), 438-439.

Includes 18th century editions.

Voltaire, Francois

6348 Baumgartner, G. "Voltaire auf der englischen Buhne des 18 Jahrhunderts." Inaugural Dissertation. Strasburg, 1913.

6349 Bruce, Harold Lawton. "The Period of Greatest Popularity of
Voltaire's Plays on the English Stage." Modern Language Notes,
XXXI (1918), 20-23.

A refutation of Professor Lounsbury's statement that the
period of greatest popularity of Voltaire's plays on the English
stage was 1729-1744 (Shakespeare and Voltaire). Proves with
the help of Genest that the period of greatest popularity was
the third quarter of the century.

6350 -----. Voltaire on the English Stage. Berkeley: University of
California Press, 1918. 152 pp.

Reviews sixteen English adaptations of Voltaire plays in the
18th century from the standpoint of stage history, publishing
history, and a comparison of the original and the adaptation.
Concludes that Voltaire as dramatist was long a presence on
the English stage but not an influence. English authors considered: Duncombe, Hill, Miller and Hoadly, Murphy, Francklin,
Colman, Macklin, Celesia, Cradock, Ayscough.

6351 Fenger, H. "Voltaire et le Théâtre Anglais." Orbis Litterarum,
VII (1949), 161-287.

A thorough analysis, noting particularly Voltaire's reading
of the Elizabethan and Jacobean dramatists, and the influence
on his plays of Dryden, Otway, Lee and others.

Wales

6352 Price, Cecil. The English Theatre in Wales in the Eighteenth and
Early Nineteenth Centuries. Cardiff: University of Wales Press,
1948. xii, 202 pp.

A detailed study of the provincial theatres and itinerant performers, casting light on the social conditions and status of
actors during the period and on the tastes of provincial audiences.

Walker, Robert

6353 Dawson, Giles E. "Robert Walker's Editions of Shakespeare."
Studies in the English Renaissance Drama: In Memory of Karl
Julius Holzknecht. Edited by Josephine W. Bennett, Oscar Car-
gill, and Vernon Hall, Jr. (New York: New York University
Press, 1959), 58-81.

An historical treatment of Walker's 1734-35 edition of Shakespeare's Works, including a very detailed discussion of the con-

troversy over this edition between Walker and Tonson.

Walker, Thomas

6354 Lawrence, W. J. "Thomas Walker in Dublin." Notes and Queries,
       10th Ser., II (September 24, 1904), 247.
       A correction of Fitzgerald Molloy's Romance of the Irish
       Stage: Walker could not have been manager of a Dublin theatre
       in 1732, as from 1730-33, he was acting in London under Rich.

Waller, Edmund

6355 Deas, M. C. "A Study of the Life and Poetry of Edmund Waller."
       Ph.D. Cambridge University (Newnham), 1931.

Walpole, Miss

6356 Hudleston, C. Roy. "Miss Walpole." Notes and Queries, CXC
       (April 6, 1946), 153.
       Additions to G. O. Rickword's note, 23 February, 1946.
6357 Rickword, G. O. "Miss Walpole c. 1778." Notes and Queries,
       CXC (February 23, 1946), 80.
       Asks for information about Miss Walpole, who played Cor-
       poral Williams in Tickell's The Camp, 1778.

Walpole, Horace

letters

6358 Walpole, Horace. Supplement to the Letters of Horace Walpole,
       chronologically arranged and edited with Notes and Indices.
       Vol. III, 1744-97. Edited by Paget Toynbee. Oxford: Clarendon
       Press, 1925. xxxi, 450 pp.
       Contains 105 new letters, a few of them containing theatrical
       and dramatic references, plus upwards of one hundred and fifty
       to Walpole between 1735 and 1796.
6359 -----. Correspondence with Thomas Gray, Richard West and
       Thomas Ashton. Edited by Wilmarth Sheldon Lewis, George L.
       Lam and Charles H. Bennett. 2 vols. New Haven: Yale Uni-
       versity Press, 1948. (The Yale Edition of Horace Walpole's
       Correspondence, XIII, XIV).
       Contains numerous references to drama and theatrical af-
       fairs, especially in the Gray correspondence.

biography and criticism

6360 Stuart, Dorothy Margaret. Horace Walpole. London: Macmillan,
       1927. x, 229 pp. (English Men of Letters, New Series).
       Biography, with a brief discussion of The Mysterious Mother.
6361 Holzknecht, Karl J. "Horace Walpole as Dramatist." South Atlantic
       Quarterly, XXVIII (April, 1929), 174-189.
       The work Walpole wrought most seriously was his unacted
       drama, an outgrowth of his love of the eccentric and medieval.
6362 Stein, Jess M. "Horace Walpole and Shakespeare." Studies in
       Philology, XXXI (1934), 51-68.
       This paper proposes to discuss Walpole'a attitude toward
       Shakespeare, Shakespeare's influence on Walpole's play and
       novel, and Walpole's criticism of Shakespeare. Walpole ap-
       parently worshipped Shakespeare as a native genius; he criti-
       cized Voltaire's strictures on Shakespeare; and he was influenced
       only incidentally by Shakespeare in his own compositions.
6363 Kilby, Clyde S. "Horace Walpole on Shakespeare." Studies in
       Philology, XXXVIII (July, 1941), 480-493.
       Based on unpublished material in Walpole's notebooks.
6364 Brandenburg, Alice S. "The Theme of The Mysterious Mother."
       Modern Language Quarterly, X (1949), 464-474.
       Argues that Walpole "was attempting to treat incest as a
       tragic subject and not merely as a device for achieving a cheap
       sensationalism." Explores other 18th-century uses of the in-
       cest theme.
6365 Bateson, F.W., ed. "Exhumations II: Horace Walpole's 'Thoughts
       on Comedy.'" Essays in Criticism, XV (1965), 162-170.
       Reprints Walpole's 1775-1776 essay on the comedy of man-
       ners, first published in 1798.
6366 Parlakian, Nishan. "The Image of Sir Robert Walpole in English
       Drama, 1728-1742." Ph.D. Columbia University, 1967. (Order
       No. 67-14,076).
       The image of Walpole can be found in the plot, character,
       dianoia, and diction of more than fifty plays written during the
       period. Special attention is given to Gay's The Beggar's Opera.

Warburton, William

6367 Sherbo, Arthur. "Warburton and the 1745 Shakespeare." Journal
       of English and Germanic Philology, LI (1952), 71-82.
       The theory of Warburton's close connection with the 1745
       edition, as suggested by Giles Dawson ("Warburton, Hanmer,
       and the 1745 Edition of Shakespeare," Studies in Bibliography,
       II [1949-50], 35-48), is highly questionable.

6368 McAleer, John J. "William Warburton--Editor Ex Cathedra."
      Shakespeare Newsletter, XVII (1967), 40.
            A brief biography of Warburton that discusses his edition of
      Shakespeare.

Ward, John

6369 Price, Cecil. "John Ward, Stroller." Theatre Notebook, I (January,
      1946), 10-12.
            A biographical study of the actor.
6370 Kennedy-Skipton, A.L.D. "John Ward and Restoration Drama."
      Shakespeare Quarterly, XI (1960), 493-494.
            Relates two passages in the notebooks of the Rev. John Ward
      --one telling of the revels of the Prince de la Grange at Lincoln's
      Inn Fields on Jan. 6 [1661/2] and one telling of a 1662 performance
      of The Alchemist.
6371 -----. "A Footnote to 'John Ward and Restoration Drama.'" Shake-
      speare Quarterly, XII (1961), 353.
            See also his earlier article, "John Ward and Restoration Drama."
      Shakespeare Quarterly, XI (1960), 493-494.

Ward, Ned

6372 Ward, Ned. The London Spy. Edited by Arthur L. Hayward. New
      York: George H. Doran, 1927. x, 309 pp.
            An expurgated edition. Contains numerous dramatic references
      1698-1703.

Wargrave

6373 C., R.L. "Private Theatres in England." Notes and Queries, 12th
      Ser., XI (December, 1922), 457.
            Information concerning the theatre at Wargrave in the 18th
      century.

Warton, Thomas

6374 Wilson, Robert H. "Reed and Warton on the Old Wives Tale."
      Publications of the Modern Language Association, LV (June,
      1940), 605-608.
            Argues that Thomas Warton "plagiarized" from Joseph Reed
      in his comments on The Old Wives Tale in his edition of the
      minor poems of Milton (1785).
6375 Kirchbaum, Leo. "The Imitations of Thomas Warton the Elder."
      Philological Quarterly, XXII (April, 1943), 119-124.

Quotes parallel passages to show that Warton echoes Shakespeare, Jonson, Milton, Denham, and Dryden. Kirchbaum
believes that Warton is more important historically than has been
recognized.

6376 Brown, Ernest A. "A Study of the Materials on the History of the
Drama in Warton's History of English Poetry." Ph.D. University
of North Carolina, 1952. 278 pp.

Analyzes Warton's comments on the drama and its history.

Weaver, John

6377 Cohen, Selma Jeanne. "Theory and Practice of Theatrical Dancing
in England in the Restoration and Early Eighteenth Century as
Seen in the Lives and Works of Josias Priest, John Weaver,
and Hester Santlow, Part II." Bulletin of the New York Public
Library, XLIV (1960), 41-54.

A history of the career of John Weaver, "choreographer,
historian and theorist, who attempted to revive the art of Roman pantomime and created a new form of dramatic dance."

Webb, John

6378 Keith, William Grant. "The Designs for the First Movable Scenery
on the English Stage." Burlington Magazine, XXV (1914), 29-33,
85-89.

A study of Webb's sketches for the scenery of The Siege of
Rhodes at Rutland House and of Mustapha, produced 1666 at
Whitehall before the Court.

6379 -----. "John Webb and the Court Theatre of Charles II." Architectural Review, LVII (1925), 49-55.

A discussion of Webb's work as Inigo Jones's successor,
with plans of the stage at Whitehall, 1665, and several reproductions of scenes from Mustapha, designed by Webb (1666).

Webster, Benjamin

6380 Downer, Alan S. "The Diary of Benjamin Webster." Theatre
Annual (1945), 47-64.

Reprints some comments on Garrick, Goldsmith and the
eighteenth century stage made in his diary by Benjamin Webster,
the nineteenth century manager.

Webster, John

6381 Moore, Don D. John Webster and His Critics, 1617-1964. Baton

Rouge: Louisiana State University Press, 1966. 199 pp.
Chapter 1, "Early Stagings and Scholarship," concerns
Webster's reception in the 17th and 18th centuries.

Wedding

6382 W.J.L. [W. J. Lawrence]. Note on the Ballad Opera The Wedding.
The Musical Antiquary, II (April, 1911), 184.
Does not believe that The Wedding and The Country Wedding
are the same, as Baker (Biographia Dramatica) asserted. If
the pieces are the same, the first performance was May 6,
1729, at Lincoln's Inn Fields.

Welsh Players

6383 Jones, T. J. R. "Welsh Interlude Players of the Eighteenth Century."
Theatre Notebook, II (July, 1948), 62-66.
Traditional folk plays discussed.

Wessex

6384 Hare, Arnold. The Georgian Theatre in Wessex. With twelve pages
of plates. London: Phoenix House, 1958. 228 pp. Index.
The scope is limited to the 18th century, and the first decade
of the nineteenth, and covers the regions of Wiltshire and Hampshire, West Sussex, East Dorset, and East Sussex.

West, Thomas

6385 Bulloch, J. M. "Colonel Temple West of the Surrey Theatre." Notes
and Queries, CLVI (February 2, 1929), 80.
A biographical sketch of one of the men responsible for building the Surrey Theatre (1782).

Whig Propaganda

6386 Ramsland, Clement. "Whig Propaganda in the Theatre, 1700-1742."
Ph.D. University of Minnesota, 1940.

Whitefield, George

6387 King, C. Harold. "George Whitefield: Dramatic Evangelist."
Quarterly Journal of Speech, XIX (1933), 165-175.

Whitehead, William

6388 Dobson, Austin. "Laureate Whitehead." Kensington Palace and
      Other Papers. (London: Chatto and Windus, 1910), 140-172.
          Sketch of life and works with some attention to Whitehead's
      two tragedies, The Roman Father and Creusa, and his senti-
      mental comedy, School for Lovers, in all of which Garrick
      acted.
6389 Plattner, H. William Whitehead, His Life and His Two Dramas,
      "The Roman Father" and "Creusa." Zurich, 1914.
6390 Bitter, August. William Whitehead--poeta laureatus; eine Studie
      zu den Literarischen Strömungen um die mitte des 18 Jahrhundert
      Halle (Saale): M. Niemeyer, 1933. 105 pp.
          The fourth chapter discusses his dramatic works, dramatic
      traditions, and the public.
6391 Neebe, Frederick Louis. "William Whitehead: a Study of His Life
      and His Place in His Day and His Works." Ph.D. University
      of Missouri, 1947.

Whitier, Walter

6392 Muir, Kenneth. "Shakespeare's Imagery--Then and Now." Shake-
      speare Survey, XVIII (1965), 46-57.
          Includes an analysis of Rev. Walter Whiter's A Specimen of a
      Commentary on Shakespeare published in 1794.
6393 Bell, Mary. "Walter Whiter's Notes on Shakespeare." Shakespeare
      Survey, XX (1967), 83-94.
          A selection and discussion of notes not included in Walter
      Whiter's Specimen of a Commentary on Shakespeare (1794).

Wilkes, Thomas

6394 Miller, William Hubert. "The Authorship of 'A General View of
      the Stage.'" Modern Language Notes, LVI (December, 1941),
      612-614.
          Brings evidence to show that A General View (1759) was
      written by Thomas Wilkes and not by Samuel Derrick, to
      whom it is generally ascribed.

Wilkinson, Tate

6395 Wright, Louis B. "A Note on Dramatic Piracy." Modern Language
      Notes, XLIII (April, 1928), 256-258.
          Three quotations from Tate Wilkinson's theatrical memoirs,
      showing how plays were reproduced from the memory of actors

in certain parts with the gaps otherwise supplied.

Wilmot, John

works

6396 Wilmot, John, Earl of Rochester. Collected Works. Edited by
      John Hayward. London: Nonesuch Press, 1926. xlix, 404 pp.
          A biographical introduction and textual and explanatory
      notes. Includes the text of Valentinian, A Tragedy (acted 1683,
      printed 1685).

biography and criticism

6397 Longueville, Thomas. Rochester and Other Literary Rakes at the
      Court of Charles II, with Some Account of Their Surroundings.
      London: Longmans, Green, and Co., 1903. x, 330 pp.
          An account of the social and literary milieu of the court of
      Charles II, centering upon Rochester as characteristic of a type,
      but touching on other literary men such as Etherege, Wycherley,
      Davenant, and St. Evremond.
6398 Prinz, Johannes. John Wilmot, Earl of Rochester: His Life and
      Writings. Leipzig: Mayer and Müller, 1927. (No. 154 in the
      Palaestra Series). 460 pp.
          Includes a full selection of letters and other documents,
      and a very thorough bibliography. Prinz accepts the principle
      that Restoration drama was intended to inculcate vice, and con-
      siders Rochester a prime representative of his period. Treats
      at length his involvement in the theatre, including the production
      of Valentinian.
6399 Williamson, George. "The Restoration Petronius." University of
      California Chronicle, XXIX (1927), 273-280.
          A sketch of his life and career.
6400 Nicoll, Allardyce. "The First Baconian." Times Literary Supple-
      ment, February 25, 1932, p. 128.
          The article states that Bacon's authorship of Shakespeare's
      plays was first suggested by an Englishman of the 18th-century,
      the Rev. James Wilmott, D.D., Rector of Barton on Heath,
      near Stratford.
6401 Wilson, John Harold. "The Dating of Rochester's 'Scaen.'" Review
      of English Studies, XIII (1937), 455-458.
          To complete his play, The Conquest of China by the Tartars,
      Sir Robert Howard invited the collaboration of Rochester in
      1678 and not earlier.
6402 -----. "Rochester's 'Valentinian,' and Heroic Sentiment." English

Literary History, IV (1937), 265-273.
> Rochester adapted the original play by Fletcher according to "contemporary neo-classic ideals," and to the concept of heroic sentiment he probably derived from d'Urfé's L'Astrée.

6403 -----. "Satiric Elements in Rochester's 'Valentinian.'" Philological Quarterly, XVI (1937), 41-48.
> Rochester's style in his adaptation of Fletcher's play (performed 1684) is revealed in his satiric portrait of Charles II as Valentinian.

6404 Murdock, Kenneth B. The Sun at Noon: Three Biographical Sketches. New York: Macmillan, 1939. viii, 327 pp.
> Includes a brief life of John Wilmot, Earl of Rochester.

6405 Hook, Lucyle. "The Publication Date of Rochester's 'Valentinian.'" Huntington Library Quarterly, XIX (1956), 401-407.
> Probably before December 6, 1684, although the imprint says 1685.

6406 Bror, Danielsson, and David M. Vieth, eds. The Gyldenstolpe Manuscript Miscellany of Poems by John Wilmot, Earl of Rochester, and Other Restoration Authors. Stockholm Studies in English, XVII. (Acta Universitatis Stockholmiensis). Stockholm: Almqvist and Wiksells, 1967.

Wilson, John

dramatic works

6407 Wilson, John. The Dramatic Works of John Wilson. Edited by James Maidment and W. H. Logan. New York: Benjamin Blom, 1967. 418 pp.
> A reprint of the 1874 edition contains four plays including The Cheats (1662).

individual texts

6408 -----. The Cheats. Edited by Milton C. Nahm. Oxford: Blackwell, 1935. ix, 280 pp.
> An authoritative scholarly edition with a detailed historical and bibliographical introduction and a text based on a collation of the MS. with the quarto editions.

biography and criticism

6409 Hollstein, E. Verhaltnis von Ben Johnson's [sic!] "The Devil Is an Ass" und John Wilson's "Belphegor, or The Marriage and the Devil" zu Machiavelli's Novelle vom Belfayor. Inaugural Dissertation. Halle, 1901. 52 pp.

6410 Faber, Karl. John Wilsons Dramen: eine Quellenstudie. Wies-
baden: Buchdruckerei von C. Ritter, 1904.

6411 Boas, F. S. "Stage Censorship under Charles II." Times Literary
Supplement, April 15, 1920, p. 238; April 22, 1920, p. 254.
Discusses censorship by Sir Henry Herbert, Master of the
Revels, of John Wilson's The Cheats.

6412 Flood, W. H. Grattan. "John Wilson (Author of 'The Cheats'),
Recorder of Londonderry." Times Literary Supplement, July
28, 1921.
Correction of the dates given by Boas for Wilson's term as
recorder; Flood indicates that Wilson held the post from 1667/8
to 1682.

6413 Nahm, Milton C. "John Wilson and his 'Some Few Plays.'" Review
of English Studies, XIV (1938), 143-154.
Wilson wrote Andronicus in 1644, published it in 1661, then
revised the play and printed it as Andronicus Comnenius in 1664.

Winston

6414 Hogan, Charles Beecher. "The Manuscript of Winston's Theatric
Tourist." Theatre Notebook, I (April, 1947), 86-95.
On the discovery of the notebook, with editorial comment by
Sybil Rosenfeld and Richard Southern.

Wit

6415 Fujimura, Thomas H. "The Comedy of Wit, 1660-1710." Ph.D.
Columbia University, 1950. 314 pp. (Publication No. 1850).
Restoration comedy should be described as "witty, natural-
istic, and hedonic."

6416 -----. The Restoration Comedy of Wit. Princeton: Princeton University Press, 1952. 232 pp.
Restoration comedy is "a witty presentation of a naturalistic
outlook on life."

6417 Milburn, D. Judson. The Age of Wit, 1650-1750. New York: Macmillan; London: Collier-Macmillan, 1966. 348 pp.
Attempts to identify and describe contexts for meanings of
wit by which the age understood itself. Includes references to
the period's drama, and a part of Chapter Seven is given to a
study of the caricature of wit in Wycherley's The Country Wife.

Wits

6418 Praz, Mario. "Poets and Wits of the Restoration." English Studies,

X (April, 1928), 41-53.

Remarks occasioned by recent studies of Etherege, Sedley, Rochester, and Marvell. Praz sees the new interest in the Restoration wits as an indication that the post-war era has much in common with that of the 17th century. Believes that the editors have minimized too much the licentiousness of the age.

6419 Wilson, John Harold. The Court Wits of the Restoration, an Introduction. Princeton: Princeton University Press, 1948. x, 264 pp.

Studies the court wits as a group, against their social background. Incidental comments on the drama and the theatre are found throughout.

Woffington, Peg

6420 Dobson, Austin. "Mrs. Woffington." Side-Walk Studies. (Oxford: Oxford University Press, 1902), 1-32. Second edition, 1903.

A short biographical sketch of Mrs. Woffington including some of her roles on the 18th century stage.

6421 Lawrence, W. J. "Peg Woffington's Sister." Notes and Queries, 9th Ser., XII (October 17, 1903), 309-310.

A biographical note on Mary Woffington Cholmondeley.

6422 L., F.F. "Peg Woffington's Letter." Notes and Queries, 10th Ser., I (February 13, 1904), 124.

Attempts to discredit the authenticity of a letter reputed to be of Peg Woffington's signature; the letter is printed in Notes and Queries, 3rd Ser., XII, p. 430.

6423 Lawrence, W. J. "TheWoffingtons of Dublin, Some Records of an Old Musical Family." The Musical Antiquary, III (1911-1912), 215-219.

The Protestant branch of the family, musicians and musical instrument makers, traced from 1720 to 1836. Wonders about, but is unable to establish, a connection with Spencer Woffington and his Patagonian Theatre at 27 Capel Street and Miss Woffington, performer on the musical glasses.

6424 Trowbridge, W.R.H. Daughters of Eve. London: Chapman and Hall, Ltd., 1911. xii, 315, [1] pp. [Also, New York: Brentano's, 1911].

Biographical sketches of five women of 18th-century Europe and England. Pages 123-175 are devoted to the theatrical experiences of the "merry magdalen with the heart of gold," Peg Woffington: her first stage experiences in Dublin at Mme. Violante's Booth, at Smock Alley, the Theatre Royal in Aungier Street, at Covent Garden and Drury Lane; her affaire with Garrick; and her skirmishes with Kitty Clive, Mrs. Cibber, and

George Anne Bellamy.

6425 Dobson, Austin. "Peg Woffington." Sidewalk Studies. (London
      and Oxford: Humphrey Milford, Oxford University Press,
      1924), 1-32.
          Biographical sketch of Margaret "Peg" Woffington, the
      actress. The first edition of this book was 1902, the second
      edition, 1903; the second edition was re-issued by Oxford
      University Press in 1923 and reprinted by World's Classics,
      1924.

6426 "The Merry Wives of Windsor." Theatre Arts Monthly, X (July,
      1926), 480.
          Portraits of Edward Shuter and Peg Woffington.

6427 Hanbury-Williams, John. "Peg Woffington and Her Portraits."
      Connoisseur, CVI (1940), 227-233, 266.
          Ten paintings reproduced for this article; includes poems
      written to her.

6428 de C[astro], J.P. "'Peg Woffington's Cottages,' Teddington."
      Notes and Queries, CLXXXIII (1942), 84.
          There is no evidence that the traditionally pious Peg Wof-
      fington ever built almshouses.

6429 Seton-Anderson, James. "Peg Woffington and Mrs. Cholmondeley."
      Notes and Queries, CLXXXIII (October 24, 1942), 264.

6430 Lucey, Janet Camden. Lovely Peggy: The Life and Times of
      Margaret Woffington. London: Hurst and Blackett, 1952. 268
      pp.
          An attempt to make the life of Mrs. Woffington, "more
      human and understandable." Basically a biographical novel
      with scanty documentation.

6431 Scott, W. S. "Peg Woffington and Her Circle." The New Rambler,
      Serial No. C. II (January, 1967), 14-23.
          A brief biography of the Irish actress who played roles in
      Gay's The Beggar's Opera, Farquhar's Constant Couple, and
      Steele's Conscious Lovers.

Women Dramatists

6432 Raeburn, Eleanor. "Early Feminine Dramatists." Theatre,
      XVIII (December, 1913), 194-196.
          Very short summaries of the work of women dramatists
      of the 16th and 17th centuries, including Catharine Philips;
      Margaret Cavendish, Duchess of Newcastle; Frances Boothby;
      Aphra Behn; Mary Pix; Mrs. Manley; and Catharine Cockburn.

Wordsworth, William

6433 Campbell, Oscar James, and Paul Mueschke. "'Guilt and Sorrow':
A Study in the Genesis of Wordsworth's Aesthetic." Modern
Philology, XXIII (May, 1926), 465-482.
    The play "throws light upon the extraordinary transformation
which took place in Wordsworth's aesthetic principles during
the obscure years from 1793 to 1797."

6434 de Selincourt, Edward. "The Hitherto Unpublished Preface to
Wordsworth's 'Borderers.'" Nineteenth Century and After, C
(November, 1926), 723-741.
    This recently discovered Preface to Wordsworth's only play
(written 1795-96 and published 1842) throws light on the changes
of character Wordsworth underwent during his residence in
France because of the collapse of the Revolution and the ex-
cesses of the Reign of Terror, but not because of Annette Vallon.

Worthing

6435 Odell, Mary Theresa. More about the Old Theatre, Worthing,
1807-1855. Worthing: Aldridge Bros., for the Worthing Art
Development Scheme, 1945.

Wren, Christopher

6436 Milman, Lena. Sir Christopher Wren. New York: Charles
Scribner's Sons, 1911.

6437 Bell, Hamilton. "On Three Plans by Sir Christopher Wren."
Architectural Record, XXX (1913), 359-369.
    This is part of a series entitled Contributions to the History
of the English Playhouse. The article reveals at least a partial
plan--executed by Wren--of the Duke's Theatre, Dorset Gardens.

6438 Whitaker-Wilson, C. Sir Christopher Wren. London: Methuen
& Co., 1932. 268 pp.
    Attempts to provide the first complete account of Wren's
character, his friends and enemies, his creations, and aspects
of the 17th century relevant to a study of Wren. The chapter
on "The Secular Buildings" deals with his theatres.

6439 Bolton, [John Robert] Glorney. Sir Christopher Wren. London:
Hutchinson, 1956. 191 pp.
    Although the book covers Wren's life, it centers mainly
around St. Paul's, with only a few lines devoted to the
Sheldonian Theatre at Oxford.

6440 Furst, Viktor. The Architecture of Sir Christopher Wren. London: Lund Humphries, 1956. [12], 244 pp.

157 plates, photographs, or drawings. Excellent notes.
Page 3 gives a picture of the Sheldonian Theatre, south front.
The notes on p. 182 discuss the theatre.

6441 Sekler, Eduard. Wren and His Place in European Architecture.
London: Faber and Faber [1956]. 217, [80] pp.
Eighty pages of plates, including two plates of the Sheldonian
Theatre at Oxford. His probable design of the Theatre Royal,
Drury Lane (1674) is mentioned.

6442 Gregory, William Earnest. "The Theatre Architecture of Sir
Christopher Wren." M.S. University of Oregon, 1966.

6443 Mullin, Donald C. and Bruce Koenig. "Christopher Wren's Theatre
Royal." Theatre Notebook, XXI (Summer, 1967), 180-187.
Uses memorabilia from the period to trace the development
of Wren's original design.

Writing

6444 Beauchamp, George Emerson. "The Profession of Writing in England from 1660 to 1740." Ph.D. Northwestern University,
1943-44.

Wycherley, William

works

6445 Wycherley, William. Works. Edited with introduction and notes
by W. C. Ward. New edition. London: T. Fisher Unwin, 1900.
xlviii, 508 pp.
Text based on first editions collated with the 1713 edition
and Hunt's edition of 1849; includes general introduction and
biographical sketch of Wycherley, as well as introductions
to the individual plays.

6446 -----. The Complete Works of William Wycherley. Edited by
Montague Summers. 4 vols. London: The Nonesuch Press,
1924.
The introduction consists of a biography of Wycherley, followed by an extensive analysis of his plays, including attention
to sources, background, and details of early performances.

dramas

6447 -----. The Country Wife and the Plain Dealer. With Life and
Introduction by George B. Churchill. Boston: Belles Lettres
Series, 1924.
The "Life" is a biographical sketch of Wycherley; the "Intro-

duction" is a discussion of the background of the Restoration
theatre and of the dates of composition and backgrounds of the
plays.

6448 [Wycherley, William]. William Wycherley. Edited with an introduction and notes by W. C. Ward. London: T. Fischer Unwin,
Ltd., etc., etc. [1927]. xlviii, 508 pp. (The Mermaid Series.)
The complete plays preceded by an introduction on Restoration comedy and Wycherley's place in it.

6449 Wycherley, William. The Complete Plays. Edited by Gerald Weales.
Garden City, N.Y.: Doubleday and Company, 1966. (The Anchor
Seventeenth-Century Series).
Includes introduction, notes, and variants.

individual texts

6450 -----. The Country Wife. Edited with a critical introduction,
notes, and appendices, by Ursula Todd-Naylor. Northampton,
Mass.: Smith College, 1931. lix, 108 pp. (Smith College Studies
in Modern Languages, 1931).

6451 -----. The Country Wife, A Comedy. New York: Random House,
1936. 125 pp.
Evidently intended for the mass market, this edition contains
what is apparently an early text of the play, but there is no
statement about the text and no mention of the editing, if any.

6452 -----. The Country Wife. Edited and with an introduction by
Steven H. Rubin. San Francisco: Chandler [1961]. xii, 100 pp.
(Chandler Editions in Drama).
The introduction covers Wycherley's life and gives an analysis
of the plot of the play. This is followed by the text based on the
1675 quarto. Few notes.

6453 -----. The Country Wife. Edited by Thomas H. Fujimura. (Regents
Restoration Drama Series). Lincoln: University of Nebraska
Press, 1965.
Includes critical introduction, notes, and bibliography.

6454 -----. The Plain-dealer, a Comedy. London: Printed by T. N. for
James Magnes, etc., 1677; [New York: H. Holt & Co., 1931?].
67 pp.
Issued separately as an addition to MacMillan's Plays of the
Restoration and 18th Century. An edition based on the 1677
edition, preceded by a two-page introduction on Wycherley's
life and critical reputation.

6455 -----. The Plain Dealer. Edited by Leo Hughes. (Regents Restoration Drama Series). Lincoln: University of Nebraska Press,
1967.
Includes introduction, notes, and chronology.

translation

6456 -----. "Fragment de L'Homme Franc." Théâtre, II (1945), 99-118.

A French translation of part of The Plain-Dealer.

biography and criticism

6457 Churchill, George B. "The Relation of Dryden's State of Innocence to Milton's Paradise Lost and Wycherley's Plain Dealer, an Inquiry into Dates." Modern Philology, IV (1906), 381-388.

Contends Wycherley's Plain Dealer was not produced in 1674 but probably as late as 1676, and that the 1677 edition of The State of Innocence is the first.

6458 Ferchlandt, H. Molière's Misanthrop und seine englische Nachahmungen. Inaugural Dissertation. Halle, 1907.

Molière's La critique de l'école des femmes was used by Wycherley in a scene of The Plain Dealer. The main plot of The Plain Dealer is quite obviously founded on Le misanthrope.

6459 Quaas, Curt. "William Wycherley als Mensch und Dichter; Ein Beitrag zur englischen Literaturgeschichte des Restaurationszeitalters." Inaugural Dissertation, Rostock, 1907.

Wycherley's life, character, and works.

6460 Shrimpton, R. A. "Wycherley's Place of Birth." Notes and Queries, 11th Ser., IX (March 7, 1914), 186-187.

Corrects entry in D.N.B. of c. 1640 at Clive, Shropshire. Finds entry in Church register of Whitchurch, Hampshire, April 8, 1641. Apparently born at residence of maternal grandfather, William Shrimpton.

6461 Perromat, Charles. William Wycherley, Sa Vie, Son Oeuvre. Paris, Librairie Felix Alian, 1921. 468 pp.

A presentation of Wycherley's life and character, followed by a brief general consideration of his works and an individual treatment of each play. Finally, an analysis of Wycherley's dramatic technique and style, his morality and his influence.

6462 Churchill, G. B. "The Originality of William Wycherley." Schelling Anniversary Papers, by His Former Students. (New York: The Century Co,, 1923), 65-85.

A consideration of Wycherley's dependence on Molière's L'Ecole des Maris for The Country Wife and on Le Misanthrope for Plain Dealer.

6463 F., R. "William Wycherley." Notes and Queries, 12th Ser., VI (1924), 70.

Identification of an allusion to Mustard Alley in The Gentleman Dancing-Master.

6464 Tyrrell, T. W. "William Wycherley." Notes and Queries, Ser.
12, VI (1924), 103.
Discussion of an allusion to Mustard Alley in The Gentleman Dancing-Master.

6465 MacCarthy, Desmond. "The Gentleman Dancing Master." New
Statesman, XXVI (December 26, 1925), 332.
Wycherley's comedy is a poor repetition of his own The
Country Wife. Reviews the Phoenix Society performance.

6466 H.[orsnell] H.[orace]. "Period Farce." Outlook (London), LVIII
(December 18, 1926), 609.
A review of the Everyman Theatre (Hampstead) production
and a brief essay on the dull cuckoldry of Restoration comedy.

6467 Boswell, Eleanore. "Wycherley and the Countess of Drogheda."
Times Literary Supplement, November 28, 1929, pp. 1001-
1002.
Replies to W. G. Hargest (TLS Nov. 21, 1929). The documents reported by Hargest had been independently discovered
by Boswell. She adds details from other sources.

6468 -----. "'Young Mr. Cartwright.'" Modern Language Review,
XXIV (April, 1929), 125-142.
An account of actor William Cartwright, one of the original
members of the King's Company immediately after the Restoration.

6469 Connely, Willard. "Mr. Wycherley." Times Literary Supplement,
May 23, 1929, p. 420.
A Mr. Wycherley accompanying Sir Richard Fanshawe,
British Ambassador, to Madrid in 1664 and 1665 may have been
the dramatist.

6470 Hargest, W. G. "Wycherley and the Countess of Drogheda."
Times Literary Supplement, November 21, 1929, p. 960.
The records of a lawsuit cast light on Wycherley's "romance"
and help date his marriage to the Countess.

6471 [Wycherley]. Notes and Queries, CLVII (November 30, 1929), 380.
Reprints a notice from the Country Journal (Nov. 29, 1729)
of Pope's edition of Wycherley's Posthumous Works.

6472 Connely, Willard. Brawny Wycherley, First Master in English
Modern Comedy. New York: Scribner's, 1930. x, 352 pp.
This study sees Wycherley as establishing and maturing
conventions now traditional in the comedy of manners.

6473 Granville-Barker, Harley. "Wycherley and Dryden." On Dramatic
Method. (London: Sidgwick and Johnson, Ltd. [1931]), 113-155.
Wycherley is the most skillful of the flatterers, as seen in
an analysis of The Plain Dealer, and Dryden, the most "in-
teresting" of the heroic play writers, as seen in a study of
Aureng-Zebe.

6474 Jones, Howard Mumford. "Wycherley, Montaigne, Tertullian, and Mr. Summers." Modern Language Notes, XLVII (April, 1932), 244-245.

Wycherley's two-line Latin quotation from Tertullian, cited in the dedication of The Plain Dealer, but borrowed from Montaigne's Essais (Livre III, Chapitre 5), illustrated the profound effect upon Wycherley of Montaigne's cynicism on the sexual nature of women.

6475 Vincent, Howard P. "The Date of Wycherley's Birth." Times Literary Supplement, March 3, 1932, p. 155.

Discusses the accuracy of the traditionally assigned date, 1640.

6476 -----. "The Death of William Wycherley." Harvard Studies and Notes in Philology and Literature, XV (1933), 219-242.

6477 Allen, Robert J. "Two Wycherley Letters." Times Literary Supplement, April 18, 1935, p. 257.

Prints two letters from Wycherley to the Earl of Mulgrave dated 1677 and 1687.

6478 Cory, Herbert Ellsworth. "William Wycherley: The Plain Dealer." Representative English Comedies. Vol. IV: Dryden and His Contemporaries: Cowley to Farquhar. Edited by Charles Mills Gayley and Alwin Thaler. (New York: The Macmillan Company, 1936), 257-271.

Biography of Wycherley; treats The Plain Dealer by attempting to refute critical charges against it. The text of the play, edited by Alexandre Beljame and Harold S. Symmes, follows.

6479 Seely, Frederick F. "The Last Eighteenth Century Performance of Wycherley's The Country Wife." Philological Quarterly, XVI (1937), 217-218.

The last performance was "probably" on November 7, 1753.

6480 Wyatt, Euphemia Van R. "Wycherley." Catholic World, CXLIV (1937), 467-468.

Brief notice of a Broadway performance of The Country Wife, which the reviewer finds "incredibly vile."

6481 Williams, Edwin E. "Furetière and Wycherley: 'Le Roman Bourgeois' in Restoration Comedy." Modern Language Notes, LIII (1938), 98-104.

Points out reminiscences of Le Roman Bourgeois in Wycherley's Plain Dealer, Gentleman Dancing Master, and Country Wife.

6482 Avery, Emmett L. "The Country Wife in the Eighteenth Century." Research Studies of the State College of Washington, X (1942), 141-172.

Surveys "the enduring popularity of The Country Wife, in the original and in altered form."

6483 Varm, Tamara. "The Relation of Wycherley's Comedies to Ben

Jonson's and Molière's: A Comparative Study." M.A. University of Oregon, 1942.

6484 Avery, Emmett L. "The Plain Dealer in the Eighteenth Century." Research Studies of the State College of Washington, XI (1943), 234-256.

6485 Vincent, Howard P. "William Wycherley's 'Posthumous Works.'" Notes and Queries, CLXXXV (July 3, 1943), 12-13.
      Discusses the acquisition of the MSS. and Theobald's connection with the publication.

6486 Abegglen, Homer N. "The Premiere of Wycherley's Plain Dealer at the Theatre Royal." Ph.D. Western Reserve University, 1944.

6487 Avery, Emmett L. "The Reputation of Wycherley's Comedies as Stage Plays in the Eighteenth Century." Research Studies of the State College of Washington, XII (September, 1944), 131-154.

6488 Le Theatre anglais d'hier et d'aujourd'hui. [Paris]: Editions du pavais [1945]. 227 pp.
      Contains an essay on Wycherley which is essentially a translation of six scenes from The Plain Dealer.

6489 Heiland, Hugh George. "A Production and Prompt Book of William Wycherley's The Country Wife." M.A. Miami University, 1947.

6490 Chorney, Alexander H. "Wycherley's Manly Reinterpreted." Essays Critical and Historical Dedicated to Lily B. Campbell (Berkeley and Los Angeles: University of California Press, 1950), 161-169.
      Manly is a "humours" character whose plain-dealing is an object of satire.

6491 Humbert, Beate. "Die Lustspiele Wycherleys und Shadwells in ihrer Beziehung zu den Komödien Molieres." Inaugural Dissertation. Hamburg, 1950.

6492 Megaw, Robert N. E. "Notes on Restoration Plays: (1) The Two 1695 Editions of Wycherley's Country Wife." Studies in Bibliography, III (1950-1951), 252-253.
      Bibliographical note to state that the Woodward and McManaway order of the editions should be reversed.

6493 Feltham, Frederik G. "The Quality of the Wit in Comedies of Etheredge, Wycherley, Congreve, and Shadwell." Ph.D. University of Chicago, 1951.

6494 Bowman, John Stewart. "The Dramaturgy of William Wycherley." Honors Thesis. Harvard University, 1953. v, 46 pp.
      A discussion of the realistic and artificial in Wycherley's plays; also considers how Wycherley embodied his ideas in characters and how his morality was dynamically resolved in the conflict of the drama.

6495 Carstens, William Frederick. "Wycherley and the Critics: A

Survey of the Dramatist's Reputation as Reflected in Some Important Critical Writings Appearing in English to 1952." Ph.D.
University of Iowa, 1954. 301 pp.

Criticism has never neglected Wycherley, but has not
rendered a final verdict on him.

6496 Vahl, Wolfgang. "Wycherley und Molière." Inaugural Dissertation.
Frankfurt, 1954.

6497 Cecil, C. D. "Restoration Comic Diction: Modes of Speech in
Etherege, Wycherley, and Congreve." B. Litt. Oxford University (Wadham), 1955-1956.

6498 Dalldorff, Horst. "Die Welt der Restaurationskomödie. Ein Quer-
schnitt durch die Lustspiele Hauptsaechlich von Etherege,
Wycherley und Congreve zur Erfassung ihrer Stofflichen
Wesenszüge." Kiel Dissertation, 1956.

6499 Holland, Norman Norwood, Jr. "A Critical Reading of the Comedies
of Etherege, Wycherley, and Congreve." Ph.D. Harvard University, 1956.

6500 Dessen, Alan Charles. "William Wycherley and the Comedy of
Manners." Honors Thesis. Harvard University, 1957. ii, 34 pp.

Insists that Wycherley was not writing comedy of manners,
because his plays are intellectual, but that he can only be
understood in relation to the comedy of manners and the conventions of that form which he employed.

6501 Freeman, Phyllis. "Two Fragments of Walsh Manuscripts." Review of English Studies, VIII (1957), 390-401.

Includes letter to Wycherley.

6502 Hart, Jeffrey P. "T. S. Eliot: His Use of Wycherley and Pope."
Notes and Queries, CCII (1957), 389-390.

There is an echo of Wycherley in Eliot's "Portrait of a
Lady" and of Pope in "Gerontion."

6503 Taylor, Archer. "Proverbs in the Plays of William Wycherley."
Southern Folklore Quarterly, XXI (1957), 213-217.

Most of the proverbs were widely current.

6504 Chinol, Elio, ed. La Commedia della Restaurazione; Etherege,
Wycherley, Congreve. Collona di Letterature Moderne, 3.
Napoli: Edizioni scientifiche italiane [1958]. 534 pp.

A long introduction making stylistic remarks on Dryden,
Vanbrugh and Farquhar as well as the three dramatists of the
title; includes English texts of Etherege's Man of Mode,
Wycherley's Plain Dealer, and Congreve's Way of the World,
with notes primarily glossing the text.

6505 "'The Country Wife': No Place to Hide." Notes and Queries,
New Ser., V (1958), 250-251.

Brief discussion of theme of disguise, literal and figurative.

6506 Gjerset, Ava. "An Interpretative Analysis and Comparison of

The Plain Dealer, by William Wycherley and Le Misanthrope, by Jean Baptiste Poquelin (Molière)." M.F.A. University of Oklahoma, 1958.

6507 Korninger, Siegfried. "Wycherleys satirische Methode." Anglistische Studien: Festschrift zum 70, Geburtstag von Professor Friedrich Wild (Wiener Beiträge zur Englischen Philologie, Vol. LXVI). Edited by Karl Brunner, Herbert Koziol, and Siegfried Korninger. W. Braumüller, 1958. pp. 110-126.

6508 O'Regan, M. J. "Furetière and Wycherley." Modern Language Review, LIII (1958), 77-81.

Le Roman bourgeois as a source of The Plain Dealer.

6509 Taylor, Archer. "The Country Wife." Theatre Arts Monthly, XLIII (February, 1958), 23.

Adverse criticism of revival.

6510 Thomas, Mary Jean. "William Wycherley's The Gentleman Dancing Master: A Thesis Production for the Arena Stage." M.S. Kansas State College, 1958.

6511 Holland, Norman N. The First Modern Comedies: The Significance of Etherege, Wycherley, and Congreve. Cambridge: Harvard University Press, 1959. iv, 274 pp.

The comedies are about the difference between appearance and reality.

6512 Craik, T. W. "Some Aspects of Satire in Wycherley's Plays." English Studies, XLI (June, 1960), 168-179.

This provides a detailed analysis of Wycherley's four comedies and suggests that if Wycherley is indeed a satirist, he seeks to do little more than amuse since his satire "does not spring from a consistently moral view of society."

6513 Swarr, Roberta. "William Wycherley: A Study of the Influence which the Society and Stage of London during the Period of the Restoration Proper had on his Dramatic Works and Techniques." M.A. Smith College, 1960.

6514 Zimbardo, Rose A. "The Comedy of William Wycherley a Study in Pre-Augustan Satire." Ph.D. Yale University, 1960.

6515 Gable, Carl Irwin. "William Wycherley; the Interaction of Theme and Form in The Country Wife." Honors Thesis. Harvard University, 1961. 30 [2] pp.

Asserts that The Country Wife contains "implicit judgments which close investigation shows to be ethical according to modern values."

6516 Rogers, K. M. "Fatal Inconsistency: Wycherley and The Plain Dealer." English Literary History, XXVIII (1961), 148-162.

Feels that "the play is written from two incompatible levels of reality," because he never made up his mind what he wished to do.

6517 Zimbardo, Rose A. "The Satiric Design in The Plain Dealer."
Studies in English Literature, I (Summer, 1961), 1-18.
  Analysis in terms of "satirist" and "adversarius" and the
technique of formal satire.

6518 Auffret, J. "Wycherley et ses maîtres les Moralistes." Etudes
Anglais, XV (1962), 375-387.
  Wycherley is not a "repressed Puritan" as John Palmer suggests, but a moralist interested in human psychology and understanding human nature.

6519 Brown, T. J. "English Literary Autograph XLI: William Wycherley,
1640?-1716, Sir John Vanbrugh, 1664-1726." Book Collector,
XI (1962), 63.

6520 Gibb, Carson. "Figurative Structre in Restoration Comedy." Ph.D.
University of Pennsylvania, 1962. (Order No. 63-4153).
  Figurative structure results from the juxaposition of apparently
unrelated actions in selected plays of Dryden, Etherege, and
Wycherley.

6521 Jenkins, E. Valerie. "Plans for the Production of William Wycherley's
The Plain Dealer." M.A. Kent State University, 1962.

6522 Sinko, Grzegorz. Angielska komedia Restauracji: G. Etherege, W.
Wycherley, W. Congreve. Przelozyl i opracowal. Wroclaw:
Zaklad Narodowy Im. Ossolinskich [1962]. lxiii, 559 pp. (Biblio-
teka narodowa. Ser II, 133).
  Introduction, giving historical background. Polish transla-
tions of Etherege's She Would, If She Could, Wycherley's The
Country Wife, and Congreve's The Way of the World.

6523 Bowman, John S. "Dance, Chant and Mask in the Plays of Wycherley." Drama Survey, III (1963), 181-205.
  Concerns Wycherley's use of dance, chant and masks to
project the ideas of his plays. The devices also demonstrate
the significance of the plays for Restoration society.

6524 Foxon, David. "Libertine Literature in England, 1660-1745, I."
Book Collector, XII (1963), 21-36.
  Allusions to Continental pornographic writings in the plays
of Wycherley indicate that these writings were more widely
known than is generally assumed.

6525 Germer, Erich. Sentimentale Züge in den Lustspielgestalten
Ethereges, Wycherleys, Congreves, Vanbrughs und Farquhars.
Inaugural Dissertation. Münster, 1963. 164 pp.
  Appearance and treatment of types of sentimentalism in
Restoration comedy.

6526 Shepherd, James L. "Molière and Wycherley's Plain Dealer:
Further Observations." South Central Bulletin Studies, XXIII
(1963), 37-40.
  Shows the influence of L'Ecole des Femmes on Wycherley's
hero and comic technique.

6527 Wooton, Carl. "The Country Wife and Contemporary Comedy:
      A World Apart." Drama Survey, II (1963), 333-343.
          Compares the moral attitude of The Country Wife with that
      of three modern plays written on the same theme: George
      Axelrod's The Seven Year Itch, Tennessee Williams's Baby
      Doll, and Terrence Rattigan's Tea and Sympathy.
6528 Hymas, Scott Simpson. "The Satiric Attitude: Rejection in the
      Comedies of Wycherley and Etherege." Ph.D. Western Reserve
      University, 1964. (Order No. 65-2325).
          Seeks to discover that the dramas of Wycherley and Etherege
      are "more expressive of the rejection of the satiric attitude
      than the acceptance of the comic."
6529 Mercier, Vivian. "From Myth to Idea and Back." Ideas in the
      Drama: Selected Papers from the English Institute. Edited by
      John Gassner. (New York: Columbia University Press, 1964),
      42-70.
          Restoration comedy cannot be considered a part of the drama
      of ideas since it lacks "a fair confrontation of ideals." Its "one-
      sidedness" is best illustrated in the antiorthodoxy of Wycherley's
      The Country Wife.
6530 Wilkinson, D.R.M. The Comedy of Habit: An Essay on the Use of
      Courtesy Literature in a Study of Restoration Comic Drama.
      (Leidse Germanistische en Anglistiche Reehs von de Ryksuni-
      versiteit Leiden, 4). The Hague: Martinus Nijhoff, 1964. 190 pp.
          Uses Francis Osborne's Advice to a Son (1656-1658) and
      other contemporary courtesy literature to examine the wit and
      characterization of the gallant, particularly in the plays of
      Etherege and Wycherley.
6531 Lagarde, Fernand. "Wycherley et Webster." Caliban, New Ser.,
      I (1965), 33-45.
          Wycherley's indebtedness to Webster and other Jacobean
      playwrights.
6532 Swander, Homer. "Morality in the Theatre: The Country Wife."
      California English Journal, I, iii (1965), 17-24.
6533 Vernon, P.F. William Wycherley. London: Longman's Green
      and Company (for the British Council and the National Book
      League), 1965. 44 pp.
          Brief introduction to Wycherley's life and art with special
      emphasis on the nature of his satiric temperament and social
      criticism.
6534 Zimbardo, Rose. Wycherley's Drama: A Link in the Development
      of English Satire. New York: Yale University Press, 1965.
      174 pp.
          An investigation of Wycherley's position in the Roman-
      Anglo-Saxon-Elizabethan satiric tradition. Reviewed by Paul

Parnell, RECTR, IV, 2 (November, 1965), 58-61.
6535 Auffret, J. M. "The Man of Mode and The Plain Dealer: Common
        Origin and Parallels." Etudes Anglais, XIX (1966), 209-222.
6536 Holland, Norman N. "The Country Wife." Restoration Drama:
        Modern Essays in Criticism. (A Galaxy Book). Edited by John
        Loftis. (New York: Oxford University Press, 1966), 82-96.
        Reprinted from The First Modern Comedies (Cambridge,
        Mass.: Harvard University Press, 1959), pp. 73-85. The
        significance of the play lies in the contrast and interaction of
        its three closely woven lines of intrigue.
6537 Mukherjee, Sujit. "Marriage as Punishment in the Plays of Wycher-
        ley." Review of English Literature (Leeds), VII, iv (1966), 61-
        64.
        Wycherley uses marriage as an instrument of poetic justice;
        it is "the life sentence given to erring human beings."
6538 Righter, Anne. "William Wycherley." Restoration Theatre. Edited
        by John Russell Brown and Bernard Harris. (Stratford-Upon-
        Avon Studies, 6). (London: Edward Arnold, 1965; New York: St.
        Martin's Press, 1965), 71-91. Also in Restoration Dramatists:
        A Collection of Critical Essays. (Twentieth Century Views).
        Edited by Earl Miner. (Englewood Cliffs, N.J.: Prentice Hall,
        Inc., 1966), 105-122.
        Traces Wycherley's development from his indebtedness to
        Etherege to his movement toward sentimentalism and a kind of
        "dark comedy."
6539 -----. "William Wycherley." Restoration Dramatists. A Collec-
        tion of Critical Essays. Edited by Earl Miner. (Englewood
        Cliffs, New Jersey: Prentice-Hall, Inc., 1966), 105-122.
        From Restoration Theatre (Edward Arnold, Ltd., 1965).
        Wycherley is partly responsible for the new directions taken
        by comedy in the later Restoration.
6540 Vernon, P. F. "Wycherley's First Comedy and Its Spanish Source."
        Comparative Literature, XVIII (1966), 132-144.
        Wycherley's borrowings from Calderon's Mananas de abril y
        mayo for his Love in a Wood shows that he borrowed with dis-
        crimination to create an English courtship comedy fused with
        realistic social satire.
6541 Vieth, David M. "Wycherley's The Country Wife: An Anatomy of
        Masculinity." Papers on Language and Literature, II (1966),
        335-350.
        The play's central concern is with providing a definition of
        masculinity.
6542 Weales, Gerald. "A Wycherley Prologue." The Library Chronicle,
        XXXII (1966), 101-104.
        Reprints and discusses the prologue written by Wycherley

for Agnes de Castro (1696) by Catharine Trotter.

6543 Zimbardo, Rose A. "The Satiric Design in The Plain Dealer."
Restoration Dramatists. A Collection of Critical Essays.
Edited by Earl Miner. (Englewood Cliffs, New Jersey: Prentice-
Hall, Inc., 1966), 123-138.

From Studies in English Literature, I (1961), 1-18.

6544 Berman, Ronald. "The Ethic of The Country Wife." Texas Studies
in Literature and Language, IX (1967), 47-55.

Studies the ethical system in which the action occurs, what
institutions are recognized and encountered, and what relationship exists between ideals and reality in the play.

6545 Birdsall, Virginia Ogden. "The English Comic Spirit on the Restoration Stage." Ph.D. Brown University, 1967. (Order No. 68-
1439).

The immorality and libertinism of comic protagonists are
an essential part of their nature and relate them to an English
comic tradition that always takes sides with the individual
against the group. The study concentrates on Etherege,
Wycherley, and Congreve.

6546 Donaldson, Ian. "'Tables Turned': The Plain Dealer." Essays
in Criticism, XVII (1967), 304-321.

The ambilvalence in Manly's character and the contradic-
toriness of the play are deliberate and controlled, the sources
of the play's energy and brilliance. The Plain Dealer, not The
Country Wife, was considered his best play by Wycherley's
friends and contemporaries.

6547 Friedson, A. M. "Wycherley and Molière: Satirical Point of View
in The Plain Dealer." Modern Philology, LXIV (1967), 189-
197.

An analysis of The Plain Dealer and a comparison of this
play with Molière's Le Misanthrope show that particular
social follies, and not the subsidiary comedy of Manly's
humor, are the main object of Wycherley's satire.

6548 Held, George M. C. "The Use of Comic Conventions in the Plays
of William Wycherley." Ph.D. Rutgers, 1967. (Order No. 68-
4539).

Wycherley uses conventions characteristic not only of
Restoration drama but of the comedy of humours and romantic
comedy as well.

6549 Matlack, Cynthia Sutherland. "Dramatic Techniques in the Plays
of William Wycherley." Ph.D. University of Pennsylvania,
1967. (Order No. 68-9223).

Challenges the common and oversimplified criticisms of
the plays' craft and content. Special attention is given to
Wycherley's use of the technique of breaking the dramatic
illusion.

6550 Wolper, Roy S. "The Temper of The Country Wife." Humanities Association Bulletin, XVIII (1967), 69-74.

Wynne

6551 Freemantle, Anne, ed. The Wynne Diaries. Vol. I, 1789-1794. London: Oxford University Press, 1935. xvi, 376 pp.
Includes some contemporary comment about plays and the provincial theatre.

Yearsley, Ann

6552 Tompkins, J. M. S. The Polite Marriage, also the Didactic Lyre, The Bristol Milkwoman, The Scotch Parents, Clio in Motley, and Mary Hays, Philosophress. Cambridge: Cambridge University Press, 1938. vii, 209 pp.
Essays on some minor literary figures of the 18th century. The only dramatist included is Ann Yearsley, the Bristol Milkwoman, who is presented in her relationship to her patroness, Hannah More.

Young, Edward

6553 Kind, John Louis. Edward Young in Germany: Historical Surveys, Influence upon German Literature, Bibliography. New York: The Columbia University Press, The Macmillan Company, agents (etc., etc.) 1906. xiv, 186 pp.

6554 Thomas, Walter. Le poète Edward Young (1683-1765) étude sur sa vie et ses oeuvres. Paris: Hachette et cie, 1911. xii, 663, [2] pp.

6555 Shelley, Henry C. The Life and Letters of Edward Young. London: Sir Isaac Pitman and Sons, Ltd., 1914. xi, 289 pp.
A biography of Young presenting his life in sharply divided segments. The chapter covering 1719-1726 is devoted to Young as dramatist and discusses his plays Busiris, The Revenge, and The Brothers and some of the circumstances of their production.

6556 Boas, F. S. "A Manuscript Copy of Edward Young's Busiris." Times Literary Supplement, May 22, 1930, p. 434.
A description of the manuscript. Boas does not believe it is an autograph copy.

6557 Wicker, C. V. Edward Young and the Fear of Death; A Study in Romantic Melancholy. Albuquerque: University of New Mexico Press, 1952. 108 pp.

Zoffany, John

6558 Manners, Lady Victoria, and Dr. G. C. Williamson. John Zoffany,
        R.A. London: John Lane, 1920. 331 pp.
            A biography of the theatrical portrait painter.
6559 Gosse, Edmund. "Zoffany." Books on the Table. (London: W.
        Heinemann [1921]), 139-145.
            An essay on Zoffany, the eighteenth-century theatrical
        painter.

Zuccarelli, Francesco

6560 Levey, Michael. "Francesco Zuccarelli in England." Italian Studies,
        XIV (1959), 1-20.